The Mitchell Beazley
New Concise Atlas
of the
Earth

The Mitchell Beazley
New Concise Atlas of the Earth

With a foreword by the late Sir Julian Huxley, FRS

Mitchell Beazley Publishers Limited with George Philip
in association with Rand McNally and Company

Chief Editorial Consultants and Advisers

B. W. Atkinson, Ph.D., B.Sc.,
Dept. of Geography, Queen Mary College, University of London
Prof. K. F. Bowden, D.Sc., S.Inst.P.,
Professor of Oceanography, University of Liverpool
Graham Chedd, B.A.,
Life Science Editor, *New Scientist*
Miss A. Coleman, M.A.,
Reader in Geography, King's College, University of London
R. Dearnley, Ph.D., B.Sc., F.G.S.,
Principal Geologist, Institute of Geological Sciences, London
Prof. A. N. Duckham, C.B.E., F.I.Biol.,
Professor Emeritus, Dept. of Agriculture, University of Reading
F. W. Dunning, B.Sc., F.G.S.,
Curator, Geological Museum, London
David Fishlock,
Science Editor, *Financial Times*
Harold Fullard, M.Sc.,
Cartographic Director, George Philip and Son Limited
Ken Gatland, F.R.A.S., F.B.I.S.,
Aerospace Consultant, Vice President, British Interplanetary Society
Arch C. Gerlach, Ph.D.,
lately Chief Geographer, U.S. Geological Survey
Prof. G. Melvyn Howe, Ph.D., M.Sc., F.R.G.S., F.R.Met.Soc.,
Professor of Geography, University of Strathclyde
Prof. Emrys Jones, Ph.D., M.Sc., F.R.G.S.,
Professor of Geography, London School of Economics
Patrick Moore, O.B.E., F.R.A.S.
A. Mountjoy, M.C., M.A., F.R.G.S.,
Reader in Geography, Bedford College, University of London
National Aeronautics and Space Administration
Prof. Sir Alan S. Parkes, C.B.E., Ph.D., D.Sc., Sc.D., F.R.S.,
Chairman, The Galton Foundation, London
Brian Stafford,
Industrial Consultant
Margaret Walters, Ph.D., B.Sc.,
formerly of Chester Beatty Research Institute, London

For Rand McNally and Company
Cartographic and Design Director : Chris Arvetis
Cartographic Editor : Jon M. Leverenz
Editorial Direction : Russell L. Voisin

Contents

The Mitchell Beazley Concise Atlas of the Earth
Copyright © Mitchell Beazley Publishers Limited 1973
Fully revised 1977, © Mitchell Beazley Publishers Limited.
The Good Earth pages 1–65 ©
Mitchell Beazley Publishers Limited 1973 and 1976. **World Atlas** pages
68–190, World Political Information Tables and Index pages 191–240,
© Rand McNally and Company from *The International Atlas* © 1969
Rand McNally and Company, and © Rand McNally and Company 1977.
ISBN O 85533 134 8.

Foreword by the late
Sir Julian Huxley, FRS

The Concise Atlas is
not merely a collection of
maps, but an Encyclopaedia,
dealing with the formation of
the Earth and its oceans,
the environment they provide
for the vast and varied
assemblage of their animal
and plant inhabitants; the
origin of life, and its
history during the
huge span of evolutionary time.

Sir Julian Huxley, F.R.S.
One of this century's most distinguished
zoologists, the late Sir Julian Huxley,
grandson of T. H. Huxley, was born in 1887.
In the course of an outstanding academic
career he received honours from universities
throughout the world, and was also famous
as a scientific writer for popular audiences.
Toward the end of his life he dedicated
himself in particular to wildlife conservation.

It also deals with the origin of our own species, with the history of its achievements and with some of the problems now besetting it—violence and pollution, disunity and over-population.

As a scientific naturalist interested in human affairs as well as biology and geology, I welcome this splendid work, for only by understanding and knowledge shall we be able to cope with our enormous responsibility —for avoiding disaster to this planet and its inhabitants and for guiding its future towards greater sanity and greater achievement.

The mass of facts and ideas assembled in this *Atlas* was not handed to us on a plate: it needed millennia of thought and experiment, of intellectual and moral striving.

Let me attempt a brief history of this great adventure. Although some Greek philosophers concluded that the Earth was spherical, almost everyone in early times thought it was flat, and it was not until the great voyagers of the 16th and 17th centuries proved the Earth's sphericity by sailing round it that the theory was accepted. These bold adventurers made possible accurate maps and also discovered new animals and plants, new tribes and new nations with their own customs and legends.

But this was just one part of the struggle for knowledge. Early in this century, the German geologist Wegener propounded the theory of continental drift—the idea that all the Earth's land was originally one single mass, and that about 180 million years ago it started to split up, forming the separate continents we know today. We have also now discovered that the Earth's axis has shifted, so that different parts of the world have been exposed to Arctic and Antarctic cold at different periods—a fact brought home to me personally by seeing coal-mines in Spitzbergen.

The drifting is made possible by huge cracks or rifts, some in the ocean bed, others on land, such as the Great Rift of Africa and Palestine, and all, especially those in the oceans, constantly enlarging their diameter. We now know that Europe and North America are drifting further apart by nearly an inch every year.

When large chunks of crust drift against each other, as happened when India moved against Central Asia, the belt of contact is squashed up into great mountains—here the Karakoram and Himalayas. There are also interesting consequences of drift— animal and plant forms originally inhabiting part of the mass are now found in its separated regions—thus the beautiful Protea plants grown in South Africa and Australia, and the southern beech in Australia and the northern part of South America.

In addition to rocks upwelling in molten form below the surface, others are sedimentary, deposited by fresh water, such as clays, or on the ocean bed, such as chalk, made of shells of microscopic floating organisms. The sedimentary rocks are laid down in bands or strata, and often contain fossilized organisms—for example, ammonites, mammoth skeletons or petrified wood.

It was soon found that fossils in later deposited strata were more like existing species than those of earlier date, and that fossil types change gradually during geological time. In other words, life evolves. But what brings evolution about? There were many suggestions. At the beginning of the 19th century,

Jean Lamarck (1744-1829)

Georges Cuvier (1769-1832)

Charles Darwin (1808-1882)

Gregor Mendel (1822-1884)

Alfred Wallace (1823-1913)

T. H. Huxley (1825-1895)

Cuvier, the great French zoologist, believed that each major epoch was brought to a close by some world-wide catastrophe and then the Almighty created a set of new types. This was soon found to be impossible. Meanwhile Lamarck, his contemporary, thought that structure was changed by individual effort—for instance that, when the ancestral giraffe stretched its neck to reach higher foliage, some of the extra height was inherited by the next generation. This too wouldn't work—characters acquired by the individual are not, and cannot be, inherited by its descendants. Finally, in 1858, two Englishmen, Charles Darwin and Alfred Russel Wallace, provided the answer: 'Natural selection', operating through the slight advantage enjoyed by those individuals best able to survive and reproduce themselves in a given environment.

Darwin and his adherents, like my grandfather T. H. Huxley, soon converted the majority of scientists, and eventually laymen, to this new view, which dispensed with cataclysms and divine intervention and worked automatically, producing delicate adaptations to the conditions of life, and also the sexual adornments, such as the peacock's tail, which promote success in mating. Here clearly was the key to evolution. But it worked through inheritance, and the mechanism of inheritance was still a puzzle.

I am old enough to remember how the puzzle was solved—by the rediscovery of the Abbé Mendel's work, showing that inheritance of a given character was due to a particular unit or set of units in the hereditary mechanism; and the later proof by T. H. Morgan that these units were parts of the visible chromosomes in the body's organs and reproductive cells that we call genes. Then the discovery that mutation-changes in the properties and effects of genes were taking place all the time, and H. J. Muller's demonstration that external agencies, such as X-rays and certain chemicals, could cause new mutations to occur.

Darwin also studied the development of 'mind', including instinct. This led on to modern psychology with its various types—extraverts and introverts, gifted and less gifted; and also to social anthropology and sociology—the study of human societies, their variety, their central systems of ideas, their change or evolution during historic times.

This *Atlas* also deals with the most important factors in man's present existence—his religion, his technology, the spread of pollution and its counter-measure, conservation. It also discusses population-increase, that most urgent of human problems. I commend it to every intelligent human being— especially to the younger generation, for it is they who will have to continue man's efforts to cope with the ever-increasing challenge of the future—to keep our world fit to live in.

There are people who maintain that the evolution of man and his societies has reached an impasse. I do not believe this. Faith, goodwill and purposeful intelligence can overcome our problems, and knowledge helps us to understand them. This *Atlas* contributes both to our knowledge and understanding, and spurs us to action.

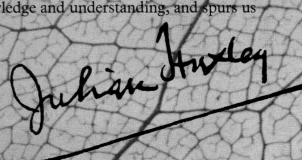

The Planet Earth

Our home the Earth is a small planet revolving round the Sun. The Sun is a star, but only one of the hundred thousand million which exist in the local system of stars, or galaxy, of which we are a part. Our own galaxy, we now know, is just one of millions of other galaxies in the universe, all almost unbelievably remote. The light now reaching us from the most distant observable star-systems began its journey towards us even before the Earth came into existence more than 4500 million years ago.

It is inconceivable that other stars in the universe do not have planetary systems like our own Sun. Although our neighbours in the Sun's family seem barren of life, some of those planets in other systems must support life in some form. Yet, barring some revolutionary new insight into the problems of time and space travel, it is difficult to believe that man will ever be able to explore the depths of the universe to find such life. So far as we can now see, we on this Earth are alone.

Nebula in Sagittarius
The Trifid nebula in the constellation Sagittarius is so called because dark dust clouds appear to divide the glowing gas into three segments. The Trifid, which forms a typical emission nebula, contains hot early-type stars. Its distance from us is 2300 light-years.

The Sun in the Galaxy

Less than 2500 years ago the Greeks thought of the Earth as the centre of all creation, and of the Sun as a bright body not more than 2ft (0.6m) across. Today we know that the Sun, although it is 864,950 mi (1,392,000 km) across, is merely one star among 100,000 million in a spiral organization of stars known as our galaxy; and this in turn is merely one among thousands of millions of other galaxies which make up the entire visible universe. The diagrams on these pages afford at least an indication of the relative sizes of stars, galaxies and the known universe. What nobody can yet answer with any precision is just how big the universe is, or what lies beyond it. Such problems are increasingly extending the mind of man. Complete answers will probably never be known. At present the universe is regarded as a three-dimensional space which seems to be swiftly expanding.

Scale of the universe *right*
On a cosmological scale, man's knowledge is extremely limited and fragmentary. So large is the observable universe that it is geometrically impossible to link it by diagrams with a familiar object except by introducing separate and increasing exaggerations of scale. The large box contains our local group of galaxies, with our own looking like a catherine wheel at the centre. Each galaxy, whether a spiral, a barred spiral or irregular in form, contains thousands of millions of stars. Some idea of the scale of this box is given by the fact that even with the fastest Moon rocket it would take more than 60000 million years to cross from our own galaxy to a similar one, M31 in the constellation of Andromeda, seen in the left of the box. Even the nearest objects known to lie outside our galaxy, the small and large Magellanic Clouds (SMC and LMC), which are really small galaxies of irregular shape, are so far away that no man is ever likely to visit them. But our local group is only one amongst millions that go to make up the universe that has been observed by successive generations of increasingly powerful telescopes and other analytical instruments. We now know that even what can be seen is far from being a static situation: the most distant objects that we can see appear to be receding from us; and, the farther away they are, the faster this 'speed of recession' becomes. In fact, the universe appears to be an expanding sphere, as if the whole of creation had once exploded from a central point. Nevertheless we can, by taking a tremendous leap in scale, portray our visible universe, as shown in the chart above the large box, although at this point our local galaxies (see small box projected into the centre) have become no more than a pin-prick. On the chart, the innermost coloured ring, A, marks the limit of objects that astronomers can see with optical telescopes; ring B contains the furthest objects detected by radio telescopes; and, finally, ring C is the radius at which objects appear to be moving from the Earth at a speed equal to that of light. This represents the limit to our observations; nothing can ever be seen from the Earth beyond C. The distance to this point, the supposed limit of the universe, is 10000 million light-years, or 120,000,000,000,000,000,000 mi (193 x 10²¹km).

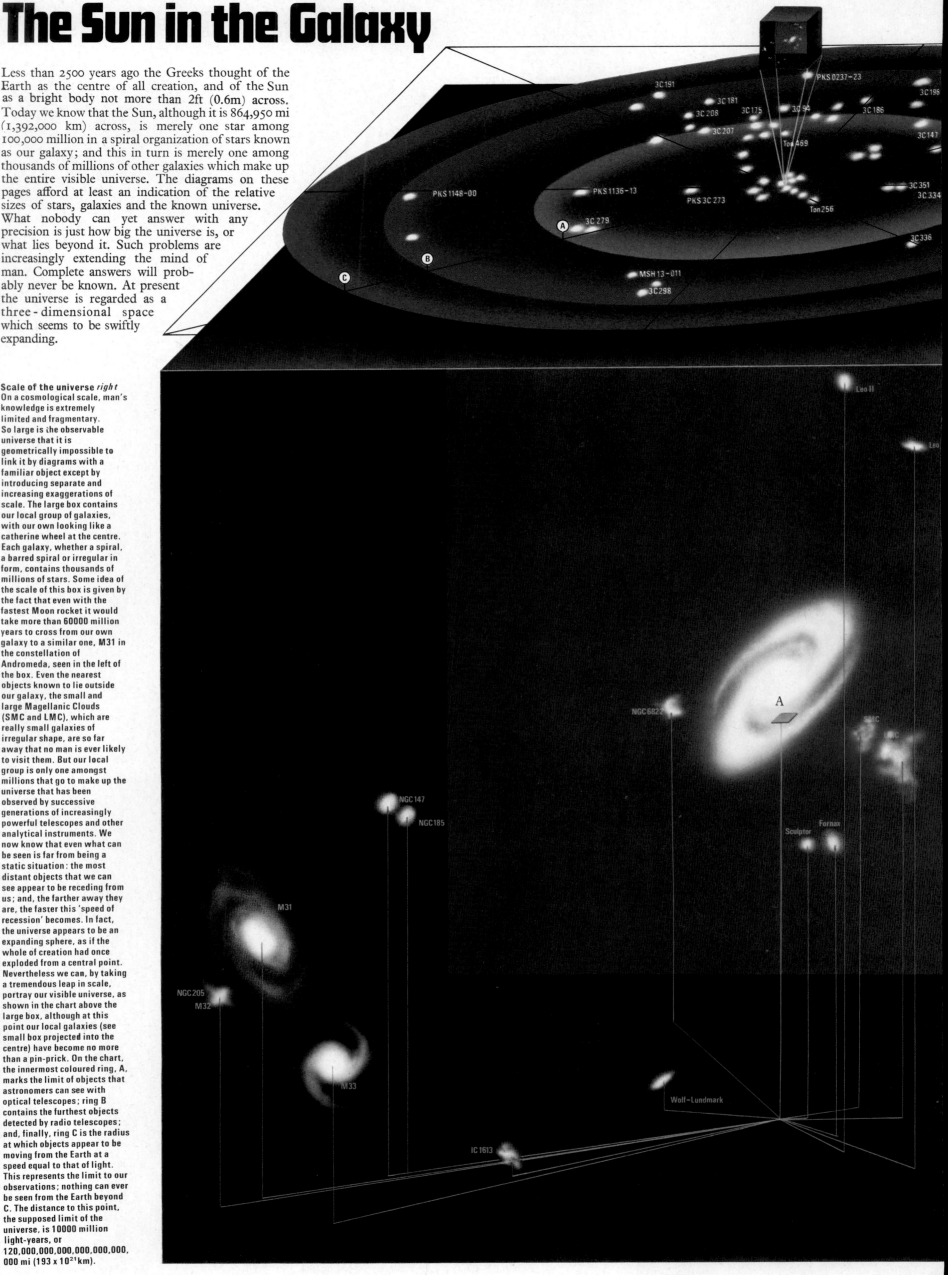

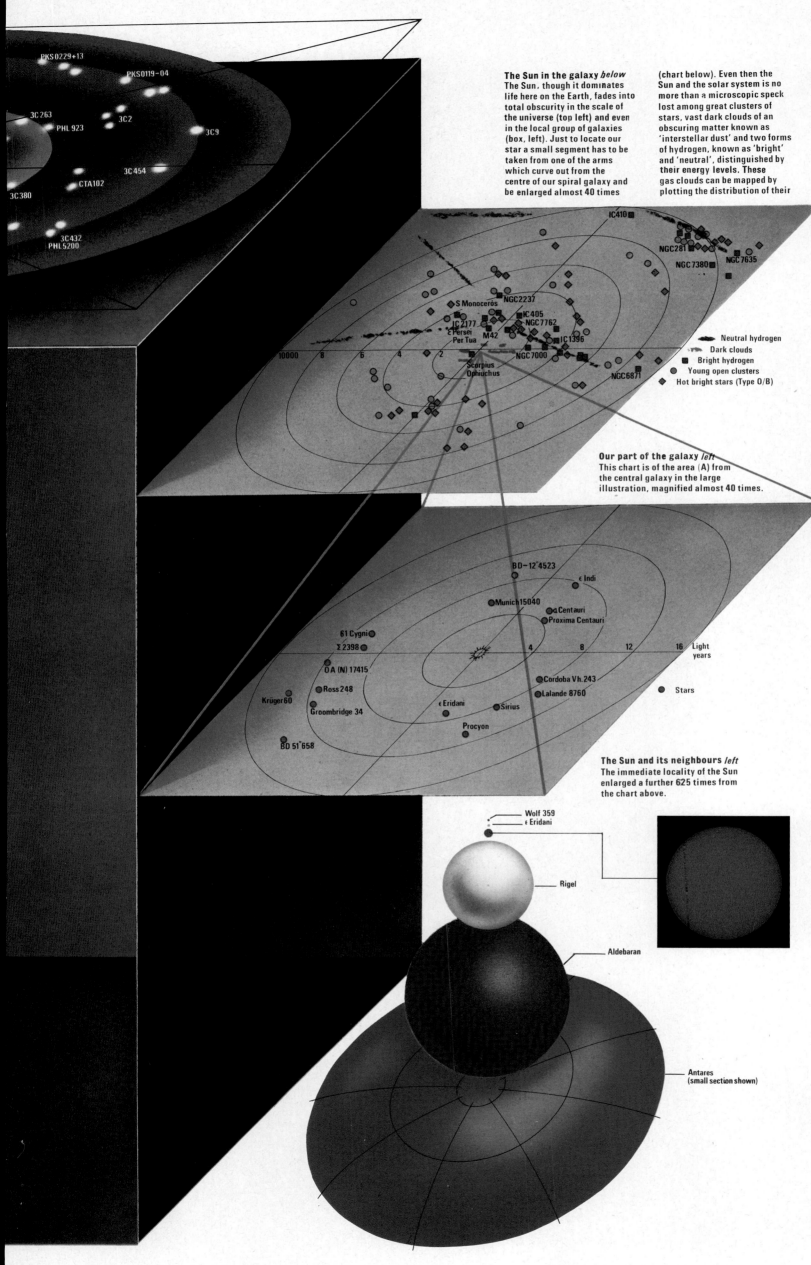

PKS 0229+13
PKS 0119-04
3C 263
PHL 923
3C 2
3C 9
3C 454
CTA 102
3C 380
3C 432
PHL 5200

The Sun in the galaxy *below*
The Sun, though it dominates life here on the Earth, fades into total obscurity in the scale of the universe (top left) and even in the local group of galaxies (box, left). Just to locate our star a small segment has to be taken from one of the arms which curve out from the centre of our spiral galaxy and be enlarged almost 40 times

(chart below). Even then the Sun and the solar system is no more than a microscopic speck lost among great clusters of stars, vast dark clouds of an obscuring matter known as 'interstellar dust' and two forms of hydrogen, known as 'bright' and 'neutral', distinguished by their energy levels. These gas clouds can be mapped by plotting the distribution of their

radiation. This section is 20000 light-years across (the scale is given in the prominent concentric rings) and its focal point, the Sun, is approximately 30000 light-years from the centre of the galaxy. Still the Sun is invisible. To see it, much greater magnification of the surrounding areas is needed. With a further enlargement of 625 times the Sun at last becomes visible along with other stars in its neighbourhood (lower chart). The radius chosen for this chart is 16 light-years, or some 10^{13}mi (1.6×10^{13}km). The most remarkable fact is that this distance is not sufficient to capture a single giant star. Indeed, of all the stars included, only three— Sirius, Procyon and the brighter member of the double star Proxima Centauri—are more luminous than the Sun; and even Sirius, with 26 times the luminosity of the Sun, is classified by astronomers as a dwarf star. Most of the other near neighbours are faint red dwarfs much less powerful than the Sun. One, Munich 15040, more commonly known as Barnard's star, is thought to be accompanied by two planets each about the size of Jupiter, which cause disturbances in its motion sufficiently large to be measured by astronomers. Even where such changes in motion have not been observed this does not necessarily mean that other neighbouring stars do not also have planetary systems similar to our own. At present, no way exists of finding out. Certainly there is little hope of man ever being able to visit them. It would take the fastest Moon rocket about 120,000 years to reach the nearest star, Proxima Centauri. If we return now to the large box, itself a minute part of the entire observable universe, we can realise something of the vastness of space and the place of the Sun and therefore the planet Earth within it.

Our part of the galaxy *left*
This chart is of the area (A) from the central galaxy in the large illustration, magnified almost 40 times.

Legend:
Neutral hydrogen
Dark clouds
Bright hydrogen
Young open clusters
Hot bright stars (Type O/B)

IC410, NGC281, NGC7380, NGC7635, S Monoceros, NGC2237, IC405, NGC7762, IC2177, Per Tua, Persei, M42, IC1396, Scorpius, Ophiuchus, NGC7000, NGC6871

The Sun and its neighbours *left*
The immediate locality of the Sun enlarged a further 625 times from the chart above.

BD-12°4523, ε Indi, Munich 15040, α Centauri, Proxima Centauri, 61 Cygni, Σ 2398, O A (N) 17415, Ross 248, Krüger 60, Groombridge 34, ε Eridani, Sirius, Procyon, Cordoba Vh.243, Lalande 8760, BD 51°658, Stars, Light years

The size of our Sun *left*
With distances as immense as those in the universe, it seems natural that the sizes of its stars should also be immense. The diameter of our Sun, for example, is equal to 109 Earths placed side by side. However, we know from observations of other stars that its size is not fixed and will change with time. A star follows an evolutionary sequence, in the course of which it changes dramatically in size, surface temperature and luminosity. The star is probably formed in a nebula as a result of coalescing interstellar material. After about 100,000 years the young star joins the 'main sequence' as a very bright body with a surface temperature of some 40000°C. It grows in size and luminosity, sending out energy at a very high rate from its internal conversion of hydrogen to helium. Gradually it swells to a size 100 or more times larger than the Sun, cooling and becoming dulled. It finishes as a reddish dwarf and ultimately probably loses all luminosity. Wolf 359 is a faint red dwarf. Epsilon (ε) Eridani, a near neighbour of the Sun, is smaller and cooler than the Sun and may have a planetary system. Rigel is at the peak of its career. Aldebaran is a moderate example of a red giant. Antares, the largest red giant known, is so vast (250 million miles across) that only a very small segment of it can be shown.

Wolf 359
ε Eridani
Rigel
Aldebaran
Antares
(small section shown)

11

The Life and Death of the Earth

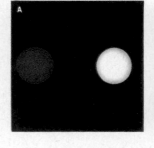
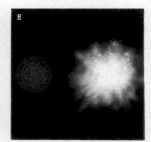

3 The gas cloud begins to assume the form of a regular disk. The infant Sun begins to shine - by the energy from gravitational shrinkage.

4 Material is thrown off from the Sun to join that already in the solar cloud, whose condensations have become more noticeable.

1 According to the most widely accepted theory, (the 'accretion' theory) the solar system originally consisted only of a mass of tenuous gas, and dust. There was no true Sun, and there was no production of nuclear energy. The gas was made up chiefly of hydrogen, with occasional random condensations.

2 Gravitational forces now cause the cloud to shrink and assume a more regular shape. Its density and mass near the centre increase, but there are still no nuclear processes.

How did the Earth come into existence? This question has intrigued mankind for centuries but it was not until the start of true science that plausible theories were advanced. Although some theories held sway for many years, they were eventually deposed by the discovery of some fatal flaw. Even today, it is impossible to be sure that the main problem has been solved, but at least some concrete facts exist as a guide. It is now reasonably certain that the age of the Earth is of the order of 4550-4700 million years. The other planets are presumably about the same age, since they were probably formed by the same process in the same epoch.

Several centuries ago Archbishop Ussher of Armagh maintained that the world had come into being at a definite moment in the year 4004 BC. This estimate was made on purely religious grounds, and it soon became clear that the Earth is much older. In 1796 the French astronomer Laplace put forward the famous Nebular Hypothesis, according to which the Sun and the planets were formed from a rotating cloud of gas which shrank under the influence of gravitation. As it shrank, the cloud shed gaseous rings, each of which condensed into a planet. This would mean that the outer planets were older than those closer to the Sun which itself would represent the remaining part of the gas cloud.

The Nebular Hypothesis was accepted for many years, but eventually serious mathematical weaknesses were found in it. Next came a number of tidal theories according to which the Earth and other planets were formed from a cigar-shaped tongue of matter torn from the Sun by the gravitational pull of a passing star. The first plausible theory of this kind came from the English astronomer Sir James Jeans, but this too was found to be mathematically untenable and the idea had to be given up.

Most modern theories assume that the planets were formed by accretion from a rotating solar cloud of gas and finely-dispersed dust. If the Sun were originally attended by such a cloud, this cloud would, over a sufficiently long period of time, become a flat disk.

If random concentration had become sufficiently massive, it would draw in extra material by virtue of its gravitational attraction, forming 'proto-planets'. When the Sun began to radiate strongly, part of the mass of each proto-planet would be driven off due to the high temperatures, leaving a solar system of the kind that exists today.

The fact that such an evolutionary sequence can be traced emphasizes that in talking about the origin of the Earth we are considering only a small part of a continuous story. What will become of the Earth in the far future? The Sun is radiating energy because of the nuclear process within it: hydrogen is being converted into helium causing mass to be lost with a resulting release of energy. However, when the supply of hydrogen begins to run low, the Sun must change radically. It will move towards a red giant stage swelling and engulfing the Earth. Fortunately, this will not happen for at least another 6000 million years, but eventually the Sun which sustains our planet will finally destroy it.

Alternative theories

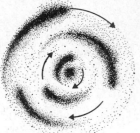

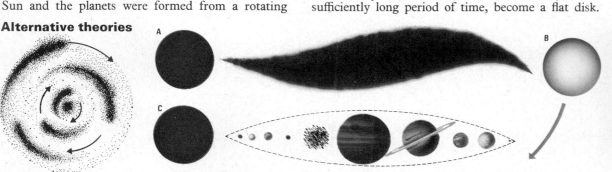

Contracting nebula *above* Laplace suggested that a contracting nebula might shed gas which then condensed.

Tidal theories *above* In 1901 Sir James Jeans postulated that Sun A was attracted to another star B which passed at close range. A cloud of matter was drawn off by their gravitational attraction. Star B moved on while the cloud condensed to form planets circling our Sun at C.

A violent beginning *above* One of the theories of how the solar system came to be formed assumes that the Sun once had a binary companion star. This exploded as a supernova (above) and was blown off as a white dwarf

16 As the 'fuel' runs out, the radiation pressure falls, and under internal gravity the Sun will collapse inwards changing in only 50000 years from a red giant into a super-dense white dwarf.

17 As a white dwarf, the Sun will continue to radiate feebly for an immense period. At last all radiation must cease, and the Sun will remain as a dead, dark globe - a black dwarf.

15 By now all the inner planets will have long since been destroyed. The Sun will become unstable, reaching the most violent stage of its career as a red giant, with a vast, relatively cool surface and an intensely hot, dense core.

14 When the centre of the Sun has reached another critical temperature, the helium will begin to 'burn' giving the so-called 'helium flash'. After a temporary contraction the Sun will then swell out to a diameter 400 times that at present.

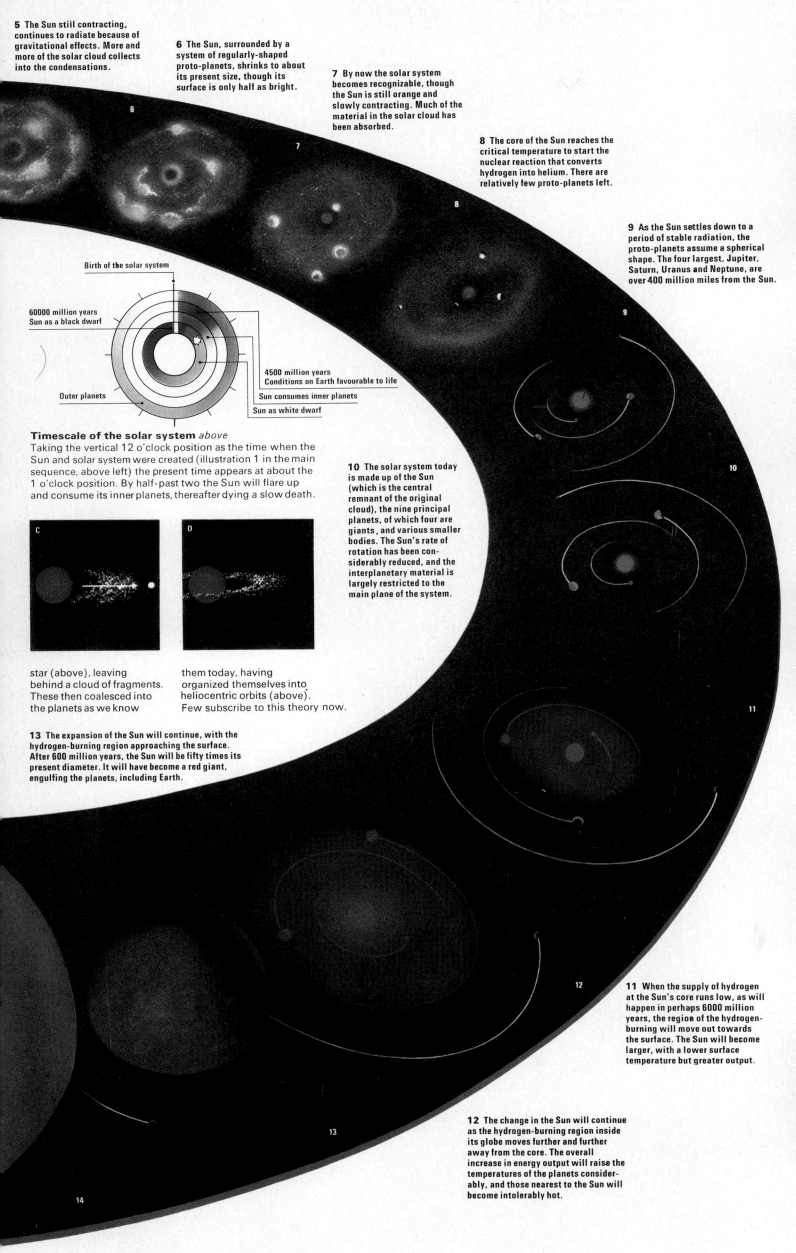

5 The Sun still contracting, continues to radiate because of gravitational effects. More and more of the solar cloud collects into the condensations.

6 The Sun, surrounded by a system of regularly-shaped proto-planets, shrinks to about its present size, though its surface is only half as bright.

7 By now the solar system becomes recognizable, though the Sun is still orange and slowly contracting. Much of the material in the solar cloud has been absorbed.

8 The core of the Sun reaches the critical temperature to start the nuclear reaction that converts hydrogen into helium. There are relatively few proto-planets left.

9 As the Sun settles down to a period of stable radiation, the proto-planets assume a spherical shape. The four largest, Jupiter, Saturn, Uranus and Neptune, are over 400 million miles from the Sun.

Birth of the solar system

60000 million years
Sun as a black dwarf

Outer planets

4500 million years
Conditions on Earth favourable to life

Sun consumes inner planets

Sun as white dwarf

Timescale of the solar system *above*
Taking the vertical 12 o'clock position as the time when the Sun and solar system were created (illustration 1 in the main sequence, above left) the present time appears at about the 1 o'clock position. By half-past two the Sun will flare up and consume its inner planets, thereafter dying a slow death.

star (above), leaving behind a cloud of fragments. These then coalesced into the planets as we know them today, having organized themselves into heliocentric orbits (above). Few subscribe to this theory now.

10 The solar system today is made up of the Sun (which is the central remnant of the original cloud), the nine principal planets, of which four are giants, and various smaller bodies. The Sun's rate of rotation has been considerably reduced, and the interplanetary material is largely restricted to the main plane of the system.

13 The expansion of the Sun will continue, with the hydrogen-burning region approaching the surface. After 600 million years, the Sun will be fifty times its present diameter. It will have become a red giant, engulfing the planets, including Earth.

11 When the supply of hydrogen at the Sun's core runs low, as will happen in perhaps 6000 million years, the region of the hydrogen-burning will move out towards the surface. The Sun will become larger, with a lower surface temperature but greater output.

12 The change in the Sun will continue as the hydrogen-burning region inside its globe moves further and further away from the core. The overall increase in energy output will raise the temperatures of the planets considerably, and those nearest to the Sun will become intolerably hot.

The lifespan of the Earth

The Earth was produced from the solar cloud (1-6 on main diagram). It had no regular form, but, as more and more material was drawn in, it began to assume a spherical shape (7-8).

When it had reached its present size (9), the Earth had a dense atmosphere; not the original hydrogen atmosphere but one produced by gas from the interior. Life had not started.

The Earth today (10), moving in a stable orbit, has an equable temperature and oxygen-rich atmosphere, so that it alone of all the planets in the solar system is suitable for life.

When the Sun nears the red giant stage (11-13), the Earth will be heated to an intolerable degree. The atmosphere will be driven off, the oceans will boil and life must come to an end.

As the Sun reaches the peak of its violence (14-15), it will swell out until the Earth is engulfed. Its life-expectation is probably no more than 8000 million years: its end is certain

The Solar System

The Sun is the controlling body of the solar system and is far more massive than all its planets combined. Even Jupiter, much the largest of the planets, has a diameter only about one-tenth that of the Sun. The solar system is divided into two main parts. The inner region includes four relatively small, solid planets: Mercury, Venus, the Earth and Mars. Beyond the orbit of Mars comes a wide gap in which move many thousands of small minor planets or asteroids, some of which are little more than rocks. Further out come the four giants: Jupiter, Saturn, Uranus and Neptune. Pluto, on the fringe of the system, is a curious little planet; it appears to be in a class of its own, but at present very little is known about it and even its size is a matter for conjecture. Maps of the solar system can be misleading in that they tend to give a false idea about distance. The outer planets are very widely separated. For example, Saturn is further away from Uranus than it is from the Earth.

The contrasting planets

The inner, or terrestrial, planets have some points in common, but a greater number of differences. Mercury, the planet closest to the Sun, has no atmosphere and that of Mars is very thin; but Venus, strikingly similar to the Earth in size and mass, has a dense atmosphere made up chiefly of carbon dioxide, and a surface temperature of over 400°C. The giant planets are entirely different. At least in their outer layers they are made up of gas, like a star; but, unlike a star, they have no light of their own, and shine only by reflecting the light of their star, the Sun. Several of the planets have moons. The Earth has one (or it may be our partner in a binary system), Jupiter has 14, Saturn 10 (discounting its rings), Uranus five and Neptune two. Mars also has two satellites, but these are less than 15 miles (24 km) in diameter and of a different type from the Earth's Moon. The Earth is unique in the solar system in having oceans on its surface and an atmosphere made up chiefly of nitrogen and oxygen. It is the only planet suited to life of terrestrial type. It is not now believed that life can exist on any other planet in the Sun's family, though it is still possible that some primitive vegetation may grow on Mars.

Observing the planets

Five of the planets, Mercury, Venus, Mars, Jupiter and Saturn, were known to the inhabitants of the Earth in very ancient times. They are starlike in aspect but easy to distinguish because, unlike the stars, they seem to wander slowly about the sky whereas the true stars appear to hold their position for century after century. The so-called proper motions of the stars are too slight to be noticed by the naked eye, but they can be measured by modern techniques. Mercury and Venus always appear to be in the same part of the sky as the Sun. Mercury is never prominent but Venus is dazzlingly bright, partly because its upper clouds are highly reflective and partly because it is close; it can come within 25,000,000 mi (40,000,000 km), only about 100 times as far as the Moon. Jupiter is generally very bright, as is Mars when it is well placed. Saturn is also conspicuous to the naked eye, but Uranus is only just visible and Neptune and Pluto are much fainter.

The Sun's active surface *right*

The structure of a star, such as the Sun, is immensely complex. The very concept of its surface is hard to define, and the size of the Sun depends on the wavelength of the light with which it is viewed. Using the 'hydrogen alpha' wavelength the bright surface of the Sun, known as the photosphere, appears as shown right, above. The surface, at about 6000°C, is dotted with light and dark patches as a result of the violent upcurrents of hotter gas and cooler areas between them. Larger, darker regions are sunspots (right), temporary but very large disturbances.

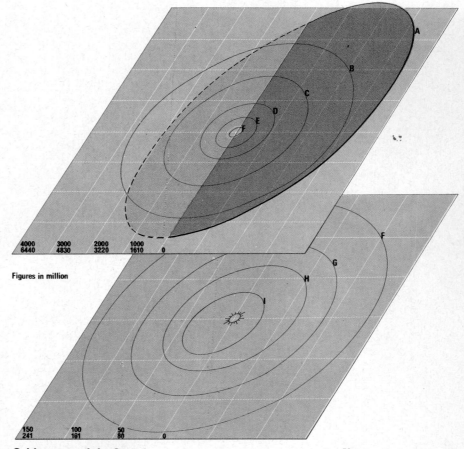

Figures in million

4000	3000	2000	1000	0
6440	4830	3220	1610	

150	100	50	0
241	161	80	

Orbits around the Sun *above*
The Sun's nine known planets, and the asteroids, describe heliocentric orbits in the same direction. But some planetary orbits are highly eccentric, while some asteroids are both eccentric and steeply inclined. The outermost planet, Pluto, passes within the orbit of Neptune, while one asteroid reaches almost to the radius of Saturn. Over 350 years ago Johannes Kepler showed that the planets do not move in perfect circles, and found that the line joining each planet to the Sun sweeps out a constant area in a given time. so that speed is greatest close to the Sun.

A	Pluto
B	Neptune
C	Uranus
D	Saturn
E	Jupiter
F	Mars
G	Earth
H	Venus
I	Mercury

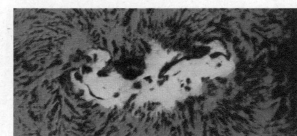

The Sun's structure *right*
The Sun is made up of highly dissimilar regions. This narrow sector includes the inner part of the corona (A) which, though very diffuse, has a temperature of some 1,000,000°C. Into it leap solar prominences, 'flames' thousands of miles long which arch along the local magnetic field from the chromosphere (B), the outer layer of the Sun proper, which covers the visible photosphere with a layer of variable, highly mobile and rarefied gas about 6000 mi (10000 km) thick. Inside the Sun the outer layer (C) of gas is in constant movement and transfers heat from the interior. Inner region D is thought to transfer energy mainly by radiation. The innermost zone of all (E), the conditions of which can only be surmised but are thought to include a temperature of some 14,000,000°C, sustains the energy of the Sun (and its planets) by continuous fusion of hydrogen into helium.

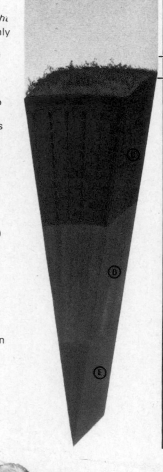

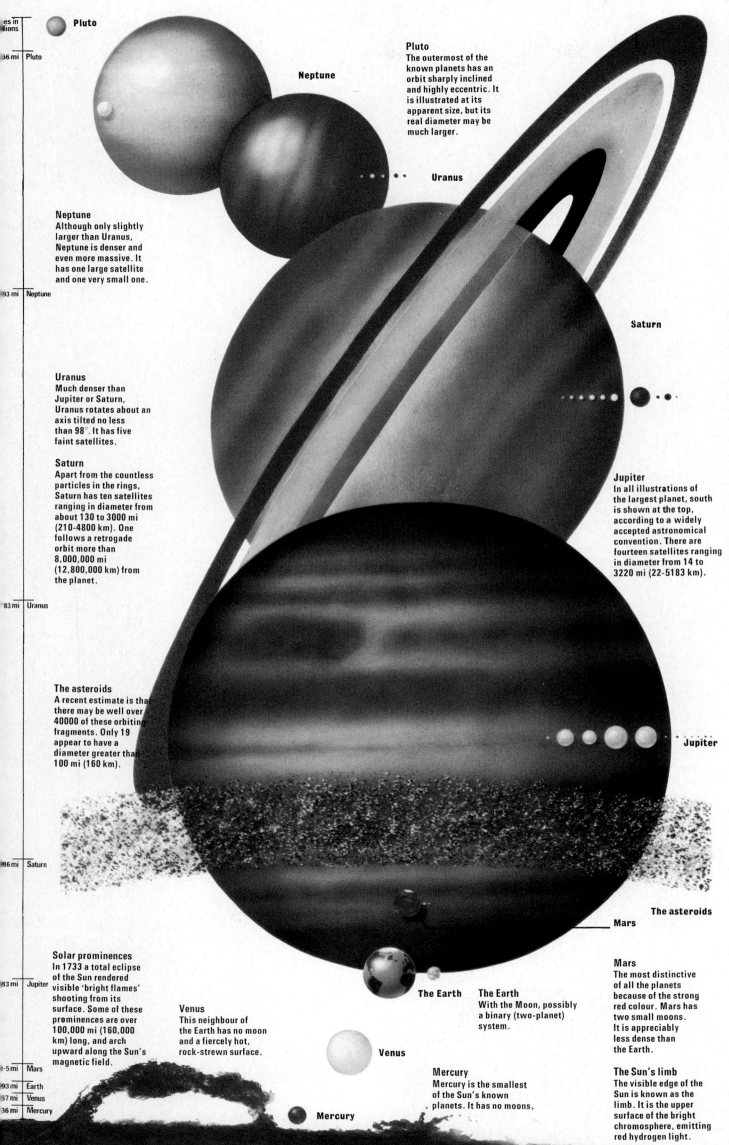

Pluto

Neptune

Pluto
The outermost of the known planets has an orbit sharply inclined and highly eccentric. It is illustrated at its apparent size, but its real diameter may be much larger.

Uranus

Neptune
Although only slightly larger than Uranus, Neptune is denser and even more massive. It has one large satellite and one very small one.

Saturn

Uranus
Much denser than Jupiter or Saturn, Uranus rotates about an axis tilted no less than 98°. It has five faint satellites.

Saturn
Apart from the countless particles in the rings, Saturn has ten satellites ranging in diameter from about 130 to 3000 mi (210-4800 km). One follows a retrograde orbit more than 8,000,000 mi (12,800,000 km) from the planet.

Jupiter
In all illustrations of the largest planet, south is shown at the top, according to a widely accepted astronomical convention. There are fourteen satellites ranging in diameter from 14 to 3220 mi (22-5183 km).

The asteroids
A recent estimate is that there may be well over 40000 of these orbiting fragments. Only 19 appear to have a diameter greater than 100 mi (160 km).

Jupiter

The asteroids

Mars

Solar prominences
In 1733 a total eclipse of the Sun rendered visible 'bright flames' shooting from its surface. Some of these prominences are over 100,000 mi (160,000 km) long, and arch upward along the Sun's magnetic field.

Venus
This neighbour of the Earth has no moon and a fiercely hot, rock-strewn surface.

The Earth

Venus

The Earth
With the Moon, possibly a binary (two-planet) system.

Mars
The most distinctive of all the planets because of the strong red colour. Mars has two small moons. It is appreciably less dense than the Earth.

Mercury
Mercury is the smallest of the Sun's known planets. It has no moons.

Mercury

The Sun's limb
The visible edge of the Sun is known as the limb. It is the upper surface of the bright chromosphere, emitting red hydrogen light.

The solar system *left*
The Sun is the major body in the solar system. It lies 30000 light-years from the center of our galaxy and takes 225 million years to complete one journey around it. There are nine planets and their satellites in the system, as well as comets and various minor bodies such as meteoroids. The diagram on the left shows the upper limb of the Sun (bottom) and the main constituent members of the solar system very greatly condensed into a smaller space. To indicate the amount of the radial compression, the limb of the Sun is drawn for a near-sphere of 5 ft (1.52 m) diameter. On this scale the Earth would be about 420 ft (127 m) away and the outermost planet Pluto, no less than 3 mi (4.9 km) distant.

Pluto, discovered in 1930, has a very eccentric orbit, with a radius varying between 2766 and 4566 million mi (4500 and 7400 million kilometers). Being so far from the Sun, it is extremely cold, and probably has no atmosphere.

Neptune, discovered in 1846, has a diameter of 31500 mi (50700 km) and is made up of gas, although little is known of its interior. It orbits the Sun once in 164¾ years. Seen through binoculars it is a small bluish disk.

Uranus, discovered in 1781, is apparently similar to Neptune, but less massive. Although faintly visible to the naked eye, even large telescopes show little detail upon its greenish surface.

Saturn is the second largest planet, its equatorial diameter being 75100 mi (122,300 km). Visually it is unlike any other heavenly body, because of its equatorial system of rings made up of particles of various sizes. The planet itself is less dense than water and at least its outer layers are gaseous.

Jupiter, the largest planet, has an equatorial diameter of 88700 mi (142,750 km), but its rapid spin, once every 9¾ hours, makes it very flattened at the poles. It appears to have cloud belts, possibly of liquid ammonia, and various spots, of which the great red spot seems to be semi-permanent.

The asteroids, a mass of apparent planetary material ranging in size from dust up to one lump about as large as the British Isles, orbit mainly between Mars and Jupiter, though some have eccentric orbits which approach the Earth.

Mars is about 4200 mi (6760 km) in diameter. It has a thin atmosphere, mainly of carbon dioxide, and its surface is pitted with Moon-like craters. It is not thought today that the planet contains any life.

The Earth/Moon system is today regarded as a double planet rather than a planet and satellite. The Moon has an average distance from Earth of 239,000 mi (385,000 km) and it is now known that it has never contained life.

Venus is almost the twin of the Earth in size and mass. It is too hot to contain life, and its very dense atmosphere is mainly carbon dioxide. It has a 'year' of 224¾ Earth days, and it spins on its axis once every 243 Earth days.

Mercury, the innermost planet, is only about 3000 mi (4800 km) in diameter, and has lost whatever atmosphere it had. Like Venus it shows phases, but it is always close to the Sun when viewed from the Earth and cannot be seen clearly.

es in
lions

36 mi | Pluto

93 mi | Neptune

83 mi | Uranus

86 mi | Saturn

83 mi | Jupiter

5 mi | Mars

93 mi | Earth
67 mi | Venus
36 mi | Mercury

Earth's Companion: The Moon

The Moon is our companion in space. Its mean distance from the Earth is less than a quarter of a million miles – it varies between 221,460 miles (356,410 km) and 252,700 miles (406,685 km) – and it was the first world other than our Earth to come within the range of man's space probes. At first mere masses, these then became instrument packages and finally spacecraft carrying men. With their aid our knowledge of the Moon has been vastly increased in the past decade. Astronauts Neil Armstrong and Edwin Aldrin made the first human journey to the lunar surface in July 1969, and the Moon has since been subjected to detailed and direct investigation.

The mean diameter of the Moon is 2158 miles (3473 km), and its mass is 1/81st as much as that of the Earth. Despite this wide difference the ratio is much less than that between other planets and their moons, and the Earth/Moon system is now widely regarded as a double planet rather than as a planet and satellite. The Moon's mean density is less than that of the Earth, and it may lack a comparable heavy core. Escape velocity from the lunar surface is only 1.5 mi/sec (2.4 km/sec), and this is so low that the Moon has lost any atmosphere it may once have had. To Earth life it is therefore an extremely hostile world. Analysis of lunar rock brought back to Earth laboratories and investigated by Soviet probes on the Moon has so far revealed no trace of any life. The Moon appears to have always been sterile.

Much of the surface of the Moon comprises large grey plains, mis-called 'mare' (seas), but most of it is extremely rough. There are great ranges of mountains, isolated peaks and countless craters which range from tiny pits up to vast enclosures more than 150 miles (240 km) in diameter. Many of the craters have central mountains or mountain-groups. Some of

Full Moon *below*
This striking photograph was taken by the *Apollo 11* astronauts in July 1969. It shows parts of both the Earth-turned and far hemispheres. The dark plain near the centre is the Mare Crisium.

the larger craters show signs of having been produced by volcanic action, while others appear to have resulted from the impacts of meteorites.

The Moon rotates slowly, performing one complete turn on its axis every 27.3 days. This is the same as its period of revolution around the Earth, so it always presents the same face to us. But in October 1959 the Soviet probe *Lunik 3* photographed the hidden rear hemisphere and it has since been mapped in detail. It contains no large 'seas'. The appearance of the lunar surface depends strongly on the angle at which it is viewed and the direction of solar illumination. In the photograph on the right, taken from a height of about 70 miles (115 km) with the Earth having once more come into full view ahead, the lunar surface looks deceptively smooth; in fact, there is practically no level ground anywhere in the field of vision. The lunar horizon is always sharply defined, because there is no atmosphere to cause blurring or distortion. For the same reason, the sky seen from the Moon is always jet black.

Earthrise *above*
This view of the Earth rising was visible to the crew of
Apollo 10 in May 1969 as they orbited the Moon 70 miles
(115 km) above the surface. They had just come round
from the Moon's rear hemisphere.

Eclipses

Once regarded as terrifying actions of angry gods,
eclipses are today merely useful. They provide a
different view of the Sun and Moon that opens up
fresh information. In a lunar eclipse the Earth passes
directly between the Sun and Moon; in a solar eclipse
the Moon passes between Sun and Earth. Both the
Earth and Moon constantly cast a shadow comprising
a dark inner cone surrounded by a region to which
part of the sunlight penetrates. A body passing
through the outer shadow experiences a partial
eclipse, while the inner cone causes a total eclipse in
which all direct sunlight is cut off.

A total solar eclipse is magnificent. The bright star
is blocked out by a black Moon, but around it the
Sun's atmosphere flashes into view. The pearly
corona of thin gas can be seen extending a million
miles from the Sun. Closer to the surface huge
'prominences' of red hydrogen leap into space and
curve back along the solar magnetic field. In a partial
solar eclipse these things cannot be seen, while in a
total eclipse caused by the Moon at its greatest
distance from Earth a ring of the Sun is left visible.
As the Moon's orbit is not in the same plane as the
Earth's, total solar eclipses occur very rarely, on
occasions when the tip of the Moon's dark shadow
crosses the Earth as a spot 169 miles (272 km) wide.

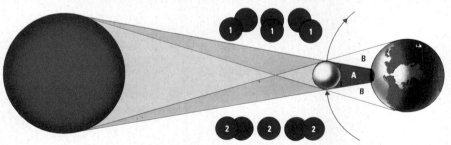

Eclipses *left and below*
When the Moon passes in
front of the Sun as in
sequence 1 its shadow B
causes a partial solar
eclipse (below, left, taken
21 November 1966).
But in the case of sequence
2, shadow cone A gives a
total eclipse (below, right,
15 February 1961).

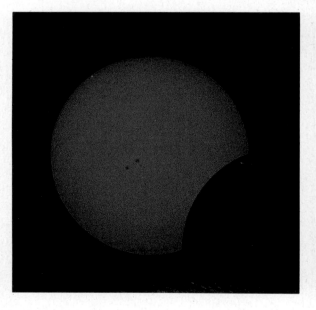

Anatomy of the Earth

A fundamental mystery that still confronts science even today is the detailed internal structure of the planet on which we live. Although Jules Verne's intrepid Professor Otto Lindenbrock was able to journey to the centre of the Earth, this is one scientific fantasy that will never be achieved. The deepest boreholes and mines do little more than scratch the surface and so, deprived of direct observation, the geologist is forced to rely almost entirely on indirect evidence to construct his picture of the Earth's anatomy. In spite of these drawbacks, he can outline with some confidence the story of the planet's development from the time of its formation as a separate body in space some 4550 million years ago.

Since that time the Earth has been continuously evolving. The crust, mantle and inner core developed during its first 1000 million years, but there is only scant evidence of how they did so. Probably the original homogenous mass then partly or completely melted, whereupon gravitational attraction caused the densest material to form a part-liquid, part-solid central core overlain by the less dense mantle. The extremely thin outermost layer of 'scum' began to form at an early stage and as long ago as 3500 million years parts of it had reached almost their present state. But most of the crust evolved in a complex way through long-term cyclic changes spanning immense periods of time. The evidence of today's rocks can be interpreted in different ways; for example, the core, mantle and crust could have separated out quickly at an early stage or gradually over a longer period.

Today's restless Earth

Many of the changes which have taken place in the Earth's structure and form have been very gradual. For example, although it may well be that our planet has been getting larger (as illustrated below), the rate of increase in radius has been no more rapid than 2½ inches (65 mm) per century. But this does not alter the fact that the Earth is very far from being a mere inert sphere of matter. Although it is not possible faithfully to portray it, almost the whole globe is at brilliant white heat. If the main drawing were true to life it would contain no colour except for a thin band, about as thick as cardboard, around the outer crust in which the colour would change from white through yellow and orange to red. With such high temperatures the interior of the Earth is able to flow under the influence of relatively small differences in density and stress. The result is to set up convection currents which are now believed to be the main driving force behind the formation of mountain ranges and the drifting apart of continents. But the fact remains that our knowledge of the interior of our planet is derived almost entirely from indirect evidence, such as the passage of earthquake shock waves through the mantle. Direct exploration is confined to the surface and to boreholes which so far have never penetrated more than about five miles (8 km) into the crust. It is difficult to imagine how man could ever devise experiments that would greatly enhance and refine his knowledge of the Earth's interior. Indeed, he knows as much about the Moon and other much more distant heavenly bodies as he does about the Earth below a depth of a mere 20 miles (32 km).

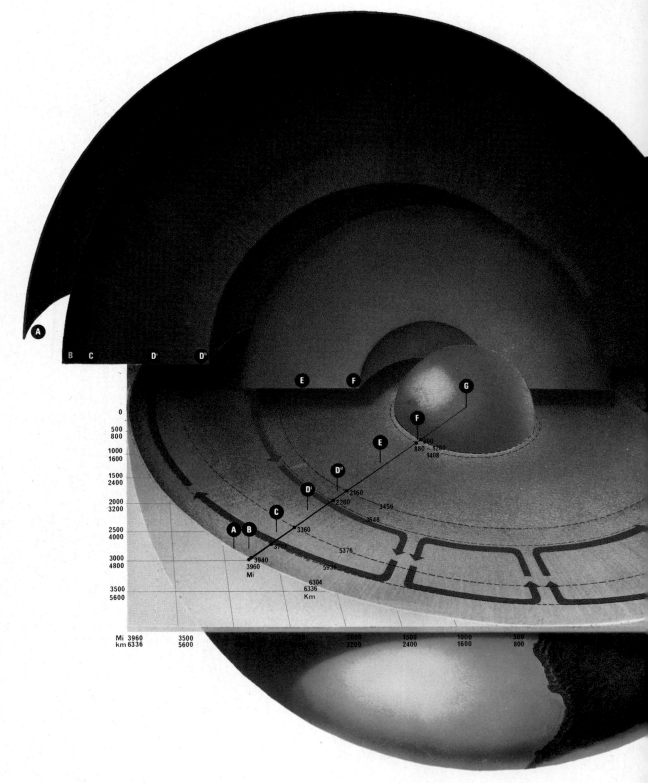

The crust (A)
This varies in thickness from 25 miles (40 km) in continental regions, where it is largely granitic, to 3 miles (5 km) under the oceans, where it is basaltic.

The upper mantle (B, C)
From the crust down to 375 miles (600 km), this layer is divided into an upper and a lower zone with differing P wave speeds.

The lower mantle (D1, D2)
Made of peridotite, as is the upper mantle, this zone extends down to a depth of 1800 miles (2900 km). P wave speeds increase still further.

The outer core (E, F)
Largely iron and nickel, this molten zone reaches to 2900 miles (4700 km). Dynamo action of convection currents may cause the Earth's magnetic field.

Not a true sphere *below*
The Earth's shape is controlled by equilibrium between inward gravitational attraction and outward centrifugal force. This results in the average radius at the equator of 3963 miles (6378 km) slightly exceeding that at the poles of 3950 miles (6356 km).

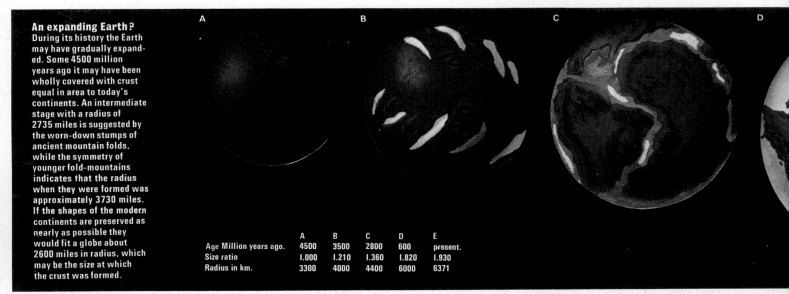

An expanding Earth?
During its history the Earth may have gradually expanded. Some 4500 million years ago it may have been wholly covered with crust equal in area to today's continents. An intermediate stage with a radius of 2735 miles is suggested by the worn-down stumps of ancient mountain folds, while the symmetry of younger fold-mountains indicates that the radius when they were formed was approximately 3730 miles. If the shapes of the modern continents are preserved as nearly as possible they would fit a globe about 2600 miles in radius, which may be the size at which the crust was formed.

	A	B	C	D	E
Age Million years ago.	4500	3500	2800	600	present.
Size ratio	1.000	1.210	1.360	1.820	1.930
Radius in km.	3300	4000	4400	6000	6371

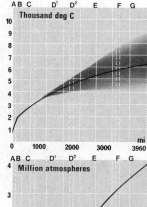

Temperature *left*
Temperature inside the Earth increases with depth, initially at a rate of 48°C per mile (30°C/km) so that 60 miles (100 km) down it is white hot. The rate of increase then falls, and the shaded area indicates how uncertain is man's knowledge at great depths.

Pressure *left*
This likewise increases with depth. Only 200 miles (320 km) down it reaches 100,000 atmospheres, 1200 times the pressure at the deepest point in the ocean. A change of state at the discontinuity between the mantle and core shows as a kink on the graph.

O₂	OXYGEN	
Si	SILICON	
Al	ALUMINIUM	
Fe	IRON	
Ni	NICKEL	
Co	COBALT	
Mg	MAGNESIUM	
Ca	CALCIUM	
Na	SODIUM	
K	POTASSIUM	

Key: O₂ OXYGEN, Si SILICON, Al ALUMINIUM, Fe IRON, Ni NICKEL, Co COBALT, Mg MAGNESIUM, Ca CALCIUM, Na SODIUM, K POTASSIUM

Chemical composition *above*
The crust is made of mainly light elements and has relatively low density. Towards the base of the crust the composition is probably richer in iron and magnesium. The mantle is principally metallic and the core is predominantly of iron and nickel.

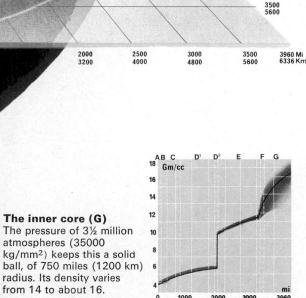

The inner core (G)
The pressure of 3½ million atmospheres (35000 kg/mm²) keeps this a solid ball, of 750 miles (1200 km) radius. Its density varies from 14 to about 16.

Density *left*
Virtually all man's knowledge of the interior of the Earth stems from measuring the transit of earthquake waves. The resulting data indicate sharp increases in density at the boundaries of both the outer core and the 'solid' inner core, with several intermediate zones.

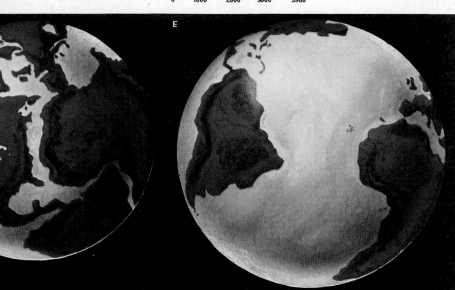

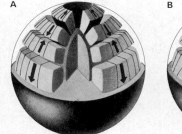 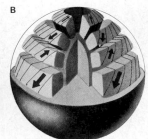

Convection currents
The fundamental pattern of movement in the mantle (A) is modified by the Earth's rotation (B) and also by friction between adjacent cells as shown in the main figure, below, in which core (X) and mantle (Y) are shown but crust (Z) is removed.

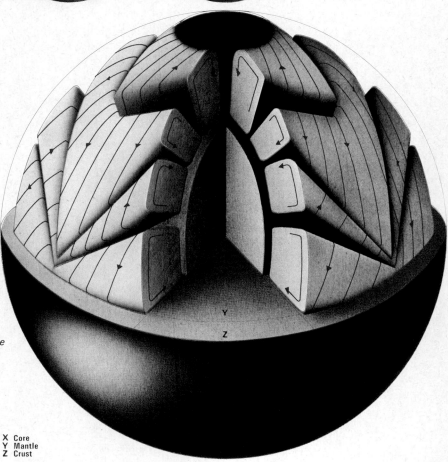

X Core
Y Mantle
Z Crust

Convection theory
Geologists and geophysicists are not unanimous on the question of whether there are convection currents present in the Earth's mantle or not, nor on the part these could play in providing the driving mechanism for major movements of the continents. Slow movement of 'solid' rocks can occur over long periods of time when the temperature is high and only relatively small density differences would be required to trigger them. Another matter for debate is whether convection is confined to the upper mantle or is continuous throughout the whole. It is not certain whether changes of physical state at different levels would constitute barriers to mantle-wide convection. The convection schemes above are highly schematic but could largely explain the formation of some of the major geosynclinal fold mountains in the crust over the past thousand million years. Large-scale convection current systems in the mantle could also be the driving force for sea floor spreading and the associated continental drift.

The watery Earth *below*
Almost three quarters of the Earth is covered by water. Basically the continents are rafts of relatively light crust 'floating' on generally denser oceanic crust. They comprise not only the visible land but also the adjacent continental shelves covered by shallow water. Oceanic crust underlies the deep sea platforms and ocean trenches. The areas of the major lands and seas (below, left) do not take into account the continental shelves but are the gross areas reckoned in terms of the land and water distribution at mean sea level. Extra area due to terrain is not included.

The watery Earth *right*
Key to numbered areas.

Oceans	Area (x1000) Sq mi	km²
1 Arctic	5541	14350
2 Pacific	63986	165750
3 Atlantic	31530	81660
4 Indian	28350	73430

Continents	Sq mi	km²
5 Americas	16241	42063
6 Europe (excluding USSR)	1903	4929
7 Asia (excluding USSR)	10661	27611
8 USSR	8649	22402
9 Africa	11683	30258
10 Oceania	3286	8510
11 Antarctica	5500	14245

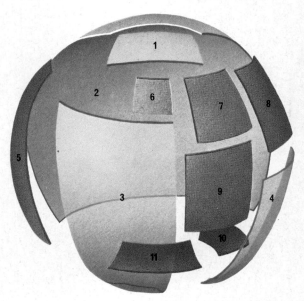

19

The Active Earth

Man's most powerful nuclear weapons pale into insignificance beside the violence of an earthquake or the destructive and indiscriminate force of a volcano. These cataclysmic phenomena frequently occur along the same belts of instability in the Earth's crust and are often only different manifestations of the same fundamental processes. About 800 volcanoes are known to have been active in historical times, and many are extremely active today. All the mid-ocean ridges are volcanic in origin, and many underwater eruptions occur along these submarine mountain ranges. Spectacular volcanic eruptions sometimes break the ocean surface, such as during the formation in 1963 of the island of Surtsey, south of Iceland (photograph, right). Some islands, such as Iceland itself, are the products of continued outpourings of lava along the crest of the mid-ocean ridge.

Oceanic earthquakes caused by sudden sea-floor displacements may result in tsunamis or giant sea waves. About 80 per cent of the shallow earthquakes and almost all deep ones take place along the belt around the Pacific. Clear evidence of the large scale movements of the mantle are provided by the zones within which earthquake shocks are generated along some Pacific island arc systems. These zones plunge down from sea-floor level to depths of 440 miles (700 km) beneath the adjacent continents and mark the positions of downward flow of the mantle convection currents (page 19). The corresponding upwelling regions lie along the mid-ocean ridges, where new basic volcanic material is continually being added to the ocean crust as outward movement takes place away from the ridges.

These sea-floor spreading movements act as 'conveyor belts' for the continents, and constitute the basic mechanism for the large displacements involved in continental drifting. Geological data confirm the former close fits of the margins of the reassembled continental jig-saw puzzle, and also corroborate the detailed palaeomagnetic evidence visible in today's rocks of the movements of the continents relative to the geographic poles.

Geysers
Ground water and mud heated by volcanic activity can lie on the surface as puddles and hot springs, rendered colourful by dissolved minerals, or be pumped out in the form of geysers. The latter are connected to extensive underground reservoirs in which steam pressure builds up above the hot water. Intermittently the system discharges high into the air.

Fissure eruption
In this type of eruption freely flowing molten basaltic material exudes from apertures forced in the crust. The surface crack may be several miles in length and the more or less horizontal flow has on occasion covered more than 200 square miles (500 km²).

Hawaiian-type eruption
In this case large, shallow cones, often containing lakes of molten lava, generally release gas and vapour in a relatively passive way. But sometimes glowing lava is expelled as a fine spray which in a high wind can be drawn out into fine threads called Pelée's hair.

Emissions
Incandescent lava issues from the main cone or from side vents, while dense vapours pour from every crevice. Water vapour is the main gaseous component, but nitrogen and sulphur dioxide are also important.

Layering
Most volcanoes have a history extending back thousands or even millions of years. Over this time the main cone has built up in many stratified layers, sometimes of contrasting types of lava. Each fresh eruption produces at least one additional layer.

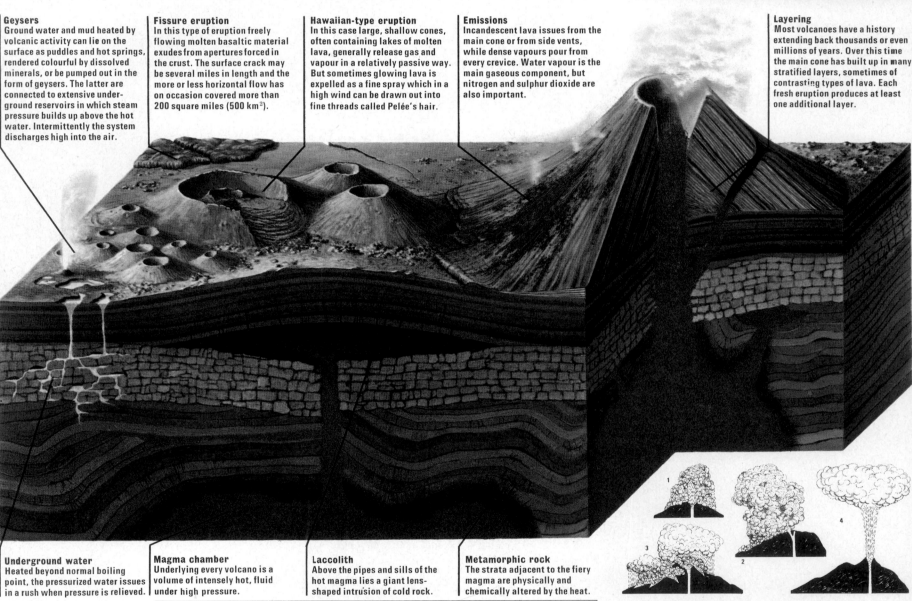

Underground water
Heated beyond normal boiling point, the pressurized water issues in a rush when pressure is relieved.

Magma chamber
Underlying every volcano is a volume of intensely hot, fluid under high pressure.

Laccolith
Above the pipes and sills of the hot magma lies a giant lens-shaped intrusion of cold rock.

Metamorphic rock
The strata adjacent to the fiery magma are physically and chemically altered by the heat.

Where the Earth seems active *right*
Although we live on a white-hot globe with a thin cool crust, the fierce heat and energy of the interior is manifest only along fairly clearly defined belts. Around the Pacific, volcanoes and earthquakes are frequent. Another belt traverses the mountains from south-east Asia through the Middle East to the Mediterranean. Every site is an external expression of activity within the crust and upper mantle. The underlying cause is a slow flowing of the rocks of the mantle in response to changes in temperature and density.

● Volcanoes
● Earthquake foci

Types of eruption *above*
Volcanic cones differ in both shape and activity. The Strombolian (1) erupts every few minutes or hours; the Peléan form (2) gives a hot avalanche; the Vesuvian (3) is a fierce upwards expulsion, while the Plinian (4) is the extreme form.

A caldera *left*
Expulsion of lava (A) from the magma chamber (B) may leave the central core (C) without support. A collapse results in a large, steep-sided caldera (D). The magma chamber may cool and solidify (E), allowing water to collect inside the caldera (F).

Earthquake *right*
Along lines of potential
movement, such as fault
planes, stresses may build
up over many years until
the breaking strength of
some part of the rock is
exceeded (A). A sudden
break occurs and the two
sides of the fault line
move, generating shock-
waves which travel
outwards in all directions
from the focus at the
point of rupture (B). The
point on the surface
directly above the focus is
the 'epicentre' (C). While
the fault movement reaches
its fullest extent, the
shockwaves reach the
surface (D). Far right the
aftermath of an earthquake.

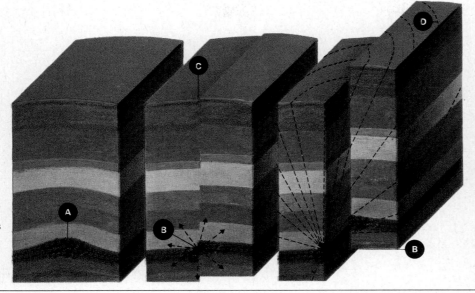

Destructive waves *right*
The Japanese, who have
suffered severely from
them, have given the name
tsunami to the terrifying
waves which follow
earthquakes. Their
character depends on the
cause. In the case of a
sudden rift and slump in
the ocean bed (A) the
wave at the surface is
initially a trough, which
travels away to both sides
followed by a crest and
subsequent smaller waves
(B). A fault causing a
sudden changed level of
sea bed (C) can generate
a tsunami that starts with a
crest (D). Travelling at
400 miles (650 km) per
hour or more the tsunami
arrives at a beach as a
series of waves up to
200 feet (60 m) high (E),
the 'trough first' variety
being heralded by a sudden
withdrawal of the ocean
from the shore. Warning
stations ring the Pacific
(far right) and the
concentric rings show
tsunamic travel time from
an earthquake site to
Hawaii at the centre.

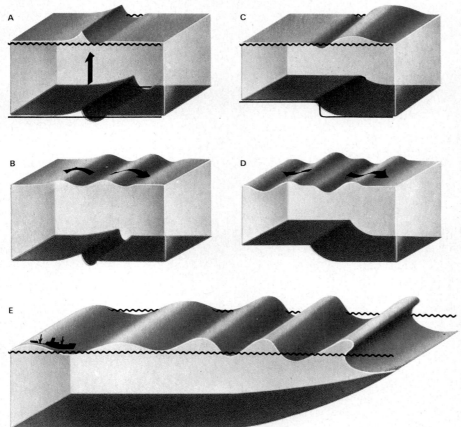

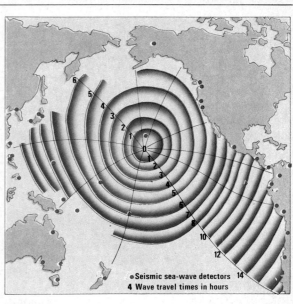

Tsunami warning *above*
Numerous seismographic warning stations around the
earthquake belt of the Pacific Ocean maintain a
continuous alert for earthquake shocks and for the
tsunami waves that may follow it. Possible recipients of
such waves plot a series of concentric rings, such as
these centred on the Hawaiian Islands, which show the
time in hours that would be taken for a tsunami to
travel from any earthquake epicentre. Aircraft and
satellites are increasingly helping to create a globally
integrated life-saving system.

Seismic waves *right*
An earthquake caused by
a sudden movement in the
crust at the focus (A)
sends out a pattern of
shock waves radiating like
ripples in a pond. These
waves are of three kinds.
Primary (P) waves (full
lines) vibrate in the
direction of propagation,
and thus are a rapid
succession of high and low
pressures. Secondary (S)
waves (broken lines),
which travel only 60 per
cent as fast, shake from
side to side. Long waves
(L) travel round the crust.
In a belt around the
world only waves of the
L-type occur, giving
rise to the concept of a
shadow zone (B and shaded
belt in inset at lower right).
But intermittent records of P
waves in this zone led
seismologists to the belief
that the Earth must have a
very dense fluid core (D, lower
drawing) capable of strongly
refracting P waves like a lens.
Seismic waves are almost
man's only source
of knowledge about
the Earth's interior.

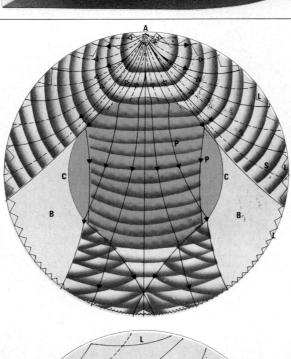

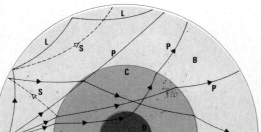

Seismology *right*
Seismic waves of all three
types (P, S and L) are
detected and recorded by
seismographs. Usually these
contain a sprung mass
which, when an earthquake
shock passes, stays still
while the rest of the
instrument moves. Some
seismographs detect
horizontal waves (A) while
others detect vertical ones
(B). The pen in the instrument leaves a distinctive
trace (P-S-L). P (primary)
waves are a succession of
rarefactions and compres-
sions, denoted by the packing
of the dots; S (secondary)
waves are a sideways
shaking, shown here in
plan view.

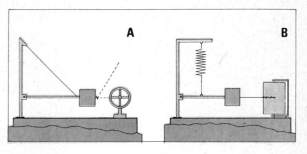

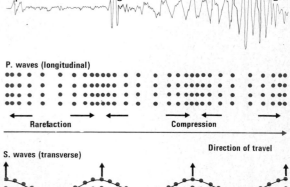

P. waves (longitudinal)

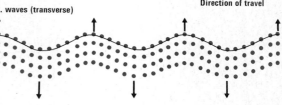

S. waves (transverse)

21

The Evolution of Land and Sea

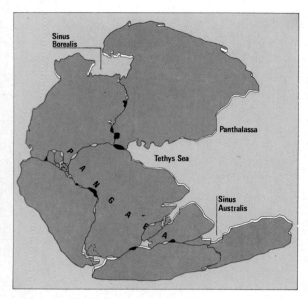

Pangaea *above*
About 200 million years ago there was only a single land mass on Earth, named Pangaea. The map shows how today's continents can be fitted together, with the aid of a computer, at the edge of the continental shelf at a depth of 1000 fathoms (6000 ft, 1830 m).

Although land and water first appeared on the Earth's surface several thousand million years before anyone could be there to watch, modern man has a very good idea of how it came about. The Earth's gravitational field caused the lighter, more volatile elements gradually to move outwards through the mantle and form a solid crust on the surface. By far the largest proportion of material newly added to the crust is basaltic volcanic rock derived from partial melting of the mantle beneath; in fact the oceanic crust which underlies the Earth's great water areas is made of almost nothing else. So the earliest crust to form was probably volcanic and of basaltic composition.

Air and water appear
The earliest records of the existence of an atmosphere of air and a hydrosphere of water are to be found in sediments laid down some 3300 million years ago from the residue of erosion of previously existing rocks. These sediments could not have been formed without atmospheric weathering, water transport and water deposition. The atmosphere was probably originally similar to the fumes which today issue from volcanoes and hot springs and which are about three-quarters water vapour. Once formed, the primitive atmosphere and oceans could erode the crust to produce vast layers of sediments of new chemical compositions. Gradually the oceans deepened and the land took on a more varied form. Convection in the mantle produced mountain ranges which in turn eroded to generate new sedimentary rocks. The ceaseless cycles of growth and decay had started, causing continually changing patterns of seas, mountains and plains. And in the past few years man has discovered how the continents and oceans have developed over the most recent 200 million years of geological time. The results of this research are to be seen in the maps on this page.

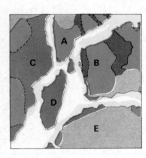

Another arrangement *left*
India (A) may have been separated by Australia (B) from East Antarctica (E) rather more than 200 million years ago on the evidence of today's geological deposition zones. Africa (C) and Madagascar (D) complete this convincing fit.

Migrant Australia *left*
By measuring the direction of magnetization of old Australian rocks it is possible to trace successive positions of that continent. It appears to have moved across the world and back. These movements cover a period throughout the past 1000 million years.

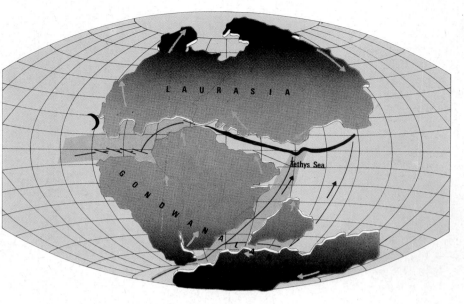

180 million years ago
At this time the original Pangaea land mass had just begun to break up. The continents first split along the lines of the North Atlantic and Indian Oceans. North America separated from Africa and so did India and Antarctica. The Tethyan Sea, between Africa and Asia, closed somewhat, and the super continents of Laurasia to the north and Gondwanaland to the south became almost completely separated. In effect the Earth possessed three super landmasses, plus an India that had already begun to move strongly northward.

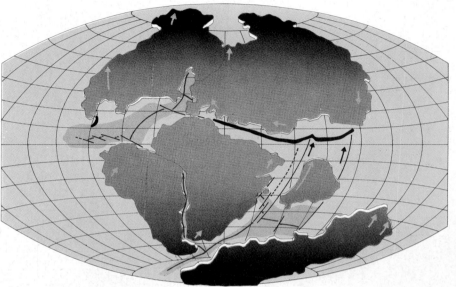

135 million years ago
After a further 45 million years of drifting, the world map had still not taken on a form that looks familiar today. But the two original splits, the North Atlantic and the Indian Ocean, have continued to open out. The North Atlantic is now about 600–650 miles (1000 km) wide. Rifting is extending towards the split which opened up the Labrador Sea and this will eventually separate Greenland from North America. India has firmly launched itself on its collision course with the southern coast of Asia, which is still 2000 miles (3200 km) away.

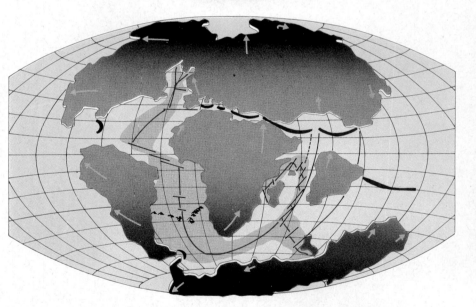

65 million years ago
Some 135 million years after the start of the drifting process the continents have begun to assume their present configuration. South America has at last separated from Africa and in Gondwanaland only Australia and Antarctica have yet to move apart. A continuation of the North Atlantic rifting will shortly bring about another big separation in Laurasia. Greenland will move apart from Europe and eventually North America will separate completely from the Eurasian landmass. The pink area shows the extent of the crustal movements.

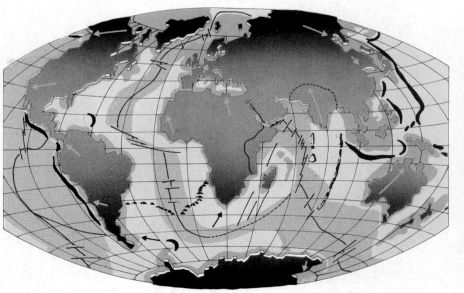

Today's positions
The Atlantic is now a wide ocean from Arctic to Antarctic, the Americas have joined and Australia has separated from Antarctica and moved far to the north. India has likewise moved northwards and its collision with Asia and continued movement has given rise to the extensive uplift of the Himalayas. All the continents which formerly made up the great land mass of Pangaea are now separated by wide oceans. Comparison of areas shows how much of India has been submerged by sliding underneath the crust of Asia (see facing page, far right).

Plate tectonics

This theory has revolutionized the way the Earth's crust – continents and oceans – is interpreted on a global scale. The crust is regarded as being made up of huge plates which converge or diverge along margins marked by earthquakes, volcanoes and other seismic activity. Major divergent margins are the mid-ocean ridges where molten lava forces its way out and wedges the plates apart. This causes vast regions of crust to move apart at a rate of an inch or two (some centimetres) per year. When sustained for up to 200 million years this means movements of thousands of miles or kilometres. The process can be seen in operation today in and around Iceland. Oceanic trenches are margins where the plates are moving together and the crust is consumed downwards. The overall result is for the crustal plates to move as relatively rigid entities, carrying the continents along with them as if they were on a giant conveyor belt. Over further considerable periods of geologic time this will markedly change today's maps.

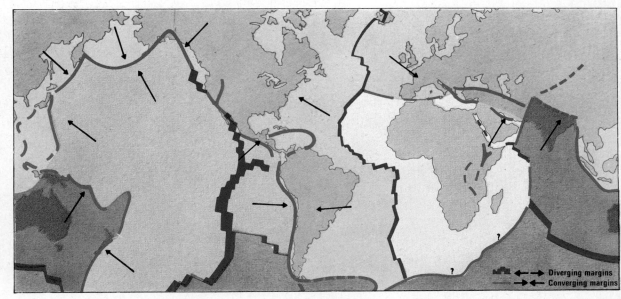

← → Diverging margins
→ ← Converging margins

Sea-floor spreading *left*
Arrows show how the lava flows on the ocean bed spread out on each side of a mid-ocean ridge. Evidence for such movement is provided by the fact the rock is alternately magnetized in opposing directions (coloured stripes).

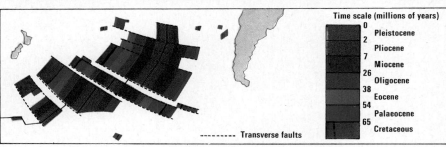

Time scale (millions of years)

0	
	Pleistocene
2	
	Pliocene
7	
	Miocene
26	
	Oligocene
38	
	Eocene
54	
	Palaeocene
65	
	Cretaceous

-------- Transverse faults

Plate movements
above and left
The Earth's crust is a series of large plates 'floating' on the fluid mantle. At their edges the plates are either growing or disappearing. Magnetic measurements in the S. Pacific (left) show rock ages on each side of the mid-ocean ridges.

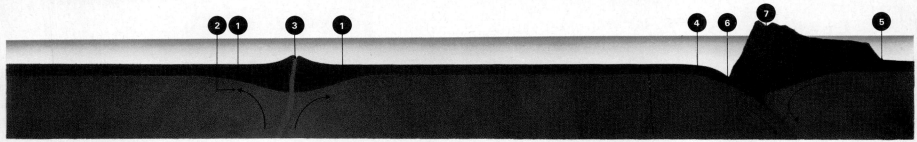

Plate movements in cross-section *above*
The basic mechanism of plate movements is illustrated above in simplified form with the vertical scale greatly exaggerated. This figure is explained in detail in both of the captions below.

Crustal divergence
above and right
The Earth's crust (1) behaves as a series of rigid plates which move on top of the fluid mantle (2). At their mating edges some of these plates are moving apart (3). This was the mechanism that separated North America (A) from Europe (B). The plates moved to the north and also away from each other under the influence of convection currents in the mantle (C). Between the land areas appeared an oceanic gap with a mid-ocean ridge (D) and lateral ridges (E). The movements continued for some 200 million years, fresh volcanoes being generated by igneous material escaping through the plate joint (F) to add to the lateral ridges which today cross the Atlantic (G). The volcanoes closest to the median line in mid-Atlantic are still young and active — as witness the scene on page 18 — whereas those nearer to the continents are old and extinct.

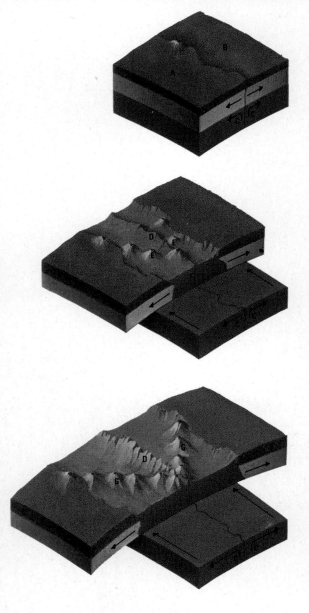

Crustal convergence
above and right
Diverging plate margins occur only in the centres of the major oceans (see map above) but plates are converging on both sea and land. Where an oceanic plate (4, above) is under-riding a continental plate (5) a deep ocean trench is the result (6). Such trenches extend around much of the Pacific; those around the north-west Pacific include the deepest on Earth where the sea bed is almost seven miles below the ocean surface. The continental margin is squeezed upwards to form mountains such as the Andes or Rockies (7). If continental masses converge, such as India (A, right) and Asia (B), the convection in the mantle (C) pulls the plates together so hard that the upper crust crumples (D). Sedimentary deposits between the plates (E) are crushed and squeezed out upwards (F), while the mantle on each side is turned downwards, one side being forced under the other (G). Continued movement causes gross deformation at the point of collision. The static or slow-moving crust is crushed and tilted, and giant young mountains (the Himalayas, H) are thrust upwards along the collision just behind the edge of the crumpled plate.

The Earth under the Sea

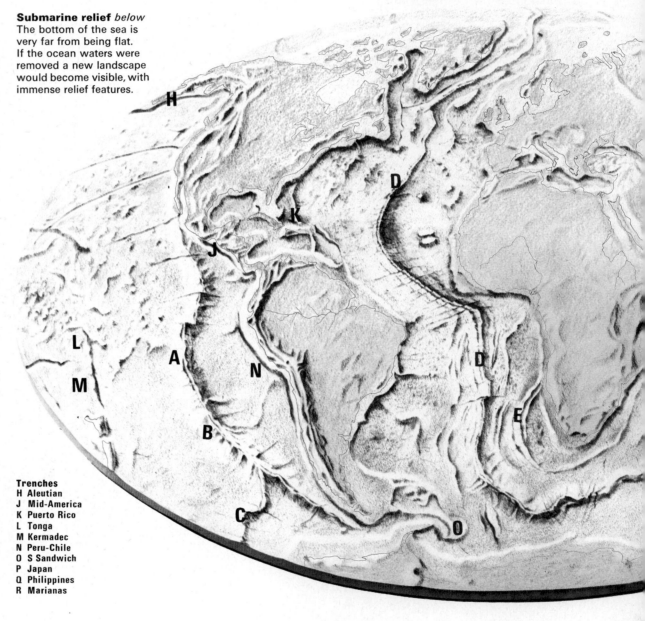

Comparison of drained areas. (A) and ocean areas (B)
Areas in million sq mls (black) million sq km (blue)

Indian Ocean 6·5 / 17
28·6 / 74
Atlantic Ocean 25·9 / 67
41·3 / 107
Pacific Ocean 69·5 / 180
6·9 / 18

a Shelf and slope
b Continental rise
c Ocean basin
d Volcano, volcanic ridge
e Rise and ridge
f Trench

9·1% 5·7% 5·4% 0·3%
49·2% 30·2%
19·4% 8·5% 2·1% 0·7%
38·0% 31·2%
13·1% 2·7% 2·5% 2·9%
43·0% 35·9%

The water planet *left*
From directly over Tahiti the Earth appears to be covered by water. The Pacific averages 2.5 miles (4 km) deep, with great mountains and trenches.

Ocean drainage *above*
The ratio between the areas of the oceans and the land they drain varies greatly. Many large rivers feed the Atlantic but few discharge into the Pacific.

Ocean proportions *above*
The major oceans show a similarity in the proportions of their submarine topography. By far the greatest areas contain deep plains with rises and ridges. More prominent features, the mid-ocean volcanic ridges and trenches, occupy much smaller areas. About one tenth of each ocean is continental shelf.

At present the sea covers about 71 per cent of the Earth's surface. But if the continents could be sliced away and put into the deep oceans to make a perfectly uniform sphere the sea would have an average depth of about 8000 feet (2500 m) over the whole planet. In the distant past the level of the sea has fluctuated violently. The main cause has been the comings and goings of the ice ages. Glaciers and ice-caps lock up enormous volumes of water and the advance and recession of ice has alternately covered the continental shelves with shallow seas and revealed them as dry land. If the Earth's present polar ice-caps and glaciers were to melt, the mean sea level would rise by about 200 feet (60 m), which would submerge half the world's population. Average depth of the sea is more than 12000 feet (3600 m), five times the average height of the land above sea level.

The deep oceans
Below the level of the continental shelf lies the deep ocean floor with great topographical contrasts ranging from abyssal plains at a depth of about 13000 feet (4 km) to towering submarine mountain ranges of the mid-ocean ridges which reach far up towards the surface. Great advances have recently been made in exploring the ocean floors which were previously unknown. Most of the ocean area is abyssal plain which extends over about 78 million square miles (200 million km²). But a more remarkable feature of the deep ocean is the almost continuous mid-ocean mountain range which sweeps 40000 miles (64000 km) around the globe and occasionally – as at Iceland – is seen above sea level in the form of isolated volcanic islands. The basic symmetry of the oceans is the central ridge flanked by abyssal plain sloping up to the continental shelves. On the deep floor sediments accumulate at a rate of 30–35 feet (10 m) per million years; they also build up more slowly at the central ridges. No ocean sediments have been found older than 150 million years, which suggests that the material which now makes up the floors of the deep oceans was formed comparatively recently. Exploration and detailed mapping of the ocean bed is still in its infancy.

Submarine landscape
Principal features of the bed of the oceans can be grouped into a much smaller space than they would actually occupy. Although each ocean differs in detail, all tend to conform to the general layout of a central volcanic ridge (which can break the surface in places), broad abyssal plains with occasional deep trenches and shallow slopes and shelves bordering the continents.

Submarine relief *below*
The bottom of the sea is very far from being flat. If the ocean waters were removed a new landscape would become visible, with immense relief features.

Trenches
H Aleutian
J Mid-America
K Puerto Rico
L Tonga
M Kermadec
N Peru-Chile
O S Sandwich
P Japan
Q Philippines
R Marianas

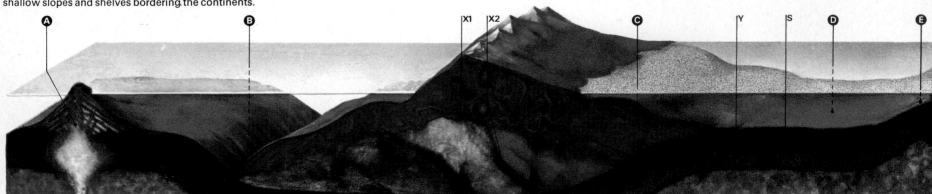

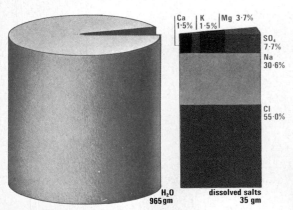

	Ca 1·5%	K 1·5%	Mg 3·7%
			SO₄ 7·7%

Ca 1·5% | K 1·5% | Mg 3·7%
SO₄ 7·7%
Na 30·6%
Cl 55·0%

H₂O 965 gm   dissolved salts 35 gm

Composition of sea-water *above*
The water of the Earth's oceans is an exceedingly complex solution of many organic and inorganic salts, together with suspended solid matter. In a typical kilogramme of sea-water there are 35 grammes of chlorine, sodium, sulphates, magnesium, potassium and calcium.

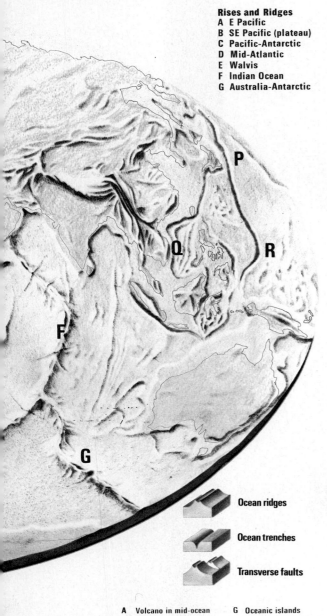

Rises and Ridges
A E Pacific
B SE Pacific (plateau)
C Pacific-Antarctic
D Mid-Atlantic
E Walvis
F Indian Ocean
G Australia-Antarctic

◻ Ocean ridges

◻ Ocean trenches

◻ Transverse faults

A Volcano in mid-ocean ridge
B Deep oceanic trench
C Continental shelf
D Abyssal plain
E Mid-ocean ridge
F Guyots
G Oceanic islands
X1 Upper granitic crust and sediments
X2 Lower granitic crust
Y Basaltic crust
Z Mantle

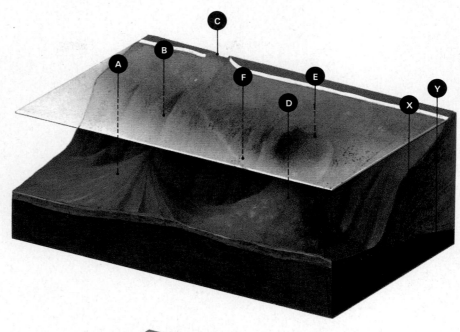

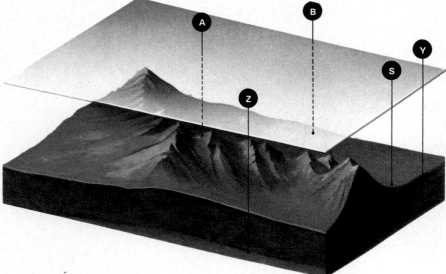

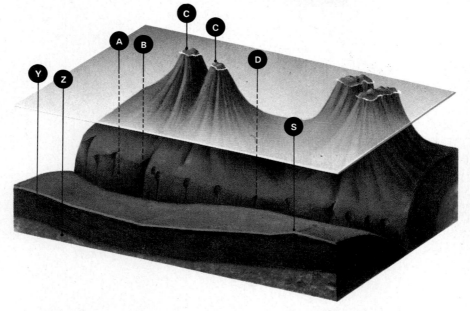

Continental shelf *left*
The submerged continental fringes lie at depths to about 450 feet (135 m) and have a total area of some 11 million square miles (28 million km²). The surface of the land is eroded and carried by rivers to form sedimentary deposits on the shelf. At its outer margin it slopes down to the abyssal plains of the deep ocean at about 2½ miles (4 km) below sea level.

A Scree fan
B Gully opposite river
C River delta
D Slump (turbidite) mass
E Scar left by (D)
F Continental slope
X Granite
Y Basalt

Mid-ocean ridge *left*
Well-marked ridges are found along the centres of the major oceans and form an extensive worldwide system. The central part of the ridge may have a double crest with an intervening deep trough forming a rift valley, or there may be several ridges. They are volcanic in nature and along them is generated new basaltic ocean crust. The volcanoes become progressively younger as the mid-ocean ridge is approached.

A Mid-ocean ridge
B Abyssal plain
S Ocean floor sediments
Y Basalt crust
Z Mantle

Oceanic trench *left*
These long and relatively narrow depressions are the deepest portions of the oceans, averaging over 30,000 feet (10 km) below sea level. Around the Pacific they lie close to the continental margins and in the western Pacific are often associated with chains of volcanic islands. Some trenches are slowly becoming narrower as the ocean floor plates on either side converge.

A Trench wall
B Canyon
C Island arc
D Trench
S Sediment
Y Basalt
Z Mantle

A sinking island *below*
A pre-requisite to the formation of a coral atoll is an island that is becoming submerged by the sea. Such islands are formed by the peaks of the volcanic mountains which are found on the flanks of the great mid-oceanic ridges.

Coral grows *below*
Millions of polyps, small marine animals, secrete a substance which forms the hard and often beautiful coral. The structure grows round the island in shallow water and extends above the sinking island to form an enclosed and shallow salt-water lagoon.

The mature atoll *below*
Continued submergence of the volcano results in the disappearance of the original island, but the upward growth of the coral continues unabated. The reef is then worn away by the sea and the coral debris fills in the central part of the lagoon.

A guyot *below*
Eventually the coral atoll itself begins to sink beneath the ocean surface. By this time the lagoon is likely to have become completely filled in by debris eroded from the reef, and the result is a submerged flat island, known as a guyot.

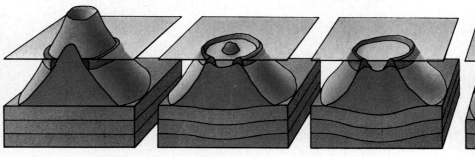

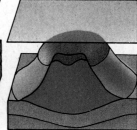

The Atmosphere

A thin coating *left*
The protective atmospheric shell around the Earth is proportionately no thicker than the skin of an apple. Gravity compresses the air so that half its mass lies within 3.5 miles (5.5 km) of the surface and all the weather within an average depth of 12 miles (20 km).

Space exploration has enabled man to stand back and take a fresh look at his Earth. Even though we, like all Earth life, have evolved to suit the Earth environment, we can see today as never before how miraculous that environment is. And by far the most important single factor in determining that environment is the atmosphere.

The Earth orbits round the Sun in a near-total vacuum. So rarefied is the interplanetary medium that it contains little heat energy, but the gas molecules that are present are vibrating so violently that their individual temperature is over 2000°C. And the surface of the Sun, at some 6000°C, would melt almost everything on the surface of the Earth, while the tenuous chromosphere around the Sun is as hot as 1,000,000°C. From the chromosphere, and from millions of other stars and heavenly objects, come radio waves. Various places in the universe, most of them far beyond the solar system, send us a penetrating kind of radiation known as cosmic rays. The Earth also receives gamma rays, X-rays and ultraviolet radiation, and from the asteroid belt in the solar system (see pages 14-15) comes a stream of solid material. Most of these are small micrometeorites, no more than flying specks, but the Earth also receives meteors and meteorites.

A meteorite is a substantial mass that strikes the Earth; fortunately, none has yet hit in a populous area. Apart from these extremely rare objects, every other influence from the environment that would be dangerous to life is filtered out by the atmosphere. Meteors burn up through friction as they plunge into the upper parts of the atmosphere. To avoid burning up in the same way, spacecraft designed to return to the Earth from lunar or interplanetary flight require a special re-entry shield.

Much of the ultraviolet radiation is arrested many miles above the Earth and creates ionized layers known as the ionosphere which man uses to reflect radio waves. Much of the infra-red (heat) radiation is likewise absorbed, lower down in the atmosphere, and most of the cosmic radiation is broken up by collisions far above the ground into such particles as 'mu-mesons'. Only a few cosmic rays, harmless radio waves and visible light penetrate the blanket of air to reach the planetary surface and its teeming life.

Credit for our vital atmosphere rests with the Earth's gravitational attraction, which both prevents the molecules and atoms in the atmosphere from escaping into space and also pulls them down tightly against the Earth. As a result nearly all the atmosphere's mass is concentrated in a very thin layer; three-quarters of it lies below 29000 feet (8840 m), the height of Mount Everest. The highest-flying aircraft, 19 miles (30 km) up, are above 99 per cent of the atmosphere. The total weight of the atmosphere is of the order of 5000 million million tons. In the lower parts are some 17 million million tons of water vapour.

The water vapour plays a great part in determining the weather on Earth, the only way in which the atmosphere consciously affects daily human life. All the weather is confined to the lower parts of the atmosphere below the tropopause. In this region, called the troposphere, temperature falls away sharply with increasing altitude. The Sun heats up the Earth's surface, water is evaporated from the surface of the oceans and an immensely complicated pattern of global and local weather systems is set up. Every part of the air in the troposphere is in motion. Sometimes the motion is so slow as to be barely perceptible, while on other occasions, or at the same time in other places, the air roars over the surface with terrifying force at speeds of 200 miles (320 km) per hour or more. It erodes the land, lashes the surface with rain and clogs cold regions with snow. Yet it is man's shield against dangers, an ocean of air without which we could not exist.

Characteristics of the atmosphere *right*
Basically the Earth's atmosphere consists of a layer of mixed gases covering the surface of the globe which, as a result of the Earth's gravitational attraction, increases in density as the surface is approached. But there is very much more to it than this. Temperature, composition and physical properties vary greatly through the depth of the atmosphere. The Earth's surface is assumed to lie along the bottom of the illustration, and the various major regions of the atmosphere—which imperceptibly merge into each other—are indicated by the numbers on the vertical scale on the facing page.

Exosphere (1)
This rarefied region is taken to start at a height of some 400 miles (650 km) and to merge above into the interplanetary medium. Atomic oxygen exists up to 600 mi (1000 km); from there up to about 1500 mi (2400 km) helium and hydrogen are approximately equally abundant, with hydrogen becoming dominant above 1500 mi. The highest auroras are found in this region. Traces of the exosphere extend out to at least 5000 mi (8000 km).

Ionosphere (2)
This contains electrically conducting layers capable of reflecting radio waves and thus of enabling radio signals to be received over great distances across the Earth. The major reflecting layers, designated D, E, F1 and F2, are at the approximate heights shown. Meteors burn up brightly at heights of around 100 mi (160 km). Charged particles coming in along the lines of force of the Earth's magnetic field produce aurorae in the ionosphere at high latitudes, some of them of the corona type with a series of radial rays; and the ionosphere's structure alters from day to night and according to the influence of the solar wind and incoming streams of other particles and radiation.

Stratosphere (3)
This lies above the tropopause which varies in altitude from about 10 mi (16 km) over the equator to just below 7 mi (11 km) in temperate latitudes. The lower stratosphere has a constant temperature of -56°C up to 19 mi (30 km); higher still the 'mesosphere' becomes warmer again. One of the vital properties of the stratosphere is its minute ozone content which shields the Earth life from some harmful short-wave radiations which, before the Earth's atmosphere had developed, penetrated to the surface.

Troposphere (4)
Within this relatively very shallow layer is concentrated about 80 per cent of the total mass of the atmosphere, as well as all the weather and all the Earth's life. The upper boundary of the troposphere is the tropopause, which is about 36000 ft (11000 m) above the surface in temperate latitudes; over the tropics it is higher, and therefore colder, while it is at a lower altitude over the poles. Air temperature falls uniformly with increasing height until the tropopause is reached; thereafter it remains constant in the stratosphere. Composition of the troposphere is essentially constant, apart from the vital factor of clouds and humidity.

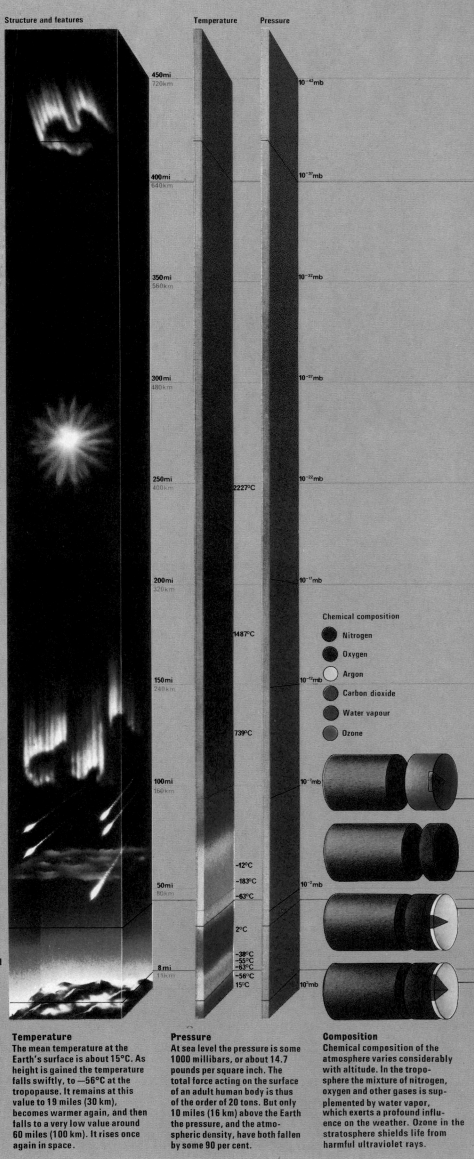

Structure and features

Temperature   Pressure

450mi / 720km 10^{-43}mb

400mi / 640km 10^{-35}mb

350mi / 560km 10^{-32}mb

300mi / 480km 10^{-27}mb

250mi / 400km   2227°C 10^{-22}mb

200mi / 320km 10^{-17}mb

1487°C

150mi / 240km   739°C 10^{-10}mb

100mi / 160km

-12°C

50mi / 80km   -183°C 10^{-3}mb

-63°C

2°C

-38°C / -55°C / -63°C
8mi / 11km   -56°C 10^{0}mb
15°C

Chemical composition
- Nitrogen
- Oxygen
- Argon
- Carbon dioxide
- Water vapour
- Ozone

Temperature
The mean temperature at the Earth's surface is about 15°C. As height is gained the temperature falls swiftly, to −56°C at the tropopause. It remains at this value to 19 miles (30 km), becomes warmer again, and then falls to a very low value around 60 miles (100 km). It rises once again in space.

Pressure
At sea level the pressure is some 1000 millibars, or about 14.7 pounds per square inch. The total force acting on the surface of an adult human body is thus of the order of 20 tons. But only 10 miles (16 km) above the Earth the pressure, and the atmospheric density, have both fallen by some 90 per cent.

Composition
Chemical composition of the atmosphere varies considerably with altitude. In the troposphere the mixture of nitrogen, oxygen and other gases is supplemented by water vapor, which exerts a profound influence on the weather. Ozone in the stratosphere shields life from harmful ultraviolet rays.

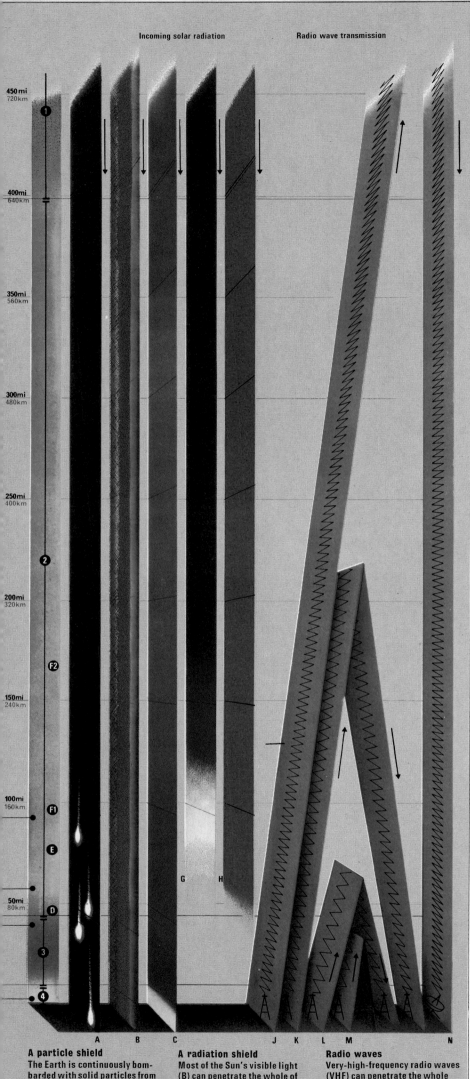

Incoming solar radiation   Radio wave transmission

450mi
720km

400mi
640km

350mi
560km

300mi
480km

250mi
400km

200mi
320km

150mi
240km

100mi
160km

50mi
80km

A   B   C   J K L M   N

The circulation of the atmosphere *left*
The atmosphere maintains its equilibrium by transferring heat, moisture and momentum from low levels at low latitudes to high levels at high latitudes where the heat is radiated to space. This circulation appears to comprise three distinct 'cells' in each hemisphere. In the tropical (A) and polar (B) cells the circulations are thermally direct – warm air rises and cold air sinks – but the mid-latitude circulation, the Ferrel cell (C), is distorted by the polar front as shown in greater detail below.

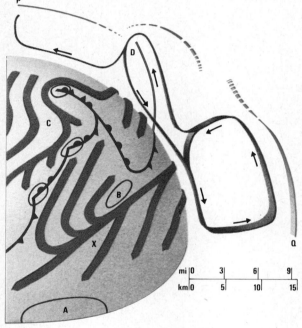

P

D

C

B

X

Q

A

mi 0   3   6   9
km 0   5   10   15

Warm front   A Area of low pressure   D Polar front
Cold front   B Area of high pressure   P Polar cell tropopause
                 C Area of low pressure   Q Tropical tropopause

Frontal systems *left*
Although the figure above shows a true general picture, the actual circulation is more complicated. A portion of the Earth on a larger scale shows how frontal systems develop between the polar and tropical air masses. The tropopause, the demarcation between the troposphere in which temperature falls with height, and the stratosphere above, is much higher in the tropics than in the polar cell. Between the cells the polar front causes constant successions of warm and cold fronts and changeable weather. Surface winds are shown, together with areas of low pressure and high pressure. The scale along the bottom, although exaggerated, indicates the greater height of the tropical tropopause compared with that in polar regions. Conventional symbols indicate warm and cold fronts.

A particle shield
The Earth is continuously bombarded with solid particles from elsewhere in the solar system and possibly from more distant parts of the universe. Only the largest meteors (A) reach the surface. Small meteorites generally burn up through friction caused by passage through the thin air more than 40 miles (65 km) up.

A radiation shield
Most of the Sun's visible light (B) can penetrate the whole of the atmosphere right down to the Earth's surface, except where cloud intervenes. But only some of the infra-red radiation gets through (C); the rest (G) is cut off, along with the harmful ultraviolet radiation (H), by atmospheric gases.

Radio waves
Very-high-frequency radio waves (VHF) can penetrate the whole depth of the atmosphere (J), but short-wave transmissions are reflected by the Appleton F2 layer (K). Medium (L) and long waves (M) are reflected at lower levels by the D, E or F1 layers. Yet radio waves from distant stellar sources can be received (N).

Precipitation *left*
This map shows the mean annual rain, hail and snow over the Earth.

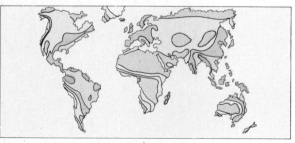

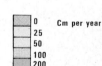

0
25   Cm per year
50
100
200

Evaporation *left*
Accurate estimates of evaporation can be made only over the oceans.

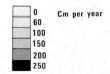

0
60   Cm per year
100
150
200
250

Net surface radiation *left*
Variations in heat output over the Earth's surface drive air and ocean circulations.

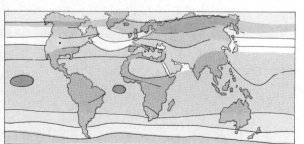

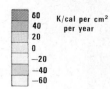

60   K/cal per cm²
40   per year
20
0
−20
−40
−60

27

The Structure of Weather Systems

Until recently there were few scientists in the tropics or the polar regions, and the science of meteorology therefore evolved in the mid-latitudes. Likewise, the early concepts of meteorology were all based on observations of the mid-latitude atmosphere. Originally only two types of air mass were recognized: polar and tropical. Today a distinct equatorial air mass has been identified, as well as Arctic and Antarctic masses at latitudes even higher than the original polar ones. The concept of a 'front' between dissimilar air masses dates from as recently as 1919, and three years later the development of a cyclone – a large system of air rotating around an area of low pressure– was first described. Today satellite photographs have confirmed the validity of these early studies and enable the whole Earth's weather to be watched as it happens on daily computer processed photo-charts.

Why the weather varies
Anywhere in the Earth's mid-latitudes the climate is determined mainly by the frequency and intensity of the cyclones, with their frontal systems and contrasting air masses, which unceasingly alter the local temperature, wind velocity, air pressure and humidity. In turn, the frequency of the cyclonic visits is governed principally by the behaviour of the long waves in the upper westerlies. When these waves change their shape and position the cyclonic depressions follow different paths. The major changes are seasonal, but significant variations also occur on a cycle of 5–6 weeks. It is still proving difficult to investigate the long wave variations. As a front passes, a fairly definite sequence of cloud, wind, humidity, temperature, precipitation and visibility can be seen. The most obvious change is the type of cloud, of which nine are shown opposite. Each cyclone contains numerous cloud types in its structure. Within these clouds several forms of precipitation can form; raindrops are the most common, but ice precipitation also forms, with snow in winter and hail in the summer when intense atmospheric instability produces towering cumulonimbus clouds topped by an 'anvil' of ice crystals.

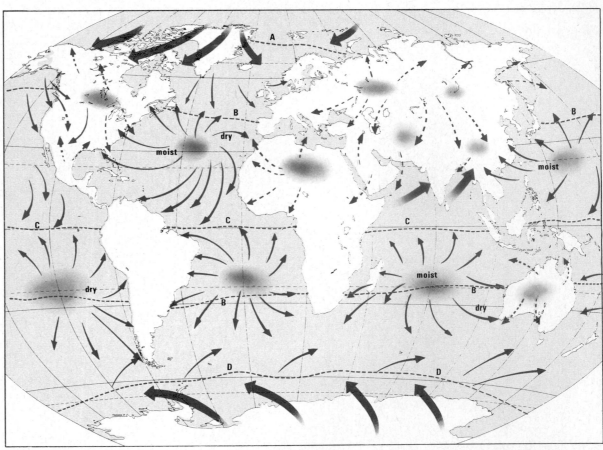

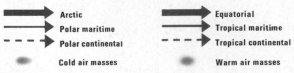

Air masses and convergences *above*
An air mass is an extensive portion of the atmosphere in which, at any given altitude, the moisture and temperature are almost uniform. Such a mass generally arises when the air rests for a time on a large area of land or water which has uniform surface conditions. There are some 20 source regions throughout the world. A second pre-requisite is large-scale subsidence and divergence over the source region. The boundary between air masses is a convergence or front. (A Arctic, B Polar, C Equatorial, D Antarctic.) The polar front is particularly important in governing much of the weather in mid-latitudes. The pattern depicted provides a raw framework for the world's weather. It is considerably modified by the air's vertical motion, by surface friction, land topography, the Earth's rotation and other factors.

➡ Arctic		➡ Equatorial
→ Polar maritime		→ Tropical maritime
--- Polar continental		--- Tropical continental
Cold air masses		Warm air masses

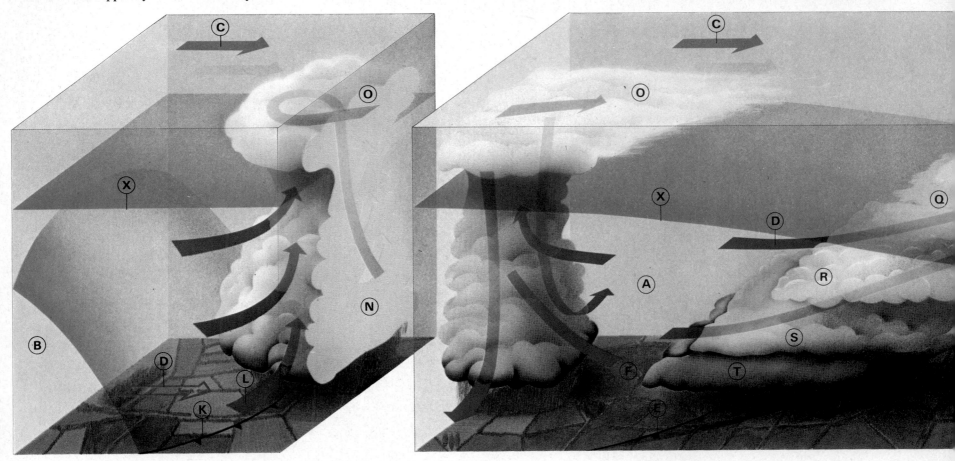

Anatomy of a depression
Seen in cross section, a mature mid-latitude cyclone forms a large system which always follows basically the same pattern. Essentially it comprises a wedge of warm air (A) riding over, and being undercut by, cold air masses (B). The entire cyclone is moving from left to right, and this is also the basic direction of the winds (C) and (D). To an observer on the ground the warm front (E) may take 12-24 hours to pass, followed by the warm sector (F) perhaps 180 miles (300 km) wide.

The warm front (E)
The front is first heralded by cirrus clouds (P), followed by cirrostratus (Q), altocumulus (R), stratus (S) and finally nimbostratus (T). The descending layers are due partly to humidity distribution and partly to the warm air rising over the sloping frontal surface. Precipitation may be steady and last for hours. Alternatively some warm fronts have a predominantly subsident air motion, with the result that there is only a little thin cloud and negligible precipitation. Air temperature increases as the front passes.

The cold front (K)
As this narrow front zone, some mile (1–2 km) wide, passes overhead the direction of the wind alters (L) and precipitation (M) pours from cumuliform clouds (N). If the air above the frontal surface is moving upwards then giant cumulonimbus (O) may grow, with heavy rain or hail. Cirrus clouds then form in air above the freezing level (X). Sometimes the front is weak with subsidence of air predominant on both sides of it. In this case there is little cloud development and near-zero surface precipitation.

Development of a depression *right*

Most mid-latitude depressions (cyclones) develop on the polar front (map above). An initial disturbance along this front causes a fall in pressure and a confluence at the surface, deforming the front into a wave (1, right). The confluence and thermal structure accelerate the cyclonic spin into a fully developed depression (2). The depression comprises a warm sector bounded by a sharp cold front (A) and warm front (B). The fast-moving cold front overtakes the warm front and eventually the warm sector is lifted completely clear of the ground resulting in an occlusion (3). The continued overlapping of the two wedges of cold air eventually fills up the depression and causes it to weaken and disperse (4). By the time this occurs the warm sector has been lifted high in the atmosphere. In this way, depressions fulfil an essential role in transferring heat from low to high levels and from low to high latitudes.

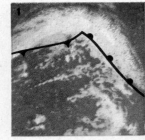

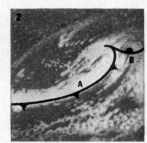

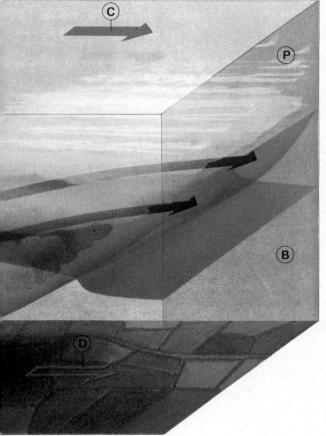

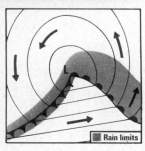

Plan view *left*

A developing cyclone will appear this way on the 'synoptic' weather chart. Lines of equal pressure (isobars) are nearly straight within the warm sector but curve sharply in the cold sector to enclose the low pressure focus of the system.

Rain limits

Examples of the three major cloud groups

Low cloud *top*

Stratocumulus (1) is a grey or white layer of serried masses or rolls. Cumulus (2) is the familiar white cauliflower. It can develop into cumulonimbus (3), a large, threatening cloud, characterized by immense vertical development topped by an 'anvil' of ice crystals. These produce heavy rain or hail.

Medium cloud *left*

Nimbostratus (4) is a ragged grey layer producing drizzle or snow. Altocumulus (5) comprises rows of 'blobs' of ice and water forming a sheet at a height of 1.5-4.5 miles (2-7 km). Altostratus (6) occurs at similar heights but is a water/ice sheet either uniform, striated or fibrous in appearance.

High cloud *right*

Cirrus (7) is the highest cloud and appears as fine white ice filaments at 8–10 miles (13–16 km), often hair-like or silky. Cirro-cumulus (8) forms into thin white layers made up of very numerous icy globules or ripples. Cirrostratus (9) is a high-level veil of ice crystals often forming a halo round the Sun.

Four kinds of precipitation

Rain
Although raindrops are often melted snow, most rain results from the coalescence of micro-scopic droplets (1) which are condensed from vapour on to nuclei such as small particles of salt from sea spray. The repeated merging eventually forms water droplets (2) which are too large to be kept up by the air currents.

Glaze
In completely undisturbed air it is possible for water to remain liquid even at temperatures well below freezing point. So air above the freezing level (X) may contain large quantities of this 'supercooled water'. This can fall as rain and freeze on impact with objects, coating them with ice.

Dry snow
The origin of snow differs from that of rain in that the vapour droplets (1) settle on microscopic crystals of ice and freeze. The result is the growth of a white or translucent ice crystal having a basically hexagonal form (photomicrograph below). The crystals then agglomerate into flakes (2).

Hail
In cumulonimbus clouds raindrops (formed at 1,2) may encounter up-currents strong enough to lift them repeatedly back through a freezing level (X). On each pass (3) a fresh layer of ice is collected. The hailstone builds up like an onion until it is so heavy (4) that it falls to the ground.

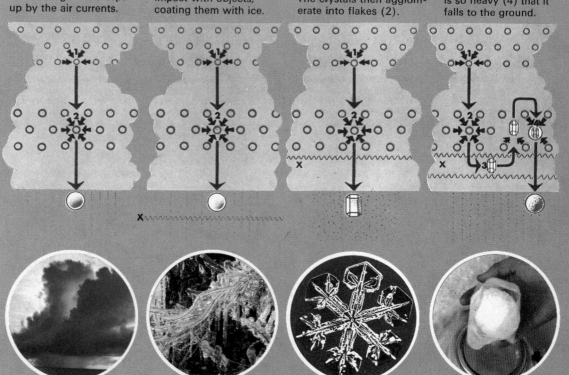

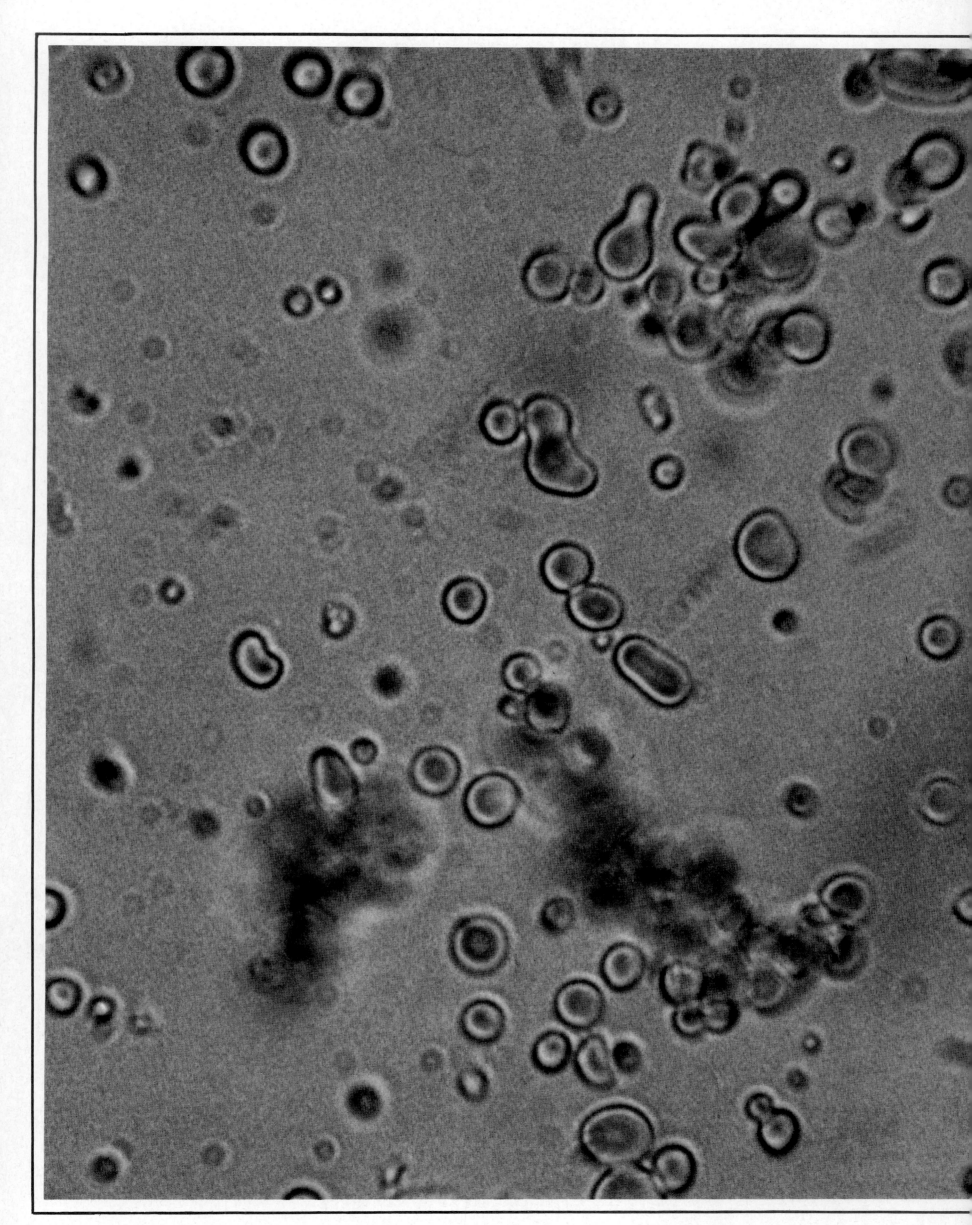

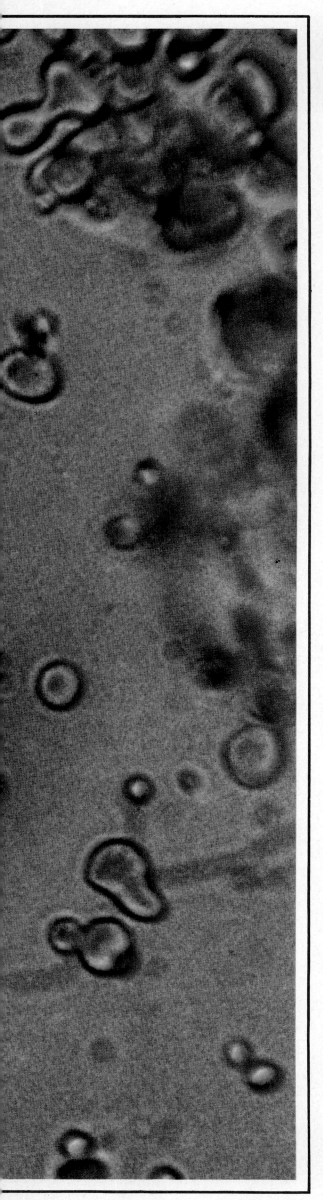

Life on Earth

No one will ever know exactly how or when life first appeared on Earth. But one thing is certain : the planet upon which life glimmered into being was very different from the world we know now. Barren rock, heaving with earthquakes and volcanic eruptions ; the shores echoing discordantly to the crash of a sterile sea ; violent thunderstorms and heavy cloud flickering across the face of a harsh, blinding Sun ; and a choking, noxious atmosphere : these are the fierce and unlikely conditions that nourished life into existence. Ironically, they were tamed by those first primitive specks of living matter to which they had given birth. With agonizing slowness, through hundreds of millions of years, life gradually began to fashion its own environment. The struggle to stay alive produced new plants and animals of many millions of varieties, from the tiniest bug to giant whales and from speck-like algae to towering trees, crowded together into a thin film of life smeared over the surface of the planet. And it was into this world that man eventually emerged.

The dawn of life
Exactly how, where and when terrestrial life began will
probably never be known. But it is certain that all Earth
life stemmed from primitive cells such as these
microspheres grown in the laboratory from artificial
chains of amino-acids. (Magnified over 5000 times)

Life Begins

Dawn of life *left*
It was probably upon primitive estuarine shores such as these that most of the key chemical reactions which were to precede the emergence of life took place. Chain-like chemicals dissolved in the seas were concentrated in and upon the mud of such estuaries. Here the alternation of wet and dry, the fierce heat of an unshielded Sun and the catalytic effects of the mud combined to promote the chemical rearrangements needed to make primeval proteins and nucleic acids. Associations of such molecules then formed the first primitive living cells.

For something like half of its existence the Earth has been devoid of life. Perhaps the most important characteristic of the primitive Earth was that its atmosphere contained no oxygen, the vital element that makes today's life possible. It was this absence during at least the first 2000 million years of the Earth's history that allowed the chemical reactions to take place that were necessary for life to evolve.

The primordial atmosphere contained such gases as methane and ammonia which, under the action of a glaring Sun, formed new compounds, including the poisonous hydrogen cyanide, which could link together to form chemical chains. These then dissolved in the oceans and became concentrated in the sea foam and on the shores. Some of these chain-like chemicals must have been similar to present-day proteins, which play such an important role in living things. Other primordial molecules were undoubtedly crude versions of the so-called nucleic acids, the best known of which – DNA, deoxyribonucleic acid – functions as the material of inheritance as illustrated in the main figure opposite.

Over millions of years such chemicals were made and destroyed under the fierce rays of the Sun. But, as time went by, some of these molecules acquired a totally new characteristic: they became able to an increasing degree to organize their own manufacture. Such molecules, which were probably nucleic acids, fared better than the others which were made completely by accident, and so increased at the latter's expense. Then some of these nucleic acids became able to use proteins in constructing themselves, and began to organize them also. Thus a close and interdependent relationship sprang up between the two classes of molecule. Separated from the rest of the world by their surrounding membrane, such interrelated proteins and nucleic acids formed the first living cells.

Certain cells, by making a dye known as chlorophyll, became able to use sunlight more efficiently and in so doing pumped oxygen into the atmosphere. For 1000 million years this oxygen was soaked up by the rocks of the Earth; then it slowly began to accumulate in the atmosphere. Oxygen that rose to great altitudes became converted by the Sun into ozone which gradually formed a protective screen for the Earth by filtering out some of the Sun's harshest rays which previously reached the surface. At this point life began in earnest. The oxygen went on increasing, and evolutionary expansion had begun.

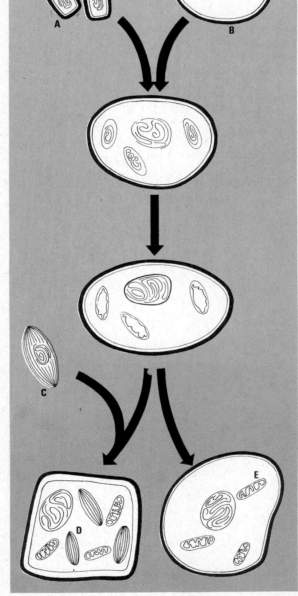

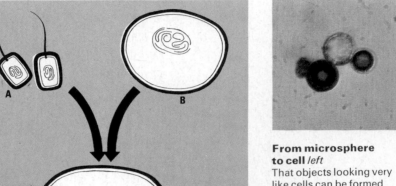

From microsphere to cell *left*
That objects looking very like cells can be formed merely by dissolving protein-like molecules in water is shown by the photograph of a 'microsphere' (above). Of course, such microspheres lack the complex internal organization of real cells (right), many of which contain a nucleus and other internal structures or 'organelles'. Nuclei were formed by creating a wall around the hereditary material, the DNA, but the organelles were probably acquired by engulfing other types of cell (left). Some of these were bacteria (A) very efficient at burning sugars to produce energy. Their engulfment by larger cells (B) meant that they were assured of a steady sugar supply, and the cells were in turn provided with built-in miniature 'power plants'. The organelles descended from these bacteria are mitochondria. Algae (C) taken into the cell were able to make sugars using the energy of the Sun and gave rise to chloroplasts (D). Animal cells contain mitochondria (E) only; plant cells may contain chloroplasts as well.

The living cell *above*
Cells are the basic building blocks from which all but the most primitive forms of Earth life are constructed. Strictly speaking, a bird's egg could be defined as a cell, but most cells are microscopic. The illustration above is 100,000 times life size.

The struggle for life *right*
This time scale shows the gradual evolution of terrestrial life forms from simple chemicals, and the concomitant evolution of the Earth's atmosphere. The primitive atmosphere was totally devoid of oxygen, and consisted almost entirely of methane and ammonia. It was life itself, by producing oxygen which became ozone, that made conditions safer for life.

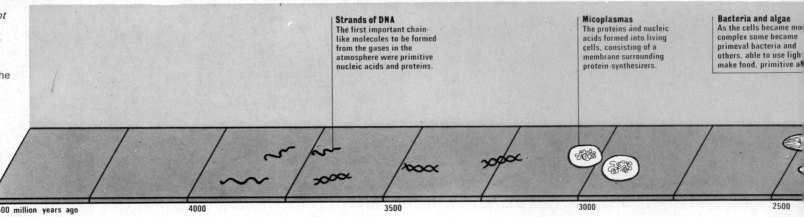

Strands of DNA
The first important chain-like molecules to be formed from the gases in the atmosphere were primitive nucleic acids and proteins.

Micoplasmas
The proteins and nucleic acids formed into living cells, consisting of a membrane surrounding protein-synthesizers.

Bacteria and algae
As the cells became more complex some became primeval bacteria and others, able to use light make food, primitive al

4500 million years ago   4000   3500   3000   2500

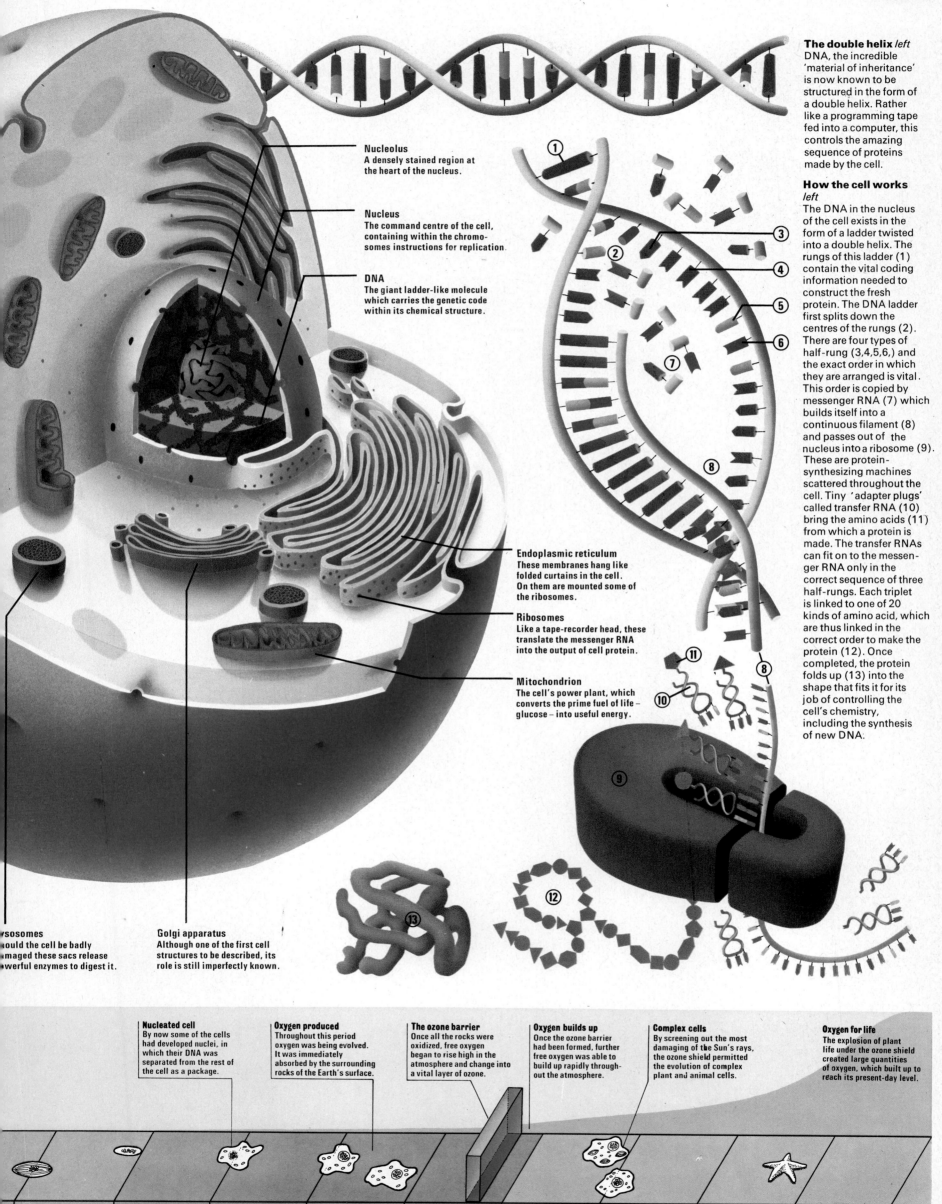

Nucleolus
A densely stained region at the heart of the nucleus.

Nucleus
The command centre of the cell, containing within the chromo-somes instructions for replication.

DNA
The giant ladder-like molecule which carries the genetic code within its chemical structure.

Endoplasmic reticulum
These membranes hang like folded curtains in the cell. On them are mounted some of the ribosomes.

Ribosomes
Like a tape-recorder head, these translate the messenger RNA into the output of cell protein.

Mitochondrion
The cell's power plant, which converts the prime fuel of life – glucose – into useful energy.

...sosomes
...ould the cell be badly ...maged these sacs release ...werful enzymes to digest it.

Golgi apparatus
Although one of the first cell structures to be described, its role is still imperfectly known.

The double helix *left*
DNA, the incredible 'material of inheritance' is now known to be structured in the form of a double helix. Rather like a programming tape fed into a computer, this controls the amazing sequence of proteins made by the cell.

How the cell works
left
The DNA in the nucleus of the cell exists in the form of a ladder twisted into a double helix. The rungs of this ladder (1) contain the vital coding information needed to construct the fresh protein. The DNA ladder first splits down the centres of the rungs (2). There are four types of half-rung (3,4,5,6,) and the exact order in which they are arranged is vital. This order is copied by messenger RNA (7) which builds itself into a continuous filament (8) and passes out of the nucleus into a ribosome (9). These are protein-synthesizing machines scattered throughout the cell. Tiny 'adapter plugs' called transfer RNA (10) bring the amino acids (11) from which a protein is made. The transfer RNAs can fit on to the messen-ger RNA only in the correct sequence of three half-rungs. Each triplet is linked to one of 20 kinds of amino acid, which are thus linked in the correct order to make the protein (12). Once completed, the protein folds up (13) into the shape that fits it for its job of controlling the cell's chemistry, including the synthesis of new DNA.

Nucleated cell
By now some of the cells had developed nuclei, in which their DNA was separated from the rest of the cell as a package.

Oxygen produced
Throughout this period oxygen was being evolved. It was immediately absorbed by the surrounding rocks of the Earth's surface.

The ozone barrier
Once all the rocks were oxidized, free oxygen began to rise high in the atmosphere and change into a vital layer of ozone.

Oxygen builds up
Once the ozone barrier had been formed, further free oxygen was able to build up rapidly through-out the atmosphere.

Complex cells
By screening out the most damaging of the Sun's rays, the ozone shield permitted the evolution of complex plant and animal cells.

Oxygen for life
The explosion of plant life under the ozone shield created large quantities of oxygen, which built up to reach its present-day level.

2000   1500   1000   500   present day

33

The Ocean Cradle

Early life probably derived its energy not directly from the Sun or atmosphere, but by breaking down compounds as some bacteria do today. The arrival of chlorophyll marked the appearance of the first real plants able to synthesize food out of sunlight, carbon dioxide and water. Thereafter there was abundant food on the Earth to support all types of animals. Some fed directly on, or in, the plants. Others fed on the plant-eaters, or in them as parasites. The result was a vast chain of animal energy-dissipators all depending on the primary producers, the green plants.

Since the lack of oxygen in the primeval atmosphere meant that the surface of the Earth was flooded with far more ultraviolet light from the Sun than it is today, early life could not leave the protection of the water. So the first great evolution of living things was confined to the oceans – not the great depths where there is no light, but the surface, inshore waters and tidal pools. Later even the depths could be colonized, as life near the surface became so abundant that dead plants and animals, mainly microscopic, perpetually rained down into the depths to provide food there.

A few fossils, mainly algae, are known to date from 2700 million years ago. But the earliest plentiful fossils, in the Cambrian rocks, are already highly evolved: true arthropods (jointed-legged animals), true molluscs, true echinoderms (related to starfish), rather odd corals and other forms all nearing the end of their branches on the evolutionary thicket. Even today it is tempting to think of mammals, birds and perhaps reptiles as the higher animals and to dismiss fishes and the remainder as very lowly. But within that remainder there is far more diversity than within all the vertebrates.

True vertebrates appear in the fossil record only in the Ordovician (about 400 million years ago). But their evolution is then rapid, and by the Devonian (300 million) true sharks, bony fishes and lung fishes have appeared. Quickly thereafter (250 million) the first four-legged beasts are abundant. They first appeared at the end of the Carboniferous, when the advance to the land had begun.

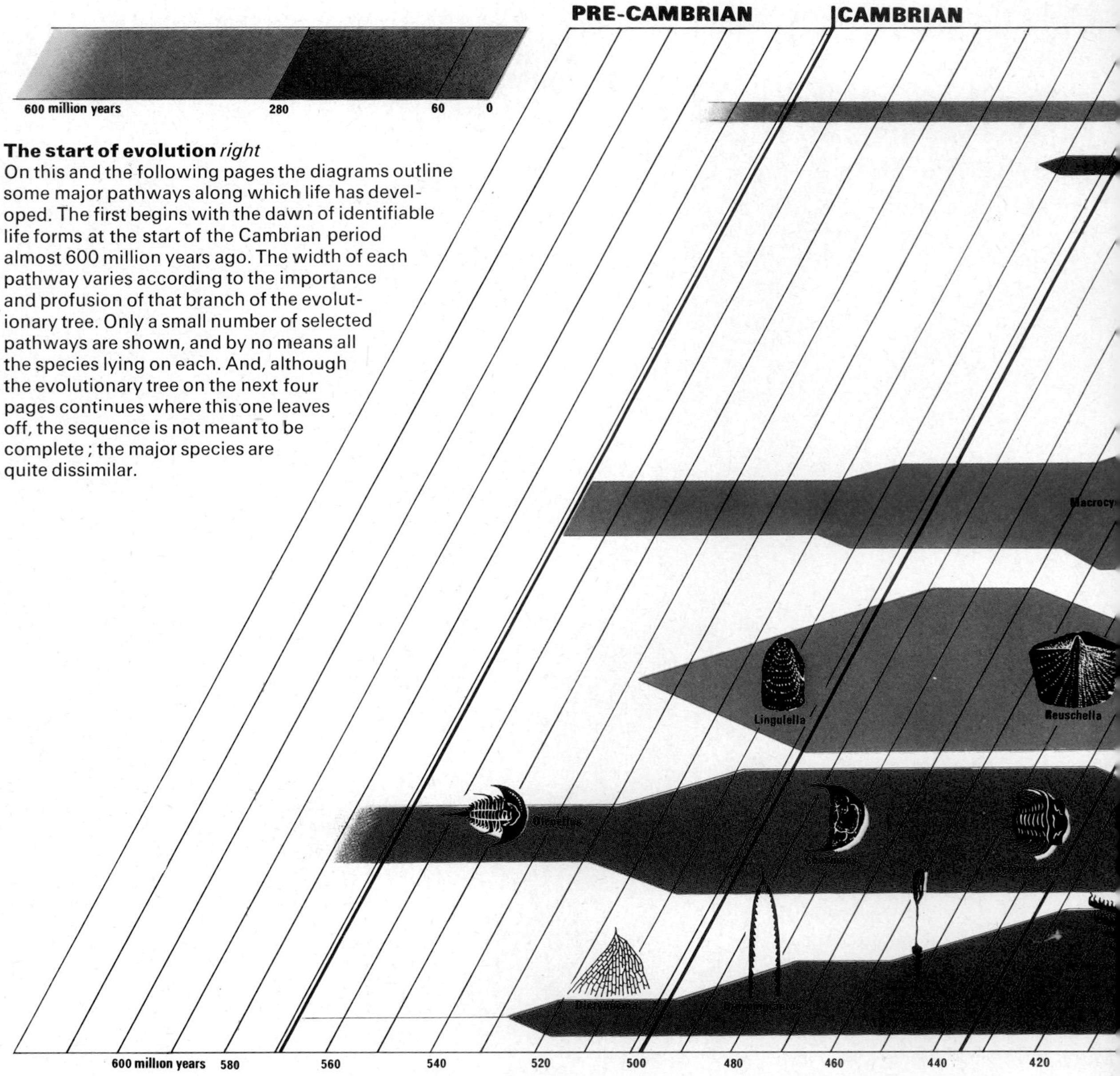

The start of evolution *right*
On this and the following pages the diagrams outline some major pathways along which life has developed. The first begins with the dawn of identifiable life forms at the start of the Cambrian period almost 600 million years ago. The width of each pathway varies according to the importance and profusion of that branch of the evolutionary tree. Only a small number of selected pathways are shown, and by no means all the species lying on each. And, although the evolutionary tree on the next four pages continues where this one leaves off, the sequence is not meant to be complete; the major species are quite dissimilar.

PRE-CAMBRIAN | **CAMBRIAN**

600 million years   280   60   0

The primeval sea *below*
For a period approaching 200 million years all life on the Earth was confined to the water. At first simple single-celled creatures dominated the scene but gradually life evolved giving rise to multicellular plants and animals such as jellyfish, polyps, segmented worms, free-swimming molluscs and other hard-shelled animals.

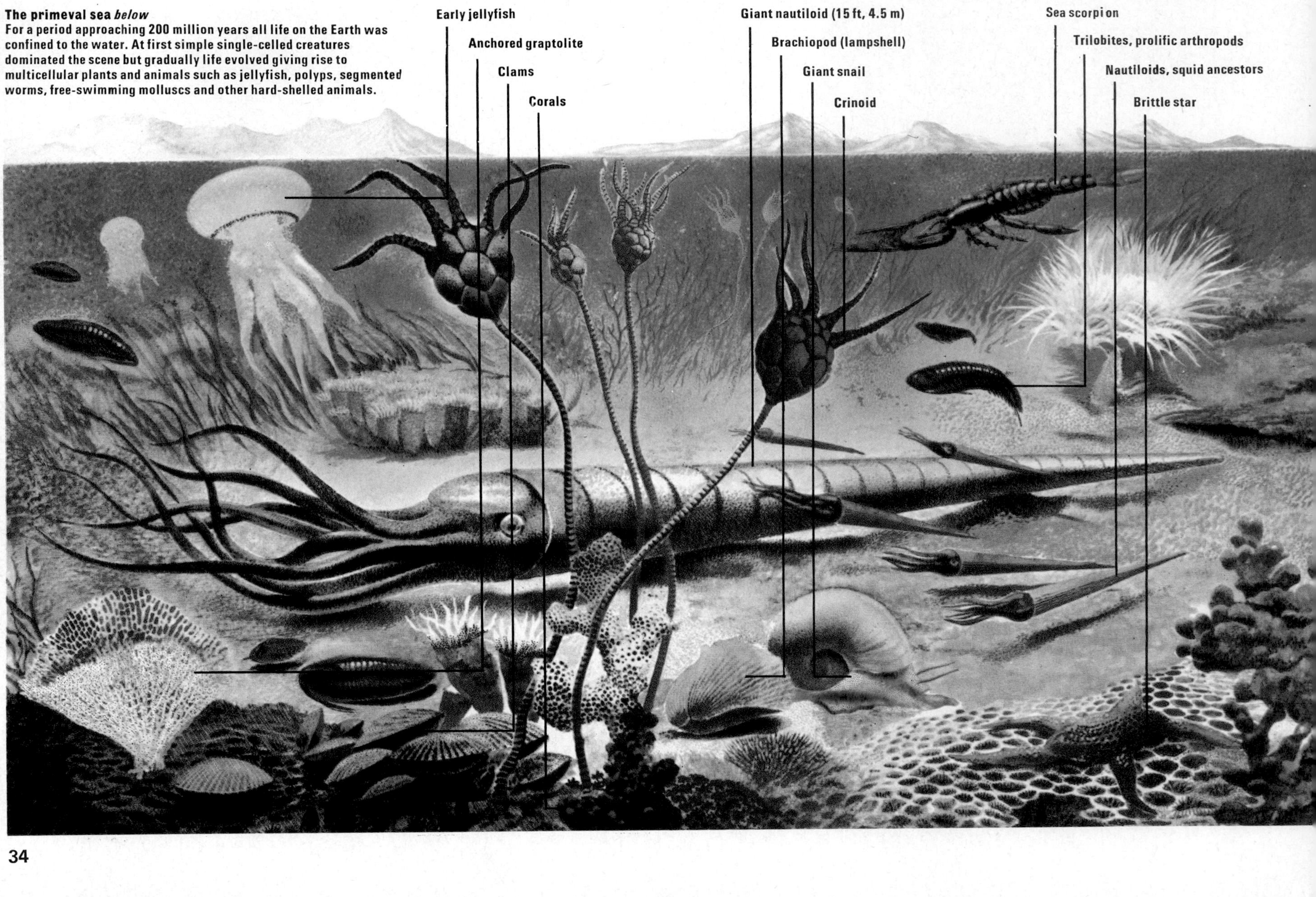

Early jellyfish
Anchored graptolite
Clams
Corals
Giant nautiloid (15 ft, 4.5 m)
Brachiopod (lampshell)
Giant snail
Crinoid
Sea scorpion
Trilobites, prolific arthropods
Nautiloids, squid ancestors
Brittle star

600 million years   580   560   540   520   500   480   460   440   420

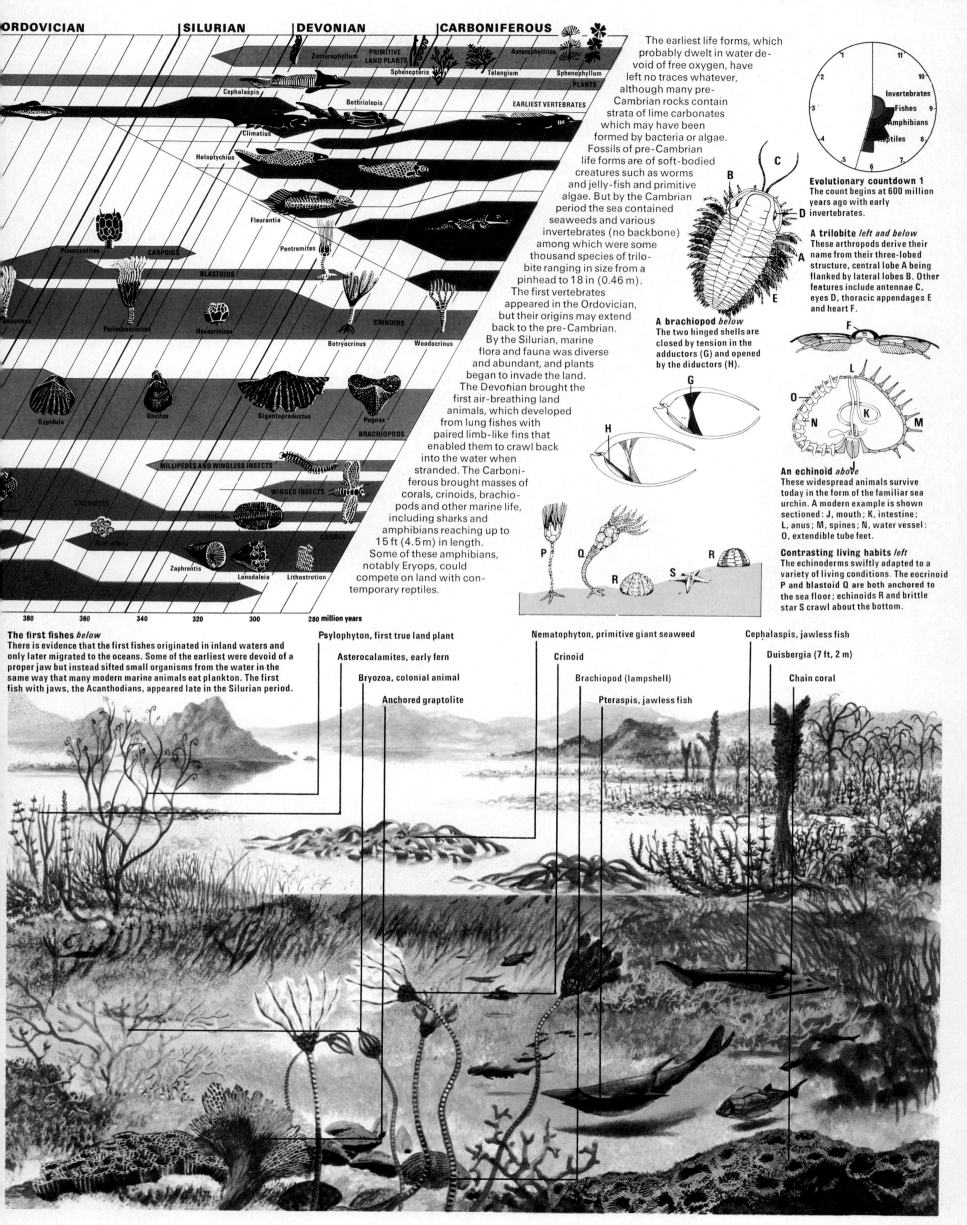

ORDOVICIAN | SILURIAN | DEVONIAN | CARBONIFEROUS

Zosterophyllum | PRIMITIVE LAND PLANTS | Asterophyllites
Sphenopteris | Telangium | Sphenophyllum
PLANTS

Cephalaspis
Bothriolepis   EARLIEST VERTEBRATES
Climatius
Holoptychius
Fleurantia
Pentremites
Placocystites   CARPOIDS
BLASTOIDS
Periechocrinites   Hexacrinites
CRINOIDS
Botryocrinus   Woodocrinus
Gypidula   Uncites   Gigantoproductus   Pugnax
BRACHIOPODS
MILLIPEDES AND WINGLESS INSECTS
WINGED INSECTS
TRILOBITES
Griffithides
CORALS
Zaphrentis   Lonsdaleia   Lithostrotion

380   360   340   320   300   280 million years

The earliest life forms, which probably dwelt in water devoid of free oxygen, have left no traces whatever, although many pre-Cambrian rocks contain strata of lime carbonates which may have been formed by bacteria or algae. Fossils of pre-Cambrian life forms are of soft-bodied creatures such as worms and jelly-fish and primitive algae. But by the Cambrian period the sea contained seaweeds and various invertebrates (no backbone) among which were some thousand species of trilobite ranging in size from a pinhead to 18 in (0.46 m).
The first vertebrates appeared in the Ordovician, but their origins may extend back to the pre-Cambrian. By the Silurian, marine flora and fauna was diverse and abundant, and plants began to invade the land. The Devonian brought the first air-breathing land animals, which developed from lung fishes with paired limb-like fins that enabled them to crawl back into the water when stranded. The Carboniferous brought masses of corals, crinoids, brachiopods and other marine life, including sharks and amphibians reaching up to 15 ft (4.5 m) in length. Some of these amphibians, notably Eryops, could compete on land with contemporary reptiles.

Evolutionary countdown 1
The count begins at 600 million years ago with early invertebrates.

Invertebrates
Fishes
Amphibians
Reptiles

A trilobite *left and below*
These arthropods derive their name from their three-lobed structure, central lobe A being flanked by lateral lobes B. Other features include antennae C, eyes D, thoracic appendages E and heart F.

A brachiopod *below*
The two hinged shells are closed by tension in the adductors (G) and opened by the diductors (H).

An echinoid *above*
These widespread animals survive today in the form of the familiar sea urchin. A modern example is shown sectioned : J, mouth ; K, intestine ; L, anus ; M, spines ; N, water vessel ; O, extendible tube feet.

Contrasting living habits *left*
The echinoderms swiftly adapted to a variety of living conditions. The eocrinoid P and blastoid Q are both anchored to the sea floor ; echinoids R and brittle star S crawl about the bottom.

The first fishes *below*
There is evidence that the first fishes originated in inland waters and only later migrated to the oceans. Some of the earliest were devoid of a proper jaw but instead sifted small organisms from the water in the same way that many modern marine animals eat plankton. The first fish with jaws, the Acanthodians, appeared late in the Silurian period.

Psylophyton, first true land plant

Asterocalamites, early fern

Bryozoa, colonial animal

Anchored graptolite

Nematophyton, primitive giant seaweed

Crinoid

Brachiopod (lampshell)

Pteraspis, jawless fish

Cephalaspis, jawless fish

Duisbergia (7 ft, 2 m)

Chain coral

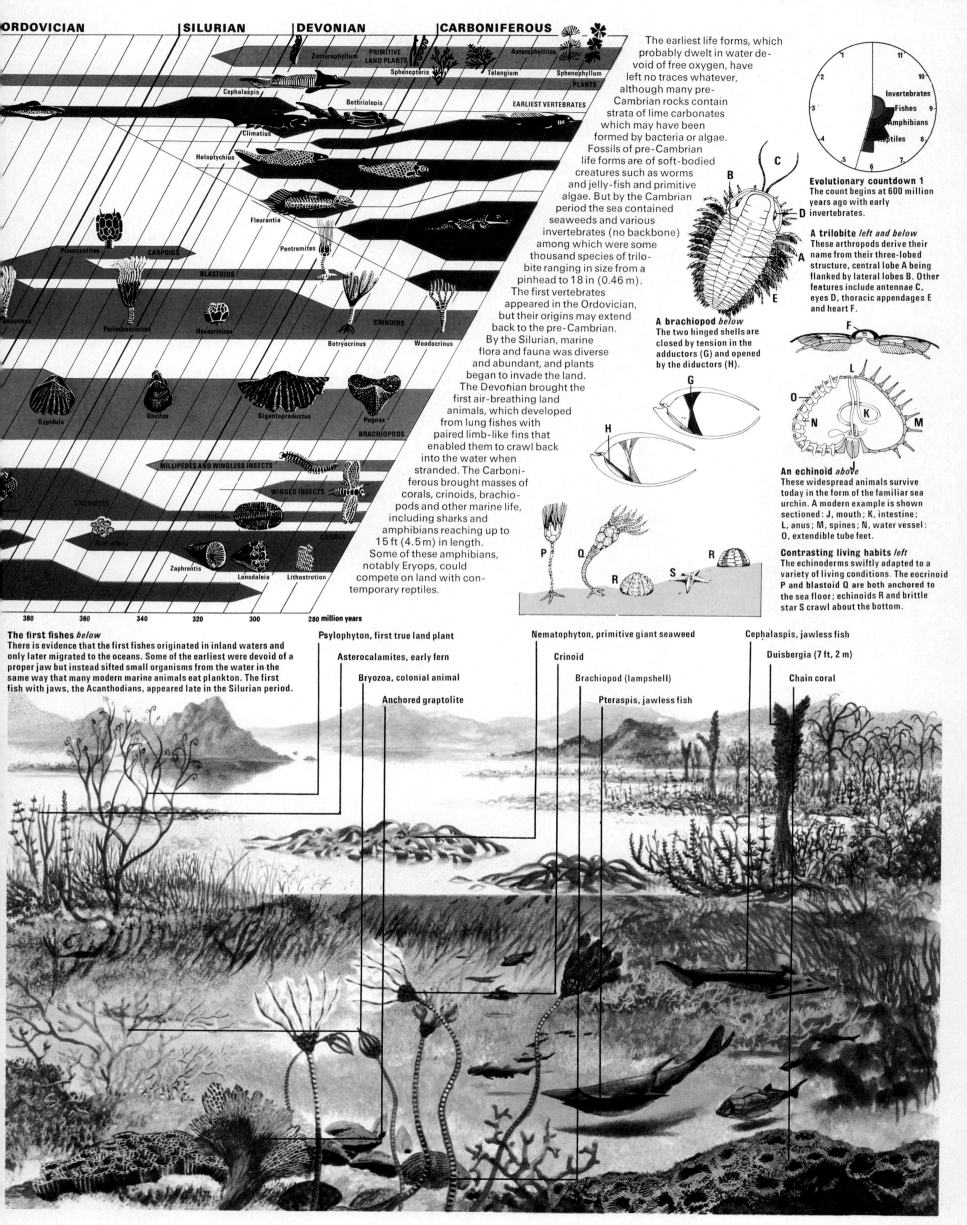

Advance to the Land

As soon as the land was inhabitable it was invaded by many different sorts of living things. First came the essential plants; as the vegetation spread it was followed by animals. Fresh water had been colonized early on and some animals came to the land from there instead of directly from the seas. In swampy places in the Carboniferous period tree-ferns, horsetails and clubmosses had produced real forests. These supported many insects, some scorpions, myriapods and other jointed-legged animals. There were probably worms and other soil animals, but these are not easily fossilized. The advance to the land happened many times over, in many groups. For example, the land snails belong to at least two distinct stocks, one of which invaded the land via fresh water while the other, related to the winkles, may have come straight from the sea.

Primitive fishes possibly evolved under fresh water or estuarine conditions, and invaded the sea soon after. As early as the Devonian period amphibians had been produced, resembling fishes but with four legs instead of paired fins. They probably arose in rivers and pools subjected to seasonal drought, and it has been suggested that their legs were just for walking to the next puddle. By the Carboniferous they had given rise to the reptiles, which produce eggs that can develop on land.

The reptiles soon split up into diverse types, filling all the places that mammals do today. They produced everything from tiny lizards to immense plant-eating armoured monsters and carnivores of all sizes up to the huge Tyrannosaurus. Many of the earlier carnivores and herbivores that flourished in the Permian and Triassic periods died out, but not before they had given rise to successful lines of descendants leading to today's mammals. The later ones include the two main groups of dinosaurs, as well as the flying pterodactyls, the marine ichthyosaurs – so like modern porpoises and dolphins – and the fish- or mollusc-eating plesiosaurs which resembled large turtles with long necks. Crocodile-like forms were produced several times independently, and from one of the primitive dinosaur stocks arose the true birds.

Life inherits the land *below*
The first life forms to colonize the land were probably marine plants, perhaps seaweeds growing at the water's edge, which were forced to survive periods when the water was absent. By 250 million years ago the Earth was clothed in green, mainly as a result of soft, pithy trees and giant ferns. Amphibians, reptiles and flying insects appeared.

The age of giant reptiles *right*
While the Earth erupted in volcanic activity, folded into huge young mountains and became covered with primitive trees and shrubs, the life of the land slowly gave rise to amphibians and then to reptiles larger than any earlier form. For a remarkable 100 million years the giant reptiles ruled the land. Today it is tempting to regard these huge beasts as failures, because they do not exist today; but very few of today's life forms have a 100 million year history, and man has existed for much less than one per cent as long a time.

PERMIAN TRIASS

600 million years   280   60   0

VERY PRIMITIVE FISH
Cleithrolepis
PRIMITIVE AMPHIBIANS
Chelonia
Euparkeria
VERY PRIMITIVE DINOSAURS
COTYLOSAURS
PELYCOSAURS   Edaphosaurus   Herbivores
Dimetrodon   Carnivores
Opthalmosaurus
ICHTHYOSAUR

280 million years   260   240   220   200   180   160

Sigillaria, early tree
Lepidodendron (over 120 ft, 37 m)
Sphenacodon, probable carnivore
Meganeuron, giant dragonfly

Edaphosaurus, a 'finback' herbivore
Seymouria, only about 30 in (0.75 m)
Calamites
Dimetrodon, hunter of Edaphosaurus

Eryops, dwelt mainly on land
Limnoscelis
Araucarioxylon, a conifer

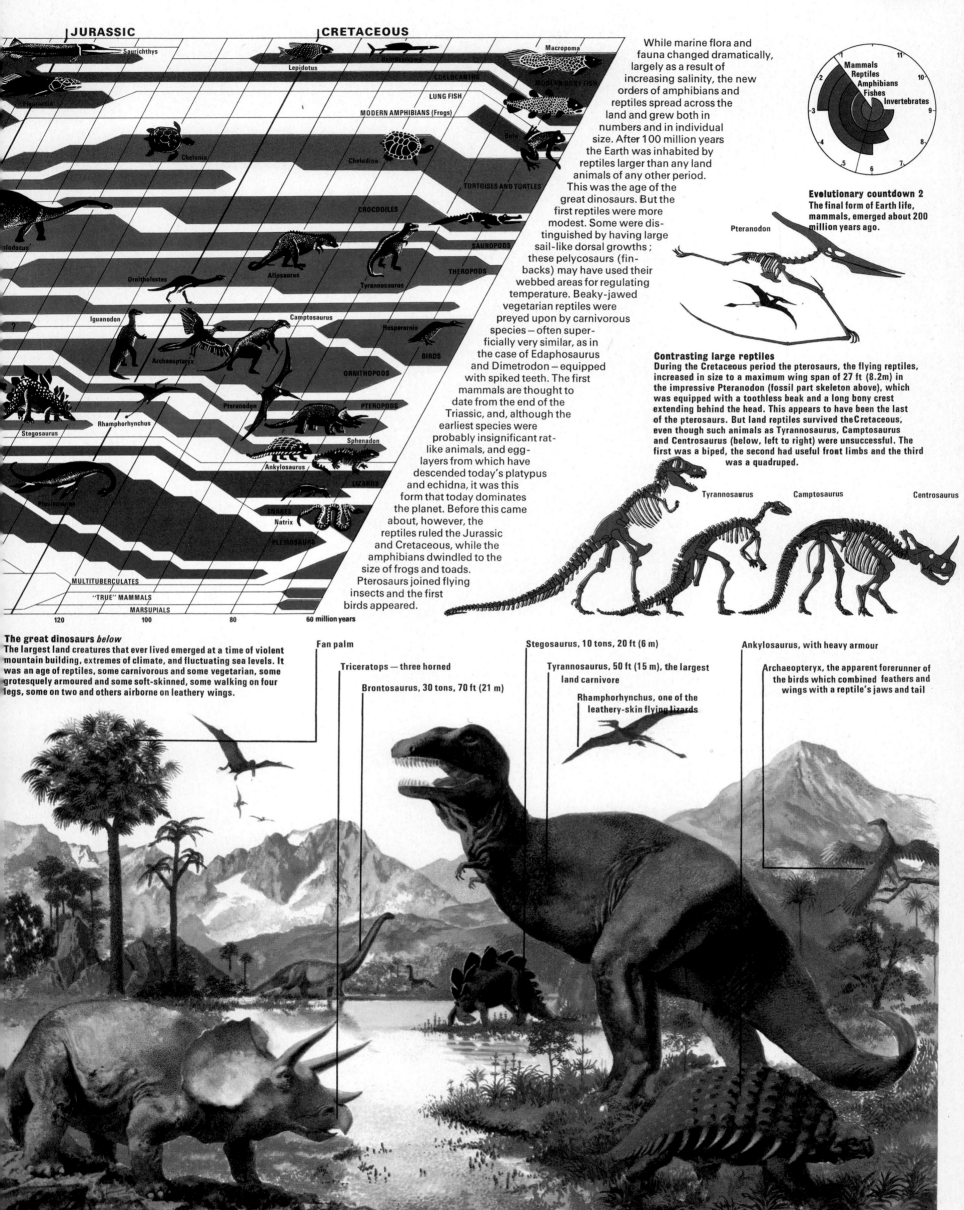

JURASSIC　　　CRETACEOUS

Saurichthys
Lepidotus
Macropoma
MODERN BONY FISH
COELOCANTHS
LUNG FISH
MODERN AMPHIBIANS (Frogs)
Chelonia
Chelodina
TORTOISES AND TURTLES
CROCODILES
SAUROPODS
Ornitholestes
Allosaurus
THEROPODS
Tyrannosaurus
Iguanodon
Camptosaurus
Hesperornis
BIRDS
Archaeopteryx
ORNITHOPODS
Pteranodon
PTEROPODS
Rhamphorhynchus
Stegosaurus
Sphenodon
Ankylosaurus
LIZARDS
Plesiosaurus
SNAKES
Natrix
PLESIOSAURS
MULTITUBERCULATES
"TRUE" MAMMALS
MARSUPIALS
120　100　80　60 million years

While marine flora and fauna changed dramatically, largely as a result of increasing salinity, the new orders of amphibians and reptiles spread across the land and grew both in numbers and in individual size. After 100 million years the Earth was inhabited by reptiles larger than any land animals of any other period. This was the age of the great dinosaurs. But the first reptiles were more modest. Some were distinguished by having large sail-like dorsal growths; these pelycosaurs (finbacks) may have used their webbed areas for regulating temperature. Beaky-jawed vegetarian reptiles were preyed upon by carnivorous species — often superficially very similar, as in the case of Edaphosaurus and Dimetrodon — equipped with spiked teeth. The first mammals are thought to date from the end of the Triassic, and, although the earliest species were probably insignificant rat-like animals, and egg-layers from which have descended today's platypus and echidna, it is this form that today dominates the planet. Before this came about, however, the reptiles ruled the Jurassic and Cretaceous, while the amphibians dwindled to the size of frogs and toads. Pterosaurs joined flying insects and the first birds appeared.

Evolutionary countdown 2
The final form of Earth life, mammals, emerged about 200 million years ago.

Mammals
Reptiles
Amphibians
Fishes
Invertebrates

Pteranodon

Contrasting large reptiles
During the Cretaceous period the pterosaurs, the flying reptiles, increased in size to a maximum wing span of 27 ft (8.2m) in the impressive Pteranodon (fossil part skeleton above), which was equipped with a toothless beak and a long bony crest extending behind the head. This appears to have been the last of the pterosaurs. But land reptiles survived the Cretaceous, even though such animals as Tyrannosaurus, Camptosaurus and Centrosaurus (below, left to right) were unsuccessful. The first was a biped, the second had useful front limbs and the third was a quadruped.

Tyrannosaurus　　Camptosaurus　　Centrosaurus

The great dinosaurs *below*
The largest land creatures that ever lived emerged at a time of violent mountain building, extremes of climate, and fluctuating sea levels. It was an age of reptiles, some carnivorous and some vegetarian, some grotesquely armoured and some soft-skinned, some walking on four legs, some on two and others airborne on leathery wings.

Fan palm

Triceratops — three horned

Brontosaurus, 30 tons, 70 ft (21 m)

Stegosaurus, 10 tons, 20 ft (6 m)

Tyrannosaurus, 50 ft (15 m), the largest land carnivore

Rhamphorhynchus, one of the leathery-skin flying lizards

Ankylosaurus, with heavy armour

Archaeopteryx, the apparent forerunner of the birds which combined feathers and wings with a reptile's jaws and tail

The Age of Mammals

At the end of the Cretaceous period something happened that involved a great change in the environment – a change so far-reaching that all the large reptiles died out. However, snakes, lizards, turtles, crocodiles and birds survived, and so did the primitive small mammals who now got the chance of their evolutionary life. They blossomed out into all the modes of life of the great reptiles, as well as into new ones. Plant eaters, carnivores, insectivores and omnivores (plant and meat eaters) arose in all sizes. By this time the continents had drifted far apart, so that usually only very small mammals could disperse across the sea on driftwood. As a result the mammals show many examples of 'convergent evolution' in which different species in widely separated but similar places become remarkably alike.

For example, S America was for about 70 million years an island continent. It had vacancies for horses, for camels, for elephants, for pigs of all kinds, and for lions and tigers to eat them. What actually happened was that three or four sorts of primitive mammals managed to get in, and proceeded to evolve to fill all these niches, independently of how they were being filled elsewhere. A one-toed horse and a three-toed variety thus appeared in S America quite independently of the evolution, from a similar stock, of the 'true' horses in N America. Even more remarkable was the emergence of 'weasels', 'dogs' and 'cats' – even 'great cats' and a 'sabre-tooth tiger' – from a stock of primitive marsupials (pouched mammals) that reached there very early on. Similarly, in Australia the marsupials independently produced forms that resembled cats, dogs, wolves, rabbits, shrews and moles, as well as all the wallabies and kangaroos. And in Madagascar the lemurs produced independent goat-like and chimpanzee-like forms.

When S America became joined to N America vast invasions took place and most of the S American specialities became extinct. Then came the great ice ages, shaking the whole world including the tropics, and many more mammals vanished. Only in small parts of Africa can we today get any idea of what evolution has produced in the mammal line.

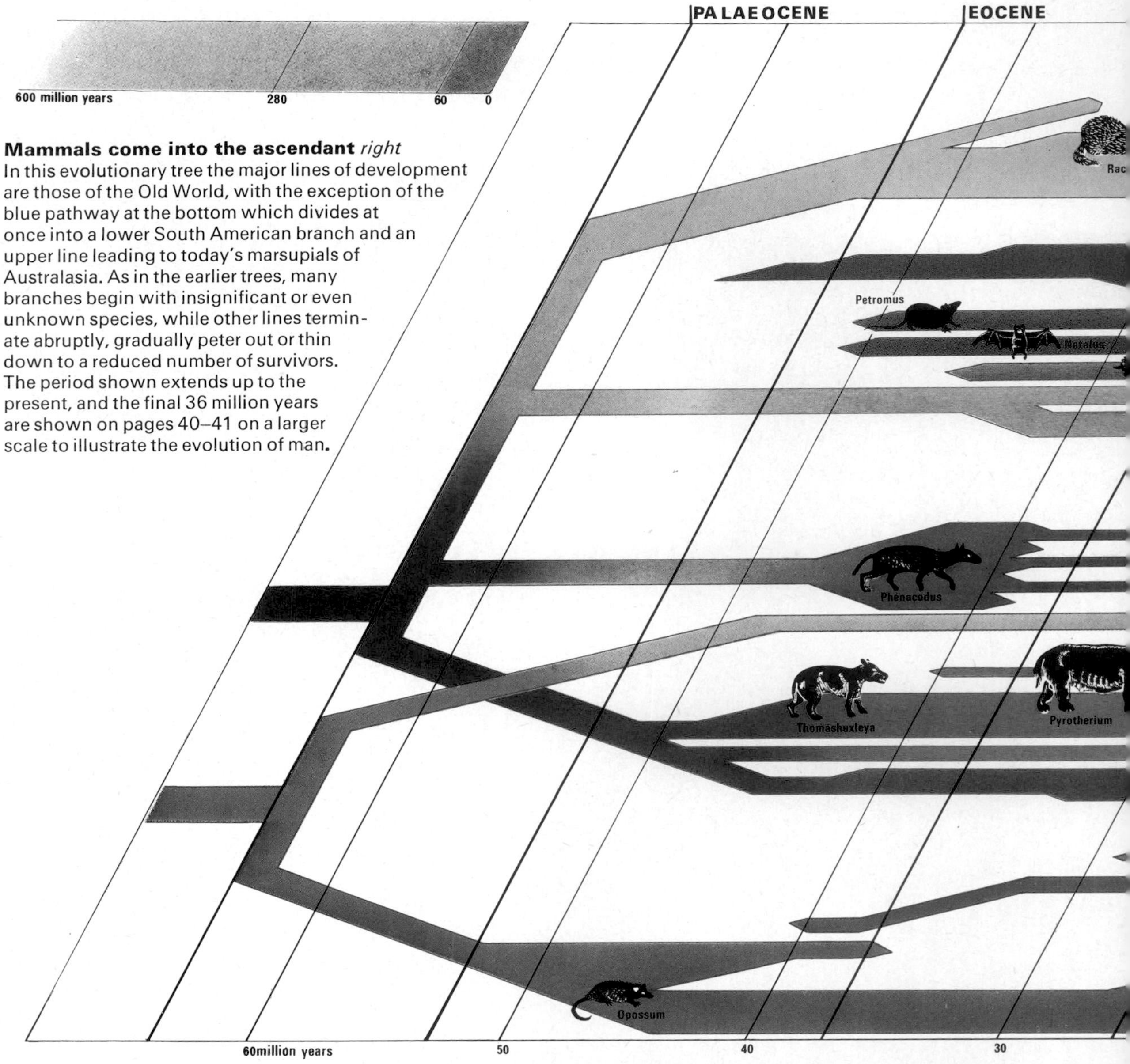

Replacing the reptiles *below*
As the Palaeocene epoch dawned, the life of the land underwent a great change. After dominating their rivals for the remarkable period of over 100 million years, the dinosaurs faded away almost completely. In their place developed a new major group: the warm-blooded mammals, bearing living young. But there was no clue to the development of man.

Mammals come into the ascendant *right*
In this evolutionary tree the major lines of development are those of the Old World, with the exception of the blue pathway at the bottom which divides at once into a lower South American branch and an upper line leading to today's marsupials of Australasia. As in the earlier trees, many branches begin with insignificant or even unknown species, while other lines terminate abruptly, gradually peter out or thin down to a reduced number of survivors. The period shown extends up to the present, and the final 36 million years are shown on pages 40–41 on a larger scale to illustrate the evolution of man.

600 million years   280   60   0

PALAEOCENE   EOCENE

Racoon

Petromus

Natalus

Phenacodus

Thomashuxleya   Pyrotherium

Opossum

60 million years   50   40   30

Diatryma, a 7 ft (2 m) bird

Mesonyx, a successful carnivore

Palaeosyops, unsuccessful herbivore

Eohippus, ancestor of the horse (see facing page)

Uintatherium, a herbivore with many horns

Coryphodon, an ungulate (hoofed animal)

Hyrachyus, ancestor of the rhino

Eocene trees were in many respects the same as those of today, although grass did not evolve until later

38

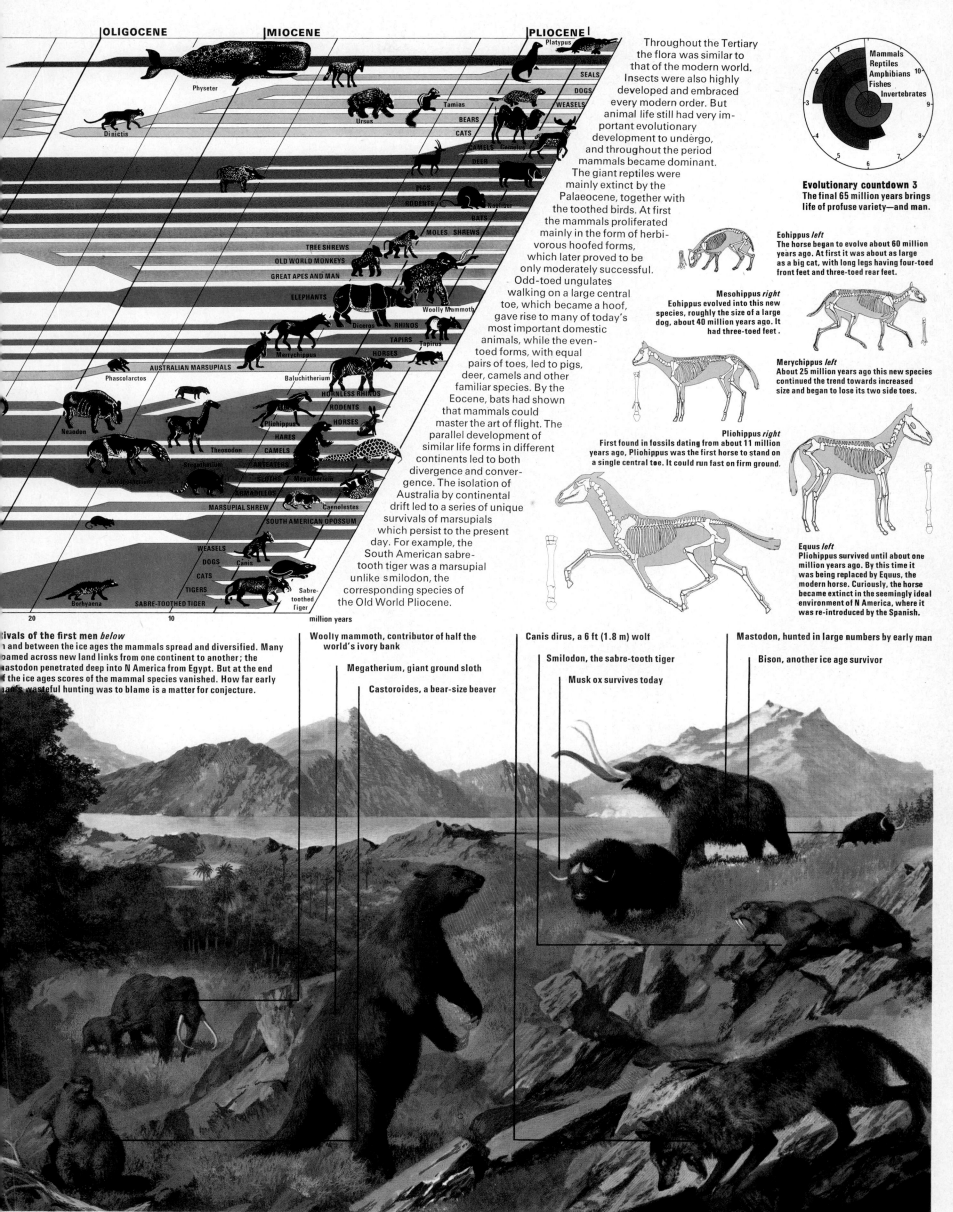

OLIGOCENE	MIOCENE	PLIOCENE

Physeter

Dinictis

Platypus

SEALS

DOGS

WEASELS

Tamias

Ursus

BEARS

CATS

CAMELS Camelus

DEER

PIGS

RODENTS

BATS

MOLES SHREWS

TREE SHREWS

OLD WORLD MONKEYS

GREAT APES AND MAN

ELEPHANTS

Woolly Mammoth

Diceros RHINOS

TAPIRS Tapirus

Merrychippus HORSES

AUSTRALIAN MARSUPIALS

Phascolarctos

Baluchitherium

HORNLESS RHINOS

RODENTS

Pliohippus HORSES

Nesodon

HARES

Theosodon CAMELS

Stegotherium ANTEATERS

Astrapotherium SLOTHS Megatherium

ARMADILLOS

MARSUPIAL SHREW

Caenolestes

SOUTH AMERICAN OPOSSUM

WEASELS

DOGS Canis

CATS

TIGERS

Borhyaena SABRE-TOOTHED TIGER

Sabre-toothed Tiger

```
20          10          million years
```

Throughout the Tertiary the flora was similar to that of the modern world. Insects were also highly developed and embraced every modern order. But animal life still had very important evolutionary development to undergo, and throughout the period mammals became dominant. The giant reptiles were mainly extinct by the Palaeocene, together with the toothed birds. At first the mammals proliferated mainly in the form of herbivorous hoofed forms, which later proved to be only moderately successful. Odd-toed ungulates walking on a large central toe, which became a hoof, gave rise to many of today's most important domestic animals, while the even-toed forms, with equal pairs of toes, led to pigs, deer, camels and other familiar species. By the Eocene, bats had shown that mammals could master the art of flight. The parallel development of similar life forms in different continents led to both divergence and convergence. The isolation of Australia by continental drift led to a series of unique survivals of marsupials which persist to the present day. For example, the South American sabre-tooth tiger was a marsupial unlike smilodon, the corresponding species of the Old World Pliocene.

Evolutionary countdown 3
The final 65 million years brings life of profuse variety—and man.

Mammals
Reptiles
Amphibians
Fishes
Invertebrates

Eohippus *left*
The horse began to evolve about 60 million years ago. At first it was about as large as a big cat, with long legs having four-toed front feet and three-toed rear feet.

Mesohippus *right*
Eohippus evolved into this new species, roughly the size of a large dog, about 40 million years ago. It had three-toed feet.

Merychippus *left*
About 25 million years ago this new species continued the trend towards increased size and began to lose its two side toes.

Pliohippus *right*
First found in fossils dating from about 11 million years ago, Pliohippus was the first horse to stand on a single central toe. It could run fast on firm ground.

Equus *left*
Pliohippus survived until about one million years ago. By this time it was being replaced by Equus, the modern horse. Curiously, the horse became extinct in the seemingly ideal environment of N America, where it was re-introduced by the Spanish.

Rivals of the first men *below*
...n and between the ice ages the mammals spread and diversified. Many ...oamed across new land links from one continent to another; the ...astodon penetrated deep into N America from Egypt. But at the end ...f the ice ages scores of the mammal species vanished. How far early ...an's wasteful hunting was to blame is a matter for conjecture.

Woolly mammoth, contributor of half the world's ivory bank

Megatherium, giant ground sloth

Castoroides, a bear-size beaver

Canis dirus, a 6 ft (1.8 m) wolf

Smilodon, the sabre-tooth tiger

Musk ox survives today

Mastodon, hunted in large numbers by early man

Bison, another ice age survivor

The Evolution of Man

Man has a history of at least 70 million years of development. During the first half of this period various monkey groups evolved, and probably about 35 million years ago one of the more advanced of these gave rise to the first hominoids, the primitive stock from which sprang today's pongids (great apes) and hominids (humans). Practically no fossil record survives of this period, but fragments exist of Ramapithecus, a probable hominid dating from 14 million years ago found in India and Africa. Then there is a gap until the first undeniable hominid group, Australopithecus, is found from five to three million years ago. He was an ape-man who may have lingered on until 500,000 years ago or later.

During this group's evolutionary lifetime major structural changes occurred which were critical to the success and survival of the hominids. These changes were centred in the regions of the pelvis, thighs, feet and head, and resulted in the great advantage of up-right stance. Although there was at this stage little parallel advance in brain power, the improved skeleton led about 500,000 years ago to a new stock, *Homo erectus*. He did show a marked advance in brain size, and he also used well-shaped stone tools and roasted his meat by the fire. By 250,000 years ago a further advance had taken place, as exemplified by the Swanscombe skull from the Thames Valley and the Steinheim skull from Germany. The immediate forebears of *Homo sapiens* are still unknown. The final forms of *Homo erectus* could have given rise to the Upper Palaeolithic people; equally, it could have been the large-brained Neanderthal man.

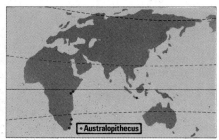

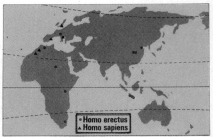

Australopithecus *left*
Man did not suddenly appear; many kinds of men evolved in many places over several million years. Remains of the earliest indisputable hominid group, Australopithecus, were discovered first in S Africa. So far, only one find, still disputed, is outside Africa.

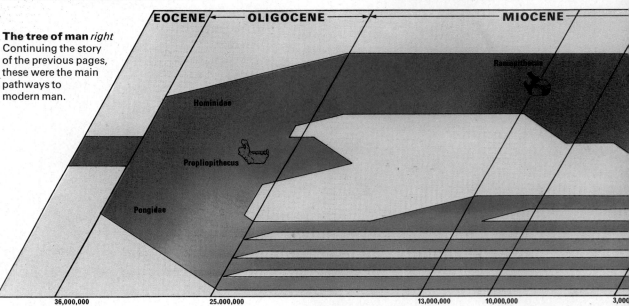

The tree of man *right*
Continuing the story of the previous pages, these were the main pathways to modern man.

EOCENE — OLIGOCENE — MIOCENE

36,000,000 25,000,000 13,000,000 10,000,000 3,000

Early Australopithecus
2,500,000 years ago
Ten million and more years later than Ramapithecus and other 'ape men', the Australopithecines were the first true hominids. They walked upright, lived on the ground and used primitive tools such as the broken piece of bone below. While hominids are all erect man-like creatures, Australopithecus is more correctly described as a pre-man, for he lacked modern man's brain-power and versatility. Knowledge of the earliest hominids is sparse. Their remains are usually in deep strata, and their tools difficult to distinguish from natural bones and stones. But the finds that have been made cover a very wide area of the Earth, mainly in Africa, and have revealed some sub-species differing in body size, possibly in diet and certainly in jaw and skull geometry and chewing strength.

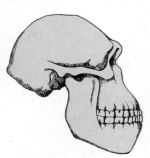

A primitive skull
In 1925 Raymond Dart discovered a human ancestor who had a small brain-case; previously, a large brain was thought to be a fundamental characteristic of man. Dart had found the earliest Pleistocene hominid yet known: *Australopithecus africanus,* shown above.

Late Australopithecus
1,000,000 years ago
Another 1½ million years of development brought great advances and further diversification. *Australopithecus robustus,* whose massive dental equipment suggested he was a vegetarian, proved to be an evolutionary dead-end; but *A. africanus* and other early hominid lines appear to have become progressively larger in stature and particularly improved in brain size and power. Some of the most significant finds of these later Australopithecines have been made in Olduvai Gorge, Tanzania, where there is ready access to strata extending down over 300 feet (100 m), representing a time-span of more than 2,000,000 years. Forty years ago Louis Leakey found chipped stones in this gorge which he judged could not have happened by accident: they were apparently the oldest shaped tools on Earth.

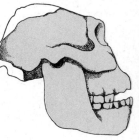

Cranium and mandible
The skull of *Australopithecus robustus* from Swartkrans, in South Africa, has been assembled from a cranium and mandible from two individuals of the same period. The main difference seen in *A. robustus* is a dental one, the cheek teeth being massive.

Homo erectus
500,000 years ago
There is no sharp dividing line between apes and men, but *Homo erectus* is possibly the first human ancestor that would be universally regarded by modern men as one of their own kind. First found, in differing forms, in Java and near Peking, his bones are much closer in geometry and proportion to those of modern man than are those of his predecessors. His lower legs, thighs, pelvic girdle and head are fully adapted to a life spent in an upright posture. His brain shows further growth, falling midway in capacity between that of a chimpanzee and that of an advanced modern man. His greatest known achievements are that he used fire and appears to have lived in communities larger than the family.

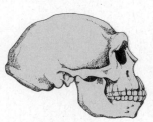

Peking man
Most initial finds of *Homo erectus* come from the neighbourhood of Peking. This skull was found at Lower Cave, Choukoutien, and dates from about 450,000 years ago.

The first men *left*
In 1891 fragments of an ape-man skeleton found in Java caused a sensation. They are now seen as the first clue to *Homo erectus* who has since been dug up in China and Tanzania. But his successor, *Homo sapiens*, was discovered first in Britain and Germany.

Neanderthal man *left*
The best-known of primitive men, he dates from 110,000 to 35000 years ago and was found from the Atlantic to Iraq. Solo and Rhodesian man were his contemporaries. These men were thoughtful, superstitious, skilful and often artistic.

Cro-Magnon man *left*
Over 25000 years ago these men sheltered from the Upper Palaeolithic ice in caves which preserved their remains for research today. While the greatest finds have been in the Dordogne, scattered caves have been found elsewhere, inhabited by related men.

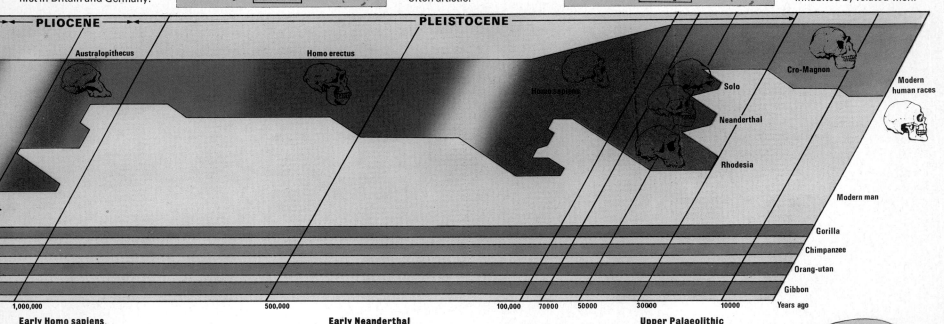

Early Homo sapiens
200,000 years ago
Man was not the first animal to walk on two legs, but he remains the only species to do so while retaining the full use of powerful and dextrous hands. This, allied with his great brain power, enabled him to become the most widespread and dominant species on Earth. Of all his manifold assets one of the greatest is his capacity to think. *Homo sapiens* ('thinking man') is the species from which all modern men have sprung; indeed, all humans today are members of the high-browed subspecies *Homo sapiens sapiens*, no matter what their colour. Solo man and Rhodesian man are examples of extinct species of *Homo sapiens*, but the illustration below is based on Swanscombe man who, with his contemporaries found at Steinheim and Montmaurin, shows many modern features.

Steinheim man
The oldest fossils that can claim to be *Homo sapiens* were fragments found in Germany and in Kent.

Early Neanderthal
70,000 years ago
By this time man's history was becoming varied and complex. The people known as Neanderthal, from the German town where the first primitive man's skull was found, lived from 110,000 to 35000 years ago and were widely distributed throughout Europe and the Middle East, and to a lesser degree in N Africa and the Near East. Many sub-types of Neanderthaler are known. Most appear to have been squat, thick-set and powerful, with a craggy, beetled-browed face and a brain sometimes larger than that of modern men. The Neanderthaler is the archetype of Stone Age man. He was very far from being a crude, ignorant brute. Typically, he dwelt in a cave, wore clothing of skins and used highly sophisticated tools and weapons. He was the first man to leave behind substantial culture.

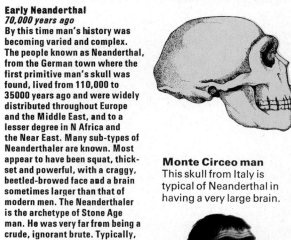

Monte Circeo man
This skull from Italy is typical of Neanderthal in having a very large brain.

Upper Palaeolithic
30,000 years ago
The later forms of Neanderthal man were replaced by Cro-Magnon man a little more than 30000 years ago. Much of our knowledge of this period stems from a unique assortment of caves and other dwellings as in the Dordogne, in France (Cro-Magnon = big grotto). Here men have lived for more than 30000 years, and traces of their culture are everywhere. The man illustrated is not quite Cro-Magnon but is drawn from early skulls found in Eastern Europe. He wears a fur coat, skin shoes and leather girdle, and his dwelling and tools show marked advance on everything that went before. In cave paintings, the manufacture of ornaments and the use of early jewellery, the period is often remarkable. There is evidence such men had devised religions, and almost certainly spoken language.

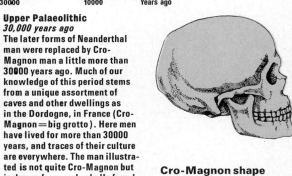

Cro-Magnon shape
His skull differed from our own only in detail.

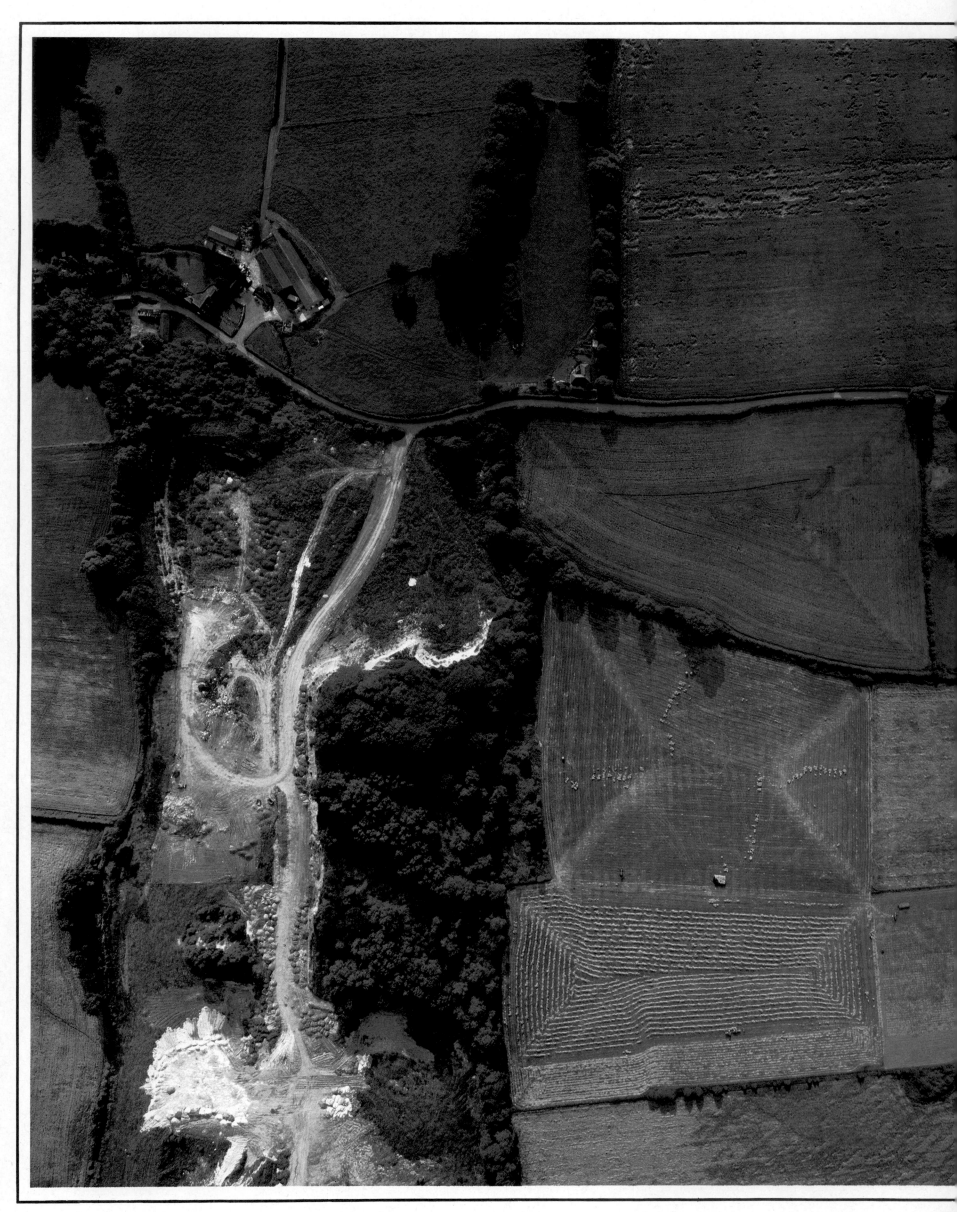

Man on Earth

The vast geographical expanse of the Earth has beguiled man into believing that its resources could never be exhausted. Only with the dramatic growth in man's industrial and agricultural demands has it become obvious that not only does his home planet have limits, but in some instances these limits are being fast approached. Of course some new supplies remain to be discovered and others will be replaced from man-made sources, but there is no room for complacency when man continues to squander his terrestrial heritage. If all nations were ever to enjoy the same standard of life as the privileged few, the demand for energy and minerals would generate an industrial 'famine' that would bring a world-wide crisis. Already excessive demands have led in some instances to over-exploitation and dereliction of the land. If a world disaster is to be averted, man must discover a new relationship with the Earth and learn to manage and to conserve its vital resources.

Monitoring Earth's resources
With Earth's known resources under pressure, a complete global picture of them, using techniques such as infra-red photography shown here, becomes urgent. In the photo, healthy vegetation is red, stubble in a harvested field pink, whilst roads and buildings are blue.

Patterns of Land Use

Land-use surveys are inventories of the Earth intended both to increase academic knowledge and to resolve practical planning problems. Some have been of a specialized nature, such as detailed surveys made of dereliction in the English Midlands and of neglected land around Ottawa, but most are general and comprehensive. The first national survey in history was that of Britain directed by L. D. Stamp to study the plight of farming during the depression of the 1930s. It soon proved to have many unexpected uses. Its detailed record of farmscape aided the plough-up campaign during World War II; its urban findings stimulated the growth of government planning; its wildscape commentary spurred the conservation movement and its derived statistics proved more accurate than many official records. A great advantage is the complete overview such surveys give.

Today most countries have undertaken detailed land-use surveys, using increasingly modern methods to secure more information. Aerial photography, using colour and infra-red film, and other data-gathering methods are integrated to create a map recording vast amounts of factual data. Such maps have proved far more useful than generalized ones because different users can extract particular sets of information for their own analysis. Thus one user can trace the spread of crop disease while another designs the restoration of open-cast coal pits and quarries. Now the whole world is being surveyed in a series of maps by the UN Food and Agriculture Organization which will not merely record how man uses the Earth but will help him to use it better.

Confined valley *above*
Pontypridd typifies land use in the Welsh valleys. Communications are confined to the valley sides. Coalmining and engineering industries completely fill the valley floor, and marginal land outside the valley is either waste or used for rough sheep grazing.

Wide open spaces *above*
Affording a total contrast with the Welsh valley, the region around the border between Alberta and Saskatchewan (left and right of vertical broken grey line) is vast and open. Roads run straight, north/south or east/west, and the fields show the large-scale

rectilinear pattern of N American farming. Dark areas are spring wheat, pale regions grass for mixed farming and red lines the borders of co-operative pastures. Along the Red Deer and Saskatchewan rivers are natural, irregular scrub woodlands (green).

A dam and its problems

In 1954 the decision was taken to build the largest rockfill dam in the world near a small earlier dam at Aswan. The completion of this, one of man's greatest engineering triumphs, has brought many economic rewards—a vast increase in arable area, good flood control and a huge output of electricity. But there are many inherent environmental problems in a dam of this size—among others nutrient and silt holdback, bilharzia increase and a build-up of toxic mineral salts. The future will tell if these outweigh the advantages

Building the dam *left*
This 1965 photograph shows concreting in progress on the main dam (left) with the power station in front. Three of the 12 turbine water tunnels, each 50 ft (15 m) in diameter, can be seen in the floor. Right, a plan of the dam site.

Abu Simbel *left*
The 3200-year-old temple of Rameses II was raised 200 ft at a cost of $40m.

The lake (1-4)
The High Dam (1) now permits multiple crops to be grown on formerly one-crop land in Upper Egypt. Floods are eliminated, new land irrigated.

Lake Nasser (2) will be 310 miles (500 km) long and should hold 157000 million m³. Filling is slowed by evaporation losses (3) and underground seepage (4).

Egypt's fisheries (5)
Nutrient losses have badly damaged offshore sardine fisheries, but by stocking coastal lakes and Lake Nasser the potential annual catch will be over 50000 tons.

The displaced people (6)
Villagers made homeless by the rising waters have all been resettled, 50000 Egyptians in Kom Ombo, Kalabsha and Nasser City, 50000 Sudanese in Kashm el Girba.

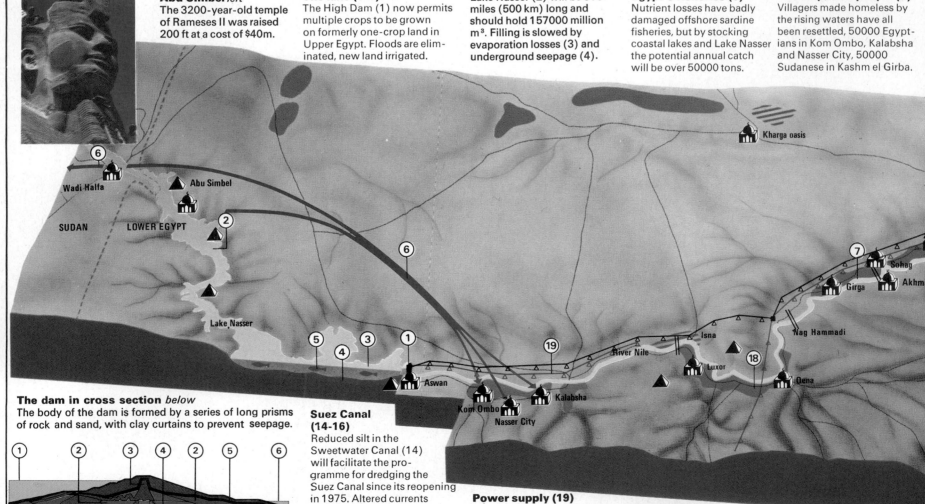

The dam in cross section *below*
The body of the dam is formed by a series of long prisms of rock and sand, with clay curtains to prevent seepage.

① Storage level (182m)
② Stone and sand
③ Clay cone
④ Injection curtain (180m)
⑤ Clay blanket
⑥ River level (85m)

Suez Canal (14-16)
Reduced silt in the Sweetwater Canal (14) will facilitate the programme for dredging the Suez Canal since its reopening in 1975. Altered currents and the apparent reduction of the saline barrier of the Bitter Lakes (15) may allow northward migration of Red Sea species (16).

Power supply (19)
Once the power station is in full operation the annual power out-put will be 10000 million kilowatt hours. Although the project initially cost $1000 million, Egypt, already the second most industrialised country in Africa, is assured of a firm basis for development.

Hostilities (17)
Reclamation projects on the Sinai coast were halted by the wars in 1967 and 1973.

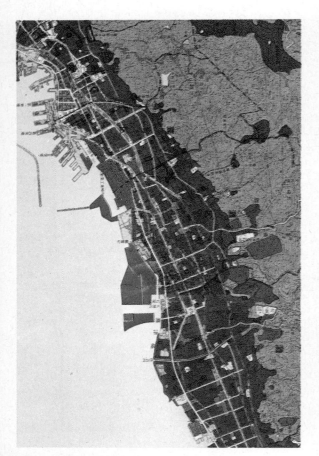

Crowded coast *left*
Japan's dense population is confined to a coastal strip by the steep, heavily forested hinterland (pale brown). The Hanshin urban region just west of the city of Kobe has large docks, a dense residential area (red), heavy industries (bright blue) and city-centre offices (purple).

Tyneside *right*
This area in NE England has both river banks completely devoted to heavy industry, as they have been for 150 years. Residential areas are set back from the river, and to the south are small mixed arable/cattle farms on scrubland and some market gardening.

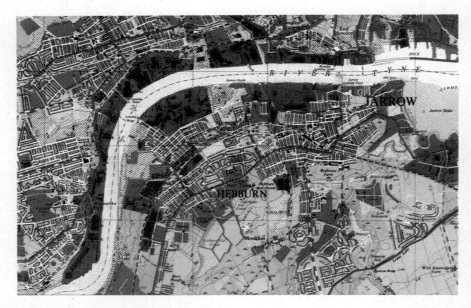

The fens *left*
The low-lying flat country of East Anglia, England, was among the first ever to be artificially drained to avoid flooding and maintain high-yield arable land. Downham Market grew from a compact mediaeval village, and is surrounded by a varied pattern of fields all deline-ated by the drainage control scheme. The region produces vegetables, fruit, poultry, pigs and cereals, the latter on the larger, more modern fields which without drainage would be too wet. Many of the older plots still have the form of long, narrow rectangles of small area.

New and old *left and right*
The Aswan High Dam (under construction, left) succeeds 6000 or more years of irrigation by wells and the Archimedean screw (right). Hydro-electric power drives the new large pumps needed to handle the new irrigation flow.

Nile delta *right*
Throughout much longer than recorded history the delta of the Nile has been naturally fertile, in sharp contrast to the Sinai desert seen in the background beyond the Gulf of Suez. The dam promises to bring fertility to the arid Upper Nile region.

Control barrages (7)
Existing and proposed barrages help slow down bank erosion.

Erosion (8)
Where bank erosion at flood time was formerly balanced by silt deposition, the steady fast flow of the Nile all the year round is causing problems. Three new barrages are proposed to slow down the flow of water.

The delta (10, 11 and 13)
Fertility of delta soil (10) is now maintained not by silt but by chemical fertilizers. Plant at Aswan, Kafr-el-Zayat (13) and Suez produce 60% of requirements and it is hoped that enough fresh water will soon be available for a rice crop from a million acres of extra land (11).

Hazards (12 and 18)
Soil sterility due to accumulation of mineral salts must be avoided by installing adequate drainage in irrigated areas (12). Bilhartzia (18), a disease carried by fresh-water snails, will increase but should be contained at a tolerable level.

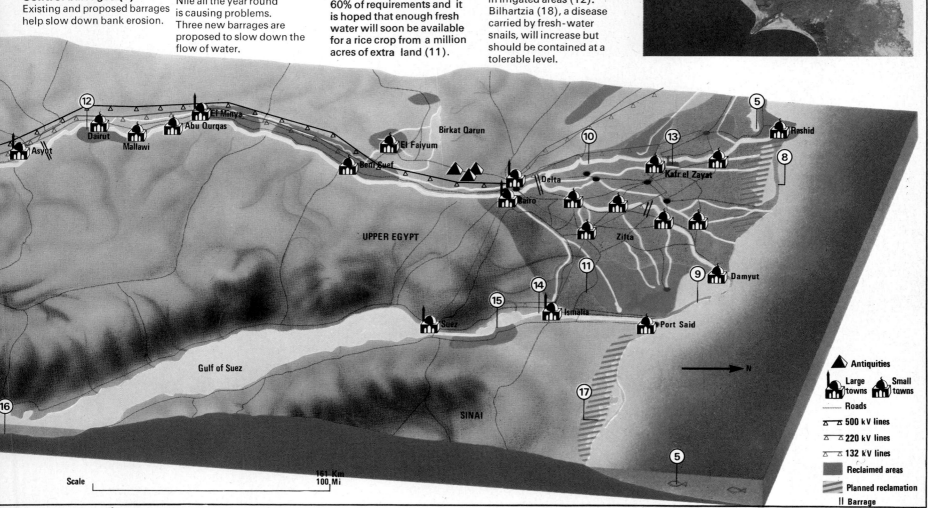

Scale | 161 Km / 100 Mi

Antiquities
Large towns / Small towns
Roads
500 kV lines
220 kV lines
132 kV lines
Reclaimed areas
Planned reclamation
Barrage

Earth's Water Resources

Without water there would be no life as we know it on the Earth. Life began in the oceans (p.34) and the life of the land, both plant and animal, still remains utterly dependent on water for its survival. The atmosphere plays a vital role in the terrestrial water system. Spurred by the energy of the Sun, the moist layer surrounding the globe forms a vast heat engine, operating at a rate of billions of horsepower. All the exposed water surface is constantly being converted into vapour. Eventually the air holding the vapour cools, and the vapour condenses as rain, hail or snow. Most of this precipitation falls into the sea, but nearly a quarter of it falls on the land. Altogether about two-thirds of it evaporates back into the air, or is transpired by plants; the rest runs off in rivers, or filters through the ground to the water table beneath.

Satisfying the collective thirst of man and his industry grows daily more difficult. Almost always the demand is for fresh water; but the proportion of the Earth's water in rivers and streams is less than one part in a million. If the Antarctic ice cap were to melt, it would feed all the rivers for 800 years. Although schemes have been suggested for towing giant freshwater icebergs from Antarctica to the Californian coast, man is unlikely to make extensive use of the ice cap. Far more promising is the large supply of subterranean water. At the same time great strides are being made in desalination of sea water, using a variety of methods. Management of the Earth's water resources is seen ever more clearly as a technical challenge of the greatest magnitude.

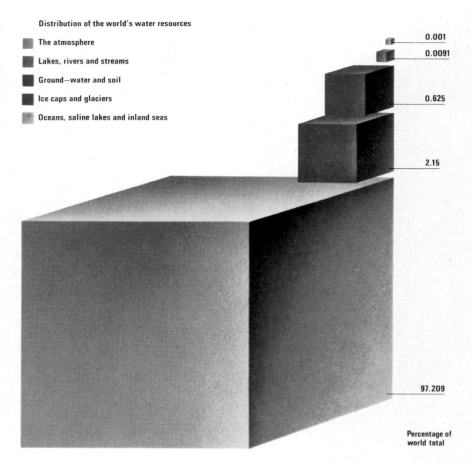

Distribution of the world's water resources

- The atmosphere
- Lakes, rivers and streams
- Ground-water and soil
- Ice caps and glaciers
- Oceans, saline lakes and inland seas

0.001
0.0091
0.625
2.15
97.209

Percentage of world total

The world's water *left*
The total volume of the Earth's water is 317 million cubic miles (1330 million km³). Practically all of it is in the oceans, in a form rich in dissolved salts. Solar heating is constantly evaporating this mass, converting it ultimately into precipitation of fresh water which falls back to the surface Run-off from the surface in rivers and streams is one of the forms of terrestrial water most visible to man, but it accounts for a negligible fraction of the total. Some 80 times as much water lies in salt lakes and inland seas, 90 times as much in fresh-water lakes, more than 6000 times as much in ground water beneath the land surface, and almost a quarter-million times as much in ice caps and glaciers. So far man has made little attempt to use these sources of fresh water. Instead he interrupts the hydrologic cycle in the easy places: the rivers and lakes, where, because of the small volumes and flows available, he causes significant pollution.

A valued resource *above*
Shiupur head, the head-waters of the Gang canal in Rajasthan province, India. This and other canal systems are gradually bringing to this arid province an assured supply of irrigation water from the Himalayas.

The hydrologic cycle *left*
This diagram is drawn for United States, but the basic features of the cycle are common to most of the Earth's land. Just over three quarters of the rain, snow and hail falls on the oceans. The usual measure for water in huge quantities is the acre-foot (one acre of water, one foot deep). Each year about 300 thousand million acre-feet of water falls on the oceans and 80 thousand million on the land. In the diagram all the figures are percentages. In the US, which is not unusual in its proportion of farmland, less than one-quarter of the water falling on the land falls directly on crops or pasture. A greater amount falls into rivers and streams, from which man takes varying small fractions for his own purposes. It can be seen that, even in the US, the total quantity of water withdrawn for use is only 7.3 per cent of the fraction of water falling on the land. Yet, to attain even this performance, Americans spend more than $10000 million each year on improving their water supplies.

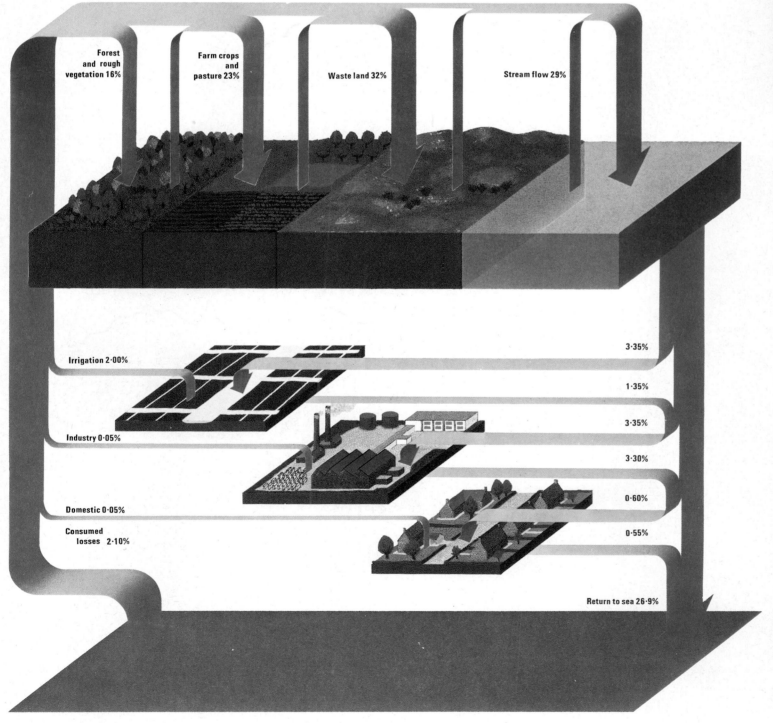

Annual precipitation 100%

Forest and rough vegetation 16%

Farm crops and pasture 23%

Waste land 32%

Stream flow 29%

Irrigation 2·00%

Industry 0·05%

Domestic 0·05%

Consumed losses 2·10%

3·35%
1·35%
3·35%
3·30%
0·60%
0·55%

Return to sea 26·9%

Domestic use of water

In some countries the total consumption of water is less than one gallon per head, but in the United States more than 70 US gallons is consumed by each person daily, on average, in domestic use alone. The way this consumption is split up varies greatly, but these percentages, for 'an average home in Akron, Ohio' are typical for modern urban areas having piped water to flush toilets. Total domestic water consumption in the industrially advanced countries is usually between five and 30 per cent of the national total.

Flushing toilet
41%

Washing and bathing 37%

No car without water
Most cars need intermittent supplies of water for cooling and washing. But every car consumes vast quantities of water during its processes of manufacture. These figures are typical.

	Process	Requirement
1	Family car	100,000 gals
2	Filling radiator	2 gals
3	One gallon of petrol	70 gals
4	One tyre	42 000 gals
5	One ton of steel	44 000 gals
6	One ton of glass	130 gals

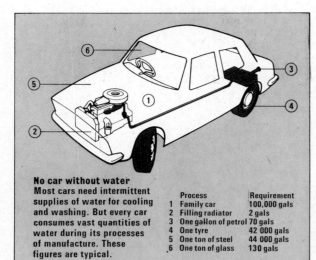

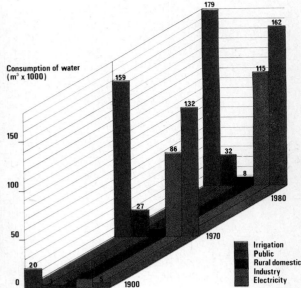

Consumption of water (m³ x 1000)

Rising demand *above*
Civilized man needs more water every year. Plotted graphically, the rising demand for water in the United States is startling ; the rate of increase is about three times the rate of population growth. Rural domestic supplies are from wells ; others are piped.

Irrigation *below*
Irrigation of land by man is at least 7000 years old, yet still in its infancy. The grey areas on the world map are virtually without irrigation. The last column of data shows the percentage of each continent irrigated. Only Japan and the UAR exceed 50 per cent.

Kitchen use 6%

Drinking 5%

Laundry 4%

Household cleaning 3%

Garden 3%

Cleaning car 1%

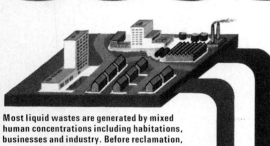

Most liquid wastes are generated by mixed human concentrations including habitations, businesses and industry. Before reclamation, any wastes having excessive or toxic mineral content must be segregated from the main flow.

Liquid wastes from residential and business areas normally comprise sewage suitable for reclamation without pre-treatment or segregation.

Oilfields on the land invariably generate large and varied liquid wastes, particularly including concentrated brines, which must be excluded from conventional reclamation processes.

This water reclamation plant supplies water to the city (above) and to agriculture and industry (below, right). Sludge and grease are returned to the sewer (route, far right).

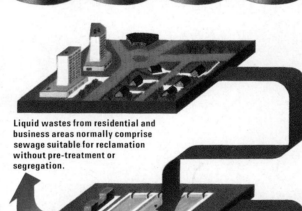

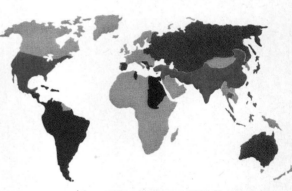

Continent	Area : million acres (1 acre = 4047m²)			Ratio of B to A (x 100)
	Total	Cultivated (A)	Irrigated (B)	
Africa	898	37	11.2	30
Asia	5062	1289	296.9	23
Australia	1900	38	3	8
Europe	288	122	5.8	5
N America	2809	485	49	10
S America	4620	187	13	7
USSR	5540	568	23	4
Grand total	21117	2726	401.9	15

This water reclamation plant accepts mainly residential effluent. Water reclaimed is returned for re-use, while sludge and grease are returned to the sewer and piped to the main sewage treatment plant. A proportion of the output is supplied to spreading grounds at the coast (below) to replenish the ground water table.

Reclaimed waters may be used to maintain underground supplies by spreading them on percolation beds (above), where the water filters down to the storage basin.

Below, the main sewage treatment plant can operate by a variety of methods, including long-term open storage, aeration, mechanical filtration and softening.

Desalination
Man's growing demand for fresh water cannot readily be met without an enormous increase in his capacity to desalinate the oceans. A choice between several ways of doing this is invariably made on economic grounds. Nearly all the large installations in use are multi-stage flash evaporators in which some form of heat – if possible, heat otherwise wasted - is used to convert sea water to steam which is condensed by the incoming salt water. But in some circumstances more economic results can be obtained by freezing, reverse osmosis or other methods.

GROWTH OF DESALTING CAPACITY 1961 TO 1968

Year Ending	Municipal water use M gal per day	Industrial/other uses M gal per day	Total
1961	17.6	42.2	59.8
1962	20.9	45.5	66.4
1963	28.4	50.4	78.8
1964	32.5	53.5	86.0
1965	39.3	58.9	98.2
1966	52.6	101.6	154.2
1967	102.2	115.3	217.5
1968	121.4	125.8	247.2
Historical annual growth %	32	17	23
Projection to 1975	835	415	1250
Projected annual growth %	32	19	26

SIZE RANGES OF THE WORLD'S DESALTING PLANTS

Size range M gal per day	Number of Plants	Total capacity M gal per day
0.025—0.1	351	17.8
0.1—0.3	218	35.3
0.3—0.5	34	13.0
0.5—1.0	31	21.3
1.0—5.0	46	95.4
5.0—7.5	3	17.5
over 7.5	3	46.9
TOTAL	686	247.2

Reclaiming used water
In almost every country the quality of the water pumped into domestic supplies is subject to precise controls, and the proportion of some substances may not exceed one or two parts per million. National water systems make maximum use of water reclaimed close to the point of consumption by plant which returns the heavy sludges and greases to the sewer for treatment at a large sewage works. This facilitates effluent quality control and also provides an emergency outlet for a temporarily overloaded or faulty reclamation plant. In the example here the main treatment plant discharges wastes into an ocean outfall (left), while the fresh water spreading grounds just inshore replenish the water table and thus prevent infiltration by the ocean water.

Minerals under the Land

Of about 2000 minerals in the Earth's crust only 100 or so are of economic importance. These are distributed very irregularly, so that no country today can boast all the minerals it needs. As a result minerals are a source of great national wealth, exploitation and even of rivalry. And the strife is likely to intensify as man's demands grow, because the total of the Earth's minerals is limited.

Against this background of uneven distribution, economic warfare and sharply increasing demand, man's use of minerals constantly changes. Coal, in 1920 the most important mineral in the world on a tonnage basis, is today unable to compete in several of its former markets because of the high cost of transporting it, and its use is increasingly changing from that of a fuel to that of a raw material for plastics and chemicals. Nitrates for fertilizers and explosives sustained the economy of Chile until 1914, when Germany found a way to 'fix' nitrogen from the atmosphere. Aluminium, one of the most abundant minerals, was costly and little used until a large-scale refining process was discovered which made use of cheap hydro-electricity.

Taking the broad view, the Earth's minerals are seen as a stern test of man's ability to make proper use of the resources available to him. Already some nations have amassed enormous stockpiles of what are today considered to be strategically important minerals. Nickel is one such metal, and the bulk of the world's supply comes from Canada. Another is manganese, and in this case the dominant supplier is the Soviet Union; but manganese is one of the many minerals which might be dredged from the sea bed.

Uneven distribution of minerals is paralleled by uneven consumption. Paradoxically, the industrialized countries which owed their original development to the presence of mineral resources, particularly iron and coal, now rely for their continued prosperity on developing nations. If the latter were to develop a similar demand for materials a mineral famine would ensue which would have repercussions throughout the world.

World output *right*
The most important commercial minerals and main producers. At the foot of each column is annual world output in millions of long tons. Precious mineral outputs (asterisked) are : gold 52 million fine troy ounces ; silver 240 m.f.t.o. ; platinum 3.4 m.f.t.o. ; diamonds 30 million metric carats.

Key to mineral producers

1 Soviet Union	15 Zambia
2 USA	16 Australia
3 France	17 Spain
4 S Africa	18 Italy
5 Philippines	19 Malaysia
6 Congo (Kinshasa)	20 United Kingdom
7 Canada	21 Thailand
8 Morocco	22 Argentina
9 Brazil	23 Uganda
10 Chile	24 India
11 New Caledonia	25 Mexico
12 SW Africa	26 Peru
13 Finland	27 Congolese Rep.
14 China (People's Rep.)	28 Ghana

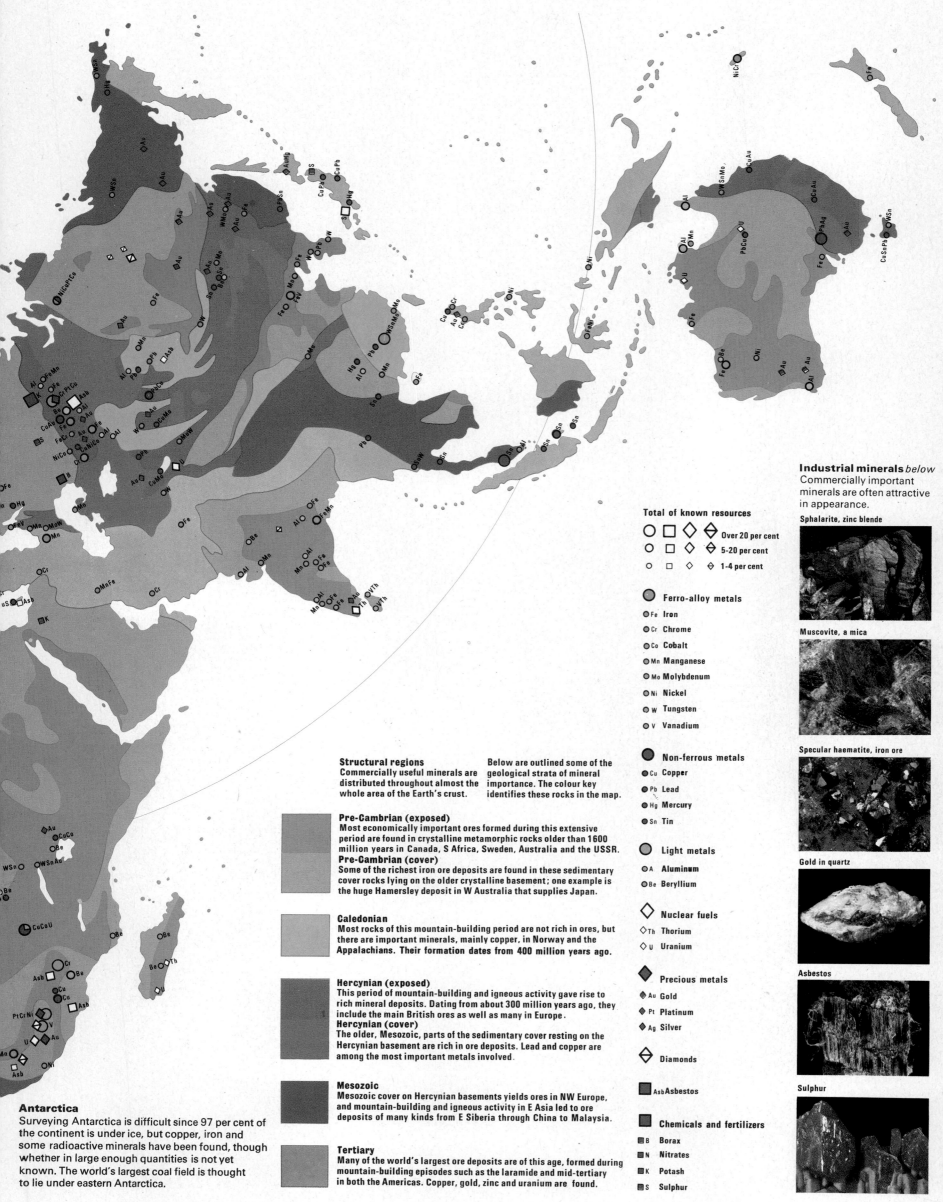

Total of known resources

○	□	◇	⬦ Over 20 per cent
○	□	◇	⬦ 5-20 per cent
○	□	◇	⬦ 1-4 per cent

◉ Ferro-alloy metals

- ⊙ Fe Iron
- ⊙ Cr Chrome
- ⊙ Co Cobalt
- ⊙ Mn Manganese
- ⊙ Mo Molybdenum
- ⊙ Ni Nickel
- ⊙ W Tungsten
- ⊙ V Vanadium

◉ Non-ferrous metals

- ⊙ Cu Copper
- ⊙ Pb Lead
- ⊙ Hg Mercury
- ⊙ Sn Tin

◉ Light metals

- ⊙ A Aluminum
- ⊙ Be Beryllium

◇ Nuclear fuels

- ◇ Th Thorium
- ◇ U Uranium

◆ Precious metals

- ◆ Au Gold
- ◆ Pt Platinum
- ◆ Ag Silver

◇ Diamonds

▪ Asb Asbestos

▪ Chemicals and fertilizers

- ▪ B Borax
- ▪ N Nitrates
- ▪ K Potash
- ▪ S Sulphur

Structural regions

Commercially useful minerals are distributed throughout almost the whole area of the Earth's crust.

Below are outlined some of the geological strata of mineral importance. The colour key identifies these rocks in the map.

Pre-Cambrian (exposed)
Most economically important ores formed during this extensive period are found in crystalline metamorphic rocks older than 1600 million years in Canada, S Africa, Sweden, Australia and the USSR.

Pre-Cambrian (cover)
Some of the richest iron ore deposits are found in these sedimentary cover rocks lying on the older crystalline basement; one example is the huge Hamersley deposit in W Australia that supplies Japan.

Caledonian
Most rocks of this mountain-building period are not rich in ores, but there are important minerals, mainly copper, in Norway and the Appalachians. Their formation dates from 400 million years ago.

Hercynian (exposed)
This period of mountain-building and igneous activity gave rise to rich mineral deposits. Dating from about 300 million years ago, they include the main British ores as well as many in Europe.

Hercynian (cover)
The older, Mesozoic, parts of the sedimentary cover resting on the Hercynian basement are rich in ore deposits. Lead and copper are among the most important metals involved.

Mesozoic
Mesozoic cover on Hercynian basements yields ores in NW Europe, and mountain-building and igneous activity in E Asia led to ore deposits of many kinds from E Siberia through China to Malaysia.

Tertiary
Many of the world's largest ore deposits are of this age, formed during mountain-building episodes such as the laramide and mid-tertiary in both the Americas. Copper, gold, zinc and uranium are found.

Antarctica

Surveying Antarctica is difficult since 97 per cent of the continent is under ice, but copper, iron and some radioactive minerals have been found, though whether in large enough quantities is not yet known. The world's largest coal field is thought to lie under eastern Antarctica.

Industrial minerals *below*

Commercially important minerals are often attractive in appearance.

Sphalarite, zinc blende

Muscovite, a mica

Specular haematite, iron ore

Gold in quartz

Asbestos

Sulphur

Earth's Energy Resources

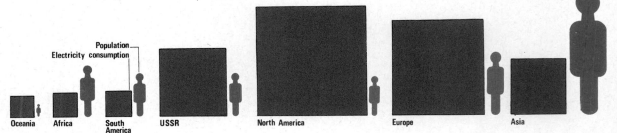

Energy consumption
kilograms
per capita

The concept of energy arose only very recently in the period of man's life on Earth, but already it dominates the whole quality of this life. Early man had no mechanical energy but that of his muscles. By about 2500 years ago he had learned to harness draught animals, such as the ox and horse, and to devise crude water wheels to harness part of the energy of the flow of water in a river. Soon afterwards he added sails to make the fickle wind propel his ships, and by 1000 years ago had started to dot his landscape with windmills. By this time he was adept at burning combustible materials, and during the past 500 years his energy has been increasingly based upon fire, first using wood, and subsequently coal, gas made from coal, petroleum, and natural gas.

All these energy sources, including animal muscle and the wind, are based on the energy radiated by the Sun. Although modern man has begun to use this energy directly in a few trivial installations in hot countries, almost all his energy is derived from solar heat locked up in fossil fuels. The known reserves of these fuels are tending to increase, as a result of prospecting, even faster than man is burning them up. But if no more were discovered most of man's world would come to a halt inside 20 years.

But there should be no energy gap. The promise of nuclear energy is such that, by using fast reactors that breed more fuel than they consume, energy should become one of the very few really plentiful and cheap commodities in man's world of the future. The challenges reside in extracting the fuels and using them effectively.

Power and people *above*
World consumption of energy is very uneven. One way of measuring it is to reduce all forms of energy to an equivalent weight of coal burned. The columns on the world map are proportional to the 'coal equivalent' of selected national consumptions expressed in kilogrammes per head. Electricity consumption is even more disproportionate, as witness the square areas and figure heights immediately above.

Fuels and energy *right*
The calorific value of a fuel is the quantity of heat generated by burning a unit mass. Figures are in British Thermal Units per pound. The surrounding curve shows the increase in the rate at which man is consuming energy; one joule (j) per second is equal to one watt.

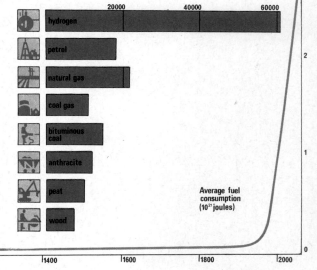

Sources of power *below*
For many centuries the only alternative sources of power to muscles were wood fires, waterwheels and windmills — and the latter had too slight an effect to be shown on the figure below. The left portion shows the way in which, since 1850, the United States has enjoyed successive new sources of energy. In 1920 the US economy was not untypical in being based on coal, but since then more energetic, cleaner and more efficiently used fuels have dominated the picture. In the future, nuclear power, shown in the right-hand figure, promises to make good shortages of fossil fuels.

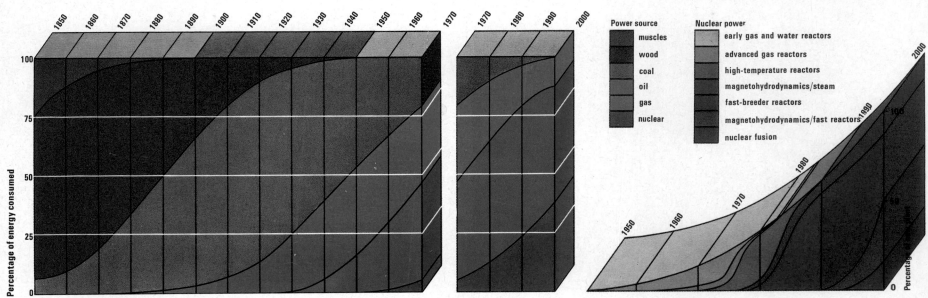

Power source	Nuclear power
muscles	early gas and water reactors
wood	advanced gas reactors
coal	high-temperature reactors
oil	magnetohydrodynamics/steam
gas	fast-breeder reactors
nuclear	magnetohydrodynamics/fast reactors
	nuclear fusion

Coal into electricity
To reduce costs modern coal-fired generating stations are sited on coalfields ; Lea Hall colliery feeds Rugeley power station (background).

Flare in the desert
Once oil has been struck, harmful gases are burned off in the atmosphere. Similar 'flares' are a prominent feature of petroleum refineries.

Drilling for gas
To reach natural gas trapped in submarine strata a drill rig is used to bore a hole at a location determined by the prospectors.

Nuclear power station
Nearly all today's nuclear energy is used to generate electricity. One of the largest stations is Wylfa, Wales, rated at 1180 million watts.

Coal

For three centuries the most important of the fossil fuels, coal is the result of some 300 million years of subterranean decay of vegetation. Many thousands of generations of the Carboniferous trees have become compressed and hardened, first into peat, then into lignite, then into bituminous coal and finally into anthracite. Until this century coal was used inefficiently as a source of heat. Today it is becoming equally important as a raw material producing plastics, heavy chemicals, insecticides, perfumes, antiseptics, road surfaces and many other products. Great advances have been made in automating the mining of coal, but it remains a labour-intensive task and is therefore becoming increasingly expensive. However, coal remains a worldwide industry that passes on to modern man the products of the solar energy captured by a younger Earth.

Petroleum

Like coal, oil is a mixture of fossil remains, but yields few clues as to its origin. Crude oil, from the locations shown on the map at right, is carried by tanker ships to refineries in the user countries. Here it is heated in pipe stills until the various constituent 'fractions' are boiled off. The result is a wide range of products from petrol through kerosene and gas oil to heavy fuel oils, lubricants and vaseline, with a wide range of other by-products used in many thousands of chemicals and plastics materials. Petroleum fuels are replacing coal in heating and transport applications, partly owing to their easier handling and partly to reduce air pollution by sulphurous compounds. LPG, liquefied petroleum gas, is even cleaner burning and may become more important than petrols and kerosenes in road vehicles and aircraft over the next 25 years.

Gas

In 1807 a London street was lit by town gas, a mixture of hydrogen (about 50%), methane, carbon monoxide and dioxide and other gases, formed by cooking coal at high temperature in a retort. By 1950 this manufactured gas was an important fuel, but in many advanced countries its place is now being taken by natural gas, a primary fuel consisting mainly of methane piped straight from deposits sometimes conveniently sited from the user's point of view (right). Intensive prospecting is discovering natural gas faster than it is being used, and during the past 20 years natural gas has become man's largest single source of energy. In refrigerated form, as a compact liquid, it promises to become an attractive fuel for transport vehicles. A major benefit is that the exhaust from such a vehicle would contain less pollutants than from those using petrol.

Nuclear energy

In 1956 Britain opened the world's first electricity generating station using the heat of nuclear fission. It was fuelled with rods of natural uranium, a heavy silvery metal containing a small proportion of atoms capable of spontaneous fission when struck by a free neutron. Fission releases further neutrons capable of sustaining a continuous chain reaction. Such a reaction generates heat which is used to provide steam for turbines. The prime advantage of nuclear power is that the fuel is used extremely slowly. Now the fast reactor, which uses raw 'fast' neutrons instead of ones artificially slowed down, has been developed. Not only can the fast reactor generate great energy from a small bulk but it creates fresh fuel faster than the original (plutonium) fuel is consumed. Fast re-actors, using uranium from granite, could provide limitless cheap energy.

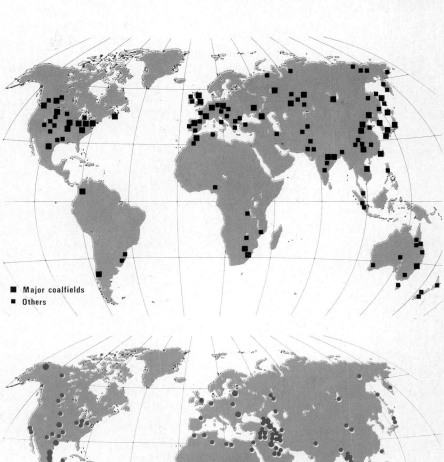

■ Major coalfields
■ Others

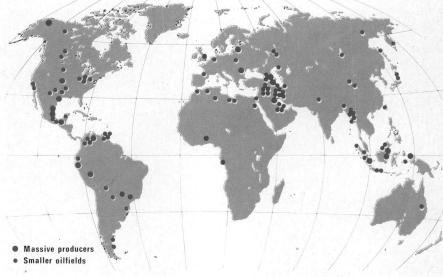

● Massive producers
● Smaller oilfields

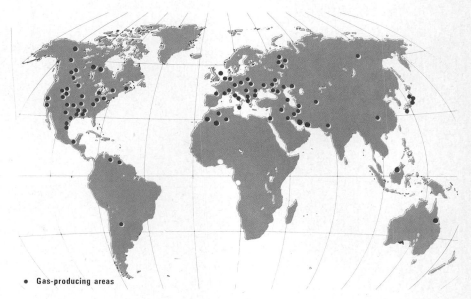

● Gas-producing areas

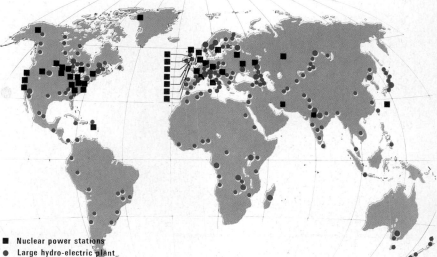

■ Nuclear power stations
● Large hydro-electric plant
● Smaller hydro schemes

The Oceans' Living Resources

Fish and shellfish were probably the first marine resources to be exploited by man. Many of his early settlements in coastal and estuarine areas bear witness to this with their ancient mounds of oyster and mussel shells. Even now, coastal fisheries remain a vital source of high quality protein for numerous primitive communities. And yet, in spite of this long history of coastal fishing, the commercial fisheries have been dominated by a mere handful of nations until recent times. Three-quarters of the world fish catch is still accounted for by only 14 countries.

The world fish catch is the only source of food that has managed to increase dramatically since the end of World War 2. In the decade from 1958-68 alone, it rose from below 34 million tons to 64 million tons. Although the catch fell by two per cent in 1969, it is expected to continue to improve and may even top the 120 million ton mark by the mid-1980s.

The steady growth of the commercial fisheries since the war has relied on improvements in technology and boats, and the spread of these modern techniques from traditional northern fisheries to newer ones being developed in the southern oceans. Peru, for example, now has the world's largest single species fishery, catching some 10 million tons of anchoveta a year: in 1958 the catch was only 960,000 tons. However, the time is fast approaching when few fish stocks will remain unexploited.

Already many established fisheries are beginning to suffer from the effects of over-fishing with too many boats pursuing too few fish, leading to the capture of younger, smaller fish and a decline in the fish stocks and the fisheries that they. support. Only the briefest respite may be needed for the fish to recover: a single female fish can lay thousands of eggs in a single season. Over-exploitation of the whales and turtles is a much more serious matter. Already several species of whale are on the verge of extinction and, with one young born to a female every two years, the prospects for their recovery are poor.

The living resources of the oceans must be conserved and managed if they are to continue to provide mankind with food. It is now clear that the world fish catch has a finite limit, possibly about 200 million tons. With adequate international agreement and controls, this limit might one day be approached. The productivity of the oceans could be increased further only by harvesting animals lower than fish in the marine food chain or by artificially fertilizing and farming the seas. Some of the first steps in this direction are now in progress. Perhaps in the future a new pattern of exploitation will emerge, with fleets harvesting the oceanic fish while other fish, shellfish and crustaceans such as lobster and prawn are farmed in the shallow coastal waters.

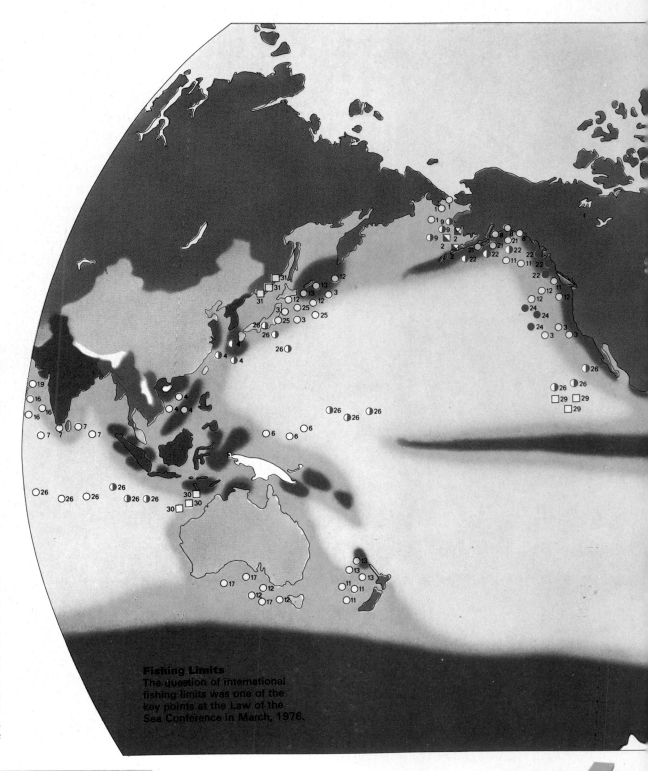

Fishing Limits
The question of international fishing limits was one of the key points at the Law of the Sea Conference in March, 1976.

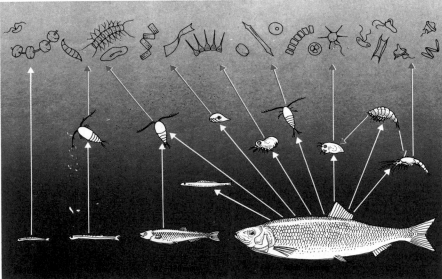

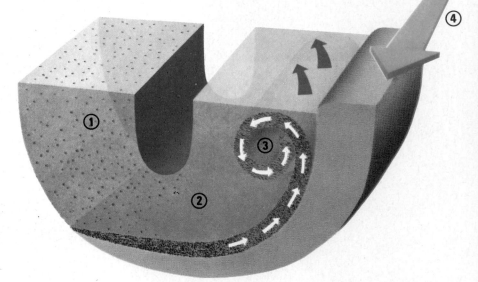

Marine food web *above*
The path leading to food fish such as the herring involves a succession of feeding and energy levels. The plants drifting in the plankton first convert the Sun's energy into a usable form through the process of photosynthesis (top band). The plants are then eaten by small planktonic animals (middle band). These in turn are eaten by the fish during its growth (bottom band). However, as the arrows indicate, the path from plant to fish is far from simple. At each point in the web, energy is exchanged and lost so that the adult fish receives less than a thousandth of the original energy captured in photosynthesis. This loss of energy has prompted suggestions for short-circuiting the process by harvesting members of the plankton itself – either the plants or the small crustaceans and other animals that feed on them.

Upwelling *above*
Most of the world's great fisheries occur in regions of upwelling where nutrient-rich water rises to the surface and supports prolific marine life. Deep ocean waters accumulate the remains of dead and decaying organisms (1) that rain down from the surface. When this nutrient-rich water (2) rises to the surface (3) it contains all the minerals and salts necessary for plant growth in approximately the ratio best suited to stimulate maximum growth. The actual mechanism which causes the water to rise to the surface can vary, but a common source is the interaction between surface winds and ocean currents running along the edge of continents. The wind (4) causes the surface water to move away from the coast, enabling the deep water to swirl up to the surface where it renews the supplies of plant nutrients.

World fisheries *left*
With more nations claiming a share of the oceans' living resources few productive regions remain unexplored by fishing fleets. Already many fisheries show signs of over-exploitation and some coastal states are demanding exclusive rights to very large areas of sea, e.g. Iceland's demand for a 50 mile limit.

Biological productivity

■ Very favourable conditions for the growth of marine life

■ Moderately favourable conditions for the growth of marine life

Exploitation of fish stocks

● Over-exploited by 1949

◑ Over-exploited by 1968

○ Under-exploited

Exploitation of crustaceans

◪ Over-exploited by 1968

□ Under-exploited

Key to numbers

1 Alaska pollack	16 Pelagic
2 Anchoveta	17 Pilchard
3 Anchovy	18 Plaice
4 Demersal fish	19 Pomfret
5 Capelin	20 Red fish
6 Carangidae	21 Rock fish
7 Clupeidae	22 Salmon
8 Cod	23 Sand eel
9 Flat fish	24 Sardine
10 Haddock	25 Saury
11 Hake	26 Tuna
12 Herring	27 King crab
13 Jack Mackerel	28 Krill
14 Mackerel	29 Crab
15 Menhaden	30 Shrimp
	31 Squid

Fishing limits

■ Nations claiming a 3 mile exclusive zone

■ Nations claiming a 6 mile exclusive zone

■ Nations claiming a 12 mile exclusive zone

■ Nations claiming more than 12 miles

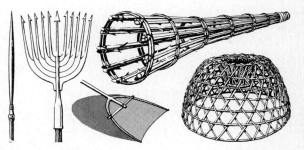

Fishing gear
Primitive fisheries use a wide range of techniques (above) including spears, nets and basket traps.

Mainstays of the modern commercial fisheries (below) are the gill net (top), the seine net and the otter trawl (bottom).

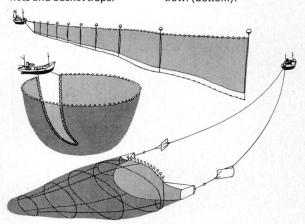

Anchoveta — 5 in, 13 cm 2-3 oz, 85 g

Herring — 12 in, 30 cm 8 oz, 227 g

Commercial fish
Although the oceans contain many thousands of different fish species, very few of these support large commercial fisheries. The anchoveta supplies the largest single species fishery in the world with an annual catch of about 10 million tons. This is slightly greater than the total catch of the other species illustrated here.

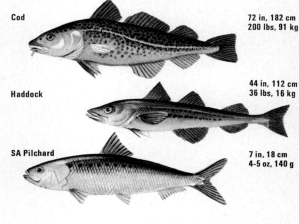

Cod — 72 in, 182 cm 200 lbs, 91 kg

Haddock — 44 in, 112 cm 36 lbs, 16 kg

SA Pilchard — 7 in, 18 cm 4-5 oz, 140 g

The first marine farms, *right*
An early use of marine stockades was to keep alive fish caught at sea until they were needed for eating (A). An advance on this is to catch young fish and then fatten them in fertile coastal waters (B). But marine farming really begins with the production of 'seed fish' which can be reared until they are large enough to survive at sea (C). Such a scheme was proposed in the early 1900s as a means of increasing the productivity of the North Sea fisheries. The proposal was rejected, although marine fish hatcheries existed at the time. These hatcheries, however, were unable to feed their young fish once the yolk sacs had become exhausted. Success became possible with the discovery that brine shrimps, hatched in large numbers, could be used as fish food and that antibiotics would prevent marine bacteria from coating the eggs and killing or weakening the fish embryos inside. The point has now been reached at which fish farming is possible, although fish reared in this way are still too expensive to compete with those caught at sea. In one scheme, eggs collected from adult fish kept in ponds are hatched and the young fed on diatoms and brine shrimps until large enough to be put into marine enclosures (D).

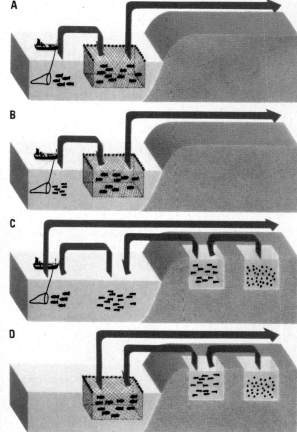

A

B

C

D

Enriching the sea *right, below*
Some marine farms in the future will exploit the store of nutrients that lie in the cold, deep ocean water. The value of this marine 'fertilizer' is clearly seen in areas where deep water rises to the surface. One project to create an artificial upwelling was started in the Virgin Islands in 1970. When completed it could include both a marine farm and provide fresh water supplies. In this system the cold nutrient-rich water (1) would be raised to the surface by a pump (2) driven by the warm, humid, prevailing winds (3). The cold water would then pass through a condenser (4) where it would be used to cool the wind and release its store of fresh water (5). Finally, the water, now warmed to the temperature of the surface waters, would be used to promote the growth of marine plants and animals such as shellfish, prawn and valuable food fish within net enclosures in the lagoon (6). Deep ocean water may also be used to combat thermal pollution, particularly in tropical areas where marine organisms live close to their upper temperature limit. The cold water would cool down the warm effluent discharged from power stations as well as provide valuable nutrients for marine aquiculture.

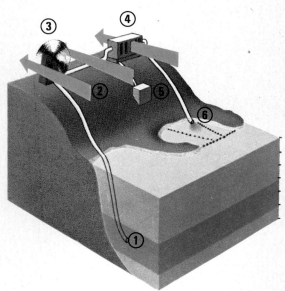

The Food Resource: 1

Combine harvester discharging wheat into trailer

Agriculture has always been a cornerstone of human civilization. Until man was able to give up the life of a nomadic hunter he could not be called civilized, and it was the settled life based on the land which enabled progress towards modern society to begin. Today agriculture is the occupation of more people than all other industries, but the pattern of their work varies greatly. In poor or developing lands as many as 90 per cent of the population live directly off the land, whereas in the most industrialized countries the proportion can be as low as three per cent.

The underlying purpose of farming is to convert the energy of sunlight into a form in which it can be assimilated by humans. Initially this can be done only by photosynthesis in green plants, and here the efficiency of the conversion process – expressed in terms of assimilable food energy obtained from a given amount of sunlight – varies from about two per cent down to less than one part in 1000. Further stages involve the consumption of plants by livestock to provide meat and other food for man, or the direct consumption of fruit, vegetables and cereals by man himself. Each additional step in this food chain involves large losses in energy, lowering the overall 'efficiency' of the process.

For many years research has led to improved methods of producing crops, by developing new plant strains with a higher edible yield or greater resistance to disease, by increasing both the area of land under cultivation and the nutritional value of the soil, by devising swifter and surer techniques of cultivation and by reducing the labour effort needed. Improved methods are especially needed in regions of poor farming. The 'Green Revolution' of SE Asia has already shown how yields can be increased dramatically, although at a greater cost in terms of agricultural chemicals and water supplies. Another promising way of increasing food supplies is to extract protein from plants such as soyabean and even grass, and to convert them into forms that have the texture and taste of meat. For the more distant future there are prospects of growing single-cell protein and other revolutionary foods which in theory could at least double the Earth's ability to produce food.

World crop production and trade *right above*
In the large map, symbols and shading indicate the pattern of distribution of a selection of the most important crops used for human food The distribution shown is that of growing area. This is often far removed from the plant's original centre, and today the world crop pattern is being subjected to dramatic changes. For example, enormous increases have taken place in Italy's yield of maize (corn) and the United States' production of rice. Pie diagrams are used to show world crop trade, the pie area giving output and the colour segments the products (key, far right).

Some important crops *right*
Eight of the world's chief human food crops are described individually at right. The figure below the name is the aggregate world production expressed in metric tons (1 m. ton is 0.984 British ton and 1.12 US tons). The pie diagrams in the form of segmented drums show the percentage of the world total raised by the three largest producing countries (in each case China is the People's Republic). The sketches illustrate the mature plant and its fruit, a form often unfamiliar to consumers. Similar panels on the next two pages deal with livestock, fish and oils.

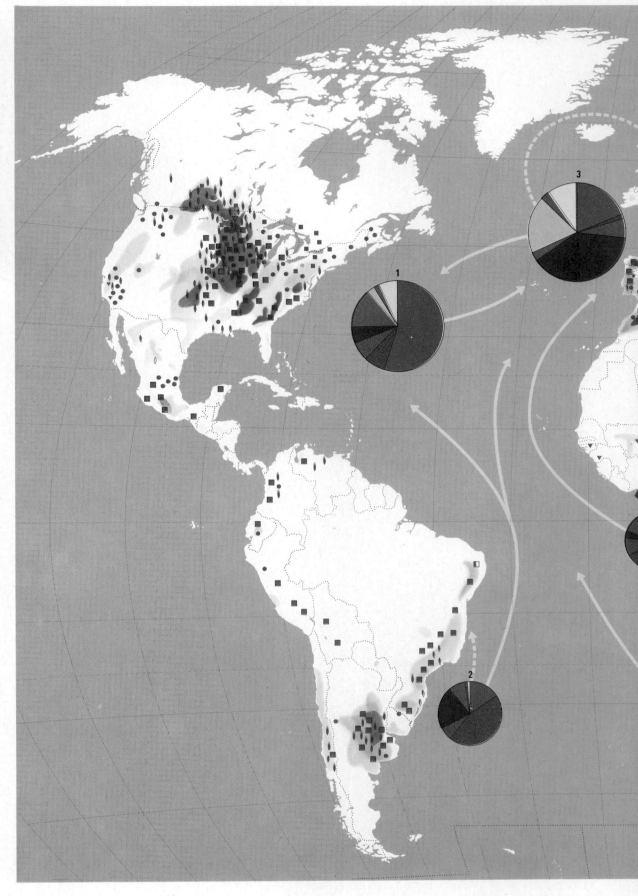

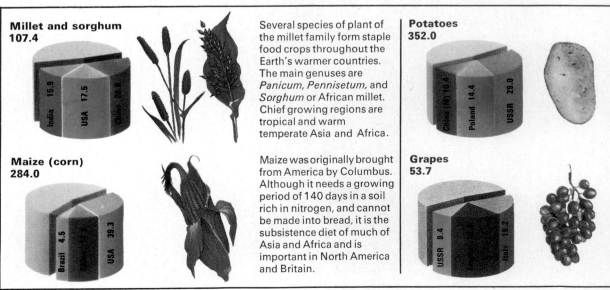

Millet and sorghum
107.4

India 15.9 | USA 17.5 | China 30.8

Several species of plant of the millet family form staple food crops throughout the Earth's warmer countries. The main genuses are *Panicum, Pennisetum,* and *Sorghum* or African millet. Chief growing regions are tropical and warm temperate Asia and Africa.

Maize (corn)
284.0

Brazil 4.5 | Bahong 7.5 | USA 39.3

Maize was originally brought from America by Columbus. Although it needs a growing period of 140 days in a soil rich in nitrogen, and cannot be made into bread, it is the subsistence diet of much of Asia and Africa and is important in North America and Britain.

Potatoes
352.0

China (M) 10.4 | Poland 14.4 | USSR 29.0

Grapes
53.7

USSR 8.4 | France | Italy 19.2

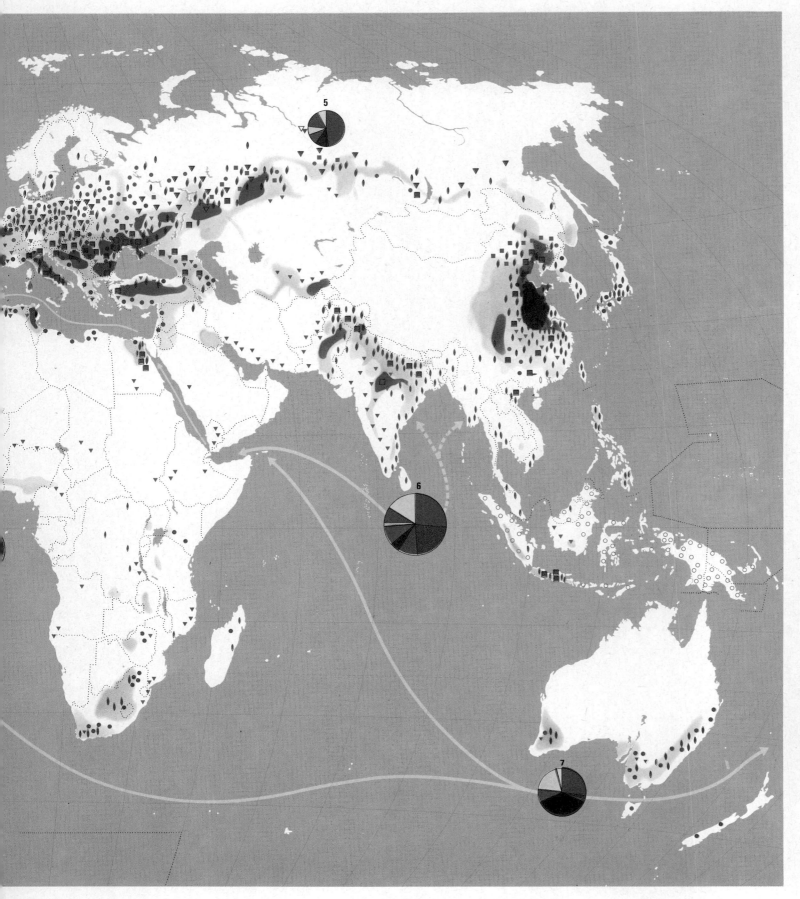

The circular 'pie diagrams'
depict world trade in selected
agricultural products in 1968:
1 N and Central America;
2 S America; 3 Europe, 4 Africa;
5 Soviet Union, 6 Asia;
7 Oceania. Products considered
are cereals, beverages, meat
and meat products, fish and fish
products, dairy products, fruit
and vegetables, vegetable oils
and sugar.

Cereals
Beverages
Fruit
Meat and meat products
Sugar
Dairy products
Vegetable oils
Fish and fish products

Total trade US$ million

5000

2500

1250

Native to South America,
the potato was introduced
by Spanish explorers to an
intrigued Europe about
1572. Although it needs a
long, cool growing season,
and a high nutrient level. it
yields more food per area of
land than cereals. They are
a source of alcohol.

The vine thrives in warm,
temperate areas, although
the quality of its rootstock
is critical to its nutrient
demand and its resistance
to disease and drought.
About 80 per cent of the
world crop is made into
wine, but large quantities
are dried for raisins.

Rice
284.2

Rye
33.4

Grown in Asia for at least
5000 years, rice was
introduced into Europe by
the Arabs. Irrigation or a
very heavy rainfall is
essential for growing rice,
with the fields being flooded
for most of the season. The
main source of vitamins, the
husk, is removed in milling.

Gradually giving way to
other cereals, rye is
important where soils are
sandy and acid and the
winters long and harsh.
From Britain deep into
Siberia it remains a staple
foodstuff used for animal
feeds, for various forms of
bread and for whisky.

Wheat
332.5
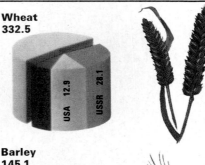

Barley
145.1
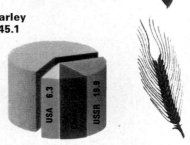

Wheat is the most basic
human food of the
temperate zone. It flourishes
in well-drained, fertile
conditions, but can rapidly
exhaust the soil. New breeds
have been genetically
tailored to improve yield
and resistance to disease.

Barley has a very short
growing season and so can
be produced further north
and at a higher altitude than
any other cereal. It needs
good drainage and non-
acid soil. More than half the
world crop is eaten by
livestock, and 12 per cent
goes into making beer.

The Food Resource:2

Unloading frozen lamb carcases.

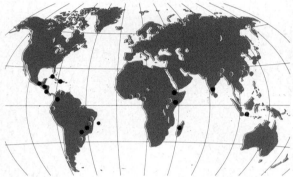

Beverages
Coffee, cocoa and tea are grown in the tropics for export to economically advanced countries, where their chief role is to add flavour rather than to provide nutrition. Tea is the cheapest at present.

- ● Coffee
- ● Cocoa
- ● Tea

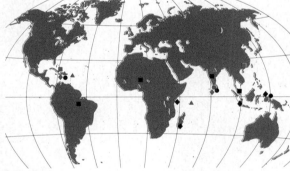

Spices
Invariably these are pungent, aromatic vegetable products. They have been important European imports since pre-Roman times, and a major source today is Indonesia. Spices are extracted from buds, bark and pods.

- ■ Pimento
- ▲ Ginger
- ◆ Nutmeg
- ● Mace
- ■ Pepper
- ◆ Cloves
- ● Cinnamon
- ■ Cassia
- ▲ Vanilla

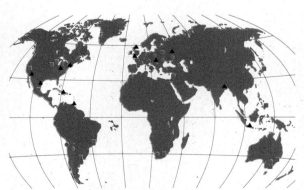

Alcohol and tobacco
Originally native to South America, tobacco was brought to Europe by the Spanish 400 years ago. Today, it is grown all over the world in various climates and soils. The US is the biggest producer.

- ■ Beer
- ● Wine
- ▲ Spirits
- ◆ Tobacco

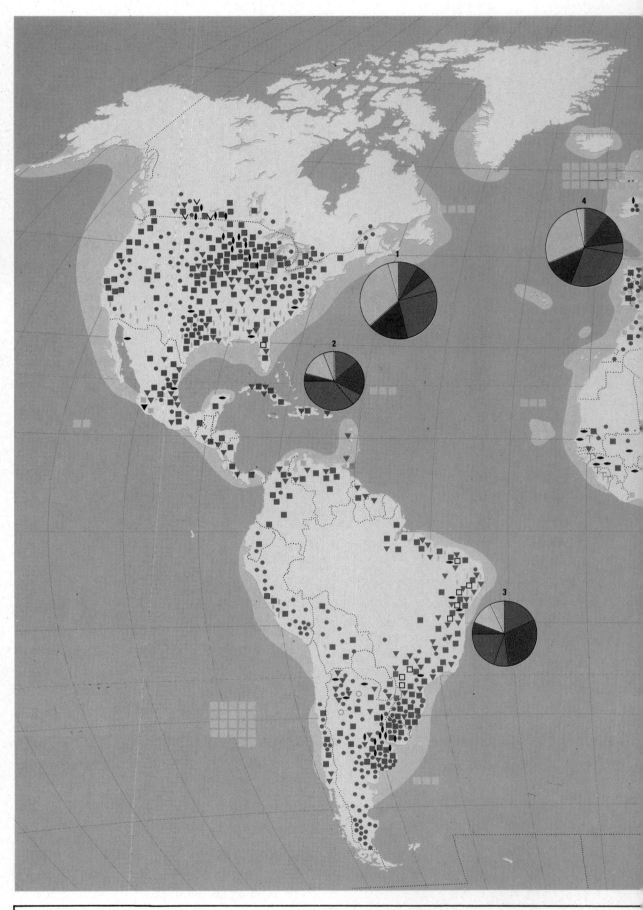

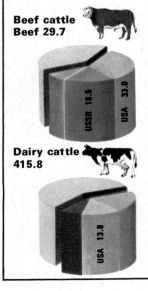

**Beef cattle
Beef 29.7**

The two principal types of domestic cattle, the Eurpopean and the tropical Zebu or humped type, are found all over the world in every type of climate. There is an urgent need in the developing countries for better breeding, disease control and management.

**Dairy cattle
415.8**

Specialized dairy farming takes place mainly near densely populated urban areas with a high standard of living, though there is an increasing trend towards combined milk/meat herds. Various forms of processing, such as canning and freezing, extend product life.

**Sheep
Mutton 4.5**

Sheep are kept mainly for meat and wool, although in southern Europe they may be milked and in the tropics the hides are the most important product. Sheep do not lend themselves readily to 'factory farming' and are raised on marginal land only.

**Pigs
Pork 24.5**

Because they are often kept indoors, the distribution of pigs depends more on food supply than on the climate. They are usually found on mixed farms where they are fed on by-products such as skim milk. Their breeding cycle is complete in about six months.

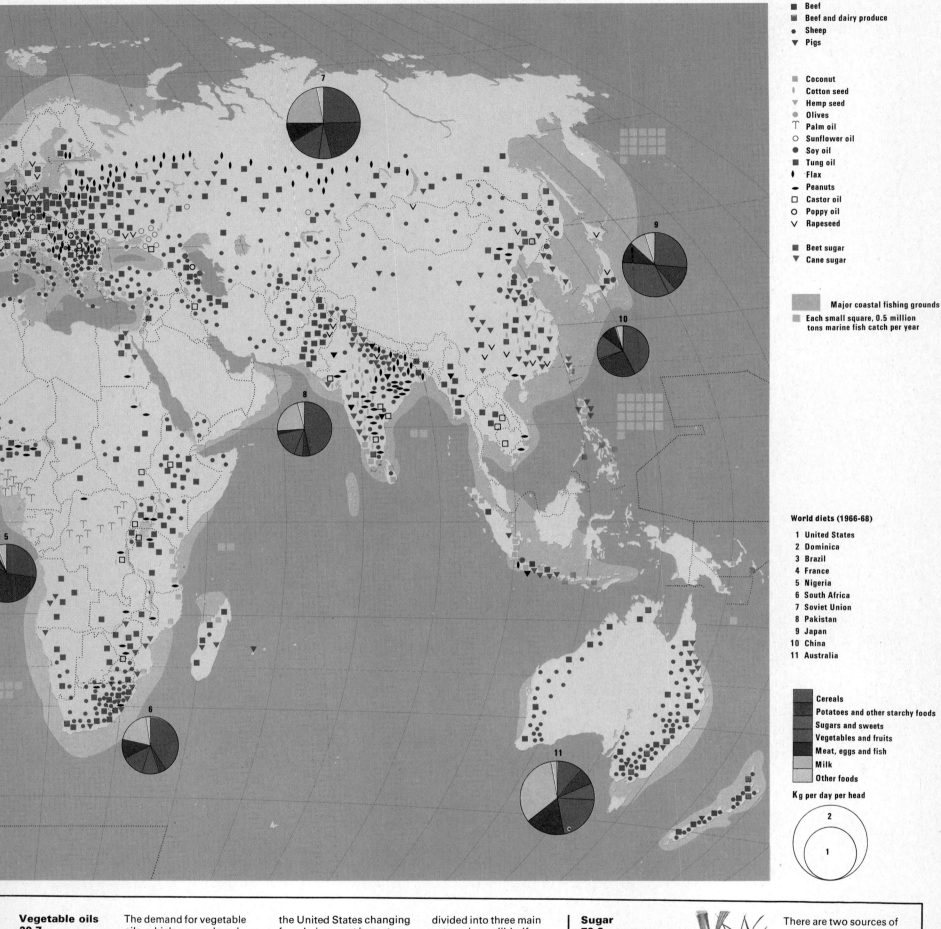

- ■ Beef
- ▦ Beef and dairy produce
- ● Sheep
- ▼ Pigs

- ▪ Coconut
- | Cotton seed
- ▼ Hemp seed
- ⊤ Olives
- ⊤ Palm oil
- ○ Sunflower oil
- ● Soy oil
- ■ Tung oil
- ◆ Flax
- ◗ Peanuts
- □ Castor oil
- ○ Poppy oil
- ∨ Rapeseed

- ■ Beet sugar
- ▼ Cane sugar

Major coastal fishing grounds

Each small square, 0.5 million tons marine fish catch per year

World diets (1966-68)

1 United States
2 Dominica
3 Brazil
4 France
5 Nigeria
6 South Africa
7 Soviet Union
8 Pakistan
9 Japan
10 China
11 Australia

- Cereals
- Potatoes and other starchy foods
- Sugars and sweets
- Vegetables and fruits
- Meat, eggs and fish
- Milk
- Other foods

Kg per day per head

2

1

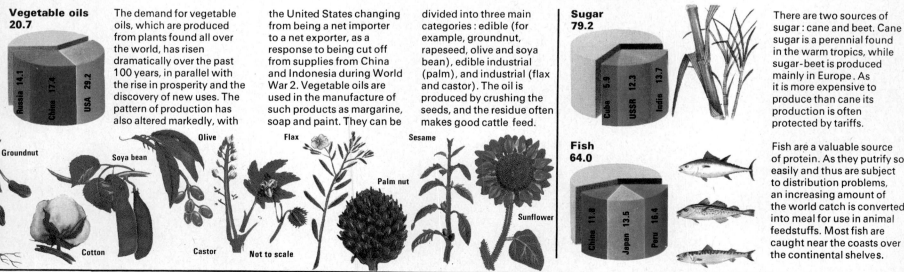

Vegetable oils
20.7

Russia 14.1   China 17.4   USA 29.2

The demand for vegetable oils, which are produced from plants found all over the world, has risen dramatically over the past 100 years, in parallel with the rise in prosperity and the discovery of new uses. The pattern of production has also altered markedly, with the United States changing from being a net importer to a net exporter, as a response to being cut off from supplies from China and Indonesia during World War 2. Vegetable oils are used in the manufacture of such products as margarine, soap and paint. They can be divided into three main categories : edible (for example, groundnut, rapeseed, olive and soya bean), edible industrial (palm), and industrial (flax and castor). The oil is produced by crushing the seeds, and the residue often makes good cattle feed.

Groundnut   Soya bean   Olive   Flax   Sesame

Cotton   Castor   Palm nut   Not to scale   Sunflower

Sugar
79.2

Cuba 5.9   USSR 12.3   India 13.7

There are two sources of sugar : cane and beet. Cane sugar is a perennial found in the warm tropics, while sugar-beet is produced mainly in Europe. As it is more expensive to produce than cane its production is often protected by tariffs.

Fish
64.0

China 11.8   Japan 13.5   Peru 16.4

Fish are a valuable source of protein. As they putrify so easily and thus are subject to distribution problems, an increasing amount of the world catch is converted into meal for use in animal feedstuffs. Most fish are caught near the coasts over the continental shelves.

The Abuse of the Earth

Pollution is harmful waste. All living creatures produce waste, often with marked effects on the environment. Pine leaves blanket out the flowers which would otherwise grow on the forest floor; the droppings of seabirds can cover nesting islands metres deep in guano. Plants as well as road vehicles give off carbon dioxide; volcanoes as well as power stations emit sulphur dioxide.

What turns man's waste into pollution? First, we produce too much waste: only man lives in such vast communities that his excreta de-oxygenates whole rivers. Secondly, the unwanted by-products of man's industrial metabolism change so rapidly that the environment has little hope of accommodating it. African grassland has evolved over millions of years to accept piles of elephant dung, with many species of animals specially adapted to living inside dungheaps and helping to decompose them. But the ecosystem is often unable to cope with our latest pollutants: few bacteria are able to digest plastics. Thirdly, man's waste is often extremely persistent: DDT may remain unchanged for decades, passing from one animal to another, poisoning and weakening them all.

Pollution may harm man directly: smoke causes bronchitis, and fouled drinking water can spread typhoid. Pollution may harm us indirectly, reducing the capacity of the land, rivers and seas to supply us with food. But perhaps the most insidious effects are the least obvious. Small doses of separate pollutants, each harmless by itself, may together weaken wild populations of animals so that they cannot recover from natural disasters. Acute pollution kills tens of thousands of animals; chronic pollution gradually reduces the quality of the entire human environment.

Pollution is wasteful. Too often modern technology painstakingly extracts a metal from the crust, uses it once and then discards it. For example, once unwanted chromium or mercury is released into the seas it will be diluted many millions of times and is unlikely ever to be recoverable except at prohibitive expense. If man is not to face raw material famines in the foreseeable future, he must learn to recycle everything from air and water to the rarer elements.

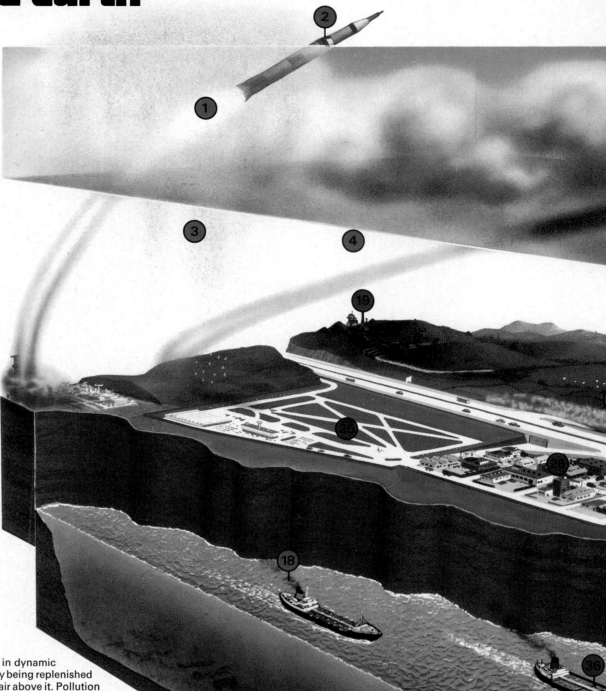

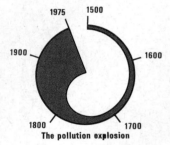

The pollution explosion

Pollution of the land
The soil is a living organic layer, in dynamic equilibrium with, and continually being replenished by, the rocks beneath it and the air above it. Pollution affects it in many ways. The farmer who sprays plants with insecticides may leave residues in the soil for 30 years, impoverishing the micro-organisms which contribute to the ecology on which his crops depend. The delicate chemical balance of the soil may be disrupted by rain loaded with nitrates and sulphates from polluted air. But the land is also a de-pollutant. Some substances can be buried in the knowledge that before they can re-appear they will have been oxidized to harmless compounds.

Pollution of the air

1 Rocket exhaust contains a variety of combustion products.

2 Space launchings leave jettisoned propellants and other debris orbiting above the atmosphere.

3 Nuclear weapon testing can leave fall-out on a global scale.

4 Modern aircraft generate intense noise pollution over wide areas.

5 Jet efflux contains kerosene combustion products, unburned fuel and particles of soot.

6 Nuclear weapons can cause radioactive contamination; together with chemical and biological devices they could eradicate all life on Earth.

7 Jet aircraft cause intense local noise, and supersonic aircraft create a shock-wave boom.

8 Large-scale aerial transport of pollutants distributes particles and gaseous matter.

9 Carbon dioxide build-up and 'greenhouse effect' traps solar heat within the atmosphere.

10 Pesticide spraying can cause widespread contamination, and organochlorine residues (such as DDT) can build up in animals and disrupt natural food chains.

11 Nuclear power station is potential source of escaping radio-active or liquid coolant.

12 Thermal (coal or oil fired) power station causes thermal and chemical pollution from exhaust stacks.

13 Power station cooling towers transfer waste heat to the air.

14 Sulphur dioxide from high roof-level chimneys falls into 'canyon streets' causing irritation to eyes and lungs.

15 Refinery waste gases burned in the air cause heavy pollution unless the flame is extremely hot.

16 Road vehicle exhausts and crankcase gases contain lead, unburned hydrocarbons, carbon monoxide and oxides of nitrogen, and can cause widespread pollution; action of sunlight on nitrogen oxides causes smog.

17 Most domestic fuels are very inefficiently burned, causing smoke and chemical pollution.

18 Steam boilers or diesel smoke can cause persistent trails of gaseous and particulate matter.

Pollution of the land

19 Coal mining leaves unsightly and potentially dangerous tips.

20 Electricity transmission pylons are a classic of visual pollution.

21 Powerful air-conditioning cools buildings in summer by heating the immediate surroundings.

22 Visual pollution of highways is accentuated by hoardings.

23 Unreclaimed wastes are often dumped and not recycled.

24 Quarrying leaves unsightly scars.

25 Growth of air traffic is reflected in increasing size and number of airports which occupy otherwise valuable land.

26 Even modern industrial estates invariably cause chemical and thermal pollution, and pose waste-disposal problems.

27 Large motorways, especially intersections, occupy large areas of land.

28 Caravan and chalet sites may cause severe local chemical, as well as visual, pollution.

29 Modern litter includes high proportion of non-biodegradable plastics materials.

Pollution of the water

30 Nuclear power station discharges waste heat into river and can cause radioactive contamination.

31 Industrial wastes are often poured into rivers without treatment.

32 Cooling water from thermal power stations can cause very large-scale heating of rivers changing or destroying the natural fauna and flora.

33 Refinery and other chemical plants generate waste heat and liquid refuse which may be discharged direct into the river.

34 Oil storage installation can cause intermittent pollution.

35 When it reaches the sea the river is heavily polluted by nitrates and phosphates from fertilizers and treated sewage, as well as by heavy toxic metals.

36 Tanker too close inshore risks severe beach pollution from accidental release of cargo.

37 Radioactive and corrosive wastes often dumped without detailed knowledge of local conditions to ensure steel drums or concrete containers will not leak before contents have decomposed; nothing should be dumped on continental shelf and adequate dilution is essential.

38 The main influx of pollutants into the sea is via rivers; typical categories include agricultural and industrial chemicals, waste heat, treated and untreated sewage and solid matter.

39 Excess nutrients from untreated sewage, agricultural chemicals and nuclear wastes can lead to 'blooms' of toxic marine plankton or, through their oxidation and decay, to severely reduced oxygen levels in the water.

40 Sewage sludge dumped at sea contains persistent chemicals such as PCB (polychlorinated biophenyl) compounds, toxic heavy metals and nutrients.

41 Large oil slicks are released by tanker accidents or deliberate washing at sea, and by oil-rig blow-outs.

42 Sediments stirred by mineral exploitation, dumped from ships or carried by rivers may form thick layers on the ocean floor which suffocate the organisms living there.

43 Clouds of particulate matter, both organic and inorganic wastes, reduce the penetration of sunlight and sharply curtail marine productivity.

44 Oil rigs suffer explosive blow-outs, a serious problem off the California coast.

45 In some waters wrecks, many of them uncharted, pose hazards to shipping which may lead to further pollution.

Pollution of the air

Most atmospheric pollutants are gases or dusts emitted when coal, oil or natural gas are burned. DDT and other organochlorine pesticides are distributed mainly by air, since they readily evaporate but are extremely insoluble in water. Some pollutants, such as the particles of carbon we call smoke, fall to the ground within 100 mi (160 km) of emission. Others, particularly minute radio-active particles, can circle the globe for months. Some pollutants undergo chemical change in the air; sulphur dioxide is oxidized and then hydrolized to fall in rain as dilute sulphuric acid.

Pollution of the water

Water is a great transporter. Agricultural run-off joins sewage and industrial effluent down the rivers. While some organic pollutants decay or settle into mud, most end up in lakes, estuaries and shallow seas. These are the very waters which have the highest productivity, and already the spawning grounds of fish and shellfish have been seriously damaged in some enclosed waters. Today man treats the deep seas as his final dustbin. Radio-active wastes are dumped in containers, and drums of sulphuric acid are tipped overboard. The sea is also the main transport route for bulk materials, notably crude petroleum. As the size and speed of bulk carriers increase, so does accidental pollution of busy waterways become more frequent and more severe. Exploitation of submarine minerals will pose yet another pollution hazard involving new materials and locations.

46 Apart from the direct effect of pollutants on marine life, many are less obvious. For example, traces of organic chemicals may confuse or disrupt the mating behaviour of fish that normally make use of related chemicals that occur naturally.

Human Nutrition

Man's existence depends on his capacity to produce, store, process and distribute food. Technically, an agreeable food consists of the non-toxic, socially acceptable, digestible, palatable and nutritive parts of plants and animals. At least 43 chemical compounds and elements are required in the human diet. Of these essential nutrients 17 are minerals such as calcium, iron and magnesium, while the remainder fall within four main groups: carbohydrates (sugars and starch); fats and fatty acids; proteins; and vitamins.

Proteins provide the very stuff of life—the variety of tissues that make up the healthy individual. For example, proteins are the key substance of heart and other muscles and of the corpuscles in the blood. They and their products are essential for digestion and many other body functions. Man needs protein to replace daily wear and tear and to repair tissues damaged by accident or disease. Pregnant women and growing children need extra protein to meet the demands of pregnancy, lactation and growth. Unfortunately, proteins vary in quality—measured in terms of the amino-acids of which they consist. Since the body cannot synthesize all these chemicals, some essential amino-acids must be received in the diet either as plants which can make them or as the meat of animals that have previously consumed them. Therefore meat products generally have a higher protein quality than plant foods, some of which are deficient in essential amino-acids. Vitamins and minerals are also essential in small amounts; and deficits lead to specific deficiency diseases. Energy foods—carbohydrates, fats and, if necessary, proteins —provide the power for internal work, such as pumping blood, and external work.

Human foods differ widely in their palatability and in their content of proteins, vitamins, minerals and energy sources. People can suffer from deficiencies in their diet simply because the staple food lacks essential nutritive ingredients. A good diet should be a mixture of food which is neither too bulky nor too liquid, is appetizing, and easy to cook and prepare for the table. This increases the likelihood that it will supply a balanced intake of the needed nutrients.

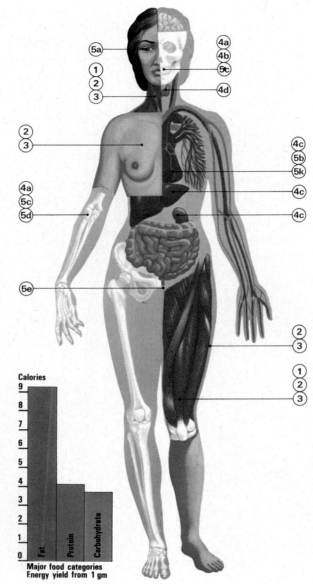

Calories
9
8
7
6
5
4
3
2
1
0

Fat | Protein | Carbohydrate

Major food categories
Energy yield from 1 gm

1	Protein	Meats, eggs, fish, milk	Basic body structural material: growth and repair of muscles and tissue: control of metabolism and muscular energy
2	Fats	Animal and vegetable oils, animal fats, fish oils, butter	Body fat provides, with sugars, basic source of energy for body; also provides energy store and heat insulation
3	Carbohydrates	Starches, such as potatoes, sugars	Starch yields glycogen, mainly stored in liver and muscle; sugar is basic source of body energy
4	Minerals	4a Calcium: peas, beans, milk, meat, cheese	Essential for bone formation, including nails and teeth.
		4b Phosphorus: cheese, liver, eggs	Essential for energy transfer and health of teeth
		4c Iron: green vegetables	Blood haemoglobin, energy transport, liver and kidney function
		4d Iodine: fish, water	Thyroid gland; prevents goitre and cretinism
5	Vitamins	5a Animal fats, fish oils,	Eyes
	Note: 5a=Vitamin A; 5k=Vitamin K	5b Grain products, meat, milk	Growth, circulatory system
		5c Fruit, vegetables	Bones, teeth, child growth
		5d Cod liver oil, liver of tuna, halibut	Bones, child skeletal development
		5e Fat content of food, egg yolks, liver	
		5k Green plants, liver	Blood clotting

How we use our food *left and below*
Human food is composed of at least 43 chemical elements and compounds, all of which are needed to sustain a healthy individual. Of these essential constituents, 17 are minerals ; the rest are carbohydrates and fats (needed in substantial bulk) and proteins and vitamins (specialized chemicals needed in much smaller quantities yet nonetheless vital). The table below lists the principal constituents of each class of food and the parts of the body for which they are particularly needed ; these locations are indicated in the keyed illustration of a typical white adult. In fact, of course, the interaction between food and the body is usually almost unbelievably complicated.

Physique and food *below*
Although there are numerous exceptions, human body shape is in general adapted to climate. The Watussi (below, right) from Entebbe, Uganda, is tall and slender, whereas the Eskimo from Angmagssalik is rotund and better shaped for conserving heat energy and avoiding frostbite.

Temperature contrast
Temperature variation at Entebbe (A) is near zero, unlike Angmagssalik (B).

Kwashiorkor *above*
Widespread in Africa and SE Asia, this protein-deficiency disease is characterized by swollen stomach, wasted muscles and general retardation and susceptibility to other afflictions. The name means 'first-second', signifying a disease of the first child when the second is near.

The deficient profile *right*
Although malnutrition causes ill-health and death, large numbers of children (and adults) still die from a lack of food. This state of undernourishment, called marasmus, is reflected in the emaciated body. Gradually the body ceases to function and ultimately diarrhoea and vomiting cause death from dehydration. In many cases, however, the sufferer falls victim to infections against which the weakened body no longer has any defence.

What do we need? *right*
Human need for food depends on our body size, how warm it is and what energy we expend in our daily life. Shown here are the daily requirements for different people in terms of kilogramme calories of energy and grammes per day of protein.

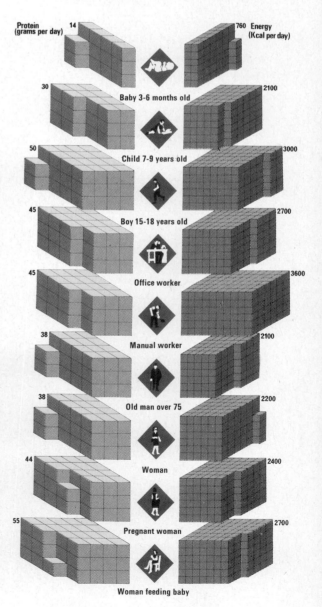

Protein (grams per day) | Energy (Kcal per day)

14 / 760

30 / 2100 — Baby 3-6 months old

50 / 3000 — Child 7-9 years old

45 / 2700 — Boy 15-18 years old

45 / 3600 — Office worker

38 / 2100 — Manual worker

38 / 2200 — Old man over 75

44 / 2400 — Woman

55 / 2700 — Pregnant woman

Woman feeding baby

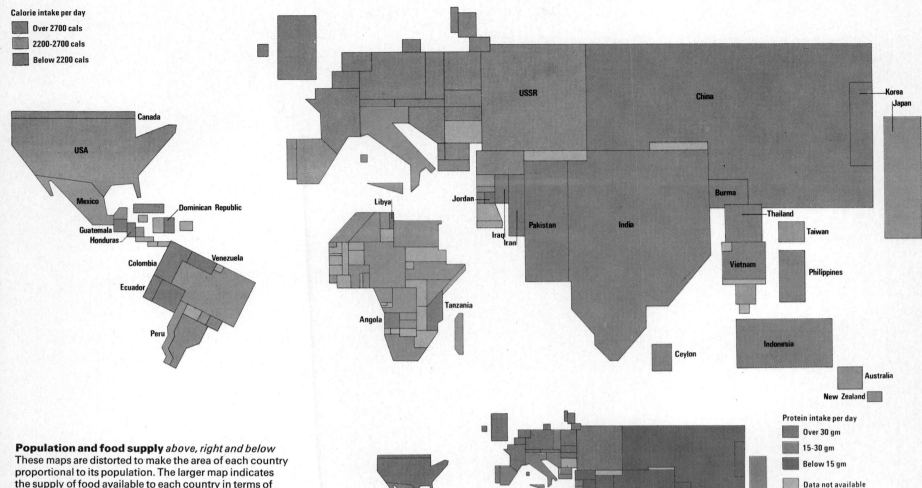

Calorie intake per day
- Over 2700 cals
- 2200-2700 cals
- Below 2200 cals

Labels on map: Canada, USA, Mexico, Dominican Republic, Guatemala, Honduras, Colombia, Venezuela, Ecuador, Peru, USSR, China, Korea, Japan, Libya, Jordan, Iraq, Iran, Pakistan, India, Burma, Thailand, Taiwan, Vietnam, Philippines, Angola, Tanzania, Ceylon, Indonesia, Australia, New Zealand

Protein intake per day
- Over 30 gm
- 15-30 gm
- Below 15 gm
- Data not available

Population and food supply *above, right and below*
These maps are distorted to make the area of each country proportional to its population. The larger map indicates the supply of food available to each country in terms of calories per head per day; the smaller map shows available protein in terms of weight. Countries with little food also generally suffer from a poor quality diet, with ample starchy food but little meat; there is a sharp contrast in animal protein figures (below). Although some countries with modest food supplies do have adequate protein (Japan is one), others such as Spain and the Soviet Union still lack protein despite ample supplies of food.

Daily protein and calorie consumption per head

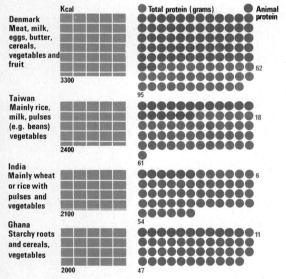

	Kcal	Total protein (grams)	Animal protein
Denmark Meat, milk, eggs, butter, cereals, vegetables and fruit	3300	95	62
Taiwan Mainly rice, milk, pulses (e.g. beans) vegetables	2400	61	18
India Mainly wheat or rice with pulses and vegetables	2100	54	6
Ghana Starchy roots and cereals, vegetables	2000	47	11

Food and nutrition

All man's food depends ultimately on the capture of the Sun's energy by plants via the process of photosynthesis. When man eats these plants, he makes efficient use of the Earth's resources in terms of energy conversion. In fact, poorer peoples generally have little other choice, but richer ones favour meat in their diet. Not only do the animals consume foods unpalatable to man but their meat also has a much greater nutritive value, at the expense of an inefficient energy-conversion process. The basic energy released by eating food is expressed in calories. Different people need different amounts of energy (see facing page). In many countries hardly anyone can attain even this basic energy level. In most of the world stomachs are filled, but a more subtle form of hunger remains. Unless the body also receives adequate quantities of certain constituents of proteins, minerals and vitamins it cannot function properly. Disorders and disease are the inevitable result of this malnutrition.

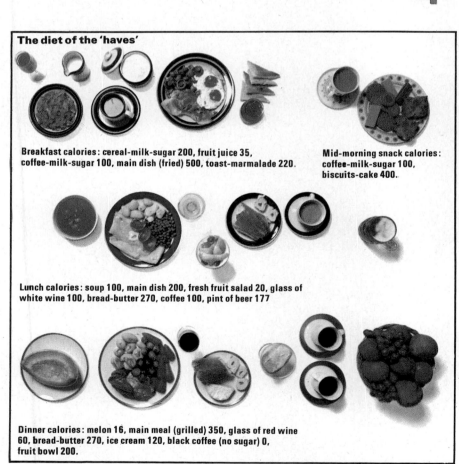

The diet of the 'haves'

Breakfast calories: cereal-milk-sugar 200, fruit juice 35, coffee-milk-sugar 100, main dish (fried) 500, toast-marmalade 220.

Mid-morning snack calories: coffee-milk-sugar 100, biscuits-cake 400.

Lunch calories: soup 100, main dish 200, fresh fruit salad 20, glass of white wine 100, bread-butter 270, coffee 100, pint of beer 177

Dinner calories: melon 16, main meal (grilled) 350, glass of red wine 60, bread-butter 270, ice cream 120, black coffee (no sugar) 0, fruit bowl 200.

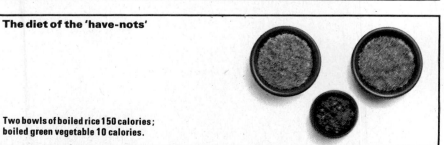

The diet of the 'have-nots'

Two bowls of boiled rice 150 calories; boiled green vegetable 10 calories.

The haves and have-nots

Throughout a large and growing part of the Earth man is often found to suffer from a form of malnutrition caused not by starvation but by overeating. It is manifest in gross build-up of body fat leading to increased effort in walking and movement. In turn this leads to greater stress on the heart and a shorter life span. The food shown at left is not untypical of the daily consumption of adults in the world's more prosperous societies. The total number of calories is 3538, probably double the energy input needed and used mainly in new tissue formation. Protein input is substantially above requirement, and all vitamins are abundant. Vitamin A total amounts to more than 4000 international units, and thiamine, riboflavine, nicotinamide and ascorbic acid are all included in amounts which in aggregate are about double the body's needs. In contrast, the world's less advanced, poorer and hungrier nations have a diet that results in the more common type of malnutrition. Two small bowls of rice and a small quantity of vegetable such as cabbage, pulses or lentils form a common daily intake over a wide belt of tropical countries. Such fare is uninteresting, lacking in energy content and grossly deficient in proteins and vitamin content.

The Population Problem

In the year 1000 there were about 300 million people. In the last century the population reached 1000 million. Today it exceeds 3600 million. In 2000 it is predicted to reach 7000 million, and in 2050 something between 12000 and 20000 million. The main reason is that in spite of generally improved survival rates for children, little attempt has been made in many countries to curb the size of families.

The distribution of humans over the Earth has always been grossly uneven, and it appears likely to stay that way. While man has never ceased to open up and exploit new regions, a process of urbanization has become more clearly evident in recent years. The more advanced the development of a nation, the more its cities attract people from the surrounding countryside. In most industrialized countries the proportion of the population living in cities has risen to 60 or 70 per cent. Modern cities pose severe social problems; they have to be considered as living, adaptable organisms in themselves if human life is not to become increasingly frustrating.

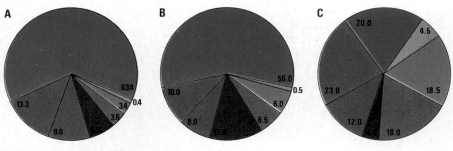

People and land area *left*
Nearly two-thirds of the births (percentages per continent, A) and half the population (B) are in only quarter of the area (C).

World population density *below*
Humanity is distributed over the Earth's land surface in a most uneven way. Dividing the population of each country by its area yields such diverse figures (for 1965) as 3.8 inhabitants per square mile for Australia and almost 10000 per square mile for Hong Kong (1.46 and 3900 per square kilometer, respectively). This map indicates density in proportion to the heights of the columns.

North America and Europe
Europe has for centuries housed about one-sixth of the world's population, but the developing countries are reducing this proportion. Despite massive migrations and wars, the pattern of settlement has changed little in 500 years. In contrast North America was almost uninhabited 200 years ago; but the westward migration of the white man opened up the continent. But most of the population is still concentrated round the coasts and Great Lakes.

Latin America
In 1750 Central and South America had more than six times as many inhabitants as the north. Although North America stormed past in 1860, S America is today the fastest growing continent in the world, mainly on or near the coast.

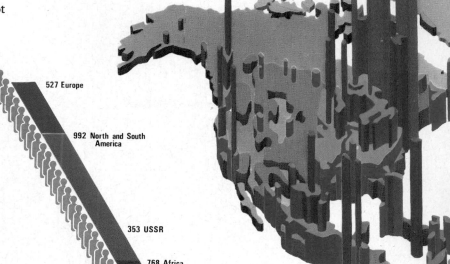

An overcrowded world *right and above*
Of all the problems facing man today the most intractable and persistent is the basic fact that his numbers are growing in an excessive and uncontrolled manner. When the total human population is plotted graphically the result is frightening in its implications. Cold statistics (right), even projected to the year 2000, do not bring home the desperate problems of an overcrowded world.

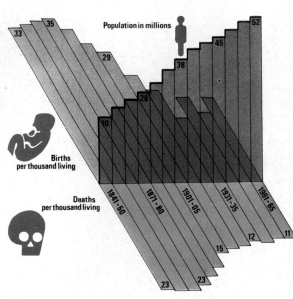

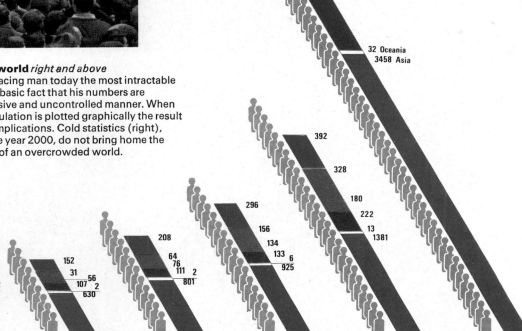

1750   1800   1850   1900   1950   2000

UK births and deaths *left*
The basic reason for the population explosion is an excess of births over deaths. In the UK both birth and death rates have declined during the past 100 years, but over five year periods births have always exceeded deaths, though in the 1930s the margin was very small.

Age distribution *right*
British population growth is about 0.5 per cent, or 250,000 people, per year. This is a modest rate and gives an age distribution where the old are almost as numerous as the young (right above). Sweden (far right) is an even more marked case of slow growth.

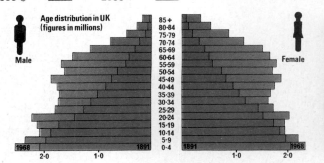

Age distribution in UK (figures in millions)

Male   Female

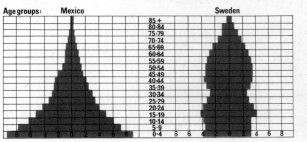

Age groups: Mexico   Sweden

Large families *above*
Big families are no longer common in Britain. But in many parts of the world the tradition of large families persists. Allied with much lower child mortality, the result is booming population. The age distribution then looks like that of Mexico (left).

Europe

Population per sq mi
- 0–5
- 5–25
- 25–250
- over 250

Migration to the cities
In every part of the world people are congregating in the cities, searching for a better standard of living. Many of the world's larger cities, unable to accommodate this rapid influx, have become marred by largely unplanned settlements. The most densely packed city in the world, Hong Kong, is home to over three million people. The fortunate ones live in tenements (right); the rest have built shanties (left). Man's population is thus increasingly becoming an urban one.

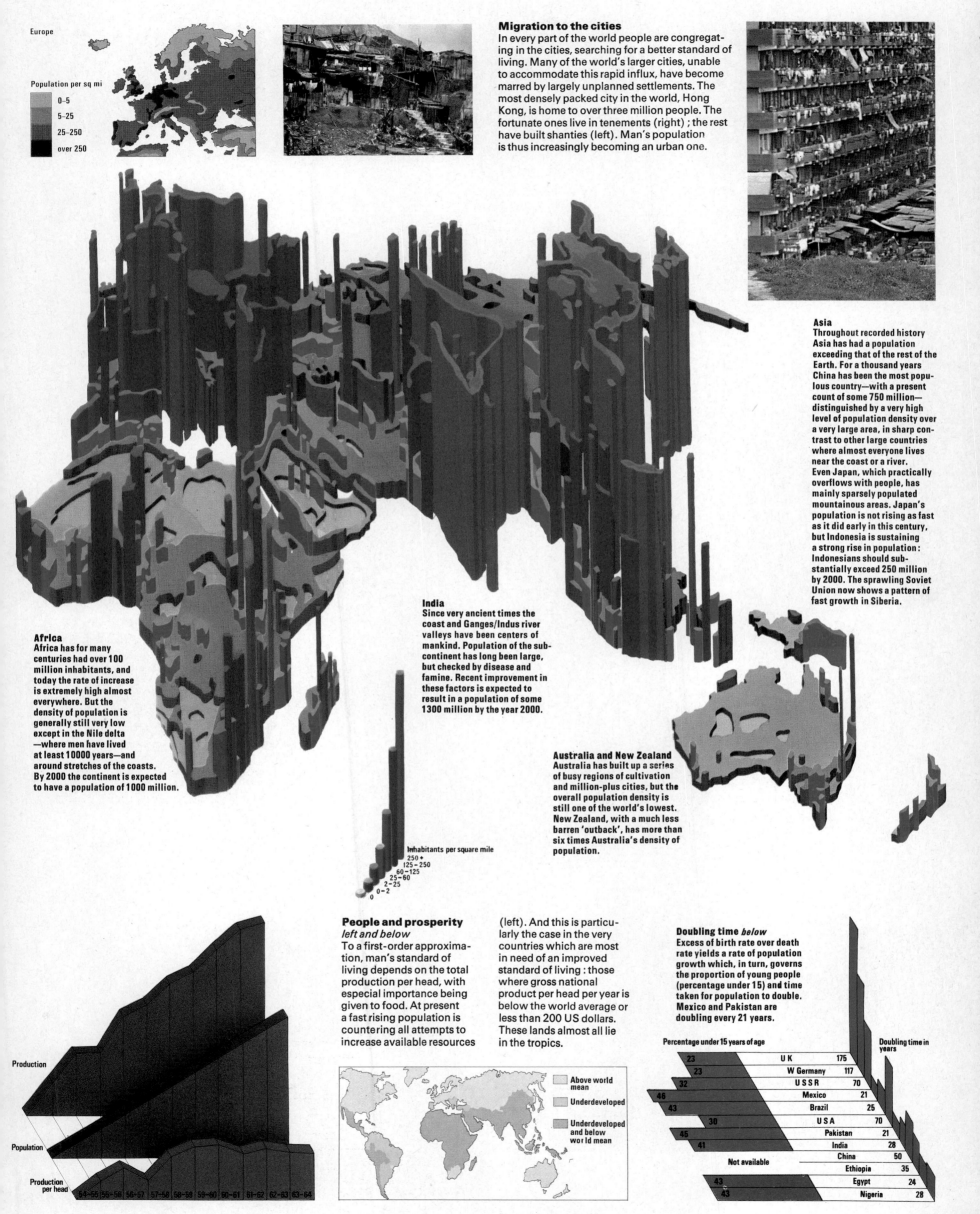

Asia
Throughout recorded history Asia has had a population exceeding that of the rest of the Earth. For a thousand years China has been the most populous country—with a present count of some 750 million—distinguished by a very high level of population density over a very large area, in sharp contrast to other large countries where almost everyone lives near the coast or a river. Even Japan, which practically overflows with people, has mainly sparsely populated mountainous areas. Japan's population is not rising as fast as it did early in this century, but Indonesia is sustaining a strong rise in population : Indonesians should substantially exceed 250 million by 2000. The sprawling Soviet Union now shows a pattern of fast growth in Siberia.

India
Since very ancient times the coast and Ganges/Indus river valleys have been centers of mankind. Population of the subcontinent has long been large, but checked by disease and famine. Recent improvement in these factors is expected to result in a population of some 1300 million by the year 2000.

Africa
Africa has for many centuries had over 100 million inhabitants, and today the rate of increase is extremely high almost everywhere. But the density of population is generally still very low except in the Nile delta —where men have lived at least 10000 years—and around stretches of the coasts. By 2000 the continent is expected to have a population of 1000 million.

Australia and New Zealand
Australia has built up a series of busy regions of cultivation and million-plus cities, but the overall population density is still one of the world's lowest. New Zealand, with a much less barren 'outback', has more than six times Australia's density of population.

Inhabitants per square mile
- 250 +
- 125–250
- 60–125
- 25–60
- 2–25
- 0–2

People and prosperity
left and below
To a first-order approximation, man's standard of living depends on the total production per head, with especial importance being given to food. At present a fast rising population is countering all attempts to increase available resources (left). And this is particularly the case in the very countries which are most in need of an improved standard of living : those where gross national product per head per year is below the world average or less than 200 US dollars. These lands almost all lie in the tropics.

Production
Population
Production per head

54–55 55–56 56–57 57–58 58–59 59–60 60–61 61–62 62–63 63–64

- Above world mean
- Underdeveloped
- Underdeveloped and below world mean

Doubling time *below*
Excess of birth rate over death rate yields a rate of population growth which, in turn, governs the proportion of young people (percentage under 15) and time taken for population to double. Mexico and Pakistan are doubling every 21 years.

Percentage under 15 years of age		Doubling time in years
23	U K	175
23	W Germany	117
32	U S S R	70
46	Mexico	21
43	Brazil	25
30	USA	70
45	Pakistan	21
41	India	28
Not available	China	50
	Ethiopia	35
43	Egypt	24
43	Nigeria	28

Religion

The earliest religions, still strong among pre-civilized peoples, were animistic and identified with the forces of nature. Even when these have crystallized into systems of beliefs centred on gods there often is still a close identification with a restricted territory. These ethnic religions are confined to specific peoples having a limited range of movement. Such a territorial concept of a deity is apparent in the earlier parts of Jewish and Christian scripture. In the religions of the East beliefs of this kind became more diffuse and the system more philosophical. The teaching of Gautama Buddha (563-483 BC) was a denial of materialism, in the face of the miseries of life in a part of the world where existence is still equated with hardship. Confucius (551-478 BC) was more concerned with defining social relationships and was able to absorb primitive ancestor worship, which still survives. In India Hinduism is a comprehensive system embracing a range of beliefs in numbers of gods but welding the whole together by fundamental attitudes such as the doctrine of rebirth, worship of cattle and the caste system. The last is a practical social element based on occupation and very different from the philosophical elements of Hinduism.

Ethnic religions in the Near East took on a totally different aspect by becoming monotheistic: the tribal god of the Jews became for them the only god. To Christianity, which emerged from Judaism, monotheism was central, and so it became in Islam, which owed much to both Judaism and Christianity. Judaism was dispersed, but retained its strength until Israel was re-established in 1948. But Christianity and Islam became the great 'saving' religions whose aim was the conversion of mankind. The early history of Christianity is of proselytizing, and later of conquest. And within a short time of the death of Mohammed (AD 632), his beliefs also had been carried far.

But a characteristic of both these religions is the deep schisms which have appeared. In Islam there is sharp disagreement between Sunni and Shia. Equally marked is the division of Christianity into Roman Catholics and Protestants, with a strong third element in the Greek Orthodox Church.

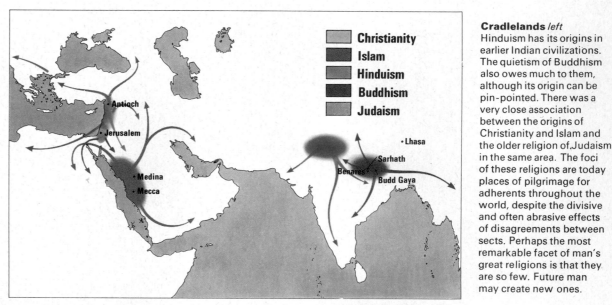

Christianity
Islam
Hinduism
Buddhism
Judaism

Cradlelands *left*
Hinduism has its origins in earlier Indian civilizations. The quietism of Buddhism also owes much to them, although its origin can be pin-pointed. There was a very close association between the origins of Christianity and Islam and the older religion of Judaism in the same area. The foci of these religions are today places of pilgrimage for adherents throughout the world, despite the divisive and often abrasive effects of disagreements between sects. Perhaps the most remarkable facet of man's great religions is that they are so few. Future man may create new ones.

Hindu *left*
While most Hindus worship at home, often to local or to family deities, they may passively watch ceremonies conducted by priests in temples for their gods. In Jinja, Uganda, priests pour ghee (clarified butter) into a fire in supplication to the terrible god Amba (Durga).

Islam *left*
Seated in the open courtyard of a mosque an Indian reads the Koran. This holy book, about as long as the Christian New Testament, is the scripture revealed to Mohammed. It is the basis of Moslem teaching and social behaviour; mosques are also schools.

Buddhism *left*
Buddhist temples are ornate and richly decorated. Here in Singapore an assistant priest studies the scriptures. His white robe distinguishes him from a monk who would wear saffron yellow (and be prohibited from having any possessions apart from vestments, razor and bowl).

Christianity *left*
The Christian church is an institution that impinges upon the individual at the major milestones of life: baptism (shown here), marriage and burial. Everyone can take part in any church service, but usually the organization is in the hands of the priesthood.

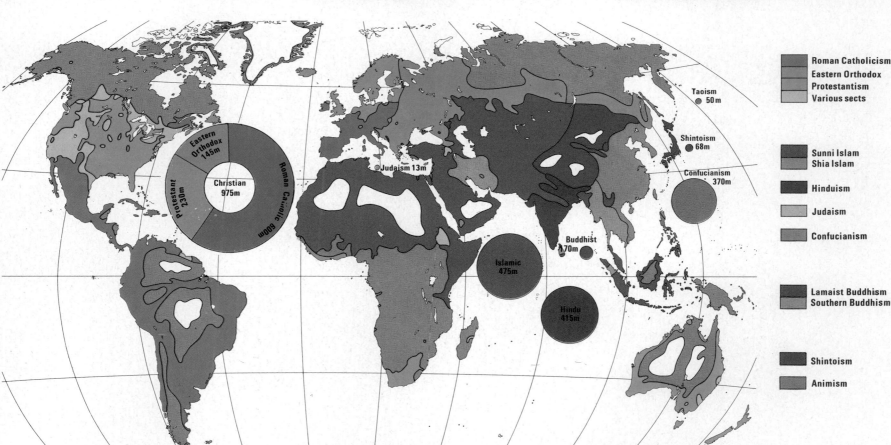

Roman Catholicism
Eastern Orthodox
Protestantism
Various sects

Sunni Islam
Shia Islam

Hinduism

Judaism

Confucianism

Lamaist Buddhism
Southern Buddhism

Shintoism

Animism

Contrasting beliefs
Christianity is numerically the strongest religion, with Roman Catholicism the largest of its many sects. Islam is next largest (overwhelmingly Sunni), and Hinduism is growing with the Indian population. Animism and ethnic religions prevail where Western influences are slight or where, as in Central Africa, there is a very large indigenous population. The most remarkable spread has been that of the great proselytizing religions, Christianity and Islam. The former is world-wide, while the latter is restricted to hot, dry lands of the Old World. Many minor sects are urban.

Shinto *left*
This religion is based on a multitude of small shrines dedicated to numerous deities. Its priests were government officials until 1945. The Japanese temple in the background contains an inner sanctuary where these priests recite, pray and conduct the purification rites.

Judaism *left*
Inside the West London Synagogue the Rabbi holds up the richly decorated Torah (Law) which contains the five Books of Moses. Behind him is the Ark. Judaism emphasizes the transcendence of God, whose name it avoids by substituting some epithet (such as 'the Holy One').

Language

Of all those things which tend to divide mankind into groups, language is possibly the most important. While it binds together those who speak a common language, it imposes a major handicap upon communication between different groups. Language is the medium by which ideas are transmitted, and this tends to give a cultural homogeneity to each language group. For example, the 'English-speaking world' identifies people with common culture and sympathetic beliefs. Language also has very strong emotional connotations, because it is associated with the individual's earliest memories. Consequently a great amount of tension can arise between contiguous language groups, or when a majority language is given precedence in a multi-language state. The subdivision of India, largely on a language basis, produced many riots. The dividing line between Flemish and Walloon in Belgium is marked by constant tensions. Language is the main basis of the claims of the French Canadians to independence.

World languages and their distribution are extremely complex. Even the major groups of languages, such as Latin or Teutonic, do not mean much in practical terms because to the layman it is the minor differences which count and not the basic similarities. Differences even of dialect are enough to divide people: the least nuance will serve to identify group antipathies. 'Speaking another language' can apply to subtleties of meaning even within one language. One way of overcoming this problem is to encourage second languages of international standing. Many of the world's peoples are bilingual—a fact which makes the mapping of distributions very difficult. Even so it is difficult to overcome a person's emotional link with his first language. There are over 30 languages in Europe alone. Many of the minor languages are in danger of disappearing. This is partly because they cannot cope with the language of modern technology, and partly because fluent knowledge of a major language is an essential. Within the British Isles, for example, the Celtic languages could not hope to compete with English and some such as Cornish and Manx have virtually disappeared.

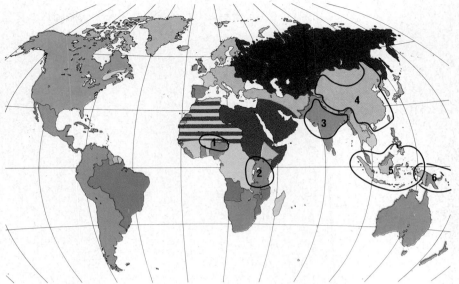

International languages
Superimposed on the thousands of local languages and dialects round the world are six major international languages—those of the colonialist powers. They are used for ease of communication in government and business, for example, India's retention of English as the official language.

Spanish — English
French — Portuguese
Russian — Arabic

1 Hausa   4 Chinese
2 Swahili   5 Malay
3 Hindi/Urdu 6 Melanesian pidgin

The written word
left and foot of page
The invention of writing has proved one of the most potent of all human tools. Some of the earliest written forms show clear derivation from pictures; indeed Nasi (foot of page) is still a major language in the Yunnan province of China. But most modern languages have become streamlined into simpler forms. Even Chinese is being simplified, although its hieroglyphic form remains. Modern Burmese, based on curved characters, contrasts with the angular Sanskrit which is an ancient script pictorially resembling Hindi and other languages of modern India.

Russian
Идея использования квантовых систем для ге радиоволн оказалась весьма плодотворной и недостижимые для обычной радиотехники резу.

Burmese
ဖြစ်ပ စံစည်းကရ်ယာ၊ပျား ရ္ဖြို့ပြိုပြင်လေသည်။ အလယ် ၊င်ရ ပၢ်ကိုလ်ပျားအတွက် အထူးသင်တန်းပျား

Greek
'Ο 'Οδυσσεὺς καὶ οἱ σύντροφοι αὐτοῦ πλοῖα, τὰ ὁποῖα ἦσαν πλήρη λαφύρων, ἀι Τρωάδος, ἐπιθυμοῦντες νὰ φθάσωσιν ὅσο

Hebrew
: יְהוּדִים שְׁמְּרְדוּ בָּךְ. כֵּן שֶהָגִיעַ לְאָנְטִפַטְרֶם זַרְחָה
רָן שֶׁרָאָה אֵת שִׁמְעוֹן הַצַּדִּיק יָרַד מִמֶּרְכַּבְתּוֹ וְהִשְׁתַּחֲוָה

Sanskrit
संस्कृत नाम देवी वाग् अन्वाख्याता महर्षिभिः । तद्वचस् तत्समो देशीत्य मनेफ़:
प्राकृतक्रम्॥ श्रीभेगदिगिर: काव्यध्वश्वं इति समता । शास्त्रे तु संस्कृताद् मन्यद् श्रप्रोक्ष्णयोदितम् ॥ लोक: प्रसाद: समता माधुर्य सुकुमारता । अर्थव्यपितर

Chinese
是
帶所及,使英國人的生活習慣也起了變化。
館子吃一頓的,現在大多數改爲吃自助餐,
習慣,一星期中,捱了幾天牛油麵包或三文
被迫產生的節約風氣所造成的後果是帶來不
至殃及學生們在假期中找臨時工作的出路。
貶值以來,英國的經濟衰退情形更嚴重。人
情況都還不錯的華僑們所開設的中國
停業。光是倫敦一地,過去一年來停

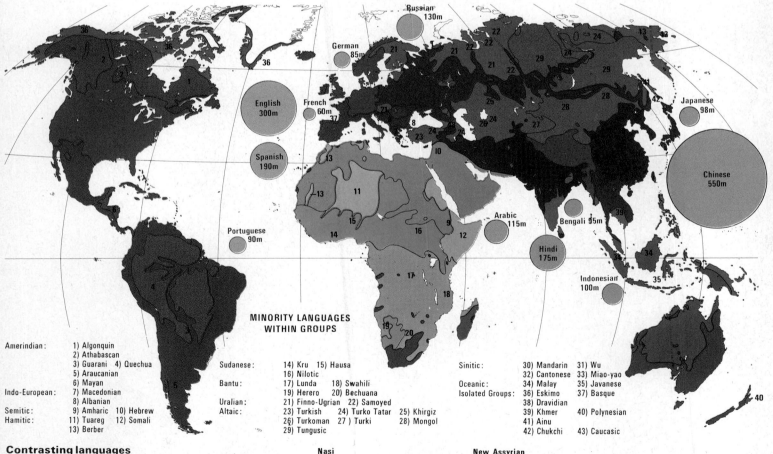

Russian 130m
German 85m
English 300m
French 60m
Spanish 190m
Portuguese 90m
Arabic 115m
Hindi 175m
Bengali 85m
Indonesian 100m
Japanese 98m
Chinese 550m

MINORITY LANGUAGES WITHIN GROUPS

Teutonic
Latin
Slavonic
Indo-Iranian
Indo-Aryan
Amerindian
Semitic
Hamitic
Sudanese
Bantu
Bushman-Hottentot
Uralian
Altaic (Turkish and dialects)
Altaic (Mongol)
Korean-Japanese
Tibetan-Burman
Sinitic
Thai
Oceanic
Melanesian
Papuan aborigine
Australian aborigine
Isolated groups

Amerindian:
1) Algonquin
2) Athabascan
3) Guarani 4) Quechua
5) Araucanian
6) Mayan

Indo-European:
7) Macedonian
8) Albanian

Semitic:
9) Amharic 10) Hebrew

Hamitic:
11) Tuareg 12) Somali
13) Berber

Sudanese:
14) Kru 15) Hausa
16) Nilotic

Bantu:
17) Lunda 18) Swahili
19) Herero 20) Bechuana

Uralian:
21) Finno-Ugrian 22) Samoyed

Altaic:
23) Turkish 24) Turko Tatar 25) Khirgiz
26) Turkoman 27) Turki 28) Mongol
29) Tungusic

Sinitic:
30) Mandarin 31) Wu
32) Cantonese 33) Miao-yao

Oceanic:
34) Malay 35) Javanese

Isolated Groups:
36) Eskimo 37) Basque
38) Dravidian
39) Khmer 40) Polynesian
41) Ainu
42) Chukchi 43) Caucasic

Contrasting languages
The biggest language group is Chinese, but this is really a profusion of dialects. English, Spanish and Portuguese have spread with colonization, while Russian has become a uniform language from Europe to the Pacific. Easy communications will increase the domination of the great international languages for education, commerce and cultural exchange. This means that many more people will have to become at least bilingual, although minor languages may survive indefinitely. It is unlikely that cultural diversity, which depends so much on language, will be submerged.

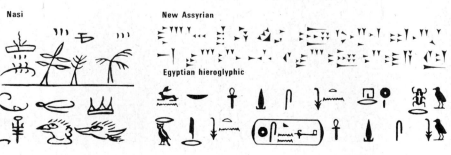

Nasi

New Assyrian

Egyptian hieroglyphic

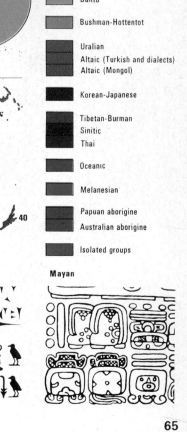

Mayan

Great Cities of the Earth

Legend to Maps

Inhabited Localities

The symbol represents the number of inhabitants within the locality

o	10,000—25,000
⊙	25,000—100,000
⊡	100,000—250,000
▣	250,000—1,000,000
■	>1,000,000

The size of type indicates the relative economic and political importance of the locality

Écommoy   **Rouen**
Trouville
Lisieux   **PARIS**

Hollywood   ■ Section of a City,
Westminster   Neighborhood

Northland   ■ Major Shopping Center
Center

Urban Area (area of continuous industrial, commercial, and residential development)

Major Industrial Area

Wooded Area

Local Park or Recreational Area

Political Boundaries

International (First-order political unit)

Demarcated, Undemarcated, and Administrative

Demarcation Line

Internal

State, Province, etc. (Second-order political unit)

County, Oblast, etc. (Third-order political unit)

Okrug, Kreis, etc. (Fourth-order political unit)

City or Municipality (may appear in combination with another boundary symbol)

Capitals of Political Units

BUDAPEST   Independent Nation

Recife   State, Province, etc.

White Plains   County, Oblast, etc.

Iserlohn   Okrug, Kreis, etc.

Transportation

Road

PASSAIC EXPWY.   (1-80)   Primary

BERLINER RING   Secondary

Tertiary

Railway

CANADIAN NATIONAL   Primary

Secondary

Rapid Transit

Airport

LONDON (HEATHROW) AIRPORT

Rail or Air Terminal

SÜD BAHNHOF

REICHS-BRÜCKE   Bridge

GREAT ST. BERNARD TUNNEL   Tunnel

Houston Ship Channel   Shipping Channel

Canal du Midi   Navigable Canal

TO MALMÖ   Ferry

Hydrographic Features

Shoreline

Undefined or Fluctuating Shoreline

Amur   River, Stream

Intermittent Stream

Rapids, Falls

SALTO ANGEL   Navigable Canal
Canal du Midi

Irrigation or Drainage Canal

Los Angeles Aqueduct   Aqueduct

Pier, Breakwater

GREAT BARRIER REEF   Reef

L. Victoria   Lake, Reservoir

Intermittent Lake

The Everglades   Swamp

Miscellaneous Cultural Features

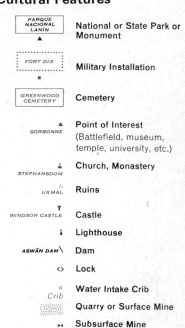

PARQUE NACIONAL LANIN   ▲ National or State Park or Monument

FORT DIX   Military Installation

GREENWOOD CEMETERY   Cemetery

SORBONNE   ▲ Point of Interest (Battlefield, museum, temple, university, etc.)

STEPHANSDOM   Church, Monastery

UXMAL   Ruins

WINDSOR CASTLE   Castle

Lighthouse

ASWĀN DAM   Dam

<>   Lock

Crib   Water Intake Crib

Quarry or Surface Mine

Subsurface Mine

Topographic Features

Mt. Kenya 5199   △ Elevation Above Sea Level

Elevations are given in meters

* Rock

A N D E S Mountain Range, Plateau,
KUNLUNSHANMAI   Valley, etc.

BAFFIN ISLAND   Island

POLUOSTROV KAMČATKA   Peninsula, Cape, Point, etc.
CABO DE HORNOS

67

London

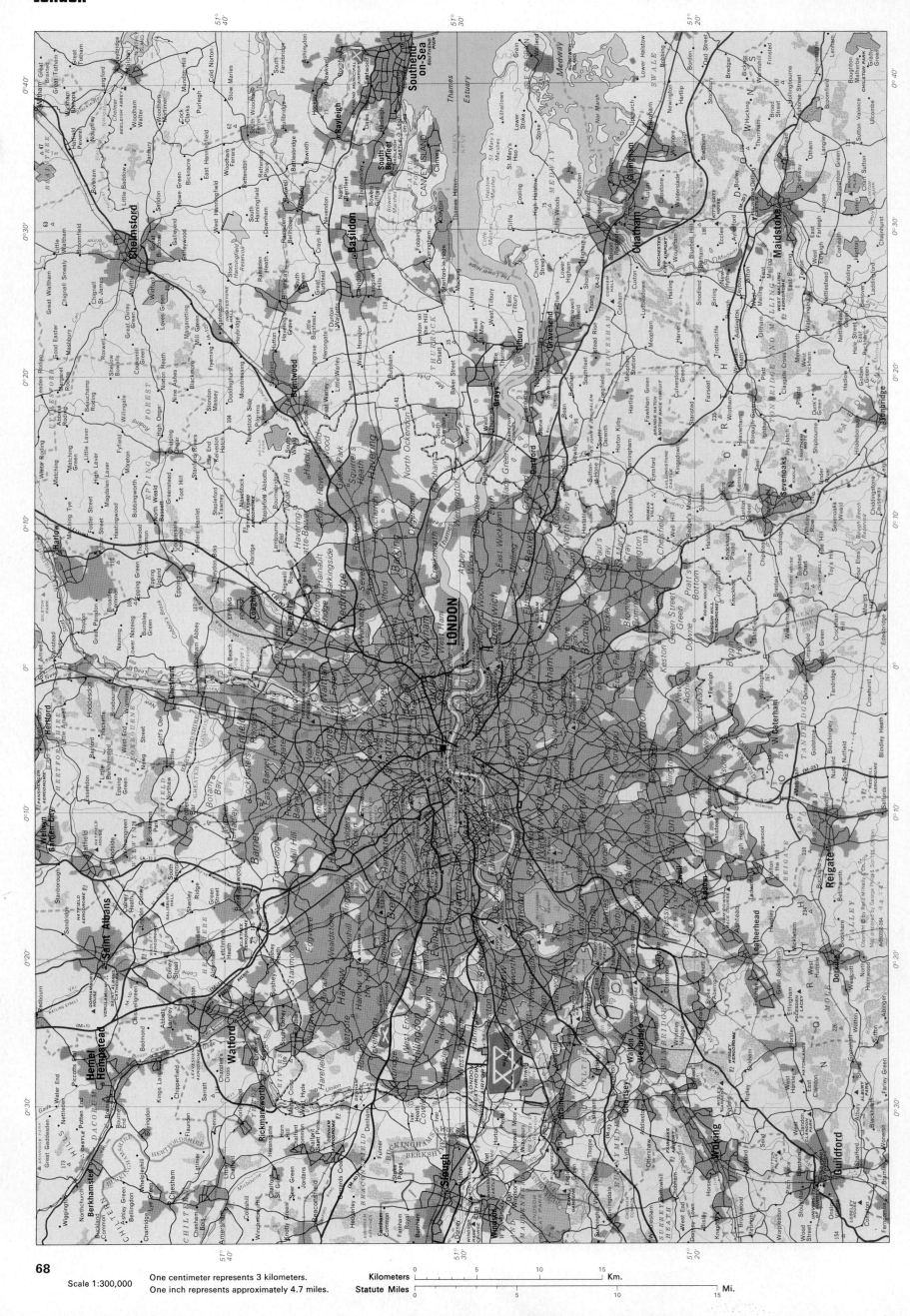

Scale 1:300,000

One centimeter represents 3 kilometers.
One inch represents approximately 4.7 miles.

Kilometers

Statute Miles

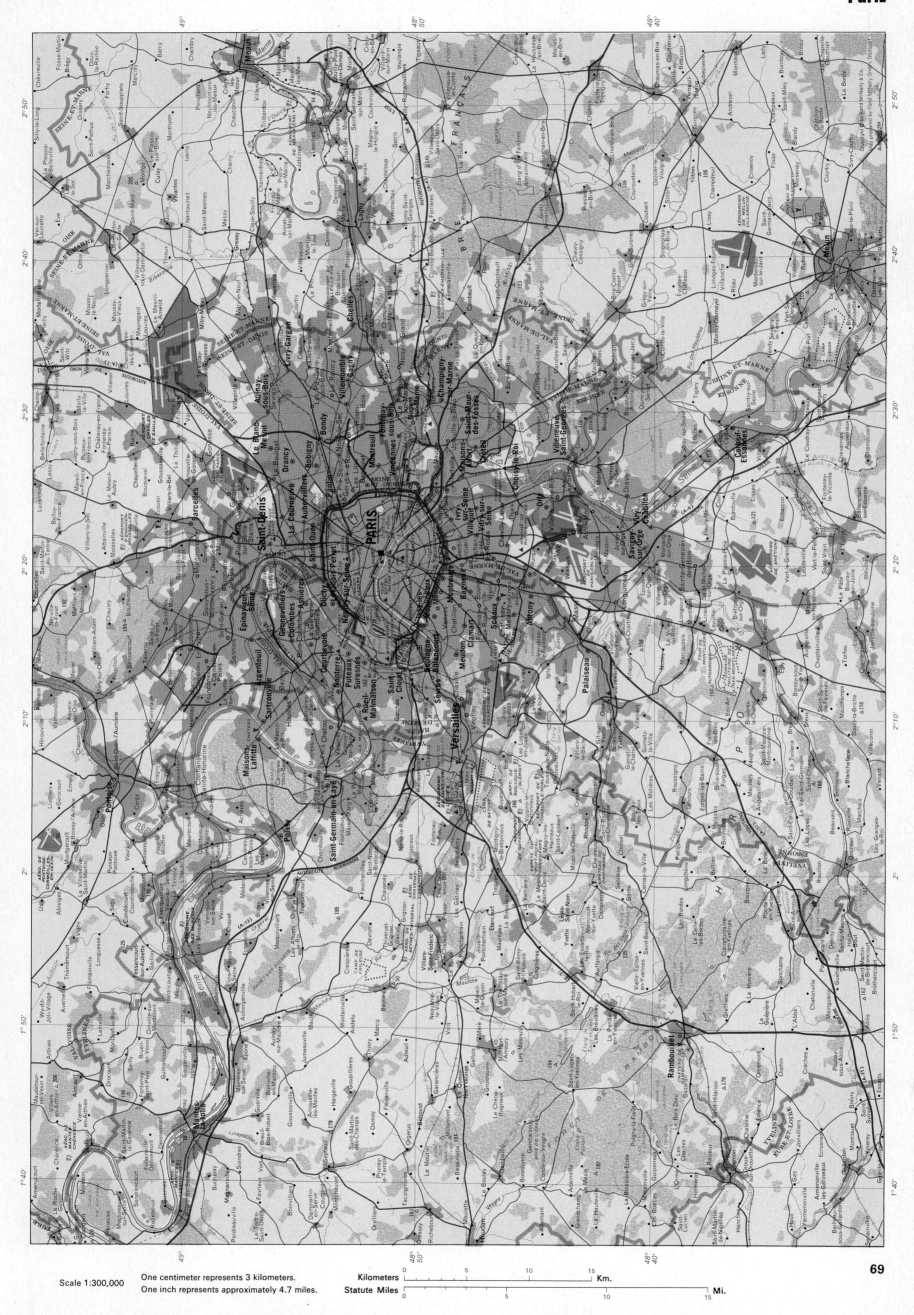

Scale 1:300,000
One centimeter represents 3 kilometers.
One inch represents approximately 4.7 miles.

Kilometers

Km.

Statute Miles

Mi.

0   5   10   15

Amsterdam—'s-Gravenhage (The Hague)—Rotterdam

Scale 1:300,000
One centimeter represents 3 kilometers.
One inch represents approximately 4.7 miles.

Kilometers
Statute Miles

Scale 1:300,000   One centimeter represents 3 kilometers.
One inch represents approximately 4.7 miles.

Kilometers
Statute Miles

Berlin · Wien · Budapest

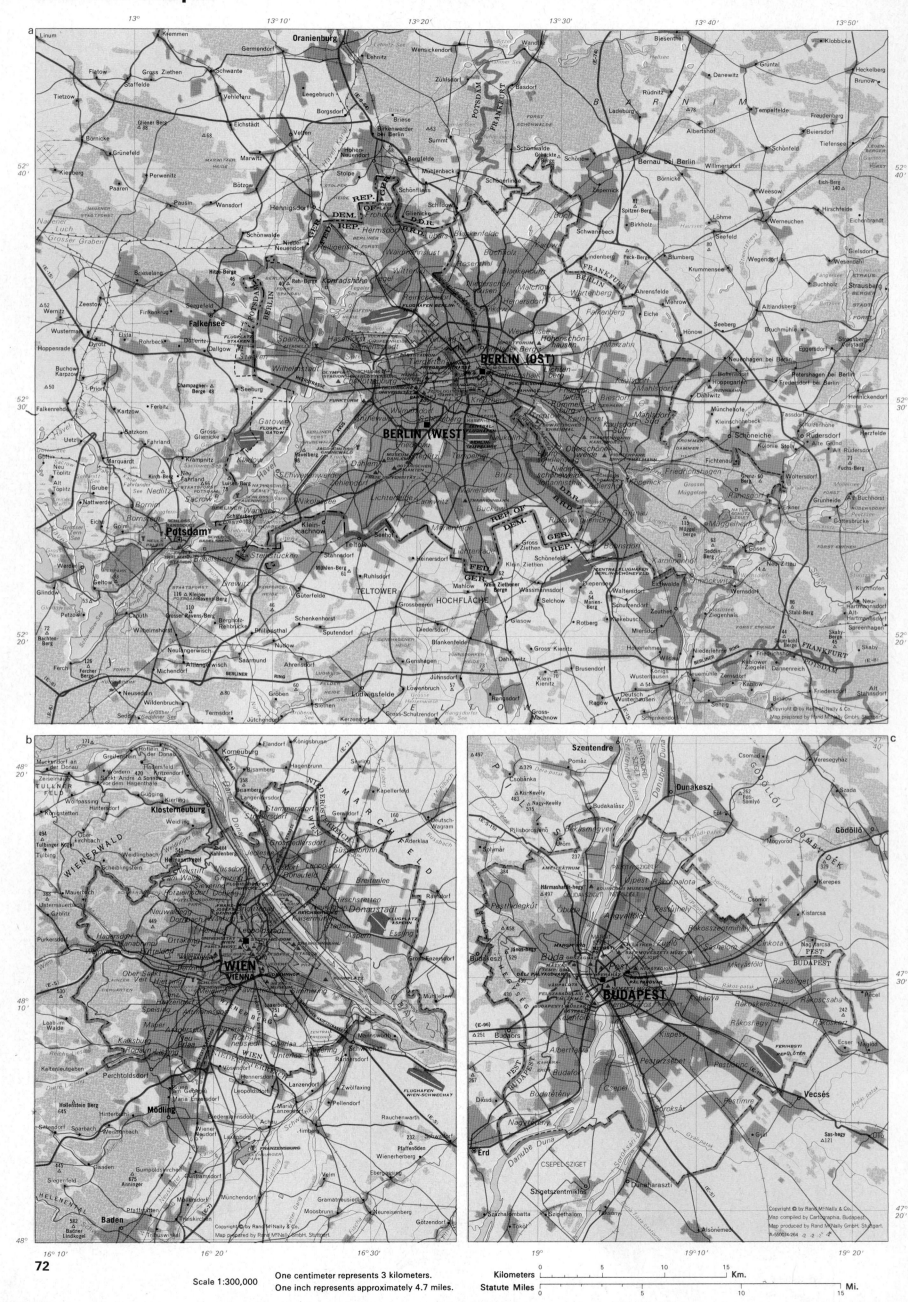

Scale 1:300,000

One centimeter represents 3 kilometers.
One inch represents approximately 4.7 miles.

Kilometers

Statute Miles

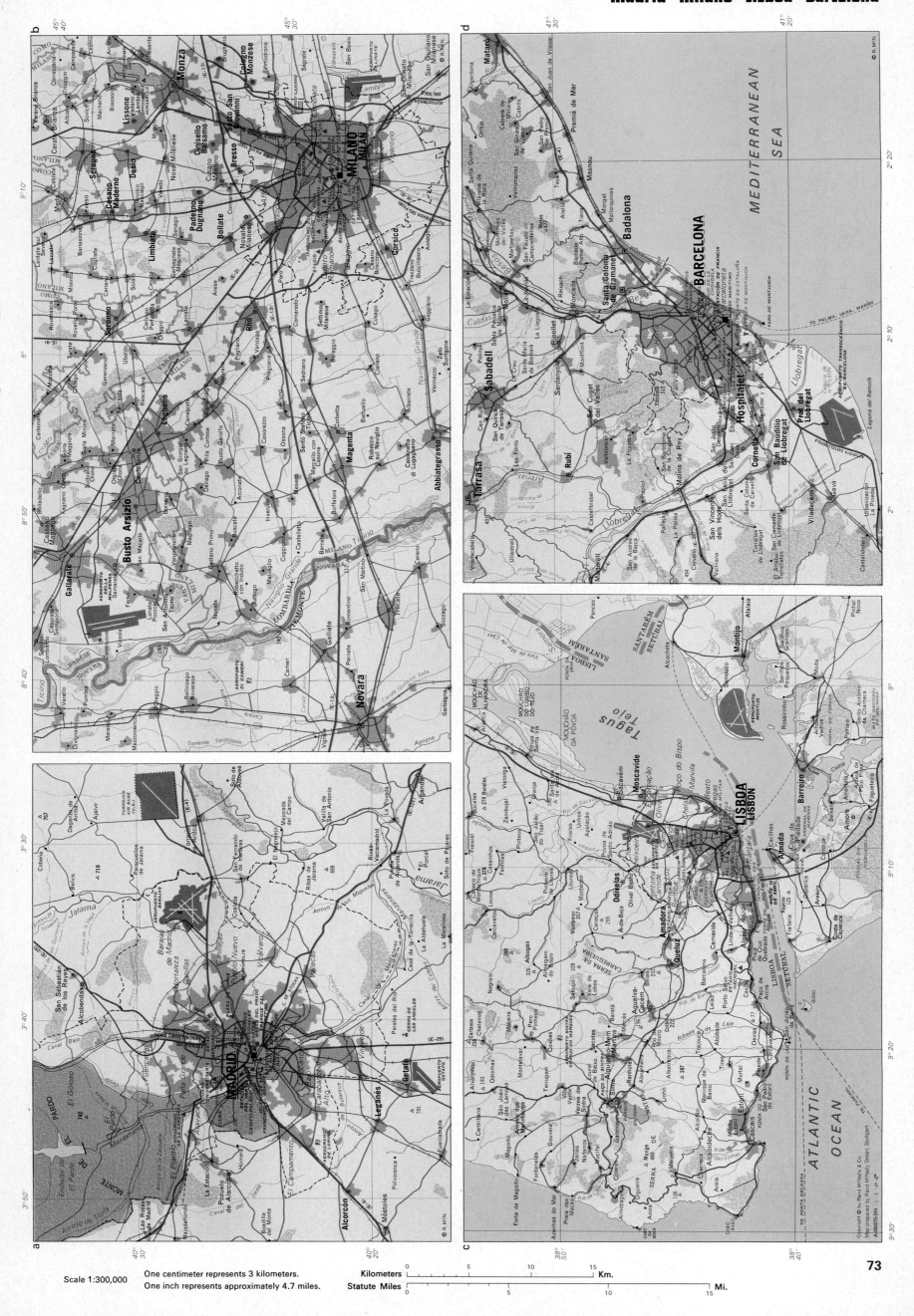

Scale 1:300,000

One centimeter represents 3 kilometers.
One inch represents approximately 4.7 miles.

Kilometers

Statute Miles

Km.

Mi.

Roma · Athínai · İstanbul · Tehrān

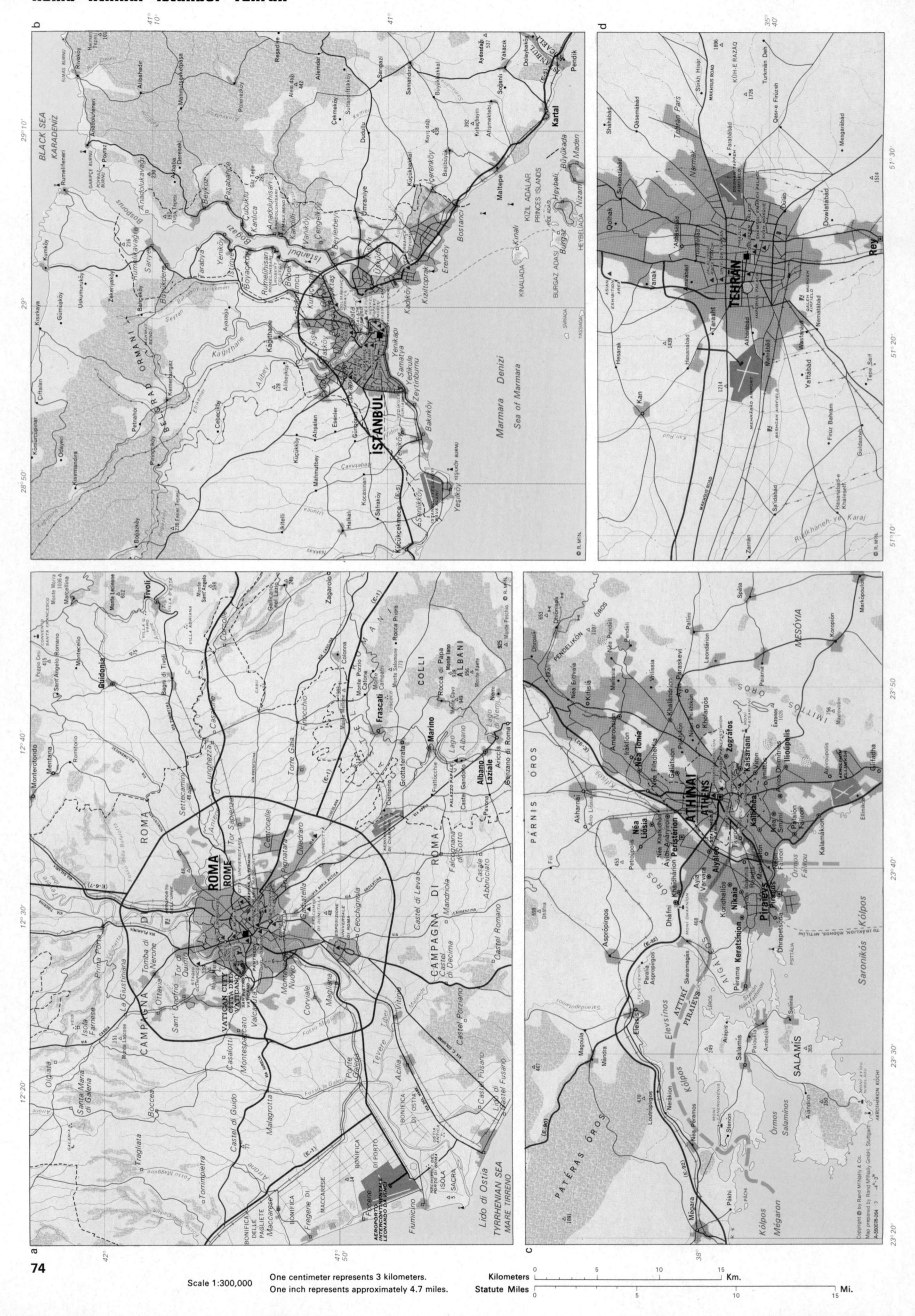

Scale 1:300,000
One centimeter represents 3 kilometers.
One inch represents approximately 4.7 miles.

Kilometers
Statute Miles
Km.
Mi.

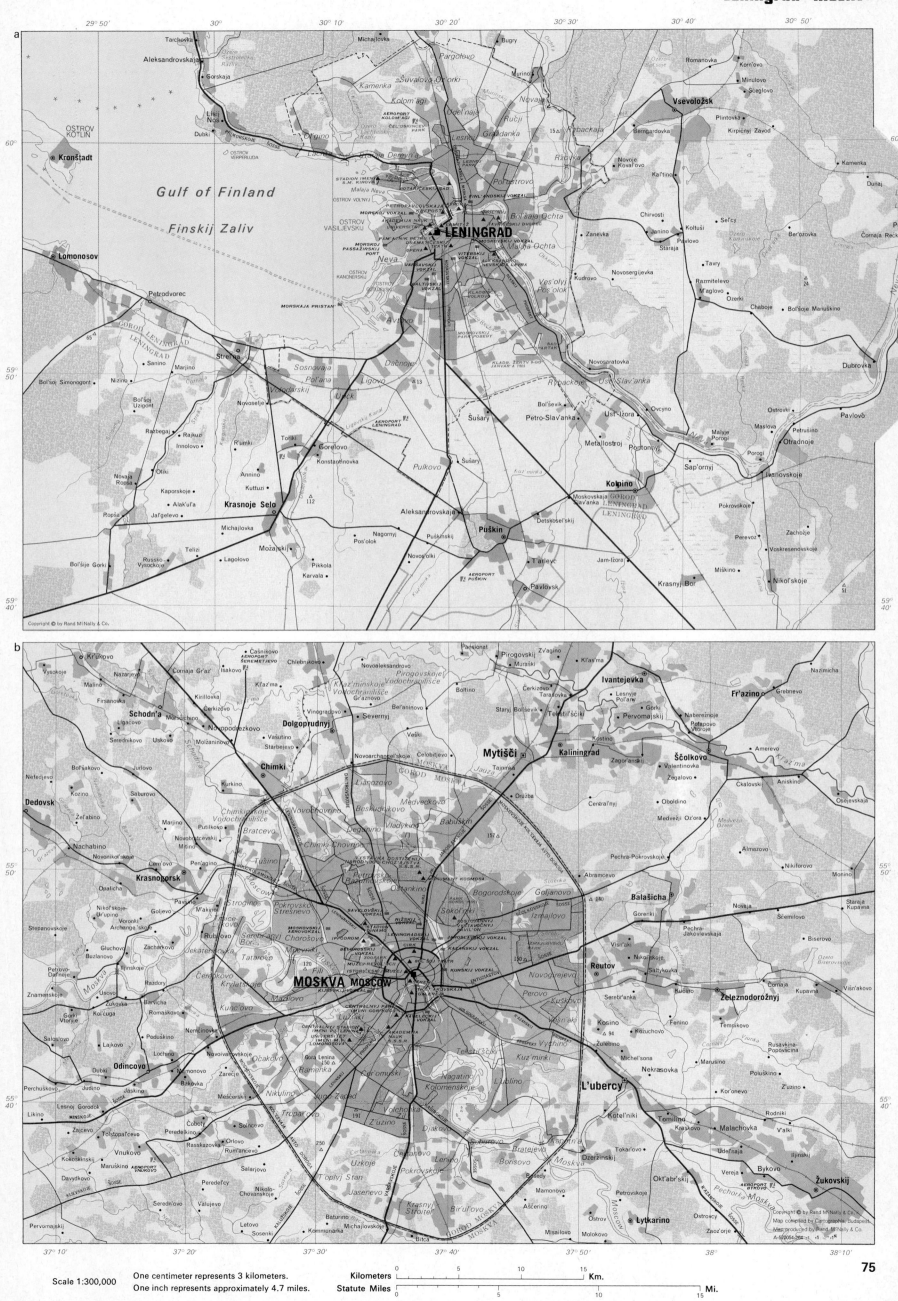

Scale 1:300,000

One centimeter represents 3 kilometers.
One inch represents approximately 4.7 miles.

Kilometers

Km.

Statute Miles

Mi.

0   5   10   15

0   5   10   15

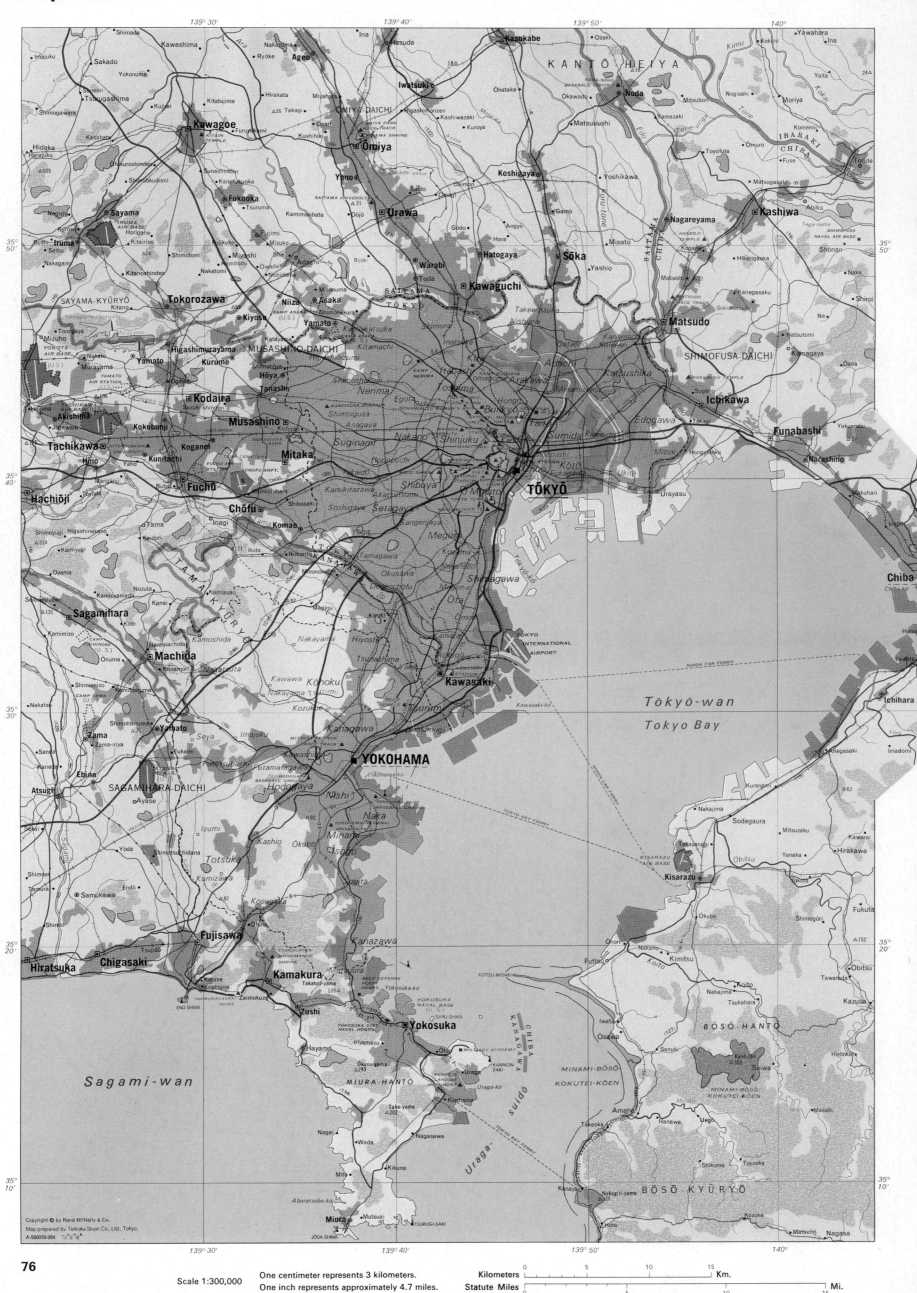

Scale 1:300,000

One centimeter represents 3 kilometers.
One inch represents approximately 4.7 miles.

Kilometers

Statute Miles

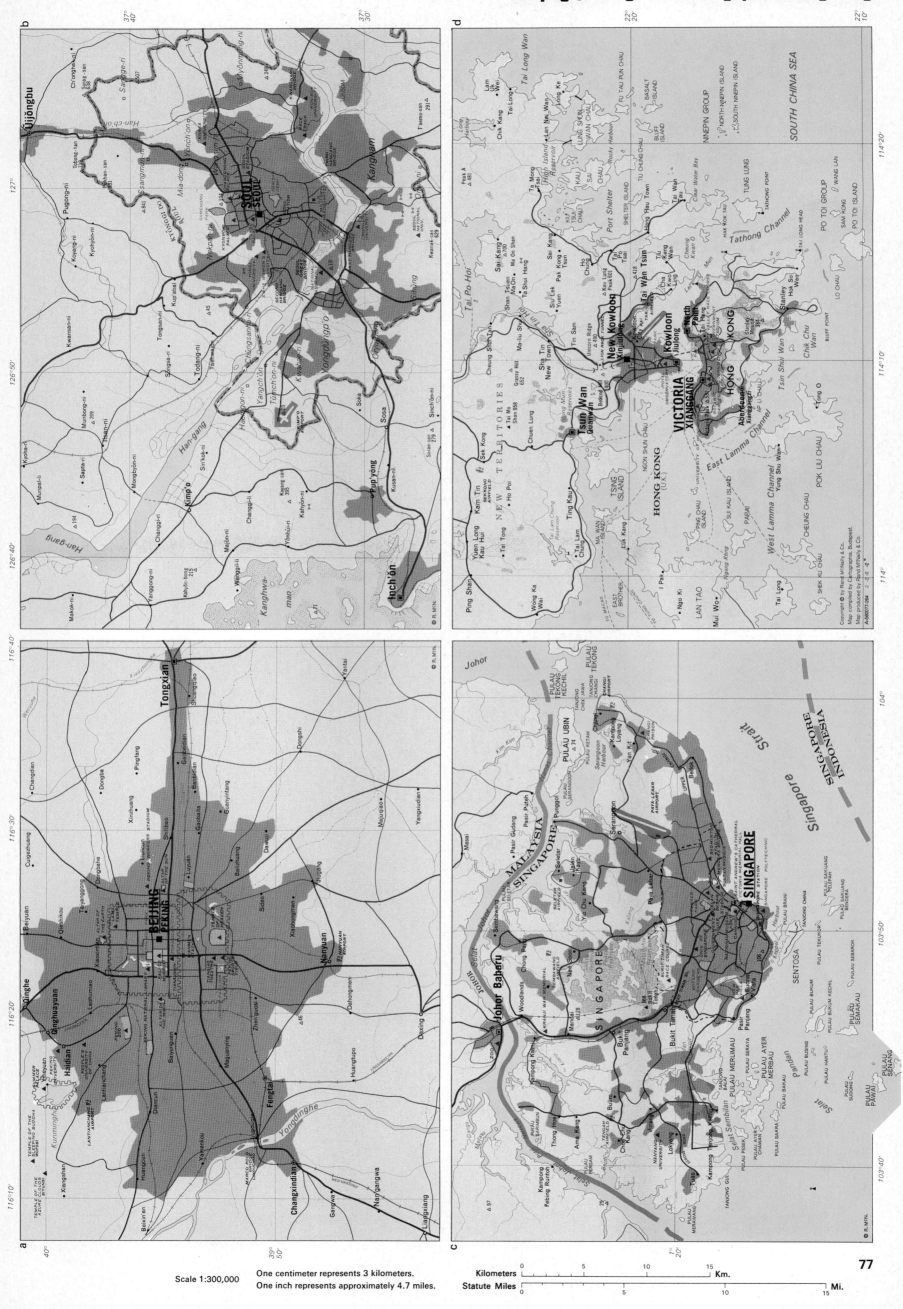

Scale 1:300,000

One centimeter represents 3 kilometers.
One inch represents approximately 4.7 miles.

Kilometers
Statute Miles

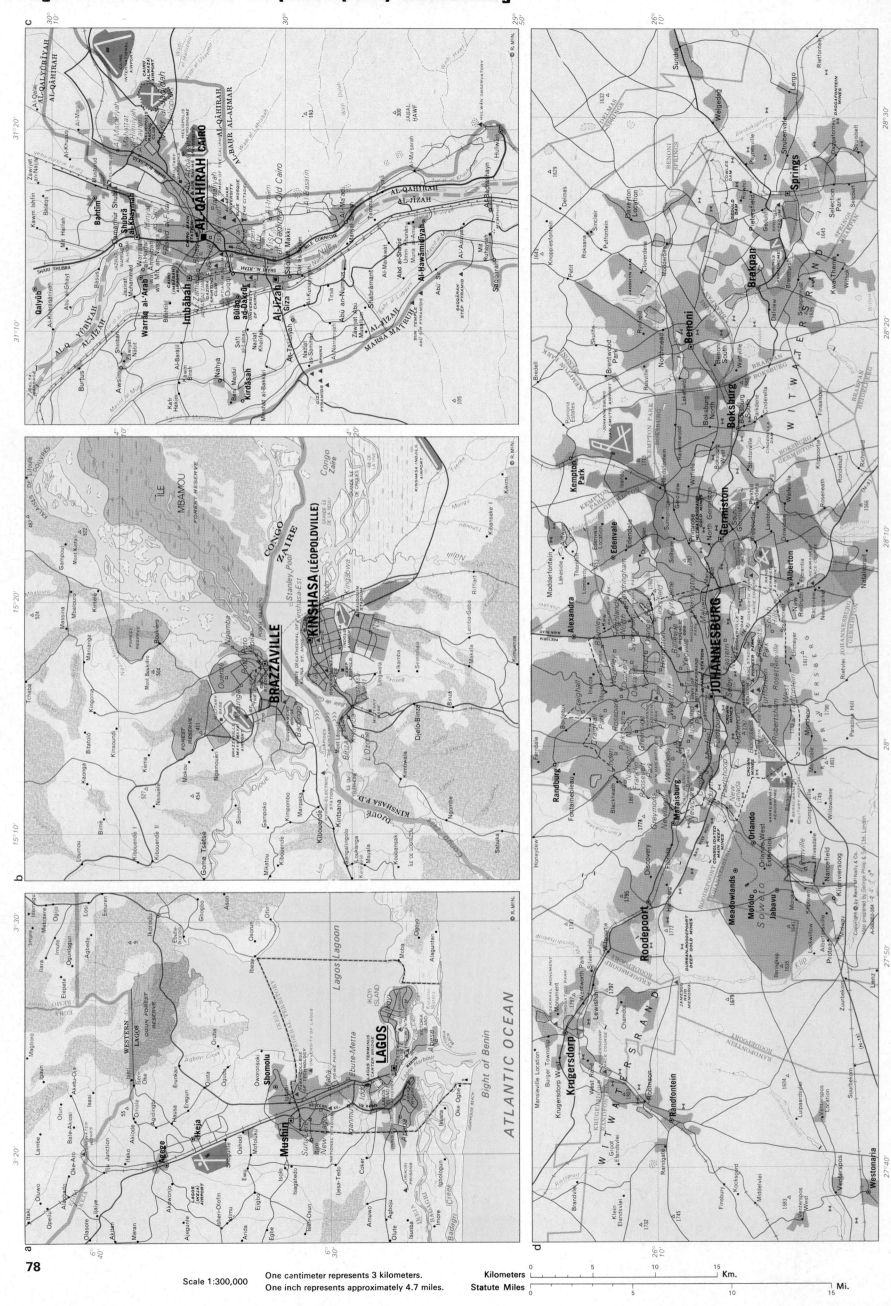

Scale 1:300,000

One centimeter represents 3 kilometers.
One inch represents approximately 4.7 miles.

Kilometers

Statute Miles

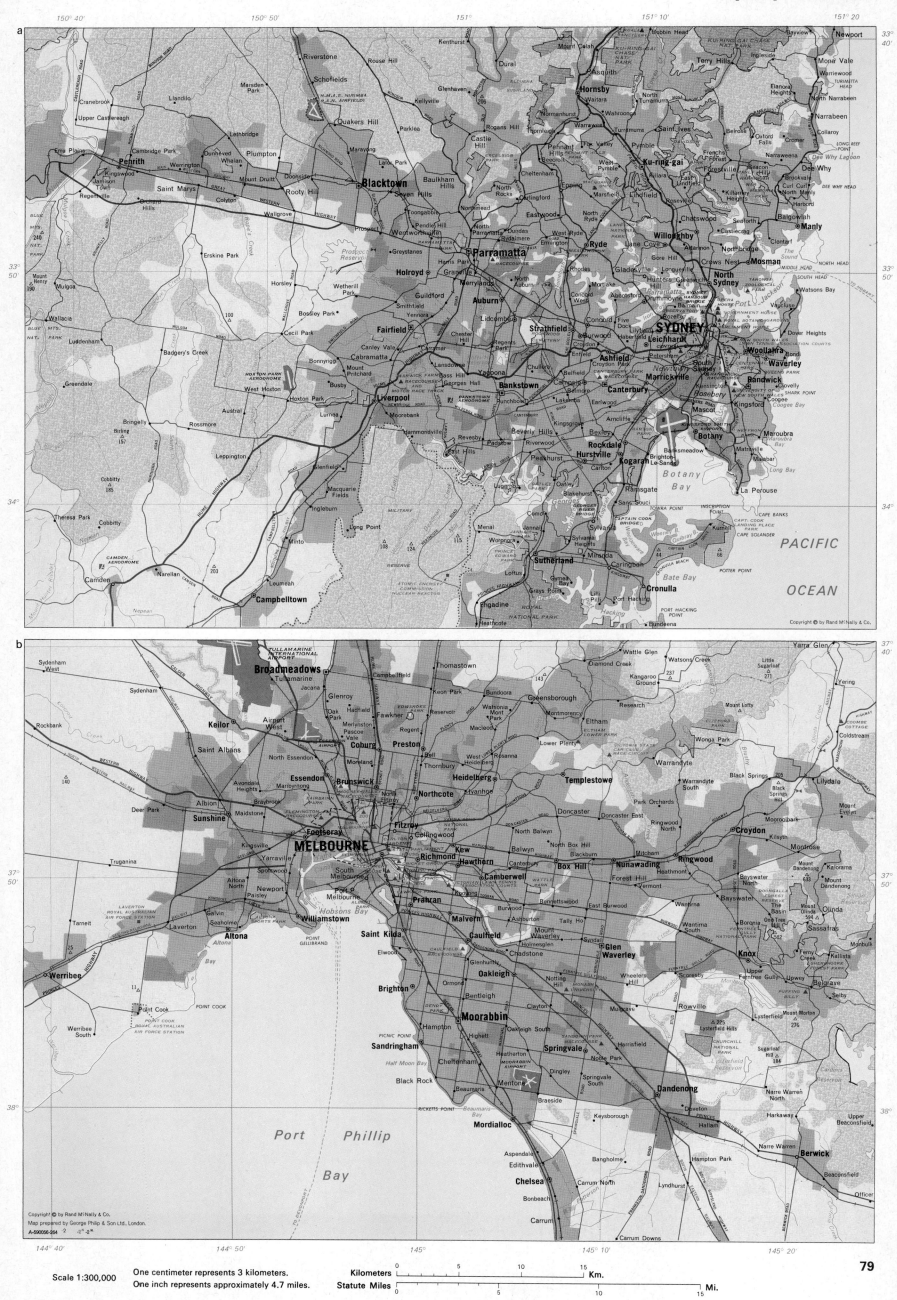

Scale 1:300,000

One centimeter represents 3 kilometers.
One inch represents approximately 4.7 miles.

Kilometers

Statute Miles

Scale 1:300,000

One centimeter represents 3 kilometers.
One inch represents approximately 4.7 miles.

Kilometers

Statute Miles

The Face of the Earth

For many centuries, each new voyage of discovery left the impression that our earthly home was expanding. In recent years, with the coming of air and space travel, it has seemed to shrink. Now it can be encircled in minutes and full views of our planet have become familiar sights.

This section opens with a world physical map at the scale of 1:75,000,000. There follow maps of Antarctica, at a scale of 1:24,000,000 (as it appears from about 4,000 miles in space); of the Atlantic, at 1:48,000,000 (the largest scale at which such a body of water can be portrayed); and then 1:24,000,000 maps of Europe and Africa, North America, South America, Asia, and Australia and Oceania.

The legend below shows how terrains and vegetation have been represented.

Submarine Features

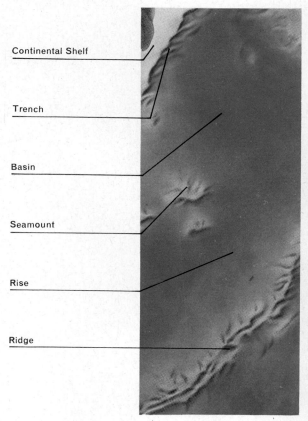

Continental Shelf

Trench

Basin

Seamount

Rise

Ridge

Land Features

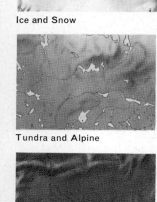

Ice and Snow

High Barren Area

Tundra and Alpine

Needleleaf Trees

Broadleaf Trees

Tropical Rainforest

Grassland

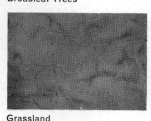

Dry Scrub

Desert

The Spherical Earth Flattened
The curved surface of the Earth is transferred to a flat surface by means of a projection. This is an orderly system of parallels and meridians upon which a map can be drawn. Many different map projections are used today, and the most appropriate ones have been chosen for the maps that follow. The Azimuthal Equal–Area projection is used for the 1:24,000,000 maps, the scale being approximately that of a globe 20 inches in diameter.

World: Physical

Kilometers 0 1000 2000 3000 Km.

Statute Miles 0 1000 2000 3000 Mi.

One centimeter represents 750 kilometers.
One inch represents approximately 1200 miles.
Robinson Projection
Scale 1:75,000,000

Scale 1:48,000,000
One centimeter represents 480 kilometers.
One inch represents approximately 760 miles.
Modified Cylindrical Projection

Copyright © by Rand McNally & Co.
Map prepared by Rand McNally & Co.
A-513700-764

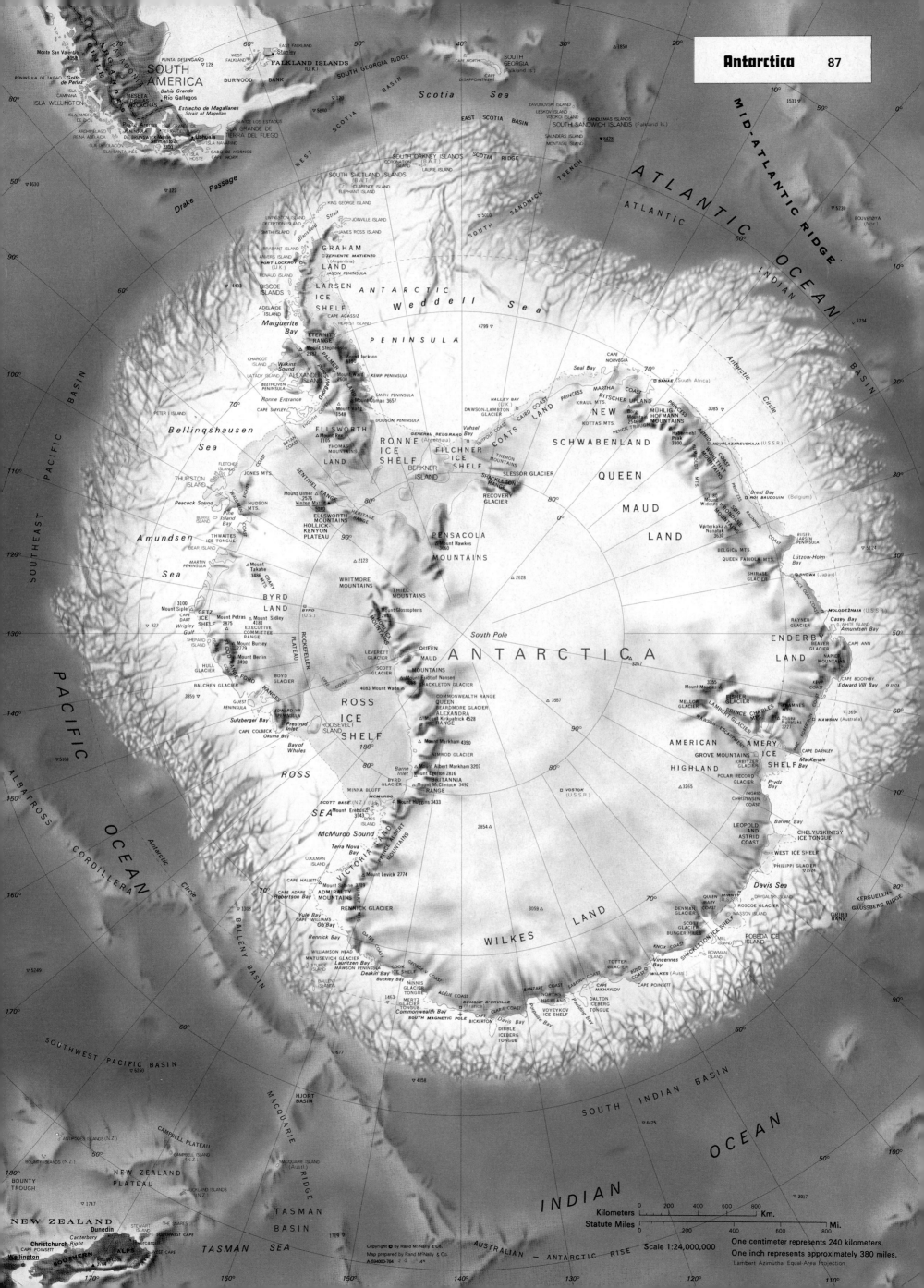

Scale 1:24,000,000

One centimeter represents 240 kilometers.
One inch represents approximately 380 miles.
Lambert Azimuthal Equal-Area Projection

Copyright © by Rand McNally & Co.
Map prepared by Rand McNally & Co.
A-594000-764

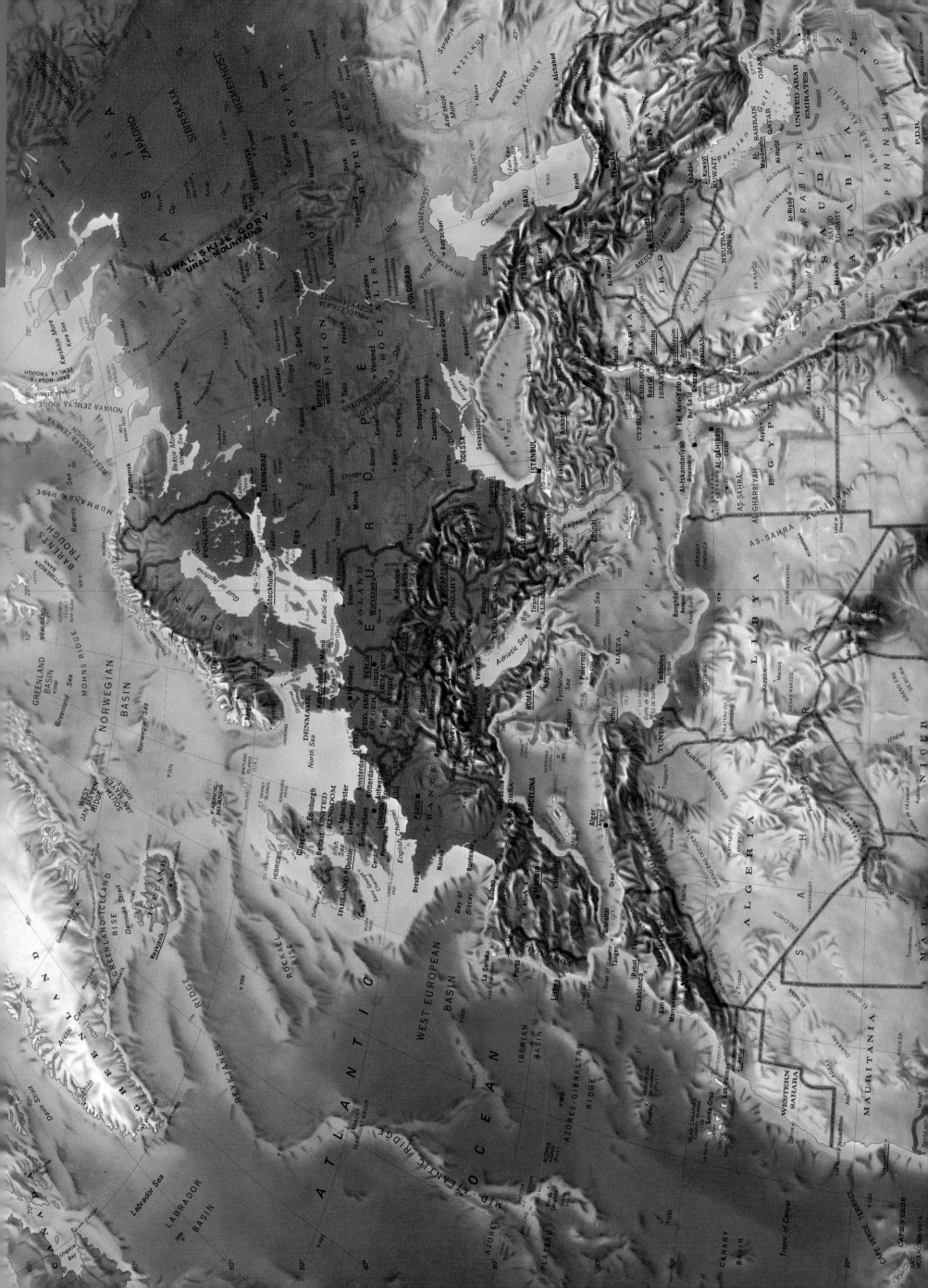

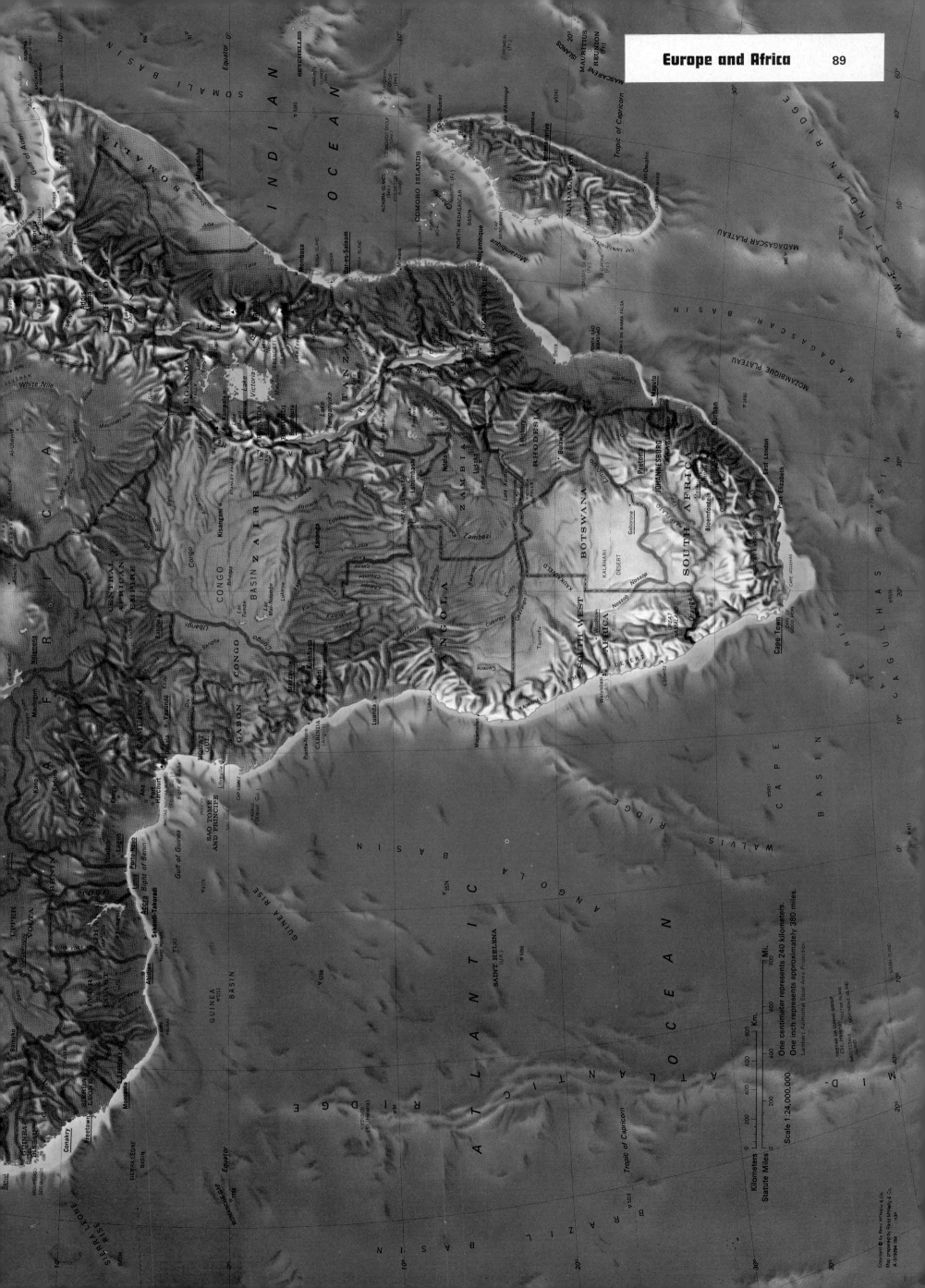

SOMALI BASIN

INDIAN OCEAN

SEYCHELLES

MASCARENE ISLANDS
MAURITIUS (Fr.)
REUNION (Fr.)

Tropic of Capricorn

MADAGASCAR

MADAGASCAR PLATEAU

MADAGASCAR BASIN

W. IND. INDIAN RIDGE

Gulf of Aden

SOMALIA

Mogadishu

Juba

COMORO ISLANDS

NORTH MADAGASCAR BASIN

Mozambique

ETHIOPIA

Addis Ababa

White Nile

Mountain Nile

UGANDA

Lake Victoria

Kampala

RWANDA

BURUNDI

Lake Tanganyika

KENYA

Mombasa

Dar-es-Salaam

TANZANIA

SERENGETI

Lake Eyasi

MALAWI

MOZAMBIQUE

Beira

Mozambique

CENTRAL AFRICAN EMPIRE

ZAIRE

CONGO BASIN

Kisangani

Kananga

Congo

Lualaba

KATANGA

Lubumbashi

ZAMBIA

Lusaka

RHODESIA

Salisbury

Bulawayo

Zambezi

BOTSWANA

Gaborone

KALAHARI DESERT

KAUKAUVELD

Pretoria

JOHANNESBURG

Bloemfontein

SOUTH AFRICA

Durban

East London

Port Elizabeth

CAPE OF GOOD HOPE

Cape Town

CAPE AGULHAS

AGULHAS BASIN

A F R I C A

GABON

CONGO

Brazzaville

Kinshasa

Matadi

CABINDA (Angola)

ANGOLA

Luanda

SOUTH WEST AFRICA

NAMIB DESERT

Walvis Bay (S. Af.)

Lüderitz

GREAT KARROO

Orange

Nossob

KALAHARI DESERT

CAMEROON

Yaoundé

Libreville

EQUAT. GUI.

SAO TOME AND PRINCIPE

Gulf of Guinea

CAPE BASIN

WALVIS RIDGE

ANGOLA BASIN

GUINEA BASIN

SAINT HELENA (U.K.)

ATLANTIC OCEAN

ATLANTIC OCEAN

BRAZIL BASIN

MID-ATLANTIC RIDGE

GUINEA RISE

GUINEA BASIN

Lagos

BENIN

Porto-Novo

Bight of Benin

Accra

Sekondi-Takoradi

Abidjan

IVORY COAST

UPPER VOLTA

SIERRA LEONE BASIN

GUINEA

Bamako

Conakry

Freetown

SIERRA LEONE

Monrovia

LIBERIA

Equator

Kilometers
Statute Miles

One centimeter represents 240 kilometers.
One inch represents approximately 380 miles.

Lambert Azimuthal Equal-Area Projection.

Scale 1:24,000,000

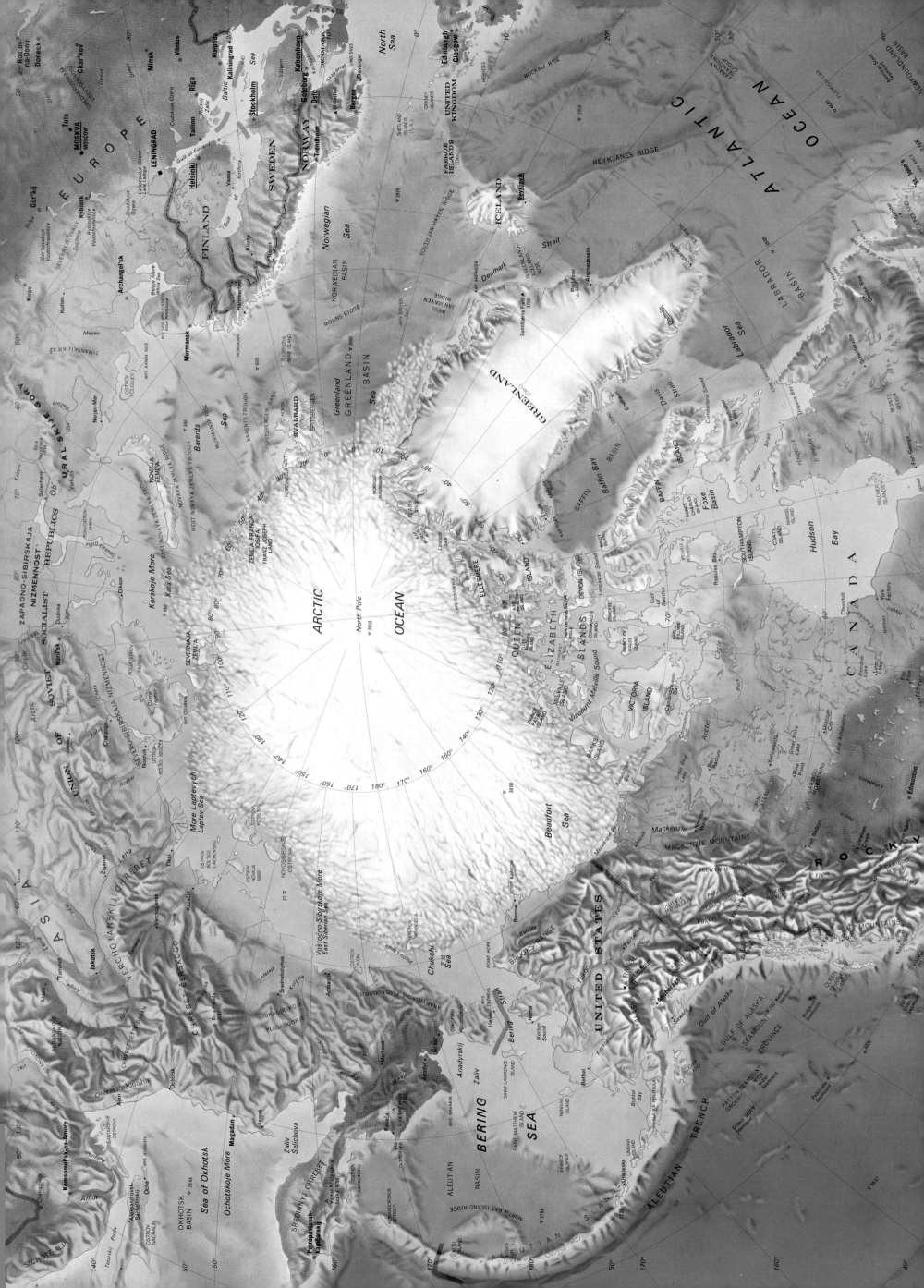

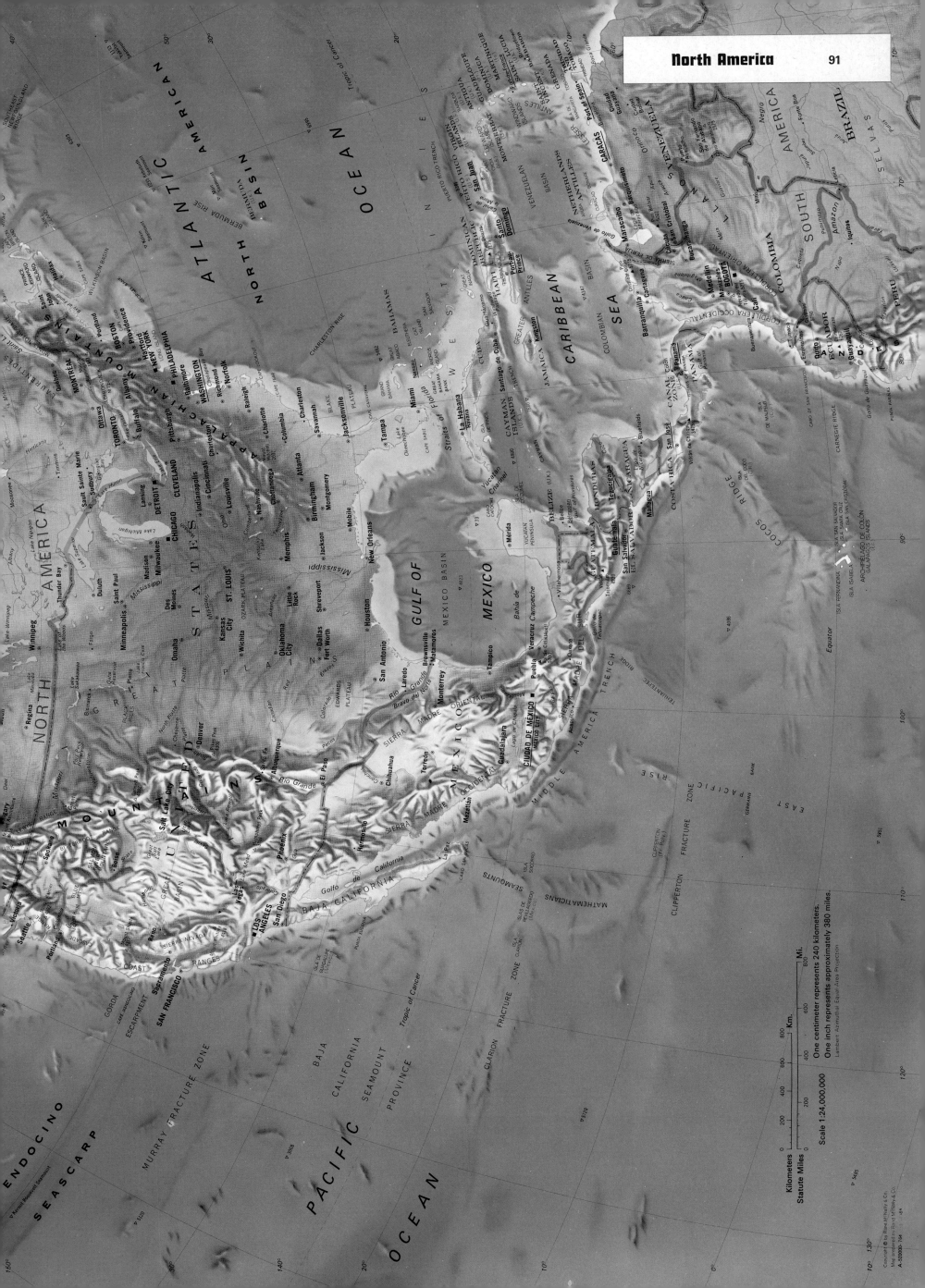

NORTH AMERICA

UNITED STATES

ATLANTIC OCEAN

MID-ATLANTIC RIDGE

NORTH AMERICAN BASIN

CANARY BASIN

CAPE VERDE BASIN

GUIANA BASIN

SOUTH AMERICA

BRAZIL

CARIBBEAN SEA

GULF OF MEXICO

MEXICO

WEST INDIES

LESSER ANTILLES

GREATER ANTILLES

VENEZUELA

COLOMBIA

PERU

ECUADOR

GUYANA

SURINAM

FRENCH GUIANA

PANAMA

COSTA RICA

NICARAGUA

HONDURAS

EL SALVADOR

GUATEMALA

BELIZE

CUBA

JAMAICA

HAITI

DOMINICAN REPUBLIC

HISPANIOLA

PUERTO RICO

BAHAMAS

VIRGIN ISLANDS (U.K. and U.S.)

ANGUILLA (U.K.)

ANTIGUA (U.K.)

GUADELOUPE (Fr.)

DOMINICA (U.K.)

MARTINIQUE (Fr.)

SAINT LUCIA (U.K.)

SAINT VINCENT (U.K.)

BARBADOS

GRENADA

TRINIDAD AND TOBAGO

NETHERLANDS ANTILLES

ROCKY MOUNTAINS

APPALACHIAN MOUNTAINS

SIERRA MADRE ORIENTAL

SIERRA MADRE DEL SUR

ANDES

CORDILLERA OCCIDENTAL

CORDILLERA ORIENTAL

LLANOS

SELVAS

GREAT PLAINS

OZARK PLATEAU

EDWARDS PLATEAU

BERMUDA RISE

BERMUDA (U.K.)

CAYMAN ISLANDS (U.K.)

AZORES (Port.)

AZORES RIDGE

CAYMAN TRENCH

PUERTO RICO TRENCH

MIDDLE AMERICA TRENCH

COCOS RIDGE

CARNEGIE RIDGE

CHARLESTON RISE

BLAKE PLATEAU

SOUTHEAST NEWFOUNDLAND RIDGE

Straits of Florida

Yucatan Channel

Gulf of Honduras

ISTHMUS OF PANAMA

CANAL ZONE

Equator

Tropic of Cancer

New York
Philadelphia
Baltimore
WASHINGTON
Richmond
Norfolk
Raleigh
Charleston
Savannah
Jacksonville
Tampa
Miami
Atlanta
Montgomery
Birmingham
Memphis
Nashville
Louisville
Cincinnati
Pittsburgh
Cleveland
CHICAGO
Des Moines
Omaha
Kansas City
ST. LOUIS
Wichita
Little Rock
Jackson
Mobile
New Orleans
Houston
Fort Worth
Dallas
San Antonio
Laredo
Brownsville
Matamoros
Monterrey
Denver
Oklahoma City

MEXICO CITY
Guadalajara
Torreón
Tampico
Veracruz
Puebla
Mérida
Campeche

Guatemala
San Salvador
Tegucigalpa
Managua
San José
Panamá

La Habana
Santiago de Cuba
Nassau
Port-au-Prince
Kingston
Santo Domingo
San Juan
Fort-de-France
Bridgetown
Port of Spain

CARACAS
Maracaibo
Barquisimeto
Barcelona
Ciudad Bolívar
Ciudad Guayana
Georgetown
Paramaribo
Cayenne

BOGOTÁ
Barranquilla
Cartagena
Medellín
Manizales
Cali
Cúcuta
Bucaramanga
Buenaventura

QUITO
Guayaquil

LIMA

Manaus
Boa Vista
Belém
São Luís
Teresina
Fortaleza
Natal
João Pessoa
Recife
Maceió
Salvador
Campina Grande

Mississippi
Rio Grande
Orinoco
Amazon
Negro
Branco

GALÁPAGOS ISLANDS
ARCHIPIÉLAGO DE COLÓN

AKARAIMA MTS.
WILHELMINA MTS.
ACARAI MTS.
GUIANA HIGHLANDS

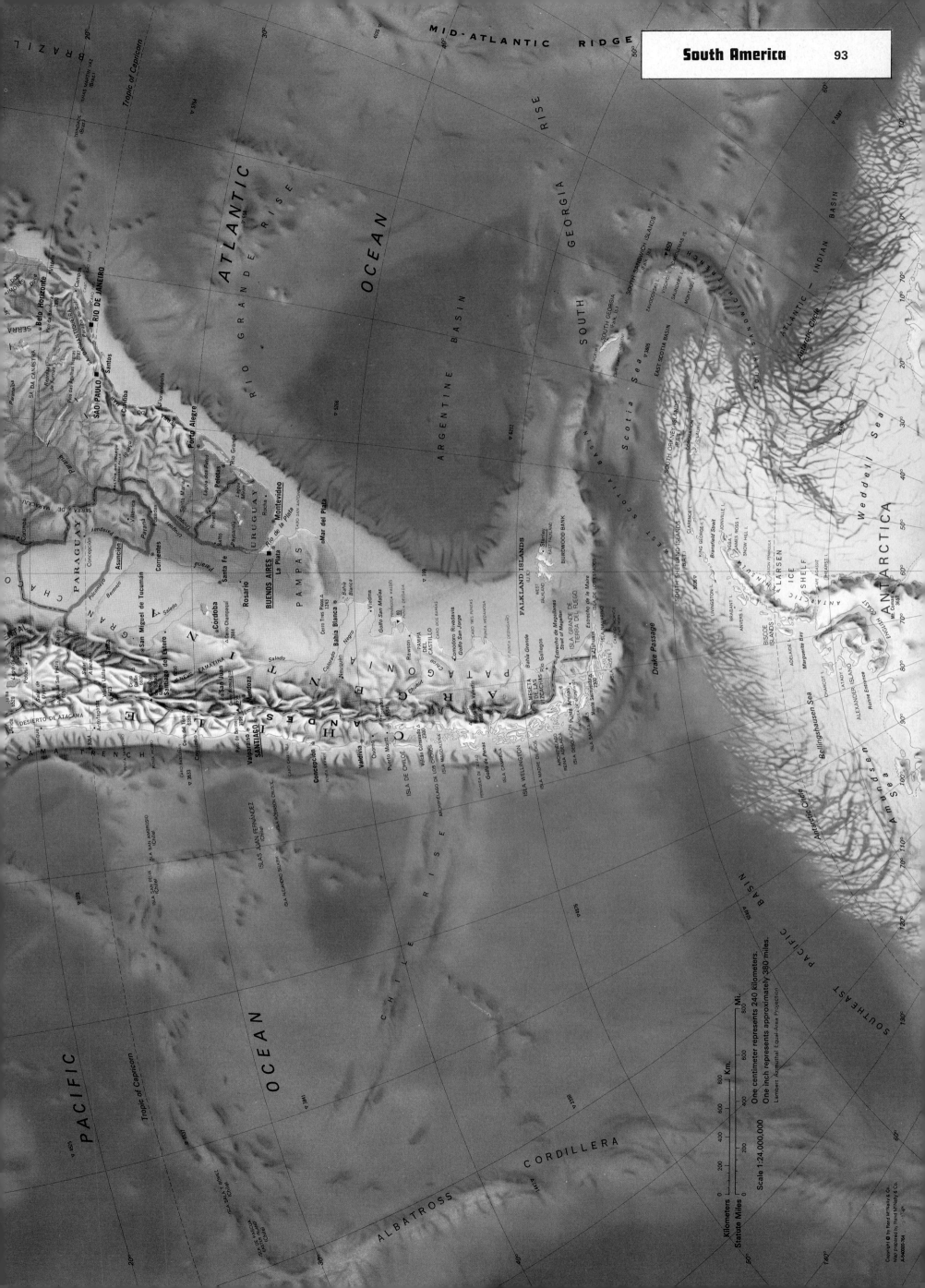

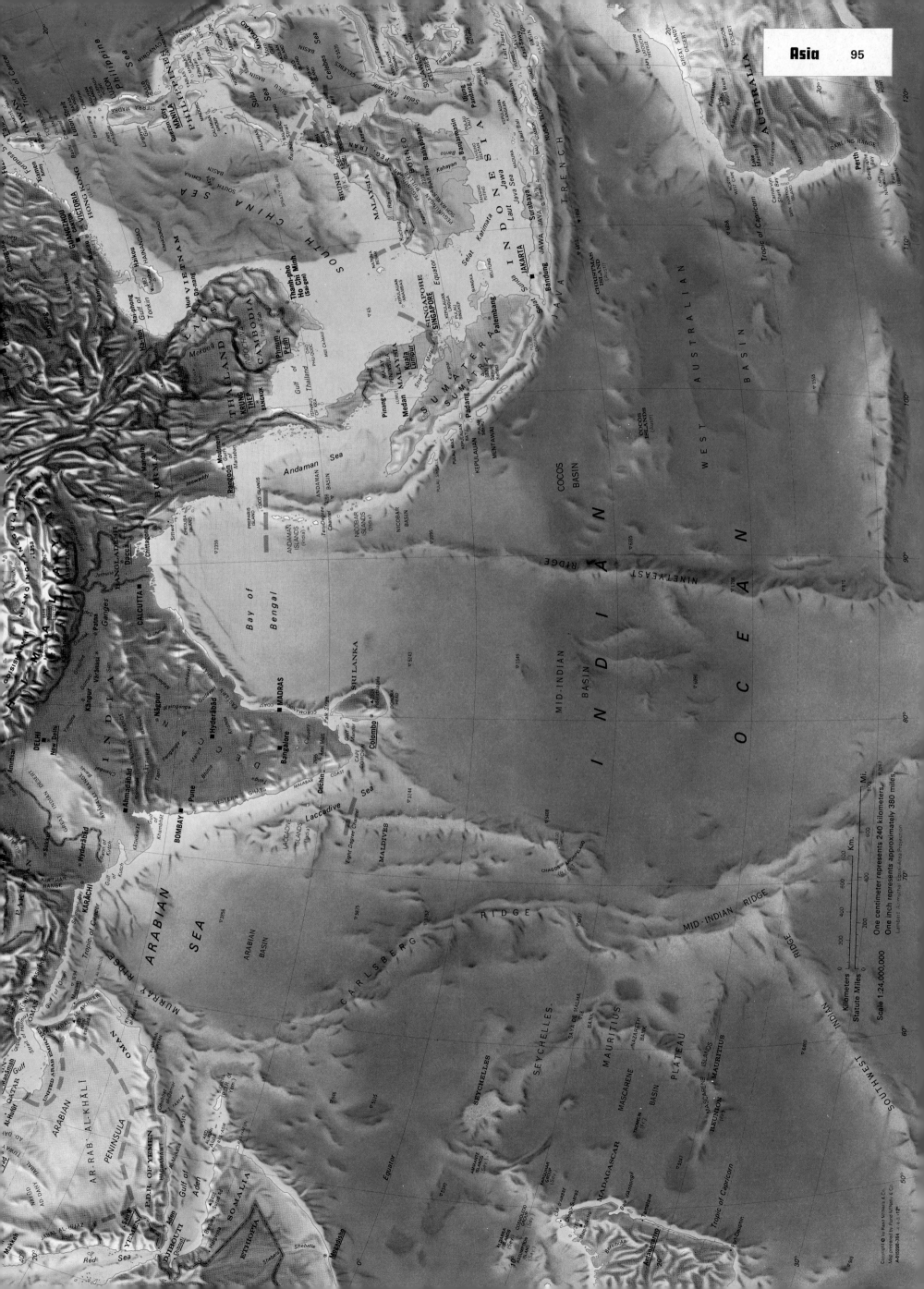

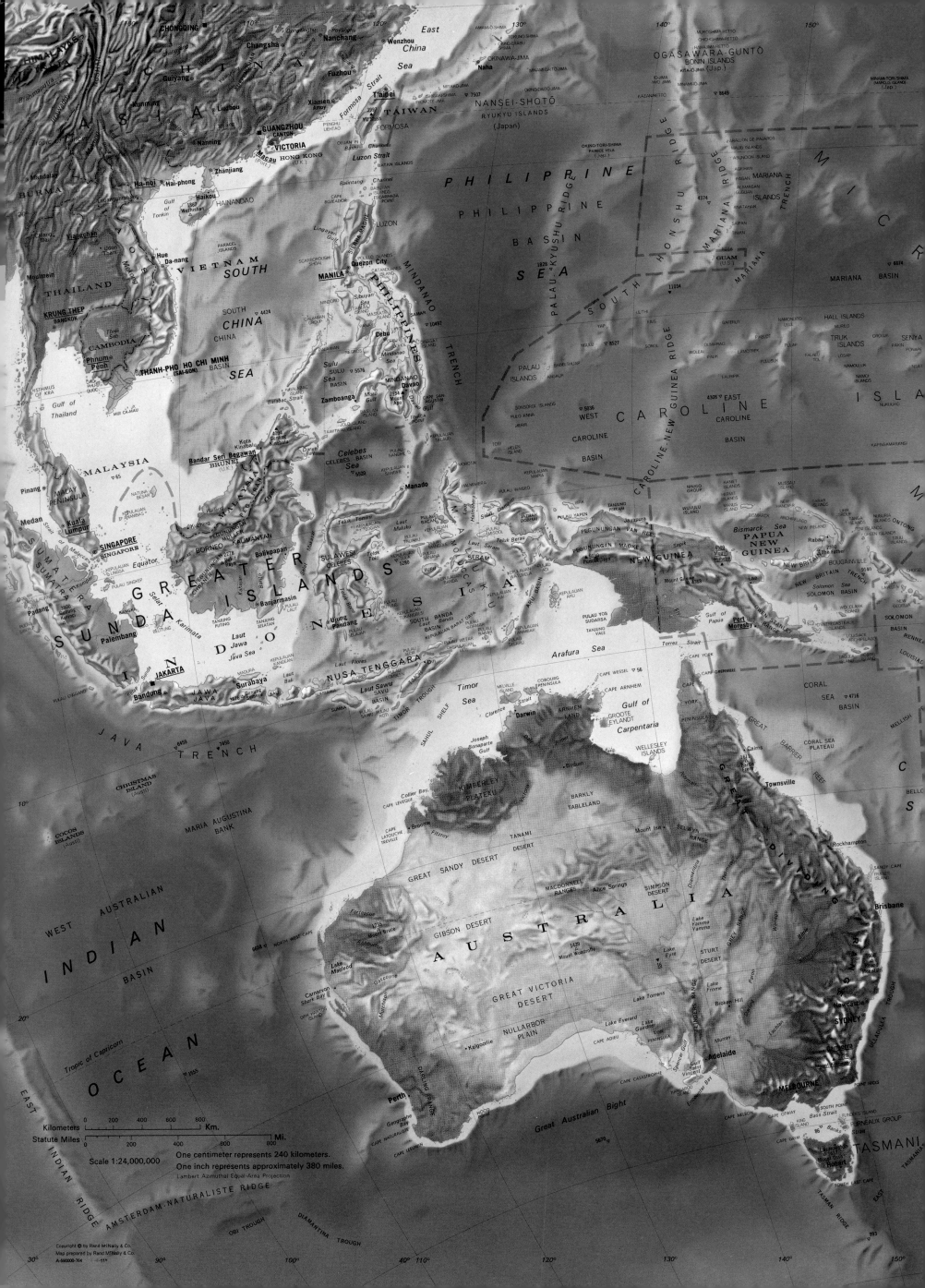

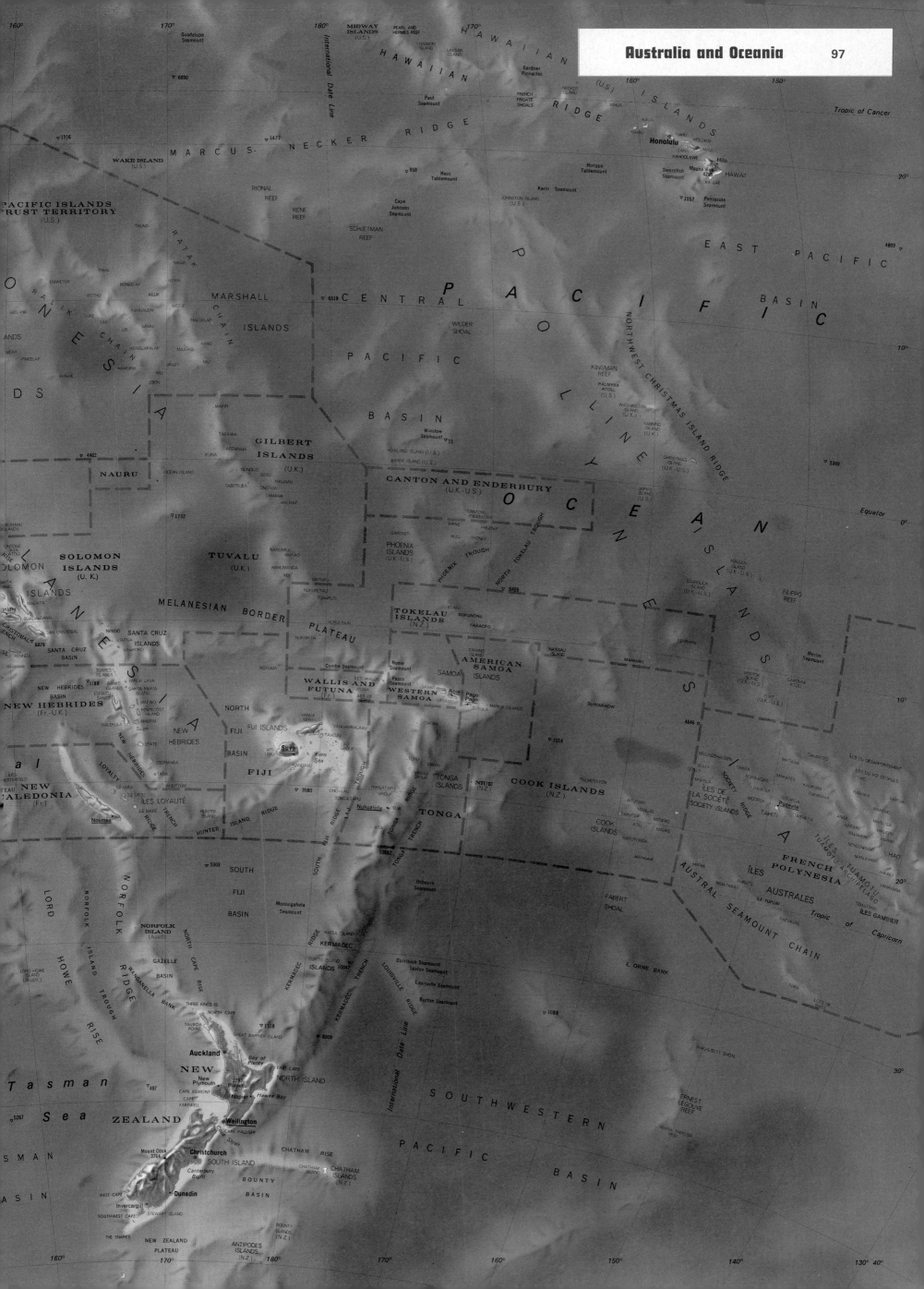

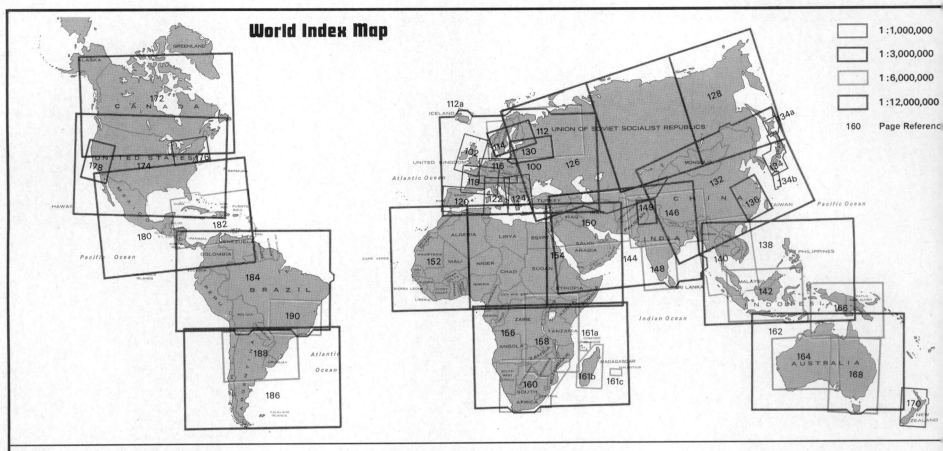

World Index Map

1:1,000,000
1:3,000,000
1:6,000,000
1:12,000,000

160 Page Reference

Legend to Maps

Inhabited Localities

The symbol represents the number of inhabitants within the locality

1:1,000,000	• 0—10,000	1:12,000,000	• 0—50,000
1:3,000,000	○ 10,000—25,000		⊙ 50,000—100,000
1:6,000,000	⊙ 25,000—100,000		⊡ 100,000—250,000
	⊡ 100,000—250,000		▣ 250,000—1,000,000
	▣ 250,000—1,000,000		■ >1,000,000
	■ >1,000,000		

▨ Urban Area (area of continuous industrial, commercial, and residential development)

The size of type indicates the relative economic and political importance of the locality

Écommoy	Lisieux	**Rouen**
Trouville	**Orléans**	**PARIS**

Hollywood ○ Section of a City, Neighborhood
Westminster

Bi'r Safâjah ○ Inhabited Oasis   Kumdah ○ Uninhabited Oasis

Capitals of Political Units

BUDAPEST Independent Nation

Cayenne Dependency (Colony, protectorate, etc.)

GALAPAGOS Administering Country
(Ecuador)

Villarica State, Province, etc.

White Plains County, Oblast, etc.

Alternate Names

Basel	**MOSKVA**	English or second official language names are shown
Bâle	'MOSCOW	in reduced size lettering
Ventura	Volgograd	Historical or other alternates in the local language
(San Buenaventura)	(Stalingrad)	are shown in parentheses

Political Boundaries

International (First-order political unit)

1:1,000,000	1:3,000,000	1:6,000,000	1:12,000,000	
				Demarcated, Undemarcated, and Administrative
				Disputed de jure
				Indefinite or Undefined
				Demarcation Line

Internal

State, Province, etc. (Second-order political unit)

County, Oblast, etc. (Third-order political unit)

ANDALUCIA Historical Region (No boundaries indicated)

Transportation

1:12,000,000	1:1,000,000 / 1:3,000,000	1:6,000,000	
			Primary Road
			Secondary Road
			Minor Road, Trail
			Primary Railway
			Airport

MACKINAC BRIDGE Bridge   Shipping Channel
GREAT ST. BERNARD TUNNEL Tunnel   Canal du Midi Navigable Canal
TO CALAIS Ferry   Intracoastal Waterway

Metric-English Equivalents

Areas represented by one square centimeter at various map scales

1:3,000,000 900 km² 348 square miles	1:6,000,000 3,600 km² 1,390 square miles	1:12,000,000 14,400 km² 5,558 square miles

Meter=3.28 feet   Meter² (m²)=10.76 square feet
Kilometer=0.62 mile   Kilometer² (km²)=0.39 square mile

Miscellaneous Cultural Features

PARQUE NACIONAL CANAIMA ▲ National or State Park or Monument   TANGLEWOOD ▲ Point of Interest (Battlefield, cave historical site, etc.)

FORT CLATSOP NAT. MEM. ▲ National or State Historic(al) Site, Memorial   STEINHAUSEN ⚓ Church, Monastery

BLACKFOOT IND. RES. Indian Reservation   UXMAL ⊻ Ruins

FORT DIX ■ Military Installation   WINDSOR CASTLE ⊻ Castle

AMISTAD DAM ⁄ Dam

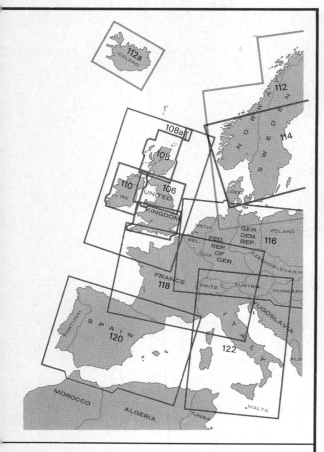

Systematic Atlas of the Earth

Hydrographic Features

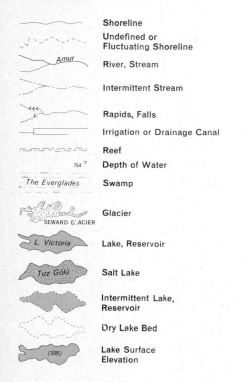

	Shoreline
	Undefined or Fluctuating Shoreline
Amur	River, Stream
	Intermittent Stream
	Rapids, Falls
	Irrigation or Drainage Canal
	Reef
764 ▽	Depth of Water
The Everglades	Swamp
SEWARD GLACIER	Glacier
L. Victoria	Lake, Reservoir
Tuz Gölü	Salt Lake
	Intermittent Lake, Reservoir
	Dry Lake Bed
(395)	Lake Surface Elevation

Topographic Features

Mt. Kenya △ 5199	Elevation Above Sea Level
76 ▽	Elevation Below Sea Level
Mount Cook ▲ 3764	Highest Elevation in Country
Khyber Pass ≍ 1067	Mountain Pass
133 ▼	Lowest Elevation in Country

Elevations and depths are given in meters
Highest Elevation and Lowest Elevation of a continent are underlined

	Lava		Sand Area
	Salt Flat		
ANDES KUNLUNSHANMAI	Mountain Range, Plateau, Valley, etc.	BAFFIN ISLAND NUNIVAK ISLAND	Island
POLUOSTROV KAMČATKA CABO DE HORNOS	Peninsula, Cape. Point, etc.		

For as long as man has followed his instinct to travel and explore he has attempted to record his journeys, both for himself and for those who would follow.

Though the first maps were fanciful, inaccurate and highly coloured by superstition and legend, the map-maker's art has developed apace with man's soaring technology.

Today, distances of many miles may be measured to an accuracy of a few centimetres; high-altitude aircraft and satellites can photograph areas of more than a million square miles and our maps, the most sophisticated ever compiled, are beautiful, accurate and packed with a wealth of detail.

In the Systematic Atlas which follows the world is mapped at the scales 1:1,000,000; 1:3,000,000; 1:6,000,000 and 1:12,000,000. It is thus a comprehensive work of reference to the physical, cultural and political face of the modern world.

Kilometers |0   200   400   600| Km.

Statute Miles |0   200   400   600| Mi.

Scale 1:12,000,000   One centimeter represents 120 kilometers.
                       One inch represents approximately 190 miles.
                       Miller Oblated Stereographic Projection

101

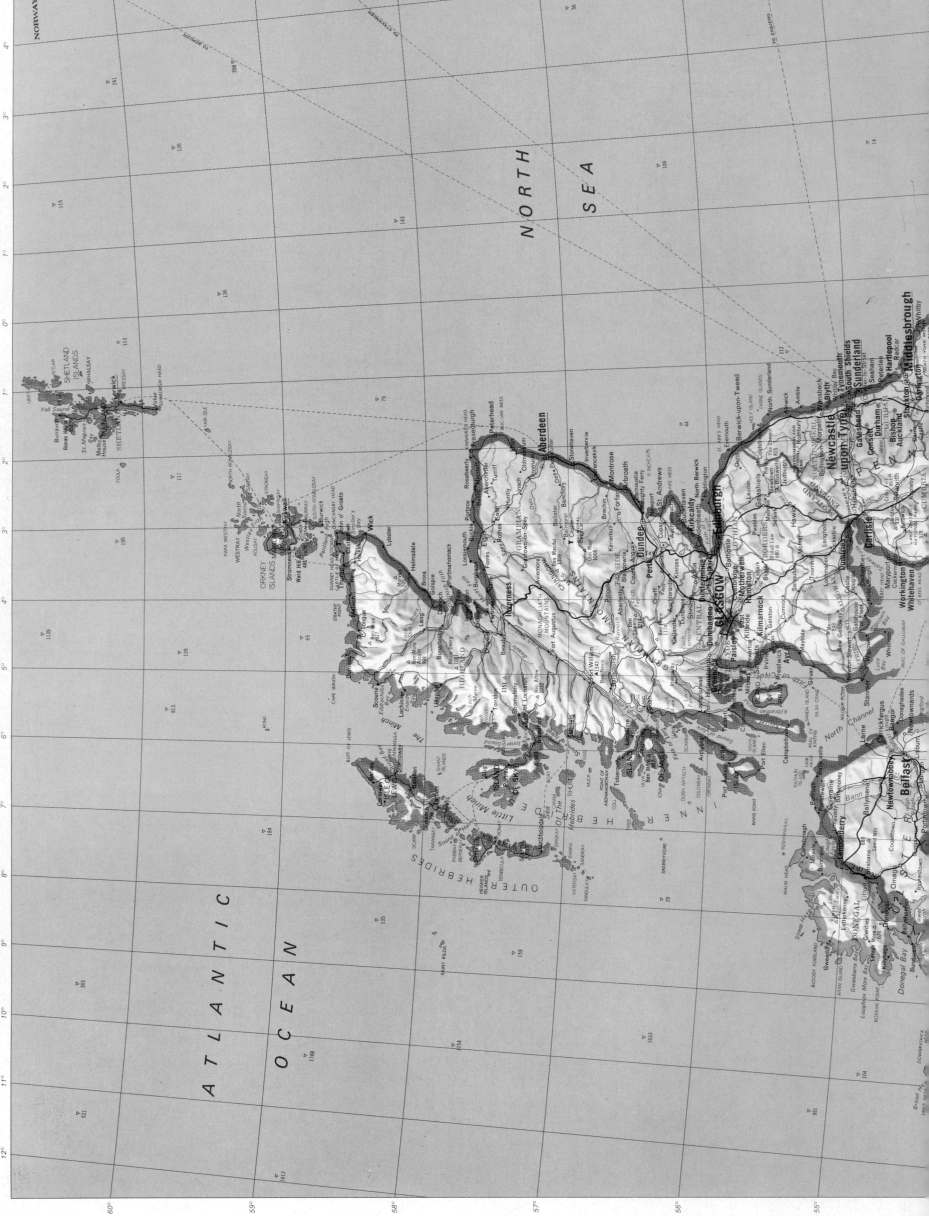

Kilometers

Statute Miles

Scale 1:3,000,000

One centimeter represents 30 kilometers.
One inch represents approximately 47 miles.
Conic Projection, Two Standard Parallels

Southern England

Kilometers |0 10 20 30 40 Km.
Statute Miles |0 10 20 30 40 50 Mi.

Scale 1:1,000,000

One centimeter represents 10 kilometers.
One inch represents approximately 16 miles.

Lambert Conformal Conic Projection

105

107

Kilometers
Statute Miles

Scale 1:1,000,000   One centimeter represents 10 kilometers.
One inch represents approximately 16 miles.
Lambert Conformal Conic Projection

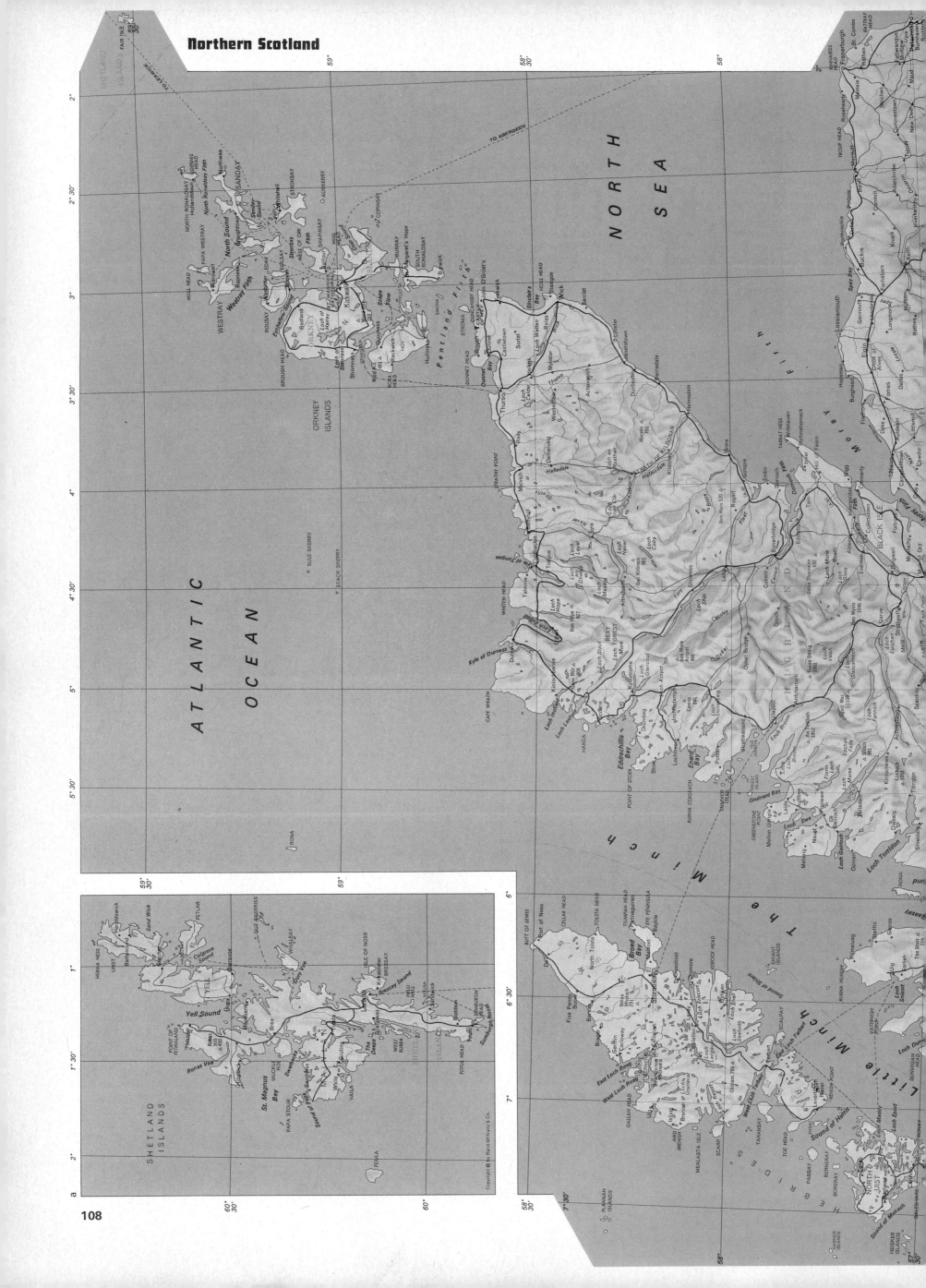

109

Kilometers 0 10 20 30 40 50 Km.

Statute Miles 0 10 20 30 40 50 Mi.

Scale 1:1,000,000

One centimeter represents 10 kilometers.
One inch represents approximately 16 miles.

Lambert Conformal Conic Projection

Kilometers

Statute Miles

Scale 1:1,000,000

One centimeter represents 10 kilometers.
One inch represents approximately 16 miles.

Lambert Conformal Conic Projection

111

BARENTS SEA
BARENC'OVO MORE
PEČORSKOJE MORE

S E A
M O R E

Murmansk
Severomorsk

Apatity Kirovsk
Kandalakša

White Sea
Bel Belaja

Kem
Segeža

Archangel'sk
Severodvinsk

Onega

Petrozavodsk

Kondopoga

Vorkuta

Inta

URAL MOUNTAINS
URALSKIJE GORY

Pečora

Uchta Sosnogorsk

Syktyvkar

Kotlas
Velikij Ust'ug

Solikamsk

Kudymkar

Kirov Kirovo-Čepeck

Glazov

Votkinsk

Iževsk

Sarapul

Možga

LENINGRAD

Volchov

Vologda

Čerepovec
Rybinskoje
Vodochranilišče

Rybinsk
Kostroma

Jaroslavl'

Kinešma

Joškar-Ola

Kazan'

Čeboksary

Zelenodol'sk

Čistopol'

Al'met'evsk

Leninogorsk

Bugul'ma

Staraja Russa

Vyšnij Voloček

Ivanovo

GOR'KIJ GORKY
Bor

Dzeržinsk

Vladimir

Kovrov

Murom
Arzamas

Alatyr'

Uljanovsk

Dimitrovgrad

Toljatti

KUJBYŠEV

Novokujbyševsk

Syzran'

Kalinin

Klin

Zagorsk

MOSKVA MOSCOW

Podol'sk

Kolomna

Serpuchov

Kaluga

Tula

Smolensk

Velikije Luki

Copyright © by Rand McNally & Co.
Map compiled by Rand McNally GmbH, Stuttgart
Manufactured by Rand McNally & Co.
A-570000-264

Kilometers 0   100   200   300   Km.
Statute Miles 0   100   200   300   Mi.

Scale 1:6,000,000   One centimeter represents 60 kilometers.
One inch represents approximately 95 miles.
Lambert Conformal Conic Projection

113

Kilometers 0 50 100 150 Km.

Statute Miles 0 50 100 150 Mi.

Scale 1:3,000,000
One centimeter represents 30 kilometers.
One inch represents approximately 47 miles.
Conic Projection, Two Standard Parallels

NORTH SEA

Kilometers
Statute Miles

Scale 1:3,000,000

One centimeter represents 30 kilometers.
One inch represents approximately 47 miles.
Conic Projection, Two Standard Parallels.

117

119

Kilometers 0 50 100 150 Km.

Statute Miles 0 50 100 150 Mi.

Scale 1:3,000,000

One centimeter represents 30 kilometers.
One inch represents approximately 47 miles.
Lambert Conformal Conic Projection

MEDITERRANEAN SEA

ISLAS BALEARES
BALEARIC ISLANDS

Golfe du Lion

Barcelona
Valencia
Zaragoza
Toulouse
Marseille
Nice
Palma
Alicante
Murcia
Cartagena
Oran
ALGER
ALGIERS

121

Scale 1:3,000,000
One centimeter represents 30 kilometers.
One inch represents approximately 47 miles.
Conic Projection, Two Standard Parallels

Kilometers
Statute Miles
Km.
Mi.

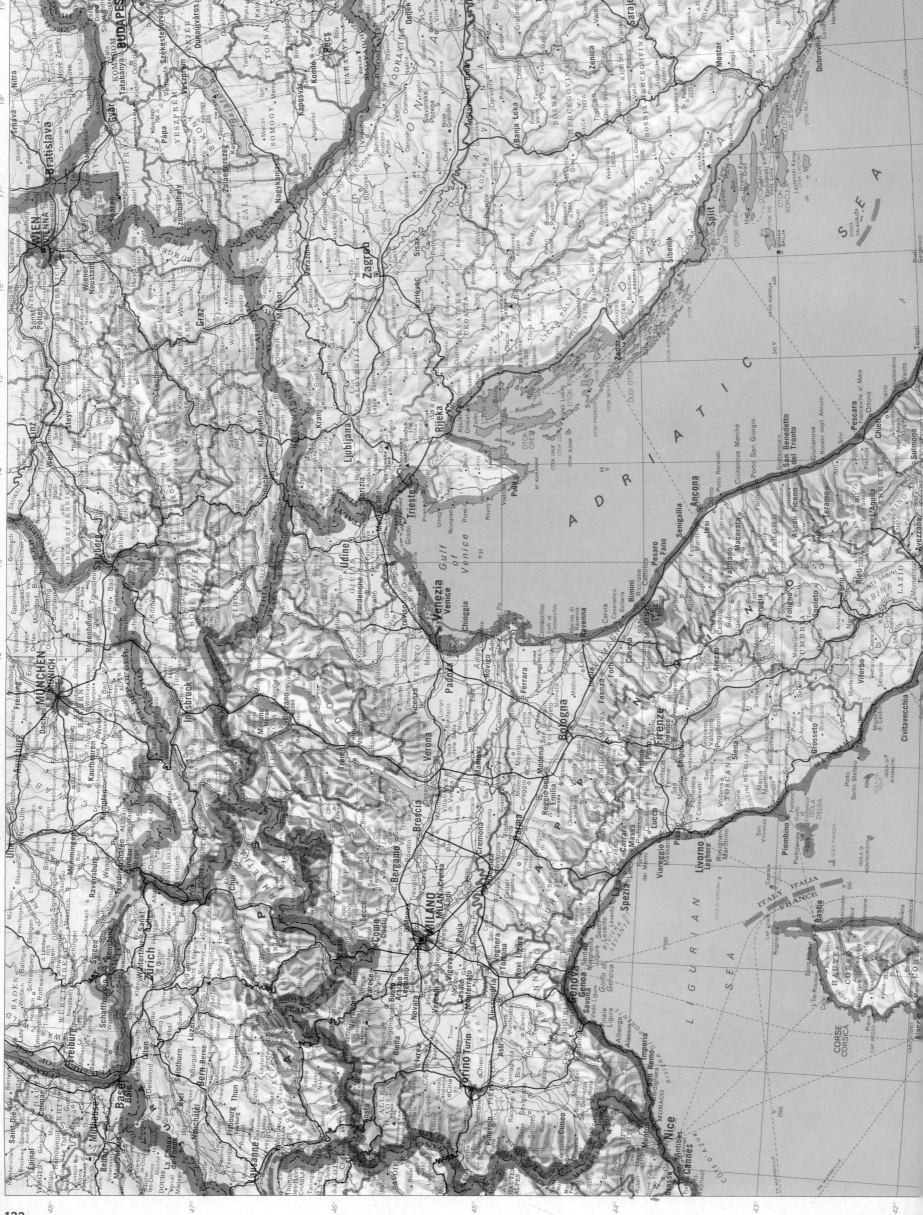

Strait of Otranto

Brindisi

IONIAN SEA

Taranto

Golfo di Taranto

Crotone

Golfo di Squillace

Catanzaro

CALABRIA

Reggio di Calabria

Stretto di Messina

Messina

Taormina

Acireale

Catania

Golfo di Catania

Augusta

Siracusa

Golfo di Noto

PUGLIA

Bari

Molfetta

Bisceglie

Andria

Barletta

Manfredonia

Golfo di Manfredonia

BASILICATA

LUCANIA

Matera

Potenza

Cosenza

CAMPANIA

Salerno

Golfo di Salerno

Caserta

Benevento

NAPLES

NAPOLI

Pozzuoli

Gaeta

Golfo di Gaeta

Ischia

Capri

Roma

Latina

TYRRHENIAN SEA

MARE TIRRENO

ISOLE EOLIE

ISOLA DI USTICA

SICILIA

SICILY

Palermo

Golfo di Palermo

Bagheria

Trapani

Marsala

Mazara del Vallo

Sciacca

Agrigento

Porto Empedocle

Caltanissetta

Gela

Golfo di Gela

Ragusa

Vittoria

Modica

Capo Passero

MEDITERRANEAN

Strait of Sicily

ITALY ITALIA

ITALY ITALIA

TUNISIA TUNISIE

MALTA

Valletta

ISOLA DI PANTELLERIA

ISOLE PELAGE

ISOLA DI LAMPEDUSA

SEA

Annaba

(Bône)

Bizerte

Bizerte

Menzel Bourguiba

TUNIS

Tunis

Golfe de Tunis

Cap Bon

Golfe de Hammamet

Nabeul

Hammamet

Sousse

El Mahdia

KAIROUAN

BIZERTE

BÉJA

JENDOUBA

Guelma

Souk Ahras

Tébessa

KASSERINE

ALGERIA ALGÉRIE

TUNISIA TUNISIE

FRANCE

ITALY

SARDEGNA

SARDINIA

Sassari

Alghero

Nuoro

Oristano

Iglesias

Carbonia

Cagliari

Golfo di Cagliari

Golfo di Palmas

Capo Spartivento

123

Kilometers |0 50 100 150| Km.

Statute Miles |0 50 100 150| Mi.

Scale 1:3,000,000

One centimeter represents 30 kilometers.
One inch represents approximately 47 miles.

Conic Projection, Two Standard Parallels.

Copyright © by Rand McNally & Co.
Map prepared by Karl Wenschow GmbH, Stuttgart

ADRIATIC

Marmara Denizi
Sea of Marmara

İSTANBUL

Bursa

Bandırma

Çanakkale

Edremit

Balıkesir

Akhisar

Manisa

İzmir

Turgutlu

Uşak

Denizli

Söke

TURKEY
GREECE ELLÁS
TURKEY TÜRKIYE

Ródhos
Rhodes

RÓDHOS
RHODES

KÁRPATHOS
Kárpathos

DHODHEKÁNISOS
DODECANESE

Kırklareli

Lüleburgaz

Tekirdağ

Edirne

Keşan

Haskovo

Kŭrdžali

Komotiní

Xánthi

Alexandroúpolis

SAMOTHRÁKI
SAMOTHRACE

LÍMNOS

LÉSVOS
LESBOS

Mitilíni

KHÍOS
CHIOS

SÁMOS

IKARÍA

KIKLÁDHES
CYCLADES

NÁXOS

PÁROS

Thrakikón
Pélagos

THÁSOS

Drama

Kaválla

ÁYION
ÓROS

Sérrai

Skopje

Bitola

Thessaloníki
Salonika

Kateríni

Vólos

Lárisa

Lamía

Tríkala

Karpenísion

Agrínion

Ioánnina

Prévesa

KÉRKIRA
CORFU

Tiranë

Elbasan

Berat

Vlorë

AEGEAN

SEA

EVVOIA

Khalkís

ATHÍNAI
ATHENS

Piraiévs

ÁNDROS

TÍNOS

SÝROS

MÍLOS

Kiritikón Pélagos
Sea of Crete

KRÍTI
CRETE

Khaniá

Réthimnon

Iráklion

ANTIKÍTHIRA

KÍTHIRA

Spárti

Kalámai

Kalamata

Pátrai

PELOPONNESUS

Kórinthos

Argolikós
Kólpos

Mirtóön
Pélagos

IONIAN

SEA

IÓNIOI NÍSOI
IONIAN ISLANDS

KEFALLINÍA

ZÁKINTHOS

ITALY

Strait of Otranto

MEDITERRANEAN SEA

125

Kilometers

Statute Miles

Scale 1:3,000,000

One centimeter represents 30 kilometers.
One inch represents approximately 47 miles.
Lambert Conformal Conic Projection

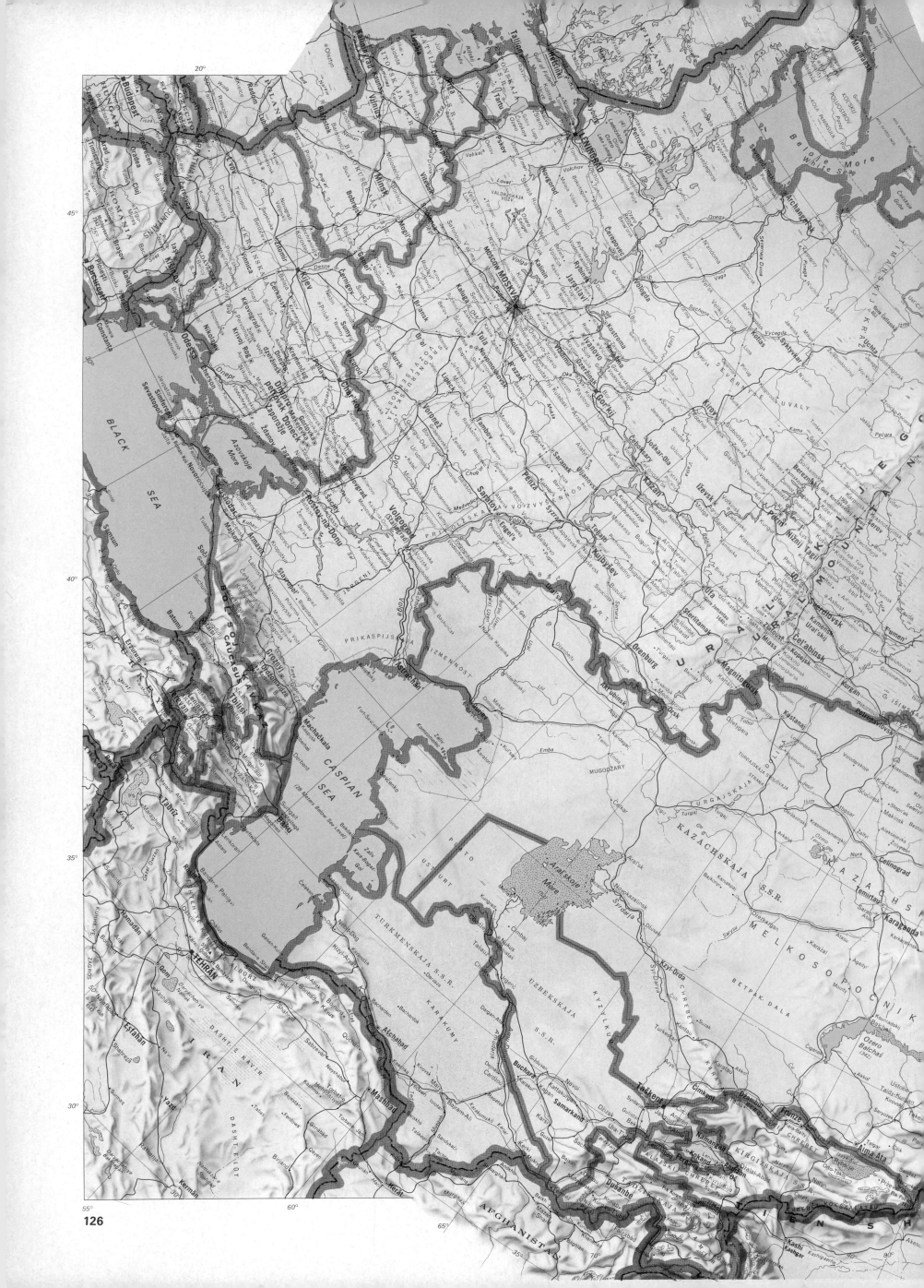

126

Kilometers

Statute Miles

0   200   400   600   Km.

0   200   400   600   Mi.

Scale 1:12,000,000

One centimeter represents 120 kilometers.
One inch represents approximately 190 miles.

Lambert Conformal Conic Projection

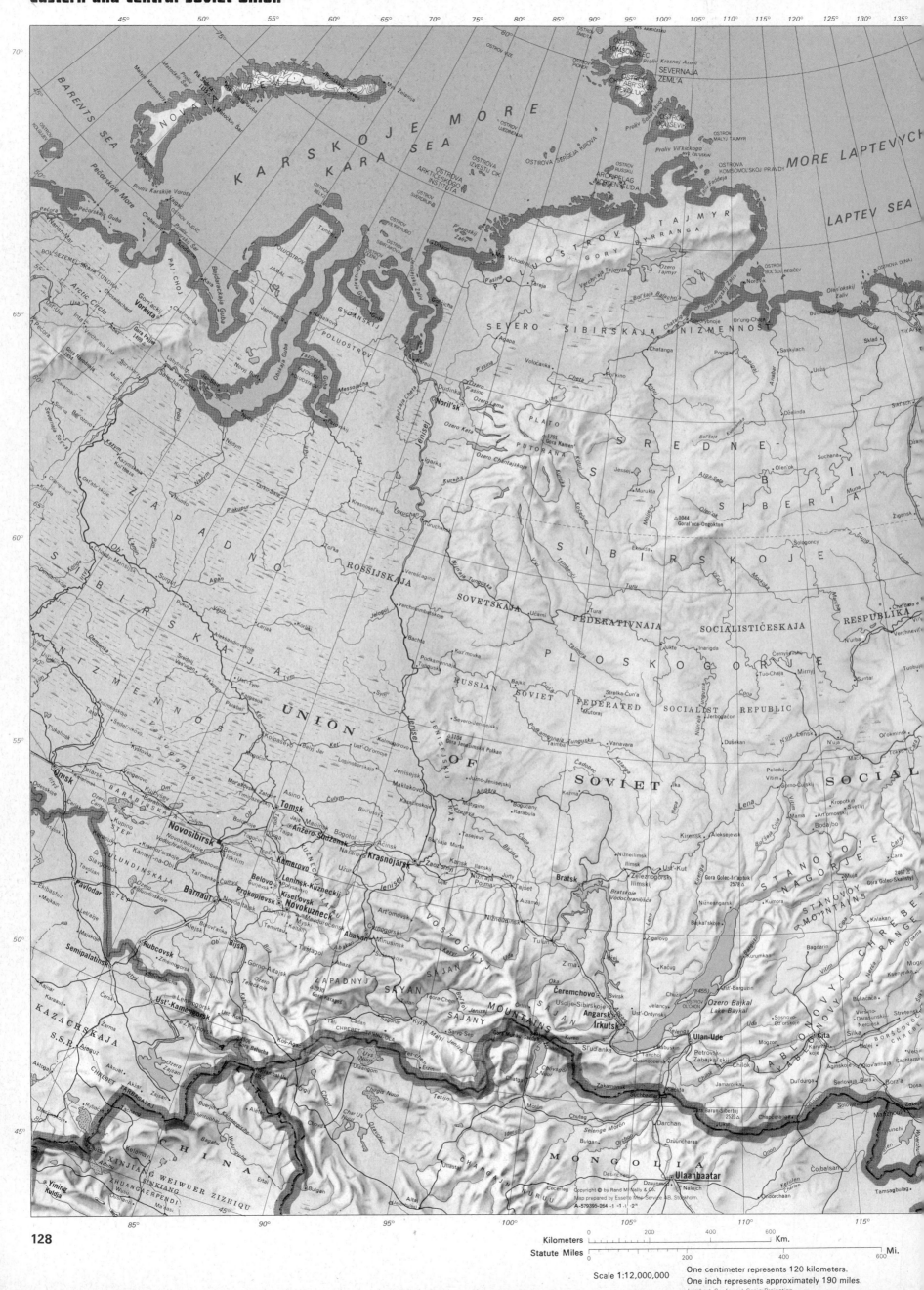

Kilometers
Statute Miles

Km.
Mi.

Scale 1:12,000,000

One centimeter represents 120 kilometers.
One inch represents approximately 190 miles.
Lambert Conformal Conic Projection

The annexation of Lithuania, Latvia, and Estonia in 1940 by the Soviet Union has never been officially recognized by the United States Government.

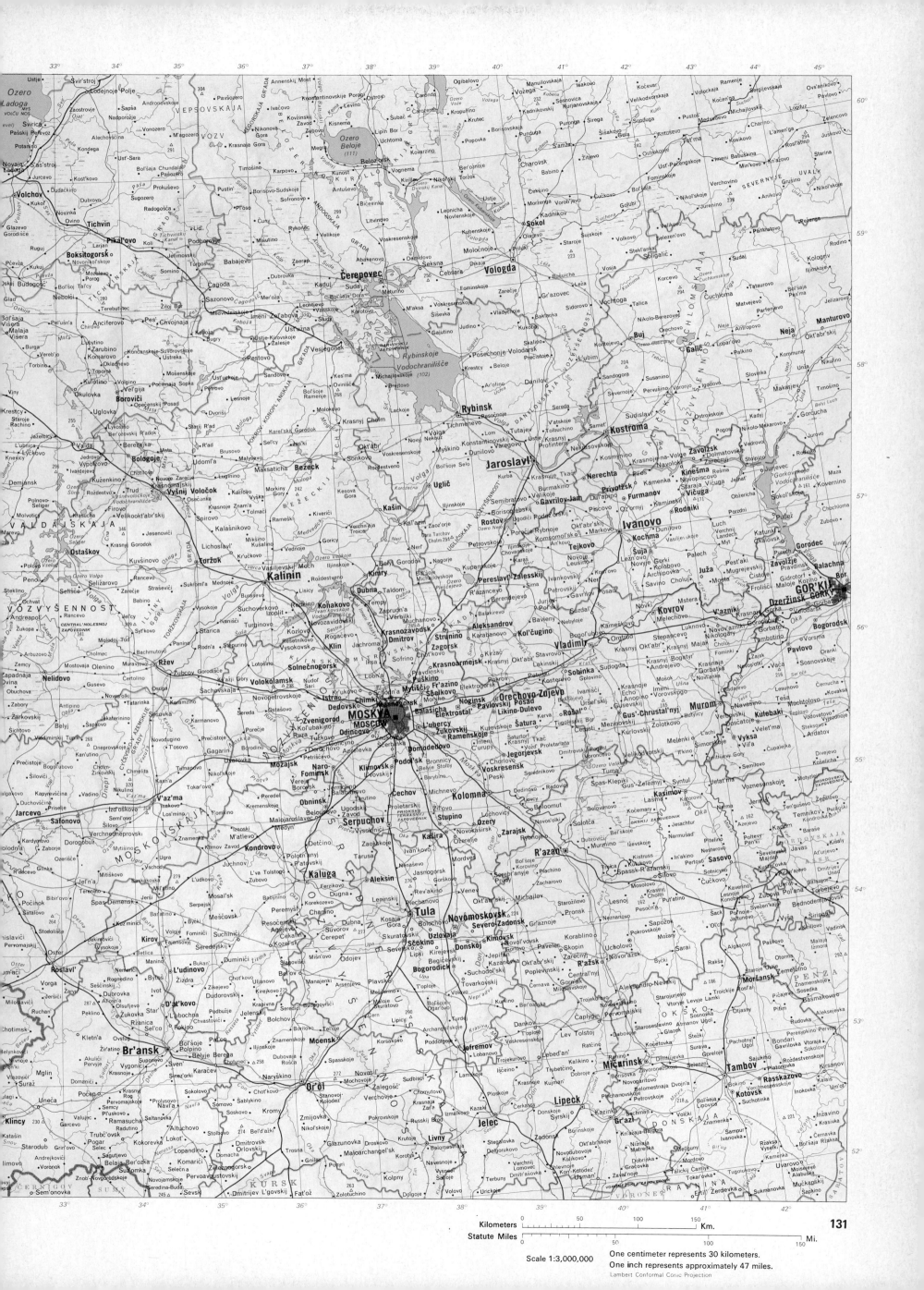

Kilometers

Statute Miles

Scale 1:3,000,000 One centimeter represents 30 kilometers.
One inch represents approximately 47 miles.
Lambert Conformal Conic Projection

133

Kilometers
0   200   400   600
Km.

Statute Miles
0   200   400   600
Mi.

Scale 1:12,000,000
One centimeter represents 120 kilometers.
One inch represents approximately 190 miles.
Lambert Conformal Conic Projection

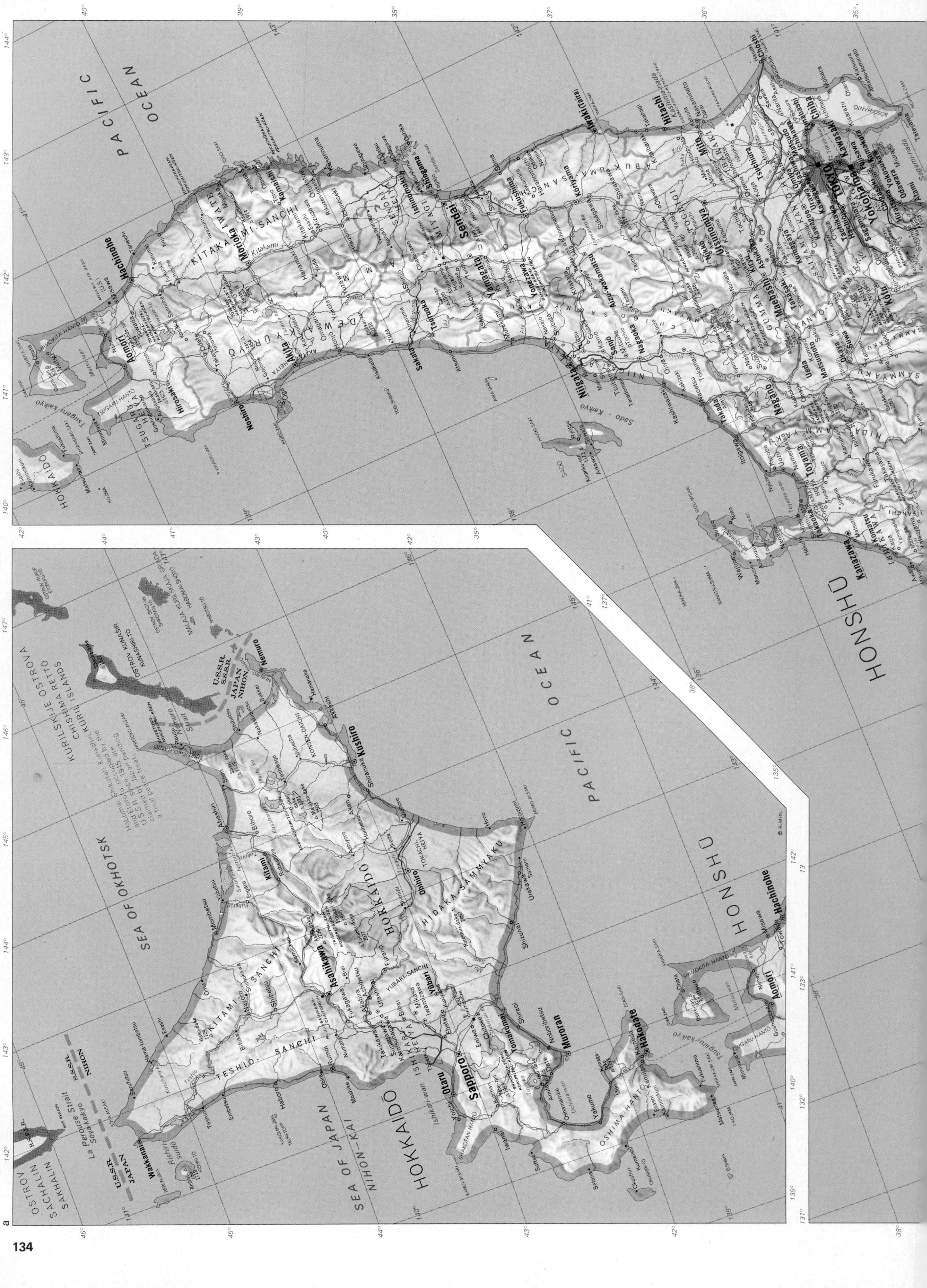

PACIFIC OCEAN

HOKKAIDŌ

Hachinohe

KITAKAMI

KITAKAMI SANCHI

Morioka

Kitakami

Aomori

Hirosaki

Noshiro

Akita

Sakata

DEWA

TSUGARU-HANTŌ

Tsugaru-kaikyō

SHIMOKITA-HANTŌ

Kamaishi

Ishinomaki

Shiogama

MIYAGI

Sendai

Yamagata

Tsuruoka

Yonezawa

Niigata

Sanjo

Nagaoka

SADO

Sado-kaikyō

Takada

Nagano

Ueda

Matsumoto

Toyama

Kanazawa

Komatsu

HONSHŪ

Chōshi

Hitachi

Mito

IBARAKI

Tsuchiura

Utsunomiya

Nikkō

Ashikaga

GUMMA

Maebashi

Takasaki

SAITAMA

TOKYO

Chiba

BŌSŌ-HANTŌ

Yokohama

Kawasaki

Kawagoe

Hachiōji

Odawara

Hiratsuka

KANTŌ

KAI

SAMMYAKU

HIDA-SAMMYAKU

PACIFIC OCEAN

SEA OF OKHOTSK

OSTROV SACHALIN SAKHALIN

KURILSKIJE OSTROVA CHISHIMA RETTO KURIL ISLANDS

OSTROV KUNAŠIR KUNASHIR-TŌ

MALAJA KURILSKAJA GRJADA

U.S.S.R. S.S.S.R.

JAPAN NIHON

Nemuro

Kushiro

KONSEN-DAICHI

TOKACHI-HEIYA

Obihiro

HIDAKA-SAMMYAKU

Abashiri

Kitami

KITAMI-SANCHI

Asahikawa

Rumoi

TESHIO-SANCHI

YUBARI-SANCHI

Yubari

Otaru

Sapporo

ISHIKARI

Tomakomai

Muroran

Hakodate

OSHIMA-HANTŌ

HOKKAIDŌ

SEA OF JAPAN

NIHON-KAI

Wakkanai

RISHIRI

U.S.S.R. S.S.S.R.

La Perouse Strait Sōyakaikyō

JAPAN NIHON

R.S.F.S.R.

HONSHŪ

Hachinohe

Aomori

SHIMOKITA-HANTŌ

Tsugaru-kaikyō

TSUGARU-HANTŌ

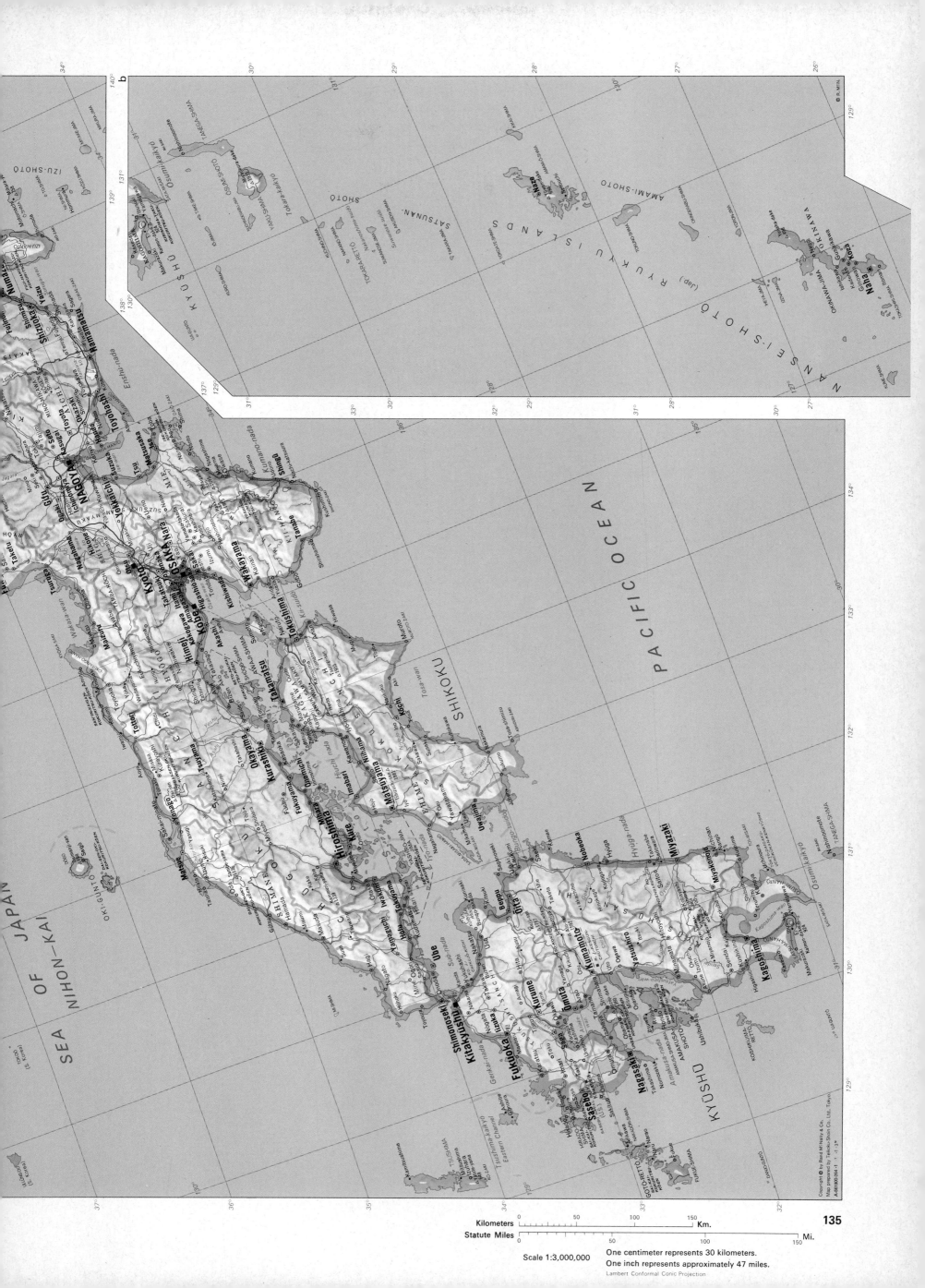

SEA OF JAPAN
NIHON-KAI

PACIFIC OCEAN

NANSEI-SHOTO RYUKYU ISLANDS (Jap.)

AMAMI-SHOTO

SATSUNAN-SHOTO

KYŪSHŪ

SHIKOKU

KYŪSHŪ

NAGOYA
OSAKA
KYŌTO
KŌBE
Himeji
Hiroshima
Takamatsu
Matsuyama
Kōchi
Ōita
Kumamoto
Kagoshima
Miyazaki
Nobeoka
Beppu
Fukuoka
Kitakyūshū
Shimonoseki
Nagasaki
Sasebo
Kurume
Ōmuta
Ube
Yamaguchi
Okayama
Kurashiki
Fukuyama
Onomichi
Kure
Iwakuni
Tottori
Matsue
Matsusaka
Wakayama
Tokushima
Hamamatsu
Shizuoka

Naha
Naze

IZU-SHOTO

Copyright © by Rand McNally & Co.
Map prepared by Teikoku-Shoin Co., Ltd., Tokyo

135

Kilometers
Statute Miles

0   50   100   150   Km.
0   50   100   150   Mi.

Scale 1:3,000,000
One centimeter represents 30 kilometers.
One inch represents approximately 47 miles.
Lambert Conformal Conic Projection

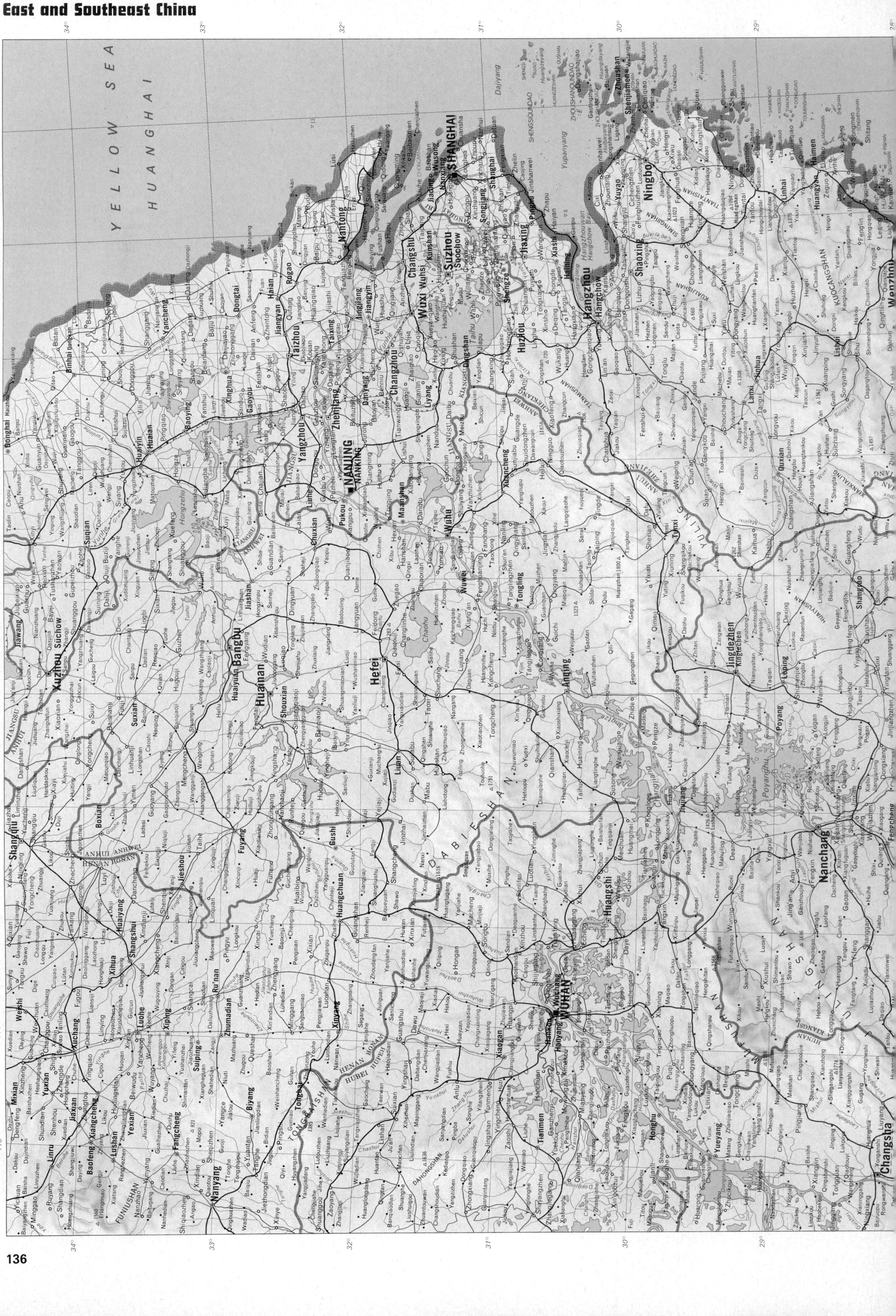

YELLOW SEA

HUANGHAI

SHANGHAI

NANJING / NANKING

Suzhou / Soochow

Wuxi

Changzhou

Zhenjiang

Yangzhou

Hangzhou

Shaoxing

Ningbo

Wenzhou

Huzhou

Jiaxing

Kunshan

Songjiang

Nantong

Taizhou

Jiangyan

Gaoyou

Huaiyin

Yancheng

Binhai

Dongtai

Dongbai

Xuzhou / Suchow

Suqian

Suixian

Bengbu

Huainan

Huaiyuan

Shouxian

Hefei

Lu'an

Wuhu

Maanshan

Tongling

Anqing

Chuxian

Pukou

Pengpu

Kuzhou / Suchow

Shangqiu

Boxian

Fuyang

Gushi

Zhumadian

Xuchang

Luohe

Xiping

Suiping

Xihua

Huaiyang

Shangshui

Ru'nan

Xinyang

Biyang

Tongbai

Nanyang

Fangcheng

Baofeng

Lushan

Yexian

Linru

Mixian

Yuxian

Jiaxian

Wanxi

WUHAN

Hanyang

Wuchang

Xiaogan

Tianmen

Honghu

Yueyang

Changsha

Nanchang

Jiujiang

Poyang

Jingdezhen / Kingtehchen

Leping

Quxian

Jinhua

Lishui

DABIESHAN

TONGBAISHAN

DAHONGSHAN

WUYISHAN

HUANGSHAN

TIANMUSHAN

KUOCANGSHAN

YULING

NANLING

Tai Hu

Hongze Hu

Chao Hu

Poyang Hu

JIANGSU / KIANGSU

ANHUI / ANHWEI

HENAN / HONAN

HUBEI / HUPEH

ZHEJIANG / CHEKIANG

JIANGXI / KIANGSI

Yangtze

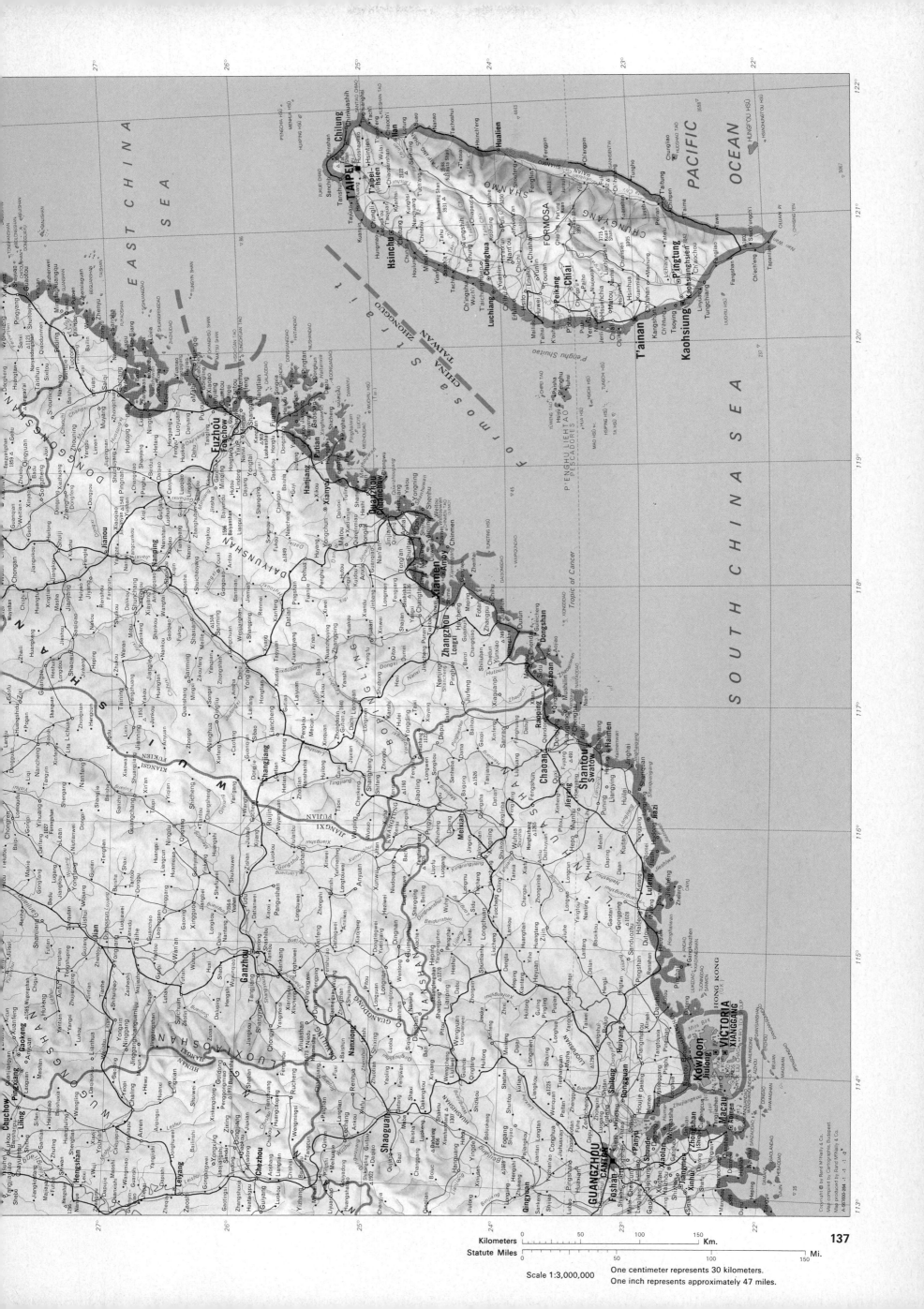

Kilometers
Statute Miles

0   50   100   150 Km.
0   50   100   150 Mi.

Scale 1:3,000,000

One centimeter represents 30 kilometers.
One inch represents approximately 47 miles.

137

120°   125°   130°   135°   140°   145°

Tropic of Cancer

TAIWAN
Chiai
Yu Shan △3997
FORMOSA
nan
Pingtung
MUNG

OUAN PI
Bashi Channel
Luzon
YAMI ISLAND
ITBAYAT ISLAND
Strait
BATAN ISLANDS
Basco
BATAN ISLAND
Balintang Channel
BABUYAN ISLAND
CALAYAN ISLAND
DALUPIRI
ISLAND
CAMIGUIN ISLAND
FUGA
ISLAND
BABUYAN ISLANDS
CAPE BOJEADOR
ESCARPADA
POINT
Laoag
Aparri
Tuguegarao
Vigan
San Fernando
Bayombong
Baguio
San Carlos
MADRE
Angeles
Tarlac
Cabanatuan
MANILA
Quezon City
Cavite
Dingalan Bay
Lucena
Lamon Bay
San Pablo
Tagaytay
Batangas
Naga
Virac
CATANDUANES ISLAND
Mindoro
San Jose
Mayon Volcano
MINDORO
Calapan
Sorsogon
Bernardino Strait
Masbate
SIBUYAN
ISLAND
SAMAR
Calbayog
Catbalogan
MASBATE
Roxas
Kalibo
Tacloban
PANAY
LEYTE
Guiuan
Iloilo
Bacolod
Leyte Gulf
Cebu
BOHOL
DINAGAT ISLAND
NEGROS
SIARGAO ISLAND
Dumaguete
Surigao
Tandag
Mindanao Sea
Dipolog
Cagayan
de Oro
Malaybalay
Bislig
Ozamiz
Pagan
MINDANAO
Zamboanga
Moro Gulf
Cotabato
Davao
BASILAN ISLAND
Mount Apo △2954
Davao
Gulf
Lebak
Kiamba
CAPE SAN AGUSTIN
SULU ARCHIPELAGO
Jolo
TINACA POINT
PULAU MANGAS
SARANGANI ISLANDS

PHILIPPINE

SEA

PACIFIC OCEAN

OKINO-TORI-SHIMA
(Japan)

FARALLON DE PAJAROS
MAUG ISLANDS
ASUNCION ISLAND
AGRIHAN
PAGAN
ALAMAGAN
MARIANA ISLANDS
GUGUAN
PACIFIC ISLANDS TRUST TERRITORY
(U.S.)
SARIGAN
ANATAHAN
FARALLON DE MEDINILLA
SAIPAN
TINIAN
AGUIJAN
ROTA

Agana
GUAM
(U.S.)

ULITHI
YAP
FAIS
GAFERUT
KAYANGEL ISLANDS
PALAU ISLANDS
BABELTHUAP
URUKTHAPEL
Koror
NGULU
SOROL
FARAULEP
PELELIU
EIL MALK
ANGAUR
WOLEAI
FALALIS
EAURIPIK
OLIMARAO

CAROLINE   ISLANDS

ZSONSOROL ISLANDS
PACIFIC ISLANDS TRUST TERRITORY
(U.S.)

PULO ANNA
MERIR

CELEBES
SEA
PULAU-PULAU NANUSA
PULAU KARAKELONG
KEPULAUAN TALAUD
PULAU
SALEBABU
Tahuna
PULAU SANGHE
KEPULAUAN TANGUT
PULAU KABURUANG

TOBI
HELEN ISLAND

SANGIHE
PULAU SIAU
PULAU TAHULANDANG
PULAU BIARO
MOROTAI
Wayabula
Waha
Galela
MINAHASA
Tobelo
Manado
Gunung Klabat
Butung
2022
Jailolo
Tondano
KEPULAUAN ASIA
KEPULAUAN
MAPIA
Kotamobagu
Ternate
Gorontalo
Tidore
HALMAHERA
Weda
KEPULAUAN AYU
Equator

LAUT MALUKU
MOLUCCA SEA
PULAU GEBE
PULAU WAIGEO
Teluk Tomini
PULAU KASIPUTA
Laut
Halmahera
PULAU MANDIOLI
Halmahera
Sea
Luwuk
PULAU MACAN
Selat Dampier
Sorong
BIAK
Bosnik
Posu
PULAU OBILATU
PULAU BISA
Salawati
Manokwari
NINIGO GROUP
Danau
Poso
KEPULAUAN
BANGGAI
Banggai
PULAU MANGOLE
PULAU
OBI
BATANTA
PULAU NUMFOR
WUVULU ISLAND
Teluk
Tolo
PULAU TALIABU
KEPULAUAN
OBI
Teminabuan
PULAU YAPEN
Sarmi
KEPULAUAN
SULA
PULAU GANANA
PULAU MISOOL
Inanwatan
Teluk
Cenderawasih
Wareh
Demta
Jayapura (Sukarnapura)
PAPUA
NEW GUINEA
LAUT SERAM
CERAM SEA
Teluk Berau
FAKFAK
Babo
Wasior
Nabire
Yamimo
Aitape
Wewak
Namlea
PULAU MANUK
Kairatu
Bula
JAZIRAH
SERAM
CERAM
SOMBEREP
Karufa
Kaimana
PEGUNUNGAN
MAOKE
Angoram
MANAM
ISLAND
BURU
Ambon
Geser
Modowi
5030△
Puncak Jaya
Ambunti
Sepik
PULAU AMBON
Kokonau
4750△
Puncak Trikora
Maramuni
Mount
Wilhelm
PULAU AMBELAU
KEPULAUAN
WATUBELA
Nabire
4760△
Puncak
Mandala
PEGUNUNGAN VAN REES
Mamberamo
NEW
KEPULAUAN KAI
Tual
Telefomin
4509△
Mount
Giluwe
KEPULAUAN
LUOPARA
KEPULAUAN
PENYU
KAI KECIL
KAI BESAR
Dobo
PULAU WOKAM
GUINEA
Mount Bosavi
△2397
LAUT BANDA
BANDA SEA
PULAU SERUA
KEPULAUAN
ARU
PULAU KOBROOR
Kepi
Mount
Murray
DAYA
PULAU
NILA
PULAU MAIKOR
PULAU YAMDENA
KEPULAUAN TANIMBAR
PULAU
YOS
SUDARSA
BARAT
PULAU
WULIARU
Saumlaki
BOGA
ISLAND
WARRIOR REEF
KEPULAUAN
LETI
PULAU DAMAR
PULAU LARAT
Okababa
SABAI ISLAND
PULAU WETAR
PULAU ROMANG
PULAU
SELU
PULAU SELARU
Merauke
Gulf
of Papua
FLORES
PULAU KAMBING
KEPULAUAN
BABAR
TANJUNG VALS
Dili
Ende
PULAU SERMATA
ARAFURA   SEA
MIAI ISLAND
GGARA
DA ISLANDS
Laut Sawu
Savu Sea
Waingapu
TIMOR
Torres Strait
PRINCE OF WALES ISLAND
SUMBA
Kupang
Soe
PULAU SEMAU
CAPE YORK
GREAT
PULAU ROTI
TIMOR   SEA
AUSTRALIA
CAPE WESSEL
CAPE CROKER
CAPE YORK
PENINSULA
Endeavour Strait

120°   125°   130°   135°   140°   145°

Kilometers |0 200 400 600| Km.

Statute Miles |0 200 400 600| Mi.

139

Scale 1:12,000,000
One centimeter represents 120 kilometers.
One inch represents approximately 190 miles.
Lambert Conformal Conic Projection

HUNAN

GUIZHOU / KWEICHOW

GUANGXI ZHUANGZU / KWANGSI

GUANGDONG / KWANGTUNG

YUNNAN

HAINANDAO

GULF OF TONKIN

SOUTH CHINA SEA

VIETNAM

LAOS

THAILAND

BURMA / MYANMAR

BANGLADESH

INDIA

ASSAM

MIZORAM

CHIN HILLS

NAGA HILLS

SHAN

KACHIN

ARAKAN YOMA

PEGU YOMA

BAY OF BENGAL

Gulf of Martaban

Mouths of the Irrawaddy

Guiyang (Kweiyang)
Guilin (Kweilin)
Kunming
Nanning
Wuzhou (Wuchow)
Zhanjiang
Haikou
Da-nang
Hue
Myitkyina
Mandalay
Monywa
Pakokku
Chauk
Yenangyaung
Prome (Pye)
RANGOON
Bassein
Henzada
Pegu
Thaton
Moulmein
Tavoy
Chittagong
Cox's Bazar
Sittwe (Akyab)
Imphal
Chiang Mai
Lampang
Phitsanulok
Nakhon Sawan
Nakhon Ratchasima
Khon Kaen
Udon Thani
Nong Khai
Viangchan (Vientiane)
Louangphrabang
Louang Namtha
Phongsali
Hanoi
Hai-duong
Nam-dinh
Thanh-hoa
Vinh
Son-tay
Viet-tri
Thai-nguyen
Bac-ninh
Nakhon Pathom
Ratchaburi
Ubon Ratchathani

Irrawaddy
Salween
Chindwin
Mekong
Chao Phraya

COCO ISLANDS

Preparis North Channel
Preparis South Channel
Coco Channel

Tropic of Cancer

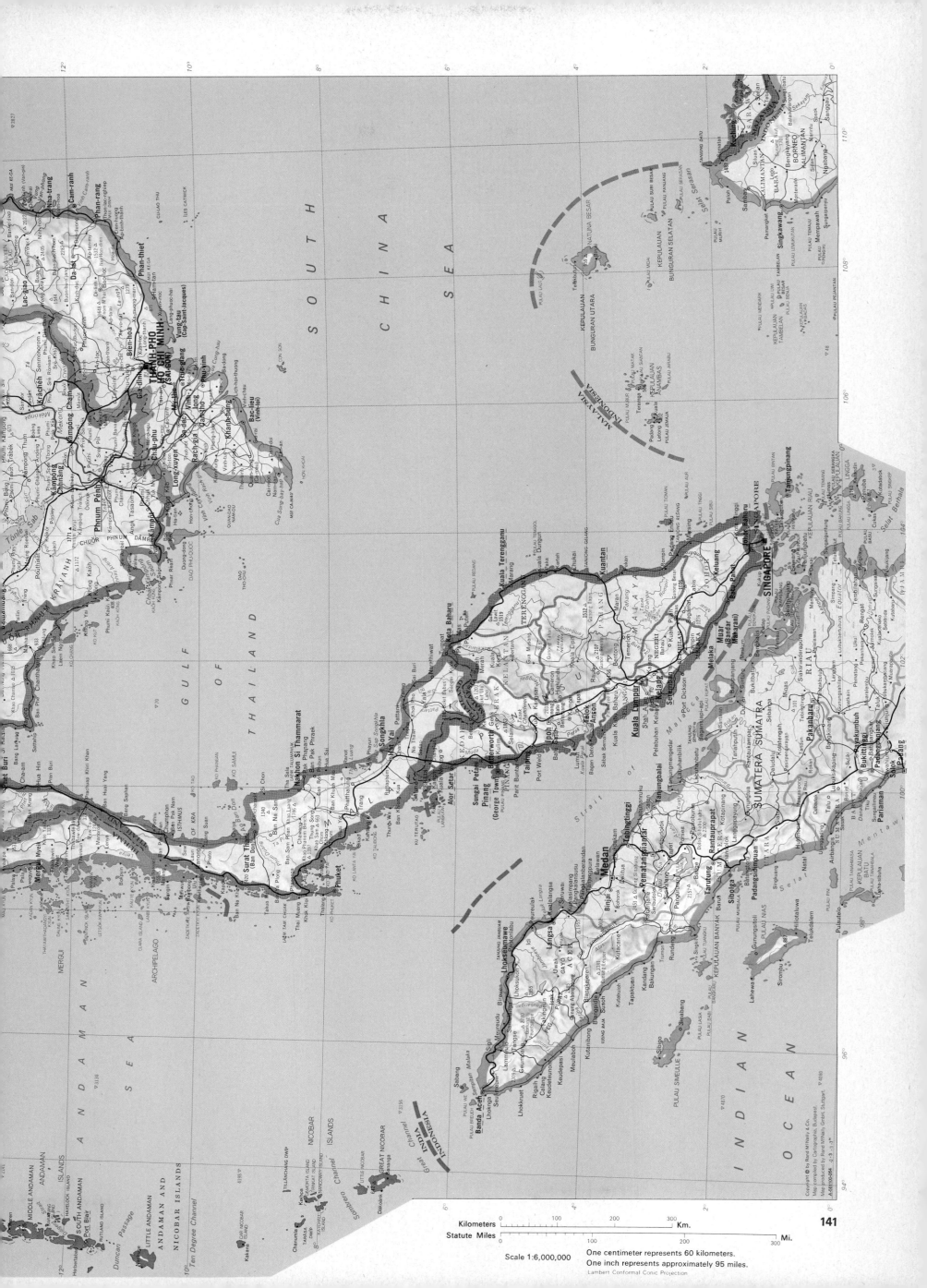

141

Kilometers 0 100 200 300
Km.

Statute Miles 0 100 200 300
Mi.

Scale 1:6,000,000   One centimeter represents 60 kilometers.
One inch represents approximately 95 miles.
Lambert Conformal Conic Projection

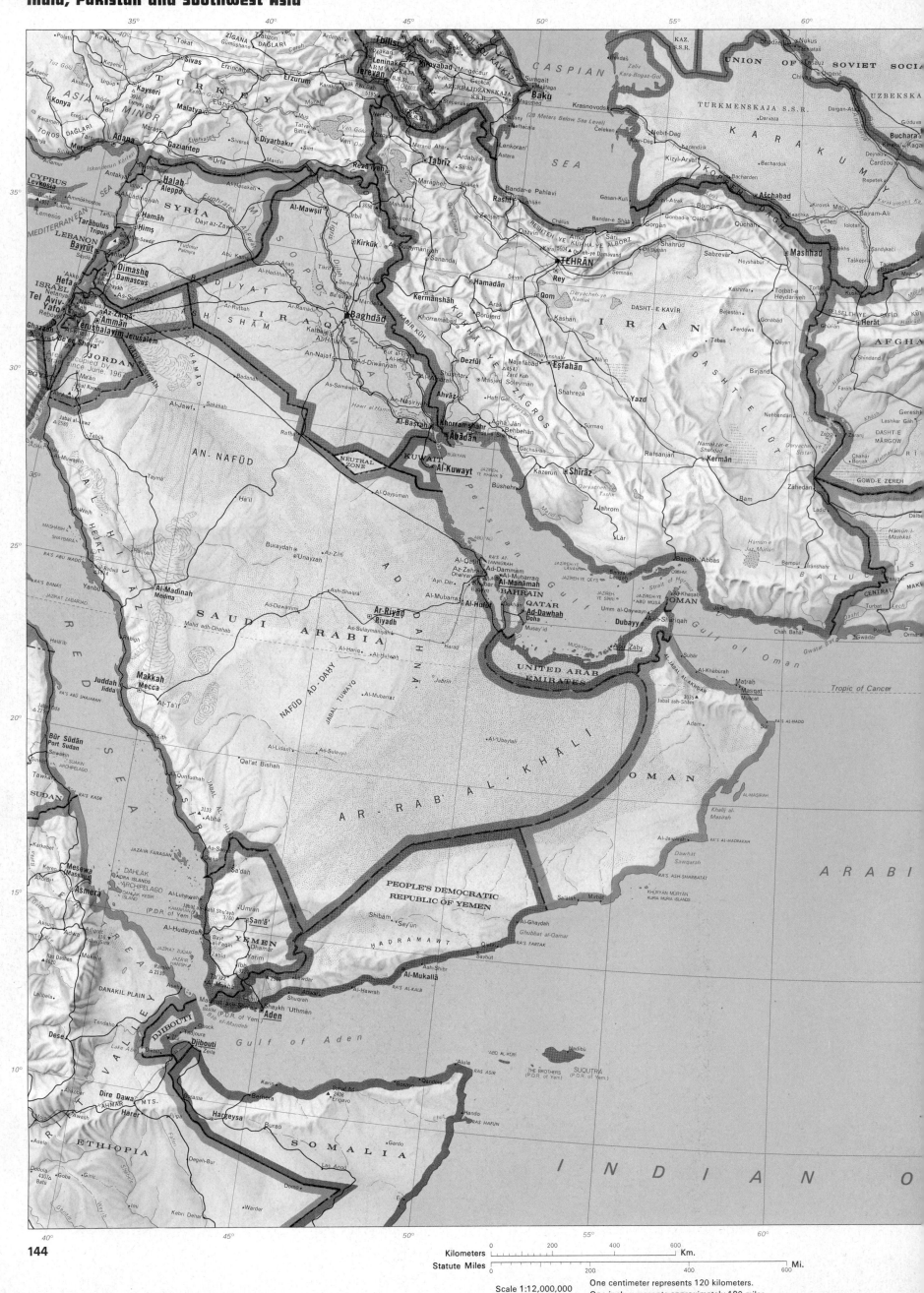

Kilometers

Statute Miles

Scale 1:12,000,000

One centimeter represents 120 kilometers.
One inch represents approximately 190 miles.
Lambert Conformal Conic Projection

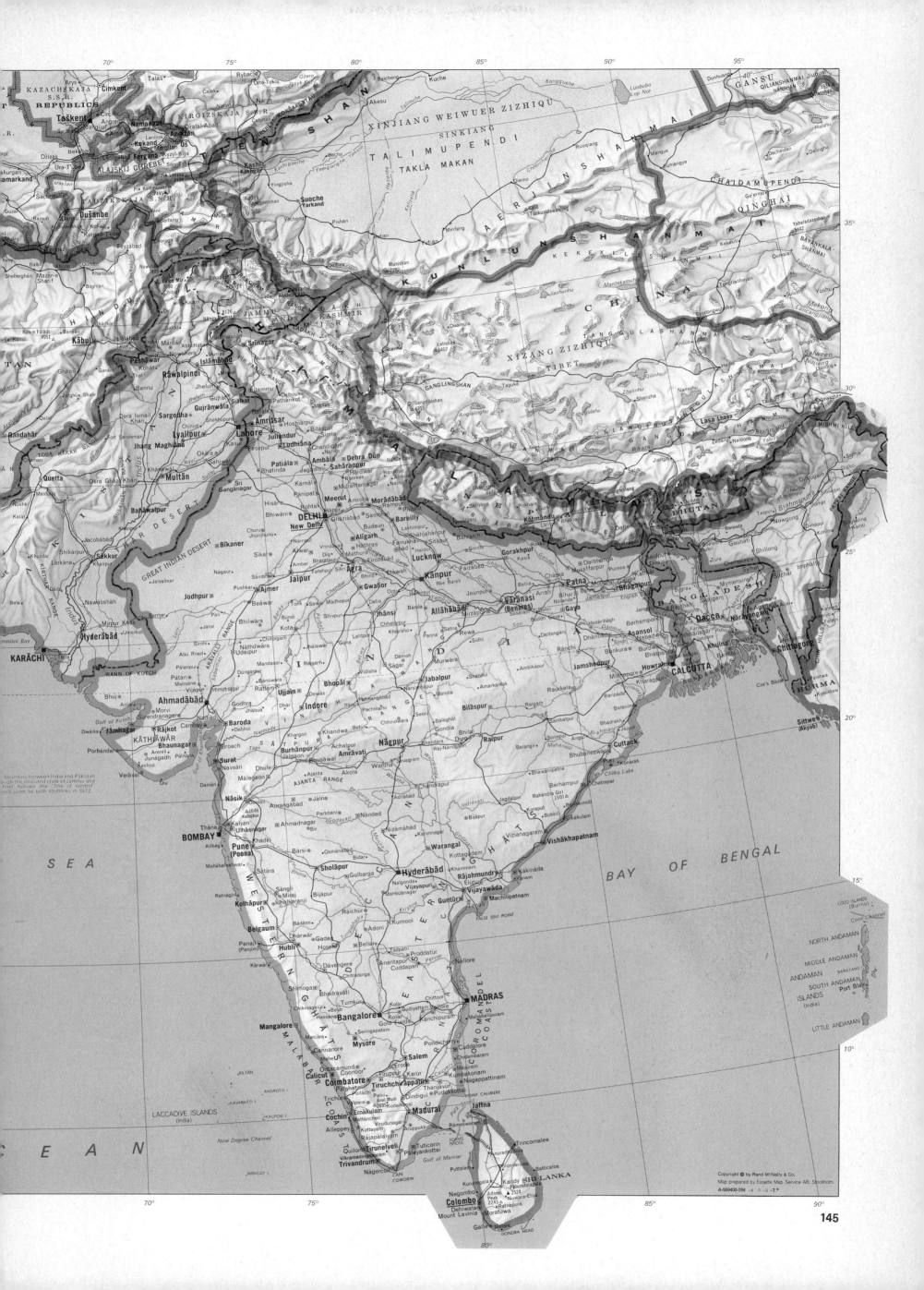

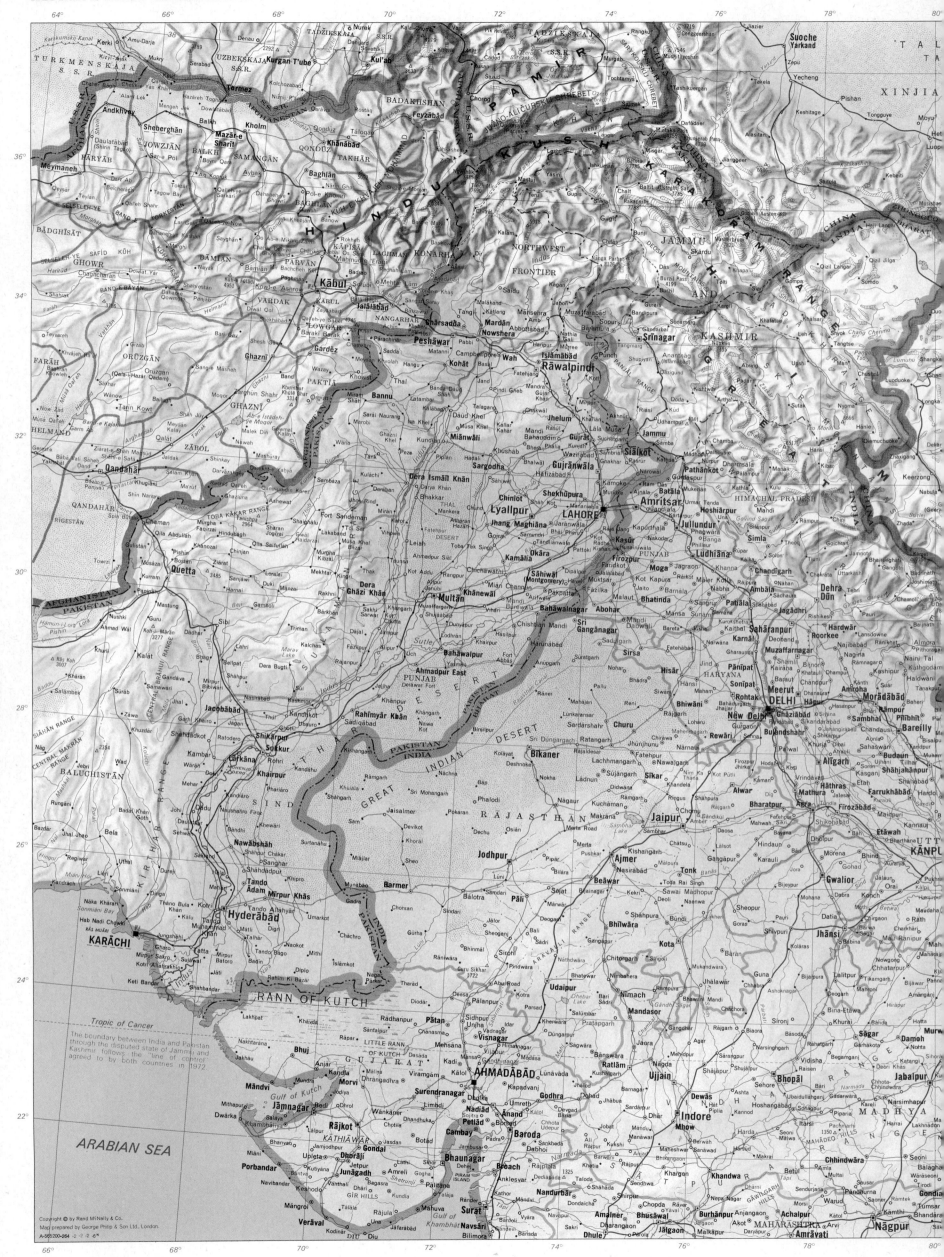

The boundary between India and Pakistan through the disputed state of Jammu and Kashmir follows the "line of control" agreed to by both countries in 1972.

ARABIAN SEA

BAY OF BENGAL

Mouths of the Ganges

CALCUTTA

Scale 1:6,000,000

Kilometers 0 100 200 300 Km.

Statute Miles 0 100 200 300 Mi.

One centimeter represents 60 kilometers.
One inch represents approximately 95 miles.

Lambert Conformal Conic Projection

147

Southern India and Sri Lanka

Kilometers

Statute Miles

Scale 1:8,000,000

One centimeter represents 60 kilometers.
One inch represents approximately 95 miles.
Lambert Conformal Conic Projection

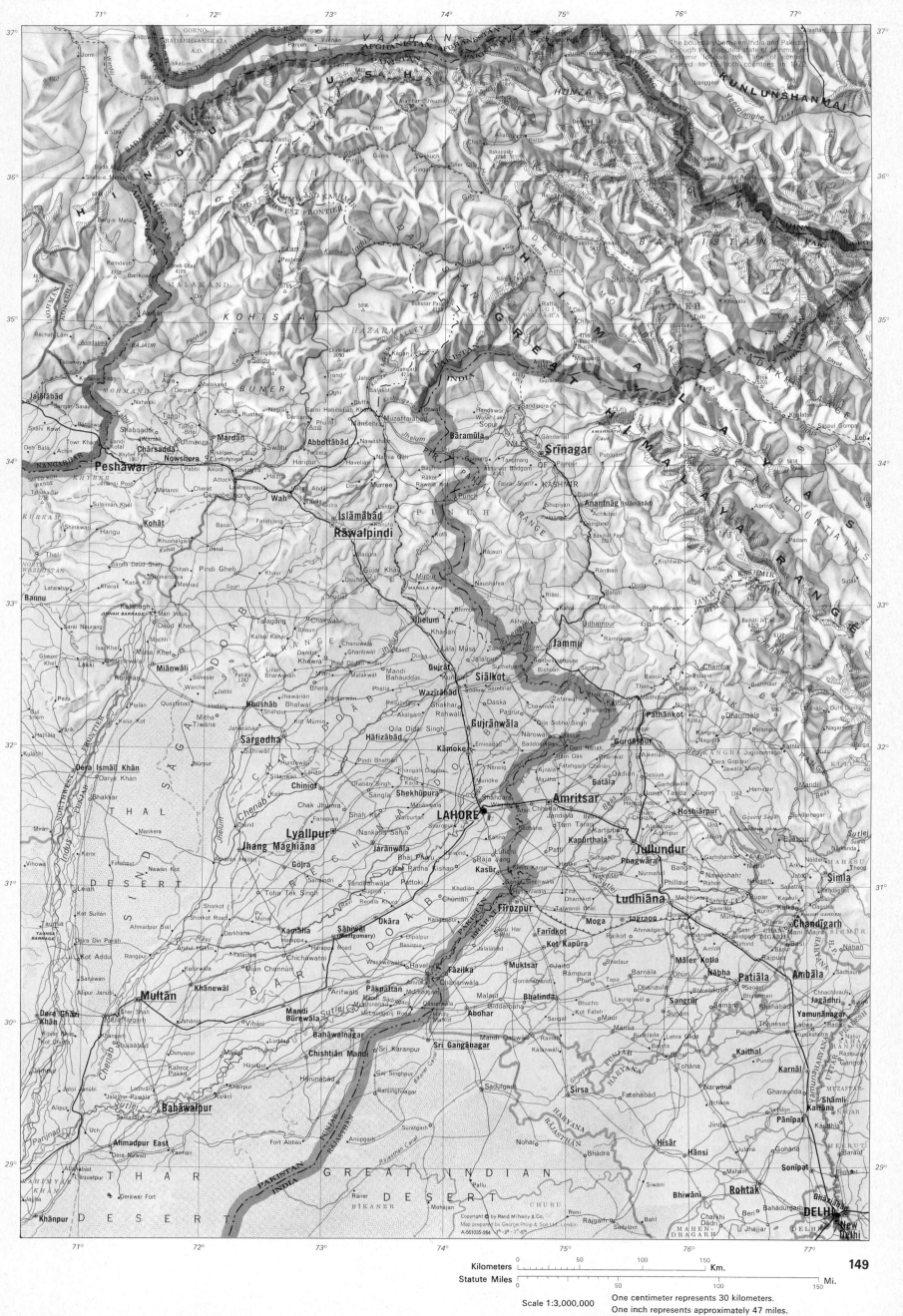

Kilometers

Km.

Statute Miles

Mi.

Scale 1:3,000,000

One centimeter represents 30 kilometers.
One inch represents approximately 47 miles.
Lambert Conformal Conic Projection

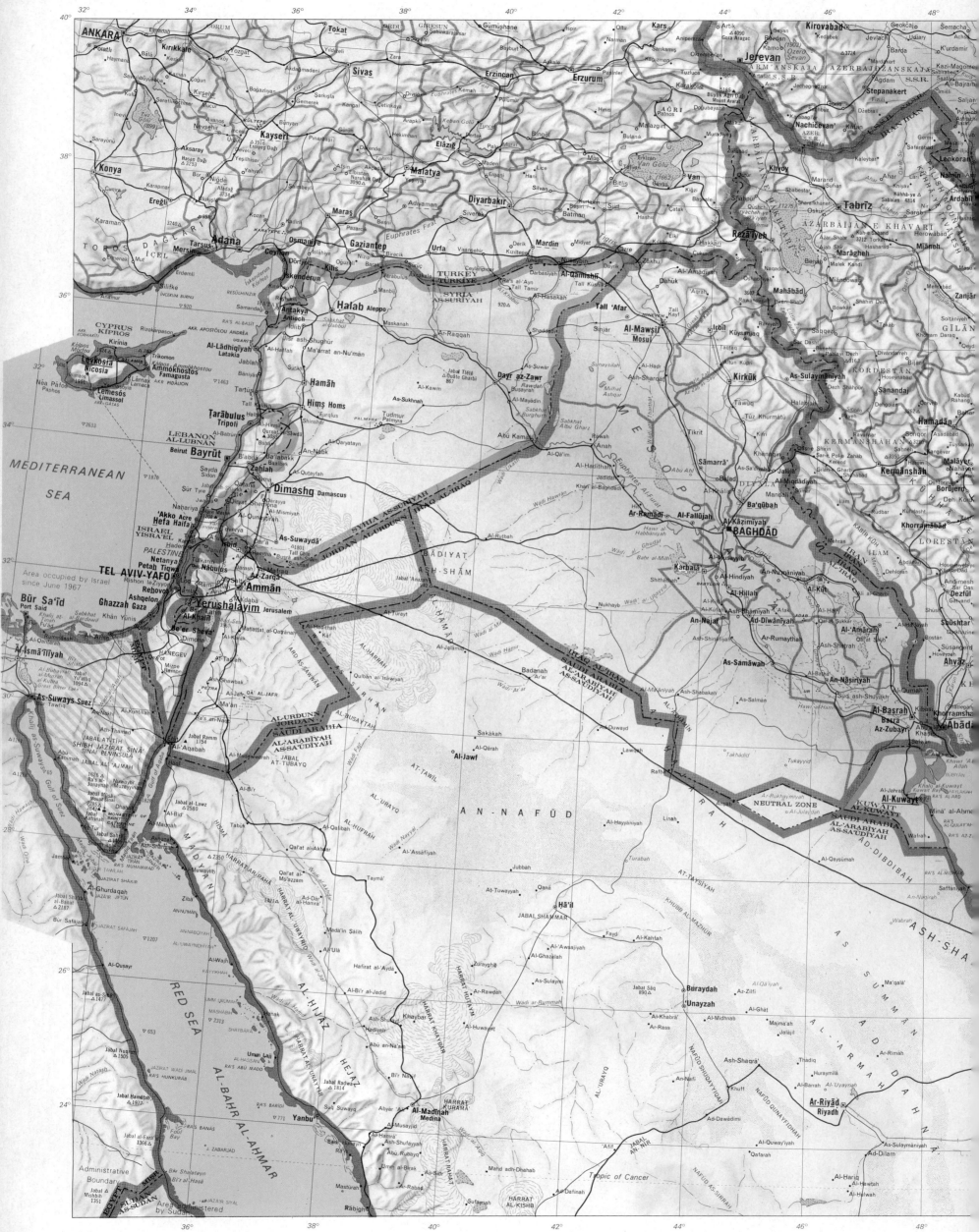

151

Kilometers
0   100   200   300 Km.

Statute Miles
0   100   200   300 Mi.

Scale 1:6,000,000
One centimeter represents 60 kilometers.
One inch represents approximately 95 miles.
Lambert Conformal Conic Projection

Copyright © by Rand McNally & Co.
Map prepared by George Philip & Son Ltd. London
A-569495-264 -2°, -2°-2° -6°

Western Sahara has been occupied
by Morocco and Mauritania

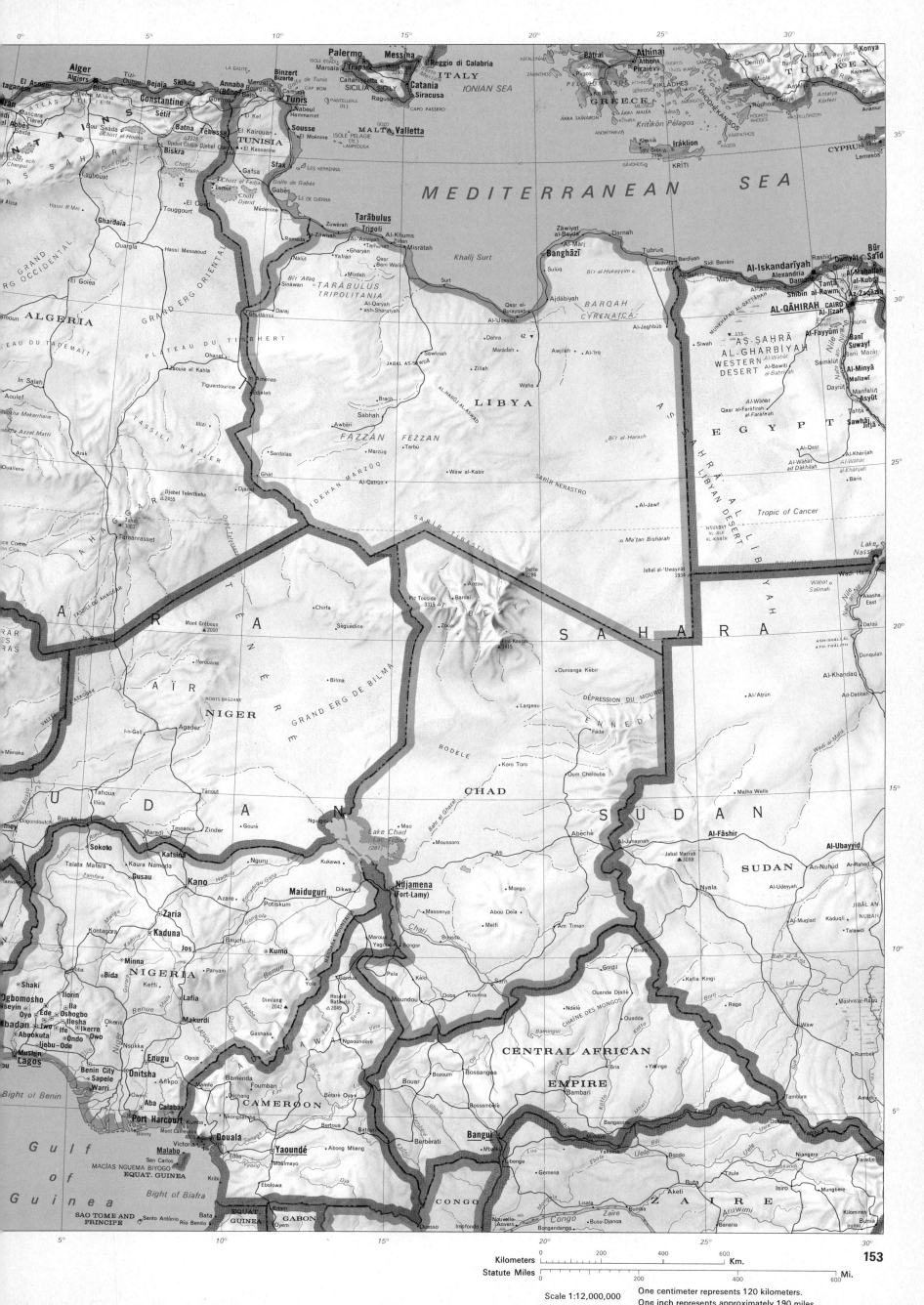

MEDITERRANEAN SEA

ALGERIA

TUNISIA

LIBYA

TARĀBULUS
TRIPOLITANIA

FAZZAN   FEZZAN

EGYPT

AŞ-ṢAḤRĀ
AL-GHARBĪYAH
WESTERN
DESERT

S A H A R A

NIGER

CHAD

SUDAN

SUDAN

NIGERIA

CAMEROON

CENTRAL AFRICAN

EMPIRE

Gulf
of
Guinea

EQUAT. GUINEA

SAO TOME AND
PRINCIPE

EQUAT.
GUINEA   GABON

CONGO

ZAIRE

Bangui

Yaoundé

Tropic of Cancer

153

Kilometers
Km.
0   200   400   600

Statute Miles
Mi.
0   200   400   600

Scale 1:12,000,000
One centimeter represents 120 kilometers.
One inch represents approximately 190 miles.
Miller Oblated Stereographic Projection

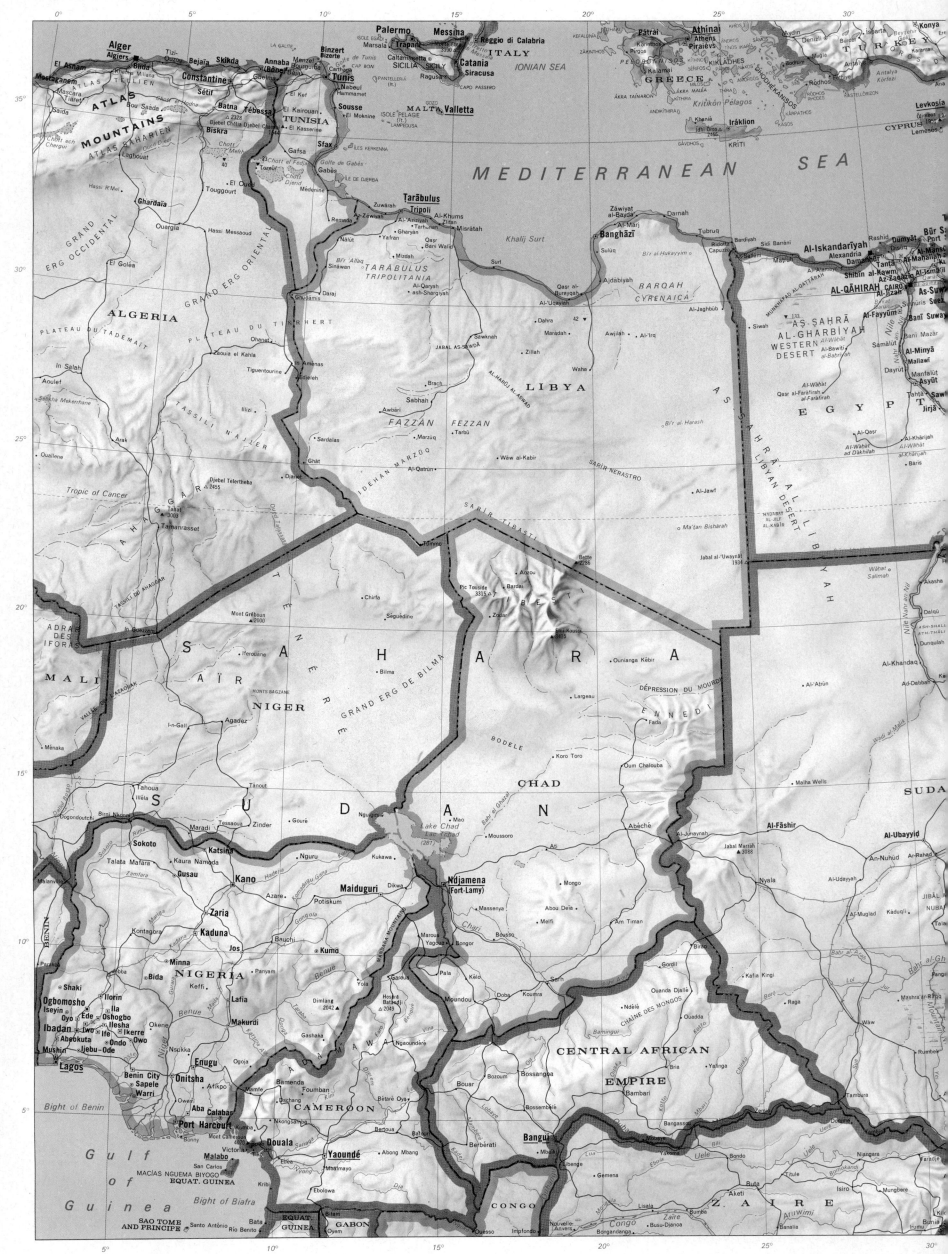

Kilometers 0   200   400   600 Km.

Statute Miles 0   200   400   600 Mi.

Scale 1:12,000,000

One centimeter represents 120 kilometers.
One inch represents approximately 190 miles.

Miller Oblated Stereographic Projection

Copyright © by Rand McNally & Co.
Map prepared by Esselte Map Service AB, Stockholm.
A-589391 -264- ½ ⁵ ½ ¹ ⁶ ⁵

The United Nations declared an end to the mandate of South Africa over South West Africa in October, 1966. Administration of the territory by South Africa is not recognized by the United Nations.

SOMALIA

Brava

Equator

INDIAN OCEAN

KENYA

Nairobi

SEYCHELLES
PRASLIN
ISLAND • LA DIGUE
SILHOUETTE • Victoria
MAHE ISLAND

Mombasa

MASAI
STEPPE

AMIRANTE ISLANDS
(Sey.)
• ÎLE DESROCHES
(Sey.)
PLATTE ISLAND (Sey.)

TANZANIA

Zanzibar
Dar-es-Salaam

ALPHONSE ISLAND (Sey.)

COETIVY ISLAND
(Sey.)

ULUGURU
MOUNTAINS

KIPENGERE RANGE

PROVIDENCE ISLAND
(Sey.)

ALDABRA ISLANDS
(Sey.)
COSMOLEDO GROUP
(Sey.)
SAINT PIERRE ISLAND
(Sey.)
CERF ISLAND
(Sey.)

ASSUMPTION ISLAND
(Sey.)
ASTOVE ISLAND
(Sey.)
FARQUHAR GROUP
(Sey.)

Lake Nyasa

AGALEGA ISLANDS
(Mauritius)

MALAWI

GRANDE COMORE
Moroni
Fomboni
MOHELI
COMORO ISLANDS
Mutsamudu
ANJOUAN
BANC DU GEYSER
ÎLES GLORIEUSES
(Mad.)
CAP D'AMBRE
SAINT-SÉBASTIEN CAP
Diégo-Suarez

MAYOTTE
(Fr.)
Dzaoudzi
NOSY MITSIO
NOSY-BE
Hell-Ville
Ambilobe
Vohémar

Zomba
Blantyre

Porto Amélia

MOZAMBIQUE

MADAGASCAR

Majunga

CAP SAINT-ANDRÉ

Tamatave

Antananarivo

Antsirabe

Beira

Tropic of Capricorn

Tuléar

Fianarantsoa

Port Louis
Curepipe
Mahébourg
Saint-Denis
MAURITIUS
Le Port
Saint-Paul
RÉUNION
Saint-Pierre
(Fr.)

MASCARENE
ISLANDS

Mozambique Channel

Rhodesia unilaterally
declared its independence
from the United Kingdom
on November 11, 1965.

Fort-Dauphin
CAP SAINTE-MARIE

INDIAN OCEAN

Copyright © by Rand McNally & Co.
Map prepared by Esselte Map Service AB, Stockholm.
A-589200-264 -4 -5 -5 -10°

157

Kilometers

Statute Miles

Scale 1:12,000,000

One centimeter represents 120 kilometers.
One inch represents approximately 190 miles.
Miller Oblated Stereographic Projection

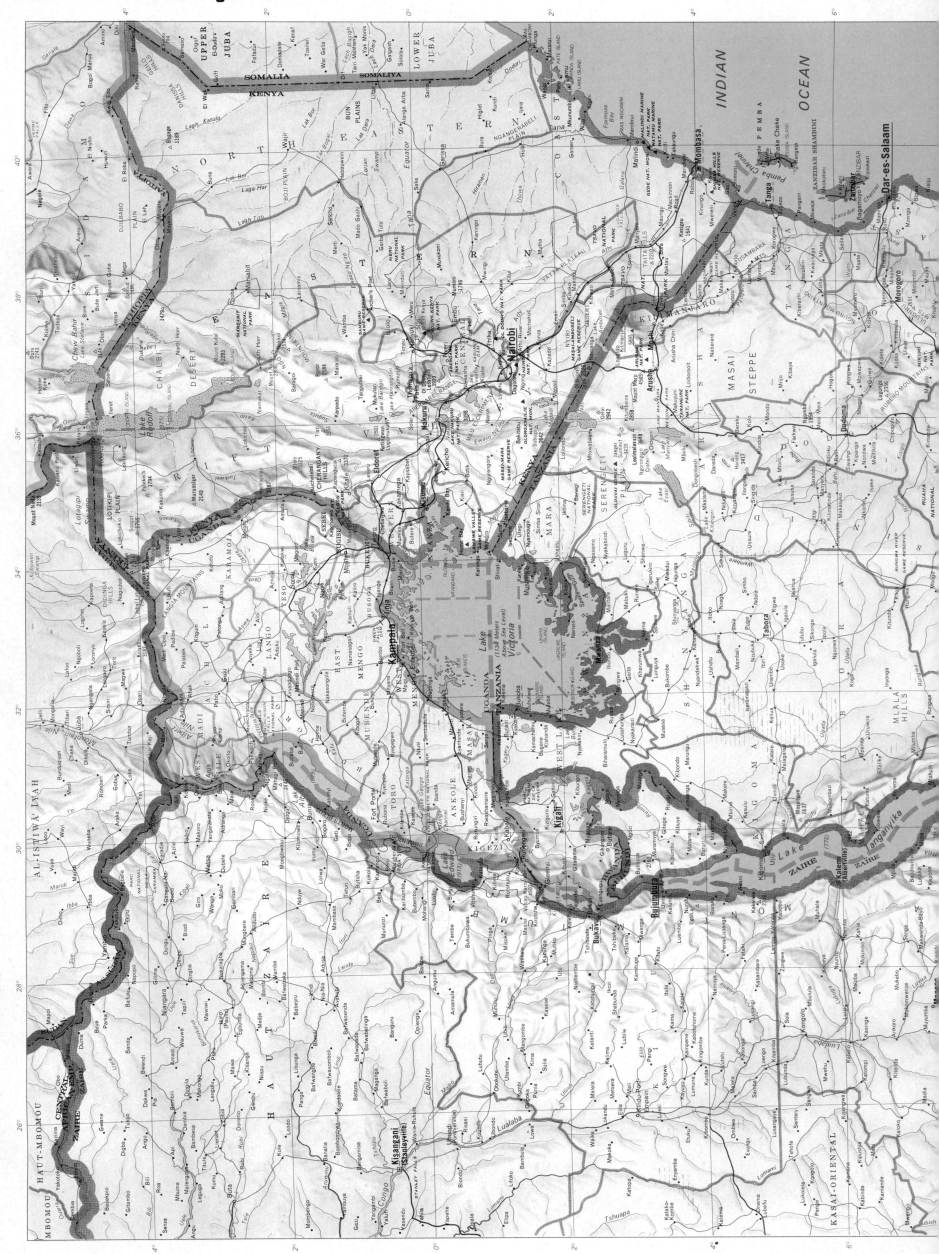

MOZAMBIQUE CHANNEL

159

Rhodesia unilaterally declared its
independence from the United Kingdom
on November 11, 1965.

Kilometers
Statute Miles

Scale 1:6,000,000

One centimeter represents 60 kilometers.
One inch represents approximately 95 miles.
Lambert Azimuthal Equal-Area Projection

Kilometers

Statute Miles

Scale 1:6,000,000

One centimeter represents 60 kilometers.
One inch represents approximately 95 miles.
Lambert Azimuthal Equal-Area Projection

The United Nations
declared an end to the
mandate of South Africa
over South West Africa
in October, 1966. Administration
of the territory by South
Africa is not recognized
by the United Nations

Copyright © by Rand McNally & Co.
Map prepared by George Philip & Son Ltd, London.
A-689292-264

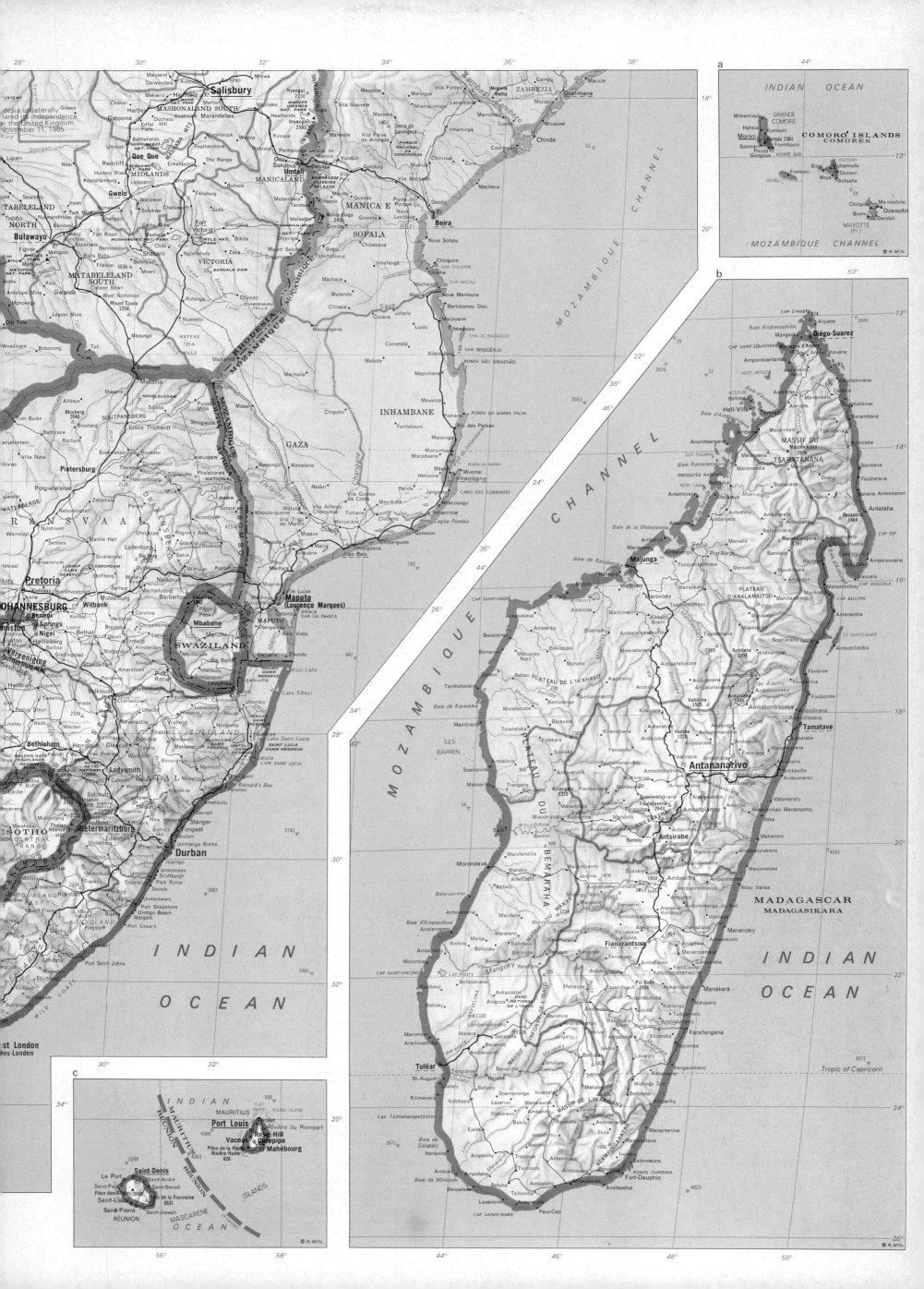

163

Kilometers 0 200 400 600 Km.
Statute Miles 0 200 400 600 Mi.

Scale 1:12,000,000
One centimeter represents 120 kilometers.
One inch represents approximately 190 miles.
Lambert Conformal Conic Projection

INDIAN OCEAN

GREAT SANDY DESERT

GIBSON DESERT

WESTERN AUSTRALIA

Tropic of Capricorn

Perth
Fremantle
Geraldton
Carnarvon
Bunbury
Albany
Kalgoorlie

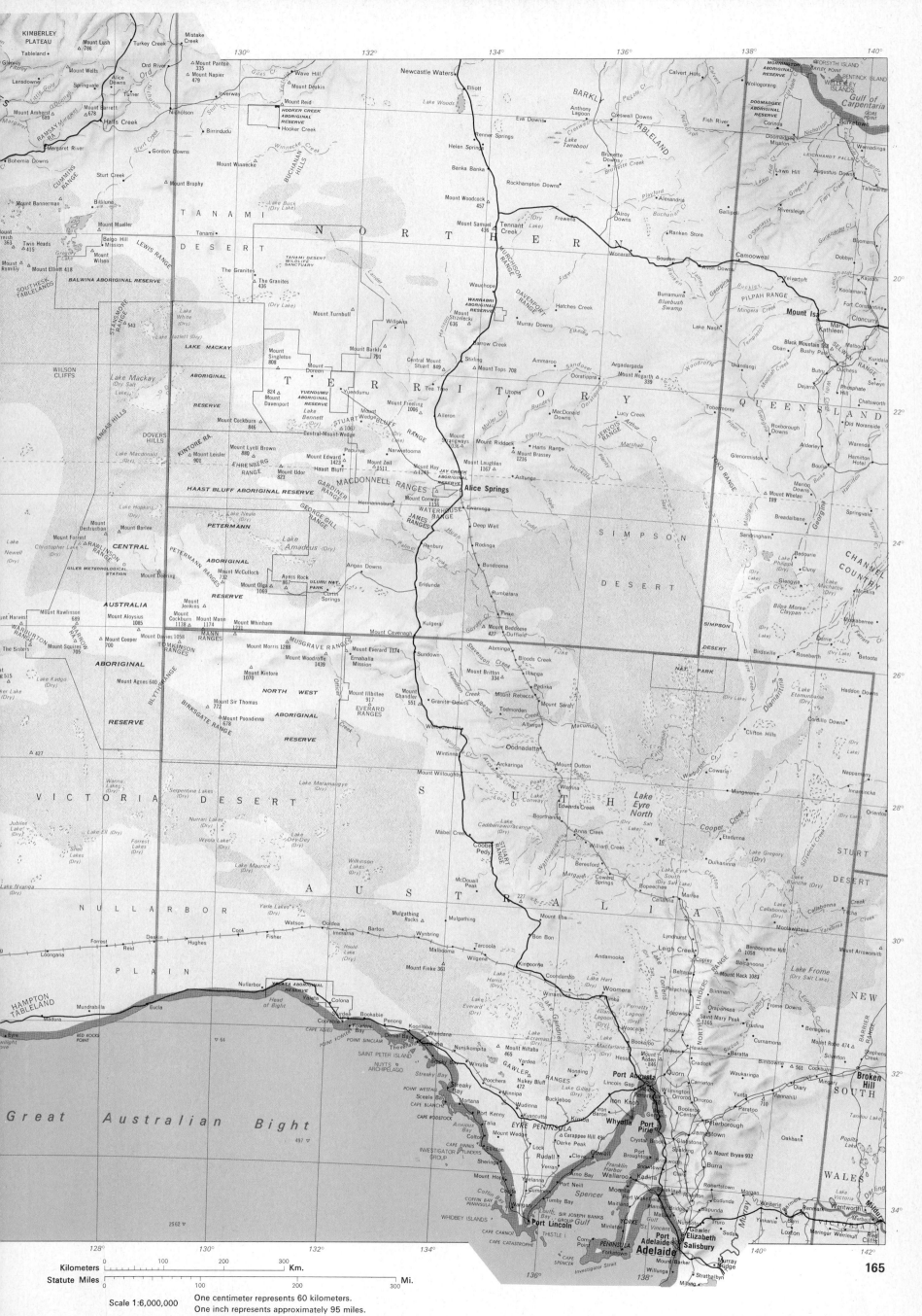

KIMBERLEY
PLATEAU
Mount Lush △786 Turkey Creek Mistake Creek
Mount Wells Ord River Wave Hill
Springvale Turner Inverway Mount Deakin
Lansdowne Nicholson Mount Reid Newcastle Waters Elliott BARKLY Calvert Hills Calvert MORNINGTON ABORIGINAL RESERVE FORSYTH ISLAND BAYLEY POINT GORE POINT WELLESLEY ISLANDS Gulf of Carpentaria
Mount Amherst △589 RAMSAY RA Mount Barrett △678 Halls Creek Hooker Creek ABORIGINAL RESERVE Hooker Creek Lake Woods Anthony Lagoon Creswell Downs Fish River DOOMADGEE ABORIGINAL RESERVE Corinda Doomadgee Mission BENTINCK ISLAND Burketown
Margaret River Birrindudu Renner Springs Eva Downs Brunette Downs Wologorang Wernadinga
Bohemia Downs Gordon Downs Helen Springs TABLELAND Brunette Creek Lawn Hill Augustus Downs Talawanta
CUMMINS RANGE Sturt Creek Banka Banka Alroy Downs Gregory Riversleigh Dobbyn
Mount Bannerman Billiluna Mount Brophy Mount Woodcock 457 Rockhampton Downs Alexandria Buchanan Ck Souden Ranken Store Camooweal PILPAH RANGE Fort Constantine Koolamarra
Mount Mueller TANAMI Tanami Mount Samuel △436 Tennant Creek Frewena Wauchope Argadargada Urandangi Butru Mount Isa Mary Kathleen Cloncurry
Twin Heads △415 DESERT The Granites MURCHISON RANGE DAVENPORT RANGE Hatches Creek Mount Hogarth 339 Tobermorey Oban Black Mountain 909 Bushy Park Duchess Selwyn Kuridala
Balgo Hill Mission Mount Wilson TANAMI DESERT WILDLIFE SANCTUARY WARRABRI ABORIGINAL RESERVE Lake Nash Templeton Mingera Creek Dajarra Phosphate Hill Chatsworth
SOUTHESK TABLELANDS Mount Elliott 418 Mount Romilly BALWINA ABORIGINAL RESERVE Willowra Mount Strezlecki 636 Murray Downs Elkedra Sandover Roxborough Downs Glenormiston Boulia Hamilton Hotel QUEENSLAND
WILSON CLIFFS STANSMORE RANGE △543 Mount Turnbull Barrow Creek Stirling Mount Tops 708 Ammaroo Woodroffe Marion Downs Warenda
Lake White Mount Barkly △791 Central Mount Stuart 849 Mount Doreen Utopia MacDonald Downs Lucy Creek Arthur Ck Sandringham Old Noranside
Lake Mackay Mount Singleton 808 Tea Tree JERVOIS RANGE Marshall Mount Whelan △189 Springvale Breadalbane
Mount Davenport △824 YUENDUMU ABORIGINAL RESERVE Yuendumu TERRITORY Bundey Plenty Ck TOKO RANGE Georgina
ABORIGINAL Lake Bennett Mount Freeling 1006 Aileron Mount Strangways 1036 Mount Riddock Harts Range 1216 Glenormiston
Mount Cockburn 846 RESERVE Mount Wedge Narwietooma Mount Brassey 1216
ANGAS HILLS DOVERS HILLS KINTORE RA Mount Leisler 901 Mount Lyell Brown 880 Stuart BLUFF RANGE Papunya Mount Laughlen 1167 CHANNEL COUNTRY
Lake Macdonald (Dry) EHRENBERG RANGE Mount Edward 1423 Mount Zeil △1511 Mount Hay △1249 JAY CREEK ABORIGINAL RESERVE Aritunga
Mount Udor 823 Haast Bluff GARDINER RANGE MACDONNELL RANGES Hermannsburg Alice Springs SIMPSON Lake Philippi
HAAST BLUFF ABORIGINAL RESERVE Mount Conway 1138 WATERHOUSE RANGE Ewaninga Mount Whelan DESERT Lake Machattie (Dry) Bilpa Morea (Dry) Claypan
PETERMANN GEORGE GILL RANGE JAMES RANGES Deep Well Hale Todd Bedourie Cluny
Lake Neale (Dry) Lake Amadeus (Dry) Henbury Rodinga Finke Sandringham Birdsville
CENTRAL Mount Destruction Mount Barlee Palmer Hugh Bundooma Roseberth Betoota
Mount Forrest Christopher Lake (Dry) RAWLINSON RA GILES METEOROLOGICAL STATION Mount McCulloch 732 Angas Downs Erldunda Rumbatara NAT PARK Lake Eyre (Dry Lake)
Lake Newell (Dry) Mount Deering PETERMANN RANGES Ayers Rock 867 ULURU NAT PARK Curtin Springs Finke SIMPSON DESERT Clifton Hills
Mount Olga 1069 RESERVE Mount Beddome 427 Duffield Lake Eyre North Haddon Downs
AUSTRALIA Mount Rawlinson 689 Mount Jenkins Kulgera Stevenson Ck Abminga Bloods Creek Cordillo Downs
Mount Harvest Mount Aloysius 1085 Mount Cockburn 1138 Mount Mann 1174 Mount Whinham 1231 Mount Cavenagh Sundown Mount Britton 334 Ilbunga Pedirka Macumba
WARBURTON RANGES Mount Davies 1058 MANN RANGES Mount Morris 1288 Mount Everard 1174 Mount Rebecca Mount Sarah Warburton Ck
BARROW RANGE Mount Cooper 700 TOMKINSON RANGES MUSGRAVE RANGES Ernabella Mission Todmorden Diamantina Lake Etamunbanie (Dry) Lake Pure (Dry)
Mount Squires 705 Mount Woodroffe 1439 Albinga Oodnadatta Birdsville
Lake Kadgo (Dry) BLYTH RANGE Mount Kintore 1070 NORTH WEST Mount Illbillee 917 Mount Chandler 551 Granite Downs Arckaringa Welbourn Hill Mount Dutton
ABORIGINAL Mount Agnes 640 BIRKSGATE RANGE Mount Sir Thomas 772 EVERARD RANGES Oldea Ck Warrina
Mount Poondinna 678 RESERVE ABORIGINAL Officer Wintinna Lake Cadibarrawirracanna (Dry) Lake Conway Cowarie Mungeranie Innamincka Orientos
△427 RESERVE Mount Willoughby Mabel Creek Anna Creek Etadunna STURT DESERT
Wanna Lakes (Dry) Serpentine Lakes (Dry) Lake Meramangye (Dry) Boorthanna William Creek Coward Springs Lake Gregory (Dry) Lake Blanche (Dry)
VICTORIA DESERT SOUTH Lake Eyre South Margaret Beresford Callanna Callabonna Creek
Jubilee Lake (Dry) Lake Ell (Dry) Nurrari Lakes (Dry) Lake Dey-Dey (Dry) Lake Maurice (Dry) Coober Pedy STUART RANGE Bopeechee Marree Lake Callabonna (Dry Salt Lake)
Shell Lakes (Dry) Wyola Lake (Dry) Wilkinson Lakes (Dry) McDouall Peak △227 Lyndhurst Mount Arrowsmith
Lake Nyanga (Dry) NULLARBOR Yarle Lakes (Dry) AUSTRALIA Mount Eba Bon Bon Copley Leigh Creek Benboayathie Hill 1058 NEW
Mulgathing Rocks Mulgathing Tarcoola Andamooka Balcanoona Mount Hack 1083
Watson Ooldea Immarna Barton Wynbring Kingoonya Woomera Beltana Mount Painter FLINDERS RANGE
Loongana Reid Deakin Hughes Fisher Malbooma Wilgena Lake Harris (Dry) Coondambo Pernatty Lagoon Parachilna Blinman Frome Downs
Forrest Mount Finke 361 Lake Everard (Dry) Wirraminna NORTH Beda Nackara Saint Mary Peak 1165 Orapanna Benagerie
HAMPTON TABLELAND YALATA ABORIGINAL RESERVE Kingoonya Lake Gairdner Umba Pernatty Hookina Edeowie Mount Rose 474 △ STURT
Eucla Nullarbor Yalata Colona Koonibba Wirrulla Lake Gilles Iron Knob Pimba Carrapee Hill Wilson Hawker Curnamona Silverton
Mundrabilla Madura RED ROCKS POINT Fowlers Bay Penong Bookabie Lake Macfarlane (Dry) Port Augusta Quorn Carrieton Wilmington Cradock Bimbowrie △501 Cockburn Broken Hill
Eyre CAPE ADIEU Point Fowler Point Sinclair Denial Bay Nunjikompita GAWLER RANGES Nonning Whyalla Iron Baron Orroroo Baratta SOUTH
SAINT PETER ISLAND Thevenard Ceduna Wirrulla Mount Hiltaba 465 Nukey Bluff 472 Cowell Peterborough Waukaringa WALES
NUYTS ARCHIPELAGO Streaky Bay Poochera Minnipa Lincoln Gap Gladstone Yunta Mannahill Olary
△64 Streaky Bay Wudinna Kimba Crystal Brook Jamestown Oakbank Popilah Lake
CAPE BLANCHE Mortana Port Kenny Kyancutta Port Pirie Spalding Burra Terowie
Great Australian Bight Talia Lock Verran Arno Bay Cleve Port Broughton Broken Hill
CAPE FINNISS Elliston Rudall Wallaroo Moonta Robertstown Morgan Renmark Paringa
497 ▽ INVESTIGATOR GROUP Mount Wedge Cummins Port Neil Kadina Balaklava Eudunda Waikerie Berri
CAPE RADSTOCK Coffin Bay Tumby Bay SPENCER Port Broughton Maitland Hamley Bridge Gawler Truro Loxton
Coulta Yorke Gulf Port Wakefield Tanunda Nuriootpa Waikerie
Coffin Bay Coobowie Minlaton Port Adelaide Elizabeth Salisbury Meningie
2562 ▽ WHIDBEY ISLANDS CAPE CARNOT Port Lincoln THISTLE I. SIR JOSEPH BANKS GROUP YORKE PENINSULA Edithburgh Adelaide Murray Bridge VICTORIA
CAPE CATASTROPHE EYRE PENINSULA Corny Point YORKE PENINSULA Cape Jervis Willunga Strathalbyn Red Cliffs
CAPE SPENCER Investigator Strait Milang Mildura

Kilometers 0 100 200 300 Km.
Statute Miles 0 100 200 300 Mi.

Scale 1:6,000,000
One centimeter represents 60 kilometers.
One inch represents approximately 95 miles.
Lambert Conformal Conic Projection

PACIFIC OCEAN

MANUS

BISMARCK ARCHIPELAGO

BISMARCK SEA

INDONESIA
PAPUA NEW GUINEA

Jayapura
(Sukarnapura)

NEW IRELAND

NEW
HANOVER

Rabaul

NEW GUINEA

WEST SEPIK

EAST SEPIK

Wewak

Madang

WEST
BRITAIN

EAST
NEW BRITAIN

NEW
BRITAIN

WESTERN
HIGHLANDS

MADANG

SOUTHERN
HIGHLANDS

CHIMBU

EASTERN
HIGHLANDS

HUON
PENINSULA

Finschhafen

Lae

SOLOMON SEA

MOROBE

Morobe

INDONESIA
PAPUA NEW GUINEA

GULF

WESTERN

Gulf of Papua

TROBRIAND
ISLANDS

D'ENTRECASTEAUX
ISLANDS

WOODLARK
ISLAND

Kerema

Kokoda

Popondetta

NORTHERN

MILNE BAY

Port Moresby

CENTRAL

STANLEY
RANGE

LOUISIADE ARCHIPELAGO

Torres Strait

Thursday Island

PAPUA NEW GUINEA
AUSTRALIA

CORAL

CAPE
YORK

SEA

PENINSULA

QUEENSLAND

GREAT DIVIDING RANGE

Cooktown

Cairns

CORAL SEA ISLANDS TERRITORY

167

Copyright © by Rand McNally & Co.
Map prepared by George Philip & Son Ltd. London
A-593000-264

Kilometers
Statute Miles

Scale 1:6,000,000
One centimeter represents 60 kilometers.
One inch represents approximately 95 miles.
Lambert Conformal Conic Projection

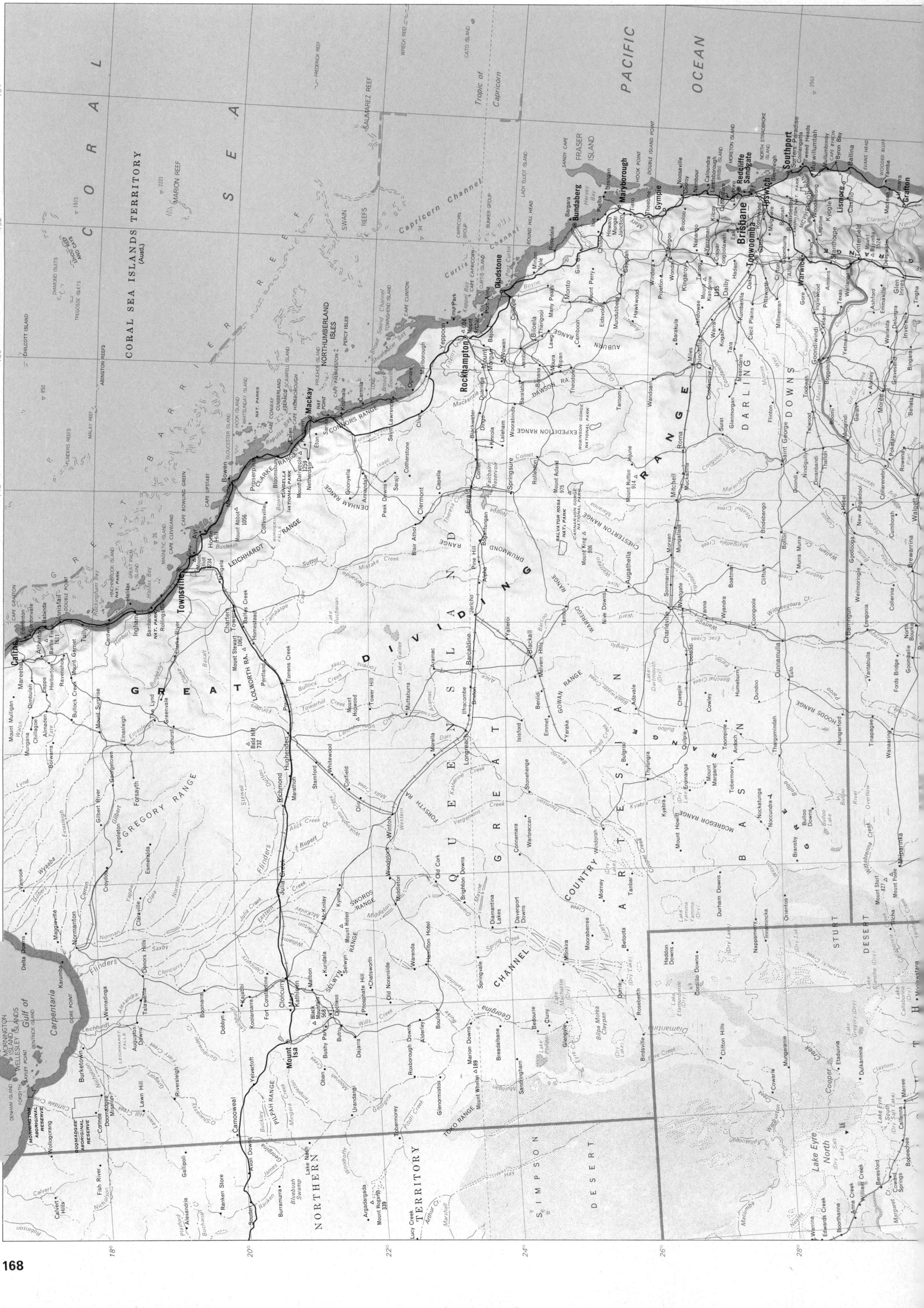

PACIFIC OCEAN

CORAL SEA

CORAL SEA ISLANDS TERRITORY (Aust.)

GREAT BARRIER REEF

Gulf of Carpentaria

GREAT DIVIDING RANGE

QUEENSLAND

NORTHERN TERRITORY

GREAT ARTESIAN BASIN

CHANNEL COUNTRY

SIMPSON DESERT

STURT DESERT

DARLING DOWNS

Tropic of Capricorn

Brisbane
Ipswich
Toowoomba
Southport
Redcliffe
Sandgate
Warwick
Maryborough
Bundaberg
Gladstone
Rockhampton
Mackay
Townsville
Cairns
Charters Towers
Hughenden
Richmond
Mount Isa
Cloncurry
Longreach
Barcaldine
Blackall
Roma
Gympie
Lismore
Grafton

Kilometers

Statute Miles

Km.

Mi.

0   100   200   300

0   100   200   300

Scale 1:6,000,000

One centimeter represents 60 kilometers.
One inch represents approximately 95 miles.

Lambert Conformal Conic Projection

Copyright © by Rand McNally & Co.

Map prepared by George Philip & Son, Ltd., London.

A-580309-364

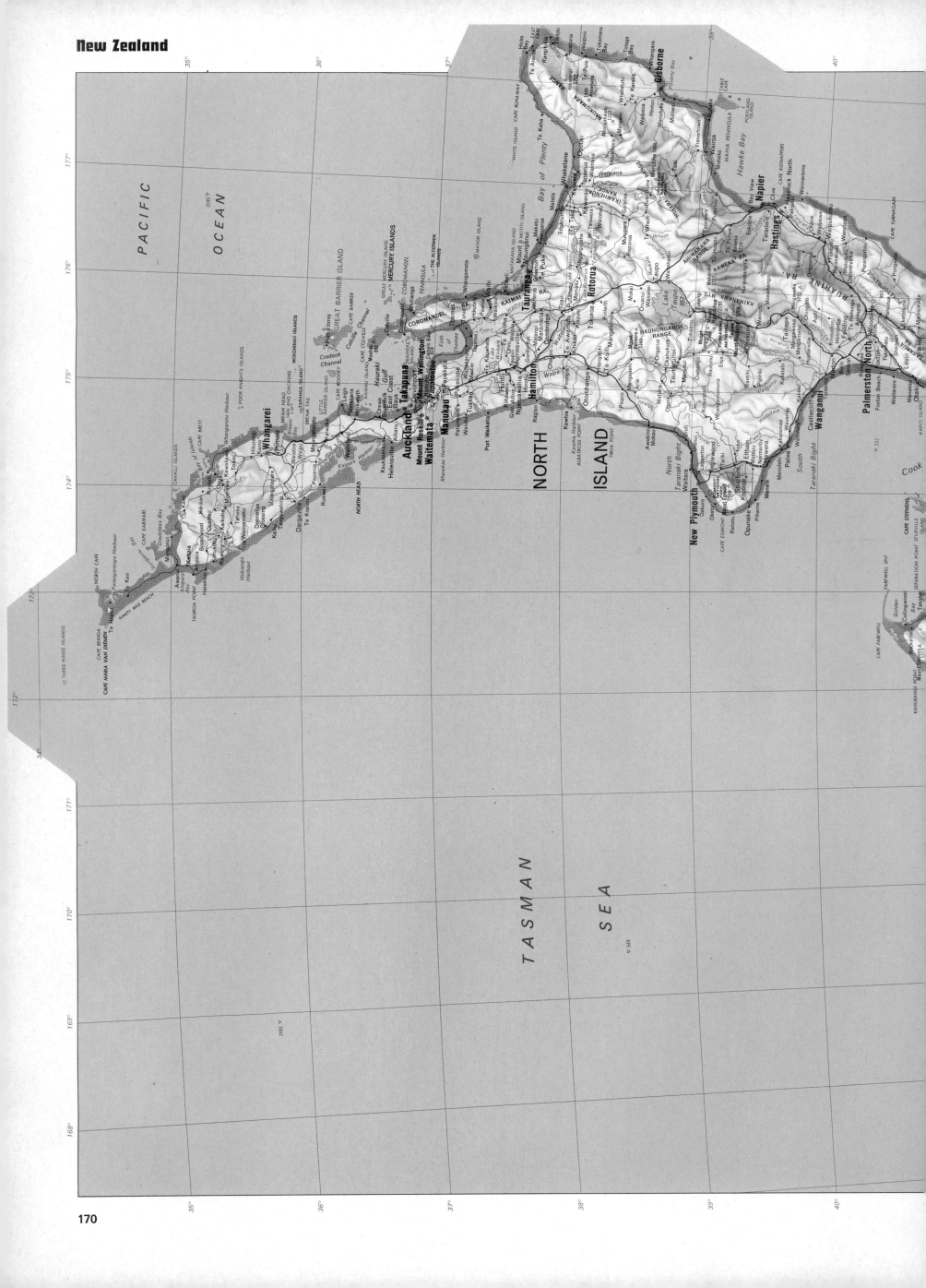

PACIFIC

OCEAN

NORTH

ISLAND

North
Taranaki Bight

South
Taranaki Bight

TASMAN

SEA

Cook

Whangarei

Auckland
Mount Roskill
Waitemata
Takapuna
Mount Wellington
Papatoetoe
Manukau

Hamilton

Tauranga
Rotorua

Gisborne

Napier
Hastings

New Plymouth

Wanganui
Palmerston North

COROMANDEL

GREAT BARRIER ISLAND

MERCURY ISLANDS

Bay of Plenty

Hawke Bay

RUAHINE

Lake
Taupo

NORTH CAPE

CAPE REINGA
CAPE MARIA VAN DIEMEN

THREE KINGS ISLANDS

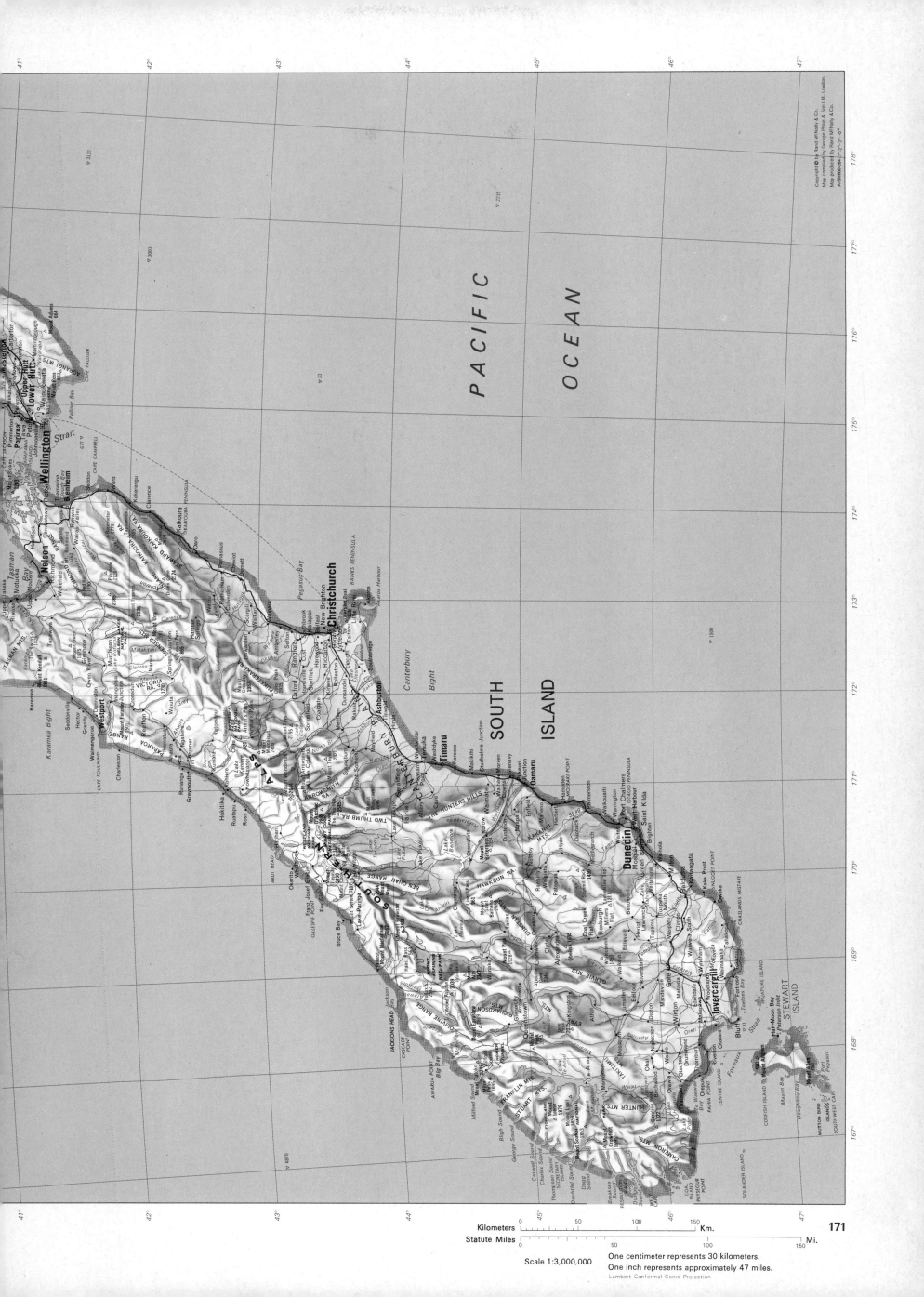

PACIFIC

OCEAN

SOUTH

ISLAND

STEWART
ISLAND

Wellington
Blenheim

Nelson
Tasman
Bay

Westport

Greymouth
Hokitika

Christchurch
New Brighton

Timaru

Oamaru

Dunedin

Invercargill
Bluff

Canterbury
Bight

SOUTHERN
ALPS

KAIKOURA RA.

TASMAN MTS.

VICTORIA RA.

PAPAROA RANGE

Kilometers
0   50   100   150   Km.

Statute Miles
0   50   100   150   Mi.

Scale 1:3,000,000   One centimeter represents 30 kilometers.
One inch represents approximately 47 miles.

Lambert Conformal Conic Projection

Kilometers

Km.

Statute Miles

Mi.

Scale 1:12,000,000   One centimeter represents 120 kilometers.
One inch represents approximately 190 miles.

Lambert Conformal Conic Projection

PACIFIC

OCEAN

Tropic of Cancer

175

Kilometers |0| |200| |400| |600| Km.

Statute Miles |0| |200| |400| |600| Mi.

Scale 1:12,000,000   One centimeter represents 120 kilometers.
One inch represents approximately 190 miles.

Albers Conical Equal-Area Projection

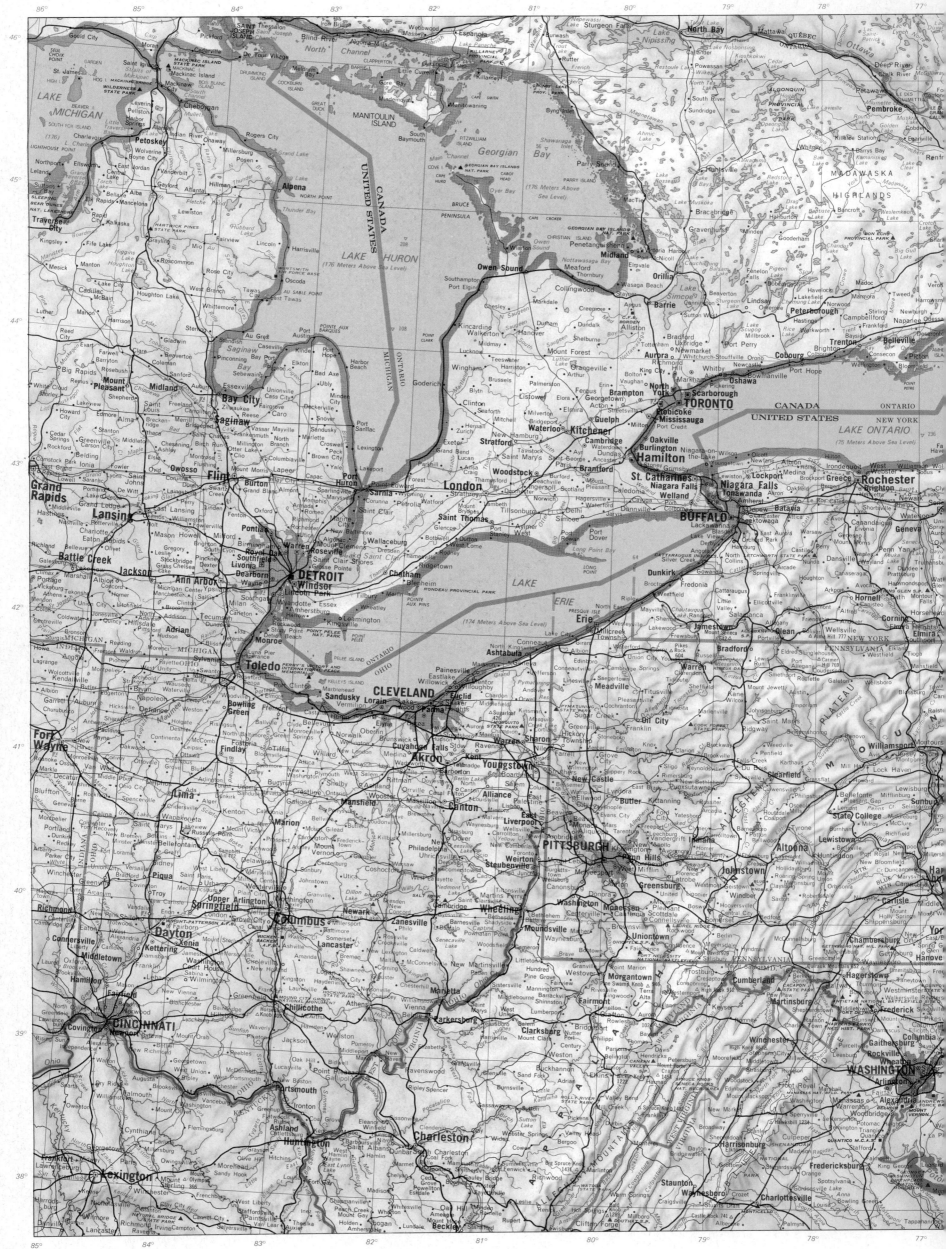

177

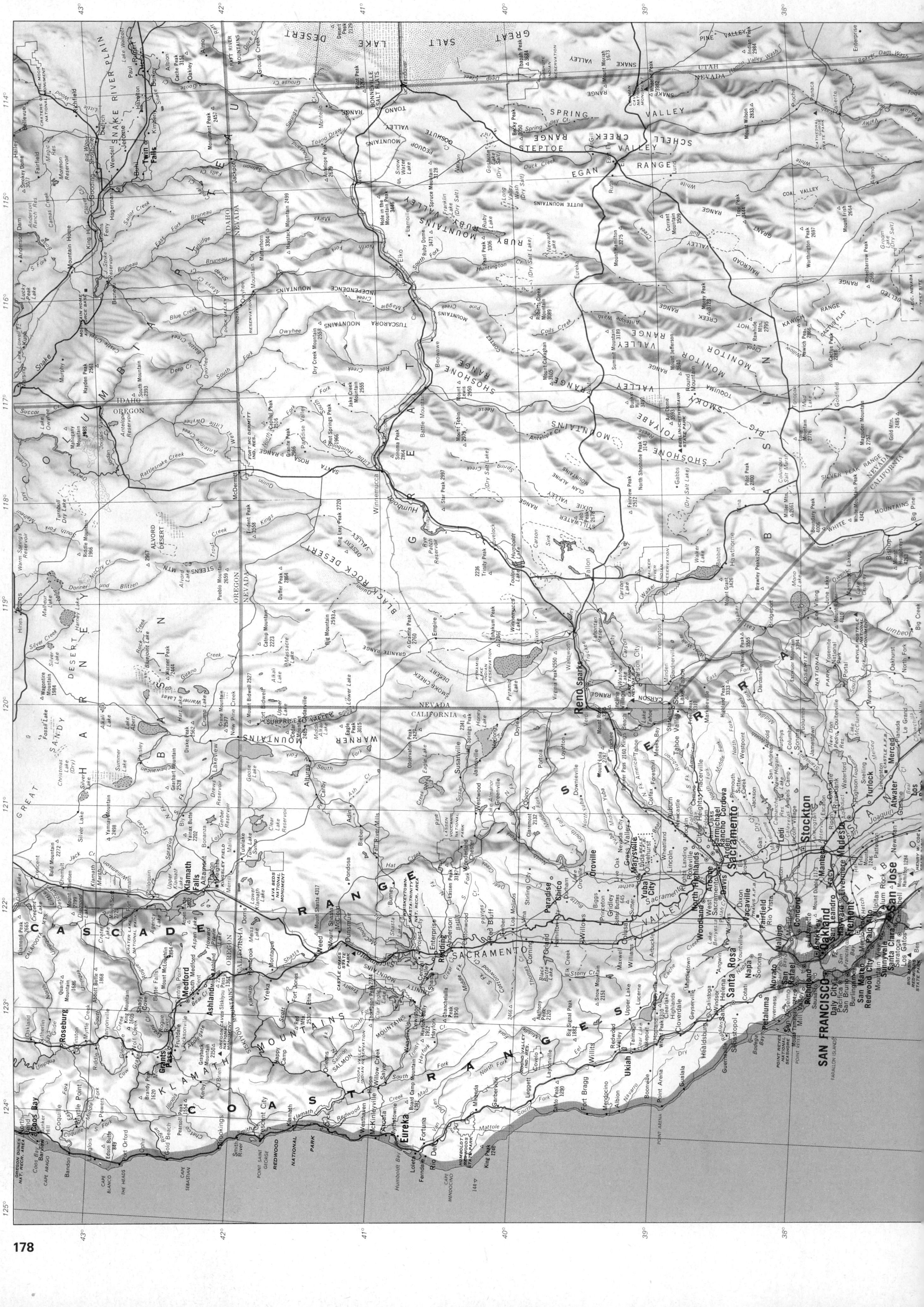

California, Nevada and Hawaii

SAN FRANCISCO · Oakland · San Jose · Sacramento · Stockton · Modesto · Santa Rosa · Napa · Reno · Sparks · Carson City · Klamath Falls · Medford · Ashland · Roseburg · Grants Pass · Eureka · Redding · Chico · Oroville · Marysville · Twin Falls · Ukiah · Fort Bragg · San Rafael · Palo Alto · Fremont · Merced

GREAT SALT LAKE DESERT · UTAH · NEVADA · IDAHO · OREGON · CALIFORNIA · COLUMBIA PLATEAU · GREAT BASIN · SIERRA NEVADA · CASCADE RANGE · KLAMATH MOUNTAINS · COAST RANGES · SACRAMENTO VALLEY · SNAKE RIVER PLAIN · RUBY MOUNTAINS · SHOSHONE RANGE · TOIYABE RANGE · MONITOR RANGE · EGAN RANGE · SCHELL CREEK RANGE · SANTA ROSA RANGE · WARNER MOUNTAINS · BLACK ROCK DESERT · STEENS MTN · ALVORD DESERT · SMOKE CREEK DESERT

179

Kilometers 0 50 100 150 Km.
Statute Miles 0 50 100 150 Mi.

Scale 1:3,000,000   One centimeter represents 30 kilometers.
                      One inch represents approximately 47 miles.

Albers Conical Equal-Area Projection

ATLANTIC OCEAN

CARIBBEAN SEA

WEST INDIES

GREATER ANTILLES

LESSER ANTILLES

Tropic of Cancer

BAHAMAS

BERMUDA (U.K.)   Hamilton

TURKS AND CAICOS ISLANDS (U.K.)

CUBA

La Habana   Havana
Matanzas
Cárdenas
Mariango
Pinar del Río
Santa Clara
Cienfuegos
Sancti Spíritus
Ciego de Ávila
Camagüey
Holguín
Manzanillo
Santiago de Cuba
Guantánamo

ISLA DE PINOS

JAMAICA
Montego Bay
Kingston

CAYMAN IS. (U.K.)

HAITI
Port-au-Prince
HISPANIOLA

DOMINICAN REPUBLIC
Santo Domingo

PUERTO RICO (U.S.)
San Juan
Mayagüez   Ponce

VIRGIN ISLANDS
Charlotte Amalie

ANTIGUA (U.K.)
St. Johns

GUADELOUPE (Fr.)
Basse-Terre

DOMINICA
Roseau

MARTINIQUE (Fr.)
Fort-de-France

SAINT LUCIA
Castries

BARBADOS
Bridgetown

SAINT VINCENT
Kingstown

GRENADA
St. George's

TRINIDAD AND TOBAGO
Port of Spain

NETHERLANDS ANTILLES
Willemstad
Oranjestad

VENEZUELA
Caracas
Maracaibo
Valencia
Barquisimeto
Ciudad Bolívar
Ciudad Guayana
Barcelona
Cumaná
Maturín

COLOMBIA
Bogotá
Medellín
Cali
Barranquilla
Cartagena
Santa Marta
Cúcuta
Bucaramanga
Manizales
Pereira
Armenia

NICARAGUA
COSTA RICA
San José

PANAMA
CANAL ZONE (U.S.)
Colón

GUYANA
LA GRAN SABANA

BRAZIL

FLORIDA
Miami
Tampa
St. Petersburg
Sarasota
West Palm Beach
Fort Lauderdale
Daytona Beach
Orlando
Jacksonville
Key West

GEORGIA
Atlanta
Savannah
Augusta
Macon
Columbus

SOUTH CAROLINA
Columbia
Charleston

NORTH CAROLINA
Charlotte
Greensboro
Raleigh
Durham
Wilmington

VIRGINIA
Norfolk
Newport News
Roanoke

KENTUCKY

Nassau
NEW PROVIDENCE

181

Kilometers 0   200   400   600   Km.
Statute Miles 0   200   400   600   Mi.

Scale 1:12,000,000

One centimeter represents 120 kilometers.
One inch represents approximately 190 miles.

Oblique Conic Conformal Projection

Caribbean Region

GULF OF MEXICO

PACIFIC OCEAN

CARIBBEA

CUBA

GREATER

UNITED STATES

BAHAMA

Copyright © by Rand McNally & Co.
Map prepared by Rand McNally & Co.
A-530100 264

182

Kilometers

Statute Miles

Scale 1:12,000,000

One centimeter represents 120 kilometers.
One inch represents approximately 190 miles.
Oblique Conic Conformal Projection

ATLANTIC OCEAN

BARBADOS
getown

AGO

Georgetown
Charity
Hydro Park
Parika
Bartica
Rosignol
Rockstone
Mackenzie
Skeldon
New Amsterdam
Nieuw Nickerie

GUYANA

Paramaribo
Totness
Nieuw Amsterdam
Moengo
Kwakoegron
Brokopondo
Saint-Élie
Matoury
Cayenne
ÎLE DU DIABLE

SURINAM
WILHELMINA GEBERGTE
Julianatop
1280

FRENCH
GUIANA
Saint-Georges
Oiapoque

TUMUC-HUMAC MOUNTAINS

CABO ORANGE

Saül
930

Cunani

Calçoene

Amapá

ILHA DE MARACÁ

Serra do Navio

Macapá
Mazagão

ILHA CAVIANA
ILHA MEXIANA

ILHA DE MARAJÓ

CABO MAGUARINHO

Equator

Belém

Amazon

Santarém

Parintins

Faro

Óbidos
Alenquer
Monte Alegre

São Luís

Teresina

Fortaleza

Natal

João Pessoa

Olinda
Recife
Caruaru

Maceió

Aracaju

Salvador

B R A Z I L

PLANALTO DO
MATO GROSSO

Cuiabá

Corumbá

Brasília
Goiânia
Anápolis

PLANALTO

CENTRAL

Belo
Horizonte

Vitória
da Conquista

Ilhéus
Itabuna

Governador
Valadares

Vitória

Campo Grande

São José
do Rio Prêto

Araçatuba

Presidente Prudente

Uberlândia

Uberaba

Ribeirão
Prêto

Campinas

São Paulo

Santos

RIO DE JANEIRO
Niterói

Tropic of Capricorn

185

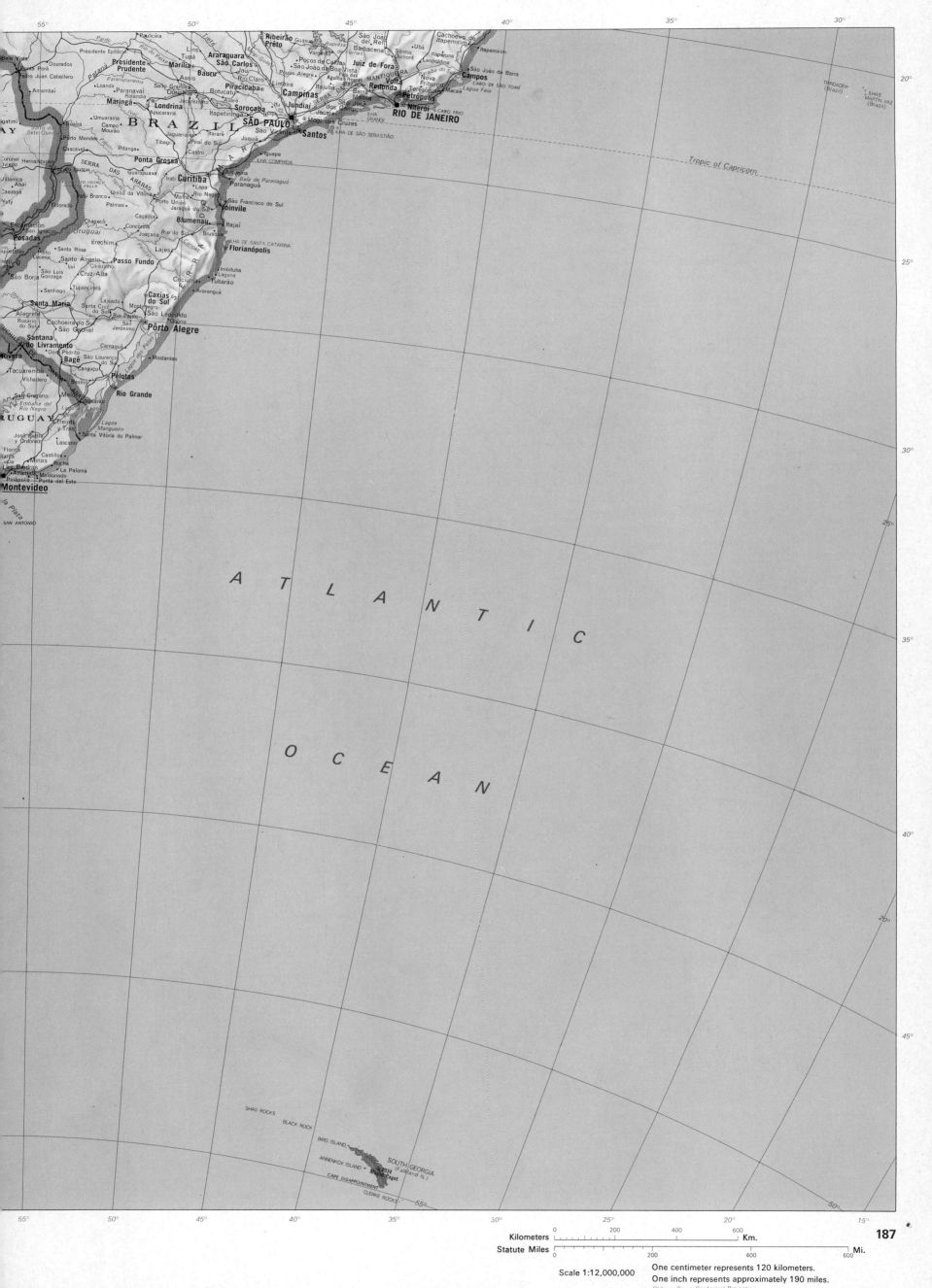

ATLANTIC

OCEAN

BRAZIL

Tropic of Capricorn

RIO DE JANEIRO

SÃO PAULO

Santos

Curitiba

Florianópolis

Pôrto Alegre

Rio Grande

Pelotas

Montevideo

SHAG ROCKS   BLACK ROCK

SOUTH GEORGIA

187

Scale 1:12,000,000

One centimeter represents 120 kilometers.

One inch represents approximately 190 miles.

Oblique Conic Conformal Projection

ATLANTIC

OCEAN

Kilometers 0 100 200 300 Km.

Statute Miles 0 100 200 300 Mi.

Scale 1:6,000,000
One centimeter represents 60 kilometers.
One inch represents approximately 95 miles.
Oblique Conic Conformal Projection

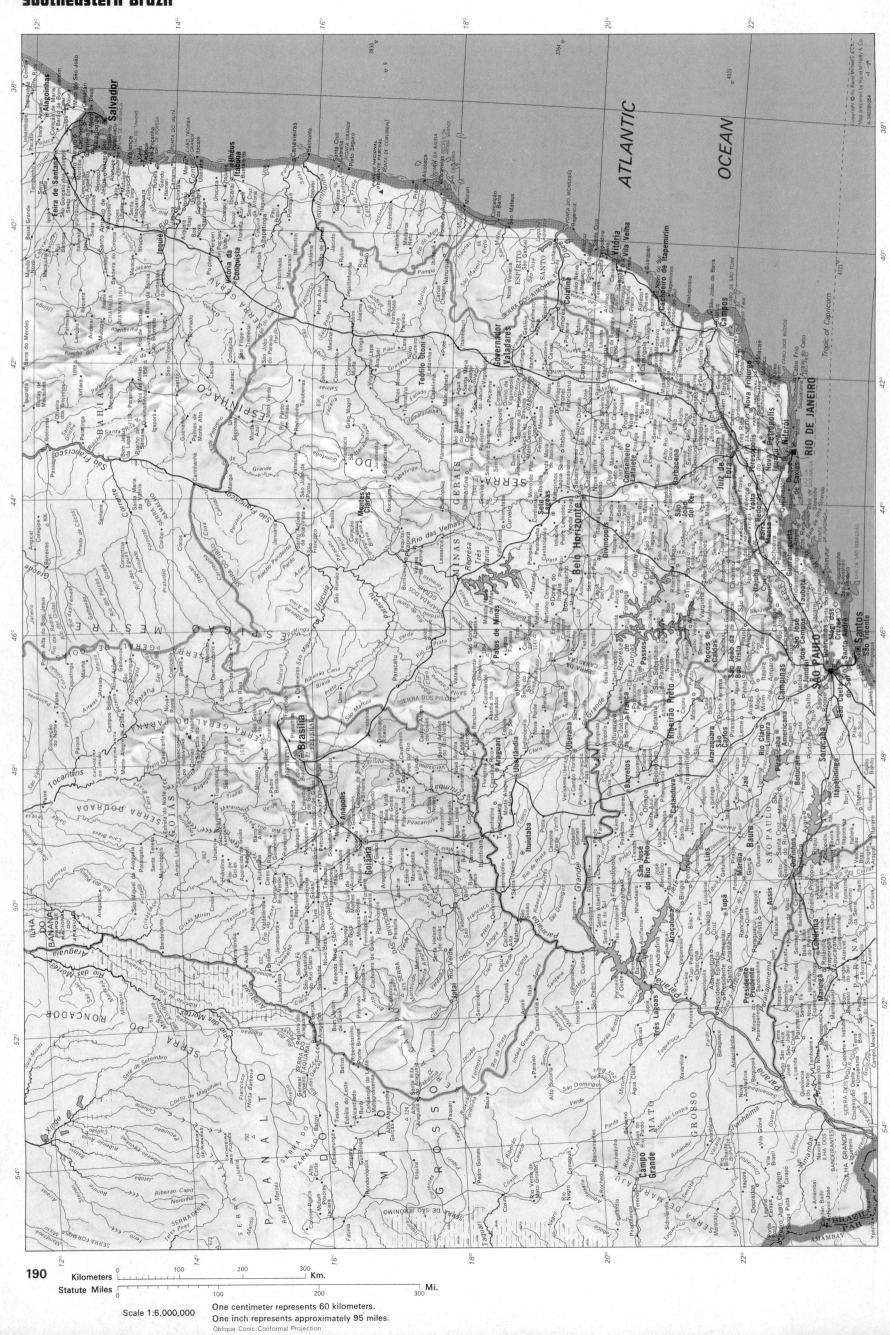

Kilometers 0 100 200 300 Km.

Statute Miles 0 100 300 Mi.

Scale 1:6,000,000

One centimeter represents 60 kilometers.
One inch represents approximately 95 miles.
Oblique Conic Conformal Projection

World Political Information Table

This table lists all countries and dependencies in the world, U.S. States, Canadian provinces, and other important regions and political subdivisions. Besides specifying the form of government for all political areas, the table classifies them into six groups according to their political status. Units labeled **A** are independent sovereign nations. Units labeled **B** are independent as regards internal affairs, but for purposes of foreign affairs they are under the protection of another country. Areas under military government are also labeled **B**. Units labeled **C** are colonies, overseas territories, dependencies,

etc., of other countries. Together the **A**, **B**, and **C** areas comprise practically the entire inhabited area of the world. The areas labeled **D** are physically separate units, such as groups of islands, which are *not* separate countries, but form part of a nation or dependency. Units labeled **E** are States, provinces, Soviet Republics, or similar major administrative subdivisions of important countries. Units in the table with no letter designation are regions or other areas that do not constitute separate political units by themselves.

Region or Political Division	Area in sq. miles	Estimated Population 1/1/77	Pop. per sq. mi.	Form of Government and Ruling Power	Capital; Largest City (unless same)	Predominant Languages
Afars & Issas, see Djibouti						
Afghanistan†	250,000	20,010,000	80	Republic..........................A	Kābul	Dari, Pushtu
Africa	11,706,727	420,700,000	36		........; Al-Qāhirah (Cairo)	
Alabama	51,609	3,667,300	71	State (U.S.)...................E	Montgomery; Birmingham	
Alaska	586,412	367,400	0.6	State (U.S.)...................E	Juneau; Anchorage	English, Indian, Eskimo
Albania†	11,100	2,580,000	232	People's Republic.................A	Tiranë	Albanian
Alberta	255,285	1,835,000	7.2	Province (Canada)................E	Edmonton	English
Algeria†	919,595	17,535,000	19	Republic.......................A	Alger (Algiers)	Arabic, French, Berber
American Samoa	76	28,000	368	Unincorporated Territory (U.S.).....C	Pago Pago	Polynesian, English
Andaman & Nicobar Is.	3,202	145,000	45	Territory (India)................D	Port Blair	Andaman, Nicobar Malay
Andorra	175	27,000	154	Principality.....................A	Andorra	Catalan, Spanish, French
Angola†	481,353	7,205,000	15	People's Republic.................A	Luanda	Portuguese, native languages
Anguilla	35	15,000	429	Colony (U.K.)..................C	The Valley; South Hill	English
Antarctica	5,100,000					
Antigua (incl. Barbuda)	171	73,000	427	Associated State (U.K.)...........B	St. Johns	English
Arabian Peninsula	1,142,050	19,112,000	17		........; Al-Kuwayt	Arabic
Argentina†	1,072,162	25,880,000	24	Federal Republic..................A	Buenos Aires	Spanish
Arizona	113,909	2,333,700	20	State (U.S.)...................E	Phoenix	
Arkansas	53,104	2,132,800	40	State (U.S.)...................E	Little Rock	
Arm'anskaja (Armenia) S.S.R.	11,500	2,835,000	247	Soviet Socialist Republic (U.S.S.R.)....E	Jerevan	Armenian, Russian
Aruba	69	64,000	928	Division of Netherlands Antilles (Neth.)..D	Oranjestad	Dutch, Spanish, English, Papiamento
Ascension I.	34	1,200	35	Dependency of St. Helena (U.K.).......D	Georgetown	English
Asia	17,085,000	2,405,300,000	141		........; Tōkyō	
Australia†	2,967,909	13,760,000	4.6	Monarchy (Federal) (Comm. of Nations)....A	Canberra; Sydney	English
Australian Capital Territory	939	205,000	218	Federal Territory (Australia)..........E	Canberra	English
Austria†	32,374	7,540,000	233	Federal Republic..................A	Wien (Vienna)	German
Azerbajdžanskaja (Azerbaidzhan) S.S.R.	33,450	5,700,000	170	Soviet Socialist Republic (U.S.S.R.)......E	Baku	Turkic languages, Russian, Armenian
Azores Is.	905	280,000	309	Part of Portugal (3 Districts)........D	........; Ponta Delgada	Portuguese
Baden-Württemberg	13,803	9,165,000	664	State (Germany, Federal Republic of)....E	Stuttgart	German
Bahamas†	5,380	215,000	40	Parliamentary State (Comm. of Nations).....A	Nassau	English
Bahrain†	240	275,000	1,146	Emirate.......................A	Al-Manāmah	Arabic
Balearic Is.	1,936	585,000	302	Part of Spain (Baleares Province)......D	Palma	Catalan, Spanish
Baltic Republics	67,150	7,320,000	109	Union of Soviet Socialist Republics........E	........; Rīga	Lithuanian, Latvian, Estonian, Russian
Bangladesh†	55,126	79,550,000	1,443	Republic (Comm. of Nations).........A	Dacca	Bangla, English
Barbados†	166	245,000	1,476	Parliamentary State (Comm. of Nations).....A	Bridgetown	English
Basutoland, see Lesotho						
Bayern (Bavaria)	27,239	10,775,000	396	State (Germany, Federal Republic of)......E	München (Munich)	German
Bechuanaland, see Botswana						
Belgium†	11,781	9,845,000	836	Monarchy......................A	Bruxelles (Brussels)	Dutch, French
Belize	8,867	146,000	16	Colony (U.K.)..................C	Belmopan; Belize	English, Spanish, Indian languages
Belorusskaja (Byelorussia) S.S.R.†	80,150	9,490,000	118	Soviet Socialist Republic (U.S.S.R.).......E	Minsk	Byelorussian, Polish
Benelux	28,549	24,030,000	842		Bruxelles (Brussels)	Dutch, French, Luxembourgish
Benin (Dahomey)†	43,484	3,230,000	74	Republic.......................A	Porto Novo; Cotonou	French, native languages
Berlin, West	185	2,010,000	10,865	State (Germany, Federal Republic of).......E	Berlin (West)	German
Bermuda	21	57,000	2,714	Colony (U.K.)..................C	Hamilton	English
Bhutan†	18,200	1,210,000	66	Monarchy (Indian protection)..........B	Paro and Thimbu	Tibetan dialects
Bismarck Archipelago	18,965	300,000	16	Part of Papua New Guinea............D	........; Rabaul	Malay-Polynesian and Papuan languages
Bolivia†	424,164	5,865,000	14	Republic.......................A	Sucre and La Paz; La Paz	Spanish, Quechua, Aymará
Borneo, Indonesian (Kalimantan)	208,286	5,880,000	28	Part of Indonesia.................D	........; Banjarmasin	Bahasa Indonesia (Indonesian)
Botswana (Bechuanaland)†	231,805	715,000	3.0	Republic (Comm. of Nations).........A	Gaborone; Francistown	English, Setswana
Brazil†	3,286,487	112,670,000	34	Federal Republic..................A	Brasília; São Paulo	Portuguese
Bremen	156	720,000	4,615	State (Germany, Federal Republic of)......E	Bremen	German
British Antarctic Territory (excl. Antarctic mainland)	2,040	Winter pop. 75	....	Colony (U.K.)..................C	Stanley, Falkland Islands	
British Columbia	366,255	2,505,700	6.8	Province (Canada)................E	Victoria; Vancouver	English
British Guiana, see Guyana						
British Honduras, see Belize						
British Indian Ocean Territory	18	900	50	Colony (U.K.)..................C	Administered from London	English
Brunei	2,226	160,000	72	Sultanate (U.K. protection).........B	Bandar Seri Begawan	Malay-Polynesian languages, English
Bulgaria†	42,823	8,790,000	205	People's Republic.................A	Sofija (Sofia)	Bulgarian
Burma†	261,790	32,570,000	124	Federal Republic..................A	Rangoon	Burmese, English
Burundi (Urundi)†	10,747	3,880,000	361	Republic.......................A	Bujumbura	Kirundi, French, Swahili
California	158,693	21,491,300	135	State (U.S.)...................E	Sacramento; Los Angeles	
Cambodia†	69,898	8,440,000	121	People's Republic.................A	Phnum Pénh	Cambodian (Khmer), French
Cameroon†	183,569	6,575,000	36	Federal Republic..................A	Yaoundé; Douala	French, English, native languages
Canada†	3,851,809	23,270,000	6.0	Monarchy (Federal) (Comm. of Nations)......A	Ottawa; Montréal	English, French
Canal Zone	553	43,000	78	Under U.S. Jurisdiction...........C	Balboa Heights; Balboa	English, Spanish
Canary Is.	2,808	1,310,000	467	Part of Spain (2 Provinces).........D	........; Las Palmas de Gran Canaria	Spanish
Canton & Enderbury	27	....	....	U.K.-U.S. Administration.........C	Canton Island	Malay-Polynesian languages, English
Cape Verde†	1,557	305,000	196	Republic.......................A	Praia; Mindelo	Portuguese
Caroline Is.	463	75,000	162	Part of U.S. Pacific Is. Trust Ter. (4 Districts).D		Malay-Polynesian languages, English
Cayman Is.	100	12,000	120	Colony (U.K.)..................C	Georgetown	English
Celebes (Sulawesi)	72,987	9,735,000	133	Part of Indonesia.................D	........; Ujung Pandang	Malay-Polynesian languages, Indonesian
Central African Empire	240,535	2,760,000	11	Empire.......................A	Bangui	French, native languages
Central America	202,063	19,454,000	96		........; Guatemala	Spanish, Indian languages
Central Asia, Soviet	493,950	23,310,000	47	Union of Soviet Socialist Republics	........; Taškent	Uzbek, Russian, Kirghiz, Turkoman, Tadzhik
Ceylon, see Sri Lanka						
Chad†	495,800	4,150,000	8.4	Republic.......................A	Ndjamena	French, native languages
Channel Is. (Guernsey, Jersey, etc.)	75	131,000	1,747		........; St. Helier	English, French
Chile†	292,258	10,510,000	36	Republic.......................A	Santiago	Spanish
China (excl. Taiwan)†	3,691,500	859,480,000	233	People's Republic.................A	Beijing (Peking); Shanghai	Chinese, Mongolian, Turkish, Tungus
China (Nationalist), see Taiwan						
Christmas I. (Indian Ocean)	52	3,400	65	External Territory (Australia).........C		Chinese, Malay, English
Cocos (Keeling) Is.	5	700	120	External Territory (Australia).........C		Malay, English

† Member of the United Nations (1977).

191

Region or Political Division	Area in sq. miles	Estimated Population 1/1/77	Pop. per sq. mi.	Form of Government and Ruling Power	Capital; Largest City (unless same)	Predominant Languages
Colombia†	439,737	24,495,000	56	Republic...A	Bogotá	Spanish
Colorado	104,247	2,587,200	25	State (U.S.)...E	Denver	....
Commonwealth of Nations	10,713,229	967,928,000	90		London	
Comoro Is.†	694	290,000	418	Republic...A	Moroni	Malagasy, French
Congo†	132,000	1,405,000	11	Republic...A	Brazzaville	French, native languages
Congo, The, see Zaire						
Connecticut	5,009	3,106,800	620	State (U.S.)...E	Hartford	
Cook Is.	93	17,000	183	Self-governing Territory, (New Zealand)...C	Avarua	Malay-Polynesian languages
Corsica	3,352	220,000	66	Part of France (2 Departments)...D	............; Bastia	French, Italian
Costa Rica†	19,600	2,045,000	104		San José	Spanish
Cuba†	44,218	9,645,000	218	People's Republic...A	La Habana (Havana)	Spanish
Curaçao	173	160,000	925	Division of Netherlands Antilles (Neth.)...D	Willemstad	Dutch, Spanish, English, Papiamento
Cyprus†	3,572	630,000	176	Republic (Comm. of Nations)...A	Levkósia	Greek, Turkish, English
Czechoslovakia†	49,373	14,975,000	303	People's Republic...A	Praha (Prague)	Czech, Slovak
Dahomey, see Benin						
Delaware	2,057	584,600	284	State (U.S.)...E	Dover;Wilmington	
Denmark†	16,629	5,085,000	306	Monarchy...A	København (Copenhagen)	Danish
Denmark and Possessions	857,169	5,177,000	6.0		København (Copenhagen)	Danish, Faeroese, Greenlandic
District of Columbia	67	707,000	10,552	District (U.S.)...E	Washington	
Djibouti†	8,900	110,000	12	Republic...A	Djibouti	Arabic, French
Dominica	290	77,000	266	Associated State (U.K.)...B	Roseau	English, French
Dominican Republic†	18,816	4,905,000	261	Republic...A	Santo Domingo	Spanish
Ecuador†	109,483	6,945,000	63	Republic...A	Quito; Guayaquil	Spanish, Quechua
Egypt†	386,661	38,890,000	101	Republic‡‡...A	Al-Qāhirah (Cairo)	Arabic
Ellice Is., see Tuvalu						
El Salvador†	8,260	4,190,000	507	Republic...A	San Salvador	Spanish
England (excl. Monmouthshire)	50,332	46,490,000	924	United Kingdom...A	............; London	English
England & Wales	58,348	49,255,000	844	Administrative division of United Kingdom...E	London	English, Welsh
Equatorial Guinea†	10,830	320,000	30	Republic...A	Malabo	Spanish, native languages
Estonskaja (S.S.R.)	17,400	1,445,000	83	Soviet Socialist Republic (U.S.S.R.)...E	Tallinn	Estonian, Russian
Ethiopia†	471,778	29,010,000	61	Provisional Military Government...A	Addis Abeba	Amharic, Arabic, Hamitic dialects
Eurasia	20,910,000	3,055,900,000	146		..........; Tōkyō	....
Europe	3,825,000	650,600,000	170		............; London	....
Faeroe Is.	540	41,000	76	Self-governing Territory (Denmark)...B	Tórshavn	Danish, Faeroese
Falkland Is. (excl. Deps)	4,618	1,900	0.4	Colony (U.K.)...C	Stanley	English
Fernando Poo, see Macías Nguema Biyogo						
Fiji†	7,055	590,000	84	Monarchy (Federal) (Comm. of Nations)...A	Suva	English, Fijian, Hindustani
Finland†	130,120	4,765,000	37	Republic...A	Helsinki (Helsingfors)	Finnish, Swedish
Florida	58,560	8,749,000	149	State (U.S.)...E	Tallahassee; Miami	
France†	211,207	53,290,000	252	Republic...A	Paris	French
France and Possessions	229,981	55,039,000	239		Paris	
Franklin	549,253	9,000	0.02	District of Northwest Territories, Canada...E	..........; Cambridge Bay	English, Eskimo, Indian
French Guiana	35,100	65,000	1.9	Overseas Department (France)...C	Cayenne	French
French Polynesia	1,550	134,000	86	Overseas Territory (France)...C	Papeete	Malay-Polynesian languages, French
French Somaliland, see Djibouti						
French Southern & Antarctic Ter. (excl. Adélie Coast)	2,918	200	0.07	Overseas Territory (France)...C	....	French
French West Indies	1,112	740,000	665	...........................A	............; Fort-de-France	French
Gabon†	103,347	535,000	5.2	Republic...A	Libreville	French, native languages
Galápagos Is. (Colon, Archipélago de)	3,075	4,200	1.3	Province (Ecuador)...D	Puerto Baquerizo Moreno	Spanish
Gambia†	4,361	535,000	123	Republic (Comm. of Nations)...A	Banjul	English, native languages
Georgia	58,876	5,014,000	85	State (U.S.)...E	Atlanta	
Germany (Entire)	137,727	78,335,000	569		.........; Essen	German
German Democratic Republic†	41,768	16,745,000	401	People's Republic...A	Berlin (East)	German
Germany, Federal Republic of (incl. West Berlin)†	95,968	61,590,000	642	Federal Republic...A	Bonn; Essen	German
Ghana†	92,100	10,250,000	111	Republic (Comm. of Nations)...A	Accra	English, native languages
Gibraltar	2	31,000	15,500	Colony (U.K.)...C	Gibraltar	Spanish, English
Gilbert Islands	331	55,000	166	Colony (U.K.)...C	Bairiki	Malay-Polynesian languages, English
Great Britain & Northern Ireland, see United Kingdom						
Greece†	50,944	9,165,000	180	Republic...A	Athínai (Athens)	Greek
Greenland	840,000	51,000	0.06	Overseas Territory (Denmark)...C	Godthåb	Greenlandic, Danish, Eskimo
Grenada	133	111,000	835	Parliamentary State (Comm. of Nations)...A	Saint George's	English
Gruzinskaja (Georgia) S.S.R.	26,900	5,000,000	186	Soviet Socialist Republic (U.S.S.R.)...E	Tbilisi	Georgic, Armenian, Russian
Guadeloupe (incl. Dependencies)	687	365,000	531	Overseas Department (France)...C	Basse-Terre; Pointe-à-Pitre	French
Guam	212	116,000	547	Unincorporated Territory (U.S.)...C	Agana	English, Chamorro
Guatemala†	42,042	6,065,000	144	Republic...A	Guatemala	Spanish, Indian languages
Guernsey (incl. Dependencies)	30	56,000	1,867	Bailiwick (U.K.)...C	St. Peter Port	English, French
Guinea†	94,964	4,585,000	48	Republic...A	Conakry	French, native languages
Guinea-Bissau†	13,948	535,000	38	Republic...A	Bissau	Portuguese, native languages
Guyana†	83,000	820,000	9.9	Republic (Comm. of Nations)...A	Georgetown	English
Haiti†	10,714	4,690,000	438	Republic...A	Port-au-Prince	Creole, French
Hamburg	288	1,725,000	5,990	State (Germany, Federal Republic of)...E	Hamburg	German
Hawaii	6,450	882,200	137	State (U.S.)...E	Honolulu	English, Japanese, Hawaiian
Hessen (Hesse)	8,150	5,535,000	679	State (Germany, Federal Republic of)...E	Wiesbaden; Frankfurt am Main	German
Hispaniola	29,530	9,595,000	325		..........; Santo Domingo	French, Spanish
Holland, see Netherlands						
Honduras†	43,277	2,945,000	68	Republic...A	Tegucigalpa	Spanish
Hong Kong	403	4,580,000	11,365	Colony (U.K.)...C	Victoria (Xianggang)	Chinese, English
Hungary†	35,920	10,625,000	296	People's Republic...A	Budapest	Hungarian
Iceland†	39,800	225,000	5.7	Republic...A	Reykjavík	Icelandic
Idaho	83,557	853,000	10	State (U.S.)...E	Boise (Boise City)	
Illinois	56,400	11,139,000	198	State (U.S.)...E	Springfield; Chicago	
India (incl. part of Kashmir)†	1,269,210	615,860,000	485	Republic (Comm. of Nations)...A	New Delhi; Calcutta	Hindi and other Indo-Aryan languages, Dravidian languages, English
Indiana	36,291	5,325,800	147	State (U.S.)...E	Indianapolis	
Indonesia (incl. West Irian)†	753,271	136,920,000	182	Republic...A	Jakarta	Bahasa Indonesia (Indonesian), Chinese, English
Iowa	56,290	2,886,000	51	State (U.S.)...E	Des Moines	
Iran (Persia)†	636,300	34,325,000	54	Monarchy...A	Tehrān	Farsi, Turkish dialects, Kurdish
Iraq†	167,925	11,650,000	69	Republic...A	Baghdād	Arabic, Kurdish
Ireland†	27,137	3,200,000	118	Republic...A	Dublin (Baile Átha Cliath)	English, Irish
Isle of Man	227	59,000	260	Possession (U.K.)...C	Douglas	English
Israel†	8,019	3,550,000	443	Republic‡‡...A	Yerushalayim; Tel Aviv-Yafo	Hebrew, Arabic, English
Italy†	116,304	56,450,000	485	Republic...A	Roma (Rome); Milano	Italian
Ivory Coast†	124,504	7,040,000	57	Republic...A	Abidjan	French, native languages

† Member of the United Nations (1977).
‡‡ Areas for Egypt, Israel, Jordan and Syria do not reflect de facto changes which took place during 1967.

Region or Political Division	Area in sq. miles	Estimated Population 1/1/77	Pop. per sq. mi.	Form of Government and Ruling Power	Capital; Largest City (unless same)	Predominant Languages
Jamaica†	4,232	2,075,000	490	Parliamentary State (Comm. of Nations)........A	Kingston	English
Japan†	143,751	113,750,000	791	Monarchy................................A	Tōkyō	Japanese
Java (Jawa) (incl. Madura)	51,033	86,850,000	1,702	Part of Indonesia (5 Provinces)...............D	........; Jakarta	Bahasa Indonesia (Indonesian), Chinese, English
Jersey	45	75,000	1,667	Bailiwick (U.K.)........................C	St. Helier	English, French
Jordan†	37,738	3,505,000	93	Monarchy‡‡..............................A	'Ammān	Arabic
Kansas	82,264	2,724,200	28	State (U.S.)...........................E	Topeka; Wichita	
Kashmir, Jammu &	86,024	5,225,000	61	In dispute (India & Pakistan).................	Srinagar	Kashmiri, Punjabi
Kazachskaja (Kazakh) S.S.R.	1,048,300	14,415,000	14	Soviet Socialist Republic (U.S.S.R.)..........E	Alma-Ata	Turkic languages, Russian
Keewatin	228,160	4,000	0.02	District of Northwest Territories, Canada......E	........; Baker Lake	English, Eskimo, Indian
Kentucky	40,395	3,457,500	86	State (U.S.)...........................E	Frankfort; Louisville	
Kenya†	224,960	14,115,000	63	Republic (Comm. of Nations)................A	Nairobi	English, Swahili, native languages
Kerguélen	2,700	90	0.03	Part of French Southern & Antarctic Ter. (Fr.)..D	....	French
Kirgizskaja (Kirghiz) S.S.R.	76,650	3,350,000	44	Soviet Socialist Republic (U.S.S.R.)..........E	Frunze	Turkic languages, Persian
Korea (Entire)‡	85,052	51,950,000	611		........; Sŏul (Seoul)	Korean
Korea, North	46,540	16,465,000	354	People's Republic........................A	P'yŏngyang	Korean
Korea, South	38,025	35,485,000	933	Republic..............................A	Sŏul (Seoul)	Korean
Kuwait†	6,880	1,080,000	157	Sheikdom.............................A	Al-Kuwayt	Arabic
Labrador	112,826	35,000	0.3	Part of Newfoundland Province, Canada........D	........; Labrador City	English, Eskimo
Laos†	91,429	3,375,000	37	People's Republic ....A	Viangchan (Vientiane)	Lao, French
Latin America	7,924,731	332,884,000	42		........; Ciudad de México (Mexico City)	
Latvijskaja (Latvia) S.S.R.	24,600	2,525,000	103	Soviet Socialist Republic (U.S.S.R.)..........E	Rīga	Latvian, Russian
Lebanon†	4,015	3,005,000	748	Republic..............................A	Bayrūt (Beirut)	Arabic, French, English
Lesotho (Basutoland)†	11,720	1,075,000	92	Monarchy (Comm. of Nations)...............A	Maseru	English, Sesotho
Liberia†	43,000	1,770,000	41	Republic..............................A	Monrovia	English, native languages
Libya†	679,362	2,580,000	3.8	Republic..............................A	Tarābulus (Tripoli)	Arabic
Liechtenstein	62	25,000	403	Principality............................A	Vaduz	German
Litovskaja (Lithuania) S.S.R.	25,150	3,350,000	133	Soviet Socialist Republic (U.S.S.R.)..........E	Vilnius	Lithuanian, Polish, Russian
Louisiana	48,523	3,818,900	79	State (U.S.)...........................E	Baton Rouge; New Orleans	
Luxembourg†	998	370,000	371	Grand Duchy...........................A	Luxembourg	French, German, Luxembourgish
Macau	6	280,000	46,667	Overseas Province (Portugal)................C	Macau	Chinese, Portuguese
Macías Nguema Biyogo	785	79,000	101	Part of Equatorial Guinea..................D	Malabo	Spanish, native languages
Mackenzie	527,490	27,000	0.05	District of Northwest Territories, Canada......E	........; Yellowknife	English, Eskimo, Indian
Madagascar (Malagasy Republic)†	226,658	7,770,000	34	Republic..............................A	Antananarivo	French, Malagasy
Madeira Is.	308	260,000	844	Part of Portugal (Funchal District)............D	Funchal	Portuguese
Maine	33,215	1,075,800	32	State (U.S.)...........................E	Augusta; Portland	
Malawi (Nyasaland)†	45,747	5,225,000	114	Republic (Comm. of Nations)................A	Lilongwe; Blantyre	Chichewa, English
Malaya	50,700	10,380,000	205	Part of Malaysia........................	........; Kuala Lumpur	Malay, Chinese, English
Malaysia†	128,430	12,315,000	96	Constitutional Monarchy (Comm. of Nations)...A	Kuala Lumpur	Malay, Chinese, English
Maldives†	115	145,000	1,261	Republic..............................A	Male	Divehi, Arabic
Mali†	478,655	5,925,000	12	Republic..............................A	Bamako	French, Bambara
Malta†	122	275,000	2,254	Republic (Comm. of Nations)................A	Valletta	English, Maltese
Manitoba	251,000	1,035,000	4.1	Province (Canada).......................E	Winnipeg	English
Mariana Is. (excl. Guam)	184	15,000	82	District of U.S. Pacific Is. Trust Ter............D	Saipan	Malay-Polynesian languages, English
Maritime Provinces (excl. Newfoundland)	51,963	1,655,000	32	Canada...............................	........; Halifax	English
Marshall Is.	70	25,000	357	District of U.S. Pacific Is. Trust Ter............D	Majuro	Malay-Polynesian languages, English
Martinique	425	375,000	882	Overseas Department (France)...............C	Fort-de-France	French
Maryland	10,577	4,130,000	390	State (U.S.)...........................E	Annapolis; Baltimore	
Massachusetts	8,257	5,854,700	709	State (U.S.)...........................E	Boston	
Mauritania†	397,950	1,405,000	3.5	Republic..............................A	Nouakchott	Arabic, French
Mauritius (incl. Dependencies)†	789	905,000	1,147	Parliamentary State (Comm. of Nations).......A	Port Louis	Indo-Aryan languages, French, Creole, English
Mayotte	144	31,000	215	Overseas Territory (France)..................C	Dzaoudzi	French
Mexico†	761,604	63,170,000	83	Federal Republic........................A	Ciudad de México (Mexico City)	Spanish
Michigan	58,216	9,221,800	158	State (U.S.)...........................E	Lansing; Detroit	
Middle America	1,054,731	110,384,000	105		........; Ciudad de México (Mexico City)	
Midway Is.	2	2,100	1,050	Possession (U.S.).......................C		English
Minnesota	84,068	3,957,400	47	State (U.S.)...........................E	St. Paul; Minneapolis	
Mississippi	47,716	2,372,600	50	State (U.S.)...........................E	Jackson	
Missouri	69,686	4,777,900	69	State (U.S.)...........................E	Jefferson City; St. Louis	
Moldavskaja (Moldavia) S.S.R.	13,000	3,895,000	300	Soviet Socialist Republic (U.S.S.R.)..........E	Kišin'ov (Kishinev)	Moldavian, Russian, Ukrainian
Monaco	0.6	26,000	43,333	Principality............................A	Monaco	French, Italian
Mongolia†	604,200	1,500,000	2.5	People's Republic.......................A	Ulaanbaatar (Ulan Bator)	Mongolian
Montana	147,138	763,300	5.2	State (U.S.)...........................E	Helena; Billings	
Montserrat	39	12,000	308	Colony (U.K.)..........................C	Plymouth	English
Morocco†	172,415	18,010,000	104	Monarchy.............................A	Rabat; Casablanca	Arabic, Berber, French
Mozambique†	302,329	9,560,000	32	People's Republic.......................A	Maputo (Lourenço Marques)	Portuguese, native languages
Nauru	8	7,300	913	Republic (Comm. of Nations)............... A		Nauruan, English
Nebraska	77,227	1,559,000	20	State (U.S.)...........................E	Lincoln; Omaha	
Nepal†	54,362	12,950,000	238	Monarchy.............................A	Kātmāndu	Nepali, Tibeto-Burman languages
Netherlands†	15,770	13,815,000	876	Monarchy.............................A	Amsterdam and s'-Gravenhage (The Hague); Amsterdam	Dutch
Netherlands and Possessions	16,141	14,055,000	871		Amsterdam and s'-Gravenhage; Amsterdam	
Netherlands Antilles	371	240,000	647	Self-governing Territory (Netherlands)..........C	Willemstad	Dutch, Spanish, English, Papiamento
Netherlands Guiana, see Surinam						
Nevada	110,540	619,200	5.6	State (U.S.)...........................E	Carson City; Las Vegas	
New Brunswick	28,354	695,000	25	Province (Canada).......................E	Fredericton; Saint John	English, French
New Caledonia (incl. Deps.)	7,358	144,000	20	Overseas Territory (France)..................C	Nouméa	Malay-Polynesian languages, French
New England	66,608	12,268,000	184	United States...........................	........; Boston	English
Newfoundland	156,185	560,000	3.6	Province (Canada).......................E	St. John's	English
Newfoundland (excl. Labrador)	43,359	525,000	12		........; St. John's	English
New Hampshire	9,304	836,000	90	State (U.S.)...........................E	Concord; Manchester	
New Hebrides	5,700	99,000	17	Condominium (France-U.K.).................C	Vila	Malay-Polynesian languages, French, English
New Jersey	7,836	7,333,900	936	State (U.S.)...........................E	Trenton; Newark	
New Mexico	121,666	1,185,800	9.7	State (U.S.)...........................E	Santa Fe; Albuquerque	
New South Wales	309,433	4,870,000	16	State (Australia).........................E	Sydney	English
New York	49,576	18,138,900	366	State (U.S.)...........................E	Albany; New York	
New Zealand†	103,736	3,180,000	31	Monarchy (Comm. of Nations)...............A	Wellington; Auckland	English
Nicaragua†	50,200	2,275,000	45	Republic..............................A	Managua	Spanish
Niedersachsen (Lower Saxony)	18,299	7,220,000	395	State (Germany, Federal Republic of)..........E	Hannover	German
Niger†	489,200	4,805,000	9.8	Republic..............................A	Niamey	Hausa, Arabic, French
Nigeria†	356,669	65,400,000	183	Republic (Comm. of Nations)................A	Lagos	Hausa, Ibo, Yoruba, English
Niue	100	3,100	31	Island Territory (New Zealand)...............C	Alofi	Malay-Polynesian languages, English
Nordrhein-Westfalen (North Rhine Westphalia)	13,145	17,110,000	1,302	State (Germany, Federal Republic of)..........E	Düsseldorf; Essen	German
Norfolk Island	14	2,400	171	External Territory (Australia)................C	Kingston	English

† Member of the United Nations (1977).
‡ Includes 487 sq. miles of demilitarized zone, not included in North or South Korea figures.
‡‡ Areas for Egypt, Israel, Jordan and Syria do not reflect de facto changes which took place during 1967.

Region or Political Division	Area in sq. miles	Estimated Population 1/1/77	Pop. per sq. mi.	Form of Government and Ruling Power	Capital; Largest City (unless same)	Predominant Languages
North America................	9,420,000	349,300,000	37		........; New York	
North Borneo, see Sabah...........						
North Carolina................	52,586	5,558,500	106	State (U.S.)...............................E	Raleigh; Charlotte	
North Dakota.................	70,665	640,500	9.1	State (U.S.).................................E	Bismarck; Fargo	
Northern Ireland................	5,463	1,525,000	279	Administrative division of United Kingdom.....E	Belfast	English
Northern Rhodesia, see Zambia.....						
Northern Territory..............	520,280	100,000	0.2	Territory (Australia)...........................E	Darwin	English, Aboriginal languages
North Polar Regions.............						
Northwest Territories.............	1,304,903	40,000	0.03	Territory (Canada)..........................E	Yellowknife	English, Eskimo, Indian
Norway†......................	125,181	4,045,000	32	Monarchy.....................................A	Oslo	Norwegian (Riksmål and Landsmål)
Nova Scotia..................	21,425	840,000	39	Province (Canada)............................E	Halifax	English
Nyasaland, see Malawi...........						
Oceania (incl. Australia)..........	3,295,000	21,600,000	6.6		........; Sydney	
Ohio........................	41,222	10,781,400	262	State (U.S.)..................................E	Columbus; Cleveland	
Oklahoma....................	69,919	2,760,300	39	State (U.S.).................................E	Oklahoma City	
Oman†......................	82,030	815,000	9.9	Sultanate.....................................A	Masqaṭ; Maṭraḥ	Arabic
Ontario.....................	412,582	8,390,000	20	Province (Canada)............................E	Toronto	English
Oregon.....................	96,981	2,339,200	24	State (U.S.)..................................E	Salem; Portland	
Orkney Is...................	376	18,000	48	Part of Scotland, U.K........................D	Kirkwall	English
Pacific Islands Trust Territory......	717	115,000	160	Trust Territory (U.S.)........................C	Saipan	Malay-Polynesian languages, English
Pakistan (incl. part of Kashmir)†....	345,753	74,620,000	216	Federal Republic..............................A	Islāmābād; Karāchī	Urdu, English
Panama†....................	29,209	1,745,000	60	Republic......................................A	Panamá	Spanish
Papua New Guinea†..............	178,260	2,920,000	16	Republic (Comm. of Nations)...................A	Port Moresby	Papuan and Negrito languages, English
Paraguay†...................	157,048	2,840,000	18	Republic......................................A	Asunción	Spanish, Guaraní
Pennsylvania.................	45,333	11,792,000	260	State (U.S.).................................E	Harrisburg; Philadelphia	
Persia, see Iran...............						
Peru†.......................	496,224	16,600,000	33	Republic......................................A	Lima	Spanish, Quechua
Philippines†..................	116,000	43,365,000	374	Republic......................................A	Manila	Pilipino, English
Pitcairn (excl. Dependencies).......	2	100	50	Colony (U.K.).................................C	Adamstown	English
Poland†.....................	120,725	34,520,000	286	People's Republic.............................A	Warszawa (Warsaw); Katowice	Polish
Portugal†....................	35,553	8,730,000	246	Republic......................................A	Lisboa (Lisbon)	Portuguese
Portugal and Possessions..........	35,559	9,010,000	253		Lisboa (Lisbon)	
Portuguese Guinea, see Guinea-Bissau...............						
Prairie Provinces...............	757,985	3,815,000	5.0	Canada......................................	........; Winnipeg	English
Prince Edward Island...........	2,184	120,000	55	Province (Canada)............................E	Charlottetown	English
Puerto Rico..................	3,435	3,190,000	929	Commonwealth (U.S.)..........................C	San Juan	Spanish, English
Qatar†......................	4,247	97,000	23	Emirate.......................................A	Ad-Dawḥah (Doha)	Arabic
Quebec.....................	594,860	6,285,000	11	Province (Canada)............................E	Québec; Montréal	French, English
Queensland..................	667,000	2,035,000	3.0	State (Australia).............................E	Brisbane	English
Reunion.....................	969	520,000	537	Overseas Department (France)..................C	St. Denis	French
Rheinland-Pfalz (Rhineland-Palatinate)................	7,657	3,665,000	479	State (Germany, Federal Republic of)..........E	Mainz	German
Rhode Island.................	1,214	917,600	756	State (U.S.)..................................E	Providence	
Rhodesia....................	150,804	6,625,000	44	Self-governing Colony (U.K.)*.................C	Salisbury	English, native languages
Rio Muni, see Equatorial Guinea....						
Rodrigues...................	42	27,000	643	Dependency of Mauritius (U.K.)................D	Port Mathurin	English, French
Romania†....................	91,699	21,575,000	235	People's Republic.............................A	Bucureşti (Bucharest)	Romanian, Hungarian
Rossijskaja Sovetskaja Federativnaja Socialističeskaja Respublika.................	6,592,850	136,170,000	21	Soviet Federated Socialist Republic (U.S.S.R.)..E	Moskva (Moscow)	Russian, Finno-Ugric languages, various Turkic, Iranian, and Mongol languages
Rossijskaja S.F.S.R. in Europe......	1,527,350	100,070,000	66	Union of Soviet Socialist Republics..............	........; Moskva (Moscow)	Russian, Finno-Ugric languages
Rwanda†....................	10,169	4,330,000	426	Republic......................................A	Kigali	French, Kinyarwanda
Saarland (Saar)................	992	1,095,000	1,104	State (Germany, Federal Republic of)..........E	Saarbrücken	German
Sabah (North Borneo)...........	29,388	815,000	28	Administrative division of Malaysia..............C	Kota Kinabalu; Sandakan	Malay, Chinese, English
St. Helena (incl. Dependencies)....	162	6,900	43	Colony (U.K.).................................C	Jamestown	English
St. Kitts-Nevis................	103	62,000	602	Associated State (U.K.).......................B	Basseterre	English
St. Lucia....................	238	115,000	483	Associated State (U.K.).......................B	Castries	English
St. Pierre & Miquelon............	93	6,100	66	Overseas Territory (France)...................C	St. Pierre	French
St. Vincent..................	150	109,000	727	Associated State (U.K.).......................B	Kingstown	English
Samoa (Entire)...............	1,173	193,000	165		........; Apia	Malay-Polynesian languages, English
San Marino..................	24	21,000	875	Republic......................................A	San Marino	Italian
Sao Tome & Principe†...........	372	82,000	220	Republic......................................A	São Tomé	Portuguese, native languages
Sarawak....................	48,342	1,120,000	23	Administrative division of Malaysia..............E	Kuching	Malay, Chinese, English
Sardinia....................	9,301	1,575,000	169	Part of Italy.................................D	Cagliari	Italian
Saskatchewan................	251,700	945,000	3.8	Province (Canada)............................E	Regina	English
Saudi Arabia†................	830,000	9,380,000	11	Monarchy.....................................A	Ar-Riyāḍ (Riyadh)	Arabic
Scandinavia (incl. Finland and Iceland)...................	509,899	22,419,000	44		........; København (Copenhagen)	Swedish, Danish, Norwegian, Finnish, Icelandic
Schleswig-Holstein..............	6,046	2,570,000	425	State (Germany, Federal Republic of)...........E	Kiel	German
Scotland....................	30,414	5,190,000	171	Administrative division of United Kingdom.....E	Edinburgh; Glasgow	English, Gaelic
Senegal†....................	75,750	4,375,000	58	Republic......................................A	Dakar	French, native languages
Seychelles†..................	156	59,000	378	Republic (Comm. of Nations)...................A	Victoria	English, Creole
Shetland Is..................	550	19,000	35	Part of Scotland, U.K........................D	Lerwick	English
Siam, see Thailand.............						
Sicily......................	9,926	4,925,000	496	Part of Italy (Sicilia Autonomous Region)......D	Palermo	Italian
Sierra Leone†................	27,699	3,150,000	114	Republic (Comm. of Nations)...................A	Freetown	English, native languages
Singapore†..................	224	2,360,000	10,536	Republic (Comm. of Nations)...................A	Singapore	Chinese, Malay, English
Solomon Is. (Papua New Guinea)...	4,100	120,000	30	Part of Papua New Guinea....................D	Sohano; Kieta	Malay-Polynesian languages, English
Solomon Is..................	10,983	200,000	18	Protectorate (U.K.)...........................D	Honiara	Malay-Polynesian languages, English
Somalia†....................	246,201	3,290,000	13	Republic......................................A	Mogadisho	Somali
South Africa (incl. Walvis Bay)†....	471,879	26,335,000	56	Federal Republic..............................A	Pretoria, Cape Town, Bloemfontein; Johannesburg	English, Afrikaans, native languages
South America................	6,870,000	222,500,000	32		........; São Paulo	
South Australia...............	380,070	1,250,000	3.3	State (Australia).............................E	Adelaide	English
South Carolina...............	31,055	2,884,700	93	State (U.S.).................................E	Columbia	
South Dakota................	77,047	686,700	8.9	State (U.S.)..................................E	Pierre; Sioux Falls	
Southern Rhodesia, see Rhodesia...						
Southern Yemen, see Yemen, People's Democratic Republic of..						
South Georgia................	1,450	20	0.01	Dependency of Falkland Is. (U.K.)..............D	Grytviken	English, Norwegian

† Member of the United Nations (1977).
* Rhodesia unilaterally declared its independence from the United Kingdom on November 11, 1965.
‡ Areas for Egypt, Israel, Jordan and Syria do not reflect de facto changes which took place during 1967.

World Political Information Table (Continued)

Region or Political Division	Area in sq. miles	Estimated Population 1/1/77	Pop. per sq. mi.	Form of Government and Ruling Power	Capital; Largest City (unless same)	Predominant Languages
South Polar Regions	....	....	....	....	....	....
South West Africa (excl. Walvis Bay)†	317,827	900,000	2.8	Under South African Administration** ... C	Windhoek	Afrikaans, English, German, native languages
Spain†	194,885	35,890,000	184	Monarchy ... A	Madrid	Spanish, Catalan, Galician, Basque
Spain and Possessions	194,897	36,006,000	185	....	Madrid	....
Spanish Possessions in North Africa	12	116,000	9,667	Five Possessions (no central government) (Spain) ... C	........; Ceuta	Spanish, Arabic, Berber
Spitsbergen, see Svalbard	....	....	....	....	....	....
Sri Lanka (Ceylon)†	25,332	14,505,000	573	Republic (Comm. of Nations) ... A	Colombo	Sinhala, Tamil, English
Sudan†	967,499	18,415,000	19	Republic ... A	Al-Khurṭūm (Khartoum)	Arabic, native languages, English
Sumatra (Sumatera)	182,860	23,755,000	130	Part of Indonesia (6 Provinces) ... D	........; Medan	Bahasa Indonesia, English, Chinese
Surinam (Neth. Guiana)†	63,037	520,000	8.2	Republic ... A	Paramaribo	Dutch, Creole
Svalbard (Spitsbergen) and Jan Mayen	24,102	Winter pop. 3,000	....	Dependency (Norway) ... C	Longyearbyen	Norwegian, Russian
Swaziland†	6,705	520,000	78	Monarchy (Comm. of Nations) ... A	Mbabane	English, siSwati
Sweden†	173,732	8,255,000	48	Monarchy ... A	Stockholm	Swedish
Switzerland	15,941	6,290,000	395	Federal Republic ... A	Bern (Berne); Zürich	German, French, Italian
Syria†	71,498	7,700,000	108	Republic‡‡ ... A	Dimashq (Damascus)	Arabic, French
Tadžikskaja (Tadzhik) S.S.R.	55,250	3,455,000	63	Soviet Socialist Republic (U.S.S.R.) ... E	Dušhanbe	Tadzhik, Turkic languages, Russian
Taiwan (Formosa) (Nationalist China)	13,885	16,575,000	1,194	Republic ... A	T'aipei	Chinese
Tanganyika, see Tanzania	....	....	....	....	....	....
Tanzania (Tanganyika & Zanzibar)†	364,900	15,755,000	43	Republic (Comm. of Nations) ... A	Dar-es-Salaam	Swahili, English
Tasmania	26,383	415,000	16	State (Australia) ... E	Hobart	English
Tennessee	42,244	4,253,500	101	State (U.S.) ... E	Nashville; Memphis	....
Texas	267,339	12,545,400	47	State (U.S.) ... E	Austin; Houston	....
Thailand (Siam)†	198,500	43,290,000	218	Monarchy ... A	Krung Thep (Bangkok)	Thai, Chinese
Tibet (Xizang Zizhiqu)	471,700	1,545,000	3.3	Autonomous Region (China) ... E	Lasa (Lhasa)	Tibetan, Chinese
Togo†	21,600	2,300,000	106	Republic ... A	Lomé	Native languages, French
Tokelau (Union) Is.	4	1,500	375	Island Territory (New Zealand) ... C	........; Fakaofu	Malay-Polynesian languages, English
Tonga	270	100,000	370	Monarchy (Comm. of Nations) ... A	Nukualofa	Tongan, English
Transcaucasia	71,850	13,535,000	188	Union of Soviet Socialist Republics	........; Baku	....
Trinidad & Tobago†	1,980	1,110,000	561	Parliamentary State (Comm. of Nations) ... A	Port of Spain	English, Spanish
Tristan da Cunha	40	300	7.5	Dependency of St. Helena (U.K.) ... D	Edinburgh	English
Trucial States, see United Arab Emirates	....	....	....	....	....	....
Tunisia†	63,170	5,995,000	95	Republic ... A	Tunis	Arabic, French
Turkey†	301,382	40,550,000	135	Republic ... A	Ankara; İstanbul	Turkish, Kurdish, Arabic
Turkey in Europe	9,121	3,500,000	384	Turkey	........; İstanbul	Turkish
Turkmenskaja (Turkmen) S.S.R.	188,450	2,555,000	14	Soviet Socialist Republic (U.S.S.R.) ... E	Aščhabad	Turkic languages, Russian
Turks & Caicos Is.	166	5,000	30	Colony (U.K.) ... C	Grand Turk	English
Tuvalu (Ellice Is.)	9.5	5,600	589	Colony (U.K.) ... C	Funafuti	Malay-Polynesian languages, English
Uganda†	91,134	12,115,000	133	Republic (Comm. of Nations) ... A	Kampala	English, Swahili
Ukrainskaja (Ukraine) S.S.R.†	233,100	49,715,000	213	Soviet Socialist Republic (U.S.S.R.) ... E	Kijev (Kiev)	Ukrainian, Russian
Union of Soviet Socialist Republics (Soviet Union)†	8,649,500	257,850,000	30	Federal Soviet Republics ... A	Moskva (Moscow)	Russian and other Slavic languages, various Finno-Ugric, Turkic and Mongol languages, Caucasian languages, Persian
Union of Soviet Socialist Republics in Europe	1,920,750	170,490,000	89	Union of Soviet Socialist Republics	........; Moskva (Moscow)	Russian, Ruthenian, various Finno-Ugric and Caucasian languages
United Arab Emirates (Trucial States)†	32,278	235,000	7.3	Self-governing Union ... A	Abū Ẓaby; Dubayy	Arabic
United Kingdom of Great Britain & Northern Ireland†	94,227	55,970,000	594	Monarchy (Comm. of Nations) ... A	London	English, Welsh, Gaelic
United Kingdom & Possessions	288,049	68,618,000	238	....	London	....
United States†	*3,675,545	215,625,800	59	Federal Republic ... A	Washington; New York	English
United States and Possessions	3,680,713	219,227,500	60	....	Washington; New York	English, Spanish
Upper Volta†	105,800	6,230,000	59	Republic ... A	Ouagadougou	French, native languages
Uruguay†	68,536	2,785,000	41	Republic ... A	Montevideo	Spanish
Utah	84,916	1,246,100	15	State (U.S.) ... E	Salt Lake City	....
Uzbekskaja (Uzbek) S.S.R.	173,600	13,950,000	80	Soviet Socialist Republic (U.S.S.R.) ... E	Taškent	Turkic languages, Sart, Russian
Vatican City (Holy See)	0.2	1,000	5,000	Ecclesiastical State ... A	Città del Vaticano (Vatican City)	Italian, Latin
Venezuela†	352,144	12,555,000	36	Federal Republic ... A	Caracas	Spanish
Vermont	9,609	477,100	50	State (U.S.) ... E	Montpelier; Burlington	....
Victoria	87,884	3,730,000	42	State (Australia) ... E	Melbourne	English
Vietnam†	128,402	47,785,000	372	People's Republic ... A	Ha-noi; Thanh-pho Ho Chi Minh (Sai-gon)	Vietnamese
Virginia	40,817	5,058,800	124	State (U.S.) ... E	Richmond; Norfolk	....
Virgin Is., British	59	9,000	152	Colony (U.K.) ... C	Road Town	English
Virgin Is. of the U.S.	133	99,000	744	Unincorporated Territory (U.S.) ... C	Charlotte Amalie	English
Wake I.	3	1,000	333	Possession (U.S.) ... C	....	English
Wales (incl. Monmouthshire)	8,016	2,765,000	345	United Kingdom	Cardiff	English, Welsh
Wallis & Futuna	77	9,400	122	Overseas Territory (France) ... C	Mata-Utu	Malay-Polynesian languages, French
Washington	68,192	3,604,800	53	State (U.S.) ... E	Olympia; Seattle	....
Western Australia	975,920	1,155,000	1.2	State (Australia) ... E	Perth	English
Western Sahara	102,700	131,000	1.3	Administered by Morocco and Mauritania ... C	El Aaiún	Arabic
Western Samoa†	1,097	165,000	150	Constitutional Monarchy (Comm. of Nations) ... A	Apia	Samoan, English
West Indies	92,041	27,760,000	302	....	........; La Habana (Havana)	....
West Virginia	24,181	1,824,000	75	State (U.S.) ... E	Charleston	....
White Russia, see Belorusskaja	....	....	....		....	....
Wisconsin	56,154	4,661,700	83	State (U.S.) ... E	Madison; Milwaukee	....
World	57,280,000	4,070,000,000	71	....	........; Tōkyō	....
Wyoming	97,914	388,800	4.0	State (U.S.) ... E	Cheyenne	....
Yemen†	75,300	5,450,000	72	Republic ... A	Ṣan'ā'	Arabic
Yemen, People's Democratic Republic of,†	111,075	1,780,000	16	People's Republic ... A	Aden	Arabic, English
Yugoslavia†	98,766	21,645,000	219	Socialist Federal Republic ... A	Beograd (Belgrade)	Serbo-Croatian, Slovenian, Macedonian
Yukon	207,076	20,000	0.09	Territory (Canada) ... E	Whitehorse	English, Eskimo, Indian
Zaire (Congo, The)†	905,567	25,915,000	29	Republic ... A	Kinshasa	French, native languages
Zambia (Northern Rhodesia)†	290,586	5,115,000	18	Republic (Comm. of Nations) ... A	Lusaka	English, native languages
Zanzibar	950	435,000	458	Part of Tanzania ... D	Zanzibar	Arabic, English

† Member of the United Nations (1977).
‡‡ Areas for Egypt, Israel, Jordan and Syria do not reflect de facto changes which took place during 1967.
* Total area of the United States includes 3,536,855 square miles of land; 78,268 square miles of inland water; and 60,422 square miles of Great Lakes area, not included in any state.
** The United Nations declared an end to the mandate of South Africa over South West Africa in October 1966. Administration of the territory by South Africa is not recognized by the United Nations.

Largest Metropolitan Areas of the World, 1977

This table lists the major metropolitan areas of the world according to their estimated population on January 1, 1977. For convenience in reference, the areas are grouped by major region, and the number of areas in each region and size group is given.

There are 24 areas with more than 5,000,000 population each; these are listed in rank order of estimated population, with the world rank given in parentheses following the name. For example, New York's 1975 rank is second. Below the 5,000,000 level, the metropolitan areas are listed alphabetically within region, not in order of size.

For ease of comparison, each metropolitan area has been defined by Rand McNally & Company according to consistent rules. A metropolitan area includes a central city, neighboring communities linked to it by continuous built-up areas, and more distant communities if the bulk of their population is supported by commuters to the central city. Some metropolitan areas have more than one central city, for example Tōkyō-Yokohama or San Francisco-Oakland-San Jose.

POPULATION CLASSIFICATION	UNITED STATES and CANADA	LATIN AMERICA	EUROPE (excl. U.S.S.R.)	U.S.S.R.	ASIA	AFRICA–OCEANIA
Over 15,000,000 (3)	New York (2)				Tōkyō–Yokohama (1) Osaka–Kōbe–Kyoto (3)	
10,000,000–15,000,000 (5)		Ciudad de México (Mexico City) (4) São Paulo (7)	London (5)	Moskva (Moscow) (6)	Calcutta (8)	
5,000,000–10,000,000 (16)	Los Angeles (12) Chicago (17) Philadelphia (23)	Buenos Aires (9) Rio de Janeiro (13)	Paris (10) Essen–Dortmund–Duisburg (The Ruhr) (21)	Leningrad (24)	Sŏul (Seoul) (11) Bombay (15) Shanghai (16) Jakarta (18) Manila (19) Delhi (20) Beijing (Peking) (22)	Al-Qāhirah (Cairo) (14)
3,000,000–5,000,000 (27)	Boston Detroit–Windsor San Francisco–Oakland–San Jose Washington	Bogotá Caracas Lima Santiago	Athínai (Athens) Barcelona Berlin İstanbul Madrid Milano (Milan) Roma (Rome)		Baghdād Chongqing (Chungking) Karāchi Krung Thep (Bangkok) Madras Nagoya Shenyang (Mukden) T'aipei (Taipei) Tehrān Tianjin (Tientsin) Victoria Wuhan	
2,000,000–3,000,000 (38)	Cleveland Dallas–Fort Worth Houston Miami–Fort Lauderdale Montréal Pittsburgh St. Louis Toronto	Belo Horizonte Guadalajara Recife	Birmingham Bruxelles (Brussel) (Brussels) Budapest Hamburg Katowice–Bytom–Gliwice Manchester Napoli (Naples)	Doneck (Donetsk)–Makejevka Kijev (Kiev)	Ahmādābād Bangalore Dacca Guangzhou (Canton) Haerbin (Harbin) Hyderābād Lahore Pusan Rangoon Singapore Surabaya Thanh–pho Ho Chi Minh (Sai-gon)	Alexandria Alger (Algiers) Johannesburg Kinshasa Melbourne Sydney
1,500,000–2,000,000 (39)	Atlanta Baltimore Buffalo Minneapolis–St. Paul San Diego–Tijuana Seattle–Tacoma	La Habana (Havana) Medellín Monterrey Montevideo Pôrto Alegre	Amsterdam Bucureşti (Bucharest) Frankfurt am Main Glasgow København (Copenhagen) Köln (Cologne) Leeds–Bradford Lisboa (Lisbon) Liverpool München (Munich) Stuttgart Torino (Turin) Warszawa (Warsaw) Wien (Vienna)	Baku Char'kov (Kharkov) Gor'kij (Gorki) Taškent (Tashkent)	Ankara Chengdu (Chengtu) Colombo Kānpur Kitakyūshū Nanjing (Nanking) Taiyuan Xi'an (Sian)	Casablanca Lagos
1,000,000–1,500,000 (75)	Cincinnati Denver El Paso–Ciudad Juárez Hartford Indianapolis Kansas City Milwaukee New Orleans Phoenix Portland Vancouver	Cali Córdoba Fortaleza Guatemala Guayaquil Salvador San Juan	Antwerpen (Anvers) (Antwerp) Beograd (Belgrade) Düsseldorf Hannover Lille Lyon Mannheim Marseille Newcastle–Sunderland Nürnberg Praha (Prague) Rotterdam Sofija (Sofia) Stockholm Valencia	Čel'abinsk (Chelyabinsk) Dnepropetrovsk Jerevan (Yerevan) Kazan' Kujbyšev (Kuybyshev) Minsk Novosibirsk Odessa Omsk Perm Rostov-na-Donu Saratov Sverdlovsk Tbilisi Volgograd	Anshan Bandung Bayrūt (Beirut) Changchun (Hsinking) Chittagong Dimashq (Damascus) Fukuoka Fushun Hiroshima–Kure Jinan (Tsinan) Kaohsiung Kunming Lanzhou (Lanchow) Lüda (Dairen) Nāgpur Pune P'yŏngyang Qingdao (Tsingtao) Sapporo Taegu Tel Aviv-Yafo Zhengzhou (Chengchow)	Addis Abeba (Addis Ababa) Brisbane Cape Town Durban Tunis
Total by Region (203)	33	23	46	23	64	14

Introduction to the Index

The index includes in a single alphabetical list some 39,000 names appearing on the maps. Each name is followed by a page reference and by the location of the feature on the map. The map location is designated by latitude and longitude coordinates. If a page contains several maps, a lowercase letter identifies the inset map. The page reference for two-page maps is always to the left hand page.

Most map features are indexed to the largest-scale map on which they appear. Countries, mountain ranges, and other extensive features are generally indexed to the map that shows them in their entirety.

The features indexed are of three types: *point*, *areal*, and *linear*. For *point* features (for example, cities, mountain peaks, dams), latitude and longitude coordinates give the location of the point on the map. For *areal* features (countries, mountain ranges, etc.), the coordinates generally indicate the approximate center of the feature. For *linear* features (rivers, canals, aqueducts), the coordinates locate a terminating point—for example, the mouth of a river, or the point at which a feature reaches the map margin.

NAME FORMS Names in the Index, as on the maps, are generally in the local language and insofar as possible are spelled according to official practice. Diacritical marks are included, except that those used to indicate tone, as in Vietnamese, are usually not shown. Most features that extend beyond the boundaries of one country have no single official name, and these are usually named in English. Many conventional English names and former names are cross referenced to the primary map name. All cross references are indicated by the symbol→. A name that appears in a shortened version on the map due to space limitations is given in full in the Index, with the portion that is omitted on the map enclosed in brackets, for example, Acapulco [de Juárez].

TRANSLITERATION For names in languages not written in the Roman alphabet, the locally official transliteration system has been used where one exists. Thus, names in the Soviet Union and Bulgaria have been transliterated according to the systems adopted by the academies of science of these countries. Similarly, the transliteration for mainland Chinese names follows the Pinyin system, which has been officially adopted in mainland China. For languages with no one locally accepted transliteration system, notably Arabic, transliteration in general follows closely a system adopted by the United States Board on Geographic Names.

ALPHABETIZATION Names are alphabetized in the order of the letters of the English alphabet. Spanish *ll* and *ch*, for example, are not treated as distinct letters. Furthermore, diacritical marks are disregarded in alphabetization—German or Scandinavian *ä* or *ö* are treated as *a* or *o*.

The names of physical features may appear inverted, since they are always alphabetized under the proper, not the generic, part of the name, thus: "Gibraltar, Strait of ∪." Otherwise every entry, whether consisting of one word or more, is alphabetized as a single continuous entity. "Lakeland," for example, appears after "La Crosse" and before "La Salle." Names beginning with articles (Le Havre, Den Helder, Al-Qāhirah, As-Suways) are not inverted. Names beginning "Mc" are alphabetized as though spelled "Mac," and names beginning "St." and "Sainte" as though spelled "Saint."

In the case of identical names, towns are listed first, then political divisions, then physical features. Entries that are completely identical (including symbols, discussed below) are distinguished by abbreviations of their official country names and are sequenced alphabetically by country name. The many duplicate names in Canada, the United Kingdom, and the United States are further distinguished by abbreviations of the names of their primary subdivisions. (See list of abbreviations on pages 202 and 203).

ABBREVIATION AND CAPITALIZATION Abbreviation and styling have been standardized for all languages. A period is used after every abbreviation even when this may not be the local practice. The abbreviation "St." is used only for "Saint." "Sankt" and other forms of the term are spelled out.

All names are written with an initial capital letter except for a few Dutch names, such as 's-Gravenhage. Capitalization of noninitial words in a name generally follows local practice.

SYMBOL The symbols that appear in the Index graphically represent the broad categories of the features named, for example, ∧ for mountain (Everest, Mount ∧). Superior numbers following some symbols in the Index indicate finer distinctions, for example, $\wedge^1$ for volcano (Fuji-san $\wedge^1$). A complete list of the symbols and those with superior numbers is given on page 198.

LIST OF ABBREVIATIONS

	LOCAL NAME	ENGLISH
Afg.	Afghānestān	Afghanistan
Afr.	—	Africa
Ala., U.S.	Alabama	Alabama
Alaska, U.S.	Alaska	Alaska
Alg.	Algérie	Algeria
Alta., Can.	Alberta	Alberta
Am. Sam.	American Samoa	American Samoa
And.	Andorra	Andorra
Ang.	Angola	Angola
Anguilla	Anguilla	Anguilla
Ant.	—	Antarctica
Antig.	Antigua	Antigua
Arc. O.	—	Arctic Ocean
Arg.	Argentina	Argentina
Ariz., U.S.	Arizona	Arizona
Ark., U.S.	Arkansas	Arkansas
Ar. Sa.	Al-'Arabīyah as-Sa'ūdīyah	Saudi Arabia
As.	—	Asia
Atl. O.	—	Atlantic Ocean
Austl.	Australia	Australia
Ba.	Bahamas	Bahamas
Baḥr.	Al-Baḥrayn	Bahrain
Barb.	Barbados	Barbados
B.A.T.	British Antarctic Territory	British Antarctic Territory
B.C., Can.	British Columbia	British Columbia
Bdi.	Burundi	Burundi
Bel.	Belgique België	Belgium
Belize	Belize	Belize
Benin	Benin	Benin
Ber.	Bermuda	Bermuda
Ber. S.	—	Bering Sea
Bhārat	Bhārat	India
B.I.O.T.	British Indian Ocean Territory	British Indian Ocean Territory
Blg.	Bâlgarija	Bulgaria
Bngl.	Bangladesh	Bangladesh
Bol.	Bolivia	Bolivia
Bots.	Botswana	Botswana
Bra.	Brasil	Brazil
B.R.D.	Bundesrepublik Deutschland	Federal Republic of Germany
Bru.	Brunei	Brunei
Br. Vir. Is.	British Virgin Islands	British Virgin Islands
Calif., U.S.	California	California
Cam.	Cameroun	Cameroon
Can.	Canada	Canada
Can./End.	Canton and Enderbury	Canton and Enderbury
Carib. S.	—	Caribbean Sea
Cay. Is.	Cayman Islands	Cayman Islands
Centraf.	Centrafricaine Empire	Central African Empire
Česko.	Československo	Czechoslovakia
Chile	Chile	Chile
Christ. I.	Christmas Island	Christmas Island
C. Iv.	Côte d'Ivoire	Ivory Coast
C.M.I.K.	Chosŏn Minjujuŭi In'min Konghwaguk	North Korea
Cocos Is.	Cocos (Keeling) Islands	Cocos (Keeling) Islands
Col.	Colombia	Colombia
Colo., U.S.	Colorado	Colorado
Comoros	Comoros	Comoros
Congo	Congo	Congo
Conn., U.S.	Connecticut	Connecticut
Cook Is.	Cook Islands	Cook Islands
C.R.	Costa Rica	Costa Rica
Cuba	Cuba	Cuba
C.V.	Cabo Verde	Cape Verde
C.Z.	Canal Zone	Canal Zone
Dan.	Danmark	Denmark
D.C., U.S.	District of Columbia	District of Columbia
D.D.R.	Deutsche Demokratische Republik	German Democratic Republic
Del., U.S.	Delaware	Delaware
Den.	Danmark	Denmark
Djibouti	Djibouti	Djibouti
Dom.	Dominica	Dominica
D.Y.	Druk-Yul	Bhutan
Ec.	Ecuador	Ecuador
Eire	Eire	Ireland
Ellás	Ellás	Greece
El Sal.	El Salvador	El Salvador
Eng., U.K.	England	England
Esp.	España	Spain
Eur.	—	Europe
Falk. Is.	Falkland Islands	Falkland Islands (Islas Malvinas)
Fiji	Fiji	Fiji
Fla., U.S.	Florida	Florida
Før.	Føroyar	Faeroe Islands
Fr.	France	France
Ga., U.S.	Georgia	Georgia
Gabon	Gabon	Gabon
Gam.	Gambia	Gambia
Gaza	—	Gaza Strip
Ghana	Ghana	Ghana
Gib.	Gibraltar	Gibraltar
Gilb. Is.	Gilbert Islands	Gilbert Islands
Gren.	Grenada	Grenada
Grn.	Grønland	Greenland
Guad.	Guadeloupe	Guadeloupe
Guam.	Guam	Guam
Guat.	Guatemala	Guatemala
Guer.	Guernsey	Guernsey
Gui.-B.	Guinea-Bissau	Guinea-Bissau
Gui. Ecu.	Guinea Ecuatorial	Equatorial Guinea
Guinée	Guinée	Guinea
Guy.	Guyana	Guyana
Guy. fr.	Guyane française	French Guiana
Haï.	Haïti	Haiti
Haw., U.S.	Hawaii	Hawaii
H.K.	Hong Kong	Hong Kong
Hond.	Honduras	Honduras
H. Vol.	Haute-Volta	Upper Volta
Idaho, U.S.	Idaho	Idaho
I.I.A.	Ittiḥād al-Imārāt al-'Arabīyah	United Arab Emirates
Ill., U.S.	Illinois	Illinois
Ind., U.S.	Indiana	Indiana
Ind. O.	—	Indian Ocean
Indon.	Indonesia	Indonesia
I. of Man	Isle of Man	Isle of Man
Iowa, U.S.	Iowa	Iowa
Īrān	Īrān	Iran
'Irāq	Al-'Irāq	Iraq
Ísland	Ísland	Iceland
It.	Italia	Italy
Jam.	Jamaica	Jamaica
Jersey	Jersey	Jersey
Jugo.	Jugoslavija	Yugoslavia
Kam.	Kampuchea	Cambodia
Kans., U.S.	Kansas	Kansas
Kenya	Kenya	Kenya
Kípros	Kípros Kıbrıs	Cyprus
Kuwayt	Al-Kuwayt	Kuwait
Ky., U.S.	Kentucky	Kentucky
La., U.S.	Louisiana	Louisiana
Lao	Lao	Laos
Leso.	Lesotho	Lesotho
Liber.	Liberia	Liberia
Lībiyā	Lībiyā	Libya
Liech.	Liechtenstein	Liechtenstein
Lubnān	Al-Lubnān	Lebanon
Lux.	Luxembourg	Luxembourg
Macau	Macau	Macau
Madag.	Madagasikara	Madagascar
Magreb	Al-Magreb	Morocco
Magy.	Magyarország	Hungary
Maine, U.S.	Maine	Maine
Malawi	Malawi	Malawi
Malay.	Malaysia	Malaysia
Mald.	Maldives	Maldives
Mali	Mali	Mali
Malta	Malta	Malta
Man., Can.	Manitoba	Manitoba
Mart.	Martinique	Martinique
Mass., U.S.	Massachusetts	Massachusetts
Maur.	Mauritanie	Mauritania
Maus.	Mauritius	Mauritius
Md., U.S.	Maryland	Maryland
Medit. S.	—	Mediterranean Sea
Méx.	México	Mexico
Mich., U.S.	Michigan	Michigan
Mid. Is.	Midway Islands	Midway Islands
Minn., U.S.	Minnesota	Minnesota
Miṣr	Miṣr	Egypt
Miss., U.S.	Mississippi	Mississippi
Mo., U.S.	Missouri	Missouri
Moç.	Moçambique	Mozambique
Monaco	Monaco	Monaco
Mong.	Mongol Ard Uls	Mongolia
Mont., U.S.	Montana	Montana
Monts.	Montserrat	Montserrat
Mya.	Myanma	Burma
N.A.	—	North America
Nauru	Nauru	Nauru
N.B., Can.	New Brunswick	New Brunswick
N.C., U.S.	North Carolina	North Carolina
N. Cal.	Nouvelle-Calédonie	New Caledonia
N. Dak., U.S.	North Dakota	North Dakota
Nebr., U.S.	Nebraska	Nebraska
Ned.	Nederland	Netherlands
Ned. Ant.	Nederlandse Antillen	Netherlands Antilles
Nepāl	Nepāl	Nepal
Nev., U.S.	Nevada	Nevada
Newf., Can.	Newfoundland	Newfoundland
N.H., U.S.	New Hampshire	New Hampshire
N. Heb.	New Hebrides Nouvelles-Hébrides	New Hebrides
Nic.	Nicaragua	Nicaragua
Nig.	Nigeria	Nigeria
Niger	Niger	Niger
Nihon	Nihon	Japan
N. Ire., U.K.	Northern Ireland	Northern Ireland
Niue	Niue	Niue
N.J., U.S.	New Jersey	New Jersey
N. Mex., U.S.	New Mexico	New Mexico
Nor.	Norge	Norway
Norf. I.	Norfolk Island	Norfolk Island
N.S., Can.	Nova Scotia	Nova Scotia
N.W. Ter., Can.	Northwest Territories	Northwest Territories
N.Y., U.S.	New York	New York
N.Z.	New Zealand	New Zealand
Oc.	—	Oceania
Ohio, U.S.	Ohio	Ohio
Okla., U.S.	Oklahoma	Oklahoma
Ont., Can.	Ontario	Ontario
Oreg., U.S.	Oregon	Oregon
Öst.	Österreich	Austria
Pa., U.S.	Pennsylvania	Pennsylvania
Pac. O.	—	Pacific Ocean
Pāk.	Pākistān	Pakistan
Pan.	Panamá	Panama
Pap. N. Gui.	Papua New Guinea	Papua New Guinea
Para.	Paraguay	Paraguay
P.E.I., Can.	Prince Edward Island	Prince Edward Island
Perú	Perú	Peru
Pil.	Pilipinas	Philippines
Pit.	Pitcairn	Pitcairn
P.I.T.T.	Pacific Islands Trust Territory	Pacific Islands Trust Territory
Pol.	Polska	Poland
Poly. fr.	Polynésie française	French Polynesia
Port.	Portugal	Portugal
P.R.	Puerto Rico	Puerto Rico
P.S.N.Á.	Plazas de Soberanía en el Norte de África	Spanish North Africa
Qaṭar	Qaṭar	Qatar
Que., Can.	Québec	Quebec
Rep. Dom.	República Dominicana	Dominican Republic
Réu.	Réunion	Reunion
Rh.	Rhodesia	Rhodesia
R.I., U.S.	Rhode Island	Rhode Island
Rom.	România	Romania
Rw.	Rwanda	Rwanda
S.A.	—	South America
S. Afr.	South Africa Suid-Afrika	South Africa
Sah. Occ.	Sahara Occidentale	Western Sahara
Sask., Can.	Saskatchewan	Saskatchewan
S.C., U.S.	South Carolina	South Carolina
S. Ch. S.	—	South China Sea
Schw.	Schweiz; Suisse; Svizzera	Switzerland
Scot., U.K.	Scotland	Scotland
S. Dak., U.S.	South Dakota	South Dakota
Sén.	Sénégal	Senegal
Sey.	Seychelles	Seychelles
Shq.	Shqipëri	Albania
Sing.	Singapore	Singapore
S.L.	Sierra Leone	Sierra Leone
S. Lan.	Sri Lanka	Sri Lanka
S. Mar.	San Marino	San Marino
Sol. Is.	Solomon Islands	Solomon Islands
Som.	Somaliya	Somalia
Sp.	España	Spain
S.S.R.	Sovetskaja Socialističeskaja Respublika	Soviet Socialist Republic
S.S.S.R.	Sojuz Sovetskich Socialističeskich Respublik	Union of Soviet Socialist Republics
St. Hel.	St. Helena	St. Helena
St. K.-N.	St. Kitts-Nevis	St. Kitts-Nevis
St. Luc.	St. Lucia	St. Lucia
S. Tom./P.	São Tomé e Príncipe	Sao Tome and Principe
St. P./M.	St.-Pierre-et-Miquelon	St. Pierre and Miquelon
St. Vin.	St. Vincent	St. Vincent
Sūd.	As-Sūdān	Sudan
Suomi	Suomi	Finland
Sur.	Suriname	Surinam
Sūrīy.	As-Sūrīyah	Syria
Sval.	Svalbard og Jan Mayen	Svalbard and Jan Mayen
Sve.	Sverige	Sweden
S.W. Afr.	South West Africa	South West Africa
Swaz.	Swaziland	Swaziland
T.a.a.f.	Terres australes et antarctiques françaises	French Southern and Antarctic Territories
Taehan	Taehan-Min'guk	South Korea
T'aiwan	T'aiwan	Taiwan
Tan.	Tanzania	Tanzania
Tchad	Tchad	Chad
T./C. Is.	Turks and Caicos Islands	Turks and Caicos Islands
Tenn., U.S.	Tennessee	Tennessee
Tex., U.S.	Texas	Texas
Thai.	Prathet Thai	Thailand
Togo	Togo	Togo
Tok. Is.	Tokelau Islands	Tokelau Islands
Tonga	Tonga	Tonga
Trin.	Trinidad and Tobago	Trinidad and Tobago
Tun.	Tunisie	Tunisia
Tür.	Türkiye	Turkey
Tuvalu	Tuvalu	Tuvalu
Ug.	Uganda	Uganda
U.K.	United Kingdom	United Kingdom
'Umān	'Umān	Oman
Ur.	Uruguay	Uruguay
Urd.	Al-Urdunn	Jordan
U.S.	United States	United States

Introduction to the Index

LIST OF ABBREVIATIONS CON'T.

	LOCAL NAME	ENGLISH
U.S.S.R.	Sojuz Sovetskich Socialističeskich Respublik	Union of Soviet Socialist Republics
Utah, U.S.	Utah	Utah
Va., U.S.	Virginia	Virginia
Vat.	Città del Vaticano	Vatican City
Ven.	Venezuela	Venezuela
Viet.	Viet-nam	Vietnam
Vir. Is., U.S.	Virgin Islands	Virgin Islands (U.S.)
Vt., U.S.	Vermont	Vermont
Wake I.	Wake Island	Wake Island
Wales, U.K.	Wales	Wales
Wal./F.	Wallis et Futuna	Wallis and Futuna
Wash., U.S.	Washington	Washington
Wis., U.S.	Wisconsin	Wisconsin
W. Sam.	Western Samoa	Western Samoa
W. Va., U.S.	West Virginia	West Virginia
Wyo., U.S.	Wyoming	Wyoming
Yai.	Yaitopya	Ethiopia
Yaman	Al-Yaman	Yemen
Yam. S.	Al-Yaman ash-Sha'bīyah	People's Democratic Republic of Yemen
Yis.	Yisra'el	Israel
Yukon, Can.	Yukon	Yukon
Zaïre	Zaïre	Zaire
Zam.	Zambia	Zambia
Zhg.	Zhongguo	China

KEY TO SYMBOLS

- ∧ **Mountain**
- ∧[1] Volcano
- ∧[2] Hill
- ⋏ **Mountains**
- ⋏[1] Plateau
- ⋏[2] Hills
-)(**Pass**
- ∨ **Valley, Canyon**
- ≚ **Plain**
- ≚[1] Basin
- ≚[2] Delta
- ≻ **Cape**
- ≻[1] Peninsula
- ≻[2] Spit, Sand Bar
- I **Island**
- I[1] Atoll
- I[2] Rock
- II **Islands**
- II[1] Rocks
- ⊥ **Other Topographic Features**
- ⊥[1] Continent
- ⊥[2] Coast, Beach
- ⊥[3] Isthmus
- ⊥[4] Cliff
- ⊥[5] Cave, Caves
- ⊥[6] Crater
- ⊥[7] Depression
- ⊥[8] Dunes
- ⊥[9] Lava Flow
- ≃ **River**
- ≃[1] River Channel
- ≅ **Canal**
- ≅[1] Aqueduct
- ⌞ **Waterfall, Rapids**
- ⋓ **Strait**
- C **Bay, Gulf**
- C[1] Estuary
- C[2] Fjord
- C[3] Bight
- ⊜ **Lake, Lakes**
- ⊜[1] Reservoir
- ≡ **Swamp**
- ◺ **Ice Features, Glacier**
- ⊤ **Other Hydrographic Features**
- ⊤[1] Ocean
- ⊤[2] Sea
- ⊤[3] Anchorage
- ⊤[4] Oasis, Well, Spring
- ⊹ **Submarine Features**
- ⊹[1] Depression
- ⊹[2] Reef, Shoal
- ⊹[3] Mountain, Mountains
- ⊹[4] Slope, Shelf
- □ **Political Unit**
- □[1] Independent Nation
- □[2] Dependency
- □[3] State, Canton, Republic
- □[4] Province, Region, Oblast
- □[5] Department, District, Prefecture
- □[6] County
- □[7] City, Municipality
- □[8] Miscellaneous
- □[9] Historical
- ♉ **Cultural Institution**
- ♉[1] Religious Institution
- ♉[2] Educational Institution
- ♉[3] Scientific, Industrial Facility
- ⊥ **Historical Site**
- ♠ **Recreational Site**
- ⊠ **Airport**
- ▪ **Military Installation**
- ⟜ **Miscellaneous**
- ⟜[1] Region
- ⟜[2] Desert
- ⟜[3] Forest, Moor
- ⟜[4] Reserve, Reservation
- ⟜[5] Transportation
- ⟜[6] Dam
- ⟜[7] Mine, Quarry
- ⟜[8] Neighborhood
- ⟜[9] Shopping Center

Index

Name	Page	Lat°′	Long°′
A			
Aachen	116	50.47 N	6.05 E
Aaiun → El Aaiún	152	27.09 N	13.12 W
Aalen	116	48.50 N	10.05 E
Aalst	116	50.56 N	4.02 E
Äänekoski	114	62.36 N	25.44 E
Aarau	118	47.23 N	8.03 E
Aarburg	118	47.19 N	7.54 E
Aarschot	116	50.59 N	4.50 E
Aba, Nig.	152	5.06 N	7.21 E
Aba, Zaïre	158	3.52 N	30.14 E
Aba, Zhg.	132	33.06 N	101.59 E
Abacaxis ≃	184	3.54 S	58.47 W
Ābādān	150	30.20 N	48.16 E
Ābādeh	150	31.10 N	52.37 E
Abaeté	190	19.09 S	45.27 W
Abaetetuba	184	18.02 S	45.12 W
Abagaqi	132	43.41 N	114.40 E
Abaj	126	49.38 N	72.52 E
Abakan	128	53.43 N	91.26 E
Abakan ≃	128	53.43 N	91.30 E
Abancay	184	13.35 S	72.55 W
Abashiri	134a	44.01 N	144.17 E
Abasolo	178	32.39 N	115.21 W
Abatiá	190	23.19 S	50.18 W
Abau	166	10.11 S	148.42 E
Abaya, Lake ⊜	154	6.20 N	37.55 E
Abayita, Lake ⊜	154	7.37 N	38.35 E
Abaza	126	52.39 N	90.06 E
Abbert ≃	110	53.26 N	9.54 W
Abbeville	118	50.06 N	1.50 E
Abbeydorney	110	52.19 N	9.41 W
Abbeyfeale	110	52.24 N	9.18 W
Abbey Head ≻	106	54.46 N	3.58 W
Abbeyleix	110	52.55 N	7.20 W
Abbey Peak ∧	166	14.18 S	144.29 E
Abbey Town	106	54.50 N	3.17 W
Abbiategrasso	122	45.24 N	8.54 E
Abbotsbury	104	50.40 N	2.36 W
Abbots Langley	104	51.43 N	0.25 W
Abbottābād	149	34.09 N	73.13 E
Abbott Butte ∧	178	42.57 N	122.33 W
'Abd al-Kūrī I	144	12.12 N	52.15 E
'Abd Allāh, Khawr ⋓	150	29.50 N	48.20 E
Abdulino	126	53.42 N	53.40 E
Abe, Lake ⊜	154	11.06 N	41.50 E
Abéché	154	13.49 N	20.49 E
Abemama I[1]	96	0.21 N	173.51 E
Abengourou	152	6.44 N	3.29 W
Åbenrå	114	55.02 N	9.26 E
Abensberg	116	48.49 N	11.51 E
Abeokuta	152	7.10 N	3.26 E
Aberaman	104	51.42 N	3.25 W
Aberayron	104	52.15 N	4.15 W
Abercarn	104	51.39 N	3.08 W
Aberchirder	108	57.33 N	2.38 W
Abercorn → Mbala	158	8.50 S	31.22 E
Aberdare	104	51.43 N	3.27 W
Aberdaron	104	52.49 N	4.43 W
Aberdeen, S. Afr.	160	32.29 S	24.04 E
Aberdeen, Scot., U.K.	108	57.10 N	2.04 W
Aberdeen, Md., U.S.	176	39.30 N	76.10 W
Aberdeen, S. Dak., U.S.	174	45.28 N	98.29 W
Aberdeen, Wash., U.S.	174	46.59 N	123.50 W
Aberdeen Lake ⊜	172	64.27 N	99.00 W
Aberdour	108	56.03 N	3.19 W
Aberdovey	104	52.33 N	4.02 W
Aberdulais	104	51.41 N	3.48 W
Aberfeldy	108	56.37 N	3.54 W
Aberfoyle	108	56.11 N	4.23 W
Abergavenny	104	51.50 N	3.00 W
Abergele	106	53.17 N	3.34 W
Abergwynfi	104	51.40 N	3.35 W
Abergynolwyn	104	52.40 N	3.58 W
Aberlour	108	57.28 N	3.14 W
Abernethy	108	56.20 N	3.19 W
Aberporth	104	52.09 N	4.33 W
Abersoch	104	52.50 N	4.29 W
Abersychan	104	51.44 N	3.04 W
Abert, Lake ⊜	178	42.38 N	120.13 W
Abertillery	104	51.45 N	3.09 W
Aberuthven	108	56.19 N	3.39 W
Aberystwyth	104	52.25 N	4.05 W
Abez'	112	66.32 N	61.42 E
Abhā	144	18.13 N	42.30 E
Abhar	150	36.09 N	49.13 E
Abidjan	152	5.19 N	4.02 W
Abilene	174	32.27 N	99.44 W
Abingdon	104	51.41 N	1.17 W
Abington Reefs ⊹[2]	168	18.00 S	149.36 E
Āb-i-Panja (P'andž) ≃	126	37.06 N	68.20 E
Abitau ≃	172	59.53 N	109.03 W
Abitibi ≃	172	51.03 N	80.55 W
Abitibi, Lake ⊜	172	48.42 N	79.45 W
Ablis	118	48.31 N	1.50 E
Abminga	164	26.07 S	134.52 E
Åbo → Turku	114	60.27 N	22.17 E
Abohar	149	30.09 N	74.11 E
Abomey	152	7.11 N	1.59 E
Abongabong, Gunung ∧	140	4.15 N	96.48 E
Abong Mbang	152	3.59 N	13.10 E
Abony	116	47.11 N	20.01 E
Aborigen, Pik ∧	128	61.59 N	149.19 E
Abou Deïa	154	11.27 N	19.17 E
Aboyne	108	57.05 N	2.50 W
Abra Pampa	188	22.43 S	65.42 W
Abriachan	108	57.22 N	4.24 W
Abruzzi □[4]	122	42.20 N	13.45 E
Absaroka Range ⋏	174	44.45 N	109.50 W
Absecon	176	39.26 N	74.30 W
Abtenau	116	47.33 N	13.21 E
Abū 'Alī I	150	27.20 N	49.33 E
Abū al-Khaṣīb	150	30.27 N	47.59 E
Abū Ḥamad	154	19.32 N	33.19 E
Abū Kamāl	150	34.27 N	40.55 E
Abukuma ≃	134	38.02 N	140.56 E
Abukuma-sanchi ⋏	134	37.30 N	140.45 E
Abū Madd, Ra's ≻	150	24.50 N	37.07 E
Abū Mūsā, Jazīreh-ye I	150	25.52 N	55.03 E
Abunã	184	9.42 S	65.23 W
Abuná ≃	184	9.41 S	65.23 W
Abu Road	144	24.29 N	72.47 E
Abū Shajarah, Ra's ≻	154	21.04 N	37.14 E
Abuta	134a	42.33 N	140.46 E
Abū Ẓaby	150	24.28 N	54.22 E
Abū Żanīmah	150	29.03 N	33.06 E
Abydos	164	21.25 S	118.54 E
Acajutla	180	13.36 N	89.50 W
Acámbaro	180	20.02 N	100.44 W
Acaponeta	180	22.30 N	105.22 W
Acapulco [de Juárez]	180	16.51 N	99.55 W
Acarai Mountains ∧	184	1.50 N	57.40 W
Acaraú	184	2.53 S	40.07 W
Acarigua	184	9.33 N	69.12 W
Acay, Nevado de ∧	188	24.22 S	66.10 W
Accra	152	5.33 N	0.13 W
Accrington	106	53.46 N	2.21 W
Acerra	122	40.57 N	14.22 E
Achacachi	184	16.03 S	68.43 W
Achalpur	146	21.16 N	77.31 E
Acharacle	108	56.44 N	5.47 W
Achavanich	108	58.22 N	3.24 W
Acheng	132	45.32 N	126.59 E
Achill Head ≻	110	53.59 N	10.13 W
Achill Island I	110	54.00 N	10.00 W
Achill Sound	110	53.55 N	9.58 W
Achnasaul	108	56.58 N	4.59 W
Achnasheen	108	57.35 N	5.06 W
Acholi □[5]	158	3.00 N	32.30 E
Achosnich	108	56.45 N	6.06 W
Achtyrka	126	50.19 N	34.55 E
Ačinsk	128	56.17 N	90.30 E
Acireale	122	37.37 N	15.10 E
Ačisaj	126	43.35 N	68.53 E
Acklins, The Bight of C[3]	182	22.25 N	74.10 W
Acklins Island I	182	22.25 N	74.00 W
Acland, Mount ∧	168	24.55 S	148.05 E
Acle	104	52.38 N	1.33 E
Aconcagua □[4]	188	32.15 S	70.50 W
Aconcagua, Cerro ∧	188	32.39 S	70.00 W
Aconquija, Sierra del ⋏	188	27.10 S	66.00 W
Acores (Azores), Arquipélago dos II	88	38.30 N	28.00 W
Acornhoek	160	24.37 S	31.02 E
Acoyapa	182	11.57 N	85.12 W
Acqui Terme	122	44.41 N	8.28 E
Acraman, Lake ⊜	164	32.02 S	135.26 E
Acre → 'Akko	150	32.55 N	35.05 E
Acre ≃	184	8.45 S	67.22 W
Acton	176	43.37 N	80.02 W
Acton Turville	104	51.32 N	2.17 W
Acton Vale	176	45.39 N	72.34 W
Ada, Jugo.	124	45.48 N	20.08 E
Ada, Ohio, U.S.	176	40.46 N	83.49 W
Ada, Okla., U.S.	174	34.46 N	96.41 W
Adair, Cape ≻	172	71.24 N	71.13 W
Ādam	144	22.24 N	57.32 E
Adam, Mount ∧	186	51.34 S	60.04 W
Adamantina	190	21.42 S	51.04 W
Adamawa ⋏	152	7.00 N	12.00 E
Adaminaby	168	36.03 S	148.43 E
Adams, Mass., U.S.	176	42.37 N	73.07 W
Adams, N.Y., U.S.	176	43.49 N	76.01 W
Adams, Mount ∧	174	46.12 N	121.28 W
Adams Bridge ⊹[2]	148	9.04 N	79.37 E
Adams Lake ⊜	172	51.13 N	119.33 W
Adams Peak ∧	148	6.48 N	80.30 E
Adana	150	37.01 N	35.18 E
Adarama	154	17.05 N	34.54 E
Adare	110	52.34 N	8.48 W
Adare, Cape ≻	87	71.17 S	170.14 E
Adavale	168	25.55 S	144.36 E
Ad-Dabbah	154	18.03 N	30.57 E
Ad-Dahnā' ⟜[2]	150	24.30 N	48.10 E
Ad-Dāmir	154	17.35 N	33.58 E
Ad-Dammām	150	26.26 N	50.07 E
Ad-Dawādimī	150	24.28 N	44.18 E
Ad-Dawḥah (Doha)	150	25.17 N	51.32 E
Adderbury	104	52.00 N	1.17 W
Ad-Dilam	150	23.59 N	47.12 E
Addingham	106	53.57 N	1.53 W
Addis Abeba	154	9.00 N	38.50 E
Addison	176	41.59 N	84.21 W
Ad-Dīwānīyah	150	31.59 N	44.56 E
Ad-Duwaym	154	14.00 N	32.19 E
Adelaide, Austl.	168	34.55 S	138.35 E
Adelaide, Ba.	182	25.00 N	77.31 W
Adelaide, S. Afr.	160	32.42 S	26.20 E
Adelaide Island I	87	67.15 S	68.30 W
Adelaide Peninsula ≻[1]	172	68.09 N	97.45 W
Adelaide River	166	13.15 S	131.06 E
Adélie Coast ⊥[2]	87	67.00 S	139.00 E
Adelong	168	35.19 S	148.03 E
Aden	144	12.45 N	45.12 E
Aden, Gulf of C	88	12.30 N	48.00 E
Adendorp	160	32.20 S	24.33 E
Adi, Pulau I	166	4.18 S	133.26 E
Adieu, Cape ≻	164	31.59 S	132.09 E
Adigrat	154	14.18 N	39.31 E
Ādilābād	148	19.40 N	78.32 E
Adimi	128	47.20 N	138.56 E
Adin	178	41.12 N	120.57 W
Adirondack Mountains ⋏	176	44.00 N	74.00 W
Adıyaman	150	37.46 N	38.17 E
Adlington	106	53.37 N	2.36 W
Admiralty Gulf C	166	14.20 S	125.50 E
Admiralty Inlet C	172	73.00 N	86.00 W
Admiralty Island I, N.W. Ter., Can.	172	69.30 N	101.00 W
Admiralty Island I, Alaska, U.S.	172	57.50 N	134.30 W
Admiralty Islands II	166	2.10 S	147.00 E
Admiralty Mountains ⋏	87	71.45 S	168.30 E
Adonara, Pulau I	142	8.20 S	123.10 E
Ādoni	148	15.38 N	77.17 E
Adour ≃	118	43.32 N	1.32 E
Adra	120	36.44 N	3.01 W
Adrano	122	37.40 N	14.50 E
Adrar ⟜[1]	152	20.30 N	13.30 W
Adria	122	45.03 N	12.03 E
Adrian, Mich., U.S.	176	41.54 N	84.02 W
Adrian, W. Va., U.S.	176	38.54 N	80.17 W
Adriatic Sea ⊤[2]	100	42.30 N	16.00 E
Adrigole	110	51.40 N	9.42 W
Adur ≃	104	50.49 N	0.16 W
Advie	108	57.23 N	3.27 W
Adwa	154	14.10 N	38.55 E
Adwick le Street	106	53.34 N	1.11 W
Adyča ≃	128	68.13 N	134.41 E
Ae, Water of ≃	106	55.08 N	3.27 W
Aegean Sea ⊤[2]	124	38.30 N	25.00 E
A'erjinshanmai ⋏	132	37.30 N	86.30 E
Aeron ≃	104	52.14 N	4.16 W
Ærøskøbing	114	54.53 N	10.25 E
Aershan	132	47.11 N	119.57 E
Afándou	124	36.17 N	28.10 E
Affric ≃	108	57.19 N	4.50 W
Affric, Glen ∨	108	57.17 N	4.56 W
Afghanistan □[1]	144	33.00 N	65.00 E
Afgoi	154	2.10 N	45.09 E
Afikpo	152	5.53 N	7.56 E
Åfjord	114	63.58 N	10.12 E
Afmadu	156	0.32 N	42.10 E
Afonso Cláudio	190	20.05 S	41.08 W
Africa ⊥[1]	88	10.00 N	22.00 E
Afton	176	42.14 N	75.32 W
'Afula	150	32.36 N	35.17 E
Aga	114	60.18 N	6.36 E
Agadez	152	16.58 N	7.59 E
Agadir	152	30.26 N	9.36 W
Agadyr'	126	48.17 N	72.53 E
Agalega Islands II	156	10.24 S	56.37 E
Agalta, Cordillera de ⋏	182	15.00 N	85.53 W
Agan ≃	126	61.23 N	74.35 E
Agana	138	13.28 N	144.45 E
Agano ≃	134	37.57 N	139.08 E
Agapa	128	71.27 N	89.15 E
Agartala, Bhārat	144	23.50 N	91.16 E
Agartala, Bhārat	146	23.49 N	91.16 E
Agassiz, Cape ≻	87	68.29 S	62.56 W
Agboville	152	5.56 N	4.13 W
Agdam	150	39.59 N	46.57 E
Agde	118	43.19 N	3.28 E
Agde, Cap d' ≻	118	43.16 N	3.30 E
Agen	118	44.12 N	0.37 E
Agency Lake ⊜	178	42.32 N	121.58 W
Aggteleki Barlang ⊥[5]	116	48.30 N	20.32 E
Āghā Jārī	150	30.42 N	49.50 E
Aghleam	110	54.08 N	10.07 W
Aginskoje	128	55.15 N	94.55 E
Agira	122	37.39 N	14.32 E
Agly ≃	118	42.47 N	3.02 E
Agnes, Mount ∧	164	26.51 S	128.59 E
Agnew	164	28.01 S	120.30 E
Agnews Hill ∧[2]	110	54.50 N	6.54 W
Ago	134	34.20 N	136.51 E
Agordat → Akordat	154	15.35 N	37.54 E
Agout ≃	118	43.47 N	1.41 E
Āgra	146	27.11 N	78.01 E
Agri → Karaköse	150	39.44 N	43.03 E
Agrigento	122	37.18 N	13.35 E
Agrihan I	138	18.46 N	145.40 E
Agrínion	124	38.37 N	21.24 E
Agro Pontino ⟜[1]	122	41.25 N	12.55 E
Agryz	112	56.33 N	53.00 E
Aguada de Pasajeros	182	22.23 N	80.51 W
Aguadas	184	5.37 N	75.27 W
Aguadilla	182	18.26 N	67.09 W
Água Doce	188	27.00 S	51.33 W
Aguaí	190	22.04 S	46.58 W
Aguán ≃	182	15.58 N	85.44 W
Aguanus ≃	172	50.13 N	62.05 W
Agua Prieta	180	31.18 N	109.34 W
Aguaray Guazú ≃	188	24.05 S	56.40 W
Aguarico ≃	184	0.59 S	75.11 W
Aguascalientes	180	21.53 N	102.18 W
Águas Formosas	190	17.05 S	40.57 W
Agu Bay C	172	70.18 N	86.30 W
Agudo	188	29.38 S	53.15 W
Agudos	190	22.28 S	49.00 W
Águeda	120	40.34 N	8.27 W
Águeda ≃	120	41.02 N	6.56 W
Aguijan I	138	14.51 N	145.34 E
Aguilar	120	37.31 N	4.39 W
Aguilar, Salar de ≚	188	25.49 S	68.53 W
Aguilares	188	27.26 S	65.35 W
Águilas	120	37.24 N	1.35 W
Agulhas, Cape ≻	160	34.52 S	20.00 E
Agulhas Basin ⊹[1]	84	45.00 S	25.00 E
Agulhas Negras, Pico das ∧	190	22.23 S	44.38 W
Agusan ≃	138	9.00 N	125.31 E
Agustín Codazzi	182	10.02 N	73.14 W
Ahaggar ⋏	152	23.00 N	6.30 E
Ahaggar, Tassili du ⋏[1]	152	21.00 N	6.00 E
Aha Hills ⋏[2]	160	19.45 S	21.10 E
Ahar	150	38.28 N	47.04 E
Ahascragh	110	53.24 N	8.20 W
Ahaura	170	42.21 S	171.32 E
Ahfir	120	34.57 N	2.17 W
Ahipara	170	35.10 S	173.10 E
Ahlen	116	51.46 N	7.53 E
Ahmadābād	146	23.02 N	72.37 E
Ahmadnagar	148	19.05 N	74.44 E
Ahmadpur East	149	29.09 N	71.16 E
Ahmar Mountains ⋏	154	9.15 N	41.00 E
Ahmic Lake ⊜	176	45.37 N	79.42 W
Ahrensburg	116	53.40 N	10.14 E
Ähtärinjärvi ⊜	114	62.40 N	24.03 E
Ähtävänjoki ≃	114	63.38 N	22.48 E
Ahu	136	34.27 N	118.39 E
Ahuacatlán	180	21.03 N	104.29 W
Ahumada	178	32.30 N	115.30 W
Ahun	118	46.05 N	2.05 E
Ahunui I[1]	96	19.39 S	140.25 W
Ahuriri ≃	170	44.33 S	170.11 E
Ahvāz	150	31.19 N	48.42 E
Ahvenanmaa □[4]	114	60.15 N	20.00 E
Ahvenanmaa (Åland) II	114	60.15 N	20.00 E
Aḥwar	144	13.31 N	46.42 E
Aibihu ⊜	132	44.55 N	82.55 E
Aichi □[5]	134	35.00 N	137.15 E
Aide ≃	104	52.10 N	1.27 E
Aiea	179a	21.23 N	157.56 W
Aigre	118	45.54 N	0.01 E
Aigues-Mortes	118	43.34 N	4.11 E
Aihun	132	50.13 N	127.33 E
Aijal	146	23.44 N	92.43 E
Aikawa	134	38.02 N	138.15 E
Aiken	174	33.34 N	81.43 W
Ailaoshan ⋏	140	24.08 N	101.25 E
Aileron	164	22.39 S	133.20 E
Ailigandí	182	9.13 N	78.04 W
Ailinglapalap I[1]	96	7.23 N	168.46 E
Ailsa Craig	176	43.08 N	81.33 W
Ailsa Craig I	106	55.16 N	5.07 W
Aim	128	58.50 N	134.12 E
Aimorés	190	19.30 S	41.04 W
Ain □[5]	118	46.10 N	5.20 E
Ain ≃	118	45.48 N	5.10 E
Aïn Berda	122	36.39 N	7.35 E
Ainsdale	106	53.36 N	3.02 W
Aioi	134	34.48 N	134.28 E
Aïr ⋏	152	18.00 N	8.30 E
Airabu, Pulau I	142	2.46 N	106.14 E
Airdrie	108	55.52 N	3.59 W
Aire ≃, Fr.	118	49.19 N	4.49 E
Aire ≃, Eng., U.K.	106	53.44 N	0.54 W
Aire-sur-l'Adour	118	43.42 N	0.16 W
Air Force Island I	172	67.55 N	74.10 W
Airolo	118	46.32 N	8.37 E
Airor	108	57.04 N	5.46 W
Airvault	118	46.50 N	0.08 W
Aisch ≃	116	49.46 N	11.01 E
Aishihik Lake ⊜	172	61.25 N	137.06 W
Aisne □[5]	118	49.30 N	3.30 E
Aïssa, Djebel ∧	152	32.51 N	0.30 W
Aitape	166	3.08 S	142.21 E
Aith	108	60.16 N	1.23 W
Aitolikón	124	38.27 N	21.22 E
Aitutaki I[1]	96	18.52 S	159.45 W
Ait Youssef ou Ali	120	35.13 N	3.55 W
Aiud	124	46.19 N	23.44 E
Aiuruoca	190	21.58 S	44.36 W
Aix-en-Provence	118	43.32 N	5.26 E
Aix-la-Chapelle → Aachen	116	50.47 N	6.05 E
Aix-les-Bains	118	45.42 N	5.55 E
Aíyina	124	37.44 N	23.27 E
Aiyínion	124	40.30 N	22.33 E
Aíyion	124	38.15 N	22.05 E
Aizu-bange	134	37.34 N	139.49 E
Aizu-wakamatsu	134	37.30 N	139.56 E
Ajaccio	122	41.55 N	8.44 E
Ajaguz	128	47.56 N	80.23 E
Ajan	128	56.27 N	138.10 E
Ajan ≃	128	70.10 N	95.50 E
Ajanta	144	20.30 N	75.48 E
Ajanta Range ⋏	148	20.30 N	76.00 E
Ajax	176	43.51 N	79.02 W
Ajdābiyah	154	30.48 N	20.14 E
Ajigasawa	134	40.47 N	140.12 E
Ajjer, Tassili n' ⋏[1]	152	25.10 N	8.00 E
'Ajmah, Jabal al- ⋏	150	29.12 N	34.02 E
Ajmer	146	26.27 N	74.38 E
Ajo, Cabo de ≻	120	43.31 N	3.35 W
Ajon, Ostrov I	128	69.50 N	168.40 E
Ajtos	124	42.42 N	27.15 E
Ajusco	178	31.35 N	116.25 W
Aka ≃	134	38.54 N	139.50 E
Akabira	134a	43.34 N	142.03 E
Akademii, Zaliv C	128	54.15 N	138.05 E
Akagi-san ∧	134	36.33 N	139.11 E
Akaishi-sammyaku ⋏	134	35.18 N	138.07 E
Akalkot	148	17.32 N	76.13 E
Akan	134a	43.06 N	144.10 E
Akaroa	170	43.48 S	172.58 E
'Akasha East	154	21.05 N	30.43 E
Akashi	134	34.38 N	134.59 E
Aken	116	51.51 N	12.02 E
Akershus □[6]	114	60.00 N	11.10 E
Akesu	132	41.10 N	80.20 E
Aketi	154	2.44 N	23.46 E
Akharnaí	124	38.05 N	23.44 E
Aki	134	33.30 N	133.54 E
Akimiski Island I	172	53.00 N	81.20 W
Akita	134	39.43 N	140.07 E
Akita-heiya ≚	134	39.45 N	140.10 E
Akjoujt	152	19.45 N	14.23 W
Akkeshi	134a	43.02 N	144.51 E
'Akko (Acre)	150	32.55 N	35.05 E
Akkol', S.S.S.R.	126	43.25 N	70.47 E
Akkol', S.S.S.R.	126	45.02 N	75.40 E
Aklavik	172	68.12 N	135.00 W
Akō	134	34.45 N	134.24 E
Akobo ≃	154	7.47 N	33.01 E
Akola	148	20.44 N	77.00 E
Akordat	154	15.35 N	37.54 E
Akot	146	21.11 N	77.04 E
Akpatok Island I	172	60.25 N	68.00 W
Åkrafjorden C[2]	114	59.46 N	6.06 E
Akranes	112a	64.18 N	22.02 W
Akron, N.Y., U.S.	176	43.01 N	78.30 W
Akron, Ohio, U.S.	176	41.05 N	81.31 W
Akron, Pa., U.S.	176	40.09 N	76.12 W
Aksaray	150	38.23 N	34.03 E
Aksarka	128	66.36 N	67.46 E
Akşehir	144	38.21 N	31.25 E
Aksuat	128	47.48 N	82.50 E
Aksum	154	14.08 N	38.48 E
Aktogaj	128	46.57 N	79.40 E
Akt'ubinsk	126	50.17 N	57.10 E
Akune	134	32.01 N	130.11 E
Akureyri	112a	65.44 N	18.08 W
Akuseki-shima I	135b	29.27 N	129.37 E
Akžar	128	47.35 N	83.42 E
Alabama □[3]	174	32.50 N	87.00 W
Alagoa Grande	184	7.03 S	35.38 W
Alagoinhas	190	12.07 S	38.26 W
Alagón	120	41.46 N	1.07 W
Alajskij Chrebet ⋏	126	39.45 N	72.00 E
Alajuela	182	10.01 N	84.13 W
Alakol', Ozero ⊜	128	46.10 N	81.45 E
Alalakeiki Channel ⋓	179a	20.35 N	156.30 W
Al-'Alamayn	154	30.49 N	28.57 E
Al-'Amādīyah	150	37.06 N	43.29 E
Alamagan I	138	17.36 N	145.50 E
Al-'Amārah	150	31.50 N	47.09 E
Alameda, Esp.	120	37.12 N	4.39 W
Alameda, Calif., U.S.	178	37.46 N	122.16 W
Alamein → Al-'Alamayn	154	30.49 N	28.57 E
Alamo	178	37.22 N	115.10 W
Alamo ≃	178	33.14 N	115.39 W
Alamogordo	174	32.54 N	105.57 W
Alamosa	174	37.28 N	105.52 W
Alanäs	114	64.10 N	15.42 E
Aland Sea ⊤[2]	114	60.00 N	19.30 E
Alanson	176	45.27 N	84.47 W
Alanya	144	36.33 N	32.01 E
Alaotra, Lac ⊜	161b	17.30 S	48.30 E
Alapajevsk	126	57.52 N	61.42 E
Al-'Aqabah	150	29.31 N	35.00 E
Alarcón	120	39.33 N	2.05 W
Alarcón, Embalse de ⊜[1]	120	39.36 N	2.10 W
Al-'Arīsh	154	31.08 N	33.48 E
Alasdair, Sgurr ∧	108	57.12 N	6.14 W
Alashanyouqi	132	40.02 N	103.33 E
Alaska □[3]	90	64.00 N	150.00 W
Alaska, Gulf of C	172	58.00 N	146.00 W
Alaska Range ⋏	172	62.30 N	150.00 W
Alassio	122	44.00 N	8.10 E
Alat, S.S.S.R.	150	39.26 N	63.48 E
Al'at, S.S.S.R.	150	39.57 N	49.25 E
Al-'Aṭrūn	154	18.11 N	26.36 E
Alatyr'	112	54.51 N	46.36 E
Alausí	184	2.12 S	78.50 W
Alava □[4]	120	42.50 N	2.45 W
Alavus	114	62.35 N	23.37 E
Alaw ≃	106	53.18 N	4.32 W
Alaw, Llyn ⊜[1]	106	53.20 N	4.22 W
Alazeja ≃	128	70.51 N	153.34 E
Al-'Azīzīyah	154	32.32 N	13.01 E
Alba, It.	122	44.42 N	8.02 E
Alba, Mich., U.S.	176	44.59 N	84.58 W
Alba □[4]	124	46.15 N	23.30 E
Albacete	120	38.59 N	1.51 W
Alba-Iulia	124	46.04 N	23.35 E
Alban	118	43.54 N	2.28 E
Albanel, Lac ⊜	172	50.55 N	73.12 W
Albania □[1]	100	41.00 N	20.00 E
Albano Laziale	122	41.44 N	12.39 E
Albany, Austl.	164	35.02 S	117.53 E
Albany, N.Z.	170	36.43 S	174.42 E
Albany, Ga., U.S.	174	31.35 N	84.10 W
Albany, Ind., U.S.	176	40.18 N	85.14 W
Albany, N.Y., U.S.	176	42.39 N	73.45 W
Albany, Ohio, U.S.	176	39.14 N	82.12 W
Albany ≃	172	52.17 N	81.31 W
Albardón	188	31.26 S	68.30 W
Al-Başrah (Basra)	150	30.30 N	47.47 E
Albatross Bay C	166	12.45 S	141.43 E
Albatross Cordillera ⊹[3]	87	62.00 S	155.00 W
Al-Bawīṭī	154	28.21 N	28.52 E
Albemarle Sound ⋓	174	36.03 N	76.12 W
Albenga	122	44.03 N	8.13 E
Alberene	176	37.53 N	78.37 W
Alberga Creek ≃	164	27.06 S	135.33 E
Albert	118	50.00 N	2.39 E
Albert, Lake ⊜, Afr.	158	1.40 N	31.00 E
Albert, Lake ⊜, Austl.	168	35.38 S	139.17 E
Alberta □[4]	172	54.00 N	113.00 W
Albert Edward, Mount ∧	166	8.23 S	147.24 E
Albert Edward Bay C	172	69.32 N	103.00 W
Albertinia	160	34.13 S	21.36 E
Albertirsa	116	47.15 N	19.38 E
Albert Lea	174	43.39 N	93.22 W
Albert Markham, Mount ∧	87	81.23 S	158.12 E
Albert Nile ≃	158	3.36 N	32.02 E
Albertville, Fr.	118	45.41 N	6.23 E
Albertville → Kalemi, Zaïre	158	5.56 S	29.12 E
Albi	118	43.56 N	2.09 E
Albina	184	5.30 N	54.03 W
Albino	122	45.46 N	9.47 E
Albion, Calif., U.S.	178	39.13 N	123.46 W
Albion, Idaho, U.S.	178	42.25 N	113.35 W
Albion, Ind., U.S.	176	41.24 N	85.25 W
Albion, Mich., U.S.	176	42.15 N	84.45 W
Albion, N.Y., U.S.	176	43.15 N	78.12 W
Albion, Pa., U.S.	176	41.53 N	80.22 W
Alborán, Isla de I	120	35.58 N	3.02 W
Ålborg	114	57.03 N	9.56 E
Alborz, Reshteh-ye Kūhhā-ye ⋏	150	36.00 N	53.00 E
Albrighton	104	52.38 N	2.16 W
Albufeira	120	37.05 N	8.15 W
Ālbū Gharz, Sabkhat ⊜	150	34.45 N	41.15 E
Albuquerque	174	35.05 N	106.40 W
Albuquerque, Cayos de II	182	12.10 N	81.50 W
Alburg	176	44.59 N	73.18 W
Alburquerque	120	39.13 N	7.00 W
Albury	168	36.05 S	146.55 E
Alcains	120	39.55 N	7.27 W
Alcalá de Guadaira	120	37.20 N	5.50 W
Alcalá de Henares	120	40.29 N	3.22 W
Alcalá la Real	120	37.28 N	3.56 W
Alcamo	122	37.59 N	12.58 E
Alcañiz	120	41.03 N	0.08 W
Alcântara	184	2.24 S	44.24 W
Alcántara, Embalse de ⊜[1]	120	39.45 N	6.25 W
Alcantarilla	120	37.58 N	1.13 W
Alcarrache ≃	120	38.16 N	7.24 W
Alcázar de San Juan	120	39.24 N	3.12 W
Alcester	104	52.13 N	1.52 W
Alcira	120	39.09 N	0.26 W
Alcobaça, Bra.	190	17.30 S	39.13 W
Alcobaça, Port.	120	39.33 N	8.59 W
Alcobendas	120	40.32 N	3.38 W
Alcolea del Piuar	120	41.02 N	2.28 W
Alconbury Brook ≃	104	52.19 N	0.12 W
Alcorta	188	33.32 S	61.08 W
Alcoy	120	38.42 N	0.28 W
Alcudia, Bahía de C	120	39.48 N	3.13 E
Aldabra Islands I[1]	156	9.25 S	46.22 E
Aldan	128	58.37 N	125.24 E
Aldan ≃	128	63.28 N	129.35 E
Aldanskoje Nagorje ⋏[1]	128	57.00 N	127.00 E
Aldbourne	104	51.31 N	1.37 W
Aldbrough	106	53.50 N	0.07 W
Aldbury	104	51.48 N	0.36 W
Alde ≃	102	52.03 N	1.28 E
Aldeburgh	104	52.09 N	1.35 E
Aldeia Nova de Santo Bento	120	37.55 N	7.25 W
Alder, Ben ∧	108	56.48 N	4.28 W
Alderley	168	22.39 S	139.44 E
Alderley Edge	106	53.18 N	2.15 W
Aldermaston	104	51.23 N	1.09 W
Alderney I	105b	49.43 N	2.12 W
Aldershot	104	51.15 N	0.47 W
Aldridge	104	52.36 N	1.55 W
Aled Om	104	53.14 N	3.34 W
Aleg	152	17.03 N	13.55 W
Alegre	190	20.46 S	41.32 W
Alegrete	188	29.46 S	55.46 W
Alejandro Roca	188	33.20 S	63.43 W
Alejandro Selkirk, Isla (Isla Más Afuera) I	186	33.45 S	80.46 W
Alejsk	128	52.58 N	82.45 E
Aleksandrov	130	56.24 N	38.43 E
Aleksandrovsk	126	48.35 N	39.12 E
Aleksandrovskoje	128	60.26 N	77.50 E
Aleksandrovsk-Sachalinskij	128	50.54 N	142.10 E
Aleksejevka	126	51.59 N	70.59 E
Aleksejevsk	128	57.50 N	108.23 E
Aleksin	130	54.31 N	37.05 E
Aleksinac	124	43.32 N	21.43 E
Alemania, Arg.	188	25.35 S	65.40 W
Alemania, Chile	188	25.10 S	69.55 W
Alençon	118	48.26 N	0.05 E
Alenquer	184	1.56 S	54.46 W

Symbols in the index entries are identified on page 198.

Arch – Baja

Name	Page	Lat °′	Long °′
Archangel → Archangel'sk	112	64.34 N	40.32 E
Archangel'sk	112	64.34 N	40.32 E
Archbold	176	41.31 N	84.18 W
Archer, Mount ∧	168	23.20 S	150.34 E
Archer Bay C	166	13.25 S	141.43 E
Archiac	118	45.31 N	0.18 W
Arckaringa	164	27.56 S	134.45 E
Arckaringa Creek ≃	164	28.10 S	135.22 E
Arco de Baúlhe	120	41.29 N	7.58 W
Arcos	190	20.17 S	45.32 W
Arcos de la Frontera	120	36.45 N	5.48 W
Arcot	148	12.54 N	79.20 E
Arcoverde	184	8.25 S	37.04 W
Arctic Bay	172	73.02 N	85.11 W
Arctic Ocean ▼1	90	85.00 N	170.00 E
Arctic Red ≃	172	67.27 N	133.46 W
Arcturus	158	17.47 S	31.20 E
Ard, Loch ⊜	108	56.11 N	4.28 W
Arda ≃	124	41.39 N	26.29 E
Ardabīl	150	38.15 N	48.18 E
Ardagh	110	52.28 N	9.04 W
Ardahan	144	41.07 N	42.41 E
Ardakān	150	32.19 N	53.59 E
Ardalanish, Rubh' ➤	108	56.17 N	6.18 W
Årdalsfjorden C2	114	61.12 N	7.30 E
Årdalstangen	114	61.14 N	7.43 E
Ardara	110	54.46 N	8.25 E
Ardarroch	108	57.25 N	5.38 W
Ardbeg	108	55.39 N	6.05 W
Ardcharnich	108	57.51 N	5.05 W
Ardèche □5	118	44.40 N	4.20 E
Ardee	110	53.52 N	6.33 W
Arden	178	38.36 N	121.23 W
Arden, Forest of ◆3	104	52.23 N	1.42 W
Arden, Mount ∧	168	32.09 S	137.59 E
Ardennes □5	118	49.40 N	4.40 E
Ardennes ◆1	116	50.10 N	5.45 E
Ardentinny	108	56.03 N	4.55 W
Arderin ∧2	110	53.02 N	7.40 W
Ardfern	108	56.10 N	5.32 W
Ardglass	110	54.16 N	5.36 W
Ardgroom	110	51.42 N	9.52 W
Ardila ≃	120	38.12 N	7.28 W
Ardlethan	168	34.21 S	146.54 E
Ardlui	108	56.18 N	4.43 W
Ardlussa	108	56.02 N	5.47 W
Ardmolich	108	56.49 N	5.41 W
Ardmore, Eire	110	51.57 N	7.43 W
Ardmore, Okla., U.S.	174	34.10 N	97.08 W
Ardmore, Pa., U.S.	176	40.01 N	75.18 W
Ardmore Point ➤, Scot., U.K.	108	56.39 N	6.07 W
Ardmore Point ➤, Scot., U.K.	108	55.42 N	6.01 W
Ardnamurchan ➤1	108	56.43 N	6.00 W
Ardnamurchan, Point of ➤	108	56.44 N	6.13 W
Ardnaree	110	54.06 N	9.08 W
Ardnave Point ➤	108	55.44 N	6.20 W
Ardoch	168	27.26 S	144.08 E
Ardrishaig	108	56.01 N	5.27 W
Ardrossan	108	55.39 N	4.49 W
Ardsley	106	53.32 N	1.28 W
Ardtalnaig	108	56.31 N	4.06 W
Åre	114	63.24 N	13.04 E
Areado	190	21.21 S	46.09 W
Arecibo	182	18.28 N	66.43 W
Areia Branca	184	4.56 S	37.07 W
Arena, Point ➤	178	38.57 N	123.44 W
Arena de la Ventana, Punta ➤	174	24.04 N	109.52 W
Arenas, Punta de ➤	182	10.29 N	64.14 W
Arenas de San Pedro	120	40.12 N	5.05 W
Arendal	114	58.27 N	8.48 E
Arennig Fawr ∧	104	52.55 N	3.45 W
Arenys de Mar	120	41.35 N	2.33 E
Arequipa	184	16.24 S	71.33 W
Arequito	188	33.10 S	61.29 W
Arero	158	4.42 N	38.47 E
Arès	118	44.46 N	1.08 W
Arezzo	122	43.25 N	11.53 E
Argadargada	168	21.40 S	136.40 E
Argamasilla de Alba	120	39.07 N	3.06 W
Arga-Sala ≃	128	68.30 N	112.12 E
Argelès-Gazost	118	43.01 N	0.06 E
Argelès-sur-Mer	118	42.33 N	3.01 E
Argent, Côte d' ⊥2	120	43.30 N	1.30 W
Argenta	122	44.37 N	11.50 E
Argentan	118	48.45 N	0.01 W
Argentat	118	45.06 N	1.56 E
Argenteuil	102	48.57 N	2.15 E
Argentina □1	186	34.00 S	64.00 W
Argentine Basin ∻1	92	45.00 S	45.00 W
Argentino, Lago ⊜	186	50.15 S	72.25 W
Argeș □4	124	45.00 N	24.45 E
Arghandāb ≃	144	31.27 N	64.23 E
Argolikós Kólpos C	124	37.33 N	22.45 E
Argonne ◆1	118	49.30 N	5.00 E
Árgos	124	37.39 N	22.44 E
Árgos Orestikón	124	40.28 N	21.16 E
Argostólion	124	38.10 N	20.30 E
Arguello, Point ➤	178	34.35 N	120.39 W
Argun' (Eergu'nahe) ≃	128	53.20 N	121.28 E
Argyle, Lake ⊜1	166	16.15 S	128.45 E
Århus	114	56.09 N	10.13 E
Ariake-wan C	134	31.28 N	131.08 E
Ariana	122	36.52 N	10.12 E
Ariano Irpino	122	41.09 N	15.05 E
Arica, Chile	184	18.29 S	70.20 W
Arica, Col.	184	2.08 S	71.47 W
Arid, Cape ➤	164	34.00 S	123.09 E
Arida	134	34.05 N	135.07 E
Ariège □5	118	43.00 N	1.30 E
Ariège ≃	118	43.31 N	1.25 E
Ārifwāla	149	30.17 N	73.04 E
Ariguaní ≃	182	9.35 N	73.50 W
Arīḥā (Jericho)	150	31.52 N	35.27 E
Arikawa	134	32.59 N	129.07 E
Arima	182	10.38 N	61.17 W
Arinagour	108	56.37 N	6.31 W
Ariquemes	184	9.56 S	63.04 W
Arisaig	108	56.51 N	5.51 W
Arisaig, Sound of C	108	56.51 N	5.51 W
'Arīsh, Wādī al- V	150	31.09 N	33.49 E
Arizaro, Salar de ≚	188	24.40 S	67.55 W
Arizgoiti	120	43.01 N	2.24 W
Arizona	188	35.49 S	65.20 W
Arizona □3	174	34.00 N	112.00 W
Årjäng	114	59.23 N	12.08 E
Arjona	182	10.15 N	75.21 W
Arka	128	60.03 N	142.12 E
Arkadelphia	174	34.07 N	93.04 W
Arkaig, Loch ⊜	108	56.58 N	5.08 W
Arkalyk	126	50.13 N	66.50 E
Arkansas □3	174	34.50 N	93.40 W
Arkansas ≃	174	33.48 N	91.04 W
Arkansas City	174	37.04 N	97.02 W
Arklow	110	52.48 N	6.09 W
Arkona, Kap ➤	116	54.41 N	13.26 E
Arkonam	148	13.06 N	79.40 E
Arkport	176	42.24 N	77.42 W
Arktičeskij, Mys ➤	128	81.15 N	95.45 E
Arktičeskogo Instituta, Ostrova II	128	75.20 N	81.55 E
Arlanc	118	45.25 N	3.44 E
Arles	118	43.40 N	4.38 E
Arlington, S. Afr.	160	28.06 S	27.54 E
Arlington, Ohio, U.S.	176	40.54 N	83.39 W
Arlington, Vt., U.S.	176	43.05 N	73.09 W
Arlington, Va., U.S.	176	38.52 N	77.05 W
Arlon	116	49.41 N	5.49 E
Arltunga	164	23.26 S	134.41 E
Armada	176	42.51 N	82.53 W
Armadale, Austl.	164	32.09 S	116.00 E
Armadale, Scot., U.K.	108	55.54 N	3.42 W
Armagh	110	54.21 N	6.39 W
Armançon ≃	118	47.57 N	3.30 E
Arm'anskaja Sovetskaja Socialističeskaja Respublika □3	126	40.00 N	45.00 E
Armavir	126	45.00 N	41.08 E
Armazém	188	28.16 S	49.01 W
Armenia	184	4.31 N	75.41 W
Armentières	118	50.41 N	2.53 E
Armidale	168	30.31 S	151.39 E
Armit Lake ⊜	172	64.10 N	91.32 W
Armona	178	36.19 N	119.42 W
Armstrong	188	32.50 S	61.35 W
Armstrong, Mount ∧	172	63.12 N	133.16 W
Armstrong Station	172	50.18 N	89.02 W
Armthorpe	106	53.32 N	1.03 W
Arnaud ≃	172	59.59 N	69.46 W
Arnay-le-Duc	118	47.08 N	4.29 E
Arney ≃	110	54.16 N	7.37 W
Arnhem	116	51.59 N	5.55 E
Arnhem, Cape ➤	166	12.21 S	136.21 E
Arnhem Bay C	166	12.20 S	136.12 E
Arnhem Land ◆1	166	13.10 S	134.30 E
Arno I1	96	7.05 N	171.41 E
Arno ≃	122	43.41 N	10.17 E
Arno Bay	168	33.54 S	136.34 E
Arnold, Eng., U.K.	104	53.00 N	1.08 W
Arnold, Calif., U.S.	178	38.15 N	120.21 W
Arnold ≃	166	15.19 S	134.06 E
Arnprior	172	45.26 N	76.21 W
Arnsberg	116	51.24 N	8.03 E
Arnstadt	116	50.50 N	10.57 E
Aroa	182	10.26 N	68.54 W
Aroa ≃	182	10.40 N	68.19 W
Aroab	160	26.47 S	19.40 E
Arona	122	45.46 N	8.34 E
Arorae I	96	2.38 S	176.49 E
Arosa	118	46.47 N	9.41 E
Arowhana ∧	170	38.07 S	177.52 E
Ar-Rab' al-Khālī ◆2	144	20.00 N	51.00 E
Ar-Rābi', Ash-Shallāl ↳	154	18.47 N	32.03 E
Arrah	146	25.34 N	84.40 E
Ar-Rahad	154	12.43 N	30.39 E
Arraial do Cabo	190	22.58 S	42.01 W
Arraias	190	12.56 S	46.57 W
Ar-Ramādī	150	33.25 N	43.17 E
Arran, Island of I	108	55.36 N	5.15 W
Ar-Rank	154	11.45 N	32.48 E
Ar-Raqqah	150	35.56 N	39.01 E
Arras	118	50.17 N	2.47 E
Arrats ≃	118	44.06 N	0.52 E
Arrecifes	188	34.05 S	60.05 W
Arrée, Montagnes d' ⋀	118	48.26 N	3.55 W
Ar-Riyāḍ (Riyadh)	150	24.38 N	46.43 E
Arrochar	108	56.12 N	4.44 W
Arroio Grande	188	32.14 S	53.05 W
Arronches	120	39.07 N	7.17 W
Arroux ≃	118	46.29 N	3.58 E
Arrow ≃, Eng., U.K.	104	52.09 N	1.53 W
Arrow ≃, Eng., U.K.	104	52.12 N	2.43 W
Arrow, Lough ⊜	110	54.04 N	8.21 W
Arrowsmith, Mount ∧	168	30.09 S	141.50 E
Arrowsmith Bay C	172	68.00 N	95.15 W
Arroyo de la Luz	120	39.29 N	6.35 W
Arroyo Grande	178	35.07 N	120.34 W
Ar-Rukhaymīyah ▼4	150	29.14 N	45.35 E
Ar-Ruṣayriṣ	154	11.51 N	34.23 E
Ar-Ruṭbah	150	33.02 N	40.17 E
Arsenjev	128	44.10 N	133.15 E
Árta	124	39.09 N	20.59 E
Artemisa	182	22.49 N	82.46 W
Artesia	174	32.51 N	104.24 W
Arthabaska	176	46.02 N	71.55 W
Arthur	176	43.50 N	80.32 W
Arthur ≃	168	41.03 S	144.40 E
Arthur Creek ≃	168	22.55 S	136.45 E
Arthur Fiord C2	172	76.33 N	93.11 W
Arthur's Pass	170	42.57 S	171.34 E
Arthurs Town	182	24.38 N	75.42 W
Artibonite ≃	182	19.15 N	72.46 W
Artigas	188	30.24 S	56.28 W
Artik	150	40.35 N	43.52 E
Artillery Lake ⊜	172	63.09 N	107.52 W
Artney, Glen V	108	56.20 N	4.04 W
Artois □9	118	50.30 N	2.30 E
Art'om	128	43.22 N	132.13 E
Art'omovsk	128	54.21 N	93.26 E
Art'omovskij, S.S.S.R.	126	57.21 N	61.54 E
Art'omovskij, S.S.S.R.	128	58.12 N	114.45 E
Artur de Paiva	156	14.28 S	16.20 E
Artvin	126	41.11 N	41.49 E
Artyk	128	64.12 N	145.06 E
Aru, Kepulauan II	166	6.00 S	134.30 E
Aru, Tanjung ➤	142	2.10 S	116.34 E
Arua	154	3.01 N	30.55 E
Aruanã	190	14.54 S	51.05 W
Aruângua (Luangwa) ≃	158	15.36 S	30.25 E
Aruba I	182	12.30 N	69.58 W
Aru Basin ∻1	96	5.30 S	133.30 E
Arun ≃	102	50.48 N	0.33 W
Arunachal Pradesh □8	146	28.30 N	95.00 E
Arundel	104	50.51 N	0.34 W
Aruppukkottai	148	9.31 N	78.06 E
Arusha	158	3.22 S	36.41 E
Arusha □4	158	4.00 S	36.15 E
Aruwimi ≃	158	1.13 N	24.10 E
Arvagh	110	53.55 N	7.34 W
Arvajcheer	132	46.15 N	102.45 E
Arvi	146	20.59 N	78.14 E
Arvida	172	48.25 N	71.11 W
Arvidsjaur	112	65.35 N	19.07 E
Arvika	114	59.39 N	12.36 E
Arvin	178	35.12 N	118.50 W
Àrvorezinha	188	28.53 S	52.10 W
Arys'	126	42.26 N	68.48 E
Arzamas	112	55.23 N	43.50 E
Arzew	120	35.51 N	0.19 W
Arzignano	122	45.31 N	11.20 E
Aš	116	50.10 N	12.10 E
Aša	126	55.00 N	57.16 E
Asadābād	146	34.52 N	71.09 E
Asahi	134	35.43 N	140.39 E
Asahi ≃	134	34.36 N	133.58 E
Asahi-dake ∧	134a	43.40 N	142.51 E
Asahigawa → Asahikawa	134a	43.46 N	142.22 E
Asahikawa	134a	43.46 N	142.22 E
Asahi-sanchi ⋀	134	38.25 N	139.50 E
Asamankese	152	5.52 N	0.42 W
Asama-yama ∧	134	36.24 N	138.31 E
Asansol	146	23.41 N	86.59 E
Asbesberge ⋀	160	28.55 S	23.15 E
Asbest	126	57.00 N	61.30 E
Asbestos	172	45.46 N	71.57 W
Asbury Park	176	40.13 N	74.01 W
Ascension I	88	7.57 S	14.22 W
Ascensión, Bahía de la C	182	19.38 N	87.35 W
Aš̌chabad	150	37.57 N	58.23 E
Aschaffenburg	116	49.59 N	9.09 E
Aschersleben	116	51.45 N	11.27 E
Ascoli Piceno	122	42.51 N	13.34 E
Ascona	118	46.09 N	8.46 E
Ascot	104	51.25 N	0.41 W
Ascotán	188	21.44 S	68.18 W
Aseb	154	13.00 N	42.45 E
Asela	154	7.59 N	39.08 E
Åsele	114	64.10 N	17.20 E
Asenovgrad	124	42.01 N	24.52 E
Åsgårdstrand	114	59.21 N	10.28 E
Ash, Eng., U.K.	104	51.15 N	0.44 W
Ash, Eng., U.K.	104	51.17 N	1.16 E
Ash ≃	104	51.48 N	0.02 W
Ashbourne, Eire	110	53.31 N	6.24 W
Ashbourne, Eng., U.K.	104	53.02 N	1.44 W
Ashburton, N.Z.	170	43.55 S	171.45 E
Ashburton, Eng., U.K.	104	50.31 N	3.45 W
Ashburton ≃	164	21.40 S	114.56 E
Ashburton, North Branch ≃	170	43.54 S	171.44 E
Ashburton, South Branch ≃	170	43.44 S	171.32 E
Ashby-de-la-Zouch	104	52.46 N	1.28 W
Ash Creek ≃	178	41.05 N	121.08 W
Ashdown Forest ◆3	104	51.04 N	0.03 E
Asheville	174	35.34 N	82.33 W
Asheweig ≃	172	54.17 N	87.12 W
Ashford, Austl.	168	29.20 S	151.06 E
Ashford, Eng., U.K.	102	51.26 N	0.27 W
Ashford, Eng., U.K.	104	51.08 N	0.53 E
Ashibe	134	33.48 N	129.46 E
Ashibetsu	134a	43.31 N	142.11 E
Ashikaga	134	36.20 N	139.27 E
Ashington	106	55.12 N	1.35 W
Ashio	134	36.38 N	139.27 E
Ashiyoro	134a	43.15 N	143.30 E
Ashizuri-zaki ➤	134	32.44 N	133.01 E
Ashland, Ky., U.S.	176	38.28 N	82.38 W
Ashland, N.H., U.S.	176	43.42 N	71.38 W
Ashland, Ohio, U.S.	176	40.52 N	82.19 W
Ashland, Oreg., U.S.	178	42.12 N	122.42 W
Ashland, Pa., U.S.	176	40.47 N	76.21 W
Ashland, Wis., U.S.	174	46.35 N	90.53 W
Ashland, Mount ∧	178	42.05 N	122.43 W
Ashley, Austl.	168	29.19 S	149.49 E
Ashley, Mich., U.S.	176	43.11 N	84.29 W
Ashley, Ohio, U.S.	176	40.25 N	82.57 W
Ashley ≃	170	43.16 S	172.43 E
Ashmore Islands II	162	12.14 S	123.05 E
Ashoknagar	146	24.34 N	77.43 E
Ashqelon	150	31.40 N	34.35 E
Ash-Shaqrā'	150	25.15 N	45.15 E
Ash-Shāriqah	150	25.22 N	55.23 E
Ash-Sharqāṭ	150	35.27 N	43.16 E
Ash-Shaṭrah	150	31.25 N	46.10 E
Ash-Shiḥr	144	14.44 N	49.35 E
Ashtabula	176	41.52 N	80.48 W
Ashtead	104	51.19 N	0.18 W
Ashton	160	33.50 S	20.05 E
Ashton-in-Makerfield	106	53.29 N	2.39 W
Ashton-under-Lyne	106	53.29 N	2.06 W
Ashuanipi Lake ⊜	172	52.35 N	66.10 W
Ashuelot ≃	176	42.46 N	72.29 W
Ashville	176	39.43 N	82.57 W
Ashwater	104	50.44 N	4.16 W
Asia ⊥1	94	50.00 N	100.00 E
Asia, Kepulauan II	138	1.03 N	131.18 E
Asia Minor ◆1	144	39.00 N	32.00 E
Asilah	152	35.32 N	6.00 W
Asino	128	57.00 N	86.09 E
'Asīr ◆1	144	19.00 N	42.00 E
Asir, Ras ➤	144	11.48 N	51.22 E
Askeaton	110	52.36 N	8.58 W
Askern	106	53.37 N	1.09 W
Askham	160	26.59 S	20.47 E
Askival ∧	108	56.59 N	6.17 W
Askja ∧1	112a	65.00 N	16.48 W
Askrigg	106	54.19 N	2.04 W
Āsmār	149	35.02 N	71.22 E
Asmera	154	15.20 N	38.53 E
Åsnen ⊜	114	56.38 N	14.42 E
Asosa	154	10.03 N	34.32 E
Aso-san ∧	134	32.53 N	131.06 E
Aspatria	106	54.46 N	3.20 W
Aspe	120	38.21 N	0.46 W
Aspen	174	39.11 N	106.49 W
Aspen Butte ∧	178	42.19 N	122.05 W
Aspen Lake ⊜	178	42.18 N	122.00 W
Aspiring, Mount ∧	170	44.23 S	168.44 E
Asprópotamos ≃	124	40.52 N	21.41 E
As-Sablūkah, Ash-Shallāl ↳	154	16.20 N	32.42 E
Aṣ-Ṣabyā	144	17.09 N	42.37 E
Aṣ-Ṣaḥrā'al-Gharb1yah (Western Desert) ◆2	154	27.00 N	27.00 E
Aṣ-Ṣaḥrā' al-Lībīyah (Libyan Desert) ◆2	154	24.00 N	25.00 E
Aṣ-Ṣaḥrā'ash-Sharq1yah (Eastern Desert) ◆2	154	28.00 N	32.00 E
Assai	190	23.22 S	50.49 W
As-Sallūm	154	31.34 N	25.09 E
As-Salṭ	150	32.03 N	35.44 E
Assam □3	146	26.00 N	92.00 E
As-Samāwah	150	31.18 N	45.17 E
Assateague Island I	176	38.05 N	75.10 W
Asse	116	50.55 N	4.12 E
Assen	116	52.59 N	6.34 E
Assens	114	55.16 N	9.55 E
Assiniboia	172	49.38 N	105.59 W
Assiniboine, Mount ∧	172	50.52 N	115.39 W
Assis	190	22.40 S	50.25 W
Assisi	122	43.04 N	12.37 E
As-Sulaymānīyah, Ar. Sa.	150	24.09 N	47.19 E
As-Sulaymānīyah, 'Irāq	150	35.33 N	45.26 E
As-Sulaymī	150	26.17 N	41.21 E
As-Sulayyil	144	20.27 N	45.34 E
Assumption Island I	156	9.45 S	46.30 E
As-Suwaydā'	150	32.42 N	36.34 E
As-Suways (Suez)	154	29.58 N	32.33 E
Assynt, Loch ⊜	108	58.11 N	5.06 W
Astaffort	118	44.04 N	0.40 E
Astakós	124	38.32 N	21.05 E
Āstārā, Īrān	150	38.26 N	48.52 E
Astara, S.S.S.R.	126	38.28 N	48.52 E
Asti	122	44.54 N	8.12 E
Astolfo Dutra	190	21.19 S	42.52 W
Aston Clinton	104	51.48 N	0.44 W
Astorga, Bra.	190	23.13 S	51.40 W
Astorga, Esp.	120	42.27 N	6.03 W
Astoria	174	46.11 N	123.50 W
Astove Island I	156	10.06 S	47.45 E
Astrachan'	126	46.21 N	48.03 E
Astrolabe Bay C	166	5.20 S	145.50 E
Asturias □9	120	43.20 N	6.00 W
Asunción	188	25.16 S	57.40 W
Asuncion Island I	138	19.40 N	145.24 E
Aswān	154	24.05 N	32.53 E
Asyūṭ	154	27.11 N	31.11 E
Aszód	116	47.39 N	19.31 E
Ata I	96	22.20 S	176.12 W
Atacama □4	188	27.30 S	70.00 W
Atacama, Desierto de ◆2	92	22.30 S	69.15 W
Atacama, Puna de ⋀1	188	25.00 S	68.00 W
Atacama, Salar de ≚	188	23.30 S	68.15 W
Atacama Trench ∻1	92	21.00 S	72.00 W
Atafu I1	96	8.33 S	172.30 W
Atakpamé	152	7.32 N	1.08 E
Atalándi	124	38.39 N	23.00 E
Atambua	142	9.07 S	124.54 E
Atami	134	35.05 N	139.04 E
Atapupu	142	9.00 S	124.51 E
Atar	152	20.31 N	13.03 W
Atascadero	178	35.29 N	120.40 W
Atasu	126	48.42 N	71.38 E
'Aṭbarah	154	17.42 N	33.59 E
'Aṭbarah (Atbara) ≃	154	17.40 N	33.56 E
Atbasar	126	51.48 N	68.20 E
Atchison	174	39.34 N	97.07 W
Ath	118	50.38 N	3.47 E
Athabasca	172	54.43 N	113.17 W
Athabasca ≃	172	58.40 N	110.50 W
Athabasca, Lake ⊜	172	59.07 N	110.00 W
Athboy	110	53.37 N	6.55 W
Athea	110	52.28 N	9.17 W
Athenry	110	53.18 N	8.45 W
Athens, Ont., Can.	176	44.38 N	75.57 W
Athens → Athínai, Ellás	124	37.58 N	23.43 E
Athens, Ga., U.S.	174	33.57 N	83.23 W
Athens, Maine, U.S.	176	44.55 N	69.41 W
Athens, Mich., U.S.	176	42.05 N	85.14 W
Athens, N.Y., U.S.	176	42.16 N	73.49 W
Athens, Ohio, U.S.	176	39.20 N	82.06 W
Athens, Pa., U.S.	176	41.57 N	76.31 W
Athens, Tenn., U.S.	174	35.27 N	84.36 W
Atherstone	104	52.35 N	1.31 W
Atherton, Austl.	168	17.16 S	145.29 E
Atherton, Eng., U.K.	106	53.31 N	2.31 W
Athínai (Athens)	124	37.58 N	23.43 E
Athleague	110	53.34 N	8.15 W
Athlone	110	53.25 N	7.56 W
Athni	148	16.44 N	75.04 E
Athol, N.Z.	170	45.31 S	168.35 E
Athol, Mass., U.S.	176	42.36 N	72.14 W
Atholl, Forest of ◆3	108	56.50 N	4.00 W
Áthos ∧	124	40.09 N	24.19 E
Ath-Thālith, Ash-Shallāl ↳	154	19.49 N	30.19 E
Ath-Thamad	150	29.41 N	34.18 E
Athy	110	53.00 N	7.00 W
Ati	154	13.13 N	18.20 E
Atibaia ≃	190	22.42 S	47.17 W
Atikokan	172	48.45 N	91.37 W
Atikonak Lake ⊜	172	52.40 N	64.30 W
Atka	128	60.50 N	151.48 E
Atkarsk	126	51.52 N	45.00 E
Atlanta, Ga., U.S.	174	33.45 N	84.23 W
Atlanta, Mich., U.S.	176	45.00 N	84.09 W
Atlantic City	176	39.22 N	74.26 W
Atlantic-Indian Basin ∻1	87	60.00 S	15.00 E
Atlantic Indian Ridge ∻3	84	54.00 S	20.00 E
Atlántico □5	182	10.45 N	45.00 W
Atlantic Ocean ▼1	84	0.00	25.00 W
Atlántida	188	34.46 S	55.45 W
Atlas Mountains ⋀	152	33.00 N	2.00 W
Atlasova, Ostrov I	128	50.53 N	155.27 E
Atlas Saharien ⋀	152	33.25 N	1.20 E
Atlas Tellien ⋀	152	36.00 N	3.00 E
Atlin	172	59.35 N	133.42 W
Atmore	174	31.02 N	87.29 W
Atna ≃	114	61.44 N	10.49 E
Atnosen	114	61.44 N	10.49 E
Atrå	114	59.59 N	8.45 E
Atrak (Atrek) ≃	150	37.28 N	53.57 E
Ätran ≃	114	56.53 N	12.30 E
Atrato ≃	184	8.17 N	76.58 W
Atrek (Atrak) ≃	150	37.28 N	53.57 E
Atsugi	134	35.27 N	139.22 E
Atsumi, Nihon	134	34.37 N	137.07 E
Atsumi, Nihon	134	38.37 N	139.35 E
Atsumi-hantō ➤1	134	34.39 N	137.15 E
Aṭ-Ṭā'if	144	21.16 N	40.24 E
Attapu	140	14.48 N	106.50 E
Attawapiskat	172	52.55 N	82.26 W
Attawapiskat ≃	172	52.57 N	82.18 W
Attawapiskat Lake ⊜	172	52.18 N	87.54 W
Attersee	116	47.55 N	13.33 E
Attica, N.Y., U.S.	176	42.52 N	78.17 W
Attica, Ohio, U.S.	176	41.04 N	82.53 W
Attleboro	176	41.56 N	71.17 W
Attleborough	104	52.31 N	1.01 E
Attnang	116	48.01 N	13.43 E
Attow, Ben ∧	108	57.13 N	5.18 W
Āttūr, Bhārat	148	11.36 N	78.37 E
Aṭ-Ṭūr, Miṣr	150	28.14 N	33.37 E
Attymon	110	53.19 N	8.35 W
Atuel ≃	188	36.17 S	66.50 W
Atwater	178	37.21 N	120.36 W
Auasberge ⋀	160	22.45 S	17.22 E
Auau Channel ⩌	179a	20.51 N	156.45 W
Aubagne	118	43.17 N	5.34 E
Aube □5	118	48.15 N	4.05 E
Aube ≃	118	48.34 N	3.43 E
Aubrac ⋀	118	44.40 N	3.00 E
Aubry Lake ⊜	172	67.23 N	126.30 W
Auburn, Ala., U.S.	174	32.36 N	85.29 W
Auburn, Calif., U.S.	178	38.54 N	121.04 W
Auburn, Ind., U.S.	176	41.22 N	85.04 W
Auburn, Maine, U.S.	176	44.06 N	70.14 W
Auburn, Mass., U.S.	176	42.12 N	71.50 W
Auburn, Mich., U.S.	176	43.36 N	84.04 W
Auburn, N.Y., U.S.	176	42.56 N	76.34 W
Auburn Heights	176	42.41 N	83.15 W
Auburn Range ⋀	168	25.10 S	150.30 E
Aubusson	118	45.57 N	2.11 E
Auch	118	43.39 N	0.35 E
Auchenblae	108	56.54 N	2.26 W
Auchinleck	108	55.28 N	4.17 W
Auchterarder	108	56.18 N	3.43 W
Auchterderran	108	56.09 N	3.16 W
Auchtermuchty	108	56.17 N	3.15 W
Auckland	170	36.52 S	174.46 E
Auckland Islands II	87	50.40 S	166.30 E
Aude □5	118	43.05 N	2.30 E
Aude ≃	118	43.13 N	3.14 E
Audierne	118	48.01 N	4.32 W
Audincourt	118	47.29 N	6.50 E
Aue	116	50.35 N	12.42 E
Auerbach	116	50.41 N	12.54 E
Augathella	168	25.48 S	146.35 E
Augher	110	54.26 N	7.09 W
Aughnacloy	110	54.25 N	6.58 W
Aughrim	110	52.51 N	6.17 W
Aughty, Slieve ⋀	110	53.05 N	8.35 W
Auglaize ≃	176	41.17 N	84.21 W
Augrabies Falls National Park ♦	160	28.35 S	20.19 E
Augrabiesvalle ↳	160	28.35 S	20.19 E
Au Gres	176	44.03 N	83.42 W
Au Gres ≃	176	44.02 N	83.40 W
Au Gres, East Branch ≃	176	44.05 N	83.41 W
Augsburg	116	48.23 N	10.53 E
Augusta, Austl.	164	34.19 S	115.10 E
Augusta, It.	122	37.13 N	15.13 E
Augusta, Ga., U.S.	174	33.29 N	81.57 W
Augusta, Ky., U.S.	176	38.46 N	84.00 W
Augusta, Maine, U.S.	176	44.19 N	69.47 W
Augustów	116	53.51 N	22.59 E
Augustowski, Kanał ≃	130	53.54 N	23.26 E
Augustus, Mount ∧	164	24.20 S	116.50 E
Augustus Downs	168	18.33 S	139.52 E
Augustus Island I	166	15.20 S	124.30 E
Auld, Lake ⊜	164	22.32 S	123.44 E
Auldearn	108	57.34 N	3.49 W
Aulestad	114	61.13 N	10.17 E
Aulitivik Island I	172	69.32 N	67.50 W
Aulnay	118	46.01 N	0.21 W
Aulne ≃	118	48.17 N	4.16 W
Ault	118	50.06 N	1.27 E
Aultbea	108	57.50 N	5.35 W
Aumale	118	49.46 N	1.45 E
Auneau	118	48.27 N	1.46 E
Auning	114	56.26 N	10.23 E
Auob ≃	160	26.25 S	20.35 E
Aurangābād	148	19.53 N	75.20 E
Auray	118	47.40 N	2.59 W
Aurdal	114	60.56 N	9.24 E
Aure ≃	166	7.05 S	145.19 E
Aurich	116	53.28 N	7.29 E
Auriflama	190	20.41 S	50.34 W
Aurillac	118	44.56 N	2.26 E
Aurlandsfjorden C2	114	61.05 N	7.02 E
Aurlandsvangen	114	60.54 N	7.11 E
Aurora, Ont., Can.	172	44.00 N	79.28 W
Aurora, S. Afr.	160	32.42 S	18.29 E
Aurora, Colo., U.S.	174	39.44 N	104.52 W
Aurora, Ill., U.S.	174	42.46 N	88.19 W
Aurora, Ind., U.S.	176	39.04 N	84.54 W
Aurora, N.Y., U.S.	176	42.46 N	76.42 W
Aurora, Ohio, U.S.	176	41.19 N	81.21 W
Aurora, W. Va., U.S.	176	39.19 N	79.33 W
Aursunden ⊜	114	62.40 N	11.40 E
Aurukun Mission	166	13.19 S	141.45 E
Aus	160	26.40 S	16.15 E
Ausable ≃, Ont., Can.	176	43.19 N	81.46 W
Au Sable ≃, Mich., U.S.	176	44.25 N	83.20 W
Au Sable, North Branch ≃	176	44.40 N	84.23 W
Au Sable, South Branch ≃	176	44.40 N	84.23 W
Au Sable Forks	176	44.27 N	73.41 W
Au Sable Point ➤	176	44.20 N	83.20 W
Ausangate, Nevado ∧	184	13.47 S	71.13 W
Auschwitz → Oświęcim	116	50.03 N	19.12 E
Auskerry I	108	59.02 N	2.34 W
Aust-Agder □6	114	58.50 N	8.00 E
Austin, Minn., U.S.	174	43.40 N	92.59 W
Austin, Nev., U.S.	178	39.30 N	117.04 W
Austin, Pa., U.S.	176	41.38 N	78.05 W
Austin, Tex., U.S.	174	30.16 N	97.45 W
Austin, Lake ⊜	164	27.40 S	118.00 E
Austin Channel ⩌	172	75.35 N	103.25 W
Austintown	176	41.06 N	80.46 W
Australes, Îles II	96	23.00 S	150.00 W
Australia □1	162	25.00 S	135.00 E
Australian-Antarctic Rise ∻3	87	50.00 S	130.00 E
Australian Capital Territory □8	168	35.30 S	149.00 E
Austral Seamount Chain ∻3	96	24.00 S	150.00 W
Austråt	114	63.43 N	9.45 E
Austria □1	100	47.20 N	13.20 E
Austvågøya I	112	68.20 N	14.36 E
Authie ≃	118	50.21 N	1.38 E
Autlán de Navarro	180	19.46 N	104.22 W
Autun	118	46.57 N	4.18 E
Auvergne	166	15.41 S	130.01 E
Auvergne □9	118	45.25 N	2.30 E
Auvézère ≃	118	45.12 N	0.51 E
Aux Barques, Pointe ➤	176	44.04 N	82.58 W
Auxerre	118	47.48 N	3.34 E
Auxier	176	37.44 N	82.46 W
Auxi-le-Château	118	50.14 N	2.07 E
Auyán-Tepuí ∧	184	5.55 N	62.32 W
Avai	190	22.08 S	49.22 W
Avaloirs, Les ∧2	118	48.28 N	0.07 W
Avalon	178	33.49 N	118.16 W
Avan ≃	104	51.35 N	3.48 W
Avaré	190	23.05 S	48.55 W
Ave ≃	120	41.20 N	8.45 W
Avebury	104	51.27 N	1.51 W
Aveiro	120	40.38 N	8.39 W
Avellaneda, Arg.	188	34.40 S	58.20 W
Avellaneda, Arg.	188	29.07 S	59.40 W
Avellino	122	40.54 N	14.47 E
Avenal	178	36.00 N	120.08 W
Aversa	122	40.58 N	14.12 E
Aves, Islas de II	184	12.00 N	67.30 W
Avesta	114	60.09 N	16.12 E
Aveyron □5	118	44.15 N	2.40 E
Aveyron ≃	118	44.05 N	1.16 E
Avezzano	122	42.02 N	13.25 E
Avich, Loch ⊜	108	56.16 N	5.20 W
Aviemore	108	57.12 N	3.50 W
Avignon	118	43.57 N	4.49 E
Ávila	120	40.39 N	4.42 W
Ávila, Sierra de ⋀	120	40.35 N	5.08 W
Avilés	120	43.33 N	5.55 W
Avis	176	41.11 N	77.19 W
Avlum	114	56.16 N	8.48 E
Avoca, Austl.	168	37.05 S	143.28 E
Avoca, N.Y., U.S.	176	42.25 N	77.25 W
Avoca ≃	110	52.48 N	6.09 W
Avola	122	36.54 N	15.09 E
Avon	176	42.55 N	77.45 W
Avon □6	102	51.30 N	2.40 W
Avon ≃, Eng., U.K.	102	52.25 N	1.31 W
Avon ≃, Eng., U.K.	102	50.43 N	1.46 W
Avon ≃, Eng., U.K.	104	51.30 N	2.43 W
Avon ≃, Eng., U.K.	104	51.59 N	2.10 W
Avon ≃, Eng., U.K.	104	50.17 N	3.52 W
Avon ≃, Scot., U.K.	108	56.00 N	3.40 W
Avon ≃, Scot., U.K.	108	57.25 N	3.23 W
Avon, Ben ∧	108	57.05 N	3.27 W
Avondale	158	17.43 S	30.58 E
Avon Downs	168	20.05 S	137.30 E
Avon Lake	176	41.30 N	82.01 W
Avonmore	176	40.32 N	79.28 W
Avonmore ≃	110	52.50 N	6.13 W
Avonmouth	104	51.31 N	2.42 W
Avontuur	160	33.44 S	23.11 E
Avon Water ≃	108	55.47 N	4.01 W
Avranches	118	48.41 N	1.22 W
Avre ≃	118	49.53 N	2.20 E
Awaji	134	34.35 N	135.01 E
Awaji-shima I	134	34.21 N	134.51 E
Awakino	170	38.39 S	174.38 E
Awal Edo	158	4.14 N	40.39 E
Awanui	170	35.03 S	173.15 E
Awara, Nihon	134	36.13 N	136.12 E
Awara, Yai.	158	5.25 N	39.58 E
Awash	154	8.59 N	40.10 E
Awash ≃	154	11.45 N	41.05 E
Awa-shima I	134	38.27 N	139.14 E
Awaso	152	6.14 N	2.16 W
Awatere ≃	170	41.37 S	174.10 E
Awbārī	154	26.35 N	12.46 E
Awe, Loch ⊜	108	56.15 N	5.17 W
Awjilah	154	29.09 N	21.15 E
Axbridge	104	51.18 N	2.49 W
Axe ≃, Eng., U.K.	104	51.19 N	2.59 W
Axe ≃, Eng., U.K.	104	50.42 N	3.03 W
Axel Heiberg Island I	90	80.30 N	92.00 W
Axim	152	4.52 N	2.14 W
Axiós (Vardar) ≃	124	40.31 N	22.43 E
Ax-les-Thermes	118	42.43 N	1.50 E
Axminster	104	50.47 N	3.00 W
Axmouth	104	50.42 N	3.02 W
Ayabe	134	35.18 N	135.15 E
Ayacucho, Arg.	188	37.10 S	58.30 W
Ayacucho, Perú	184	13.07 S	74.13 W
Ayamonte	120	37.13 N	7.24 W
Ayapel	184	8.19 N	75.09 W
Ayaviri	184	14.52 S	70.35 W
Āybak	146	36.16 N	68.01 E
Ayer	176	42.34 N	71.35 W
Ayers Rock ∧	164	25.23 S	131.05 E
Áyios Kírikos	124	37.37 N	26.14 E
Áyios Nikólaos	124	35.11 N	25.42 E
Aylesbury, Eng., U.K.	102	51.18 N	0.29 E
Aylesbury, Eng., U.K.	104	51.50 N	0.50 W
Aylesford	104	51.18 N	0.29 E
Aylesham	104	51.13 N	1.13 E
Aylmer East	176	45.24 N	75.51 W
Aylmer Lake ⊜	172	64.05 N	108.30 W
Aylmer West	176	42.46 N	80.59 W
Aylsham	104	52.49 N	1.15 E
'Ayn Dār	150	25.59 N	49.23 E
'Ayoûn el 'Atroûs	152	16.40 N	9.37 W
Ayr, Austl.	168	19.35 S	147.24 E
Ayr, Ont., Can.	176	43.17 N	80.27 W
Ayr, Scot., U.K.	106	55.28 N	4.38 W
Ayr ≃	106	55.29 N	4.28 W
Ayre, Point of ➤	106	54.26 N	4.22 W
Ayrolle, Étang de l' ⊜	118	43.05 N	3.03 E
Aysgarth	106	54.17 N	2.00 W
Ayton	166	15.56 S	145.22 E
Ayu, Kepulauan II	138	0.28 N	131.03 E
Ayutla	180	20.07 N	104.22 W
Azambuja	120	39.04 N	8.52 W
Azamgarh	146	26.04 N	83.11 E
Azaouak, Vallée de l' V	152	15.30 N	3.18 E
Azare	152	11.40 N	10.11 E
Āžar Shahr	150	37.45 N	45.59 E
Azerbajdžanskaja Sovetskaja Socialističeskaja Respublika □3	126	40.30 N	47.30 E
Azogues	184	2.44 S	78.50 W
Azores → Açores, Arquipélago dos II	88	38.30 N	28.00 W
Azores-Gibraltar Ridge ∻3	88	38.00 N	19.00 W
Azores Plateau ∻3	88	38.30 N	30.00 W
Azov	126	47.07 N	39.25 E
Azov, Sea of → Azovskoje More ▼2	126	46.00 N	36.00 E
Azovskoje More ▼2	126	46.00 N	36.00 E
Azua	182	18.27 N	70.44 W
Azuaga	120	38.16 N	5.41 W
Azuero, Península de ➤1	180	7.40 N	80.30 W
Azul	188	36.45 S	59.50 W
Azul, Cerro ∧	182	9.55 N	85.18 W
Azul, Cordillera ⋀	184	9.00 S	76.00 W
Azur, Côte d' ⊥2	118	43.30 N	7.00 E
Aẓ-Ẓahrān (Dhahran)	150	26.18 N	50.08 E
Az-Zaqāzīq	154	30.35 N	31.31 E
Az-Zarqā'	150	32.05 N	36.06 E
Az-Zāwiyah	154	32.45 N	12.44 E
Azzel Matti, Sebkha ≚	152	25.55 N	0.56 E
Az-Zilfī	150	26.18 N	44.48 E
Az-Zubayr	150	30.23 N	47.43 E
B			
Ba ≃	140	13.02 N	109.03 E
Ba, Loch ⊜	108	56.36 N	4.44 W
Baa	142	10.43 S	123.03 E
Baarn	116	52.13 N	5.16 E
Babaeski	124	41.26 N	27.06 E
Babahoyo	184	1.49 S	79.31 W
Babakin	164	32.07 S	118.01 E
Babar, Kepulauan II	166	7.50 S	129.45 E
Babar, Pulau I	166	7.55 S	129.45 E
Babbacombe Bay C	104	50.30 N	3.25 W
Babbitt	178	38.39 N	118.37 W
B'abdā	150	33.50 N	35.32 E
Babelthuap I	138	7.30 N	134.36 E
Babinda	168	17.20 S	145.55 E
Babine Lake ⊜	172	54.45 N	126.00 W
Babo	166	2.33 S	133.25 E
Bābol	150	36.34 N	52.42 E
Bābol Sar	150	36.43 N	52.39 E
Babuškin	128	51.41 N	105.54 E
Babuyan Island I	138	19.32 N	121.57 E
Babuyan Islands II	138	19.10 N	121.40 E
Bacabal	184	4.14 S	44.47 W
Bacan, Pulau I	166	0.35 S	127.30 E
Bacău	124	46.34 N	26.55 E
Bacău □4	124	46.30 N	26.45 E
Bacchus Marsh	168	37.41 S	144.27 E
Bac-giang	140	21.16 N	106.12 E
Bachaquero	182	9.56 N	71.08 W
Bacharden	150	38.26 N	57.25 E
Bachardok	150	38.46 N	58.30 E
Bachta	128	62.28 N	89.00 E
Bachu	132	39.50 N	78.20 E
Back ≃	172	67.15 N	95.15 W
Bačka ◆1	124	45.50 N	19.30 E
Bac-kan	140	22.08 N	105.50 E
Bačka Palanka	124	45.15 N	19.24 E
Bačka Topola	124	45.49 N	19.38 E
Back Creek ≃	176	38.02 N	79.54 W
Backnang	116	48.56 N	9.25 E
Backstairs Passage ⩌	168	35.42 S	138.05 E
Bac-lieu (Vinh-loi)	140	9.17 N	105.44 E
Bac-ninh	140	21.11 N	106.03 E
Bacolod	138	10.40 N	122.57 E
Bácsalmás	124	46.08 N	19.20 E
Bács-Kiskun □6	116	46.30 N	19.25 E
Bacton	104	52.52 N	1.28 E
Bacup	106	53.43 N	2.12 W
Bad ≃	176	43.18 N	84.06 W
Badagara	148	11.36 N	75.35 E
Badajia	136	33.57 N	120.17 E
Badajoz	120	38.53 N	6.58 W
Badakhshan □4	146	36.45 N	72.00 E
Badalona	120	41.27 N	2.15 E
Bādāmi	144	15.58 N	75.45 E
Badanah	150	30.59 N	41.02 E
Bad Axe	176	43.48 N	83.00 W
Bad Doberan	116	54.06 N	11.53 E
Bad Dürkheim	116	49.28 N	8.10 E
Bad Ems	116	50.20 N	7.43 E
Baden, Öst.	116	48.00 N	16.14 E
Baden, Schw.	118	47.29 N	8.18 E
Baden-Baden	116	48.46 N	8.14 E
Badenoch ◆1	108	56.57 N	4.19 W
Baden-Württemberg □3	116	48.30 N	9.00 E
Badenyon	108	57.15 N	3.05 W
Bad Freienwalde	116	52.47 N	14.01 E
Bādghīsāt □4	150	35.00 N	63.45 E
Bad Harzburg	116	51.53 N	10.33 E
Bad Hersfeld	116	50.52 N	9.42 E
Bad Homburg [vor der Höhe]	116	50.13 N	8.37 E
Bad Honnef	116	50.39 N	7.13 E
Bad Ischl	116	47.43 N	13.37 E
Bad Kissingen	116	50.12 N	10.04 E
Bad Kreuznach	116	49.52 N	7.51 E
Badlands ⋀	174	46.45 N	103.30 W
Bad Langensalza	116	51.06 N	10.38 E
Bad Liebenwerda	116	51.31 N	13.23 E
Bad Mergentheim	116	49.30 N	9.46 E
Bad Nauheim	116	50.22 N	8.44 E
Badnera	148	20.52 N	77.44 E
Bad Oeynhausen	116	52.12 N	8.48 E
Bad Oldesloe	116	53.48 N	10.22 E
Bad Pyrmont	116	51.59 N	9.15 E
Bad Reichenhall	116	47.43 N	12.52 E
Badrīnāth	144	30.44 N	79.30 E
Bad Sachsa	116	51.36 N	10.32 E
Bad Salzuflen	116	52.05 N	8.44 E
Bad Salzungen	116	50.48 N	10.13 E
Bad Schwartau	116	53.55 N	10.40 E
Bad Segeberg	116	53.56 N	10.17 E
Bad Tölz	116	47.46 N	11.34 E
Badu Island I	166	10.07 S	142.08 E
Badulla	148	6.59 N	81.03 E
Baena	120	37.37 N	4.19 W
Baependi	190	21.57 S	44.53 W
Bafatá	152	12.10 N	14.40 W
Baffin Basin ∻1	90	73.00 N	68.00 W
Baffin Bay C	90	73.00 N	66.00 W
Baffin Island I	172	68.00 N	70.00 W
Bafing ≃	152	13.49 N	10.50 W
Bafoulabé	152	13.48 N	10.50 W
Bafwasende	158	1.05 N	27.16 E
Bagaces	182	10.31 N	85.15 W
Bagaha	146	27.06 N	84.05 E
Bagahu ⊜	126	46.57 N	87.27 E
Bāgalkot	148	16.11 N	75.42 E
Bagamoyo	158	6.26 S	38.54 E
Bagansiapi-api	142	2.09 N	100.49 E
Bagdad → Baghdād	150	33.21 N	44.25 E
Bagdarin	128	54.26 N	113.36 E
Bagé	188	31.20 S	54.06 W
Bagenkop	114	54.45 N	10.41 E
Baggy Point ➤	104	51.09 N	4.16 W
Baghdād	150	33.21 N	44.25 E
Bagheria	122	38.05 N	13.30 E
Baghlān	146	36.13 N	68.46 E
Baghlīn	146	36.14 N	65.55 E
Bagnara Cálabra	122	38.18 N	15.49 E
Bagnères-de-Bigorre	118	43.04 N	0.09 E
Bagnères-de-Luchon	118	42.47 N	0.36 E
Bagnols-sur-Cèze	118	44.10 N	4.37 E
Bagshot	104	51.22 N	0.42 W
Baguio	138	16.25 N	120.36 E
Bagur, Cabo ➤	120	41.57 N	3.14 E
Bagzane, Monts ⋀	152	17.43 N	8.45 E
Bahādurgarh	149	28.41 N	76.55 E
Bahamas □1	180	24.15 N	76.00 W
Bahār	150	34.54 N	48.26 E
Bahāwalnagar	149	29.59 N	73.16 E
Bahāwalpur	149	29.24 N	71.41 E
Bahia → Salvador	190	12.59 S	38.31 W
Bahia □3	190	12.00 S	42.00 W
Bahía, Islas de la II	182	16.20 N	86.30 W
Bahía Blanca	188	38.44 S	62.16 W
Bahía de Caráquez	184	0.36 S	80.25 W
Bahir Dar	154	11.35 N	37.28 E
Bahoruco, Sierra de ∧	182	18.20 N	71.35 W
Bahraich	146	27.36 N	81.36 E
Bahrain □1	144	26.00 N	50.30 E
Baia-Mare	124	47.40 N	23.35 E
Baicheng, Zhg.	132	41.46 N	81.52 E
Baicheng, Zhg.	132	45.38 N	122.46 E
Baidoa	154	3.04 N	43.48 E
Baie-Comeau	172	49.13 N	68.10 W
Baiersbronn	116	48.30 N	8.22 E
Baie-Saint-Paul	172	47.27 N	70.30 W
Baiju	136	33.04 N	120.20 E
Baildon	106	53.52 N	1.46 W
Bailén	120	38.06 N	3.46 W
Băilești	124	44.02 N	23.21 E
Bailieborough	110	53.54 N	6.59 W
Baillie ≃	172	65.10 N	104.24 W
Baillie-Hamilton Island I	172	75.53 N	94.35 W
Baillie Islands II	172	70.33 N	128.10 W
Bailongjiang ≃	132	32.18 N	105.42 E
Bailundo	156	12.12 S	15.52 E
Bain ≃	104	53.05 N	0.12 W
Bainbridge, Ga., U.S.	174	30.54 N	84.34 W
Bainbridge, N.Y., U.S.	176	42.18 N	75.29 W
Bainbridge, Ohio, U.S.	176	39.14 N	83.16 W
Bain-de-Bretagne	118	47.50 N	1.41 W
Baing	138	10.14 S	120.34 E
Bains-les-Bains	118	48.00 N	6.16 E
Baipu	136	32.15 N	120.46 E
Baird Peninsula ➤1	172	69.00 N	75.15 W
Bairnsdale	168	37.50 S	147.38 E
Bais	118	48.15 N	0.22 W
Baise	132	23.57 N	106.26 E
Baïse ≃	118	44.07 N	0.17 E
Baisha	140	19.17 N	109.27 E
Baishanji	136	33.48 N	116.40 E
Baishuijiang	132	33.29 N	106.01 E
Baituzhen	136	31.59 N	119.21 E
Baiyinchang	132	36.47 N	104.07 E
Baiyunebo	132	41.58 N	110.02 E
Baja	116	46.11 N	18.57 E
Baja California ➤1	180	27.30 N	113.00 W
Baja California Norte □3	178	30.00 N	115.00 W
Baja California Seamount Province ∻	90	26.00 N	124.00 W
Bajada del Agrio	188	38.24 S	70.02 W
Bajanaul	126	50.47 N	75.42 E
Bajanchongor	132	46.10 N	100.45 E
Bajawa	142	8.47 S	120.59 E

Symbols in the index entries are identified on page 198.

Name	Page	Lat °′	Long °′
Bajdarackaja Guba C	126	69.00 N	67.30 E
Bajimba, Mount ∧	168	29.18 S	152.07 E
Bajkal, Ozero (Lake Baykal) ⊜	128	53.00 N	107.40 E
Bajkal'skoje	128	55.21 N	109.12 E
Bajkit	128	61.41 N	96.25 E
Bajkonyr	126	47.50 N	66.03 E
Bajmak	126	52.36 N	58.19 E
Bajmok	124	45.58 N	19.25 E
Bajool	168	23.39 S	150.39 E
Bajos de Haina	182	18.25 N	70.01 W
Bajram-Ali	150	37.37 N	62.10 E
Bajsun	126	38.14 N	67.12 E
Bakel	152	14.54 N	12.27 W
Baker, Calif., U.S.	178	35.16 N	116.04 W
Baker, Mont., U.S.	174	46.22 N	104.17 W
Baker, Oreg., U.S.	174	44.47 N	117.50 W
Baker, Mount ∧	174	48.47 N	121.49 W
Baker Island I	96	0.15 N	176.27 W
Baker Lake	172	64.15 N	96.00 W
Baker Lake ⊜	172	64.10 N	95.30 W
Bakersfield	178	35.23 N	119.01 W
Bakerville	160	26.00 S	26.06 E
Bakewell	106	53.13 N	1.40 W
Bakhtegān, Daryācheh-ye ⊜	150	29.20 N	54.05 E
Bakırköy	124	40.59 N	28.52 E
Bakkaflói C	112a	66.10 N	14.45 W
Bako	154	5.50 N	36.40 E
Bakony ⩕	116	46.55 N	17.40 E
Bakoye ≃	152	13.49 N	10.50 W
Baku	150	40.23 N	49.51 E
Bala	104	52.54 N	3.35 W
Balabac Island I	142	7.57 N	117.01 E
Balabac Strait ⊔	138	7.35 N	117.00 E
Ba'labakk (Baalbek)	150	34.00 N	36.12 E
Balad'ok	128	53.41 N	133.07 E
Bālāghāt	146	21.48 N	80.11 E
Balagne ⇠[1]	122	42.30 N	8.50 E
Balaklava	168	34.09 S	138.25 E
Balakovo	126	52.02 N	47.47 E
Balallan	108	58.05 N	6.35 W
Balambangan, Pulau I	142	7.15 N	116.55 E
Bālā Morghāb	150	35.35 N	63.20 E
Balāngīr	148	20.43 N	83.29 E
Balaraja	142	6.12 S	106.27 E
Bālārampuram	148	8.26 N	77.03 E
Balašicha	130	55.49 N	37.58 E
Balasore	146	21.30 N	86.56 E
Balašov	126	51.32 N	43.08 E
Balassagyarmat	116	48.05 N	19.18 E
Balaton ⊜	116	46.50 N	17.45 E
Balboa	182	8.57 N	79.34 W
Balboa Heights	180	8.58 N	79.35 W
Balbriggan	110	53.37 N	6.11 W
Balcanoona	168	30.31 S	139.18 E
Balcarce	188	37.52 S	58.15 W
Balchaš	126	46.49 N	74.59 E
Balchaš, Ozero ⊜	126	46.00 N	74.00 E
Balchen Glacier ⊽	87	76.46 S	145.30 W
Balclutha	170	46.14 S	169.44 E
Balcombe	104	51.04 N	0.08 W
Balcosna	188	27.54 S	65.43 W
Bald Eagle Creek ≃	176	41.08 N	77.24 W
Balderton	104	53.03 N	0.47 W
Bald Hill ∧[2]	168	20.18 S	144.06 E
Bald Island I	164	34.55 S	118.27 E
Bald Knob ∧	176	37.56 N	79.51 W
Bald Mountain ∧, Conn., U.S.	176	41.59 N	72.25 W
Bald Mountain ∧, N.J., U.S.	176	41.07 N	74.12 W
Bald Mountain ∧, Oreg., U.S.	178	43.16 N	121.21 W
Baldock	104	51.59 N	0.12 W
Baldock Lake ⊜	172	56.33 N	97.57 W
Baldoyle	110	53.24 N	6.08 W
Baldwinsville	176	43.09 N	76.20 W
Baldwinville	176	42.36 N	72.05 W
Baldy Peak ∧	174	33.55 N	109.35 W
Bâle → Basel	118	47.33 N	7.35 E
Baleares □[4]	120	39.30 N	3.00 E
Baleares, Islas (Balearic Islands) II	120	39.30 N	3.00 E
Balearic Islands → Baleares, Islas II	120	39.30 N	3.00 E
Baleine, Rivière à la ≃	172	58.15 N	67.40 W
Balej	128	51.36 N	116.38 E
Balen	116	51.10 N	5.09 E
Baleshare I	108	57.31 N	7.22 W
Balestrand	114	61.12 N	6.32 E
Balfate	182	15.48 N	86.25 W
Balfes Creek	168	20.13 S	145.55 E
Balfour, S. Afr.	160	26.44 S	28.45 E
Balfour, Scot., U.K.	108	59.01 N	2.55 W
Balfour Downs	164	22.50 S	120.50 E
Balgo Hill Mission	164	20.09 S	127.48 E
Bali I	142	8.20 S	115.00 E
Bali, Laut (Bali Sea) ⊤[2]	142	7.45 S	115.30 E
Bali, Selat ⊔	142	8.18 S	114.25 E
Balikpapan	142	1.17 S	116.50 E
Balikun	132	43.50 N	93.30 E
Balin	132	48.19 N	122.19 E
Balingen	116	48.16 N	8.51 E
Balingup	164	33.48 S	115.58 E
Balintang Channel ⊔	138	19.49 N	121.40 E
Balinzuoqi	132	44.00 N	119.00 E
Balkan Mountains → Stara Planina ⩕	124	43.15 N	25.00 E
Balkh	146	36.46 N	66.54 E
Balkhash, Lake → Balchaš, Ozero ⊜	126	46.00 N	74.00 E
Balla	110	53.48 N	9.09 W
Balla Balla	158	20.26 S	29.02 E
Ballachulish	108	56.40 N	5.10 W
Balladonia	164	32.27 S	123.51 E
Ballagh	110	52.35 N	7.59 W
Ballaghaderreen	110	53.55 N	8.36 W
Ballālpur	148	19.50 N	79.22 E
Ballangen	112	68.20 N	16.50 E
Ballantrae	106	55.06 N	5.00 W
Ballarat	168	37.34 S	143.52 E
Ballard, Lake ⊜	164	29.27 S	120.55 E
Ballater	108	57.03 N	3.03 W
Ballaugh	106	54.20 N	4.32 W
Ballenita, Punta ≻	188	25.46 S	70.44 W
Balleny Islands II	87	66.35 S	162.50 E
Balleroy	118	49.11 N	0.50 W
Ballı	124	40.50 N	27.03 E
Ballia	146	25.45 N	84.10 E
Ballina, Austl.	168	28.52 S	153.33 E
Ballina, Eire	110	52.49 N	8.26 W
Ballinakill	110	52.53 N	7.18 W
Ballinalack	110	53.37 N	7.28 W
Ballinascarty	110	51.40 N	8.51 W
Ballinasloe	110	53.20 N	8.13 W
Ballindine	110	53.39 N	8.59 W
Ballineen	110	51.44 N	8.56 W
Ballingarry	110	52.29 N	8.52 W
Ballingeary	110	51.49 N	9.13 W
Ballinluig	108	56.38 N	3.39 W
Ballinrobe	110	53.37 N	9.13 W
Ballinskelligs Bay C	110	51.50 N	10.15 W
Ballintoy	110	55.14 N	6.21 W
Ballintra	110	54.35 N	8.08 W
Balloch	108	57.29 N	4.07 W
Balls Pyramid I	162	31.45 S	159.15 E
Ballston Spa	176	43.00 N	73.51 W
Ballville	176	41.20 N	83.09 W
Ballybay	110	54.08 N	6.54 W
Ballybofey	110	54.57 N	7.47 W
Ballybogey	110	55.07 N	6.34 W
Ballybunion	110	52.31 N	9.40 W
Ballycanew	110	52.36 N	6.19 W
Ballycastle, Eire	110	54.16 N	9.23 W
Ballycastle, N. Ire., U.K.	110	55.12 N	6.15 W
Ballyclare	110	54.46 N	6.01 W
Ballyconneely	110	53.26 N	10.02 W
Ballyconnell	110	54.07 N	7.35 W
Ballycotton	110	51.50 N	8.01 W
Ballycroy	110	54.01 N	9.51 W
Ballyduff, Eire	110	52.09 N	8.03 W
Ballyduff, Eire	110	52.27 N	9.40 W
Ballyferriter	110	52.09 N	10.26 W
Ballyfinboy ≃	110	53.02 N	8.15 W
Ballygar	110	53.32 N	8.20 W
Ballygawley	110	54.28 N	7.02 W
Ballygorman	110	55.22 N	7.21 W
Ballyhaise	110	54.03 N	7.19 W
Ballyhalbert	110	54.30 N	5.28 W
Ballyhaunis	110	53.46 N	8.46 W
Ballyhoura Hills ⩕[2]	110	52.20 N	8.35 W
Ballyjamesduff	110	53.52 N	7.12 W
Ballylongford	110	52.33 N	9.28 W
Ballymacoda	110	51.57 N	7.54 W
Ballymahon	110	53.34 N	7.45 W
Ballymakeery (Ballyvourney)	110	51.55 N	9.09 W
Ballymena	110	54.52 N	6.17 W
Ballymoe	110	53.42 N	8.29 W
Ballymoney	110	55.04 N	6.31 W
Ballymote	110	54.06 N	8.31 W
Ballymurray	110	53.35 N	8.08 W
Ballynahinch	110	54.24 N	5.54 W
Ballyneety	110	52.35 N	8.33 W
Ballynoe	110	52.03 N	8.05 W
Ballyquintin Point ≻	110	54.20 N	5.29 W
Ballyragget	110	52.47 N	7.20 W
Ballysadare	110	54.13 N	8.31 W
Ballyshannon	110	54.30 N	8.11 W
Ballyvaughan	110	53.07 N	9.07 W
Ballyvoy	110	55.12 N	6.11 W
Ballywalter	110	54.33 N	5.30 W
Balmaceda	186	45.55 S	71.41 W
Balmerino	108	56.24 N	3.02 W
Balmoral Castle	108	57.20 N	3.15 W
Balnacra	108	57.28 N	5.23 W
Balonne ≃	168	28.47 S	147.56 E
Bālotra	146	25.50 N	72.14 E
Balovale	156	13.33 S	23.06 E
Balrāmpur	146	27.26 N	82.11 E
Balranald	168	34.38 S	143.33 E
Balsam Lake ⊜	176	44.35 N	78.50 W
Balsas	184	7.31 S	46.02 W
Balsas ≃	180	17.55 N	102.10 W
Balsham	104	52.08 N	0.20 E
Balta	126	47.55 N	29.37 E
Baltasar Brum	188	30.44 S	57.19 W
Baltasound	108a	60.45 N	0.52 W
Baltic Sea ⊤[2]	112	57.00 N	19.00 E
Baltijsk	130	54.39 N	19.55 E
Baltijskaja Kosa ≻[2]	116	54.25 N	19.35 E
Baltimore, Eire	110	51.29 N	9.22 W
Baltimore, S. Afr.	160	23.15 S	28.20 E
Baltimore, Md., U.S.	176	39.17 N	76.37 W
Baltimore, Ohio, U.S.	176	39.51 N	82.36 W
Baltinglass	110	52.55 N	6.41 W
Baluchistan □[9]	150	28.00 N	63.00 E
Bālurghāt	146	0.00	0.00
Balvicar	108	56.14 N	5.38 W
Balygyčan	128	63.56 N	154.12 E
Balykši	126	47.05 N	51.54 E
Bam	150	29.06 N	58.21 E
Bama	140	24.21 N	107.08 E
Bamaga	166	10.52 S	142.24 E
Bamako	152	12.39 N	8.00 W
Bamba	152	17.02 N	1.24 W
Bambana ≃	182	13.27 N	83.45 W
Bambari	154	5.45 N	20.40 E
Bambaroo	168	18.52 S	146.12 E
Bamberg	116	49.53 N	10.53 E
Bamboesberg ⩕	160	31.30 S	26.10 E
Bamboo Creek	164	20.56 S	120.13 E
Bambuí	190	20.01 S	45.58 W
Bamburgh	106	55.36 N	1.42 W
Bamenda	152	5.56 N	10.10 E
Bāmīān	146	34.50 N	67.50 E
Bāmīān □[4]	146	34.45 N	67.15 E
Bamingui ≃	154	8.33 N	19.05 E
Bampton, Eng., U.K.	104	51.00 N	3.29 W
Bampton, Eng., U.K.	104	51.44 N	1.33 W
Bampūr	150	27.12 N	60.27 E
Baña, Punta de la ≻	120	40.34 N	0.38 E
Banagher	110	53.11 N	7.59 W
Banalia	158	1.33 N	25.20 E
Banana, Austl.	168	24.28 S	150.07 E
Banana, Zaïre	156	6.01 S	12.24 E
Bananal	190	22.41 S	44.19 W
Bananal, Ilha do I	190	11.30 S	50.15 W
Banarlı	124	41.04 N	27.20 E
Banās ≃	146	25.54 N	76.45 E
Banās, Ra's ≻	154	23.54 N	35.48 E
Banat ⇠[1]	124	45.20 N	20.40 E
Banbridge	110	54.21 N	6.16 W
Banbury	104	52.04 N	1.20 W
Banchory	108	57.30 N	2.30 W
Bancroft, Ont., Can.	172	45.03 N	77.51 W
Bancroft → Chililabombwe, Zam.	158	12.18 S	27.43 E
Bānda	146	25.29 N	80.20 E
Banda, Kepulauan II	166	4.35 S	129.55 E
Banda, Laut (Banda Sea) ⊤[2]	138	5.00 S	128.00 E
Banda Aceh	140	5.34 N	95.20 E
Banda del Rio Salí	188	26.50 S	65.10 W
Bandai-san ∧	134	37.36 N	140.04 E
Bandak ⊜	114	59.24 N	8.15 E
Bandama ≃	152	5.10 N	5.00 W
Bandama Blanc ≃	152	6.54 N	5.31 W
Bandama Rouge ≃	152	6.54 N	5.31 W
Bandar 'Abbās	150	27.11 N	56.17 E
Bandar-e Lengeh	150	26.33 N	54.53 E
Bandar-e Māh Shahr	150	30.33 N	49.12 E
Bandar-e Pahlavī	150	37.28 N	49.27 E
Bandar-e Shāh	150	36.56 N	54.06 E
Bandar-e Shāhpūr	150	30.25 N	49.05 E
Bandar Seri Begawan	142	4.56 N	114.55 E
Bandeira, Pico da ∧	190	20.26 S	41.47 W
Bandeirantes	190	23.06 S	50.21 W
Bandeli	161a	12.55 S	45.13 E
Bandera	188	28.53 S	62.16 W
Bandera, Alto de la ∧	182	18.50 N	70.35 W
Bandiantaolehai	132	41.41 N	104.06 E
Bandon, Eire	110	51.45 N	8.45 W
Bandon, Oreg., U.S.	178	43.07 N	124.25 W
Bandon ≃	110	51.42 N	8.30 W
Bandundu	156	3.18 S	17.20 E
Bandung	142	6.54 S	107.36 E
Banes	182	20.58 N	75.43 W
Banff, Alta., Can.	172	51.10 N	115.34 W
Banff, Scot., U.K.	108	57.40 N	2.33 W
Banga	149	31.11 N	75.59 E
Bangala Dam ⇠[6]	158	20.40 S	31.15 E
Bangalore	148	12.59 N	77.35 E
Bangaon	146	23.04 N	88.49 E
Bangassou	154	4.50 N	23.07 E
Bangbu	132	32.58 N	117.24 E
Banggai, Kepulauan II	142	1.30 S	123.15 E
Banggi, Pulau I	142	7.17 N	117.12 E
Banghāzī	154	32.07 N	20.04 E
Bangil	142	7.36 S	112.47 E
Bangka I	142	2.15 S	106.00 E
Bangka, Selat ⊔	142	2.20 S	105.45 E
Bangkalan	142	7.02 S	112.44 E
Bangkinang	142	0.21 N	101.02 E
Bangko	142	2.05 S	102.17 E
Bangkok → Krung Thep	140	13.45 N	100.31 E
Bangladesh □[1]	144	24.00 N	90.00 E
Bang Mun Nak	140	16.02 N	100.23 E
Bangor, Wales, U.K.	106	53.13 N	4.08 W
Bangor, Maine, U.S.	176	44.49 N	68.47 W
Bangor, Pa., U.S.	176	40.52 N	75.13 W
Bangor Erris	110	54.09 N	9.45 W
Bangs, Mount ∧	178	36.48 N	113.51 W
Bangui	154	4.22 N	18.35 E
Bangweulu, Lake ⊜	158	11.05 S	29.45 E
Bangweulu Swamp ☷	158	11.30 S	30.15 E
Ban Hat Yai → Hat Yai	140	7.01 N	100.28 E
Ban Houayxay	138	20.18 N	100.26 E
Baní	182	18.17 N	70.20 W
Bani ≃	152	14.30 N	4.12 W
Baniara	166	9.46 S	149.53 E
Banī Mazār	154	28.30 N	30.48 E
Banī Suwayf	154	29.05 N	31.05 E
Banja Luka	122	44.46 N	17.11 E
Banjarmasin	142	3.20 S	114.35 E
Banjul	152	13.28 N	16.39 W
Banka Banka	164	18.48 S	134.01 E
Bankfoot	108	56.30 N	3.30 W
Banks Island I, B.C., Can.	172	53.25 N	130.10 W
Banks Island I, N.W. Ter., Can.	172	73.15 N	121.30 W
Banks Islands II	96	13.50 S	167.30 E
Banks Peninsula ≻[1]	170	43.45 S	173.00 E
Banks Strait ⊔	168	40.40 S	148.07 E
Bānkura	146	23.15 N	87.04 E
Bann ≃	110	55.10 N	6.45 W
Ban Na San	140	8.48 N	99.22 E
Bannerman, Mount ∧[2]	164	19.26 S	127.10 E
Banning	178	33.56 N	116.52 W
Bannockburn, Rh.	158	20.16 S	29.51 E
Bannockburn, Scot., U.K.	108	56.06 N	3.55 W
Bannu	149	32.59 N	70.36 E
Baños	184	1.24 S	78.25 W
Baños de Cerrato	120	41.55 N	4.28 W
Ban Pak Phraek	140	8.13 N	100.12 E
Ban Pong	140	13.49 N	99.53 E
Banqiao	136	30.06 N	120.27 E
Banqiaoji	136	32.19 N	116.37 E
Bansha	110	52.28 N	8.04 W
Banská Bystrica	116	48.44 N	19.07 E
Banská Štiavnica	116	48.28 N	18.56 E
Banstead	104	51.19 N	0.12 W
Bānswāra	146	23.33 N	74.27 E
Banteer	110	52.07 N	8.54 W
Bantry	110	51.41 N	9.27 W
Bantry Bay C	110	51.38 N	9.48 W
Banwell	104	51.20 N	2.52 W
Banwy ≃	104	52.42 N	3.16 W
Banyak, Kepulauan II	140	2.10 N	97.15 E
Banyuwangi	142	8.12 S	114.21 E
Baoan	136	22.34 N	114.07 E
Baode	132	39.06 N	111.11 E
Baoding	132	38.52 N	115.29 E
Baofeng	136	33.55 N	113.02 E
Bao-ha	140	22.11 N	104.21 E
Baoji	132	34.22 N	107.14 E
Bao-loc	140	11.32 N	107.48 E
Baoshan, Zhg.	136	31.25 N	121.29 E
Baoshan, Zhg.	140	25.09 N	99.09 E
Baoting	140	18.42 N	109.45 E
Baotou	132	40.40 N	109.59 E
Baoying	136	33.16 N	119.20 E
Bāpatla	148	15.54 N	80.28 E
Bapaume	118	50.06 N	2.51 E
Baptiste Lake ⊜	176	45.07 N	78.02 W
Ba'qūbah	150	33.45 N	44.38 E
Baquedano	188	23.20 S	69.51 W
Bar	124	42.05 N	19.05 E
Barabinsk	128	55.21 N	78.21 E
Barabinskaja Step' ≚	128	55.00 N	79.00 E
Baracoa	182	20.21 N	74.30 W
Baradero	188	33.50 S	59.30 W
Barakī Barak	146	33.56 N	68.55 E
Barakula	168	26.26 S	150.31 E
Baralaba	168	24.11 S	149.49 E
Baram ≃	142	4.36 N	113.59 E
Bārāmati	148	18.09 N	74.35 E
Bāramūla	149	34.12 N	74.21 E
Bārān	146	25.06 N	76.31 E
Baranagar	146	22.38 N	88.22 E
Barania Góra ∧	116	49.37 N	19.00 E
Baranoa	182	10.48 N	74.55 W
Baranof Island I	172	56.45 N	135.10 W
Baranoviči	130	53.08 N	26.02 E
Baranya □[6]	116	46.05 N	18.15 E
Barão de Cocais	190	19.56 S	43.28 W
Barão de Melgaço	184	16.13 S	55.58 W
Baraoltului, Munții ⩕	124	46.15 N	25.45 E
Baraque de Fraiture ∧	116	50.15 N	5.44 E
Baratang Island I	140	12.13 N	92.45 E
Barat Daya, Kepulauan II	138	7.25 S	128.00 E
Baratta	168	31.59 S	139.06 E
Baraut	149	29.06 N	77.16 E
Barbacena	190	21.14 S	43.46 W
Barbacoas	184	1.41 N	78.09 W
Barbadillo del Mercado	120	42.02 N	3.21 W
Barbados □[1]	180	13.10 N	59.32 W
Barbar	154	18.01 N	33.59 E
Barbaros	124	40.54 N	27.27 E
Barbas, Cabo ≻	152	22.18 N	16.41 W
Barbastro	120	42.02 N	0.08 E
Barbate de Franco	120	36.12 N	5.55 W
Barbeau Peak ∧	90	81.54 N	75.01 W
Barberton, S. Afr.	160	25.48 S	31.03 E
Barberton, Ohio, U.S.	176	41.01 N	81.36 W
Barbil	148	22.06 N	85.20 E
Barboursville	176	38.24 N	82.18 W
Barbuda I	182	17.38 N	61.48 W
Barby	116	51.58 N	11.53 E
Barcaldine	168	23.33 S	145.17 E
Barcellona Pozzo di Gotto	122	38.09 N	15.13 E
Barcelona, Esp.	120	41.23 N	2.11 E
Barcelona, Ven.	184	10.08 N	64.42 W
Barcelos	184	0.58 S	62.57 W
Barcoo ≃	168	25.30 S	142.50 E
Barcs	116	45.58 N	17.28 E
Barda	150	40.23 N	47.08 E
Bardaï	154	21.22 N	16.59 E
Bardawīl, Sabkhat al- ☷	150	31.10 N	33.10 E
Bardejov	116	49.18 N	21.16 E
Bárdenas Reales ⩕[1]	120	42.10 N	1.25 W
Bardera	154	2.21 N	42.20 E
Bardīyah	154	31.46 N	25.06 E
Bardney	106	53.12 N	0.21 W
Bardoc	164	30.20 S	121.17 E
Bardsey Island I	104	52.45 N	4.45 W
Bardsey Sound ⊔	104	52.47 N	4.45 W
Bareilly	146	28.21 N	79.25 E
Barentsøya I	88	78.27 N	21.15 E
Barents Sea (Barenc'ovo More) ⊤[2]	112	69.00 N	40.00 E
Barents Trough ✣[1]	88	74.00 N	28.00 E
Barfleur, Pointe de ≻	118	49.42 N	1.16 W
Bargara	168	24.49 S	152.27 E
Bargarh	146	21.20 N	83.37 E
Bargoed	104	51.43 N	3.15 W
Barguzin ≃	128	53.27 N	109.00 E
Bar Harbor	176	44.23 N	68.13 W
Bari	122	41.07 N	16.52 E
Bariloche → San Carlos de Bariloche	186	41.08 S	71.15 W
Barīm I	144	12.40 N	43.25 E
Barinas	184	8.38 N	70.12 W
Baring, Cape ≻	172	70.05 N	117.20 W
Baring Channel ⊔	172	73.48 N	98.50 W
Baripāda	146	21.56 N	86.43 E
Bariri	190	22.04 S	48.44 W
Bārīs	154	24.40 N	30.36 E
Barisāl	146	22.42 N	90.22 E
Barisan, Pegunungan ⩕	142	3.00 S	102.15 E
Barito ≃	142	3.32 S	114.29 E
Barjac	118	44.18 N	4.21 E
Barjols	120	43.33 N	6.00 E
Barka ∨	154	18.13 N	37.35 E
Barking ⇠[8]	104	51.33 N	0.06 E
Bark Lake ⊜	176	45.27 N	77.51 W
Barkley, Lake ⊜[1]	180	36.40 N	87.55 W
Barkley Sound ⊔	172	48.53 N	125.20 W
Barkly, Mount ∧[2]	164	21.34 S	132.28 E
Barkly East	160	30.58 S	27.33 E
Barkly Tableland ⩕[1]	164	18.00 S	136.00 E
Barkly West	160	28.05 S	24.31 E
Barlby	106	53.48 N	1.03 W
Bar-le-Duc	118	48.47 N	5.10 E
Barlee, Lake ⊜	164	29.10 S	119.30 E
Barlee, Mount ∧[2]	164	24.37 S	128.06 E
Barletta	122	41.19 N	16.17 E
Barmedman	168	34.09 S	147.23 E
Barmer	146	25.45 N	71.23 E
Barmera	168	34.15 S	140.28 E
Barmouth	104	52.43 N	4.03 W
Barmouth Bay C	104	52.42 N	4.08 W
Barnāla	149	30.23 N	75.33 E
Barnard Castle	106	54.33 N	1.55 W
Barnaul	128	53.22 N	83.45 E
Barnegat	176	39.45 N	74.13 W
Barnegat Bay C	176	39.52 N	74.07 W
Barnesboro	176	40.40 N	78.47 W
Barnesville	176	39.59 N	81.11 W
Barnet ⇠[8]	104	51.40 N	0.13 W
Barnetby le Wold	106	53.35 N	0.25 W
Barneville-Carteret	118	49.23 N	1.47 W
Barnoldswick	106	53.55 N	2.11 W
Barnsley	106	53.34 N	1.28 W
Barnstable	176	41.42 N	70.18 W
Barnstaple	104	51.05 N	4.04 W
Barnstaple Bay C	104	51.05 N	4.20 W
Barnt Green	104	52.22 N	1.59 W
Baro ≃	154	8.26 N	33.13 E
Baroda, Bhārat	144	25.30 N	76.40 E
Baroda, Bhārat	148	22.18 N	73.12 E
Baroe	160	33.13 S	24.33 E
Barotseland □[9]	156	16.00 S	24.00 E
Barpeta	146	26.19 N	91.00 E
Barqah (Cyrenaica) ⇠[1]	154	31.00 N	22.30 E
Barque Canada Reef ✣[2]	138	8.12 N	113.19 E
Barquisimeto	184	10.04 N	69.19 W
Barra	184	11.05 S	43.10 W
Barra I	108	56.58 N	7.29 W
Barra, Ponta da ≻	160	23.45 S	35.30 E
Barra, Sound of ⊔	108	57.05 N	7.25 W
Barraba	168	30.22 S	150.36 E
Barracão	188	26.15 S	53.38 W
Barrackville	176	39.30 N	80.10 W
Barra do Corda	184	5.30 S	45.15 W
Barra do Garças	190	15.53 S	52.15 W
Barra do Mendes	190	11.43 S	42.04 W
Barra do Piraí	190	22.28 S	43.49 W
Barra do Ribeiro	188	30.18 S	51.18 W
Barra Falsa, Ponta da ≻	160	22.55 S	35.37 E
Barrafranca	122	37.23 N	14.13 E
Barra Head ≻	108	56.46 N	7.38 W
Barra Mansa	190	22.32 S	44.11 W
Barranca	184	10.42 S	77.45 W
Barrancabermeja	184	7.03 N	73.52 W
Barrancas, Chile	188	33.27 S	70.46 W
Barrancas, Col.	182	10.57 N	72.50 W
Barrancas, Ven.	184	8.42 N	62.11 W
Barranco do Velho	120	37.14 N	7.56 W
Barranqueras	188	27.30 S	58.55 W
Barranquilla	184	10.59 N	74.48 W
Barras	184	4.15 S	42.18 W
Barraza	188	30.38 S	71.26 W
Barre, Mass., U.S.	176	42.26 N	72.06 W
Barre, Vt., U.S.	174	44.12 N	72.30 W
Barre des Écrins ∧	118	44.55 N	6.22 E
Barreiras	190	12.08 S	45.00 W
Barreiro	120	38.40 N	9.04 W
Barreiros	184	8.49 S	35.12 W
Barren, Îles II	161b	18.25 S	43.40 E
Barren Islands II	172	58.55 N	152.15 W
Barretos	190	20.33 S	48.33 W
Barrett, Mount ∧	164	18.10 S	127.33 E
Barrhead	108	55.48 N	4.24 W
Barrhill	106	55.07 N	4.46 W
Barrie	172	44.24 N	79.40 W
Barrie Island I	176	45.55 N	82.40 W
Barrier, Cape ≻	170	36.21 S	175.31 E
Barrier Range ⩕	168	31.25 S	141.25 E
Barrier Reef ✣[2]	166	11.36 S	153.00 E
Barrington Tops ∧	168	32.00 S	151.28 E
Barringun	168	29.01 S	145.43 E
Barrow ≃	110	52.15 N	7.00 W
Barrow Creek	164	21.33 S	133.53 E
Barrowford	106	53.52 N	2.13 W
Barrow-in-Furness	106	54.07 N	3.14 W
Barrow Island I	164	20.48 S	115.23 E
Barrow Strait ⊔	172	74.21 N	94.10 W
Barry	104	51.24 N	3.18 W
Barrys Bay	176	45.29 N	77.41 W
Barryton	176	43.45 N	85.09 W
Bārsi	148	18.14 N	75.42 E
Barstow	178	34.54 N	117.01 W
Bar-sur-Seine	118	48.07 N	4.22 E
Bartang	126	38.05 N	71.51 E
Barth	116	54.22 N	12.43 E
Bartica	184	6.24 N	58.37 W
Bartle Frere ∧	168	17.23 S	145.49 E
Bartlesville	174	36.45 N	95.59 W
Bartlett	176	44.05 N	71.17 W
Bartolomeu Dias	160	21.10 S	35.09 E
Barton, Austl.	164	30.31 S	132.39 E
Barton, Vt., U.S.	176	44.45 N	72.11 W
Barton Mills	104	52.20 N	0.31 E
Barton-under-Needwood	104	52.45 N	1.43 W
Barton-upon-Humber	106	53.41 N	0.27 W
Bartoszyce	116	54.16 N	20.49 E
Bāruni	146	25.29 N	85.59 E
Barun-Šibertuj, Gora ∧	128	49.42 N	109.59 E
Baruun Urt	132	46.40 N	113.12 E
Barvas	108	58.22 N	6.32 W
Barview	178	43.21 N	124.18 W
Barwāni	146	22.02 N	74.54 E
Barwell	104	52.32 N	1.21 W
Barwidgee	164	27.02 S	120.54 E
Barwon ≃	168	30.00 S	148.05 E
Baryš	112	53.39 N	47.08 E
Basalt ≃	168	19.38 S	145.52 E
Basankusu	156	1.14 N	19.48 E
Basatongwulashan ∧	146	33.05 N	91.30 E
Basco	138	20.27 N	121.58 E
Bascuñán, Cabo ≻	188	28.51 S	71.30 W
Basel (Bâle)	118	47.33 N	7.35 E
Basey	138	11.17 N	125.04 E
Bashākerd, Kūhhā-ye ⩕	150	26.42 N	59.00 E
Bashee ≃	160	32.15 S	28.53 E
Bashi Channel ⊔	138	22.00 N	121.00 E
Basi	149	30.41 N	76.24 E
Basilan	138	6.42 N	121.58 E
Basilan Island I	142	6.34 N	122.03 E
Basildon	104	51.35 N	0.25 E
Basilicata □[4]	122	40.30 N	16.10 E
Basílio	188	31.53 S	53.01 W
Basingstoke	104	51.15 N	1.05 W
Basīrhāt	146	22.40 N	88.53 E
Baška	122	44.58 N	14.46 E
Baskahegan Lake ⊜	176	45.30 N	67.48 W
Baskatong, Réservoir ⊜[1]	172	46.48 N	75.50 W
Baslow	106	53.15 N	1.38 W
Basmat	148	19.19 N	77.10 E
Basoko	156	1.14 N	23.36 E
Basra → Al-Başrah	150	30.30 N	47.47 E
Bas-Rhin □[5]	118	48.35 N	7.40 E
Bass, Îlots de II	96	27.55 S	143.26 W
Bassano del Grappa	122	45.46 N	11.44 E
Bassari	152	9.15 N	0.47 E
Bassas da India ✣[2]	156	21.25 S	39.42 E
Bassein	140	16.47 N	94.44 E
Bassenthwaite	106	54.41 N	3.12 W
Bassenthwaite Lake ⊜	106	54.38 N	3.13 W
Basses-Pyrénées □[5]	118	43.15 N	0.50 W
Basse-Terre, Guad.	182	16.00 N	61.44 W
Basseterre, St. K.-N.	182	17.18 N	62.43 W
Basse-Terre I	182	16.10 N	61.40 W
Bass Harbor	176	44.16 N	68.19 W
Bass Strait ⊔	168	39.20 S	145.30 E
Bästad	114	56.26 N	12.51 E
Basti	146	26.48 N	82.43 E
Bastia	118	42.42 N	9.27 E
Bastogne	116	50.00 N	5.43 E
Bastrop	174	32.47 N	91.55 W
Bata	156	1.51 N	9.45 E
Batabanó, Golfo de C	182	22.15 N	82.30 W
Batagaj	128	67.38 N	134.38 E
Batagaj-Alyta	128	67.48 N	130.25 E
Bataguaçu	190	21.42 S	52.22 W
Batai Kandao)(	146	33.23 N	70.19 E
Bataiporã	190	22.20 S	53.17 W
Batajsk	126	47.10 N	39.44 E
Batak, Jazovir ⊜[1]	124	41.59 N	24.11 E
Batāla	149	31.48 N	75.12 E
Batalha ≃	190	21.42 S	49.10 W
Batamaj	128	63.31 N	129.27 E
Batan	136	34.10 N	120.04 E
Batang	132	30.02 N	99.02 E
Batangas	138	13.45 N	121.03 E
Batanghari ≃	142	1.16 S	104.05 E
Batan Island I	138	20.26 N	121.58 E
Batan Islands II	138	20.30 N	121.50 E
Batanta, Pulau I	166	0.50 S	130.40 E
Bátaszék	116	46.12 N	18.44 E
Batatais	190	20.53 S	47.37 W
Batavia, N.Y., U.S.	176	43.00 N	78.11 W
Batavia, Ohio, U.S.	176	39.05 N	84.11 W
Batchelor	166	13.04 S	131.01 E
Bătdâmbâng	140	13.06 N	103.12 E
Batemans Bay	168	35.43 S	150.11 E
Bath, Eng., U.K.	104	51.23 N	2.22 W
Bath, Maine, U.S.	176	43.55 N	69.49 W
Bath, N.Y., U.S.	176	42.20 N	77.19 W
Bathgate	108	55.55 N	3.39 W
Bathurst, Austl.	168	33.25 S	149.35 E
Bathurst, N.B., Can.	172	47.36 N	65.39 W
Bathurst → Banjul, Gam.	152	13.28 N	16.39 W
Bathurst, S. Afr.	160	33.30 S	26.50 E
Bathurst, Cape ≻	172	70.35 N	128.00 W
Bathurst Inlet	172	66.50 N	108.01 W
Bathurst Inlet C	172	68.10 N	108.50 W
Bathurst Island I, Austl.	166	11.37 S	130.23 E
Bathurst Island I	90	76.00 N	100.30 W
Bāţin, Wādī al- ∨	150	29.35 N	47.00 E
Batley	106	53.44 N	1.37 W
Batlow	168	35.31 S	148.09 E
Batman	150	37.52 N	41.07 E
Batna	152	35.34 N	6.11 E
Baton Rouge	174	30.23 N	91.11 W
Batouri	152	4.26 N	14.22 E
Batovi	190	15.53 S	53.24 W
Battambang → Bătdâmbâng	140	13.06 N	103.12 E
Batticaloa	148	7.43 N	81.42 E
Battle	104	50.55 N	0.29 E
Battle ≃	172	52.42 N	108.15 W
Battle Creek	176	42.19 N	85.11 W
Battle Creek ≃, Calif., U.S.	178	40.21 N	122.11 W
Battle Creek ≃, Idaho, U.S.	178	42.14 N	116.32 W
Battle Creek, North Fork ≃	178	40.26 N	122.00 W
Battle Creek, South Fork ≃	178	40.26 N	122.00 W
Battlefields	158	18.31 S	29.52 E
Battle Harbour	172	52.16 N	55.35 W
Battle Mountain	178	40.38 N	116.56 W
Batu ∧	154	6.55 N	39.46 E
Batu, Kepulauan II	140	0.18 S	98.28 E
Batu Gajah	142	4.28 N	101.03 E
Batumi	126	41.38 N	41.38 E
Batu Pahat	142	1.51 N	102.56 E
Baturaja	142	4.08 S	104.10 E
Baturité	184	4.20 S	38.53 W
Batusangkar	142	0.27 S	100.35 E
Baubau	142	5.28 S	122.38 E
Bauchi	152	10.19 N	9.50 E
Baud	118	47.52 N	3.01 W
Baudouinville	158	7.04 S	29.46 E
Bauld, Cape ≻	172	51.38 N	55.25 W
Baume-les-Dames	118	47.21 N	6.22 E
Baun	142	10.18 S	123.43 E
Bauru	190	22.19 S	49.04 W
Bautzen	116	51.11 N	14.26 E
Baviaanskloofberge ⩕	160	33.35 S	24.10 E
Bawdeswell	104	52.45 N	1.01 E
Bawean, Pulau I	138	5.46 S	112.40 E
Bawtry	106	53.26 N	1.01 W
Bay, Laguna de ⊜	138	14.23 N	121.15 E
Bayamo	182	20.23 N	76.39 W
Bayamón	182	18.24 N	66.09 W
Bayan	142	8.16 S	116.26 E
Bayanhaote	132	38.50 N	105.41 E
Bayankalashanmai ⩕	132	33.48 N	98.10 E
Bayano ≃	182	9.00 N	79.08 W
Bayard	176	39.16 N	79.22 W
Bayble	108	58.12 N	6.13 W
Bayburt	150	40.16 N	40.15 E
Bay City, Mich., U.S.	176	43.36 N	83.53 W
Bay City, Tex., U.S.	174	28.59 N	95.58 W
Bayern □[9]	116	49.00 N	11.30 E
Bayeux	118	49.16 N	0.42 W
Bayhead	108	57.33 N	7.24 W
Bayiji	136	34.18 N	117.41 E
Bayley Point Of	166	16.56 S	139.02 E
Bayon	118	48.29 N	6.19 E
Bayonne	118	43.29 N	1.29 W
Bayovar	184	5.50 S	81.03 W
Bay Port	176	43.51 N	83.23 W
Bayreuth	116	49.57 N	11.35 E
Bayrūt (Beirut)	150	33.53 N	35.30 E
Bays, Lake of ⊜	176	45.15 N	79.04 W
Bay Shore	176	40.44 N	73.15 W
Bayside	176	44.07 N	77.30 W
Bayt al-Faqīh	144	14.32 N	43.20 E
Bayt Laḩm	150	31.43 N	35.12 E
Baytown	174	29.44 N	94.58 W
Bay View	170	39.25 S	176.53 E
Baza	120	37.29 N	2.46 W
Baza, Sierra de ⩕	120	37.15 N	2.45 W
Bazargic → Tolbuhin	124	43.34 N	27.50 E
Bazaruto, Ilha do I	160	21.40 S	35.28 E
Bazas	118	44.26 N	0.13 W
Beach Haven	176	39.34 N	74.14 W
Beachport	168	37.30 S	140.01 E
Beachville	176	43.05 N	80.49 W
Beachy Head ≻	102	50.44 N	0.16 E
Beacon, Austl.	164	30.26 S	117.51 E
Beacon, N.Y., U.S.	176	41.30 N	73.58 W
Beacon Hill ∧[2]	104	52.23 N	3.12 W
Beaconsfield, Austl.	168	41.12 S	146.48 E
Beaconsfield, Eng., U.K.	104	51.37 N	0.39 W
Beagh, Slieve ∧[2]	110	54.21 N	7.12 W
Beagle Bay Mission	164	16.58 S	122.40 E
Beagle Gulf C	166	12.00 S	130.20 E
Bealanana	161b	14.33 S	48.44 E
Beaminster	104	50.49 N	2.45 W
Bear ≃	178	38.57 N	121.35 W
Bear Bay C	172	75.47 N	87.00 W
Bear Creek ≃	178	42.26 N	122.58 W
Beardmore	172	49.36 N	87.57 W
Beardmore Glacier ⊽	87	83.45 S	171.00 E
Bear Island I	110	51.40 N	9.48 W
Bear Lake ⊜	174	42.00 N	111.20 W
Béarn ⇠[1]	118	43.20 N	0.45 W
Bearsden	108	55.56 N	4.20 W
Beās ≃	149	31.10 N	74.59 E
Beata, Cabo ≻	182	17.35 N	71.25 W
Beata, Isla I	182	17.34 N	71.31 W
Beatrice, Rh.	158	18.15 S	30.55 E
Beatrice, Nebr., U.S.	174	40.16 N	96.44 W
Beatrice, Cape ≻	166	14.15 S	136.59 E
Beattock	106	55.18 N	3.28 W
Beatton ≃	172	56.10 N	120.25 W
Beatty	178	36.54 N	116.46 W
Beaucaire	118	43.48 N	4.38 E
Beauce ⇠[1]	118	48.22 N	1.50 E
Beauceville-Est	176	46.12 N	70.46 W
Beaudesert	168	27.59 S	153.00 E
Beaufort, Malay.	142	5.20 N	115.45 E
Beaufort, S.C., U.S.	174	32.26 N	80.40 W
Beaufort, Cape ≻	164	34.26 S	115.32 E
Beaufort Sea ⊤[2]	172	73.00 N	140.00 W
Beaufort West	160	32.18 S	22.36 E
Beaugency	118	47.47 N	1.38 E
Beauharnois	176	45.19 N	73.52 W
Beaujolais, Monts du ⩕	118	46.00 N	4.30 E
Beaulieu	104	50.49 N	1.27 W
Beauly	108	57.29 N	4.29 W
Beauly ≃	108	57.28 N	4.28 W
Beauly Firth C[1]	108	57.30 N	4.23 W
Beaumaris	106	53.16 N	4.05 W
Beaumont, Fr.	118	48.13 N	0.08 E
Beaumont, N.Z.	170	45.49 S	169.32 E
Beaumont, Calif., U.S.	178	33.56 N	116.58 W
Beaumont, Tex., U.S.	174	30.05 N	94.06 W
Beaumont Hill ∧[2]	168	31.33 S	145.13 E
Beaumont-sur-Sarthe	118	48.13 N	0.08 E
Beaune	118	47.02 N	4.50 E
Beaune-la-Rolande	118	48.04 N	2.26 E
Beaupré	172	47.03 N	70.54 W
Beaurepaire	118	45.20 N	5.03 E
Beausejour	172	50.04 N	96.33 W
Beauvais	118	49.26 N	2.05 E
Beauville	118	44.17 N	0.52 E
Beauvoir-sur-Mer	118	46.55 N	2.02 W
Beaver	176	40.42 N	80.18 W
Beaver ≃, Can.	172	54.30 N	107.45 W
Beaver ≃, Can.	172	59.43 N	124.16 W
Beaver ≃, N.Y., U.S.	176	43.54 N	75.30 W
Beaver ≃, Pa., U.S.	176	40.40 N	80.18 W
Beaver Falls	176	40.46 N	80.19 W
Beaver Island I	176	45.40 N	85.31 W
Beaverton	176	43.53 N	84.29 W
Beāwar	146	26.06 N	74.19 E
Bebedouro	190	20.56 S	48.28 W
Bebington	106	53.23 N	3.01 W
Bécancour ≃	176	46.22 N	72.27 W
Beccles	104	52.28 N	1.34 E
Bečej	124	45.37 N	20.03 E
Béchar	152	31.37 N	2.13 W
Bechuanaland ⇠[1]	160	27.30 S	22.30 E
Beckington	104	51.16 N	2.18 W
Beckley	174	37.46 N	81.13 W
Beckum	116	51.45 N	8.02 E
Becky Peak ∧	178	39.58 N	114.36 W
Bedale	106	54.17 N	1.35 W
Bédarieux	118	43.37 N	3.09 E
Beddgelert	106	53.01 N	4.06 W
Beddome, Mount ∧	164	25.50 S	134.22 E
Bedele	154	8.33 N	36.23 E
Bedford, Qué., Can.	176	45.07 N	72.59 W
Bedford, S. Afr.	160	32.41 S	26.05 E
Bedford, Eng., U.K.	104	52.08 N	0.29 W
Bedford, Pa., U.S.	176	40.01 N	78.30 W
Bedford, Cape ≻	166	15.14 S	145.21 E
Bedford Harbour C	164	33.35 S	120.35 E
Bedford Level ≚	104	52.27 N	0.02 W
Bedfordshire □[6]	102	52.05 N	0.30 W
Bedi	146	22.30 N	70.02 E
Bedourie	168	24.21 S	139.28 E
Bedwas	104	51.35 N	3.13 W
Bedworth	104	52.28 N	1.29 W
Beechworth	168	36.22 S	146.41 E
Beela ≃	106	54.13 N	2.47 W
Beenleigh	168	27.43 S	153.12 E
Beeringgnurding ∧	164	29.53 S	117.55 E
Beersheba → Be'er Sheva'	150	31.14 N	34.47 E
Be'er Sheva'	150	31.14 N	34.47 E
Beeskow	116	52.10 N	14.14 E
Beestekraal	160	25.23 S	27.38 E
Beeston	104	52.56 N	1.12 W
Beethoven Peninsula ≻[1]	87	71.40 S	73.45 W
Beeville	174	28.24 N	97.45 W
Befale	156	0.28 N	20.58 E
Befandriana, Malg.	161b	22.06 S	43.54 E
Befandriana, Malg.	161b	15.16 S	48.32 E
Bega	168	36.40 S	149.50 E
Bega (Begej) ≃	124	45.13 N	20.19 E
Begej (Bega) ≃	124	45.13 N	20.19 E
Begi	154	9.16 N	34.33 E
Beglés	118	44.47 N	0.34 W
Begusarai	146	25.25 N	86.08 E
Behbehān	150	30.35 N	50.14 E
Behshahr	150	36.43 N	53.34 E
Beian	132	48.15 N	126.30 E
Beianfeng	136	33.06 N	120.08 E
Beibaozhen	136	31.33 N	121.38 E
Beihai (Pakhoi)	140	21.29 N	109.05 E
Beijiang ≃	132	23.09 N	112.48 E
Beijing (Peking)	132	39.55 N	116.25 E
Beijing Shih □[7]	132	40.15 N	116.30 E
Beiliu	140	22.42 N	110.22 E
Beipanjiang ≃	140	25.05 N	106.00 E
Beipiao	132	41.49 N	120.46 E
Beira	160	19.49 S	34.52 E
Beira Baixa □[9]	120	39.45 N	7.30 W
Beira Litoral □[9]	120	40.15 N	8.25 W
Beirut → Bayrūt	150	33.53 N	35.30 E
Beishanmai ⩕	132	41.12 N	97.05 E
Beitbridge	156	22.13 S	30.00 E
Beith	108	55.45 N	4.38 W
Beitstadfjorden C[2]	114	63.53 N	11.00 E
Beiwudu	136	33.39 N	113.39 E
Beja, Port.	120	38.01 N	7.52 W
Béja, Tun.	152	36.44 N	9.11 E
Bejaïa	152	36.45 N	5.05 E
Béjar	120	40.23 N	5.46 W
Bejestān	150	34.31 N	58.10 E
Bejuma	182	10.11 N	68.16 W
Bekabad	126	40.13 N	69.14 E
Bekdaš	126	41.34 N	52.32 E
Békés	116	46.46 N	21.08 E
Békés □[6]	116	46.46 N	21.08 E
Békéscsaba	116	46.41 N	21.06 E
Bekily	161b	24.13 S	45.19 E
Bekkai	134a	43.23 N	145.17 E
Bela, Bhārat	146	25.56 N	81.59 E
Bela, Pāk.	146	26.14 N	66.19 E
Bélâbre	118	46.33 N	1.09 E
Bela Crkva	124	44.54 N	21.26 E
Belaga	138	2.42 N	113.47 E
Bel Air	176	39.32 N	76.21 W
Belaja ≃	126	56.00 N	54.32 E
Belaja Cerkov'	126	49.49 N	30.07 E
Belambanganumpu	142	4.54 S	105.03 E
Belampalli	148	19.02 N	79.30 E
Bela Vista, Bra.	188	22.06 S	56.31 W
Bela Vista, Moç.	160	26.20 S	32.40 E
Bela Vista de Goiás	190	16.58 S	48.57 W
Bela Vista do Paráiso	190	23.00 S	51.12 W
Belawan	138	3.47 N	98.41 E
Belayan ≃	142	0.14 S	116.36 E
Belcher Islands II	172	56.20 N	79.30 W
Belcoo	110	54.17 N	7.52 W
Bel'cy	126	47.46 N	27.56 E
Belding	176	43.06 N	85.14 W
Belebej	126	54.07 N	54.07
Beled Weyne	154	4.47 N	45.12 E
Belém	184	1.27 S	48.29 W
Belén, Arg.	188	27.40 S	67.05 W
Belén, Nic.	182	11.30 N	85.53 W
Belén, Para.	188	23.30 S	57.06 W
Belen, N. Mex., U.S.	174	34.40 N	106.46 W
Belesar, Embalse de ⊜[1]	120	42.45 N	7.40 W
Belfast, S. Afr.	160	25.43 S	30.03 E
Belfast, N. Ire., U.K.	110	54.35 N	5.55 W
Belfast, Maine, U.S.	176	44.27 N	69.01 W
Belfast Lough C	110	54.40 N	5.36 W
Belford	106	55.36 N	1.49 W
Belfort	118	47.38 N	6.52 E
Belgaum	148	15.52 N	74.30 E
Belgium □[1]	100	50.50 N	4.00 E
Belgodere	122	42.35 N	9.01 E
Belgorod	126	50.36 N	36.35 E
Belgorod-Dnestrovskij	126	46.12 N	30.20 E
Belgrade → Beograd	124	44.50 N	20.30 E
Beli Drim ≃	124	42.06 N	20.25 E
Belin	118	44.30 N	0.47 W
Belington	176	39.01 N	79.56 W
Belitung I	142	2.50 S	107.55 E
Belize	180	17.30 N	88.12 W
Belize □[2]	180	17.15 N	88.45 W
Bel'kovskij, Ostrov ≃	128	75.32 N	135.44 E
Bell ≃	172	49.48 N	77.38 W
Bella Bella	172	52.09 N	128.07 W
Bella Coola	172	52.22 N	126.46 W
Bellahy	110	53.58 N	8.48 W
Bellaire, Mich., U.S.	176	44.59 N	85.13 W
Bellaire, Ohio, U.S.	176	40.02 N	80.45 W
Bellary	148	15.09 N	76.56 E
Bellata	168	29.55 S	149.47 E
Bella Unión	188	30.15 S	57.35 W
Bella Vista, Arg.	188	27.02 S	65.19 W
Bella Vista, Arg.	188	28.30 S	59.00 W
Bellavista, Perú	184	4.54 S	80.42 W
Bellavista, Perú	184	6.58 S	76.32 W
Bellbrook	168	30.49 S	152.31 E
Bell Crags ∧[2]	106	55.03 N	2.22 W
Belle	176	38.14 N	81.32 W
Belle ≃	176	42.43 N	82.30 W
Belleek	110	54.28 N	8.06 W
Bellefontaine	176	40.22 N	83.46 W

Symbols in the index entries are identified on page 198.

Name	Page	Lat	Long
Bolsward	116	53.03 N	5.31 E
Bolton, Ont., Can.	176	43.53 N	79.44 W
Bolton, Eng., U.K.	106	53.35 N	2.26 W
Bolton Abbey	106	53.59 N	1.53 W
Bolton Bridge	106	53.58 N	1.57 W
Bolton-le-Sands	106	54.06 N	2.47 W
Bolton upon Dearne	106	53.31 N	1.19 W
Boluo	136	23.11 N	114.17 E
Bolus Head ↗	110	51.46 N	10.21 W
Bolwarra	168	17.24 S	144.11 E
Bolzano (Bozen)	122	46.31 N	11.22 E
Boma	156	5.51 S	13.03 E
Bomaderry	168	34.51 S	150.37 E
Bombala	168	36.54 S	149.14 E
Bombay	148	18.58 N	72.50 E
Bomberai, Jazirah ↗1	166	3.00 S	133.00 E
Bom Despacho	190	19.43 S	45.15 W
Bom Jesus da Lapa	190	13.15 S	43.25 W
Bømlafjorden ⊂2	114	59.39 N	5.20 E
Bømlo I	114	59.46 N	5.12 E
Bomnak	128	54.46 N	128.51 E
Bomokandi ≈	158	3.39 N	26.08 E
Bon, Cap ↗	152	37.05 N	11.03 E
Bonaire I	182	12.10 N	68.15 W
Bonanza, Nic.	182	13.57 N	84.32 W
Bonanza, Oreg., U.S.	178	42.12 N	121.24 W
Bonao	182	18.56 N	70.25 W
Bonarbridge	108	53.33 N	4.21 W
Bonavista	172	48.39 N	53.07 W
Bonavista Bay ⊂	172	48.45 N	53.20 W
Bonawe	108	56.26 N	5.13 W
Bon Bon	164	30.26 S	135.28 E
Bonchester Bridge	108	55.24 N	2.40 W
Bondeno	122	44.53 N	11.25 E
Bondo	154	3.49 N	23.40 E
Bondoukou	152	8.02 N	2.48 W
Bondowoso	142	7.55 S	113.49 E
Bône → Annaba, Alg.	152	36.54 N	7.46 E
Bone → Watampone, Indon.	142	4.32 S	120.20 E
Bone, Teluk ⊂	142	4.00 S	120.40 E
Bo'ness	108	56.01 N	3.37 W
Bonete, Cerro ∧	188	27.51 S	68.48 W
Bonfinópolis	190	16.38 S	48.58 W
Bongor	154	10.17 N	15.22 E
Bonham	174	33.35 N	96.11 W
Bonham, Pic ∧	182	19.05 N	72.15 W
Bonifacio	118	41.23 N	9.10 E
Bonifacio, Strait of ⋃	122	41.20 N	9.15 E
Bonin Islands → Ogasawara-guntō II	96	27.00 N	142.10 E
Bonito, Pico ∧	182	15.38 N	86.55 W
Bonn	116	50.44 N	7.05 E
Bonnechere ≈	176	45.31 N	76.33 W
Bonnétable	118	48.11 N	0.26 E
Bonneville	118	46.05 N	6.25 E
Bonneville Salt Flats	178	40.45 N	113.52 W
Bonney, Lake ⊜	168	37.48 S	140.22 E
Bonnie Rock	164	30.32 S	118.21 E
Bonnievale	160	33.57 S	20.06 E
Bonny	152	4.27 N	7.10 E
Bonnyrigg	108	55.52 N	3.08 W
Bonsecours	118	49.26 N	1.08 E
Bonthain	142	5.32 S	119.56 E
Bonthe	152	7.32 N	12.30 W
Bontoc	138	17.05 N	120.58 E
Bonyhád	116	46.19 N	18.32 E
Boogardie	164	28.02 S	117.47 E
Bookabie	164	31.50 S	132.41 E
Bookaloo	168	31.55 S	137.22 E
Booleroo Centre	168	32.53 S	138.21 E
Booligal	168	33.52 S	144.53 E
Boologooro	164	24.21 S	114.02 E
Boom	116	51.05 N	4.22 E
Boomarra	168	19.33 S	140.02 E
Boomer	176	38.09 N	81.17 W
Boomi	168	28.44 S	149.35 E
Boonah	168	28.00 S	152.41 E
Boone	174	42.04 N	93.53 W
Boonsboro	176	39.30 N	77.39 W
Boonville, Calif., U.S.	178	39.00 N	123.22 W
Boonville, N.Y., U.S.	176	43.29 N	75.20 W
Booroorban	168	34.56 S	144.46 E
Boorowa	168	34.26 S	148.43 E
Boot	106	54.24 N	3.17 W
Boothbay Harbor	176	43.51 N	69.38 W
Boothby, Cape ↗	87	66.34 S	57.16 E
Boothia, Gulf of ⊂	172	71.00 N	91.00 W
Boothia Peninsula ↗1	172	70.00 N	95.00 W
Bootle	106	53.28 N	3.00 W
Booué	156	0.06 S	11.56 E
Bopeechee	168	29.36 S	137.23 E
Boquerón ⊡5	188	21.30 S	60.00 W
Boquete	182	8.46 N	82.27 W
Bor, Jugo.	124	44.05 N	22.07 E
Bor, S.S.S.R.	130	56.22 N	44.05 E
Bor, Sud.	154	6.12 N	31.33 E
Bor, Tür.	150	37.54 N	34.34 E
Bora-Bora I	96	16.30 S	151.45 W
Borah Peak ∧	174	44.08 N	113.48 W
Borama	154	9.58 N	43.07 E
Borås	114	57.43 N	12.55 E
Borāzjān	150	29.16 N	51.12 E
Borba	190	4.24 S	59.35 W
Borborema	190	21.37 S	49.04 W
Borda, Cape ↗	168	35.45 S	136.34 E
Bordeaux	118	44.50 N	0.34 W
Borden	108	54.35 S	118.16 E
Borden Peninsula ↗1	172	73.00 N	83.00 W
Borders ⊡4	108	55.37 N	3.15 W
Bordertown	168	36.19 S	140.47 E
Bordighera	122	43.46 N	7.39 E
Bordj Bou Arreridj	120	36.04 N	4.46 E
Bordj Menaïel	120	36.44 N	3.43 E
Bore	158	4.40 N	37.40 E
Borehamwood	104	51.40 N	0.16 W
Boreray I	108	57.42 N	7.18 W
Borgå (Porvoo)	114	60.24 N	25.40 E
Borgarnes	112a	64.35 N	21.53 W
Borger	174	35.39 N	101.24 W
Borgholm	114	56.53 N	16.39 E
Borghorst	116	52.07 N	7.23 E
Borg Mountain ∧	87	72.42 S	3.30 W
Borgosesia	122	45.42 N	8.16 E
Borgosesia	122	45.43 N	8.16 E
Borisoglebsk	126	51.23 N	42.06 E
Borisov	130	54.15 N	28.30 E
Borjas Blancas	120	41.31 N	0.52 E
Borkum	116	51.51 N	6.41 E
Borlänge	114	60.29 N	15.25 E
Borna	116	51.19 N	13.11 E
Borne	116	52.18 N	6.45 E
Borneo (Kalimantan) I	142	0.30 N	114.00 E
Bornholm I	114	55.10 N	15.00 E
Bornos, Embalse de ⊜1	120	36.50 N	5.30 W
Boro ≈	154	8.52 N	26.11 E
Borogoncy	128	62.42 N	131.08 E
Boron	178	34.60 N	117.39 W
Boroughbridge	106	54.06 N	1.24 W
Borough Green	104	51.17 N	0.19 E
Borovičí	130	58.24 N	33.55 E
Borovi'anka	128	52.38 N	84.29 E
Borrazópolis	190	23.56 S	51.36 W
Borris	110	52.35 N	6.06 W
Borrisokane	110	52.59 N	8.07 W
Borrisoleigh	110	52.44 N	7.57 W
Borrowdale	106	54.31 N	3.10 W
Borsa	124	47.39 N	24.40 E
Borşad	146	22.26 N	72.54 E
Borščovčnyj Chrebet ⋌	128	52.00 N	117.00 E
Borsod-Abaúj-Zemplén ⊡6	116	48.15 N	21.00 E
Borth	104	52.29 N	4.03 W
Borthwick Water ≈	108	55.24 N	2.50 W
Bort-les-Orgues	118	45.24 N	2.30 E
Borūjen	150	31.59 N	51.18 E
Borūjerd	150	33.54 N	48.46 E
Borve	108	56.58 N	7.32 W
Borz'a	128	50.38 N	115.38 E
Bosanska Dubica	122	45.11 N	16.49 E
Bosanska Gradiška	122	45.09 N	17.15 E
Bosanski Novi	122	45.03 N	16.23 E
Bosanski Petrovac	122	44.33 N	16.22 E
Bosanski Šamac	124	45.03 N	18.28 E
Bosansko Grahovo	122	44.11 N	16.22 E
Bosaso	154	11.13 N	49.08 E
Bosavi, Mount ∧	166	6.35 S	142.50 E
Boscastle	104	50.41 N	4.42 W
Bose	140	23.57 N	106.26 E
Boshan	132	36.29 N	117.50 E
Boshoek	160	25.30 S	27.09 E
Boshof	160	28.34 S	25.04 E
Bositenghu	132	42.00 N	87.00 E
Bosna ≈	124	45.04 N	18.29 E
Bosnik	166	1.10 S	136.14 E
Bōsō-hantō ↗1	134	35.18 N	140.10 E
Bosporus → İstanbul Boğazı ⋃	124	41.06 N	29.04 E
Bossangoa	154	6.29 N	17.27 E
Bossembélé	154	5.16 N	17.39 E
Bossier City	174	32.31 N	93.43 W
Bosso, Dallol ∨	152	12.25 N	2.50 E
Bossut, Cape ↗	164	18.43 S	121.38 E
Bostan	146	30.26 N	67.02 E
Boston, Eng., U.K.	104	52.59 N	0.01 W
Boston, Mass., U.S.	176	42.21 N	71.04 W
Boston Mountains ⋌	174	35.50 N	93.20 W
Boswell	176	40.10 N	79.02 W
Botād	146	22.10 N	71.40 E
Boteti ≈	160	20.08 S	23.23 E
Botha's Hill	160	29.45 S	30.45 E
Bothaville	160	27.27 S	26.36 E
Bothnia, Gulf of ⊂	114	63.00 N	20.00 E
Bothwell, Austl.	168	42.23 S	147.00 E
Bothwell, Ont., Can.	176	42.38 N	81.52 W
Botkins	176	40.28 N	84.11 W
Botley	104	50.56 N	1.18 W
Botoşani	124	47.45 N	26.40 E
Botoşani ⊡4	124	48.00 N	26.45 E
Botrange ∧	116	50.30 N	6.08 E
Botswana ⊡1	156	22.00 S	24.00 E
Bottenhavet (Selkämeri) ⊂	114	62.00 N	20.00 E
Bottenviken (Perämeri) ⊂	114	65.00 N	23.00 E
Bottesford	104	52.56 N	0.48 W
Bottineau	174	48.50 N	100.27 W
Bottrop	116	51.31 N	6.55 E
Botucatu	190	22.52 S	48.26 W
Botwood	172	49.09 N	55.21 W
Bouaflé	152	6.59 N	5.45 W
Bouaké	152	7.41 N	5.02 W
Bouar	154	5.57 N	15.36 E
Bouches-du-Rhône ⊡5	118	43.30 N	5.00 E
Bougainville I	96	6.00 S	155.00 E
Bougainville, Cape ↗	164	13.54 S	126.06 E
Bougainville Reef ↗2	166	15.30 S	147.06 E
Boughton Street	104	51.18 N	0.59 E
Bougouni	152	11.25 N	7.29 W
Bouillon	116	49.48 N	5.04 E
Bouira	120	36.23 N	3.54 E
Boulay-Moselle	118	49.11 N	6.30 E
Boulder, Austl.	164	30.47 S	121.29 E
Boulder, Colo., U.S.	174	40.01 N	105.17 W
Boulder City	178	35.59 N	114.50 W
Boulia	168	22.54 S	139.54 E
Boulogne-Billancourt	118	48.50 N	2.15 E
Boulogne-sur-Mer	118	50.43 N	1.37 E
Bouloire	118	47.58 N	0.33 E
Boulsworth Hill ∧	106	53.48 N	2.06 W
Bouna	152	9.16 N	3.00 W
Boundary Peak ∧	178	37.51 N	118.21 W
Bounty Basin ↗1	84	46.30 S	178.00 E
Bounty Islands II	96	47.42 S	179.04 E
Bounty Trough ↗1	87	46.30 S	178.00 E
Bourbon-Lancy	118	46.37 N	3.46 E
Bourbonnais ↗9	118	46.30 N	3.00 E
Bourbonne-les-Bains	118	47.57 N	5.45 E
Bourem	152	16.57 N	0.21 W
Bourganeuf	118	45.57 N	1.46 E
Bourg-en-Bresse	118	48.50 N	2.15 E
Bourges	118	47.05 N	2.24 E
Bourget	176	45.26 N	75.09 W
Bourget, Lac du ⊜	118	45.44 N	5.52 E
Bourg-Lastic	118	45.39 N	2.33 E
Bourgneuf-en-Retz	118	47.02 N	1.57 W
Bourgogne ⊡9	118	47.00 N	4.30 E
Bourgogne, Canal de ⑃	118	47.58 N	3.30 E
Bourgoin	118	45.35 N	5.17 E
Bourg-Saint-Andéol	118	44.22 N	4.39 E
Bourg-Saint-Maurice	118	45.37 N	6.46 E
Bourke	168	30.05 S	145.56 E
Bourne	104	52.46 N	0.23 W
Bournemouth	104	50.43 N	1.54 W
Bourton-on-the-Water	104	51.53 N	1.45 W
Bou Saâda	152	35.12 N	4.11 E
Bouse	178	33.56 N	113.60 W
Boussu	158	10.29 N	16.43 E
Boussu	116	50.26 N	3.48 E
Boultmit	152	17.33 N	14.42 W
Bouvard, Cape ↗	164	32.41 S	115.37 E
Bouvetøya I	87	54.26 S	3.24 E
Bøvågen	114	60.40 N	4.58 E
Bøverdal	114	61.43 N	8.21 E
Bovey	118	50.34 N	3.47 W
Bovey Tracey	104	50.36 N	3.40 W
Bovingdon	104	51.44 N	0.32 W
Bow ≈, Austl.	168	32.41 S	149.27 E
Bow ≈, Alta., Can.	172	49.56 N	111.42 W
Bow Brook ≈	104	52.04 N	2.07 W
Bowelling	164	33.25 S	116.29 E
Bowen, Arg.	188	35.00 S	67.32 W
Bowen, Austl.	168	20.01 S	148.15 E
Bowgreave	106	53.52 N	2.45 W
Bowie	174	33.34 N	97.51 W
Bowland, Forest of ↗3	106	53.58 N	2.32 W
Bowling Green, Ky., U.S.	174	37.00 N	86.27 W
Bowling Green, Ohio, U.S.	176	41.22 N	83.39 W
Bowling Green, Va., U.S.	176	38.03 N	77.21 W
Bowling Green, Cape ↗	168	19.19 S	147.25 E
Bowman	174	46.10 N	103.24 W
Bowman Bay ⊂	172	65.30 N	73.40 W
Bowmanville	176	43.55 N	78.41 W
Bowmont Water ≈	106	55.34 N	2.09 W
Bowmore	108	55.45 N	6.17 W
Bowness-on-Windermere	106	54.22 N	2.55 W
Bowral	168	34.28 S	150.25 E
Bowraville	168	30.39 S	152.51 E
Bowwood	160	17.05 S	26.17 E
Box	104	51.26 N	2.15 W
Boxholm	114	58.12 N	15.03 E
Boxian	132	33.53 N	115.46 E
Boxtel	116	51.35 N	5.19 E
Boyalık	124	41.33 N	28.37 E
Boyanup	164	33.29 S	115.44 E
Boyd ≈	168	29.22 S	152.35 E
Boyd Glacier ⛰	87	77.14 S	145.25 W
Boyertown	176	40.20 N	75.38 W
Boyle	110	53.58 N	8.18 W
Boyne ≈, Austl.	168	23.58 S	151.12 E
Boyne ≈, Ont., Can.	176	44.10 N	79.49 W
Boyne City	176	45.13 N	85.01 W
Boyup Brook	164	33.50 S	116.24 E
Boz Burun ↗	124	40.32 N	28.46 E
Bozel	118	45.27 N	6.39 E
Bozeman	174	45.41 N	111.02 W
Bozen → Bolzano	122	46.31 N	11.22 E
Bozhen	132	38.06 N	116.33 E
Bozouls	118	44.28 N	2.44 E
Bozoum	154	6.19 N	16.23 E
Bra	122	44.42 N	7.51 E
Braan ≈	108	56.33 N	3.35 W
Brabant Island I	87	64.15 S	62.20 W
Bracadale, Loch ⊂	108	57.19 N	6.30 W
Bracebridge	176	45.02 N	79.19 W
Bracebridge Heath	106	53.13 N	0.32 W
Brach	154	27.32 N	14.16 E
Bräcke	114	62.43 N	15.27 E
Brackley	104	52.02 N	1.09 W
Bracknell	104	51.26 N	0.45 W
Braco	108	56.15 N	3.53 W
Braço do Norte	188	28.17 S	49.11 W
Brad	124	46.08 N	22.47 E
Bradenton	174	27.29 N	82.34 W
Bradford, Ont., Can.	176	44.07 N	79.34 W
Bradford, Eng., U.K.	106	53.48 N	1.45 W
Bradford, Ohio, U.S.	176	40.08 N	84.26 W
Bradford, Pa., U.S.	176	41.58 N	78.39 W
Bradford-on-Avon	104	51.20 N	2.15 W
Brading	104	50.41 N	1.09 W
Bradley Institute	158	17.02 S	31.27 E
Bradwell-on-Sea	104	51.44 N	0.54 E
Bradworthy	104	50.54 N	4.22 W
Brae	108a	60.23 N	1.21 W
Braeside	164	21.12 S	121.01 E
Brăila	124	45.16 N	27.58 E
Brăila ⊡4	124	45.00 N	27.40 E
Brain ≈	104	51.48 N	0.39 E
Braine-l'Alleud	116	50.41 N	4.22 E
Braine-le-Comte	116	50.36 N	4.08 E
Brainerd	174	46.21 N	94.12 W
Braintree	104	51.53 N	0.32 E
Brak ≈	160	29.35 S	22.55 E
Brake	116	53.19 N	8.28 E
Brakpan	160	26.13 S	28.20 E
Bramford	104	52.04 N	1.06 E
Bramming	114	55.28 N	8.42 E
Brampton, Ont., Can.	176	43.41 N	79.46 W
Brampton, Eng., U.K.	106	54.57 N	2.43 W
Brancaster	104	52.58 N	0.39 E
Brancaster Roads ↗3	104	53.05 N	0.45 W
Branco ≈	184	1.24 S	61.51 W
Brandberg ∧	160	21.10 S	14.33 E
Brandenburg	116	52.24 N	12.32 E
Brandenburg ⊡9	116	52.00 N	13.00 E
Brandfort	160	28.41 S	26.30 E
Brandon, Man., Can.	172	49.50 N	99.57 W
Brandon, Eng., U.K.	104	52.27 N	0.37 E
Brandon, Eng., U.K.	106	54.46 N	1.39 W
Brandon Bay ⊂	110	52.16 N	10.05 W
Brandon Head ↗	110	52.16 N	10.14 W
Brandon Mountain ∧	110	52.14 N	10.15 W
Brandvlei	160	30.25 S	20.30 E
Brandy Peak ∧	178	42.36 N	123.53 W
Brandýs nad Labem	116	50.10 N	14.41 E
Bransby	168	28.14 S	142.04 E
Bransfield Strait ⋃	87	63.00 S	59.00 W
Br'ansk	130	53.15 N	34.22 E
Brantford	172	43.08 N	80.16 W
Branxholme	168	37.51 S	141.47 E
Bras d'Or Lake ⊜	172	45.52 N	60.50 W
Brasília	190	11.00 S	68.44 W
Brasília, Bra.	190	16.12 S	44.26 W
Brasília, Bra.	190	15.47 S	47.55 W
Braşov	124	45.39 N	25.37 E
Braşov ⊡4	124	45.45 N	25.15 E
Brassey, Mount ∧	164	23.05 S	134.38 E
Brates, Lacul ⊜	124	45.30 N	28.05 E
Bratislava	116	48.09 N	17.07 E
Bratsk	128	56.05 N	101.48 E
Bratskoje Vodochranilišče ⊜1	128	56.10 N	102.10 E
Brattleboro [am Inn]	176	42.51 N	72.34 W
Braunau [am Inn]	116	48.15 N	13.02 E
Braunschweig	116	52.16 N	10.31 E
Braunton	104	51.07 N	4.10 W
Brava	154	1.05 N	44.02 E
Brava, Costa ↗2	120	41.45 N	3.04 E
Brava, Punta ↗	190	34.56 S	56.10 W
Brave	176	39.44 N	80.16 W
Bravo del Norte (Rio Grande) ≈	174	25.57 N	97.09 W
Brawley	178	32.59 N	115.31 W
Brawley Peaks ⋌	178	38.15 N	118.55 W
Bray, Bel.	116	50.26 N	4.06 E
Bray, Eire	110	53.12 N	6.06 W
Bray ≈	104	50.44 N	1.09 W
Bray Head ↗	110	51.53 N	10.26 W
Bray Island I	172	69.20 N	76.45 W
Brazeau ≈	172	52.55 N	115.15 W
Brazil ⊡1	184	10.00 S	55.00 W
Brazil Basin ↗1	84	15.00 S	25.00 W
Brazos ≈	174	28.53 N	95.23 W
Brazzaville	156	4.16 S	15.17 E
Brčko	124	44.53 N	18.48 E
Brea	188	33.55 N	117.54 W
Breadalbane ↘	168	23.49 S	139.35 E
Bream Bay ⊂	170	35.55 S	174.30 E
Bream Head ↗	170	35.50 S	174.36 E
Bream's Eaves	104	51.45 N	2.34 W
Bream Tail ↗	170	36.03 S	174.35 E
Brebes	142	6.53 S	109.03 E
Brécey	118	48.44 N	1.10 W
Brechfa	104	51.54 N	4.06 W
Brechin	108	56.44 N	2.39 W
Breckenridge	178	43.24 N	84.29 W
Breckland ↘1	104	52.28 N	0.42 E
Břeclav	116	48.46 N	16.53 E
Brecon	104	51.57 N	3.24 W
Brecon Beacons ∧	104	51.53 N	3.31 W
Breda	116	51.35 N	4.46 E
Bredasdorp	160	34.32 S	20.02 E
Bredon Hill ∧2	104	52.03 N	2.03 W
Bredstedt	116	54.37 N	8.57 E
Brée ≈	160	34.24 S	20.50 E
Breedoge ≈	110	53.55 N	8.27 W
Breeza Plains	168	14.50 S	144.07 E
Bregenz	116	47.30 N	9.46 E
Bréhal	118	48.54 N	1.31 W
Breidafjörður ⊂	112a	65.15 N	23.15 W
Breil-sur-Roya	118	43.56 N	7.31 E
Brejo	190	3.41 S	42.47 W
Brejões	190	13.06 S	39.48 W
Brejo da Madre de Deus	190	8.09 S	36.22 W
Brekstad	114	63.41 N	9.40 E
Bremangerlandet I	114	61.48 N	5.00 E
Bremen, B.R.D.	116	53.04 N	8.49 E
Bremen, Ohio, U.S.	176	39.42 N	82.26 W
Bremerhaven	116	53.33 N	8.34 E
Bremerton	174	47.34 N	122.38 W
Bremervörde	116	53.29 N	9.08 E
Brendon Hills ∧2	104	51.07 N	3.25 W
Brenish	108	58.08 N	7.06 W
Brenish, Aird ↗	108	58.08 N	7.08 W
Brenner Pass ⫶	116	47.00 N	11.30 E
Brent ≈8	104	51.28 N	0.18 W
Brentwood, Eng., U.K.	104	51.38 N	0.18 E
Brentwood, N.Y., U.S.	176	40.47 N	73.14 W
Brescia	122	45.33 N	10.13 E
Breslau → Wrocław	116	51.06 N	17.00 E
Bressanone	122	46.43 N	11.39 E
Bressay I	108a	60.08 N	1.05 W
Bressay Sound ⋃	108a	60.07 N	1.09 W
Brest, Fr.	118	48.24 N	4.29 W
Brest, S.S.S.R.	130	52.06 N	23.42 E
Bretagne ⊡9	118	48.00 N	3.00 W
Breteuil	118	48.50 N	0.55 E
Breteuil-sur-Iton	118	48.50 N	1.04 E
Breton, Pertuis ⋃	118	46.25 N	1.42 W
Brett, Cape ↗	170	35.10 S	174.20 E
Breuelh, Pulau I	140	5.18 N	95.06 E
Brevoort Island I	172	63.30 N	64.20 W
Brewarrina	168	29.57 S	146.52 E
Brewer	176	44.48 N	68.46 W
Brewood	104	52.41 N	2.10 W
Brewster	176	41.24 N	73.37 W
Brewster, Kap ↗	90	70.19 N	22.05 W
Brewster, Lake ⊜	168	33.28 S	146.00 E
Brewster, Mount ∧	170	44.04 S	169.27 E
Breyten	160	26.16 S	30.00 E
Brežice	122	45.54 N	15.36 E
Brezno	116	48.50 N	19.39 E
Bria	154	6.32 N	21.59 E
Briançon	118	44.54 N	6.39 E
Brickaville	161b	18.49 S	49.04 E
Bride	106	54.22 N	4.22 W
Bride ≈	110	52.04 N	7.52 W
Bridgend, Scot., U.K.	108	55.48 N	6.16 W
Bridgend, Wales, U.K.	104	51.31 N	3.35 W
Bridge of Allan	108	56.09 N	3.57 W
Bridge of Gaur	108	56.41 N	4.27 W
Bridge of Orchy	108	56.30 N	4.46 W
Bridge of Weir	108	55.52 N	4.35 W
Bridge Point ↗	182	25.35 N	76.42 W
Bridgeport, Ont., Can.	176	43.29 N	80.29 W
Bridgeport, Calif., U.S.	178	38.15 N	119.13 W
Bridgeport, Conn., U.S.	176	41.11 N	73.11 W
Bridgeport, Mich., U.S.	176	43.22 N	83.53 W
Bridgeport, W. Va., U.S.	176	39.17 N	80.15 W
Bridgeton	176	39.26 N	75.14 W
Bridgetown, Austl.	164	33.57 S	116.08 E
Bridgeville	176	38.45 N	75.36 W
Bridgewater, N.S., Can.	172	44.23 N	64.31 W
Bridgewater, Mass., U.S.	176	41.59 N	70.58 W
Bridgewater, Va., U.S.	176	38.18 N	78.59 W
Bridgnorth	104	52.33 N	2.25 W
Bridgwater	104	51.08 N	3.00 W
Bridgwater Bay ⊂	104	51.16 N	3.12 W
Bridlington	106	54.05 N	0.12 W
Bridlington Bay ⊂	106	54.04 N	0.08 W
Bridport	104	50.44 N	2.46 W
Brie ≈1	118	48.40 N	3.20 E
Briec	118	48.06 N	4.00 W
Brienne-le-Château	118	48.24 N	4.32 E
Brienz	118	46.46 N	8.03 E
Brierfield	106	53.50 N	2.14 W
Brierley Hill	104	52.29 N	2.07 W
Briey	118	49.15 N	5.56 E
Brig	118	46.19 N	8.00 E
Brigg	106	53.34 N	0.30 W
Brigham City	174	41.31 N	112.01 W
Brighouse	106	53.42 N	1.47 W
Brighstone	104	50.38 N	1.24 W
Bright	168	36.44 S	146.58 E
Brightlingsea	104	51.49 N	1.02 E
Brighton, Ont., Can.	176	44.02 N	77.44 W
Brighton, Eng., U.K.	104	50.50 N	0.08 W
Brighton, Mich., U.S.	176	42.32 N	83.47 W
Brighton, N.Y., U.S.	176	43.08 N	77.34 W
Brighton Downs	168	23.22 S	141.34 E
Brignoles	118	43.24 N	6.04 E
Brig o' Turk	108	56.13 N	4.22 W
Brikama	152	13.15 N	16.39 W
Brilhante ≈	190	21.58 S	54.18 W
Brill	104	51.49 N	1.03 W
Brilon	116	51.24 N	8.34 E
Brimfield	104	52.18 N	2.42 W
Brimington	106	53.16 N	1.23 W
Brindisi	122	40.38 N	17.56 E
Brinje	122	45.00 N	15.08 E
Brinkworth	168	33.42 S	138.24 E
Brinyan	108	59.07 N	2.59 W
Brione	104	49.12 N	0.43 E
Brioude	118	45.18 N	3.23 E
Brisbane	168	27.28 S	153.02 E
Bristol, Eng., U.K.	104	51.27 N	2.35 W
Bristol, Conn., U.S.	176	41.41 N	72.57 W
Bristol, N.H., U.S.	176	43.36 N	71.44 W
Bristol, Pa., U.S.	176	40.06 N	74.52 W
Bristol, R.I., U.S.	176	41.40 N	71.16 W
Bristol, Vt., U.S.	176	44.08 N	73.05 W
Bristol Channel ⋃	104	51.20 N	4.00 W
Bristol Lake ⊜	178	34.28 N	115.41 W
Britannia Range ⋌	87	80.00 S	158.00 E
British Antarctic Territory ⊡2	87	60.00 S	45.00 W
British Columbia ⊡4	172	54.00 N	125.00 W
British Indian Ocean Territory ⊡2	94	7.00 S	72.00 E
British Mountains ⋌	172	69.00 N	140.20 W
Briton Ferry	104	51.38 N	3.49 W
Brits	160	25.37 S	27.45 E
Britstown	160	30.37 S	23.30 E
Brittany → Bretagne ⊡9	118	48.00 N	3.00 W
Britton	174	45.47 N	97.45 W
Brive-la-Gaillarde	118	45.10 N	1.32 E
Brixham	104	50.24 N	3.30 W
Brixton	168	23.32 S	144.57 E
Brixworth	104	52.20 N	0.54 W
Brno	116	49.12 N	16.37 E
Broach ≈	146	21.42 N	72.58 E
Broad Arrow	164	30.28 S	121.20 E
Broadback ≈	172	51.21 N	78.52 W
Broad Bay ⊂	108	58.15 N	6.15 W
Broad Chalke	104	51.02 N	1.58 W
Broad Chyst	104	50.46 N	3.26 W
Broadford	108	57.14 N	5.54 W
Broad Haven ⊂	110	54.19 N	9.55 W
Broad Law ∧	108	55.30 N	3.22 W
Broad Sound ⋃	168	22.10 S	149.45 E
Broadstairs	104	51.21 N	1.27 E
Broadway, Eng., U.K.	104	52.02 N	1.51 W
Broadway, Va., U.S.	176	38.36 N	78.48 W
Broadwindsor	104	50.49 N	2.48 W
Brochel	108	57.26 N	6.01 W
Brock ≈	106	53.52 N	2.47 W
Brockenhurst	104	50.49 N	1.34 W
Brockman, Mount ∧	164	22.28 S	117.18 E
Brockport	176	43.13 N	77.56 W
Brocks Creek	166	13.28 S	131.25 E
Brockton	176	42.05 N	71.01 W
Brockville	176	44.35 N	75.41 W
Brockworth	104	51.51 N	2.09 W
Brocton	176	42.23 N	79.27 W
Brodeur Peninsula ↗1	172	73.00 N	88.00 W
Brodick	108	55.35 N	5.09 W
Broken Bay ⊂	168	33.34 S	151.18 E
Broken Hill, Austl.	168	31.57 S	141.27 E
Broken Hill → Kabwe, Zam.	156	14.27 S	28.27 E
Brokopondo	190	5.03 N	54.59 W
Bromborough	106	53.20 N	3.00 W
Bromley ≈8	104	51.24 N	0.02 E
Brompton	106	54.22 N	1.25 W
Bromsgrove	104	52.20 N	2.03 W
Bromyard	104	52.11 N	2.30 W
Brønderslev	114	57.16 N	9.58 E
Bronllys	104	52.01 N	3.15 W
Bronlund Peak ∧	172	57.26 N	126.38 W
Brønnøysund	114	65.28 N	12.13 E
Bronson	178	41.52 N	85.12 W
Bronte Park	168	42.08 S	146.30 E
Brookeborough	110	54.19 N	7.24 W
Brookhaven	174	31.35 N	90.26 W
Brookings, Oreg., U.S.	178	42.03 N	124.17 W
Brookings, S. Dak., U.S.	174	44.18 N	96.48 W
Brookland	104	50.59 N	0.49 E
Brooklyn	164	32.06 N	84.15 W
Brooks, Alta., Can.	172	50.35 N	111.53 W
Brooks Range ⋌	174	68.00 N	154.00 W
Brooksville	174	28.32 N	82.23 W
Brookville, Ind., U.S.	176	39.25 N	85.00 W
Brookville, Pa., U.S.	176	41.09 N	79.05 W
Brookville Lake ⊜	176	39.30 N	85.00 W
Brooloo	168	26.29 S	152.42 E
Broom, Little Loch ⊂	108	57.54 N	5.22 W
Broom, Loch ⊂	108	57.52 N	5.08 W
Broome	164	17.58 S	122.14 E
Brora	108	58.01 N	3.51 W
Brora ≈	108	58.01 N	3.52 W
Broseley	104	52.37 N	2.29 W
Brosna ≈	110	53.13 N	7.58 W
Brossac	118	45.20 N	0.03 W
Brotton	106	54.34 N	0.56 W
Brough, Eng., U.K.	106	54.32 N	2.19 W
Brough, Eng., U.K.	106	53.44 N	0.35 W
Brough, Scot., U.K.	108	58.39 N	3.20 W
Brough Head ↗	108	59.08 N	3.17 W
Broughshane	110	54.54 N	6.12 W
Broughton, Eng., U.K.	104	52.23 N	0.46 W
Broughton, Scot., U.K.	108	55.37 N	3.25 W
Broughton in Furness	106	54.17 N	3.12 W
Broughton Island I	172	67.35 N	63.50 W
Broughtown	108	59.15 N	2.36 W
Broughty Ferry	108	56.28 N	2.53 W
Brovst	114	57.06 N	9.32 E
Brown City	176	43.13 N	82.59 W
Brown Clee Hill ∧2	104	52.28 N	2.35 W
Browne ≈	164	21.15 S	128.15 E
Browne Gelly ∧2	104	50.32 N	4.32 W
Brownhills	104	52.39 N	1.55 W
Brown Lake ⊜	172	65.55 N	91.15 W
Brown Mountain ∧	168	35.41 N	117.01 W
Brownsburg	176	39.51 N	74.25 W
Brownsville, Pa., U.S.	176	40.01 N	79.53 W
Brownsville, Tex., U.S.	174	25.54 N	97.30 W
Brownville	176	45.18 N	69.02 W
Brownville Junction	176	45.21 N	69.03 W
Brown Willy ∧2	104	50.35 N	4.36 W
Brownwood	174	31.43 N	98.59 W
Bruay-en-Artois	118	50.29 N	2.33 E
Bruce, Mount ∧	164	22.36 S	118.08 E
Bruce Bay	170	43.35 S	169.41 E
Bruce Peninsula ↗1	176	44.50 N	81.20 W
Bruce Rock	164	31.53 S	118.09 E
Bruchsal	116	49.07 N	8.35 E
Bruck an der Mur	116	47.25 N	15.16 E
Brue ≈	104	51.13 N	3.00 W
Bruff	110	52.29 N	8.33 W
Bruges → Brugge	116	51.13 N	3.14 E
Brugg	118	47.29 N	8.12 E
Brugge	116	51.13 N	3.14 E
Brumado, Lac ⊜	118	52.17 N	63.52 W
Brumath	118	48.43 N	7.43 E
Brummen	116	52.05 N	6.09 E
Brumunddal	114	60.53 N	10.56 E
Bruneau	178	42.53 N	115.48 W
Bruneau ≈	178	42.57 N	115.58 W
Bruneau, East Fork ≈	178	42.34 N	115.38 W
Brunei → Bandar Seri Begawan	138	4.56 N	114.55 E
Brunei ⊡1	138	4.30 N	114.40 E
Brunei, Teluk ⊂	138	5.00 N	115.00 E
Brunette Downs	166	18.38 S	135.57 E
Brunkeberg	114	59.26 N	8.29 E
Brunner	170	42.27 S	171.19 E
Brunsbüttel	116	53.54 N	9.07 E
Brunswick → Braunschweig, B.R.D.	116	52.16 N	10.31 E
Brunswick, Ga., U.S.	174	31.10 N	81.29 W
Brunswick, Maine, U.S.	176	43.55 N	69.58 W
Brunswick, Md., U.S.	176	39.19 N	77.37 W
Brunswick, Ohio, U.S.	176	41.14 N	81.50 W
Brunswick, Peninsula de ↗1	186	53.25 S	71.25 W
Brunswick Junction	164	33.15 S	115.51 E
Bruntál	116	49.59 N	17.28 E
Brus, Laguna de ⊜	182	15.50 N	84.35 W
Brus Laguna	182	15.47 N	84.35 W
Brusque	188	27.06 S	48.56 W
Brussels → Bruxelles, Bel.	116	50.50 N	4.20 E
Brussels, Ont., Can.	176	43.44 N	81.15 W
Bruthen	168	37.43 S	147.48 E
Bruton	104	51.07 N	2.27 W
Brüx → Most	116	50.32 N	13.38 E
Bruxelles (Brussel)	116	50.50 N	4.20 E
Bryan, Ohio, U.S.	176	41.28 N	84.33 W
Bryan, Tex., U.S.	174	30.40 N	96.22 W
Bryan Coast ≈2	87	73.45 S	82.00 W
Bryant Mountain ∧2	178	42.28 N	72.58 W
Bryher I	104a	49.57 N	6.20 W
Brymbo	104	53.06 N	3.04 W
Brynamman	104	51.49 N	3.52 W
Bryncethin	104	51.32 N	3.34 W
Bryn-mawr	104	51.48 N	3.11 W
Bryson	176	45.41 N	76.37 W
Brzeg	116	49.12 N	16.37 E
Brześć Nad Bugiem → Brest	130	52.06 N	23.42 E
Brzesko	116	49.59 N	20.36 E
Bua Yai	140	15.35 N	102.25 E
Buayan	138	6.07 N	125.11 E
Bubanza	158	3.06 S	29.23 E
Bubiyān I	150	29.47 N	48.10 E
Bubye ≈	160	22.18 S	31.00 E
Bucaramanga	184	7.08 N	73.09 W
Buchanan	152	5.57 N	10.02 W
Buchanan Creek ≈	168	21.35 S	145.52 E
Buchan Gulf ⊂	172	71.47 N	74.16 W
Buchan Ness ↗	108	57.28 N	1.46 W
Buchans	172	48.49 N	56.52 W
Bucharest → București	124	44.26 N	26.06 E
Buchon, Point ↗	178	35.15 N	120.54 W
Buchs	118	47.10 N	9.28 E
Buchy	118	49.35 N	1.22 E
Buck, Lake ⊜	166	14.38 S	133.00 E
Buckden, Eng., U.K.	104	52.17 N	0.16 W
Buckden, Eng., U.K.	106	54.13 N	2.05 W
Bückeburg	116	52.15 N	9.03 E
Buckeye Lake	176	39.55 N	82.29 W
Buckfastleigh	104	50.29 N	3.46 W
Buckhaven	108	56.11 N	3.02 W
Buckie	108	57.40 N	2.58 W
Buckingham, Qué., Can.	176	45.35 N	75.25 W
Buckingham, Eng., U.K.	104	52.00 N	0.59 W
Buckinghamshire ⊡6	104	51.45 N	0.48 W
Buckland Brewer	104	50.58 N	4.14 W
Bucklands	160	25.53 S	23.44 E
Bucklebo	168	32.54 S	136.12 E
Buckley	104	53.10 N	3.05 W
Buckley Bay ⊂	168	30.18 S	148.17 E
Buckow	116	52.33 N	14.04 E
Buckskin Mountains ⋌	178	34.10 N	113.48 W
București (Bucharest)	124	44.26 N	26.06 E
Bucyrus	176	40.48 N	82.58 W
Bud	114	62.54 N	6.55 E
Budapest	116	47.30 N	19.05 E
Budaun	146	28.03 N	79.07 E
Bud Coast ≈2	87	68.30 S	112.30 E
Buddh Gaya	146	24.42 N	84.59 E
Bude	104	50.50 N	4.33 W
Bude Bay ⊂	104	50.50 N	4.37 W
Büdir	112a	64.57 N	14.13 W
Budleigh Salterton	104	50.38 N	3.19 W
→ České Budějovice	116	48.59 N	14.28 E
Buea	152	4.09 N	9.14 E
Buena Esperanza	188	34.45 S	65.15 W
Buenaventura, Col.	184	3.53 N	77.04 W
Buenaventura, Méx.	180	29.51 N	107.29 W
Buena Vista, Méx.	178	27.28 N	114.28 W
Buenavista, Cerro ∧	182	9.33 N	83.45 W
Buena Vista, Cordillera de ∧	182	10.40 N	70.10 W
Buena Vista Lake Bed ⊜	178	35.11 N	119.17 W
Buendia, Embalse de ⊜1	120	40.25 N	2.43 W
Buenópolis	190	17.54 S	44.11 W
Buenos Aires, Arg.	188	34.36 S	58.27 W
Buenos Aires, C.R.	182	9.10 N	83.20 W
Buenos Aires ⊡4	188	36.00 S	60.00 W
Buerarema	190	14.57 S	39.19 W
Buffalo, N.Y., U.S.	176	42.54 N	78.53 W
Buffalo, Ohio, U.S.	176	39.55 N	81.31 W
Buffalo ≈, S. Afr.	160	28.43 S	30.37 E
Buffalo Lake ⊜	160	28.45 S	21.11 E
Buffels ≈	160	29.36 S	17.16 E
Bug ≈	100	52.31 N	21.05 E
Buga	184	3.54 N	76.17 W
Buganga	158	0.03 S	31.59 E
Bugibu ⊡5	104	51.45 N	1.59 E
Bugibu ⊡5	104	50.24 N	4.47 W
Bugojno	122	44.03 N	17.27 E
Buguldeila	128	52.32 N	104.13 E
Buguma	112	69.58 N	29.39 E
Bugsuk Island I	138	8.15 N	117.18 E
Bugul'ma	112	54.33 N	52.48 E
Bugulunskaja	126	53.39 N	52.26 E
Buhl	178	42.36 N	114.46 W
Buhuşi	124	46.43 N	26.41 E
Buie, Loch ⊂	108	56.20 N	5.52 W
Builth Wells	104	52.09 N	3.24 W
Buin	188	33.44 S	70.45 W
Buir Nuur ⊜	132	47.48 N	117.42 E
Buji	138	58.30 N	41.30 E
Bujalance	120	37.54 N	4.22 W
Bujnaksk	126	42.49 N	47.07 E
Bukačača	128	52.59 N	116.55 E
Bukama	158	9.12 S	25.51 E
Bukavu	158	2.30 S	28.52 E
Bukedi ⊡5	158	0.50 N	34.00 E
Bukhara → Buchara	150	39.48 N	64.25 E
Bukittinggi	142	0.19 S	100.22 E
Bukoba	158	1.20 S	31.49 E
Bukovina ⊡9	124	48.00 N	25.30 E
Bula	166	3.06 S	130.30 E
Bulan	138	12.40 N	123.52 E
Bulandshahr	146	28.24 N	77.51 E
Bulawayo	156	20.09 S	28.36 E
Bulgan, Mong.	132	46.53 N	91.05 E
Bulgan, Mong.	132	48.52 N	103.34 E
Bulgaria ⊡1	124	43.00 N	25.00 E
Bulgroo	168	25.27 N	75.39 E
Bulkington	104	52.29 N	1.25 W
Bulkley ≈	172	55.13 N	127.40 W
Bullabulling	164	31.01 S	120.32 E
Bullara	164	22.40 S	114.03 E
Bull Creek ≈	178	38.40 N	115.40 W
Buller, Mount ∧	168	37.09 S	146.26 E
Bullfinch	164	30.59 S	119.06 E
Bullhead City	178	35.08 N	114.34 W
Bullock Creek	168	17.43 S	144.31 E
Bulloo ≈	168	28.43 S	142.30 E
Bulloo Downs	168	28.31 S	142.57 E
Bull Shoals Lake ⊜1	174	36.30 N	92.50 W
Bulnes	188	36.44 S	72.18 W
Bulsår	148	20.38 N	72.56 E
Bultfontein	160	28.16 S	26.05 E
Bulubulawang ≈	142	47.15 N	87.20 W
Bulun-Tuochai ⊜	132	47.15 N	87.20 W
Bulyee	164	32.22 S	117.31 E
Bumba	154	2.11 N	22.28 E
Bumpus, Mount ∧2	172	69.33 N	112.40 W
Bunbury	164	33.19 S	115.38 E
Bunclody	110	52.38 N	6.40 W
Buncrana	110	55.08 N	7.27 W
Bundaberg	168	24.52 S	152.21 E
Bundarra	168	30.10 S	151.05 E
Bündi	146	25.27 N	75.39 E
Bundooma	166	24.46 S	134.16 E
Bundoran	110	54.28 N	8.17 W
Bunduqiyah	150	34.32 N	50.53 E
Bungay	104	52.28 N	1.26 E
Bungendore	168	35.15 S	149.27 E
Bunger Hills ↗2	87	66.17 S	100.47 E
Bungo-suidō ⋃	134	33.00 N	132.13 E
Bunguran Selatan, Kepulauan II	142	2.45 N	109.00 E
Bunguran Utara, Kepulauan II	142	4.40 N	108.00 E
Bunia	158	1.34 N	30.15 E
Buntingford	104	51.57 N	0.01 W
Bunyoro ⊡5	158	1.40 S	31.40 E
Buolkalach	128	72.56 N	119.50 E
Buor-Chaja, Guba ⊂	128	71.30 N	131.00 E
Buor-Chaja, Mys ↗	128	71.56 N	132.40 E
Bura, Kenya	158	1.06 S	39.57 E
Bura, Kenya	158	3.30 S	38.19 E
Burakin	164	30.31 S	117.10 E
Burao	154	9.29 N	45.32 E
Buraydah	150	26.20 N	43.59 E
Burco	158	9.32 N	45.33 E
Burdekin ≈	168	19.39 S	147.30 E
Burdekin Falls ⛰	168	20.39 S	147.11 E
Burdwan	146	23.15 N	87.51 E
Burdwood Bank ↗4	186	54.00 S	60.00 W
Bureinskij Chrebet ⋌	128	50.00 N	133.35 E
Burford, Eng., U.K.	104	51.49 N	1.38 W
Burford, Eng., U.K.	104	52.16 N	2.40 W
Bür Fu'ād	150	31.15 N	32.19 E
Burg [bei Magdeburg]	116	52.16 N	11.51 E
Bur Gavo	158	1.08 S	41.51 E
Burgdorf, Schw.	118	47.04 N	7.37 E
Burgenland ⊡3	116	47.30 N	16.25 E
Burgersdorp	160	31.00 S	26.20 E
Burgess, Mount ∧2	172	60.30 N	139.00 W
Burgess Hill	104	50.57 N	0.08 W
Burghausen	116	48.10 N	12.50 E
Burgh le Marsh	106	53.11 N	0.15 E
Burgos	120	42.21 N	3.42 W
Burgsteinfurt	116	52.09 N	7.20 E
Burgsvik	114	57.03 N	18.16 E
Burgundy → Bourgogne ⊡9	118	47.00 N	4.30 E
Burhanpur	146	21.18 N	76.14 E
Burias Island I	138	12.50 N	123.07 E
Burica, Punta ↗	182	8.03 N	82.53 W
Buriram	140	14.60 N	103.07 E
Buriti Alegre	190	18.09 S	49.03 W
Burjasot	120	39.31 N	0.25 W
Burke ≈	168	23.12 S	139.33 E
Burketown	168	17.45 S	139.33 E
Burkina Faso ⊡1	152	13.00 N	2.00 W
Burlada	120	42.49 N	1.36 W
Burley, Eng., U.K.	106	53.55 N	1.46 W
Burley, Idaho, U.S.	178	42.32 N	113.47 W
Burlington, Ont., Can.	176	43.19 N	79.47 W
Burlington, Iowa, U.S.	174	40.48 N	91.06 W
Burlington, Vt., U.S.	176	44.28 N	73.12 W
Burma ⊡1	140	22.00 N	98.00 E
Burnet	174	30.45 N	98.13 W
Burnett ≈	168	24.46 S	152.25 E
Burnett Bay ⊂	172	73.53 N	124.40 W
Burney	178	40.53 N	121.40 W

Burn – Cass

Name	Page	Lat °′	Long °′
Burnham, Eng., U.K.	104	51.33 N	0.39 W
Burnham, Pa., U.S.	176	40.38 N	77.34 W
Burnham Market	104	52.57 N	0.44 E
Burnham-on-Crouch	104	51.38 N	0.49 E
Burnham-on-Sea	104	51.15 N	3.00 W
Burnhaven	108	57.29 N	1.47 W
Burnie	168	41.04 S	145.54 E
Burnley	106	53.48 N	2.14 W
Burnmouth	108	55.50 N	2.04 W
Burns	178	43.35 N	119.03 W
Burnside ≃	172	66.51 N	108.04 W
Burns Lake	172	54.14 N	125.46 W
Burnsville	176	38.51 N	80.40 W
Burnt ≃	176	44.35 N	78.46 W
Burntisland	108	56.03 N	3.15 W
Burntwood ≃	172	56.08 N	96.30 W
Burra	168	33.40 S	138.56 E
Burragorang, Lake ⊜	168	33.58 S	150.25 E
Burramurra	168	20.30 S	137.20 E
Burravoe	108a	60.32 N	1.28 W
Burray I	108	58.51 N	2.54 W
Burrel	124	41.37 N	20.00 E
Burren Junction	168	30.06 S	148.58 E
Burriana	120	39.53 N	0.05 W
Burrinjuck Reservoir ⊜1	168	35.00 S	148.45 E
Burrow Head ≻	106	54.41 N	4.24 W
Burrundie	166	13.32 S	131.42 E
Burruyacú	188	26.30 S	64.45 W
Burry Holms I	104	51.37 N	4.18 W
Burry Port	104	51.42 N	4.15 W
Būr Sa'īd (Port Said)	154	31.16 N	32.18 E
Burscough	106	53.35 N	2.51 W
Bursey, Mount ∧	87	76.00 S	132.40 W
Burslem	104	53.02 N	2.12 W
Būr Sūdān (Port Sudan)	154	19.37 N	37.14 E
Būr Tawfīq	150	29.57 N	32.34 E
Burt Lake ⊜	176	45.27 N	84.40 W
Burton	176	43.02 N	83.36 W
Burton Fleming	106	54.08 N	0.20 W
Burton Latimer	104	52.23 N	0.41 W
Burton Seamount ✧3	96	32.00 S	171.55 W
Burton-upon-Trent	104	52.49 N	1.36 W
Burtville	164	28.47 S	122.39 E
Buru I	138	3.24 S	126.40 E
Burundi □1	156	3.15 S	30.00 E
Bururi	158	3.57 S	29.37 E
Burwash	176	46.19 N	80.48 W
Burwell	104	52.16 N	0.19 E
Burwick	108	58.44 N	2.57 W
Bury, Eng., U.K.	104	50.54 N	0.34 W
Bury, Eng., U.K.	106	53.36 N	2.17 W
Bury Saint Edmunds	104	52.15 N	0.43 E
Busanga Swamp ☷	158	14.10 S	25.50 E
Būshehr	150	28.59 N	50.50 E
Bushey	104	51.39 N	0.22 W
Bushimaie ≃	156	6.02 S	23.45 E
Bushman Land □9	160	29.15 S	20.00 E
Bushmills	110	55.12 N	6.32 W
Bushy Park	168	21.16 S	139.43 E
Buskerud □6	114	60.25 N	9.12 E
Busko Zdrój	116	50.28 N	20.44 E
Busoga □5	158	0.40 N	33.30 E
Busselton	164	33.39 S	115.20 E
Bussum	116	52.16 N	5.10 E
Busto Arsizio	122	45.37 N	8.51 E
Busuanga Island I	138	12.05 N	120.05 E
Busu-Djanoa	156	1.43 N	21.23 E
Buta	158	2.48 N	24.44 E
Buta Ranquil	188	37.04 S	69.50 W
Butare	158	2.36 S	29.44 E
Bute, Island of I	108	55.50 N	5.06 W
Bute, Kyles of ⋈	108	55.53 N	5.13 W
Bute, Sound of ⋈	108	55.44 N	5.12 W
Butehaqi	132	48.02 N	122.43 E
Bute Inlet C	172	50.37 N	124.53 W
Bute Jarti	158	4.34 N	37.48 E
Butere	158	0.13 N	34.30 E
Butha Buthe	160	28.45 S	28.15 E
Butiá	188	30.07 S	51.58 W
Butler, Ind., U.S.	176	41.26 N	84.52 W
Butler, Ohio, U.S.	176	40.35 N	82.26 W
Butler, Pa., U.S.	176	40.52 N	79.54 W
Butlers Bridge	110	54.02 N	7.22 W
Bütow → Bytów	116	54.11 N	17.30 E
Butru	168	21.30 S	139.43 E
Butte	174	46.00 N	112.32 W
Butte Creek ≃	178	39.12 N	121.59 W
Butte Falls	178	42.33 N	122.34 W
Butte Mountains ⋀	178	39.50 N	115.05 W
Buttermere	106	54.33 N	3.17 W
Butterwick	104	52.59 N	0.05 E
Butterworth, Malay.	142	5.25 N	100.24 E
Butterworth, S. Afr.	160	32.23 S	28.04 E
Buttevant	110	52.14 N	8.40 W
Button Islands II	172	60.35 N	64.45 W
Buttonwillow	178	35.24 N	119.28 W
Butuan	138	8.57 N	125.33 E
Butung, Pulau I	142	5.00 S	122.55 E
Butzbach	116	50.26 N	8.40 E
Bützow	116	53.50 N	11.59 E
Buxtehude	116	53.28 N	9.41 E
Buxton, S. Afr.	160	27.38 S	24.42 E
Buxton, Eng., U.K.	106	53.15 N	1.55 W
Buxy	118	46.43 N	4.41 E
Büyük Ağrı Dağı (Mount Ararat) ∧	150	39.42 N	44.18 E
Büyükçekmece	124	41.01 N	28.34 E
Büyük Doğanca	124	41.11 N	26.25 E
Büyükkarıştıran	124	41.18 N	27.32 E
Buzançais	118	46.53 N	1.25 E
Buzău	124	45.09 N	26.49 E
Buzău □4	124	47.40 N	23.00 E
Buzen	134	33.40 N	131.18 E
Búzi ≃	160	19.50 S	34.43 E
Buziji	136	33.49 N	118.14 E
Buzuluk	126	52.47 N	52.15 E
Bwana Mkubwa	158	13.01 S	28.42 E
Bwlch	104	51.54 N	3.15 W
Byam Channel ⋈	172	75.20 N	105.20 W
Byam Martin Channel ⋈	172	75.45 N	104.00 W
Byam Martin Island I	172	75.15 N	104.00 W
Bydalen	114	63.06 N	13.47 E
Bydgoszcz	116	53.08 N	18.00 E
Byesville	176	39.58 N	81.32 W
Byfield	104	52.11 N	1.14 W
Byfleet	104	51.20 N	0.29 W
Bygdin ⊜	114	61.21 N	8.36 E
Byglandsfjord	114	58.41 N	7.48 E
Byglandsfjorden ⊜	114	58.48 N	7.50 E
Bylot Island I	172	73.13 N	78.34 W
Byng Inlet	176	45.46 N	80.33 W
Byrd Glacier ⛛	87	80.15 S	160.20 E
Byrd Land ⟜1	87	80.00 S	120.00 W
Byro	164	26.05 S	116.09 E
Byrock	168	30.40 S	146.24 E
Byron, Cape ≻	168	28.39 S	153.38 E
Byron, Isla I	186	47.45 S	75.11 W
Byron Bay	168	28.39 S	153.37 E
Byrranga, Gory ⋀	128	75.00 N	104.00 E
Bystrzyca ≃	116	51.13 N	16.54 E
Bytantaj ≃	128	68.46 N	134.20 E
Bytom (Beuthen)	116	50.22 N	18.54 E
Bytów	116	54.11 N	17.30 E
Byumba	158	1.35 S	30.04 E
Byxelkrok	114	57.20 N	17.00 E

C

Name	Page	Lat °′	Long °′
Ca ≃	140	18.46 N	105.47 E
Caacupé	188	25.23 S	57.09 W
Caaguazú □5	188	25.00 S	55.45 W
Caazapá	188	26.09 S	56.24 W
Caazapá □5	188	26.10 S	56.00 W
Cabaiguán	182	22.05 N	79.30 W
Caballería, Cabo de ≻	120	40.05 N	4.05 E
Cabanatuan	138	15.29 N	120.58 E
Cabano	172	47.41 N	68.53 W
Cabedelo	184	6.58 S	34.50 W
Cabeza del Buey	120	38.43 N	5.13 W
Cabildo, Arg.	188	38.30 S	61.55 W
Cabildo, Chile	188	32.26 S	71.05 W
Cabimas	184	10.23 N	71.28 W
Cabinda	156	5.33 S	12.12 E
Cabinda □5	156	5.00 S	12.30 E
Cabo Blanco	186	47.15 S	65.45 W
Cabo Delgado □5	158	12.35 S	39.00 E
Cabonga, Réservoir ⊜1	172	47.20 N	76.35 W
Caboolture	168	27.05 S	152.57 E
Caborca	180	30.37 N	112.06 W
Cabot, Mount ∧	176	44.31 N	71.24 W
Cabot Head ≻	176	45.14 N	81.17 W
Cabot Strait ⋈	172	47.20 N	59.30 W
Cabo Verde	190	21.28 S	46.24 W
Cabra	120	37.28 N	4.27 W
Cabral	182	18.15 N	71.13 W
Cabrera I	120	39.09 N	2.56 E
Cabrera ≃	120	42.25 N	6.49 W
Cabrera, Sierra de la ⋀	120	42.12 N	6.40 W
Cabriel ≃	120	39.14 N	1.03 W
Cabure	182	11.08 N	69.38 W
Caçador	188	26.47 S	51.00 W
Čačak	124	43.53 N	20.21 E
Caçapava	190	23.06 S	45.42 W
Caçapava do Sul	188	30.30 S	53.30 W
Cacapon ≃	176	39.37 N	78.16 W
Cacequi	188	29.53 S	54.49 W
Cáceres	120	39.29 N	6.22 W
Cacharí	188	36.23 S	59.29 W
Cache Creek ≃	178	38.42 N	121.42 W
Cache Peak ∧	178	42.11 N	113.40 W
Cachimbo, Serra do ⋀	184	8.30 S	55.50 W
Cachoeira	190	12.36 S	38.58 W
Cachoeira Alta	190	18.48 S	50.58 W
Cachoeira do Sul	188	30.02 S	52.54 W
Cachoeira Paulista	190	22.40 S	45.01 W
Cachoeiras de Macacu	190	22.28 S	42.39 W
Cachoeiro de Itapemirim	190	20.51 S	41.06 W
Cachos, Punta ≻	188	27.39 S	71.02 W
Cachuma, Lake ⊜1	178	34.35 N	119.55 W
Cacólo	156	10.07 S	19.17 E
Caconda	156	13.43 S	15.06 E
Cactus Flat ≚	178	37.45 N	116.45 W
Cactus Peak ∧	178	37.47 N	116.53 W
Caculé	190	14.30 S	42.13 W
Čadan	128	51.17 N	91.35 E
Čadca	116	49.26 N	18.48 E
Cader Bronwyn ∧	104	52.54 N	3.22 W
Cader Idris ∧	104	52.42 N	3.54 W
Cadibarrawirracanna, Lake ⊜	164	28.52 S	135.27 E
Cadillac	176	44.15 N	85.24 W
Cádiz, Esp.	120	36.32 N	6.18 W
Cadiz, Ohio, U.S.	176	40.16 N	81.00 W
Cádiz, Bahía de C	120	36.32 N	6.16 W
Cádiz, Golfo de C	120	36.50 N	7.10 W
Cadiz Lake ⊜	178	34.18 N	115.24 W
Cadnam	104	50.55 N	1.35 W
Čadobec ≃	128	58.40 N	98.50 E
Cadoux	164	30.47 S	117.08 E
Caen	118	49.11 N	0.21 W
Caergwrle	104	53.07 N	3.03 W
Caerleon	104	51.37 N	2.57 W
Caernarvon	104	53.08 N	4.16 W
Caernarvon Bay C	104	53.05 N	4.30 W
Caernarvon Castle ⊥	106	53.08 N	4.16 W
Caerphilly	104	51.35 N	3.14 W
Caersws	104	52.31 N	3.25 W
Caeté	190	19.54 S	43.40 W
Caetité	190	14.04 S	42.29 W
Cafayate	188	26.06 S	65.57 W
Cagayan ≃	138	18.22 N	121.37 E
Cagayan de Oro	138	8.29 N	124.39 E
Cagayan Islands II	138	9.40 N	121.16 E
Cagayan Sulu Island I	142	7.01 N	118.30 E
Čagda	128	58.45 N	130.37 E
Cagliari	122	39.20 N	9.00 E
Cagnes	118	43.40 N	7.09 E
Čagoda	130	59.10 N	35.17 E
Cagoyan ≃	132	18.22 N	121.37 E
Cagua	182	10.11 N	67.27 W
Caguas	182	18.14 N	66.02 W
Caha Mountains ⋀	110	51.45 N	9.45 W
Caher	110	52.21 N	7.56 W
Caherdaniel	110	51.45 N	10.05 W
Cahirciveen	110	51.57 N	10.13 W
Cahore Point ≻	110	52.34 N	6.11 W
Cahors	118	44.27 N	1.26 E
Cahto Peak ∧	178	39.41 N	123.35 W
Caí ≃	188	29.56 S	51.16 W
Caia ≃	120	38.50 N	7.05 W
Caiapônia	190	16.57 S	51.49 W
Caibarién	182	22.31 N	79.28 W
Caicara	184	7.37 N	66.10 W
Caicara de Maturín	182	9.49 N	63.36 W
Caicó	184	6.27 S	37.06 W
Caicos Islands II	182	21.50 N	71.50 W
Caicos Passage ⋈	182	22.15 N	72.40 W
Caimanera	182	19.59 N	75.09 W
Cain ≃	104	52.46 N	3.08 W
Caird Coast ⟜2	87	76.00 S	24.30 W
Cairndow	108	56.15 N	4.56 W
Cairngorm Mountains ⋀	108	57.04 N	3.50 W
Cairns	168	16.55 S	145.46 E
Cairnsmore of Carsphairn ∧	106	55.15 N	4.12 W
Cairnsmore of Fleet ∧	106	54.59 N	4.20 W
Cairn Table ∧	106	55.29 N	4.02 W
Cairn Water ≃	106	55.07 N	3.45 W
Cairo → Al-Qāhirah, Miṣr	154	30.03 N	31.15 E
Cairo, Ill., U.S.	180	37.00 N	89.11 W
Cairo, W. Va., U.S.	176	39.13 N	81.09 W
Cairo Montenotte	122	44.24 N	8.16 E
Caister-on-Sea	104	52.39 N	1.44 E
Caistor	106	53.30 N	0.20 W
Caiundo	156	15.46 S	17.28 E
Cajamarca	184	7.10 S	78.31 W
Cajarc	118	44.29 N	1.50 E
Cajàzeiras	184	6.54 S	38.34 W
Čajek	126	41.56 N	74.30 E
Čajkovskij	112	56.40 N	54.10 E
Čajniče	124	43.33 N	19.04 E
Cajon Summit)(	178	34.21 N	117.27 W
Čakovec	122	46.23 N	16.26 E
Cala, Embalse de ⊜1	120	37.50 N	6.00 W
Calabar	152	4.57 N	8.19 E
Calabozo	184	8.56 N	67.26 W
Calabozo, Ensenada de C	182	11.30 N	71.45 W
Calabria □4	122	39.00 N	16.30 E
Calafate	186	50.20 S	72.16 W
Calahorra	120	42.18 N	1.58 W
Calais, Fr.	118	50.57 N	1.50 E
Calais, Maine, U.S.	176	45.11 N	67.17 W
Calais, Pas de (Strait of Dover) ⋈	102	51.00 N	1.30 E
Calalaste, Sierra de ⋀	188	25.30 S	67.30 W
Calama	188	22.28 S	68.56 W
Calamar	184	10.15 N	74.55 W
Calamian Group II	138	12.00 N	120.00 E
Calapan	138	13.25 N	121.10 E
Calapooya Mountains ⋀	178	43.30 N	122.50 W
Călărași	124	44.11 N	27.20 E
Cala Ratjada	120	39.42 N	3.25 E
Calatayud	120	41.21 N	1.38 W
Calaveras ≃	178	38.12 N	120.41 W
Calayan Island I	138	19.20 N	121.27 E
Calbayog	138	12.04 N	124.36 E
Calbe	116	51.54 N	11.46 E
Calçoene	184	2.30 N	50.57 W
Calcutta	146	22.32 N	88.22 E
Caldas	190	21.56 S	46.23 W
Caldas da Rainha	120	39.24 N	9.08 W
Caldas de Reyes	120	42.36 N	8.38 W
Caldeirão, Serra do ⋀	120	37.42 N	8.21 W
Calder ≃	106	53.44 N	1.21 W
Calder, Loch ⊜	108	58.31 N	3.36 W
Caldera	188	27.04 S	70.50 W
Calder Bridge	106	54.27 N	3.29 W
Caldew ≃	106	54.54 N	2.56 W
Caldey Island I	104	51.38 N	4.41 W
Caldicot	104	51.36 N	2.45 W
Caldwell, Idaho, U.S.	174	43.40 N	116.41 W
Caldwell, Ohio, U.S.	176	39.45 N	81.31 W
Cale ≃	104	50.59 N	2.20 W
Caledon	160	34.12 S	19.23 E
Caledon ≃	160	30.31 S	26.05 E
Caledonia, Ont., Can.	176	43.04 N	79.56 W
Caledonia, N.Y., U.S.	176	42.58 N	77.51 W
Caledonia, Ohio, U.S.	176	40.38 N	82.58 W
Caledonian Canal ≍	108	56.50 N	5.06 W
Calexico	178	32.40 N	115.30 W
Calf of Man I	106	54.03 N	4.48 W
Calfpasture ≃	176	37.58 N	79.28 W
Calgary	172	51.03 N	114.05 W
Cali	184	3.27 N	76.31 W
Calicut	148	11.15 N	75.46 E
Caliente	178	37.37 N	114.31 W
California	176	40.04 N	79.53 W
California □3	174	37.30 N	119.30 W
California, Golfo de C	180	28.00 N	112.00 W
California Aqueduct ≍1	178	33.52 N	117.12 W
Calilegua	188	23.47 S	64.46 W
Calingiri	164	31.06 S	116.27 E
Calipatria	178	33.08 N	115.31 W
Calistoga	178	38.35 N	122.35 W
Calitzdorp	160	33.33 S	21.42 E
Callabonna, Lake ⊜	168	29.45 S	140.04 E
Callabonna Creek ≃	168	29.38 S	140.08 E
Callaghan, Mount ∧	178	39.42 N	116.57 W
Callan	110	52.33 N	7.23 W
Callander, Ont., Can.	176	46.13 N	79.23 W
Callander, Scot., U.K.	108	56.15 N	4.14 W
Callanish	108	58.12 N	6.43 W
Callanna	168	29.38 S	137.55 E
Callao	184	12.02 S	77.05 W
Callington	104	50.30 N	4.18 W
Calliope	168	24.00 S	151.12 E
Callosa de Ensarriá	120	38.39 N	0.07 W
Callosa de Segura	120	38.08 N	0.52 W
Calne	104	51.27 N	2.00 W
Caloosahatchee ≃	182	26.31 N	82.01 W
Caloundra	168	26.48 S	153.09 E
Calshot	104	50.49 N	1.19 W
Calstock	104	50.30 N	4.12 W
Caltagirone	122	37.14 N	14.31 E
Caltanissetta	122	37.29 N	14.04 E
Caltra	110	53.26 N	8.25 W
Calunda	156	12.06 S	23.23 E
Calvados □5	118	49.10 N	0.30 W
Calvert ≃	168	16.30 S	137.30 E
Calvert Hills	168	17.15 S	137.20 E
Calvi	118	42.34 N	8.45 E
Calvinia	160	31.25 S	19.45 E
Calw	116	48.43 N	8.44 E
Calwa	178	36.42 N	119.46 W
Cam ≃	102	52.21 N	0.15 E
Camabatela	156	8.11 S	15.22 E
Camaçari	190	12.41 S	38.18 W
Camagüey	182	21.23 N	77.55 W
Camaiore	122	43.56 N	10.18 E
Camajuaní	182	22.28 N	79.44 W
Camamu	190	13.57 S	39.07 W
Camaná	184	16.36 S	72.40 W
Camanche Reservoir ⊜1	178	38.13 N	120.58 W
Camapuã	190	19.30 S	54.05 W
Camaquã	188	30.51 S	51.49 W
Camaquã ≃	188	31.17 S	51.47 W
Camará	184	3.55 S	62.44 W
Camarat, Cap ≻	118	43.12 N	6.41 E
Camarès	118	43.49 N	2.53 E
Camargue ⟜1	118	43.34 N	4.34 E
Camarón, Cabo ≻	182	16.00 N	85.04 W
Camarones	186	44.45 S	65.40 W
Camas	120	37.24 N	6.02 W
Camas Creek ≃	178	43.20 N	114.24 W
Ca-mau → Quan-long	140	9.11 N	105.08 E
Ca-mau, Mui ≻	140	8.38 N	104.44 E
Cambará	190	23.03 S	50.05 W
Cambay	146	22.18 N	72.37 E
Camberley	104	51.21 N	0.45 W
Cambo	106	55.10 N	1.57 W
Cambodia □1	138	13.00 N	105.00 E
Cambois	106	55.10 N	1.31 W
Camboriú	188	27.01 S	48.38 W
Camboriú, Ponta do ≻	188	25.10 S	47.55 W
Camborne, Eng., U.K.	104	50.12 N	5.19 W
Camborne, Eng., U.K.	118	52.13 N	0.08 E
Cambrai	118	50.10 N	3.14 E
Cambria	178	35.34 N	121.05 W
Cambrian Mountains ⋀	104	52.35 N	3.35 W
Cambridge, Ont., Can.	172	43.22 N	80.19 W
Cambridge, N.Z.	170	37.53 S	175.28 E
Cambridge, Eng., U.K.	104	52.13 N	0.08 E
Cambridge, Md., U.S.	176	38.34 N	76.04 W
Cambridge, Mass., U.S.	176	42.22 N	71.06 W
Cambridge, N.Y., U.S.	176	43.02 N	73.23 W
Cambridge, Ohio, U.S.	176	40.02 N	81.35 W
Cambridge Bay	172	69.03 N	105.05 W
Cambridge City	176	39.49 N	85.10 W
Cambridge Fiord C2	172	71.20 N	74.44 W
Cambridge Gulf C	166	14.55 S	128.15 E
Cambridgeshire □6	104	52.20 N	0.05 E
Cambridge Springs	176	41.48 N	80.04 W
Cambuí	190	22.37 S	46.04 W
Camden, Austl.	168	34.03 S	150.42 E
Camden, Ark., U.S.	174	33.35 N	92.50 W
Camden, Del., U.S.	176	39.07 N	75.33 W
Camden, Maine, U.S.	176	44.12 N	69.04 W
Camden, N.J., U.S.	174	39.57 N	75.07 W
Camden, N.Y., U.S.	176	43.02 N	75.45 W
Camden, Ohio, U.S.	176	39.38 N	84.39 W
Camden ⟜8	104	51.33 N	0.10 W
Camel ≃	104	50.33 N	4.55 W
Camelford	104	50.37 N	4.41 W
Camels Hump ∧	176	44.19 N	72.53 W
Cameron	176	39.50 N	80.34 W
Cameron Highlands	142	4.29 N	101.27 E
Cameron Hills ⋀2	172	59.48 N	118.00 W
Cameroon □1	152	6.00 N	12.00 E
Cameroun → Cameroon □1	152	6.00 N	12.00 E
Cameroun, Mont ∧	152	4.12 N	9.11 E
Cametá	184	2.15 S	49.30 W
Camfield	166	17.09 S	131.21 E
Camiguin Island I	138	18.56 N	121.55 E
Camino	178	38.44 N	120.41 W
Camiranga	184	1.48 S	46.17 W
Camiri	184	20.03 S	63.31 W
Camlad ≃	104	52.36 N	3.10 W
Çamlıca	124	40.46 N	26.39 E
Camocim	184	2.54 S	40.50 W
Camooweal	168	19.55 S	138.07 E
Camorta Island I	140	8.08 N	93.30 E
Camowen ≃	110	54.36 N	7.18 W
Campagna di Roma ⟜1	122	41.50 N	12.35 E
Campana	188	34.10 S	58.57 W
Campana, Isla I	186	48.25 S	75.20 W
Campania □4	122	41.00 N	14.30 E
Campbell, S. Afr.	160	28.48 S	23.44 E
Campbell, Calif., U.S.	178	37.17 N	121.57 W
Campbellford	176	44.18 N	77.48 W
Campbell Hill ∧2	176	40.22 N	83.43 W
Campbell Island I	87	52.30 S	169.05 E
Campbell Plateau ✧3	87	56.00 S	165.00 E
Campbellpore	149	33.46 N	72.22 E
Campbell Rise ✧3	84	56.00 S	165.00 E
Campbell River	172	50.01 N	125.15 W
Campbells Bay	176	45.44 N	76.36 W
Campbellton, N.B., Can.	172	48.00 N	66.40 W
Campbellton, Newf., Can.	172	49.17 N	54.56 W
Campbell Town, Austl.	168	41.56 S	147.29 E
Campbelltown, Austl.	168	34.04 S	150.49 E
Campbelltown, Scot., U.K.	108	57.34 N	4.02 W
Campbeltown	106	55.26 N	5.36 W
Campeche	180	19.51 N	90.32 W
Campeche, Bahía de C	180	20.00 N	94.00 W
Campechuela	182	20.14 N	77.17 W
Camperdown	168	38.14 S	143.09 E
Cam-pha	140	21.01 N	107.19 E
Camp Hill	176	40.14 N	76.55 W
Campidano ⟜1	122	39.30 N	8.50 E
Campillo de Llerena	120	38.30 N	5.50 W
Campina ⟜1	120	37.45 N	4.45 W
Campina Grande	184	7.13 S	35.53 W
Campinas	190	22.54 S	47.05 W
Campoalegre	184	2.41 N	75.20 W
Campo Alegre de Goiás	184	22.54 S	47.05 W
Campobasso	122	41.34 N	14.39 E
Campo Belo	190	20.53 S	45.16 W
Campo de Criptana	120	39.24 N	3.07 W
Campo de la Cruz	182	10.23 N	74.53 W
Campo Erê	188	26.23 S	53.03 W
Campo Florido	190	19.47 S	48.35 W
Campo Gallo	188	26.35 S	62.50 W
Campo Grande	190	20.27 S	54.37 W
Campo Largo	188	25.26 S	49.32 W
Campo Maior	184	4.49 S	42.10 W
Campo Mourão	190	24.03 S	52.22 W
Campo Nôvo	188	27.42 S	53.48 W
Campo Quijano	188	24.54 S	65.40 W
Campos	190	21.45 S	41.18 W
Campos Altos	190	19.41 S	46.10 W
Campos do Jordão	190	22.44 S	45.35 W
Campos Gerais	190	21.14 S	45.46 W
Campos Novos	188	27.24 S	51.12 W
Camps-en-Amiénois	102	49.52 N	1.58 E
Campsie Fells ⋀2	108	56.02 N	4.12 W
Campton	176	37.44 N	83.33 W
Cam-ranh	140	11.54 N	109.09 E
Camrose, Alta., Can.	172	53.01 N	112.50 W
Camrose, Wales, U.K.	104	51.51 N	5.01 W
Camsell ≃	172	65.40 N	118.07 W
Can ≃	104	51.48 N	0.25 E
Canaan, Conn., U.S.	176	42.02 N	73.20 W
Canaan, Vt., U.S.	176	45.00 N	71.32 W
Canada □1	172	60.00 N	95.00 W
Cañada de Gómez	188	32.49 S	61.25 W
Cañada Honda	188	32.00 S	68.33 W
Canadian ≃	174	35.27 N	95.03 W
Canajoharie	176	42.54 N	74.35 W
Çanakkale Boğazı (Dardanelles) ⋈	124	40.15 N	26.25 E
Canal Fulton	176	40.54 N	81.36 W
Canals	188	33.34 S	62.53 W
Canal Winchester	176	39.51 N	82.48 W
Canal Zone □2	180	9.10 N	79.48 W
Canandaigua	176	42.54 N	77.17 W
Cananea	180	30.57 N	110.18 W
Cananéia	188	25.01 S	47.57 W
Canápolis	190	18.44 S	49.13 W
Canarias, Islas (Canary Islands) II	88	28.00 N	15.30 W
Canarreos, Archipiélago de los II	182	21.50 N	82.30 W
Canary Basin ✧1	92	27.00 N	25.00 W
Cañas	182	10.25 N	85.07 W
Canaseraga	176	42.28 N	77.47 W
Canastota	176	43.10 N	75.45 W
Canaveral, Cape ≻	174	28.27 N	80.32 W
Canavese ⟜1	122	45.20 N	7.40 E
Canavieiras	190	15.39 S	38.57 W
Canbelego	168	31.33 S	146.19 E
Canberra	168	35.17 S	149.08 E
Canby	178	41.27 N	120.52 W
Cancale	118	48.41 N	1.51 W
Cancún, Punta ≻	182	21.08 N	86.45 W
Candeias	190	12.40 S	38.33 W
Candelária, Bra.	188	29.40 S	52.48 W
Candelaria, Cuba	182	22.44 N	82.58 W
Candelo	168	36.46 S	149.42 E
Candia → Iráklion	124	35.20 N	25.09 E
Cândido de Abreu	188	24.35 S	51.20 W
Candlemas Islands II	92	57.03 S	26.43 W
Candlewood, Lake ⊜	176	41.32 N	73.27 W
Candor	176	42.14 N	76.21 W
Candover	160	27.28 S	31.57 E
Cane ≃	164	21.33 S	115.23 E
Canea → Khaniá	124	35.31 N	24.02 E
Canela	188	29.22 S	50.50 W
Canelles, Embalse de ⊜1	120	42.10 N	0.30 E
Canelones	188	34.32 S	56.17 W
Cañete, Chile	188	37.48 S	73.24 W
Cañete, Perú	184	13.08 S	76.28 W
Cangas de Narcea	120	43.11 N	6.33 W
Cangas de Onís	120	43.21 N	5.07 W
Cangkuang, Tanjung ≻	142	6.51 S	105.15 E
Cangombe	156	14.24 S	19.59 E
Canguçu	188	31.24 S	52.41 W
Cangyuan	140	23.12 N	99.16 E
Cangzhou	132	38.19 N	116.51 E
Caniapiscau ≃	172	57.40 N	69.30 W
Caniapiscau, Lac ⊜	172	54.10 N	69.55 W
Canicatti	122	37.21 N	13.51 E
Canigou, Pic du ∧	120	42.31 N	2.27 E
Canisp ∧	108	58.07 N	5.03 W
Canisteo	176	42.16 N	77.36 W
Canisteo ≃	176	42.07 N	77.08 W
Canna I	108	57.04 N	6.34 W
Canna, Sound of ⋈	108	56.59 N	6.40 W
Cannanore	148	11.51 N	75.22 E
Cannel City	176	37.47 N	83.17 W
Cannes	118	43.33 N	7.01 E
Cannich	108	57.21 N	4.46 W
Cannich ≃	108	57.21 N	4.44 W
Cannington, Ont., Can.	176	44.21 N	79.02 W
Cannington, Eng., U.K.	104	51.09 N	3.04 W
Cannock	104	52.42 N	2.09 W
Cann River	168	37.34 S	149.10 E
Canoas	188	29.56 S	51.11 W
Canoas ≃	188	27.36 S	51.25 W
Canoinhas	188	26.10 S	50.24 W
Canonbie	106	55.05 N	2.57 W
Canon City	174	38.27 N	105.14 W
Canonsburg	176	40.16 N	80.11 W
Canora	172	51.37 N	102.26 W
Canosa [di Puglia]	122	41.13 N	16.04 E
Canouan I	182	12.43 N	61.20 W
Canowindra	168	33.34 S	148.38 E
Cantábrica, Cordillera ⋀	120	43.00 N	5.00 W
Cantal □5	118	45.05 N	2.45 E
Cantal ⋀	118	45.10 N	2.40 E
Cantaura	184	9.19 N	64.21 W
Canterbury	104	51.17 N	1.05 E
Canterbury Bight C3	170	44.15 S	171.38 E
Canterbury Plains ≚	170	44.00 S	171.45 E
Canterbury Station	176	45.53 N	67.29 W
Can-tho	140	10.02 N	105.47 E
Canton, Maine, U.S.	176	44.28 N	70.19 W
Canton, Miss., U.S.	174	32.37 N	90.02 W
Canton, N.Y., U.S.	176	44.36 N	75.10 W
Canton, Ohio, U.S.	176	40.48 N	81.22 W
Canton, Pa., U.S.	176	41.39 N	76.51 W
Canton → Guangzhou, Zhg.	136	23.06 N	113.16 E
Canton I	96	2.50 S	171.41 W
Canton and Enderbury □2	96	2.50 S	171.40 W
Cantù	122	45.44 N	9.08 E
Cantu ≃	188	24.46 S	52.54 W
Cañuelas	188	35.03 S	58.44 W
Canutama	184	6.32 S	64.20 W
Canvastown	170	41.18 S	173.40 E
Canvey	104	51.32 N	0.36 E
Canvey Island I	104	51.33 N	0.34 E
Čany, Ozero ⊜	128	54.50 N	77.30 E
Canyon	174	34.59 N	101.55 W
Canyon Creek ≃	178	42.59 N	115.59 W
Canyonville	178	42.56 N	123.17 W
Cao-bang	138	22.40 N	106.15 E
Caolisport, Loch C	108	55.54 N	5.37 W
Caoqiao	136	31.32 N	119.59 E
Cap, Pointe du ≻	182	14.07 N	60.57 W
Capac	176	43.01 N	82.56 W
Čapajevsk	112	52.58 N	49.41 E
Capanaparo ≃	184	7.01 N	67.07 W
Capanema	188	25.40 S	53.48 W
Capão Bonito	190	24.01 S	48.20 W
Capão Doce, Morro do ∧	188	26.43 S	51.25 W
Capatárida	182	11.11 N	70.37 W
Cape Barren Island I	168	40.25 S	148.12 E
Cape Basin ✧1	88	35.00 S	5.00 E
Cape Breton Island I	172	46.00 N	60.30 W
Cape Coast	152	5.05 N	1.15 W
Cape Cod Bay C	176	41.52 N	70.22 W
Cape Dorset	172	64.14 N	76.32 W
Cape Elizabeth	176	43.34 N	70.12 W
Cape Girardeau	174	37.19 N	89.32 W
Cape Johnson Seamount ✧3	96	17.00 N	177.20 W
Capel Curig	104	53.06 N	3.54 W
Capelinha	190	17.42 S	42.31 W
Capella	168	23.05 S	148.02 E
Cape May	176	38.56 N	74.55 W
Cape May Court House	176	39.05 N	74.50 W
Cape of Good Hope (Kaap) □4	160	31.00 S	23.00 E
Cape Porpoise	176	43.22 N	70.26 W
Cape Rise ✧3	88	41.00 S	13.00 E
Capesterre	182	16.03 N	61.34 W
Cape Town (Kaapstad)	160	33.55 S	18.22 E
Cape Verde □1	152	16.00 N	24.00 W
Cape Verde Basin ✧1	92	14.00 N	33.00 W
Cape Verde Islands → Cape Verde □1	152	16.00 N	24.00 W
Cape Verde Terrace ✧3	88	18.30 N	22.00 W
Cape Vincent	176	44.08 N	76.20 W
Cape York Peninsula ≻1	166	14.00 S	142.30 E
Cap-Haïtien	182	19.45 N	72.15 W
Capilla del Monte	188	30.50 S	64.32 W
Capinópolis	190	18.41 S	49.35 W
Capinzal	188	27.20 S	51.36 W
Capitán Bermúdez	188	32.50 S	60.40 W
Capitola	178	36.59 N	121.57 W
Capitol Peak ∧	178	41.50 N	117.18 W
Capivari	190	23.00 S	47.31 W
Capiz → Roxas	138	11.35 N	122.45 E
Cappamore	110	52.37 N	8.20 W
Cappercleuch	106	55.29 N	3.12 W
Cappoquin	110	52.08 N	7.50 W
Capreol	172	46.43 N	80.56 W
Capri, Isola di I	122	40.33 N	14.13 E
Capricorn, Cape ≻	168	23.30 S	151.13 E
Capricorn Channel ⋈	168	23.00 S	152.20 E
Capricorn Group II	168	23.28 S	152.00 E
Caprivi Strip (Caprivizipfel) □9	160	17.59 S	23.00 E
Cap-Saint-Jacques → Vung-tau	140	10.21 N	107.04 E
Captain Cook	179a	19.30 N	155.55 W
Captains Flat	168	35.35 S	149.27 E
Captieux	118	44.18 N	0.16 W
Captina Creek ≃	176	39.52 N	80.48 W
Capua	122	41.06 N	14.12 E
Caquetá (Japurá) ≃	184	3.08 S	64.46 W
Car, Slieve ∧	110	54.03 N	9.40 W
Čara	128	56.54 N	118.12 E
Čara ≃	128	60.22 N	120.50 E
Carabobo □3	182	10.10 N	68.05 W
Caracal	124	44.07 N	24.21 E
Caracaraí	184	1.50 N	61.08 W
Caracas	184	10.30 N	66.56 W
Carache	182	9.38 N	70.14 W
Caracol	188	22.01 S	57.02 W
Caragh, Lough ⊜	110	52.03 N	9.52 W
Caraghnan Mountain ∧	168	31.20 S	149.03 E
Caraguatatuba	190	23.37 S	45.25 W
Caraí	190	17.12 S	41.42 W
Caraïbes, Îles des → West Indies II	180	19.00 N	70.00 W
Carandaí	190	20.57 S	43.48 W
Carangola	190	20.44 S	42.02 W
Caransebeș	124	45.25 N	22.13 E
Carapó	190	22.38 S	54.48 W
Carappee Hill ∧2	168	33.26 S	136.16 E
Caraș-Severin □4	124	45.00 N	22.00 E
Caratasca, Laguna de C	182	15.20 N	83.50 W
Caratinga	190	19.47 S	42.08 W
Carauari	184	4.52 S	66.54 W
Caravaca	120	38.06 N	1.51 W
Caravaggio	122	45.30 N	9.38 E
Caravelas	190	17.45 S	39.15 W
Caràzinho	188	28.18 S	52.48 W
Carberry	172	49.52 N	99.20 W
Carbon-Blanc	118	44.53 N	0.31 W
Carbondale, Ill., U.S.	174	37.44 N	89.13 W
Carbondale, Pa., U.S.	176	41.35 N	75.30 W
Carbonear	172	47.44 N	53.13 W
Carboneras de Guadazaon	120	39.53 N	1.48 W
Carbonia	122	39.11 N	8.32 E
Carbost	108	57.18 N	6.22 W
Carcagente	120	39.08 N	0.27 W
Carcajou ≃	172	65.37 N	128.43 W
Carcans, Étang de C	118	45.08 N	1.08 W
Carcassonne	118	43.13 N	2.21 E
Carcross	172	60.10 N	134.42 W
Cardabia	164	23.06 S	113.48 E
Cardamum Island I	148	11.14 N	72.47 E
Cardeña	120	38.13 N	4.19 W
Cárdenas	182	23.05 N	81.10 W
Cárdenas, Bahía de C	182	23.05 N	81.09 W
Cardiel, Lago ⊜	186	48.55 S	71.10 W
Cardiff	104	51.29 N	3.13 W
Cardigan	104	52.06 N	4.40 W
Cardigan Bay C	104	52.30 N	4.20 W
Cardigan Island I	104	52.08 N	4.41 W
Cardinal	176	44.47 N	75.23 W
Cardington	176	40.30 N	82.53 W
Cardston	172	49.12 N	113.18 W
Cardwell	168	18.16 S	146.02 E
Čardžou	150	39.06 N	63.34 E
Čardžou □4	150	38.51 N	63.34 E
Carei	124	47.42 N	22.28 E
Carén	188	30.51 S	70.47 W
Carey	176	40.57 N	83.23 W
Carey, Lake ⊜	164	29.05 S	122.15 E
Carey Downs	164	25.38 S	115.27 E
Cargados Carajos Shoals II	94	16.38 S	59.38 E
Cargill	108	56.30 N	3.22 W
Carhaix-Plouguer	118	48.17 N	3.35 W
Cariacica	190	20.16 S	40.25 W
Cariaco	182	10.29 N	63.33 W
Cariaco, Golfo de C	182	10.30 N	64.00 W
Caribbean Sea ⚲2	84	15.00 N	73.00 W
Cariboo Mountains ⋀	172	53.00 N	121.00 W
Caribou	174	46.52 N	68.01 W
Caribou ≃	172	59.20 N	94.44 W
Caribou Mountain ∧	176	45.26 N	70.38 W
Caribou Mountains ⋀	172	59.12 N	115.40 W
Carinda	168	30.28 S	147.41 E
Carinhanha	190	14.18 S	43.47 W
Carini	122	38.08 N	13.11 E
Carinish	108	57.31 N	7.18 W
Caripe	182	10.12 N	63.29 W
Caripito	184	10.08 N	63.06 W
Carisbrooke	104	50.41 N	1.19 W
Carleton	176	42.04 N	83.23 W
Carleton, Mount ∧	172	47.23 N	66.53 W
Carleton Place	176	45.08 N	76.09 W
Carletonville	160	26.23 S	27.22 E
Carlin	178	40.43 N	116.07 W
Carlisle, Eng., U.K.	106	54.54 N	2.55 W
Carlisle, Ky., U.S.	176	38.19 N	84.02 W
Carlisle, Pa., U.S.	176	40.12 N	77.12 W
Carlópolis, Bra.	188		
	190	23.25 S	49.41 W
Carlos Barbosa	188	29.18 S	51.30 W
Carlos Casares	188	35.37 S	61.22 W
Carlow	110	52.50 N	6.55 W
Carlow □6	110	52.50 N	7.00 W
Carloway	108	58.17 N	6.48 W
Carlsbad → Karlovy Vary, Česko.	116	50.11 N	12.52 E
Carlsbad, Calif., U.S.	178	33.10 N	117.21 W
Carlsbad, N. Mex., U.S.	174	32.25 N	104.14 W
Carlsberg Ridge ✧3	94	4.00 N	65.00 E
Carlton	104	52.58 N	1.05 W
Carluke	108	55.45 N	3.51 W
Carmacks	172	62.05 N	136.18 W
Carmagnola	122	44.51 N	7.43 E
Carman	172	49.32 N	98.00 W
Carmarthen	104	51.52 N	4.19 W
Carmarthen Bay C	104	51.40 N	4.30 W
Carmaux	118	44.03 N	2.09 E
Carmel, Calif., U.S.	178	36.33 N	121.55 W
Carmel, N.Y., U.S.	176	41.26 N	73.41 W
Carmel Head ≻	106	53.24 N	4.34 W
Carmelo	188	34.00 S	58.17 W
Carmel Valley	178	36.29 N	121.43 W
Carmel Woods	178	36.34 N	121.54 W
Carmen, Isla I	180	25.55 N	111.10 W
Carmen, Río del ≃	188	28.45 S	70.30 W
Carmen Alto	188	23.11 S	69.40 W
Carmen de Patagones	186	40.48 S	63.00 W
Carmer Hill ∧2	176	41.54 N	77.58 W
Carmichael	178	38.38 N	121.19 W
Carmichael Point ≻	182	21.11 N	73.23 W
Carmila	168	21.55 S	149.25 E
Carmo	190	21.56 S	42.37 W
Carmona	120	37.28 N	5.38 W
Carmópolis de Minas	190	20.33 S	44.38 W
Carnamah	164	29.42 S	115.53 E
Carnarvon, Austl.	164	24.53 S	113.40 E
Carnarvon, S. Afr.	160	30.56 S	22.08 E
Carnatic ⟜1	144	12.30 N	78.15 E
Carncastle	110	54.54 N	5.53 W
Carndonagh	110	55.15 N	7.15 W
Carnedd Llewelyn ∧	104	53.10 N	3.58 W
Carnedd Wen ∧	104	52.41 N	3.35 W
Carnegie	164	25.43 S	122.59 E
Carnegie, Lake ⊜	164	26.10 S	122.30 E
Carnegie Ridge ✧3	92	1.30 S	85.00 W
Carnew	110	52.43 N	6.30 W
Carnforth	106	54.08 N	2.46 W
Carniche, Alpi ⋀	122	46.40 N	13.00 E
Car Nicobar Island I	140	9.10 N	92.47 E
Carnlough	110	54.59 N	5.59 W
Carno	104	52.33 N	3.31 W
Carnot, Cape ≻	168	34.57 S	135.38 E
Carnoustie	108	56.30 N	2.44 W
Carnsore Point ≻	110	52.10 N	6.22 W
Carnwath	108	55.43 N	3.38 W
Carnwath ≃	172	68.26 N	128.50 W
Caro	176	43.29 N	83.24 W
Carolina, Bra.	184	7.20 S	47.28 W
Carolina, S. Afr.	160	26.05 S	30.06 E
Caroline Atoll I1	96	9.58 S	150.13 W
Caroline Islands II	96	8.00 N	147.00 E
Caroline-New Guinea Ridge ✧3	96	4.00 N	141.30 E
Caroline Peak ∧	170	45.56 S	167.13 E
Caroní ≃	184	8.21 N	62.43 W
Carora	184	10.11 N	70.05 W
Carp	176	45.21 N	76.02 W
Carp ≃	176	46.02 N	84.42 W
Carpathian Mountains ⋀	100	48.00 N	24.00 E
Carpații Meridionali ⋀	124	45.30 N	24.15 E
Carpentaria, Gulf of C	168	17.00 S	140.00 E
Carpentras	118	44.03 N	5.03 E
Carpi	122	44.47 N	10.53 E
Carpinteria	178	34.24 N	119.31 W
Carpolac	168	36.44 S	141.19 E
Carra, Lough ⊜	110	53.42 N	9.16 W
Carradale	108	55.35 N	5.28 W
Carrantuohill ∧	110	52.00 N	9.45 W
Carranza, Cabo ≻	188	35.36 S	72.38 W
Carrara	122	44.05 N	10.06 E
Carrathool	168	34.24 S	145.26 E
Carrbridge	108	57.17 N	3.49 W
Carreria	188	21.59 S	58.35 W
Carreta, Punta ≻	184	14.12 S	76.17 W
Carriacou I	182	12.25 N	61.30 W
Carrickart	110	55.10 N	7.47 W
Carrickfergus	110	54.43 N	5.49 W
Carrickmacross	110	53.58 N	6.43 W
Carrick-on-Shannon	110	53.57 N	8.05 W
Carrick-on-Suir	110	52.21 N	7.25 W
Carrieton	168	32.26 S	138.32 E
Carrigahorig	110	53.04 N	8.09 W
Carrigaline	110	51.48 N	8.24 W
Carrigallen	110	53.59 N	7.39 W
Carrington	174	47.27 N	99.08 W
Carrión ≃	120	41.53 N	4.32 W
Carrión de los Condes	120	42.20 N	4.36 W
Carrizal Bajo	188	28.05 S	71.10 W
Carrizo Wash ∨	178	33.05 N	115.56 W
Carrollton, Mich., U.S.	176	43.27 N	83.54 W
Carrollton, Ohio, U.S.	176	40.34 N	81.05 W
Carrolltown	176	40.36 N	78.43 W
Carron ≃, Scot., U.K.	108	57.25 N	5.27 W
Carron ≃, Scot., U.K.	108	57.53 N	4.21 W
Carron ≃, Scot., U.K.	108	56.02 N	3.44 W
Carron, Loch C	108	57.22 N	5.31 W
Carronbridge	106	55.16 N	3.48 W
Carron Valley Reservoir ⊜1	108	56.02 N	4.05 W
Carrot ≃	172	53.50 N	101.17 W
Carrouges	102	48.34 N	0.09 W
Carrowmore Lake ⊜	110	54.12 N	9.47 W
Carry Falls Reservoir ⊜1	176	44.25 N	74.45 W
Carsaig	108	56.17 N	6.00 W
Čarsk	128	49.35 N	81.05 E
Carson ≃	178	39.45 N	118.40 W
Carson, East Fork ≃	178	39.00 N	119.49 W
Carson City, Mich., U.S.	176	43.11 N	84.51 W
Carson City, Nev., U.S.	178	39.10 N	119.46 W
Carson Lake ⊜	178	39.19 N	118.43 W
Carson Range ⋀	178	39.15 N	120.20 W
Carson Sink ⊜	178	39.45 N	118.30 W
Carstairs	108	55.42 N	3.42 W
Carstensz-Toppen → Jaya, Puncak ∧	166	4.05 S	137.11 E
Cartagena, Chile	188	33.33 S	71.37 W
Cartagena, Col.	184	10.25 N	75.32 W
Cartagena, Esp.	120	37.36 N	0.59 W
Cartago, Col.	184	4.45 N	75.55 W
Cartago, C.R.	182	9.52 N	83.55 W
Carterton	170	41.02 S	175.31 E
Carthage, Tun.	152	36.51 N	10.21 E
Carthage, Mo., U.S.	174	37.11 N	94.19 W
Carthage, N.Y., U.S.	176	43.59 N	75.37 W
Cartier Island I	162	12.32 S	123.32 E
Cartwright	172	53.42 N	57.01 W
Caruaru	184	8.17 S	35.58 W
Carúpano	184	10.40 N	63.14 W
Carutapera	184	1.13 S	46.01 W
Carvin	118	50.29 N	2.58 E
Carvoeiro	184	1.24 S	61.59 W
Carvoeiro, Cabo ≻	120	39.21 N	9.24 W
Cary ≃	104	51.09 N	2.59 W
Casablanca (Dar-el-Beida)	152	33.39 N	7.35 W
Casa Branca	190	21.46 S	47.04 W
Casale Monferrato	122	45.08 N	8.27 E
Casanare ≃	184	6.02 N	69.51 W
Casanay	182	10.30 N	63.25 W
Casarano	122	40.00 N	18.10 E
Casar de Cáceres	120	39.34 N	6.25 W
Casas Ibáñez	120	39.17 N	1.28 W
Casca	188	28.34 S	51.59 W
Cascade Range ⋀	174	49.00 N	120.00 W
Cascais	120	38.42 N	9.25 W
Cascavel	188	24.57 S	53.28 W
Cascina	122	43.41 N	10.33 E
Casco Bay C	176	43.40 N	70.00 W
Caserta	122	41.04 N	14.20 E
Caseville	176	43.56 N	83.16 W
Casey Bay C	87	67.20 S	48.00 E
Cashel, Eire	110	53.25 N	9.48 W
Cashel, Eire	110	52.31 N	7.53 W
Cashmere Downs	164	28.58 S	119.35 E
Casilda	188	33.03 S	61.10 W
Casino	168	28.52 S	153.03 E
Casiquiare, Brazo ≃	184	2.01 N	67.07 W
Čáslav	116	49.54 N	15.23 E
Casper	174	42.51 N	106.19 W
Caspian Sea ⚲2	126	42.00 N	50.30 E
Cass ≃	176	43.23 N	83.59 W
Cassai (Kasai) ≃	156	3.06 S	16.57 E
Cassano allo Ionio	122	39.47 N	16.20 E
Cass City	176	43.36 N	83.10 W
Casselman	176	45.19 N	75.05 W
Cássia	190	20.36 S	46.56 W

Symbols in the index entries are identified on page 198.

Name	Page	Lat °′	Long °′
Cassiar	172	59.16 N	129.40 W
Cassiar Mountains ⛰	172	59.00 N	129.00 W
Cassinga	156	15.08 S	16.05 E
Cassino, Bra.	188	32.11 S	52.10 W
Cassino, It.	122	41.30 N	13.49 E
Cassley ≃	108	57.58 N	4.35 W
Castalia	176	41.24 N	82.48 W
Castel	105b	49.28 N	2.34 W
Castelfranco Veneto	122	45.40 N	11.55 E
Castellamare del Golfo	122	38.01 N	12.53 E
Castellammare [di Stabia]	122	40.42 N	14.29 E
Castellane	118	43.51 N	6.31 E
Castellaneta	122	40.37 N	16.57 E
Castellón □4	120	40.10 N	0.10 W
Castellón de la Plana	120	39.59 N	0.02 W
Castellote	120	40.48 N	0.19 W
Castelmoron-sur-Lot	118	44.24 N	0.30 E
Castelnaudary	118	43.19 N	1.57 E
Castelnau-Montratier	118	44.16 N	1.21 E
Castelo	190	20.36 S	41.12 W
Castelo Branco	120	39.49 N	7.30 W
Castelsarrasin	118	44.02 N	1.06 E
Castelvetrano	122	37.41 N	12.47 E
Casterton	168	37.35 S	141.24 E
Castets	118	43.53 N	1.09 W
Castile	176	42.38 N	78.03 W
Castilla	184	5.12 S	80.38 W
Castilla, Playa de ⩡2	120	37.00 N	6.33 W
Castilla la Nueva □9	120	40.00 N	3.45 W
Castilla la Vieja □9	120	41.30 N	4.00 W
Castillo, Pampa del ⏝	186	45.58 S	68.24 W
Castillon-la-Bataille	118	44.51 N	0.03 W
Castillos	188	34.12 S	53.50 W
Castine	176	44.23 N	68.48 W
Castle Acre	104	52.42 N	0.41 E
Castlebar	110	53.52 N	9.17 W
Castlebay	108	56.57 N	7.28 W
Castlebellingham	110	53.54 N	6.23 W
Castleblayney	110	54.07 N	6.44 W
Castle Cary	104	51.06 N	2.31 W
Castlecliff	170	39.57 S	174.59 E
Castlecomer	110	52.48 N	7.12 W
Castle Creek ≃	178	43.06 N	116.16 W
Castlederg	110	54.42 N	7.36 W
Castledermot	110	52.55 N	6.50 W
Castle Dome Peak ∧	178	33.05 N	114.08 W
Castle Donington	104	52.51 N	1.19 W
Castle Douglas	106	54.57 N	3.56 W
Castlefin	110	54.47 N	7.35 W
Castleford	106	53.44 N	1.21 W
Castlegar	172	49.19 N	117.40 W
Castleisland	110	52.14 N	9.27 W
Castlemaine, Austl.	168	37.04 S	144.13 E
Castlemaine, Eire	110	52.09 N	9.43 W
Castlemartyr	110	51.55 N	8.03 W
Castle Mountain ∧	172	64.35 N	135.55 W
Castlepoint	170	40.54 S	176.13 E
Castlepollard	110	53.40 N	7.17 W
Castlerea	110	53.46 N	8.29 W
Castlereagh	110	54.33 N	5.48 W
Castlereagh ≃	168	30.12 S	147.32 E
Castle Rock ∧	176	37.57 N	78.44 W
Castleside	106	54.50 N	1.52 W
Castleton, Eng., U.K.	106	53.21 N	1.46 W
Castleton, Eng., U.K.	106	54.28 N	0.56 W
Castleton, Vt., U.S.	176	43.37 N	73.11 W
Castletown, Eire	110	53.26 N	7.38 W
Castletown, I. of Man	106	54.04 N	4.40 W
Castletown, Scot., U.K.	108	58.35 N	3.23 W
Castletown Bere (Castletown Bearhaven)	110	51.39 N	9.55 W
Castletownroche	110	52.10 N	8.28 W
Castletownshend	110	51.32 N	9.11 W
Castlewellan	110	54.16 N	5.57 W
Castres	118	43.36 N	2.15 E
Castries	182	14.01 N	61.00 W
Castro, Bra.	188	24.47 S	50.00 W
Castro, Chile	186	42.29 S	73.46 W
Castro del Río	120	37.41 N	4.28 W
Castro Marim	120	37.13 N	7.26 W
Castro-Urdiales	120	43.23 N	3.13 W
Castro Verde	120	37.42 N	8.05 W
Castrovillari	122	39.49 N	16.13 E
Castroville	178	36.46 N	121.45 W
Castuera	120	38.43 N	5.33 W
Catacamas	182	14.54 N	85.56 W
Catacaos	184	5.15 S	80.42 W
Cataguases	190	21.24 S	42.41 W
Catalão	190	18.10 S	47.57 W
Çatalca	124	41.09 N	28.27 E
Catalina	188	25.13 S	69.43 W
Cataluña □9	120	42.00 N	2.00 E
Catamarca	188	28.30 S	65.45 W
Catamarca □4	188	27.00 S	67.00 W
Catanduanes Island I	138	13.45 N	124.15 E
Catanduva	190	21.08 S	48.58 W
Catania	122	37.30 N	15.06 E
Catanzaro	122	38.54 N	16.36 E
Catarman	138	12.30 N	124.38 E
Catarroja	120	39.24 N	0.24 W
Catastrophe, Cape ≻	168	34.59 S	136.00 E
Catatumbo ≃	182	9.22 N	71.45 W
Catbalogan	138	11.46 N	124.53 E
Caterham	104	51.17 N	0.04 W
Catete	156	9.06 S	13.43 E
Cathcart	160	32.18 S	27.09 E
Cathedral City	178	33.47 N	116.28 W
Cat Island I	182	24.30 N	75.30 W
Catlettsburg	176	38.25 N	82.36 W
Catlins ≃	170	46.29 S	169.43 E
Catlodge	108	57.00 N	4.15 W
Catnip Mountain ∧	178	41.52 N	119.23 W
Catoche, Cabo ≻	180	21.36 N	87.07 W
Cato Island I	168	23.15 S	155.32 E
Catonsville	176	39.16 N	76.44 W
Catriló	188	36.23 S	63.24 W
Catrine	108	55.30 N	4.20 W
Catskill	176	42.13 N	73.52 W
Catskill Creek ≃	176	42.12 N	73.51 W
Catskill Mountains ⛰	176	42.10 N	74.30 W
Cattaraugus	176	42.20 N	78.52 W
Cattaraugus Creek ≃	176	42.35 N	79.10 W
Catterick	106	54.22 N	1.38 W
Catterick Camp	106	54.22 N	1.43 W
Cattolica	122	43.58 N	12.44 E
Catton	106	54.55 N	2.15 W
Catu	190	12.21 S	38.23 W
Catus	118	44.34 N	1.20 E
Čatyrtaš	126	40.55 N	76.26 E
Cauca ≃	184	8.54 N	74.28 W
Caucasus → Bol'šoj Kavkaz ⛰	126	42.30 N	45.00 E
Cauldcleuch Head ∧	106	55.18 N	2.51 W
Caulkerbush	106	54.54 N	3.40 W
Caúngula	156	8.25 S	18.40 E
Čaunskaja Guba ⊂	128	69.20 N	170.00 E
Cauquenes	188	35.58 S	72.21 W
Caura ≃	184	7.38 N	64.53 W
Caussade	118	44.10 N	1.32 E
Cautín □4	188	39.00 S	72.30 W
Cauto ≃	182	20.33 N	77.15 W
Cauvery ≃	148	11.09 N	79.52 E
Caux, Pays de ←1	118	49.40 N	0.40 E
Cava [de'Tirreni]	122	40.42 N	14.42 E
Cavaillon	118	43.50 N	5.02 E
Cavalaire-sur-Mer	118	43.10 N	6.32 E
Cavalcante	190	13.48 S	47.30 W
Cavalheiro	190	17.15 S	48.02 W
Cavalla (Cavally) ≃	152	4.22 N	7.32 W
Cavalli Islands II	170	34.58 S	173.58 E
Cavan	110	54.00 N	7.21 W
Cavan □6	110	53.55 N	7.30 W
Cave	170	44.19 S	170.57 E
Caveiras ≃	188	27.35 S	50.56 W
Cavendish	168	37.31 S	142.02 E
Cavite	138	14.29 N	120.55 E
Cawdor	108	57.31 N	3.56 W
Cawood	106	53.50 N	1.07 W
Cawston	104	52.46 N	1.10 E
Caxambu	190	21.59 S	44.56 W
Caxias	184	4.50 S	43.21 W
Caxias do Sul	188	29.10 S	51.11 W
Caxito	156	8.33 S	13.36 E
Cayambe	184	0.03 N	78.08 W
Cayambe ∧1	184	0.02 N	77.59 W
Cayenne	184	4.56 N	52.20 W
Cayey	182	18.07 N	66.10 W
Cayman Brac I	182	19.43 N	79.49 W
Cayman Islands □2	180	19.30 N	80.40 W
Cayman Trench ⌁1	90	19.00 N	80.00 W
Cayucos	178	35.27 N	120.54 W
Cayuga	176	42.56 N	79.51 W
Cayuga Heights	176	42.28 N	76.30 W
Cayuga Lake ⊜	176	42.45 N	76.45 W
Cayuta Creek ≃	176	41.59 N	76.30 W
Cazalla de la Sierra	120	37.56 N	5.45 W
Cazaux, Étang de ⊂	118	44.30 N	1.10 W
Cazenovia	176	42.56 N	75.51 W
Cazères	118	43.13 N	1.05 E
Cazombo	156	11.54 S	22.52 E
Cazorla, Sierra de ⛰	120	37.55 N	2.55 W
Cchinvali	126	42.13 N	43.56 E
Cea ≃	120	42.00 N	5.36 W
Ceanannus M ⊤	110	53.44 N	6.53 W
Ceará-Mirim	184	5.38 S	35.26 W
Čeboksary	112	56.09 N	47.15 E
Cebollar	188	29.06 S	66.34 W
Cebreros	120	40.27 N	4.28 W
Cebu	138	10.18 N	123.54 E
Cebu I	138	10.20 N	123.45 E
Cecerleg	132	48.55 N	101.09 E
Čechy □9	116	49.50 N	14.00 E
Cecil Plains	168	27.32 S	151.12 E
Cecina	122	43.19 N	10.31 E
Cedar ≃, Mich., U.S.	176	43.53 N	84.29 W
Cedar ≃, N.Y., U.S.	176	43.51 N	74.11 W
Cedar Creek ≃	178	42.24 N	114.49 W
Cedar Falls	174	42.32 N	92.27 W
Cedar Grove	176	38.13 N	81.26 W
Cedar Lake ⊜	176	46.02 N	78.30 W
Cedar Lake ⊜1	172	53.10 N	100.00 W
Cedar Mountain ∧	178	41.36 N	120.16 W
Cedar Rapids	174	41.59 N	91.40 W
Cedar Springs	176	43.13 N	85.33 W
Cedarville, S. Afr.	160	30.23 S	29.03 E
Cedarville, Calif., U.S.	178	41.32 N	120.10 W
Cedarville, Mich., U.S.	176	46.00 N	84.22 W
Cedarville, N.J., U.S.	176	39.20 N	75.12 W
Cedillo, Embalse de ⊜1	120	39.40 N	7.25 E
Cedros, Isla I	180	28.10 N	115.15 W
Ceduna	164	32.07 S	133.40 E
Cefalù	122	38.02 N	14.01 E
Cefni ≃	106	53.12 N	4.23 W
Čegdomyn	128	51.07 N	133.05 E
Cegléd	116	47.10 N	19.48 E
Ceglie Messapico	122	40.39 N	17.31 E
Cehegín	120	38.06 N	1.48 W
Ceheng	140	25.10 N	105.48 E
Ceiriog ≃	104	52.57 N	3.02 W
Ceirw ≃	104	52.59 N	3.27 W
Cela	156	11.25 S	15.07 E
Čel'abinsk	126	55.10 N	61.24 E
Celaya	180	20.31 N	100.37 W
Cele	146	37.00 N	80.47 E
Celebes → Sulawesi I	142	2.00 S	121.00 E
Celebes Basin ⌁1	94	4.00 N	122.00 E
Celebes Sea ⊤2	142	3.00 N	122.00 E
Čeleken	150	39.26 N	53.07 E
Celina	176	40.33 N	84.34 W
Celinograd	126	51.10 N	71.30 E
Celje	122	46.14 N	15.16 E
Čelkar	126	47.50 N	59.36 E
Cellar Head ≻	108	58.26 N	6.10 W
Celldömölk	116	47.16 N	17.09 E
Celle	116	52.37 N	10.05 E
Celorico da Beira	120	40.38 N	7.23 W
Čel'uskin, Mys ≻	128	77.45 N	104.20 E
Cemaes Head ≻	104	52.07 N	4.44 W
Čemerno	122	43.11 N	18.37 E
Cemmaes	104	52.37 N	3.42 W
Cenderawasih, Teluk ⊂	166	2.30 S	135.20 E
Centenario	188	38.48 S	68.08 W
Centenário do Sul	190	22.48 S	51.37 W
Centerburg	176	40.18 N	82.42 W
Center Moriches	176	40.48 N	72.48 W
Centerville, Ind., U.S.	176	39.49 N	85.00 W
Centerville, Pa., U.S.	176	41.44 N	79.46 W
Cento	122	44.43 N	11.17 E
Central □4, Kenya	158	0.45 S	37.00 E
Central □4, Malawi	158	13.00 S	34.00 E
Central □4, Scot., U.K.	108	56.05 N	4.20 W
Central □4, Zam.	158	15.00 S	29.00 E
Central □5, Bots.	160	21.30 S	26.00 E
Central □5, Para.	188	25.30 S	57.30 W
Central, Cordillera ⛰, Bol.	184	18.30 S	64.55 W
Central, Cordillera ⛰, Col.	184	5.00 N	75.00 W
Central, Cordillera ⛰, Perú	184	8.00 S	77.00 W
Central, Cordillera ⛰, P.R.	182	18.08 N	66.35 W
Central, Cordillera ⛰, Rep. Dom.	182	19.15 N	71.00 W
Central, Massif ⛰	118	45.00 N	3.10 E
Central, Planalto ⛰1	184	18.00 S	47.00 W
Central, Sistema ⛰	120	40.30 N	5.00 W
Central African Empire □1	154	7.00 N	21.00 E
Central City	176	40.06 N	78.48 W
Centralia	174	46.43 N	122.58 W
Central Lake	176	45.04 N	85.16 W
Central Makrān Range ⛰	146	26.40 N	64.30 E
Central Mount Wedge ∧	164	22.51 S	131.50 E
Central Pacific Basin ⌁1	96	7.00 N	176.00 W
Central Point	178	42.23 N	122.57 W
Central Range ⛰, Leso.	160	29.35 S	28.35 E
Central Range ⛰, Pap. N. Gui.	166	5.00 S	142.30 E
Central Square	176	43.17 N	76.09 W
Central Valley	178	40.41 N	122.22 W
Centreville, Md., U.S.	176	39.03 N	76.04 W
Centreville, Mich., U.S.	176	41.55 N	85.32 W
Century	176	39.06 N	80.11 W
Cepu	142	7.09 S	111.35 E
Ceram → Seram I	166	3.00 S	129.00 E
Ceram Sea → Seram, Laut ⊤2	138	2.30 S	128.00 E
Cère ≃	118	44.55 N	1.53 E
Čeremchovo	128	53.09 N	103.05 E
Čerepanovo	128	54.13 N	83.22 E
Čerepovec	130	59.08 N	37.54 E
Ceres, Arg.	188	29.50 S	61.55 W
Ceres, S. Afr.	160	33.21 S	19.18 E
Cerf Island I	156	9.32 S	50.59 E
Ceri ≃	104	52.03 N	4.29 W
Cerignola	122	41.16 N	15.54 E
Cérilly	118	46.37 N	2.49 E
Cerisiers	118	48.08 N	3.29 E
Čerkassy	126	49.26 N	32.04 E
Čerkessk	126	44.14 N	42.04 E
Çerkezköy	124	41.17 N	28.00 E
Cerknica	122	45.48 N	14.22 E
Čerlak	128	54.09 N	74.48 E
Čern'achovsk (Insterburg)	130	54.38 N	21.49 E
Černá hora ∧	116	48.58 N	13.48 E
Cernăuţi → Černovcy	124	48.18 N	25.56 E
Cernavodă	124	44.21 N	28.01 E
Cernay	118	47.49 N	7.10 E
Cerne Abbas	104	50.49 N	2.29 W
Černigov	126	51.30 N	31.18 E
Černogorsk	128	53.49 N	91.18 E
Černovcy	124	48.18 N	25.56 E
Černyševskij	128	63.00 N	112.15 E
Cerralvo, Isla I	180	24.17 N	109.52 W
Cerrigydrudion	104	53.02 N	3.33 W
Cërrik	124	41.02 N	19.57 E
Cerrillos	188	24.55 S	65.29 W
Cerritos	180	22.26 N	100.17 W
Cerro Azul, Arg.	188	27.33 S	55.29 W
Cêrro Azul, Bra.	188	24.50 S	49.15 W
Cerro de Pasco	184	10.41 S	76.16 W
Cêrro Largo	188	28.09 S	54.45 W
Cerro Moreno	188	23.26 S	70.26 W
Cerro Prieto	178	32.27 N	115.17 W
Čerskij	128	68.45 N	161.45 E
Čerskogo, Chrebet ⛰	128	52.00 N	114.00 E
Červen Brjag	124	43.16 N	24.06 E
Cervera del Río Alhama	120	42.01 N	1.57 W
Cervera de Pisuerga	120	42.52 N	4.30 W
Cervia	122	44.15 N	12.22 E
Cervione	122	42.20 N	9.31 E
Červonograd	126	50.24 N	24.14 E
César ≃	182	9.00 N	73.58 W
Cesena	122	44.08 N	12.15 E
Cēsis	130	57.18 N	25.15 E
Česká Lípa	116	50.42 N	14.32 E
Česká Socialistická Republika □3	116	49.40 N	15.10 E
Česká Třebová	116	49.54 N	16.27 E
České Budějovice	116	48.59 N	14.28 E
Českomoravská vrchovina ⛰1	116	49.20 N	15.30 E
Český Těšín	116	49.45 N	18.37 E
Češskaja Guba ⊂	112	67.30 N	46.30 E
Cessnock	168	32.50 S	151.21 E
Cestos ≃	152	5.40 N	9.10 W
Cetinje	124	42.23 N	18.55 E
Ceuta	120	35.53 N	5.19 W
Cévennes ←1	118	44.00 N	3.30 E
Ceyhan	150	37.04 N	35.47 E
Ceylon → Sri Lanka □1	148	7.00 N	81.00 E
Chabanais	118	45.52 N	0.43 E
Chabarovo	126	69.39 N	60.24 E
Chabarovsk	128	48.27 N	135.06 E
Chabás	188	33.15 S	61.20 W
Chabeuil	118	44.54 N	5.01 E
Chabjuwardoo Bay ⊂	164	22.57 S	113.48 E
Chablais ←1	118	46.18 N	6.39 E
Chacabuco	188	34.38 S	60.29 W
Chacewater	104	50.15 N	5.10 W
Chachani, Nevado ∧	184	16.12 S	71.32 W
Chachapoyas	184	6.10 S	77.50 W
Chachoengsao	140	13.42 N	101.05 E
Chaco □4	188	26.25 S	60.30 W
Chaco Austral ←1	188	26.30 S	61.30 W
Chaco Boreal ←1	188	23.00 S	60.00 W
Chaco Central ←1	188	25.00 S	59.45 W
Chad □1	154	15.00 N	19.00 E
Chad, Lake (Lac Tchad) ⊜	154	13.20 N	14.00 E
Chadderton	106	53.33 N	2.08 W
Chadileuvú ≃	188	37.46 S	66.00 W
Chadiza	158	14.05 S	32.28 E
Chadron	174	42.50 N	102.60 W
Chāgai Hills ⛰2	150	29.30 N	64.15 E
'Chaghcharān	146	34.32 N	65.15 E
Chagny	118	46.55 N	4.45 E
Chaguaramas	182	9.20 N	66.16 W
Chāh Bahār	150	25.18 N	60.37 E
Chaibāsā	148	22.34 N	85.49 E
Chaidamupendi ⏝1	146	37.00 N	95.00 E
Chaillé-les-Marais	118	46.24 N	1.01 W
Chaîne Annamitique ⛰	140	17.00 N	106.00 E
Chaîne des Mongos ⛰	154	8.40 N	22.25 E
Chaiqiao	136	29.51 N	121.56 E
Chaiyaphum	138	15.48 N	102.02 E
Chajarí	188	30.45 S	57.59 W
Chajian	136	32.40 N	118.46 E
Chaka	158	4.49 N	31.14 E
Chake Chake	158	5.15 S	39.46 E
Chak Jhumra	149	31.34 N	73.11 E
Chakwāl	149	32.56 N	72.52 E
Chalais	118	45.16 N	0.02 E
Chalbi Desert ←2	154	3.00 N	37.20 E
Chalfont Saint Peter	104	51.37 N	0.33 W
Chalford	104	51.45 N	2.09 W
Chaling	136	26.47 N	113.33 E
Chālisgaon	148	20.28 N	75.01 E
Chalk River	176	46.01 N	77.27 W
Chal'mer-Ju	112	67.58 N	64.50 E
Châlons-sur-Marne	118	48.57 N	4.22 E
Chalon-sur-Saône	118	46.47 N	4.51 E
Châlus, Fr.	118	45.39 N	0.59 E
Chālūs, Īrān	150	36.38 N	51.26 E
Cham	116	49.13 N	12.41 E
Chaman	146	30.55 N	66.22 E
Chamba	149	32.34 N	76.08 E
Chambal ≃	146	26.30 N	79.15 E
Chamberlain	174	43.49 N	99.20 W
Chamberlain ≃	166	15.08 S	128.06 E
Chambersburg	176	39.56 N	77.39 W
Chambéry	118	45.34 N	5.56 E
Chambeshi ≃	158	11.21 S	30.37 E
Chambi, Djebel ∧	152	35.11 N	8.42 E
Chambishi	158	12.40 S	28.03 E
Chambley-Bussières	118	49.03 N	5.54 E
Chambon-sur-Voueize	118	46.11 N	2.25 E
Chamical (Gobernador Gordillo)	188	30.22 S	66.19 W
Chamonix-Mont-Blanc	118	45.55 N	6.52 E
Chāmpa	148	22.03 N	82.39 E
Champagne □9	118	49.00 N	4.30 E
Champagne Castle ∧	160	29.06 S	29.20 E
Champagnole	118	46.45 N	5.55 E
Champaign	174	40.07 N	88.14 W
Champaquí, Cerro ∧	188	31.58 S	64.56 W
Champasak	140	14.53 N	105.52 E
Champdeniers	118	46.29 N	0.24 W
Champdoré, Lac ⊜	172	55.55 N	65.49 W
Champéry	118	46.10 N	6.52 E
Champion	176	41.17 N	80.51 W
Champlain	176	44.59 N	73.27 W
Champlain, Lake ⊜	176	44.45 N	73.15 W
Champlitte-et-le-Prélot	118	47.37 N	5.31 E
Champotón	180	19.21 N	90.43 W
Chānanwāla	149	30.22 N	73.57 E
Chañaral	188	26.21 S	70.37 W
Chanch	132	51.30 N	100.40 E
Chanchelulla Peak ∧	178	40.28 N	122.59 W
Chanco	188	35.44 S	72.32 W
Chandalar ≃	172	66.36 N	145.48 W
Chandausi	146	28.27 N	78.46 E
Chandīgarh	149	30.44 N	76.55 E
Chandler's Ford	104	50.59 N	1.23 W
Chandos Lake ⊜	176	44.49 N	78.00 W
Chāndpur	146	23.13 N	90.39 E
Chandrapur	148	19.57 N	79.18 E
Chandyga	128	62.40 N	135.36 E
Chang, Ko I	140	12.05 N	102.20 E
Changajn Nuruu ⛰	132	47.30 N	100.00 E
Changanācheri	148	9.28 N	76.33 E
Changane ≃	160	24.43 S	33.32 E
Changbaishan ⛰	132	42.05 N	128.00 E
Changchou → Zhangzhou	136	24.33 N	117.39 E
Changchow → Changzhou	136	31.47 N	119.57 E
Changchun	132	43.53 N	125.19 E
Changde	132	28.55 N	111.38 E
Changdu	132	31.11 N	97.15 E
Changgou	136	34.15 N	113.50 E
Changhua, T'aiwan	136	24.05 N	120.32 E
Changhua, Zhg.	136	30.11 N	119.13 E
Changji	132	44.01 N	87.19 E
Changjiang, Zhg.	136	25.52 N	116.20 E
Changjiang, Zhg.	140	19.17 N	109.02 E
Changjiang (Yangtze) ≃	132	31.48 N	121.10 E
Changle	136	26.00 N	119.31 E
Changli	132	39.43 N	119.11 E
Changlinhe	136	31.40 N	117.29 E
Changning	140	24.55 N	99.35 E
Changokurt	126	61.58 N	64.18 E
Changsha	136	28.11 N	113.01 E
Changshan	136	28.55 N	118.30 E
Changshu	136	31.39 N	120.45 E
Changxing	136	31.01 N	119.54 E
Changzhi	132	36.11 N	113.08 E
Changzhou (Changchow)	136	31.47 N	119.57 E
Chanka, Ozero (Xingkathu) ⊜	132	45.00 N	132.24 E
Channapatna	148	12.39 N	77.13 E
Channel Country ←1	168	24.45 S	141.00 E
Channel Islands II, Eur.	102	49.20 N	2.20 W
Channel Islands II, Calif., U.S.	178	34.00 N	120.00 W
Channel-Port-aux-Basques	172	47.34 N	59.09 W
Chantada	120	42.37 N	7.46 W
Chantajskoje, Ozero ⊜	128	68.20 N	91.00 E
Chanthaburi	140	12.36 N	102.09 E
Chantilly	118	49.12 N	2.28 E
Chantrey Inlet ⊂	172	67.48 N	96.20 W
Chanty-Mansijsk	128	61.00 N	69.06 E
Chanute	174	37.41 N	95.27 W
Chaoan	136	23.41 N	116.38 E
Ch'aochou	136	22.33 N	120.32 E
Chaohu ⊜	136	31.31 N	117.33 E
Chao Phraya ≃	140	13.32 N	100.36 E
Chaoxian	136	31.36 N	117.52 E
Chaoyang, Zhg.	132	41.35 N	128.08 E
Chaoyang, Zhg.	136	23.17 N	116.37 E
Chapala, Lago de ⊜	180	20.15 N	103.00 W
Chaparra	182	21.10 N	76.29 W
Chaparral	184	3.43 N	75.28 W
Chapčeranga	128	49.42 N	112.24 E
Chapecó	188	27.06 S	52.36 W
Chapel-en-le-Frith	106	53.20 N	1.54 W
Chapelfell Top ∧	106	54.41 N	2.13 W
Chapel Point ≻	104	50.16 N	4.46 W
Chapleau	172	47.50 N	83.24 W
Chapman, Cape ≻	172	69.12 N	88.59 W
Chapmanville	176	37.58 N	82.01 W
Chāpra, Bhārat	144	23.31 N	88.33 E
Chāpra, Bhārat	146	25.46 N	84.45 E
Chapultepec, Méx.	178	31.50 N	116.38 W
Chapultepec, Méx.	178	32.22 N	115.05 W
Chapultepec ∧	174	23.27 N	103.04 W
Char ≃	104	50.44 N	2.53 W
Charadai	188	27.40 S	59.55 W
Charata	188	27.15 S	61.15 W
Charbala	128	64.07 N	120.19 E
Chard	104	50.53 N	2.58 W
Chardon	176	41.35 N	81.12 W
Charente □5	118	45.40 N	0.10 E
Charente ≃	118	45.57 N	1.05 W
Charente-Maritime □5	118	45.30 N	0.45 W
Chari ≃	154	12.58 N	14.31 E
Chārīkār	146	35.01 N	69.11 E
Charing	104	51.13 N	0.48 E
Charity	184	7.24 N	58.36 W
Charkhi Dādri	149	28.37 N	76.16 E
Char'kov	126	50.00 N	36.15 E
Charlbury	104	51.53 N	1.29 W
Charleroi	116	50.25 N	4.26 E
Charles City	174	43.04 N	92.40 W
Charles Island I	172	62.40 N	74.15 W
Charles Point ≻	166	12.23 S	130.36 E
Charles Sound ⊍	170	45.02 S	167.04 E
Charleston, N.Z.	170	41.54 S	171.26 E
Charleston, S.C., U.S.	174	32.48 N	79.57 W
Charleston, W. Va., U.S.	174	38.21 N	81.38 W
Charleston Peak ∧	178	36.16 N	115.42 W
Charleston Rise ⌁3	90	30.00 N	75.00 W
Charlestown, Eire	110	53.57 N	8.49 W
Charlestown, St. K.-N.	182	17.08 N	62.37 W
Charlestown, S. Afr.	160	27.30 S	29.55 E
Charlestown, N.H., U.S.	176	43.14 N	72.26 W
Charles Town, W. Va., U.S.	176	39.17 N	77.52 W
Charlesville	156	5.27 S	20.58 E
Charleville	168	26.24 S	146.15 E
Charleville-Mézières	118	49.46 N	4.43 E
Charlevoix	176	45.19 N	85.16 W
Charlevoix, Lake ⊜	176	45.15 N	85.08 W
Charlieu	118	46.10 N	4.10 E
Charlotte, Mich., U.S.	176	42.36 N	84.50 W
Charlotte, N.C., U.S.	174	35.14 N	80.50 W
Charlotte Amalie	182	18.21 N	64.56 W
Charlotte Harbor ⊂	182	26.45 N	82.12 W
Charlottenberg	114	59.53 N	12.17 E
Charlottesville	174	38.02 N	78.29 W
Charlottetown	172	46.14 N	63.08 W
Charlton	168	36.16 S	143.21 E
Charlton Island I	172	52.00 N	79.30 W
Charlton Kings	104	51.53 N	2.03 W
Charmes	118	48.22 N	6.17 E
Charminster	104	50.43 N	2.28 W
Charmouth	104	50.45 N	2.55 W
Charnley ≃	166	16.25 S	124.57 E
Charnwood Forest ←3	104	52.43 N	1.15 W
Charolles	118	46.26 N	4.17 E
Chārsadda	149	34.09 N	71.44 E
Charters Towers	168	20.05 S	146.16 E
Chartres	118	48.27 N	1.30 E
Char Us Nuur ⊜	132	48.00 N	92.10 E
Chasavjurt	126	43.15 N	46.37 E
Chascomús	188	35.35 S	58.00 W
Chase, Mount ∧	176	46.07 N	68.29 W
Chasefu Mission	158	11.55 S	33.08 E
Chasetown	104	52.41 N	1.56 W
Chaslands Mistake ≻	170	46.38 S	169.22 E
Chatanbulag	132	43.11 N	109.10 E
Chatanga	128	71.58 N	102.30 E
Chatanga ≃	128	72.55 N	106.00 E
Chatangskij Zaliv ⊂	128	73.30 N	109.00 E
Chatanika ≃	172	65.04 N	149.18 W
Châteaubriant	118	47.43 N	1.23 W
Château-Chinon	118	47.04 N	3.56 E
Château d'Oex	118	46.28 N	7.08 E
Château-du-Loir	118	47.42 N	0.25 E
Châteaudun	118	48.05 N	1.20 E
Chateaugay	176	44.56 N	74.05 W
Château-Gontier	118	47.50 N	0.42 W
Château-la-Vallière	118	47.33 N	0.19 E
Châteaulin	118	48.12 N	4.05 W
Châteauneuf	118	43.23 N	5.10 E
Châteauneuf-sur-Charente	118	45.36 N	0.03 W
Châteauneuf-sur-Loire	118	47.52 N	2.14 E
Châteauneuf-sur-Sarthe	118	47.41 N	0.30 W
Châteauroux	118	46.49 N	1.42 E
Château-Salins	118	48.49 N	6.30 E
Château-Thierry	118	49.03 N	3.24 E
Châtellerault	118	46.49 N	0.33 E
Châtel-sur-Moselle	118	48.18 N	6.24 E
Chatgal	132	50.26 N	100.07 E
Chatham, N.B., Can.	172	47.02 N	65.28 W
Chatham, Ont., Can.	172	42.24 N	82.11 W
Chatham, Eng., U.K.	104	51.23 N	0.32 E
Chatham, Mass., U.S.	176	41.41 N	69.58 W
Chatham, N.Y., U.S.	176	42.22 N	73.36 W
Chatham Island I	96	43.55 S	176.30 W
Chatham Rise ⌁3	96	43.30 S	178.00 W
Chatham Strait ⊍	172	57.30 N	134.45 W
Châtillon-en-Bazois	118	47.03 N	3.49 E
Châtillon-sur-Seine	118	47.51 N	4.33 E
Chatrapur	144	19.21 N	85.00 E
Chatsworth, Austl.	168	21.58 S	140.19 E
Chatsworth, Rh.	158	19.38 S	31.13 E
Chattahoochee ≃	174	30.52 N	84.57 W
Chattanooga	174	35.03 N	85.19 W
Chatteris	104	52.27 N	0.03 E
Chatton	106	55.33 N	1.55 W
Chatyrka	128	62.03 N	175.15 E
Chaudes-Aigues	118	44.51 N	3.00 E
Chauk	140	20.54 N	94.50 E
Chaumont	118	48.07 N	5.08 E
Chaumont-en-Vexin	118	49.16 N	1.53 E
Chaumont-Porcien	118	49.39 N	4.15 E
Chauncey	176	39.24 N	82.08 W
Chauny	118	49.37 N	3.13 E
Chau-phu	140	10.42 N	105.07 E
Chaussin	118	46.58 N	5.25 E
Chautauqua Lake ⊜	176	42.12 N	79.27 W
Chauvigny	118	46.34 N	0.39 E
Chavakkad	148	10.32 N	76.06 E
Chavanges	118	48.31 N	4.34 E
Chaves	120	41.44 N	7.28 W
Chayuanpu	136	27.40 N	112.57 E
Chazy	176	44.53 N	73.26 W
Cheadle	104	52.59 N	1.59 W
Cheadle Hulme	106	53.22 N	2.12 W
Cheat, Shavers Fork ≃	176	39.06 N	79.33 W
Cheb	116	50.01 N	12.25 E
Cheboygan	176	45.39 N	84.29 W
Chech, Erg ←2	152	25.00 N	2.15 W
Chechaouene	120	35.10 N	5.16 W
Cheddar	104	51.17 N	2.46 W
Cheduba Island I	140	18.48 N	93.38 E
Cheektowaga	176	42.55 N	78.46 W
Cheepie	168	26.39 S	145.01 E
Cheerchenghe ≃	132	39.25 N	88.20 E
Chef-Boutonne	118	46.07 N	0.04 W
Cheiron, Cimedu ∧	118	43.49 N	6.58 E
Cheju	132	33.31 N	126.32 E
Cheju-do I	132	33.20 N	126.30 E
Chelghoum el Aïd	120	36.10 N	6.10 E
Chélia, Djebel ∧	152	35.19 N	6.42 E
Chellaston	104	52.53 N	1.27 W
Chełm	116	51.10 N	23.28 E
Chelmer ≃	104	51.48 N	0.40 E
Chełmno	116	53.22 N	18.26 E
Chelmsford	104	51.44 N	0.28 E
Chełmża	116	53.12 N	18.37 E
Chelsea, Mich., U.S.	176	42.19 N	84.01 W
Chelsea, Vt., U.S.	176	43.59 N	72.27 W
Cheltenham	104	51.54 N	2.04 W
Chelyan	176	38.12 N	81.30 W
Chemax	182	20.39 N	87.56 W
Chemillé	118	47.13 N	0.44 W
Chemnitz → Karl-Marx-Stadt	116	50.50 N	12.55 E
Chemult	178	43.13 N	121.47 W
Chemung Lake ⊜	176	44.25 N	78.22 W
Chenāb ≃	149	29.23 N	71.02 E
Chenachane	152	26.00 N	4.15 E
Chenango ≃	176	42.05 N	75.55 W
Chenango Bridge	176	42.10 N	75.52 W
Chencun	136	22.58 N	113.13 E
Chendai	136	23.48 N	117.24 E
Chénéville	176	45.53 N	75.03 W
Cheney	174	47.29 N	117.34 W
Chengannur	148	9.20 N	76.38 E
Chengde	132	40.58 N	117.53 E
Chengdu	132	30.39 N	104.04 E
Chenghai	136	23.30 N	116.46 E
Chengjiang	140	24.45 N	102.54 E
Chengmai	140	19.48 N	110.02 E
Chengshanjiao ≻	132	37.23 N	122.39 E
Chengtu → Chengdu	132	30.39 N	104.04 E
Chenmu	136	31.10 N	120.53 E
Chepén	184	7.15 S	79.25 W
Chepes	188	31.21 S	66.40 W
Chépica	188	34.44 S	71.17 W
Chepo	182	9.11 N	79.06 W
Chepstow	104	51.39 N	2.41 W
Cher □5	118	47.05 N	2.30 E
Cher ≃	118	47.21 N	0.29 E
Cherbourg	118	49.39 N	1.39 W
Cherchell	120	36.36 N	2.12 E
Cherepovets → Čerepovec	130	59.08 N	37.54 E
Chergui, Chott ech ⊜	152	34.21 N	0.30 E
Cheribon → Cirebon	142	6.44 S	108.34 E
Cherokee Sound	182	26.17 N	77.02 W
Cherquenco	188	38.41 S	72.00 W
Cherrabun	164	18.29 S	125.19 E
Cherrapunji	144	25.17 N	91.44 E
Cherry Hill	176	39.55 N	75.01 W
Cherson	126	46.38 N	32.35 E
Chertsey	104	51.24 N	0.30 W
Cherwell ≃	104	51.44 N	1.15 W
Chesaning	176	43.11 N	84.07 W
Chesapeake	174	36.43 N	76.15 W
Chesapeake Bay ⊂	174	38.40 N	76.25 W
Chesapeake Beach	176	38.41 N	76.32 W
Chesapeake City	176	39.32 N	75.49 W
Chesham	104	51.43 N	0.38 W
Cheshire	176	42.34 N	73.10 W
Cheshire □6	102	53.23 N	2.30 W
Cheshire Plain ⏝	106	53.17 N	2.40 W
Cheshunt	104	51.43 N	0.02 W
Chesil Beach ⩡2	104	50.38 N	2.33 W
Chesley	176	44.17 N	81.05 W
Chest Creek ≃	176	40.53 N	78.44 W
Chester, Eng., U.K.	106	53.12 N	2.54 W
Chester, Calif., U.S.	178	40.19 N	121.14 W
Chester, Pa., U.S.	176	39.51 N	75.21 W
Chester, Vt., U.S.	176	43.16 N	72.36 W
Chesterfield	106	53.15 N	1.25 W
Chesterfield, Île I	156	16.20 S	43.58 E
Chesterfield, Îles II	162	19.30 S	158.00 E
Chesterfield Inlet	172	63.21 N	90.42 W
Chesterfield Inlet ⊂	172	63.25 N	90.45 W
Chesterhill	176	39.29 N	81.52 W
Chester-le-Street	106	54.52 N	1.34 W
Chestertown	176	39.13 N	76.04 W
Chesterville	176	45.06 N	75.14 W
Chesuncook Lake ⊜	176	46.00 N	69.20 W
Chet ≃	104	52.33 N	1.32 E
Cheta ≃	128	71.54 N	102.06 E
Chetco ≃	178	42.03 N	124.16 W
Cheval Blanc, Pointe du ≻	182	19.41 N	73.27 W
Chevington Drift	106	55.17 N	1.36 W
Cheviot, N.Z.	170	42.49 S	173.16 E
Cheviot, Ohio, U.S.	176	39.11 N	84.35 W
Chew Bahir (Lake Stefanie) ⊜	154	4.40 N	36.50 E
Chew Magna	104	51.22 N	2.35 W
Cheyenne	174	41.08 N	104.49 W
Cheyenne ≃	174	44.40 N	101.15 W
Cheyne Bay ⊂	164	34.35 S	118.50 E
Chezhou	136	25.48 N	112.59 E
Chhatarpur	146	24.55 N	79.36 E
Chheharta	149	31.38 N	74.48 E
Chhindwāra	146	22.04 N	78.56 E
Chi ≃	140	15.11 N	104.43 E
Chiai	136	23.29 N	120.27 E
Chiali	136	23.10 N	120.11 E
Chiamboni, Ras ≻	158	1.38 S	41.36 E
Chian → Ji'an	136	27.07 N	114.58 E
Chiang Khan	140	17.52 N	101.36 E
Chiang Mai	140	18.47 N	98.59 E
Chiang Rai	140	19.54 N	99.50 E
Chiari	122	45.32 N	9.56 E
Chiavari	122	44.19 N	9.19 E
Chiba	134	35.36 N	140.07 E
Chibi	158	20.19 S	30.30 E
Chibiribira Falls ↳	158	21.14 S	32.20 E
Chibougamau	172	49.55 N	74.22 W
Chibuto	160	24.44 S	33.33 E
Chibuzhangchuhu ⊜	146	33.25 N	90.15 E
Chicago	174	41.53 N	87.38 W
Chicapa ≃	156	6.26 S	20.47 E
Chichagof Island I	172	57.30 N	135.30 W
Chīchāwatni	149	30.32 N	72.42 E
Chichester	104	50.50 N	0.48 W
Chichester Range ⛰	164	22.00 S	118.50 E
Chichi	136	23.50 N	120.46 E
Chichibu	134	35.59 N	139.05 E
Chichiriviche	182	10.56 N	68.16 W
Chichishima-rettō II	96	27.06 N	142.12 E
Chickasha	174	35.02 N	97.58 W
Chickerell	104	50.37 N	2.30 W
Chiclana de la Frontera	120	36.25 N	6.08 W
Chiclayo	184	6.46 S	79.50 W
Chico	178	39.44 N	121.50 W
Chico ≃, Arg.	186	50.00 S	68.30 W
Chico ≃, Arg.	186	43.50 S	66.25 W
Chicoa	158	15.37 S	32.24 E
Chicopee	176	42.10 N	72.36 W
Chicoutimi	172	48.26 N	71.04 W
Chidambaram	148	11.24 N	79.42 E
Chidley, Cape ≻	172	60.23 N	64.26 W
Chiemsee ⊜	116	47.54 N	12.29 E
Chiengi	158	8.39 S	29.10 E
Chieri	122	45.01 N	7.49 E
Chieti	122	42.21 N	14.10 E
Chieveley	104	51.27 N	1.19 W
Chifeng	132	42.18 N	119.00 E
Chigasaki	134	35.19 N	139.24 E
Chigwell	104	51.38 N	0.05 E
Chihli, Gulf of → Bohai ⊂	132	38.30 N	120.00 E
Ch'ihu, T'aiwan	136	23.58 N	120.28 E
Chihu, Zhg.	136	24.07 N	117.51 E
Chihuahua	180	28.38 N	106.05 W
Chik Ballāpur	148	13.28 N	77.44 E
Chikmagalūr	148	13.19 N	75.47 E
Chikoa	158	13.24 S	32.07 E
Chikugo ≃	134	33.09 N	130.21 E
Chikuma ≃	134	36.59 N	138.35 E
Chilakalūrupet	148	16.05 N	80.10 E
Chilanga	158	15.34 S	28.17 E
Chilās	144	35.26 N	74.05 E
Chilcotin ≃	172	51.45 N	122.24 W
Chilcott Island I	168	16.58 S	149.58 E
Childers	168	25.14 S	152.17 E
Childress	174	34.25 N	100.13 W
Chile	188	25.09 S	69.54 W
Chile □1	186	30.00 S	71.00 W
Chile Chico	186	46.33 S	71.44 W
Chilecito	188	29.10 S	67.30 W
Chile Rise ⌁3	92	42.00 S	90.00 W
Chilete	184	7.14 S	78.51 W
Chilham	104	51.15 N	0.57 E
Chilia, Braţul ≃1	124	45.18 N	29.40 E
Chililabombwe (Bancroft)	158	12.18 S	27.43 E
Chilka Lake ⊜	148	19.46 N	85.20 E
Chilko Lake ⊜	172	51.20 N	124.05 W
Chillagoe	168	17.09 S	144.32 E
Chillán	188	36.36 S	72.07 W
Chillicothe, Mo., U.S.	174	39.48 N	93.33 W
Chillicothe, Ohio, U.S.	176	39.20 N	82.59 W
Chilliwack	172	49.10 N	121.57 W
Chilloa, Ciénaga ⊜	182	9.10 N	74.05 W
Chiloé, Isla de I	186	42.30 S	73.55 W
Chilok	128	51.21 N	110.28 E
Chilok ≃	128	51.19 N	106.59 E
Chilonga	158	12.03 S	31.21 E
Chiloquin	178	42.35 N	121.52 W
Chilpancingo	180	17.33 N	99.30 W
Chiltern Hills ⛰2	104	51.42 N	0.48 W
Chiluage	156	9.30 S	21.47 E
Chilubula Mission	158	10.09 S	31.00 E
Chilung	136	25.08 N	121.44 E
Chilwa, Lake ⊜	158	15.12 S	35.50 E
Chimbarongo	188	34.42 S	71.03 W
Chimbas	188	31.28 S	68.30 W
Chimborazo ∧1	184	1.28 S	78.48 W
Chimbote	184	9.05 S	78.36 W
Chimichagua	182	9.15 N	73.49 W
Chimkent → Čimkent	126	42.18 N	69.36 E
Chimpembe	158	9.31 S	29.33 E
Chin □8	140	22.00 N	93.30 E
China □1	132	35.00 N	105.00 E
China Lake ⊜	178	35.46 N	117.39 W
Chinandega	182	12.37 N	87.09 W
Chincha, Islas de II	184	13.39 S	76.24 W
Chincha Alta	184	13.27 S	76.08 W
Chinchaga ≃	172	58.50 N	118.20 W
Chinchiang → Quanzhou	136	24.54 N	118.35 E
Chinchilla	168	26.45 S	150.38 E
Chinchón	120	40.08 N	3.25 W
Chinchorro, Banco ⌁4	180	18.35 N	87.20 W
Chincilla de Monte Aragón	120	38.55 N	1.55 W
Chincolco	188	32.13 S	70.50 W
Chincoteague	176	37.56 N	75.23 W
Chinde	160	18.37 S	36.24 E
Chindwin ≃	140	21.26 N	95.15 E
Ch'ingchiang → Huaiyin	136	33.35 N	119.02 E
Chingleput	148	12.42 N	79.59 E
Chingola	158	12.32 S	27.52 E
Chingoni	161a	12.48 S	45.08 E
Ch'ingshui	136	24.15 N	120.35 E
Chinguetti	152	20.27 N	12.22 W
Chinhae	132	35.09 N	128.40 E
Chin Hills ⛰2	140	22.30 N	93.30 E
Chiniot	149	31.43 N	72.59 E
Chinju	132	35.11 N	128.05 E
Chinkiang → Zhenjiang	136	32.13 N	119.26 E
Chinko ≃	154	4.50 N	23.53 E
Chinkuashih	136	25.08 N	121.51 E
Chinmen	136	24.27 N	118.21 E
Chinnor	104	51.43 N	0.56 W
Chino	178	34.01 N	117.42 W
Chinon	118	47.10 N	0.15 E
Chinsali	158	10.34 S	32.03 E
Chintāmani	148	13.24 N	78.04 E
Chinú	182	9.06 N	75.24 W
Chioggia	122	45.13 N	12.17 E
Chios → Khíos I	124	38.22 N	26.00 E
Chipata (Fort Jameson)	158	13.39 S	32.40 E
Chippenham	104	51.28 N	2.07 W
Chippewa ≃, Mich., U.S.	176	43.35 N	84.17 W
Chippewa ≃, Wis., U.S.	174	44.25 N	92.10 W
Chippewa Falls	174	44.56 N	91.24 W
Chipping Campden	104	52.03 N	1.46 W
Chipping Norton	104	51.56 N	1.32 W
Chipping Ongar	104	51.43 N	0.15 E
Chipping Sodbury	104	51.33 N	2.24 W
Chiquimula	180	14.48 N	89.33 W
Chiquinquirá	184	5.37 N	73.50 W
Chīrāla	148	15.49 N	80.21 E
Chiramba	158	16.55 S	34.39 E
Chire (Shire) ≃	158	17.42 S	35.19 E
Chiredzi	158	21.03 S	31.45 E
Chirfa	152	20.57 N	12.21 E
Chirgis Nuur ⊜	132	49.12 N	93.24 E
Chiricahua Peak ∧	174	31.52 N	109.20 W
Chirigua ≃	182	8.54 N	67.58 W
Chiriguaná	182	9.22 N	73.36 W
Chiriquí, Golfo de ⊂	180	8.00 N	82.20 W
Chiriquí, Laguna de ⊂	182	9.02 N	82.00 W
Chiriquí, Volcán de (Volcán Barú) ∧1	182	8.49 N	82.32 W
Chiriquí Grande	182	8.57 N	82.07 W
Chirk	104	52.56 N	3.03 W
Chirnside	108	55.48 N	2.13 W
Chiromo	158	16.33 S	35.08 E
Chirripó ≃	182	10.41 N	83.41 W
Chirripó, Cerro ∧	182	9.29 N	83.29 W
Chisamba	158	14.58 S	28.23 E
Chiseldon	104	51.31 N	1.44 W
Ch'ishan	136	22.53 N	120.29 E
Chisholm	176	44.29 N	70.12 W
Chishtiān Mandi	149	29.48 N	72.52 E
Chitado	156	17.20 S	13.54 E
Chita-hantō ≻1	134	34.50 N	136.53 E
Chitembo	156	13.34 S	16.40 E
Chitipa	158	9.43 S	33.16 E
Chitorgarh	146	24.53 N	74.38 E
Chitose	134a	42.49 N	141.39 E
Chitradurga	148	14.14 N	76.24 E
Chitrāl	144	35.51 N	71.47 E
Chitré	180	7.58 N	80.26 W
Chittagong	146	22.20 N	91.50 E
Chittering	164	31.29 S	116.06 E
Chittoor	148	13.12 N	79.07 E
Chittūr	148	10.42 N	76.45 E
Chiuchiu	188	22.21 S	68.39 W
Chiumbe ≃	156	7.00 S	21.12 E
Chiúta	158	15.34 S	33.17 E
Chiuta, Lake ⊜	158	14.55 S	35.50 E
Chiva	126	41.24 N	60.22 E
Chivacoa	182	10.10 N	68.54 W
Chivasso	122	45.11 N	7.53 E
Chivilcoy	188	34.52 S	60.02 W
Chizu	134	35.16 N	134.14 E
Chkalov → Orenburg	126	51.54 N	55.06 E
Chloride	178	35.25 N	114.19 W
Chmel'nickij	126	49.25 N	27.00 E
Choapa ≃	188	31.38 S	71.34 W
Chobe □5	160	18.30 S	25.00 E
Chobe (Linyanti) ≃	160	17.50 S	25.05 E
Chochis, Cerro ∧	184	18.10 S	59.53 W
Chocolate Mountains ⛰, Ariz., U.S.	178	33.10 N	114.25 W
Chocolate Mountains ⛰, Calif., U.S.	178	33.20 N	115.15 W
Chocope	184	7.47 S	79.12 W
Chodžejli	126	42.48 N	59.25 E
Chodzież	116	52.59 N	16.56 E
Choele-Choel	188	39.15 S	65.30 W
Choiseul I	162	7.05 S	157.00 E
Chojnice	116	53.42 N	17.34 E
Chojnów	116	51.17 N	15.56 E
Chōkai-zan ∧	134	39.06 N	140.03 E
Cholame Creek ≃	178	35.39 N	120.22 W
Cholet	118	47.04 N	0.53 W
Cholmsk	128	47.03 N	142.03 E
Cholo	158	16.10 S	35.10 E
Cholsey	104	51.34 N	1.10 W
Choluteca	182	13.18 N	87.12 W

Symbols in the index entries are identified on page 198.

Symbols in the index entries are identified on page 198.

Name	Page	Lat	Long
Corrientes	184	17.38 S	55.08 W
Corrientes, Cabo, Col.	184	5.30 N	77.34 W
Corrientes, Cabo, Cuba	182	21.45 N	84.31 W
Corrientes, Cabo, Méx.	180	20.25 N	105.42 W
Corrientes, Ensenada de	182	21.50 N	84.35 W
Corrigin	164	32.21 S	117.52 E
Corry	176	41.56 N	73.39 W
Corryvreckan, Gulf of	108	56.09 N	5.44 W
Corse	122	42.00 N	9.00 E
Corse (Corsica) I	122	42.00 N	9.00 E
Corse, Cap	118	43.00 N	9.25 E
Corserine	106	55.09 N	4.22 W
Corsham	104	51.26 N	2.11 W
Corsica → Corse	122	42.00 N	9.00 E
Corsicana	174	32.06 N	96.28 W
Corsock	106	55.04 N	3.57 W
Cortachy	108	56.43 N	2.58 W
Cort Adelaer, Kap	172	62.00 N	42.00 W
Corte	122	42.18 N	9.08 E
Cortez	174	37.21 N	108.35 W
Cortez Mountains	178	40.20 N	116.20 W
Cortina d'Ampezzo	122	46.32 N	12.08 E
Cortland, N.Y., U.S.	176	42.36 N	76.11 W
Cortland, Ohio, U.S.	176	41.20 N	80.44 W
Corton	104	52.32 N	1.44 E
Cortona	122	43.16 N	11.59 E
Corubal	152	11.57 N	15.06 W
Çoruh	126	41.36 N	41.35 E
Corumbá	184	19.01 S	57.39 W
Corumbaíba	190	18.09 S	48.34 W
Corumbataí	188	23.55 S	51.57 W
Corunna, Ont., Can.	176	42.53 N	82.26 W
Corunna → La Coruña, Esp.	120	43.22 N	8.23 W
Corunna, Mich., U.S.	176	42.59 N	84.07 W
Corunna Downs	164	21.28 S	119.51 E
Corvallis	174	44.34 N	123.16 W
Corve	104	52.22 N	2.43 W
Corve Dale	104	52.30 N	2.40 W
Corvo I	88	39.42 N	31.06 W
Corwen	104	52.59 N	3.22 W
Cos → Kos I	124	36.50 N	27.10 E
Cosby	104	52.33 N	1.11 W
Coseley	104	52.33 N	2.06 W
Cosenza	122	39.17 N	16.15 E
Coshocton	176	40.16 N	81.51 W
Cosmoledo Group II	156	9.43 S	47.35 E
Cosne-sur-Loire	118	47.24 N	2.55 E
Cosquín	188	31.25 S	64.25 W
Cossé-le-Vivien	102	47.57 N	0.55 W
Cosson	118	47.30 N	1.15 E
Costa Mesa	178	33.39 N	117.55 W
Costa Rica	180	10.00 N	84.00 W
Costelloe	110	53.17 N	9.32 W
Costermansville → Bukavu	158	2.30 S	28.52 E
Costessey	104	52.40 N	1.11 E
Cosumnes	178	38.16 N	121.26 W
Cosumnes, Middle Fork	178	38.33 N	120.51 W
Cosumnes, North Fork	178	38.33 N	120.51 W
Coswig	116	51.53 N	12.26 E
Cotabambas	184	13.45 S	72.20 W
Cotabato	138	7.13 N	124.15 E
Cotati	178	38.20 N	122.42 W
Coteaux	182	18.12 N	74.02 W
Côte-d'Or	118	47.30 N	4.50 E
Côte-d'Or	116	47.30 N	4.50 E
Cotentin	118	49.30 N	1.30 W
Côtes-du-Nord	118	48.25 N	2.40 W
Cotherstone	168	22.37 S	148.14 E
Cothi	104	51.52 N	4.10 W
Cotonou	152	6.21 N	2.26 E
Cotopaxi	184	0.40 S	78.26 W
Cotswold Hills	102	51.45 N	2.10 W
Cottbus	116	51.45 N	14.19 E
Cottbus	116	51.45 N	14.00 E
Cottenham	104	52.18 N	0.09 E
Cottiennes, Alpes (Alpi Cozie)	122	44.45 N	7.00 E
Cottingham (Haltemprice)	106	53.47 N	0.24 W
Cottonwood	178	40.23 N	122.17 W
Cottonwood Creek, Middle Fork	178	40.23 N	122.20 W
Cottonwood Creek, South Fork	178	40.23 N	122.20 W
Cottonwood Wash	178	36.19 N	113.59 W
Cotui	182	19.03 N	70.09 W
Coubre, Pointe de la	118	45.41 N	1.13 W
Couchiching, Lake	176	44.40 N	79.23 W
Coudersport	176	41.46 N	78.01 W
Coulommiers	118	48.49 N	3.05 E
Coulonge-Est	176	46.06 N	76.43 W
Coulta	168	34.23 S	135.29 E
Coulterville	178	37.43 N	120.12 W
Council Bluffs	174	41.16 N	95.52 W
Coupar Angus	108	56.33 N	3.17 W
Courantyne (Corantijn)	184	5.55 N	57.05 W
Courcelles	116	50.28 N	4.22 E
Courchevel	118	45.25 N	6.38 E
Courpière	118	45.45 N	3.33 E
Courtalain	118	48.05 N	1.09 E
Courtenay	172	49.41 N	125.00 W
Courtmacsherry	110	51.38 N	8.43 W
Courtmacsherry Bay	110	51.35 N	8.40 W
Courtown Harbour	110	52.38 N	6.13 W
Courtrai → Kortrijk	116	50.50 N	3.16 E
Coutances	118	49.03 N	1.26 W
Coutras	118	45.02 N	0.08 W
Couture, Lac	172	60.07 N	75.20 W
Covasna	124	46.00 N	26.00 E
Cove	108	57.51 N	5.42 W
Cove Island I	176	45.17 N	81.44 W
Covelo	178	39.48 N	123.15 W
Coventry	104	52.25 N	1.30 W
Cover	106	54.17 N	1.46 W
Covilhã	120	40.17 N	7.30 W
Covington, Ky., U.S.	176	39.05 N	84.30 W
Covington, Ohio, U.S.	176	40.07 N	84.21 W
Cowal	108	56.05 N	5.08 W
Cowal, Lake	168	33.35 S	147.25 E
Cowan, Lake	164	31.50 S	121.50 E
Cowansville	176	45.12 N	72.45 W
Cowaramup	164	33.52 S	115.05 E
Coward Springs	168	29.24 S	136.49 E
Cowarie	168	27.43 S	138.20 E
Cowbridge	104	51.28 N	3.27 W
Cowcowing Lakes	164	31.01 S	117.18 E
Cow Creek	178	42.57 N	123.20 W
Cowdenbeath	108	56.07 N	3.21 W
Cowell	168	33.41 S	136.55 E
Cowen	176	38.25 N	80.34 W
Cowes	104	50.45 N	1.18 W
Cow Green Reservoir	106	54.40 N	2.18 W
Cowie Water	108	56.58 N	2.12 W
Cowley, Austl.	168	26.54 S	144.49 E
Cowley, Eng., U.K.	104	51.43 N	1.12 W
Cowpasture	176	37.48 N	79.45 W
Cowplain	104	50.54 N	1.01 W
Cowra	168	33.50 S	148.41 E
Cox, Mount	164	24.55 S	125.36 E
Coxim	190	18.30 S	54.45 W
Coxsackie	176	42.21 N	73.48 W
Cox's Bāzār	144	21.26 N	91.59 E
Coya Sur	188	22.25 S	69.38 W
Coyhaique	186	45.34 S	72.04 W
Coyle, Water of	108	55.28 N	4.32 W
Coyote Creek	178	33.13 N	116.13 W
Coyote Lake	178	35.04 N	116.45 W
Coyuca de Catalán	180	18.20 N	100.39 W
Cozes	118	45.35 N	0.50 W
Cozie, Alpi (Alpes Cottiennes)	122	44.45 N	7.00 E
Cozumel	182	20.31 N	86.55 W
Cozumel, Isla de I	180	20.25 N	86.55 W
Cracovie → Kraków	116	50.03 N	19.58 E
Cradock, Austl.	168	32.04 S	138.30 E
Cradock, S. Afr.	160	32.08 S	25.36 E
Craig, Point	164	26.51 S	126.19 E
Craighouse	108	55.51 N	5.57 W
Craigmore	158	20.28 S	32.50 E
Craignish Point	108	56.07 N	5.37 W
Craignure	108	56.28 N	5.42 W
Craigsville	176	40.47 N	85.06 W
Crail	108	56.16 N	2.38 W
Crailsheim	116	49.08 N	10.04 E
Craiova	124	44.19 N	23.48 E
Crake	106	54.14 N	3.03 W
Cramlington	106	55.05 N	1.36 W
Cranberry Lake	176	44.10 N	74.50 W
Cranborne Chase	104	50.55 N	2.05 W
Cranbrook, Austl.	164	34.18 S	117.32 E
Cranbrook, B.C., Can.	172	49.31 N	115.46 W
Cranbrook, Eng., U.K.	104	51.06 N	0.33 E
Crane	178	32.42 N	114.40 W
Crane Mountain	178	42.04 N	120.13 W
Cranfield	104	52.05 N	0.35 W
Cranleigh	104	51.09 N	0.30 W
Cranston	176	41.47 N	71.26 W
Craon	118	47.51 N	0.57 W
Craonne	118	49.27 N	3.47 E
Crasna (Kraszna)	124	48.09 N	22.20 E
Crater Lake	178	42.56 N	122.06 W
Cratéus	184	5.10 S	40.40 W
Crathie	108	57.02 N	3.12 W
Crato	184	7.14 S	39.23 W
Crauford, Cape	172	73.43 N	84.50 W
Craughwell	110	53.13 N	8.43 W
Craven Arms	104	52.26 N	2.50 W
Crawford	106	55.28 N	3.40 W
Crawley	104	51.07 N	0.12 W
Cray	104	51.55 N	3.36 W
Creagan	108	56.33 N	5.17 W
Creagorry	108	57.26 N	7.19 W
Crécy-en-Brie	118	48.51 N	2.55 E
Crediton	104	50.47 N	3.39 W
Cree, Sask., Can.	172	59.00 N	105.47 W
Cree, Scot., U.K.	106	54.52 N	4.20 W
Cree Lake	172	57.30 N	106.30 W
Creemore	176	44.19 N	80.06 W
Cregganbaun	110	53.42 N	9.51 W
Creil	118	49.16 N	2.29 E
Crema	122	45.22 N	9.41 E
Crémieu	118	45.43 N	5.15 E
Cremona	122	45.07 N	10.02 E
Crépy-en-Valois	118	49.14 N	2.54 E
Creran, Loch	108	56.31 N	5.20 W
Cresaptown	176	39.36 N	78.50 W
Crescent	178	43.29 N	121.41 W
Crescent City	178	41.45 N	124.12 W
Crescent Group II	138	16.31 N	111.38 E
Crescent Lake	178	48.05 N	123.50 W
Crespo	188	32.02 S	60.20 W
Cresson	176	40.28 N	78.35 W
Cressy	168	38.02 S	143.38 E
Crestline, Calif., U.S.	178	34.14 N	117.17 W
Crestline, Ohio, U.S.	176	40.47 N	82.44 W
Creston	172	49.06 N	116.31 W
Creswell	106	53.16 N	1.12 W
Creswell Bay	172	72.35 N	93.25 W
Creswick	168	37.26 S	143.54 E
Crete → Kriti I	124	35.29 N	24.42 E
Creus, Cabo de	120	42.19 N	3.19 E
Creuse	118	46.05 N	2.00 E
Creuse	118	47.00 N	0.34 E
Creussen	116	49.51 N	11.37 E
Crevillente	120	38.15 N	0.48 W
Crewe	102	53.05 N	2.27 W
Crewkerne	104	50.53 N	2.48 W
Crianlarich	108	56.23 N	4.36 W
Criccieth	104	52.55 N	4.14 W
Criciúma	188	28.40 S	49.23 W
Crick	104	52.21 N	1.07 W
Crickhowell	104	51.53 N	3.07 W
Cricklade	104	51.39 N	1.51 W
Cridersville	176	40.39 N	84.09 W
Crieff	108	56.23 N	3.52 W
Crikvenica	122	45.11 N	14.42 E
Crimea → Krymskij Poluostrov	126	45.00 N	34.00 E
Crimmitschau	116	50.49 N	12.23 E
Crinan	108	56.05 N	5.35 W
Crisfield	176	37.59 N	75.51 W
Crissiumal	188	27.30 S	54.07 W
Cristal, Sierra del	182	20.33 N	75.30 W
Cristalina	190	16.45 S	47.36 W
Cristóbal	182	9.20 N	79.55 W
Cristóbal Colón, Pico	184	10.50 N	73.45 W
Crișu Alb	124	46.42 N	21.17 E
Crișu Negru	124	46.42 N	21.16 E
Crișu Repede (Sebes Körös)	124	46.55 N	20.59 E
Črnomelj	122	45.34 N	15.11 E
Croachy	108	57.19 N	4.14 W
Crocketford	106	55.02 N	3.50 W
Crocus Hill → The Valley	182	18.13 N	63.04 W
Croggan	108	56.22 N	5.42 W
Croghan	176	43.54 N	75.24 W
Croglin	106	54.49 N	2.39 W
Croick	108	57.53 N	4.35 W
Croker, Cape, Austl.	166	10.58 S	132.35 E
Croker, Cape, Ont., Can.	176	44.58 N	80.59 W
Croker Island I	166	11.12 S	132.32 E
Cromarty	108	57.40 N	4.02 W
Cromarty Firth	108	57.41 N	4.07 W
Cromer	104	52.56 N	1.18 E
Cromore	108	58.09 N	6.29 W
Cromwell	170	45.03 S	169.12 E
Cronadun	170	42.02 S	171.52 E
Crook	106	54.43 N	1.44 W
Crooked Creek	176	40.45 N	79.33 W
Crooked Island I	182	22.45 N	74.12 W
Crooked Island Passage	182	23.00 N	74.30 W
Crook of Alves	108	57.38 N	3.27 W
Crookston	174	47.47 N	96.37 W
Crookstown	110	51.50 N	8.50 W
Crooksville	176	39.46 N	82.06 W
Crookwell	168	34.28 S	149.28 E
Croom	110	52.31 N	8.42 W
Crosby	106	53.30 N	3.02 W
Crossbost	108	58.08 N	6.23 W
Cross Creek	178	36.08 N	119.38 W
Cross Fell	106	54.42 N	2.29 W
Crossgar	110	54.24 N	5.45 W
Crosshaven	110	51.48 N	8.17 W
Crosshill	108	55.19 N	4.39 W
Cross Lake	172	54.45 N	97.30 W
Crossmaglen	110	54.05 N	6.37 W
Crossman Peak	178	34.32 N	114.07 W
Crossmolina	110	54.06 N	9.20 W
Cross Sound	172	58.10 N	136.30 W
Croswell	176	43.16 N	82.37 W
Crotch Lake	176	44.55 N	76.48 W
Crotone	122	39.05 N	17.07 E
Crouch	104	51.37 N	0.57 E
Crowborough	104	51.03 N	0.09 E
Crowe	176	44.22 N	77.46 W
Crowfoot, Mount	170	45.33 S	167.03 E
Crowland	104	52.41 N	0.11 W
Crowl Creek	168	31.58 S	144.53 E
Crowle	106	53.37 N	0.49 W
Crowley	174	30.13 N	92.22 W
Crowley, Lake	178	37.37 N	118.44 W
Crowlin Islands II	108	57.20 N	5.44 W
Crown Point	176	43.57 N	73.25 W
Crown Prince Frederick Island I	172	70.02 N	86.50 W
Crowthorne	104	51.23 N	0.49 W
Croxley Green	104	51.39 N	0.27 W
Croy	108	57.31 N	4.02 W
Croyde	104	51.07 N	4.13 W
Croydon	168	18.12 S	142.14 E
Croydon	104	51.23 N	0.06 W
Croydon Peak	176	43.28 N	72.13 W
Crozet	176	38.04 N	78.42 W
Crozon	118	48.15 N	4.29 W
Cruachan, Ben	108	56.25 N	5.08 W
Cruces	182	22.21 N	80.16 W
Crucible	176	39.57 N	79.58 W
Cruden Bay	108	57.25 N	1.50 W
Crudgington	104	52.46 N	2.33 W
Crumlin	110	54.37 N	6.14 W
Crummock Water	106	54.34 N	3.18 W
Crump Lake	178	42.17 N	119.50 W
Crusheen	110	52.58 N	8.53 W
Cruz, Cabo	182	19.51 N	77.44 W
Cruz Alta	188	28.39 S	53.36 W
Cruz del Eje	188	30.44 S	64.49 W
Cruzeiro	190	22.34 S	44.58 W
Cruzeiro do Oeste	190	23.46 S	53.04 W
Cruzeiro do Sul	184	7.38 S	72.36 W
Cruz Grande	188	29.25 S	71.18 W
Cruzília	190	21.50 S	44.48 W
Cruz Machado	188	26.01 S	51.21 W
Crymmych	104	51.59 N	4.40 W
Crysler	176	45.13 N	75.09 W
Crystal Brook	168	33.21 S	138.13 E
Crystal City	174	28.41 N	99.50 W
Cserhát	116	47.55 N	19.30 E
Csorna	116	47.37 N	17.16 E
Csurgó	116	46.16 N	17.06 E
Ču	126	43.36 N	73.45 E
Ču	126	45.00 N	67.44 E
Cúa	182	10.10 N	66.54 W
Cuando (Kwando)	156	18.27 S	23.32 E
Cuangar	156	17.36 S	18.39 E
Cuango	156	6.17 S	16.41 E
Cuango (Kwango)	156	3.14 S	17.23 E
Cuanza	156	9.19 S	13.08 E
Cuarto	188	33.28 S	63.04 W
Cuba	176	42.13 N	78.17 W
Cuba	180	21.30 N	80.00 W
Cubagua, Isla I	182	10.48 N	64.10 W
Cubango (Okavango)	156	18.50 S	22.25 E
Cucalaya	182	13.34 N	83.40 W
Cuckfield	104	51.00 N	0.09 W
Cuckney	106	53.15 N	1.08 W
Cúcuta	184	7.54 N	72.31 W
Cuddalore	148	11.45 N	79.45 E
Cuddapah	148	14.28 N	78.49 E
Cuddeback Lake	178	35.18 N	117.28 W
Cudworth	106	53.35 N	1.25 W
Cue	164	27.25 S	117.54 E
Cuenca, Ec.	184	2.53 S	78.59 W
Cuenca, Esp.	120	40.04 N	2.08 W
Cuencamé	180	24.53 N	103.42 W
Cuernavaca	180	18.55 N	99.15 W
Cuervos	178	32.38 N	114.52 W
Cuesta Pass	178	35.21 N	120.38 W
Cueto	182	20.39 N	75.56 W
Cuevas del Almanzora	120	37.18 N	1.53 W
Cuffley	104	51.47 N	0.07 W
Cuiabá	184	15.35 S	56.05 W
Cuilcagh	110	54.10 N	7.48 W
Cuilo (Kwilu)	156	3.22 S	17.22 E
Cuito	156	18.01 S	20.48 E
Cuito-Cuanavale	156	15.10 S	19.10 E
Cuitzeo, Lago de	180	19.55 N	101.05 W
Cuixi	136	28.16 N	117.10 E
Čukotskij, Mys	128	64.14 N	173.10 W
Čukotskij Poluostrov	128	66.00 N	175.00 W
Culcairn	168	35.40 S	147.03 E
Culdaff	110	55.18 N	7.11 W
Culdaff Bay	110	55.17 N	7.10 W
Culebra, Isla de I	182	18.19 N	65.18 W
Culebra, Sierra de la	120	41.54 N	6.20 W
Culgoa	168	29.56 S	146.20 E
Culiacán	180	24.48 N	107.24 W
Cúllar de Baza	120	37.35 N	2.34 W
Cullen	108	57.41 N	2.49 W
Cullen Point	166	11.57 S	141.54 E
Cullera	120	39.10 N	0.15 W
Cullicudden	108	57.39 N	4.13 W
Cullin, Lough	110	53.57 N	9.12 W
Cullinan	160	25.41 S	28.31 E
Cullin Hills	108	57.15 N	6.15 W
Cullman	174	34.11 N	86.51 W
Cullompton	104	50.52 N	3.24 W
Culm	104	50.46 N	3.31 W
Čul'man	128	56.52 N	124.52 E
Culpeper	176	38.28 N	77.53 W
Culrain	108	57.55 N	4.24 W
Cults	108	57.07 N	2.10 W
Culvain	108	56.56 N	5.17 W
Culver, Point	164	32.54 S	124.43 E
Culverden	170	42.46 S	172.51 E
Čulym	128	55.06 N	80.58 E
Čulym	128	57.43 N	83.51 E
Cumaná	184	10.28 N	64.10 W
Cumanacoa	182	10.15 N	63.55 W
Cumari	190	18.16 S	48.11 W
Cumbal, Volcán de	184	0.57 N	77.52 W
Cumberland	176	39.39 N	78.46 W
Cumberland	174	37.09 N	88.25 W
Cumberland Islands II	168	20.40 S	149.09 E
Cumberland Peninsula	172	66.50 N	64.00 W
Cumberland Plateau	174	36.00 N	85.00 W
Cumberland Sound	172	65.10 N	65.30 W
Cumbernauld	108	55.58 N	3.59 W
Cumborah	168	29.44 S	147.46 E
Cumbria	102	54.30 N	3.00 W
Cumbrian Mountains	106	54.30 N	3.05 W
Čumikan	128	54.42 N	135.19 E
Cuminestown	108	57.32 N	2.20 W
Cummins	168	34.16 S	135.44 E
Cumnock	106	55.27 N	4.16 W
Cumnor	104	51.44 N	1.20 W
Cumwhinton	106	54.52 N	2.51 W
Čumyš	128	53.31 N	83.10 E
Čun'a, S.S.S.R.	128	61.36 N	96.30 E
Čuna, S.S.S.R.	128	57.47 N	95.26 E
Cunani	184	2.52 N	51.06 W
Cunco	188	38.55 S	72.02 W
Cuncumén	188	31.53 S	70.38 W
Cunderdin	164	31.39 S	117.15 E
Cunene	156	17.20 S	11.50 E
Cuneo	122	44.23 N	7.32 E
Cunha Porã	188	26.54 S	53.09 W
Cunlhat	118	45.38 N	3.35 E
Cunnamulla	168	28.04 S	145.41 E
Cunninghame	108	55.40 N	4.30 W
Cuokkaraš'ša	112	69.57 N	24.32 E
Cupar	108	56.19 N	3.01 W
Curaçao I	182	12.11 N	69.00 W
Curacautín	188	38.26 S	71.53 W
Curacaví	188	33.24 S	71.09 W
Curanilahue	188	37.28 S	73.21 W
Curanipe	188	35.50 S	72.38 W
Čurapča	128	62.00 N	132.24 E
Curaray	184	2.20 S	74.05 W
Curepipe	161c	20.19 S	57.31 E
Curepto	188	35.05 S	72.01 W
Curiapo	182	8.33 N	61.00 W
Curicó	188	34.59 S	71.14 W
Curinhuás	182	12.46 N	83.40 W
Curious, Mount	164	27.28 S	114.20 E
Curitiba	188	25.25 S	49.15 W
Curitibanos	188	27.18 S	50.36 W
Curiúva	190	24.02 S	50.27 W
Curlewis	168	31.07 S	150.16 E
Curnamona	168	31.39 S	139.32 E
Currais Novos	184	6.15 S	36.31 W
Curralinho	184	1.48 S	49.47 W
Currant Mountain	178	38.55 N	115.25 W
Curreeney	110	52.43 N	8.08 W
Currie, Austl.	168	39.56 S	143.52 E
Currie, Scot., U.K.	108	55.54 N	3.20 W
Currituck Seamount	96	30.05 S	173.25 W
Curry Rivel	104	51.02 N	2.52 W
Curtea-de-Argeș	124	45.08 N	24.41 E
Curtin Springs	164	25.20 S	131.45 E
Curtis, Port	168	24.00 S	151.30 E
Curtis Channel	168	23.30 S	151.45 E
Curtis Island I	168	23.38 S	151.09 E
Curtis Lake	172	66.38 N	89.02 W
Čurug	124	45.29 N	20.04 E
Curup	142	3.28 S	102.32 E
Cururupu	184	1.50 S	44.52 W
Curuzú-Cuatiá	188	29.50 S	58.05 W
Curvelo	190	18.45 S	44.25 W
Curwensville	176	40.58 N	78.32 W
Cusco → Cuzco	184	13.31 S	71.59 W
Cushendall	110	55.06 N	6.04 W
Cushendun	110	55.08 N	6.02 W
Cushina	110	53.11 N	7.05 W
Čusovoj	126	58.17 N	57.49 E
Cust	170	43.19 S	172.22 E
Cutler, Calif., U.S.	178	36.31 N	119.17 W
Cutler, Maine, U.S.	176	44.40 N	67.12 W
Cutral-Có	188	38.58 S	69.15 W
Cutro	122	39.02 N	16.59 E
Cuttack	146	20.30 N	85.50 E
Cuvier, Cape	164	24.05 S	113.22 E
Cuvo	156	10.50 S	13.47 E
Cuxhaven	116	53.52 N	8.42 E
Cuyahoga Falls	176	41.08 N	81.29 W
Cuyama	178	34.54 N	120.18 W
Cuyamaca Peak	178	32.57 N	116.36 W
Cuyo Islands II	138	11.04 N	120.57 E
Cuyuni	184	6.23 N	58.41 W
Cuzco	184	13.31 S	71.59 W
Cuzcuz	188	31.39 S	71.14 W
Cwmbran	104	51.39 N	3.00 W
Cyangugu	158	2.29 S	28.54 E
Cynin	104	51.48 N	4.29 W
Cynthiana	176	38.23 N	84.18 W
Cynwyl Elfed	104	51.55 N	4.22 W
Cyprus	100	35.00 N	33.00 E
Cyrus Field Bay	172	62.50 N	64.55 W
Czechoslovakia	100	49.30 N	17.00 E
Czechowice-Dziedzice	116	49.54 N	19.00 E
Częstochowa	116	50.49 N	19.06 E
D			
Daan	140	23.19 N	110.34 E
Dabajuro	182	11.02 N	70.40 W
Dabashan	132	31.55 N	109.05 E
Dabhoi	146	22.11 N	73.26 E
Dabieshan	136	31.00 N	115.40 E
Dabola	152	10.45 N	11.07 W
Dacca	146	23.43 N	90.25 E
Dachaidan	146	37.53 N	95.07 E
Dachau	116	48.15 N	11.27 E
Dadou	118	43.44 N	1.49 E
Dādu	146	26.44 N	67.47 E
Daduhe	132	29.33 N	103.45 E
Daerhanmaoming'anqi	132	41.42 N	110.23 E
Daet	138	14.05 N	122.55 E
Dafeng (Dazhongji)	136	33.12 N	120.30 E
Dagana	152	16.31 N	15.30 W
Dagang, Zhg.	136	32.12 N	119.39 E
Dagang, Zhg.	136	33.12 N	120.07 E
Dagang, Zhg.	136	22.49 N	113.23 E
Dagg Sound	170	45.23 S	166.46 E
Dagua	166	3.25 S	143.20 E
Dagupan	138	16.03 N	120.20 E
Dahlak Archipelago II	154	15.45 N	40.30 E
Dahlak Kebir Island I	154	15.38 N	40.11 E
Dahomey → Benin	152	9.30 N	2.15 E
Dahra	154	29.34 N	17.50 E
Dahy, Nafūd ad-	144	22.20 N	45.35 E
Daibu	136	31.18 N	119.30 E
Daijiayao	136	32.56 N	120.44 E
Daimanji-san	134	36.15 N	133.19 E
Daimiel	120	39.04 N	3.37 W
Dainan	136	32.43 N	120.06 E
Daingean	110	53.18 N	7.17 W
Daintree	166	16.15 S	145.19 E
Daiō-zaki	134	34.17 N	136.54 E
Daireaux	188	36.37 S	61.45 W
Dairsie	108	56.20 N	2.56 W
Dairy	108	55.43 N	4.43 W
Dai-sen	134	35.22 N	133.33 E
Daiyunshan	136	25.46 N	118.16 E
Dajabón	182	19.34 N	71.43 W
Dajarra	168	21.41 S	139.31 E
Dajianshan	140	26.42 N	103.34 E
Dajishan	136	24.38 N	114.26 E
Dakar	152	14.40 N	17.26 W
Dak-gle	138	15.11 N	107.48 E
Dakhla	152	23.43 N	15.57 W
Đakovica	124	42.23 N	20.25 E
Đakovo	124	45.19 N	18.25 E
Dalälven	114	60.38 N	17.27 E
Dalandzadgad	132	43.35 N	104.30 E
Dalane	114	58.35 N	6.20 E
Dalarna	114	61.01 N	14.04 E
Da-lat	140	11.56 N	108.25 E
Dalatando	156	9.18 S	14.54 E
Dālbandin	150	28.53 N	64.25 E
Dalbeattie	106	54.56 N	3.49 W
Dalby	168	27.11 S	151.16 E
Dalch	104	50.52 N	3.47 W
Dale, Nor.	114	61.22 N	5.25 E
Dale, Wales, U.K.	104	51.43 N	5.11 W
Dale Lake	178	34.08 N	115.42 W
Dalgaranga	164	27.46 S	117.02 E
Dalgaranger	164	27.51 S	117.06 E
Dalgety Brook	164	25.07 S	115.47 E
Dalgety Downs	164	25.17 S	116.15 E
Dalhalvaig	108	58.28 N	3.54 W
Dalhart	174	36.04 N	102.31 W
Dalhousie, Bhārat	144	32.32 N	75.59 E
Dalhousie, N.B., Can.	172	48.04 N	66.23 W
Dalhousie, Cape	172	70.14 N	129.42 W
Dali	140	25.38 N	100.09 E
Daliangshan	132	28.00 N	103.00 E
Daliji	136	33.48 N	117.48 E
Dalkeith	108	55.54 N	3.04 W
Dallas, Scot., U.K.	108	57.33 N	3.28 W
Dallas, Pa., U.S.	176	41.20 N	75.58 W
Dallas, Tex., U.S.	174	32.47 N	96.48 W
Dall Island I	172	54.50 N	132.55 W
Dalmacija	122	43.00 N	17.00 E
Dalmally	108	56.24 N	4.58 W
Dalmatia → Dalmacija	122	43.00 N	17.00 E
Dalmellington	106	55.19 N	4.24 W
Dalnaspidal	108	56.50 N	4.14 W
Daloa	152	6.53 N	6.27 W
Dalqū	154	20.07 N	30.37 E
Dalry, Scot., U.K.	106	55.07 N	4.10 W
Dalry, Scot., U.K.	108	55.43 N	4.44 W
Dalsland	114	58.30 N	12.50 E
Dalton, Ga., U.S.	174	34.47 N	84.58 W
Dalton, Mass., U.S.	176	42.29 N	73.09 W
Dalton, Pa., U.S.	176	41.32 N	75.45 W
Daltonganj	146	24.03 N	84.04 E
Dalton Iceberg Tongue	87	66.15 S	121.30 E
Dalton-in-Furness	106	54.09 N	3.11 W
Dalupiri Island I	138	19.05 N	121.14 E
Dalvík	112a	65.59 N	18.32 W
Dalwallinu	164	30.17 S	116.40 E
Dalwhinnie	108	56.56 N	4.14 W
Daly	166	13.20 S	130.19 E
Daly Bay	172	64.00 N	89.40 W
Daly City	178	37.42 N	122.29 W
Daly Lake	172	56.33 N	105.40 W
Daly River	166	13.45 S	130.50 E
Daly Waters	166	16.15 S	133.22 E
Damān	144	20.25 N	72.50 E
Damanhūr	154	31.02 N	30.28 E
Damar, Pulau I	138	7.09 S	128.40 E
Damaraland	160	22.34 S	17.06 E
Damariscotta	176	44.02 N	69.32 W
Damascus → Dimashq, Sūrīy.	150	33.30 N	36.18 E
Damascus, Md., U.S.	176	39.17 N	77.12 W
Damāvand, Qolleh-ye	150	35.56 N	52.08 E
Damba	156	6.41 S	15.08 E
Damerham	104	50.57 N	1.52 W
Dāmghān	150	39.09 N	54.22 E
Damiaoshan	140	25.06 N	109.15 E
Dammartin-en-Goële	118	49.03 N	2.41 E
Dāmodar	146	22.17 N	88.05 E
Damoh	146	23.50 N	79.27 E
Dampier	164	20.39 S	116.45 E
Dampier, Cape	166	6.02 S	151.02 E
Dampier, Selat	166	0.40 S	130.40 E
Dampier Archipelago II	164	20.35 S	116.35 E
Dampier Land	164	17.30 S	122.55 E
Dampier Strait	166	5.36 S	148.12 E
Danakil Plain	154	12.25 N	40.30 E
Da-nang	140	16.04 N	108.13 E
Danbury, Eng., U.K.	104	51.44 N	0.33 E
Danbury, Conn., U.S.	176	41.23 N	73.27 W
Danby Lake	178	34.14 N	115.07 W
Dancheng	136	33.39 N	115.11 E
Dandaragan	164	30.40 S	115.42 E
Dandenong	168	37.59 S	145.12 E
Dane	106	53.15 N	2.31 W
Danforth	176	45.40 N	67.52 W
Dangé	118	46.56 N	0.36 E
Danger Point	160	34.40 S	19.17 E
Dangla	154	11.18 N	36.54 E
Dangshan	136	34.26 N	116.21 E
Dangtu	136	31.34 N	118.30 E
Danielskuil	160	28.11 S	23.33 E
Danielson	176	41.48 N	71.53 W
Danilov	130	58.12 N	40.12 E
Danjo-guntō II	134	32.02 N	128.23 E
Danlí	182	14.00 N	86.35 W
Dannemora	176	44.43 N	73.43 W
Dannevirke	170	40.12 S	176.07 E
Dannhauser	160	28.04 S	30.04 E
Danshui	136	22.49 N	114.27 E
Dansville	176	42.34 N	77.42 W
Danube	100	45.20 N	29.40 E
Danube, Mouths of the	124	45.10 N	29.50 E
Danville, Qué., Can.	176	45.47 N	72.01 W
Danville, Ill., U.S.	174	40.08 N	87.37 W
Danville, Ky., U.S.	176	37.39 N	84.46 W
Danville, Pa., U.S.	176	40.57 N	76.37 W
Danville, Vt., U.S.	176	44.25 N	66.09 W
Danville, Va., U.S.	174	36.35 N	79.24 W
Danxian	132	34.48 N	116.03 E
Danyang	136	32.00 N	119.35 E
Danzig → Gdańsk	116	54.23 N	18.40 E
Danzig, Gulf of	116	54.40 N	19.15 E
Dâo	120	40.20 N	8.11 W
Daocheng	132	29.06 N	100.38 E
Daoxian	140	25.35 N	111.27 E
Dapango	152	10.52 N	0.12 E
Dapu	136	24.32 N	116.42 E
Daqiao	136	32.21 N	119.41 E
Dar'ā	150	32.37 N	36.06 E
Dārāb	150	28.45 N	54.34 E
Darabani	124	48.11 N	26.35 E
Daraj	154	30.09 N	10.26 E
Darbhanga	146	26.10 N	85.54 E
Darby	176	39.54 N	75.15 W
Darchan	132	49.28 N	105.56 E
Dardanelle	178	38.20 N	119.50 W
Dardanelles → Çanakkale Boğazı	124	40.15 N	26.25 E
Dar-el-Beida → Casablanca	152	33.39 N	7.35 W
Darent	104	51.28 N	0.13 E
Dar-es-Salaam	158	6.48 S	39.17 E
Dargan-Ata	128	40.29 N	62.10 E
Dargaville	170	35.56 S	173.53 E
Dargle	110	53.11 N	6.04 W
Dari	132	33.55 N	99.54 E
Darién, Cordillera de	182	12.55 N	85.30 W
Dariganga	132	45.21 N	113.38 E
Darjeeling	146	27.02 N	88.16 E
Darkan	164	33.20 S	116.44 E
Darke Peak	168	33.28 S	136.12 E
Darlaston	104	52.34 N	2.02 W
Darling	160	33.23 S	18.23 E
Darling	168	34.07 S	141.55 E
Darling Range	164	32.00 S	116.00 E
Darlington	106	54.31 N	1.34 W
Darlot, Lake	164	27.48 S	121.35 E
Darłowo	116	54.26 N	16.23 E
Darmstadt	116	49.53 N	8.40 E
Darnah	154	32.46 N	22.39 E
Darnall	160	29.23 S	31.18 E
Darnétal	118	49.27 N	1.09 E
Darnick	168	32.51 S	143.37 E
Darnley, Cape	87	67.43 S	69.30 E
Darnley Bay	172	69.35 N	123.30 W
Darr	168	23.39 S	143.50 E
Darregueira	188	37.40 S	63.10 W
Darreh Gaz	150	37.27 N	59.07 E
Darsser Ort	116	54.29 N	12.31 E
Dart	104	50.20 N	3.33 W
Dart, Cape	87	73.06 S	126.20 W
Dartford	104	51.27 N	0.14 E
Dartmoor	168	37.55 S	141.17 E
Dartmoor	102	50.35 N	4.00 W
Dartmouth, N.S., Can.	172	44.40 N	63.34 W
Dartmouth, Eng., U.K.	104	50.21 N	3.35 W
Dartmouth, Lake	168	26.04 S	145.18 E
Darton	106	53.36 N	1.32 W
Dartuch, Cabo	120	39.56 N	3.48 E
Daru	166	9.04 S	143.21 E
Daruvar	122	45.36 N	17.13 E
Darvaza	150	40.11 N	58.24 E
Darvel	108	55.37 N	4.18 W
Darwen	106	53.42 N	2.28 W
Darwen	106	53.45 N	2.41 W
Darwendale	158	17.43 S	30.33 E
Darwin	166	12.28 S	130.50 E
Darwin, Monte	186	55.00 S	69.50 W
Darwin River	166	12.49 S	130.58 E
Darya Khān	149	31.48 N	71.06 E
Dasht	150	25.10 N	61.40 E
Dašinčilen	132	47.51 N	104.03 E
Daska	149	32.20 N	74.21 E
Dasseneiland I	160	33.26 S	18.04 E
Dassow	116	53.50 N	10.59 E
Date	134a	42.27 N	140.51 E
Datia	146	25.41 N	78.28 E
Datian	136	25.42 N	117.49 E
Datong	132	40.08 N	113.13 E
Datonghe	132	36.20 N	102.55 E
Datu, Tanjung	142	2.06 N	109.39 E
Datuan	136	30.58 N	121.44 E
Datu Piang	142	7.01 N	124.30 E
Daua (Dawa)	158	4.11 N	42.06 E
Dāūd Khel	149	32.53 N	71.34 E
Daugava (Zapadnaja Dvina)	130	57.04 N	24.03 E
Daugavpils	130	55.53 N	26.32 E
Daulatābād (Shirin Tagāo)	146	36.26 N	64.55 E
Daule	184	2.10 S	79.52 W
Dauphin	172	51.09 N	100.03 W
Dauphiné	118	44.50 N	6.00 E
Dauphin Lake	172	51.17 N	99.48 W
Dāvangere	148	14.28 N	75.55 E
Davao	142	7.04 N	125.36 E
Davao Gulf	142	6.40 N	125.55 E
Davel	160	26.24 S	29.40 E
Davenham	106	53.14 N	2.31 W
Davenport, Iowa, U.S.	174	41.32 N	90.41 W
Davenport, Wash., U.S.	174	47.39 N	118.09 W
Davenport Downs	168	24.08 S	141.07 E
Daventry	104	52.16 N	1.09 W
Davey, Port	168	43.19 S	145.55 E
David	180	8.25 N	82.27 W
Davies, Mount	164	26.14 S	129.16 E
Davington	108	55.18 N	3.12 W
Daviot	108	57.25 N	4.08 W
Davis, Calif., U.S.	178	38.33 N	121.44 W
Davis, W. Va., U.S.	176	39.08 N	79.28 W
Davis	164	21.42 S	121.05 E
Davis, Mount	176	39.47 N	79.10 W
Davis Bay	87	66.08 S	134.05 E
Davis Dam	178	35.15 N	114.35 W
Davis Mountains	174	30.35 N	104.00 W
Davis Sea	87	66.00 S	92.00 E
Davis Strait	172	67.00 N	57.00 W
Davlekanovo	126	54.13 N	55.03 E
Davos	118	46.48 N	9.50 E
Dawa (Daua)	158	4.11 N	42.06 E
Dawley	104	52.40 N	2.28 W
Dawlish	104	50.35 N	3.28 W
Dawna Range	140	16.50 N	98.15 E
Dawson	172	64.04 N	139.25 W
Dawson	168	23.38 S	149.46 E
Dawson, Isla I	186	54.00 S	70.40 W
Dawson Creek	172	55.46 N	120.14 W
Dawson Inlet	172	61.50 N	93.25 W
Dawson-Lambton Glacier	87	76.15 S	27.30 W
Dawson Range	172	62.40 N	139.00 W
Dawu	136	31.34 N	114.06 E
Dax	118	43.43 N	1.03 W
Daxian	132	31.18 N	107.30 E
Daxing'anlingshanmai	132	49.40 N	122.00 E
Daxueshan	132	30.10 N	101.50 E
Daya	136	25.24 N	114.22 E
Dayao	140	25.43 N	101.13 E
Dayboro	168	27.11 S	152.50 E
Daye	136	30.06 N	114.57 E
Dayingjiang (Taping)	140	24.17 N	97.14 E
Daylesford	168	37.21 S	144.09 E
Dayr az-Zawr	150	35.20 N	40.09 E
Dayrūṭ	154	27.33 N	30.49 E
Dayton, Ohio, U.S.	176	39.45 N	84.15 W
Dayton, Pa., U.S.	176	40.53 N	79.15 W
Dayton, Va., U.S.	176	38.25 N	78.56 W
Daytona Beach	174	29.12 N	81.00 W
Dayuling	136	25.20 N	114.16 E
De Aar	160	30.39 S	24.00 E
Deadman Hill	164	23.48 S	119.25 E
Deadmans Cay	182	23.14 N	75.14 W
Dead Sea	150	31.30 N	35.30 E
Deadwood	174	44.23 N	103.44 W
Deakin	164	30.46 S	128.58 E
Deakin Bay	87	68.23 S	150.10 E
Deal	104	51.14 N	1.24 E
Deale	176	38.47 N	76.33 W
Dealesville	160	28.40 S	25.37 E
Deal Island	176	38.09 N	75.56 W
Dean	136	29.20 N	115.46 E
Dean	106	53.20 N	2.14 W
Dean, Forest of	104	51.48 N	2.30 W
Dean Channel	172	52.33 N	127.13 W
Deán Funes	188	30.25 S	64.20 W
Deans Dundas Bay	172	72.15 N	118.25 W
Dearborn	176	42.18 N	83.10 W
Dearg, Beinn	108	57.47 N	4.56 W
Dearne	106	53.30 N	1.16 W
Dear Reservoir	106	55.20 N	3.37 W
Dease	172	59.54 N	128.30 W
Dease Arm	172	66.52 N	119.37 W
Dease Strait	172	68.40 N	108.00 W
Death Valley	178	36.18 N	116.25 W
Death Valley	178	36.30 N	117.00 W
Deauville	118	49.22 N	0.04 E
Debar	124	41.31 N	20.30 E
Deben	104	51.58 N	1.24 E
Debenham	104	52.13 N	1.11 E
Debica	116	50.04 N	21.24 E
De Bilt	116	52.06 N	5.10 E
Deblin	116	51.35 N	21.50 E
Deborah West, Lake	164	30.45 S	119.07 E
Debrecen	116	47.32 N	21.38 E
Debre Markos	154	10.20 N	37.45 E
Debre Tabor	154	11.50 N	38.05 E
Decatur, Ala., U.S.	174	34.36 N	86.59 W
Decatur, Ill., U.S.	174	39.51 N	89.32 W
Decatur, Ind., U.S.	176	40.50 N	84.56 W
Decazeville	118	44.34 N	2.15 E
Deccan	148	14.00 N	77.00 E
Deception Island I	87	62.57 S	60.38 W
Děčín	116	50.48 N	14.13 E
Decize	118	46.50 N	3.27 E
Deckerville	176	43.32 N	82.44 W
Decorah	174	43.18 N	91.48 W
Decs	116	46.17 N	18.46 E
Deddington	104	51.59 N	1.19 W
Dédougou	152	12.28 N	3.28 W
Dee, Eire	110	53.52 N	6.21 W
Dee, U.K.	104	53.10 N	2.50 W
Dee, Eng., U.K.	106	54.18 N	2.32 W
Dee, Scot., U.K.	108	57.09 N	2.07 W
Dee, Wales, U.K.	106	53.20 N	3.18 W
Dee, Loch	106	55.05 N	4.24 W
Deep Creek	178	42.15 N	116.40 W
Deeping Fen	104	52.44 N	0.13 W
Deep River, Ont., Can.	172	46.06 N	77.30 W
Deep River, Conn., U.S.	176	41.23 N	72.26 W
Deepwater	168	29.27 S	151.51 E
Deep Well	164	24.25 S	134.05 E
Deer	176	44.55 N	74.43 W
Deer Creek, U.S.	176	39.37 N	76.09 W
Deer Creek, Calif., U.S.	178	39.56 N	122.04 W
Deer Creek, Ohio, U.S.	176	39.27 N	83.00 W
Deering, Mount	164	24.53 S	129.04 E
Deer Isle	176	44.13 N	68.41 W
Deer Lake	172	49.10 N	57.26 W
Deer Lodge	174	46.24 N	112.44 W
Deer Mountain	176	45.01 N	70.56 W
Deerpass Bay	172	65.56 N	122.25 W
Deer Sound	108	58.58 N	2.48 W
Defiance	176	41.17 N	84.22 W
Deganwy	106	53.18 N	3.47 W
Dege	132	31.50 N	98.40 E
Degeberga	114	55.50 N	14.05 E
Degeh-Bur	154	8.14 N	43.35 E
Degerfors	114	59.14 N	14.26 E
Deggendorf	116	48.51 N	12.59 E
Degh	149	31.25 N	74.04 E
De Graff	176	40.19 N	83.55 W
De Grey	164	20.10 S	119.12 E
De Grey	164	20.12 S	119.11 E
Degt'arsk	126	56.42 N	60.06 E
Dehej	148	21.42 N	72.35 E
Dehiwala-Mount Lavinia	148	6.51 N	79.52 E
Deh Kord	150	33.49 N	48.53 E
Dehra Dūn	146	30.19 N	78.02 E
Dehri	146	24.52 N	84.11 E
Dehua	136	25.32 N	118.15 E
Dehui	132	44.34 N	125.43 E
Deinze	116	50.59 N	3.32 E
Dej	124	47.09 N	23.52 E
Deje	114	59.36 N	13.28 E
Dejnau	150	39.15 N	63.11 E
Deka, Afr.	160	18.03 S	26.44 E
Deka, Rh.	158	18.03 S	26.44 E
Dekese	156	3.27 S	21.24 E
Delabole	104	50.37 N	4.42 W
Delamere	166	15.45 S	131.33 E
Delamere Forest	106	53.14 N	2.38 W
Delanggu	142	7.37 S	110.41 E
Delano	178	35.41 N	119.15 W
Delareyville	160	26.44 S	25.29 E
Delaware	176	40.18 N	83.04 W
Delaware	174	39.10 N	75.30 W
Delaware	176	39.20 N	75.25 W
Delaware, East Branch	176	41.55 N	75.17 W
Delaware, West Branch	176	41.56 N	75.17 W
Delaware Bay	176	39.05 N	75.15 W
Delaware City	176	39.34 N	75.36 W
Delegate	168	37.03 S	148.58 E
Delémont	118	47.22 N	7.21 E
Delft	116	52.00 N	4.21 E
Delfzijl	116	53.19 N	6.46 E
Delgado, Cabo	158	10.40 S	40.35 E
Delhi, Bhārat	146	28.40 N	77.13 E
Delhi, Ont., Can.	176	42.51 N	80.30 W
Delhi, N.Y., U.S.	176	42.17 N	74.55 W
Delicias	180	28.13 N	105.28 W
Delingha	132	37.14 N	97.11 E
Delitua	140	3.30 N	98.41 E
Delitzsch	116	51.31 N	12.20 E
Dell	108	58.30 N	6.20 W
Dellys	120	36.55 N	3.55 E
Del Mar, Calif., U.S.	178	32.58 N	117.16 W
Delmar, Del., U.S.	176	38.27 N	75.34 W
Delmenhorst	116	53.03 N	8.38 E
De-Longa, Ostrova II	128	76.30 N	153.00 E
De-Long-Strasse → Longa, Proliv	128	70.20 N	178.00 E
Deloraine	168	41.31 S	146.39 E
Delorme, Lac	172	54.31 N	69.52 W
Delphos	176	40.50 N	84.20 W
Delportshoop	160	28.22 S	24.20 E
Delray Beach	182	26.28 N	80.04 W
Del Rio	174	29.22 N	100.54 W
Delta, Méx.	178	32.22 N	115.12 W

Symbols in the index entries are identified on page 198.

Name	Page	Lat °′	Long °′
Delta, Ohio, U.S.	176	41.34 N	84.00 W
Delta Amacuro □8	182	8.30 N	61.30 W
Delta Downs	168	17.00 S	141.18 E
Delta Peak ▲	172	56.39 N	129.34 W
Delungra	168	29.39 S	150.50 E
Delvin	110	53.36 N	7.05 W
Delvinë	124	39.57 N	20.06 E
Demak	142	6.53 S	110.38 E
Demarcation Point >	172	69.40 N	141.15 W
Demba	156	5.30 S	22.16 E
Dembia	158	5.07 N	24.25 E
Dembidolo	154	8.30 N	34.48 E
Deming	174	32.16 N	107.45 W
Demir Kapija V	124	41.24 N	22.15 E
Demirköy	124	41.49 N	27.45 E
Demjanka ≃	128	59.34 N	69.17 E
Demjanskoje	128	59.36 N	69.18 E
Demmin	116	53.54 N	13.02 E
Dempo, Gunung ▲	142	4.02 S	103.09 E
Dempster, Point >	164	33.39 S	123.52 E
Denain	118	50.20 N	3.23 E
Denau	126	38.16 N	67.54 E
Denbigh	106	53.11 N	3.25 W
Den Burg	116	53.03 N	4.48 E
Denby Dale	106	53.35 N	1.38 W
Dendermonde	116	51.02 N	4.07 E
Denge Marsh ☷	104	50.57 N	0.55 E
Dengfeng	136	34.29 N	113.04 E
Denham	164	25.55 S	113.32 E
Denham, Mount ▲	182	18.13 N	77.32 W
Denham Island I	168	16.43 S	139.09 E
Denham Range ⋀	168	21.55 S	147.46 E
Denham Sound 𝔘	164	25.40 S	113.15 E
Den Helder	116	52.54 N	4.45 E
Denial Bay	164	32.06 S	133.32 E
Deniliquin	168	35.32 S	144.58 E
Denison	174	33.45 N	96.33 W
Denmark	164	34.57 S	117.21 E
Denmark □1	100	56.00 N	10.00 E
Denmark Bay C	172	70.33 N	103.20 W
Denmark Strait 𝔘	88	67.00 N	25.00 W
Dennis Head >	108	59.23 N	2.23 W
Dennison	176	40.24 N	81.19 W
Dennis Port	176	41.39 N	70.08 W
Denniston	170	41.44 S	171.48 E
Denny	108	56.02 N	3.55 W
Denpasar	142	8.39 S	115.13 E
Denton, Eng., U.K.	106	53.27 N	2.07 W
Denton, Md., U.S.	176	38.53 N	75.50 W
Denton, Tex., U.S.	174	33.13 N	97.08 W
D'Entrecasteaux, Point >	164	34.50 S	116.00 E
D'Entrecasteaux Islands II	166	9.30 S	150.40 E
Denver, Colo., U.S.	174	39.43 N	105.01 W
Denver, Pa., U.S.	176	40.14 N	76.08 W
Deolāli	148	19.57 N	73.50 E
Depew	176	42.54 N	78.42 W
Deposit	176	42.04 N	75.25 W
Depuch Island I	164	20.38 S	117.43 E
Deqin	132	28.38 N	98.52 E
Deqing	136	30.33 N	120.05 E
Dera, Lak (Lach Dera) ≃	158	0.15 N	42.17 E
Derac	182	19.41 N	71.48 W
Dera Ghāzi Khān	149	30.03 N	70.38 E
Dera Ismāīl Khān	149	31.50 N	70.54 E
Derbent	126	42.03 N	48.18 E
Derby, Austl.	164	17.18 S	123.38 E
Derby, Austl.	168	41.09 S	147.47 E
Derby, Eng., U.K.	104	52.55 N	1.29 W
Derby, Maine, U.S.	176	45.14 N	68.59 W
Derby, N.Y., U.S.	176	42.41 N	78.58 W
Derby Line	176	45.00 N	72.06 W
Derbyshire □6	104	53.00 N	1.33 W
Derdepoort	160	24.42 S	26.20 E
Dereköy	124	41.56 N	27.21 E
Derg ≃	110	54.44 N	7.25 W
Derg, Lough ⊜, Eire	110	54.36 N	7.53 W
Derg, Lough ⊜, Eire	110	53.00 N	8.20 W
Déroute, Passage de la 𝔘	105b	49.25 N	2.00 W
Derravaragh, Lough ⊜	110	53.40 N	7.24 W
Derry	176	42.53 N	71.19 W
Derrybrien	110	53.04 N	8.36 W
Derrykeevan	110	55.08 N	6.29 W
Derryveagh Mountains ⋀	110	55.00 N	8.05 W
Dersingham	104	52.51 N	0.30 E
De Rust	160	33.30 S	22.32 E
Derval	118	47.40 N	1.40 W
Derventa	124	44.58 N	17.55 E
Derwent ≃, Eng., U.K.	104	52.50 N	1.15 W
Derwent ≃, Eng., U.K.	106	53.45 N	0.57 W
Derwent ≃, Eng., U.K.	106	54.38 N	3.34 W
Derwent ≃, Eng., U.K.	106	54.57 N	1.41 W
Derwent Bridge	168	42.08 S	146.13 E
Derwent Reservoir ⊜1	106	54.50 N	2.00 W
Derwent Water ⊜	106	54.34 N	3.08 W
Deržavinskij	126	51.03 N	66.19 E
Desaguadero ≃, Arg.	188	34.13 S	66.47 W
Desaguadero ≃, Bol.	184	18.24 S	67.05 W
Désappointement, Îles du II	96	14.10 S	141.20 W
Desborough	104	52.27 N	0.49 W
Descabezado Grande, Volcán ▲1	188	35.36 S	70.45 W
Descanso, Bra.	188	26.50 S	53.35 W
Descanso, Calif., U.S.	178	32.51 N	116.37 W
Descanso, Punta >	178	32.15 N	117.00 W
Deschambault Lake ⊜	172	54.40 N	103.35 W
Deschênes	176	45.23 N	75.48 W
Deschutes ≃	174	45.38 N	120.54 W
Dese	154	11.05 N	39.41 E
Deseado ≃	186	47.45 S	65.50 W
Desengaño, Punta >	186	49.15 S	67.35 W
Desenzano del Garda	122	45.28 N	10.32 E
Deseronto	176	44.12 N	77.03 W
Desert Hot Springs	178	33.58 N	116.30 W
Desert Lake ⊜	178	37.58 N	115.15 W
Desert Peak ▲	178	41.11 N	113.22 W
Desert Valley V	178	41.15 N	118.20 W
Desford	104	52.39 N	1.17 W
Deshler	176	41.12 N	83.54 W
Des Moines	174	41.35 N	93.37 W
Des Moines ≃	174	40.22 N	91.26 W
Desna ≃	126	50.33 N	30.32 E
Desolación, Isla I	186	53.00 S	74.10 W
Despatch	160	33.46 S	25.30 E
Despeñaperros, Desfiladero de)(	120	38.24 N	3.30 W
Dessau	116	51.50 N	12.14 E
Destruction, Mount ▲2	164	24.35 S	127.59 E
Destruction Bay	172	61.15 N	138.48 W
Detmold	116	51.56 N	8.52 E
De Tour Village	176	46.00 N	83.53 W
Detrital Wash V	178	36.02 N	114.28 W
Detroit	176	42.20 N	83.03 W
Detroit Beach	176	41.55 N	83.20 W
Dett	158	18.38 S	26.50 E
Deurne	116	51.28 N	5.47 E
Deutsche Bucht C	116	54.30 N	7.30 E
Deutschlandsberg	116	46.49 N	15.13 E
Deux-Sèvres □5	118	46.30 N	0.20 W
Deva	124	45.53 N	22.55 E
Devakottai	148	9.57 N	78.49 E
Dévaványa	116	47.02 N	20.58 E
Devecser	116	47.06 N	17.26 E
Deventer	116	52.15 N	6.10 E
Deveron ≃	108	57.40 N	2.31 W
Devès, Monts du ⋀	118	45.00 N	3.45 E
Devil River Peak ▲	170	40.58 S	172.39 E
Devil's Island → Diable, Île du I	184	5.18 N	52.35 W
Devils Lake	174	48.07 N	98.59 W
Devil's Bridge	104	52.23 N	3.51 W
Devil's Water ≃	106	54.58 N	2.02 W
Devizes	104	51.22 N	1.59 W
Devoll ≃	124	40.49 N	19.51 E
Devon □6	102	50.45 N	3.50 W
Devon ≃, Eng., U.K.	104	53.04 N	0.43 W
Devon ≃, Scot., U.K.	108	56.07 N	3.51 W
Devon Island I	90	75.00 N	87.00 W
Devonport, Austl.	168	41.11 S	146.21 E
Devonport, N.Z.	170	36.49 S	174.48 E
Devonport, Eng., U.K.	104	50.22 N	4.10 W
Devoto	188	31.25 S	62.20 W
Devure ≃	158	19.50 S	31.45 E
Dewa-kyūryō ⋀2	134	39.05 N	140.10 E
Dewās	146	22.58 N	76.04 E
Dewetsdorp	160	29.33 S	26.34 E
De Witt, Mich., U.S.	176	42.51 N	84.34 W
De Witt, N.Y., U.S.	176	43.02 N	76.04 W
Dewsbury	106	53.42 N	1.37 W
Dexing	136	28.54 N	117.36 E
Dexter, Maine, U.S.	176	45.01 N	69.18 W
Dexter, Mich., U.S.	176	42.20 N	83.53 W
Dexter, N.Y., U.S.	176	44.01 N	76.03 W
Dexterity Fiord C2	172	71.11 N	73.03 W
Dey-Dey, Lake ⊜1	164	29.12 S	131.04 E
Dezfūl	150	32.23 N	48.24 E
Dezhou	132	37.27 N	116.18 E
Dežneva, Mys >	128	66.06 N	169.45 W
Dhahab	150	28.29 N	34.32 E
Dhahran → Az-Zahrān	150	26.18 N	50.08 E
Dhamār	144	14.46 N	44.23 E
Dhamtari	148	20.41 N	81.34 E
Dhanaula	149	30.17 N	75.35 E
Dhānbād	146	23.48 N	86.27 E
Dhangarhi	132	28.41 N	80.36 E
Dhār	146	22.36 N	75.18 E
Dharangaon	146	21.01 N	75.16 E
Dhārāpuram	148	10.44 N	77.31 E
Dharmapuri	148	12.08 N	78.10 E
Dharmavaram	148	14.26 N	77.43 E
Dharmsāla	149	32.13 N	76.19 E
Dhārwār	148	15.28 N	75.01 E
Dhaulāgiri ▲	146	28.42 N	83.30 E
Dherue, Loch an ⊜	108	58.25 N	4.27 W
Dheskáti	124	39.55 N	21.49 E
Dhidhimótikhon	124	41.21 N	26.30 E
Dhodhekánisos (Dodecanese) II	124	36.30 N	27.00 E
Dholka	146	22.43 N	72.28 E
Dhomhnull, Sgurr ▲	108	56.45 N	5.27 W
Dhorāji	146	21.44 N	70.27 E
Dhoxáton	124	41.05 N	24.14 E
Dhubri	146	26.01 N	89.59 E
Dhule	146	20.54 N	74.47 E
Dhūri	149	30.22 N	75.52 E
Diabaig	108	57.34 N	5.40 W
Diable, Île du I	184	5.18 N	52.35 W
Diablo, Mount ▲	178	37.53 N	121.55 W
Diablo Range ⋀	178	37.00 N	121.20 W
Diablotin, Morne ▲	182	15.30 N	61.24 W
Diaka ≃1	152	15.13 N	4.14 W
Diamante	188	32.05 S	60.35 W
Diamante ≃	188	34.31 S	66.56 W
Diamantina	190	18.15 S	43.36 W
Diamantina ≃	168	26.45 S	139.10 E
Diamantina Lakes	168	23.46 S	141.09 E
Diamantina Trough ≃1	96	37.00 S	105.00 E
Diamond Harbour	146	0.00	0.00
Diamond Islets II	168	17.25 S	150.58 E
Diamond Lake ⊜	178	43.10 N	122.09 W
Diamond Peak ▲	178	43.33 N	122.09 W
Diana, Baie C	172	60.50 N	69.50 W
Dianalund	114	55.32 N	11.30 E
Dianbai (Shuidong)	140	21.33 N	111.16 E
Dianchi ⊜	140	24.50 N	102.42 E
Dibaya	156	6.30 S	22.57 E
Dibeng	160	27.35 S	22.54 E
Dibi	158	4.12 N	41.58 E
Dibrugarh	146	27.29 N	94.54 E
Dickinson	174	46.53 N	102.47 W
Didbiran	128	51.58 N	139.20 E
Didcot	104	51.37 N	1.15 W
Didinga Hills ⋀	158	4.20 N	33.35 E
Die	118	44.45 N	5.22 E
Die Berg ▲	160	25.12 S	30.09 E
Diego de Almagro, Isla I	186	51.25 S	75.10 W
Diego de Ocampo, Pico ▲	182	19.36 N	70.45 W
Diego Garcia I	94	7.20 S	72.25 E
Diego Ramírez, Islas II	186	56.30 S	68.44 W
Diégo-Suarez	161b	12.16 S	49.17 E
Diégo-Suarez □4	161b	13.00 S	49.00 E
Dien-bien-phu	138	21.23 N	103.01 E
Dieppe	118	49.56 N	1.05 E
Diest	116	50.59 N	5.03 E
Dietrich	178	42.55 N	114.16 W
Dif	158	1.00 N	41.00 E
Differdange	116	49.32 N	5.52 E
Dig	146	27.28 N	77.20 E
Digboi	146	27.23 N	95.38 E
Digby	172	44.37 N	65.46 W
Digges Islands II	172	62.35 N	77.50 W
Digne	118	44.06 N	6.14 E
Digoin	118	46.29 N	3.59 E
Digos	142	6.45 N	125.20 E
Digras	148	20.07 N	77.43 E
Digul ≃	166	7.07 S	138.42 E
Dijon	118	47.19 N	5.01 E
Dikala	158	4.41 N	31.23 E
Dikhil	154	11.06 N	42.22 E
Diksmuide (Dixmude)	116	51.02 N	2.52 E
Dikson	128	73.30 N	80.35 E
Dikwa	152	12.02 N	13.56 E
Dili	142	8.33 S	125.34 E
Dillenburg	116	50.44 N	8.17 E
Dillon	174	45.13 N	112.38 W
Dillon Cone ▲	170	42.16 S	173.13 E
Dillon Lake ⊜1	176	40.02 N	82.10 W
Dilolo	156	10.42 S	22.20 E
Dimāpur	144	25.54 N	93.45 E
Dimashq (Damascus)	150	33.30 N	36.18 E
Dimboola	168	36.27 S	142.02 E
Dîmbovița □4	124	45.00 N	25.30 E
Dimbulah	168	17.09 S	145.07 E
Dimitrovgrad, Blg.	124	42.03 N	25.36 E
Dimitrovgrad, Jugo.	124	43.01 N	22.47 E
Dimitrovo → Pernik	124	42.36 N	23.02 E
Dimlang ▲	152	8.24 N	11.47 E
Dimona	150	31.04 N	35.02 E
Dinagat Island I	142	10.12 N	125.35 E
Dinājpur	146	25.38 N	88.38 E
Dinan	118	48.27 N	2.02 W
Dinant	116	50.16 N	4.55 E
Dinara ⋀	122	43.50 N	16.35 E
Dinard	118	48.38 N	2.04 W
Dinaric Alps → Dinara ⋀	122	43.50 N	16.35 E
Dinas	104	52.00 N	4.54 W
Dinas Head >	104	52.02 N	4.55 W
Dinas Powis	104	51.26 N	3.14 W
Dindigul	148	10.21 N	77.57 E
Dingalan Bay C	138	15.18 N	121.25 E
Dingan	140	19.44 N	110.21 E
Dingle	110	52.08 N	10.15 W
Dingle Bay C	110	52.05 N	10.15 W
Dingle Peninsula >1	110	52.12 N	10.05 W
Dingnan	136	24.48 N	114.59 E
Dingo	168	23.39 S	149.20 E
Dingolfing	116	48.38 N	12.31 E
Dingqing	146	31.32 N	95.27 E
Dingri	146	28.35 N	87.05 E
Dingshan	136	31.17 N	119.50 E
Dingwall	108	57.35 N	4.29 W
Dingxi	132	35.38 N	104.29 E
Dingxian	132	38.32 N	114.59 E
Dingyuan	136	32.32 N	117.40 E
Dinh-lap	140	21.33 N	107.06 E
Dinin ≃	110	52.43 N	7.18 W
Dinkelsbühl	116	49.04 N	10.19 E
Dinnet	108	57.03 N	2.54 W
Dinnington	106	53.22 N	1.12 W
Dinuba	178	36.32 N	119.23 W
Diois □9	118	44.40 N	5.20 E
Dionisio Cerqueira	188	26.15 S	53.38 W
Diourbel	152	14.40 N	16.15 W
Dipolog	138	8.35 N	123.20 E
Dippoldiswalde	116	50.54 N	13.40 E
Dipton	170	45.54 S	168.22 E
Dir	144	35.12 N	71.53 E
Direction, Cape >	166	12.51 S	143.32 E
Dire Dawa	154	9.37 N	41.52 E
Diriamba	182	11.53 N	86.15 W
Dirico	156	17.58 S	20.47 E
Dirk Hartog Island I	164	25.48 S	113.00 E
Dirranbandi	168	28.35 S	148.14 E
Disappointment, Cape >, Falk. Is.	186	54.53 S	36.07 W
Disappointment, Cape >, Wash., U.S.	174	46.18 N	124.03 W
Disappointment, Lake ⊜	164	23.30 S	122.50 E
Disaster Bay C	168	37.17 S	150.00 E
Discovery Bay C	168	38.12 S	141.07 E
Discovery Tablemount ≃3	86	42.00 S	0.05 E
Disko I	172	69.50 N	53.30 W
Disko Bugt C	172	69.15 N	52.00 W
Dismal Lakes ⊜	172	67.26 N	117.07 W
Disraëli	176	45.54 N	71.21 W
Diss	104	52.23 N	1.07 E
Distington	106	54.36 N	3.32 W
District of Columbia □5	174	38.54 N	77.01 W
Distrito Federal □5, Bra.	190	15.45 S	47.45 W
Distrito Federal □5, Ven.	182	10.30 N	66.55 W
Disūq	154	31.08 N	30.39 E
Dithmarschen ⊹1	116	54.05 N	9.00 E
Ditton Priors	104	52.30 N	2.35 W
Diu	146	20.42 N	70.59 E
Dives ≃	118	49.19 N	0.05 W
Divilican Bay C	132	17.25 N	122.19 E
Divinópolis	190	20.09 S	44.54 W
Divisor, Serra do ⋀1	184	8.20 S	73.30 W
Dixfield	176	44.32 N	70.27 W
Dixie Valley V	178	39.50 N	117.55 W
Dixon	178	38.27 N	121.49 W
Dixon Entrance 𝔘	172	54.25 N	132.30 W
Diyālā (Sirvān) ≃	150	33.14 N	44.31 E
Diyarbakir	150	37.55 N	40.14 E
Dizzard Point >	104	50.45 N	4.38 W
Dja ≃	152	2.02 N	15.12 E
Djakarta → Jakarta	142	6.10 S	106.48 E
Djambala	156	2.33 S	14.45 E
Djanet	152	24.34 N	9.29 E
Djawa, Laut (Java Sea) ≃2	138	5.00 S	110.00 E
Djedi, Oued V	152	34.28 N	6.05 E
Djelfa	100	34.40 N	3.15 E
Djemmal	122	35.37 N	10.46 E
Djenné	152	13.54 N	4.33 W
Djerba, Île de I	152	33.48 N	10.54 E
Djerem ≃	152	5.20 N	13.24 E
Djerid, Chott ☷	152	33.42 N	8.26 E
Djibouti	154	11.36 N	43.09 E
Djibouti □2	154	11.30 N	43.00 E
Djidjelli	120	36.48 N	5.46 E
Djilbabo Plain ≃	158	4.00 N	39.10 E
Djougou	152	9.42 N	1.40 E
Dmitrija Lapteva, Proliv 𝔘	128	73.00 N	142.00 E
Dnepr ≃	112	54.10 N	30.20 E
Dneprodzeržinsk	126	48.30 N	34.37 E
Dnepropetrovsk	126	48.27 N	34.59 E
Dnestr ≃, S.S.S.R.	88	48.21 N	28.10 E
Dnestr ≃, S.S.S.R.	126	46.18 N	30.17 E
Dnieper → Dnepr ≃	112	54.10 N	30.20 E
Dniester → Dnestr ≃	126	46.18 N	30.17 E
Dno	130	57.50 N	29.59 E
Doany	161b	14.22 S	49.31 E
Doba	154	19.50 N	18.30 E
Dobbyn	168	19.48 S	140.00 E
Döbeln	116	51.07 N	13.07 E
Doberai, Jazirah (Vogelkop) >1	166	1.30 S	132.30 E
Dobo	166	5.46 S	134.13 E
Doboj	124	44.44 N	18.06 E
Dobr'anka	126	52.04 N	31.11 E
Dobrudžansko plato ⋀1	124	43.32 N	27.50 E
Dobruš	130	52.25 N	31.19 E
Doce Leguas, Cayos de las II	182	20.55 N	79.05 W
Dochart ≃	108	56.28 N	4.20 W
Docking	104	52.55 N	0.38 E
Dod Ballāpur	148	13.18 N	77.32 E
Dodecanese → Dhodhekánisos II	124	36.30 N	27.00 E
Dodge City	174	37.45 N	100.01 W
Dodman Point >	104	50.13 N	4.48 W
Dodola	154	7.02 N	39.07 E
Dodoma	156	6.11 S	35.45 E
Dodoma □4	158	6.00 S	36.00 E
Dodson Peninsula >1	87	75.46 S	62.50 W
Doetinchem	116	51.58 N	6.17 E
Dōgo I	134	36.15 N	133.16 E
Dogondoutchi	152	13.38 N	4.02 E
Doha → Ad-Dawḥah	150	25.17 N	51.32 E
Dohad	146	22.50 N	74.16 E
Doiran, Lake ⊜	124	41.13 N	22.44 E
Dokkum	116	53.19 N	6.00 E
Dolbeau	172	48.53 N	72.14 W
Dole	118	47.06 N	5.30 E
Dolgarrog	106	53.11 N	3.51 W
Dolgellau	104	52.44 N	3.53 W
Dolgeville	176	43.06 N	74.46 W
Dolinsk	128	47.21 N	142.48 E
Dolisie	156	4.12 S	12.41 E
Dolj □4	124	44.15 N	23.45 E
Dollar	108	56.09 N	3.41 W
Dollar Law ▲	108	55.33 N	3.17 W
Dolo	154	4.13 N	42.08 E
Dolomites → Dolomiti ⋀	122	46.25 N	11.50 E
Dolomiti ⋀	122	46.25 N	11.50 E
Dolores, Arg.	188	36.19 S	57.40 W
Dolores, Esp.	120	38.08 N	0.46 W
Dolores, Ur.	188	33.33 S	58.13 W
Dolphin and Union Strait 𝔘	172	69.05 N	114.45 W
Dolton	104	50.53 N	4.01 W
Dolwyddelan	104	53.03 N	3.53 W
Domadare	158	1.48 N	41.13 E
Dombarovskij	126	50.46 N	59.32 E
Dombås	114	62.05 N	9.08 E
Dombes ⊹1	118	46.00 N	5.03 E
Dombóvár	116	46.23 N	18.08 E
Domeyko	188	28.57 S	70.54 W
Domeyko, Cordillera ⋀	188	24.30 S	69.00 W
Dominica □1	180	15.30 N	61.20 W
Dominica Channel 𝔘	182	15.10 N	61.15 W
Dominican Republic □1	180	19.00 N	70.40 W
Dominion, Cape >	172	66.13 N	74.28 W
Domo	154	7.54 N	46.52 E
Domodedovo	130	55.26 N	37.46 E
Domodossola	122	46.07 N	8.17 E
Domoni	161a	12.15 S	44.32 E
Dom Pedrito	188	30.59 S	54.40 W
Dompu	142	8.32 S	118.28 E
Domuyo, Volcán ▲1	188	36.37 S	70.28 W
Don ≃, S.S.S.R.	126	47.04 N	39.18 E
Don ≃, Eng., U.K.	106	53.39 N	0.58 W
Don ≃, Scot., U.K.	108	57.08 N	2.05 W
Donaghadee	110	54.39 N	5.33 W
Donaghmore	110	54.32 N	6.49 W
Donald	168	36.22 S	143.00 E
Donard, Slieve ▲	110	54.11 N	5.55 W
Donaueschingen	116	47.57 N	8.29 E
Donauwörth	116	48.43 N	10.46 E
Don Benito	120	38.57 N	5.52 W
Doncaster	106	53.32 N	1.07 W
Dondo, Ang.	156	9.38 S	14.25 E
Dondo, Moç.	160	19.36 S	34.44 E
Dondra Head >	148	5.55 N	80.35 E
Doneck	126	48.00 N	37.48 E
Donegal	110	54.39 N	8.07 W
Donegal □6	110	54.50 N	8.00 W
Donegal Bay C	110	54.30 N	8.30 W
Doneraile	110	52.13 N	8.35 W
Donetsk → Doneck	126	48.00 N	37.48 E
Donga ≃	152	8.19 N	9.58 E
Dongara	164	29.15 S	114.56 E
Dongba	136	31.18 N	119.03 E
Dongchuan	140	26.10 N	103.01 E
Dongen	116	51.37 N	4.56 E
Dongfang (Basuo)	140	19.05 N	108.39 E
Donggala	142	0.40 S	119.44 E
Donggou, Zhg.	136	33.38 N	119.40 E
Donggou, Zhg.	136	32.16 N	119.00 E
Dongguan	136	23.03 N	113.46 E
Donghai (Haizhou)	136	34.34 N	119.11 E
Donghaidao I	140	21.02 N	110.25 E
Dong-hoi	140	17.29 N	106.36 E
Dongjiang ≃	136	23.06 N	114.00 E
Donglong	136	23.36 N	116.50 E
Dong-nai ≃	140	10.45 N	106.46 E
Dongpushi	136	30.03 N	120.34 E
Dongshajiao	136	30.19 N	122.09 E
Dongshan	136	23.46 N	117.31 E
Dongshaqundao (Pratas Islands) II	132	20.42 N	116.43 E
Dongshi	136	24.42 N	118.27 E
Dongtai	136	32.51 N	120.20 E
Dongtinghu ⊜	136	29.20 N	112.54 E
Dongwe ≃	158	13.58 S	23.53 E
Dongxiang	136	28.13 N	116.35 E
Dongyang	136	29.16 N	120.14 E
Donington	104	52.55 N	0.12 W
Donjek ≃	172	62.35 N	140.00 W
Donji Vakuf	122	44.09 N	17.25 E
Donnellys Crossing	170	35.43 S	173.37 E
Donner Pass)(	178	39.19 N	120.20 W
Donner und Blitzen ≃	178	43.17 N	118.49
Donnybrook, Austl.	164	33.35 S	115.49 E
Donnybrook, S. Afr.	160	30.00 S	29.48 E
Donora	176	40.11 N	79.52 W
Donors Hills	168	18.42 S	140.33 E
Donoughmore	110	51.57 N	8.45 W
Dooagh	110	53.59 N	10.09 W
Doomadgee Mission	168	17.56 S	138.49 E
Doon ≃	108	55.26 N	4.38 W
Doon, Loch ⊜	106	55.15 N	4.22 W
Doonbeg	110	52.44 N	9.32 W
Doonbeg ≃	110	52.44 N	9.34 W
Doondi	168	28.15 S	148.28 E
Dora, Lake ⊜	164	22.05 S	122.55 E
Dorāh Ān)(	149	36.07 N	71.15 E
Dorain, Beinn ▲	108	56.30 N	4.42 W
Dorback Burn ≃	108	57.31 N	3.40 W
Dorchester, Ont., Can.	176	42.59 N	81.04 W
Dorchester, Eng., U.K.	104	50.43 N	2.26 W
Dorchester, Eng., U.K.	104	51.39 N	1.10 W
Dorchester, Cape >	172	65.29 N	77.30 W
Dordogne □5	118	45.10 N	0.45 E
Dordogne ≃	118	45.02 N	0.35 W
Dordon	104	52.36 N	1.37 W
Dordrecht, Ned.	116	51.49 N	4.40 E
Dordrecht, S. Afr.	160	31.20 S	27.03 E
Dore	104	51.57 N	2.52 W
Dore, Monts ⋀	118	45.30 N	2.45 E
Doré Lake ⊜	172	54.46 N	107.17 W
Dores	108	57.22 N	4.15 W
Dores do Indaiá	190	19.27 S	45.36 W
Dori	152	14.02 N	0.02 W
Dorking	104	51.14 N	0.20 W
Dormans	118	49.04 N	3.38 E
Dornbirn	116	47.25 N	9.44 E
Dornie	108	57.17 N	5.31 W
Dornoch	108	57.52 N	4.02 W
Dornoch Firth C1	108	57.53 N	4.00 W
Dorog	116	47.43 N	18.44 E
Dorohoi	124	47.57 N	26.24 E
Dorotea	114	64.16 N	16.24 E
Dorre Island I	164	25.09 S	113.07 E
Dorridge	104	52.22 N	1.45 W
Dorrigo	168	30.21 S	152.43 E
Dorris	178	41.58 N	121.55 W
Dorset □6	102	50.47 N	2.20 W
Dorset Peak ▲	176	43.19 N	73.02 W
Dortmund	116	51.31 N	7.28 E
Doruma	158	4.44 N	27.42 E
Dosatuj	128	50.23 N	118.28 E
Dos Bahías, Cabo >	186	44.55 S	65.32 W
Dos Hermanas	120	37.17 N	5.55 W
Dos Palos	178	36.59 N	120.37 W
Dos Reyes, Punta >	188	24.33 S	70.35 W
Dossor	126	47.32 N	53.01 E
Dothan	174	31.13 N	85.24 W
Douai	118	50.22 N	3.04 E
Douala	152	4.03 N	9.42 E
Douarnenez	118	48.06 N	4.20 W
Double Island Point >	168	25.56 S	153.11 E
Double Point >	168	17.39 S	146.09 E
Doubs ≃	118	47.10 N	6.25 E
Doubtful Sound 𝔘	170	45.17 S	166.51 E
Doubtless Bay C	170	34.55 S	173.25 E
Doudeville	118	49.43 N	0.48 E
Douentza	152	15.00 N	2.57 W
Douglas, I. of Man	106	54.09 N	4.28 W
Douglas, S. Afr.	160	29.04 S	23.46 E
Douglas, Scot., U.K.	108	55.33 N	3.51 W
Douglas, Ariz., U.S.	180	31.21 N	109.33 W
Douglas ≃	106	53.43 N	2.50 W
Douglas, Mount ▲2	164	28.39 S	123.53 E
Douglas Channel 𝔘	172	53.30 N	129.12 W
Douglas Water ≃	108	55.38 N	3.46 W
Doune	108	56.12 N	4.05 W
Dour	116	50.24 N	3.47 E
Dourado ≃	190	21.22 S	49.41 W
Dourados	190	22.13 S	54.48 W
Dourdou ≃	118	44.00 N	2.41 E
Douro (Duero) ≃	120	41.08 N	8.40 W
Douze ≃	118	43.54 N	0.30 W
Dove ≃, Eng., U.K.	104	52.50 N	1.35 W
Dove ≃, Eng., U.K.	106	54.12 N	0.54 W
Dove Creek ≃	178	41.42 N	113.22 W
Dover, Austl.	168	43.19 S	147.01 E
Dover, Eng., U.K.	104	51.08 N	1.19 E
Dover, Del., U.S.	176	39.10 N	75.32 W
Dover, N.H., U.S.	176	43.12 N	70.56 W
Dover, N.J., U.S.	176	40.53 N	74.34 W
Dover, Ohio, U.S.	176	40.32 N	81.29 W
Dover, Point >	164	32.32 S	125.32 E
Dover, Strait of (Pas de Calais) 𝔘	102	51.00 N	1.30 E
Dovercourt	104	51.56 N	1.16 E
Dover-Foxcroft	176	45.11 N	69.13 W
Dovey Valley V	104	52.35 N	3.50 W
Dovrefjell ⋀	114	62.06 N	9.25 E
Dowally	108	56.36 N	3.37 W
Dowerin	164	31.12 S	117.02 E
Downham	104	52.26 N	0.15 E
Downham Market	104	52.36 N	0.23 E
Downieville	178	39.34 N	120.50 W
Downingtown	176	40.00 N	75.42 W
Downpatrick	110	54.20 N	5.43 W
Downpatrick Head >	110	54.20 N	9.20 W
Downsville	176	42.05 N	75.00 W
Downton	104	51.00 N	1.44 W
Dow Rūd	150	33.28 N	49.04 E
Doyle	178	40.02 N	120.06 W
Doylestown, Ohio, U.S.	176	40.58 N	81.42 W
Doylestown, Pa., U.S.	176	40.19 N	75.08 W
Dra, Hamada du ⊹2	152	29.00 N	6.45 W
Drâa, Oued V	152	28.43 N	11.09 W
Drac ≃	118	45.13 N	5.41 E
Dracena	190	21.32 S	51.32 W
Drachten	116	53.06 N	6.06 E
Dracut	176	42.40 N	71.18 W
Drăgășani	124	44.40 N	24.16 E
Drag Lake ⊜	176	45.05 N	78.24 W
Dragonera, Isla I	120	39.35 N	2.19 E
Draguignan	118	43.32 N	6.28 E
Drakensberg ⋀	160	27.00 S	30.00 E
Drake Passage 𝔘	92	58.00 S	70.00 W
Drake Peak ▲	178	42.19 N	120.07 W
Dráma	124	41.09 N	24.08 E
Drammen	114	59.44 N	10.15 E
Draperstown	110	54.48 N	6.47 W
Drās	149	34.27 N	75.59 E
Drau (Drava) (Dráva) ≃	122	45.33 N	18.55 E
Drava (Drau) (Dráva) ≃	122	45.33 N	18.55 E
Dravinja ≃	122	46.22 N	15.57 E
Dravograd	122	46.35 N	15.01 E
Drayton Valley	172	53.13 N	114.59 W
Dresden, Ont., Can.	176	42.35 N	82.11 W
Dresden, D.D.R.	116	51.03 N	13.44 E
Dresden, Ohio, U.S.	176	40.07 N	82.01 W
Dresden □5	116	51.10 N	14.00 E
Dreux	118	48.44 N	1.22 E
Drews Reservoir ⊜1	178	42.10 N	120.40 W
Driffield	106	54.00 N	0.27 W
Drimnin	108	56.36 N	6.00 W
Drimoleague	110	51.38 N	9.14 W
Drin ≃	124	41.17 N	20.02 E
Drina ≃	124	44.53 N	19.21 E
Drinit, Pellg i C	124	41.45 N	19.28 E
Drobeta-Turnu-Severin	124	44.38 N	22.39 E
Drogheda	110	53.43 N	6.21 W
Droichead Nua	110	53.11 N	6.48 W
Droitwich	104	52.16 N	2.09 W
Dromahair	110	54.14 N	8.19 W
Dromcolliher	110	52.20 N	8.54 W
Drôme □5	118	44.35 N	5.10 E
Drôme ≃	118	44.35 N	5.10 E
Dromod	110	53.51 N	7.55 W
Dromore	110	54.25 N	6.09 W
Dromore West	110	54.15 N	8.53 W
Dronfield	106	53.19 N	1.27 W
Dronne ≃	118	45.02 N	0.09 W
Drumbeg	108	58.14 N	5.12 W
Drumcliffe	110	54.20 N	8.30 W
Drumheller	172	51.28 N	112.42 W
Drumlish	110	53.48 N	7.46 W
Drummond	170	46.09 S	168.09 E
Drummond Island I	176	46.00 N	83.40 W
Drummondville	172	45.53 N	72.29 W
Drummore	106	54.42 N	4.54 W
Drumquin	110	54.37 N	7.30 W
Drumshanbo	110	54.02 N	8.02 W
Družba	128	45.15 N	82.26 E
Družina	128	68.14 N	145.18 E
Dry ≃	166	14.54 S	132.24 E
Dry Bay C	172	59.08 N	138.25 W
Dry Creek ≃, Calif., U.S.	178	38.35 N	122.51 W
Dry Creek ≃, Calif., U.S.	178	38.14 N	121.24 W
Dry Creek ≃, Oreg., U.S.	178	43.34 N	117.21 W
Dry Creek Mountain ▲	178	41.22 N	116.22 W
Dryden	172	49.47 N	92.50 W
Dryfe Water ≃	106	55.08 N	3.26 W
Drymen	108	56.04 N	4.27 W
Dry Ridge	176	38.41 N	84.35 W
Drysdale ≃	166	13.59 S	126.51 E
Dry Tortugas II	182	24.38 N	82.55 W
Dschang	152	5.27 N	10.04 E
Duan	140	24.06 N	108.10 E
Duaringa	168	23.43 S	149.40 E
Duarte, Pico ▲	182	19.00 N	71.00 W
Duartina	190	22.24 S	49.25 W
Dubai → Dubayy	150	25.18 N	55.18 E
Dubawnt ≃	172	64.33 N	100.06 W
Dubawnt Lake ⊜	172	63.08 N	101.30 W
Dubayy	150	25.18 N	55.18 E
Dubbo	168	32.15 S	148.36 E
Dubh Artach I1	108	56.08 N	6.40 W
Dublin (Baile Átha Cliath), Eire	110	53.20 N	6.15 W
Dublin, Ga., U.S.	174	32.32 N	82.54 W
Dublin □6	110	53.20 N	6.15 W
Dublin Bay C	110	53.20 N	6.06 W
Du Bois	176	41.07 N	78.46 W
Dubovka	126	49.03 N	44.50 E
Dubréka	152	9.48 N	13.31 W
Dubrovnik	124	42.38 N	18.07 E
Dubuque	174	42.30 N	90.41 W
Duchang	136	29.15 N	116.12 E
Duchess	168	21.22 S	139.52 E
Duchess Hill	158	18.08 S	30.13 E
Duck Creek ≃	178	40.06 N	114.43 W
Du Couedic, Cape >	168	36.04 S	136.42 E
Duddington	104	52.36 N	0.32 W
Duddon ≃	106	54.15 N	3.13 W
Dudelange	116	49.28 N	6.05 E
Duderstadt	116	51.31 N	10.16 E
Dudinka	128	69.25 N	86.15 E
Dudley	104	52.30 N	2.05 W
Dudweiler	116	49.17 N	7.02 E
Duero (Douro) ≃	120	41.08 N	8.40 W
Duffer Peak ▲	178	41.40 N	118.44 W
Duffield	164	25.50 S	134.40 E
Dufftown	108	57.26 N	3.08 W
Dufour Spitze ▲	118	45.55 N	7.52 E
Dugi Otok I	122	44.00 N	15.04 E
Dugort	110	54.01 N	10.01 W
Du Gué ≃	172	57.21 N	70.45 W
Duich, Loch C	108	57.14 N	5.30 W
Duifken Point >	166	12.33 S	141.38 E
Duirinish	108	57.19 N	5.41 W
Duisburg	116	51.25 N	6.46 E
Duitama	184	5.50 N	73.02 W
Duiwelskloof	160	23.42 S	30.06 E
Duke of York Bay C	172	65.25 N	84.50 W
Duk Fadiat	154	7.45 N	31.25 E
Dukhān	150	25.25 N	50.48 E
Dulais ≃	104	51.41 N	3.47 W
Dulan	132	36.16 N	98.28 E
Dulas ≃, Wales, U.K.	104	52.36 N	3.50 W
Dulas ≃, Wales, U.K.	104	52.16 N	3.22 W
Dulas Bay C	106	53.23 N	4.15 W
Dul'durga	128	50.41 N	113.36 E
Duleek	110	53.39 N	6.25 W
Dulgalach ≃	128	67.44 N	133.12 E
Dulkaninna	168	29.01 S	138.27 E
Dullstroom	160	25.27 S	30.07 E
Dülmen	116	51.51 N	7.16 E
Dulnain Bridge	108	57.16 N	3.41 W
Dulnan ≃	108	57.18 N	3.40 W
Duluth	174	46.47 N	92.06 W
Dulverton	104	51.03 N	3.33 W
Dūmā, Sūrīy.	150	33.35 N	36.24 E
Duma, Zaïre	158	4.47 N	27.19 E
Dumaguete	142	9.18 N	123.18 E
Dumai	142	1.41 N	101.27 E
Dumaran Island I	138	10.33 N	119.51 E
Dumaresq ≃	168	28.40 S	150.28 E
Dumaring	138	1.36 N	118.12 E
Dumbarton	108	55.57 N	4.35 W
Dumbleyung	164	33.19 S	117.44 E
Dume, Point >	178	34.00 N	118.48 W
Dumfries	106	55.04 N	3.37 W
Dumfries and Galloway □4	106	55.00 N	4.00 W
Dumoine ≃	176	46.13 N	77.51 W
Dumont, Lac ⊜	176	46.04 N	76.27 W
Dumyāṭ	154	31.25 N	31.48 E
Dumyāṭ, Maṣabb ≃1	150	31.32 N	31.52 E
Duna → Danube ≃	100	45.20 N	29.40 E
Dunaff Head >	110	55.17 N	7.33 W
Dunaharaszti	116	47.21 N	19.05 E
Dunaj → Danube ≃	100	45.20 N	29.40 E
Dunaj, Ostrova II	128	73.52 N	124.29 E
Dunajec ≃	116	50.15 N	20.44 E
Dunakeszi	116	47.38 N	19.08 E
Dunărea → Danube ≃	100	45.20 N	29.40 E
Dunas	188	31.45 S	52.11 W
Dunaújváros	116	46.58 N	18.57 E
Dunav → Danube ≃	100	45.20 N	29.40 E
Dunbar, Scot., U.K.	108	56.00 N	2.31 W
Dunbar, W. Va., U.S.	176	38.22 N	81.45 W
Dunbeath	108	58.15 N	3.25 W
Dunblane	108	56.12 N	3.59 W
Duncan, B.C., Can.	172	48.47 N	123.42 W
Duncan, Okla., U.S.	174	34.30 N	97.57 W
Duncannon	176	40.23 N	77.02 W
Duncansby Head >	108	58.39 N	3.02 W
Dunchurch	104	52.20 N	1.16 W
Duncormick	110	52.14 N	6.39 W
Dundalk, Ont., Can.	176	44.10 N	80.24 W
Dundalk, Eire	110	54.01 N	6.25 W
Dundalk, Md., U.S.	176	39.15 N	76.31 W
Dundalk Bay C	110	53.57 N	6.17 W
Dundas	172	76.34 N	68.48 W
Dundas, Lake ⊜	164	32.35 S	121.50 E
Dundas Peninsula >1	172	74.50 N	111.30 W
Dundee, S. Afr.	160	28.12 S	30.16 E
Dundee, Scot., U.K.	108	56.28 N	3.00 W
Dundee, Mich., U.S.	176	41.57 N	83.40 W
Dundee, N.Y., U.S.	176	42.31 N	76.59 W
Dundoo	168	27.39 S	144.39 E
Dundrum, Eire	110	53.17 N	6.15 W
Dundrum, N. Ire., U.K.	110	54.16 N	5.51 W
Dundrum Bay C	110	54.14 N	5.45 W
Duneaton Water ≃	108	55.32 N	3.42 W
Dunedin	170	45.52 S	170.30 E
Dunedoo	168	32.01 S	149.24 E
Dunfanaghy	110	55.11 N	7.59 W
Dunfermline	108	56.04 N	3.29 W
Dungannon	110	54.31 N	6.46 W
Dungarvan	110	52.05 N	7.37 W
Dungarvan Harbour C	110	52.10 N	7.35 W
Dungeness >	102	50.55 N	0.58 E
Dungiven	110	54.55 N	6.55 W
Dungloe	110	54.57 N	8.22 W
Dungog	168	32.24 S	151.46 E
Dunhua	132	43.21 N	128.13 E
Dunhuang	132	40.12 N	94.41 E
Dunkeld	108	56.34 N	3.35 W
Dunkellin ≃	110	53.12 N	8.54 W
Dunkerque	118	51.03 N	2.22 E
Dunkerrin	110	52.55 N	7.55 W
Dunkery Hill ▲2	104	51.11 N	3.35 W
Dunkineely	110	54.38 N	8.23 W
Dunkirk → Dunkerque, Fr.	118	51.03 N	2.22 E
Dunkirk, Ind., U.S.	176	40.23 N	85.13 W
Dunkirk, N.Y., U.S.	176	42.29 N	79.20 W
Dunkirk, Ohio, U.S.	176	40.48 N	83.39 W
Dunkwa	152	5.22 N	1.12 W
Dún Laoghaire	110	53.17 N	6.08 W
Dunlavin	110	53.02 N	6.41 W
Dunleer	110	53.50 N	6.24 W
Dunlop	108	55.43 N	4.32 W
Dunloy	110	55.01 N	6.25 W
Dunmanus Bay C	110	51.35 N	9.45 W
Dunmanway	110	51.43 N	9.06 W
Dunmarra	166	16.42 S	133.25 E
Dunmore, Eire	110	53.36 N	8.46 W
Dunmore, Pa., U.S.	176	41.25 N	75.38 W
Dunmore Cave ⊹5	110	52.44 N	7.15 W
Dunmore East	110	52.09 N	7.00 W
Dunmore Town	182	25.30 N	76.39 W
Dunmurry	110	54.33 N	6.01 W
Dunnamanagh	110	54.52 N	7.18 W
Dunnet	108	58.31 N	3.20 W
Dunnet Bay C	108	58.37 N	3.24 W
Dunnet Head >	108	58.40 N	3.24 W
Dunnville	176	42.54 N	79.36 W
Dunqulah	154	19.10 N	30.29 E
Dun Rig ▲	108	55.34 N	3.10 W
Duns	108	55.47 N	2.20 W
Dunsandel	170	43.40 S	172.11 E
Dunsford	104	50.41 N	3.40 W
Dunsmuir	178	41.13 N	122.16 W
Dunstable	104	51.53 N	0.32 W
Dunster	104	51.12 N	3.27 W
Duntelchaig, Loch ⊜	108	57.20 N	4.18 W
Dunton Green	104	51.18 N	0.11 E
Duntroon	170	44.52 S	170.41 E
Dunvegan	108	57.26 N	6.35 W
Dunvegan, Loch C	108	57.28 N	6.40 W
Dunvegan Head >	108	57.31 N	6.43 W
Duolun	132	33.25 N	93.54 E
Duomaer	132	34.15 N	79.45 E
Duomula	132	34.07 N	82.30 E
Duque de Caxias	190	22.47 S	43.18 W
Duque de York, Isla I	186	50.37 S	75.25 W
Durack ≃	166	15.33 S	127.52 E
Durack Range ⋀	166	16.30 S	128.00 E
Durance ≃	118	44.35 N	5.10 E
Durand	176	42.55 N	83.59 W
Durango, Esp.	120	43.10 N	2.37 W
Durango, Méx.	180	24.02 N	104.40 W
Durango, Colo., U.S.	174	37.16 N	107.53 W
Durant	174	34.00 N	96.23 W
Duras	118	44.41 N	0.11 E
Durazno	188	33.22 S	56.31 W
Durazzo → Durrës	124	41.19 N	19.26 E
Durban	160	29.55 S	30.56 E
Durbin	176	38.33 N	79.50 W
Đurđevac	122	46.03 N	17.04 E
Düren	116	50.48 N	6.28 E
Durg	146	21.11 N	81.17 E
Durgāpur	146	23.29 N	87.20 E
Durham, Ont., Can.	176	44.10 N	80.49 W
Durham, Eng., U.K.	106	54.47 N	1.34 W
Durham, Calif., U.S.	178	39.39 N	121.48 W
Durham, N.H., U.S.	176	43.08 N	70.56 W
Durham, N.C., U.S.	174	35.59 N	78.54 W
Durham □6	102	54.45 N	1.45 W
Durham Downs	168	27.05 S	141.54 E
Durham Heights ▲	172	71.08 N	122.56 W
Durmitor ▲	124	43.08 N	19.01 E
Durness	108	58.33 N	4.45 W
Durness, Kyle of C	108	58.34 N	4.49 W
Dürnkrut	116	48.28 N	16.51 E
Durrës	124	41.19 N	19.26 E
Durrie	168	25.38 S	140.16 E
Durrington	104	51.13 N	1.45 W
Durris	108	57.03 N	2.22 W
Durrow	110	52.50 N	7.22 W
Dursey Head >	110	51.35 N	10.14 W
Dursley	104	51.42 N	2.21 W
Duru ▲	158	5.30 N	37.10 E
Dury Voe C	108a	60.20 N	1.08 W
Dušanbe	126	38.35 N	68.48 E
Dušekan	128	60.39 N	109.03 E
Dushan	140	25.53 N	107.30 E
Dushanzi	132	44.20 N	84.51 E
Dushore	176	41.31 N	76.24 W
Dusky Sound 𝔘	170	45.47 S	166.28 E
Düsseldorf	116	51.12 N	6.47 E
Duston	104	52.14 N	0.56 W
Dutou	136	22.54 N	115.12 E
Dutton	176	42.39 N	81.30 W
Duval, Lac ⊜	176	46.19 N	76.55 W
Duvno	122	43.43 N	17.14 E
Duxun	136	23.55 N	117.37 E
Dvinsk → Daugavpils	130	55.53 N	26.32 E
Dvuch Cirkoje, Gora ▲	128	67.35 N	168.07 E
Dvůr Králové [nad Labem]	116	50.26 N	15.48 E
Dwārka	146	22.14 N	68.58 E
Dwyfor ≃	104	52.55 N	4.17 W
Dyce	108	57.12 N	2.11 W
Dyer, Cape >	172	66.37 N	61.18 W
Dyer Bay C	176	45.10 N	81.18 W
Dyersburg	174	36.03 N	89.23 W
Dyfed □6	104	52.00 N	4.30 W
Dyfi ≃	104	52.32 N	4.03 W
Dyje (Thaya) ≃	116	48.37 N	16.56 E
Dyke	108	57.36 N	3.41 W
Dymchurch	104	51.02 N	1.00 E
Dymock	104	51.59 N	2.26 W
Dyrnesvågen	114	63.26 N	7.51 E
Dysart	108	56.08 N	3.08 W
Dysselsdorp	160	33.34 S	22.28 E
Dysynni ≃	104	52.36 N	4.05 W
Džalal-Abad	126	40.56 N	73.00 E
Džalinda	128	53.29 N	123.54 E
Džambejty	126	50.16 N	52.35 E
Džambul	126	42.54 N	71.22 E
Džankoj	126	45.43 N	34.24 E
Džanybek	126	49.25 N	46.51 E
Dzaoudzi	161a	12.47 S	45.17 E
Džardžan	128	68.43 N	124.02 E
Dzavchan ≃	132	48.54 N	93.23 E
Dželinda	128	70.08 N	114.00 E
Dzeržinsk	130	56.15 N	43.24 E
Dzeržinskoje	128	45.50 N	81.07 E
Džetygara	126	52.11 N	61.12 E
Džezkazgan	126	47.47 N	67.46 E
Dzierżoniów (Reichenbach)	116	50.44 N	16.39 E
Džizak	126	40.06 N	67.50 E
Džugdžur, Chrebet ⋀	128	58.00 N	136.00 E
Džul'fa	150	38.58 N	45.38 E
Džungarskij Alatau, Chrebet ⋀	126	45.00 N	80.00 E
Džusaly	126	45.28 N	64.05 E
Dzüüncharaa	132	48.52 N	106.28 E
Dzuunmod	132	47.45 N	106.58 E

Symbols in the index entries are identified on page 198.

Eagl – Exet

Name	Page	Lat °′	Long °′
E			
Eagle ≃	172	53.35 N	57.25 W
Eagle Creek ≃	176	38.36 N	85.04 W
Eagle Lake ⊜	178	40.39 N	120.44 W
Eagle Mountain	178	33.49 N	115.27 W
Eagle Pass	174	28.43 N	100.30 W
Eagle Peak ∧	178	41.17 N	120.12 W
Eaglesfield	106	55.03 N	3.12 W
Eaglesham	108	55.44 N	4.18 W
Ealing -•[8]	104	51.31 N	0.20 W
Eamont ≃	106	54.40 N	2.39 W
Earaheedy	164	25.34 S	121.39 E
Earby	106	53.56 N	2.08 W
Eardisley	104	52.08 N	2.59 W
Earlimart	178	35.53 N	119.16 W
Earlish	108	57.34 N	6.23 W
Earls Colne	104	51.56 N	0.42 E
Earl Shilton	104	52.35 N	1.20 W
Earl Soham	104	52.14 N	1.16 E
Earlston	108	55.39 N	2.40 W
Earlville	176	42.44 N	75.33 W
Earn ≃	108	56.21 N	3.19 W
Earn, Loch ⊜	108	56.23 N	4.14 W
Earnslaw, Mount ∧	170	44.37 S	168.24 E
Earsdon	106	55.03 N	1.29 W
Easington	106	54.47 N	1.19 W
Easingwold	106	54.07 N	1.11 W
Eask, Lough ⊜	110	54.41 N	8.03 W
Easky	110	54.18 N	8.58 W
East ≃	176	45.20 N	79.17 W
East Aberthaw	104	51.23 N	3.22 W
East Allen ≃	106	54.55 N	2.19 W
East Alligator ≃	166	12.08 S	132.42 E
East Angus	176	45.29 N	71.40 W
East Aurora	176	42.46 N	78.37 W
East Berlin → Berlin (Ost)	116	52.30 N	13.20 E
East Berlin, Pa., U.S.	176	39.56 N	76.59 W
Eastbourne, N.Z.	170	41.18 S	174.54 E
Eastbourne, Eng., U.K.	104	50.46 N	0.17 E
East Brady	176	40.59 N	79.37 W
East Caicos I	182	21.40 N	71.32 W
East Calder	108	55.54 N	3.27 W
East Canada Creek ≃	176	43.00 N	74.45 W
East Cape ≻	170	37.41 S	178.33 E
East Caroline Basin ÷[1]	96	3.00 N	147.00 E
East China Sea ▾[2]	132	30.00 N	126.00 E
Eastchurch	104	51.25 N	0.52 E
East Cleddau ≃	104	51.46 N	4.52 W
East Coast Bays	170	36.45 S	174.46 E
East Corinth	176	45.00 N	69.01 W
East Dereham	104	52.41 N	0.56 E
East Ely	178	39.15 N	114.53 W
Easter Island → Pascua, Isla de I	92	27.08 S	109.23 W
Eastern □[4], Kenya	158	0.05 N	38.00 E
Eastern □[4], Zam.	158	13.00 S	32.15 E
Eastern Caprivi Strip □[5]	160	17.45 S	24.00 E
Eastern Ghāts ⛰	148	14.00 N	78.50 E
Eastern Highlands □[5]	166	6.30 S	145.15 E
Eastern Isles II	104a	49.57 N	6.15 W
Eastern Sayans → Vostočnyj Sajan ⛰	128	53.00 N	97.00 E
East Falkland I	186	51.45 S	58.50 W
East Germany → German Democratic Republic □[1]	100	52.00 N	12.30 E
East Glacier Park	174	48.27 N	113.13 W
East Grand Rapids	176	42.56 N	85.35 W
East Greenwich	176	41.40 N	71.27 W
East Grinstead	104	51.08 N	0.01 W
Easthampton	176	42.16 N	72.40 W
East Harling	104	52.26 N	0.55 E
East Hoathly	104	50.55 N	0.10 E
East Horsley	104	51.15 N	0.26 W
East Ilsley	104	51.32 N	1.17 W
East-Indian Ridge ÷[3]	84	15.00 S	88.00 E
East Jordan	176	45.10 N	85.07 W
East Kilbride	108	55.46 N	4.10 W
Eastlake	176	41.34 N	81.35 W
East Lansing	176	42.44 N	84.29 W
Eastleigh	104	50.58 N	1.22 W
East Linton	108	55.59 N	2.39 W
East Liverpool	176	40.38 N	80.35 W
East Loch Roag C	108	58.14 N	6.48 W
East Loch Tarbert C	108	57.52 N	6.45 W
East London (Oos-Londen)	160	33.00 S	27.55 E
East Longmeadow	176	42.04 N	72.31 W
East Loof	104	50.22 N	4.27 W
East Lynn Lake ⊜[1]	176	38.05 N	82.20 W
East Machias	176	44.44 N	67.24 W
Eastmain	172	52.15 N	78.30 W
Eastmain ≃	172	52.15 N	78.35 W
East Markham	106	53.15 N	0.54 W
East Mengo □[5]	158	1.00 N	32.30 E
East Millinocket	176	45.37 N	68.35 W
East Novaya Zemlya Trough ÷[1]	88	74.00 N	62.00 E
Easton, Eng., U.K.	104	50.32 N	2.26 W
Easton, Md., U.S.	176	38.46 N	76.04 W
Easton, Pa., U.S.	176	40.42 N	75.12 W
East Orne Bank ÷[4]	96	27.45 S	157.25 W
East Pacific Basin ÷[1]	96	12.00 N	150.00 W
East Palestine	176	40.50 N	80.33 W
East Peckham	104	51.15 N	0.23 E
Eastport	176	44.54 N	67.00 W
East Porterville	178	36.04 N	118.56 W
East Retford	106	53.19 N	0.56 W
Eastry	104	51.15 N	1.18 E
East Saint Louis	174	38.38 N	96.08 W
East Scotia Basin ÷[1]	87	57.00 S	35.00 W
East Sister Island I	168	39.39 S	148.00 E
East Stour ≃	104	51.08 N	0.53 E
East Stroudsburg	176	41.00 N	75.11 W
East Sullivan	176	44.30 N	68.09 W
East Tasmania Rise ÷[3]	96	43.00 S	152.00 E
East Tawas	176	44.17 N	83.29 W
East Walker ≃	178	38.53 N	119.10 W
East Wittering	104	50.41 N	0.53 W
Eastwood	106	53.01 N	1.18 W
Eaton Rapids	176	42.36 N	84.39 W
Eaton Socon	104	52.13 N	0.18 W
Eau ≃	106	53.31 N	0.44 W
Eau Claire	174	44.49 N	91.31 W
Eau-Claire, Lac à l' ⊜	172	56.10 N	74.25 W
Eauripik I[1]	138	6.42 N	143.03 E
Eauze	118	43.52 N	0.06 E
Ebbw ≃	104	51.33 N	2.59 W
Ebbw Vale	104	51.47 N	3.12 W
Ebeltoft	114	56.12 N	10.41 E
Ebensburg	176	40.29 N	78.44 W
Ebensee	116	47.48 N	13.46 E
Eberbach	116	49.28 N	8.59 E
Ebermannstadt	116	49.23 N	11.13 E
Ebern	116	50.05 N	10.47 E
Ebersberg	116	48.05 N	11.58 E
Eberstein	116	46.48 N	14.34 E
Eberswalde	116	52.50 N	13.49 E
Ebetsu	134a	43.07 N	141.34 E
Ebingen	116	48.13 N	9.01 E
Ebola ≃	154	3.20 N	20.57 E
Eboli	122	40.37 N	15.04 E
Ebolowa	152	2.54 N	11.09 E
Ebon I[1]	96	4.35 N	168.44 E
Ebro ≃	120	40.43 N	0.54 E
Ebro, Delta del ≚[2]	120	40.43 N	0.54 E
Ebro, Embalse del ⊜[1]	120	43.00 N	3.58 W
Ecclefechan	106	55.03 N	3.17 W
Eccles	106	53.29 N	2.21 W
Ecclesfield	106	53.27 N	1.27 W
Eccleshall	104	52.52 N	2.15 W
Echaporã	190	22.26 S	50.12 W
Echeng	136	30.24 N	114.51 E
Echigo-sammyaku ⛰	134	37.50 N	139.50 E
Echt, Ned.	116	51.06 N	5.52 E
Echt, Scot., U.K.	108	57.08 N	2.26 W
Echuca	168	36.08 S	144.46 E
Écija	120	37.32 N	5.05 W
Eck, Loch ⊜	108	56.05 N	5.00 W
Eckernförde	116	54.28 N	9.50 E
Eckington	106	53.19 N	1.21 W
Eclipse Sound ⩌	172	72.38 N	79.00 W
Ečmiadzin	126	40.10 N	44.18 E
Ecuador □[1]	184	2.00 S	77.30 W
Écueillé	118	47.05 N	1.21 E
Ed	114	58.55 N	11.55 E
Edah	164	28.17 S	117.10 E
Edam	116	52.31 N	5.03 E
Eday I	108	59.11 N	2.47 W
Edderton	108	57.50 N	4.10 W
Eddleston	108	55.43 N	3.13 W
Eddrachillis Bay C	108	58.18 N	5.15 W
Eddystone Rocks II[1]	102	50.12 N	4.15 W
Ede, Ned.	116	52.03 N	5.40 E
Ede, Nig.	152	7.44 N	4.27 E
Edéa	152	3.48 N	10.08 E
Edehon Lake ⊜	172	60.25 N	97.15 W
Eden, Austl.	168	37.04 S	149.54 E
Eden, N. Ire., U.K.	110	54.43 N	5.47 W
Eden ≃, Eng., U.K.	102	54.57 N	3.01 W
Eden ≃, Eng., U.K.	104	51.10 N	0.11 E
Eden ≃, Scot., U.K.	108	56.22 N	2.50 W
Eden ≃, Wales, U.K.	104	52.48 N	3.53 W
Edenbridge	104	51.12 N	0.04 E
Edenburg	160	29.45 S	25.56 E
Edendale, N.Z.	170	46.19 S	168.47 E
Edendale, S. Afr.	160	29.39 S	30.18 E
Edenderry	110	53.21 N	7.35 W
Eden Hill ∧[2]	176	41.20 N	73.19 W
Edenside ∨	106	54.40 N	2.35 W
Edenville	160	27.37 S	27.34 E
Edeowie	168	31.27 S	138.27 E
Ederny	110	54.32 N	7.39 W
Edgartown	176	41.23 N	70.31 W
Edge Hill ∧[2]	104	52.08 N	1.27 W
Edgemont	174	43.18 N	103.50 W
Edgeroi	168	30.07 S	149.48 E
Edgerton	176	41.27 N	84.45 W
Edgewood	176	39.25 N	76.18 W
Edgeworthstown	110	53.42 N	7.36 W
Édhessa	124	40.48 N	22.03 E
Edievale	170	45.48 S	169.22 E
Edinboro	176	41.52 N	80.08 W
Edinburg, Tex., U.S.	174	26.18 N	98.10 W
Edinburg, Va., U.S.	176	38.49 N	78.34 W
Edinburgh	108	55.57 N	3.13 W
Edirne	124	41.40 N	26.34 E
Edirne □[4]	124	41.15 N	26.40 E
Edith River	166	14.11 S	132.02 E
Edjeleh	152	27.38 N	9.50 E
Edjudina	164	29.48 S	122.23 E
Edmondbyers	106	54.51 N	1.58 W
Edmonton, Austl.	166	17.01 S	145.45 E
Edmonton, Alta., Can.	172	53.33 N	113.28 W
Edmore	176	43.25 N	85.03 W
Edmund	164	23.46 S	116.02 E
Edmundston	172	47.22 N	68.20 W
Edrengijn Nuruu ⛰	132	44.15 N	97.45 E
Edsbro	114	59.54 N	18.29 E
Edsbruk	114	58.02 N	16.28 E
Edsbyn	114	61.23 N	15.49 E
Edson	172	53.35 N	116.26 W
Edson Butte ∧	178	42.52 N	124.20 W
Eduardo Castex	188	35.55 S	64.20 W
Edward, Lake ⊜	158	0.25 S	29.30 E
Edwards	176	44.20 N	75.15 W
Edwards Creek	168	28.21 S	135.51 E
Edwards Plateau ⛰[1]	174	31.20 N	101.00 W
Edward VIII Bay C	87	66.50 S	57.00 E
Edward VII Peninsula ≻[1]	87	77.40 S	155.00 W
Edwinstowe	106	53.12 N	1.04 W
Edzell	108	56.48 N	2.39 W
Eeklo	116	51.11 N	3.34 E
Eel ≃	178	40.40 N	124.20 W
Eel, Middle Fork ≃	178	39.42 N	123.21 W
Eel, North Fork ≃	178	39.57 N	123.26 W
Eel, South Fork ≃	178	40.22 N	123.55 W
Eergu'nahe (Argun') ≃	128	53.20 N	121.28 E
Efate I	96	17.40 S	168.25 E
Egadi, Isole II	122	37.56 N	12.16 E
Egan Range ⛰	178	39.00 N	115.00 W
Eganville	176	45.32 N	77.06 W
Egede og Rothes Fjord C[2]	172	66.00 N	38.00 W
Egedesminde	172	68.42 N	52.45 W
Eger	116	47.54 N	20.23 E
Egersund	114	58.27 N	6.00 E
Egerton, Mount ∧	87	80.50 S	158.50 E
Egg Harbor City	176	39.32 N	74.39 W
Egg Lagoon	168	39.39 S	143.58 E
Egham	104	51.26 N	0.34 W
Egilsay I	108	59.09 N	2.56 W
Égletons	118	45.24 N	2.03 E
Eglinton	110	55.01 N	7.11 W
Egloskerry	104	50.39 N	4.27 W
Egmont, Cape ≻	170	39.17 S	173.45 E
Egremont	106	54.29 N	3.33 W
Egton	106	54.26 N	0.45 W
Egtved	114	55.37 N	9.18 E
Egvekinot	128	66.19 N	179.10 E
Egypt □[1]	154	27.00 N	30.00 E
Ehen ≃	106	54.25 N	3.30 W
Ehime □[5]	134	33.40 N	132.50 E
Ehingen	116	48.17 N	9.43 E
Ehrenberg	178	33.36 N	114.31 W
Ei	134	31.12 N	130.30 E
Éibar	120	43.11 N	2.28 W
Eichstätt	116	48.54 N	11.12 E
Eidfjord	114	60.28 N	7.05 E
Eidsvåg	114	60.27 N	5.21 E
Eidsvold	168	25.22 S	151.07 E
Eidsvoll	114	60.19 N	11.14 E
Eifel ⛰	116	50.15 N	6.45 E
Eiffel Flats	158	18.15 S	29.59 E
Eigg I	108	56.54 N	6.10 W
Eigg, Sound of ⩌	108	56.51 N	6.13 W
Eighe, Carn ∧	108	57.17 N	5.07 W
Eight Degree Channel ⩌	148	8.00 N	73.00 E
Eights Coast _•[2]	87	73.30 S	93.00 W
Eighty Mile Beach _•[2]	164	19.45 S	121.00 E
Eikeren ⊜	114	59.38 N	9.58 E
Eikesdalsvatnet ⊜	114	62.34 N	8.11 E
Eil	154	8.00 N	49.51 E
Eildon	168	37.14 S	145.56 E
Eildon, Lake ⊜[1]	168	37.11 S	145.55 E
Eilenburg	116	51.27 N	12.37 E
Eil Malk I	138	7.09 N	134.22 E
Einasleigh	168	18.31 S	144.05 E
Einasleigh ≃	168	17.30 S	142.17 E
Einbeck	116	51.49 N	9.52 E
Eindhoven	116	51.26 N	5.28 E
Einsiedeln	118	47.08 N	8.45 E
Eire → Ireland □[1]	100	53.00 N	8.00 W
Eisenach	116	50.59 N	10.19 E
Eisenberg	116	50.58 N	11.53 E
Eisenerz	116	47.33 N	14.53 E
Eisenerzer Alpen ⛰	116	47.28 N	14.45 E
Eisenhüttenstadt	116	52.10 N	14.39 E
Eisenkappel	124	46.29 N	14.36 E
Eisenstadt	116	47.51 N	16.32 E
Eishken	108	58.01 N	6.32 W
Eishort, Loch C	108	57.10 N	5.59 W
Eisleben	116	51.31 N	11.32 E
Eislingen	116	48.42 N	9.42 E
Eithon ≃	104	52.12 N	3.27 W
Eitorf	116	50.46 N	7.26 E
Ejea de los Caballeros	120	42.08 N	1.08 W
Ejinaqi	132	41.50 N	100.50 E
Ekenäs (Taamisaari)	114	59.58 N	23.26 E
Ekeren	116	51.17 N	4.25 E
Eketahuna	170	40.39 S	175.42 E
Ekiatapskij Chrebet ⛰	128	68.30 N	179.00 E
Ekibastuz	128	51.42 N	75.22 E
Ekimčan	128	53.04 N	132.58 E
Ekonda	128	65.47 N	105.17 E
Eksjö	114	57.40 N	14.57 E
Ekwan ≃	172	53.14 N	82.13 W
El- → Ad-, Al-, An-, Ar-, As-, Ash-, At-, Az-			
El Aaiún	152	27.09 N	13.12 W
El Aguilar	188	23.15 S	65.40 W
El Álamo	178	31.34 N	116.02 W
Elands ≃	160	25.10 S	29.10 E
Elandsvlei	160	32.19 S	19.33 E
El Arahal	120	37.16 N	5.33 W
El Asnam	152	36.10 N	1.20 E
Elassón	124	39.54 N	22.11 E
Elat	150	29.33 N	34.57 E
Elat, Gulf of → Aqaba, Gulf of C	150	29.00 N	34.40 E
Elâziğ	150	38.41 N	39.14 E
Elba, Isola d' I	122	42.46 N	10.17 E
El Banco	184	9.00 N	73.58 W
El Barco de Avila	120	40.21 N	5.31 W
El Barco de Valdeorras	120	42.25 N	6.59 W
Elbasan	124	41.06 N	20.05 E
El Baúl	182	8.57 N	68.17 W
Elbe (Labe) ≃	116	53.50 N	9.00 E
Elbe-Havel-Kanal ≖	116	52.24 N	12.23 E
Elbert, Mount ∧	174	39.07 N	106.27 W
Elbeuf	118	49.17 N	1.00 E
Elbing → Elblag	116	54.10 N	19.25 E
Elblag (Elbing)	116	54.10 N	19.25 E
El Bluff	182	11.59 N	83.40 W
Elbow Cay I	182	23.55 N	80.25 W
El'brus, Gora ∧	126	43.21 N	42.26 E
Elbrus, Mount → El'brus, Gora ∧	126	43.21 N	42.26 E
El Burgo de Osma	120	41.35 N	3.04 W
Elburz Mountains → Alborz, Reshteh-ye Kūhhā-ye ⛰	150	36.00 N	53.00 E
El Cajon	178	32.48 N	116.58 W
El Calvario	182	8.59 N	67.00 W
El Capitan ∧	174	46.01 N	114.23 W
El Carmen, Arg.	188	24.24 S	65.15 W
El Carmen, Col.	184	8.30 N	73.27 W
El Carmen de Bolívar	182	9.43 N	75.08 W
El Castillo	182	11.01 N	84.25 W
El Cenajo, Embalse de ⊜[1]	120	38.25 N	2.00 W
El Centinela	178	32.38 N	115.40 W
El Centro	178	32.48 N	115.34 W
El César □[5]	182	10.00 N	73.40 W
Elche	120	38.15 N	0.42 W
Elche de la Sierra	120	38.27 N	2.03 W
El Ciprés	178	31.50 N	116.38 W
El Colorado	188	26.20 S	59.20 W
El Cóndor, Cerro ∧	188	26.39 S	68.24 W
El Corpus	182	13.16 N	87.03 W
Elda	120	38.29 N	0.47 W
El Descanso	178	32.12 N	116.55 W
El'dikan	128	60.48 N	135.11 E
El Djouf -•[2]	152	20.30 N	8.00 W
Eldorado, Arg.	188	26.26 S	54.40 W
Eldorado, Bra.	188	24.32 S	48.06 W
El Dorado, Ark., U.S.	174	33.13 N	92.40 W
El Dorado, Kans., U.S.	174	37.49 N	96.52 W
Eldoret	156	0.31 N	35.17 E
Eldred	176	41.57 N	78.23 W
El-Dudu	158	2.40 N	41.46 E
Eleanor	176	38.32 N	81.56 W
Elefantes, Rio dos (Olifants) ≃	160	24.10 S	32.40 E
Elektrostal'	130	55.47 N	38.28 E
El Encanto	184	1.37 S	73.14 W
Elephant Butte Reservoir ⊜[1]	174	33.19 N	107.10 W
Elephant Island I	87	61.10 S	55.14 W
Elephant Mountain ∧	176	44.46 N	70.46 W
El Eulma	120	36.08 N	5.40 E
Eleuthera I	182	25.15 N	76.20 W
Eleuthera Point ≻	182	24.40 N	76.11 W
Elevsís	124	38.02 N	23.32 E
Elevtheroúpolis	124	40.55 N	24.16 E
El Ferrol del Caudillo	120	43.29 N	8.14 W
El Galpón	188	25.24 S	64.39 W
Elgin, Scot., U.K.	108	57.39 N	3.20 W
Elgin, Ill., U.S.	174	42.02 N	88.17 W
Elgol	108	57.09 N	6.06 W
El Goléa	152	30.30 N	2.50 E
El Golfo de Santa Clara	178	31.34 N	114.19 W
Elgon, Mount ∧	158	1.08 N	34.33 E
El Guamo	182	10.02 N	74.59 W
El Guapo	182	10.09 N	65.58 W
Elham	104	51.10 N	1.07 E
El Hank _•[4]	152	24.30 N	7.00 W
Elhovo	124	42.10 N	26.34 E
Elia	182	20.59 N	77.26 W
Elías Piña	182	18.53 N	71.42 W
Elila ≃	158	2.45 S	25.53 E
Elinghu ⊜	132	34.50 N	97.35 E
Eliot	176	43.09 N	70.48 W
Élisabethville → Lubumbashi	158	11.40 S	27.28 E
Elista	126	46.16 N	44.14 E
Elizabeth, Austl.	168	34.43 S	138.40 E
Elizabeth, N.J., U.S.	176	40.40 N	74.11 W
Elizabeth, W. Va., U.S.	176	39.04 N	81.24 W
Elizabeth City	174	36.18 N	76.14 W
Elizabeth Reef I[1]	162	29.56 S	159.04 E
Elizabethtown, N.Y., U.S.	176	44.13 N	73.36 W
Elizabethtown, Pa., U.S.	176	40.09 N	76.36 W
El-Jadida	152	33.16 N	8.30 W
Ełk	116	53.50 N	22.22 E
Elk ≃	176	38.21 N	81.38 W
El Kairouan	152	35.41 N	10.07 E
El Kala	122	36.50 N	8.30 E
El Kasserine	152	35.11 N	8.48 E
Elk Creek	178	39.36 N	122.32 W
Elkedra ≃	164	21.08 S	136.22 E
El Kef	122	36.11 N	8.43 E
Elk Grove	178	38.25 N	121.22 W
Elkhart	174	41.41 N	85.58 W
Elkins	176	38.55 N	79.51 W
Elkland	176	41.59 N	77.21 W
Elko	178	40.50 N	115.46 W
Elk Rapids	176	44.54 N	85.25 W
Elkton, Md., U.S.	176	39.36 N	75.50 W
Elkton, Mich., U.S.	176	43.49 N	83.11 W
Elkton, Va., U.S.	176	38.25 N	78.38 W
Ell, Lake ⊜	164	29.13 S	127.46 E
Elland	106	53.41 N	1.50 W
Ellavalla	164	25.05 S	114.22 E
Ellef Ringnes Island I	90	78.30 N	104.00 W
El Leh	158	3.48 N	39.48 E
Elleker	164	35.00 S	117.43 E
Ellen ≃	106	54.43 N	3.30 W
Ellendale, Austl.	164	17.56 S	124.48 E
Ellendale, N. Dak., U.S.	174	46.06 N	98.32 W
Ellensburg	174	47.00 N	120.32 W
Ellenville	176	41.43 N	74.28 W
Ellesmere	104	52.54 N	2.54 W
Ellesmere Island I	90	81.00 N	80.00 W
Ellesmere Port	106	53.17 N	2.54 W
Ellice ≃	172	68.02 N	103.26 W
Ellice Islands → Tuvalu □[2]	96	8.00 S	178.00 E
Ellicott City	176	39.16 N	76.48 W
Ellicottville	176	42.17 N	78.40 W
Ellington	106	55.13 N	1.34 W
Elliot	160	31.18 S	27.50 E
Elliotdale	160	31.55 S	28.38 E
Elliot Lake	172	46.23 N	82.39 W
Elliott	166	17.33 S	133.32 E
Elliott, Mount ∧	164	20.29 S	126.37 E
Ellisras	160	23.40 S	27.46 E
Elliston	162	33.39 S	134.55 E
Ellon	108	57.22 N	2.05 W
Ellore → Elūru	148	16.42 N	81.06 E
Ellsworth, Maine, U.S.	176	44.33 N	68.26 W
Ellsworth, Mich., U.S.	176	45.10 N	85.15 W
Ellsworth Land -•[1]	87	75.30 S	80.00 W
Ellsworth Mountains ⛰	87	79.00 S	85.00 W
Ellwangen	116	48.57 N	10.07 E
Ellwood City	176	40.50 N	80.17 W
Elm	104	52.38 N	0.10 E
El Mahdia	122	35.30 N	11.04 E
El Maneadero	178	31.45 N	116.35 W
Elmer	176	39.36 N	75.10 W
Elmira, Ont., Can.	176	43.36 N	80.33 W
Elmira, N.Y., U.S.	176	42.06 N	76.49 W
El Mirage Lake ⊜	178	34.38 N	117.35 W
Elmira Heights	176	42.08 N	76.49 W
El Moknine	152	35.38 N	10.54 E
El Monte	188	33.41 S	71.01 W
Elmore, Austl.	168	36.30 S	144.37 E
Elmore, Ohio, U.S.	176	41.29 N	83.18 W
El Mreyyé -•[1]	152	19.30 N	7.00 W
Elmshorn	116	53.45 N	9.39 E
Elmswell	104	52.15 N	0.53 E
Elmvale	176	44.35 N	79.52 W
Elne	118	42.36 N	2.58 E
El Nevado, Cerro ∧	184	3.59 N	74.04 W
El Niybo	158	4.32 N	39.59 E
Elobey, Islas II	156	0.59 N	9.30 E
Elora	176	43.41 N	80.26 W
Elortondo	188	33.45 S	61.35 W
El Oued	152	33.20 N	6.58 E
El Palqui	188	30.45 S	70.59 W
El Pao	182	9.38 N	68.08 W
El Paradero	182	10.38 N	69.32 W
El Paso	174	31.45 N	106.29 W
El Paso Peaks ⛰	178	35.28 N	117.43 W
Elphin	110	53.51 N	8.12 W
El Pilar	182	10.32 N	63.09 W
El Piñón	182	10.24 N	74.50 W
El Portal	178	37.41 N	119.47 W
El Porvenir	178	32.05 N	116.38 W
El Puente del Arzobispo	120	39.48 N	5.10 W
El Puerto de Santa María	120	36.36 N	6.13 W
Elqui ≃	188	29.54 S	71.17 W
El Rastro	182	9.03 N	67.27 W
El Reno	174	35.32 N	97.57 W
El Rio	178	34.14 N	119.10 W
Elsa	172	63.55 N	135.28 W
El Salto	180	23.47 N	105.22 W
El Salvador □[1]	180	13.50 N	88.55 W
El Sauce	182	12.53 N	86.32 W
El Sauzal	178	31.54 N	116.41 W
El Seibo	182	18.46 N	69.02 W
Elsie	176	43.05 N	84.23 W
Elsinore → Helsingør	114	56.02 N	12.37 E
Elsinore, Lake ⊜[1]	178	33.39 N	117.21 W
Elsmere	176	39.44 N	75.36 W
El Socorro	182	8.59 N	65.44 W
El Sombrero	182	9.23 N	67.03 W
Elspe	116	51.09 N	8.04 E
Elstead	104	51.11 N	0.43 W
Elsterwerda	116	51.28 N	13.31 E
Elstree	104	51.39 N	0.16 W
Eltham	170	39.26 S	174.18 E
El Tigre	184	8.55 N	64.15 W
Eltmann	116	49.58 N	10.40 E
El Toco	188	22.05 S	69.35 W
El Tocuyo	182	9.47 N	69.48 W
El Tofo	188	29.27 S	71.15 W
El Tranco, Embalse de ⊜[1]	120	38.10 N	2.45 W
El Tránsito	188	28.52 S	70.17 W
El Triunfo	182	15.46 N	87.26 W
El Turbio	186	51.41 S	72.05 W
Elūru	148	16.42 N	81.06 E
Elvas	120	38.53 N	7.10 W
Elven	118	47.44 N	2.35 W
Elverum	114	60.53 N	11.34 E
El Viejo	182	12.38 N	87.11 W
El Volcán	188	33.49 S	70.11 W
El-Wak	158	2.50 N	41.03 E
Elwy ≃	106	53.16 N	3.26 W
Ely, Eng., U.K.	104	52.24 N	0.16 E
Ely, Nev., U.S.	178	39.15 N	114.53 W
Ely, Isle of -•[1]	104	52.24 N	0.10 E
Elyria	176	41.22 N	82.06 W
Emba	126	48.50 N	58.08 E
Emba ≃	126	46.38 N	53.14 E
Embarcación	188	23.15 S	64.10 W
Embetsu	134a	44.44 N	141.47 E
Embleton	106	55.30 N	1.37 W
Embo	108	57.54 N	3.59 W
Embrun, Ont., Can.	176	45.16 N	75.17 W
Embrun, Fr.	118	44.34 N	6.30 E
Embu	158	0.32 S	37.27 E
Emden	116	53.22 N	7.12 E
Emerald	168	23.32 S	148.10 E
Emilia-Romagna □[4]	122	44.35 N	11.00 E
Emlembe ∧	160	25.57 S	31.11 E
Emlenton	176	41.11 N	79.43 W
Emmaus	176	40.32 N	75.30 W
Emmen	116	52.47 N	7.00 E
Emmendingen	116	48.07 N	7.50 E
Emmerich	116	51.50 N	6.15 E
Emmet	168	24.40 S	144.28 E
Emmiganūru	148	15.44 N	77.29 E
Emmitsburg	176	39.42 N	77.20 W
Emneth	104	52.38 N	0.11 E
Emőd	116	47.56 N	20.49 E
Empalme	180	27.58 N	110.51 W
Empangeni	160	28.50 S	31.48 E
Empedrado, Arg.	188	27.55 S	58.45 W
Empedrado, Chile	188	35.36 S	72.17 W
Empire, Nev., U.S.	178	40.37 N	119.21 W
Empire, Oreg., U.S.	178	43.23 N	124.17 W
Empoli	122	43.43 N	10.57 E
Emporia	174	38.24 N	96.11 W
Emporium	176	41.31 N	78.14 W
Emsdetten	116	52.10 N	7.31 E
Emsworth	104	50.51 N	0.56 W
Emukae	134	33.18 N	129.38 E
Emu Park	168	23.15 S	150.50 E
Emyvale	110	54.20 N	6.59 W
En (Inn) ≃	118	48.35 N	13.28 E
Enard Bay C	108	58.05 N	5.20 W
Enborne ≃	104	51.24 N	1.06 W
Encantado	188	29.15 S	51.53 W
Encinitas	178	33.03 N	117.17 W
Encontrados	184	9.03 N	72.14 W
Encounter Bay C	168	35.35 S	138.44 E
Encruzilhada do Sul	188	30.32 S	52.31 W
Encs	116	48.20 N	21.08 E
Ende	142	8.50 S	121.39 E
Endeavour Strait ⩌	166	10.50 S	142.15 E
Enderbury I[1]	96	3.08 S	171.05 W
Enderby	104	52.36 N	1.12 W
Enderby Land -•[1]	87	67.30 S	53.00 E
Endicott	176	42.06 N	76.03 W
Ene ≃	184	11.10 S	74.18 W
Eneabba	164	29.50 S	115.20 E
Enez	124	40.44 N	26.04 E
Enfer, Pointe d' ≻	182	14.22 N	60.52 W
Enfield	176	43.34 N	71.57 W
Enfield -•[8]	104	51.40 N	0.05 W
Engaño, Cabo ≻	182	18.40 N	68.20 W
Engaru	134a	44.03 N	143.31 E
Engcobo	160	31.37 S	28.00 E
Engel's	126	51.30 N	46.07 E
Enggano, Pulau I	142	5.24 S	102.16 E
England □[8]	102	52.30 N	1.30 W
Englefield, Cape ≻	172	69.51 N	85.39 W
Englehart	172	47.49 N	79.52 W
English ≃, Ont., Can.	172	50.12 N	95.00 W
English ≃, N.A.	176	45.13 N	73.50 W
English Bāzār	146	25.00 N	88.09 E
English Channel (La Manche) ⩌	102	50.20 N	1.00 W
English Coast _•[2]	87	73.45 S	73.00 W
Enid	174	36.19 N	97.48 W
Eniwa	134a	42.45 N	141.33 E
Eniwetok I[1]	96	11.30 N	162.15 E
Enkeldoorn	158	19.01 S	30.53 E
Enkhuizen	116	52.42 N	5.17 E
Enköping	114	59.38 N	17.04 E
Enmelen	128	65.01 N	175.54 W
Enna	122	37.34 N	14.17 E
Ennadai Lake ⊜	172	60.53 N	101.15 W
Ennedi ⛰[1]	154	17.15 N	22.00 E
Ennell, Lough ⊜	110	53.28 N	7.24 W
Ennerdale Water ⊜	106	54.31 N	3.23 W
Enngonia	168	29.19 S	145.51 E
Ennis	110	52.50 N	8.59 W
Enniscorthy	110	52.30 N	6.34 W
Enniskillen	110	54.21 N	7.38 W
Ennistymon	110	52.57 N	9.15 W
Enns	116	48.13 N	14.29 E
Enns ≃	116	48.14 N	14.32 E
Enon	176	39.53 N	83.56 W
Enontekiö	112	68.23 N	23.38 E
Enosburg Falls	176	44.55 N	72.48 W
Enrekang	142	3.34 S	119.47 E
Enriquillo	182	17.54 N	71.14 W
Enriquillo, Lago ⊜	182	18.30 N	71.37 W
Ensay	168	37.23 S	147.50 E
Ensay I	108	57.46 N	7.05 W
Enschede	116	52.12 N	6.53 E
Ensenada, Arg.	188	34.51 S	57.55 W
Ensenada, Méx.	180	31.52 N	116.37 W
Enshi	132	30.17 N	109.19 E
Enshū-nada ▾[2]	134	34.27 N	137.38 E
Entebbe	158	0.04 N	32.28 E
Enterprise, Calif., U.S.	178	39.32 N	121.22 W
Enterprise, Utah, U.S.	178	37.34 N	113.43 W
Entinas, Punta ≻	120	36.41 N	2.46 W
Entrepeñas, Embalse de ⊜[1]	120	40.34 N	2.42 W
Entre Rios, Bra.	190	11.56 S	38.05 W
Entre-Rios, Moç.	158	14.57 S	37.20 E
Entre Ríos □[4]	188	32.00 S	59.20 W
Enugu	152	6.27 N	7.27 E
Enurmino	128	66.57 N	171.49 W
Envalira, Port d')(	120	42.35 N	1.45 E
Envermeu	118	49.54 N	1.16 E
Enys, Mount ∧	170	43.14 S	171.38 E
Eo ≃	120	43.28 N	7.03 W
Eolie, Isole II	122	38.30 N	15.00 E
Epanomi	124	40.26 N	22.56 E
Épernay	118	49.03 N	3.57 E
Ephraim	174	39.22 N	111.35 W
Ephrata	176	40.11 N	76.10 W
Epi I	96	16.43 S	168.15 E
Épinal	118	48.11 N	6.27 E
Eport, Loch C	108	57.33 N	7.11 W
Epping, Eng., U.K.	104	51.43 N	0.07 E
Epping, N.H., U.S.	176	43.02 N	71.04 W
Epping Forest -•[3]	104	51.40 N	0.03 E
Epsom	104	51.20 N	0.16 W
Epte ≃	118	49.04 N	1.37 E
Epukiro	160	21.41 S	19.08 E
Epukiro ≃	160	20.45 S	21.05 E
Epworth	106	53.32 N	0.49 W
Equatorial Guinea □[1]	156	2.00 N	9.00 E
Eradu	164	28.41 S	115.02 E
Erba	122	45.48 N	9.15 E
Erciyeş Dağı ∧	150	38.32 N	35.28 E
Érd	116	47.23 N	18.56 E
Erdene	132	44.40 N	111.05 E
Erding	116	48.18 N	11.54 E
Erebus, Mount ∧	87	77.32 S	167.09 E
Erechim	188	27.38 S	52.17 W
Ereğli	150	37.31 N	34.04 E
Erétria	124	38.24 N	23.48 E
Erfoud	152	31.28 N	4.10 W
Erfurt	116	50.58 N	11.01 E
Erfurt □[5]	116	51.20 N	10.50 E
Ergene ≃	124	41.01 N	26.22 E
Erges (Erjas) ≃	120	39.40 N	7.01 E
Erhai ⊜	140	25.48 N	100.11 E
Erhlin	136	23.54 N	120.22 E
Eriboll	108	58.28 N	4.41 W
Eriboll, Loch C	108	58.31 N	4.41 W
Erice	122	38.02 N	12.36 E
Erichsen Lake ⊜	172	70.38 N	80.21 W
Ericht, Loch ⊜	108	56.48 N	4.24 W
Erie	176	42.08 N	80.04 W
Erie, Lake ⊜	174	42.15 N	81.00 W
Erie Canal → New York State Barge Canal ≖	176	43.05 N	78.43 W
Erigavo	154	10.37 N	47.24 E
Erimanthos ∧	124	37.59 N	21.51 E
Erimo-misaki ≻	134a	41.55 N	143.15 E
Erin	176	43.45 N	80.07 W
Eriskay I	108	57.04 N	7.18 W
Erisort, Loch C	108	58.07 N	6.24 W
Erithrai	124	38.13 N	23.19 E
Eritrea □[9]	154	15.20 N	39.00 E
Erivan → Jerevan	150	40.11 N	44.30 E
Erjas (Erges) ≃	120	39.40 N	7.01 W
Erjia	136	32.02 N	121.13 E
Erkelenz	116	51.05 N	9.19 E
Erkina ≃	110	52.51 N	7.23 W
Erlangen	116	49.36 N	11.01 E
Erldunda	164	25.14 S	133.12 E
Erlian	132	43.46 N	112.05 E
Erlistoun	164	28.20 S	122.08 E
Erme ≃	104	50.18 N	3.56 W
Ermelo	160	26.34 S	29.58 E
Ermoúpolis	124	37.26 N	24.56 E
Ernaballa Mission	164	26.17 S	132.07 E
Ernākulam	148	9.59 N	76.17 E
Erne ≃	110	54.30 N	8.16 W
Erne, Lower Lough ⊜	110	54.26 N	7.46 W
Erne, Upper Lough ⊜	110	54.14 N	7.32 W
Ernée	118	48.18 N	0.56 W
Ernest Legouve Reef ÷[2]	96	35.10 S	150.40 W
Erode	148	11.21 N	77.44 E
Eromanga	168	26.40 S	143.16 E
Eromanga I	96	18.45 S	169.05 E
Errabiddy	164	25.28 S	117.07 E
Errigal ∧	110	55.02 N	8.07 W
Erris Head ≻	110	54.19 N	10.00 W
Errochty, Loch ⊜	108	56.45 N	4.12 W
Errogie	108	57.16 N	4.22 W
Ersekë	124	40.20 N	20.41 E
Erskine Inlet C	172	76.15 N	102.20 W
Ertai	132	46.07 N	90.06 E
Erua	170	39.14 S	175.24 E
Erudina	168	31.28 S	139.23 E
Erval	188	32.02 S	53.24 W
Erval d'Oeste	188	27.13 S	51.34 W
Erzgebirge (Krušné hory) ⛰	116	50.30 N	13.10 E
Erzin	128	50.15 N	95.10 E
Erzincan	150	39.44 N	39.29 E
Erzurum	150	39.55 N	41.17 E
Esa-Ala	166	9.44 S	150.49 E
Esan-saki ≻	134a	41.49 N	141.11 E
Esashi, Nihon	134	39.12 N	141.09 E
Esashi, Nihon	134	41.52 N	140.07 E
Esashi, Nihon	134a	44.56 N	142.35 E
Esbjerg	114	55.28 N	8.27 E
Escalon	178	37.48 N	120.60 W
Escalona	120	40.10 N	4.24 W
Escanaba	174	45.45 N	87.04 W
Escarpada Point ≻	138	18.31 N	122.13 E
Escaut (Schelde) ≃	116	51.22 N	4.15 E
Esch-sur-Alzette	116	49.30 N	5.59 E
Eschwege	116	51.11 N	10.04 E
Eschweiler	116	50.49 N	6.16 E
Esclave, Grand Lac de l'→ Great Slave Lake ⊜	172	61.30 N	114.00 W
Escocesa, Bahía C	182	19.20 N	69.40 W
Escondido	178	33.07 N	117.05 W
Escondido ≃	182	12.10 N	83.42 W
Escrick	106	53.53 N	1.02 W
Escuinapa	180	22.51 N	105.48 W
Escuintla	180	14.18 N	90.47 W
Eşfahān (Isfahan)	150	32.40 N	51.38 E
Esgueva ≃	120	41.40 N	4.43 W
Eshan	140	24.11 N	102.22 E
Esher	104	51.23 N	0.22 W
Eshowe	160	28.58 S	31.29 E
Esk ≃, Eng., U.K.	106	54.29 N	0.37 W
Esk ≃, Eng., U.K.	106	54.21 N	3.23 W
Esk ≃, Scot., U.K.	108	55.57 N	3.03 W
Eskdale	176	38.05 N	81.27 W
Eskdale ∨	106	55.10 N	3.00 W
Eskifjörður	112a	65.04 N	13.59 W
Eskilstuna	114	59.22 N	16.30 E
Eskimo Lakes ⊜	172	69.15 N	132.17 W
Eskimo Point	172	61.07 N	94.03 W
Eskişehir	94	39.46 N	30.32 E
Esmeralda, Austl.	168	18.50 S	142.34 E
Esmeralda, Cuba	182	21.51 N	78.07 W
Esmeralda, Isla I	186	48.55 S	75.25 W
Esmeraldas	184	0.59 N	79.42 W
Esmeraldas ≃	184	0.58 N	79.38 W
Espada, Punta ≻	182	12.00 N	71.08 W
Espalion	118	44.31 N	2.46 E
Espanola	172	46.15 N	81.46 W
Esparta	182	9.59 N	84.40 W
Espejo	120	37.41 N	4.33 W
Espelkamp	116	52.25 N	8.36 E
Esperance	164	33.51 S	121.53 E
Esperance Bay C	164	33.51 S	121.53 E
Esperanza, Arg.	188	31.30 S	60.55 W
Esperanza, S. Afr.	160	30.21 S	30.40 E
Espevær	114	59.36 N	5.10 E
Espichel, Cabo ≻	120	38.25 N	9.13 W
Espinhaço, Serra do ⛰	190	17.30 S	43.30 W
Espinho	120	41.00 N	8.39 W
Espírito Santo □[3]	190	19.30 S	40.30 W
Espiritu Santo I	96	15.50 S	166.50 E
Espíritu Santo, Bahía del C	182	19.20 N	87.35 W
Espíritu Santo, Isla del I	180	24.30 N	110.20 W
Esplanada	190	11.47 S	37.57 W
Espoo (Esbo)	114	60.13 N	24.40 E
Esposende	120	41.32 N	8.47 W
Espumoso	188	28.44 S	52.51 W
Espungabera	160	20.29 S	32.48 E
Esquel	186	42.55 S	71.20 W
Esquina	188	30.00 S	59.30 W
Essaouira	152	31.30 N	9.47 W
Essen	116	51.28 N	7.01 E
Essendon, Mount ∧	164	24.59 S	120.28 E
Essequibo ≃	184	6.50 N	58.30 W
Essex, Ont., Can.	176	42.10 N	82.49 W
Essex, Md., U.S.	176	39.18 N	76.29 W
Essex □[6]	102	51.48 N	0.40 E
Essex Junction	176	44.29 N	73.07 W
Essexvale	158	20.18 S	28.56 E
Essexville	176	43.37 N	83.50 W
Esslingen	116	48.45 N	9.16 E
Essonne □[5]	118	48.36 N	2.20 E
Essoyes	118	48.04 N	4.32 E
Est, Cap ≻	161b	15.16 S	50.29 E
Est, Pointe de l' ≻	172	49.08 N	61.41 W
Estaca de Bares, Punta de la ≻	120	43.46 N	7.42 W
Estacado, Llano ≚	174	33.30 N	103.00 W
Estados, Isla de los I	186	54.45 S	64.20 W
Eşţahbānāt	150	29.08 N	54.04 E
Estância	184	11.16 S	37.26 W
Estats, Pique d' ∧	120	42.40 N	1.24 E
Estcourt	160	29.01 S	29.52 E
Este	122	45.14 N	11.39 E
Esteio	188	29.51 S	51.10 W
Estelí	182	13.05 N	86.23 W
Estepona	120	36.26 N	5.08 W
Estevan	172	49.07 N	103.05 W
Estissac	118	48.16 N	3.49 E
Eston, Sask., Can.	172	51.10 N	108.46 W
Eston, Eng., U.K.	106	54.34 N	1.07 W
Estonskaja Sovetskaja Socialističeskaja Respublika □[3]	130	59.00 N	26.00 E
Estrêla	188	29.29 S	51.58 W
Estrela ∧	120	40.19 N	7.37 W
Estrela, Serra da ⛰	120	40.20 N	7.38 W
Estrella, Punta ≻	178	30.55 N	114.43 W
Estremadura □[9]	120	39.15 N	9.10 W
Esztergom	116	47.48 N	18.45 E
Étables	118	48.38 N	2.50 W
Etadunna	168	28.43 S	138.38 E
Etah	90	78.19 N	72.38 W
Étampes	118	48.26 N	2.09 E
Etamunbanie, Lake ⊜	168	26.15 S	139.44 E
Étaples	118	50.31 N	1.39 E
États-Unis → United States □[1]	174	38.00 N	97.00 W
Etāwah, Bhārat	144	25.33 N	76.22 E
Etāwah, Bhārat	146	26.46 N	79.02 E
Eten	184	6.55 S	79.50 W
Eternity Range ⛰	87	69.46 S	64.34 W
Ethel Creek	164	22.54 S	120.09 E
Ethiopia □[1]	154	8.00 N	38.00 E
Etive, Loch ⊜	108	56.29 N	5.09 W
Etna	178	41.27 N	122.54 W
Etna, Monte ∧[1]	122	37.46 N	15.00 E
Etne	114	59.40 N	5.56 E
Eton, Austl.	168	21.16 S	148.58 E
Eton, Eng., U.K.	104	51.31 N	0.37 W
Etoshapan ≚	160	18.45 S	16.15 E
Ettelbruck	116	49.52 N	6.05 E
Etten-Leur	116	51.34 N	4.38 E
Ettington	104	52.09 N	1.36 W
Ettlingen	116	48.56 N	8.24 E
Ettrick Forest -•[3]	108	55.30 N	3.00 W
Ettrick Pen ∧	108	55.22 N	3.16 W
Ettrick Water ≃	106	55.31 N	2.55 W
Eu	118	50.03 N	1.25 E
Eua I	96	21.22 S	174.56 W
Eucla	164	31.43 S	128.52 E
Euclid	176	41.34 N	81.32 W
Eucumbene, Lake ⊜	168	36.05 S	148.45 E
Eudunda	168	34.11 S	139.04 E
Eugene	174	44.02 N	123.05 W
Eugenia, Punta ≻	180	27.50 N	115.03 W
Eugênio Bustos	188	33.45 S	69.03 W
Eugênio Penzo	188	22.13 S	55.53 W
Eugowra	168	33.26 S	148.23 E
Eulo	168	28.10 S	145.03 E
Eumungerie	168	31.57 S	148.37 E
Eupen	116	50.38 N	6.02 E
Euphrates (Firat) (Al-Furāt) ≃	150	31.00 N	47.25 E
Eure □[5]	118	49.10 N	1.00 E
Eure ≃	118	49.18 N	1.12 E
Eure-et-Loir □[5]	118	48.30 N	1.30 E
Eureka, Calif., U.S.	178	40.47 N	124.09 W
Eureka, Nev., U.S.	178	39.31 N	115.58 W
Eurinilla Creek ≃	164	30.50 S	140.01 E
Euroa	168	36.45 S	145.35 E
Europa, Île I	156	22.20 S	40.22 E
Europa, Picos de ⛰	120	43.12 N	4.48 W
Europa Point ≻	120	36.10 N	5.22 W
Europe _•[1]	84	50.00 N	28.00 E
Euskirchen	116	50.39 N	6.47 E
Euston	168	34.35 S	142.44 E
Eutin	116	54.08 N	10.37 E
Eutsuk Lake ⊜	172	53.20 N	126.44 W
Eva Downs	164	18.01 S	134.52 E
Evandale	168	41.34 S	147.14 E
Evans, Lac ⊜	172	50.55 N	77.00 W
Evans City	176	40.45 N	80.03 W
Evans Creek ≃	178	42.25 N	123.11 W
Evans Strait ⩌	172	63.15 N	82.00 W
Evanston, Ill., U.S.	174	42.03 N	87.42 W
Evanston, Wyo., U.S.	174	41.16 N	110.58 W
Evansville	174	37.58 N	87.35 W
Evanton	108	57.40 N	4.20 W
Evart	176	43.54 N	85.08 W
Evaton	160	26.31 S	27.54 E
Evenlode ≃	104	51.47 N	1.21 W
Evensk	128	61.57 N	159.14 E
Everard, Lake ⊜	164	31.25 S	135.05 E
Everard, Mount ∧	164	26.16 S	132.04 E
Evercreech	104	51.09 N	2.30 W
Everest, Mount (Zhumulangmafeng) ∧	146	27.59 N	86.56 E
Everett, Pa., U.S.	176	40.01 N	78.23 W
Everett, Wash., U.S.	174	47.59 N	122.31 W
Everett, Mount ∧	176	42.06 N	73.25 W
Everett Mountains ⛰	172	62.45 N	67.12 W
Evergem	116	51.07 N	3.42 E
Everglades	182	25.52 N	81.23 W
Evergreen	178	35.54 N	120.26 W
Evesham	104	52.06 N	1.56 W
Evesham, Vale of ∨	104	52.06 N	1.50 W
Évian-les-Bains	118	46.23 N	6.35 E
Evijärvi	114	63.22 N	23.29 E
Evisa	122	42.15 N	8.47 E
Évora	120	38.34 N	7.54 W
Évreux	118	49.01 N	1.09 E
Évros (Marica) (Meriç) ≃	124	40.52 N	26.12 E
Évry	118	48.38 N	2.27 E
Ewa	179a	21.21 N	158.02 W
Ewaninga	164	23.58 S	133.58 E
Ewe, Loch C	108	57.48 N	5.40 W
Ewes Water ≃	106	55.08 N	3.00 W
Ewo	156	0.53 S	14.49 E
Excelsior	160	28.56 S	27.06 E
Excelsior Mountain ∧	178	38.02 N	119.18 W
Exe ≃	102	50.37 N	3.25 W
Executive Committee Range ⛰	87	76.50 S	126.00 W
Exeter, Ont., Can.	176	43.21 N	81.29 W
Exeter, Eng., U.K.	104	50.43 N	3.31 W
Exeter, Calif., U.S.	178	36.18 N	119.09 W
Exeter, N.H., U.S.	176	42.59 N	70.57 W
Exeter ≃	176	43.02 N	70.55 W

Symbols in the index entries are identified on page 198.

Name	Page	Lat	Long
Exeter Sound ᴜ	172	66.14 N	62.00 W
Exford	104	51.08 N	3.38 W
Exminster	104	50.41 N	3.29 W
Exmoor ~3	104	51.10 N	3.45 W
Exmouth, Austl.	164	21.56 S	114.07 E
Exmouth, Eng., U.K.	104	50.37 N	3.25 W
Exmouth Gulf	164	22.23 S	114.07 E
Exmouth Gulf C	164	22.00 S	114.20 E
Expedition Range	162	24.30 S	149.05 E
Extrema	190	22.51 S	46.19 W
Extremadura □9	122	39.00 N	6.00 W
Exuma Sound ᴜ	182	24.00 N	76.00 W
Eyam	108	53.17 N	1.41 W
Eyasi, Lake	158	3.40 S	35.05 E
Eydehavn	114	58.31 N	8.53 E
Eye, Eng., U.K.	104	52.35 N	0.10 W
Eye, Eng., U.K.	104	52.19 N	1.09 E
Eyemouth	108	55.52 N	2.06 W
Eye Peninsula >1	108	58.13 N	6.13 W
Eye Water	108	55.53 N	2.06 W
Eylar Mountain ʌ	178	37.28 N	121.33 W
Eynhallow Sound ᴜ	108	59.08 N	3.06 W
Eynort, Loch C	108	57.13 N	7.18 W
Eynsham	104	51.48 N	1.22 W
Eyre	164	32.15 S	126.18 E
Eyre, Lake	96	28.40 S	137.10 E
Eyrecourt	104	53.11 N	8.07 W
Eyre Creek	168	26.40 S	139.00 E
Eyre Mountains ʌ	170	45.20 S	168.30 E
Eyre Peninsula >1	168	34.00 S	135.45 E
Eyre South, Lake	168	29.30 S	137.20 E
Eythorne	104	51.11 N	1.17 E
F			
Fåberg	114	61.10 N	10.24 E
Faber Lake	172	63.56 N	117.15 W
Fabert Shoal ~2	96	24.30 S	158.05 W
Fabriano	122	43.20 N	12.54 E
Factoryville	176	41.34 N	75.47 W
Fada	154	17.14 N	21.33 E
Fada N'gourma	152	12.04 N	0.21 E
Fadd	128	46.28 N	18.50 E
Faddeja, Zaliv C	128	76.40 N	107.20 E
Faenza	122	44.17 N	11.53 E
Faeroe Islands □2	100	62.00 N	7.00 W
Faeröerne → Faeroe Islands □2	100	62.00 N	7.00 W
Fafadun	158	2.11 N	41.32 E
Fåfjärås	154	6.07 N	44.20 E
Făgăras	124	45.51 N	24.58 E
Fagerås	114	60.59 N	9.15 E
Fagersta	114	60.00 N	15.47 E
Faguibine, Lac ⊜	152	16.45 N	3.54 W
Fahan	110	55.05 N	7.28 W
Faial	88	38.34 N	28.42 W
Failsworth	106	53.31 N	2.09 W
Fairbanks	172	64.51 N	147.43 W
Fairbourne	104	52.41 N	4.03 W
Fairbury	174	40.08 N	97.11 W
Fairchance	176	39.49 N	79.45 W
Fairfax, Vt., U.S.	176	44.40 N	73.01 W
Fairfax, Va., U.S.	176	38.51 N	77.18 W
Fairfield, Calif., U.S.	178	38.15 N	122.03 W
Fairfield, Idaho, U.S.	178	43.21 N	114.48 W
Fairfield, Maine, U.S.	176	44.35 N	69.36 W
Fairfield, Ohio, U.S.	176	39.20 N	84.33 W
Fairford	104	51.44 N	1.47 W
Fairgrove	176	43.31 N	83.33 W
Fairhaven, Mass., U.S.	176	41.39 N	70.54 W
Fair Haven, N.Y., U.S.	176	43.19 N	76.42 W
Fair Haven, Vt., U.S.	176	43.36 N	73.16 W
Fair Head >	110	55.14 N	6.09 W
Fair Isle I	108	59.32 N	1.39 W
Fairlie, N.Z.	170	44.06 S	170.50 E
Fairlie, Scot., U.K.	108	55.46 N	4.51 W
Fairlight	104	53.10 N	0.40 E
Fairmont, Minn., U.S.	174	43.39 N	94.28 W
Fairmont, W. Va., U.S.	174	39.29 N	80.09 W
Fair Ness >	172	63.24 N	72.05 W
Fair Oaks	178	38.39 N	121.16 W
Fairport	176	43.06 N	77.26 W
Fairport Harbor	176	41.45 N	81.17 W
Fairview, Austl.	168	15.33 S	144.19 E
Fairview, Mich., U.S.	176	44.44 N	84.03 W
Fairview, Mont., U.S.	174	47.51 N	104.03 W
Fairview, W. Va., U.S.	176	39.36 N	80.15 W
Fairview Peak ʌ	178	39.14 N	118.08 W
Fairweather, Cape >	172	58.45 S	137.75 W
Fairweather, Mount ʌ	172	58.54 N	137.32 W
Fairy Water ≈	110	54.37 N	7.20 W
Fais I	138	9.46 N	140.31 E
Faizabad, Afg.	126	37.06 N	70.34 E
Faizābād, Bhārat	146	26.47 N	82.08 E
Fajardo	182	18.20 N	65.39 W
Fakako I¹	96	18.20 S	171.14 W
Fakarava	96	16.20 S	145.37 W
Fakenham	104	52.50 N	0.51 E
Fakfak	166	2.55 S	132.18 E
Faku	132	42.30 N	123.24 E
Fal ≈	104	50.08 N	5.02 W
Falaise	118	48.54 N	0.12 W
Falalu I	96	7.38 N	151.41 E
Falam	140	22.55 N	93.40 E
Falcón □3	182	11.00 N	69.50 W
Falconara Marittima	122	43.37 N	13.24 E
Falcon Heights	174	44.59 N	93.10 W
Falcon Reservoir ⊜1	174	26.37 N	99.11 W
Falémé ≈	152	14.46 N	12.14 W
Falkenberg, D.D.R.	116	51.35 N	13.14 E
Falkenberg, Sve.	114	56.54 N	12.28 E
Falkensee	116	52.33 N	13.04 E
Falkenstein, B.R.D.	116	49.06 N	12.30 E
Falkenstein, D.D.R.	116	50.29 N	12.22 E
Falkirk	108	56.00 N	3.48 W
Falkland	108	56.15 N	3.12 W
Falkland Islands (Islas Malvinas) □2	186	51.45 S	59.00 W
Falkland Rise ~3	84	54.50 S	50.00 W
Falkland Sound ᴜ	186	51.45 S	59.25 W
Fallbrook	178	33.23 N	117.15 W
Fallon	178	39.28 N	118.47 W
Fall River	176	41.43 N	71.08 W
Fall River Mills	178	41.00 N	121.26 W
Falls Creek	176	41.09 N	78.48 W
Falmouth, Jam.	182	18.30 N	77.40 W
Falmouth, Eng., U.K.	104	50.08 N	5.04 W
Falmouth, Ky., U.S.	176	38.40 N	84.20 W
Falmouth, Maine, U.S.	176	43.44 N	70.15 W
Falmouth, Va., U.S.	176	38.19 N	77.28 W
Falmouth Bay C	104	50.07 N	3.36 W
False Divi Point >	148	15.43 N	80.49 E
Falso, Cabo >	182	11.45 N	71.40 W
Falster I	114	54.48 N	11.58 E
Fălticeni	124	47.28 N	26.18 E
Falun	114	60.36 N	15.38 E
Famagusta → Ammókhostos	150	35.07 N	33.57 E
Famaillá	188	27.05 S	65.25 W
Famatina, Nevado de ʌ	188	29.00 S	67.51 W
Fanad Head >	110	55.16 N	7.38 W
Fanchang	136	31.07 N	118.12 E
Fane ≈	110	53.56 N	6.23 W
Fangak	154	9.04 N	30.53 E
Fangcheng	136	33.16 N	112.59 E
Fangshan ʌ	136	33.16 N	111.52 E
Fannich, Loch ⊜	108	57.38 N	5.00 W
Fanning Island I¹	96	3.52 N	159.20 W
Fano	122	43.50 N	13.01 E
Fanshan	132	32.40 N	119.42 E
Fan-si-pan ʌ	140	22.15 N	103.46 E
Faoileann, Bágh nam C			
Farāàn, Jazā'ir II	144	16.48 N	41.54 E
Faraday Seamount Group ~3	88	49.00 N	28.00 W
Faradje	158	3.44 N	29.43 E
Farafangana	161b	22.49 S	47.50 E
Farāh	150	32.22 N	62.07 E
Farāh □3	150	31.29 N	61.24 E
Farà'id, Jabal al- ʌ	150	23.31 N	25.20 E
Farallon de Medinilla I	138	16.01 N	146.04 E
Farallon de Pajaros I	138	20.32 N	144.54 E
Farallon Island II	178	37.43 N	123.03 W
Faranah	152	10.02 N	10.44 W
Faraulep I¹	138	8.36 N	144.33 E
Fardes ≈	120	37.35 N	3.00 W
Fareham	104	50.51 N	1.10 W
Farewell, Cape >	170	40.30 S	172.41 E
Fargo	174	46.52 N	96.48 W
Faribault	174	44.18 N	93.16 W
Faribault, Lac ⊜	172	56.19 N	72.00 W
Faridkot	146	30.40 N	74.45 E
Faridpur	146	23.36 N	89.50 E
Farilhões II	120	39.28 N	9.34 W
Faringdon	104	51.40 N	1.35 W
Fāriskür	150	31.20 N	31.43 E
Farmington, Maine, U.S.	176	44.40 N	70.09 W
Farmington, N.H., U.S.	176	43.24 N	71.04 W
Farmington, N. Mex., U.S.	174	36.44 N	108.12 W
Farnborough	104	51.17 N	0.46 W
Farne Islands II	102	55.38 N	1.38 W
Farnham, Qué., Can.	176	45.17 N	72.59 W
Farnham, Eng., U.K.	106	51.13 N	0.49 W
Farnworth	106	53.33 N	2.24 W
Faro	120	37.01 N	7.56 W
Faro ≈	152	12.00 N	12.55 E
Faro, Punta >	182	11.06 N	74.50 W
Fårön I	114	57.56 N	19.08 E
Farquhar, Cape >	164	23.37 S	113.37 E
Farquhar Group II	156	10.10 S	51.10 E
Farrar ≈	108	57.24 N	4.12 W
Farrars	108	57.24 N	4.50 W
Farrell	176	41.13 N	80.30 W
Farrukhābād	146	27.24 N	79.34 E
Fårsala	124	39.17 N	22.23 E
Farsø	114	56.47 N	9.21 E
Fartak, Ra's >	144	15.38 N	52.15 E
Farvel, Kap >	172	59.45 N	44.00 W
Farwell	176	43.50 N	84.52 W
Fasā	150	28.56 N	53.42 E
Fasano	122	40.50 N	17.22 E
Fastnet Rock I2	110	51.24 N	9.35 W
Fatehabad	146	29.31 N	75.27 E
Fatehpur	146	27.59 N	74.57 E
Fatehpur Sikri	144	27.06 N	77.40 E
Fatshan → Foshan	136	23.03 N	113.09 E
Faucilles, Monts ʌ	118	48.07 N	6.16 E
Fauldhouse	108	55.50 N	3.37 W
Faure Island I	164	25.51 S	113.52 E
Fauresmith	160	49.42 S	25.21 E
Fauske	112	67.15 N	15.24 E
Favara	122	37.19 N	13.40 E
Faverges	118	45.45 N	6.18 E
Faversham	104	51.20 N	0.53 E
Fawley	104	50.49 N	1.20 W
Fawn ≈	172	55.22 N	88.20 W
Faxaflói C	112a	64.25 N	23.00 W
Faxinal	190	23.59 S	51.22 W
Faxinal do Soturno	188	29.37 S	53.26 W
Fayence	118	43.37 N	6.41 E
Fayette	176	41.40 N	84.20 W
Fayetteville, Ark., U.S.	174	36.04 N	94.10 W
Fayetteville, N.C., U.S.	174	35.03 N	78.54 W
Fayetteville, W. Va., U.S.	176	38.03 N	81.06 W
Fayl-Billot	118	47.47 N	5.36 E
Fāzilka	146	30.24 N	74.02 E
Fazzān (Fezzan) →1	154	26.00 N	14.00 E
Fderik	152	22.41 N	12.43 W
Feale ≈	110	52.28 N	9.40 W
Feather ≈	178	38.47 N	121.36 W
Feather, Middle Fork ≈	178	39.34 N	125.26 W
Feather, North Fork ≈	178	39.34 N	121.28 W
Feather, North Fork, East Branch ≈	178	40.01 N	121.13 W
Feather, South Fork ≈	178	39.33 N	121.28 W
Featherston	170	41.07 S	175.20 E
Featherstone, Rh.	158	18.42 S	30.49 E
Featherstone, Eng., U.K.	106	53.41 N	1.21 W
Feathertop, Mount ʌ	168	36.54 S	147.08 E
Fécamp	118	49.45 N	0.22 E
Fedala → Mohammedia	152	33.44 N	7.24 W
Federación	188	31.00 S	57.55 W
Federal	188	30.55 S	58.45 W
Federalsburg	176	38.42 N	75.47 W
Fedjadj, Chott el ⅏	122	33.55 N	9.10 E
Feeagh, Lough ⊜	110	53.55 N	9.36 W
Fehérgyarmat	116	48.00 N	22.32 E
Fehmarn I	116	54.27 N	11.09 E
Fehmarn Belt ᴜ	116	54.36 N	11.20 W
Feia, Lagoa ⊜	190	22.00 S	41.20 W
Feidong (Dianbu)	136	31.52 N	117.29 E
Feigumfossen ᴸ	114	61.23 N	7.26 E
Feilding	170	40.13 S	175.34 E
Feio ≈	190	21.03 S	51.47 W
Feira	158	15.37 S	30.25 E
Feira de Santana	184	12.15 S	38.57 W
Feistritz ≈	116	47.10 N	16.08 E
Feixi	136	31.42 N	117.10 E
Fejér □6	116	47.10 N	18.35 E
Feldbach	116	46.57 N	15.53 E
Feldkirch	116	47.14 N	9.36 E
Felipe Carrillo Puerto	180	19.35 N	88.03 W
Felix, Cape >	172	69.56 N	97.51 W
Felixburg	158	19.29 S	30.51 E
Felixstowe	104	51.58 N	1.20 E
Felixton	160	28.50 S	31.53 E
Fellbach	116	48.48 N	9.15 E
Felletin	118	45.53 N	2.10 E
Felling	106	54.57 N	1.33 W
Felpham	104	50.47 N	0.39 W
Feltre	122	46.01 N	11.54 E
Femunden ⊜	114	62.12 N	11.52 E
Fen Ditton	104	52.13 N	0.10 E
Fenelon Falls	176	44.32 N	78.45 W
Fénérive	161b	17.22 S	49.25 E
Fengcheng, Zhg.	136	40.28 N	124.00 E
Fengcheng, Zhg.	136	28.12 N	115.46 E
Fengdu	132	29.58 N	107.41 E
Fengfeng	132	36.28 N	114.14 E
Fenggang	132	36.24 N	121.24 E
Fenghua	136	29.39 N	121.24 E
Fenghuanjing	136	31.11 N	117.49 E
Fenghuizhen	136	30.05 N	113.18 E
Fengkou	136	30.05 N	113.18 E
Fenglin, T'aiwan	136	23.44 N	121.27 E
Fenglin, Zhg.	136	28.19 N	120.06 E
Fengshun	136	23.48 N	116.11 E
Fengtai	136	30.04 N	116.43 E
Fengting	136	25.16 N	118.54 E
Fengxian	136	30.55 N	121.27 E
Fengxin	136	28.43 N	115.23 E
Fengyang	132	32.52 N	117.34 E
Fengzhen	132	40.24 N	113.09 E
Fenhe ≈	132	37.19 N	112.05 E
Fenny Compton	104	52.09 N	1.20 W
Fenny Stratford	104	52.00 N	0.43 W
Feno, Capo di >	122	41.57 N	8.36 E
Fensfjorden C2	114	60.51 N	4.55 E
Fenshui	136	32.18 N	119.25 E
Fenton	176	42.48 N	83.42 W
Fenwick	176	38.14 N	80.35 W
Fenyang	132	37.18 N	111.41 E
Fenyi	136	27.47 N	114.42 E
Feodosija	128	45.02 N	35.23 E
Ferbane	110	53.15 N	7.49 W
Ferdows	150	34.00 N	58.09 E
Fère-en-Tardenois	118	49.12 N	3.31 E
Fergana	126	40.23 N	71.46 E
Fergus	176	43.42 N	80.02 W
Fergus Falls	174	46.17 N	96.04 W
Ferlach	116	46.31 N	14.18 E
Ferlo, Vallée du V	152	15.42 N	15.30 W
Fermanagh □6	110	54.21 N	7.40 W
Fermoy	110	52.08 N	8.16 W
Fernández	188	27.55 S	63.54 W
Fernando de Noronha, Ilha I	184	3.51 S	32.25 W
Fernando Póo → Macías Nguema Biyogo I	152	3.30 N	8.40 E
Fernán-Núñez	120	37.40 N	4.43 W
Ferndale, Calif., U.S.	178	40.35 N	124.16 W
Ferndale, Mich., U.S.	176	42.28 N	83.08 W
Ferndown	104	50.48 N	1.55 W
Fernley	178	39.36 N	119.15 W
Ferns	110	52.35 N	6.31 E
Ferokh	148	11.11 N	75.51 E
Ferrara	122	44.50 N	11.35 E
Ferreñafe	184	6.35 S	79.45 W
Ferryhill	106	54.41 N	1.33 W
Fès	152	34.05 N	4.57 W
Feshi	156	6.07 S	18.10 E
Feshie ≈	108	57.08 N	3.55 W
Fetcham	104	51.17 N	0.22 W
Fetesti	124	44.23 N	27.50 E
Fethaland, Point of >	108a	60.38 N	1.18 W
Fethard	110	52.27 N	7.41 W
Fetisovo	126	42.46 N	52.38 E
Fetlar I	108a	60.37 N	0.52 W
Fetterangus	108	57.33 N	2.01 W
Fettercairn	108	56.51 N	2.34 W
Feucht	116	49.22 N	11.13 E
Feuilles, Baie aux C	172	58.55 N	69.20 W
Feuilles, Rivière aux ≈	172	58.47 N	70.04 W
Fevik	114	58.23 N	8.42 E
Feyzābād	146	37.06 N	70.34 E
Fez → Fès	152	34.05 N	4.57 W
Ffestiniog	104	52.58 N	3.55 W
Fforest Fawr ʌ1	104	51.52 N	3.36 W
Fianarantsoa	161b	21.26 S	47.05 E
Fianarantsoa □4	161b	22.00 S	47.00 E
Fichtelberg ʌ	116	50.26 N	12.57 E
Ficksburg	160	28.57 S	27.52 E
Fidenza	122	44.52 N	10.03 E
Fier	124	40.43 N	19.34 E
Fiery Creek ≈	168	18.23 S	139.52 E
Fiesch	118	46.20 N	8.10 E
Fife □4	108	56.13 N	3.02 W
Fife Lake	176	44.35 N	85.21 W
Fie Ness >	108	56.17 N	2.36 W
Figeac	118	44.37 N	2.02 E
Figtree	158	20.24 S	28.21 E
Figueira da Foz	120	40.09 N	8.52 W
Figueras	120	42.16 N	2.58 E
Fiji □1	96	18.00 S	178.00 E
Fiji Islands II	96	18.00 S	178.00 E
Filchner Ice Shelf ⛵	87	79.00 S	40.00 W
Filey	106	54.12 N	0.17 W
Filey Bay C	106	54.12 N	0.16 W
Filiatrá	124	37.10 N	21.35 E
Filippo Reef ~2	96	6.30 S	151.50 W
Fillmore	178	34.24 N	118.55 W
Filton	104	51.31 N	2.35 W
Fimi ≈	156	3.01 S	16.58 E
Finale Ligure	122	44.10 N	8.20 E
Fincham	104	52.37 N	0.30 E
Findhorn	108	57.39 N	3.38 W
Findhorn ≈	108	57.38 N	3.38 W
Findlay	176	41.02 N	83.39 W
Findon	104	52.20 N	0.39 W
Fingal	110	41.39 S	147.58 E
Fingoè	158	15.12 S	31.50 E
Finisk ≈	110	52.07 N	7.50 W
Finistère □5	118	48.20 N	4.00 W
Finisterre, Cabo de >	120	42.53 N	9.16 W
Finisterre Range ʌ	166	5.50 S	146.05 E
Finke	164	25.34 S	134.35 E
Finke ≈	164	26.20 S	136.00 E
Finke, Mount ʌ	164	30.55 S	134.02 E
Finland □1	100	64.00 N	26.00 E
Finland, Gulf of (Suomenlahti) (Finskij Zaliv) C	114	60.00 N	27.00 E
Finlas, Loch ⊜	108	55.15 N	4.25 W
Finlay ≈	172	57.00 N	125.05 W
Finley	178	39.00 N	123.07 W
Finnie Bay C	156	65.13 N	72.30 W
Finnigan, Mount ʌ	168	15.49 S	145.17 E
Finnis, Cape >	164	33.38 S	134.51 E
Finnmark □6	112	70.00 N	25.00 E
Finno ʌ2	112	66.00 N	13.00 E
Fins	146	3.27 N	41.32 E
Finschhafen	166	6.35 S	147.52 E
Finspáng	114	58.43 N	15.47 E
Finsterwalde	116	51.38 N	13.42 E
Fintona	110	54.30 N	7.19 W
Fintown	110	54.52 N	8.08 W
Fionn Loch ⊜	108	57.46 N	5.29 W
Firbaugh	178	36.52 N	120.27 W
Firenze (Florence)	122	43.46 N	11.15 E
Firmat	188	33.25 S	61.30 W
Firminy	118	45.23 N	4.18 E
Firozābād	146	27.09 N	78.25 E
Firozpur	146	30.55 N	74.36 E
First King	138	31.49 S	124.21 E
Firth ≈	172	69.32 N	139.20 W
Fischbacher Alpen ʌ	116	47.28 N	15.30 E
Fish ≈	160	28.07 S	17.45 E
Fishbourne	104	50.44 N	1.12 W
Fish Creek ≈	178	43.04 N	84.51 W
Fisher ≈	164	30.33 S	150.58 E
Fisher Glacier ⛵	87	73.15 S	66.00 E
Fisher Strait ᴜ	172	63.15 N	83.30 W
Fishguard	104	51.59 N	4.59 W
Fishing Creek	176	38.20 N	76.14 W
Fishtoft	106	52.58 N	0.02 E
Fitchburg	176	42.35 N	71.48 W
Fitful Head >	108a	59.54 N	1.23 W
Fittleworth	104	50.58 N	0.35 W
Fitu	158	5.05 N	40.42 E
Fitzmaurice ≈	166	14.50 S	129.44 E
Fitzroy	166	17.00 S	67.15 W
Fitzroy, Monte (Cerro Chaltel) ʌ	186	49.17 S	73.05 W
Fitzroy Crossing	164	18.11 S	125.35 E
Fitzwilliam Island I	176	45.30 N	81.45 W
Fiume → Rijeka	122	45.20 N	14.27 E
Fivemiletown	110	54.23 N	7.18 W
Five Penny Borve	108	58.25 N	6.25 W
Fiwila Mission	158	13.58 S	29.36 E
Fizi	158	4.18 S	28.57 E
Fjærlandsfjorden C2	114	61.17 N	6.40 E
Fjerritslev	114	57.05 N	9.16 E
Flagstaff, S. Afr.	160	31.05 S	29.29 E
Flagstaff, Ariz., U.S.	174	35.12 N	111.39 W
Flagstaff Lake ⊜	176	45.10 N	70.15 W
Flám	114	60.50 N	7.07 E
Flamborough Head >	102	54.07 N	0.04 W
Flaming	116	52.00 N	12.30 E
Flaming Gorge Reservoir ⊜1	174	41.15 N	109.30 W
Flannan Islands II	108	58.18 N	7.36 W
Flat ≈, N.W. Ter., Can.	168	61.33 N	125.18 W
Flat ≈, Mich., U.S.	176	43.00 N	85.20 W
Flateyri	112a	65.59 N	23.42 W
Flathead Lake ⊜	174	47.52 N	114.08 W
Flat Holm I	104	51.23 N	3.08 W
Flat Island I	161c	19.52 S	57.42 E
Flat Rock	176	42.06 N	83.17 W
Flattery, Cape >, Austl.	166	14.58 S	145.21 E
Flattery, Cape >, Wash., U.S.	174	48.23 N	124.43 W
Flatwoods	176	38.31 N	82.43 W
Fleet	104	51.17 N	0.50 W
Fleet ≈	108	57.57 N	4.05 W
Fleetwood, Eng., U.K.	106	53.56 N	3.01 W
Fleetwood, Pa., U.S.	176	40.27 N	75.49 W
Flemingsburg	176	38.25 N	83.44 W
Flemish Cap ~3	90	48.00 N	45.00 W
Flers	118	48.45 N	0.34 W
Fletcher Islands II	87	72.40 S	94.10 W
Fletcher Pond ⊜1	176	45.00 N	83.52 W
Fleury-sur-Andelle	118	49.22 N	1.21 E
Flimby	106	54.41 N	3.31 W
Flinders ≈	166	17.36 S	140.36 E
Flinders Bay C	164	34.23 S	115.19 E
Flinders Island I	166	39.45 S	148.00 E
Flinders Range ʌ	168	31.25 S	138.45 E
Flinders Reefs ~2	168	17.37 S	148.31 E
Flin Flon	172	54.46 N	101.53 W
Flint, Wales, U.K.	106	53.15 N	3.07 W
Flint, Mich., U.S.	176	43.01 N	83.41 W
Flint I	96	11.26 S	151.48 W
Flint ≈, Ga., U.S.	174	30.52 N	84.38 W
Flint ≈, Mich., U.S.	172	69.10 N	74.20 W
Flint Lake ⊜	172	69.10 N	74.20 W
Flinton	168	27.53 S	149.34 E
Flitwick	104	52.00 N	0.29 W
Flize	118	49.42 N	4.46 E
Flodden	106	55.38 N	2.10 W
Flor de Chile	188	25.19 S	69.50 W
Florence → Firenze, It.	122	43.46 N	11.15 E
Florence, Ala., U.S.	174	34.49 N	87.40 W
Florence, S.C., U.S.	174	34.12 N	79.46 W
Florencia	184	1.36 N	75.36 W
Florenville	118	49.42 N	5.18 E
Flores	184	7.51 S	37.59 W
Flores I, Indon.	166	8.30 S	121.00 E
Flores I, Port.	88	39.26 N	31.13 W
Flores, Laut (Flores Sea) ~2	142	8.00 S	120.00 E
Flores da Cunha	188	29.02 S	51.11 W
Floresta Azul	184	14.51 S	39.41 W
Floriano	184	6.47 S	43.01 W
Florianópolis	188	27.35 S	48.34 W
Florida, Cuba	182	21.32 N	78.14 W
Florida, Ur.	188	34.06 S	56.13 W
Florida □3	174	28.00 N	82.00 W
Florida Keys II	174	24.45 N	81.00 W
Floridia	122	37.04 N	15.10 E
Florina	124	40.47 N	21.24 E
Florø	114	61.36 N	5.00 E
Florvåg	114	60.25 N	5.14 E
Flotta I	108	58.50 N	3.07 W
Flushing → Vlissingen, Ned.	116	51.26 N	3.35 E
Flushing, Mich., U.S.	176	43.04 N	83.51 W
Flushing, Ohio, U.S.	176	40.09 N	81.04 W
Fluvia ≈	120	42.12 N	3.07 E
Fly ≈	166	8.30 S	143.41 E
Flying Fish Cove	166	10.25 S	105.43 E
Foca	124	43.31 N	18.46 E
Fochabers	108	57.37 N	3.05 W
Fochville	160	26.30 S	27.30 E
Focsani	124	45.41 N	27.11 E
Foelsche ≈	166	16.03 S	136.50 E
Foggia	122	41.27 N	15.33 E
Foggo	152	14.55 N	24.25 W
Fogo I	152	49.40 N	54.13 W
Fohnsdorf	116	47.13 N	14.41 E
Foix	118	42.58 N	1.36 E
Foix ʌ1	118	43.00 N	1.40 E
Fokino	130	53.00 N	34.24 E
Folarskardhuten ʌ	114	60.37 N	7.45 E
Foley Island I	172	68.35 N	75.10 W
Folgares	156	14.54 S	15.08 E
Folgefonni ⛵	114	60.00 N	6.20 E
Foligno	122	42.57 N	12.42 E
Folkestone	104	51.05 N	1.11 E
Folkingham	106	52.54 N	0.24 W
Follatosa	118	63.59 N	11.06 E
Follonica	122	42.55 N	10.43 E
Follonica, Golfo di C	122	42.54 N	10.40 E
Folsom	178	38.41 N	121.15 W
Folsom Lake ⊜1	178	38.43 N	121.08 W
Fomboni	161a	12.16 S	43.45 E
Fonda	176	42.57 N	74.22 W
Fond du Lac, Sask., Can.	172	59.19 N	107.10 W
Fond du Lac, Wis., U.S.	174	43.47 N	88.27 W
Fond du Lac ≈	172	59.17 N	106.00 W
Fondi	122	43.08 N	7.04 W
Fonsagrada	120	43.08 N	7.04 W
Fonseca	184	10.54 N	72.51 W
Fonseca, Golfo de C	180	13.08 N	87.40 W
Font ≈	106	57.00 N	1.44 W
Fontainebleau	118	48.24 N	2.42 E
Fontana	178	34.06 N	117.26 W
Fontas ≈	172	58.16 N	121.48 W
Fontenay-le-Comte	118	46.28 N	0.48 W
Fontur >	112a	66.23 N	14.30 W
Foochow → Fuzhou	136	26.06 N	119.17 E
Forbach	118	49.11 N	6.54 E
Forbes	168	33.23 S	148.01 E
Forcalquier	118	43.58 N	5.47 E
Forchheim	116	49.43 N	11.04 E
Ford ≈	108	56.10 N	5.26 W
Ford, Cape >	166	13.25 S	129.52 E
Ford City, Calif., U.S.	178	35.09 N	119.27 W
Ford City, Pa., U.S.	176	40.46 N	79.32 W
Ford Dry Lake ⊜	178	33.38 N	115.00 W
Forde	114	59.36 N	5.29 E
Førdefjorden C2	114	61.27 N	5.25 E
Forden	104	52.36 N	3.08 W
Fordingbridge	104	50.56 N	1.47 W
Fords Bridge	168	29.45 S	145.26 E
Forel, Mont ʌ	172	66.56 N	37.00 W
Foreland Point >	104	51.15 N	3.47 W
Forest, Ont., Can.	176	43.06 N	82.00 W
Forest, Miss., U.S.	174	32.22 N	89.28 W
Forest City	174	41.39 N	78.25 W
Foresthill	178	39.01 N	120.49 W
Forestier Peninsula >1	168	42.57 S	147.55 E
Forest Row	104	51.05 N	0.03 E
Forez, Monts du ʌ	118	45.35 N	3.48 E
Forfar	108	56.38 N	2.54 W
Forggensee ⊜	116	47.36 N	10.44 E
Forli	122	44.13 N	12.03 E
Formby	106	53.34 N	3.05 W
Formby Point >	106	53.33 N	3.06 W
Formentera I	120	38.43 N	1.28 E
Formentor, Cabo de >	120	39.58 N	3.12 E
Formia	122	41.15 N	13.37 E
Formiga	190	20.27 S	45.25 W
Formosa, Arg.	188	26.10 S	58.11 W
Formosa, Bra.	190	15.32 S	47.20 W
Formosa I	184	28.25 S	83.08 W
Formosa I	120	37.00 N	7.51 W
Formosa Strait ᴜ	136	24.00 N	119.00 E
Forres	108	57.37 N	3.38 W
Forrest	164	30.51 S	128.06 E
Forrest City	174	35.01 N	90.47 W
Forrest Lakes ⊜	164	29.25 S	128.46 E
Forsayth	168	18.35 S	143.36 E
Forsby	114	60.09 N	21.23 E
Forser	114	59.31 N	12.58 E
Forster	168	32.11 S	152.31 E
Forsyth Island I	164	34.23 S	115.19 E
Forsyth Range ʌ	168	22.45 S	143.15 E
Fort Albany	172	52.15 N	81.37 W
Fortaleza	184	3.43 S	38.30 W
Fort-Archambault → Sarh	154	9.09 N	18.23 E
Fort Augustus	108	57.09 N	4.41 W
Fort Beaufort	160	32.46 S	26.40 E
Fort Bidwell	178	41.52 N	120.09 W
Fort Bragg	178	39.26 N	123.48 W
Fort-Chimo	172	58.06 N	68.25 W
Fort Chipewyan	172	58.46 N	111.09 W
Fort Collins	174	40.35 N	105.05 W
Fort Constantine	168	20.28 S	140.17 E
Fort-Coulonge	176	45.51 N	76.44 W
Fort Covington	176	44.59 N	74.30 W
Fort-Dauphin	161b	25.02 S	47.00 E
Fort-de-France	182	14.36 N	61.05 W
Fort Dodge	174	42.30 N	94.10 W
Fort Edward	176	43.16 N	73.35 W
Fort Erie	176	42.54 N	78.56 W
Fortescue ≈	164	21.20 S	116.06 E
Fortevoit	108	56.21 N	3.32 W
Fort Fitzgerald	172	59.53 N	111.37 W
Fort Frances	172	48.36 N	93.24 W
Fort Franklin	172	65.11 N	123.46 W
Fort Gay	176	38.07 N	82.36 W
Fort-George	172	53.50 N	79.00 W
Fort Good Hope	172	66.15 N	128.38 W
Forth	108	55.47 N	3.41 W
Forth ≈	108	56.03 N	3.44 W
Forth, Carse of V	108	56.08 N	4.05 W
Forth, Firth of C	108	56.10 N	2.45 W
Forthill	108	57.42 N	2.00 W
Fort Hill → Chitipa	158	9.43 S	33.16 E
Fort Jones	178	41.36 N	122.51 W
Fort Klamath	178	42.42 N	122.00 W
Fort-Lamy → Ndjamena	154	12.07 N	15.03 E
Fort Lauderdale	174	26.07 N	80.08 W
Fort Liard	172	60.15 N	123.28 W
Fort Loramie	176	40.21 N	84.22 W
Fort Macleod	172	49.43 N	113.25 W
Fort Madison	174	40.38 N	91.27 W
Fort McMurray	172	56.44 N	111.23 W
Fort McPherson	172	67.27 N	134.53 W
Fort Morgan	174	40.15 N	103.48 W
Fort Myers	174	26.37 N	81.54 W
Fort Nelson	172	58.49 N	122.39 W
Fort Nelson ≈	172	59.30 N	124.00 W
Fort Norman	172	64.54 N	125.34 W
Fort Peck Lake ⊜1	174	47.45 N	106.50 W
Fort Pierce	174	27.27 N	80.20 W
Fort Plain	176	42.56 N	74.38 W
Fort Portal	158	0.40 N	30.17 E
Fort Providence	172	61.21 N	117.39 W
Fort Qu'Appelle	172	50.56 N	103.09 W
Fort Recovery	176	40.25 N	84.47 W
Fort Reliance	172	62.42 N	109.08 W
Fort Resolution	172	61.10 N	113.40 W
Fort Rixon	158	20.01 S	29.18 E
Fortrose, N.Z.	170	46.34 S	168.48 E
Fortrose, Scot., U.K.	108	57.35 N	4.08 W
Fort-Rousset	156	0.29 S	15.55 E
Fort Saint James	172	54.26 N	124.15 W
Fort Saint John	172	56.15 N	120.51 W
Fort Sandeman	146	31.20 N	69.27 E
Fort-Sevčenko	126	44.31 N	50.16 E
Fort Severn	172	56.00 N	87.38 W
Fort Simpson	172	61.52 N	121.23 W
Fort Smith, N.W. Ter., Can.	172	60.00 N	111.53 W
Fort Smith, Ark., U.S.	174	35.23 N	94.25 W
Fort Stockton	174	30.53 N	102.53 W
Fortuna	178	40.36 N	124.09 W
Fortune Bay C	172	47.25 N	55.25 W
Fort Vermilion	172	58.24 N	116.00 W
Fort Victoria	158	20.05 S	30.50 E
Fort Walton Beach	174	30.25 N	86.36 W
Fort Wayne	176	41.04 N	85.09 W
Fort William → Thunder Bay, Ont., Can.	172	48.23 N	89.15 W
Fort William, Scot., U.K.	108	56.49 N	5.07 W
Fort Worth	174	32.45 N	97.20 W
Forty Foot Drain: ≈	104	52.28 N	0.05 W
Fort Yukon	172	66.34 N	145.17 W
Foshan	136	23.03 N	113.09 E
Foss	108	56.41 N	3.58 W
Foss ≈	106	53.57 N	1.06 W
Fossano	122	44.33 N	7.43 E
Fossil Downs	164	18.08 S	125.28 E
Fossil Lake ⊜	168	43.18 N	120.15 W
Fossombrone	122	43.41 N	12.48 E
Foster	168	38.39 S	146.12 E
Foster ≈	176	45.47 N	105.49 W
Fostoria	176	41.09 N	83.25 W
Fotan	136	24.12 N	117.53 E
Fothergill	158	16.29 S	28.18 E
Fouesnant	118	47.54 N	4.01 W
Fougamou	156	1.13 S	10.36 E
Fougères	118	48.21 N	1.12 W
Foula I	108a	60.08 N	2.05 W
Foul Bay C	150	23.30 N	35.39 E
Foulness	178	33.36 N	119.14 W
Foulness Island I	102	53.36 N	0.55 E
Foulness Point >	104	51.37 N	0.57 E
Foulsham	104	52.48 N	1.01 E
Foulwind, Cape >	170	41.45 S	171.28 E
Foumban	154	5.43 N	10.55 E
Foumbouni	161a	11.50 S	43.30 E
Fountain Peak ʌ	178	34.57 N	115.32 W
Fouriesburg	160	28.38 S	28.14 E
Fourmies	118	50.00 N	4.03 E
Fournaise, Piton de la ʌ	161c	21.14 S	55.43 E
Fouta Djallon ʌ1	152	11.30 N	12.30 W
Foveran	108	57.18 N	2.02 W
Fowey	104	50.20 N	4.38 W
Fowler, Calif., U.S.	178	36.38 N	119.41 W
Fowler, Mich., U.S.	176	43.00 N	84.44 W
Fowler, Point >	164	32.02 S	132.29 E
Fowlers Bay	164	31.59 S	132.27 E
Fowlerville	176	42.40 N	84.04 W
Fowliang → Jingdezhen	136	29.16 N	117.11 E
Foxborough	176	42.04 N	71.15 W
Foxe Basin C	172	68.25 N	77.00 W
Foxe Channel ᴜ	172	64.30 N	80.00 W
Foxe Peninsula >1	172	65.00 N	76.00 W
Foxford	110	53.59 N	9.06 W
Fox Glacier	170	43.28 S	170.00 E
Foxholes	106	54.08 N	0.24 W
Foyers	108	57.15 N	4.28 W
Foyle, Lough C	110	55.06 N	7.08 W
Foynes	110	52.37 N	9.06 W
Foz do Cunene	156	17.16 S	11.50 E
Foz do Iguaçu	188	25.33 S	54.35 W
Framingham	176	42.17 N	71.25 W
Framlingham	104	52.13 N	1.21 E
Frames Mountains ʌ	87	67.50 S	62.35 E
Frampton on Severn	104	51.46 N	2.22 W
Franca	190	20.32 S	47.24 W
Francavilla Fontana	122	40.31 N	17.35 E
Frances Creek	166	13.35 S	131.52 E
Frances Lake	172	61.25 N	129.30 W
Francés Viejo, Cabo >	182	19.40 N	70.00 W
Franceville	156	1.38 S	13.35 E
Franche-Comté □9	118	47.00 N	6.00 E
Francisca, Punta >	182	21.34 N	87.21 W
Francis Case, Lake ⊜1	174	43.15 N	99.00 W
Francisco Beltrão	188	26.05 S	53.04 W
Francisco Zarco	180	24.06 N	116.30 W
Francistown	160	21.11 S	27.32 E
Francofonte	122	37.13 N	14.53 E
François Lake	172	54.00 N	125.40 W
Francs Peak ʌ	174	43.58 N	109.20 W
Frankenberg	116	51.03 N	13.02 E
Frankenmuth	176	43.20 N	83.44 W
Frankford	176	38.29 N	84.52 W
Frankfort, Ky., U.S.	174	38.12 N	84.52 W
Frankfort, N.Y., U.S.	176	43.02 N	75.04 W
Frankfort, Ohio, U.S.	176	39.24 N	83.11 W
Frankfurt am Main	116	50.07 N	8.40 E
Frankfurt an der Oder	116	52.20 N	14.33 E
Fränkische Alb ʌ	116	49.00 N	11.30 E
Franklin, S. Afr.	160	30.18 S	24.49 E
Franklin, Maine, U.S.	176	44.35 N	68.13 W
Franklin, N.H., U.S.	176	43.26 N	71.39 W
Franklin, Pa., U.S.	176	41.24 N	79.49 W
Franklin, Ohio, U.S.	176	39.33 N	84.18 W
Franklin, Va., U.S.	176	36.41 N	76.55 W
Franklin □5	172	72.00 N	96.00 W
Franklin Bay C	172	69.45 N	126.00 W
Franklin Harbor C	168	33.42 S	136.56 E
Franklin Lake ⊜, Nev., U.S.	178	40.24 N	115.12 W
Franklin Lake ⊜, N.W. Ter., Can.	172	66.56 N	96.03 W
Franklin Mountains ʌ, N.W. Ter., Can.	172	64.00 N	125.30 W
Franklin Mountains ʌ, N.Z.	170	44.55 S	167.45 E
Franklin Strait ᴜ	172	72.00 N	96.00 W
Franklinville	176	42.20 N	78.28 W
Frankton	170	45.00 S	168.44 E
Frankton	158	17.36 S	31.02 E
Frannshoek	160	33.55 S	19.09 E
Franz	172	48.28 N	84.25 W
Franz Josef Glacier	170	43.24 S	170.11 E
Frascati	122	41.48 N	12.41 E
Fraser ≈, B.C., Can.	172	49.09 N	123.12 W
Fraser ≈, Newf., Can.	172	56.35 N	61.55 W
Fraser, Mount ʌ	164	25.39 S	118.23 E
Fraserburg	160	31.55 S	21.30 E
Fraserburgh	108	57.42 N	2.00 W
Fraser Island I	168	25.15 S	153.10 E
Fraser Plateau ʌ1	172	51.30 N	122.00 W
Fraser Range	164	32.03 S	122.48 E
Frauenfeld	118	47.34 N	8.54 E
Fray Bentos	188	33.08 S	58.18 W
Fr'azino	130	55.58 N	38.04 E
Frechilla	120	42.08 N	4.50 W
Frechen	116	50.55 N	6.49 E
Fredericia	114	55.35 N	9.46 E
Frederick	176	39.25 N	77.25 W
Frederick Island I	164	34.04 S	122.00 E
Fredericksburg	174	38.18 N	77.29 W
Fredericktown	174	40.29 N	90.25 W
Frederico Westphalen	188	27.22 S	53.24 W
Fredericton	172	45.58 N	66.39 W
Fredericton Junction	172	45.40 N	66.37 W
Frederikshåb	114	62.00 N	49.43 W
Frederikshavn	114	57.26 N	10.32 E
Frederiksted	182	17.43 N	64.53 W
Frederiksværk	114	55.58 N	12.02 E
Fredonia	176	42.27 N	79.20 W
Fredrika	114	64.05 N	18.24 E
Fredrikstad	114	59.13 N	10.57 E
Freehold	176	40.16 N	74.17 W
Freeland, Mich., U.S.	176	43.32 N	84.07 W
Freel Peak ʌ	178	38.52 N	119.54 W
Freels, Cape >	172	49.15 N	53.28 W
Freeman	174	43.21 N	97.26 W
Freemount	110	52.16 N	8.53 W
Freeport, Ba.	182	26.30 N	78.45 W
Freeport, Maine, U.S.	176	43.51 N	70.06 W
Freeport, N.Y., U.S.	176	43.09 N	73.35 W
Freeport, Pa., U.S.	176	40.40 N	79.41 W
Freeport, Tex., U.S.	174	28.58 N	95.22 W
Freetown	152	8.30 N	13.15 W
Fregenal de la Sierra	120	38.10 N	6.39 W
Freiberg	116	50.54 N	13.20 E
Freiburg → Fribourg	118	46.48 N	7.09 E
Freiburg [im Breisgau]	116	47.59 N	7.51 E
Freirina	188	28.30 S	71.06 W
Freistadt	116	48.23 N	11.44 E
Freital	116	48.31 N	14.31 E
Frejus	116	43.26 N	6.44 E
Fremantle	164	32.03 S	115.45 E
Fremington	104	51.04 N	4.07 W
Fremont, Calif., U.S.	178	37.34 N	122.01 W
Fremont, Ind., U.S.	176	41.44 N	84.56 W
Fremont, Nebr., U.S.	174	41.26 N	96.30 W
Fremont, Ohio, U.S.	176	41.21 N	83.07 W
French ≈	176	45.56 N	80.54 W
Frenchburg	176	37.57 N	83.37 W
French Frigate Shoals ~2	96	23.45 N	166.10 W
French Guiana □2	184	4.00 N	53.00 W
Frenchman Bay C	176	44.25 N	68.10 W
Frenchman Flat ≈	178	36.50 N	115.55 W
Frenchmans Cap ʌ	168	42.18 S	145.48 E
Frenchpark	110	53.52 N	8.26 W
French Pass	170	40.56 S	173.50 E
French Polynesia □2	96	15.00 S	140.00 W
French Southern and Antarctic Territories □2	84	49.30 S	69.30 E
Freshwater	104	50.43 N	1.31 W
Fresnillo	180	23.10 N	102.53 W
Fresno	178	36.45 N	119.45 W
Fresno, Portillo del >	120	42.38 N	3.46 W
Freswick	108	58.35 N	3.05 W
Freu, Cabo del >	120	39.45 N	3.27 E
Freudenstadt	116	48.28 N	8.25 E
Frew ≈	166	20.00 S	135.38 E
Frewash ≈	106	52.53 N	1.14 W
Frewena	166	19.25 S	135.25 E
Freycinet, Cape >	164	34.06 S	114.59 E
Freycinet Peninsula >1	168	42.13 S	148.18 E
Freyre	188	31.10 S	62.05 W
Fria	152	10.22 N	13.32 W
Fria, Cape >	156	18.30 S	12.01 E
Frias	188	28.39 S	65.56 W
Friant	178	36.59 N	119.43 W
Fribourg (Freiburg)	118	46.48 N	7.09 E
Fridaythorpe	106	54.01 N	0.40 W
Fridtjof Nansen, Mount ʌ	87	85.21 S	167.33 W
Friedberg, B.R.D.	116	50.20 N	8.45 E
Friedberg, B.R.D.	116	50.21 N	8.45 E
Friedrichshafen	116	54.22 N	9.28 E
Friedrichstadt	116	54.22 N	9.06 E
Friendship	176	43.28 N	77.00 W
Friesach	116	46.57 N	14.24 E
Friesland □9	116	53.00 N	6.00 E
Frinton-on-Sea	104	51.50 N	1.14 E
Friockheim	108	56.38 N	2.35 W
Frisa, Loch C	108	56.34 N	6.05 W
Friesian Islands II	100	53.35 N	6.40 E
Friuli-Venezia-Giulia □4	122	46.00 N	13.00 E
Friza, Proliv ᴜ	132	45.30 N	149.10 E
Frizington	106	54.32 N	3.30 W
Frobisher Bay	172	63.44 N	68.28 W
Frobisher Bay C	172	62.30 N	66.00 W
Frodsham	106	53.18 N	2.44 W
Frohavet C	114	63.56 N	9.05 E
Frolovo	128	49.46 N	43.39 E
Frolovo ≈	114	60.51 N	11.01 E
Frome	104	51.14 N	2.20 W
Frome ≈, Austl.	168	29.08 S	137.52 E
Frome ≈, Eng., U.K.	104	50.41 N	2.04 W
Frome Downs	168	31.13 S	139.46 E
Front Royal	176	38.55 N	78.11 W
Frosinone	122	41.38 N	13.19 E
Frosolone	122	41.36 N	14.27 E
Frösön	114	63.11 N	14.32 E
Frostburg	176	39.39 N	78.56 W
Frövi	114	59.28 N	15.22 E
Frøya I	114	63.43 N	8.42 E
Fruges	118	50.31 N	2.08 E
Fruitdale	176	38.19 N	75.37 W
Frutal	190	20.02 S	48.55 W
Frýdek-Místek	116	49.41 N	18.22 E
Fryeburg	176	44.01 N	70.59 W
Fuchū	136	34.34 N	133.14 E
Fuchun → Fuzhou	136	28.01 N	116.20 E
Fuchunjiang ≈	136	30.10 N	120.09 E
Fuday	108	56.59 N	7.24 W
Fuding	136	27.15 N	120.12 E
Fuente de Cantos	120	38.15 N	6.18 W
Fuenta-obejuna	120	38.16 N	5.25 W
Fuente de Ebro	120	41.31 N	0.38 W
Fuerte ≈	180	25.54 N	109.22 W
Fuerte Olimpo	188	21.02 S	57.54 W
Fuerteventura I	152	28.26 N	14.00 W
Fuji → Fuji-san	134	35.22 N	138.44 E
Fujian □4	136	26.00 N	118.00 E
Fujieda	134	34.52 N	138.16 E
Fujin	132	47.16 N	132.01 E
Fujinomiya	134	35.13 N	138.38 E
Fuji-san ʌ1	134	35.22 N	138.44 E
Fuji-yoshida	134	35.29 N	138.41 E
Fukagawa	134	43.43 N	142.03 E
Fukuchiyama	134	35.18 N	135.07 E
Fukue	134	32.41 N	128.50 E

Symbols in the index entries are identified on page 198.

Name	Page	Lat ° ′	Long ° ′
Fukue-shima I	134	32.40 N	128.45 E
Fukui	134	36.04 N	136.13 E
Fukuoka, Nihon	134	33.35 N	130.24 E
Fukuoka, Nihon	134	40.16 N	141.18 E
Fukuroi	134	34.45 N	137.55 E
Fukushima, Nihon	134	37.45 N	140.28 E
Fukushima, Nihon	134a	41.29 N	140.15 E
Fukuyama	134	34.29 N	133.22 E
Fūlādī, Kūh-e ∧	146	34.38 N	67.32 E
Fulaerji	132	47.13 N	123.39 E
Fulda	116	50.33 N	9.41 E
Fuliji	136	33.46 N	116.58 E
Fuling	132	29.42 N	107.21 E
Fullarton ≃	168	20.15 S	141.10 E
Fullerton	178	33.52 N	117.55 W
Fulpmes	116	47.10 N	11.21 E
Fulton	176	43.19 N	76.25 W
Fulwood	106	53.47 N	2.41 W
Fumay	118	49.59 N	4.42 E
Fumel	118	44.29 N	0.57 E
Fumin	140	25.16 N	102.26 E
Funabashi	134	35.42 N	139.59 E
Funafuti I	96	8.31 S	179.13 E
Funan, Zhg.	132	22.32 N	107.56 E
Funan, Zhg.	136	32.39 N	115.32 E
Funchal	88	32.38 N	16.54 W
Fundación	184	10.31 N	74.11 W
Fundy, Bay of C	172	45.00 N	66.00 W
Funhalouro	160	23.03 S	34.25 E
Funing	136	33.47 N	119.48 E
Funiushan ⋀	136	33.40 N	112.30 E
Funshinagh, Lough ⊜	110	53.31 N	8.07 W
Funyan Goba	158	4.22 N	37.58 E
Fuqing	136	25.44 N	119.22 E
Furano	134a	43.21 N	142.24 E
Furmanov	130	57.15 N	41.07 E
Furnace	108	56.09 N	5.10 W
Furnas, Represa de ⊜[1]	190	20.45 S	46.00 W
Furneaux Group II	168	40.10 S	148.05 E
Furnes → Veurne	116	51.04 N	2.40 E
Furness Fells ⋀[2]	106	54.18 N	3.07 W
Fürstenberg/Havel	116	53.11 N	13.08 E
Fürstenfeldbruck	116	48.10 N	11.15 E
Fürstenwalde	116	52.21 N	14.04 E
Fürth	116	49.28 N	10.59 E
Furth im Wald	116	49.18 N	12.51 E
Furudal	114	61.10 N	15.08 E
Furukawa	134	38.34 N	140.58 E
Fury and Hecla Strait ⩌	172	69.56 N	84.00 W
Fushan	136	31.49 N	120.46 E
Fushun	132	41.52 N	123.53 E
Füssen	116	47.34 N	10.42 E
Futuna I	96	14.15 S	178.09 W
Fuxian, Zhg.	132	39.37 N	122.01 E
Fuxian, Zhg.	132	36.02 N	109.13 E
Fuxianhu ⊜	140	24.30 N	102.55 E
Fuxinshi	132	42.03 N	121.46 E
Fuyang, Zhg.	136	30.03 N	119.57 E
Fuyang, Zhg.	136	32.52 N	115.42 E
Fuyu	132	45.10 N	124.50 E
Fuyuan	140	25.39 N	104.12 E
Fuzhong	140	24.28 N	111.22 E
Fuzhou (Foochow), Zhg.	136	26.06 N	119.17 E
Fuzhou, Zhg.	136	28.01 N	116.20 E
Fyfield	104	51.45 N	0.16 E
Fylde ≻[1]	106	53.47 N	2.56 W
Fyn I	114	55.20 N	10.30 E
Fyne, Loch C	108	55.56 N	5.24 W
Fyresvatn ⊜	114	59.06 N	8.12 E
Fyvie	108	57.25 N	2.23 W
G			
Gabas ≃	118	43.46 N	0.42 W
Gabbs	178	38.52 N	117.55 W
Gabela	156	10.48 S	14.20 E
Gaberones → Gaborone	160	24.45 S	25.55 E
Gabès	152	33.53 N	10.07 E
Gabès, Golfe de C	152	34.00 N	10.25 E
Gablonz → Jablonec nad Nisou	116	50.44 N	15.10 E
Gabon □[1]	156	1.00 S	11.45 E
Gaborone	160	24.45 S	25.55 E
Gabriel Strait ⩌	172	61.45 N	65.30 W
Gabriel y Galan, Embalse de ⊜[1]	120	40.15 N	6.15 W
Gabrovo	124	42.52 N	25.19 E
Gacé	118	48.48 N	0.18 E
Gachsārān	150	30.12 N	50.47 E
Gacko	124	43.10 N	18.32 E
Gadag	148	15.25 N	75.37 E
Gäddede	114	64.30 N	14.09 E
Gádor	120	36.57 N	2.29 W
Gádor, Sierra de ⋀	120	36.54 N	2.47 W
Gadsden, Ala., U.S.	174	34.02 N	86.02 W
Gadsden, Ariz., U.S.	178	32.33 N	108.47 W
Gaer (Geeryasha)	146	31.44 N	80.21 E
Gaerwen	106	53.13 N	4.16 W
Gaeta	122	41.12 N	13.35 E
Gaferut I	138	9.14 N	145.23 E
Gafsa	152	34.25 N	8.48 E
Gaggenau	116	48.48 N	8.19 E
Gagnoa	152	6.08 N	5.56 W
Gagnon	172	51.53 N	68.10 W
Gagnon, Lac ⊜	176	46.07 N	75.07 W
Gago Coutinho	156	14.08 S	21.25 E
Gagra	126	43.20 N	40.15 E
Gahini	158	1.50 S	30.30 E
Gail ≃	116	46.36 N	13.53 E
Gaillac	118	43.54 N	1.55 E
Gaillon	118	49.10 N	1.20 E
Gailtaler Alpen ⋀	118	46.42 N	13.00 E
Gainesville, Fla., U.S.	174	29.40 N	82.20 W
Gainesville, Ga., U.S.	174	34.18 N	83.50 W
Gainesville, Tex., U.S.	174	33.37 N	97.08 W
Gainford	106	54.32 N	1.44 W
Gainsborough	106	53.24 N	0.46 W
Gaiping	132	40.24 N	122.22 E
Gairdner, Lake ⊜	168	31.35 S	136.00 E
Gairloch	108	57.42 N	5.40 W
Gairloch, Loch C	108	57.44 N	5.44 W
Gairn ≃	108	57.03 N	3.05 W
Gaithersburg	176	39.09 N	77.12 W
Gajny	112	60.15 N	54.15 E
Gakarosa ∧	160	27.50 S	23.38 E
Gal, Punta de ≻	120	39.10 N	1.05 E
Galán, Cerro ∧	188	25.55 S	66.52 W
Galana ≃	158	3.09 S	40.08 E
Galapagos Islands → Colón, Archipiélago de II	84	0.30 S	90.30 W
Galaroza	120	37.55 N	6.42 W
Galashiels	108	55.37 N	2.49 W
Galatea	170	38.25 S	176.45 E
Galați	124	45.26 N	28.03 E
Galați □[4]	124	45.45 N	27.45 E
Galatina	122	40.10 N	18.10 E
Galatz → Galați	124	45.26 N	28.03 E
Gala Water ≃	108	55.37 N	2.47 W
Galaxidhion	124	38.22 N	22.23 E
Galdhøpiggen ∧	114	61.37 N	8.17 E
Galela	138	1.50 N	127.50 E
Galena, Austl.	164	27.50 S	114.41 E
Galena, Ill., U.S.	174	42.25 N	90.26 W
Galeota Point ≻	182	10.08 N	61.00 W
Galera, Punta ≻	186	39.59 S	73.43 W
Galera Point ≻	182	10.49 N	60.55 W
Galesburg, Ill., U.S.	174	40.57 N	90.22 W
Galesburg, Mich., U.S.	176	42.14 N	85.25 W
Galeton	176	41.44 N	77.39 W
Galgash	158	0.14 N	41.37 E
Galgate	106	54.00 N	2.47 W
Galič	130	58.23 N	42.21 E
Galicia □[9], Esp.	120	43.00 N	8.00 W
Galicia □[9], Eur.	116	49.50 N	21.00 E
Galilee, Lake ⊜	168	22.21 S	145.48 E
Galion	176	40.44 N	82.47 W
Galka'yo	154	6.49 N	47.23 E
Gallan Head ≻	108	58.14 N	7.03 W
Gallarate	122	45.40 N	8.47 E
Gallatin	174	36.24 N	86.27 W
Galle	148	6.02 N	80.13 E
Galley Head ≻	110	51.30 N	8.57 W
Gallinas, Punta ≻	184	12.25 N	71.40 W
Gallipoli, Austl.	168	19.10 S	137.55 E
Gallipoli, It.	122	40.03 N	17.58 E
Gallipoli → Gelibolu, Tür.	124	40.24 N	26.40 E
Gallipolis	176	38.49 N	82.12 W
Gällivare	112	67.07 N	20.45 E
Galloo Island I	176	43.54 N	76.25 W
Galloway □[9]	106	55.00 N	4.25 W
Galloway, Mull of ≻	106	54.38 N	4.50 W
Gallup	174	35.32 N	108.44 W
Gallura ⊸[1]	122	41.05 N	9.15 E
Galston	108	55.36 N	4.24 W
Galt	178	38.15 N	121.18 W
Galtür	116	46.58 N	10.11 E
Galtymore ∧	110	52.22 N	8.10 W
Galty Mountains ⋀	110	52.25 N	8.10 W
Galvarino	188	38.24 S	72.47 W
Galveston	174	29.18 N	94.48 W
Gálvez	188	32.02 S	61.15 W
Galway	110	53.16 N	9.03 W
Galway □[6]	110	53.20 N	9.00 W
Galway Bay C	110	53.10 N	9.15 W
Gamagōri	134	34.50 N	137.14 E
Gamarra	184	8.20 N	73.45 W
Gambela	154	8.18 N	34.37 E
Gambell	128	63.46 N	171.46 W
Gambia □[1]	152	13.25 N	16.00 W
Gambia (Gambie) ≃	152	13.28 N	16.34 W
Gambier	176	40.23 N	82.24 W
Gambier, Îles II	96	21.20 S	136.30 W
Gamboa	182	9.05 N	79.40 W
Gamboma	156	1.53 S	15.51 E
Gamka ≃	160	33.18 S	21.39 E
Gamleby	114	57.54 N	16.24 E
Gamoep	160	29.55 S	18.25 E
Gamph, Slieve ⋀	110	54.05 N	9.00 W
Gamtoos ≃	160	33.58 S	25.01 E
Gamud ∧	158	4.05 N	38.03 E
Gananoque	172	44.20 N	76.10 W
Gand → Gent	116	51.03 N	3.43 E
Gandak ≃	146	25.39 N	85.13 E
Gandavaroyi Falls ʟ	158	17.17 S	29.07 E
Gander	172	48.57 N	54.37 W
Ganderkesee	116	53.02 N	8.32 E
Gandía	120	38.58 N	0.11 W
Ganga → Ganges ≃	146	23.22 N	90.32 E
Gangaw	132	22.11 N	94.07 E
Gangdisishan ∧	146	31.29 N	80.45 E
Gangdisishanmai ⋀	146	29.30 N	87.00 E
Ganges (Ganga) (Padma) ≃	146	23.22 N	90.32 E
Ganges, Mouths of the ≃[1]	146	22.00 N	89.00 E
Gangkov	136	29.32 N	118.56 E
Ganglingshan ⋀	136	32.00 N	83.00 E
Gangoh	149	29.46 N	77.15 E
Gangotri	144	30.56 N	79.02 E
Gangtok	144	27.20 N	88.37 E
Gangu	132	34.38 N	105.27 E
Ganhe ≃	128	49.12 N	125.03 E
Ganjiang ≃	136	29.12 N	116.00 E
Gannett Peak ∧	174	43.11 N	109.39 W
Ganos Dağı ∧	124	40.47 N	27.16 E
Gansbaai	160	34.35 S	19.22 E
Gansu □[4]	132	37.00 N	103.00 E
Gantang	136	26.56 N	119.40 E
Gantheaume, Cape ≻	168	36.05 S	137.27 E
Gantheaume Bay C	164	27.44 S	114.07 E
Ganu Mór ∧	108	58.25 N	4.53 W
Ganyesa	160	26.35 S	24.10 E
Ganzhenyi	136	30.33 N	113.21 E
Ganzhou	136	25.54 N	114.55 E
Ganzi	132	31.40 N	100.01 E
Gao	152	16.16 N	0.03 W
Gaoan	136	28.25 N	115.22 E
Gaochun	136	31.20 N	118.52 E
Gaogou	136	34.03 N	119.15 E
Gaohe	136	22.47 N	112.57 E
Gaokeng	136	27.40 N	113.58 E
Gaoshan	136	25.29 N	119.34 E
Gaoyou	136	32.47 N	119.27 E
Gaoyouhu ⊜	136	32.50 N	119.20 E
Gaozhou	140	21.55 N	110.50 E
Gap	118	44.34 N	6.05 E
Gara, Lough ⊜	110	53.55 N	8.25 W
Garah	168	29.04 S	149.38 E
Garamba ≃	158	3.53 N	29.12 E
Garanhuns	184	8.54 S	36.29 W
Garberville	178	40.06 N	123.48 W
Garboldisham	104	52.24 N	0.56 E
Garça	190	22.14 S	49.37 W
García de Sola, Embalse de ⊜[1]	120	39.15 N	5.05 W
Gard □[5]	118	44.00 N	4.00 E
Gard ≃	118	43.51 N	4.37 E
Garda, Lago di ⊜	122	45.40 N	10.41 E
Gardelegen	116	52.31 N	11.23 E
Garden City	174	37.58 N	100.53 W
Garden Grove	178	33.46 N	117.57 W
Garden Island I, Austl.	164	32.13 S	115.41 E
Garden Island I, Mich., U.S.	176	45.49 N	85.30 W
Garden Reach	146	22.33 N	88.17 E
Gardēz	146	33.37 N	69.07 E
Gardiner	176	44.14 N	69.46 W
Gardiner Range ⋀	164	23.50 S	131.46 E
Gardiners Bay C	176	41.08 N	72.10 W
Gardner	176	42.34 N	71.60 W
Gardner I[1]	96	4.40 S	174.32 W
Gardnerville	178	38.56 N	119.45 W
Gardo	154	9.30 N	49.03 E
Gardone Val Trompia	122	45.41 N	10.11 E
Gardunha, Serra da ⋀	120	40.05 N	7.31 W
Garelochhead	108	56.05 N	4.50 W
Garešnica	122	45.35 N	16.56 E
Garforth	106	53.48 N	1.22 W
Gargaliánoi	124	37.04 N	21.39 E
Gargrave	106	53.59 N	2.06 W
Garibaldi	188	29.15 S	51.32 W
Garies	160	30.30 S	18.00 E
Garinin	108	58.21 N	6.50 W
Garissa	158	0.28 S	39.38 E
Garlieston	106	54.48 N	4.22 W
Garm	126	39.02 N	70.22 E
Garmisch-Partenkirchen	116	47.29 N	11.05 E
Garmouth	108	57.40 N	3.07 W
Garnet Bay C	172	65.17 N	75.15 W
Garnock ≃	108	55.38 N	4.42 W
Garnpung, Lake ⊜	168	33.30 S	143.12 E
Garonne ≃	118	45.02 N	0.36 W
Garoua	152	9.18 N	13.24 E
Garrett	176	41.21 N	85.08 W
Garrison	110	54.25 N	8.05 W
Garron Point ≻	110	55.03 N	5.55 W
Garros	108	57.37 N	6.11 W
Garry ≃	108	56.43 N	3.47 W
Garry Bay C	172	68.55 N	85.05 W
Garry Lake ⊜	172	66.00 N	100.00 W
Garsdale Head	106	54.19 N	2.20 W
Garsen	158	2.16 S	40.07 E
Garstang	106	53.55 N	2.47 W
Gartempe ≃	118	46.48 N	0.50 E
Garut	142	7.13 S	107.54 E
Garve	108	57.37 N	4.42 W
Garvellachs II	108	56.14 N	5.47 W
Garvie Mountains ⋀	170	45.30 S	168.50 E
Gary	174	41.36 N	87.20 W
Garzón	184	2.12 N	75.38 W
Gasan-Kuli	150	37.27 N	53.59 E
Gascoyne ≃	164	24.52 S	113.37 E
Gascoyne, Mount ∧	164	24.58 S	116.38 E
Gash (Al-Qash) ≃	154	16.48 N	35.51 E
Gashaka	152	7.21 N	11.27 E
Gasherbrum ∧	149	35.40 N	76.40 E
Gashunhu ⊜	132	42.22 N	100.34 E
Gaspar	188	26.56 S	48.58 W
Gaspé	172	48.50 N	64.29 W
Gas-san ∧	134	38.32 N	140.01 E
Gassaway	176	38.40 N	80.47 W
Gastonia	174	35.16 N	81.11 W
Gastoúni	124	37.51 N	21.16 E
Gastre	186	42.17 S	69.15 W
Gästrikland □[9]	114	60.30 N	16.27 E
Gata, Cabo de ≻	120	36.43 N	2.12 W
Gata, Sierra de ⋀	120	40.14 N	6.45 W
Gatčina	130	59.34 N	30.08 E
Gatehouse of Fleet	106	54.53 N	4.11 W
Gateshead	106	54.58 N	1.37 W
Gateshead Island I	172	70.22 N	100.27 W
Gaths Mine	158	20.00 S	30.31 E
Gatineau	176	45.29 N	75.38 W
Gatineau ≃	172	45.27 N	75.40 W
Gatooma	158	18.21 S	29.55 E
Gatton	168	27.33 S	152.17 E
Gatun Lake ⊜[1]	182	9.10 N	79.55 W
Gauer Lake ⊜	172	57.00 N	97.50 W
Gauhāti	146	26.11 N	91.44 E
Gauley ≃	176	38.10 N	81.12 W
Gauley Bridge	176	38.10 N	81.11 W
Gaunless ≃	106	54.40 N	1.41 W
Gaurama	188	27.34 S	52.03 W
Gauri Sankar ∧	146	27.57 N	86.21 E
Gausta ∧	114	59.50 N	8.35 E
Gavà	120	41.18 N	2.01 E
Gave d'Aspe ≃	118	43.12 N	0.36 W
Gävle	114	60.40 N	17.10 E
Gävleborgs Län □[6]	114	61.30 N	16.15 E
Gavrilov-Jam	130	57.18 N	39.51 E
Gawler	168	34.37 S	138.44 E
Gawler Ranges ⋀	164	32.30 S	136.00 E
Gaya	146	24.47 N	85.00 E
Gaylord	176	45.02 N	84.40 W
Gayndah	168	25.37 S	151.36 E
Gayton	104	52.45 N	0.34 E
Gaywood	104	52.46 N	0.26 E
Gaza □[5]	160	23.30 S	32.45 E
Gazelle Basin ✧[1]	96	32.00 S	170.00 E
Gaziantep	150	37.05 N	37.22 E
Gbarnga	152	7.00 N	9.29 W
Gdańsk (Danzig)	116	54.23 N	18.40 E
Gdov	130	58.44 N	27.48 E
Gdynia	116	54.32 N	18.33 E
Gearhart Mountain ∧	178	42.30 N	120.53 W
Gêba ≃	152	11.46 N	15.36 W
Gebe, Pulau I	166	0.05 S	129.20 E
Gebweiler → Guebwiller	118	47.55 N	7.12 E
Geel	116	51.10 N	5.00 E
Geelong	168	38.08 S	144.21 E
Geelvink Channel ⩌	164	28.30 S	114.10 E
Geer	132	31.44 N	80.21 E
Ge'ermu	132	36.23 N	94.50 E
Geesthacht	116	53.26 N	10.22 E
Geeveston	168	43.10 S	146.55 E
Geikie ≃	172	57.45 N	103.52 W
Geisenfeld	116	48.41 N	11.37 E
Geislingen	116	48.37 N	9.51 E
Geistown	176	40.17 N	78.52 W
Geita	158	2.52 S	32.10 E
Gejiu (Kokiu)	140	23.22 N	103.06 E
Gela	122	37.03 N	14.15 E
Gelai ∧[1]	158	2.33 S	36.05 E
Gelasa, Selat ⩌	142	2.40 S	107.15 E
Geldrop	118	51.25 N	5.33 E
Geleen	116	50.58 N	5.52 E
Gelibolu	124	40.24 N	26.40 E
Gelibolu Yarımadası (Gallipoli Peninsula) ≻[1]	124	40.20 N	26.30 E
Gélise ≃	118	44.11 N	0.17 E
Gellibrand	168	38.32 S	143.32 E
Gelsenkirchen	116	51.31 N	7.07 E
Gelt ≃	106	54.56 N	2.47 W
Gembloux	116	50.34 N	4.41 E
Gembrook	168	37.57 S	145.33 E
Gemena	154	3.15 N	19.46 E
Gemert	116	51.34 N	5.40 E
Genale ≃	154	5.43 N	40.53 E
Gending	142	7.48 S	113.18 E
General Acha	188	37.20 S	64.35 W
General Alvear	188	34.59 S	67.42 W
General Cabrera	188	32.49 S	63.52 W
General Câmara	188	29.54 S	51.46 W
General Conesa	188	36.30 S	57.19 W
General Enrique Mosconi	188	22.36 S	63.49 W
General Guido	188	36.40 S	57.45 W
General Gutiérrez	188	32.58 S	68.45 W
General Juan Madariaga	188	37.00 S	57.05 W
General La Madrid	188	37.15 S	61.16 W
General Levalle	188	34.00 S	63.55 W
General Machado	156	12.03 S	17.30 E
General Manuel Belgrano, Cerro ∧	188	29.02 S	67.51 W
General Martín Miguel de Güemes	188	24.40 S	65.00 W
General Paz, Arg.	188	35.32 S	58.18 W
General Paz, Arg.	188	27.45 S	57.40 W
General Pico	188	35.38 S	63.46 W
General Pinedo	188	27.20 S	61.20 W
General Roca	188	39.02 S	67.33 W
General Rondon	188	24.34 S	54.04 W
General San Martín	188	34.35 S	58.30 W
General Santos	142	6.07 N	125.11 E
General Vargas	188	29.42 S	54.40 W
General Viamonte (Los Toldos)	188	35.00 S	61.05 W
General Villegas	188	35.02 S	63.02 W
Geneseo	176	42.48 N	77.49 W
Geneva → Genève, Schw.	118	46.12 N	6.09 E
Geneva, Ind., U.S.	176	40.36 N	84.58 W
Geneva, N.Y., U.S.	176	42.52 N	77.00 W
Geneva, Ohio, U.S.	176	41.48 N	80.57 W
Geneva, Lake ⊜	118	46.25 N	6.30 E
Genève	118	46.12 N	6.09 E
Gengma	140	23.34 N	99.06 E
Genhe ≃	128	50.16 N	119.22 E
Genk	116	50.58 N	5.30 E
Genkai-nada ⫪[2]	134	34.00 N	130.00 E
Genlis	118	47.14 N	5.13 E
Gennes	118	47.20 N	0.14 W
Genoa, Austl.	168	37.29 S	149.35 E
Genoa → Genova, It.	122	44.25 N	8.57 E
Genoa, Ohio, U.S.	176	41.31 N	83.22 W
Genova (Genoa)	122	44.25 N	8.57 E
Genrijetty, Ostrov I	128	77.06 N	156.30 E
Gent (Gand)	116	51.03 N	3.43 E
Genthin	116	52.24 N	12.09 E
Geographe Bay C	164	33.35 S	115.15 E
Geographe Channel ⩌	164	24.40 S	113.20 E
Geokčaj	150	40.39 N	47.44 E
George	160	33.58 S	22.24 E
George ≃, Austl.	164	20.50 S	117.28 E
George ≃, Qué., Can.	172	58.49 N	66.10 W
George, Lake ⊜, Austl.	168	35.05 S	149.25 E
George, Lake ⊜, Ug.	158	0.02 N	30.12 E
George, Lake ⊜, N.Y., U.S.	176	43.35 N	73.35 W
George Gill Range ⋀	164	24.15 S	131.36 E
Georges Bank ✧[4]	90	41.00 N	67.00 W
George Sound ⩌	170	44.50 S	167.23 E
Georgetown, Austl.	168	18.18 S	143.33 E
George Town, Austl.	168	41.06 S	146.50 E
Georgetown, Ont., Can.	172	43.39 N	79.55 W
Georgetown, Cay. Is.	182	19.18 N	81.23 W
Georgetown, Gam.	152	13.30 N	14.47 W
Georgetown, Guy.	184	6.48 N	58.10 W
George Town → Pinang, Malay.	142	5.25 N	100.20 E
Georgetown, St. Vin.	182	13.16 N	61.08 W
Georgetown, Del., U.S.	176	38.42 N	75.23 W
Georgetown, Ky., U.S.	176	38.13 N	84.33 W
Georgetown, Ohio, U.S.	176	38.52 N	83.54 W
Georgetown, S.C., U.S.	174	33.23 N	79.17 W
George V Coast ⏚[2]	87	68.30 S	147.30 E
George VI Sound ⩌	87	71.00 S	68.00 W
Georgia □[3]	174	32.50 N	83.15 W
Georgia, Strait of ⩌	172	49.00 N	123.20 W
Georgian Bay C	172	45.15 N	80.50 W
Georgijevsk	126	44.09 N	43.28 E
Georgina ≃	168	23.30 S	139.47 E
Georgiu-Dež	126	50.59 N	39.30 E
Gera	116	50.52 N	12.04 E
Gera □[5]	116	51.08 N	10.56 E
Geraardsbergen	118	50.46 N	3.52 E
Geral, Serra ⏚[4]	188	26.30 S	50.30 W
Geraldton, Austl.	164	28.46 S	114.36 E
Geraldton, Ont., Can.	172	49.44 N	86.57 W
Gerard, Mount ∧	164	27.13 S	122.41 E
Gérardmer	118	48.04 N	6.53 E
Gerber	178	40.03 N	122.09 W
Gerber Reservoir ⊜[1]	178	42.12 N	121.06 W
Gerdine, Mount ∧	172	61.35 N	152.26 W
Gereshk	146	31.48 N	64.34 E
Gerik	142	5.25 N	101.08 E
Gerlachovský Štít ∧	116	49.12 N	20.08 E
Germaine Bank ✧[4]	90	5.05 N	107.35 W
German Democratic Republic (East Germany) □[1]	100	52.00 N	12.30 E
Germany, Federal Republic of (West Germany) □[1]	100	51.00 N	9.00 E
Germiston	160	26.15 S	28.05 E
Gero	134	35.48 N	137.14 E
Gerona	120	41.59 N	2.49 E
Gerrei ⊸[1]	122	39.28 N	9.20 E
Gers □[5]	118	43.40 N	0.30 E
Gers ≃	118	44.09 N	0.39 E
Geser	166	3.53 S	130.54 E
Getafe	120	40.18 N	3.43 W
Gettysburg	176	39.50 N	77.14 W
Getulina	190	21.49 S	49.55 W
Getz Ice Shelf ◸	87	75.00 S	129.00 W
Gévora ≃	120	38.53 N	6.57 W
Geyser, Banc du ✧[2]	156	12.25 S	46.25 E
Geyserville	178	38.42 N	122.54 W
Ghāghra ≃	146	25.47 N	84.37 E
Ghakhar	149	32.18 N	74.09 E
Ghana □[1]	152	8.00 N	2.00 W
Ghanzi □[5]	160	22.00 S	23.00 E
Gharaunda	149	29.33 N	76.58 E
Ghardaïa	152	32.31 N	3.37 E
Gharyān	154	32.10 N	13.01 E
Ghāt	154	24.58 N	10.11 E
Ghawdex I	122	36.03 N	14.15 E
Ghazāl, Baḥr al- ≃	154	9.31 N	30.25 E
Ghazal, Baḥr el ≃	154	13.01 N	15.28 E
Ghazaouet	120	35.06 N	1.51 W
Ghāziābād	149	28.40 N	77.26 E
Ghāzīpur	146	25.35 N	83.34 E
Ghaznī	146	33.33 N	68.26 E
Ghaznī □[4]	146	33.00 N	68.00 E
Ghazzah (Gaza)	150	31.30 N	34.28 E
Ghent → Gent	116	51.03 N	3.43 E
Gheorghe Gheorghiu-Dej	124	46.14 N	26.44 E
Gheorgheni	124	46.43 N	25.36 E
Ghlò, Beinn a ∧	108	56.50 N	3.43 W
Ghowr □[4]	150	34.00 N	65.00 E
Ghudāmis	154	30.08 N	9.30 E
Ghūrīān, Afg.	144		
	150	34.21 N	61.30 E
Gia-dinh	140	10.48 N	106.42 E
Giant Mountain ∧	176	44.10 N	73.44 W
Giant's Castle ∧	160	29.20 S	29.30 E
Gibara	182	21.07 N	76.08 W
Gibb River	166	15.39 S	126.38 E
Gibeon	160	25.09 S	17.43 E
Gibeon □[5]	160	25.00 S	19.00 E
Gibraltar	120	36.09 N	5.21 W
Gibraltar □[2]	100	36.11 N	5.22 W
Gibraltar, Strait of (Estrecho de Gibraltar) ⩌	120	35.57 N	5.36 W
Gibraltar Point ≻	102	53.05 N	0.19 E
Gibson	164	33.39 S	121.48 E
Gibsonburg	176	41.23 N	83.19 W
Gibson Desert ⊸[2]	164	24.30 S	126.00 E
Giddarbāha	149	30.12 N	74.40 E
Gidgee	164	27.16 S	119.22 E
Gidgi, Lake ⊜	164	29.16 S	126.03 E
Gien	118	47.42 N	2.38 E
Giessen	116	50.35 N	8.40 E
Gifford ≃	172	70.21 N	83.05 W
Gifford Creek	164	24.05 S	116.11 E
Gifford Fjord C[2]	172	69.57 N	81.55 W
Gifhorn	116	52.29 N	10.33 E
Gifu	134	35.25 N	136.45 E
Giggleswick	106	54.04 N	2.17 W
Gigha, Sound of ⩌	108	55.41 N	5.42 W
Gigha Isles II	108	55.41 N	5.46 W
Gijón	120	43.32 N	5.40 W
Gikongoro	158	2.29 S	29.34 E
Gila ≃	174	32.43 N	114.33 W
Gila Bend	174	32.57 N	112.43 W
Gilbert ≃	168	16.35 S	141.15 E
Gilbert Islands □[2]	96	4.00 S	175.00 E
Gilbert Islands II	96	0.30 S	174.00 E
Gilbert River	168	18.09 S	142.52 E
Gilbert Seamount ✧[3]	90	52.50 N	150.05 W
Gilbués	184	9.50 S	45.21 W
Giles Creek ≃	164	17.25 S	130.50 E
Gilford	110	54.23 N	6.22 W
Gilgai	164	31.15 S	119.56 E
Gilgandra	168	31.42 S	148.39 E
Gil Gil Creek ≃	168	29.10 S	148.51 E
Gilgit	149	35.55 N	74.18 E
Gilgit ≃	149	35.44 N	74.38 E
Gill, Lough ⊜	110	54.16 N	8.24 W
Gillam	172	56.21 N	94.43 W
Gilleleje	114	56.07 N	12.19 E
Gillen, Lake ⊜	164	26.11 S	124.38 E
Gilles, Lake ⊜	168	32.50 S	136.45 E
Gillian, Lake ⊜	172	69.32 N	75.23 W
Gillingham, Eng., U.K.	104	51.24 N	0.33 E
Gillingham, Eng., U.K.	104	51.02 N	2.17 W
Gilo ≃	154	8.10 N	33.15 E
Gilroy	178	37.00 N	121.43 W
Gil'uj ≃	128	53.58 N	127.30 E
Giluwe, Mount ∧	166	6.05 S	143.50 E
Gilwern	104	51.51 N	3.06 W
Gimie, Mount ∧	182	13.51 N	61.00 W
Gimli	172	50.38 N	96.59 W
Gimone ≃	118	44.00 N	1.06 E
Gimont	118	43.38 N	0.53 E
Gin Gin	168	25.00 S	151.58 E
Ginir	154	7.07 N	40.46 E
Ginosa	122	40.34 N	16.46 E
Ginowan	135b	26.17 N	127.46 E
Gioia del Colle	122	40.48 N	16.56 E
Gioia Tauro	122	38.26 N	15.54 E
Gipping ≃	104	52.04 N	1.10 E
Giralia	164	22.41 S	114.21 E
Girard, Ohio, U.S.	176	41.10 N	80.42 W
Girard, Pa., U.S.	176	42.00 N	80.19 W
Girardot	184	4.18 N	74.48 W
Girgarre	168	36.24 S	144.59 E
Girilambone	168	31.15 S	146.54 E
Gironde □[5]	118	44.45 N	0.35 W
Girou ≃	118	43.46 N	1.23 E
Giru	168	19.31 S	147.06 E
Giruá	188	28.02 S	54.21 W
Girvan	106	55.15 N	4.51 W
Girvan, Water of ≃	108	55.15 N	4.51 W
Girwa ≃	146	28.17 N	81.07 E
Gisborne	170	38.40 S	178.01 E
Gisenyi	158	1.42 S	29.15 E
Gislaved	114	57.18 N	13.32 E
Gitarama	158	2.07 S	29.45 E
Gitega	158	3.26 S	29.56 E
Giugliano [in Campania]	122	40.56 N	14.12 E
Giulianova	122	42.45 N	13.57 E
Giurgiu	124	43.53 N	25.57 E
Give	114	55.51 N	9.15 E
Givors	118	45.35 N	4.46 E
Givry	118	46.47 N	4.45 E
Giyon	154	8.30 N	38.00 E
Giza → Al-Jīzah	154	30.01 N	31.13 E
Giždüvan	150	40.06 N	64.41 E
Gižiga	128	62.03 N	160.30 E
Gižiginskaja Guba C	128	61.30 N	158.00 E
Gizo	162	8.06 S	156.51 E
Giżycko	116	54.03 N	21.47 E
Gjelma	154	36.28 N	7.26 E
Gjirokastër	124	40.05 N	20.10 E
Gjoa Haven	172	68.38 N	95.57 W
Gjøvik	114	60.48 N	10.42 E
Gjuhëzës, Kep i ≻	124	40.25 N	19.18 E
Glace Bay	172	46.12 N	59.57 W
Glacier Bay C	172	58.40 N	136.00 W
Gladbach → Mönchengladbach	116	51.12 N	6.28 E
Gladbeck	116	51.34 N	6.59 E
Gladstone, Austl.	168	33.17 S	138.22 E
Gladstone, Austl.	168	23.51 S	151.16 E
Gladwin	176	43.59 N	84.29 W
Gláma ∧	112a	65.47 N	23.00 W
Glåma ≃	114	59.12 N	10.57 E
Glamis	108	56.36 N	3.00 W
Glamoč	122	44.03 N	16.51 E
Glamsbjerg	114	55.16 N	10.07 E
Glanamman	104	51.48 N	3.54 W
Glarner Alpen ⋀	118	46.55 N	9.00 E
Glarus	118	47.02 N	9.04 E
Glascarnoch, Loch ⊜	108	57.40 N	4.50 W
Glasgow, Scot., U.K.	108	55.53 N	4.15 W
Glasgow, Ky., U.S.	174	37.00 N	85.55 W
Glasgow, Mont., U.S.	174	48.12 N	106.38 W
Glaslyn ≃	104	52.56 N	4.06 W
Glas Maol ∧	108	56.52 N	3.22 W
Glass, Loch ⊜	108	57.43 N	4.30 W
Glassboro	176	49.32 N	99.15 W
Glasson	110	53.28 N	7.52 W
Glastonbury	104	51.06 N	2.43 W
Glauchau	116	50.49 N	12.32 E
Glaven ≃	104	52.58 N	1.03 E
Glazov	112	58.09 N	52.40 E
Gleinalpe ⋀	116	47.15 N	15.03 E
Gleiwitz → Gliwice	116	50.17 N	18.40 E
Glemsford	104	52.06 N	0.41 E
Glen ≃, Eire	110	54.38 N	8.40 W
Glen ≃, Eng., U.K.	104	52.51 N	0.06 W
Glen Afton	170	37.37 S	175.02 E
Glenamaddy	110	53.37 N	8.35 W
Glenamoy	110	54.14 N	9.42 W
Glenarm	110	54.58 N	5.57 W
Glenavy	110	54.35 N	6.13 W
Glenbeigh	110	52.02 N	9.58 W
Glen Burnie	176	39.10 N	76.37 W
Glencoe, Ont., Can.	176	42.45 N	81.43 W
Glencoe, S. Afr.	160	28.12 S	30.07 E
Glencolumbkille	110	54.43 N	8.45 E
Glencoul, Loch C	108	58.14 N	4.58 W
Glen Cove	176	40.52 N	73.37 W
Glendale, Rh.	158	17.21 S	31.04 E
Glendale, Calif., U.S.	178	34.10 N	118.17 W
Glendale, Oreg., U.S.	178	42.44 N	123.26 W
Glendive	174	47.06 N	104.43 W
Glendoe Forest ⊸[3]	108	57.06 N	4.37 W
Glendowan	110	54.58 N	7.57 W
Glenelg	108	57.13 N	5.38 W
Glenelly ≃	110	54.44 N	7.18 W
Glenfarg	108	56.16 N	3.24 W
Glenfarne	110	54.17 N	7.59 W
Glenfield	104	52.39 N	1.12 W
Glenfinnan	108	56.52 N	5.27 W
Glen Florrie	164	22.55 S	115.59 E
Glengarriff	110	51.45 N	9.33 W
Glengyle	168	24.48 S	139.37 E
Glenhope	170	41.39 S	172.39 E
Glen Innes	168	29.44 S	151.44 E
Glenluce	106	54.53 N	4.49 W
Glen Lyon	176	41.10 N	76.05 W
Glenmorgan	168	27.15 S	149.41 E
Glenns Ferry	178	42.57 N	115.18 W
Glenorchy	170	44.51 S	168.23 E
Glenormiston	168	22.55 S	138.48 E
Glenreagh	168	30.03 S	152.59 E
Glen Robertson	176	45.21 N	74.30 W
Glen Rock	176	39.48 N	76.44 W
Glenrothes	108	56.12 N	3.10 W
Glenroy	164	21.46 S	114.49 E
Glens Falls	176	43.19 N	73.39 W
Glenshee ∨	108	56.48 N	3.30 W
Glenties	110	54.47 N	8.17 W
Glenville, Eire	110	52.03 N	8.26 W
Glenville, W. Va., U.S.	176	38.56 N	80.50 W
Glide	178	43.18 N	123.06 W
Glin	110	52.34 N	9.17 W
Glittertind ∧	88	61.39 N	8.33 E
Glittertinden ∧	114	61.39 N	8.33 E
Gliwice (Gleiwitz)	116	50.17 N	18.40 E
Globe	174	33.24 N	110.47 W
Gloggnitz	116	47.40 N	15.57 E
Głogów, Pol.	116	51.40 N	16.05 E
Głogów, Pol.	116	50.10 N	21.58 E
Glommersträsk	114	65.16 N	19.38 E
Glorieuses, Îles II	156	11.30 S	47.20 E
Glossop	106	53.27 N	1.57 W
Glossopteris, Mount ∧	87	84.44 S	113.51 W
Gloucester, Eng., U.K.	104	51.53 N	2.14 W
Gloucester, Mass., U.S.	176	42.41 N	70.39 W
Gloucester, Vale of ∨	104	51.55 N	2.10 W
Gloucester Island I	168	20.01 S	148.27 E
Gloucestershire □[6]	102	51.47 N	2.15 W
Glouster	176	39.30 N	82.05 W
Glover Reef ✧[2]	182	16.47 N	87.45 W
Gloversville	176	43.03 N	74.20 W
Głowno	116	51.58 N	19.44 E
Głuchołazy	116	50.20 N	17.22 E
Glücksburg	116	54.50 N	9.33 E
Glückstadt	116	53.47 N	9.25 E
Glyde ≃	110	53.52 N	6.21 W
Glyder Fawr ∧	104	53.06 N	4.01 W
Glyme ≃	104	51.49 N	1.22 W
Glyngøre	114	56.46 N	8.52 E
Glynneath	104	51.46 N	3.38 W
Gmunden	116	47.55 N	13.48 E
Gnalta	168	31.03 S	142.20 E
Gnaraloo	164	23.51 S	113.31 E
Gnarp	114	62.03 N	17.16 E
Gniezno	116	52.31 N	17.37 E
Gnjilane	124	42.28 N	21.29 E
Gnowangerup	164	33.56 S	117.59 E
Gō ≃	134	35.02 N	132.13 E
Goālpāra	146	26.11 N	90.37 E
Goat Fell ∧	108	55.39 N	5.11 W
Goathland	106	54.23 N	0.44 W
Goba	154	7.02 N	40.00 E
Gobabis	160	22.30 S	18.58 E
Gobabis □[5]	160	22.00 S	19.00 E
Gobernador Gregores	186	48.46 S	70.15 W
Gobernador Racedo	188	31.35 S	60.05 W
Gobur	158	4.20 N	31.04 E
Goce Delčev	124	41.34 N	23.44 E
Goch	116	51.41 N	6.10 E
Godalming	104	51.11 N	0.37 W
Godāvari ≃	148	17.00 N	81.45 E
Goderich	172	43.45 N	81.43 W
Godhavn	172	69.15 N	53.33 W
Godhra	146	22.45 N	73.38 E
Godmanchester	104	52.19 N	0.11 W
Godoy Cruz	188	32.55 S	68.50 W
Gods ≃	172	56.22 N	92.51 W
Godshill	104	50.38 N	1.14 W
Gods Lake ⊜	172	54.45 N	94.00 W
Gods Mercy, Bay of C	172	63.30 N	86.10 W
Godstone	104	51.15 N	0.04 W
Godthåb	172	64.11 N	51.44 W
Godwin Austen (K2) ∧	149	35.53 N	76.30 E
Goedgegun	160	27.06 S	31.12 E
Goéland, Lac au ⊜	172	49.47 N	76.48 W
Goélands, Lac aux ⊜	172	55.27 N	64.17 W
Goes	116	51.30 N	3.54 E
Goff	158	2.42 N	41.03 E
Goffstown	176	43.01 N	71.36 W
Gohāna	149	29.08 N	76.42 E
Goiana	184	7.33 S	34.59 W
Goianésia	190	15.18 S	49.07 W
Goiânia	190	16.40 S	49.16 W
Goiás	190	15.56 S	50.08 W
Goil, Loch C	108	56.08 N	4.52 W
Goio-Erê	188	24.12 S	53.01 W
Goio-Erê ≃	188	24.14 S	53.21 W
Gojō	134	34.21 N	135.42 E
Gojōme	134	39.56 N	140.07 E
Gojra	149	31.09 N	72.41 E
Gokāk	148	16.10 N	74.50 E
Gokase ≃	134	32.35 N	131.42 E
Gökçe	124	40.11 N	25.55 E
Gökçeada I	124	40.10 N	25.50 E
Gola I	110	55.05 N	8.22 W
Golāghāt	146	26.31 N	93.58 E
Gol'čicha	128	71.43 N	83.36 E
Golconda	178	40.57 N	117.30 W
Gold Beach	178	42.25 N	124.25 W
Gold Coast → Southport	168	27.58 S	153.25 E
Golden, B.C., Can.	172	51.18 N	116.58 W
Golden, Eire	110	52.29 N	7.58 W
Golden Bay C	170	40.40 S	172.50 E
Golden Hinde ∧	172	49.40 N	125.45 W
Golden Lake ⊜	176	45.35 N	77.20 W
Golden Valley ∨	104	52.02 N	2.56 W
Goldfield	178	37.42 N	117.14 W
Gold Mountain ∧	178	37.15 N	117.18 W
Goldsboro	180	35.23 N	77.59 W
Golec-In'aptuk, Gora ∧	126	56.22 N	110.11 E
Golec-Skalistyj, Gora ∧	128	56.24 N	119.12 E
Goleen	110	51.28 N	9.43 W
Goleniów	116	53.36 N	14.50 E
Goleta	178	34.27 N	119.50 W
Golfito	180	8.38 N	83.11 W
Goljam Perelik ∧	124	41.36 N	24.34 E
Gollel	160	27.20 S	31.55 E
Golo ≃	118	42.31 N	9.32 E
Golpāyegān	150	33.27 N	50.18 E
Golspie	108	57.58 N	3.58 W
Golyšmanovo	126	56.23 N	68.23 E
Goma	158	1.41 S	29.14 E
Gomati ≃	146	25.32 N	83.10 E
Gombe ≃	158	4.38 S	31.40 E
Gomel'	130	52.25 N	31.00 E
Gomera I	88	28.06 N	17.08 W
Gometra I	108	56.29 N	6.17 W
Gómez Palacio	180	25.34 N	103.30 W
Gona	166	8.37 S	148.17 E
Gonābād	150	34.20 N	58.42 E
Gonaïves	182	19.30 N	72.40 W
Gonam	128	57.21 N	131.12 E
Gonam ≃	128	57.21 N	131.14 E
Gonâve, Golfe de la C	182	19.20 N	73.15 W
Gonâve, Île de la I	182	18.45 N	73.00 W
Gonbad-e Qābūs	150	37.17 N	55.17 E
Gonda	146	27.08 N	81.56 E
Gondal	146	21.58 N	70.48 E
Gonder	154	12.40 N	37.30 E
Gondia	146	21.27 N	80.12 E
Gondomar	120	41.09 N	8.32 W
Gonesse	102	48.59 N	2.27 E
Gongbujiangda	132	30.01 N	93.08 E
Gongcheng	140	24.49 N	110.46 E
Gongchenqiao	136	30.20 N	120.08 E
Gonggashan ∧	132	29.35 N	101.51 E
Gonggeershan ∧	146	38.37 N	75.20 E
Gongola ≃	152	9.30 N	12.04 E
Gongping	136	23.05 N	115.24 E
Gongshui ≃	136	26.00 N	115.22 E
Gongxian	132	34.48 N	113.03 E
Gōnoura	134	33.45 N	129.41 E
Gonzales	178	36.31 N	121.32 W
González Chaves	188	38.02 S	60.05 W
González Ortega	178	32.40 N	115.23 W
Goodenough Island I	166	9.20 S	150.15 E
Gooderham	176	44.54 N	78.23 W
Good Hope	160	31.51 S	21.55 E
Good Hope, Cape of ≻	160	34.24 S	18.30 E
Good Hope Mountain ∧	172	51.09 N	124.10 W
Goodhouse	160	28.57 S	18.13 E
Gooding	178	42.56 N	114.43 W
Goodland	174	39.21 N	101.43 W
Goodooga	168	29.07 S	147.27 E
Goodwick	104	52.00 N	5.00 W
Goole	106	53.42 N	0.52 W
Goolgowi	168	33.59 S	145.42 E
Goomalling	164	31.19 S	116.49 E
Goomburra	168	28.03 S	152.07 E
Goondiwindi	168	28.32 S	150.19 E
Goonyella	168	22.42 S	147.55 E
Goose Bay	172	53.20 N	60.25 W
Goose Lake ⊜	178	41.57 N	120.25 W
Gooty	148	15.07 N	77.38 E
Gopichettipālaiyam	148	11.28 N	77.27 E
Göppingen	116	48.42 N	9.40 E
Gorakhpur	146	26.45 N	83.22 E
Gorda, Punta ≻, Cuba	182	22.24 N	82.10 W
Gorda, Punta ≻, Nic.	182	14.20 N	83.12 W
Gorda, Punta ≻, Rep. Dom.	182	19.00 N	69.00 W
Gorda Escarpment ✧[4]	90	40.20 N	127.00 W
Gordil	154	9.44 N	21.35 E
Gordon	108	55.41 N	2.34 W
Gordon, Lake ⊜[1]	168	42.42 S	146.12 E
Gordon Downs	164	18.44 S	128.35 E
Gordonsville	176	38.08 N	78.11 W
Gordonton	170	37.40 S	175.18 E
Gore, Austl.	168	28.17 S	151.29 E
Gore, N.Z.	170	46.06 S	168.58 E
Gore, Yai.	154	8.08 N	35.33 E
Gore Bay	176	45.55 N	82.28 W
Gorebridge	108	55.51 N	3.02 W
Gore Mountain ∧	176	44.55 N	71.48 W
Gorey, Eire	110	52.40 N	6.18 W
Gorey, Jersey	105b	49.12 N	2.02 W
Gorgān	150	36.50 N	54.29 E
Gorham, Maine, U.S.	176	43.41 N	70.26 W
Gorham, N.H., U.S.	176	44.23 N	71.10 W
Gori	126	41.58 N	44.07 E
Gorinchem	116	51.50 N	5.00 E
Goring	104	51.32 N	1.09 W
Goring-by-Sea	104	50.49 N	0.25 W
Goring Gap ∨	104	51.32 N	1.08 W
Goris	150	39.31 N	46.23 E
Gorizia	122	45.57 N	13.38 E
Gorj □[4]	124	45.00 N	23.20 E
Gorki → Gor'kij, S.S.S.R.	130	56.20 N	44.00 E
Gorki, S.S.S.R.	130	54.17 N	30.59 E
Gor'kij (Gorky)	130	56.20 N	44.00 E
Gorkovskoje Vodochranilišče ⊜[1]	130	57.00 N	43.10 E
Gorleston on Sea	104	52.36 N	1.43 E
Gorlice	116	49.40 N	21.10 E
Görlitz	116	53.24 N	13.54 E
Gorlovka	126	48.18 N	38.03 E
Gorm, Loch ⊜	108	55.48 N	6.25 W
Gorn'ackij	112	67.32 N	64.03 E
Gorna Dzhumaya → Blagoevgrad	124	42.01 N	23.06 E
Gorn'ak	130	53.36 N	39.29 E
Gorna Orjahovica	124	43.07 N	25.41 E
Gornji Milanovac	124	44.01 N	20.27 E
Gorno-Altajsk	128	51.58 N	85.58 E
Gorno-Čujskij	128	59.12 N	112.25 E
Gornozavodsk	128	46.34 N	141.49 E
Gorodec	130	56.38 N	43.30 E
Gorodeja	130	53.19 N	26.32 E
Goroka	166	6.05 S	145.25 E
Gorontalo	142	0.33 N	123.03 E
Gorseinon	104	51.40 N	4.02 W
Gort	110	53.04 N	8.50 W
Gortahork	110	55.08 N	8.09 W
Gorumna Island I	110	53.14 N	9.40 W
Gorzów Wielkopolski (Landsberg an der Warthe)	116	52.44 N	15.15 E
Gose	134	34.27 N	135.44 E
Gosen	134	37.44 N	139.11 E
Gosford	168	33.26 S	151.21 E
Gosforth, Eng., U.K.	106	54.26 N	3.27 W
Gosforth, Eng., U.K.	106	55.01 N	1.37 W
Goshen, Calif., U.S.	178	36.21 N	119.25 W
Goshen, N.Y., U.S.	176	41.24 N	74.20 W
Goshogawara	134	40.48 N	140.27 E
Goshute Lake ⊜	178	40.08 N	114.38 W
Goshute Valley ∨	178	40.40 N	114.30 W
Goslar	116	51.54 N	10.25 E
Gosnells	164	32.04 S	116.00 E
Gospić	122	44.33 N	15.23 E
Gosport	104	50.48 N	1.08 W
Gostivar	124	41.47 N	20.54 E
Gostyń	116	51.53 N	17.00 E
Gostynin	116	52.26 N	19.29 E
Göta älv ≃	114	57.42 N	11.52 E
Göta kanal ≊	114	58.50 N	13.58 E
Göteborg (Gothenburg)	114	57.43 N	11.58 E
Göteborgs Och Bohus län □[6]	114	58.30 N	11.30 E

Symbols in the index entries are identified on page 198.

Symbols in the index entries are identified on page 198.

Name	Page	Lat	Long
Hallowell	176	44.17 N	69.48 W
Hall Peninsula ➤¹	172	63.30 N	66.00 W
Hallsberg	114	59.04 N	15.07 E
Halls Creek	164	18.16 S	127.46 E
Hallstahammar	114	59.37 N	16.13 E
Hallstavik	114	60.03 N	18.36 E
Hallstead	176	41.58 N	75.45 W
Halluin	118	50.47 N	3.08 E
Halmahera I	138	1.00 N	128.00 E
Halmahera, Laut (Halmahera Sea) ➤²	138	1.00 S	129.00 E
Halmstad	114	56.39 N	12.52 E
Halsafjorden C²	114	63.03 N	8.11 E
Hälsingborg → Helsingborg			
Hälsingland □⁹	114	56.03 N	12.42 E
Halstead	114	51.57 N	0.38 E
Haltern	116	51.46 N	7.10 E
Haltiatunturi ∧	112	69.18 N	21.16 E
Haltwhistle	106	54.58 N	2.27 W
Halwell	104	50.22 N	3.43 W
Hamada	134	34.53 N	132.05 E
Hamadān	150	34.48 N	48.30 E
Hamāh	150	35.08 N	36.45 E
Hamamatsu	134	34.42 N	137.44 E
Hamanaka	134a	43.05 N	145.10 E
Hamana-ko	134	34.45 N	137.34 E
Hamar	114	60.48 N	11.06 E
Hamáṭah, Jabal ∧	150	24.12 N	35.00 E
Hamble	104	50.52 N	1.19 W
Hambledon	104	50.56 N	1.04 W
Hambleton Hills ∧²	106	54.16 N	1.12 W
Hamburg, B.R.D.	116	53.33 N	9.59 E
Hamburg, N.J., U.S.	176	41.09 N	74.35 W
Hamburg, N.Y., U.S.	176	42.43 N	78.50 W
Hamburg, Pa., U.S.	176	40.34 N	75.59 W
Hamden, Conn., U.S.	176	41.21 N	72.56 W
Hamden, Ohio, U.S.	176	39.10 N	82.32 W
Häme ➤¹	114	61.30 N	24.30 E
Hämeen lääni □⁴	114	61.30 N	24.30 E
Hämeenlinna	114	61.00 N	24.27 E
Hämelin Pool	164	26.26 S	114.11 E
Hameln	116	52.06 N	9.21 E
Hamer Koke	150	5.12 N	36.45 E
Hamersley Range ∧	164	21.53 S	116.46 E
Hamhŭng	132	39.54 N	127.32 E
Hami	132	42.47 N	93.32 E
Hamidiye	124	41.09 N	26.40 E
Hamilton, Austl.	168	37.45 S	142.02 E
Hamilton, Ber.	180	32.17 N	64.46 W
Hamilton, Ont., Can.	172	43.15 N	79.51 W
Hamilton, N.Z.	170	37.47 S	175.17 E
Hamilton, Scot., U.K.	108	55.47 N	4.03 W
Hamilton, N.Y., U.S.	176	42.50 N	75.33 W
Hamilton, Ohio, U.S.	176	39.26 N	84.30 W
Hamilton ≈	168	23.30 S	139.47 E
Hamilton, Mount ∧, Calif., U.S.	178	37.21 N	121.38 W
Hamilton, Mount ∧, Nev., U.S.	178	39.14 N	115.32 W
Hamilton City	178	39.45 N	122.01 W
Hamilton Creek ≈	164	26.40 S	135.19 E
Hamilton Hotel	168	22.50 S	140.35 E
Hamilton Inlet C	172	54.00 N	57.30 W
Hamilton Mountain ∧	176	43.25 N	74.22 W
Hamina	114	60.34 N	27.12 E
Hamirpur	144	25.57 N	80.09 E
Hamley Bridge	168	34.21 S	138.41 E
Hamlin	176	38.17 N	82.06 W
Hamm	116	51.41 N	7.49 E
Hammamet	152	36.24 N	10.37 E
Hammam Lif	152	36.44 N	10.20 E
Hammār, Hawr al-	150	30.50 N	47.10 E
Hammel	114	56.15 N	9.52 E
Hammerdal	114	63.36 N	15.21 E
Hammerfest	112	70.40 N	23.42 E
Hammersmith ➤⁸	104	51.30 N	0.14 W
Hammond	174	51.30 N	90.28 W
Hammond Island I	166	10.35 S	142.13 E
Hammondsport	176	42.25 N	77.13 W
Hammonton	176	39.38 N	74.48 W
Hamningberg	112	70.31 N	30.37 E
Hampden	176	44.45 N	68.50 W
Hampshire □⁶	104	51.05 N	1.15 W
Hampshire Downs ∧¹	104	51.15 N	1.17 W
Hampton, Eng., U.K.	104	51.25 N	0.22 W
Hampton, N.J., U.S.	176	40.42 N	74.58 W
Hampton, Va., U.S.	174	37.01 N	76.22 W
Hampton Bays	176	40.52 N	72.31 W
Hampton Harbour C	164	20.40 S	116.30 E
Hamra	114	61.39 N	15.00 E
Hamra, Saguia el ∨	152	27.15 N	13.21 W
Hana	179a	20.45 N	155.59 W
Han-tan	132	10.40 N	107.46 E
Hanang ∧	158	4.26 S	35.24 E
Hanapepe	179a	21.55 N	159.35 W
Hanau	152	50.08 N	8.55 E
Hanawa	134	40.11 N	140.47 E
Hanbury ≈	172	63.37 N	104.33 W
Hancheng	132	35.29 N	110.25 E
Hanchuan	136	30.39 N	113.48 E
Hancock, Md., U.S.	176	39.42 N	78.11 W
Hancock, Mich., U.S.	174	47.07 N	88.35 W
Hancock, N.Y., U.S.	176	41.57 N	75.17 W
Handa	134	34.53 N	136.56 E
Handa I	108	58.23 N	5.12 W
Handan	132	36.37 N	114.29 E
Handlová	116	48.44 N	18.46 E
Hando	154	10.37 N	50.16 E
HaNegev ➤¹	150	30.30 N	34.55 E
Hanford	178	36.20 N	119.39 W
Hangatiki	170	38.15 S	175.10 E
Hangchou → Hangzhou			
Hangington Hill ∧²	104	50.41 N	3.57 W
Hangjinhouqi	132	40.59 N	108.57 E
Hangjinqi	132	39.59 N	108.57 E
Hangklip, Kaap ➤	160	34.26 S	18.48 E
Hango (Hanko)	114	59.50 N	22.57 E
Hangu	149	33.32 N	71.04 E
Hanguang	136	24.56 N	113.08 E
Hangxian (Linping)	136	30.25 N	120.18 E
Hangzhou (Hangchow)	132	30.15 N	120.10 E
Hanish, Jazā'ir II	144	13.45 N	42.45 E
Hanjiang, Zhg.	136	25.30 N	119.06 E
Hanjiang, Zhg.	136	24.48 N	118.38 E
Hankey	160	33.50 S	24.53 E
Hankow → Wuhan			
Hann ≈	136	30.36 N	114.17 E
Hann ∧	166	17.10 S	126.10 E
Hannah Bay C	172	51.38 N	111.54 W
Hannibal	174	39.42 N	91.22 W
Hannover	116	52.22 N	9.44 E
Ha-noi	140	21.02 N	105.51 E
Hanover, Ont., Can.	176	44.09 N	81.02 W
Hanover, S. Afr.	160	31.04 S	24.29 E
Hanover, N.H., U.S.	176	43.42 N	72.17 W
Hanover, Pa., U.S.	176	39.48 N	76.59 W
Hanshan	136	31.43 N	118.06 E
Hanshui ≈	136	30.35 N	114.17 E
Hänsi	144	29.06 N	75.58 E
Hanson ≈	164	20.15 S	133.25 E
Hansthölm	114	57.07 N	8.38 E
Hantsport	176	45.04 N	64.11 W
Hantzsch ≈	172	67.22 N	19.45 E
Hanzhong	132	32.59 N	107.11 E
Hao II	96	18.15 S	140.58 W
Haparanda	114	65.50 N	24.10 E
Happy Camp	178	41.48 N	123.22 W
Hāpur	144	28.43 N	77.47 E
Harad	150	24.08 N	49.05 E
Haraiki II	96	15.43 S	144.27 W
Haranomachi	134	37.38 N	140.58 E
Harar → Harer			
Harash, Bi'r al- ➤⁴	152		
Harbin → Haerbin	132	45.45 N	126.41 E
Harbør	114	56.37 N	8.12 E
Harbor Beach	176	43.51 N	82.39 W
Harbor Springs	176	45.26 N	84.59 W
Harda	144	22.20 N	77.06 E
Hardangerfjorden C²	114	60.10 N	6.00 E
Hardangerjøkulen ⋀¹	114	60.32 N	7.26 E
Hardangervidda ⋀¹	114	60.20 N	7.30 E
Hardenberg	116	52.34 N	6.37 E
Harderwijk	116	52.21 N	5.36 E
Harding	160	30.34 S	29.58 E
Hardisty Lake ❸	172	64.30 N	117.45 W
Hardoi	146	27.24 N	80.07 E
Hardwār	146	29.58 N	78.10 E
Hardwick	104	44.30 N	72.22 W
Hardwood Ridge ∧	176	41.15 N	75.23 W
Hardy Bay C	172	75.02 N	115.16 W
Hare Bay C	172	51.18 N	55.50 W
Hare Indian ≈	172	66.18 N	128.38 W
Hareøen I	172	70.25 N	54.50 W
Harer	154	9.18 N	42.08 E
Hargeysa	154	9.30 N	44.03 E
Harghita □⁴	124	46.35 N	25.30 E
Harihar	148	14.31 N	75.48 E
Harihari	170	43.09 S	170.33 E
Haringey ➤⁸	104	51.35 N	0.07 W
Haripur	149	33.59 N	72.56 E
Harírūd ≈, As.	146	34.20 N	64.05 E
Harírūd (Tedžen) ≈, As.			
Härjedalen □⁹	114	62.20 N	13.00 E
Harlech	104	52.52 N	4.07 W
Harleston	104	52.24 N	1.18 E
Harlingen, Ned.	116	53.10 N	5.24 E
Harlingen, Tex., U.S.	174	26.11 N	97.42 W
Harlow	104	51.47 N	0.08 E
Harman	176	38.55 N	79.32 W
Harmånger	114	61.56 N	17.13 E
Harmanli	124	41.56 N	25.54 E
Harmony	176	44.58 N	69.33 W
Harney Basin ≈¹	178	43.15 N	120.40 W
Harney Lake	178	43.14 N	119.07 W
Harney Peak ∧	174	44.00 N	103.30 W
Härnösand	114	62.38 N	17.56 E
Haroldswick	108a	60.47 N	0.50 W
Harper	152	4.25 N	7.43 W
Harper Lake ❸	106	54.55 N	2.31 W
Harper Town	106	55.15 N	7.49 W
Harray, Loch of ❸	108	59.01 N	3.13 W
Harricana ≈	172	51.10 N	79.45 W
Harrietfield	108	56.25 N	3.39 W
Harrietsham	104	51.15 N	0.41 E
Harrington, Eng., U.K.	106	54.37 N	3.34 W
Harrington, Del., U.S.	176	38.56 N	75.35 W
Harrington, Maine, U.S.	176	44.37 N	67.49 W
Harris ➤¹	108	56.59 N	6.20 W
Harris, Lake ❸	164	31.08 S	135.14 E
Harris, Sound of ⨄	108	57.45 N	7.10 W
Harrisburg	174	40.16 N	76.52 W
Harrismith, Austl.	164	32.56 S	117.52 E
Harrismith, S. Afr.	160	28.18 S	29.03 E
Harrison	176	44.01 N	84.48 W
Harrison, Cape ➤	172	54.55 N	57.55 W
Harrisonburg	174	38.26 N	78.52 W
Harrison Islands II	172	69.13 N	90.30 W
Harrisville, Mich., U.S.	176	44.39 N	83.17 W
Harrisville, N.Y., U.S.	176	44.09 N	75.19 W
Harrisville, W. Va., U.S.	176	39.13 N	81.03 W
Harrodsburg	176	37.46 N	84.51 W
Harrow	104	54.00 N	1.33 W
Harrow ≈	104	42.02 N	82.55 W
Harrowsmith	176	44.24 N	76.40 W
Harstad	144	68.46 N	16.30 E
Harts Range	164	23.00 S	134.55 E
Hartsville	174	34.23 N	80.04 W
Härūnābād	149	29.37 N	73.08 E
Härūt ≈	146	31.35 N	61.18 E
Harvey, Austl.	164	33.05 S	115.54 E
Harvey, N. Dak., U.S.	174	47.47 N	99.56 W
Harwell	104	51.37 N	1.18 W
Harwich	104	51.57 N	1.17 E
Haşa, Bi'r al- ➤⁴	150	22.58 N	35.40 E
Hasaki	134	35.44 N	140.50 E
Hashā, Jabal al- ∧	144	35.19 N	136.42 E
Hashima	134	35.19 N	136.42 E
Hashimoto	134	34.19 N	135.37 E
Haskovo	124	41.56 N	25.33 E
Hasköy	124	41.38 N	26.41 E
Hasle	114	55.11 N	14.43 E
Haslemere	104	51.06 N	0.43 W
Haslev	114	55.20 N	11.58 E
Haslingden	106	53.43 N	2.18 W
Hasselt	116	50.56 N	5.20 E
Hassi el Ghella	120	35.28 N	1.03 W
Hassi Messaoud	152	31.43 N	5.59 E
Hassi R'Mel	152	32.55 N	3.24 E
Hassleholm	114	56.09 N	13.46 E
Hastings, Ont., Can.	176	44.18 N	77.57 W
Hastings, N.Z.	170	39.38 S	176.51 E
Hastings, Eng., U.K.	104	50.51 N	0.36 E
Hastings, Mich., U.S.	176	42.39 N	85.17 W
Hastings, Nebr., U.S.	174	40.35 N	98.23 W
Hatches Creek	164	20.56 S	135.12 E
Hat Creek ≈	178	40.59 N	121.33 W
Hatfield, Austl.	168	33.52 S	143.45 E
Hatfield, Eng., U.K.	104	51.46 N	0.13 W
Hatfield, Mass., U.S.	176	42.22 N	72.36 W
Hatfield Peverel	104	51.47 N	0.35 E
Hathersage	106	53.19 N	1.40 W
Hāthras	144	27.36 N	78.03 E
Ha-tien	140	10.23 N	104.29 E
Ha-tinh	140	18.20 N	105.54 E
Hato Mayor [del Rey]	182	18.46 N	69.15 W
Hatteras, Cape ➤	174	35.13 N	75.32 W
Hattiesburg	174	31.19 N	89.16 W
Hatton	106	57.25 N	1.54 W
Hatvan	116	47.40 N	19.41 E
Hat Yai	140	7.01 N	100.28 E
Haugesund	114	59.25 N	5.18 E
Haugh of Urr	106	54.58 N	3.52 W
Haugsdorf	116	48.42 N	16.05 E
Haukivesi ❸	114	62.06 N	28.28 E
Haukivuori	114	62.01 N	27.13 E
Haunstetten	116	48.18 N	10.54 E
Hauraki Gulf C	170	36.00 S	175.05 E
Hauroko, Lake ❸	170	46.00 S	167.20 E
Haut, Isle au I	176	44.03 N	68.38 W
Haut Atlas ∧	152	31.30 N	6.00 W
Haute-Garonne □⁵	118	43.25 N	1.30 E
Haute-Loire □⁵	118	45.05 N	3.50 E
Haute-Marne □⁵	118	48.05 N	5.10 E
Haute-Saône □⁵	118	47.40 N	6.10 E
Hautes-Alpes □⁵	118	44.40 N	6.30 E
Hautes Fagnes ∧	116	50.30 N	6.05 E
Hautes-Pyrénées □⁵	118	43.00 N	0.10 E
Haute-Vienne □⁵	118	45.50 N	1.15 E
Haut-Mbomou □⁵	158	5.20 N	26.00 E
Haut-Rhin □⁵	118	47.55 N	7.13 E
Hauts-de-Seine □⁵	118	48.50 N	2.11 E
Haut-Zaïre □⁵	158	2.20 N	27.20 E
Hauula	179a	21.37 N	157.55 W
Havana → La Habana	182	23.08 N	82.22 W
Havant	104	50.51 N	0.59 W
Havasu, Lake ❸¹	178	34.30 N	114.20 W
Havelli	149	30.27 N	73.42 E
Havelock	176	52.25 N	12.45 E
Havelock North	170	39.40 S	176.53 E
Haverfordwest	104	51.49 N	4.58 W
Haverhill, Eng., U.K.	104	52.05 N	0.26 E
Haverhill, Mass., U.S.	176	42.47 N	71.05 W
Häveri	148	14.48 N	75.24 E
Haverigg	106	54.11 N	3.17 W
Havering ➤⁸	104	51.34 N	0.14 E
Haverstraw	176	41.12 N	73.58 W
Havířov	116	49.47 N	18.27 E
Havlíčkův Brod	116	49.36 N	15.35 E
Havre	174	48.33 N	109.41 W
→ Le Havre, Fr.	118	49.30 N	0.08 E
Havre, Mont., U.S.	174	48.33 N	109.41 W
Havre de Grace	176	39.33 N	76.06 W
Havre-Saint-Pierre	172	50.14 N	63.36 W
Havsa	124	41.33 N	26.49 E
Hawaii □³	179a	20.00 N	157.45 W
Hawaii I	179a	19.30 N	155.30 W
Hawaiian Ridge ✳³	96	24.00 N	165.00 W
Hawarden	104	53.11 N	3.02 W
Hawashiyah, Wādī ∨	150	28.31 N	32.58 E
Hawera	170	39.35 S	174.17 E
Hawes	106	54.18 N	2.12 W
Haweswater Reservoir ❸¹			
Hawi	179a	20.14 N	155.50 W
Hawick	106	55.25 N	2.47 W
Hawke, Cape ➤	168	32.13 S	152.34 E
Hawke Bay C	170	39.20 S	177.30 E
Hawker	168	31.53 S	138.25 E
Hawkes, Mount ∧	87	83.56 S	55.45 W
Hawkesbury	172	45.36 N	74.37 W
Hawkhurst	104	51.02 N	0.30 E
Hawksbill ∧	176	38.33 N	78.23 W
Hawks Nest Point ➤	182	24.09 N	75.32 W
Hawkwood	168	25.47 S	150.50 E
Hawley	176	41.28 N	75.11 W
Hawthorne	178	38.32 N	118.38 W
Hay ≈	168	34.30 S	144.51 E
Hay ≈, Austl.	168	25.14 S	138.00 E
Hay ≈, Can.	172	60.52 N	115.44 W
Hay, Cape ➤	172	74.25 N	113.00 W
Hayachine-san ∧	134	39.34 N	141.29 E
Hayange	118	49.20 N	6.03 E
Hayden Peak ∧	178	43.33 N	116.43 W
Haydenville	176	39.20 N	82.20 W
Haydock	106	53.28 N	2.39 W
Haydon Bridge	106	54.58 N	2.14 W
Hayes ≈, Man., Can.	172	57.03 N	92.09 W
Hayes ≈, N.W. Ter., Can.	172	67.18 N	95.02 W
Hayes, Mount ∧	172	63.37 N	146.43 W
Hayford Peak ∧	178	36.40 N	115.11 W
Hayfork	178	40.33 N	123.11 W
Hayfork Bally ∧	178	40.30 N	123.13 W
Hayfork Creek ≈	178	40.37 N	123.26 W
Hay-on-Wye	104	52.04 N	3.07 W
Hayrabolu	124	41.12 N	27.06 E
Hays	174	38.53 N	99.20 W
Haystack Mountain ∧	176	43.39 N	115.38 W
Hayward	178	37.40 N	122.05 W
Haywards Heath	104	51.00 N	0.06 W
Hazārībāgh	146	23.59 N	85.21 E
Hazard	176	37.15 N	83.12 W
Hazebrouck	118	50.43 N	2.32 E
Hazel ≈	168	36.53 N	77.51 W
Hazel Grove	106	53.23 N	2.08 W
Hazelton, B.C., Can.	172	55.15 N	127.40 W
Hazelton, Idaho, U.S.	178	42.41 N	114.08 W
Hazleton	176	40.58 N	75.59 W
Hazlet, Lake ❸	164	21.30 S	128.48 E
Hazro	149	33.54 N	72.29 E
Heacham	104	52.55 N	0.30 E
Headcorn	104	51.11 N	0.37 E
Headford	110	53.28 N	9.05 W
Headington	104	51.45 N	1.13 W
Headlands	158	18.14 S	32.03 E
Headley	104	51.07 N	0.50 W
Healdsburg	178	38.37 N	122.52 W
Healesville	168	37.40 S	145.31 E
Heanor	104	53.01 N	1.22 W
Heany Junction	158	20.06 S	28.54 E
Hearst Island I	87	64.55 S	62.10 W
Heathcote	168	36.55 S	144.42 E
Heath End	104	50.59 N	0.17 E
Heathfield	104	50.58 N	0.16 E
Heathsville	176	37.55 N	76.28 W
Hebburn	106	54.59 N	1.30 W
Hebden Bridge	106	53.45 N	2.00 W
Hebei □⁴	132	39.00 N	116.00 E
Hebel	168	28.59 S	147.48 E
Heber	178	32.44 N	115.32 W
Hebi	132	35.59 N	114.11 E
Hebrides, Sea of the ➤²	108	57.00 N	6.55 W
Hebron, Newf., Can.	172	58.12 N	62.38 W
Hebron, N.D., U.S.	174	46.35 N	75.41 W
Hebron → Al-Khalīl, Urd.	150	31.32 N	35.06 E
Hecate Strait ⨄	172	53.00 N	131.00 W
Hechi	140	24.51 N	107.59 E
Hechuan	132	30.00 N	106.16 E
Heckington	104	53.00 N	0.18 W
Hector	170	41.36 S	171.53 E
Hector, Mount ∧	170	40.57 S	175.17 E
Hede	114	62.25 N	13.30 E
Hedemora	114	60.17 N	15.59 E
Hedensted	114	55.46 N	9.42 E
Hedmark □⁶	114	61.30 N	11.45 E
Hednesford	104	52.43 N	2.00 W
Hedon	106	53.44 N	0.12 W
Heerenveen	116	52.57 N	5.55 E
Heerlen	116	50.54 N	5.59 E
Hefa (Haifa)	150	32.49 N	35.00 E
Hefei	132	31.51 N	117.17 E
Heged	132	39.39 N	106.41 E
Heguaizi	132	20.43 N	96.49 E
Hei	136	24.02 N	110.17 E
Heide	116	54.12 N	9.06 E
Heidelberg, B.R.D.	116	49.25 N	8.43 E
Heidelberg, S. Afr.	160	26.32 S	28.18 E
Heidelberg, S. Afr.	160	34.06 S	20.59 E
Heidenheim	116	48.41 N	10.09 E
Heihe (Naqukê)	150	31.34 N	92.00 E
Heilbron	160	27.21 S	27.58 E
Heilbronn	116	49.08 N	9.13 E
Heiligenblut	116	47.02 N	12.50 E
Heiligenhafen	116	54.22 N	10.58 E
Heiligenstadt	116	51.23 N	10.09 E
Heilongjiang □⁴	132	48.00 N	128.00 E
Heilongjiang (Amur) ≈	128	52.56 N	141.10 E
Heilungkiang → Heilongjiang □⁴	132	48.00 N	128.00 E
Heimdal	114	63.21 N	10.22 E
Heinävesi	114	62.26 N	28.36 E
Heinola	114	61.13 N	26.02 E
Hejaz → Al-Ḥijāz ➤¹	150	24.30 N	38.30 E
Hekla ∧¹	112a	64.00 N	19.39 W
Hekou	140	22.31 N	103.57 E
Hekura-jima I	134	37.51 N	136.55 E
Helagsfjället ∧	114	62.55 N	12.27 E
Helen ∧	168	21.34 S	141.13 E
Helena, Ark., U.S.	174	34.32 N	90.35 W
Helena, Mont., U.S.	174	46.36 N	112.01 W
Helen Island I		2.58 N	131.49 E
Helensburgh	106	56.01 N	4.44 W
Helen Springs	164	18.26 S	133.52 E
Helensville	170	36.40 S	174.28 E
Helgoland I	116	54.09 N	7.53 E
Helixi	136	30.40 N	118.59 E
Hellertown	176	40.35 N	75.21 W
Hellifield	106	54.01 N	2.12 W
Hell Ness ➤	108	58.54 N	3.10 W
Hell-Ville	160	13.25 S	48.16 E
Helmand □⁴	146	31.00 N	64.10 E
Helmand ≈	146	31.12 N	61.34 E
Helmsdale	108	58.07 N	3.40 W
Helmsdale ≈	108	58.07 N	3.44 W
Helmsley	106	54.15 N	1.04 W
Helmstedt	116	52.13 N	11.00 E
Helsby	106	53.17 N	2.46 W
Helsingborg	114	56.03 N	12.42 E
Helsingfors → Helsinki			
Helsingør (Elsinore)	114	56.02 N	12.37 E
Helsinki (Helsingfors)	114	60.10 N	24.58 E
Helska, Mierzeja ➤²	116	54.45 N	18.39 E
Helston	104	50.05 N	5.16 W
Helvellyn ∧	106	54.31 N	3.01 W
Helvick Head ➤	110	52.03 N	7.33 W
Hemau	116	49.03 N	11.47 E
Hemel Hempstead	104	51.46 N	0.28 W
Hemet	178	33.45 N	116.58 W
Hempnall	104	52.30 N	1.19 E
Hemse	114	57.14 N	18.22 E
Hemsworth	106	53.38 N	1.21 W
Henan □⁴	132	34.00 N	114.00 E
Hen and Chickens II	170	35.55 S	174.45 E
Henares ≈	120	40.24 N	3.30 W
Henderson, Ky., U.S.	174	37.50 N	87.35 W
Henderson, Nev., U.S.	178	36.02 N	114.59 W
Hendricks	176	39.05 N	79.38 W
Hendrina	160	26.11 S	29.45 E
Hendy	104	51.43 N	4.04 W
Hengelo	116	52.15 N	6.45 E
Hengfeng	136	28.24 N	117.34 E
Hengoed	104	51.39 N	3.20 W
Hengshan, Zhg.	132	37.56 N	109.53 E
Hengshan, Zhg.	136	27.15 N	112.51 E
Hengxi	136	29.42 N	121.35 E
Hengxian	140	22.42 N	109.13 E
Hengyang	132	26.51 N	112.30 E
Henley-in-Arden	104	52.17 N	1.46 W
Henley-on-Thames	104	51.32 N	0.56 W
Henlopen, Cape ➤	176	38.48 N	75.05 W
Henlow	104	52.02 N	0.18 W
Hennebont	118	47.48 N	3.17 W
Hennef	116	50.46 N	7.16 E
Hennenman	160	27.59 S	27.01 E
Hennigsdorf	116	52.38 N	13.12 E
Henrietta	176	43.11 N	71.49 W
Henrietta	114	43.03 N	77.37 W
Henrietta Maria, Cape ➤	172	55.09 N	82.20 W
Henry, Point ➤	134	34.29 S	119.23 E
Henry Kater, Cape ➤	172	69.05 N	66.44 W
Hensall	176	43.26 N	81.30 W
Henshaw, Lake ❸¹	178	33.15 N	116.45 W
Henstridge	104	50.59 N	2.24 W
Henty	168	35.31 S	147.02 E
Henzada	140	17.38 N	95.28 E
Heping (Yangmingzhen)	136	24.28 N	114.58 E
Hepu (Lianzhou)	140	21.28 N	109.11 E
Heqiao	136	31.30 N	119.53 E
Heqing	140	26.30 N	100.20 E
Herāt	146	34.20 N	62.00 E
Hérault □⁵	118	43.40 N	3.30 E
Herberton	166	17.23 S	145.23 E
Herbertsdale	160	34.01 S	21.45 E
Herceg-Novi	124	42.27 N	18.32 E
Heredia	182	10.00 N	84.07 W
Hereford	104	52.04 N	2.43 W
Hereford and Worcester □⁶	102	52.10 N	2.30 W
Herekino	170	35.15 S	173.13 E
Herford	116	52.06 N	8.40 E
Herisau	118	47.23 N	9.17 E
Herkimer	176	43.02 N	74.59 W
Herlen ≈	132	48.48 N	117.00 E
Herma Ness ➤	108a	60.50 N	0.55 W
Hermann	174	38.42 N	91.26 W
Hermannsburg	164	23.57 S	132.45 E
Hermansverk	114	61.11 N	6.51 E
Hermidale	168	31.33 S	146.43 E
Hermitage	172	47.33 N	55.55 W
Hermit Islands II	166	1.30 S	145.00 E
Hermosillo	180	29.04 N	110.58 W
Hernád (Hornád) ≈	116	47.56 N	21.08 E
Hernandarias	188	25.22 S	54.45 W
Hernando	188	32.26 S	63.45 W
Herndon	176	40.43 N	76.51 W
Herne	116	51.32 N	7.13 E
Herne Bay	104	51.23 N	1.08 E
Herning	114	56.08 N	8.59 E
Herowābād	150	37.37 N	48.32 E
Herrera del Duque	120	39.10 N	5.03 W
Herrera de Pisuerga	120	42.36 N	4.20 W
Herrick	168	41.06 S	147.52 E
Hersbruck	116	49.30 N	11.26 E
Herschel	160	30.37 S	27.12 E
Herschel Island I	172	69.35 N	139.05 W
Hersham	104	51.22 N	0.23 W
Hershey	176	40.17 N	76.39 W
Herstal	116	50.40 N	5.38 E
Herstmonceux	104	50.53 N	0.20 E
Hertford	104	51.48 N	0.05 W
Hertfordshire □⁶	102	51.50 N	0.05 W
Hertzogville	160	28.08 S	25.33 E
Hervey Bay C	168	25.00 S	153.00 E
Herzberg	116	51.41 N	13.14 E
Hess ≈	172	63.34 N	133.57 W
Hessen □³	116	50.30 N	9.15 E
Hessle	106	53.44 N	0.26 W
Hess Tablemount ✳³	96	18.30 N	174.30 W
Heswall	106	53.20 N	3.06 W
Hetch Hetchy Aqueduct ☰¹	178	37.29 N	122.19 W
Hetian	176	37.08 N	79.54 E
Hetianne	132	40.30 N	80.45 E
Hetton-le-Hole	106	54.42 N	1.27 W
Hettstedt	116	51.38 N	11.30 E
Heuvelton	176	44.37 N	75.25 W
Heves	116	47.36 N	20.17 E
Heves □⁶	116	47.50 N	20.15 E
Hexham	106	54.58 N	2.06 W
Hexian, Zhg.	136	24.15 N	111.43 E
Hexian, Zhg.	136	31.43 N	118.22 E
Heybridge	104	51.44 N	0.42 E
Heyrieux	118	45.38 N	5.03 E
Heysham	106	54.02 N	2.54 W
Heywood, Austl.	168	38.08 S	141.37 E
Heywood, Eng., U.K.	106	53.36 N	2.13 W
Hialeah	174	25.49 N	80.17 W
Hibaldstow	106	53.31 N	0.31 W
Hibbing	174	47.25 N	92.56 W
Hibbs, Point ➤	168	42.38 S	145.15 E
Hickory Township	176	41.12 N	80.22 W
Hicks, Point ➤	168	37.48 S	149.17 E
Hicks Bay	170	37.36 S	178.18 E
Hicksville	176	40.46 N	73.30 W
Hidaka-sammyaku ∧	134a	42.35 N	142.45 E
Hidalgo □³	180	20.30 N	99.00 W
Hidalgo del Parral	180	26.56 N	105.40 W
Hidrolândia	190	16.58 S	49.14 W
Hierro I	152	27.45 N	18.00 W
Higashiichiki	134	31.44 N	130.20 E
Higashine	134	38.26 N	140.24 E
Higashiōsaka	134	34.39 N	135.35 E
Higgins Lake ❸	176	44.30 N	84.45 W
Higham Ferrers	104	52.19 N	0.36 W
Higham Upshire	104	51.26 N	0.28 E
High Bentham	106	54.08 N	2.31 W
Highbridge	104	51.13 N	2.59 W
Highbury	168	16.25 S	143.09 E
Highfield	106	54.38 N	3.34 W
High Force ⊔	106	54.38 N	2.18 W
Highgate	176	44.56 N	73.02 W
High Hesket	106	54.48 N	2.49 W
High Island	176	45.42 N	85.40 W
High Knob ∧	176	37.05 N	82.35 W
Highland, Calif., U.S.	178	34.08 N	117.12 W
Highland, N.Y., U.S.	176	41.43 N	73.58 W
Highland Park	176	42.11 N	87.48 W
Highland Peak ∧	178	37.34 N	118.30 W
Highlands	176	40.24 N	73.59 W
High Level	172	58.31 N	117.08 W
High Peak ∧¹	106	53.22 N	1.50 W
High Plains ≈	174	34.00 N	103.00 W
High Point ➤	176	45.19 N	84.40 W
High Point	174	35.57 N	80.00 W
High River	172	50.35 N	113.52 W
High Rock	182	26.37 N	78.58 W
High Seat ∧	106	54.23 N	2.18 W
High Street ∧	106	54.29 N	2.52 W
High Willhays ∧	104	50.41 N	4.01 W
Highworth	104	51.38 N	1.43 W
High Wycombe	104	51.38 N	0.46 W
Higüero, Punta ➤	182	18.22 N	67.16 W
Higuerote	182	10.29 N	66.06 W
Higüey	182	18.37 N	68.42 W
Hījar	120	41.10 N	0.27 W
Hijāz, Jabal al- ∧	144	19.45 N	41.55 E
Hikari	134	33.58 N	131.56 E
Hikone	134	35.15 N	136.15 E
Hikurangi I¹	96	17.36 S	142.37 W
Hikurangi	170	35.36 S	174.18 E
Hikurangi ∧	170	38.21 S	176.51 E
Hildburghausen	116	50.25 N	10.44 E
Hilden	116	51.10 N	6.56 E
Hildesheim	116	52.09 N	9.57 E
Hillaby, Mount ∧	182	13.12 N	59.35 W
Hillcrest Center	178	35.23 N	118.57 W
Hillared	114	55.56 N	12.19 E
Hillegom	116	52.18 N	4.35 E
Hillingdon ➤⁸	104	51.32 N	0.27 W
Hill Island Lake ❸	172	60.29 N	109.50 W
Hillman	176	45.04 N	83.54 W
Hillsboro, N.H., U.S.	176	43.07 N	71.54 W
Hillsboro, Ohio, U.S.	176	39.12 N	83.37 W
Hillsborough	176	54.28 N	6.05 W
Hillsdale	176	41.55 N	84.38 W
Hillside	164	21.44 S	119.23 E
Hillswick	108a	60.28 N	1.30 W
Hilo	179a	19.44 N	155.05 W
Hilo Bay C	179a	19.44 N	155.05 W
Hilpsford Point ➤	106	54.03 N	3.12 W
Hiltaba, Mount ∧	164	32.09 S	135.03 E
Hilton	176	43.17 N	77.48 W
Hilversum	116	52.14 N	5.10 E
Himalayas ∧	146	28.00 N	84.00 E
Himarë	124	40.07 N	19.44 E
Himatnagar	144	23.36 N	72.58 E
Hime-ji	134	34.49 N	134.42 E
Himi	134	36.51 N	136.59 E
Himmerland ➤¹	114	56.50 N	9.45 E
Hims (Homs)	150	34.44 N	36.43 E
Hinche	182	19.09 N	72.01 W
Hinchinbrook Island I	166	18.23 S	146.17 E
Hinckley	104	52.33 N	1.21 W
Hindhead	104	51.06 N	0.44 W
Hindley	106	53.32 N	2.35 W
Hindmarsh, Lake ❸	168	36.03 S	141.55 E
Hindon	104	51.06 N	2.08 W
Hindu Kush ∧	146	36.00 N	71.30 E
Hindupur	148	13.49 N	77.29 E
Hines	178	43.34 N	119.05 W
Hinganghāt	144	20.34 N	78.50 E
Hingham	176	42.14 N	70.53 W
Hingol ≈	146	25.23 N	65.28 E
Hingoli	148	19.43 N	77.09 E
Hinish Bay C	108	56.28 N	6.50 W
Hinkston Creek ≈	176	38.18 N	84.14 W
Hinnøya I	112	68.30 N	16.00 E
Hinojosa del Duque	120	38.30 N	5.09 W
Hinokage	134	32.39 N	131.24 E
Hinton	176	37.40 N	80.54 W
Hirado	134	33.22 N	129.33 E
Hirado-shima I	134	33.20 N	129.30 E
Hiraizumi	134	38.59 N	141.07 E
Hiram	176	43.53 N	70.49 W
Hirata	132	35.26 N	132.49 E
Hiratsuka	134	35.19 N	139.21 E
Hiroo	134a	42.17 N	143.19 E
Hirosaki	134	40.35 N	140.28 E
Hiroshima	134	34.24 N	132.27 E
Hirson	118	49.55 N	4.05 E
Hirwaun	104	51.45 N	3.30 W
Hisar	144	29.10 N	75.43 E
Hispaniola I	182	19.00 N	71.00 W
Histon	104	52.15 N	0.06 E
Hitachi	134	36.36 N	140.39 E
Hitachi-ōta	134	36.32 N	140.31 E
Hitchins	176	41.57 N	77.18 E
Hitra I	112	63.34 N	8.45 E
Hiuchiga-take ∧	134	36.57 N	139.17 E
Hiwasa	134	33.44 N	134.32 E
Hjälmaren ❸	114	59.15 N	15.45 E
Hjelmelandsvågen	114	59.14 N	6.11 E
Hjeltefjorden C²	114	60.40 N	4.55 E
Hjørring	114	57.28 N	9.59 E
Hjort Basin ≈¹	87	59.00 S	158.00 E
Hkakabo Razi ∧	140	28.20 N	97.32 E
Hkok (Kok) ≈	140	20.14 N	100.09 E
Hlatikulu	160	26.58 S	31.19 E
Hlobane	160	27.42 S	31.00 E
Hlohovec	116	48.25 N	17.47 E
Hluhluwe	160	28.01 S	32.16 E
Ho	152	6.35 N	0.30 E
Hòa-binh	140	20.50 N	105.20 E
Hoare Bay C	172	65.20 N	62.30 W
Hobart	168	42.53 S	147.19 E
Hobbs	174	32.42 N	103.08 W
Hoboken, Bel.	116	51.10 N	4.21 E
Hoboken, N.J., U.S.	176	40.45 N	74.03 W
Hochalmspitze ∧	116	47.01 N	13.19 E
Hochgolling ∧	116	47.16 N	13.45 E
Hochkönig ∧	116	47.25 N	13.04 E
Hochschwab ∧	116	47.37 N	15.09 E
Hockenheim	116	49.19 N	8.33 E
Hocking ≈	176	39.12 N	81.50 W
Hockley	104	51.37 N	0.40 E
Hodder ≈	106	53.57 N	2.27 W
Hoddesdon	104	51.46 N	0.01 W
Hodeida → Al-Ḥudaydah	144	14.48 N	42.57 E
Hodgkins Seamount ✳³	90	53.20 N	135.45 W
Hodgson	172	51.13 N	97.34 W
Hodna, Chott el ❸	152	35.25 N	4.45 E
Hodonín	116	48.51 N	17.08 E
Hoek van Holland	116	51.59 N	4.09 E
Hof	116	50.18 N	11.55 E
Höfdakaupstaður	112a	65.50 N	20.19 W
Hofei → Hefei	132	31.51 N	117.17 E
Hofheim in Unterfranken	116	50.08 N	10.31 E
Hofmeyr	160	31.39 S	25.50 E
Hofors	114	60.33 N	16.17 E
Hofsjökull ◻	112a	64.48 N	18.48 W
Höfu	134	34.03 N	131.34 E
Hofuf → Al-Hufūf	150	25.22 N	49.34 E
Hog Island I¹	176	37.25 N	75.41 W
Hogback Mountain ∧	176	42.59 N	72.55 W
Hoh ≈	178	47.45 N	124.29 W
Hohe Tauern ∧	116	47.10 N	12.30 E
Hohenau an der March	116	48.37 N	16.54 E
Hohenlimburg	116	51.20 N	7.35 E
Hohenwald	176	35.32 N	87.32 W
Hohe Venn ∧	116	50.30 N	6.05 E
Hoh Xil Shan ∧	140	35.00 N	90.00 E
Hoi-an	140	15.52 N	108.29 E
Hoima	158	1.25 N	31.21 E
Hōjō	134	33.58 N	132.46 E
Hokianga Harbour C	170	35.31 S	173.22 E
Hokitika	170	42.43 S	170.58 E
Hokkaidō I	134a	44.00 N	143.00 E
Hokkaidō □⁵	134a	43.30 N	142.45 E
Holbæk	114	55.43 N	11.43 E
Holbeach	104	52.49 N	0.01 E
Holbeach Marsh ⟺	106	52.52 N	0.05 E
Holbrook, Austl.	168	35.44 S	147.19 E
Holbrook, Ariz., U.S.	174	34.54 N	110.10 W
Holden	176	37.50 N	82.04 W
Holderness ➤¹	106	53.47 N	0.10 W
Hole in the Mountain Peak ∧	178	40.55 N	115.05 W
Holgate	176	41.15 N	84.08 W
Holguín	182	20.53 N	76.15 W
Höljes	114	60.54 N	12.36 E
Holland	160	24.45 S	14.34 E
Holland	174	42.47 N	86.07 W
→ Netherlands □¹	116	52.15 N	5.30 E
Holland, Mount ∧	164	32.12 S	119.44 E
Holland Fen ❖	104	53.00 N	0.10 W
Holland-on-Sea	104	51.48 N	1.13 E
Hollandstoun	108	59.21 N	2.26 W
Holley	176	43.14 N	78.02 W
Hollick-Kenyon Plateau ∧¹	87	79.00 S	97.00 W
Hollidaysburg	176	40.26 N	78.23 W
Hollister	178	36.51 N	121.24 W
Hollister, Mount ∧²	164	22.08 S	114.01 E
Hollum	116	53.26 N	5.35 W
Hollywood, Fla., U.S.	174	26.00 N	80.09 W
Holman Island	172	70.43 N	117.43 W
Holme ≈	106	53.41 N	1.43 W
Holmen	176	43.58 N	91.15 W
Holmes Reefs ✳²	166	16.27 S	148.00 E
Holmestrand	114	59.29 N	10.18 E
Holmfirth	106	53.35 N	1.46 W
Holmsbu	114	59.33 N	10.27 E
Holmsjön ❸	114	62.41 N	16.33 E
Holmsund	114	63.42 N	20.21 E
Holroyd ≈	166	14.10 S	141.36 E
Holstebro	114	56.21 N	8.38 E
Holsteinsborg	172	66.55 N	53.40 W
Holsworthy	104	50.49 N	4.21 W
Holt, Wales, U.K.	104	53.05 N	2.53 W
Holt, Mich., U.S.	176	42.39 N	84.31 W
Holtville	178	32.49 N	115.23 W
Holycross	110	52.38 N	7.52 W
Holyhead	106	53.19 N	4.38 W
Holyhead Bay C	106	53.23 N	4.40 W
Holy Island I, Eng., U.K.	106	55.41 N	1.48 W
Holy Island I, Scot., U.K.	108	55.32 N	5.05 W
Holy Island I, Wales, U.K.	106	53.18 N	4.37 W
Holyoke	176	42.12 N	72.37 W
Holywell	106	53.17 N	3.13 W
Holywood	110	54.38 N	5.49 W
Holzminden	116	51.50 N	9.27 E
Homalin	132	24.52 N	94.55 E
Homāyūnshahr	150	32.43 N	51.31 E
Hombori Tondo ∧	152	15.16 N	1.40 W
Hombre Muerto, Salar de ⨄	188	25.30 S	67.05 W
Homburg	116	49.19 N	7.20 E
Home Bay C	168	48.45 S	67.10 W
Home Hill	168	19.40 S	147.25 E
Homer, Alaska, U.S.	172	59.39 N	151.33 W
Homer, Mich., U.S.	176	42.09 N	84.49 W
Homer, N.Y., U.S.	176	42.38 N	76.11 W
Homer City	176	40.32 N	79.10 W
Homer Wash ∨	178	34.20 N	115.02 W
Home Seamount ✳³	96	32.30 S	176.40 W
Homestead, Austl.	166	20.22 S	145.39 E
Homestead, Fla., U.S.	174	25.28 N	80.29 W
Hommura	134	34.22 N	139.15 E
Homs → Al-Khums, Libiya	154	32.39 N	14.16 E
Homs → Ḥimş, Sūriy.	150	34.44 N	36.43 E
Honan → Henan □⁴	132	34.00 N	114.00 E
Honbetsu	134a	43.07 N	143.37 E
Honda	184	5.12 N	74.45 W
Honda, Bahía C	182	12.23 N	71.46 W
Hondadu ≈, Wales, U.K.	104	51.54 N	3.23 W
Hondeklipbaai	160	30.20 S	17.18 E
Hondo	180	30.22 N	130.12 E
Hondsrug ∧²	116	52.55 N	6.50 E
Honduras □¹	180	15.00 N	86.30 W
Honduras, Gulf of C	182	16.00 N	85.55 W
Hønefoss	114	60.10 N	10.18 E
Honey Lake ❸	178	40.13 N	120.19 W
Honfleur	118	49.25 N	0.14 E
Hon-gai	140	20.58 N	107.05 E
Honggor	132	42.09 N	113.02 E
Hongjiang	140	27.07 N	109.57 E
Hong Kong □²	136	22.15 N	114.10 E
→ Victoria	136	22.17 N	114.09 E
Hongliuyuan	132	41.02 N	95.26 E
Hongshuihe ≈	140	23.45 N	109.03 E
Hongze	132	33.18 N	118.51 E
Hongze Hu ❸	132	33.15 N	118.40 E
Honiara	96	9.26 S	159.57 E
Honiton	104	50.48 N	3.13 W
Honjō, Nihon	134	39.23 N	140.03 E
Honjō, Nihon	134	36.14 N	139.11 E
Honkanaki ∧²	179a	22.05 N	159.29 W
Honningsvåg	112	70.59 N	25.59 E
Honokaa	179a	20.05 N	155.28 W
Honolulu	179a	21.18 N	157.52 W
Honshū I	134	36.00 N	138.00 E
Honuapo Bay C	179a	19.05 N	155.33 W
Hood, Mount ∧	174	45.23 N	121.42 W
Hood Point ➤	164	34.23 S	119.34 E
Hoods Range ∧	168	24.33 S	144.30 E
Hoogeveen	116	52.44 N	6.29 E
Hoogezand	116	53.09 N	6.47 E
Hook	104	51.17 N	0.58 W
Hooker Creek	164	18.20 S	130.38 E
Hook Head ➤	110	52.07 N	6.56 W
Hoolehua	179a	21.10 N	157.06 W
Hoonah	172	58.07 N	135.26 W
Hoopa	178	41.03 N	123.40 W
Hoopstad	160	27.50 S	25.58 E
Hoorn	116	52.38 N	5.04 E
Hoosick Falls	176	42.54 N	73.21 W
Hooversville	176	40.09 N	78.55 W
Hopatcong	176	40.56 N	74.39 W
Hope, Ark., U.S.	174	33.40 N	93.36 W
Hope, B.C., Can.	172	49.23 N	121.26 W
Hope, Ben ∧	108	58.24 N	4.36 W
Hope, Loch ❸	108	58.27 N	4.38 W
Hopedale	172	55.28 N	60.13 W
Hopeh → Hebei □⁴	132	39.00 N	116.00 E
Hopelchén	180	19.46 N	89.51 W
Hopeman	108	57.42 N	3.26 W
Hopen I	88	76.35 N	25.10 E
Hopes Advance, Cap ➤	172	59.20 N	69.34 W
Hopetoun	168	35.43 S	142.22 E
Hopetown	160	29.34 S	24.03 E
Hope Valley	176	41.30 N	71.43 W
Hopewell	174	37.18 N	77.17 W
Hopewell Islands II	172	58.20 N	78.25 W
Hopkins ≈	168	38.25 S	142.00 E
Hopkinsville	174	36.52 N	87.28 W
Hopland	178	38.58 N	123.07 W
Hoquiam	178	46.58 N	123.53 W
Horasan	150	40.02 N	42.10 E
Hörby	114	55.51 N	13.39 E
Horden	106	54.46 N	1.18 W
Hordaland □⁶	114	60.15 N	6.30 E
Horezu	124	45.08 N	24.00 E
Horgen	118	47.16 N	8.36 E
Horgoš	124	46.09 N	19.59 E
Horizon Tablemount ✳³	96	19.30 N	169.00 W
Horizontina	188	27.37 S	54.19 W

Symbols in the index entries are identified on page 198.

Horl – Ista

Name	Page	Lat °′	Long °′
Horley	104	51.11 N	0.11 W
Horlick Mountains ∧∧	87	85.23 S	121.00 W
Hormoz, Jazīreh-ye I	150	27.04 N	56.28 E
Hormuz, Strait of ⩊	150	26.34 N	56.15 E
Horn ≻	112a	66.28 N	22.28 W
Horn ≃	172	61.30 N	118.01 W
Horn, Cape → Hornos Cabo de ≻	186	56.00 S	67.16 W
Horn, Ben ∧²	108	58.01 N	4.02 W
Hornád (Hernád) ≃	116	47.56 N	21.08 E
Hornaday ≃	172	69.22 N	123.50 W
Hornavan ⊜	112	66.10 N	17.30 E
Hornbrook	178	41.55 N	122.33 W
Hornby	170	43.33 S	172.32 E
Hornby Bay C	172	66.35 N	117.50 W
Horncastle	106	53.13 N	0.07 W
Horndean	104	50.55 N	1.00 W
Horne, Îles de II	96	14.16 S	178.05 W
Hornell	176	42.19 N	77.40 W
Hornepayne	172	49.13 N	84.47 W
Horn Head ≻	110	55.14 N	7.59 W
Hornindalsvatnet ⊜	114	61.56 N	6.22 E
Horn Island I	166	10.37 S	142.17 E
Hornos, Cabo de (Cape Horn) ≻	186	56.00 S	67.16 W
Horn Plateau ∧∧¹	172	62.15 N	119.15 W
Hornsea	106	53.55 N	0.10 W
Horoizumi	134a	42.01 N	143.09 E
Horoshiri-dake ∧	134a	42.43 N	142.41 E
Horotiu	170	37.43 S	175.12 E
Horqueta	188	23.24 S	56.53 W
Horrabridge	104	50.31 N	4.05 W
Horseback Knob ∧²	176	39.14 N	83.06 W
Horseheads	176	42.10 N	76.50 W
Horse Islands II	172	50.13 N	55.45 W
Horsens	114	55.52 N	9.52 E
Horse Shoe Reef ✧²	182	18.35 N	64.15 W
Horsforth	106	53.51 N	1.39 W
Horsham, Austl.	168	36.43 S	142.13 E
Horsham, Eng., U.K.	104	51.04 N	0.21 W
Horsham Saint Faith	104	52.41 N	1.16 E
Hørsholm	114	55.53 N	12.30 E
Horsted Keynes	104	51.02 N	0.01 W
Horten	114	59.25 N	10.30 E
Hortobágy □⁹	116	47.35 N	21.00 E
Horton ≃	172	70.00 N	126.53 W
Horton in Ribblesdale	106	54.09 N	2.17 W
Horton Lake ⊜	172	67.30 N	122.28 W
Horwich	106	53.37 N	2.33 W
Hosaina	154	7.38 N	37.52 E
Hoséré Batandji ∧	152	8.20 N	13.15 E
Hoshangābād	146	22.45 N	77.44 E
Hoshiārpur	149	31.32 N	75.54 E
Hospet	148	15.16 N	76.24 E
Hospital	110	52.29 N	8.25 W
Hospital de Orbigo	120	42.28 N	5.53 W
Hospitalet	120	41.22 N	2.08 E
Hossegor	118	43.40 N	1.27 W
Hoste, Isla I	186	55.10 S	69.00 W
Hotaka-dake ∧	134	36.17 N	137.39 E
Hot Creek Range ∧∧	178	38.30 N	116.25 W
Hoting	114	64.07 N	16.10 E
Hot Springs, S. Dak., U.S.	174	43.26 N	103.29 W
Hot Springs, Va., U.S.	176	38.00 N	79.50 W
Hot Springs National Park	174	34.30 N	93.03 W
Hot Springs Peak ∧, Calif., U.S.	178	40.22 N	120.07 W
Hot Springs Peak ∧, Nev., U.S.	178	41.22 N	117.26 W
Hottah Lake ⊜	172	65.04 N	118.29 W
Houeillès	118	44.12 N	0.02 E
Houei Sai	132	20.18 N	100.26 E
Houghton	176	42.25 N	78.10 W
Houghton Lake	176	44.18 N	84.45 W
Houghton Lake ⊜	176	44.20 N	84.45 W
Houghton-le-Spring	106	54.51 N	1.28 W
Houghton Regis	104	51.55 N	0.31 W
Houjie	136	22.58 N	113.39 E
Houlton	176	46.08 N	67.51 W
Houma, La., U.S.	174	29.36 N	90.43 W
Houma, Zhg.	132	35.40 N	111.29 E
Hounslow →•⁸	104	51.29 N	0.22 W
Hourn, Loch C	108	57.08 N	5.36 W
Housatonic	176	42.16 N	73.22 W
Houston	174	29.46 N	95.22 W
Hout ≃	160	23.04 S	29.36 E
Houtkraal	160	30.23 S	24.05 E
Houtman Abrolhos II	164	28.43 S	113.48 E
Houtskär I	114	60.12 N	21.22 E
Houtzdale	176	40.49 N	78.21 W
Hove	104	50.49 N	0.10 W
Hovmantorp	114	56.47 N	15.08 E
Howard, Austl.	168	25.19 S	152.34 E
Howard, Pa., U.S.	176	41.01 N	77.40 W
Howard City	176	43.24 N	85.28 W
Howardian Hills ∧∧²	106	54.07 N	1.00 W
Howard Island I	166	12.10 S	135.24 E
Howard Prairie Lake ⊜¹	178	42.15 N	122.20 W
Howden	106	53.45 N	0.52 W
Howe, Cape ≻	168	37.31 S	149.59 E
Howe Island I	176	44.17 N	76.15 W
Howell	176	42.36 N	83.55 W
Howick	160	29.28 S	30.14 E
Howitt, Mount ∧	168	37.10 S	146.40 E
Howland	176	45.14 N	68.40 W
Howland Island I	96	0.48 N	176.38 W
Howmore	108	57.18 N	7.23 W
Howrah	146	22.35 N	88.20 E
Howth	110	53.23 N	6.04 W
Höxter	116	51.46 N	9.23 E
Hoy I	108	58.51 N	3.18 W
Hoyerswerda	116	51.26 N	14.14 E
Hoylake	106	53.23 N	3.11 W
Hradec Králové	116	50.12 N	15.50 E
Hranice	116	49.33 N	17.44 E
Hronov	116	50.29 N	16.12 E
Hrubieszów	116	50.49 N	23.55 E
Hrvatska (Croatia) □³	122	45.10 N	15.30 E
Hsiamen → Xiamen	136	24.28 N	118.07 E
Hsilo	136	23.49 N	120.27 E
Hsinchu	136	24.48 N	120.58 E
Hsinghua → Xinghua	136	32.57 N	119.50 E
Hsinhua	136	23.01 N	120.20 E
Hsinkao Shan ∧	136	23.28 N	120.57 E
Hsintien	136	24.58 N	121.33 E
Hsipaw	132	22.37 N	97.18 E
Hsüehchia	136	23.14 N	120.11 E
Huaan	136	25.02 N	117.34 E
Huabu	136	29.00 N	118.20 E
Huacho	184	11.07 S	77.37 W
Huadian	132	42.58 N	126.43 E
Huagaruancha, Cerro ∧	184	10.32 S	75.56 W
Hua Hin	140	12.34 N	99.58 E
Huahua ≃	182	13.54 N	83.27 W
Huaian	136	33.32 N	119.10 E
Huaibin (Wulongji)	136	32.28 N	115.24 E
Huaide	132	43.32 N	124.50 E
Huaihe ≃	136	32.58 N	118.17 E
Huailai	132	40.23 N	115.33 E
Huainan	136	32.40 N	117.00 E
Huaining	136	30.25 N	116.38 E
Huaiyang	136	33.44 N	114.53 E
Huaiyin	136	33.35 N	119.02 E
Huaiyuan	136	32.57 N	117.12 E
Huajuapan de León	180	17.48 N	97.46 W
Hualalai ∧¹	179a	19.42 N	155.52 W
Hualañé	188	34.59 S	71.49 W
Hualapai Mountains ∧∧	178	34.50 N	113.55 W
Hualapai Peak ∧	178	35.04 N	113.54 W
Hualfín	188	27.15 S	66.50 W
Hualien	136	23.58 N	121.36 E
Huallaga ≃	184	5.07 S	75.30 W
Huallanca	184	8.50 S	77.50 W
Huamachuco	184	7.50 S	78.05 W
Huambo	156	12.44 S	15.47 E
Huancavelica	184	12.46 S	75.02 W
Huancayo	184	12.04 S	75.14 W
Huanchaca	184	20.20 S	66.39 W
Huang ≃	140	17.49 N	101.33 E
Huangchuan	136	32.09 N	115.03 E
Huangdai	136	31.26 N	120.33 E
Huangdu	136	31.16 N	121.13 E
Huanggang	136	30.27 N	114.52 E
Huanghe ≃, Zhg.	132	37.32 N	118.19 E
Huanghe ≃, Zhg.	136	32.19 N	115.02 E
Huangho → Huanghe ≃	136	32.19 N	115.02 E
Huangjinbu	136	28.27 N	116.47 E
Huangli	136	31.39 N	119.42 E
Huangling	132	35.41 N	109.09 E
Huanglong	136	23.34 N	116.58 E
Huangmei	136	30.04 N	115.56 E
Huangpi	136	30.53 N	114.22 E
Huangqi	136	26.21 N	119.54 E
Huangqiao	136	32.15 N	120.13 E
Huangshi	136	30.13 N	115.05 E
Huangyan	136	28.39 N	121.15 E
Huangyuan	132	36.42 N	101.25 E
Huangze	136	29.35 N	120.55 E
Huaning	140	24.14 N	102.56 E
Huanjiang	140	24.54 N	108.21 E
Huánuco	184	9.55 S	76.14 W
Huanuni	184	18.16 S	66.51 W
Huaral	184	11.32 S	77.13 W
Huaraz	184	9.32 S	77.32 W
Huarong	136	29.30 N	112.34 E
Huascarán, Nevado ∧	184	9.07 S	77.37 W
Huasco	188	28.28 S	71.14 W
Huasco ≃	188	28.27 S	71.13 W
Huashu	136	31.50 N	120.28 E
Huatabampo	180	26.50 N	109.38 W
Huaunta	182	13.30 N	83.32 W
Huaxian	136	23.22 N	113.12 E
Huazhou	140	21.40 N	110.33 E
Hubbard Lake ⊜	176	44.49 N	83.34 W
Hubei □⁴, Zhg.	132	31.00 N	112.00 E
Hubei □⁴, Zhg.	136	30.40 N	117.20 E
Huberdeau	176	45.58 N	74.38 W
Hubli	148	15.21 N	75.10 E
Hucclecote	104	51.51 N	2.11 W
Huckitta Creek ≃	164	22.38 S	135.30 E
Hucknall	104	53.02 N	1.11 W
Huddersfield	106	53.39 N	1.47 W
Huddinge	114	59.14 N	17.59 E
Hudiksvall	114	61.44 N	17.07 E
Hudingshan	136	33.45 N	113.17 E
Hudong	136	22.51 N	115.56 E
Hudson, Mass., U.S.	176	42.24 N	71.35 W
Hudson, Mich., U.S.	176	41.51 N	84.21 W
Hudson, N.H., U.S.	176	42.46 N	71.26 W
Hudson, N.Y., U.S.	176	42.15 N	73.47 W
Hudson, Ohio, U.S.	176	41.15 N	81.26 W
Hudson ≃	176	40.42 N	74.02 W
Hudson Bay	172	52.52 N	102.25 W
Hudson Bay C	172	60.00 N	86.00 W
Hudson Falls	176	43.18 N	73.35 W
Hudson Mountains ∧∧	87	74.32 S	99.20 W
Hudson Strait ⩊	172	62.30 N	72.00 W
Hue	140	16.28 N	107.36 E
Huehuetenango	180	15.20 N	91.28 W
Huelva	120	37.16 N	6.57 W
Huentelauquén	188	31.35 S	71.32 W
Huerta, Sierra de la ∧∧	188	31.00 S	67.30 W
Huesca	120	42.08 N	0.25 W
Huesca □⁴	120	42.05 N	0.00
Huetamo de Núñez	180	18.35 N	100.53 W
Huggins, Mount ∧	87	78.17 S	162.28 E
Hugh ≃	164	25.01 S	134.01 E
Hughenden	168	20.51 S	144.12 E
Hughes	164	30.42 S	129.31 E
Hughes, South Fork ≃	176	39.08 N	81.20 W
Hughesville	176	41.14 N	76.44 W
Hughson	178	37.36 N	120.52 W
Hugh Town	104a	49.55 N	6.17 W
Hugo	174	34.01 N	95.31 W
Hugouji	136	33.23 N	117.08 E
Huhehaote	132	40.51 N	111.40 E
Huian	136	25.04 N	118.47 E
Huiarau Range ∧∧	170	38.45 S	177.00 E
Huichang	136	25.34 N	115.49 E
Hŭich'ŏn	132	40.10 N	126.17 E
Huidong	140	26.41 N	102.36 E
Huila, Nevado del ∧	184	3.00 N	76.00 W
Huilai	136	23.04 N	116.18 E
Huili	140	26.43 N	102.10 E
Huimin	132	37.29 N	117.29 E
Huinan	132	42.40 N	126.00 E
Huinca Renancó	188	34.50 S	64.25 W
Huishui	140	26.07 N	106.24 E
Huisne ≃	118	47.59 N	0.11 E
Huittinen (Lauttakylä)	114	61.11 N	22.42 E
Huixtla	180	15.09 N	92.28 W
Huiyang (Huizhou)	136	23.05 N	114.24 E
Huize	140	26.27 N	103.09 E
Ḥukayyim, Bi'r al- ▾⁴	154	31.36 N	23.29 E
Hukeng	136	27.29 N	114.18 E
Hukou	136	29.45 N	116.13 E
Hukusima → Fukushima	134	37.45 N	140.28 E
Hulan	132	46.00 N	126.38 E
Huldrefossen ⌊	114	61.28 N	5.58 E
Hull	172	45.26 N	75.43 W
Hull I¹	96	4.29 S	172.10 W
Hull ≃	106	53.44 N	0.19 W
Hullavington	104	51.33 N	2.09 W
Hullbridge	104	51.37 N	0.38 E
Hull Glacier ⍓	87	75.05 S	137.15 W
Hultsfred	114	57.29 N	15.50 E
Hulunchi ⊜	132	49.01 N	117.32 E
Huma	132	51.43 N	126.38 E
Humacao	182	18.09 N	65.50 W
Humaerhe ≃	128	51.40 N	126.44 E
Humahuaca	188	23.12 S	65.25 W
Humaitá	188	27.03 S	58.33 W
Humansdorp	160	34.02 S	24.46 E
Humbe	156	16.40 S	14.55 E
Humbe, Serra do ∧∧	156	12.13 S	15.25 E
Humber ≃	102	53.40 N	0.10 W
Humber, Mouth of the ≃¹	106	53.32 N	0.08 E
Humberside □⁶	106	53.55 N	0.40 W
Humboldt	172	52.12 N	105.07 W
Humboldt ≃	178	40.02 N	118.31 W
Humboldt, North Fork ≃	178	40.56 N	115.32 W
Humboldt, South Fork ≃	178	40.47 N	115.53 W
Humboldt Bay C	178	40.47 N	124.11 W
Humboldt Lake ⊜	178	39.58 N	118.38 W
Humboldt Mountains ∧∧	87	71.45 S	11.30 E
Humboldt Salt Marsh ☷	178	39.50 N	117.55 W
Hume	178	36.47 N	118.55 W
Hume, Lake ⊜¹	168	36.06 S	147.05 E
Humeburn	168	27.24 S	145.14 E
Humenné	116	48.56 N	21.55 E
Hummelfjell ∧	114	62.27 N	11.17 E
Humphreys, Mount ∧	178	37.17 N	118.40 W
Humphreys Peak ∧	174	35.20 N	111.40 W
Humppila	114	60.56 N	23.22 E
Hunan □⁴	136	28.00 N	113.00 E
Hunchun	132	42.54 N	130.22 E
Hundested	114	55.58 N	11.52 E
Hundred	176	39.41 N	80.28 W
Hunedoara	124	45.45 N	22.54 E
Hunedoara □⁴	124	45.45 N	23.00 E
Hungary □¹	100	47.00 N	20.00 E
Hungerford, Austl.	168	29.00 S	144.25 E
Hungerford, Eng., U.K.	104	51.26 N	1.30 W
Hŭngnam	132	39.50 N	127.38 E
Hungry Law ≃	108	55.21 N	2.24 W
Hung-yen	140	20.39 N	106.04 E
Hunish, Rubha ≻	108	57.41 N	6.21 W
Hunjiang	132	41.56 N	126.29 E
Ḥunkurāb, Ra's ≻	150	24.34 N	35.10 E
Hunsberge ∧∧	160	27.45 S	17.12 E
Hunstanton	104	52.57 N	0.30 E
Hunter ≃	168	32.50 S	151.42 E
Hunter Island I, Austl.	168	40.32 S	144.45 E
Hunter Island I, N. Cal.	96	22.24 S	172.03 E
Hunter Island Ridge ✧³	96	21.30 S	175.00 E
Hunter Mountain ∧	176	42.10 N	74.14 W
Hunter's Quay	108	55.58 N	4.55 W
Hunters Road	158	19.09 S	29.48 E
Hunterville	170	39.56 S	175.34 E
Huntingdon, Qué., Can.	176	45.05 N	74.10 W
Huntingdon, Eng., U.K.	104	52.20 N	0.12 W
Huntingdon, Pa., U.S.	176	40.29 N	78.01 W
Huntington, Eng., U.K.	106	54.01 N	1.04 W
Huntington, N.Y., U.S.	176	40.51 N	73.25 W
Huntington, W. Va., U.S.	174	38.25 N	82.26 W
Huntington Beach	178	33.39 N	117.60 W
Huntington Creek ≃	178	40.37 N	115.43 W
Huntly, N.Z.	170	37.33 S	175.10 E
Huntly, Scot., U.K.	108	57.27 N	2.47 W
Huntsville, Ont., Can.	176	45.20 N	79.13 W
Huntsville, Ala., U.S.	174	34.44 N	86.35 W
Huntsville, Tex., U.S.	174	30.43 N	95.33 W
Hunucmá	180	21.01 N	89.52 W
Hunyani (Panhame) ≃	158	15.37 S	30.39 E
Hunyuan	132	39.48 N	113.41 E
Huonville	168	43.01 S	147.02 E
Huoqiu	136	32.20 N	116.16 E
Huoshan	136	31.25 N	116.20 E
Huotong	136	26.53 N	119.25 E
Hupu	136	31.45 N	120.54 E
Hurao	132	45.46 N	132.59 E
Hurd, Cape ≻	172	45.13 N	81.44 W
Hurdalssjøen ⊜	114	60.20 N	11.05 E
Hurlford	108	55.36 N	4.28 W
Hurliness	108	58.47 N	3.15 W
Hurlock	176	38.38 N	75.52 W
Huron, Calif., U.S.	178	36.12 N	120.06 W
Huron, Ohio, U.S.	176	41.24 N	82.33 W
Huron, S. Dak., U.S.	174	44.22 N	98.13 W
Huron ≃	176	42.03 N	83.14 W
Huron, Lake ⊜	174	44.30 N	82.15 W
Hurricane	176	38.26 N	82.01 W
Hursley	104	51.02 N	1.24 W
Hurstbourne Tarrant	104	51.17 N	1.23 W
Hurstbridge	168	37.38 S	145.12 E
Hurstpierpoint	104	50.56 N	0.11 W
Hurtado ≃	188	30.35 S	71.11 W
Hürth	116	50.52 N	6.51 E
Hurunui ≃	170	42.55 S	173.17 E
Húsavík	112a	66.04 N	17.18 W
Hushu	136	31.52 N	118.59 E
Hushuguan	136	31.23 N	120.30 E
Huşi	124	46.40 N	28.04 E
Huskvarna	114	57.48 N	14.16 E
Husum	116	54.28 N	9.03 E
Hutanopan	138	0.41 N	99.42 E
Hutchinson, S. Afr.	160	31.30 S	23.09 E
Hutchinson, Kans., U.S.	174	38.05 N	97.56 W
Huthwaite	106	53.09 N	1.17 W
Hüttental	116	50.54 N	8.02 E
Hutte Sauvage, Lac de la ⊜	172	56.15 N	64.45 W
Hutton, Mount ∧	168	25.51 S	148.20 E
Huwan	136	27.55 N	116.31 E
Huwei	136	23.42 N	120.24 E
Huwun	158	4.23 N	40.08 E
Huy	116	50.31 N	5.14 E
Huyton-with-Roby	106	53.25 N	2.52 W
Huzhen	136	28.50 N	120.15 E
Huzhou	136	30.52 N	120.06 E
Hvannadalshnúkur ∧	112a	64.01 N	16.41 W
Hveragerði	112a	64.03 N	21.10 W
Hvide Sande	114	55.59 N	8.08 E
Hwainan → Huainan	136	32.40 N	117.00 E
Hwang Ho → Huanghe ≃	132	37.32 N	118.19 E
Hyannis	176	41.39 N	70.17 W
Hyde, N.Z.	170	45.18 S	170.15 E
Hyde, Eng., U.K.	106	53.27 N	2.04 W
Hyden	164	32.27 S	118.53 E
Hyde Park, Guy.	184	6.30 N	58.16 W
Hyde Park, N.Y., U.S.	176	41.47 N	73.56 W
Hyde Park, Vt., U.S.	176	44.36 N	72.37 W
Hyderābād, Bhārat	148	17.23 N	78.28 E
Hyderābād, Pāk.	146	25.22 N	68.22 E
Hyères	118	43.07 N	6.07 E
Hyères, Îles d' II	120	43.00 N	6.20 E
Hyesan	132	41.23 N	128.12 E
Hyland ≃	172	59.50 N	128.10 W
Hylestad	114	59.05 N	7.32 E
Hyndman	176	39.49 N	78.44 W
Hyndman Peak ∧	174	43.50 N	114.10 W
Hyōgo □⁵	134	35.12 N	134.51 E
Hythe, Austl.	168	43.25 S	146.59 E
Hythe, Eng., U.K.	104	50.51 N	1.24 W
Hythe, Eng., U.K.	104	51.05 N	1.05 E
Hyūga	134	32.25 N	131.38 E
Hyūga-nada ▾²	134	32.00 N	131.35 E
Hyvinkää	114	60.38 N	24.52 E
I			
Iacanga	190	21.54 S	49.01 W
Iaco (Yaco) ≃	184	9.03 S	68.34 W
Ialomiţa □⁴	124	44.30 N	27.20 E
Iaoxing'anling-shanmai ≃	132	50.00 N	126.25 E
Iaşi	124	47.10 N	27.35 E
Iaşi □⁴	124	47.15 N	27.15 E
Ibadan	152	7.17 N	3.30 E
Ibagué	184	4.27 N	75.14 W
Ibaiti	190	23.50 S	50.10 W
Ibapah Peak ∧	178	39.50 N	113.55 W
Ibaraki □⁵	134	36.30 N	140.30 E
Ibarra	184	0.21 N	78.07 W
Ibarreta	188	25.15 S	59.51 W
Ibb	144	14.01 N	44.10 E
Ibba	158	4.48 N	29.06 E
Ibba ≃	158	5.30 N	28.41 E
Ibbenbüren	116	52.16 N	7.43 E
Iberian Basin ✧¹	88	40.00 N	16.00 W
Ibérico, Sistema ∧∧	120	41.00 N	2.30 W
Iberville	176	45.18 N	73.14 W
Iberville, Lac d' ⊜	172	55.55 N	73.15 W
Iberville, Mont d' ∧	172	58.53 N	63.43 W
Ibiá	190	19.29 S	46.32 W
Ibicaraí	190	14.51 S	39.36 W
Ibicuí ≃	188	29.25 S	56.47 W
Ibirama	188	27.04 S	49.31 W
Ibirubá	188	28.38 S	53.06 W
Ibitinga	190	21.45 S	48.49 W
Ibiza	120	38.54 N	1.26 E
Ibiza I	120	39.00 N	1.25 E
Ibo	158	12.20 S	40.35 E
Iboundji, Mont ∧	156	1.08 S	11.48 E
'Ibrī	150	23.14 N	56.30 E
İbriktepe	124	41.00 N	26.30 E
Ibstock	104	52.42 N	1.23 W
Ibusuki	134	31.16 N	130.39 E
Ica	184	14.04 S	75.42 W
Ica ≃	184	14.53 S	75.33 W
Iceland □¹	100	65.00 N	18.00 W
Ichalkaranji	148	16.42 N	74.28 E
Ich Bogd Uul ∧∧	132	44.55 N	100.20 E
Ichihara	134	35.31 N	140.05 E
Ichikawa	134	35.44 N	139.55 E
Ichilo ≃	184	15.57 S	64.42 W
Ichinohe	134	40.13 N	141.17 E
Ichinomiya, Nihon	134	32.57 N	131.07 E
Ichinomiya, Nihon	134	35.18 N	136.48 E
Ichinoseki	134	38.55 N	141.08 E
Icó	184	6.24 S	38.51 W
Icoraci	184	1.18 S	48.28 W
Icy Bay C	172	60.00 N	141.15 W
Ida	176	41.55 N	83.34 W
Ida, Mount ∧	164	29.14 S	120.25 E
Idaho □³	174	45.00 N	115.00 W
Idaho Falls	174	43.30 N	112.02 W
Idanha-a-Nova	120	39.55 N	7.14 W
Idāppādi	148	11.35 N	77.51 E
Idar-Oberstein	116	49.42 N	7.19 E
Idel'	112	64.08 N	34.14 E
Iderijn ≃	132	49.16 N	100.41 E
Idfū	154	24.58 N	32.52 E
Ídhi Óros ∧	124	35.18 N	24.43 E
Idi	140	4.57 N	97.46 E
Idiofa	156	5.02 S	19.36 E
Idlib	150	35.55 N	36.38 E
Idre	114	61.52 N	12.43 E
Idrigill Point ≻	108	57.20 N	6.35 W
Idrija	122	46.00 N	14.01 E
Iduburojo, Isla I	182	9.05 N	60.42 W
Idutywa	160	32.02 S	28.16 E
Idyllwild	178	33.45 N	116.43 W
Iepê	190	22.40 S	51.05 W
Ieper	116	50.51 N	2.53 E
Iesi	122	43.31 N	13.14 E
Ifalik I¹	138	7.15 N	144.27 E
Ife	152	7.30 N	4.30 E
Iferouâne	152	19.04 N	8.24 E
Ifni □⁹	152	29.00 N	10.00 W
Iforas, Adrar des ∧∧	152	20.00 N	2.00 E
Ifould Lake ⊜	164	30.53 S	132.09 E
Igal	116	46.31 N	17.55 E
Igarka	128	67.28 N	86.35 E
Igatimí	188	24.05 S	55.30 W
Ighil Izane	120	35.44 N	0.30 E
Iglesias	122	39.19 N	8.32 E
Iglesiente →•¹	122	39.20 N	8.40 E
Igloolik	172	69.24 N	81.49 W
İğneada	124	41.52 N	27.58 E
İğneada Burnu ≻	124	41.54 N	28.03 E
Igoumenitsa	124	39.30 N	20.16 E
Iguaçu ≃	188	25.36 S	54.36 W
Iguaçu, Saltos do (Iguassu Falls) ⌊	188	25.41 S	54.26 W
Iguaí	190	14.45 S	40.04 W
Iguala	180	18.21 N	99.32 W
Igualada	120	41.35 N	1.38 E
Iguape	188	24.43 S	47.33 W
Iguaraçu	190	23.11 S	51.50 W
Iguassu Falls → Iguaçu, Saltos do ⌊	188	25.41 S	54.26 W
Iguatemi	190	23.40 S	54.34 W
Iguatu	184	6.22 S	39.18 W
Iguéla	156	1.55 S	9.19 E
Iguidi, Erg •⁸	152	26.35 N	5.40 W
Igžej	128	53.59 N	103.10 E
Iheya-shima I	135b	27.00 N	127.56 E
Ihosy	161b	22.24 S	46.08 E
Iida	134	35.31 N	137.50 E
Iijoki ≃	114	65.20 N	25.17 E
Iisalmi	114	63.34 N	27.11 E
Iiyama	134	36.51 N	138.22 E
Iizuka	134	33.38 N	130.41 E
Ijebu-Ode	152	6.50 N	3.56 E
Ijill, Kediet ∧	152	22.38 N	12.33 W
IJmuiden	116	52.27 N	4.36 E
IJsselmeer (Zuiderzee) ▾²	116	52.45 N	5.25 E
Ijuí	188	28.23 S	53.55 W
Ika	128	59.18 N	106.12 E
Ikamatua	170	42.16 S	171.41 E
Ikaría I	124	37.41 N	26.20 E
Ikast	114	56.08 N	9.10 E
Ikeda, Nihon	134	34.01 N	133.48 E
Ikeda, Nihon	134a	42.55 N	143.27 E
Ikela	156	1.11 S	23.16 E
Ikerre	152	7.31 N	5.14 E
Iki I	134	33.47 N	129.43 E
Ikuno	134	35.10 N	134.48 E
Ila	152	8.01 N	4.55 E
Ilagan	138	17.10 N	121.54 E
Ilan	136	24.45 N	121.44 E
Ilanskij	128	56.14 N	96.03 E
Ilanz	118	46.46 N	9.12 E
Iława	116	53.37 N	19.33 E
Ilbenge	128	62.49 N	124.24 E
Ilbunga	164	26.25 S	135.03 E
Ilchester	104	51.01 N	2.41 W
Île-à-la-Crosse	172	55.27 N	107.53 W
Île-à-la-Crosse, Lac ⊜	172	55.40 N	107.45 W
Ilebo	156	4.19 S	20.35 E
Île-de-France □⁹	118	49.00 N	2.20 E
Île Desroches I	156	5.41 S	53.41 E
Ilek ≃	126	51.30 N	53.20 E
Ilen ≃	110	51.33 N	9.19 W
Ilesha	152	7.38 N	4.45 E
Ilfov □⁴	124	44.30 N	26.00 E
Ilfracombe, Austl.	168	23.30 S	144.30 E
Ilfracombe, Eng., U.K.	104	51.13 N	4.08 W
Ilhabela	190	23.47 S	45.21 W
Ilhéus	190	14.49 S	39.02 W
Ili	126	43.53 N	77.12 E
Ili ≃	132	45.24 N	74.02 E
Iliamna Lake ⊜	172	59.30 N	155.00 W
Iligan	138	8.14 N	124.14 E
Ilimsk	128	56.46 N	103.52 E
Ilion	176	43.01 N	75.02 W
Ilio Point ≻	179a	21.13 N	157.15 W
Iljinskij	128	47.58 N	142.12 E
Ilkal	148	15.58 N	76.08 E
Ilkeston	104	52.59 N	1.18 W
Ilkley	106	53.55 N	1.50 W
Illampu, Nevado ∧	184	15.50 S	68.34 W
Illapel	188	31.38 S	71.10 W
Illapel ≃	188	31.37 S	71.09 W
Illbillee, Mount ∧	164	27.02 S	132.30 E
Ille-et-Vilaine □⁵	118	48.10 N	1.30 W
Illéla	152	14.28 N	5.15 E
Illimani, Nevado ∧	184	16.39 S	67.48 W
Illinois □³	174	40.00 N	89.00 W
Illinois ≃, Ill., U.S.	174	38.58 N	90.27 W
Illinois ≃, Oreg., U.S.	178	42.33 N	124.03 W
Illizi	152	26.29 N	8.28 E
Illminster	104	50.56 N	2.55 W
Illovo	160	30.05 S	30.50 E
Il'men', Ozero ⊜	130	58.17 N	31.20 E
Ilmenau	116	50.41 N	10.55 E
Ilo	184	17.38 S	71.20 W
Iloilo	138	10.42 N	122.34 E
Ilomantsi	114	62.40 N	30.55 E
Ilondola Mission	158	10.42 S	31.47 E
Ilorin	152	8.30 N	4.32 E
Il'pyrskij	128	59.56 N	164.10 E
Ilwaki	138	7.56 S	126.26 E
Imabari	134	34.03 N	133.00 E
Imaichi	134	36.43 N	139.41 E
Iman	128	45.55 N	133.43 E
Imandra, Ozero ⊜	112	67.30 N	33.00 E
Imanombo	161b	24.26 S	45.49 E
Imari	134	33.16 N	129.53 E
Imaruí	188	28.21 S	48.49 W
Imaruí, Lagoa C	188	28.21 S	48.52 W
Imatra	114	61.10 N	28.46 E
Imbituba	188	28.14 S	48.40 W
Imbituva	188	25.12 S	50.35 W
Ime, Beinn ∧	108	56.14 N	4.49 W
Imeni Kirova	128	46.27 N	77.13 E
Imi	154	6.28 N	42.18 E
Imías	182	20.04 N	74.38 W
Imilac	188	24.14 S	68.53 W
Imlay	178	40.39 N	118.09 W
Imlay City	176	43.02 N	83.05 W
Immarna	164	30.30 S	132.09 E
Immenstadt	116	47.33 N	10.13 E
Immingham Dock	106	53.37 N	0.12 W
Imola	122	44.21 N	11.42 E
Imotski	122	43.27 N	17.13 E
Imperatriz	184	5.32 S	47.29 W
Imperia	122	43.53 N	8.03 E
Imperial	178	32.51 N	115.34 W
Imperial de Aragón, Canal ☲	120	42.02 N	1.33 W
Imperial Valley ∨	178	32.50 N	115.30 W
Impfondo	156	1.37 N	18.04 E
Imphāl	146	24.49 N	93.57 E
Imst	116	47.14 N	10.44 E
Ina, Nihon	134	35.50 N	137.57 E
In'a, S.S.S.R.	128	59.24 N	144.48 E
In'a ≃	128	59.23 N	144.54 E
Inaccessible Island I	88	37.17 S	12.45 W
In Aménas	152	28.05 N	9.30 E
Inangahua Junction	170	41.51 S	171.57 E
Inanwatan	166	2.08 S	132.10 E
Inari	112	68.54 N	27.01 E
Inari ⊜	112	69.00 N	28.00 E
Inarigda	128	63.14 N	107.27 E
Inawasiro-ko ⊜	134	37.29 N	140.06 E
Inca	120	39.43 N	2.54 E
Inca de Oro	188	26.45 S	69.54 W
Incaguasi	188	29.13 S	71.03 W
Inch	110	52.08 N	9.59 W
Inchard, Loch C	108	58.27 N	5.04 W
Inchbare	108	56.47 N	2.38 W
Inchcape I²	108	56.55 N	2.50 W
Inchmarnock I	108	55.47 N	5.09 W
Inchnadamph	108	58.09 N	4.59 W
Inch'ŏn	132	37.28 N	126.38 E
Inchture	108	56.26 N	3.10 W
Incline Village	178	39.16 N	119.56 W
Incomati (Komati) ≃	160	25.46 S	32.43 E
Incudine, l' ∧	122	41.51 N	9.12 E
Indaal, Loch C	108	55.45 N	6.21 W
Indalsälven ≃	114	62.31 N	17.27 E
Independence, Calif., U.S.	178	36.48 N	118.12 W
Independence, Kans., U.S.	174	37.13 N	95.42 W
Independence, Ky., U.S.	176	38.57 N	84.32 W
Independence ≃	176	43.45 N	75.20 W
Independence Mountains ∧∧	178	41.15 N	116.05 W
Inderborskij	126	48.33 N	51.44 E
India □¹	144	20.00 N	77.00 E
Indian ≃	176	43.58 N	75.17 W
Indiana	176	40.37 N	79.09 W
Indiana □³	174	40.00 N	86.15 W
Indianapolis	174	39.46 N	86.09 W
Indian Head	172	50.32 N	103.40 W
Indian Lake	176	43.47 N	74.16 W
Indian Ocean ▾¹	84	10.00 S	70.00 E
Indian Peak ∧	178	38.16 N	113.53 W
Indian River	176	45.25 N	84.37 W
Indian Springs	178	36.34 N	115.40 W
Indiaporã	190	19.57 S	50.17 W
Indien, territoires britanniques de l'Ocean → British Indian Ocean Territory □²	94	7.00 S	72.00 E
Indigirka ≃	128	70.48 N	148.54 E
Indio	178	33.43 N	116.13 W
Indispensable Reefs ✧²	162	12.40 S	160.25 E
Indochina →•¹	94	16.00 N	107.00 E
Indonesia □¹	138	5.00 S	120.00 E
Indore	146	22.43 N	75.50 E
Indragiri ≃	142	0.22 S	103.26 E
Indramayu	142	6.20 S	108.19 E
Indrāvati ≃	148	18.44 N	80.16 E
Indre □⁵	118	46.45 N	1.30 E
Indre ≃	118	47.16 N	0.19 E
Indre-et-Loire □⁵	118	47.15 N	0.45 E
Indus ≃	146	24.20 N	67.47 E
İnece	124	41.41 N	27.04 E
İnecik	124	40.56 N	27.16 E
Inez	176	37.52 N	82.32 W
Infanta, Kaap ≻	160	34.29 S	20.51 E
Infiernillo, Presa del ⊜¹	180	18.35 N	101.45 W
I-n-Gall	152	16.47 N	6.56 E
Ingatestone	104	51.41 N	0.22 E
Ingelheim	116	49.59 N	8.05 E
Ingende	156	0.15 S	18.57 E
Ingeniero Luiggi	188	35.25 S	64.29 W
Ingenio La Esperanza	188	24.15 S	64.51 W
Ingenio Santa Ana	188	27.25 S	65.35 W
Ingersoll	176	43.02 N	80.53 W
Ingham	168	18.39 S	146.10 E
Ingleborough ∧	106	54.11 N	2.23 W
Inglesa, Costa → English Coast •²	87	73.45 S	73.00 W
Ingleton	106	54.10 N	2.27 W
Inglewood, Austl.	168	28.25 S	151.05 E
Inglewood, N.Z.	170	39.09 S	174.12 E
Inglewood, Calif., U.S.	178	33.58 N	118.21 W
Inglewood Forest →•³	106	54.45 N	2.50 W
Ingolstadt	116	48.46 N	11.27 E
Ingrid Christensen Coast •²	87	69.30 S	76.00 E
In Guezzam	152	19.32 N	5.42 E
Ingwe	158	13.02 S	26.25 E
Inhaca, Ilha da I	160	26.03 S	32.57 E
Inhambane	160	23.51 S	35.29 E
Inhambane □⁵	160	23.00 S	34.30 E
Inhambupe	190	11.47 S	38.21 W
Inhaminga	160	18.24 S	35.00 E
Inharrime	160	24.29 S	35.01 E
Inírida ≃	184	3.55 N	67.52 W
Inishbofin I, Eire	110	55.09 N	8.11 W
Inishbofin I, Eire	110	53.37 N	10.15 W
Inisheer I	110	53.02 N	9.26 W
Inishmaan I	110	53.05 N	9.32 W
Inishmore I	110	53.07 N	9.45 W
Inishowen Peninsula ≻¹	110	55.12 N	7.20 W
Inishowen Point ≻	110	55.14 N	6.56 W
Inishshark I	110	53.37 N	10.18 W
Inishtrahull I²	110	55.26 N	7.14 W
Inishturk I	110	53.43 N	10.08 W
Inistioge	110	52.29 N	7.04 W
Injasuti ∧	160	29.09 S	29.23 E
Injune	168	25.51 S	148.34 E
Inkeroinen	114	60.42 N	26.51 E
Inle Lake ⊜	140	20.32 N	96.55 E
Inn (En) ≃	118	48.35 N	13.28 E
Innamincka	168	27.45 S	140.44 E
Innellan	108	55.54 N	4.57 W
Inner Hebrides II	108	56.30 N	6.00 W
Innerleithen	108	55.38 N	3.05 W
Inner Mongolia → Neimenggu Zizhiqu □⁴	132	43.00 N	115.00 E
Inner Sound ⩊	108	57.25 N	5.56 W
Inniscrone	110	54.12 N	9.06 W
Innisfail	168	17.32 S	146.02 E
Innoshima	134	34.20 N	133.10 E
Innsbruck	116	47.16 N	11.24 E
Innviertel →•¹	118	48.10 N	13.15 E
Inny ≃, Eire	110	53.33 N	7.48 W
Inny ≃, Eng., U.K.	104	50.35 N	4.17 W
Ino	134	33.33 N	133.26 E
Inongo	156	1.57 S	18.16 E
Inoucdjouac	172	58.27 N	78.06 W
Inowrocław	116	52.48 N	18.15 E
In Salah	152	27.12 N	2.28 E
Insch	108	57.21 N	2.37 W
Inscription, Cape ≻	164	25.29 S	112.59 E
Insein	140	16.53 N	96.07 E
Inta	112	66.02 N	60.08 E
Interlaken	118	46.41 N	7.51 E
International Falls	174	48.36 N	93.25 W
Inthanon, Doi ∧	140	18.35 N	98.29 E
Intiyaco	188	28.40 S	60.05 W
Inubō-saki ≻	134	35.42 N	140.53 E
Inuvik	172	68.25 N	133.30 W
Inver	108	57.49 N	3.55 W
Inveraray	108	56.13 N	5.05 W
Inverarity	108	56.35 N	2.53 W
Inverbervie	108	56.51 N	2.17 W
Invercargill	170	46.24 S	168.21 E
Inverdruie	108	57.10 N	3.48 W
Inverell	168	29.47 S	151.07 E
Invergarry	108	57.02 N	4.47 W
Invergordon	108	57.42 N	4.10 W
Inverkeilor	108	56.38 N	2.32 W
Inverkeithing	108	56.02 N	3.25 W
Inverkeithny	108	57.30 N	2.37 W
Invermoriston	108	57.13 N	4.38 W
Inverness, Scot., U.K.	108	57.27 N	4.15 W
Inverness, Calif., U.S.	178	38.06 N	122.51 W
Inveruglas	108	56.15 N	4.43 W
Inverurie	108	57.17 N	2.23 W
Inverway	164	17.50 S	129.38 E
Investigator Group II	164	33.45 S	134.30 E
Investigator Shoal ✧²	138	8.09 N	114.44 E
Investigator Strait ⩊	168	35.25 S	137.10 E
Inyanga	158	18.13 S	32.46 E
Inyanga Mountains ∧∧	158	18.00 S	33.00 E
Inyangani ∧	158	18.20 S	32.50 E
Inyati	158	19.39 S	28.54 E
Inyazura	158	18.43 S	32.10 E
Inyo, Mount ∧	178	36.44 N	117.59 W
Inyokern	178	35.39 N	117.49 W
Inyo Mountains ∧∧	178	36.40 N	118.10 W
Inza	112	53.51 N	46.21 E
Ioánnina	124	39.40 N	20.50 E
Iō-jima I	135b	30.48 N	130.18 E
Iolotan'	150	37.18 N	62.21 E
Iona I	108	56.19 N	6.25 W
Iona, Sound of ⩊	108	56.19 N	6.24 W
Ione	178	38.21 N	120.56 W
Ionia	176	42.59 N	85.04 W
Ionian Islands → Iónioi Nísoi II	124	38.30 N	20.30 E
Ionian Sea ▾²	100	39.00 N	19.00 E
Iónioi Nísoi II	124	38.30 N	20.30 E
Iony, Ostrov I	128	56.26 N	143.25 E
Iowa □³	174	42.15 N	93.15 W
Iowa City	174	41.40 N	91.32 W
Ipameri	190	17.43 S	48.09 W
Ipatinga	190	19.30 S	42.32 W
Ipel'(Ipoly) ≃	116	47.49 N	18.52 E
Ipiales	184	0.50 N	77.37 W
Ipiaú	190	14.08 S	39.44 W
Ipiranga	188	25.01 S	50.35 W
Ipoh	142	4.35 N	101.05 E
Ipoly (Ipel') ≃	116	47.49 N	18.52 E
Iporã, Bra.	190	23.59 S	53.37 W
Iporá, Bra.	190	16.28 S	51.07 W
İpsala	124	40.55 N	26.23 E
Ipswich, Austl.	168	27.36 S	152.46 E
Ipswich, Eng., U.K.	104	52.04 N	1.10 E
Ipswich, Mass., U.S.	176	42.41 N	70.50 W
Iquique	184	20.13 S	70.10 W
Iquitos	184	3.50 S	73.15 W
Iraí	188	27.11 S	53.15 W
Iráklion	124	35.20 N	25.09 E
Iran (Īrān) □¹	144	32.00 N	53.00 E
Iran, Pegunungan ∧∧	138	2.05 N	114.55 E
Īrānshahr	150	27.13 N	60.41 E
Irapa	182	10.34 N	62.35 W
Irapuato	180	20.41 N	101.28 W
Iraq □¹	144	33.00 N	44.00 E
Irati	188	25.27 S	50.39 W
Irazú, Volcán ∧¹	182	9.59 N	83.51 W
Irbid	150	32.33 N	35.51 E
Irbīl	150	36.11 N	44.01 E
Irbit	126	57.41 N	63.03 E
Ireland □¹	100	53.00 N	8.00 W
Irene	160	25.53 S	28.13 E
Irene, Mount ∧	170	45.10 S	167.22 E
Ireng ≃	184	3.33 N	59.51 W
Irfon ≃	104	52.09 N	3.24 W
Irgiz	126	48.37 N	61.16 E
Iri	132	35.56 N	126.57 E
Iringa	158	7.46 S	35.42 E
Iringa □⁴	158	9.00 S	35.00 E
Iriomote-jima I	132	24.20 N	123.50 E
Iriri ≃	184	3.52 S	52.37 W
Irish, Mount ∧	178	37.38 N	115.24 W
Irish Sea ▾²	102	53.30 N	5.20 W
Irishtown	168	40.55 S	145.08 E
Irkutsk	128	52.16 N	104.20 E
Irlam	106	53.28 N	2.25 W
Iroise C	118	48.15 N	4.55 W
Iron Baron	168	32.59 S	137.09 E
Iron Bridge, Ont., Can.	176	46.17 N	83.14 W
Iron Bridge, Eng., U.K.	104	52.38 N	2.29 W
Irondequoit	176	43.12 N	77.36 W
Iron Gate ∨	124	44.41 N	22.31 E
Iron Gate Reservoir ⊜¹	124	44.30 N	22.00 E
Iron Knob	168	32.44 S	137.08 E
Iron Mountain	174	45.49 N	88.04 W
Iron Range	166	12.42 S	143.18 E
Ironton	176	38.31 N	82.40 W
Ironwood	174	46.27 N	90.10 W
Iroquois	176	44.51 N	75.19 W
Irō-zaki ≻	134	34.36 N	138.51 E
Irrawaddy □⁸	140	17.00 N	95.00 E
Irrawaddy ≃	140	15.50 N	95.06 E
Irregully Creek ≃	164	23.06 S	116.21 E
Irt ≃	106	54.22 N	3.26 W
Irthing ≃	106	54.55 N	2.50 W
Irthlingborough	104	52.20 N	0.37 W
Irtyš ≃	128	61.04 N	68.52 E
Irtyšsk	128	53.21 N	75.27 E
Irumu	158	1.27 N	29.52 E
Irún	120	43.21 N	1.47 W
Irvine, Scot., U.K.	108	55.37 N	4.40 W
Irvine, Ky., U.S.	176	37.42 N	83.58 W
Irvine ≃	108	55.37 N	4.41 W
Irvinestown	110	54.28 N	7.38 W
Irwell ≃	106	53.27 N	2.17 W
Irwin	164	29.12 S	115.04 E
Irwin, Point ≻	164	35.04 S	116.56 E
Isaac ≃	168	22.52 S	149.20 E
Isabela → Basilan, Pil.	138	6.42 N	121.58 E
Isabela (Basilan), Pil.	142	6.42 N	121.58 E
Isabela, Cabo ≻	182	20.00 N	71.00 W
Isabella, Cordillera ∧∧	182	13.45 N	85.15 W
Isabella Lake ⊜¹	178	35.40 N	118.26 W
Isábena ≃	120	42.11 N	0.21 E
Ísafjörður	112a	66.08 N	23.13 W
Isahaya	134	32.50 N	130.03 E
Isak	140	4.28 N	96.55 E
Isana (Içana) ≃	184	0.26 N	67.19 W
Isar ≃	116	48.49 N	12.58 E
Isbister	108	60.36 N	1.19 W
Ischia	122	40.44 N	13.57 E
Ischia, Isola d' I	122	40.43 N	13.54 E
Isdell ≃	164	16.27 S	124.51 E
Ise	134	34.29 N	136.42 E
Iseo, Lago d' ⊜	122	45.43 N	10.04 E
Isère □⁵	118	45.10 N	5.50 E
Iserlohn	116	51.22 N	7.41 E
Isernia	122	41.36 N	14.14 E
Isesaki	134	36.19 N	139.12 E
Iset' ≃	126	56.36 N	66.24 E
Ise-wan C	134	34.43 N	136.43 E
Iseyin	152	7.58 N	3.36 E
Isfahan → Eşfahān	150	32.40 N	51.38 E
Ishigaki-shima I	132	24.24 N	124.12 E
Ishikari ≃	132	43.15 N	141.23 E
Ishikari-dake ∧	134a	44.33 N	143.02 E
Ishikari-heiya ≚	134a	43.15 N	141.23 E
Ishikari-wan C	134a	43.25 N	141.01 E
Ishikawa	135b	26.25 N	127.50 E
Ishikawa □⁵	134	36.45 N	136.45 E
Ishinomaki	134	38.25 N	141.18 E
Ishioka	134	36.11 N	140.16 E
Ishizuchi-san ∧	134	33.46 N	133.07 E
Isil'kul'	126	54.55 N	71.16 E
Išim	126	56.09 N	69.27 E
Išim ≃	128	57.45 N	71.12 E
Išimbaj	126	53.28 N	56.02 E
Išimskaja Step' ≚	126	55.00 N	70.00 E
Isimu	142	0.40 N	122.51 E
Isiolo	158	0.21 N	37.35 E
Isipingo	160	29.59 S	30.56 E
Isiro (Paulis)	158	2.47 N	27.37 E
Isis	168	25.12 S	152.13 E
Isisford	168	24.16 S	144.26 E
Iskâr, Jazovir ⊜¹	124	43.23 N	27.29 E
İskenderun	150	36.37 N	36.07 E
İskenderun Körfezi C	150	36.30 N	35.40 E
Iskitim	128	54.38 N	83.18 E
Iskut ≃	172	56.42 N	131.45 W
Isla ≃	108	57.30 N	2.47 W
Isla de Maipo	188	33.45 S	70.54 W
Islāmābād	146	33.42 N	73.10 E
Isla Mujeres	182	21.12 N	86.43 W
Island Falls	176	46.00 N	68.16 W
Island Lagoon ⊜	168	31.30 S	136.40 E
Island Lake ⊜	172	53.47 N	94.25 W
Island Pond	176	44.49 N	71.53 W
Islands, Bay of C, Newf., Can.	172	49.10 N	58.15 W
Islands, Bay Of C, N.Z.	170	35.12 S	174.10 E
Isla Vista	178	34.25 N	119.53 W
Islay I	108	55.48 N	6.12 W
Islay, Sound of ⩊	108	55.50 N	6.01 W
Isle ≃, Fr.	118	44.55 N	0.15 W
Isle ≃, Eng., U.K.	104	50.59 N	2.53 W
Isle of Man □²	100	54.15 N	4.30 W
Isle of Wight □⁶	102	50.40 N	1.20 W
Islesboro Island I	176	44.20 N	68.53 W
Isleton	178	38.10 N	121.37 W
Islington →•⁸	104	51.34 N	0.06 W
Islip	104	51.50 N	1.14 W
Islivig	108	58.05 N	7.11 W
Islón	188	29.54 S	71.12 W
Ismailia → Al-Ismā'īlīyah	154	30.35 N	32.16 E
Ismaning	116	48.14 N	11.41 E
Israel □¹	144	31.30 N	35.00 E
Israel ≃	176	44.29 N	71.35 W
Issoire	118	45.33 N	3.15 E
Issoudun	118	46.57 N	2.00 E
Is-sur-Tille	118	47.31 N	5.06 E
Issyk-Kul', Ozero ⊜	126	42.25 N	77.15 E
İstanbul	124	41.01 N	28.58 E
İstanbul □⁴	124	41.25 N	29.00 E

Symbols in the index entries are identified on page 198.

Symbols in the index entries are identified on page 198.

Name	Page	Lat ° ′	Long ° ′
Kinde	176	43.56 N	83.00 W
Kinder Scout ∧	106	53.23 N	1.52 W
Kindersley	172	51.27 N	109.10 W
Kindia	152	10.04 N	12.51 W
Kindu-Port-Empain	158	2.57 S	25.56 E
Kinel'	112	53.14 N	50.39 E
Kineo, Mount ∧	176	45.42 N	69.44 W
Kinešma	130	57.26 N	42.09 E
Kineton	104	52.10 N	1.30 W
Kinfauns	108	56.22 N	3.21 W
King, Lake ⊜	164	25.38 S	120.06 E
King, Mount ∧	168	25.10 S	147.31 E
Kingaroy	168	26.33 S	151.50 E
Kingarth	108	55.46 N	5.03 W
King City, Ont., Can.	176	43.56 N	79.32 W
King City, Calif., U.S.	178	36.13 N	121.08 W
King Edward ≃	166	14.14 S	126.35 E
Kingfield	176	44.57 N	70.09 W
King George	176	38.16 N	77.11 W
King George Island I	87	62.00 S	58.15 W
King George Islands II	172	57.20 N	78.25 W
King George Sound Ш	164	35.03 S	117.57 E
King Hill	178	43.00 N	115.12 W
Kingie ≃	108	57.04 N	5.08 W
Kingisepp	130	59.22 N	28.36 E
King Island I	168	39.50 S	144.00 E
King Lear Peak ∧	178	41.12 N	118.34 W
King Leopold Ranges ⋀	164	17.30 S	125.45 E
Kingman, Ariz., U.S.	178	35.12 N	114.04 W
Kingman, Maine, U.S.	176	45.33 N	68.12 W
Kingman Reef ✣2	96	6.24 N	162.22 W
King Mountain ∧	178	42.42 N	123.14 W
Kingoonya	164	30.54 S	135.18 E
King Peak ∧	178	40.10 N	124.08 W
Kings ≃, Calif., U.S.	178	36.03 N	119.49 W
Kings ≃, Nev., U.S.	178	41.31 N	118.08 W
Kings, Middle Fork ≃	178	36.50 N	118.52 W
Kings, North Fork ≃	178	36.52 N	119.08 W
Kingsbarns	108	56.18 N	2.39 W
Kings Beach	178	39.14 N	120.01 W
Kingsbridge	104	50.17 N	3.46 W
Kingsburg	178	36.31 N	119.33 W
Kingsbury	104	52.35 N	1.40 W
Kingsclere	104	51.20 N	1.14 W
Kingscote	168	35.40 S	137.38 E
Kingscourt	110	53.53 N	6.48 W
Kingsdown	104	51.11 N	1.25 E
Kingshouse	108	56.21 N	4.19 W
Kingskerswell	104	50.30 N	3.33 W
Kingsland	104	52.15 N	2.47 W
Kings Langley	104	51.43 N	0.28 W
Kingsley, S. Afr.	160	27.55 S	30.33 E
Kingsley, Eng., U.K.	104	53.01 N	1.59 W
Kingsley, Mich., U.S.	176	44.35 N	85.32 W
King's Lynn	104	52.45 N	0.24 E
King Sound Ш	164	17.00 S	123.30 E
Kingsport	174	36.32 N	82.33 W
King's Sutton	104	52.01 N	1.16 W
Kingsteignton	104	50.33 N	3.35 W
Kingston, Ont., Can.	176	44.18 N	76.34 W
Kingston, Jam.	182	18.00 N	76.50 W
Kingston, Eng., U.K.	102	51.25 N	0.19 W
Kingston, Mass., U.S.	176	41.59 N	70.43 W
Kingston, N.Y., U.S.	176	41.56 N	74.00 W
Kingston, Ohio, U.S.	176	39.28 N	82.55 W
Kingston, Pa., U.S.	176	41.16 N	75.54 W
Kingston ⇸8	104	51.25 N	0.19 W
Kingston Southeast	168	36.50 S	139.51 E
Kingston upon Hull (Hull)	106	53.45 N	0.20 W
Kingstown	182	13.09 N	61.14 W
Kingsville, Ont., Can.	176	42.02 N	82.45 W
Kingsville, Tex., U.S.	174	27.31 N	97.52 W
Kingswear	104	50.21 N	3.34 W
Kingswinford	104	52.29 N	2.10 W
Kingswood	104	51.27 N	2.22 W
King's Worthy	104	51.06 N	1.18 W
Kington	104	52.12 N	3.01 W
Kingussie	108	57.05 N	4.03 W
King William Island I	172	69.00 N	97.30 W
King William's Town	160	32.51 S	27.22 E
Kingwood	176	39.28 N	79.41 W
Kinkony, Lac ⊜	161b	16.08 S	45.50 E
Kinldchleven	108	56.42 N	4.58 W
Kinleith	170	38.16 S	175.54 E
Kinlochbervie	108	58.28 N	5.03 W
Kinlocheil	108	56.51 N	5.20 W
Kinlochewe	108	57.36 N	5.20 W
Kinloch Hourn	108	57.06 N	5.22 W
Kinloch Rannoch	108	56.42 N	4.11 W
Kinna	114	57.30 N	12.41 E
Kinnairds Head ≻	108	57.42 N	2.00 W
Kinnegad	110	53.26 N	7.05 W
Kinnel Water ≃	106	55.08 N	3.25 W
Kinnerley	104	52.47 N	2.59 W
Kino ≃	134	34.13 N	135.09 E
Kinosaki	134	35.37 N	134.49 E
Kinpoku-san ∧	134	38.05 N	138.22 E
Kinrola	168	23.46 S	148.45 E
Kinross	108	56.13 N	3.27 W
Kinsale	110	51.42 N	8.32 W
Kinsale, Old Head of ≻	110	51.36 N	8.32 W
Kinsale Harbour C	110	51.41 N	8.30 W
Kinsarvik	114	60.23 N	6.43 E
Kinshasa (Léopoldville)	156	4.18 S	15.18 E
Kinsman	176	41.27 N	80.36 W
Kintore	108	57.13 N	2.21 W
Kintore, Mount ∧	164	26.34 S	130.30 E
Kintyre ≻1	108	55.35 N	5.35 W
Kintyre, Mull of ≻	106	55.17 N	5.55 W
Kinvara	110	53.08 N	8.55 W
Kinver	104	52.27 N	2.14 W
Kinyeti ∧	154	3.57 N	32.54 E
Kinzua Creek ≃	176	41.47 N	78.50 W
Kiparissia	124	37.14 N	21.40 E
Kipawa, Lac ⊜	172	46.55 N	79.00 W
Kipembawe	158	7.39 S	33.24 E
Kipengere Range ⋀	158	9.10 S	34.15 E
Kipili	158	7.26 S	30.36 E
Kipini	158	2.32 S	40.31 E
Kippen	108	56.08 N	4.11 W
Kippure ∧	110	53.10 N	6.18 W
Kipushi	158	11.46 N	27.14 E
Kipushia	158	12.58 S	29.30 E
Kirbymoorside	106	54.16 N	0.55 W
Kirby Muxloe	104	52.38 N	1.13 W
Kırcasalih	124	41.23 N	26.48 E
Kirchheim	116	48.10 N	10.30 E
Kirchmöser	116	52.22 N	12.25 E
Kircubbin	110	54.24 N	5.28 W
Kirenga ≃	128	57.47 N	108.07 E
Kirensk	128	57.46 N	108.08 E
Kirgizskaja Sovetskaja Socialističeskaja Respublika □3	126	41.30 N	75.00 E
Kirgizskij Chrebet ⋀	126	42.30 N	74.00 E
Kirgiz Soviet Socialist Republic → Kirgizskaja Sovetskaja Socialističeskaja Respublika □3	126	14.30 N	75.00 E
Kiri	156	1.27 S	19.00 E
Kırıkhan	150	36.32 N	36.19 E
Kırıkkale	150	39.50 N	33.31 E
Kirin → Jilin	132	43.51 N	426.33 E
Kirinia	150	35.20 N	33.19 E
Kirishima-yama ∧	134	31.56 N	130.52 E
Kirkabister	108	60.07 N	1.08 W
Kirkbride	106	54.54 N	3.12 W
Kirkburton	106	53.37 N	1.42 W
Kirkby	106	53.29 N	2.54 W
Kirkby Lonsdale	106	54.13 N	2.36 W
Kirkby Malzeard	106	54.11 N	1.38 W
Kirkby Stephen	106	54.28 N	2.20 W
Kirkcaldy	108	56.07 N	3.10 W
Kirkcolm	106	54.58 N	5.05 W
Kirkconnel	108	55.23 N	4.00 W
Kirkcudbright	106	54.50 N	4.03 W
Kirkcudbright Bay C	106	54.48 N	4.04 W
Kirkenær	114	60.28 N	12.03 E
Kirkenes	112	69.40 N	30.03 E
Kirkham	106	53.47 N	2.53 W
Kirkhill	108	57.28 N	4.26 W
Kirkintilloch	108	55.57 N	4.10 W
Kirkland Lake	172	48.09 N	80.02 W
Kırklareli	124	41.44 N	27.12 E
Kırklareli □4	124	41.40 N	27.30 E
Kirkliston	108	55.58 N	3.25 W
Kirkmichael	108	56.43 N	3.29 W
Kirkpatrick, Mount ∧	87	84.20 S	166.19 E
Kirkstile	106	55.12 N	3.00 W
Kirksville	174	40.12 N	92.35 W
Kirkton of Culsalmond	108	57.23 N	2.34 W
Kirkton of Glenisla	108	56.44 N	3.17 W
Kirktown of Auchterless	108	57.27 N	2.28 W
Kirkūk	150	35.28 N	44.28 E
Kirkwall	108	58.59 N	2.58 W
Kirkwood	160	33.24 S	25.26 E
Kirov	130	54.05 N	34.20 E
Kirovabad	150	40.40 N	46.22 E
Kirovakan	126	40.48 N	44.30 E
Kirovgrad	126	57.26 N	60.04 E
Kirovo-Čepeck	112	58.33 N	50.01 E
Kirovograd	126	48.30 N	32.18 E
Kirovsk	150	37.42 N	60.23 E
Kirovskij, S.S.S.R.	126	44.52 N	78.12 E
Kirovskij, S.S.S.R.	128	54.18 N	155.47 E
Kirriemuir	108	56.41 N	3.01 W
Kirsanov	130	52.38 N	42.43 E
Kırşehir	150	39.09 N	34.10 E
Kīrthar Range ⋀	146	27.00 N	67.10 E
Kirtle Water ≃	106	54.58 N	3.05 W
Kirton	104	52.56 N	0.04 W
Kirton of Largo	108	56.13 N	2.55 W
Kiruna	112	67.51 N	20.16 E
Kiryū	134	36.24 N	139.20 E
Kisa	114	57.59 N	15.37 E
Kisakata	134	39.13 N	139.54 E
Kisangani (Stanleyville)	158	0.30 S	25.12 E
Kisar, Pulau I	142	8.05 S	127.10 E
Kisarazu	134	35.23 N	139.55 E
Kisel'ovsk	128	54.00 N	86.39 E
Kishanganga ≃	149	34.18 N	73.28 E
Kishangarh	146	26.34 N	74.52 E
Kishiwada	134	34.28 N	135.22 E
Kishorganj	146	24.26 N	90.46 E
Kishorn, Loch C	108	57.21 N	5.41 W
Kisii	158	0.41 S	34.46 E
Kišin'ov	126	47.00 N	28.50 E
Kiskörei-víztároló ⊜1	124	47.35 N	20.40 E
Kiskőrös	116	46.38 N	19.17 E
Kiskunfélegyháza	116	46.43 N	19.52 E
Kiskunhalas	116	46.26 N	19.30 E
Kiskunmajsa	116	46.30 N	19.45 E
Kislovodsk	126	43.55 N	42.44 E
Kismayu	156	0.23 S	42.30 E
Kiso ≃	134	35.02 N	136.45 E
Kiso-sammyaku ⋀	134	35.43 N	137.50 E
Kissidougou	152	9.11 N	10.06 W
Kississing Lake ⊜	172	55.10 N	101.20 W
Kisújszállás	116	47.13 N	20.46 E
Kisuki	134	35.17 N	132.54 E
Kisumu	158	0.06 S	34.45 E
Kisvárda	116	48.13 N	22.05 E
Kita	152	13.03 N	9.29 W
Kita-daitō-jima I	132	25.57 N	131.18 E
Kitaibaraki	134	36.48 N	140.45 E
Kita-iō-jima I	96	25.26 N	141.17 E
Kitakami	134	39.18 N	141.07 E
Kitakami ≃	134	38.25 N	141.19 E
Kitakami-sanchi ⋀	134	39.30 N	141.30 E
Kitakata	134	37.39 N	139.52 E
Kitakyūshū	134	33.53 N	130.50 E
Kitale	158	1.01 N	35.00 E
Kitami	134a	43.48 N	143.54 E
Kitami-sanchi ⋀	134a	44.22 N	142.43 E
Kitchener, Austl.	164	31.02 S	124.11 E
Kitchener, Ont., Can.	172	43.27 N	80.29 W
Kitega → Gitega	158	3.26 S	39.56 E
Kíthira I	124	36.20 N	22.58 E
Kíthnos I	124	37.25 N	24.28 E
Kitimat	172	54.03 N	128.33 W
Kitinen ≃	112	67.08 N	27.29 E
Kitsuki	134	33.25 N	131.37 E
Kittanning	176	40.49 N	79.32 W
Kittatinny Mountain ∧	149	34.18 N	73.28 E
Kittery	176	43.05 N	70.45 W
Kittery Point	176	43.05 N	70.41 W
Kittilä	112	67.40 N	24.54 E
Kitui	158	1.22 S	38.01 E
Kitwe	158	12.49 S	28.13 E
Kitzbühel	116	47.27 N	12.23 E
Kitzingen	116	49.44 N	10.09 E
Kiuruvesi	114	63.39 N	26.37 E
Kivu □4	158	2.30 S	27.00 E
Kivu, Lac ⊜	158	2.00 S	29.10 E
Kıyıköy	124	41.38 N	28.05 E
Kizel	126	59.03 N	57.40 E
Kiziguro	158	1.46 S	30.23 E
Kızıl ≃	150	40.05 N	33.45 E
Kizl'ar	126	43.50 N	46.40 E
Kiz'oma	112	61.08 N	44.50 E
Kizyl-Arvat	150	38.58 N	56.15 E
Kizyl-Atrek	150	37.36 N	54.46 E
Kjellerup	114	56.17 N	9.26 E
Kjustendil	124	42.17 N	22.41 E
Klabat, Gunung ∧	142	1.28 N	125.02 E
Klagenfurt	116	46.38 N	14.18 E
Klaipėda (Memel)	130	55.43 N	21.07 E
Klakah	142	7.59 S	113.15 E
Klamath	178	41.32 N	124.02 W
Klamath ≃	178	41.33 N	124.04 W
Klamath Falls	174	42.13 N	121.46 W
Klamath Marsh ☷	178	42.54 N	121.44 W
Klamath Mountains ⋀	178	41.40 N	123.20 W
Klamono	166	1.08 S	131.30 E
Klarälven (Trysilelva) ≃	114	59.23 N	13.32 E
Klatovy	116	49.24 N	13.18 E
Klawer	160	31.44 S	18.36 E
Kleck	130	53.04 N	26.38 E
Kleinbegin	160	28.50 S	21.36 E
Klerksdorp	160	26.58 S	26.39 E
Kleve	116	51.48 N	6.09 E
Klibreck, Ben ∧	108	58.14 N	4.22 W
Kličev	130	53.29 N	29.21 E
Klimovo	130	52.23 N	32.11 E
Klimovsk	130	55.22 N	37.32 E
Klin	130	56.20 N	36.44 E
Klincy	130	52.47 N	32.14 E
Klingenthal	116	50.21 N	12.28 E
Klintehamn	114	57.24 N	18.12 E
Klip ≃	160	27.20 S	27.10 E
Klipdale	160	34.19 S	19.57 E
Klipplaat	160	33.02 S	24.21 E
Klitmøller	114	57.02 N	8.31 E
Kłobuck	116	50.55 N	18.57 E
Kłodzko	116	50.27 N	16.39 E
Kløfta	114	60.04 N	11.09 E
Klondike □9	172	63.30 N	139.00 W
Klosterneuburg	116	48.18 N	16.20 E
Klosters	118	46.54 N	9.53 E
Klosterwappen ∧	116	47.46 N	15.48 E
Klotz, Lac ⊜	172	60.32 N	73.40 W
Klouto	152	6.57 N	0.34 E
Kluane Lake ⊜	172	61.15 N	138.40 W
Kl'učevskaja Sopka, Vulkan ∧1	128	56.04 N	160.38 E
Kl'uči	128	56.18 N	160.51 E
Kluczbork	116	50.59 N	18.13 E
Klungkung	142	8.32 S	115.24 E
Knaben gruver	114	58.39 N	7.04 E
Knaik ≃	108	56.14 N	3.52 W
Knapdale ⇸1	108	55.55 N	5.30 W
Knäred	114	56.32 N	13.19 E
Knaresborough	106	54.00 N	1.27 W
Knebworth	104	51.52 N	0.12 W
Knee Lake ⊜	172	55.03 N	94.40 W
Kneža	124	43.30 N	24.05 E
Knighton	104	52.21 N	3.03 W
Knights Landing	178	38.48 N	121.43 W
Knin	122	44.02 N	16.12 E
Knittelfeld	116	47.14 N	14.50 E
Knob, Cape ≻	164	34.32 S	119.16 E
Knobby Head ≻	164	29.40 S	114.58 E
Knoc	110	52.38 N	9.20 W
Knock	108	57.33 N	2.45 W
Knocklong	110	52.26 N	8.24 W
Knockmealdown Mountains ⋀	110	52.10 N	8.00 W
Knokke	116	51.21 N	3.17 E
Knottingley	106	53.43 N	1.14 W
Knowle	104	52.23 N	1.43 W
Knox	176	41.14 N	79.32 W
Knox, Cape ≻	172	54.11 N	133.04 W
Knoxville	174	35.58 N	83.56 W
Knutsford	106	53.19 N	2.22 W
Knysna	160	34.02 S	23.02 E
Kob'aj	128	63.34 N	126.30 E
Kobar Sink ◒7	154	14.00 N	40.30 E
Kobayashi	134	31.59 N	130.59 E
Kōbe	134	34.41 N	135.10 E
København (Copenhagen)	114	55.40 N	12.35 E
Koblenz	116	50.21 N	7.35 E
Kobowen Swamp ☷	158	5.38 N	33.54 E
Kobrin	130	52.13 N	24.21 E
Kobroor, Pulau I	166	6.12 S	134.32 E
Kočani	124	41.55 N	22.25 E
Kočečum ≃	128	64.17 N	100.10 E
Kočevje	122	45.38 N	14.52 E
Kōchi	134	33.33 N	133.33 E
Koch Island I	172	69.38 N	78.15 W
Kochma	130	56.56 N	41.06 E
Kodaikānal	144	10.14 N	77.29 E
Kodari	132	27.56 N	85.56 E
Kodok	154	9.53 N	32.07 E
Koes	160	25.59 S	19.08 E
Koffiefontein	160	29.30 S	25.00 E
Köflach	116	47.04 N	15.05 E
Koforidua	152	6.03 N	0.17 W
Kōfu	134	35.39 N	138.35 E
Koga	134	36.11 N	139.43 E
Kogaluc ≃	172	59.40 N	77.35 W
Kogaluc, Baie C	172	59.20 N	77.50 W
Kogaluk ≃	172	56.12 N	61.44 W
Kogan	168	27.03 S	150.46 E
Køge	114	55.27 N	12.11 E
Køge Bugt C	172	65.00 N	40.30 W
Kohala Mountains ⋀	179a	20.05 N	155.45 W
Kohāt	149	33.35 N	71.26 E
Kohīma	146	25.40 N	94.07 E
Kohtla-Järve	130	59.24 N	27.15 E
Kohukohu	170	35.21 S	173.32 E
Kohuratahi	170	39.06 S	174.46 E
Koide	134	37.13 N	138.57 E
Kojgorodok	112	60.26 N	50.58 E
Ko-jima I	134a	41.22 N	139.48 E
Kojonup	164	33.50 S	117.09 E
Kok (Hkok) ≃	140	20.14 N	100.09 E
Kokand	126	40.33 N	70.57 E
Kokas	166	2.42 S	132.26 E
Kokčetav	126	53.17 N	69.25 E
Kokemäki	114	61.15 N	22.21 E
Kokkola (Gamlakarleby)	114	63.50 N	23.07 E
Kokoda	166	8.52 S	147.45 E
Kokomo	174	40.29 N	86.08 W
Kokonau	166	4.43 S	136.26 E
Kokopo	166	4.20 S	152.15 E
Kokšaalatau, Chrebet ⋀	126	41.00 N	78.00 E
Koksoak ≃	172	58.32 N	68.10 W
Kokstad	160	30.32 S	29.29 E
Kokubu	134	31.44 N	130.46 E
Kolaka	138	4.03 S	121.36 E
Kolār	148	13.08 N	78.08 E
Kolār Gold Fields	148	12.55 N	78.17 E
Kolari	112	67.20 N	23.48 E
Kolárovo	116	47.52 N	18.02 E
Kolbio	158	1.10 S	41.15 E
Kol'čugino	130	56.18 N	39.23 E
Kolda	152	12.53 N	14.57 W
Kolding	114	55.31 N	9.29 E
Kolea	120	36.38 N	2.46 E
Kolgujev, Ostrov I	112	69.05 N	49.15 E
Kolhāpur	148	16.42 N	74.13 E
Kolho	114	62.08 N	24.31 E
Kolín	116	50.01 N	15.13 E
Kollegāl	148	12.09 N	77.07 E
Kolme	158	5.17 N	37.22 E
Kolmogorovo	128	59.15 N	91.20 E
Köln (Cologne)	116	50.56 N	6.59 E
Koło	116	52.12 N	18.38 E
Koloa	179a	21.55 N	159.28 W
Kolobovo	130	56.42 N	41.21 E
Kołobrzeg	116	54.12 N	15.33 E
Kolodn'a	130	54.48 N	32.09 E
Kologriv	130	58.51 N	44.17 E
Kolombangara I	162	8.00 S	157.05 E
Kolomna	130	55.05 N	38.49 E
Kolomyja	126	48.32 N	25.04 E
Kolonodale	142	2.00 S	121.19 E
Kolpaševo	128	58.20 N	82.50 E
Kolpino	130	59.45 N	30.36 E
Kolpny	130	52.15 N	37.02 E
Kol'skij Poluostrov (Kola Peninsula) ≻1	112	67.30 N	37.00 E
Kol'ubakino	130	55.40 N	36.32 E
Kolvereid	112	64.51 N	11.32 E
Kolwezi	158	10.43 S	25.28 E
Kolyma ≃	128	69.30 N	161.00 E
Kolymskaja	128	68.44 N	158.44 E
Kolymskaja Nizmennost' ≚	128	68.30 N	154.00 E
Kom → Qom	150	34.39 N	50.54 E
Kom ∧	124	43.10 N	23.03 E
Komadugu Gana ≃	152	13.05 N	12.24 E
Komadugu Yobe ≃	152	13.43 N	13.20 E
Komagane	134	35.43 N	137.55 E
Komaga-take ∧	134a	42.04 N	140.41 E
Komandorskije Ostrova II	128	55.00 N	167.00 E
Komárno	116	47.45 N	18.09 E
Komárom	116	47.44 N	18.08 E
Komárom □6	116	47.40 N	18.15 E
Komati (Incomati) ≃	160	25.46 S	32.43 E
Komatipoort	160	25.25 S	31.55 E
Komatsu	134	36.24 N	136.27 E
Komatsushima	134	34.00 N	134.35 E
Kombani	161a	11.37 S	43.23 E
Komering ≃	142	2.59 S	104.50 E
Komkans	160	31.16 S	18.09 E
Komló	116	46.12 N	18.16 E
Kommunarsk	126	48.30 N	38.47 E
Kommunizma, Pik ∧	126	38.57 N	72.01 E
Komodo, Pulau I	142	8.36 S	119.30 E
Komoé ≃	152	5.12 N	3.44 W
Komoro	134	36.19 N	138.26 E
Komotau → Chomutov	116	50.28 N	13.26 E
Komotiní	124	41.08 N	25.25 E
Kompasberg ∧	160	31.45 S	24.32 E
Komsberg ⋀	160	32.40 S	20.50 E
Komsomolec	126	53.45 N	62.02 E
Komsomolec, Ostrov I	128	80.30 N	95.00 E
Komsomolec, Zaliv C	126	45.30 N	52.45 E
Komsomol'sk-na-Amure	128	50.35 N	137.02 E
Komsomol'skoj Pravdy, Ostrova II	128	77.20 N	107.40 E
Kona Coast ◒2	179a	19.25 N	155.55 W
Konakovo	130	56.42 N	36.46 E
Konar (Kunar) ≃	149	34.26 N	70.32 E
Konārak	144	19.53 N	86.01 E
Konarha □4	146	35.15 N	71.00 E
Konda	126	61.20 N	63.58 E
Konda ≃	126	60.40 N	69.46 E
Kondinin	164	32.30 S	118.16 E
Kondoa	158	4.54 S	35.47 E
Kondopoga	112	62.12 N	34.17 E
Kondrovo	130	54.48 N	35.56 E
Kông ≃	140	13.32 N	105.58 E
Kongcheng	136	31.02 N	117.05 E
Konglong	136	29.56 N	115.54 E
Kongolo, Zaïre	158	5.23 S	27.00 E
Kongolo, Zaïre	158	5.26 S	24.49 E
Kongquehe ≃	132	40.40 N	90.10 E
Kongsvinger	114	60.12 N	12.00 E
Königsberg → Kalingrad	130	54.43 N	20.30 E
Königssee ⊜	116	47.36 N	12.59 E
Königs Wusterhausen	116	52.18 N	13.37 E
Konin	116	52.13 N	18.16 E
Konispol	124	39.39 N	20.10 E
Kónitsa	124	40.02 N	20.45 E
Konjic	124	43.39 N	17.57 E
Könkämäälv ≃	112	68.29 N	22.17 E
Konkouré ≃	152	9.58 N	13.42 W
Konnur	148	16.12 N	74.45 E
Kōnosu	134	36.03 N	139.31 E
Konotop	126	51.14 N	33.12 E
Konsen-daichi ⋀	134a	63.25 N	144.52 E
Końskie	116	51.12 N	20.26 E
Konstantinovka	126	48.32 N	37.43 E
Konstanz	116	47.40 N	9.10 E
Kontagora	152	10.24 N	5.28 E
Kontiomäki	114	64.21 N	28.09 E
Kontum	140	14.21 N	108.00 E
Konya	150	37.52 N	32.31 E
Konza	158	1.45 S	37.07 E
Konžakovskij Kamen', Gora ∧	126	59.38 N	59.08 E
Kookynie	164	29.20 S	121.29 E
Koolamarra	168	20.12 S	140.14 E
Koolatah	166	15.53 S	142.27 E
Koolau Range ⋀	179a	21.35 N	158.00 W
Kooloonong	168	34.53 S	143.09 E
Koolyanobbing	164	30.50 S	119.35 E
Koonibba	164	31.58 S	133.27 E
Koorawatha	168	34.02 S	148.33 E
Koorda	164	30.50 S	117.29 E
Kootenai ≃	172	49.18 N	117.39 W
Kootjieskolk	160	31.15 S	20.21 E
Kopargaon	148	19.53 N	74.29 E
Kópavogur	112a	64.06 N	21.50 W
Kopejsk	126	55.07 N	61.37 E
Koper	122	45.33 N	13.44 E
Köping	114	59.31 N	16.00 E
Koplik	124	42.13 N	19.26 E
Koppal	148	15.21 N	76.09 E
Koppang	114	61.34 N	11.04 E
Kopparbergs Län □6	114	61.00 N	14.30 E
Koppeh Dāgh ⋀	150	37.50 N	58.00 E
Koppies	160	27.20 S	27.30 E
Koprivnica	122	46.10 N	16.50 E
Korab ⋀	124	41.47 N	20.34 E
Kor'akskoje Nagorje ⋀	128	62.30 N	172.00 E
Koralpe ⋀	116	46.50 N	14.58 E
Koraput	144	18.48 N	82.41 E
Korbach	116	51.16 N	8.52 E
Korçë	124	40.37 N	20.46 E
Korčulanski Kanal Ш	122	43.03 N	16.40 E
Kord Kūy	150	36.48 N	54.07 E
Korea □1	84	38.00 N	127.00 E
Korea, North □1	132	40.00 N	127.00 E
Korea, South □1	132	36.30 N	128.00 E
Korea Bay C	132	39.00 N	124.00 E
Korea Strait Ш	132	34.00 N	129.00 E
Korf	128	60.19 N	165.50 E
Korfovskij	128	48.14 N	135.02 E
Korhogo	152	9.27 N	5.38 W
Kórinthos (Corinth)	124	37.56 N	22.56 E
Korínthou, Dhiórix)(	124	37.57 N	22.56 E
Koritsa → Korçë	124	40.37 N	20.46 E
Kōriyama	134	37.24 N	140.23 E
Korkino	126	54.54 N	61.23 E
Korliki	128	61.31 N	82.22 E
Körmend	116	47.01 N	16.37 E
Korneuburg	116	48.21 N	16.20 E
Kornsjø	114	58.57 N	11.39 E
Korogwe	158	5.09 S	38.29 E
Koroit	168	38.17 S	142.22 E
Koropíon	124	37.54 N	23.53 E
Koror	138	7.20 N	134.29 E
Koro Sea ▾2	96	18.00 S	179.50 E
Korosten'	126	50.57 N	28.39 E
Koro Toro	154	16.05 N	18.30 E
Korpilahti	114	62.01 N	25.33 E
Korsakov	128	46.38 N	142.46 E
Korsnäs	114	62.47 N	21.12 E
Korso	114	60.21 N	25.06 E
Korsør	114	55.20 N	11.09 E
Kortrijk (Courtrai)	116	50.50 N	3.16 E
Kos	124	36.53 N	27.18 E
Kos I	124	36.50 N	27.10 E
Kosa	112	59.56 N	54.55 E
Koš-Agač	128	50.00 N	88.40 E
Kosai	134	34.43 N	137.33 E
Kosaja Gora	130	54.07 N	37.33 E
Kosaka	134	40.19 N	140.44 E
Kosčagyl	126	46.51 N	53.48 E
Kościan	116	52.06 N	16.38 E
Kościerzyna	116	54.08 N	18.00 E
Kosciusko, Mount ∧	168	36.27 S	148.16 E
Koshikijima-rettō II	134	31.45 N	129.49 E
Kōshoku	134	36.38 N	138.06 E
Kosi, Lake ⊜	160	26.55 S	32.52 E
Košice	116	48.43 N	21.15 E
Koski	114	60.39 N	23.09 E
Koslan	126	63.28 N	48.52 E
Kosovska Mitrovica	124	42.53 N	20.52 E
Koster	160	25.57 S	26.42 E
Kostroma	130	57.46 N	40.55 E
Kostrzyn	116	52.37 N	14.39 E
Koszalin (Köslin)	116	54.12 N	16.09 E
Kőszeg	116	47.23 N	16.33 E
Kota	146	25.11 N	75.50 E
Kotaagung	142	5.30 S	104.38 E
Kota Baharu	142	6.08 N	102.15 E
Kotabaru	142	3.14 S	116.13 E
Kota Belud	138	6.00 N	116.00 E
Kotabumi	142	4.50 S	104.54 E
Kotadabok	138	0.30 S	104.33 E
Kot Addu	149	30.28 N	70.58 E
Kota Kinabalu (Jesselton)	142	5.59 N	116.04 E
Kotamobagu	142	0.46 N	124.19 E
Kotari ⋀	122	44.05 N	15.30 E
Kota Tinggi	142	1.44 N	103.54 E
Kotcho Lake ⊜	172	59.05 N	121.10 W
Kotel'nikovo	126	58.18 N	48.20 E
Kotel'nyj, Ostrov I	128	75.45 N	138.44 E
Köthen	116	51.45 N	11.58 E
Kotka	114	60.28 N	26.55 E
Kot Kapūra	149	30.35 N	74.54 E
Kotlas	112	61.16 N	46.35 E
Kotlenski prohod)(	124	42.53 N	26.27 E
Kotohira	134	34.11 N	133.49 E
Kotor	124	42.25 N	18.46 E
Kotor Varoš	122	44.37 N	17.23 E
Kotovsk	130	52.36 N	41.32 E
Kot Rādha Kishan	149	31.10 N	74.06 E
Kotri	146	25.22 N	68.18 E
Kötschach [-Mauthen]	116	46.40 N	13.00 E
Kottagūdem	148	17.33 N	80.38 E
Kottayam	148	9.35 N	76.31 E
Kotte	148	6.54 N	79.54 E
Kotto ≃	154	4.14 N	22.02 E
Kotuj ≃	128	71.55 N	102.05 E
Kötzting	116	49.11 N	12.52 E
Kouan	136	32.19 N	119.52 E
Koudougou	152	12.15 N	2.22 W
Koukdjuak ≃	172	66.45 N	73.09 W
Koula-Moutou	156	1.08 S	12.29 E
Koulikoro	152	12.53 N	7.33 W
Koumala	168	21.37 S	149.15 E
Koumi	134	36.05 N	138.29 E
Koumra	154	8.55 N	17.33 E
Kounradskij	126	46.59 N	75.00 E
Kouroussa	152	10.39 N	9.53 W
Koussi, Emi ∧	154	19.50 N	18.30 E
Koutiala	152	12.23 N	5.28 W
Kouvola	114	60.52 N	26.42 E
Kovel'	126	51.14 N	24.41 E
Kovilpatti	148	9.10 N	77.52 E
Kovno → Kaunas	130	54.54 N	23.54 E
Kovrov	130	56.22 N	41.18 E
Kovvur	148	17.01 N	81.44 E
Kowhitirangi	170	42.52 S	171.01 E
Kowkcheh ≃	146	37.10 N	69.23 E
Kowloon (Jiulong)	136	22.18 N	114.10 E
Kowt-e 'Ashrow	146	34.27 N	68.48 E
Koza	135b	26.20 N	127.50 E
Kō-zaki ≻	134	34.05 N	129.13 E
Kozan	150	37.27 N	35.49 E
Kozáni	124	40.18 N	21.47 E
Kozara ⋀	122	45.00 N	16.50 E
Kozhikode → Calicut	148	11.15 N	75.46 E
Koźle	116	50.20 N	18.08 E
Kōzu-shima I	134	34.13 N	139.10 E
Kpandu	152	7.00 N	0.18 E
Kra, Isthmus of ◒3	140	10.20 N	99.00 E
Kraai ≃	160	30.40 S	26.45 E
Krâchéh	140	12.29 N	106.01 E
Kragan	142	6.42 S	111.37 E
Kragujevac	124	44.01 N	20.55 E
Kraków	116	50.03 N	19.58 E
Kralendijk	182	12.10 N	68.17 W
Kraljevo	124	43.43 N	20.41 E
Kralupy nad Vltavou	116	50.11 N	14.18 E
Kramatorsk	126	48.43 N	37.32 E
Kramfors	114	62.56 N	17.47 E
Krångede	114	63.09 N	16.05 E
Kranidhion	124	37.22 N	23.10 E
Kranj	122	46.15 N	14.21 E
Kranskop	160	29.00 S	30.47 E
Krasneno	128	64.38 N	174.48 E
Kraśnik	116	50.56 N	22.13 E
Kraśnik Fabryczny	116	50.58 N	22.12 E
Krasnoarmejsk	130	56.08 N	38.08 E
Krasnoarmejskij	128	69.35 N	172.00 E
Krasnodar	126	45.02 N	39.00 E
Krasnogorsk, S.S.S.R.	128	48.24 N	142.06 E
Krasnogorsk, S.S.S.R.	130	55.50 N	37.20 E
Krasnoj Armii, Proliv Ш	128	80.00 N	94.35 E
Krasnojarsk	128	56.01 N	92.50 E
Krasnoje, Ozero ⊜	128	64.30 N	174.24 E
Krasnoje Selo	130	59.44 N	30.05 E
Krasnokamsk	126	58.04 N	55.48 E
Krasnosel'kup	128	65.41 N	82.28 E
Krasnoslobodsk	126	48.42 N	44.34 E
Krasnoturjinsk	126	59.46 N	60.12 E
Krasnoufimsk	126	56.37 N	57.46 E
Krasnoural'sk	126	58.21 N	60.03 E
Krasnovišersk	112	60.23 N	56.59 E
Krasnovodsk	150	40.00 N	53.00 E
Krasnozavodsk	130	56.27 N	38.25 E
Krasnoznamenskij	126	51.03 N	69.30 E
Krasnoz'orskoje	128	53.59 N	79.14 E
Krasnyj Kut	126	50.57 N	46.58 E
Krasnyj Luč	126	48.08 N	38.56 E
Krasnystaw	116	50.59 N	23.10 E
Kraszna (Crasna) ≃	124	48.09 N	22.20 E
Kratovo	124	42.05 N	22.11 E
Kraul Mountains ⋀	87	73.10 S	14.10 W
Krawang	142	6.19 S	107.17 E
Krefeld	116	51.20 N	6.34 E
Kreitzer Glacier ⚑	87	70.25 S	72.30 E
Kremenčug	126	49.04 N	33.25 E
Krems an der Donau	116	48.25 N	15.36 E
Kresta, Zaliv C	128	66.00 N	179.15 W
Krest-Major	128	67.37 N	144.45 E
Krestovaja Guba	126	74.07 N	55.33 E
Kría Vrísi	124	40.41 N	22.18 E
Kribi	152	2.57 N	9.55 E
Kričov	130	53.42 N	31.43 E
Kriens	118	47.02 N	8.17 E
Krimml	116	47.13 N	12.11 E
K▾is-hegy ∧	116	47.18 N	17.45 E
Krishna ≃	148	15.57 N	80.59 E
Krishnagiri	148	12.32 N	78.14 E
Krishnanagar	146	23.24 N	88.30 E
Kristdala	114	57.24 N	16.11 E
Kristiania → Oslo	114	59.55 N	10.45 E
Kristiansand	114	58.10 N	8.00 E
Kristianstad	114	56.02 N	14.08 E
Kristianstads Län □6	114	56.15 N	14.00 E
Kristiansund	114	63.07 N	7.45 E
Kristineberg	114	65.04 N	18.35 E
Kristinehamn	114	59.20 N	14.07 E
Kríti I	124	35.29 N	24.42 E
Kritikón Pélagos ▾2	124	35.46 N	23.54 E
Kriva Palanka	124	42.12 N	22.20 E
Krivoj Rog	126	47.55 N	33.21 E
Križevci	122	46.02 N	16.33 E
Krnov	116	50.05 N	17.41 E
Krøderen ⊜	114	60.15 N	9.38 E
Krokodil ≃, S. Afr.	160	24.12 S	26.52 E
Krokodil ≃, S. Afr.	160	25.26 S	31.58 E
Kroměříž	116	49.18 N	17.24 E
Kronach	116	50.14 N	11.20 E
Krŏng Kaôh Kŏng	140	11.37 N	102.59 E
Krŏng Kêb	140	10.29 N	104.19 E
Kronobergs Län □6	114	56.40 N	14.40 E
Kronockij Zaliv C	128	54.12 N	160.36 E
Kronoki	128	54.36 N	161.10 E
Kronštadt	130	59.59 N	29.45 E
Kroonstad	160	27.46 S	27.12 E
Kropotkin, S.S.S.R.	126	45.26 N	40.34 E
Kropotkin, S.S.S.R.	128	58.30 N	115.17 E
Krosno	116	49.42 N	21.46 E
Krotoszyn	116	51.42 N	17.26 E
Kroya	142	7.38 S	109.14 E
Krško	122	45.58 N	15.29 E
Krugersdorp	160	26.05 S	27.35 E
Krui	142	5.11 S	103.56 E
Kruidfontein	160	32.51 S	21.57 E
Kruisfontein	160	34.00 S	24.43 E
Krujë	124	41.30 N	19.48 E
Kr'ukovo	128	66.30 N	159.31 E
Krung Thep (Bangkok)	140	13.45 N	100.31 E
Kruså	114	54.50 N	9.25 E
Kruševac	124	43.35 N	21.20 E
Kruševo	124	41.22 N	21.14 E
Krušné hory (Erzgebirge) ⋀	118	50.30 N	13.15 E
Kruzenšterna, Proliv Ш	128	48.30 N	153.50 E
Kruzof Island I	172	57.10 N	135.40 W
Krymskij Poluostrov ≻1	126	45.00 N	34.00 E
Krynica	116	49.25 N	20.56 E
Ksar el Boukhari	120	35.51 N	2.52 E
Ksar-el-Kebir	152	35.01 N	5.54 W
Ksar-es-Souk	152	31.58 N	4.25 W
Ksar Hellal	122	35.39 N	10.54 E
Ksenjevka	128	53.34 N	118.44 E
Ksour Essaf	122	35.25 N	11.00 E
Kstovo	112	56.11 N	44.11 E
Kuala Dungun	142	4.47 N	103.26 E
Kuala Kangsar	142	4.46 N	100.56 E
Kualakapuas	142	3.01 S	114.21 E
Kuala Kerai	142	5.32 N	102.12 E
Kuala Kubu Baharu	142	3.34 N	101.39 E
Kualakurun	142	1.07 S	113.53 E
Kuala Lipis	142	4.11 N	102.03 E
Kuala Lumpur	142	3.10 N	101.42 E
Kuala Nerang	142	6.15 N	100.36 E
Kuala Pilah	142	2.44 N	102.15 E
Kuala Terengganu	142	5.20 N	103.08 E
Kuandang	142	0.52 N	122.55 E
Kuantan	142	3.48 N	103.20 E
Kuba	126	41.22 N	48.31 E
Kuban' ≃	126	45.20 N	37.30 E
Kubokawa	134	33.12 N	133.08 E
Kuchāman	146	27.09 N	74.52 E
Kuche	132	41.43 N	82.54 E
Kuching	142	1.33 N	110.20 E
Kuchinoerabu-jima I	135b	30.28 N	130.12 E
Kuchino-shima I	135b	29.57 N	129.57 E
Kudamatsu	134	34.00 N	131.52 E
Kudat	142	6.53 N	116.50 E
Kudus	142	6.48 S	110.50 E
Kudymkar	112	59.01 N	54.37 E
Kuerle	132	41.44 N	86.09 E
Kufstein	116	47.35 N	12.10 E
Kuhmo	114	64.08 N	29.31 E
Kuhmoinen	114	61.34 N	25.11 E
Kuitan	136	23.05 N	115.58 E
Kuiu Island I	172	57.45 N	134.10 W
Kuivaniemi	114	65.35 N	25.11 E
Kujawy ⇸1	116	52.45 N	18.30 E
Kujbyšev, S.S.S.R.	112	53.12 N	50.09 E
Kujbyšev, S.S.S.R.	128	55.27 N	78.19 E
Kujbyševskij	126	37.52 N	68.44 E
Kuji	134	40.11 N	141.46 E
Kuji ≃	134	36.29 N	140.37 E
Kujūkuri-hama ◒2	134	35.45 N	140.30 E
Kujū-san ∧	134	33.05 N	131.15 E
Kukawa	152	12.56 N	13.35 E
Kukës	124	42.05 N	20.24 E
Kula	124	45.36 N	19.32 E
Kul'ab	146	37.55 N	69.46 E
Kula Kangri ∧	146	28.03 N	90.27 E
Kulebaki	130	55.24 N	42.32 E
Kulgera	164	25.50 S	133.18 E
Kulim	142	5.22 N	100.34 E
Kulmbach	116	50.06 N	11.27 E
Kuloj	112	61.02 N	42.29 E
Kul'sary	126	46.59 N	54.01 E
Kulti	146	23.44 N	86.51 E
Kulumadau	166	9.03 S	152.43 E
Kulundinskaja Step' ≚	128	53.00 N	79.00 E
Kulundinskoje, Ozero ⊜	128	53.00 N	79.36 E
Kulunqi	132	42.44 N	121.40 E
Kuma ≃, Nihon	134	32.30 N	130.34 E
Kuma ≃, S.S.S.R.	126	44.56 N	47.00 E
Kumagaya	134	36.08 N	139.23 E
Kumaishi	134a	42.08 N	139.59 E
Kumamoto	134	32.48 N	130.43 E
Kumano	134	33.54 N	136.05 E
Kumano ≃	134	33.44 N	136.01 E
Kumano-nada ▾2	134	33.47 N	136.20 E
Kumanovo	124	42.08 N	21.43 E
Kumara	170	42.38 S	171.11 E
Kumārapālaiyam	148	11.28 N	77.43 E
Kumarl	164	32.47 S	121.33 E
Kumasi	152	6.41 N	1.35 W
Kumba	152	4.38 N	9.25 E
Kumbakonam	148	10.58 N	79.23 E
Kumbarilla	168	27.19 S	150.53 E
Kum-Dag	150	39.16 N	54.35 E
Kumertau	126	52.46 N	55.47 E
Kume-shima I	135b	26.20 N	126.47 E
Kumla	114	59.08 N	15.08 E
Kummerower See ⊜	116	53.49 N	12.52 E
Kumo	152	10.03 N	11.13 E
Kumora	128	55.53 N	111.13 E
Kumukahi, Cape ≻	179a	19.31 N	154.49 W
Kuna	178	43.30 N	116.25 W
Kunar (Konar) ≃	149	34.26 N	70.32 E
Kunašir, Ostrov (Kunashiri-tō) I	134a	44.10 N	146.00 E
Kundar ≃	146	31.56 N	69.19 E
Kundara	148	8.57 N	76.41 E
Kundiān	149	32.27 N	71.28 E
Kundiawa	166	6.00 S	145.00 E
Kundip	164	33.42 S	120.10 E
Kundūz	126	37.45 N	68.51 E
Kungälv	114	57.52 N	11.58 E
Kungrad	126	43.06 N	58.54 E
Kungsbacka	114	57.29 N	12.04 E
Kungur	126	57.25 N	56.57 E
Kungurri	168	21.05 S	148.44 E
Kunhegyes	116	47.22 N	20.38 E
Kuningan	142	6.59 S	108.29 E
Kunisaki	134	33.33 N	131.45 E
Kunisaki-hantō ≻1	134	33.30 N	131.40 E
Kunjāh	149	32.32 N	73.59 E
Kunlunshanmai ⋀	146	36.30 N	88.00 E
Kunming	140	25.05 N	102.40 E
Kunsan	132	35.58 N	126.41 E
Kunshan	136	31.23 N	120.57 E
Kununurra	166	15.47 S	128.44 E
Kuopio	114	62.54 N	27.41 E
Kuopion lääni □4	114	63.00 N	27.30 E
Kupang	142	10.10 S	123.35 E
Kup'ansk	126	49.42 N	37.38 E
Kupino	128	54.22 N	77.18 E
Küplü	124	41.07 N	26.21 E
Kupreanof Island I	172	56.50 N	133.30 W
Kura ≃	126	39.24 N	49.24 E
Kurashiki	134	34.35 N	133.46 E
Kurayoshi	134	35.26 N	133.49 E
K'urdamir	150	40.21 N	48.08 E
Kurdistan □9	144	37.00 N	45.00 E
Kure, Austl.	166	15.27 S	126.33 E
Kure, Nihon	134	34.14 N	132.34 E
Kurejka ≃	128	66.30 N	87.12 E
Kurenalus	114	65.21 N	26.59 E
Kurgan	126	55.26 N	65.18 E
Kurgan-T'ube	146	37.50 N	68.48 E
Kuria I	96	0.14 N	173.25 E
Kuria Muria Islands → Khūryān Mūryān II	144	17.30 N	56.00 E
Kuridala	168	21.17 S	140.30 E
Kurikka	114	62.37 N	22.25 E
Kuril Islands → Kuril'skije Ostrova II	128	46.10 N	152.00 E
Kuril'sk	128	45.14 N	147.53 E
Kuril'skije Ostrova (Kuril Islands) II	128	46.10 N	152.00 E
Kuril Trench ✣1	84	47.00 N	155.00 E
Kurinskaja Kosa ≻2	150	39.03 N	49.13 E
Kuripapango	170	39.23 S	176.21 E
Kuriyama	134a	43.03 N	141.47 E
Kurmuk	154	10.33 N	34.17 E
Kurnool	148	15.50 N	78.03 E
Kurobe	134	36.51 N	137.26 E
Kuroishi	134	40.38 N	140.36 E
Kuro-shima I	135b	30.50 N	129.57 E
Kurram ≃	149	32.36 N	71.20 E
Kursk	126	51.42 N	36.12 E
Kuršumlija	124	43.08 N	21.17 E
Kūrtī	154	18.07 N	31.33 E
Kurtistown	179a	19.36 N	155.04 W
Kuruman	160	27.28 S	23.28 E
Kuruman ≃	160	26.56 S	20.39 E
Kuruman Heuwells ⋀2	160	27.40 S	23.25 E
Kurume	134	33.19 N	130.31 E
Kurumkan	128	54.18 N	110.18 E
Kurunegala	148	7.29 N	80.22 E
Kusa	126	55.20 N	59.29 E
Kusaie I	96	5.19 N	162.59 E
Kusawa Lake ⊜	172	60.20 N	136.15 W
Kushikino	134	31.44 N	130.16 E
Kushima	134	31.29 N	131.14 E
Kushimoto	134	33.28 N	135.47 E
Kushiro	134a	42.58 N	144.23 E
Kushtia	146	23.55 N	89.07 E
Kushui	132	42.11 N	94.25 E
Kuška	150	35.16 N	62.20 E
Kuška ≃	150	36.00 N	62.40 E
Kuskokwim ≃	172	60.17 N	162.27 W
Kušmurun	126	52.27 N	64.36 E
Küsnacht	118	47.19 N	8.35 E
Kussharo-ko ⊜	134a	43.38 N	144.21 E
Kustanaj	126	53.10 N	63.35 E
Kūstī	154	13.10 N	32.40 E
Küstrin → Kostrzyn	116	52.37 N	14.39 E
Kusu	134	33.16 N	131.09 E
K'us'ur	128	70.39 N	127.15 E
Kušva	126	58.18 N	59.45 E
Kut, Ko I	140	11.40 N	102.35 E
Kutaisi	126	42.15 N	42.40 E
Kūt al-Imāra	144	32.25 N	45.49 E
Kutarere	170	38.03 S	177.09 E
Kutch, Gulf of C	146	22.36 N	69.30 E
Kutchan	134a	42.54 N	140.45 E
Kutcharo-ko ⊜	134a	45.09 N	142.19 E
Kutina	122	45.29 N	16.46 E
Kutná Hora	116	49.57 N	15.16 E
Kutno	116	52.15 N	19.23 E
Kuttura	112	68.24 N	26.28 E
Kuttusoja	112	67.46 N	28.50 E
Kutu	156	2.44 S	18.09 E
Kutztown	176	40.31 N	75.47 W
Kuusamo	114	65.58 N	29.11 E
Kuusankoski	114	60.54 N	26.38 E
Kuvandyk	126	51.28 N	57.21 E
Kuwait □1	144	29.30 N	47.45 E
Kuwana	134	35.04 N	136.42 E
Kuz'movka	128	62.19 N	92.02 E
Kuzneck	112	53.07 N	46.36 E
Kuzneckij Alatau ⋀	128	54.45 N	88.00 E
Kuzuryū ≃	134	36.13 N	136.08 E
Kvænangen C2	112	70.05 N	21.13 E
Kvaløya I, Nor.	112	69.40 N	18.30 E
Kvaløya I, Nor.	112	70.37 N	23.52 E
Kverkfjöll ∧	112a	64.43 N	16.38 W
Kvikkjokk	112	66.55 N	17.50 E
Kvina ≃	114	58.17 N	6.56 E
Kwajalein I1	96	9.05 N	167.20 E
Kwakoegron	184	5.12 N	55.22 W
Kwando (Cuando) ≃	156	18.27 S	23.32 E
Kwangchow → Guangzhou	136	23.06 N	113.16 E
Kwangju	132	35.09 N	126.54 E
Kwango (Cuango) ≃	156	3.14 S	17.23 E
Kwangsi Chuang Autonomous Region → Guangxi Zhuangzu Zizhiqu □4	140	24.00 N	109.00 E

Symbols in the index entries are identified on page 198.

Symbols in the index entries are identified on page 198.

Name	Page	Lat °′	Long °′
Manna	142	4.27 S	102.55 E
Mannahill	168	32.26 S	139.59 E
Mannar, Gulf of C	148	8.30 N	79.00 E
Mannārgudi	148	10.40 N	79.26 E
Mannheim	116	49.29 N	8.29 E
Mannington	176	39.32 N	80.20 W
Manningtree	104	51.57 N	1.04 E
Manokwari	166	0.52 S	134.05 E
Manono	158	7.18 S	27.25 E
Manorbier	104	51.39 N	4.48 W
Manorhamilton	110	54.18 N	8.10 W
Manosque	118	43.50 N	5.47 E
Manouane, Lac ⊜	172	50.41 N	70.45 W
Manresa	120	41.44 N	1.50 E
Mānsa, Bhārat	149	29.59 N	75.23 E
Mansa (Fort Rosebery), Zam.	158	11.12 S	28.53 E
Mānsehra	149	34.20 N	73.12 E
Mansel Island I	172	62.00 N	79.50 W
Mansfield, Eng., U.K.	106	53.09 N	1.11 W
Mansfield, Mass., U.S.	176	42.02 N	71.13 W
Mansfield, Ohio, U.S.	176	40.46 N	82.31 W
Mansfield, Pa., U.S.	176	41.48 N	77.05 W
Mansfield, Mount ∧	176	44.33 N	72.49 W
Mansfield Woodhouse	106	53.11 N	1.12 W
Mansle	118	45.53 N	0.11 E
Manta	184	0.57 S	80.44 W
Manteca	178	37.48 N	121.13 W
Mantekamuhu ⊜	146	34.30 N	89.15 E
Mantes-la-Jolie	118	48.59 N	1.43 E
Manton	176	44.24 N	85.24 W
Mantos Blancos	188	23.25 S	70.05 W
Mantova	122	45.09 N	10.48 E
Mantua, Cuba	182	22.17 N	84.17 W
Mantua, Ohio, U.S.	176	41.17 N	81.14 W
Manturovo	130	58.20 N	44.46 E
Mäntyharju	114	61.25 N	26.53 E
Mäntyluoto	114	61.35 N	21.29 E
Manu ≃	184	12.16 S	70.55 W
Manuae I[1]	96	19.21 S	158.56 W
Manua Islands II	96	14.13 S	169.35 W
Manuel Ribas	188	24.31 S	51.39 W
Manuhangi I[1]	96	19.12 S	141.16 W
Manuherikia ≃	170	45.16 S	169.24 E
Manui, Pulau I	142	3.35 S	123.08 E
Manukau	170	37.02 S	174.54 E
Manulla ≃	110	53.57 N	9.12 W
Manunui	170	38.53 S	175.20 E
Manuoha ∧	170	38.39 S	177.07 E
Manutahi	170	39.40 S	174.24 E
Manutuke	170	38.41 S	177.55 E
Manyara, Lake ⊜	158	3.35 S	35.50 E
Manyč ≃	126	47.15 N	40.00 E
Manyoni	158	5.45 S	34.50 E
Many Peaks	168	24.33 S	151.23 E
Manzanares	120	39.00 N	3.22 W
Manzanillo, Cuba	182	20.21 N	77.07 W
Manzanillo, Méx.	180	19.03 N	104.20 W
Manzanillo, Punta ≻	182	9.36 N	79.31 W
Manzanillo Bay ≃	182	19.40 N	71.45 W
Manzhouli	132	49.35 N	117.22 E
Manzini	160	26.30 S	31.25 E
Mao	154	14.07 N	15.19 E
Maoke, Pegunungan ⋀	166	4.00 S	138.00 E
Maoming	140	21.55 N	110.52 E
Maouri, Dallol V	152	12.05 N	3.32 E
Mapanza Mission	158	16.15 S	26.55 E
Mapi	166	7.07 S	139.23 E
Mapia, Kepulauan II	138	0.50 N	134.20 E
Maple ≃	176	42.59 N	84.57 W
Maple Creek	172	49.55 N	109.27 W
Mapoi	158	5.28 N	27.40 E
Maprik	166	3.40 S	143.05 E
Maputo (Lourenço Marques)	160	25.58 S	32.35 E
Maputo (Lourenço Marques) □5	160	26.00 S	32.25 E
Maputo (Great Usutu) ≃	160	26.11 S	32.42 E
Maquela do Zombo	156	6.03 S	15.07 E
Maquinchao	186	41.15 S	68.44 W
Mar, Serra do •4	186	25.00 S	48.00 W
Mara □4	158	1.45 S	34.00 E
Mara ≃	158	1.31 S	33.56 E
Marabá	184	5.21 S	49.07 W
Maracai	188	22.36 S	50.39 W
Maracaibo	184	10.40 N	71.37 W
Maracaibo, Lago de ⊜	184	9.50 N	71.30 W
Maracaju, Serra de ⋀2	190	23.57 S	55.01 W
Maracay	184	10.15 N	67.36 W
Marādah	154	29.14 N	19.13 E
Maradi	152	13.29 N	7.06 E
Marāgheh	150	37.23 N	46.13 E
Maragogipe	190	12.46 S	38.55 W
Marahuaca, Cerro ∧	184	3.34 N	65.27 W
Marajó, Baía de C	184	1.00 S	48.30 W
Marajó, Ilha de I	184	1.00 S	49.30 W
Marakabei	160	29.32 S	28.09 E
Maralal	158	1.06 N	36.42 E
Marampa	152	8.41 N	12.28 W
Maramureş □4	124	47.40 N	24.00 E
Maramureşului, Munţii ⋀	124	47.50 N	24.45 E
Maran	142	3.35 N	102.46 E
Maranalgo	164	29.23 S	117.48 E
Maranboy	166	14.30 S	132.45 E
Maranchón	120	41.03 N	2.12 W
Marand	150	38.26 N	45.46 E
Marandellas	158	18.10 S	31.36 E
Marang	142	5.12 N	103.13 E
Maranoa ≃	168	27.50 S	148.37 E
Marano [di Napoli]	122	40.54 N	14.11 E
Marañón ≃	184	4.30 S	73.35 W
Maraş	150	37.36 N	36.55 E
Marathon, Austl.	168	20.49 S	143.34 E
Marathon, Ont., Can.	172	48.40 N	86.25 W
Marathón, Ellás	124	38.10 N	23.58 E
Marathon, N.Y., U.S.	176	42.26 N	76.02 W
Marau	188	28.27 S	52.12 W
Maravilha	188	26.47 S	53.09 W
Marawī	154	18.29 N	31.49 E
Marbella	120	36.31 N	4.53 W
Marble Bar	164	21.11 S	119.44 E
Marble Hall	160	24.57 S	29.13 E
Marblehead	176	41.32 N	82.44 W
Marburg	160	30.44 S	30.26 E
Marburg an der Lahn	116	50.49 N	8.46 E
Marcal ≃	116	47.41 N	17.32 E
Marcali	116	46.35 N	17.25 E
Marcelino Ramos	188	27.28 S	51.54 W
March	104	52.33 N	0.06 E
March (Morava) ≃	116	48.10 N	16.59 E
Marcha	128	61.49 N	122.20 E
Marcha ≃	128	63.28 N	118.50 E
Marche □4	122	43.30 N	13.15 E
Marche □9	118	46.05 N	2.10 E
Marche-en-Famenne	116	50.12 N	5.20 E
Marchena	120	37.20 N	5.24 W
Mar Chiquita, Laguna ⊜	188	30.42 S	62.36 W
Marcigny	118	46.17 N	4.02 E
Marcos Juárez	188	32.42 S	62.05 W
Marcus Baker, Mount ∧	172	61.26 N	147.45 W
Marcus-Necker Ridge ⤳3	96	20.00 N	179.00 E
Marcy, Mount ∧	176	44.07 N	73.56 W
Marda	164	30.13 S	119.17 E
Mardalsfossen L	114	62.30 N	8.07 E
Mardān	149	34.12 N	72.02 E
Mar del Plata	188	38.01 S	57.35 W
Mardie	164	21.11 S	115.57 E
Mardin	150	37.18 N	40.44 E
Maré, Île I	96	21.30 S	168.00 E
Maree, Loch ⊜	108	57.42 N	5.30 W
Mareeba	168	17.00 S	145.26 E
Mareetsane	160	26.09 S	25.25 E
Mareg	154	3.47 N	47.18 E
Maremma •→1	122	42.30 N	11.30 E
Marennes	118	45.50 N	1.06 W
Marfleet	106	53.45 N	0.17 W
Mar Forest •→3	108	57.00 N	3.35 W
Margam	104	51.34 N	3.44 W
Marganec	126	47.38 N	34.40 E
Margaret Creek ≃	168	29.26 S	137.07 E
Margaret River	164	18.38 S	126.52 E
Margaretville	176	42.09 N	74.39 W
Margarita, Isla I	182	9.15 N	74.30 W
Margarita, Isla de I	184	11.00 N	64.00 W
Margate, S. Afr.	160	30.55 S	30.15 E
Margate, Eng., U.K.	104	51.24 N	1.24 E
Margate City	176	39.20 N	74.31 W
Margeride, Monts de la ⋀	118	44.50 N	3.30 E
Margherita Peak ∧	158	0.22 N	29.51 E
Margilan	126	40.28 N	71.44 E
Mārgow, Dasht-e •→2	150	30.45 N	63.10 E
Marguerite Bay C	87	68.30 S	68.30 W
Maria I[1]	96	21.48 S	154.41 W
Maria Augustina Bank ⤳4	96	14.30 S	105.40 E
María Elena	188	22.21 S	69.40 W
Maria Gail	116	46.36 N	13.52 E
María la Baja	182	9.59 N	75.17 W
Mariana	190	20.23 S	43.25 W
Mariana Basin ⤳1	96	12.00 N	154.00 E
Mariana Islands II	138	16.00 N	145.30 E
Marianao	182	23.05 N	82.26 W
Mariana Ridge ⤳3	96	17.00 N	146.00 E
Mariana Trench ⤳1	96	16.00 N	148.00 E
Mariāni	146	26.40 N	94.20 E
Marian Lake ⊜	172	63.00 N	116.10 W
Mariano Machado	156	13.02 S	14.40 E
Mariánské Lázně	116	49.59 N	12.43 E
Maria Theresa Reef ⤳2	96	37.00 S	151.15 W
Mariato, Punta ≻	180	7.11 N	80.53 W
Mariazell	116	47.47 N	15.19 E
Maribo	114	54.46 N	11.31 E
Maribor	122	46.33 N	15.39 E
Marica (Évros) (Meriç) ≃	124	40.52 N	26.12 E
Marico ≃	160	24.12 S	26.52 E
Maricopa	178	35.03 N	119.24 W
Maricourt (Wakeham Bay)	172	61.36 N	71.58 W
Maricunga, Salar de ≌	188	26.55 S	69.05 W
Marīdī	158	4.55 N	29.28 E
Maridi ≃	158	5.30 N	29.15 E
Marie-Galante I	182	15.56 N	61.16 W
Mariehamn	114	60.06 N	19.57 E
Marienburg → Malbork	116	54.02 N	19.01 E
Mariental	160	24.36 S	17.59 E
Marienville	176	41.28 N	79.07 W
Mariestad	114	58.43 N	13.51 E
Marietta, Ga., U.S.	174	33.57 N	84.33 W
Marietta, Ohio, U.S.	176	39.25 N	81.27 W
Marieville	176	45.26 N	73.10 W
Mariga ≃	152	9.40 N	5.55 E
Marignane	118	43.25 N	5.13 E
Marigot, Dom.	182	15.32 N	61.18 W
Marigot, Guad.	182	18.04 N	63.06 W
Mariinsk	128	56.13 N	87.45 E
Marília	190	22.13 S	49.56 W
Marimba	156	8.28 S	17.08 E
Marinduque Island I	138	13.24 N	121.58 E
Marine City	176	42.43 N	82.30 W
Marinette	174	45.06 N	87.38 W
Maringá	190	23.25 S	51.55 W
Maringa ≃	156	1.14 N	19.48 E
Marinha Grande	120	39.45 N	8.56 W
Marino	122	41.46 N	12.39 E
Marion, Ind., U.S.	174	40.33 N	85.40 W
Marion, Mich., U.S.	176	44.06 N	85.09 W
Marion, Ohio, U.S.	176	40.35 N	83.08 W
Marion, Lake ⊜1	174	33.30 N	80.25 W
Marion Bay C	168	42.48 S	147.55 E
Marion Downs	168	23.22 S	139.39 E
Marion Reef ⤳2	168	19.10 S	152.17 E
Mariposa	178	37.29 N	119.58 W
Mariscal Estigarribia	188	22.02 S	60.38 W
Maritime Alps ⋀	118	44.15 N	7.10 E
Mariusa, Caño ≃1	182	9.43 N	61.26 W
Marka	154	1.47 N	44.52 E
Markaryd	114	56.26 N	13.36 E
Markdale	176	44.19 N	80.39 W
Markerwaard •→1	116	52.33 N	5.15 E
Market Bosworth	104	52.37 N	1.24 W
Market Deeping	104	52.41 N	0.19 W
Market Drayton	104	52.54 N	2.29 W
Market Harborough	104	52.29 N	0.55 W
Market Lavington	104	51.18 N	1.59 W
Market Rasen	106	53.24 N	0.21 W
Market Weighton	106	53.52 N	0.40 W
Markham	176	43.52 N	79.16 W
Markham, Mount ∧	87	82.51 S	161.21 E
Markham Bay C	172	63.30 N	71.48 W
Markinch	108	56.12 N	3.08 W
Markle	176	40.50 N	85.20 W
Markleeville	178	38.41 N	119.47 W
Markovo	128	64.40 N	170.25 E
Marktredwitz	116	50.00 N	12.06 E
Marlboro	176	41.36 N	73.58 W
Marlborough, Austl.	168	22.49 S	149.53 E
Marlborough, Eng., U.K.	104	51.26 N	1.43 W
Marlborough, Mass., U.S.	176	42.21 N	71.33 W
Marlborough Downs ⋀1	104	51.30 N	1.45 W
Marle	118	49.44 N	3.46 E
Marlette	176	43.20 N	83.05 W
Marlinton	176	38.13 N	80.06 W
Marlow	104	51.35 N	0.48 W
Marmande	118	44.30 N	0.10 E
Marmara, Sea of → Marmara Denizi ⊤2	100	40.40 N	28.15 E
Marmara Denizi (Sea of Marmara) ⊤2	124	40.40 N	28.15 E
Marmara Ereğlisi	124	40.58 N	27.57 E
Marmet	176	38.15 N	81.04 W
Marmora	176	44.29 N	77.41 W
Marne □5	118	48.55 N	4.10 E
Marne ≃	118	48.49 N	2.24 E
Marne au Rhin, Canal de la ≂	118	48.35 N	7.47 E
Marnhull	104	50.58 N	2.18 W
Maroa	184	2.43 N	67.33 W
Maroantsetra	161b	15.26 S	49.44 E
Maromokotro ∧	161b	14.01 S	48.59 E
Maroni (Marowijne) ≃	184	5.45 N	53.58 W
Maros (Mureş) ≃	124	46.15 N	20.13 E
Maroua	152	10.36 N	14.20 E
Marovoay	161b	16.06 S	46.39 E
Marowijne (Maroni) ≃	184	5.45 N	53.58 W
Marple	106	53.24 N	2.03 W
Marquard	160	28.54 S	27.28 E
Marquesas Islands → Marquises, Îles II	84	9.00 S	139.30 W
Marquesas Keys II	182	24.34 N	82.08 W
Marquette	174	46.33 N	87.24 W
Marquina-Jemein	120	43.16 N	2.30 W
Marquise	118	50.49 N	1.42 E
Marquises, Îles II	84	9.00 S	139.30 W
Marra Creek ≃	168	30.05 S	147.05 E
Marrah, Jabal ∧	154	13.04 N	24.21 E
Marrakech	152	31.38 N	8.00 W
Marrawah	168	40.56 S	144.41 E
Marree	168	29.39 S	138.04 E
Marromeu	160	18.20 S	35.56 E
Mars	176	40.42 N	80.06 W
Marsabit	158	2.20 N	37.59 E
Marsala	122	37.48 N	12.26 E
Marsden	168	33.45 S	147.32 E
Marseille	118	43.18 N	5.24 E
Marseille-en-Beauvaisis	118	49.35 N	1.57 E
Marsfjället ∧	112	65.05 N	15.28 E
Marshall, Liber.	152	6.10 N	10.23 W
Marshall, Mich., U.S.	176	42.16 N	84.58 W
Marshall, Mo., U.S.	174	39.07 N	93.12 W
Marshall, Tex., U.S.	174	32.33 N	94.23 W
Marshall, Va., U.S.	176	38.52 N	77.52 W
Marshall ≃	168	22.59 S	136.59 E
Marshall Islands II	96	9.00 N	168.00 E
Marshalltown	174	42.03 N	92.55 W
Marshbrook	158	18.34 S	31.03 E
Marshfield	104	51.28 N	2.19 W
Marsh Harbour	182	26.33 N	77.03 W
Marshyhope Creek ≃	176	38.32 N	75.45 W
Marsica •→1	122	41.50 N	13.45 E
Marsing	178	43.33 N	116.48 W
Marske-by-the-Sea	106	54.36 N	1.01 W
Märsta	114	59.37 N	17.51 E
Marstal	114	54.51 N	10.31 E
Marston Moor ≌	106	53.57 N	1.17 W
Martaban	138	16.32 N	97.37 E
Martaban, Gulf of C	140	16.30 N	97.00 E
Martapura, Indon.	142	4.19 S	104.22 E
Martapura, Indon.	142	3.25 S	114.51 E
Marteg ≃	104	52.20 N	3.33 W
Martel	118	44.56 N	1.37 E
Marthaguy Creek ≃	168	30.16 S	147.35 E
Martha's Vineyard I	176	41.25 N	70.40 W
Martí	182	21.09 N	77.27 W
Martigny	118	46.06 N	7.04 E
Martigues	118	43.24 N	5.03 E
Martin, Isle I	108	57.55 N	5.14 W
Martina Franca	122	40.42 N	17.21 E
Martinborough	170	41.13 S	175.28 E
Martinez	178	37.55 N	121.55 W
Martinique □2	180	14.40 N	61.00 W
Martinniemi	114	65.13 N	25.18 E
Martinsburg, Pa., U.S.	176	40.19 N	78.20 W
Martinsburg, W. Va., U.S.	176	39.27 N	77.58 W
Martins Ferry	176	40.06 N	80.44 W
Martinsville	174	36.41 N	79.52 W
Martock	104	50.59 N	2.46 W
Marton	170	40.05 S	175.23 E
Martos	120	37.43 N	3.58 W
Martre, Lac la ⊜	172	63.15 N	116.55 W
Martti	112	67.28 N	28.28 E
Marudi	138	4.11 N	114.19 E
Marugame	134	34.17 N	133.47 E
Maruia	170	42.11 S	172.13 E
Marula	158	20.26 S	28.06 E
Marungu ⋀	158	7.42 S	30.00 E
Maruoka	134	36.09 N	136.16 E
Marutea I[1]	96	17.00 S	143.10 W
Marv Dasht	150	29.50 N	52.40 E
Marvel Loch	164	31.28 S	119.28 E
Mary	150	37.36 N	61.50 E
Mary ≃	168	25.26 S	152.55 E
Maryborough, Austl.	168	25.32 S	152.42 E
Maryborough, Austl.	168	37.03 S	143.45 E
Marydale	160	29.23 S	22.05 E
Mary Kathleen	168	20.49 S	139.58 E
Maryland	158	17.39 S	30.29 E
Maryland □3	174	39.00 N	76.45 W
Marypark	108	57.26 N	3.21 W
Maryport	106	54.43 N	3.30 W
Marys ≃	178	41.04 N	115.16 W
Marys Creek ≃	178	42.18 N	115.48 W
Marysville, Calif., U.S.	178	39.09 N	121.35 W
Marysville, Mich., U.S.	176	42.54 N	82.29 W
Marysville, Ohio, U.S.	176	40.14 N	83.22 W
Marysville, Pa., U.S.	176	40.20 N	76.56 W
Maryville	174	40.21 N	94.52 W
Marywell	108	57.02 N	2.42 W
Marzūq	154	25.55 N	13.55 E
Marzūq, Idehan •→1	154	24.30 N	13.00 E
Masai Steppe ≌	158	4.45 S	37.00 E
Masaka	158	0.20 S	31.44 E
Masaka □5	158	0.30 S	31.35 E
Masamba	142	2.32 S	120.20 E
Masan	132	35.11 N	128.32 E
Masasi	158	10.43 S	38.48 E
Masatepe	182	11.55 N	86.09 W
Masaya	182	11.59 N	86.06 W
Masbate	138	12.22 N	123.36 E
Masbate Island I	138	12.15 N	123.30 E
Mascara	152	35.45 N	0.01 E
Mascarene Basin ⤳1	94	27.00 S	55.00 E
Mascarene Islands II	161c	21.00 S	57.00 E
Maseru	160	29.28 S	27.30 E
Mashaba Mountains ⋀	158	18.45 S	30.32 E
Mashābih I	150	25.37 N	36.29 E
Masham	106	54.13 N	1.40 W
Mashan	140	23.50 N	108.16 E
Mashhad	150	36.18 N	59.36 E
Mashike	134a	43.51 N	141.31 E
Mashiko	134	36.28 N	140.06 E
Māshkel (Māshkīd) ≃	150	28.02 N	63.25 E
Māshkel, Hāmūn-i- ⊜	150	28.15 N	63.00 E
Māshkīd (Māshkel) ≃	150	28.02 N	63.25 E
Mashonaland North □4	158	16.30 S	30.00 E
Mashonaland South □4	158	18.15 S	30.45 E
Mashra'ar-Raqq	154	8.25 N	29.16 E
Mashū-ko ⊜	134a	43.35 N	144.32 E
Masi Manimba	156	4.46 S	17.55 E
Masindi	158	1.41 N	31.43 E
Maşīrah, Khalīj al- C	144	20.10 N	58.15 E
Masjed Soleymān	150	31.58 N	49.18 E
Mask, Lough ⊜	110	53.35 N	9.20 W
Masoala, Presqu'île ≻1	161b	15.40 S	50.12 E
Mason, Mich., U.S.	176	42.35 N	84.26 W
Mason, Ohio, U.S.	176	39.17 N	84.19 W
Mason, W. Va., U.S.	176	39.01 N	82.01 W
Mason, Lake ⊜	164	27.39 S	119.34 E
Mason City	174	43.09 N	93.12 W
Masontown	176	39.51 N	79.54 W
Masparro, Punta ≻	182	10.40 N	66.15 W
Masqaţ (Muscat)	150	23.37 N	58.35 E
Massa	122	44.01 N	10.09 E
Massachusetts □3	174	42.15 N	71.50 W
Massachusetts Bay C	176	42.20 N	70.50 W
Massacre Lake ⊜	178	41.39 N	119.35 W
Massafra	122	40.35 N	17.07 E
Massa Marittima	122	43.03 N	10.53 E
Massangena	160	21.32 S	32.57 E
Massarosa	122	43.52 N	10.20 E
Massaua → Mesewa	154	15.38 N	39.28 E
Massena	176	44.56 N	74.54 W
Massenya	154	11.24 N	16.10 E
Masseube	118	43.26 N	0.35 E
Massey	176	46.12 N	82.05 W
Massif Central → Central, Massif ⋀	118	45.00 N	3.10 E
Massillon	176	40.48 N	81.32 W
Massinga	160	23.20 S	35.25 E
Massive, Mount ∧	174	39.12 N	106.28 W
Maštaga	150	40.32 N	50.00 E
Masterton	170	40.57 S	175.40 E
Mastung	144	29.48 N	66.51 E
Masuda	134	34.40 N	131.51 E
Masuie	158	18.05 S	25.45 E
Mat ≃	124	41.39 N	19.34 E
Matabeleland •→1	160	19.30 S	28.00 E
Matabeleland North □4	158	19.00 S	27.15 E
Matabeleland South □4	158	21.00 S	29.15 E
Matadi	156	5.49 S	13.27 E
Matagalpa	182	12.53 N	85.57 W
Mataiva I[1]	96	14.53 S	148.40 W
Matakana	168	33.00 S	145.54 E
Matakana Island I	170	37.35 S	176.05 E
Matakitaki ≃	170	41.48 S	172.19 E
Matale	148	7.28 N	80.37 E
Matam	152	15.40 N	13.15 W
Matamata	170	37.49 S	175.47 E
Matamoras	176	41.22 N	74.42 W
Matamoros	180	25.53 N	97.30 W
Matana	158	3.46 S	29.41 E
Matandu ≃	158	8.45 S	39.19 E
Matane	172	48.51 N	67.32 W
Matanzas	182	23.03 N	81.35 W
Matapu	170	39.29 S	174.14 E
Mataquito ≃	188	34.59 S	72.12 W
Matara	148	5.56 N	80.33 E
Mataram	142	8.35 S	116.07 E
Mataranka	166	14.56 S	133.07 E
Mataró	120	41.32 N	2.27 E
Matatiele	160	30.24 S	28.43 E
Mataura	170	46.11 S	168.52 E
Matawai	170	38.21 S	177.32 E
Matehuala	180	23.39 N	100.39 W
Mateira	190	18.54 S	50.30 W
Mateke Hills ⋀2	158	21.48 S	31.00 E
Matera	122	40.40 N	16.37 E
Mátészalka	116	47.57 N	22.19 E
Mateur	122	37.03 N	9.40 E
Mathematicians Seamounts ⤳3	90	16.00 N	112.00 W
Mather	176	39.56 N	80.05 W
Mathry	104	51.57 N	5.05 W
Mathura	146	27.30 N	77.41 E
Maticora ≃	182	11.03 N	71.09 W
Matinicus Island I	176	43.54 N	68.55 W
Matlock	106	53.08 N	1.32 W
Mato, Cerro ∧	184	7.15 N	65.14 W
Matočkin Šar	126	73.16 N	56.27 E
Matočkin Šar, Proliv ⋓	126	73.20 N	55.21 E
Mato Grosso	184	15.00 S	59.57 W
Mato Grosso □3	190	16.00 S	56.00 W
Mato Grosso, Planalto do ⋀1	184	15.30 S	56.00 W
Matopo Hills ⋀2	158	20.36 S	28.28 E
Matosinhos	120	41.11 N	8.42 W
Matou, T'aiwan	136	23.11 N	120.16 E
Matou, Zhg.	136	25.14 N	118.22 E
Matoury	184	4.51 N	52.21 W
Matozinhos	190	19.35 S	44.07 W
Maţraḩ	150	23.38 N	58.34 E
Matrei in Osttirol	116	47.00 N	12.32 E
Maţrūḩ	154	31.21 N	27.14 E
Matsieng	160	29.36 S	27.32 E
Matsu → Matsu Shan I	132	26.09 N	119.56 E
Matsudo	134	35.47 N	139.54 E
Matsue	134	35.28 N	133.04 E
Matsumae	134	41.26 N	140.07 E
Matsumoto	134	36.14 N	137.58 E
Matsusaka	134	34.34 N	136.32 E
Matsu Shan I	136	26.09 N	119.56 E
Matsushima	134	38.22 N	141.04 E
Matsutō	134	36.31 N	136.34 E
Matsuura	134	33.22 N	129.42 E
Matsuyama	134	33.50 N	132.45 E
Mattagami ≃	172	50.43 N	81.29 W
Mattāncheri	148	9.59 N	76.16 E
Mattaponi ≃	176	37.51 N	77.10 W
Mattawa	172	46.19 N	78.42 W
Mattawa ≃	176	46.19 N	78.43 W
Mattawamkeag	176	45.31 N	68.21 W
Mattawamkeag ≃	176	45.30 N	68.24 W
Matterhorn ∧, Eur.	118	45.59 N	7.43 E
Matterhorn ∧, Nev., U.S.	178	41.49 N	115.23 W
Matthew Town	182	20.57 N	73.40 W
Mattighofen	116	48.06 N	13.09 E
Mattole ≃	178	40.18 N	124.21 W
Mattoon	174	39.29 N	88.22 W
Mattydale	176	43.06 N	76.09 W
Maturín	184	9.45 N	63.11 W
Matusevich Glacier ⍓	87	69.11 S	157.20 E
Maúa	158	13.51 S	37.10 E
Maubeuge	118	50.17 N	3.58 E
Ma-ubin	140	16.44 N	95.39 E
Mauchline	108	55.31 N	4.24 W
Maud	108	57.31 N	2.06 W
Maud, Point ≻	164	23.06 S	113.45 E
Maude	168	34.28 S	144.18 E
Maués	184	3.24 S	57.42 W
Maug Islands II	138	20.01 N	145.13 E
Maui I	179a	20.45 N	156.15 W
Mauke I	96	20.09 S	157.23 W
Maule □4	188	35.45 S	72.15 W
Maule ≃	188	35.19 S	72.25 W
Maule, Laguna del ⊜	188	36.04 S	70.30 W
Mauléon	118	46.56 N	0.45 W
Mauléon-Licharre	118	43.14 N	0.53 W
Maumee	176	41.34 N	83.39 W
Maumee ≃	176	41.42 N	83.28 W
Maumere	142	8.37 S	122.14 E
Maun	160	20.00 S	23.25 E
Mauna Kea ∧1	179a	19.50 N	155.28 W
Maunaloa	179a	21.08 N	157.13 W
Mauna Loa ∧1	179a	19.29 N	155.36 W
Maunath Bhanjan	146	25.57 N	83.33 E
Maungatapere	170	35.45 S	174.12 E
Maungaturoto	170	36.06 S	174.22 E
Maunoir, Lac ⊜	172	67.30 N	125.00 W
Maur	149	30.05 N	75.15 E
Maure-de-Bretagne	118	47.54 N	1.59 W
Maures ⋀	118	43.16 N	6.23 E
Maurice, Lake ⊜	164	29.28 S	130.58 E
Mauriceville	170	40.47 S	175.42 E
Mauritania □1	152	20.00 N	12.00 W
Mauritius □1	156	20.17 S	57.33 E
Mauritius I	161c	20.17 S	57.33 E
Mauron	118	48.05 N	2.18 W
Maury ≃	176	37.50 N	79.25 W
Maury Channel ⋓	172	75.44 N	94.40 W
Mauterndorf	116	47.08 N	13.40 E
Mauvezin	118	43.44 N	0.55 E
Mavinga	156	15.50 S	20.21 E
Mavuradona Mountains ⋀	158	16.30 S	31.20 E
Maw-daung Pass)(	140	11.47 N	99.39 E
Mawgan	104	50.06 N	5.06 W
Mawson Escarpment •4	87	73.05 S	68.10 E
Mawson Peninsula ≻1	87	68.35 S	154.11 E
Maw Taung ∧	140	11.39 N	99.35 E
Maxiang	136	24.41 N	118.15 E
Maxixe	160	23.51 S	35.21 E
Maxville	176	45.17 N	74.51 W
Maxwell	178	39.17 N	122.11 W
Maxwell Bay C	172	74.35 N	89.00 W
Maxwelltown	106	55.04 N	3.38 W
May, Cape ≻	176	38.58 N	74.55 W
May, Isle of I	108	56.11 N	2.34 W
Mayaguana I	182	22.21 N	73.00 W
Mayaguana Passage ⋓	182	22.25 N	73.30 W
Mayagüez	182	18.12 N	67.09 W
Mayarí	182	20.40 N	75.41 W
Maybole	106	55.21 N	4.41 W
Maydena	168	42.55 S	146.30 E
Mayen	116	50.19 N	7.13 E
Mayenne	118	48.18 N	0.37 W
Mayenne □5	118	48.05 N	0.40 W
Mayenne ≃	118	47.30 N	0.33 W
Mayfield, Eng., U.K.	104	53.01 N	1.45 W
Mayfield, Ky., U.S.	174	36.44 N	88.38 W
May Inlet C	172	76.15 N	100.45 W
Maymyo	140	22.02 N	96.28 E
Maynooth	110	53.23 N	6.35 W
Mayo	172	63.35 N	135.54 W
Mayo □6	110	53.50 N	9.30 W
Mayon Volcano ∧1	138	13.15 N	123.41 E
Mayotte □8	156	12.50 S	45.10 E
Mayotte I	161a	12.50 S	45.10 E
May Pen	182	17.58 N	77.14 W
Mayrhofen	116	47.10 N	11.52 E
Mays Landing	176	39.27 N	74.44 W
Maysville	176	38.39 N	83.46 W
Mayumba	156	3.25 S	10.39 E
Māyūram	148	11.06 N	79.40 E
Mayville, Mich., U.S.	176	43.20 N	83.21 W
Mayville, N. Dak., U.S.	174	47.30 N	97.19 W
Mayville, N.Y., U.S.	176	42.15 N	79.30 W
Maza	188	36.48 S	63.20 W
Mazabuka	158	15.51 S	27.46 E
Mazagão	184	0.07 S	51.17 W
Mazamet	118	43.30 N	2.24 E
Mazara del Vallo	122	37.39 N	12.36 E
Mazār-e Sharīf	146	36.42 N	67.06 E
Mazarrón, Golfo de C	120	37.30 N	1.18 W
Mazaruni ≃	184	6.25 N	58.35 W
Mazatenango	180	14.32 N	91.30 W
Mazatlán	180	23.13 N	106.25 W
Mazoe ≃	158	16.32 S	33.25 E
Mazunga	158	21.45 S	29.52 E
Mazury •→1	116	53.45 N	21.00 E
Mbabala Island I	158	11.18 S	29.44 E
Mbabane	160	26.18 S	31.06 E
Mbaïki	154	3.53 N	18.00 E
Mbala (Abercorn)	158	8.50 S	31.22 E
Mbale	158	1.05 N	34.10 E
Mbalmayo	152	3.31 N	11.30 E
Mbamba Bay	158	11.17 S	34.46 E
Mbandaka (Coquilhatville)	156	0.04 N	18.16 E
Mbanza-Ngungu	156	5.15 S	14.52 E
Mbarara	158	0.37 S	30.39 E
Mbari ≃	154	4.34 N	22.43 E
Mbereshi Mission	158	9.45 S	28.46 E
Mbeya	158	8.54 S	33.27 E
Mbeya □4	158	8.30 S	33.00 E
Mbeya ∧	156	8.50 S	33.22 E
Mbinda	156	2.00 S	12.55 E
Mbomou (Bomu) ≃	154	4.08 N	22.26 E
Mbout	152	16.02 N	12.35 W
Mbuji-Mayi (Bakwanga)	156	6.09 S	23.38 E
Mburucuyá	188	28.02 S	58.15 W
Mc → Mac			
M'Clintock Channel ⋓	172	71.00 N	101.00 W
M'Clure, Cape ≻	172	74.35 N	121.08 W
M'Clure Strait ⋓	172	74.30 N	116.00 W
Mead, Lake ⊜1	178	36.05 N	114.25 W
Meadie, Loch ⊜	108	58.20 N	4.33 W
Meadow Valley Wash V	178	36.39 N	114.35 W
Meadville	174	41.38 N	80.09 W
Meaford	176	44.36 N	80.35 W
Me-akan-dake ∧	134a	43.23 N	144.01 E
Mealasta Isle I	108	58.05 N	7.08 W
Mealhada	120	40.22 N	8.27 W
Méan	116	50.22 N	5.20 E
Meandarra	168	27.20 S	149.53 E
Meander River	172	59.02 N	117.42 W
Measham	104	52.43 N	1.29 W
Meath □6	110	53.35 N	6.40 W
Meath □9	110	53.36 N	6.54 W
Meaux	118	48.57 N	2.52 E
Mecca → Makkah	144	21.27 N	39.49 E
Mechanic Falls	176	44.07 N	70.24 W
Mechanicsburg, Ohio, U.S.	176	40.04 N	83.34 W
Mechanicsburg, Pa., U.S.	176	40.13 N	77.01 W
Mechanicville	176	42.54 N	73.42 W
Mechelen	116	51.02 N	4.28 E
Mechlin → Mechelen	116	51.02 N	4.28 E
Mecidiye	124	40.38 N	26.32 E
Meckering	164	31.38 S	117.01 E
Mecklenburg □9	116	53.30 N	13.00 E
Mecklenburger Bucht C	116	54.20 N	11.40 E
Medan	140	3.35 N	98.40 E
Medanosa, Punta ≻	186	48.08 S	65.58 W
Médéa	120	36.12 N	2.50 E
Medellín	184	6.15 N	75.35 W
Medelpad □9	114	62.40 N	16.15 E
Médenine	152	32.21 N	10.30 E
Medford	174	42.19 N	122.52 W
Medgidia	124	44.15 N	28.16 E
Medi	158	5.04 N	30.44 E
Media	176	39.54 N	75.23 W
Media Luna, Arrecife de la ⤳2	182	15.14 N	82.39 W
Mediaş	124	46.10 N	24.21 E
Medicine Hat	172	50.03 N	110.40 W
Medina → Al-Madīnah, Ar. Sa.	150	24.28 N	39.36 E
Medina, N.Y., U.S.	176	43.13 N	78.23 W
Medina, Ohio, U.S.	176	41.08 N	81.52 W
Medina del Campo	120	41.18 N	4.55 W
Medina de Rioseco	120	41.53 N	5.02 W
Medina-Sidonia	120	36.27 N	5.55 W
Mediterranean Sea ⊤2	88	35.00 N	20.00 E
Mednogorsk	126	51.24 N	57.37 E
Mednyj, Ostrov I	128	54.45 N	167.35 E
Médoc •→1	118	45.20 N	1.00 W
Médouneu	156	0.57 N	10.47 E
Medstead	104	51.08 N	1.04 W
Meductic	176	46.00 N	67.29 W
Medvedica ≃	126	49.35 N	42.41 E
Medvežjegorsk	112	62.55 N	34.23 E
Medvežji Ostrova II	128	70.52 N	161.26 E
Medway	176	45.37 N	68.35 W
Medway ≃	102	51.27 N	0.44 E
Meeberrie	164	26.58 S	115.58 E
Meekatharra	164	26.36 S	118.29 E
Meeks Bay	178	39.02 N	120.08 W
Meelpaeg Lake ⊜1	172	48.16 N	56.35 W
Meentheena	164	21.17 S	120.28 E
Meerane	116	50.51 N	12.28 E
Meerut	146	28.59 N	77.42 E
Meese ≃	104	52.40 N	2.39 W
Mega	158	4.07 N	38.16 E
Mega, Pulau I	142	4.00 S	101.02 E
Megálon Khoríon	124	36.27 N	27.21 E
Mégantic, Lac ⊜	176	45.32 N	70.53 W
Mégara	124	38.01 N	23.21 E
Meghna ≃	144	22.50 N	90.50 E
Mehedinţi □4	124	44.30 N	22.50 E
Mehetia I	96	17.52 S	148.03 W
Mehsāna	146	23.36 N	72.24 E
Mehtar Lām	146	34.39 N	70.10 E
Meichuan	136	30.10 N	115.36 E
Meig ≃	108	57.34 N	4.41 W
Meigle	108	56.35 N	3.09 W
Meihua	136	26.02 N	119.40 E
Meikle Millyea ∧	106	55.07 N	4.19 W
Meikle Says Law ∧	108	55.55 N	2.40 W
Meiktila	140	20.52 N	95.52 E
Meiners Oaks	178	34.30 N	119.17 W
Meiningen	116	50.34 N	10.25 E
Meiringen	118	46.43 N	8.12 E
Meissen	116	51.10 N	13.28 E
Meiss Lake ⊜	178	41.52 N	122.04 W
Meixian	136	24.21 N	116.08 E
Meizhou	136	23.50 N	117.20 E
Meizhu	136	31.16 N	119.13 E
Mejillones	188	23.06 S	70.27 W
Mejillones del Sur, Bahía de C	188	23.03 S	70.27 W
Meka	164	27.26 S	116.48 E
Mekambo	156	1.01 N	13.56 E
Mekele	154	13.33 N	39.30 E
Mekerrhane, Sebkha ≌	152	26.19 N	1.20 E
Meknès	152	33.53 N	5.37 W
Mekong ≃	94	10.33 N	105.24 E
Mékrou ≃	152	12.24 N	2.49 E
Melado ≃	188	35.43 S	71.05 W
Melaka	142	2.12 N	102.15 E
Melanesia II	96	13.00 S	164.00 E
Melanesian Border Plateau ⤳3	96	11.00 S	179.00 E
Melawi ≃	142	0.05 N	111.29 E
Melbost	108	58.15 N	6.22 W
Melbourn	104	52.05 N	0.01 E
Melbourne, Austl.	168	37.49 S	144.58 E
Melbourne, Eng., U.K.	104	52.49 N	1.25 W
Melbourne, Fla., U.S.	174	28.05 N	80.37 W
Melbourne Island I	172	68.30 N	104.45 W
Melcombe Regis	104	50.38 N	2.28 W
Melderskin ∧	114	60.01 N	6.05 E
Meldorf	116	54.05 N	9.05 E
Meldrum Bay	176	45.56 N	83.07 W
Melegnano	122	45.21 N	9.19 E
Melekess	126	54.14 N	49.39 E
Meleuz	126	52.58 N	55.55 E
Mélèzes, Rivière aux ≃	172	57.40 N	69.29 W
Melfi, It.	122	40.59 N	15.40 E
Melfi, Tchad	154	11.04 N	17.56 E
Melfort, Sask., Can.	172	52.52 N	104.36 W
Melfort, Rh.	158	17.59 S	31.19 E
Melfort, Loch C	108	56.15 N	5.31 W
Melgaço	120	42.07 N	8.16 W
Melilla	120	35.19 N	2.58 W
Melipilla	188	33.42 S	71.13 W
Melita	172	49.16 N	101.00 W
Melitopol'	126	46.50 N	35.22 E
Melksham	104	51.23 N	2.09 W
Mellansel	114	63.26 N	18.19 E
Melle	118	46.13 N	0.09 W
Mellerud	114	58.42 N	12.28 E
Mellish Reef I[1]	162	17.25 S	155.50 E
Mellish Rise ⤳3	96	17.00 S	156.00 E
Mellon Udrigle	108	57.55 N	5.39 W
Mellor Glacier ⍓	87	73.30 S	66.30 E
Melmerby	106	54.44 N	2.35 W
Melmoth	160	28.38 S	31.24 E
Mělník	116	50.20 N	14.29 E
Melo	188	32.22 S	54.11 W
Melrhir, Chott ⊜	152	34.20 N	6.20 E
Melrose, Austl.	168	32.42 S	146.58 E
Melrose	108	55.36 N	2.44 W
Melsetter	158	19.48 S	32.50 E
Meltaus	112	66.54 N	25.22 E
Melton Constable	104	52.53 N	1.01 E
Melton Mowbray	104	52.46 N	0.53 W
Melun	118	48.32 N	2.40 E
Melviag	108	57.48 N	5.49 W
Melvich	108	58.33 N	3.55 W
Melville	172	50.55 N	102.48 W
Melville, Cape ≻	166	14.11 S	144.30 E
Melville, Détroit de → Viscount Melville Sound ⋓	172	74.10 N	113.00 W
Melville, Lake ⊜	172	53.45 N	59.30 W
Melville Bugt C	90	75.30 N	63.00 W
Melville Hills ⋀2	172	69.20 N	122.00 W
Melville Island I, Austl.	166	11.40 S	131.00 E
Melville Island I	90	75.15 N	110.00 W
Melville Peninsula ≻1	172	68.00 N	84.00 W
Melville Sound ⋓	172	68.05 N	107.30 W
Melvin, Lough ⊜	110	54.26 N	8.10 W
Mélykút	116	46.13 N	19.24 E
Melzo	122	45.30 N	9.25 E
Memboro	142	9.22 S	119.32 E
Memel, S. Afr.	160	27.43 S	29.30 E
Memel → Klaipėda, S.S.S.R.	130	55.43 N	21.07 E
Memmingen	116	47.59 N	10.11 E
Memo ≃	182	9.16 N	66.40 W
Mempawah	142	0.22 N	108.58 E
Memphis, Mich., U.S.	176	42.54 N	82.46 W
Memphis, Tenn., U.S.	174	35.08 N	90.03 W
Memsie	108	57.39 N	2.02 W
Menai Bridge	106	53.14 N	4.10 W
Menai Strait ⋓	106	53.12 N	4.12 W
Ménaka	152	15.55 N	2.24 E
Menangina	164	29.50 S	121.54 E
Mendawai ≃	142	3.17 S	113.21 E
Mende	118	44.30 N	3.30 E
Menden	116	51.26 N	7.47 E
Mendi, Pap. N. Gui.	166	6.10 S	143.40 E
Mendi, Yai.	154	9.50 N	35.06 E
Mendip Hills ⋀2	102	51.15 N	2.40 W
Mendlesham	104	52.16 N	1.05 E
Mendocino	178	39.19 N	123.48 W
Mendocino, Cape ≻	178	40.25 N	124.25 W
Mendocino Seascarp ⤳4	90	41.00 N	140.00 W
Mendon	176	42.00 N	85.27 W
Mendota	178	36.45 N	120.23 W
Mendoza	188	32.54 S	68.50 W
Mendoza □4	188	34.40 S	68.30 W
Ménéac	118	48.09 N	2.28 W
Mene de Mauroa	182	10.43 N	71.01 W
Mene Grande	182	9.49 N	70.56 W
Menén	118	50.48 N	3.07 E
Menfi	122	37.36 N	12.58 E
Mengcheng	136	33.17 N	116.33 E
Menggala	142	4.28 S	105.17 E
Menghai	140	22.00 N	100.26 E
Menghe	136	32.03 N	119.47 E
Menglian	140	22.20 N	99.38 E
Mengo □5	158	0.30 N	32.15 E
Mengzhi	140	23.22 N	103.20 E
Mengzi	140	24.10 N	99.46 E
Menihek Lakes ⊜	172	54.00 N	66.35 W
Menindee	168	32.24 S	142.26 E
Menindee Lake ⊜	168	32.21 S	142.20 E
Meningie	168	35.42 S	139.20 E
Menlo Park	178	37.28 N	122.13 W
Menongue	156	14.36 S	17.48 E
Menor, Mar C	120	37.43 N	0.48 W
Menorca I	120	40.00 N	4.00 E
Mentawai, Kepulauan II	138	2.00 S	99.30 E
Mentawai, Selat ⋓	142	1.56 S	100.12 E
Menton	118	43.47 N	7.30 E
Mentor	176	41.40 N	81.20 W
Menzel Bourguiba	122	37.10 N	9.48 E
Menzies	164	29.41 S	121.02 E
Menzies, Mount ∧	87	73.30 S	61.50 E
Meon ≃	104	50.48 N	1.15 W
Meoqui	174	28.17 N	105.29 W
Mepal	104	52.24 N	0.07 E
Meppel	116	52.42 N	6.11 E
Meppen	116	52.41 N	7.17 E
Mer	118	47.42 N	1.30 E
Meramangye, Lake ⊜	164	28.25 S	132.13 E
Merano (Meran)	122	46.40 N	11.09 E
Merauke	166	8.28 S	140.20 E
Merbein	168	34.11 S	142.04 E
Mercāra	144	12.26 N	75.45 E
Merced	178	37.18 N	120.29 W
Merced ≃	178	37.21 N	120.58 W
Merced, South Fork ≃	178	37.39 N	119.53 W
Mercedario, Cerro ∧	188	31.58 S	70.07 W
Mercedes, Arg.	188	29.10 S	58.02 W
Mercedes, Arg.	188	33.40 S	65.30 W
Mercedes, Arg.	188	34.40 S	59.25 W
Mercedes, Ur.	188	33.16 S	58.01 W
Mercer, N.Z.	170	37.16 S	175.03 E
Mercer, Pa., U.S.	176	41.14 N	80.15 W
Mercersburg	176	39.50 N	77.54 W
Merchants Bay C	172	67.10 N	62.50 W
Mercury	178	36.40 N	115.59 W
Mercury Islands II	170	36.35 S	175.55 E
Mercy Bay C	172	74.05 N	119.00 W
Mere	104	51.06 N	2.16 W
Meredith	176	43.39 N	71.30 W
Merenkurkku (Norra Kvarken) ⋓	114	63.36 N	20.43 E
Mergui (Myeik)	140	12.26 N	98.36 E
Mergui Archipelago II	140	12.00 N	98.00 E
Meribah	168	34.42 S	140.51 E
Meriç (Marica) (Évros) ≃	124	40.52 N	26.12 E
Mérida, Esp.	120	38.55 N	6.20 W
Mérida, Méx.	180	20.58 N	89.37 W
Mérida, Ven.	184	8.36 N	71.08 W
Mérida, Cordillera de ⋀	184	8.40 N	71.00 W
Meriden, Eng., U.K.	104	52.26 N	1.37 W
Meriden, Conn., U.S.	176	41.32 N	72.48 W
Meridian	174	32.22 N	88.42 W
Mérignac	118	44.50 N	0.42 W
Merikarvia	114	61.51 N	21.30 E
Merimbula	168	36.53 S	149.54 E
Merín, Laguna (Lagoa Mirim) C	188	32.45 S	52.50 W
Merinda	168	20.01 S	148.10 E
Meringur	168	34.24 S	141.16 E
Merir I	138	4.19 N	132.19 E
Merkendorf	116	49.12 N	10.42 E
Merlin, Ont., Can.	176	42.14 N	82.14 W
Merlin, Oreg., U.S.	178	42.31 N	123.25 W
Mernye	116	46.30 N	17.50 E
Meron, Hare ∧	150	32.58 N	35.25 E
Merredin	164	31.29 S	118.16 E
Merrick ∧	106	55.08 N	4.29 W
Merrickville	176	44.55 N	75.50 W
Merrill, Mich., U.S.	176	43.25 N	84.20 W
Merrill, Oreg., U.S.	178	42.01 N	121.36 W
Merriott	104	50.54 N	2.48 W
Merritt	172	50.07 N	120.47 W
Merriwa	168	32.08 S	150.21 E
Merrygoen	168	31.50 S	149.14 E
Merse V	108	55.39 N	2.15 W
Mersea Island I	102	51.47 N	0.55 E
Merseburg	116	51.21 N	11.59 E
Mers el Kébir	100	35.45 N	0.43 W
Mersey ≃, Austl.	168	41.10 S	146.22 E
Mersey ≃, Eng., U.K.	106	53.25 N	3.00 W
Merseyside □6	106	53.25 N	2.50 W
Mersin	150	36.48 N	34.38 E
Mersing	142	2.26 N	103.50 E
Merthyr Tydfil	104	51.46 N	3.23 W
Mértola	120	37.38 N	7.40 W
Merton •→8	104	51.25 N	0.12 W
Mertz Glacier Tongue ⍓	87	67.40 S	144.45 E
Meru	158	0.03 N	37.39 E
Meru ∧	156	3.14 S	36.45 E
Merweville	160	32.40 S	21.31 E
Méry	118	48.30 N	3.53 E
Merzig	116	49.27 N	6.36 E
Mesa	174	33.25 N	111.50 W
Mesagne	122	40.33 N	17.49 E
Meschede	116	51.20 N	8.17 E

Symbols in the index entries are identified on page 198.

Symbols in the index entries are identified on page 198.

Name	Page	Lat	Long
Morley, Eng., U.K.	106	53.46 N	1.36 W
Morley, Mich., U.S.	176	43.29 N	85.27 W
Mormon Peak ∧	178	36.57 N	114.38 W
Mormon Reservoir ⊜¹	178	43.16 N	114.49 W
Morney	188	25.22 S	141.28 E
Morningstar	110	52.27 N	8.41 W
Mornington	184	28.13 S	145.03 E
Mornington, Isla ▮	186	49.45 S	75.20 W
Mornington Island ▮	184	16.33 S	139.24 E
Morobe	158	7.45 S	147.35 E
Morocco □¹	152	32.00 N	5.00 W
Morogoro	158	6.49 S	37.40 E
Morogoro □⁴	158	8.00 S	37.00 E
Moro Gulf C	138	6.51 N	123.00 E
Morokweng	160	26.12 S	23.45 E
Morombe	161b	21.45 S	43.22 E
Morón, Arg.	188	34.39 S	58.37 W
Morón, Cuba	182	22.06 N	78.38 W
Morón, Mong.	132	49.38 N	100.10 E
Morona, Ven.	184	4.40 S	77.10 W
Morondava	161b	20.17 S	44.17 E
Morón de Almazán	120	41.25 N	2.25 W
Morón de la Frontera	120	37.08 N	5.27 W
Moroni	161a	11.41 S	43.16 E
Morošečnoje	128	56.24 N	156.12 E
Morotai ▮	138	2.20 N	128.25 E
Morozovsk	126	48.22 N	41.50 E
Morpeth	106	55.10 N	1.41 W
Morrettes	188	25.28 S	48.49 W
Morrinhos	190	17.44 S	49.07 W
Morrinsville	170	37.39 S	175.32 E
Morris	172	49.21 N	97.22 W
Morrisburg	176	44.54 N	75.11 W
Morris Jesup, Kap ⋗	90	83.38 N	33.52 W
Morristown	176	40.48 N	74.29 W
Morrisville, N.Y., U.S.	176	42.54 N	75.39 W
Morrisville, Pa., U.S.	176	40.13 N	74.47 W
Morrisville, Vt., U.S.	176	44.34 N	72.44 W
Morro, Punta ⋗	188	27.07 S	70.57 W
Morro Bay	178	35.22 N	120.51 W
Morro do Chapéu	184	11.33 S	41.09 W
Morrosquillo, Golfo de	182	9.35 N	75.40 W
Morrumbene	160	23.39 S	35.20 E
Moršansk	130	53.26 N	41.49 E
Mortagne	118	48.31 N	0.33 E
Mortana	164	33.02 S	134.07 E
Mortara	122	45.15 N	8.44 E
Morteau	118	47.04 N	6.37 E
Morte Point ⋗	104	51.11 N	4.13 W
Morteros	188	30.40 S	62.00 W
Mortlake	168	38.05 S	142.48 E
Morton Craig Range	164	28.12 S	124.41 E
Moruya	168	35.55 S	150.05 E
Morvan ∧	118	47.05 N	4.00 E
Morven, Austl.	168	26.25 S	147.07 E
Morven ∧, Scot., U.K.	108	58.14 N	3.42 W
Morven ∧, Scot., U.K.	108	57.07 N	3.02 W
Morvi	146	22.49 N	70.50 E
Morwell	168	38.14 S	146.24 E
Morwenstow	104	50.54 N	4.33 W
Morzalândia	190	14.47 S	50.35 W
Mosbach	118	49.21 N	9.08 E
Moscow → Moskva, S.S.S.R.	130	55.45 N	37.35 E
Moscow, Idaho, U.S.	174	46.44 N	117.00 W
Mosel (Moselle) ≊	118	50.22 N	7.36 E
Moselle ▮¹	118	49.00 N	6.30 E
Moselle (Mosel) ≊	118	50.22 N	7.36 E
Mosgiel	170	45.53 S	170.21 E
Moshi	158	3.21 S	37.20 E
Moshupa	160	24.50 S	25.31 E
Mosjøen	112	65.50 N	13.10 E
Moskva (Moscow)	112	67.59 N	13.00 E
Moskva (Moscow)	130	55.45 N	37.35 E
Mosquera	184	2.30 N	78.29 W
Mosquito, Punta ⋗	182	9.08 N	77.55 W
Mosquito Creek Lake ⊜¹	176	41.22 N	80.45 W
Mosquitos, Golfo de los	190	9.00 N	81.20 W
Moss	114	59.26 N	10.42 E
Mossaka	156	1.13 S	16.48 E
Mossbank	108	60.27 N	1.12 W
Mossburn	170	45.40 S	168.15 E
Mosselbaai	160	34.11 S	22.08 E
Mossendjo	156	2.57 S	12.44 E
Mossley	106	53.32 N	2.02 W
Mossman	166	16.28 S	145.22 E
Mossoró	184	5.11 S	37.20 W
Moss Vale	168	34.33 S	150.22 E
Most	116	50.32 N	13.39 E
Mostaganem	152	35.51 N	0.07 E
Mostar	122	43.20 N	17.49 E
Mostardas	188	31.06 S	50.57 W
Møsting, Kap ⋗	172	64.00 N	41.00 W
Mostiștea ≊	124	44.15 N	27.10 E
Mostyn	106	53.19 N	3.16 W
Mosul → Al-Mawsil	148	36.20 N	43.08 E
Mota	114	59.52 N	8.05 E
Mota del Cuervo	120	39.30 N	2.52 W
Mota del Marqués	120	41.38 N	5.10 W
Motagua ≊	182	15.44 N	88.14 W
Motala	114	58.33 N	15.03 E
Motatán	182	9.24 N	70.36 W
Motherwell	108	55.48 N	4.00 W
Motilla del Palancar	120	39.34 N	1.53 W
Motomachi	134a	34.45 S	139.21 E
Motril	120	36.45 N	3.31 W
Motru ≊	124	44.44 N	23.00 E
Mottisfont	104	51.02 N	1.32 W
Motu	170	37.54 N	81.10 W
Motueka	170	41.07 S	173.00 E
Motygino	128	58.11 N	94.40 E
Motykleja	128	59.26 N	148.38 E
Mouchoir Passage ⋓	182	21.15 N	71.00 W
Moudjéria	154	17.53 N	12.20 W
Mouila	156	1.52 S	11.01 E
Moulamein	168	35.05 S	144.02 E
Moulay-Idriss	152	34.03 N	5.29 W
Moulins	118	46.34 N	3.20 E
Moulins-la-Marche	118	48.39 N	0.29 E
Moulmein	140	16.30 N	97.38 E
Moulmeingyun	140	16.23 N	95.16 E
Moulouya, Oued ≊	152	35.05 N	2.25 W
Moultrie	174	31.11 N	83.47 W
Moundou	154	8.34 N	16.05 E
Moundsville	176	39.55 N	80.44 W
Moungahaumi ∧	170	38.18 S	177.40 E
Mounier, Mont ∧	118	44.09 N	6.58 E
Mountain ≊	172	65.41 N	128.50 W
Mountain Ash	104	51.42 N	3.24 W
Mountain City	178	41.50 N	115.58 W
Mountain Home	178	43.08 N	115.41 W
Mountain Nile (Baḥr al-Jabal) ≊	154	9.30 N	30.30 E
Mountain View	178	37.23 N	122.04 W
Mount Airy	176	39.23 N	77.09 W
Mount Alida	160	29.09 S	30.18 E
Mount Aylif	160	30.54 S	29.27 E
Mount Barker	164	34.38 S	138.52 E
Mount Bellew Bridge	110	53.28 N	8.30 W
Mount Brydges	176	42.54 N	81.29 W
Mount Carmel	176	39.13 N	80.21 W
Mount Clare	176	39.13 N	80.21 W
Mount Clemens	176	42.35 N	82.52 W
Mount Desert Island ▮	176	44.20 N	68.20 W
Mount Eba	168	30.12 S	135.40 E
Mount Forest	176	43.29 N	80.44 W
Mount Frere	160	30.53 S	29.00 E
Mount Gambier	168	37.50 S	140.46 E
Mount Garnet	166	17.41 S	145.07 E
Mount Gay	176	37.51 N	82.00 W
Mount Gilead	176	40.33 N	82.50 W
Mount Hagen	158	5.50 S	144.15 E
Mount Holly Springs	176	40.07 N	77.11 W
Mount Hope, Austl.	168	34.07 S	135.23 E
Mount Hope, W. Va., U.S.	176	37.54 N	81.10 W
Mount Isa	168	20.44 S	139.30 E
Mount Jackson	176	38.45 N	78.38 W
Mount Jewett	176	41.44 N	78.38 W
Mount Kisco	176	41.12 N	73.44 W
Mount Lebanon	176	40.23 N	80.03 W
Mount Magnet	164	28.04 S	117.49 E
Mount Manara	168	32.29 S	143.56 E
Mount Margaret	168	26.54 S	143.21 E
Mount Maunganui	170	37.37 S	176.11 E
Mountmellick	110	53.07 N	7.20 W
Mount Molloy	166	16.41 S	145.20 E
Mount Monger	164	30.59 S	121.53 E
Mount Morgan	168	23.39 S	150.23 E
Mount Morris, Mich., U.S.	176	43.07 N	83.42 W
Mount Morris, N.Y., U.S.	176	42.44 N	77.53 W
Mount Mulligan	168	16.51 S	144.52 E
Mount Olivet	176	38.32 N	84.02 W
Mount Orab	176	39.02 N	83.56 W
Mount Perry	168	25.11 S	151.39 E
Mount Pleasant, Ont., Can.	176	43.05 N	80.19 W
Mount Pleasant, Mich., U.S.	176	43.35 N	84.47 W
Mount Pleasant, Pa., U.S.	176	40.09 N	79.33 W
Mount Pleasant, Tex., U.S.	174	33.09 N	94.58 W
Mount Pocono	176	41.08 N	75.22 W
Mountrath	110	53.00 N	7.27 W
Mount Rebecca	164	26.48 S	135.10 E
Mount Roskill	170	36.55 S	174.45 E
Mount Sandiman	164	24.24 S	115.23 E
Mount Savage	176	39.42 N	78.53 W
Mount's Bay C	104	50.03 N	5.25 W
Mount Selinda	160	20.25 S	32.43 E
Mount Sterling, Ky., U.S.	176	38.04 N	83.56 W
Mount Sterling, Ohio, U.S.	176	39.43 N	83.16 W
Mount Stewart	160	33.10 S	24.26 E
Mount Surprise	168	18.09 S	144.19 E
Mount Union	176	40.23 N	77.53 W
Mount Vernon, Austl.	164	24.13 S	118.14 E
Mount Vernon, Ill., U.S.	174	38.19 N	88.55 W
Mount Vernon, Ohio, U.S.	176	40.23 N	82.29 W
Mount Vernon, Wash., U.S.	178	48.25 N	122.20 W
Mount Victory	176	40.32 N	83.31 W
Mount Wedge	168	33.29 S	135.10 E
Mount Willoughby	164	27.58 S	134.08 E
Mount Wolf	176	40.04 N	76.43 W
Moura, Austl.	168	24.35 S	149.58 E
Moura, Bra.	184	1.27 S	61.38 W
Moura, Port.	120	38.08 N	7.27 W
Mourdi, Dépression du ≠¹	154	18.10 N	23.00 E
Mourne ≊	110	54.49 N	7.28 W
Mourne Beg ≊	110	54.41 N	7.39 W
Mourne Mountains ∧²	110	54.10 N	6.05 W
Mousa ▮	108	60.00 N	1.11 W
Mouscron	118	50.44 N	3.13 E
Moussoro	154	13.39 N	16.29 E
Moutier	118	47.17 N	7.23 E
Moutohora	170	38.17 S	177.32 E
Moutong	142	0.28 N	121.13 E
Mouville	110	55.11 N	7.03 W
Mowangzui	136	30.31 N	113.34 E
Mowshera	149	34.01 N	71.59 E
Moxos, Llanos de ≊	184	15.00 S	65.00 W
Moy ≊	110	54.27 N	6.42 W
Moy, Cnoc ∧²	108	54.12 N	9.08 W
Moya	108	55.22 N	5.46 W
Moyagee	164	27.45 S	117.54 E
Moyale, Kenya	158	3.32 N	39.03 E
Moyale, Yai.	158	3.30 N	39.07 E
Moyamba	152	8.10 N	12.26 W
Moycullen	110	53.21 N	9.09 W
Moyen Atlas ∧¹	152	33.30 N	5.00 W
Moyeuvre-Grande	118	49.15 N	6.02 E
Moyle ≊	110	52.24 N	7.39 W
Moyo, Pulau ▮	142	8.15 S	117.34 E
Moyobamba	184	6.02 S	76.58 W
Moyu	146	37.17 N	79.44 E
Mozajsk	130	55.30 N	36.01 E
Mozambique □¹	156	18.15 S	35.00 E
Mozambique Channel ⋓	156	19.00 S	41.00 E
Mozambique Plateau ⊹³	88	34.00 S	35.00 E
Mozdok	126	43.44 N	44.38 E
Mozga	112	56.23 N	52.17 E
Mozyr'	130	52.03 N	29.14 E
Mpanda	158	6.22 S	31.02 E
Mpika	158	11.54 S	31.26 E
Mpraeso	152	6.35 N	0.44 W
Mpulungu	158	8.46 S	31.07 E
Mpwapwa	158	6.21 S	36.29 E
Mragowo	116	53.52 N	21.19 E
Msaken	122	35.44 N	10.35 E
M'Sila	152	35.46 N	4.31 E
Msoro Mission	158	13.36 S	31.55 E
Mtamvuna ≊	160	31.06 S	30.12 E
Mtilikwe ≊	158	21.09 S	31.30 E
Mtoko	158	17.24 S	32.13 E
Mtubatuba	160	28.30 S	32.08 E
Mtwara	158	10.16 S	40.11 E
Mtwara □⁴	158	10.00 S	39.00 E
Mu, Cerro ∧	182	9.29 N	73.47 W
Muang Khammouan	140	17.24 N	104.48 E
Muang Không	140	14.07 N	105.51 E
Muang Khôngxédôn	140	15.34 N	105.49 E
Muang Pak-Lay	140	18.12 N	101.25 E
Muang Pakxan	140	18.22 N	103.39 E
Muang Sing	140	21.11 N	101.09 E
Muang Vangviang	140	18.56 N	102.27 E
Muang Xaignabouri	140	19.15 N	101.45 E
Muar (Bandar Maharani)	142	2.02 N	102.34 E
Muara	142	5.02 N	115.02 E
Muaradua	142	4.32 S	104.05 E
Muaraenim	142	3.39 S	103.48 E
Muaralabuh	142	1.29 S	101.03 E
Muaratembesi	142	1.30 S	102.26 E
Muaratewe	142	1.42 S	103.07 E
Muasdale	108	55.36 N	5.41 W
Mubende	158	0.35 N	31.23 E
Much Dewchurch	104	51.59 N	2.46 W
Muchea	164	31.35 S	115.59 E
Mücheln	116	51.18 N	11.48 E
Muchinga Escarpment ∴⁴	158	13.40 S	31.00 E
Muchinga Mountains ∧	158	12.00 S	31.45 E
Muchtolovo	130	55.27 N	43.13 E
Much Wenlock	104	52.36 N	2.34 W
Muck ▮	108	56.50 N	6.15 W
Muckadilla	168	26.35 S	148.23 E
Muckle Roe ▮	108a	60.22 N	1.27 W
Mud ≊	188	13.00 S	41.33 W
Mud ≊	176	38.25 N	82.17 W
Mu Gia, Deo)(	140	17.40 N	105.47 E
Mugodžary ∧²	126	49.00 N	58.40 E
Mugron	118	43.45 N	0.45 W
Muḥammad, Ra's ⋗	154	27.44 N	34.15 E
Muhola	114	63.20 N	25.05 E
Muhos	114	64.48 N	25.59 E
Muick, Loch ⊜	108	56.55 N	3.10 W
Muine Bheag	110	52.41 N	6.58 W
Muirdrum	108	56.31 N	2.42 W
Muirkirk	108	55.31 N	4.04 W
Muir of Ord	108	57.31 N	4.27 W
Muiron Islands ▮▮	164	21.35 S	114.20 E
Muir Seamount ⋗³	90	33.30 N	62.30 W
Muirtown	108	56.16 N	3.45 W
Muiu	158	12.06 S	24.57 E
Mujimbeji Mission	158	12.11 S	24.57 E
Mujnak	126	43.48 N	59.02 E
Mukačevo	116	48.27 N	22.45 E
Mukah	138	2.54 N	112.06 E
Mukalla → Al-Mukallā	144	14.32 N	49.08 E
Mukinbudin	164	30.54 S	118.13 E
Mukinge Hill	158	13.29 S	25.52 E
Mukomuko	142	2.35 S	101.07 E
Mukry	150	37.36 N	65.44 E
Muktsar	149	30.29 N	74.31 E
Mukutan	158	0.38 N	36.16 E
Mula	120	38.03 N	1.30 W
Mulanje	158	16.03 S	35.31 E
Mulanje Mountains ∧²	158	15.58 S	35.38 E
Mulatupo	182	8.56 N	77.46 W
Mulben	108	57.31 N	3.06 W
Mulchatna ≊	172	59.39 N	157.08 W
Mulchén	188	37.43 S	72.14 W
Mulde ≊	116	51.10 N	12.48 E
Mulga Downs	164	22.08 S	118.26 E
Mulgathing	164	30.15 S	134.00 E
Mulgowie	168	27.43 S	152.22 E
Mulgul	164	24.49 S	118.26 E
Mulhacén ∧	120	37.03 N	3.19 W
Mulhouse	118	47.45 N	7.20 E
Mulkear ≊	110	52.40 N	8.33 W
Mull, Island of ▮	108	56.25 N	5.54 W
Mull, Sound of ⋓	108	56.32 N	5.50 W
Mullagh	110	53.49 N	6.57 W
Mullaghareirk ∧	110	52.20 N	9.10 W
Mullaghcleevaun ∧	110	53.06 N	6.23 W
Mullaghmore ∧	110	54.52 N	6.50 W
Mullengudgery	168	31.41 S	147.26 E
Muller, Pegunungan ∧	142	0.40 N	113.50 E
Mullet Peninsula ⋗¹	110	54.12 N	10.00 W
Mullewa	164	28.33 S	115.31 E
Mull Head ⋗, Scot., U.K.	108	58.58 N	2.43 W
Mull Head ⋗, Scot., U.K.	108	59.23 N	2.54 W
Mullica ≊	176	39.33 N	74.25 W
Mullinahone	110	52.30 N	7.30 W
Mullinavat	110	52.21 N	7.10 W
Mullingar	110	53.32 N	7.20 W
Mullion	104	50.01 N	5.15 W
Mullumbimby	168	28.33 S	153.30 E
Multan	149	30.11 N	71.29 E
Mulungushi	158	14.40 S	28.50 E
Mumbles Head ⋗	104	51.35 N	3.59 W
Mumbwa	158	14.59 S	27.04 E
Muna ≊	140	15.19 N	105.30 E
Muna, Pulau ▮	142	5.00 S	122.30 E
Münchberg	116	50.11 N	11.47 E
München (Munich)	116	48.08 N	11.34 E
Muncie	174	40.11 N	85.23 W
Muncy	176	41.12 N	76.47 W
Mundaring	164	31.54 S	116.10 E
Münden	116	51.25 N	9.39 E
Mundesley	104	52.52 N	1.26 E
Mundo ≊	120	38.19 N	1.40 W
Mundo Novo	190	11.52 S	40.28 W
Mundrabilla	164	31.52 S	127.51 E
Mundubbera	168	25.36 S	151.18 E
Munera	120	39.02 N	2.28 W
Mungallala	168	26.27 S	147.33 E
Mungallala Creek ≊	168	28.05 S	147.15 E
Mungana	168	17.07 S	144.24 E
Mungar Junction	168	25.36 S	152.36 E
Mungbere	158	2.38 N	28.30 E
Mungeranie	168	28.00 S	138.36 E
Mungindi	168	28.58 S	148.59 E
Munhango	156	12.12 S	18.42 E
Munich → München	116	48.08 N	11.34 E
Muniesa	120	41.02 N	0.48 W
Munku-Sardyk, Gora ∧	128	51.45 N	100.32 E
Munlochy	108	57.32 N	4.15 W
Munnens Corners	176	42.35 N	76.13 W
Münster, B.R.D.	116	51.57 N	7.37 E
Münster, B.R.D.	118	52.59 N	10.05 E
Münster □⁹	110	52.25 N	8.20 W
Muntadgin	164	31.45 S	118.34 E
Muntok	142	2.04 S	105.11 E
Muonionjoki ≊	112	67.11 N	23.34 E
Muong Ngoi	140	20.43 N	102.41 E
Muong Sing	132	21.11 N	101.09 E
Muonio	112	67.57 N	23.42 E
Muoro	122	40.20 N	17.30 E
Muqayshiţ ▮	150	24.12 N	53.42 E
Mur (Mura) ≊	116	46.18 N	16.53 E
Mura (Mur) ≊	116	46.18 N	16.53 E
Murakami	134	38.14 N	139.29 E
Muramvya	158	3.16 S	29.37 E
Murana	166	3.33 S	133.49 E
Muraši	112	59.24 N	48.55 E
Murat ≊	148	38.39 N	39.50 E
Murau	116	47.07 N	14.10 E
Murayama	134	38.28 N	140.22 E
Murchison, Austl.	168	36.37 S	145.14 E
Murchison, N.Z.	170	41.48 S	172.20 E
Murchison ≊	164	27.42 S	114.09 E
Murchison, Mount ∧	158	2.17 N	31.41 E
Murchison Falls ╨	158	2.17 N	31.41 E
Murchison Range ∧	164	20.01 S	134.26 E
Murcia	120	37.59 N	1.07 W
Murcia □⁴	120	38.00 N	1.45 W
Murdo	174	43.53 N	100.43 W
Mur-de-Barrez	118	44.51 N	2.39 E
Mureck	116	46.42 N	15.46 E
Murefte	124	40.36 N	27.24 E
Mureş (Maros) ≊	124	46.35 N	20.13 E
Muret	118	43.28 N	1.21 E
Murfreesboro	174	35.51 N	86.23 W
Murgab	126	38.10 N	73.59 E
Murgab (Morghāb) ≊	150	36.50 N	61.12 E
Murgon	168	26.15 S	151.57 E
Múrgos de Paredes	120	42.57 N	2.49 W
Murilo ▮¹	96	8.40 N	152.11 E
Müritz ⊜	116	53.25 N	12.43 E
Muriwai	170	38.46 S	177.55 E
Murmansk	112	68.58 N	33.05 E
Murmansk Rise ⋗³	90	72.00 N	35.00 E
Murmino	130	54.36 N	40.03 E
Murnau	116	47.40 N	11.12 E
Muro, Capo di ⋗	122	41.44 N	8.40 E
Muroran	134a	42.18 N	140.59 E
Muros	120	42.46 N	9.02 W
Muroto-zaki ⋗	134	33.15 N	134.11 E
Murphy	178	43.13 N	116.33 W
Murphys	178	38.08 N	120.28 W
Murra Murra	168	28.16 S	146.48 E
Murray ≊	164	36.37 N	88.19 W
Murray, Lake ⊜¹	174	34.07 N	81.18 W
Murray Bay → La Malbaie	172	47.39 N	70.10 W
Murray Bridge	168	35.07 S	139.17 E
Murray City	178	39.31 N	82.10 W
Murray Downs	164	21.04 S	134.40 E
Murray Fracture Zone ⊹⁶		34.00 N	133.00 W
Murray Maxwell Bay C	172	70.00 N	80.00 W
Murray Ridge ⋗³		22.00 N	61.00 E
Murraysburg	160	31.58 S	23.47 E
Murree	149	33.54 N	73.24 E
Murrin Murrin	164	28.55 S	121.49 E
Murrumbidgee ≊	168	34.43 S	143.12 E
Murrumburrah	168	34.33 S	148.21 E
Murrurundi	168	31.46 S	150.50 E
Murska Sobota	122	46.40 N	16.10 E
Murtajāpur	148	20.44 N	77.23 E
Murtee	168	31.35 S	143.30 E
Murten	118	46.56 N	7.07 E
Murtoa	168	36.37 S	142.28 E
Murton	106	54.49 N	1.24 W
Murtosa	120	40.44 N	8.38 W
Murud, Gunong ∧	142	3.52 N	115.30 E
Murukta	128	67.46 N	102.01 E
Murupara	170	38.27 S	176.42 E
Murwāra	146	23.51 N	80.24 E
Murwillumbah	168	28.19 S	153.24 E
Mürzzuschlag	116	47.36 N	15.41 E
Muş	148	38.44 N	41.30 E
Mūsā, Jabal (Mount Sinai) ∧	154	28.32 N	33.59 E
Mūsā Khel	149	32.38 N	71.44 E
Musala ∧	124	42.11 N	23.34 E
Musay'īd	150	24.59 N	51.32 E
Muscat → Masqaţ	150	23.37 N	58.35 E
Muscat and Oman → Oman □¹	150	22.00 N	58.00 E
Muscatine	174	41.25 N	91.03 W
Mus-Chaja, Gora ∧	128	62.35 N	140.50 E
Muscongus Bay C	176	43.55 N	69.20 W
Musengezi ≊	158	15.43 S	31.14 E
Musgrave	166	14.47 S	143.30 E
Mushie	156	3.01 S	16.54 E
Mushin	158	23.36 N	117.06 E
Mushina	158	14.13 S	26.25 E
Mushin	152	6.32 N	3.22 E
Musi ≊	142	2.20 S	104.56 E
Musishan ∧	146	36.03 N	80.07 E
Muskegon	174	43.14 N	86.16 W
Muskegon ≊	176	43.25 S	85.42 W
Muskogee	174	35.45 N	95.22 W
Muskoka, Lake ⊜	176	45.00 N	79.25 W
Muskrat Lake ⊜	176	45.40 N	76.55 W
Muskwa ≊	172	58.45 N	122.35 W
Musofu Mission	158	13.31 S	29.02 E
Musoma	158	1.30 S	33.48 E
Mussau Island ▮	158	1.30 S	149.40 E
Musselburgh	108	55.57 N	3.04 W
Musselshell ≊	174	47.21 N	107.57 W
Mussomeli	122	37.35 N	13.46 E
Mussuma	156	14.14 S	21.59 E
Muswellbrook	168	32.16 S	150.53 E
Mutambara Mission	158	19.36 S	32.33 E
Mutanda Mission	158	12.24 S	26.16 E
Muthill	108	56.19 N	3.50 W
Mutoraj	128	61.20 N	100.30 E
Mutsamudu	161a	12.09 S	44.25 E
Mutsu	134	41.17 N	141.10 E
Mutsu-wan C	134	41.05 N	140.55 E
Muttaburra	168	22.36 S	144.33 E
Mutton Bird Islands ▮▮	170	47.15 S	167.24 E
Muxima	156	9.31 S	13.56 E
Muyaga	158	3.14 S	30.33 E
Muyang	136	27.06 N	119.34 E
Muyinga	158	2.51 S	30.20 E
Muyumba	158	7.15 S	26.59 E
Muzaffarābād	149	34.22 N	73.28 E
Muzaffargarh	149	30.04 N	71.12 E
Muzaffarnagar	146	29.28 N	77.41 E
Muzaffarpur	146	26.07 N	85.24 E
Muži	126	65.24 N	64.40 E
Muzillac	118	47.33 N	2.29 W
Muzoka	158	16.41 S	27.19 E
Mwadui	158	3.33 S	33.36 E
Mwanza	158	2.31 S	32.54 E
Mwanza □⁴	158	2.45 S	32.45 E
Mweelrea ∧	110	53.38 N	9.50 W
Mweka	156	4.51 S	21.34 E
Mweru, Lake ⊜	158	9.00 S	28.45 E
Mweru Wantipa, Lake ⊜	158	8.45 S	29.40 E
Mwinilunga	158	11.44 S	24.26 E
Mwombezhi ≊	158	12.52 S	25.00 E
Myanaung	140	18.17 N	95.19 E
Myaungmya	140	16.36 N	94.56 E
Mybster	108	58.27 N	3.25 W
Myerstown	176	40.22 N	76.18 W
Myingyan	140	21.28 N	95.23 E
Myitkyinā	140	25.23 N	97.24 E
Myjava	116	48.45 N	17.34 E
Myllymäki	114	62.32 N	24.18 E
Mymensingh	146	24.45 N	90.24 E
Mynfontein	160	30.55 S	23.57 E
Mynydd Bach ∧²	104	52.15 N	4.05 W
Mynydd Eppynt ∧	104	52.05 N	3.30 W
Mynydd Hiraethog ∧	104	53.05 N	3.33 W
Mynydd Pencarreg ∧²	104	52.04 N	4.04 W
Myōkō-zan ∧	134	36.52 N	138.07 E
Myroodah	164	18.08 S	124.16 E
Myrskylä (Mörskom)	114	60.40 N	25.51 E
Myrtle Creek	178	43.01 N	123.17 W
Myrtle Point	178	43.03 N	124.08 W
Myrtletowne	178	40.47 N	124.04 W
Myski	128	53.42 N	87.48 E
Mysłenice	116	49.51 N	19.56 E
Mysłowice	116	50.15 N	19.07 E
Mysore	148	12.18 N	76.39 E
Mys Smidta	128	68.56 N	179.26 W
Mys Vchodnoj	128	73.21 N	86.43 E
Mys Želanija	128	76.57 N	68.35 E
Myszków	116	50.36 N	19.20 E
My-tho	140	10.21 N	106.21 E
Mytišči	130	55.55 N	37.46 E
Mzimba	158	11.54 S	33.36 E
Mzimvubu ≊	160	31.38 S	29.32 E
Mzuzu	158	11.27 S	33.55 E
N			
Na (Tengtiaohe) ≊	140	22.05 N	103.09 E
Naab ≊	116	49.01 N	12.02 E
Naalehu	179a	19.04 N	155.35 W
Naas	110	53.13 N	6.39 W
Nabadwip	146	23.25 N	88.22 E
Nabberu, Lake ⊜	164	25.52 S	120.30 E
Nabburg	116	49.26 N	12.11 E
Naberežnyje Čelny	112	55.42 N	52.19 E
Nabeul	122	36.27 N	10.44 E
Nābha	149	30.22 N	76.09 E
Nabire	166	3.22 S	135.29 E
Nabk Shu'ayb, Jabal an- ∧	144	15.18 N	43.59 E
Nabq	150	28.04 N	34.25 E
Nābulus	150	32.13 N	35.16 E
Nacala-Velha	158	14.32 S	40.37 E
Nacereddine ∧	152	33.13 N	3.26 E
Nachičevan'	126	39.13 N	45.24 E
Nachi-katsuura	134	33.37 N	135.56 E
Nachingwea	158	10.23 S	38.46 E
Nachodka	132	42.48 N	132.52 E
Nachvak Fiord C²	172	59.03 N	63.45 W
Nacimiento	188	37.30 S	72.40 W
Nacimiento Reservoir ⊜¹	178	35.45 N	121.00 W
Nacka	114	59.18 N	18.10 E
Nacogdoches	174	31.36 N	94.39 W
Nacozari	180	30.25 N	109.38 W
Nadder ≊	104	51.03 N	1.55 W
Nador	152	35.12 N	2.55 W
Nadym ≊	126	65.12 N	72.22 E
Næstved	114	55.14 N	11.46 E
Näfels	118	47.06 N	9.04 E
Nafūd, An- ≈²	144	28.30 N	41.00 E
Naga	138	13.37 N	123.11 E
Nagahama, Nihon	134	35.23 N	136.16 E
Nagahama, Nihon	134	33.35 N	132.29 E
Naga Hills ∧²	140	26.00 N	95.00 E
Nagai	134	38.06 N	140.02 E
Nagaland □⁴	146	26.00 N	94.30 E
Nagambie	168	36.48 S	145.09 E
Nagano	134	36.39 N	138.11 E
Nagaoka	134	37.27 N	138.51 E
Nagappattinam	148	10.46 N	79.51 E
Nagara ≊	134	35.01 N	136.43 E
Nagarote	182	12.16 N	86.34 W
Nagasaki	134	32.48 N	129.55 E
Nagashima	134	34.12 N	136.20 E
Nagato	134	34.21 N	131.10 E
Nagaur	146	27.12 N	73.44 E
Nāgda	146	23.27 N	75.25 E
Nagercoil	148	8.10 N	77.26 E
Nagichot	158	4.16 N	33.34 E
Nago	135b	26.35 N	127.59 E
Nagornyj	128	55.58 N	124.57 E
Nagoya	134	35.10 N	136.55 E
Nāgpur	146	21.09 N	79.06 E
Nagua	182	19.23 N	69.50 W
Nagyatád	116	46.14 N	17.22 E
Nagykanizsa	116	46.27 N	17.00 E
Nagykőrös	116	47.02 N	19.43 E
Nagy-Milic ∧	116	48.35 N	21.28 E
Naha	135b	26.13 N	127.40 E
Nāhan	149	30.33 N	77.18 E
Nahariyya	150	33.00 N	35.05 E
Nahe ≊	116	49.58 N	7.58 E
Nahuel Huapi, Lago ⊜	186	41.00 S	71.32 W
Naidong	132	29.14 N	31.46 E
Naila	116	50.19 N	11.42 E
Nailsea	104	51.26 N	2.43 W
Nailsworth	104	51.42 N	2.14 W
Nain, Newf., Can.	172	56.32 N	61.41 W
Na'īn, Īrān	150	32.52 N	53.05 E
Naini Tāl	146	29.23 N	79.28 E
Nairn	108	57.35 N	3.53 W
Nairobi	158	1.17 S	36.49 E
Naivasha	158	0.43 S	36.26 E
Najac	118	44.17 N	2.00 E
Najafābād	150	32.37 N	51.21 E
Najasa ≊	182	20.42 N	77.58 W
Najd ∴¹	144	25.00 N	44.30 E
Najin	132	42.15 N	130.18 E
Najramdal Uul ∧	132	49.10 N	87.52 W
Naka ≊	134	36.20 N	140.36 E
Nakadōri-shima ▮	134	32.57 N	129.04 E
Nakajō	134	38.03 N	139.24 E
Nakama	134	33.50 N	130.43 E
Nakaminato	134	36.21 N	140.36 E
Nakamura	134	32.59 N	133.00 E
Nakano	134	36.45 N	138.22 E
Nakano-shima ▮	135b	29.49 N	129.52 E
Nakanoshima-suidō ⋓	135b	29.44 N	129.49 E
Nakatsu	134	33.34 N	131.13 E
Nakatsugawa	134	33.30 N	137.30 E
Nakhon Nayok	140	14.12 N	101.13 E
Nakhon Pathom	140	13.49 N	100.03 E
Nakhon Phanom	140	17.24 N	104.47 E
Nakhon Ratchasima	140	14.58 N	102.07 E
Nakhon Sawan	140	15.41 N	100.07 E
Nakhon Si Thammarat	140	8.26 N	99.58 E
Nakina	172	50.10 N	86.42 W
Nakło nad Notecią	116	53.08 N	17.35 E
Nakodar	149	31.07 N	75.29 E
Nakskov	114	54.50 N	11.09 E
Nakuru	158	0.17 S	36.04 E
Nal'čik	126	43.29 N	43.37 E
Nalgonda	148	17.03 N	79.16 E
Närke ◻⁹	114	59.00 N	15.03 E
Narmada ≊	146	21.38 N	72.36 E
Nārnaul	146	28.03 N	76.07 E
Narni	122	42.31 N	12.31 E
Naro	122	37.17 N	13.48 E
Narodnaja, Gora ∧	112	65.04 N	60.09 E
Naro-Fominsk	130	55.23 N	36.43 E
Narooma	168	36.14 S	150.08 E
Närowāl	149	32.06 N	74.52 E
Narrabri	168	30.19 S	149.47 E
Narran ≊	168	29.45 S	147.20 E
Narrandera	168	34.45 S	146.33 E
Narrogin	164	32.56 S	117.10 E
Narromine	168	32.14 S	148.15 E
Narsimhapur	146	22.57 N	79.12 E
Narsinghgarh	146	23.42 N	77.06 E
Narsipatnam	148	17.40 N	82.37 E
Narssaq	172	60.54 N	46.00 W
Naru ≊	134	32.49 N	128.56 E
Narva	130	59.23 N	28.12 E
Narvik	112	68.26 N	17.25 E
Narwāna	149	29.37 N	76.07 E
Narwietooma	164	23.15 S	132.35 E
Nar'jan-Mar	112	67.39 N	53.00 E
Naryn	132	41.26 N	75.59 E
Naryn ≊	126	40.54 N	71.45 E
Nasa ∧	112	66.29 N	15.23 E
Näsåker	114	63.26 N	16.54 E
Nase → Naze	135b	28.23 N	129.30 E
Naseby, N.Z.	170	45.02 S	170.09 E
Naseby, Eng., U.K.	104	52.24 N	0.59 W
Nash Point ⋗	104	51.24 N	3.33 W
Nashua	176	42.45 N	71.27 W
Nashville, Mich., U.S.	176	42.36 N	85.05 W
Nashville, Tenn., U.S.	174	36.09 N	86.48 W
Näsijärvi ⊜	114	61.37 N	23.42 E
Nasīrābād	146	26.18 N	74.44 E
Naskaupi ≊	172	53.47 N	60.51 W
Nass ≊	172	55.00 N	129.50 W
Nassau	182	25.05 N	77.21 W
Nassau, Bra.	190	19.41 S	43.20 W
Nassau, N.Y., U.S.	176	42.31 N	73.37 W
Nasser, Lake ⊜¹	154	22.40 N	32.00 E
Nastapoka Islands ▮▮	172	56.55 N	76.33 W
Nasu	134	37.06 N	140.03 E
Nasu-dake ∧	134	37.07 N	139.58 E
Natal, Bra.	184	5.47 S	35.13 W
Natal, Indon.	142	0.33 N	99.07 E
Natal □⁴	160	28.40 S	30.30 E
Natashquan	172	50.11 N	61.49 W
Natchez	174	31.33 N	91.23 W
Natchitoches	174	31.46 N	93.05 W
Näthdwāra	146	24.56 N	73.49 E
Natick	176	42.17 N	71.21 W
Natimuk	168	36.45 S	141.57 E
National City	178	32.40 N	117.06 W
Natron, Lake ⊜	158	2.25 S	36.00 E
Nattastunturit ∧	112	68.12 N	27.27 E
Natuna Besar ▮¹	142	4.00 N	108.15 E
Naturaliste, Cape ⋗	164	33.32 S	115.01 E
Naturaliste Channel ⋓	164	25.25 S	113.00 E
Nauen	116	52.36 N	12.52 E
Naugatuck	176	41.29 N	73.03 W
Naumburg	116	51.09 N	11.48 E
Nauru □¹	96	0.32 S	166.55 E
Naustdal	114	61.31 N	5.43 E
Nautla	180	20.13 N	96.47 W
Navalcarnero	120	40.17 N	4.00 W
Navalmoral de la Mata	120	39.54 N	5.32 W
Navalvillar de Pela	120	39.06 N	5.27 W
Navan	110	53.39 N	6.41 W
Navarin, Mys ⋗	128	62.16 N	179.10 E
Navarino, Isla ▮	186	55.05 S	67.40 W
Navarra □⁴	120	42.40 N	1.30 W
Navarro	188	35.00 S	59.16 W
Navašino	130	55.32 N	42.12 E
Navassa Island ▮	182	18.24 N	75.01 W
Navdjong	149	25.30 N	90.56 E
Navia ≊	120	43.33 N	6.44 W
Navl'a	130	52.51 N	34.30 E
Navoja	180	27.06 N	109.26 W

Name	Page	Lat ° ′	Long ° ′
Návpaktos	124	38.23 N	21.50 E
Návplion	124	37.34 N	22.48 E
Navsāri	146	20.51 N	72.55 E
Nawābganj	146	24.36 N	88.17 E
Nawābshāh	146	26.15 N	68.25 E
Nawalgarh	146	27.51 N	75.16 E
Nawāshahr	149	31.07 N	76.08 E
Náxos I	124	37.02 N	25.35 E
Nayarit	178	32.20 N	115.19 W
Nayland	104	51.59 N	0.52 E
Nayoro	134a	44.21 N	142.28 E
Nazaré, Bra.	190	13.02 S	39.00 W
Nazaré, Port.	120	39.36 N	9.04 W
Nazareth	176	40.44 N	75.19 W
Nazareth Bank ⊹[4]	94	14.30 S	60.45 E
Nazarovo	128	56.01 N	90.26 E
Nazas	180	25.14 N	104.08 W
Nazca	184	14.50 S	74.55 W
Naze	135b	28.23 N	129.30 E
N'azepetrovsk	126	56.03 N	59.36 E
Nazija	130	59.50 N	31.35 E
Nazwā	150	22.56 N	57.32 E
Nazyvajevsk	126	55.34 N	71.21 E
Nchanga	158	12.30 S	27.53 E
Nchelenge	158	9.20 S	28.50 E
Ndabala	158	13.28 S	29.50 E
Ndélé	154	8.24 N	20.39 E
Ndendé	156	2.23 S	11.23 E
Ndjamena (Fort-Lamy)	152	12.07 N	15.03 E
Ndjolé	156	0.11 S	10.45 E
Ndola	158	12.58 S	28.38 E
Nea ≃	114	63.13 N	11.02 E
Neabul Creek ≃	168	27.45 S	147.32 E
Neagh, Lough ⊜	110	54.37 N	6.25 W
Neale, Lake ⊜	164	24.22 S	130.00 E
Neales ≃	168	28.08 S	136.47 E
Neamț □[4]	124	47.00 N	26.30 E
Néa Páfos (Paphos)	150	34.45 N	32.25 E
Neápolis	124	35.15 N	25.37 E
Neath	104	51.40 N	3.48 W
Neath ≃	104	51.37 N	3.50 W
Nebine Creek ≃	168	29.07 S	146.56 E
Nebit-Dag	150	39.30 N	54.22 E
Nebolči	130	59.08 N	33.18 E
Nebraska □[3]	174	41.30 N	100.00 W
Nebraska City	174	40.41 N	95.52 W
Nechako ≃	172	53.56 N	122.42 W
Nechmeya	122	36.36 N	7.31 E
Neckar ≃	116	49.31 N	8.26 E
Neckarsulm	116	49.12 N	9.13 E
Necochea	188	38.34 S	58.45 W
Nédroma	120	35.01 N	1.45 W
Nedstrand	114	59.21 N	5.51 E
Needham Market	104	52.09 N	1.03 E
Needles	178	34.51 N	114.37 W
Ñeembucú □[5]	188	27.00 S	58.00 W
Neepawa	172	50.13 N	99.29 W
Nefern ≃	104	52.02 N	4.50 W
Neftečala	150	39.23 N	49.16 E
Nefyn	104	52.57 N	4.31 W
Negage	156	7.45 S	15.16 E
Negara	142	8.22 S	114.37 E
Negele	158	5.20 N	39.36 E
Negombo	148	7.13 N	79.50 E
Negotin	124	44.14 N	22.32 E
Negra, Cordillera ⛰	184	9.30 S	77.30 W
Negra, Laguna ⊜	188	34.03 S	53.40 W
Negra, Punta ➤	184	6.06 S	81.10 W
Negritos	184	4.36 S	81.15 W
Negro ≃, Arg.	186	41.02 S	62.47 W
Negro ≃, Bol.	184	14.11 S	63.07 W
Negro ≃, Bra.	188	26.01 S	50.30 W
Negro ≃, S.A.	184	3.06 S	59.52 W
Negro ≃, S.A.	188	33.24 S	58.22 W
Negro ≃, Ven.	182	9.36 N	72.15 W
Negros I	138	10.00 N	123.00 E
Nehbandān	150	31.32 N	60.02 E
Neheim-Hüsten	116	51.27 N	7.57 E
Neiba	182	18.28 N	71.25 W
Neiba, Bahía de C	182	18.15 N	71.00 W
Neiges, Piton des Λ	161c	21.05 S	55.29 E
Neijiang	132	29.35 N	105.03 E
Neilston	108	55.47 N	4.27 W
Neimenggu Zizhiqu (Inner Mongolia) □[4]	132	43.00 N	115.00 E
Neisse (Nysa Łużycka) (Nisa) ≃	116	52.04 N	14.46 E
Neiva	184	2.56 N	75.18 W
Neja	130	58.18 N	43.54 E
Nekemte	154	9.02 N	36.31 E
Nelidovo	130	56.13 N	32.46 E
Nel'kan	128	57.40 N	136.13 E
Nellikuppam	148	11.46 N	79.41 E
Nellore	148	14.26 N	79.58 E
Nel'ma	128	47.39 N	139.09 E
Nelson, B.C., Can.	172	49.29 N	117.17 W
Nelson, N.Z.	170	41.17 S	173.17 E
Nelson, Eng., U.K.	106	53.51 N	2.13 W
Nelson ≃	172	57.04 N	92.30 W
Nelson, Cape ➤	168	38.26 S	141.33 E
Nelson Creek ≃	178	40.36 N	114.28 W
Nelsonville	176	39.27 N	82.14 W
Nelspoort	160	32.07 S	23.01 E
Nelspruit	160	25.30 S	30.58 E
Néma	152	16.37 N	7.15 W
Nemacolin	176	39.52 N	79.56 W
Neman (Nemunas) ≃	130	55.18 N	21.23 E
Nemours	118	48.16 N	2.42 E
Nemuna, Bjeshkët e ⛰	124	42.27 N	19.47 E
Nemunas (Neman) ≃	130	55.18 N	21.23 E
Nemuro	134a	43.20 N	145.35 E
Nemuro-hantō ➤[1]	134a	43.21 N	145.42 E
Nemuro Strait ⩌	134a	44.00 N	145.20 E
Nenagh	110	52.52 N	8.12 W
Nenagh ≃	110	52.56 N	8.17 W
Nenana ≃	172	64.30 N	149.00 W
Nene ≃	104	52.48 N	0.13 E
Neneckij Nacionalnyj Okrug □[8]	112	67.30 N	54.00 E
Nengonengo I[1]	96	18.47 S	141.48 W
Néon Karlovásion	124	37.48 N	26.44 E
Nepa ≃	128	59.16 N	108.16 E
Nepal (Nepāl) □[1]	144	28.00 N	84.00 E
Nepālganj	146	28.03 N	81.37 E
Nepewassi Lake ⊜	176	46.20 N	80.40 W
Nephin Λ	110	54.01 N	9.22 W
Nephin Beg Range ⛰	110	54.00 N	9.35 W
Neptune	176	40.12 N	74.02 W
Nera ≃	124	44.49 N	21.22 E
Nérac	118	44.08 N	0.20 E
Nerastro, Sarīr ✦[2]	154	24.20 N	20.37 E
Nerča ≃	128	51.56 N	116.40 E
Nerčinsk	128	51.58 N	116.35 E
Nerčinskij Zavod	128	51.19 N	119.36 E
Nerechta	130	57.28 N	40.34 E
Neriquinha	156	15.58 S	21.42 E
Nerja	120	36.44 N	3.52 W
Nérondes	118	47.00 N	2.49 E
Nerrima	164	18.24 S	124.29 E
Nerva	120	37.42 N	6.32 W
Nes	116	53.26 N	5.45 E
Nesbyen	114	60.34 N	9.09 E
Neskaupstaður	112a	65.10 N	13.43 W
Ness, Loch ⊜	108	57.18 N	4.27 W
Nesselrode, Mount Λ	172	58.58 N	134.18 W
Nesselwang	116	47.37 N	10.30 E
Neston	106	53.18 N	3.04 W
Néstos (Mesta) ≃	124	40.41 N	24.44 E
Nesttun	114	60.19 N	5.20 E
Nesviž	130	53.13 N	26.40 E
Netanya	150	32.20 N	34.51 E
Nethan ≃	108	55.42 N	3.52 W
Netherdale	168	21.08 S	148.32 E
Netherlands □[1]	100	52.15 N	5.30 E
Netherlands Antilles □[2]	180	12.15 N	69.00 W
Nethy Bridge	108	57.16 N	3.38 W
Netley Marsh	104	50.53 N	1.21 W
Netrakona	146	24.53 N	90.43 E
Nettilling Fiord C[2]	172	66.02 N	68.12 W
Nettilling Lake ⊜	172	66.30 N	70.40 W
Nettlebed	104	51.35 N	1.00 W
Nettuno	122	41.27 N	12.39 E
Neubrandenburg	116	53.33 N	13.15 E
Neubrandenburg □[5]	116	53.30 N	13.15 E
Neuburg an der Donau	116	48.44 N	11.11 E
Neuchâtel	118	46.59 N	6.56 E
Neuf-Brisach	118	48.01 N	7.32 E
Neufchâteau	116	49.50 N	5.26 E
Neufchâtel-en-Bray	118	49.44 N	1.27 E
Neugersdorf	116	50.59 N	14.36 E
Neuillé-Pont-Pierre	118	47.33 N	0.33 E
Neu-Isenburg	116	50.03 N	8.41 E
Neumarkt [im Hausruckkreis]	116	48.16 N	13.45 E
Neumarkt in der Oberpfalz	116	49.16 N	11.28 E
Neumarkt-Sankt Veit	116	48.22 N	12.30 E
Neumünster	116	54.04 N	9.59 E
Neunburg vorm Wald	116	49.21 N	12.24 E
Neunkirchen, B.R.D.	116	49.20 N	7.10 E
Neunkirchen, Öst.	116	47.43 N	16.05 E
Neunkirchen/saar	116	49.20 N	7.10 E
Neuquén	188	39.00 S	68.05 W
Neuquén ≃	186	39.00 S	68.00 W
Neurara	188	24.10 S	68.29 W
Neuruppin	116	52.55 N	12.48 E
Neusiedler See ⊜	116	47.50 N	16.46 E
Neuss	116	51.12 N	6.41 E
Neustadt	116	50.44 N	11.44 E
Neustadt [an aisch]	116	49.34 N	10.37 E
Neustadt an der Waldnaab	116	49.44 N	12.11 E
Neustadt an der Weinstrasse	116	49.21 N	8.08 E
Neustadt in Holstein	116	54.06 N	10.48 E
Neustrelitz	116	53.21 N	13.04 E
Neutral Zone □[2]	144	29.10 N	45.30 E
Neu-Ulm	116	48.23 N	10.01 E
Neuville-de-Poitou	118	46.41 N	0.15 E
Neuville-sur-Saône	118	45.52 N	4.51 E
Neuwied	116	50.25 N	7.27 E
Nevada, Mo., U.S.	174	37.51 N	94.22 W
Nevada, Ohio, U.S.	176	40.49 N	83.08 W
Nevada □[3]	174	39.00 N	117.00 W
Nevada, Sierra ⛰, Esp.	120	37.05 N	3.10 W
Nevada, Sierra ⛰, Calif., U.S.	178	38.00 N	119.15 W
Nevada City	178	36.16 N	121.01 W
Nevada de Santa Marta, Sierra ⛰	182	10.50 N	73.40 W
Nevado, Cerro Λ	188	35.34 S	68.29 W
Nevado, Sierra del ⛰	188	35.40 S	68.30 W
Nevel'sk	128	46.40 N	141.53 E
Never	128	53.58 N	124.05 E
Nevers	118	47.00 N	3.09 E
Nevertire	168	31.52 S	147.39 E
Nevesinje	124	43.15 N	18.07 E
Nevinnomyssk	126	44.38 N	41.56 E
Nevis I	182	17.10 N	62.35 W
Nevis ≃	108	56.50 N	5.00 W
Nevis, Ben Λ	108	56.48 N	4.59 W
Nevis, Loch C	108	57.01 N	5.43 W
Nevjansk	126	57.32 N	60.13 E
Nevşehir	150	38.38 N	34.43 E
New ≃	178	33.08 N	115.44 W
New Abbey	106	54.59 N	3.38 W
New Albany	174	38.18 N	85.49 W
New Alresford	104	51.06 N	1.10 W
New Amsterdam	184	6.17 N	57.36 W
New Angledool	168	29.07 S	147.57 E
Newark, Del., U.S.	176	39.41 N	75.45 W
Newark, N.J., U.S.	176	40.44 N	74.10 W
Newark, N.Y., U.S.	176	43.03 N	77.06 W
Newark, Ohio, U.S.	176	40.04 N	82.24 W
Newark Lake ⊜	178	39.41 N	115.44 W
Newark-upon-Trent	104	53.05 N	0.49 W
Newark Valley	176	42.14 N	76.11 W
New Baltimore	176	42.41 N	82.44 W
New Bedford	176	41.38 N	70.56 W
New Bedford ≃	104	52.35 N	0.20 E
New Berlin	176	42.38 N	75.20 W
New Bern	174	35.07 N	77.03 W
Newberry	174	34.17 N	81.37 W
New Bethlehem	176	41.00 N	79.20 W
Newbiggin-by-the-Sea	106	55.11 N	1.30 W
New Bloomfield	176	40.25 N	77.11 W
Newborough	106	53.09 N	4.22 W
New Boston	176	38.45 N	82.56 W
New Bremen	176	40.26 N	84.23 W
Newbridge on Wye	104	52.13 N	3.27 W
New Brighton	170	43.31 S	172.44 E
New Britain	176	41.40 N	72.47 W
New Britain I	166	6.00 S	150.00 E
New Britain Trench ⊹[1]	96	6.00 S	152.30 E
New Brunswick	176	40.29 N	74.27 W
New Brunswick □[4]	172	46.30 N	66.15 W
Newburgh, Ont., Can.	176	44.19 N	76.52 W
Newburgh, Scot., U.K.	108	57.18 N	2.00 W
Newburgh, Scot., U.K.	108	56.20 N	3.15 W
Newburgh, N.Y., U.S.	176	41.30 N	74.01 W
Newburn	106	54.59 N	1.43 W
Newbury	104	51.25 N	1.20 W
Newburyport	176	42.49 N	70.53 W
Newby	106	54.20 N	0.28 W
Newby Bridge	106	54.16 N	2.58 W
New Caledonia □[2]	96	21.30 S	165.30 E
New Carlisle, Qué., Can.	172	48.01 N	65.20 W
New Carlisle, Ohio, U.S.	176	39.56 N	84.02 W
Newcastle, Austl.	168	32.56 S	151.46 E
Newcastle, N.B., Can.	172	47.00 N	65.34 W
Newcastle, Ont., Can.	176	43.55 N	78.35 W
Newcastle, Eire	110	52.16 N	7.48 W
Newcastle, S. Afr.	160	27.49 S	29.55 E
Newcastle, Eng., U.K.	104	52.26 N	3.06 W
Newcastle, N. Ire., U.K.	110	54.12 N	5.54 W
Newcastle, Calif., U.S.	178	38.53 N	121.08 W
New Castle, Del., U.S.	176	39.40 N	75.34 W
Newcastle, Maine, U.S.	176	44.02 N	69.33 W
New Castle, Pa., U.S.	174	41.00 N	80.20 W
Newcastle Creek ≃	166	17.20 S	133.23 E
Newcastle Emlyn	104	52.02 N	4.28 W
Newcastleton	106	55.11 N	2.49 W
Newcastle-under-Lyme	104	53.00 N	2.14 W
Newcastle upon Tyne	106	54.59 N	1.35 W
Newcastle Waters	166	17.24 S	133.24 E
Newcastle West	110	52.27 N	9.03 W
Newcestown	110	51.47 N	8.51 W
Newchurch	104	52.09 N	3.08 W
New City	176	41.09 N	73.59 W
Newcomerstown	176	40.16 N	81.36 W
New Concord	176	40.00 N	81.44 W
New Cumberland	176	40.30 N	80.36 W
New Cumnock	106	55.24 N	4.12 W
New Deer	108	57.30 N	2.12 W
Newdegate	164	33.06 S	119.01 E
New Delhi	149	28.36 N	77.12 E
New Don Pedro Reservoir ⊜[1]	178	37.43 N	120.23 W
New Egypt	176	40.04 N	74.32 W
Newell	176	40.37 N	80.36 W
Newell, Lake ⊜	164	24.50 S	126.10 E
Newent	104	51.56 N	2.24 W
Newfane, N.Y., U.S.	176	43.17 N	78.43 W
Newfane, Vt., U.S.	176	42.59 N	72.39 W
New Florence	176	40.23 N	79.05 W
New Forest ✦[3]	104	50.53 N	1.35 W
Newfoundland □[4]	172	52.00 N	56.00 W
Newfoundland I	172	48.30 N	56.00 W
Newfoundland Basin ⊹[1]	90	43.00 N	43.00 W
New Freedom	176	39.44 N	76.42 W
New Galloway	106	55.05 N	4.10 W
New Georgia I	162	8.15 S	157.30 E
New Glasgow	172	45.35 N	62.39 W
New Guinea I	166	5.00 S	140.00 E
New Guinea, Territory of → Papua New Guinea □[1]	166	6.00 S	147.00 E
Newhall, Eng., U.K.	104	52.48 N	1.34 W
Newhall, Calif., U.S.	178	34.23 N	118.31 W
Newham ✦[8]	104	51.32 N	0.03 E
New Hamburg	176	43.23 N	80.42 W
New Hampshire □[3]	174	43.35 N	71.40 W
New Hanover	160	29.28 S	30.28 E
New Hanover I	166	2.30 S	150.15 E
New Hartford	176	41.53 N	72.59 W
Newhaven, Eng., U.K.	104	50.47 N	0.03 E
New Haven, Conn., U.S.	176	41.18 N	72.56 W
New Haven, Ind., U.S.	176	41.04 N	85.01 W
New Haven, W. Va., U.S.	176	38.59 N	81.58 W
New Hebrides □[2]	96	16.00 S	167.00 E
New Hebrides II	84	16.00 S	167.00 E
New Hebrides Basin ⊹[1]	96	16.00 S	162.00 E
New Hebrides Trench ⊹[1]	96	19.00 S	168.00 E
New Hogan Lake ⊜[1]	178	38.07 N	120.50 W
New Holland, Eng., U.K.	106	53.42 N	0.22 W
New Holland, Ohio, U.S.	176	39.33 N	83.15 W
New Holland, Pa., U.S.	176	40.06 N	76.05 W
New Iberia	174	30.00 N	91.49 W
Newington	104	51.05 N	1.08 E
New Inn	110	52.26 N	7.53 W
New Ireland I	166	3.20 S	152.00 E
New Jersey □[3]	174	40.15 N	74.30 W
New Kensington	176	40.34 N	79.46 W
New Kowloon (Xinjiulong)	138	22.20 N	114.10 E
Newland Range ⛰	164	27.53 S	123.58 E
New Lexington	176	39.43 N	82.13 W
New Liskeard	172	47.30 N	79.40 W
New London, Conn., U.S.	176	41.21 N	72.07 W
New London, N.H., U.S.	176	43.25 N	71.59 W
New London, Ohio, U.S.	176	41.05 N	82.24 W
Newlyn East	104	50.22 N	5.03 W
Newmachar	108	57.16 N	2.11 W
Newman, Austl.	164	23.20 S	119.46 E
Newman, Calif., U.S.	178	37.19 N	121.01 W
Newmarket, Ont., Can.	172	44.03 N	79.28 W
Newmarket, Eire	110	52.13 N	9.00 W
Newmarket, Eng., U.K.	104	52.15 N	0.25 E
Newmarket, N.H., U.S.	176	43.05 N	70.56 W
New Market, Va., U.S.	176	38.39 N	78.40 W
Newmarket-on-Fergus	110	52.45 N	8.53 W
New Martinsville	176	39.39 N	80.52 W
New Mexico □[3]	174	34.30 N	106.00 W
New Milford, Conn., U.S.	176	41.35 N	73.25 W
New Milford, Pa., U.S.	176	41.52 N	75.44 W
New Mills	106	53.23 N	2.00 W
Newmilns	108	55.37 N	4.20 W
New Milton	104	50.44 N	1.40 W
Newnham	104	51.49 N	2.27 W
New Norcia	164	30.58 S	116.13 E
New Norfolk	168	42.47 S	147.03 E
New Orleans	174	29.58 N	90.07 W
New Oxford	176	39.52 N	77.04 W
New Paltz	176	41.45 N	74.05 W
New Paris	176	39.51 N	84.48 W
New Philadelphia	176	40.30 N	81.27 W
New Pine Creek	178	42.00 N	120.18 W
New Plymouth	170	39.04 S	174.05 E
Newport, Eire	110	52.42 N	8.24 W
Newport, Eire	110	53.53 N	9.34 W
Newport, Eng., U.K.	104	52.47 N	2.22 W
Newport, Eng., U.K.	104	50.42 N	1.18 W
Newport, Wales, U.K.	104	52.01 N	4.51 W
Newport, Wales, U.K.	104	51.35 N	3.00 W
Newport, Ky., U.S.	176	39.06 N	84.29 W
Newport, Maine, U.S.	176	44.50 N	69.17 W
Newport, N.H., U.S.	176	43.21 N	72.09 W
Newport, Pa., U.S.	176	40.29 N	77.08 W
Newport, R.I., U.S.	174	41.13 N	71.18 W
Newport, Vt., U.S.	176	44.57 N	72.12 W
Newport Beach	178	33.37 N	117.56 W
Newport News	174	37.04 N	76.28 W
Newport-on-Tay	108	56.26 N	2.55 W
Newport Pagnell	104	52.05 N	0.44 W
New Providence I	182	25.25 N	78.35 E
Newquay, Eng., U.K.	104	50.25 N	5.05 W
New Quay, Wales, U.K.	104	52.13 N	4.22 W
New Richmond	176	38.57 N	84.17 W
New Rochelle	176	40.55 N	73.47 W
New Romney	104	50.59 N	0.57 E
New Ross	110	52.24 N	6.56 W
New Rossington	106	53.29 N	1.04 W
Newry	110	54.11 N	6.20 W
New Sarum → Salisbury	104	51.05 N	1.48 W
New Schwabenland ✦[1]	87	72.30 S	1.00 E
New South Wales □[3]	168	33.00 S	146.00 E
Newton, Eng., U.K.	106	53.57 N	2.27 W
Newton, Iowa, U.S.	174	41.42 N	93.03 W
Newton, Kans., U.S.	174	38.03 N	97.21 W
Newton, Mass., U.S.	176	42.21 N	71.11 W
Newton, N.J., U.S.	176	41.03 N	74.45 W
Newton Abbot	104	50.32 N	3.36 W
Newton Arlosh	106	54.53 N	3.15 W
Newton Aycliffe	106	54.36 N	1.32 W
Newton Falls, N.Y., U.S.	176	44.13 N	74.59 W
Newton Falls, Ohio, U.S.	176	41.11 N	80.59 W
Newton Ferrers	104	50.18 N	4.02 W
Newton Flotman	104	52.32 N	1.16 E
Newtongrange	108	55.52 N	3.04 W
Newton-le-Willows	106	53.28 N	2.37 W
Newtonmore	108	57.04 N	4.08 W
Newton Stewart	106	54.57 N	4.29 W
Newtown	104	52.32 N	3.19 W
Newtownards	110	54.36 N	5.41 W
Newtownbutler	110	54.12 N	7.23 W
Newtown Crommelin	110	54.59 N	6.13 W
Newtown Forbes	110	53.46 N	7.50 W
Newtownhamilton	110	54.11 N	6.35 W
Newtown Saint Boswells	108	55.34 N	2.40 W
Newtownstewart	110	54.43 N	7.24 W
New Tredegar	104	51.43 N	3.14 W
New Ulm	174	44.19 N	94.28 W
New Vienna	176	39.19 N	83.42 W
Newville	176	40.10 N	77.24 W
New Vineyard	176	44.48 N	70.07 W
New Washington	176	40.58 N	82.51 W
New Waterford	172	46.15 N	60.05 W
New Westminster	172	49.12 N	122.55 W
New Wilmington	176	41.07 N	80.20 W
New York	176	40.43 N	74.01 W
New York □[3]	174	43.00 N	75.00 W
New York State Barge Canal ≊	176	43.05 N	78.43 W
New Zealand □[1]	170	41.00 S	174.00 E
New Zealand Plateau ⊹[3]	87	51.00 S	170.00 E
Nexon	118	45.41 N	1.11 E
Neyland	104	51.43 N	4.57 W
Neyrīz	150	29.12 N	54.19 E
Neyshābūr	150	36.12 N	58.50 E
Nežin	126	51.03 N	31.54 E
Ngabang	142	0.23 N	109.57 E
Ngahere	170	42.24 S	171.27 E
Ngami, Lake ⊜	160	20.37 S	22.40 E
Ngamiland □[5]	160	19.09 S	22.47 E
Ngangala	158	4.42 N	31.55 E
Nganjuk	142	7.36 S	111.55 E
Ngaoundéré	152	7.19 N	13.35 E
Ngapara	170	44.57 S	170.45 E
Ngaruawahia	170	37.40 S	175.09 E
Ngaruroro ≃	170	39.34 S	176.56 E
Ngatea	170	37.17 S	175.30 E
Ngatik I[1]	96	5.51 N	157.16 E
Ngauruhoe, Mount Λ	170	39.09 S	175.38 E
Ngawi	142	7.24 S	111.26 E
Ng'iro, Ewaso ≃, Kenya	158	2.04 S	36.07 E
Ng'iro, Ewaso ≃, Kenya	158	0.28 N	39.55 E
Ngiva	156	17.03 S	15.47 E
Ngoboli	158	4.57 N	32.37 E
Ngoko ≃	156	1.40 N	16.03 E
Ngoma	158	2.11 S	29.18 E
Ngomahuru	158	20.26 S	30.43 E
Ngongotaha	170	38.05 S	176.12 E
Ngosa Farm	158	12.18 S	27.28 E
Ngozi	158	2.54 S	29.50 E
Nguigmi	152	14.15 N	13.07 E
Ngulu I[1]	138	8.27 N	137.29 E
Nguru	152	12.52 N	10.27 E
Ngwakets □[5]	160	24.45 S	24.00 E
Ngwerere	158	15.18 S	28.20 E
Ngwezi ≃	158	17.40 S	25.07 E
Nhandeara	190	20.40 S	50.02 W
Nha-trang	140	12.15 N	109.11 E
Nhill	168	36.20 S	141.39 E
Niafounké	152	15.56 N	4.00 W
Niagara Falls, Ont., Can.	172	43.06 N	79.04 W
Niagara Falls, N.Y., U.S.	176	43.06 N	79.02 W
Niagara-on-the-Lake	176	43.15 N	79.04 W
Niah	138	3.52 N	113.44 E
Niamey	152	13.31 N	2.07 E
Niangara	158	3.42 N	27.52 E
Nianqingtanggula-shanmai ⛰	146	30.00 N	90.00 E
Nias, Pulau I	140	1.05 N	97.35 E
Niassa □[5]	158	13.30 S	36.00 E
Nica ≃	126	57.29 N	64.33 E
Nicaragua □[1]	180	13.00 N	85.00 W
Nicaragua, Lago de ⊜	182	11.35 N	85.25 W
Nicastro (Lamezia Terme)	122	38.59 N	16.20 E
Nice	118	43.42 N	7.15 E
Nichinan	134	31.36 N	131.23 E
Nicholas Channel ⩌	182	23.25 N	80.05 W
Nicholasville	176	37.53 N	84.34 W
Nicholson, Austl.	164	18.02 S	128.54 E
Nicholson, Pa., U.S.	176	41.38 N	75.47 W
Nicholson ≃, Austl.	164	17.34 S	128.38 E
Nicholson ≃, Austl.	168	17.31 S	139.36 E
Nicholson Range ⛰	164	27.15 S	116.45 E
Nickol Bay C	164	20.39 S	116.52 E
Nicobar Basin ⊹[1]	94	5.00 N	92.00 E
Nicobar Islands II	140	8.00 N	93.30 E
Nicolet	176	46.13 N	72.37 W
Nicolet-Sud-Ouest ≃	176	46.13 N	72.36 W
Nicolls Town	182	25.08 N	78.00 W
Nicosia, It.	122	37.45 N	14.24 E
Nicosia → Levkosia, Kípros	150	35.10 N	33.22 E
Nicoya	182	10.09 N	85.27 W
Nicoya, Golfo de C	182	9.47 N	84.48 W
Nicoya, Península de ➤[1]	182	10.00 N	85.25 W
Nidd ≃	102	54.01 N	1.12 W
Nidelva ≃	114	58.24 N	8.48 E
Nidže (Nítse Óros) ≃	124	40.58 N	21.49 E
Nidzica	116	53.22 N	20.26 E
Niebüll	116	54.48 N	8.50 E
Niederbronn-les-Bains	118	48.57 N	7.38 E
Niedere Tauern ⛰	116	47.18 N	14.00 E
Niederösterreich □[3]	116	48.20 N	15.50 E
Niedersachsen □[3]	116	52.00 N	10.00 E
Niekerkshoop	160	29.19 S	22.51 E
Nienburg	116	52.38 N	9.13 E
Nier ≃	110	52.17 N	7.48 W
Nieu Bethesda	160	31.51 S	24.34 E
Nieuw Amsterdam	184	5.53 N	55.05 W
Nieuw Nickerie	184	5.57 N	56.59 W
Nieuwoudtville	160	31.23 S	19.07 E
Nieuwpoort	116	51.08 N	2.45 E
Nièvre □[5]	118	47.05 N	3.30 E
Niğde	150	37.59 N	34.42 E
Nigel	160	26.30 S	28.28 E
Niger □[1]	152	16.00 N	8.00 E
Nigeria □[1]	152	10.00 N	8.00 E
Nigg	108	57.43 N	4.00 W
Nightcaps	170	45.58 S	168.02 E
Nightingale Island I	88	37.24 S	12.28 W
Nigríta	124	40.55 N	23.30 E
Nihing (Nahang) ≃	150	26.00 N	62.44 E
Nihommatsu	134	37.35 N	140.26 E
Nihuil, Embalse de ⊜[1]	188	35.05 S	68.40 W
Niigata	134	37.55 N	139.03 E
Niigata-heiya ≚	134	37.45 N	139.00 E
Niihama	134	33.58 N	133.16 E
Niihau I	179a	21.55 N	160.10 W
Niimi	134	34.59 N	133.28 E
Niinisalo	114	61.50 N	22.29 E
Nii-shima I	134	34.22 N	139.16 E
Niitsu	134	37.48 N	139.07 E
Nijkerk	116	52.13 N	5.30 E
Nijmegen	116	51.50 N	5.50 E
Nijvel → Nivelles	116	50.36 N	4.20 E
Nikkō	134	36.45 N	139.37 E
Nikolajev	126	46.58 N	32.00 E
Nikolajevsk-na-Amure	128	53.08 N	140.44 E
Nikol'sk	112	53.45 N	46.05 E
Nikol'skoje	128	55.12 N	166.00 E
Nikopol'	126	47.35 N	34.25 E
Nikšić	124	42.46 N	18.56 E
Nikunau I	96	1.23 S	176.26 E
Nila, Pulau I	166	6.44 S	129.31 E
Niland	178	33.14 N	115.31 W
Nile (Nahr an-Nīl) ≃	154	30.10 N	31.06 E
Niles	176	41.11 N	80.45 W
Nileshwar	148	12.15 N	75.06 E
Nilsiä	114	63.12 N	28.05 E
Nīmach	146	24.28 N	74.52 E
Nimba, Mont Λ	152	7.37 N	8.25 W
Nimba Mountains ⛰	152	7.30 N	8.30 W
Nîmes	118	43.50 N	4.21 E
Nimmitabel	168	36.31 S	149.16 E
Nimrod Glacier ◸	87	82.27 S	161.00 E
Nīmrūz □[4]	150	30.30 N	62.00 E
Nimule	154	3.36 N	32.03 E
Nina Bang Lake ⊜	172	70.51 N	79.07 W
Nindigully	168	28.21 S	148.49 E
Nine Degree Channel ⩌	148	9.00 N	73.00 E
Ninetyeast Ridge ⊹[3]	94	15.00 S	88.00 E
Ninety Mile Beach ⊥[2], Austl.	168	38.13 S	147.23 E
Ninety Mile Beach ⊥[2], N.Z.	170	34.48 S	173.00 E
Ninfield	104	50.53 N	0.25 E
Ningbo	136	29.52 N	121.31 E
Ningcheng	132	41.33 N	119.20 E
Ningde	136	26.43 N	119.33 E
Ningdu	136	26.31 N	115.58 E
Ninggang	136	26.50 N	114.02 E
Ningguo	136	30.38 N	118.58 E
Ninghai	136	29.17 N	121.25 E
Ninghua	136	26.15 N	116.38 E
Ningling	136	34.27 N	115.21 E
Ningming	140	22.07 N	107.09 E
Ningshan	132	33.04 N	108.39 E
Ningwu	132	39.01 N	112.21 E
Ningxiang	136	28.15 N	112.33 E
Ningyuan	140	25.37 N	111.46 E
Ninh-binh	140	20.15 N	105.59 E
Ninhue	188	36.24 S	72.24 W
Ninigo Group II	166	1.15 S	144.15 E
Ninnis Glacier Tongue ◸	87	68.12 S	147.12 E
Ninove	118	50.50 N	4.01 E
Nioaque	184	21.08 S	55.48 W
Niobrara ≃	174	42.45 N	98.00 W
Nioki	156	2.43 S	17.41 E
Niono	152	14.15 N	6.00 W
Nioro du Sahel	152	15.15 N	9.35 W
Niort	118	46.19 N	0.27 W
Nipan	168	24.47 S	150.01 E
Nipāni	148	16.24 N	74.23 E
Nipawin	172	53.22 N	104.00 W
Nipe, Bahía de C	182	20.47 N	75.42 W
Nipigon	172	49.01 N	88.16 W
Nipigon, Lake ⊜	172	49.50 N	88.30 W
Nipissing, Lake ⊜	172	46.17 N	80.00 W
Nipomo	178	35.03 N	120.29 W
Niquero	182	20.03 N	77.35 W
Nirasaki	134	35.42 N	138.27 E
Nirgua	182	10.09 N	68.34 W
Nirmal	148	19.06 N	78.21 E
Niš	124	43.19 N	21.54 E
Nisa	120	39.31 N	7.39 W
Nisa (Neisse) (Nysa Łużycka) ≃	116	52.04 N	14.46 E
Niscemi	122	37.08 N	14.24 E
Nishinoomote	135b	30.44 N	131.00 E
Nishio	134	34.52 N	137.03 E
Nishiwaki	134	34.59 N	134.58 E
Nisling ≃	172	62.27 N	139.30 W
Nissan ≃	114	56.40 N	12.51 E
Nisser ⊜	114	59.10 N	8.30 E
Niterói	190	22.53 S	43.07 W
Nith ≃, Ont., Can.	176	43.12 N	80.22 W
Nith ≃, Scot., U.K.	106	55.00 N	3.35 W
Nithsdale V	106	55.14 N	3.46 W
Niton	104	50.35 N	1.16 W
Nitra	116	48.20 N	18.05 E
Nitro	176	38.25 N	81.50 W
Nítse Óros (Nidže) Λ	124	40.58 N	21.49 E
Niue □[2]	96	19.02 S	169.52 W
Niut, Gunung Λ	142	1.00 N	109.55 E
Niutao I	96	6.06 S	177.17 E
Nive ≃, Austl.	168	26.02 S	146.25 E
Nive ≃, Fr.	118	43.30 N	1.29 W
Nive Downs	168	25.30 S	146.32 E
Nivelles	116	50.36 N	4.20 E
Nivernais □[9]	118	47.00 N	3.30 E
Nixon	178	39.50 N	119.21 W
Niyodo ≃	134	33.27 N	133.29 E
Nizāmābād	148	18.40 N	78.07 E
Nizhny Novgorod → Gor'kij	130	56.20 N	44.00 E
Nizip	150	37.01 N	37.46 E
Nízke Beskydy ⛰	116	49.20 N	21.30 E
Nižn'aja Peša	112	66.43 N	47.36 E
Nižn'aja Pojma	128	56.11 N	97.13 E
Nižn'aja Tunguska ≃	128	65.48 N	88.04 E
Nižn'aja Tura	126	58.37 N	59.49 E
Nižneangarsk	128	55.47 N	109.33 E
Nižneilimsk	128	57.11 N	103.16 E
Nižnekamsk	112	55.32 N	51.58 E
Nižneudinsk	128	54.54 N	99.03 E
Nižnij Kuranach	128	58.49 N	125.32 E
Nižnij P'andž	126	37.08 N	68.32 E
Nižnij Tagil	126	57.55 N	59.57 E
Njombe	158	9.20 S	34.46 E
Njombe ≃	158	6.56 S	35.06 E
Nkai	158	19.00 S	28.54 E
Nkala Mission	158	15.55 S	26.00 E
Nkhata Bay	158	11.33 S	34.18 E
Nkhota Kota	158	12.57 S	34.17 E
Nkongsamba	152	4.57 N	9.56 E
Nkwalini	160	28.45 S	31.33 E
Nmai ≃	140	25.42 N	97.30 E
Noākhāli	146	22.49 N	91.06 E
Nobeoka	134	32.35 N	131.40 E
Nōbi-heiya ≚	134	35.15 N	136.45 E
Noboribetsu	134a	42.27 N	141.11 E
Noccundra	168	27.50 S	142.36 E
Nocera [Inferiore]	122	40.44 N	14.38 E
Nockatunga	168	27.43 S	142.43 E
Noda	134	35.56 N	139.52 E
Nogales, Chile	188	32.44 S	71.15 W
Nogales, Méx.	180	31.19 N	110.56 W
Nogales, Ariz., U.S.	174	31.20 N	110.56 W
Nōgata	134	33.44 N	130.44 E
Nogent-le-Rotrou	118	48.19 N	0.50 E
Nogent-sur-Seine	118	48.29 N	3.30 E
Noginsk	130	55.51 N	38.27 E
Nogoa ≃	168	23.33 S	148.32 E
Nogoyá	188	32.22 S	59.49 W
Nógrád □[6]	116	48.00 N	19.35 E
Nohar	149	29.11 N	74.46 E
Noheji	134	40.52 N	141.08 E
Noir, Montagne ⛰	118	43.28 N	2.18 E
Noire ≃	176	45.54 N	76.57 W
Noirmoutier, Île de I	118	47.00 N	2.15 W
Nojima-zaki ➤	134	34.56 N	139.53 E
Nokia	114	61.28 N	23.30 E
Nola	122	40.55 N	14.33 E
Nombre de Dios	182	9.34 N	79.28 W
Nomgon	132	42.57 N	104.55 E
Nominingue	176	46.24 N	75.02 W
Nomozaki	134	32.35 N	129.45 E
Nonacho Lake ⊜	172	61.42 N	109.40 W
Nondalton	172	60.00 N	154.49 W
Nondweni	160	28.11 S	30.49 E
Nong'an	132	44.25 N	125.10 E
Nong Khai	140	17.52 N	102.44 E
Nonning	168	32.30 S	136.30 E
Nonoai	188	27.21 S	52.47 W
Nonouti I[1]	96	0.40 S	174.21 E
Nonthaburi	140	13.50 N	100.29 E
Nookawarra	164	26.19 S	116.52 E
Noonamah	166	12.38 S	131.04 E
Noonkanbah	164	18.30 S	124.50 E
Noordoost Polder ✦[1]	116	52.42 N	5.45 E
Noordwijk aan Zee	116	52.14 N	4.26 E
Noosaville	168	26.24 S	153.04 E
Nootka Island I	172	49.32 N	126.42 W
Nóqui	156	5.51 S	13.25 E
Nora	114	59.31 N	15.02 E
Nora Islands II	154	16.02 N	39.58 E
Noranda	172	48.15 N	79.02 W
Norberto de la Riestra	188	35.15 S	59.46 W
Norbottens Län □[6]	112	66.00 N	20.00 E
Norcott, Mount Λ	164	32.07 S	121.59 E
Nord □[5]	118	50.20 N	3.40 E
Norden	116	53.36 N	7.12 E
Nordenham	116	53.29 N	8.28 E
Nordenšel'da, Archipelag II	128	76.45 N	96.00 E
Norderney I	116	53.42 N	7.10 E
Norderstedt	116	53.43 N	10.00 E
Nordfjord C[2]	114	61.54 N	5.12 E
Nordhausen	116	51.30 N	10.47 E
Nordhorn	116	52.27 N	7.05 E
Nordkapp ➤	112	71.11 N	25.48 E
Nordkinnhalvøya ➤[1]	112	70.55 N	27.45 E
Nordland □[6]	112	67.00 N	14.40 E
Nördlingen	116	48.51 N	10.30 E
Nordmarka ✦[1]	114	60.00 N	10.25 E
Nordostrundingen ➤	90	81.36 N	12.09 W
Nord-Ostsee-Kanal ≊	116	53.53 N	9.08 E
Nordpfälzer Bergland ⛰	116	49.40 N	7.40 E
Nordre Strømfjord C[2]	172	67.50 N	52.00 W
Nordrhein-Westfalen □[3]	116	51.30 N	7.30 E
Nord-Trøndelag □[6]	114	64.25 N	12.00 E
Nordvik	128	74.02 N	111.32 E
Nore	114	60.10 N	9.01 E
Nore ≃	110	52.25 N	6.58 W
Norfolk, Nebr., U.S.	174	42.02 N	97.25 W
Norfolk, Va., U.S.	180	26.40 N	76.14 W
Norfolk □[6]	102	52.35 N	1.00 E
Norfolk Broads ✦[1]	104	52.40 N	1.30 E
Norfolk Island □[2]	96	29.02 S	167.57 E
Norfolk Island I	84	29.02 S	167.57 E
Norfolk Island Ridge ⊹[3]	84	29.00 S	167.00 E
Norfolk Island Trough ⊹[1]	96	30.00 S	165.00 E
Norfolk Ridge ⊹[3]	96	29.00 S	167.00 E
Norham	106	55.43 N	2.10 W
Norikura-dake Λ	134	36.06 N	137.33 E
Noril'sk	128	69.20 N	88.06 E
Norman	174	35.13 N	97.26 W
Norman ≃	168	17.28 S	140.49 E
Normanby ≃	166	14.25 S	144.08 E
Normandie □[9]	118	49.00 N	0.05 W
Normandie, Collines de ⛰[2]	102	48.50 N	1.00 W
Normandy → Normandie □[9]	118	49.00 N	0.05 W
Normanton, Austl.	168	17.40 S	141.05 E
Normanton, Eng., U.K.	106	53.41 N	1.27 W
Norman Wells	172	65.17 N	126.51 W
Nornalup	164	35.00 S	116.49 E
Ñorquincó	186	41.50 S	70.55 W
Norra Kvarken (Merenkurkku) ⩌	114	63.36 N	20.43 E
Norra Storfjället Λ	112	65.52 N	15.18 E
Norrbotten □[9]	114	66.45 N	23.00 E
Norrbottens Län □[6]	114	65.30 N	21.30 E
Nørresundby	114	57.04 N	9.55 E
Norridgewock	176	44.43 N	69.48 W
Norristown	176	40.07 N	75.21 W
Norrköping	114	58.36 N	16.11 E
Norrtälje	114	59.46 N	18.42 E
Norseman	164	32.12 S	121.46 E
Norsewood	170	40.04 S	176.13 E
Norsjå ⊜	114	59.18 N	9.20 E
Norsjö	114	64.55 N	19.29 E
Norsk	128	52.20 N	129.55 E
Norte, Canal do ⩌	184	0.30 N	50.30 W
North ≃	172	57.30 N	62.05 W
North, Cape ➤	92	53.58 S	37.44 W
North, Cape ⊥[2]	172	47.02 N	60.25 W
North Adams, Mass., U.S.	176	42.42 N	73.07 W
North Adams, Mich., U.S.	176	41.58 N	84.32 W
Northallerton	106	54.20 N	1.26 W
Northam, Austl.	164	31.39 S	116.40 E
Northam, S. Afr.	160	25.03 S	27.11 E
Northam, Eng., U.K.	104	51.02 N	4.12 W
North America ⊥[1]	84	45.00 N	100.00 W
North American Basin ⊹[1]	84	31.00 N	62.00 W
Northampton, Austl.	164	28.21 S	114.37 E
Northampton, Eng., U.K.	104	52.14 N	0.54 W
Northampton, Mass., U.S.	176	42.19 N	72.38 W
Northampton, Pa., U.S.	176	40.41 N	75.30 W
Northamptonshire □[6]	102	52.20 N	0.50 W
North Andaman I	140	13.15 N	92.55 E
North Anna ≃	176	37.50 N	77.29 W
North Anson	176	44.52 N	69.54 W
North Aulatsivik Island I	172	59.50 N	64.00 W
North Baltimore	176	41.11 N	83.41 W
North Battleford	172	52.47 N	108.17 W
North Bay	172	46.19 N	79.28 W
North Bend	178	43.24 N	124.14 W
North Bennington	176	42.56 N	73.15 W
North Berwick, Scot., U.K.	108	56.04 N	2.44 W
North Berwick, Maine, U.S.	176	43.17 N	70.45 W
North Bourke	168	30.03 S	145.57 E
North Branch	176	43.14 N	83.12 W
North Caicos I	182	21.55 N	71.56 W
North Canton	176	40.53 N	81.24 W
North Cape ➤	170	34.25 S	173.02 E
North Cape Rise ⊹[3]	96	32.00 S	173.00 E
North Caribou Lake ⊜	172	52.50 N	90.40 W
North Carolina □[3]	174	35.30 N	80.00 W
North Channel ⩌	172	46.02 N	82.50 W
Northcliffe	164	34.36 S	116.07 E
North College Hill	176	39.12 N	84.32 W
North Collins	176	42.36 N	78.56 W
North Conway	176	44.03 N	71.08 W
North Creek	176	43.42 N	73.59 W
North Dakota □[3]	174	47.30 N	100.15 W
North Dorset Downs ⛰[1]	104	50.47 N	2.30 W
North Down Cbangor	110	54.40 N	5.40 W
North Downs ⛰[1]	104	50.12 N	0.10 E
North East, Md., U.S.	176	39.36 N	75.56 W
North East, Pa., U.S.	176	42.13 N	79.50 W
North East □[5]	160	21.00 S	27.30 E
North Eastern □[4]	158	1.00 N	40.15 E
Northeast Harbor	176	44.18 N	68.17 W
Northeast Point ➤, Ba.	182	21.20 N	73.00 W
Northeast Point ➤, Ba.	182	22.42 N	73.50 W
Northeast Providence Channel ⩌	182	25.30 N	77.10 W
Northeim	116	51.42 N	10.00 E
North Elkhorn Creek ≃	176	38.13 N	84.48 W
Northern □[4], Malawi	158	11.00 S	34.00 E
Northern □[4], Zam.	158	11.00 S	31.00 E
Northern Dvina → Severnaja Dvina ≃	112	64.32 N	40.30 E
Northern Indian Lake ⊜	172	57.20 N	97.20 W
Northern Territory □[8]	162	21.00 S	134.00 E
North Esk ≃, Scot., U.K.	108	56.44 N	2.28 W
North Esk ≃, Scot., U.K.	108	55.54 N	3.04 W
Northfield, Mass., U.S.	176	42.42 N	72.27 W
Northfield, Minn., U.S.	174	44.27 N	93.09 W
Northfield, Vt., U.S.	176	44.09 N	72.40 W
North Fiji Basin ⊹[1]	96	17.00 S	173.00 E
Northfleet	104	51.27 N	0.21 E
North Flinders Range ⛰	168	31.00 S	139.00 E
North Foreland ➤	102	51.23 N	1.27 E
North Fork	178	37.14 N	119.31 W
North Frisian Islands II	112	54.50 N	8.12 E
North Haven	176	41.23 N	72.52 W
North Hawaiian Seamount Range ⊹[3]	84	29.00 N	163.00 W
North Henik Lake ⊜	172	61.45 N	97.40 W
North Hero	176	44.49 N	73.18 W
North Highlands	178	38.40 N	121.23 W
North Hill	104	50.34 N	4.25 W
North Hinksey	104	51.45 N	1.16 W
North Island I	170	39.00 S	176.00 E
North Kingsville	176	41.54 N	80.42 W
North Knife Lake ⊜	172	58.05 N	97.05 W
North Korea → Korea, North □[1]	132	40.00 N	127.00 E
North Lakhimpur	144	27.14 N	94.07 E
North Las Vegas	178	36.12 N	115.07 W
Northleach	104	51.51 N	1.50 W
North Luconia Shoals ⊹[2]	138	5.40 N	112.35 E
North Madagascar Basin ⊹[1]	88	14.00 S	44.00 E
North Palisade Λ	178	37.06 N	118.31 W
North Petherton	104	51.06 N	3.01 W
North Platte	174	41.08 N	100.46 W
North Platte ≃	174	41.15 N	100.45 W
North Point ➤	176	45.02 N	83.16 W
North Pole ✦	90	90.00 N	0.00
Northport	176	45.08 N	85.37 W
North Queensferry	108	56.01 N	3.25 W
North Rat Island Ridge ⊹[3]	94	54.00 N	177.00 E
North Ronaldsay I	108	59.22 N	2.26 W
North Ronaldsay Firth ⩌	108	59.20 N	2.25 W
North Saskatchewan ≃	172	53.15 N	105.06 W
North Saugeen ≃	176	44.19 N	81.17 W
North Sea ⊤[2]	100	55.20 N	3.00 E
North Seaton Colliery	106	55.11 N	1.32 W
North Shoshone Peak Λ	178	39.09 N	117.29 W
North Siberian Lowland → Severo-Sibirskaja Nizmennost' ≚	128	73.00 N	100.00 E
North Somercotes	106	53.28 N	0.08 E
North Sound ⩌, Eire	110	53.11 N	9.43 W
North Sound ⩌, Scot., U.K.	108	59.18 N	2.46 W
North Spicer Island I	172	68.30 N	78.55 W
North Stradbroke Island I	168	27.35 S	153.28 E
North Sunderland	106	55.34 N	1.39 W
North Taranaki Bight C[3]	170	38.42 S	174.15 E
North Tawton	104	50.48 N	3.53 W
North Tea Lake ⊜	176	45.56 N	79.03 W
North Thompson ≃	172	50.41 N	120.21 W
North Tidworth	104	51.16 N	1.40 W
North Tokelau Trough ⊹[1]	96	4.00 S	168.00 W
North Tolsta	108	58.20 N	6.13 W
North Troy	176	45.00 N	72.24 W
North Tyne ≃	106	54.59 N	2.08 W
North Uist I	108	57.36 N	7.18 W
Northumberland □[6]	102	55.15 N	2.05 W
Northumberland Isles II	168	21.40 S	150.00 E
Northumberland Strait ⩌	172	46.00 N	63.00 W
North Umpqua ≃	178	43.16 N	123.27 W
North Vancouver	172	49.19 N	123.04 W
North Vassalboro	176	44.29 N	69.37 W
North Vietnam → Vietnam □[1]	138	16.00 N	108.00 E
Northville	176	43.13 N	74.11 W
Northwaa	108	59.16 N	2.17 W
North Walsham	104	52.50 N	1.24 E
North Weald Bassett	104	51.43 N	0.10 E
North West Cape ➤	164	21.45 S	114.10 E
Northwest Christmas Island Ridge ⊹[3]	96	6.30 N	159.00 W
North-Western □[4]	158	13.00 S	25.00 E
Northwest Providence Channel ⩌	182	26.10 N	78.20 W
North West River	172	53.32 N	60.08 W
Northwest Territories □[4]	172	70.00 N	100.00 W
Northwich	106	53.16 N	2.32 W
North Windham	176	43.50 N	70.26 W
Northwold	104	52.33 N	0.35 E
North York Moors ⛰[2]	106	54.24 N	0.53 W

Symbols in the index entries are identified on page 198.

Nort – Ostr

Name	Page	Lat °′	Long °′
North Yorkshire □6	102	54.15 N	1.30 W
North Yuba ≃	178	39.22 N	121.08 W
Norton	106	54.09 N	0.47 W
Norton Canes	104	52.41 N	1.59 W
Norton Fitzwarren	104	51.02 N	3.09 W
Nortorf	116	54.10 N	9.50 E
Nort-sur-Erdre	118	47.26 N	1.30 W
Norvegia, Cape ≻	87	71.25 S	12.18 W
Norwalk, Conn., U.S.	176	41.07 N	73.27 W
Norwalk, Ohio, U.S.	176	41.15 N	82.37 W
Norway	176	44.13 N	70.32 W
Norway □1	100	62.00 N	10.00 E
Norway Bay C	172	71.08 N	104.35 W
Norway House	172	53.59 N	97.50 W
Norwegian Basin ∻1	88	70.00 N	5.00 E
Norwegian Sea ⊤2	88	70.00 N	2.00 E
Norwich, Ont., Can.	176	42.59 N	80.36 W
Norwich, Eng., U.K.	104	52.38 N	1.18 E
Norwich, Conn., U.S.	176	41.32 N	72.05 W
Norwich, N.Y., U.S.	176	42.32 N	75.31 W
Norwood, Ont., Can.	176	44.23 N	77.59 W
Norwood, Mass., U.S.	176	42.11 N	71.12 W
Norwood, N.Y., U.S.	176	44.45 N	75.00 W
Norwood, Ohio, U.S.	176	39.10 N	84.28 W
Nosbonsing, Lake ⊜	176	46.12 N	79.13 W
Noshiro	134	40.12 N	140.02 E
Noss, Isle of I	108a	60.09 N	1.01 W
Noss Head ≻	108	58.28 N	3.04 W
Nossob (Nossop) ≃	160	26.55 S	20.37 E
Nosy Varika	161b	20.35 S	48.32 E
Notikewin ≃	172	57.15 N	117.05 W
Noto, It.	122	36.53 N	15.05 E
Noto, Nihon	134	37.18 N	137.09 E
Noto-hantō ≻1	134	37.20 N	137.00 E
Notoro-ko ⊜	134a	44.05 N	144.10 E
Notre Dame, Monts ⋀	172	48.10 N	68.00 W
Notre Dame Bay C	172	49.45 N	55.15 W
Notre-Dame-du-Laus	176	46.05 N	75.37 W
Nottawasaga ≃	176	44.32 N	80.01 W
Nottawasaga Bay C	176	44.40	80.30 W
Nottaway ≃	172	51.22 N	79.55 W
Nottingham	104	52.58 N	1.10 W
Nottingham Island I	172	63.20 N	77.55 W
Nottingham Road	160	29.22 S	30.00 E
Nottinghamshire □6	102	53.00 N	1.00 W
Nouadhibou	152	20.54 N	17.04 W
Nouakchott	152	18.06 N	15.57 W
Nouamrhar	152	19.22 N	16.31 W
Nouméa	96	20.30 S	166.35 E
Noupoort	160	31.10 S	24.57 E
Nouveau-Québec, Cratère du •5	172	61.17 N	73.40 W
Nouvelle-Anvers	156	1.36 N	19.07 E
Nouvelle-Calédonie I	84	21.30 S	165.30 E
Nouvelle-France, Cap de ≻	172	62.27 N	73.42 W
Nova Andradina	190	22.10 S	53.15 W
Nova Caipemba	156	7.26 S	14.38 E
Nova Chaves	156	10.34 S	21.17 E
Nova Cruz	184	6.28 S	35.26 W
Nova Esperança	190	25.57 S	53.48 W
Nova Fátima	190	23.29 S	50.33 W
Nova Friburgo	190	22.16 S	42.32 W
Nova Gaia	156	10.09 S	17.31 E
Nova Goa → Panaji	148	15.29 N	73.50 E
Nova Granada	190	20.29 S	49.19 W
Nova Iguaçu	190	22.45 S	43.27 W
Novaja Kachovka	126	46.45 N	33.23 E
Novaja Ladoga	130	60.05 N	32.16 E
Novaja Sibir', Ostrov I	128	75.00 N	149.00 E
Novaja Zeml'a II	126	74.00 N	57.00 E
Nova Lima	190	19.59 S	43.51 W
Nova Lisboa → Huambo	156	12.44 S	15.47 E
Nova Mambone	160	20.59 S	35.01 E
Nova Prata	188	28.47 S	51.36 W
Novara	122	45.28 N	8.38 E
Nova Scotia □4	172	45.00 N	63.00 W
Nova Sofala	160	20.09 S	34.42 E
Novato	178	38.06 N	122.34 W
Nova Varoš	124	43.28 N	19.48 E
Nova Veneza	188	28.39 S	49.30 W
Novaya Zemlya Ridge ∻3	88	73.00 N	51.00 E
Nova Zagora	124	42.29 N	26.01 E
Nova Zembla Island I	172	72.10 N	74.50 W
Novelda	120	38.23 N	0.46 W
Nové Město nad Váhom	116	48.46 N	17.49 E
Nové Zámky	116	47.59 N	18.11 E
Novgorod	130	58.31 N	31.17 E
Novi Bečej	124	45.36 N	20.08 E
Novigrad	122	44.11 N	15.33 E
Novi Ligure	122	44.46 N	8.47 E
Novi Pazar, Blg.	124	43.21 N	27.12 E
Novi Pazar, Jugo.	124	43.08 N	20.31 E
Novi Sad	124	45.15 N	19.50 E
Novoaltajsk	128	53.24 N	83.58 E
Novoanninskij	126	50.32 N	42.41 E
Novo Aripuanã	184	5.08 S	60.22 W
Novočerkassk	126	47.25 N	40.06 E
Novogrudok	130	53.36 N	25.50 E
Nôvo Hamburgo	188	29.41 S	51.08 W
Nôvo Horizonte	190	21.28 S	49.13 W
Novokaširsk	130	54.51 N	38.15 E
Novokazalinsk	126	45.50 N	62.10 E
Novokujbyševsk	112	53.07 N	49.58 E
Novokuzneck	128	53.45 N	87.06 E
Novol'vovsk	130	53.55 N	38.47 E
Novo Mesto	122	45.48 N	15.10 E
Novomoskovsk	130	54.05 N	38.13 E
Novopetrovskoje	130	55.59 N	36.28 E
Novo Redondo	156	11.13 S	13.50 E
Novorossijsk	126	44.45 N	37.45 E
Novorybnoje	128	72.50 N	105.50 E
Novoržev	130	57.02 N	29.20 E
Novošachtinsk	126	47.47 N	39.56 E
Novosibirsk	128	55.02 N	82.55 E
Novosibirskije Ostrova II	128	75.00 N	142.00 E
Novosibirskoje Vodochranilišče ⊜1	128	54.35 N	82.35 E
Novosokol'niki	130	56.21 N	30.10 E
Novotroick	126	51.12 N	58.20 E
Novouzensk	126	50.28 N	48.08 E
Novov'atsk	112	58.29 N	49.44 E
Novovolynsk	126	50.50 N	24.05 E
Novozybkov	130	52.32 N	31.56 E
Nový Bohumín	116	49.56 N	18.20 E
Nový Jičín	116	49.36 N	18.00 E
Novyj Port	128	67.40 N	72.52 E
Nowa Ruda	116	50.35 N	16.31 E
Nowa Sól (Neusalz)	116	51.48 N	15.44 E
Nowendoc	168	31.32 S	151.43 E
Nowgong	146	26.21 N	92.40 E
Nowingi	168	34.36 S	142.14 E
Nowitna ≃	172	65.55 N	154.17 W
Nowra	168	34.53 S	150.36 E
Nowshāk ∧	149	36.26 N	71.50 E
Nowshera	146	34.01 N	71.59 E
Nowy Dwór Mazowiecki	116	52.26 N	20.43 E
Nowy Sącz	116	49.38 N	20.42 E
Nowy Targ	116	49.29 N	20.02 E
Noxen	176	41.25 N	76.03 W
Noyon	118	49.35 N	3.00 E
Nozay	118	47.34 N	1.38 W
Nsanje	158	16.55 S	35.12 E
Nsawam	152	5.50 N	0.20 W
Nsukka	152	6.52 N	7.24 E
Ntem ≃	152	2.15 N	9.45 E
Nuala	158	13.27 S	28.16 E
Nuanetsi	158	21.22 S	30.45 E
Nuanetsi ≃	160	22.40 S	31.50 E
Nūbah, Jibāl an- ⋀	154	12.00 N	30.45 E
Nubian Desert ⊸2	154	20.30 N	33.00 E
Ñuble □4	188	36.35 S	71.50 W
Ñuble ≃	188	36.39 S	72.27 W
N'uchča	112	63.27 N	46.28 E
Nudlung Fiord C2	172	68.21 N	67.22 W
Nueces ≃	174	27.50 N	97.30 W
Nueltin Lake ⊜	172	60.20 N	99.50 W
Nueva, Isla I	186	55.13 S	66.30 W
Nueva Casas Grandes	180	30.25 N	107.55 W
Nueva Esparta □3	182	11.00 N	64.00 W
Nueva Gerona	182	21.53 N	82.48 W
Nueva Imperial	188	38.44 S	72.57 W
Nueva Rosita	180	27.57 N	101.13 W
Nueve de Julio	188	35.30 S	60.50 W
Nuevitas	182	21.33 N	77.16 W
Nuevo, Golfo C	186	42.42 S	64.35 W
Nuevo Laredo	180	27.30 N	99.31 W
Nuevo Léon	178	32.20 N	115.12 W
Nuevo Mundo, Cerro ∧	184	21.55 S	66.53 W
Nûgssuaq ≻1	172	71.45 N	53.00 W
Nuguria Islands II	96	3.20 S	154.45 E
Nuhaka	170	39.03 S	177.45 E
Nui I1	96	7.15 S	177.10 E
Nuits-Saint-Georges	118	47.08 N	4.57 E
N'uja	128	60.32 N	116.14 E
N'uja ≃	128	60.32 N	116.20 E
Nukey Bluff •4	168	32.33 S	135.40 E
Nukufetau I1	96	8.00 S	178.22 E
Nukulailai I1	96	9.23 S	179.52 E
Nukumanu Islands II	96	4.30 S	159.30 E
Nukunonu I	96	9.12 S	171.54 W
Nukuoro I1	96	3.51 N	154.58 E
Nukus	126	42.50 N	59.29 E
Nules	120	39.51 N	0.09 W
Nullagine	164	21.53 S	120.06 E
Nullarbor	164	31.26 S	130.55 E
Nullarbor Plain ≚	164	31.00 S	129.00 E
Numata	134a	43.48 N	141.57 E
Numazu	134	35.06 N	138.52 E
Numbargulme, Mount ∧	166	14.56 S	145.03 E
Numfoor, Pulau I	166	1.03 S	134.54 E
Numto	128	63.40 N	71.20 E
Numurkah	168	36.06 S	145.26 E
Nunda	176	42.35 N	77.57 W
Nuneaton	104	52.32 N	1.28 W
Nunjiang	132	49.10 N	125.11 E
Nunjiang ≃	132	45.25 N	124.40 E
Nunjikompita	164	32.16 S	134.19 E
Nuominhe ≃	132	48.06 N	124.26 E
Nuoro	122	40.19 N	9.20 E
Nuqruș, Jabal ∧	150	24.49 N	34.36 E
Nura ≃	126	50.30 N	69.59 E
Nurakita I	96	10.45 S	179.30 E
N'urba	128	63.17 N	118.20 E
Nurek	146	38.23 N	69.19 E
Nuremberg → Nürnberg	116	49.27 N	11.04 E
Nuriootpa	164	34.29 S	139.00 E
Nürnberg	116	49.27 N	11.04 E
Nurra ⊸1	122	40.45 N	8.15 E
Nurrari Lakes ⊜	164	29.01 S	130.05 E
Nurri, Mount ∧	168	31.42 S	146.02 E
Nürtingen	116	48.38 N	9.20 E
Nusa Tenggara (Lesser Sunda Islands) II	138	9.00 S	120.00 E
Nusa Tenggara Barat □4	142	8.50 S	117.30 E
Nusa Tenggara Timur □4	142	9.30 S	122.00 E
Nusaybin	150	37.03 N	41.13 E
Nushan ⋀	132	26.50 N	99.03 E
Nushki	150	29.33 N	66.01 E
Nutter Fort	176	39.20 N	80.19 W
Nutwood Downs	166	15.49 S	134.10 E
Nuwara-Eliya	144	6.58 N	80.46 E
Nuwaybi' al-Muzayyinah	150	28.58 N	34.39 E
Nuwerus	160	31.08 S	18.24 E
Nuweveldberge ⋀	160	32.13 S	21.40 E
Nuyts, Point ≻	164	35.04 S	116.37 E
Nuyts Archipelago II	164	32.35 S	133.17 E
Nyabing	164	33.32 S	118.09 E
Nyack	176	41.05 N	73.55 W
Nyadiri ≃	158	16.44 S	32.33 E
Nyah West	168	35.11 S	143.22 E
Nyala	154	12.03 N	24.53 E
Nyamandhlovu	158	19.50 S	28.16 E
Nyanga, Lake ⊜	164	29.57 S	126.10 E
Nyangui ∧	158	17.53 S	32.44 E
Nyanji Mission	158	14.23 S	31.48 E
Nyanza	158	2.21 S	29.45 E
Nyanza □4	158	0.30 S	34.30 E
Nyanza-Lac	158	4.21 S	29.36 E
Nyasa, Lake (Lake Malawi) ⊜	158	12.00 S	34.30 E
Nyaunglebin	140	17.57 N	96.44 E
Nyborg	114	55.19 N	10.48 E
Nybro	114	56.45 N	15.54 E
Nyda	128	66.36 N	72.54 E
Nyenyam	146	28.11 N	85.58 E
Nyeri	158	0.25 S	36.57 E
Nyfer ≃	104	52.02 N	4.50 W
Nyimba	158	14.35 S	30.52 E
Nyíradony	116	47.41 N	21.55 E
Nyíregyháza	116	47.59 N	21.43 E
Nykøbing, Dan.	114	55.55 N	11.41 E
Nykøbing, Dan.	114	56.48 N	8.52 E
Nykøbing, Dan.	114	54.46 N	11.53 E
Nyköping	114	58.45 N	17.00 E
Nylstroom	160	24.42 S	28.20 E
Nymboida ≃	168	29.39 S	152.30 E
Nymburk	116	50.11 N	15.03 E
Nynäshamn	114	58.54 N	17.57 E
Nyngan	168	31.34 S	147.11 E
Nyon	118	46.23 N	6.14 E
Nyong ≃	152	3.17 N	9.54 E
Nysa	116	50.29 N	17.20 E
Nysa Łużycka (Neisse) (Nisa) ≃	116	52.04 N	14.46 E
Nytva	112	57.56 N	55.20 E
Nyūdō-zaki ≻	134	40.00 N	139.42 E
Nyūzen	134	36.56 N	137.30 E
Nzérékoré	152	7.45 N	8.49 W
Nzi ≃	152	5.57 N	4.50 W

O

Name	Page	Lat °′	Long °′
Oa, Mull of ≻	108	55.35 N	6.19 W
Oadby	104	52.36 N	1.04 W
Oahe, Lake ⊜1	174	45.30 N	100.25 W
Oahu I	179a	21.30 N	158.00 W
O-akan-dake ∧	134a	43.27 N	144.10 E
Oakbank	168	33.03 S	140.35 E
Oak Bluffs	176	41.27 N	70.34 W
Oakdale, Austl.	164	34.26 S	119.00 E
Oakdale, Calif., U.S.	178	37.46 N	120.51 W
Oakengates	104	52.42 N	2.28 W
Oakey	168	27.26 S	151.43 E
Oakfield, Maine, U.S.	176	46.06 N	68.10 W
Oakfield, N.Y., U.S.	176	43.04 N	78.16 W
Oakham	104	52.40 N	0.43 W
Oak Harbor	176	41.30 N	83.09 W
Oak Hill, Ohio, U.S.	176	38.54 N	82.34 W
Oak Hill, W. Va., U.S.	176	37.59 N	81.09 W
Oakhurst	178	37.19 N	119.40 W
Oak Knolls	178	34.51 N	120.27 W
Oakland, Calif., U.S.	178	37.47 N	122.13 W
Oakland, Maine, U.S.	176	44.33 N	69.43 W
Oakland, Md., U.S.	176	39.25 N	79.24 W
Oakland, Oreg., U.S.	178	43.25 N	123.18 W
Oakley	178	42.15 N	113.53 W
Oakover ≃	164	20.43 S	120.33 E
Oak Ridge	174	36.01 N	84.16 W
Oakura	170	39.07 S	173.57 E
Oak View	178	34.24 N	119.18 W
Oakville	176	43.27 N	79.41 W
Oakwood	176	41.06 N	84.23 W
Oamaru	170	45.06 S	170.58 E
Ōarai	134	36.18 N	140.34 E
Oates Coast •2	87	70.00 S	160.00 E
Oatka Creek ≃	176	43.01 N	77.44 W
Oatlands	168	42.18 S	147.21 E
Oatman	178	35.02 N	114.23 W
Oaxaca	180	17.00 N	96.30 W
Ob' ≃	126	66.45 N	69.30 E
Obama, Nihon	134	35.30 N	135.45 E
Obama, Nihon	134	32.43 N	130.13 E
Oban, Austl.	168	21.14 S	139.03 E
Oban, Scot., U.K.	108	56.25 N	5.29 W
Obanazawa	134	38.36 N	140.24 E
Obbia	154	5.20 N	48.38 E
Obelisk ∧	170	45.20 S	169.12 E
Oberá	188	27.30 S	55.07 W
Ober Ennstal ∨	116	47.28 N	14.10 E
Obergurgl	116	46.52 N	11.01 E
Oberhausen	116	51.28 N	6.50 E
Oberlin	176	41.18 N	82.13 W
Oberon	168	33.43 S	149.52 E
Oberösterreich □3	116	48.15 N	14.00 E
Oberpullendorf	116	47.31 N	16.31 E
Oberursel	116	50.11 N	8.35 E
Oberviechtach	116	49.28 N	12.25 E
Oberwart	116	47.17 N	16.13 E
Oberwölz Stadt	116	47.13 N	14.17 E
Obi, Kepulauan II	166	1.30 S	127.45 E
Obi, Pulau I	166	1.30 S	127.45 E
Óbidos	184	1.55 S	55.31 W
Obihiro	134a	42.55 N	143.12 E
Obilatu, Pulau I	138	1.25 S	127.20 E
Obira	134a	44.00 N	141.35 E
Obi Trough ∻1	96	33.00 S	98.00 E
Oblučje	128	49.03 N	131.04 E
Obninsk	130	55.05 N	36.37 E
Obo, Centraf.	158	5.24 N	26.30 E
Obo, Yai.	158	3.46 N	38.50 E
Obock	154	11.59 N	43.16 E
Obot	158	4.30 N	37.20 E
Obra ≃	116	52.36 N	15.28 E
O'brien	178	42.04 N	123.42 W
Obščij Syrt ∧	126	52.00 N	51.30 E
Observation Peak ∧	178	40.46 N	120.10 W
Observatoire, Caye de l' I	162	21.25 S	158.50 E
Obskaja Guba C	126	69.00 N	73.00 E
Obuasi	152	6.14 N	1.39 W
Ocala	174	29.11 N	82.07 W
Ocaña, Col.	184	8.15 N	73.20 W
Ocaña, Esp.	120	39.56 N	3.31 W
Occidental, Cordillera ⋀, Col.	184	5.00 N	76.00 W
Occidental, Cordillera ⋀, Perú	184	14.00 S	74.00 W
Ocean Cape ≻	172	59.30 N	139.45 W
Ocean City, Md., U.S.	176	38.20 N	75.05 W
Ocean City, N.J., U.S.	176	39.16 N	74.36 W
Ocean Falls	172	52.21 N	127.40 W
Ocean Island I	96	0.52 S	169.35 E
Oceano	178	35.06 N	120.37 W
Oceanside	178	33.12 N	117.23 W
Očer	112	57.53 N	54.42 E
Ocha	128	53.34 N	142.56 E
Ochil Hills ⋀2	108	56.14 N	3.40 W
Ochiltree	108	55.28 N	4.23 W
Ocho Rios	182	18.25 N	77.07 W
Ochota ≃	128	59.20 N	143.04 E
Ochotsk	128	59.23 N	143.18 E
Ochsenfurt	116	49.40 N	10.03 E
Ochtrup	116	52.13 N	7.11 E
Ock ≃	104	51.39 N	1.17 W
Ockelbo	114	60.53 N	16.43 E
Öckerö	114	57.43 N	11.39 E
Ocon, Bahía de C	182	18.23 N	70.40 W
Ocoña ≃	184	16.28 S	73.08 W
Ocotal	182	13.37 N	86.31 W
Ocotlán	180	20.21 N	102.46 W
Ocozingo	180	16.54 N	92.07 W
Ocreza, Ribeira da ≃	120	39.32 N	7.50 W
Ocumare del Tuy	184	10.07 N	66.46 W
Ocussi	138	9.12 S	124.21 E
Oda, Ghana	152	5.55 N	0.59 W
Ōda, Nihon	134	35.11 N	132.30 E
Oda, Jabal ∧	154	20.21 N	36.39 E
Ōdaigahara-san ∧	134	34.11 N	136.05 E
Odaka	134	37.34 N	141.00 E
Ōdate	134	40.16 N	140.34 E
Odawara	134	35.15 N	139.10 E
Odda	114	60.04 N	6.33 E
Odeleite, Ribeira de ≃	120	37.21 N	7.27 W
Odell Lake ⊜	178	45.38 N	121.32 W
Odemira	120	37.36 N	8.38 W
Odendaalsrus	160	27.48 S	26.45 E
Odense	114	55.24 N	10.23 E
Odenwald ⋀	116	49.40 N	9.00 E
Oder (Odra) ≃	116	53.32 N	14.38 E
Oderberg	116	52.52 N	14.02 E
Oderbruch ⊸1	116	52.40 N	14.15 E
Oderhaff (Zalew Szczeciński) C	116	53.46 N	14.14 E
Odessa, Ont., Can.	176	44.17 N	76.43 W
Odessa, S.S.S.R.	126	46.28 N	30.44 E
Odessa, Tex., U.S.	174	31.51 N	102.22 W
Odesskoje	128	54.13 N	72.58 E
Odienné	152	9.30 N	7.34 W
Odiham	104	51.15 N	0.57 W
Odin, Mount ∧	172	50.33 N	118.08 W
Odincovo	130	55.41 N	37.17 E
Odorheiu Secuiesc	124	46.18 N	25.18 E
Odzi	158	18.58 S	32.23 E
Odzi ≃	158	19.45 S	32.24 E
Oeiras	184	7.01 S	42.08 W
Oelde	116	51.49 N	8.08 E
Oelsnitz	116	50.24 N	12.10 E
Oenpelli Mission	166	12.20 S	133.04 E
Oettingen in Bayern	116	48.57 N	10.36 E
Offaly □6	110	53.20 N	7.30 W
Offenbach	116	50.08 N	8.47 E
Offenburg	116	48.28 N	7.57 E
Oficina Vergara	188	22.28 S	69.38 W
O'Flynn, Lough ⊜	110	53.46 N	8.40 W
Ofotfjorden C2	112	68.23 N	16.10 E
Ōfunato	134	39.04 N	141.43 E
Oga	134	39.53 N	139.51 E
Oga-hantō ≻1	134	39.55 N	139.50 E
Ōgaki	134	35.21 N	136.37 E
Ogallala	174	41.08 N	101.43 W
Ogasawara-guntō (Bonin Islands) II	96	27.00 N	142.10 E
Ogatsu	134	38.41 N	141.28 E
Ogawa	134	32.35 N	130.43 E
Ogawara-ko ⊜	134	40.47 N	141.20 E
Ogbomosho	152	8.08 N	4.15 E
Ogden	174	41.14 N	111.58 W
Ogdensburg	176	44.42 N	75.29 W
Ogilvie	164	28.09 S	114.38 E
Ogilvie Mountains ⋀	172	65.00 N	139.30 W
Ogliastra ⊸1	122	40.00 N	9.30 E
Ogmore	168	22.37 S	149.40 E
Ogmore ≃	104	51.28 N	3.38 W
Ogmore Vale	104	51.38 N	3.31 W
Ognon ≃	118	47.20 N	5.29 E
Ogoja	152	6.40 N	8.48 E
Ogoki ≃	172	51.38 N	85.57 W
Ogooué ≃	156	0.49 S	9.00 E
Ogōri	134	34.06 N	131.24 E
Ogosta ≃	124	43.45 N	23.51 E
Ogulin	122	45.16 N	15.14 E
Oguni	134	38.04 N	139.45 E
Ogunquit	176	43.16 N	70.36 W
Ohakune	170	39.25 S	175.24 E
Ohanet	152	28.45 N	8.55 E
Ōhara	134	35.15 N	140.23 E
Ōhata	134	41.24 N	141.10 E
O'Higgins □4	188	34.15 S	70.45 W
O'Higgins, Lago (Lago San Martín) ⊜	186	49.00 S	72.40 W
Ohingaiti	170	39.52 S	175.43 E
Ohio □3	174	40.15 N	82.45 W
Ohio ≃	174	36.59 N	89.08 W
Ohio City	176	40.46 N	84.37 W
Ohře ≃	116	50.32 N	14.08 E
Ohrid	124	41.07 N	20.47 E
Ohrid, Lake ⊜	124	41.02 N	20.43 E
Ohrigstad	160	24.49 S	30.33 E
Ohura	170	38.50 S	174.59 E
Ōi ≃	134	34.46 N	138.18 E
Oiapoque	184	3.50 N	51.50 W
Oil City	174	41.26 N	79.42 W
Oil Creek ≃	176	41.26 N	79.42 W
Oildale	178	35.25 N	119.01 W
Oir, Beinn an ∧	108	55.54 N	6.00 W
Oise □5	118	49.30 N	2.30 E
Oise ≃	118	49.00 N	2.04 E
Ōita	134	33.14 N	131.36 E
Ojai	178	34.27 N	119.15 W
Öje	114	60.49 N	13.51 E
Ojika-hantō ≻1	134	38.20 N	141.30 E
Ojinaga	180	29.34 N	104.25 W
Ojiya	134	37.18 N	138.48 E
Ojm'akon	128	63.28 N	142.49 E
Ojos del Salado, Cerro ∧	188	27.06 S	68.32 W
Oka ≃, S.S.S.R.	128	55.15 N	102.10 E
Oka ≃, S.S.S.R.	130	56.20 N	43.59 E
Okahandja	160	21.59 S	16.58 E
Okahandja □5	160	21.30 S	17.00 E
Okahukura	170	38.47 S	175.13 E
Okaihau	170	35.19 S	173.47 E
Okanagan Lake ⊜	172	50.00 N	119.28 W
Okanaogan ≃	174	48.06 N	119.43 W
Okāra	149	30.49 N	73.27 E
Okarito	170	43.14 S	170.11 E
Okaukuejo	160	19.10 S	15.54 E
Okavango (Cubango) ≃	156	18.50 S	22.25 E
Okavango Swamp ☷	160	18.45 S	22.45 E
Ōkawa	134	33.12 N	130.23 E
Okaya	134	36.03 N	138.03 E
Okayama	134	34.39 N	133.55 E
Okayama-heiya ≚	134	34.35 N	133.51 E
Okazaki	134	34.57 N	137.10 E
Okeechobee, Lake ⊜	174	26.55 N	80.45 W
Okehampton	104	50.44 N	4.00 W
Okement ≃	104	50.50 N	4.01 W
Okemos	176	42.43 N	84.26 W
Okene	152	7.33 N	6.15 E
Okhotsk, Sea of (Ochotskoje More) ⊤2	128	53.00 N	150.00 E
Okhotsk Basin ∻1	94	53.00 N	148.00 E
Okiep	160	29.39 S	17.53 E
Oki-guntō II	134	36.15 N	133.15 E
Okinawa □5	135b	26.31 N	127.59 E
Okinawa-jima I	135b	26.30 N	128.00 E
Okino-Daitō-jima I	132	24.28 N	131.11 E
Okino-Erabu-shima I	135b	27.22 N	128.35 E
Okino-Tori-Shima I	132	20.25 N	136.00 E
Oklahoma □3	174	35.30 N	98.00 W
Oklahoma City	174	35.28 N	97.32 W
Okmulgee	174	35.37 N	95.58 W
Oksskolten ∧	112	65.59 N	14.15 E
Okt'abr'skoje	128	62.28 N	66.03 E
Okt'abr'skoj Revol'ucii, Ostrov I	128	79.30 N	97.00 E
Ōkuchi	134	32.04 N	130.37 E
Okuku ≃	170	43.16 S	172.28 E
Okuma Bay C	87	77.48 S	158.35 W
Okushiri	134a	42.10 N	139.31 E
Okushiri-tō I	134a	42.10 N	139.27 E
Okutango-hantō ≻1	134	35.40 N	135.10 E
Ola	128	59.35 N	151.17 E
Ólafsfjörður	112a	66.06 N	18.38 W
Olancha	178	36.17 N	118.01 W
Olancha Peak ∧	178	36.16 N	118.07 W
Olanchito	182	15.30 N	86.35 W
Öland I	114	56.45 N	16.38 E
Olary	168	32.17 S	140.19 E
Olavarría	188	36.53 S	60.20 W
Oława	116	50.57 N	17.17 E
Olbia	122	40.55 N	9.29 E
Ol'chon, Ostrov I	128	53.09 N	107.24 E
Olcott	176	43.20 N	78.43 W
Old Bahama Channel ⩂	182	22.33 N	78.05 W
Old Bedford ≃	104	52.35 N	0.20 E
Old Bight	182	24.15 N	75.21 W
Oldbury	104	52.30 N	2.00 W
Oldcastle	110	53.46 N	7.10 W
Old Colwyn	106	53.18 N	3.43 W
Old Cork	168	22.56 S	141.52 E
Old Crow	172	67.35 N	139.50 W
Old Crow ≃	172	67.35 N	139.50 W
Oldebroek	116	52.26 N	5.54 E
Oldenburg	116	53.08 N	8.13 E
Oldenburg □9	116	53.00 N	8.00 E
Oldenburg [in Holstein]	116	54.17 N	10.52 E
Oldenzaal	116	52.19 N	6.56 E
Old Fletton	104	52.33 N	0.15 W
Old Forge, N.Y., U.S.	176	43.43 N	74.58 W
Old Forge, Pa., U.S.	176	41.22 N	75.44 W
Oldham	106	53.33 N	2.07 W
Old Howe ≃	106	53.57 N	0.21 W
Oldmeldrum	108	57.20 N	2.20 W
Old Mkushi	158	14.22 S	29.22 E
Old Nene ≃	104	52.40 N	0.10 E
Old Noranside	168	22.13 S	140.04 E
Old Orchard Beach	176	43.31 N	70.23 W
Olds	172	51.47 N	114.06 W
Old Saybrook	176	41.18 N	72.23 W
Old Speck Mountain ∧	176	44.34 N	70.57 W
Old Tate	160	21.22 S	27.46 E
Old Town	176	44.56 N	68.39 W
Old Wives Lake ⊜	172	50.06 N	106.00 W
Olean	176	42.05 N	78.26 W
Olenegorsk	112	68.09 N	33.15 E
Olenij, Ostrov I	128	72.25 N	77.45 E
Olen'ok	128	68.33 N	112.18 E
Olen'ok ≃	128	73.00 N	119.55 E
Olen'okskij Zaliv C	128	73.20 N	121.00 E
Oléron, Île d' I	118	45.56 N	1.15 W
Oleśnica	116	51.13 N	17.23 E
Ol'ga	128	43.45 N	135.18 E
Olga, Mount ∧	164	25.19 S	130.46 E
Ölgij	132	48.56 N	89.57 E
Olhão	120	37.02 N	8.50 W
Olifants (Rio dos Elefantes) ≃, Afr.	160	24.10 S	32.40 E
Olifants ≃, S. Afr.	156	24.10 S	32.40 E
Olifants ≃, S. Afr.	160	31.42 S	18.12 E
Olifantshoek	160	27.57 S	22.42 E
Olimarao I1	138	7.41 N	145.52 E
Ólimbos ∧, Ellás	124	40.05 N	22.21 E
Ólimbos ∧, Kípros	150	34.56 N	32.52 E
Olímpia	190	20.44 S	48.54 W
Olinda	184	8.01 S	34.51 W
Olio	168	21.54 S	143.13 E
Olite	120	42.29 N	1.39 W
Oliva, Arg.	188	32.05 S	63.35 W
Oliva, Esp.	120	38.55 N	0.07 W
Oliva de la Frontera	120	38.16 N	6.55 W
Olive Hill	176	38.16 N	83.10 W
Olivehurst	178	39.06 N	121.34 W
Oliveira	190	20.41 S	44.49 W
Olivenza	120	38.41 N	7.06 W
Olivet	176	42.27 N	84.56 W
Ollagüe	186	21.14 S	68.16 W
Ollatrim ≃	110	52.52 N	8.13 W
Ollerton	106	53.12 N	1.00 W
Olmos	184	5.59 S	79.46 W
Olney	104	52.81 N	0.43 W
Oloj ≃	128	66.29 N	159.29 E
Ol'okma ≃	128	60.22 N	120.42 E
Ol'okminsk	128	60.24 N	120.24 E
Olomouc	116	49.36 N	17.16 E
Olonec	112	61.00 N	32.57 E
Olongapo	138	14.50 N	120.16 E
Oloron, Gave d' ≃	118	43.33 N	1.05 W
Oloron-Sainte-Marie	118	43.12 N	0.36 W
Olot	120	42.11 N	2.29 E
Olov'annaja	128	50.56 N	115.35 E
Olpe	116	51.02 N	7.52 E
Olsztyn (Allenstein)	116	53.48 N	20.29 E
Olt □4	124	44.20 N	24.30 E
Olt ≃	124	43.43 N	24.51 E
Olten	118	47.21 N	7.54 E
Oltenița	124	44.05 N	26.39 E
Oluan Pi ≻	136	21.54 N	120.51 E
Ol'utorskij, Mys ≻	128	59.55 N	170.27 E
Ol'utorskij Zaliv C	128	59.55 N	170.27 E
Olympia	174	47.03 N	122.53 W
Olympus, Mount → Ólimbos ∧, Ellás	124	40.05 N	22.21 E
Olympus, Mount ∧, Ky., U.S.	176	38.03 N	83.39 W
Olympus, Mount ∧, Wash., U.S.	174	47.48 N	123.43 W
Om' ≃	128	54.59 N	73.22 E
Ōmachi	134	36.30 N	137.52 E
Omae-zaki ≻	134	34.36 N	138.14 E
Ōmagari	134	39.27 N	140.29 E
Omagh	110	54.36 N	7.18 W
Omaha	174	41.16 N	95.57 W
Omak	174	48.24 N	119.31 W
Omakau	170	45.05 S	169.36 E
Oman □1	144	22.00 N	58.00 E
Oman, Gulf of C	144	24.30 N	58.30 E
Omarama	170	44.29 S	169.58 E
Omaruru	160	21.28 S	15.56 E
Omaruru □5	160	21.00 S	15.45 E
Ōma-zaki ≻	134a	41.32 N	140.55 E
Ombersley	104	52.17 N	2.13 W
Omboué	156	1.34 S	9.15 E
Omčak	128	61.38 N	147.55 E
Ōme	134	35.47 N	139.15 E
Omegna	122	45.53 N	8.24 E
Omemee	176	44.18 N	78.33 W
Omeo	168	37.06 S	147.36 E
Ometepe, Isla de I	182	11.30 N	85.33 W
Ometepec	180	16.41 N	98.25 W
Ōmi-hachiman	134	35.08 N	136.06 E
Ōminato → Mutsu	134	41.17 N	141.10 E
Omineca ≃	172	56.05 N	124.30 W
Omineca Mountains ⋀	172	56.00 N	125.00 W
Ōmiya	134	35.54 N	139.38 E
Ommaney, Cape ≻	172	56.10 N	134.39 W
Ommanney Bay C	172	73.07 N	100.11 W
Ommen	116	52.32 N	6.25 E
Omo ≃	158	4.32 N	36.04 E
Omoloj ≃	128	71.10 N	132.08 E
Omolon ≃	128	68.42 N	158.36 E
Omono ≃	134	39.46 N	140.03 E
Omsk	128	55.00 N	73.24 E
Omsukčan	128	62.32 N	155.48 E
Ōmu	134a	44.34 N	142.58 E
Omul ∧	124	45.26 N	25.26 E
Ōmura	134	32.54 N	129.57 E
Ōmuta	134	33.02 N	130.27 E
Omutninsk	112	58.40 N	52.12 E
Onagawa	134	38.26 N	141.27 E
Onaway	176	45.21 N	84.14 W
Oncativo	188	31.55 S	63.45 W
Onda	120	39.58 N	0.15 W
Ondangua	160	17.55 S	16.00 E
Ondo, Nig.	152	7.04 N	4.47 E
Ondo, Nihon	134	34.11 N	132.32 E
Öndörchaan	132	47.19 N	110.39 E
Onega	112	63.55 N	38.05 E
Onega ≃	112	63.58 N	37.55 E
Oneida	176	43.06 N	75.39 W
Oneida Lake ⊜	176	43.13 N	76.00 W
O'Neill	174	42.27 N	98.39 W
Onekotan, Ostrov I	128	49.25 N	154.45 E
Oneonta	176	42.27 N	75.04 W
Onežskoje Ozero ⊜	126	61.30 N	35.45 E
Ongaonga	170	39.55 S	176.25 E
Ongarue	170	38.43 S	175.17 E
Ongerup	164	33.58 S	118.29 E
Ongole	148	15.31 N	80.04 E
Onich	108	56.42 N	5.13 W
Onitsha	152	6.09 N	6.47 E
Onny ≃	104	52.23 N	2.45 W
Ōno	134	35.59 N	136.29 E
Onoda	134	33.59 N	131.11 E
Ono-i-lau I	96	20.39 S	178.42 W
Onomichi	134	34.25 N	133.12 E
Onon ≃	132	51.42 N	115.50 E
Onoto	182	9.36 N	65.12 W
Onotoa I1	96	1.52 S	175.34 E
Onseepkans	160	28.46 S	19.14 E
Onset	176	41.45 N	70.39 W
Onslow	164	21.39 S	115.06 E
Ontake-san ∧	134	35.53 N	137.29 E
Ontario, Calif., U.S.	178	34.04 N	117.39 W
Ontario, Ohio, U.S.	176	40.46 N	82.39 W
Ontario, Oreg., U.S.	174	44.02 N	116.58 W
Ontario □4	172	51.00 N	85.00 W
Ontario, Lake ⊜	174	43.45 N	78.00 W
Onteniente	120	38.49 N	0.37 W
Ontong Java Rise ∻3	96	7.00 S	160.00 E
Onverwacht	184	5.35 N	55.10 W
Oobagooma	164	16.46 S	123.59 E
Oodnadatta	164	27.33 S	135.28 E
Ooldea	164	30.27 S	131.50 E
Ooratippra	164	22.00 S	136.00 E
Ooratippra Creek ≃	164	21.55 S	136.05 E
Oostelijk Flevoland ⊸1	116	52.30 N	5.45 E
Oostende (Ostende)	116	51.13 N	2.55 E
Oosterhout	116	51.38 N	4.51 E
Oost-Vlieland	116	53.17 N	5.04 E
Ootacamund	148	11.24 N	76.42 E
Ootsa Lake ⊜	172	53.49 N	126.18 W
Opala	156	0.37 S	24.21 E
Opari	158	3.56 N	32.03 E
Oparino	112	59.52 N	48.17 E
Opava	116	49.56 N	17.54 E
Opava ≃	116	49.50 N	18.13 E
Opelika	174	32.39 N	85.23 W
Opelousas	174	30.32 N	92.05 W
Opeongo ≃	176	45.30 N	77.57 W
Opeongo Lake ⊜	176	45.42 N	78.23 W
Opequon Creek ≃	176	39.35 N	77.52 W
Ophir	178	42.34 N	124.23 W
Opihikao	179a	19.26 N	154.53 W
Opinaca ≃	172	52.15 N	78.02 W
Opinan	108	57.43 N	5.47 W
Opiscotéo, Lac ⊜	172	53.10 N	68.10 W
Opladen	116	51.04 N	7.00 E
Opoczno	116	51.23 N	20.17 E
Opole (Oppeln)	116	50.41 N	17.55 E
Opotiki	170	38.00 S	177.17 E
Oppeln → Opole	116	50.41 N	17.55 E
Oppland □6	114	61.10 N	9.40 E
Opua	170	35.19 S	174.07 E
Or, Côte d' ∧	118	47.10 N	4.50 E
Ora Banda	164	30.22 S	121.04 E
Oradea	124	47.03 N	21.57 E
Öræfajökull ⊼	112a	64.03 N	16.38 W
Orai	146	25.59 N	79.28 E
Oran	152	35.43 N	0.43 W
Orange, Austl.	168	33.17 S	149.06 E
Orange, Fr.	118	44.08 N	4.48 E
Orange, Mass., U.S.	176	42.35 N	72.19 W
Orange, Tex., U.S.	174	30.01 N	93.44 W
Orange, Va., U.S.	176	38.15 N	78.07 W
Orange, Cabo ≻	184	4.24 N	51.33 W
Orangeburg	174	33.30 N	80.52 W
Orange Cove	178	36.37 N	119.19 W
Orange Free State (Oranje-Vrystaat) □3	160	28.30 S	27.00 E
Orangemouth → Oranjemund	160	28.38 S	16.24 E
Orangeville	176	43.55 N	80.06 W
Oranienburg	116	52.45 N	13.14 E
Oranje → Orange ≃	160	28.41 S	16.28 E
Oranjefontein	160	23.25 S	27.41 E
Oranje Gebergte ⋀	184	3.15 N	54.50 W
Oranjemund	160	28.38 S	16.24 E
Oranjerivier	160	29.40 S	24.12 E
Oranjestad	182	12.33 N	70.06 W
Oranmore	110	53.16 N	8.54 W
Oraparinna	168	31.22 S	138.43 E
Orăștie	124	45.50 N	23.12 E
Oravais (Oravainen)	114	63.18 N	22.23 E
Orawia	170	46.03 S	167.49 E
Orb ≃	118	43.15 N	3.18 E
Orbe	118	46.43 N	6.32 E
Orbetello	122	42.27 N	11.13 E
Orbieu ≃	118	43.14 N	2.54 E
Orbisonia	176	40.15 N	77.54 W
Orbost	168	37.42 S	148.27 E
Örbyhus	114	60.14 N	17.42 E
Orchard Park	176	42.43 N	78.45 W
Orchon ≃	132	50.21 N	106.05 E
Ord ≃	166	15.30 S	128.21 E
Ord, Mount ∧	164	17.20 S	125.34 E
Ord Mountain ∧	178	34.40 N	116.49 W
Ord River	164	17.23 S	128.51 E
Ordu	126	41.00 N	37.53 E
Ordžonikidze	126	43.03 N	44.40 E
Ore ≃	108	56.10 N	3.15 W
Örebro	114	59.17 N	15.13 E
Örebro Län □6	114	59.30 N	15.00 E
Orechovo-Zujevo	130	55.49 N	38.59 E
Oregon	176	41.38 N	83.28 W
Oregon □3	174	44.00 N	121.00 W
Oregon City	174	45.21 N	122.36 W
Orellana, Embalse de ⊜1	120	39.00 N	5.25 W
Orenburg	126	51.54 N	55.06 E
Orense	120	42.20 N	7.51 W
Orepuki	170	46.17 S	167.44 E
Orestiás	124	41.30 N	26.31 E
Oreti ≃	170	46.28 S	168.17 E
Orford	104	52.06 N	1.31 E
Orford Ness ≻	102	52.05 N	1.34 E
Orgelet	118	46.31 N	5.37 E
Orgof	158	3.03 N	43.44 E
Orgūn	146	32.51 N	69.07 E
Orick	178	41.17 N	124.04 W
Oriental, Cordillera ⋀, Col.	184	6.00 N	73.00 W
Oriental, Cordillera ⋀, Perú	184	13.00 S	72.00 W
Oriente	188	38.44 S	60.37 W
Orientos	168	28.05 S	141.14 E
Orihuela	120	38.05 N	0.57 W
Orillia	172	44.37 N	79.25 W
Orimattila	114	60.48 N	25.45 E
Orini	170	37.34 S	175.18 E
Orinoco ≃	184	8.37 N	62.15 W
Orinoco, Delta del ≚2	182	9.15 N	61.30 W
Oripää	114	60.51 N	22.41 E
Oriskany	176	43.09 N	75.20 W
Orissa □3	146	20.00 N	84.00 E
Oristano	122	40.00 N	8.40 E
Orituco ≃	182	8.45 N	67.27 W
Orivesi	114	61.41 N	24.21 E
Orivesi ⊜	114	62.16 N	29.24 E
Oriximiná	184	1.45 S	55.52 W
Orizaba	180	18.51 N	97.06 W
Ørje	114	59.29 N	11.39 E
Ork, Ness of ≻	108	59.05 N	2.48 W
Örkelljunga	114	56.17 N	13.17 E
Orkla ≃	114	63.18 N	9.50 E
Orkney	160	27.00 S	26.39 E
Orkney Islands □4	108	59.00 N	3.00 W
Orkney Islands II	108	59.00 N	3.00 W
Orland	178	39.45 N	122.11 W
Orlândia	190	20.43 S	47.53 W
Orlando	174	28.32 N	81.23 W
Orleães	188	28.21 S	49.18 W
Orléanais □9	118	47.50 N	2.00 E
Orléans, Ont., Can.	176	45.28 N	75.31 W
Orléans, Fr.	118	47.55 N	1.54 E
Orleans, Calif., U.S.	178	41.18 N	123.32 W
Orleans, Mass., U.S.	176	41.47 N	70.00 W
Orleans, Vt., U.S.	176	44.49 N	72.12 W
Orléans, Canal d' ≍	118	47.54 N	1.55 E
Orlik	128	52.30 N	99.55 E
Orlová	116	49.50 N	18.24 E
Ormāra	150	25.12 N	64.38 E
Ormesby	106	54.33 N	1.11 W
Ormesby Saint Margaret	104	52.40 N	1.42 E
Ormoc	138	11.00 N	124.37 E
Ormskirk	106	53.35 N	2.54 W
Ornans	118	47.06 N	6.09 E
Orne □5	118	48.40 N	0.05 E
Orne ≃	118	48.08 N	0.11 E
Örnsköldsvik	114	63.18 N	18.43 E
Oro, Río de ≃	182	9.06 N	72.45 W
Oročen	128	58.28 N	125.26 E
Orocué	184	4.48 N	71.20 W
Oro Grande	178	34.36 N	117.20 W
Or'ol	130	52.59 N	36.05 E
Oroluk I1	96	7.32 N	155.18 E
Oromocto	172	45.51 N	66.29 W
Oromocto Lake ⊜	176	45.36 N	67.00 W
Orono, Ont., Can.	176	43.59 N	78.37 W
Orono, Maine, U.S.	176	44.53 N	68.40 W
Oronsay I	108	56.01 N	6.16 W
Orosháza	116	46.34 N	20.40 E
Oroszlány	116	47.30 N	18.19 E
Oroville	178	39.31 N	121.33 W
Oroville, Lake ⊜1	178	39.32 N	121.25 W
Orrin, Glen ∨	108	57.30 N	4.46 W
Orrin, Loch ⊜	108	57.30 N	4.45 W
Orroroo	168	32.44 S	138.37 E
Orrs Island	176	43.46 N	69.59 W
Orrville	176	40.50 N	81.46 W
Orša	130	54.30 N	30.24 E
Orsk	126	51.12 N	58.34 E
Ørsta	114	62.12 N	6.09 E
Orta Nova	122	41.19 N	15.42 E
Ortegal, Cabo ≻	120	43.45 N	7.53 W
Ortigueira	188	24.12 S	50.55 W
Ortiz	182	9.37 N	67.17 W
Ortón ≃	184	10.50 S	66.04 W
Ortona	122	42.21 N	14.24 E
Ortonville	174	45.19 N	96.27 W
Orto-Tokoj	126	42.21 N	76.01 E
Oruanui	170	38.35 S	176.02 E
Oruro	184	17.59 S	67.09 W
Orūzgān (Qala-i-Hazār Qadam)	146	32.56 N	66.38 E
Orūzgān □4	146	33.15 N	66.00 E
Orvieto	122	42.43 N	12.07 E
Orwell	176	41.32 N	80.52 W
Orwell ≃	104	51.57 N	1.17 E
Oš	126	40.33 N	72.48 E
Osa, Península de ≻1	180	8.35 N	83.33 W
Ōsaka	134	34.40 N	135.30 E
Ōsaka-wan C	134	34.30 N	135.18 E
Osceola Mills	176	40.51 N	78.16 W
Oschatz	116	51.17 N	13.07 E
Oschersleben	116	52.01 N	11.13 E
Oscoda	176	44.26 N	83.20 W
Osen	112	64.17 N	10.30 E
Oshamambe	134a	42.30 N	140.22 E
O'Shanassy ≃	168	18.59 S	138.46 E
Oshawa	172	43.54 N	78.51 W
Oshika	134	38.16 N	141.32 E
Ōshima	134	33.03 N	129.33 E
Ō-shima I, Nihon	134	34.43 N	139.23 E
Ō-shima I, Nihon	134	33.28 N	135.50 E
Ō-shima I, Nihon	134a	41.30 N	139.22 E
Oshima-hantō ≻1	134a	42.00 N	140.30 E
Oshkosh	174	44.01 N	88.33 W
Oshogbo	152	7.47 N	4.34 E
Oshwe	156	3.24 S	19.30 E
Osijek	124	45.33 N	18.41 E
Osimo	122	43.29 N	13.29 E
Osinniki	128	53.37 N	87.21 E
Osintorf	130	54.42 N	30.39 E
Osipoviči	130	53.18 N	28.38 E
Oskaloosa	174	41.18 N	92.39 W
Oskarshamn	114	57.16 N	16.26 E
Oskarström	114	56.48 N	12.58 E
Oskū	150	37.55 N	46.06 E
Oslava ≃	116	49.05 N	16.22 E
Ösling □9	118	49.55 N	6.00 E
Oslo	114	59.55 N	10.45 E
Oslofjorden C2	114	59.20 N	10.35 E
Osmānābād	148	18.10 N	76.02 E
Osmaniye	150	37.05 N	36.14 E
Osmington	104	50.38 N	2.22 W
Osnabrück	116	52.16 N	8.02 E
Osore-san ∧	134	41.18 N	144.05 E
Osório	188	29.54 S	50.16 W
Osorno	186	40.34 S	73.09 W
Ospino	182	9.18 N	69.27 W
Osprey Reef ∻2	166	13.55 S	146.38 E
Oss	116	51.46 N	5.31 E
Ossa, Mount ∧	168	41.54 S	146.01 E
Osse ≃, Fr.	118	44.07 N	0.17 E
Osse ≃, Nig.	152	6.10 N	5.20 E
Ossett	106	53.41 N	1.35 W
Ossian	176	40.53 N	85.10 W
Ossian, Loch ⊜	108	56.46 N	4.38 W
Ossining	176	41.10 N	73.52 W
Ossipee	176	43.41 N	71.07 W
Ossjøen ⊜	114	61.13 N	11.53 E
Ossokmanuan Lake ⊜	172	53.25 N	65.00 W
Ossora	128	59.20 N	163.13 E
Ostaškov	130	57.09 N	33.06 E
Ost-Berlin	116	52.30 N	13.25 E
Ostende → Oostende	116	51.13 N	2.55 E
Østerdalen ∨	114	61.15 N	11.10 E
Östergötland □9	114	58.24 N	15.34 E
Östergötlands Län □6	114	58.25 N	15.45 E
Osterholz-Scharmbeck	116	53.14 N	8.47 E
Osterode, B.R.D.	116	51.44 N	10.11 E
Osterode → Ostróda, Pol.	116	53.43 N	19.59 E
Osterøya I	114	60.33 N	5.35 E
Österreichische Alpen ⋀	116	47.40 N	15.10 E
Östersjön → Baltic Sea ⊤2	112	57.00 N	19.00 E
Östersund	114	63.11 N	14.39 E
Osterwieck	116	51.58 N	10.42 E
Østfold □6	114	59.20 N	11.30 E
Ostfriesland □9	116	53.20 N	7.40 E
Östhammar	114	60.16 N	18.22 E
Ostrava	116	49.50 N	18.17 E
Ostredok ∧	116	48.55 N	19.04 E
Ostróda	116	53.43 N	19.59 E

Symbols in the index entries are identified on page 198.

Name	Page	Lat °′	Long °′
Ostrogożsk	126	50.52 N	39.05 E
Ostrołeka	116	53.06 N	21.34 E
Ostrov, Česko.	116	50.17 N	12.57 E
Ostrov, S.S.S.R.	130	57.20 N	28.22 E
Ostrov-Zalit	130	58.01 N	28.04 E
Ostrowiec Świętokrzyski	116	50.57 N	21.23 E
Ostrów Mazowiecka	116	52.49 N	21.54 E
Ostrów Wielkopolski	116	51.39 N	17.49 E
Ostuni	122	40.44 N	17.35 E
Osum ≃	124	40.48 N	19.52 E
Ōsumi-hantō ≻¹	134	31.20 N	130.55 E
Ōsumi-kaikyō ⊔	134	31.00 N	131.00 E
Ōsumi-shotō II	135b	30.30 N	130.00 E
Osuna	120	37.14 N	5.07 W
Osvaldo Cruz	190	21.47 S	50.50 W
Osveja	130	56.01 N	28.06 E
Oswaldtwistle	106	53.43 N	2.26 W
Oswegatchie ≃	176	44.42 N	75.30 W
Oswegatchie, West Branch ≃	176	44.18 N	75.20 W
Oswego	176	43.27 N	76.31 W
Oswego ≃	176	43.28 N	76.31 W
Oswestry	104	52.52 N	3.04 W
Oświęcim	116	50.03 N	19.12 E
Ōta	134	36.18 N	139.22 E
Otago Peninsula ≻¹	170	45.52 S	170.40 E
Otahuhu	170	36.57 S	174.51 E
Ōtake	134	34.12 N	132.13 E
Otaki	170	40.45 S	175.09 E
Otanmäki	114	64.07 N	27.06 E
Otaru	134a	43.13 N	141.00 E
Otatara	170	46.26 S	168.18 E
Otava	114	61.39 N	27.04 E
Otavalo	184	0.14 N	78.16 W
Otavi	160	19.39 S	17.20 E
Ōtawara	134	36.52 N	140.02 E
Otego Creek ≃	176	42.25 N	75.07 W
Otematata	170	44.37 S	170.16 E
Otford	104	51.19 N	0.12 E
Othery	104	51.05 N	2.53 W
Oti ≃	152	8.40 N	0.13 E
Otish, Monts ⛰	172	52.22 N	70.30 W
Otjiwarongo	160	20.29 S	16.36 E
Otjiwarongo □⁵	160	21.45 S	17.00 E
Otju □⁵	160	20.00 S	15.00 E
Otley	106	53.54 N	1.41 W
Otočac	122	44.52 N	15.14 E
Otorohanga	170	38.11 S	175.12 E
Otoskwin ≃	172	52.13 N	88.06 W
Otra ≃	114	58.09 N	8.00 E
Otradnyj	112	53.22 N	51.21 E
Otranto	122	40.09 N	18.30 E
Otranto, Strait of ≃¹	124	40.00 N	19.00 E
Otrokovice	116	49.13 N	17.31 E
Ötscher ∧	116	47.52 N	15.12 E
Otselic ≃	176	42.20 N	75.58 W
Ōtsu	134	35.00 N	135.52 E
Ōtsuchi	134	39.21 N	141.54 E
Ōtsuki	134	35.36 N	138.57 E
Otta ≃	114	61.46 N	9.31 E
Ottawa, Ont., Can.	172	45.25 N	75.42 W
Ottawa, Ill., U.S.	174	41.21 N	88.51 W
Ottawa, Kans., U.S.	174	38.37 N	95.16 W
Ottawa, Ohio, U.S.	176	41.01 N	84.03 W
Ottawa ≃	172	45.20 N	73.58 W
Ottawa Islands II	172	59.30 N	80.10 W
Ottenby	114	56.14 N	16.25 E
Otter ≃	104	50.46 N	3.17 W
Otterburn	106	55.14 N	2.10 W
Otter Creek ≃, Ont., Can.	176	42.44 N	80.51 W
Otter Creek ≃, Vt., U.S.	176	44.13 N	73.17 W
Otter Lake, Qué., Can.	176	45.51 N	76.26 W
Otter Lake, Mich., U.S.	176	43.13 N	83.28 W
Otterøya I	114	62.42 N	6.48 E
Ottery ≃	104	50.39 N	4.20 W
Ottery Saint Mary	104	50.45 N	3.17 W
Ottobrunn	116	48.04 N	11.40 E
Ottosdal	160	26.58 S	26.00 E
Ottoshoop	160	25.45 S	25.59 E
Ottoville	176	40.54 N	84.18 W
Ottumwa	174	41.01 N	92.25 W
Ottweiler	116	49.24 N	7.09 E
Otway, Cape ≻	168	38.52 S	143.31 E
Otwock	116	52.07 N	21.16 E
Ötz	122	47.12 N	10.54 E
Ötztaler Alpen ⛰	122	46.45 N	10.55 E
Ou ≃	152	9.18 N	18.14 E
Ou ≃, Lao	140	20.04 N	102.13 E
Ouachita Mountains ⛰	174	34.40 N	94.25 W
Ouadda	154	8.04 N	22.24 E
Ouagadougou	152	12.22 N	1.31 W
Ouahigouya	152	13.35 N	2.25 W
Ouaka ≃	154	4.59 N	19.56 E
Oualâta	152	17.18 N	7.02 W
Ouallene	152	24.37 N	1.14 E
Ouanda Djallé	154	8.54 N	22.48 E
Ouarane ⊸¹	152	21.00 N	10.30 W
Ouareau ≃	176	45.56 N	73.25 W
Ouareau, Lac ⊜¹	176	46.17 N	74.09 W
Ouargla	152	31.59 N	5.25 E
Ouarra ≃	158	5.05 N	24.26 E
Ouarzazate	152	30.57 N	6.50 W
Oubangui ≃	156	1.15 N	17.50 E
Ōuchi	134	34.16 N	134.18 E
Oudenaarde	116	50.51 N	3.36 E
Oudtshoorn	160	33.35 S	22.14 E
Ouémé ≃	152	6.29 N	2.32 E
Ouenza	122	35.57 N	8.04 E
Ouessant, Île d' I	118	48.28 N	5.05 W
Ouesso	156	1.37 N	16.04 E
Ouezzane	152	34.52 N	5.35 W
Oughter, Lough ⊜	110	54.00 N	7.30 W
Oughterard	110	53.25 N	9.17 W
Ouidah	152	6.22 N	2.05 E
Oujda	152	34.41 N	1.45 W
Oujiang ≃	136	28.04 N	120.35 E
Oulainen	114	64.16 N	24.48 E
Oulton Broad	104	52.31 N	1.42 E
Oulu	114	65.01 N	25.28 E
Oulujärvi ⊜	114	64.20 N	27.15 E
Oulujoki ≃	114	65.01 N	25.25 E
Oulun lääni □⁴	114	65.00 N	27.00 E
Oum Chalouba	154	15.48 N	20.46 E
Oum er Rbia, Oued ≃	152	33.19 N	8.21 W
Ounasjoki ≃	112	66.30 N	25.45 E
Oundle	104	52.29 N	0.29 W
Ounianga Kébir	154	19.04 N	20.29 E
Ourinhos	190	22.59 S	49.52 W
Ourique	120	37.39 N	8.13 W
Ouro Fino	190	22.17 S	46.22 W
Ouro Prêto	190	20.23 S	43.30 W
Ourthe ≃	116	50.38 N	5.35 E
Ōu-sammyaku ⛰	134	38.45 N	140.50 E
Ouse	168	42.29 S	146.42 E
Ouse ≃, Eng., U.K.	102	53.42 N	0.41 W
Ouse ≃, Eng., U.K.	104	50.47 N	0.03 E
Oust ≃	118	47.39 N	2.06 W
Outardes, Rivière aux ≃	172	49.04 N	68.28 W
Outeniekwaberge ⛰	160	33.53 S	22.35 E
Outer Hebrides II	108	57.45 N	7.00 W
Outer Santa Barbara Passage ⊔	178	33.10 N	118.30 W
Outjo	160	20.08 S	16.08 E
Outlook	172	51.30 N	107.03 W
Out Skerries II	108a	60.25 N	0.42 W
Outwell	104	52.37 N	0.14 E
Outwood	106	53.42 N	1.30 W
Ouyen	168	35.04 S	142.20 E
Ovalle	188	30.36 S	71.12 W
Ovamboland □⁵	160	18.00 S	16.00 E
Ovamboland □⁹	160	17.45 S	16.30 E
Ovejas	182	9.32 N	75.14 W
Overflakkee I	116	51.45 N	4.10 E
Overseal	104	52.44 N	1.34 W
Overstrand	104	52.56 N	1.20 E
Overton, Eng., U.K.	104	51.15 N	1.15 W
Overton, Nev., U.S.	178	36.33 N	114.27 W
Overton Arm C	178	36.20 N	114.25 W
Övertorneå	112	66.23 N	23.40 E
Over Wallop	104	51.09 N	1.35 W
Ovid, Mich., U.S.	176	43.01 N	84.22 W
Ovid, N.Y., U.S.	176	42.41 N	76.49 W
Oviedo	120	43.22 N	5.50 W
Oviksfjällen ⛰	114	63.02 N	13.51 E
Øvre Årdal	114	61.19 N	7.48 E
Owaka	170	46.27 S	169.40 E
Owase	134	34.04 N	136.12 E
Owbeh	150	34.22 N	63.10 E
Owego	176	42.06 N	76.16 W
Owel, Lough ⊜	110	53.34 N	7.25 W
Owenboy ≃	110	51.48 N	8.18 W
Owenea ≃	110	54.47 N	8.26 W
Owenkillew ≃	110	54.44 N	7.18 W
Owenmore ≃	110	54.07 N	9.50 W
Owens ≃	178	36.31 N	117.57 W
Owensboro	174	37.46 N	87.07 W
Owens Lake ⊜	178	36.25 N	117.56 W
Owen Sound	172	44.34 N	80.56 W
Owen Sound C	176	44.40 N	80.55 W
Owen Stanley Range ⛰	166	9.20 S	147.55 E
Owenton	176	38.32 N	84.50 W
Owerri	152	5.29 N	7.02 E
Owhango	170	39.00 S	175.23 E
Owingsville	176	38.09 N	83.46 W
Owl ≃	172	57.51 N	92.44 W
Owo	152	7.15 N	5.37 E
Owosso	176	43.00 N	84.10 W
Owyhee	178	41.57 N	116.06 W
Owyhee ≃	178	43.46 N	117.02 W
Owyhee, Lake ⊜¹	178	43.28 N	117.20 W
Owyhee, South Fork ≃	178	42.26 N	116.53 W
Oxbow	172	49.14 N	102.11 W
Oxelösund	114	58.40 N	17.06 E
Oxford, N.Z.	170	43.18 S	172.11 E
Oxford, Eng., U.K.	104	51.46 N	1.15 W
Oxford, Maine, U.S.	176	44.08 N	70.30 W
Oxford, Md., U.S.	176	38.42 N	76.10 W
Oxford, Mich., U.S.	176	42.49 N	83.16 W
Oxford, Miss., U.S.	174	34.22 N	89.32 W
Oxford, N.Y., U.S.	176	42.27 N	75.36 W
Oxford, Ohio, U.S.	176	39.30 N	84.44 W
Oxford, Pa., U.S.	176	39.47 N	75.59 W
Oxford Lake ⊜	172	54.51 N	95.37 W
Oxfordshire □⁶	102	51.50 N	1.15 W
Oxley	168	34.12 S	144.06 E
Oxnard	178	34.12 N	119.11 W
Oxted	104	51.16 N	0.01 W
Oyabe	134	36.40 N	136.52 E
Oyama	134	36.18 N	139.48 E
Oyano	134	32.35 N	130.30 E
Oyapock (Oiapoque) ≃	184	4.08 N	51.40 W
Oyem	156	1.37 N	11.35 E
Øyeren ⊜	114	59.48 N	11.14 E
Oykel ≃	108	57.56 N	4.25 W
Oykel Bridge	108	57.58 N	4.43 W
Oyo	152	7.15 N	3.56 E
Ōyodo ≃	134	31.53 N	131.28 E
Oyonnax	118	46.15 N	5.40 E
Øystese	114	60.23 N	6.13 E
Ozamiz	138	8.08 N	123.50 E
Ozark	174	31.28 N	85.38 W
Ozark Plateau ⛰¹	174	36.30 N	92.30 W
Ozarks, Lake of the ⊜¹	174	38.10 N	92.50 W
Ozbourn Seamount ⇝³	96	25.55 S	174.50 W
Ózd	116	48.14 N	20.18 E
Ozernovskij	128	51.30 N	156.31 E
Ozery	130	54.51 N	38.34 E
Ozieri	122	40.35 N	9.00 E
Ożogino, Ozero ⊜	128	69.16 N	146.36 E
Ozorków	116	51.58 N	19.19 E
Ōzu, Nihon	134	32.52 N	130.52 E
Ōzu, Nihon	134	33.30 N	132.33 E
P			
Pa-an	140	16.53 N	97.38 E
Paarl	160	33.45 S	18.56 E
Paauilo	179a	20.02 N	155.22 W
Pabbay I, Scot., U.K.	108	56.51 N	7.35 W
Pabbay I, Scot., U.K.	108	57.46 N	7.15 W
Pabianice	116	51.40 N	19.22 E
Pābna	146	24.00 N	89.15 E
Pacaembu	190	21.34 S	51.17 W
Pacaltsdorp	160	34.00 S	22.28 E
Pacasmayo	184	7.20 S	79.35 W
Pachača	128	60.34 N	169.03 E
Pachino	122	36.42 N	15.06 E
Pachitea ≃	184	8.46 S	74.33 W
Pachmarhi	144	22.28 N	78.26 E
Pachuca	180	20.07 N	98.44 W
Pacifica	178	37.38 N	122.29 W
Pacific Grove	178	36.38 N	121.56 W
Pacific Islands Trust Territory □²	96	10.00 N	155.00 E
Pacific Ocean ▾¹	84	10.00 S	150.00 W
Paciran	142	6.52 S	112.20 E
Pacitan	142	8.12 S	111.07 E
Packard Mountain ∧²	176	42.28 N	72.21 W
Pacora	182	9.05 N	79.20 W
Padang	142	0.57 S	100.21 E
Padang Endau	142	2.40 N	103.37 E
Padangpanjang	142	0.27 S	100.25 E
Padangsidempuan	140	1.22 N	99.16 E
Paddle Prairie	172	57.57 N	117.29 W
Paddock Wood	104	51.11 N	0.23 E
Paden City	176	39.36 N	80.56 W
Paderborn	116	51.43 N	8.45 E
Padiham	106	53.49 N	2.19 W
Padirac, Gouffre de •⁵	118	44.44 N	1.27 E
Padloping Island I	172	67.07 N	62.35 W
Padma → Ganges ≃	146	23.22 N	90.32 E
Padova	122	45.25 N	11.53 E
Padstow	104	50.33 N	4.56 W
Padua → Padova	122	45.25 N	11.53 E
Paducah	174	37.05 N	88.36 W
Paekakariki	170	40.59 S	174.57 E
Paektu-san ∧	132	42.00 N	128.03 E
Paengaroa	170	37.49 S	176.25 E
Paeroa	170	37.23 S	175.40 E
Pafúri	156	22.27 S	31.21 E
Pagadenbaru	142	6.28 S	107.48 E
Pagadian	138	7.49 N	123.25 E
Pagai Selatan, Pulau I	142	3.00 S	100.20 E
Pagai Utara, Pulau I	142	2.42 S	100.07 E
Pagalu I	156	1.25 S	5.36 E
Pagan I	138	18.07 N	145.46 E
Pagaralam	142	4.01 S	103.16 E
Paget, Mount ∧	186	54.26 S	36.33 W
Pagon, Bukit ∧	142	4.18 N	115.19 E
Pago Pago	96	14.16 S	170.42 W
Pahala	179a	19.12 N	155.29 W
Pahang ≃	142	3.32 N	103.28 E
Pahiatua	170	40.27 S	175.50 E
Pahoa	179a	19.28 N	154.51 W
Pahrump	178	36.12 N	115.59 W
Paignton	104	50.26 N	3.34 W
Paiguano	188	30.01 S	70.32 W
Päijänne ⊜	114	61.35 N	25.30 E
Pailolo Channel ⊔	179a	21.05 N	156.42 W
Paimboeuf	118	47.17 N	2.02 W
Paimpol	118	48.46 N	3.03 W
Painan	142	1.21 S	100.34 E
Painesville	176	41.43 N	81.15 W
Pains	190	20.22 S	45.40 W
Painscastle	104	52.07 N	3.12 W
Painswick	104	51.48 N	2.11 W
Painted Desert ⊸²	174	36.00 N	111.20 W
Paintsville	176	37.49 N	82.48 W
Paisley	108	55.50 N	4.26 W
Paisley, Oreg., U.S.	178	42.42 N	120.32 W
Paita	184	5.05 S	81.10 W
Paiton	142	7.43 S	113.30 E
Paiva ≃	120	41.04 N	8.16 W
Paizhou	136	30.13 N	113.56 E
Pajala	112	67.11 N	23.22 E
Paj-Choj ⛰²	126	69.00 N	63.00 E
Pajjer, Gora ∧	126	66.42 N	64.25 E
Pakanbaru	142	0.32 N	101.27 E
Pakaraima Mountains ⛰	184	5.30 N	60.40 W
Pakistan (Pākistān) □¹	144	30.00 N	70.00 E
Pakistan, East → Bangladesh □¹	144	24.00 N	90.00 E
Paklay	132	18.12 N	101.25 E
Pakokku	140	21.20 N	95.05 E
Pākpattan	149	30.21 N	73.24 E
Pak Phanang	140	8.21 N	100.12 E
Paks	116	46.39 N	18.53 E
Paktīā □⁴	146	33.30 N	69.30 E
P'akupur ≃	128	65.00 N	77.48 E
Pakxé	140	15.07 N	105.47 E
Pala	154	9.22 N	14.54 E
Palagonia	122	37.19 N	14.45 E
Palagruža, Otoci II	122	42.24 N	16.15 E
Palaiseau	118	48.43 N	2.15 E
Pālakollu	148	16.32 N	81.44 E
Palamás	124	39.28 N	22.05 E
Palana	128	59.07 N	159.58 E
Palangkaraya	138	2.16 S	113.56 E
Pālanpur	146	24.10 N	72.26 E
Palaoa Point ≻	179a	20.44 N	156.58 W
Palapye	160	22.37 S	27.06 E
Palas del Rey	120	42.52 N	7.52 W
Palatka, S.S.S.R.	128	60.06 N	150.54 E
Palatka, Fla., U.S.	174	29.39 N	81.38 W
Palau Islands II	138	7.30 N	134.30 E
Palau-Kyushu Ridge ⇝³	96	13.00 N	135.00 E
Palawan I	138	9.30 N	118.30 E
Pālayankottai	148	8.43 N	77.44 E
Paleleh	142	1.04 N	121.57 E
Palembang	142	2.55 S	104.45 E
Palencia	120	42.01 N	4.32 W
Palen Dry Lake ⊜	178	33.46 N	115.12 W
Palenque, Punta ≻	182	18.13 N	70.10 W
Palermo	122	38.07 N	13.21 E
Palestine	174	31.46 N	95.38 W
Paletwa	140	21.18 N	92.51 E
Pālghāt	148	10.47 N	76.39 E
Palgrave, Mount ∧	164	23.22 S	115.58 E
Pāli	146	25.46 N	73.20 E
Palit, Kep i ≻	124	41.24 N	19.24 E
Pālitāna	148	21.31 N	71.50 E
Palk Bay C	148	9.30 N	79.15 E
Palk Strait ⊔	148	10.00 N	79.45 E
Pallas Grean	110	52.33 N	8.22 W
Pallaskenry	110	52.39 N	8.52 W
Pallastunturi ∧	112	68.06 N	24.00 E
Pallinup ≃	164	34.29 S	118.54 E
Palliser, Cape ≻	170	41.37 S	175.17 E
Palma	158	10.46 S	40.29 E
Palma, Bahía de C	120	39.27 N	2.35 E
Palma del Río	120	37.42 N	5.17 W
Palma [de Mallorca]	120	39.34 N	2.39 E
Palma di Montechiaro	122	37.11 N	13.46 E
Palmar ≃	182	10.10 N	71.50 W
Palmar de Varela	182	10.45 N	74.45 W
Palmares	184	8.41 S	35.36 W
Palmares do Sul	188	30.16 S	50.31 W
Palmas	188	26.30 S	52.00 W
Palmas, Cape ≻	152	4.22 N	7.44 W
Palmas Bellas	182	9.13 N	80.06 W
Palma Soriano	182	20.13 N	76.00 W
Palm Beach	182	26.42 N	80.02 W
Palmdale	178	34.35 N	118.07 W
Palm Desert	178	33.43 N	116.22 W
Palmeira	188	25.25 S	50.00 W
Palmeira das Missões	188	27.55 S	53.17 W
Palmer	176	42.09 N	72.20 W
Palmer ≃	166	15.34 S	142.26 E
Palmer Land ⊸¹	87	71.30 S	65.00 W
Palmerston, Ont., Can.	176	43.50 N	80.51 W
Palmerston, N.Z.	170	45.29 S	170.43 E
Palmerston I¹	96	18.04 S	163.10 W
Palmerston, Cape ≻	168	21.32 S	149.29 E
Palmerston North	170	40.21 S	175.37 E
Palmerton	176	40.48 N	75.37 W
Palmerville	166	15.59 S	144.05 E
Palmi	122	38.21 N	15.51 E
Palmira, Arg.	188	33.03 S	68.34 W
Palmira, Col.	184	3.32 N	76.16 W
Palmira, Cuba	182	22.14 N	80.23 W
Palmitos	188	27.05 S	53.08 W
Palm Springs	178	33.50 N	116.33 W
Palmyra → Tudmur, Sūrīy.	150	34.33 N	38.17 E
Palmyra, N.Y., U.S.	176	43.04 N	77.14 W
Palmyra, Pa., U.S.	176	40.18 N	76.36 W
Palmyra, Va., U.S.	176	37.51 N	78.16 W
Palmyra Atoll I¹	96	5.52 N	162.06 W
Palni	148	10.28 N	77.32 E
Palo Alto	178	37.27 N	122.09 W
Paloich	154	10.28 N	32.32 E
Palojoensuu	112	68.17 N	23.05 E
Palomar Mountain ∧	178	33.22 N	116.50 W
Palo Negro	182	10.11 N	67.33 W
Palopo	142	3.00 S	120.12 E
Palos, Cabo de ≻	120	37.38 N	0.41 W
Palos Verdes Point ≻	178	33.47 N	118.26 W
Palo Verde	178	33.26 N	114.44 W
Palpalá	188	24.15 S	65.15 W
Palu	142	0.53 S	119.53 E
Pamamaroo Lake ⊜	168	32.17 S	142.27 E
Pamekasan	142	7.10 S	113.28 E
Pameungpeuk	142	7.38 S	107.43 E
Pamiers	118	43.07 N	1.36 E
Pamir ⛰, As.	126	38.00 N	73.00 E
Pamir ⛰	126	38.00 N	73.00 E
Pamlico Sound ⊔	174	35.20 N	75.55 W
Pampa	174	35.32 N	100.58 W
Pampanua	142	4.14 S	120.08 E
Pampas ≃	184	13.24 S	73.12 W
Pampas ⊸¹	188	35.00 S	63.00 W
Pamplona, Col.	184	7.23 N	72.39 W
Pamplona, Esp.	120	42.49 N	1.38 W
Pampoenpoort	160	31.03 S	22.40 E
Panaca	178	37.47 N	114.23 W
Panache, Lake ⊜	176	46.15 N	81.20 W
Panaji (Panjim)	148	15.29 N	73.50 E
Panamá	182	8.58 N	79.31 W
Panama (Panamá) □¹	180	9.00 N	80.00 W
Panama, Gulf of C	180	8.00 N	79.10 W
Panama, Isthmus of •³	182	9.20 N	79.30 W
Panama Canal ≊	182	9.00 N	79.37 W
Panama City	174	30.10 N	85.41 W
Panambi	188	28.18 S	53.30 W
Panamint Range ⛰	178	36.30 N	117.20 W
Panamint Valley V	178	36.15 N	117.20 W
Panay I	138	11.15 N	122.30 E
Panay Gulf C	138	10.15 N	122.15 E
Pančevo	124	44.52 N	20.39 E
Panda Gongoue	161a	11.50 S	43.24 E
Pandharpur	148	17.40 N	75.20 E
Pāndhurna	148	21.36 N	78.31 E
P'andž (Āb-I-Panja) ≃	126	37.06 N	68.20 E
Panevėžys	130	55.44 N	24.21 E
Panfilov	126	44.10 N	80.01 E
Pangala	156	3.19 S	14.34 E
Pangandaran	142	7.41 S	108.39 E
Pangani	158	5.26 S	38.58 E
Pangani ≃	158	5.26 S	38.58 E
Pangbourne	104	51.29 N	1.05 W
Pangi	158	3.11 S	26.38 E
Pangkajene	142	4.50 S	119.32 E
Pangkalanbuun	142	2.41 S	111.37 E
Pangkalpinang	142	2.08 S	106.08 E
Pangnirtung	172	66.08 N	65.44 W
Pangnirtung Fiord C²	172	66.06 N	65.58 W
Pangushan	136	25.46 N	115.30 E
Pangutaran Group II	142	6.15 N	120.30 E
Panhame (Hunyani) ≃	158	15.37 S	30.39 E
Paniau ∧	179a	21.57 N	160.05 W
Pānīpat	149	29.23 N	76.58 E
Panj (P'andž) ≃	146	37.06 N	68.20 E
Panjang	142	5.28 S	105.18 E
Panjgūr	150	26.58 N	64.06 E
Panna	144	24.43 N	80.12 E
Pannawonica	164	21.44 S	116.22 E
Pantar, Pulau I	142	8.25 S	124.07 E
Pantelleria, Isola di I	122	36.47 N	12.00 E
Panton, Mount ∧	164	17.21 S	129.13 E
Pánuco	180	22.03 N	98.10 W
Panulcillo	188	30.27 S	71.14 W
Panxian	140	25.50 N	104.36 E
Panyam	152	9.25 N	9.13 E
Panyu	136	22.57 N	113.20 E
Pao ≃	182	8.33 N	68.01 W
Paola	122	39.22 N	16.03 E
Paôy Pêt	138	13.39 N	102.33 E
Pápa	116	47.19 N	17.28 E
Papa, Sound of ⊔	108a	60.18 N	1.41 W
Papagayo, Golfo del C	182	10.45 N	85.45 W
Papaikou	179a	19.47 N	155.06 W
Papakura	170	37.04 S	174.57 E
Papantla	180	20.27 N	97.19 W
Paparoa	170	36.06 S	174.14 E
Papa Stour I	108a	60.20 N	1.42 W
Papatoetoe	170	36.58 S	174.52 E
Papawai Point ≻	179a	20.47 N	156.33 W
Papa Westray I	108	59.21 N	2.54 W
Papeete	96	17.32 S	149.34 W
Papenburg	116	53.05 N	7.23 E
Paphos → Néa Páfos	150	34.45 N	32.26 E
Papineau, Lac ⊜	176	45.48 N	74.46 W
Paposo	188	25.01 S	70.28 W
Paps of Jura ∧	108	55.55 N	6.00 W
Papua, Gulf of C	166	8.30 S	145.00 E
Papua New Guinea □¹	96	6.00 S	147.00 E
Papudo	188	32.31 S	71.27 W
Papun	132	18.04 N	97.27 E
Papunya	164	23.16 S	131.54 E
Paquica, Cabo ≻	188	21.54 S	70.12 W
Par	104	50.21 N	4.43 W
Pará → Belém	184	1.27 S	48.29 W
Pará ≃	184	1.30 S	48.55 W
Parabel'	128	58.43 N	81.31 E
Paraburdoo	164	23.14 S	117.48 E
Paracel Islands II	138	16.30 N	112.15 E
Parachilna	168	31.08 S	138.23 E
Pārachinār	146	33.54 N	70.06 E
Paraćin	124	43.52 N	21.24 E
Parád	116	47.55 N	20.02 E
Paradise, Calif., U.S.	178	39.46 N	121.37 W
Paradise, Nev., U.S.	178	36.09 N	115.10 W
Paradise Valley	178	41.30 N	117.32 W
Paragould	174	36.03 N	90.29 W
Paraguá ≃, Bol.	184	13.34 S	61.53 W
Paragua ≃, Ven.	184	6.55 N	62.55 W
Paraguaçu Paulista	190	22.25 S	50.34 W
Paraguaipoa	182	11.21 N	71.57 W
Paraguaná, Península de ≻¹	184	11.55 N	70.00 W
Paraguarí	188	25.38 S	57.09 W
Paraguarí □⁵	188	26.00 S	57.10 W
Paraguay □¹	186	23.00 S	58.00 W
Paraguay ≃	186	27.18 S	58.38 W
Paraibuna	190	23.23 S	45.39 W
Paraiso, C.Z.	182	9.03 N	79.38 W
Paraíso, Méx.	180	18.24 N	93.14 W
Paraíso do Norte	190	23.13 S	52.38 W
Paraisópolis	190	22.33 S	45.47 W
Parakou	152	9.21 N	2.37 E
Paramagudi	148	9.33 N	78.36 E
Paramaribo	184	5.50 N	55.10 W
Paramillo ∧	184	7.04 N	75.55 W
Paramirim	190	13.26 S	42.15 W
Paramus	176	40.57 N	74.04 W
Paramušir, Ostrov I	128	50.25 N	155.50 E
Paraná, Arg.	188	31.45 S	60.30 W
Paranã, Bra.	190	12.33 S	47.52 W
Paraná □³	188	24.00 S	51.00 W
Paranã ≃, Bra.	190	12.30 S	48.14 W
Paraná ≃, S.A.	186	33.43 S	59.15 W
Paranaguá	188	25.31 S	48.30 W
Paranaguá, Baía de C	188	25.29 S	48.33 W
Paranaíba	190	19.40 S	51.11 W
Paranam	184	5.35 N	55.10 W
Paranapanema ≃	190	22.40 S	53.09 W
Paranavaí	190	23.04 S	52.28 W
Paranhos	190	23.55 S	55.25 W
Paraopeba	190	19.18 S	44.25 W
Parapara	182	9.44 N	67.18 W
Paraparaumu	170	40.55 S	175.01 E
Paraparaumu Beach	170	40.54 S	174.59 E
Paratinga	190	12.42 S	43.10 W
Paratoo	168	32.42 S	139.22 E
Paray-le-Monial	118	46.27 N	4.07 E
Pārbati ≃	146	25.51 N	76.36 E
Pārbatipur	146	25.39 N	88.55 E
Parbhani	148	19.16 N	76.47 E
Parchim	116	53.25 N	11.51 E
Pardubice	116	50.02 N	15.47 E
Parecis, Serra dos ⛰	184	13.00 S	60.00 W
Paredes de Nava	120	42.09 N	4.41 W
Pareloup, Lac de ⊜	118	44.15 N	2.45 E
Paren'	128	62.28 N	163.05 E
Paren' ≃	128	62.25 N	163.10 E
Parent	172	47.55 N	74.37 W
Pareora	170	44.30 S	171.12 E
Parepare	142	4.01 S	119.38 E
Pargas (Parainen)	114	60.18 N	22.18 E
Pariaguán	182	8.51 N	64.43 W
Pariaman	140	0.38 S	100.08 E
Parícutin ∧¹	180	19.28 N	102.15 W
Parigi	142	0.48 S	120.10 E
Parika	184	6.51 N	58.26 W
Parikkala	114	61.33 N	29.30 E
Parima, Sierra ⛰	184	2.30 N	64.00 W
Pariñas, Punta ≻	184	4.40 S	81.20 W
Parîngul ∧	124	45.22 N	23.33 E
Parintins	184	2.36 S	56.44 W
Pariquera-Açu	188	24.43 S	47.53 W
Paris, Ont., Can.	176	43.12 N	80.23 W
Paris, Fr.	118	48.52 N	2.20 E
Paris, Ky., U.S.	176	38.13 N	84.14 W
Paris, Maine, U.S.	176	44.16 N	70.30 W
Paris, Tex., U.S.	174	33.40 N	95.33 W
Paris □⁵	118	48.52 N	2.20 E
Parit Buntar	142	5.07 N	100.30 E
Parkano	114	62.01 N	23.01 E
Parker	178	34.09 N	114.17 W
Parker, Cape ≻	172	75.04 N	79.40 W
Parker City	176	40.11 N	85.12 W
Parker Dam	178	34.17 N	114.09 W
Parker Range	164	31.38 S	119.35 E
Parkersburg	174	39.17 N	81.32 W
Parkes	168	33.08 S	148.11 E
Parkhill	176	43.09 N	81.41 W
Park Rynie	160	30.25 S	30.35 E
Parkville	176	39.23 N	76.32 W
Parlākimidi	148	18.46 N	84.05 E
Parma, It.	122	44.48 N	10.20 E
Parma, Ohio, U.S.	176	41.22 N	81.43 W
Parma ≃	122	44.56 N	10.26 E
Parnaíba	184	2.54 S	41.47 W
Parnassós ∧	124	38.32 N	22.35 E
Pärnu	130	58.24 N	24.32 E
Paro	144	27.26 N	89.25 E
Paromaj	128	52.50 N	143.02 E
Paroo	164	26.16 S	119.46 E
Paroo ≃	168	31.28 S	143.32 E
Páros I	124	37.08 N	25.12 E
Parpaillon ⛰	118	44.30 N	6.40 E
Parpik Pass)(	149	36.58 N	75.25 E
Parral	188	36.09 S	71.50 W
Parramatta	168	33.49 S	151.00 E
Parras	180	25.25 N	102.11 W
Parrett ≃	104	51.13 N	3.01 W
Parry, Cape ≻	172	70.08 N	124.24 W
Parry Bay C	172	68.07 N	82.00 W
Parry Island I	176	45.18 N	80.10 W
Parry Sound	172	45.21 N	80.02 W
Parsberg	116	49.09 N	11.43 E
Parsnip ≃	172	55.10 N	123.00 W
Parsons, Kans., U.S.	174	37.20 N	95.16 W
Parsons, W. Va., U.S.	176	39.06 N	79.41 W
Parsons Range ⛰	166	13.30 S	135.15 E
Parthenay	118	46.39 N	0.15 W
Partinico	122	38.03 N	13.07 E
Parton	106	54.34 N	3.35 W
Partree	110	53.41 N	9.19 W
Parvān □⁴	146	35.15 N	69.30 E
Pārvatīpuram	148	18.47 N	83.26 E
Parys	160	27.04 S	27.16 E
Pasadena	178	34.09 N	118.09 W
Pasaje	184	3.20 S	79.49 W
Pa Sak ≃	140	14.21 N	100.35 E
Pascagoula	174	30.23 N	88.31 W
Paşcani	124	47.15 N	26.44 E
Pasco	174	46.14 N	119.06 W
Pascoag	176	41.57 N	71.42 W
Pasco Seamount ⇝³	96	13.00 S	174.30 W
Pascua, Isla de (Easter Island) I	92	27.07 S	109.22 W
Pas-de-Calais □⁵	118	50.30 N	2.20 E
Pasewalk	116	53.30 N	14.00 E
P'asina ≃	128	73.50 N	87.10 E
P'asino, Ozero ⊜	128	69.45 N	87.45 E
P'asinskij Zaliv C	128	74.00 N	86.00 E
Pasir Mas	142	6.02 N	102.08 E
Pasirpengarayan	142	0.51 N	100.16 E
Pasir Puteh	142	5.50 N	102.24 E
Pasley, Cape ≻	164	33.57 S	123.31 E
Pasley Bay C	172	70.40 N	96.27 W
Pasmore ≃	168	31.07 S	139.48 E
Pasni	150	25.16 N	63.28 E
Paso de Indios	186	43.50 S	69.06 W
Paso de los Libres	188	29.45 S	57.05 W
Paso de los Toros	188	32.49 S	56.31 W
Paso Robles	178	35.38 N	120.41 W
Pasrūr	149	32.16 N	74.40 E
Passadumkeag	176	45.11 N	68.37 W
Passadumkeag Mountain ∧	176	45.10 N	68.20 W
Passage East	110	52.13 N	6.59 W
Passagem	190	12.11 S	43.14 W
Passage West	110	51.52 N	8.20 W
Passaic	176	40.51 N	74.08 W
Passau	116	48.35 N	13.28 E
Passero, Capo ≻	122	36.40 N	15.09 E
Passo Fundo	188	28.15 S	52.24 W
Passos	190	20.43 S	46.37 W
Passy ⊸⁸	118	48.52 N	2.17 E
Pastaza ≃	184	4.50 S	76.25 W
Pasto	184	1.13 N	77.17 W
Pasuruan	142	7.38 S	112.54 E
Pasvalys	130	56.04 N	24.24 E
Patagonia ⊸¹	186	44.00 S	68.00 W
Pātan, Bhārat	146	23.50 N	72.07 E
Patan → Lalitpur, Nepāl	146	27.41 N	85.20 E
Patargān, Daqq-e ☷	150	33.30 N	60.40 E
Patcham	104	50.52 N	0.08 W
Patchewollock	168	35.23 S	142.11 E
Patchogue	176	40.46 N	73.00 W
Patchway	104	51.32 N	2.34 W
Patea	170	39.45 S	174.28 E
Patearoa	170	45.16 S	170.03 E
Pateley Bridge	106	54.05 N	1.45 W
Patensie	160	33.46 S	24.49 E
Paterna	120	39.30 N	0.26 W
Paternò	122	37.34 N	14.54 E
Paterson, S. Afr.	160	33.26 S	25.58 E
Paterson, N.J., U.S.	176	40.55 N	74.10 W
Pathānkot	149	32.17 N	75.39 E
Pathfinder Reservoir ⊜¹	174	42.30 N	106.50 W
Pathfinder Seamount ⇝³	90	50.55 N	143.20 W
Path of Condie	108	56.15 N	3.30 W
Pati	142	6.45 S	111.01 E
Patiāla	149	30.19 N	76.24 E
P'atigorsk	126	44.03 N	43.04 E
Pātkai Range ⛰	146	27.00 N	96.00 E
Patna	146	25.36 N	85.07 E
Pato Branco	188	26.13 S	52.40 W
Patos	184	7.01 S	37.16 W
Patos, Lagoa dos C	188	31.06 S	51.15 W
Patos de Minas	190	18.35 S	46.32 W
P'atovskij	130	54.41 N	36.04 E
Patquía	188	30.02 S	66.55 W
Pátrai	124	38.15 N	21.44 E
Patricio Lynch, Isla I	186	48.35 S	75.30 W
Patrington	106	53.41 N	0.02 W
Patrocínio	190	18.57 S	46.59 W
Pattani	140	6.52 N	101.16 E
Patten	176	46.01 N	68.27 W
Patterdale	106	54.32 N	2.56 W
Patterson	178	37.28 N	121.07 W
Patterson, Mount ∧	172	64.04 N	134.39 W
Patterson Creek ≃	176	39.34 N	78.23 W
Patti	149	31.17 N	74.51 E
Pattoki	149	31.01 N	73.51 E
Patton	176	40.38 N	78.39 W
Patton Seamount Group ⇝³	90	55.30 N	149.30 W
Patuca ≃	182	15.50 N	84.18 W
Patuca, Punta ≻	182	15.50 N	84.16 W
Patuxent ≃	176	38.18 N	76.25 W
Pátzcuaro	180	19.31 N	101.36 W
Pau	118	43.18 N	0.22 W
Pau, Gave de ≃	118	43.33 N	1.12 W
Pau Brasil	190	15.27 S	39.39 W
Pauk	132	21.27 N	94.27 E
Paul	178	42.40 N	113.36 W
Paulding	176	41.08 N	84.35 W
Paulding Bay C	87	66.35 S	123.00 E
Paulicéia	190	21.17 S	51.51 W
Paulo Afonso	184	9.21 S	38.14 W
Paulpietersburg	160	27.30 S	30.51 E
Paul Roux	160	28.18 S	27.59 E
Paul Seamount ⇝³	96	18.30 N	172.30 W
Paulstown	110	52.41 N	7.01 W
Paungde	140	18.29 N	95.30 E
Pausania	122	40.55 N	9.06 E
Pavelec	130	53.50 N	39.16 E
Pavia	122	45.10 N	9.10 E
Pavlodar	128	52.18 N	76.57 E
Pavlovo	130	55.58 N	43.04 E
Pavlovskij Posad	130	55.47 N	38.40 E
Pawan ≃	142	1.51 S	109.57 E
Paw Paw	176	39.32 N	78.27 W
Pawtucket	176	41.53 N	71.23 W
Paya	182	15.37 N	85.17 W
Payakumbuh	142	0.14 S	100.38 E
Payas, Cerro ∧	182	15.45 N	84.56 W
Payeti	142	9.41 S	120.20 E
Payne	176	41.05 N	84.44 W
Payne, Bassin C	172	60.00 N	70.00 W
Payne, Lac ⊜	172	59.25 N	74.00 W
Paynes Creek ≃	178	40.16 N	122.11 W
Paynes Find	164	29.15 S	117.41 E
Paysandú	188	32.19 S	58.05 W
Pazardžik	124	42.12 N	24.20 E
Paz de Río	184	5.59 N	72.47 W
Pazin	122	45.14 N	13.56 E
Peabody	176	42.32 N	70.55 W
Peace ≃	172	59.00 N	111.25 W
Peacehaven	104	50.47 N	0.01 E
Peace River	172	56.14 N	117.17 W
Peach Creek	176	37.53 N	81.59 W
Peacock Hills ⛰²	172	66.05 N	110.45 W
Peacock Sound ⊔	87	72.55 S	100.00 W
Peak Downs	168	22.12 S	148.10 E
Peake Creek ≃	164	28.05 S	136.07 E
Peak Hill	164	25.38 S	118.43 E
Peäldoaivi ∧	112	69.11 N	26.36 E
Pearce Point ≻	166	14.25 S	129.21 E
Pearl ≃	174	30.11 N	89.32 W
Pearl Harbor C	179a	21.22 N	157.58 W
Pearl Peak ∧	178	40.14 N	115.32 W
Pearl River	176	41.04 N	74.02 W
Pearsoll Peak ∧	178	42.18 N	123.50 W
Pearston	160	32.35 S	25.09 E
Peary Land ⊸¹	90	83.00 N	35.00 W
Peat Inn	108	56.17 N	2.53 W
Pebane	158	17.10 S	38.08 E
Peć	124	42.40 N	20.19 E
Peçanha	190	18.33 S	42.34 W
Peças, Ilha das I	188	25.26 S	48.19 W
Pečenga	112	69.33 N	31.07 E
Peck	176	43.16 N	82.49 W
Pečora	112	65.10 N	57.11 E
Pečora ≃	112	68.13 N	54.15 E
Pečorskaja Guba C	112	68.40 N	54.45 E
Pečorskoje More ▾²	112	70.00 N	54.00 E
Pečory	130	57.49 N	27.36 E
Pecos	174	31.25 N	103.30 W
Pecos ≃	174	29.42 N	101.22 W
Pécs	116	46.05 N	18.13 E
Peddāpuram	148	17.05 N	82.08 E
Pedder, Lake ⊜¹	168	42.54 S	146.12 E
Peddie	160	33.12 S	27.07 E
Pedernales, Rep. Dom.	182	18.02 N	71.44 W
Pedernales, Ven.	184	9.58 N	62.16 W
Pedernales, Salar de ≚	188	26.15 S	69.10 W
Pedirka	164	26.40 S	135.14 E
Pedra Azul	190	16.01 S	41.16 W
Pedraza	182	10.11 N	74.55 W
Pedregal	182	11.01 N	70.08 W
Pedreiras	184	4.30 S	44.35 W
Pedro Afonso	184	8.59 S	48.11 W
Pedro de Valdivia	188	22.36 S	69.40 W
Pedrógão Grande	120	39.55 N	8.09 W
Pedro II	184	4.25 S	41.28 W
Pedro Juan Caballero	188	22.34 S	55.37 W
Pedro Leopoldo	190	19.38 S	44.03 W
Pedro Osório	188	31.51 S	52.45 W
Pedro R. Fernández	188	28.40 S	58.40 W
Peebinga	168	34.56 S	140.55 E
Peebles, Scot., U.K.	108	55.39 N	3.12 W
Peebles, Ohio, U.S.	176	38.57 N	83.24 W
Peedamullah	164	21.50 S	115.38 E
Pee Dee ≃	174	33.21 N	79.16 W
Peekaboo Mountain ∧²	176	45.45 N	67.53 W
Peekskill	176	41.17 N	73.55 W
Peel	106	54.13 N	4.40 W
Peel ≃	172	67.37 N	134.40 W
Peel Fell ∧	106	55.17 N	2.35 W
Peel Fell ≃	108	55.17 N	2.35 W
Peel Inlet C	164	32.35 S	115.44 E
Peel Point ≻	172	73.22 N	114.35 W
Peel Sound ⊔	172	73.15 N	96.30 W
Peene ≃	116	54.09 N	13.46 E
Pegnitz	116	49.45 N	11.33 E
Pegnitz ≃	116	49.29 N	11.00 E
Pegswood	106	55.11 N	1.38 W
Pegu	140	17.20 N	96.29 E
Pegu □⁸	140	18.00 N	96.00 E
Pegu Yoma ⛰	140	19.00 N	95.50 E
Pegwell Bay C	104	51.18 N	1.26 E
Pehčevo	124	41.46 N	22.54 E
Pehlivanköy	124	41.21 N	26.55 E
Pehuajó	188	35.45 S	61.58 W
Peikang	136	23.35 N	120.19 E
Peine	116	52.19 N	10.13 E
Peïra-Cava	122	43.56 N	7.22 E
Peixian (Yunhe)	136	34.21 N	117.59 E
Pekalongan	142	6.53 S	109.40 E
Pekin	174	40.35 N	89.40 W
Peking → Beijing	132	39.55 N	116.25 E
Pelabuhan Kelang	142	3.00 N	101.24 E
Pelabuhanratu	142	6.59 S	106.33 E
Pelagie, Isole II	122	35.40 N	12.40 E
Pelat, Mont ∧	118	44.16 N	6.42 E
Peleaga, Vîrful ∧	124	45.22 N	22.54 E
Peleduj	128	59.36 N	112.45 E
Pelée, Montagne ∧	182	14.48 N	61.10 W
Pelee, Point ≻	176	41.54 N	82.30 W
Pelee Island I	176	41.46 N	82.39 W
Peleliu I	138	7.01 N	134.15 E
Peleng, Pulau I	142	1.20 S	123.10 E
Pelhřimov	116	49.26 N	15.13 E
Pelkosenniemi	112	67.07 N	27.30 E
Pellegrini	188	36.15 S	63.10 W
Pello	112	66.47 N	24.00 E
Pellston	176	45.33 N	84.47 W
Pelly ≃	172	62.47 N	137.19 W
Pelly Bay C	172	68.53 N	89.51 W
Pelly Crossing	172	62.50 N	136.35 W
Pelly Lake ⊜	172	65.59 N	101.12 W
Pelly Mountains ⛰	172	62.00 N	133.00 W
Pelopónnisos ⊸¹	124	37.30 N	22.00 E
Pelotas	188	31.46 S	52.20 W
Pelotas ≃	188	27.28 S	51.55 W
Pelvoux, Massif du ⛰¹	118	44.55 N	6.20 E
Pemadumcook Lake ⊜	176	45.40 N	68.55 W
Pemalang	142	6.54 S	109.22 E
Pematangsiantar	140	2.57 N	99.03 E
Pemba □⁴	158	5.10 S	39.48 E
Pemba Island I	158	7.31 S	39.25 E
Pemberton	164	34.28 S	116.01 E
Pembina ≃	172	54.45 N	114.15 W
Pembrey	104	51.42 N	4.16 W
Pembroke, Ont., Can.	172	45.49 N	77.07 W
Pembroke, Wales, U.K.	104	51.41 N	4.55 W
Pembroke, Maine, U.S.	176	44.57 N	67.10 W
Pembroke, Cape ≻	172	62.56 N	81.55 W
Pembroke Dock	104	51.42 N	4.56 W
Pembuang ≃	142	3.24 S	112.33 E
Pembury	104	51.09 N	0.20 E
Pemigewasset ≃	176	43.26 N	71.40 W
Pemuco	188	36.58 S	72.06 W
Penafiel	120	41.12 N	8.17 W
Peñalara ∧	120	40.51 N	3.57 W
Penang → Pinang	142	5.25 N	100.20 E
Peñaranda de Bracamonte	120	40.54 N	5.12 W
Pen Argyl	176	40.52 N	75.16 W
Peñarroya-Pueblonuevo	120	38.18 N	5.16 W
Penarth	104	51.27 N	3.11 W
Peñas, Cabo de ≻	120	43.39 N	5.51 W
Penas, Golfo de C	186	47.20 S	75.00 W
Peñas, Punta ≻	182	10.40 N	61.40 W
Pencader	104	52.01 N	4.16 W
Pencahue	188	35.24 S	71.49 W
Penck Trough V	87	73.00 S	2.45 W
Pencoed	104	51.32 N	3.30 W
Pendembu	152	9.06 N	12.12 W
Pender Bay C	164	16.45 S	122.42 E
Pendjari ≃	152	10.54 N	0.51 E
Pendle Hill ∧²	106	53.52 N	2.17 W
Pendleton	174	45.40 N	118.47 W
Pend Oreille, Lake ⊜	174	48.10 N	116.11 W
Penebel	142	8.25 S	115.09 E
Penedo	184	10.17 S	36.36 W
Penetanguishene	176	44.47 N	79.55 W
Penfield	176	41.13 N	78.34 W
Penganga ≃	148	19.53 N	79.09 E
Penge	160	24.22 S	30.13 E
P'enghu	136	23.34 N	119.34 E
P'enghu Liehtao II	136	23.30 N	119.30 E
Pengjiachang	136	30.15 N	113.31 E
Penglai	132	37.48 N	120.42 E
Pengpu → Bangbu	132	32.58 N	117.24 E
Pengshui	132	29.18 N	108.09 E
Penguin	168	41.07 S	146.04 E
Pengxian	132	31.00 N	103.50 E
Pengze	136	29.53 N	116.33 E
Penha	188	26.46 S	48.39 W
Penhalonga	158	18.54 S	32.40 E
Peniche	120	39.21 N	9.23 W
Penicuik	108	55.50 N	3.14 W
Penistone	106	53.32 N	1.37 W
Penmaenmawr	106	53.16 N	3.54 W
Penmarc'h, Pointe de ≻	118	47.48 N	4.22 W
Penne-d'Agenais	118	44.23 N	0.49 E
Penner ≃	148	14.35 N	80.10 E
Penn Hills	176	40.28 N	79.53 W
Pennines ⛰	102	54.10 N	2.05 W
Pennines, Alpes ⛰	122	46.05 N	7.50 E
Pennsauken	176	39.58 N	75.04 W
Pennsboro	176	39.17 N	80.58 W
Penns Creek ≃	176	40.48 N	76.51 W
Penns Grove	176	39.43 N	75.28 W
Pennsylvania □³	174	40.45 N	77.30 W
Penn Yan	176	42.40 N	77.03 W
Penny Strait ⊔	172	76.30 N	97.00 W
Penobscot ≃	176	44.30 N	68.50 W
Penobscot, East Branch ≃	176	45.35 N	68.32 W
Penobscot, West Branch ≃	176	45.35 N	68.32 W
Penobscot Bay C	176	44.15 N	68.52 W
Penola	168	37.23 S	140.50 E
Penong	164	31.55 S	133.01 E
Penonomé	180	8.31 N	80.21 W
Penrhyn I¹	96	9.00 S	158.00 W
Penrhyn Bay	106	53.19 N	3.45 W
Penrhyndeudraeth	104	52.56 N	4.04 W
Penrith, Austl.	168	33.45 S	150.42 E
Penrith, Eng., U.K.	106	54.40 N	2.44 W
Penryn	104	50.09 N	5.06 W
Pensacola	174	30.25 N	87.13 W
Pensacola Mountains ⛰	87	83.45 S	55.00 W
Pensacola Seamount ⇝³	96	17.35 N	157.35 W
Penshaw	106	54.53 N	1.29 W
Pentecost Island I	96	15.42 S	168.10 E
Penticton	172	49.30 N	119.35 W
Pentire Point ≻	104	50.36 N	4.55 W
Pentland	168	20.32 S	145.24 E
Pentland Firth ⊔	108	58.44 N	3.07 W
Pentland Hills ⛰²	108	55.46 N	3.25 W
Pentraeth	106	53.17 N	4.12 W
Penuba	142	0.20 S	104.28 E

Symbols in the index entries are identified on page 198.

Name	Page	Lat °′	Long °′
Pen-y-Ghent ∧	106	54.09 N	2.14 W
Penygroes, Wales, U.K.	104	51.49 N	4.02 W
Penygroes, Wales, U.K.	106	53.04 N	4.17 W
Penyu, Kepulauan II	166	5.22 S	127.46 E
Penza	126	53.13 N	45.00 E
Penza □[4]	130	53.30 N	43.00 E
Penzance	104	50.07 N	5.33 W
Penzberg	116	47.45 N	11.23 E
Penžina ≃	128	62.28 N	165.18 E
Penžinskaja Guba C	128	61.00 N	162.00 E
Penžinskij Chrebet ∧∧	128	62.30 N	167.00 E
Peoria	174	40.42 N	89.36 W
Peqin	124	41.03 N	19.45 E
Pequop Mountains ∧∧	178	40.45 N	114.40 W
Perabumulih	138	3.27 S	104.15 E
Perak ≃	142	3.58 N	100.53 E
Peralillo	188	34.29 S	71.29 W
Perämeri (Bottenviken) C	114	65.00 N	23.00 E
Perche, Collines du ∧∧[2]	118	48.25 N	0.40 E
Perchtoldsdorf	116	48.07 N	16.17 E
Percy Isles II	168	21.39 S	150.16 E
Perdeberg	160	28.59 S	25.05 E
Perdekop	160	27.13 S	29.38 E
Perdido, Monte ∧	120	42.40 N	0.05 E
Pereira	184	4.49 N	75.43 W
Perene ≃	184	11.09 S	74.14 W
Perenjori	164	29.26 S	116.17 E
Pereslavl'-Zalesskij	130	56.44 N	38.51 E
Perg	116	48.15 N	14.37 E
Pergamino	188	33.53 S	60.36 W
Pergine Valsugana	122	46.04 N	11.14 E
Péribonca ≃	172	48.45 N	72.05 W
Périers	118	49.11 N	1.25 W
Périgord □[9]	118	45.20 N	1.00 E
Périgueux	118	45.11 N	0.43 E
Perijá, Sierra de ∧∧	184	10.00 N	73.00 W
Perim → Barīm I	144	12.40 N	43.25 E
Perito Moreno	186	46.36 S	70.56 W
Periyakulam	148	10.07 N	77.33 E
Perkam, Tanjung ≻	166	1.28 S	137.54 E
Perkasie	176	40.22 N	75.18 W
Perkiomen Creek ≃	176	40.07 N	75.28 W
Perkiomen Creek, East Branch ≃	176	40.15 N	75.27 W
Perlas, Laguna de C	182	12.35 N	83.35 W
Perleberg	116	53.04 N	11.51 E
Perm'	126	58.00 N	56.15 E
Përmet	124	40.14 N	20.21 E
Permskaja Oblast' □[4]	112	59.00 N	56.00 E
Pernambuco → Recife	184	8.03 S	34.54 W
Pernatty Lagoon ⊜	168	31.31 S	137.14 E
Pernik	124	42.36 N	23.02 E
Perpignan	118	42.41 N	2.53 E
Perranporth	104	50.20 N	5.09 W
Perris	178	33.47 N	117.14 W
Perris, Lake ⊜[1]	178	33.50 N	117.10 W
Perro, Punta del ≻	120	36.45 N	6.25 W
Perros, Bahía de C	182	22.25 N	78.36 W
Perry, Mich., U.S.	176	42.50 N	84.13 W
Perry, N.Y., U.S.	176	42.43 N	78.00 W
Perrysburg	176	41.33 N	83.38 W
Perrysville	176	40.40 N	82.19 W
Pershore	104	52.07 N	2.05 W
Persia → Iran □[1]	144	32.00 N	53.00 E
Persian Gulf C	150	27.00 N	51.00 E
Perstorp	114	56.08 N	13.23 E
Perth, Austl.	164	31.56 S	115.50 E
Perth, Ont., Can.	172	44.54 N	76.15 W
Perth, Scot., U.K.	108	56.24 N	3.28 W
Perth Amboy	176	40.31 N	74.16 W
Pertuis	118	43.41 N	5.30 E
Peru, Nebr., U.S.	174	40.29 N	95.44 W
Peru, N.Y., U.S.	176	44.35 N	73.32 W
Peru (Perú) □[1]	184	10.00 S	76.00 W
Perugia	122	43.08 N	12.22 E
Peruíbe	188	24.19 S	47.00 W
Pervomajsk	112	54.53 N	43.49 E
Pervomajskij, S.S.S.R.	112	64.26 N	40.47 E
Pervomajskij, S.S.S.R.	130	53.15 N	40.18 E
Pervoural'sk	126	56.54 N	59.58 E
Pervyj Kuril'skij Proliv ⩊	128	50.50 N	156.36 E
Pes'	130	58.55 N	34.19 E
Pesaro	122	43.54 N	12.55 E
Pescadores → P'enghu Lietao II	136	23.30 N	119.30 E
Pescara	122	42.28 N	14.13 E
Pescara ≃	122	42.28 N	14.13 E
Pescia	122	43.54 N	10.41 E
Peshāwar	149	34.01 N	71.33 E
Peshkopi	124	41.41 N	20.26 E
Peski	130	55.13 N	38.46 E
Pesmes	118	47.17 N	5.34 E
Pesočnoje	130	58.01 N	39.10 E
Peso da Régua	120	41.10 N	7.47 W
Pesqueira	184	8.22 S	36.42 W
Pessac	118	44.48 N	0.38 W
Pest □[6]	116	47.25 N	19.20 E
Pest'aki	130	56.43 N	42.40 E
Peštera	124	42.02 N	24.18 E
Pestovo	130	58.36 N	35.48 E
Petah Tiqwa	150	32.05 N	34.53 E
Petaluma	178	38.14 N	122.39 W
Petare	182	10.29 N	66.49 W
Petatlán	180	17.31 N	101.16 W
Petauke	158	14.15 S	31.20 E
Petawawa	176	45.54 N	77.17 W
Petawawa ≃	176	45.55 N	77.15 W
Peterborough, Austl.	168	32.58 S	138.50 E
Peterborough, Ont., Can.	172	44.18 N	78.19 W
Peterborough, Eng., U.K.	102	52.35 N	0.15 W
Peterborough, N.H., U.S.	176	42.53 N	71.57 W
Peterculter	108	57.05 N	2.16 W
Peterhead	108	57.30 N	1.49 W
Peter Hill ∧	108	56.58 N	2.42 W
Peter I Island I	87	68.47 S	90.35 W
Peter Lake ⊜	172	63.08 N	92.48 W
Peterlee	106	54.46 N	1.19 W
Peter Pond Lake ⊜	172	55.55 N	108.44 W
Petersburg, Alaska, U.S.	172	56.49 N	132.57 W
Petersburg, Mich., U.S.	176	41.54 N	83.43 W
Petersburg, Va., U.S.	174	37.13 N	77.24 W
Petersburg, W. Va., U.S.	176	39.00 N	79.07 W
Petersfield	104	51.00 N	0.56 W
Peterswald Hill ∧[2]	164	26.43 S	123.39 E
Petilia Policastro	122	39.07 N	16.47 E
Pétionville	182	18.31 N	72.17 W
Petite Rivière de La Baleine ≃	172	56.00 N	76.45 W
Petite Rivière Noire, Piton de la ∧	161c	20.24 S	57.24 E
Petit-Goâve	182	18.26 N	72.52 W
Petit-Mecatina, Rivière du ≃	172	50.28 N	59.35 W
Petitot ≃	172	60.14 N	123.29 W
Petit-Saint-Bernard, Col du)(	118	45.41 N	6.53 E
Petitsikapau Lake ⊜	172	54.45 N	66.25 W
Petlād	146	22.28 N	72.48 E
Peto	180	20.08 N	88.55 W
Petone	170	41.13 S	174.52 E
Petorca	188	32.15 S	70.56 W
Petoskey	176	45.22 N	84.57 W
Petras, Mount ∧	87	75.52 S	128.38 W
Petra Velikogo, Zaliv C	128	42.40 N	132.00 E
Petre, Point ≻	176	43.50 N	77.09 W
Petrič	124	41.24 N	23.13 E
Petrila	124	45.27 N	23.25 E
Petrinja	122	45.26 N	16.17 E
Petrodvorec	130	59.53 N	29.54 E
Petrograd → Leningrad	130	59.55 N	30.15 E
Petrohanski prohod)(	124	43.08 N	23.08 E
Petrolia	176	42.52 N	82.09 W
Petrolina	184	9.24 S	40.30 W
Petropavlovsk	126	54.54 N	69.06 E
Petropavlovsk-Kamčatskij	128	53.01 N	158.39 E
Petrópolis	190	22.31 S	43.10 W
Petroșani	124	45.25 N	23.22 E
Petrovsk	126	52.19 N	45.23 E
Petrovsk-Zabajkal'skij	128	51.17 N	108.50 E
Petrozavodsk	112	61.47 N	34.20 E
Petrusburg	160	29.08 S	25.27 E
Petrus Steyn	160	27.38 S	28.08 E
Petrusville	160	30.05 S	24.41 E
Petteril ≃	106	54.54 N	2.55 W
Pettigo	110	54.33 N	7.50 W
Petuchovo	126	55.06 N	67.58 E
Petworth	104	50.59 N	0.38 W
Peumo	188	34.24 S	71.10 W
Pevek	128	69.42 N	170.17 E
Pevensey	104	50.49 N	0.20 E
Pevensey Levels ≚	104	50.50 N	0.20 E
Pewsey	104	51.21 N	1.46 W
Pewsey, Vale of ∨	104	51.20 N	1.48 W
Peyruis	118	44.02 N	5.56 E
Pezinok	116	48.18 N	17.17 E
Pfaffenhofen an der Ilm	116	48.31 N	11.30 E
Pforzheim	116	48.54 N	8.42 E
Pfronten	116	47.34 N	10.33 E
Pfunds	116	46.58 N	10.33 E
Pfungstadt	116	49.48 N	8.36 E
Phagwāra	149	31.14 N	75.46 E
Phalaborwa	160	23.55 S	31.13 E
Phalodi	146	27.08 N	72.22 E
Phalsbourg	118	48.46 N	7.16 E
Phaltan	148	17.59 N	74.26 E
Phan	140	19.28 N	99.43 E
Phangan, Ko I	140	9.45 N	100.04 E
Phangnga	138	8.28 N	98.32 E
Phanom Dongrak, Thiu Khao ∧∧	140	14.25 N	103.30 E
Phan-rang	140	11.34 N	108.59 E
Phan-thiet	140	10.56 N	108.06 E
Phatthalung	140	7.37 N	100.05 E
Phayao	140	19.10 N	99.55 E
Phelps	176	42.57 N	77.03 W
Phenix City	174	32.29 N	85.01 W
Phet Buri	140	13.06 N	99.57 E
Phetchabun, Thiu Khao ∧∧	140	16.20 N	100.55 E
Philadelphia, N.Y., U.S.	176	44.09 N	75.43 W
Philadelphia, Pa., U.S.	174	39.57 N	75.07 W
Philippeville	116	50.12 N	4.32 E
Philippi	176	39.09 N	80.02 W
Philippi, Lake ⊜	168	24.22 S	139.00 E
Philippi Glacier ▽	87	66.45 S	88.20 E
Philippine Basin ⊹[1]	96	18.00 N	133.00 E
Philippines □[1]	138	13.00 N	122.00 E
Philippine Sea ▿[2]	96	20.00 N	135.00 E
Philippolis	160	30.19 S	25.13 E
Philipsburg, Ned. Ant.	182	17.59 N	63.10 W
Philipsburg, Pa., U.S.	176	40.53 N	78.05 W
Philipstown	160	30.26 S	24.29 E
Phillaur	149	31.01 N	75.47 E
Phillip Island I	168	38.29 S	145.14 E
Phillips	176	44.49 N	70.21 W
Phillipsburg	176	40.42 N	75.12 W
Philmont	176	42.15 N	73.39 W
Philo	176	39.52 N	81.55 W
Philpots Island I	172	74.48 N	80.00 W
Phimai	138	15.13 N	102.30 E
Phitsanulok	140	16.50 N	100.15 E
Phnom Penh → Phnum Pénh	140	11.33 N	104.55 E
Phnum Pénh	140	11.33 N	104.55 E
Phoenix, Ariz., U.S.	174	33.27 N	112.05 W
Phoenix, N.Y., U.S.	176	43.14 N	76.18 W
Phoenix I[1]	96	3.43 S	170.43 W
Phoenix Islands II	96	4.00 S	172.00 W
Phoenix Trough ⊹[1]	96	6.00 S	172.30 W
Phoenixville	176	40.08 N	75.31 W
Phon	140	15.49 N	102.36 E
Phôngsali	140	21.41 N	102.06 E
Phong Saly	132	21.41 N	102.06 E
Phosphate Hill	168	21.52 S	139.51 E
Phrae	140	18.09 N	100.08 E
Phra Nakhon → Krung Thep	140	13.45 N	100.31 E
Phra Nakhon Si Ayutthaya	140	14.21 N	100.33 E
Phu-cuong	140	10.58 N	106.39 E
Phuket	140	7.53 N	98.24 E
Phuket, Ko I	140	8.00 N	98.22 E
Phu-ly	140	20.32 N	105.56 E
Phumĭ Béng	140	13.05 N	104.18 E
Phumĭ Chhuk	140	10.50 N	104.28 E
Phumĭ Kâmpóng Trâbâk	140	13.06 N	105.14 E
Phuoc-binh	140	11.50 N	106.58 E
Phuoc-le	138	10.30 N	107.10 E
Phu-quoc, Dao I	140	10.12 N	104.00 E
Phu-tho	140	21.24 N	105.13 E
Phu-vinh	140	9.56 N	106.20 E
Piacenza	122	45.01 N	9.40 E
Pialba	168	25.17 S	152.51 E
Piaseczno	116	52.05 N	21.01 E
Piatra-Neamț	124	46.56 N	26.22 E
Piave ≃	122	45.32 N	12.44 E
Piawaning	164	30.51 S	116.22 E
Piazza Armerina	122	37.23 N	14.22 E
Pibor ≃	154	8.26 N	33.13 E
Pibor Post	154	6.48 N	33.08 E
Picanoc ≃	176	46.05 N	76.03 W
Picardie □[9]	118	50.00 N	3.30 E
Piccadilly Circus	158	13.56 S	29.24 E
Pichanal	188	23.20 S	64.15 W
Picheng	136	32.07 N	119.42 E
Pichilemu	188	34.23 S	72.02 W
Pickens	176	38.39 N	80.13 W
Pickerel ≃	176	45.55 N	80.50 W
Pickering, Ont., Can.	176	43.52 N	79.02 W
Pickering, Eng., U.K.	106	54.14 N	0.46 W
Pickering, Vale of ∨	106	54.12 N	0.45 W
Pickford	176	46.10 N	84.22 W
Pickle Crow	172	51.30 N	90.04 W
Pico I	88	38.28 N	28.20 W
Picos	184	7.05 S	41.28 W
Picquigny	118	49.57 N	2.09 E
Picton, Ont., Can.	176	44.00 N	77.08 W
Picton, N.Z.	170	41.18 S	174.01 E
Picton, Isla I	186	55.02 S	66.57 W
Pictou	172	45.41 N	62.43 W
Piddle ≃	104	50.42 N	2.04 W
Piddletrenthide	104	50.48 N	2.25 W
Pidurutalagala ∧	148	7.00 N	80.46 E
Pie de Palo, Sierra ∧∧	188	31.20 S	68.00 W
Piedmont Lake ⊜[1]	176	40.08 N	81.11 W
Piedra, Cerro ∧	188	37.41 S	73.07 W
Piedra del Águila	186	40.02 S	70.04 W
Piedras Negras	180	28.42 N	100.31 W
Pieksämäki	114	62.18 N	27.08 E
Pielavesi	114	63.14 N	26.45 E
Pielinen ⊜	114	63.15 N	29.40 E
Piemonte □[4]	122	45.00 N	8.00 E
Pienaarsrivier	160	25.15 S	28.18 E
Pierowall	108	59.20 N	2.59 W
Pierre	174	44.22 N	100.21 W
Pierre-Buffière	118	45.42 N	1.21 E
Piešt'any	116	48.36 N	17.50 E
Pietermaritzburg	160	29.37 S	30.16 E
Pietersburg	160	23.54 S	29.25 E
Pietrasanta	122	43.57 N	10.14 E
Piet Retief	160	27.01 S	30.50 E
Pietrosu, Vîrful ∧	124	47.36 N	24.38 E
Pigeon	176	43.50 N	83.16 W
Pigeon ≃, Mich., U.S.	176	43.56 N	83.17 W
Pigeon ≃, Mich., U.S.	176	45.27 N	84.33 W
Pigeon Lake ⊜	176	44.30 N	78.30 W
Piggs Peak	160	25.38 S	31.15 E
Pigüé	188	37.40 S	62.24 W
Pihama	170	39.30 S	173.56 E
Pihlajavesi ⊜	114	61.45 N	28.50 E
Pihtipudas	114	63.23 N	25.34 E
Pijijiapan	180	15.42 N	93.14 W
Pikal'ovo	130	59.31 N	34.06 E
Pikelot I	96	8.05 N	147.38 E
Pikes Peak ∧	174	38.51 N	105.03 W
Pikes Rock ∧[2]	176	41.56 N	79.24 W
Pikesville	176	39.23 N	76.44 W
Piketberg	160	32.54 S	18.46 E
Piketon	176	39.04 N	83.01 W
Piła (Schneidemühl)	116	53.10 N	16.44 E
Pilanesberg ∧	160	25.14 S	27.04 E
Pilar, Arg.	188	31.25 S	61.16 W
Pilar, Para.	188	26.52 S	58.23 W
Pilar de Goiás	190	14.41 S	49.27 W
Pilar do Sul	190	23.49 S	47.42 W
Pilcomayo ≃	188	25.21 S	57.42 W
Pilga	164	21.29 S	119.25 E
Pilgrim's Rest	160	24.55 S	30.44 E
Pīlībhīt	146	28.38 N	79.48 E
Pilica ≃	116	51.52 N	21.17 E
Pilliga	168	30.21 S	148.54 E
Pilot Peak ∧, Nev., U.S.	178	38.21 N	117.58 W
Pilot Peak ∧, Nev., U.S.	178	41.02 N	114.06 W
Pilpah Range ∧∧	168	20.23 S	138.34 E
Pim ≃	126	61.18 N	71.57 E
Pimba	168	31.15 S	136.47 E
Pimenta	190	20.28 S	45.48 W
Pimentel	184	6.45 S	79.55 W
Pinang (George Town)	142	5.25 N	100.20 E
Pinang, Pulau I	142	5.23 N	100.15 E
Pinar del Río	182	22.25 N	83.42 W
Pinardville	176	42.59 N	71.33 W
Pınarhisar	124	41.37 N	27.30 E
Pinas	188	31.12 S	65.28 W
Pincher Creek	172	49.29 N	113.57 W
Pinckney	176	42.27 N	83.57 W
Pinconning	176	43.51 N	83.58 W
Pindar	164	28.29 S	115.48 E
Píndhos Óros ∧∧	124	39.49 N	21.14 E
Pindi Gheb	149	33.14 N	72.16 E
Pindus Mountains → Píndhos Óros ∧∧	124	39.49 N	21.14 E
Pine ≃, B.C., Can.	172	56.08 N	120.41 W
Pine ≃, Mich., U.S.	176	44.13 N	85.53 W
Pine ≃, Mich., U.S.	176	44.26 N	83.21 W
Pine ≃, Mich., U.S.	176	46.03 N	84.40 W
Pine ≃, Mich., U.S.	176	43.35 N	84.08 W
Pine Bluff	174	34.13 N	92.01 W
Pine Bush	176	41.37 N	74.18 W
Pine Creek	166	13.49 S	131.49 E
Pine Creek ≃, Calif., U.S.	178	40.40 N	120.46 W
Pine Creek ≃, Nev., U.S.	178	40.36 N	116.10 W
Pine Creek ≃, Pa., U.S.	176	41.10 N	77.16 W
Pinedale	178	36.50 N	119.48 W
Pine Falls	172	50.35 N	96.15 W
Pine Flat Lake ⊜[1]	178	36.52 N	119.18 W
Pinega ≃	112	64.08 N	41.54 E
Pine Grove, Pa., U.S.	176	40.33 N	76.23 W
Pine Grove, W. Va., U.S.	176	39.34 N	80.41 W
Pine Hill	168	23.39 S	146.58 E
Pinehouse Lake ⊜	172	55.32 N	106.35 W
Pine Island I	182	26.35 N	82.06 W
Pine Mountain ∧	178	35.41 N	121.05 W
Pine Point	172	61.01 N	114.15 W
Pinerolo	122	44.53 N	7.21 E
Pine Swamp Knob ∧	176	39.33 N	79.31 W
Pinetown	160	29.52 S	30.46 E
Pine Valley ∨	178	38.25 N	113.40 W
Piney	118	48.22 N	4.20 E
Ping ≃	140	15.42 N	100.09 E
Pingaring	164	32.45 S	118.37 E
Pingba	140	26.22 N	106.09 E
Pingchaoshi	136	32.07 N	120.45 E
Pingdingshan	132	33.44 N	113.18 E
Pingdu	132	36.47 N	119.54 E
Pingelap I[1]	96	6.13 N	160.42 E
Pingelly	164	32.32 S	117.05 E
Pinghai	136	22.39 N	114.53 E
Pinghe	136	24.25 N	117.22 E
Pinghu	136	30.42 N	121.01 E
Pingjiang	136	28.44 N	113.34 E
Pingle	140	24.37 N	110.40 E
Pingliang	132	35.27 N	107.10 E
Pingnan	136	26.56 N	119.02 E
Pingqiao	136	33.24 N	119.13 E
Pingquan	132	40.59 N	118.34 E
Pingrup	164	33.32 S	118.31 E
Pingshan, Zhg.	136	22.59 N	114.43 E
Pingshan, Zhg.	136	23.26 N	113.15 E
Pingshi	136	32.32 N	113.03 E
Pingtan	136	25.31 N	119.47 E
P'ingtung	136	22.40 N	120.29 E
Pingwang	136	30.59 N	120.38 E
Pingwu	132	32.29 N	104.37 E
Pingxiang, Zhg.	136	27.38 N	113.50 E
Pingxiang, Zhg.	140	22.09 N	106.43 E
Pingyang	136	27.41 N	120.33 E
Pingyao	132	37.16 N	112.09 E
Pingyu	136	32.57 N	114.41 E
Pingyuan	136	24.36 N	115.54 E
Pinhal	190	22.12 S	46.45 W
Pinheiro	184	2.31 S	45.05 W
Pinheiro Machado	188	31.34 S	53.23 W
Pinhel	120	40.46 N	7.04 W
Pinhoe	104	50.44 N	3.27 W
Pini, Pulau I	140	0.08 N	98.40 E
Pinillos	182	8.55 N	74.28 W
Pinjarra	164	32.37 S	115.53 E
Pinnacle ∧	176	43.13 N	74.23 W
Pinnaroo	168	35.16 S	140.55 E
Pinneberg	116	53.40 N	9.47 E
Pinos, isla de (Isle of Pines) I	182	21.40 N	82.50 W
Pinos, Mount ∧	178	34.50 N	119.09 W
Pinrang	142	3.48 S	119.38 E
Pins, Pointe aux ≻	176	42.15 N	81.51 W
Pinsk	130	52.07 N	26.04 E
Pin'ug	126	60.15 N	47.48 E
Pinwherry	106	55.09 N	4.50 W
Pinxton	104	53.06 N	1.19 W
Pinzgau ∨	116	47.15 N	12.40 E
Pioche	178	37.56 N	114.27 W
Piombino	122	42.55 N	10.32 E
Pioneer, Austl.	164	31.48 S	121.43 E
Pioneer, Ohio, U.S.	176	41.41 N	84.33 W
Pioner, Ostrov I	128	79.50 N	92.30 E
Pionki	116	51.30 N	21.27 E
Piopio	170	38.28 S	175.01 E
Piotrków Trybunalski	116	51.25 N	19.42 E
Pipestone ≃	172	52.53 N	89.23 W
Pipinas	188	35.30 S	57.19 W
Pipmuacan, Réservoir ⊜[1]	172	49.35 N	70.30 W
Piqua	176	40.09 N	84.15 W
Piquiri ≃	188	24.03 S	54.14 W
Piracanjuba	190	17.18 S	49.01 W
Piracicaba	190	22.43 S	47.38 W
Piraeus → Piraiévs	124	37.57 N	23.38 E
Pirai do Sul	188	24.31 S	49.56 W
Piraiévs (Piraeus)	124	37.57 N	23.38 E
Piraju	190	23.12 S	49.23 W
Pirajuí	190	21.59 S	49.29 W
Piram Island I	146	21.36 N	72.41 E
Pirané	188	25.44 S	59.07 W
Piranga	190	20.41 S	43.18 W
Pirapora	190	17.21 S	44.56 W
Piraquara	188	25.26 S	49.04 W
Pirassununga	190	21.59 S	47.25 W
Piratini	188	31.27 S	53.06 W
Piratuba	188	27.27 S	51.48 W
Pirenópolis	190	15.51 S	48.57 W
Pires do Rio	190	17.18 S	48.17 W
Pírgos	124	37.41 N	21.28 E
Piriápolis	188	34.54 S	55.17 W
Píritu, Ven.	182	9.23 N	69.12 W
Píritu, Ven.	182	11.22 N	69.08 W
Pirmasens	116	49.12 N	7.36 E
Pirna	116	50.58 N	13.56 E
Pirongia	170	38.00 S	175.12 E
Pirot	124	43.09 N	22.35 E
Pīr Panjāl Range ∧∧	146	33.37 N	74.32 E
Piru	166	3.04 S	128.12 E
Piru Creek ≃	178	34.23 N	118.47 W
Pisa	122	43.43 N	10.23 E
Pisa, Mount ∧	170	44.52 S	169.11 E
Pisagua	184	19.36 S	70.13 W
Pisco	184	13.42 S	76.13 W
Písek	116	49.19 N	14.10 E
Pishan	146	37.37 N	78.18 E
Pishīn Lora (Lowrah) ≃	146	29.09 N	64.55 E
Pismo Beach	178	35.09 N	120.38 W
Pissos	118	44.19 N	0.47 W
Pisticci	122	40.23 N	16.34 E
Pistoia	122	43.55 N	10.54 E
Pit ≃	178	40.45 N	122.22 W
Pit, North Fork ≃	178	41.28 N	120.33 W
Pit, South Fork ≃	178	41.28 N	120.33 W
Pitalito	184	1.51 N	76.02 W
Pitanga	188	24.46 S	51.44 W
Piteå	114	65.20 N	21.30 E
Piteälven ≃	114	65.14 N	21.32 E
Pitești	124	44.52 N	24.52 E
Pithāpuram	148	17.07 N	82.16 E
Pithara	164	30.24 S	116.40 E
Pithiviers	118	48.10 N	2.15 E
Pitlochry	108	56.43 N	3.45 W
Pitsford Reservoir ⊜[1]	104	52.20 N	0.52 W
Pittenweem	108	56.12 N	2.44 W
Pitt Island I	172	53.35 N	129.45 W
Pittsburg	174	37.25 N	94.42 W
Pittsburgh	174	40.26 N	80.00 W
Pittsfield, Maine, U.S.	176	44.47 N	69.23 W
Pittsfield, Mass., U.S.	176	42.27 N	73.15 W
Pittsfield, N.H., U.S.	176	43.18 N	71.19 W
Pittsford	176	41.52 N	84.28 W
Pittston	176	41.19 N	75.47 W
Pittsworth	168	27.43 S	151.38 E
Pituri Creek ≃	168	22.58 S	138.50 E
Piu, Cerro ∧	182	13.38 N	84.52 W
Pium	184	10.27 S	49.11 W
Piura	184	5.12 S	80.36 W
Piute Peak ∧	178	35.27 N	118.24 W
Pivan'	128	50.29 N	137.06 E
Pivijay	182	10.28 N	74.37 W
Pixley	178	35.58 N	119.17 W
Placentia Bay C	172	47.15 N	54.30 W
Placerville	178	38.43 N	120.48 W
Placetas	182	22.19 N	79.40 W
Plain City	176	40.06 N	83.16 W
Plainfield, Conn., U.S.	176	41.41 N	71.55 W
Plainfield, N.J., U.S.	176	40.37 N	74.26 W
Plainview	174	34.11 N	101.43 W
Plaistow	176	42.50 N	71.06 W
Plampang	142	8.48 S	117.48 E
Plana, Isla I	120	38.10 N	0.28 W
Planada	178	37.18 N	120.19 W
Planalto	188	27.20 S	53.03 W
Planeta Rica	184	8.25 N	75.36 W
Plantagenet	176	45.32 N	75.00 W
Plasencia	120	40.02 N	6.05 W
Plast	126	54.22 N	60.50 E
Plata, Río de la C[1]	188	35.00 S	57.00 W
Plato	184	9.47 N	74.47 W
Platte ≃	174	39.16 N	94.50 W
Platte Island I	156	5.52 S	55.23 E
Plattling	116	48.47 N	12.53 E
Plattsburgh	176	44.42 N	73.28 W
Plauen	116	50.30 N	12.08 E
Playford ≃	168	19.05 S	136.30 E
Playgreen Lake ⊜	172	54.00 N	98.10 W
Playon Grande	182	9.30 N	78.20 W
Plaza Huincul	188	38.57 S	69.12 W
Pleasant Gap	176	40.52 N	77.45 W
Pleasant Hill	178	37.56 N	122.04 W
Pleasantville, N.J., U.S.	176	39.23 N	74.32 W
Pleasantville, Pa., U.S.	176	41.36 N	79.35 W
Pléaux	118	45.08 N	2.14 E
Pleiku	140	13.59 N	108.00 E
Pleine d'Aleria ⊸[1]	122	42.05 N	9.25 E
Plenty, Bay of C	170	37.40 S	177.00 E
Plentywood	174	48.47 N	104.34 W
Pleseck	112	62.43 N	40.20 E
Plessisville	172	46.14 N	71.47 W
Pleszew	116	51.54 N	17.48 E
Plétipi, Lac ⊜	172	51.44 N	70.06 W
Plettenbergbaai	160	34.04 S	23.22 E
Pleven	124	43.25 N	24.37 E
Pleyben	102	48.14 N	3.58 W
Plimmerton	170	41.05 S	174.52 E
Pljevlja	124	43.21 N	19.21 E
Ploaghe	122	40.40 N	8.44 E
Płock	116	52.33 N	19.43 E
Plöckenpass)(	116	46.36 N	12.58 E
Ploërmel	118	47.56 N	2.24 W
Plogastel-Saint-Germain	102	47.59 N	4.16 W
Ploiești	124	44.56 N	26.02 E
Plomárion	124	38.59 N	26.22 E
Plombières-les-Bains	118	47.58 N	6.29 E
Plön	116	54.09 N	10.25 E
Płońsk	116	52.38 N	20.23 E
Ploudalmézeau	118	48.32 N	4.39 W
Plouguenast	118	48.17 N	2.43 W
Plovdiv	124	42.09 N	24.45 E
Plumbridge	110	54.46 N	7.15 W
Plumridge Lakes ⊜	164	29.30 S	125.25 E
Plumtree	158	20.30 S	27.50 E
Pluvigner	102	47.46 N	3.01 W
Plym ≃	104	50.12 N	4.07 W
Plymouth, Monts.	182	16.42 N	62.13 W
Plymouth, Eng., U.K.	104	50.23 N	4.10 W
Plymouth, Calif., U.S.	178	38.29 N	120.51 W
Plymouth, Mass., U.S.	176	41.58 N	70.41 W
Plymouth, N.H., U.S.	176	43.45 N	71.41 W
Plymouth, Ohio, U.S.	176	40.59 N	82.40 W
Plymouth, Pa., U.S.	176	41.14 N	75.58 W
Plympton	104	50.23 N	4.03 W
Plymstock	104	50.22 N	4.04 W
Plynlimon ∧	104	52.28 N	3.47 W
Plzeň	116	49.45 N	13.23 E
Po ≃	122	44.57 N	12.04 E
Pobeda, Gora ∧	128	65.12 N	146.12 E
Pobedino	128	49.51 N	142.49 E
Pobedy, Pik ∧	126	42.02 N	80.05 E
Pocatalico ≃	176	38.29 N	81.49 W
Pocatello	174	42.52 N	112.27 W
Počep	130	52.56 N	33.27 E
Pochutla	180	15.44 N	96.28 W
Pochvistnevo	112	53.38 N	52.08 E
Pocitos	188	22.05 S	63.44 W
Pocklington	106	53.56 N	0.46 W
Poço Fundo	188	21.48 S	45.58 W
Pocomoke ≃	176	37.58 N	75.39 W
Pocomoke City	176	38.05 N	75.34 W
Pocono Mountains ∧∧[2]	176	41.10 N	75.20 W
Poços de Caldas	190	21.48 S	46.34 W
Pocrane	190	19.37 S	41.37 W
Poděbrady	116	50.08 N	15.07 E
Podensac	118	44.39 N	0.22 W
Podgorica → Titograd	124	42.26 N	19.14 E
Podkamennaja Tunguska	128	61.36 N	90.09 E
Podkamennaja Tunguska ≃	128	61.36 N	90.18 E
Podol'sk	130	55.26 N	37.33 E
Podor	152	16.40 N	14.57 W
Podporožje	112	60.53 N	34.07 E
Poel I	116	54.00 N	11.26 E
Pofadder	160	29.10 S	19.22 E
Poggibonsi	122	43.28 N	11.09 E
Pogradec	124	40.54 N	20.39 E
Pograničnyj	128	44.25 N	131.24 E
P'ohang	132	36.03 N	129.20 E
Pohjanmaa ⊸[1]	114	64.00 N	25.00 E
Pohjois-Karjalan lääni □[4]	114	63.00 N	30.00 E
Pohue Bay C	179a	19.00 N	155.48 W
Point Arena	178	38.55 N	123.41 W
Pointe-à-Pitre	182	16.14 N	61.32 W
Pointe-des-galets → Le Port	161c	20.55 S	55.18 E
Point Edward	176	43.00 N	82.24 W
Pointe-Noire	156	4.48 S	11.51 E
Point Fortin	182	10.11 N	61.41 W
Point Lake ⊜	172	65.15 N	113.04 W
Point Marion	176	39.44 N	79.53 W
Point Pleasant, N.J., U.S.	176	40.05 N	74.04 W
Point Pleasant, W. Va., U.S.	176	38.52 N	82.08 W
Point Samson	164	20.36 S	117.12 E
Poisson Blanc, Réservoir du ⊜[1]	176	46.00 N	75.45 W
Poissy	118	48.56 N	2.03 E
Poitiers	118	46.35 N	0.20 E
Poitou ⊸[1]	118	46.20 N	0.30 W
Pojarkovo	128	49.38 N	128.38 E
Pokataroo	168	29.35 S	148.42 E
Pokhara	132	28.14 N	83.59 E
Pokrovsk	128	61.29 N	129.06 E
Pokur	128	61.02 N	75.26 E
Pola de Laviana	120	43.15 N	5.34 W
Pola de Lena	120	43.10 N	5.49 W
Pola de Siero	120	43.23 N	5.40 W
Poland □[1]	100	52.00 N	19.00 E
Pol'arnyj	112	69.12 N	33.22 E
Polar Record Glacier ▽	87	69.49 S	75.30 E
Polatlı	144	39.36 N	32.09 E
Polbain	108	58.02 N	5.23 W
Polcirkeln	112	66.34 N	21.05 E
Polcura	188	37.17 S	71.43 W
Polden Hills ∧∧[2]	104	51.08 N	2.50 W
Polegate	104	50.49 N	0.15 E
Pol-e Khomrī	146	35.56 N	68.43 E
Polesje ⊸[1]	126	52.30 N	27.30 E
Polesworth	104	52.37 N	1.36 W
Polevskoj	126	56.26 N	60.11 E
Polgár	116	47.52 N	21.08 E
Police	116	53.35 N	14.33 E
Políkastron	124	41.00 N	22.34 E
Polikhnitos	124	39.05 N	26.11 E
Polillo Islands II	138	14.50 N	122.05 E
Polistena	122	38.25 N	16.05 E
Políyiros	124	40.23 N	23.27 E
Polk	176	41.22 N	79.56 W
Pol'kino	128	71.10 N	99.13 E
Pollāchi	148	10.40 N	77.01 E
Pollaphuca Reservoir ⊜[1]	110	53.08 N	6.31 W
Pöllau	116	47.18 N	15.51 E
Polock	130	55.31 N	28.46 E
Polonnaruwa	144	7.56 N	81.00 E
Polos	124	41.50 N	27.04 E
Polperro	104	50.19 N	4.31 W
Polruan	104	50.19 N	4.36 W
Poltava	126	49.35 N	34.34 E
Poltimore	176	45.47 N	75.43 W
Poluj ≃	126	66.31 N	66.33 E
Polunočnoje	126	60.52 N	60.25 E
Polvijärvi	114	62.51 N	29.22 E
Polynesia II	96	4.00 S	156.00 W
Polynésie française → French Polynesia □[2]	96	15.00 S	140.00 W
Polysajevo	128	54.35 N	86.14 E
Pomabamba	184	8.50 S	77.25 W
Pomahaka ≃	170	46.09 S	169.34 E
Pomarkku	114	61.42 N	22.00 E
Pombal	120	39.55 N	8.38 W
Pomerania □[9]	116	54.00 N	16.00 E
Pomeranian Bay C	116	54.00 N	14.15 E
Pomerode	188	26.45 S	49.11 W
Pomeroy, N. Ire., U.K.	110	54.36 N	6.56 W
Pomeroy, Ohio, U.S.	176	39.02 N	82.02 W
Pomona	178	34.04 N	117.45 W
Pomorze → Pomerania □[9]	116	54.00 N	16.00 E
Pompano Beach	182	26.15 N	80.07 W
Pompei	122	40.45 N	14.30 E
Pompéia	190	22.08 S	50.10 W
Pompton Lakes	176	41.00 N	74.17 W
Ponape I	96	6.55 N	158.15 E
Ponca City	174	36.42 N	97.05 W
Ponce	182	18.01 N	66.37 W
Pondicherry	148	11.56 N	79.53 E
Pond Inlet	172	72.41 N	78.00 W
Pond Inlet C	172	72.46 N	77.00 W
Pondoland ⊸[1]	160	31.00 S	29.30 E
Pondosa	178	41.12 N	121.41 W
Ponferrada	120	42.33 N	6.35 W
Pongaroa	170	40.33 S	176.11 E
Pongola ≃	156	26.48 S	32.23 E
Ponnūru Nidubrolu	148	16.04 N	80.34 E
Ponoj ≃	112	66.59 N	41.17 E
Ponoka	172	52.42 N	113.35 W
Ponorogo	142	7.52 S	111.27 E
Pons	118	45.35 N	0.33 W
Ponta Grossa	188	25.05 S	50.09 W
Pontalina	190	17.31 S	49.27 W
Pont-à-Mousson	118	48.54 N	6.04 E
Pontão	120	39.55 N	8.22 W
Ponta Porã	190	22.32 S	55.43 W
Pontardawe	104	51.44 N	3.51 W
Pontardulais	104	51.43 N	4.03 W
Pontarlier	118	46.54 N	6.22 E
Pontassieve	122	43.46 N	11.26 E
Pontchartrain, Lake ⊜	174	30.10 N	90.10 W
Pontchâteau	118	47.26 N	2.05 W
Pont-d'Ain	118	46.03 N	5.20 E
Pont-de-Salars	118	44.17 N	2.44 E
Pont de Suert	120	42.24 N	0.45 E
Pont-de-Vaux	118	46.26 N	4.56 E
Ponte da Barca	120	41.48 N	8.25 W
Pontedera	122	43.40 N	10.38 E
Ponte de Sor	120	39.15 N	8.01 W
Pontefract	106	53.42 N	1.18 W
Ponteland	106	55.03 N	1.44 W
Ponte Nova	190	20.24 S	42.54 W
Ponterwyd	104	52.25 N	3.50 W
Pontesbury	104	52.39 N	2.54 W
Ponte Serrada	188	26.52 S	51.58 W
Pontevedra	120	42.26 N	8.38 W
Pontgibaud	118	46.50 N	2.51 E
Pontiac	176	42.37 N	83.18 W
Pontianak	142	0.02 S	109.20 E
Pontivy	118	48.04 N	2.59 W
Pont-l'Évêque	118	49.18 N	0.11 E
Pontoise	118	49.03 N	2.06 E
Pontremoli	122	42.22 N	9.53 E
Pontresina	118	46.28 N	9.53 E
Pontrhydfendigaid	104	52.17 N	3.51 W
Pont-Scorff	102	47.50 N	3.24 W
Pont-sur-Yonne	118	48.17 N	3.12 E
Pontvallain	102	47.45 N	0.12 E
Pontyberem	104	51.17 N	4.09 W
Pontycymmer	104	51.37 N	3.34 W
Pontypool	104	51.43 N	3.02 W
Pontypridd	104	51.37 N	3.22 W
Ponziane, Isole I	122	40.55 N	12.57 E
Poochera	164	32.43 S	134.51 E
Poole	104	50.43 N	1.59 W
Poole, Mount ∧	168	29.37 S	141.46 E
Poole Bay C	104	50.42 N	1.52 W
Poolewe	108	57.45 N	5.37 W
Pooncarie	168	33.23 S	142.34 E
Poondinna, Mount ∧	164	27.20 S	129.59 E
Poopó, Lago de ⊜	184	18.45 S	67.07 W
Popayán	184	2.27 N	76.36 W
Poperinge	116	50.51 N	2.43 E
Popham Bay C	172	64.10 N	65.10 W
Popigaj	128	71.55 N	110.47 E
Popigaj ≃	128	72.54 N	106.36 E
Popilta Lake ⊜	168	33.10 S	141.43 E
Poplar ≃	172	53.00 N	97.18 W
Poplar Bluff	174	36.45 N	90.24 W
Popocatépetl, Volcán ∧[1]	180	19.02 N	98.38 W
Popokabaka	156	5.42 S	16.35 E
Popomanaseu, Mount ∧	162	9.42 S	160.04 E
Popondetta	166	8.46 S	148.14 E
Popovo	124	43.21 N	26.13 E
Poprad	116	49.03 N	20.18 E
Poprad ≃	116	49.38 N	20.42 E
Porangahau	170	40.18 S	176.37 E
Porangatu	190	13.26 S	49.10 W
Porbandar	146	21.38 N	69.36 E
Porcher Island I	172	53.57 N	130.30 W
Porcuna	120	37.52 N	4.11 W
Porcupine ≃	172	66.34 N	145.14 W
Pordenone	122	45.57 N	12.39 E
Porecatu	190	22.43 S	51.24 W
Pori	114	61.29 N	21.47 E
Porirua	170	41.08 S	174.51 E
Porkkala	114	59.59 N	24.26 E
Porlamar	184	10.57 N	63.51 W
Porlock	104	51.14 N	3.36 W
Pornic	118	47.07 N	2.06 W
Poronajsk	128	49.14 N	143.04 E
Porpoise Bay C	87	66.30 S	128.30 E
Porrentruy	118	47.25 N	7.05 E
Porsangen C[2]	112	70.58 N	27.00 E
Porsangerhalvøya ≻[1]	112	70.50 N	25.00 E
Porsgrunn	114	59.09 N	9.40 E
Portachuelo	184	17.21 S	63.24 W
Portacloy	110	54.19 N	9.48 W
Port Adelaide	168	34.51 S	138.30 E
Portadown	110	54.26 N	6.27 W
Portaferry	110	54.23 N	5.33 W
Portage	176	42.12 N	85.41 W
Portage ≃	176	41.31 N	83.05 W
Portage-la-Prairie	172	49.57 N	98.25 W
Port Alberni	172	49.14 N	124.48 W
Portalegre	120	39.17 N	7.26 W
Portales	174	34.11 N	103.20 W
Port-Alfred, Qué., Can.	172	48.19 N	70.53 W
Port Alfred (Kowie), S. Afr.	160	33.36 S	26.55 E
Port Alice	172	50.23 N	127.27 W
Port Allegany	176	41.49 N	78.17 W
Port Alma	168	23.35 S	150.51 E
Port Angeles	174	48.07 N	123.27 W
Port Antonio	182	18.10 N	76.28 W
Portarlington	110	53.10 N	7.11 W
Port Arthur, Austl.	168	43.09 S	147.51 E
Port Arthur → Thunder Bay, Ont., Can.	172	48.23 N	89.15 W
Port Arthur, Tex., U.S.	174	29.55 N	93.55 W
Port Arthur → Lüshun, Zhg.	132	38.48 N	121.16 E
Port Askaig	108	55.51 N	6.07 W
Port Augusta	168	32.30 S	137.46 E
Port-au-Prince	182	18.32 N	72.20 W
Port-au-Prince, Baie de C	182	18.40 N	72.30 W
Port Austin	176	44.03 N	83.01 W
Port Bannatyne	108	55.52 N	5.05 W
Port-Bergé	161b	15.33 S	47.40 E
Port Blair	140	11.40 N	92.45 E
Port-Bouët	152	5.15 N	3.58 W
Port Broughton	168	33.36 S	137.56 E
Port Campbell	168	38.37 S	143.00 E
Port-Cartier-Quest	172	50.01 N	66.52 W
Port Chalmers	170	45.49 S	170.37 E
Port Chester	176	41.00 N	73.40 W
Port Clinton	176	41.31 N	82.56 W
Port Clyde	176	43.56 N	69.15 W
Port Colborne	176	42.53 N	79.14 W
Port Credit	176	43.33 N	79.35 W
Port-de-Paix	182	19.57 N	72.50 W
Port Dickson	142	2.31 N	101.48 E
Port Dover	176	42.47 N	80.12 W
Porte Crayon, Mount ∧	176	38.56 N	79.27 W
Port Edward	160	31.02 S	30.13 E
Port Elgin	176	44.26 N	81.24 W
Port Elizabeth	160	33.58 S	25.40 E
Port Ellen	108	55.39 N	6.12 W
Port-en-Bessin	118	49.21 N	0.45 W
Port Erin	106	54.06 N	4.44 W
Porterville, S. Afr.	160	33.00 S	19.00 E
Porterville, Calif., U.S.	178	36.04 N	119.01 W
Portete, Bahía de C	182	12.12 N	71.56 W
Port-Étienne → Nouadhibou	152	20.54 N	17.04 W
Porteynon	104	51.33 N	4.13 W
Porteynon Point ≻	104	51.32 N	4.12 W
Port Fairy	168	38.23 S	142.14 E
Port Fitzroy	170	36.10 S	175.21 E
Port-Gentil	156	0.43 S	8.47 E
Port Germein	168	33.01 S	138.00 E
Port Glasgow	108	55.57 N	4.41 W
Portglenone	110	54.53 N	6.27 W
Porth	104	51.38 N	3.25 W
Port Harcourt	152	4.43 N	7.05 E
Porthcawl	104	51.29 N	3.43 W
Port Hedland	164	20.19 S	118.34 E
Port Henry	176	44.03 N	73.28 W
Porth Neigwl C	104	52.48 N	4.34 W
Port Hope, Ont., Can.	176	43.57 N	78.18 W
Port Hope, Mich., U.S.	176	43.57 N	82.43 W
Port Hueneme	178	34.09 N	119.12 W
Port Huron	176	42.58 N	82.27 W
Portillo	182	19.55 N	77.11 W
Portimão	120	37.08 N	8.32 W
Port Isaac	104	50.35 N	4.49 W
Portishead	104	51.30 N	2.46 W
Port Jervis	176	41.22 N	74.41 W
Port Keats Mission	166	14.13 S	129.32 E
Port Kembla	168	34.29 S	150.54 E
Port Kenny	164	33.10 S	134.42 E
Portknockie	108	57.41 N	2.51 W
Portland, Austl.	168	38.21 S	141.36 E
Portland, N.Z.	170	35.48 S	174.19 E
Portland, Ind., U.S.	176	40.26 N	84.59 W
Portland, Maine, U.S.	176	43.39 N	70.17 W
Portland, Mich., U.S.	176	42.52 N	84.54 W
Portland, Oreg., U.S.	174	45.33 N	122.36 W
Portland, Bill of ≻	102	50.31 N	2.27 W
Portland, Cape ≻	168	40.45 S	147.57 E
Portland, Isle of I	104	50.33 N	2.27 W
Portland Bight C[3]	182	17.50 N	77.05 W
Portland Point ≻	182	17.43 N	77.07 W
Portlaoghise	110	53.02 N	7.17 W
Portlaw	110	52.17 N	7.19 W
Port Leyden	176	43.35 N	75.21 W
Port Lincoln	168	34.44 S	135.52 E
Port Logan	106	54.43 N	4.56 W
Port Loko	152	8.46 N	12.47 W
Port-Louis, Fr.	118	47.43 N	3.21 W
Port Louis, Maus.	161c	20.10 S	57.30 E
Port-Lyautey → Kenitra	152	34.16 N	6.40 W
Port MacDonnell	168	38.03 S	140.42 E
Port Macquarie	168	31.26 S	152.55 E
Portmadoc	104	52.55 N	4.08 W
Portmahomack	108	57.49 N	3.50 W
Port Maria	182	18.25 N	76.55 W
Port McNicoll	176	44.45 N	79.49 W
Port Moresby	166	9.30 S	147.10 E
Portnaguiran	108	58.17 N	6.13 W
Portnahaven	108	55.41 N	6.31 W
Port Neill	168	34.07 S	136.20 E
Port Nolloth	160	29.17 S	16.51 E
Port Norris	176	39.15 N	75.02 W
Port-Nouveau-Québec	172	58.32 N	65.54 W
Porto	120	41.11 N	8.36 W
Pôrto Alegre	188	30.04 S	51.11 W
Porto Alexandre	156	15.49 S	11.53 E
Pôrto Amazonas	188	25.33 S	49.53 W
Porto Amboim	156	10.44 S	13.44 E
Porto Amélia	158	12.58 S	40.30 E
Portobello	108	55.58 N	3.07 W
Pôrto Belo, Bra.	188	27.10 S	48.33 W
Portobelo, Pan.	182	9.33 N	79.39 W
Pôrto de Moz	184	1.45 S	52.14 W
Pôrto de Pedras	184	9.10 S	35.17 W
Porto Empedocle	122	37.17 N	13.32 E
Pôrto Esperaną	184	19.37 S	57.27 W
Pôrto Esperidião	184	15.51 S	58.28 W
Pôrto Feliz	190	23.13 S	47.32 W
Pôrto Ferreira	190	21.51 S	47.28 W
Port of Ness	108	58.29 N	6.13 W
Port of Spain	182	10.39 N	61.31 W
Portogruaro	122	45.47 N	12.50 E
Portola	178	39.48 N	120.28 W
Pôrto Lucena	188	27.51 S	55.01 W
Pörtom (Pirttikylä)	114	62.42 N	21.37 E
Pôrto Mendes	188	24.30 S	54.20 W
Pôrto Murtinho	184	21.42 S	57.52 W
Pôrto Nacional	184	10.42 S	48.25 W
Porto-Novo	152	6.29 N	2.37 E
Port Orford	178	42.45 N	124.30 W
Porto San Giorgio	122	43.11 N	13.48 E
Porto Sant'Elpidio	122	43.15 N	13.45 E
Pôrto São José	190	22.43 S	53.10 W
Pôrto Seguro	190	16.26 S	39.05 W
Porto Torres	122	40.50 N	8.23 E
Pôrto União	188	26.15 S	51.05 W
Porto-Vecchio	122	41.35 N	9.16 E
Pôrto Velho	184	8.46 S	63.54 W
Portoviejo	184	1.03 S	80.27 W
Portpatrick	106	54.51 N	5.07 W
Port Perry	176	44.06 N	78.57 W
Port Phillip Bay C	168	38.07 S	144.48 E
Port Pirie	168	33.11 S	138.01 E
Port Radium	172	66.05 N	118.02 W
Portree	108	57.24 N	6.12 W
Port Rowan	176	42.37 N	80.28 W
Port Royal	176	40.32 N	77.23 W
Portrush	110	55.12 N	6.40 W
Port Said → Būr Sa'īd	154	31.16 N	32.18 E
Port Saint Johns	160	31.38 S	29.33 E
Portsalon	110	55.13 N	7.37 W
Port Sanilac	176	43.26 N	82.33 W
Port Seton	108	55.58 N	2.57 W
Port Shepstone	160	30.46 S	30.22 E
Portslade	104	50.50 N	0.11 W

Symbols in the index entries are identified on page 198.

Symbols in the index entries are identified on page 198.

Name	Page	Lat °′	Long °′
Rathkeale	110	52.32 N	8.56 W
Rathlin Island I	110	55.18 N	6.13 W
Rathlin Sound ⩊	110	55.16 N	6.17 W
Ráth Luirc	110	52.21 N	8.41 W
Rathmelton	110	55.02 N	7.38 W
Rathmore	110	52.03 N	9.13 W
Rathmullen	110	55.06 N	7.33 W
Rathnew	110	53.00 N	6.05 W
Rathowen	110	53.40 N	7.31 W
Ratingen	116	51.18 N	6.51 E
Ratisbon → Regensburg	116	49.01 N	12.06 E
Ratlām	146	23.19 N	75.04 E
Ratnāgiri	148	16.59 N	73.18 E
Ratnapura	144	6.41 N	80.24 E
Raton	174	36.54 N	104.24 W
Rattray Head ▸	108	57.37 N	1.49 W
Rättvik	114	60.53 N	15.06 E
Ratz, Mount ∧	172	57.23 N	132.19 W
Ratzeburg	116	53.42 N	10.46 E
Raub	142	3.48 N	101.52 E
Rauch	188	36.47 S	59.05 W
Raufarhöfn	112a	66.30 N	15.57 W
Rauma	114	61.08 N	21.30 E
Rauma ≃	114	62.33 N	7.43 E
Raunds	104	52.21 N	0.33 W
Raurimu	170	39.07 S	175.24 E
Raurkela	148	22.13 N	84.53 E
Rausu	134a	44.01 N	145.12 E
Ravahere I[1]	96	18.14 S	142.09 W
Ravanusa	122	37.16 N	13.58 E
Ravena	176	42.29 N	73.49 W
Ravenglass	106	54.21 N	3.24 W
Ravenna, It.	122	44.25 N	12.12 E
Ravenna, Ky., U.S.	176	37.41 N	83.57 W
Ravenna, Ohio, U.S.	176	41.09 N	81.15 W
Ravensburg	116	47.47 N	9.37 E
Ravenshoe	168	17.37 S	145.29 E
Ravensthorpe, Austl.	164	33.35 S	120.02 E
Ravensthorpe, Eng., U.K.	106	53.42 N	1.35 W
Ravenswood	176	38.57 N	81.46 W
Rāvi ≃	149	30.35 N	71.48 E
Rāwalpindi	149	33.36 N	73.04 E
Rawdon	176	46.04 N	73.44 W
Rawene	170	35.24 S	173.30 E
Rawhide Mountain ∧	178	38.17 N	116.25 W
Rawicz	116	51.37 N	16.52 E
Rawlinna	164	31.01 S	125.20 E
Rawlins	174	41.47 N	107.14 W
Rawlinson Range ⋀	164	24.51 S	128.00 E
Rawmarsh	106	53.27 N	1.21 W
Rawson, Arg.	186	43.18 S	65.06 W
Rawson, Arg.	188	34.40 S	60.02 W
Rawtenstall	106	53.42 N	2.18 W
Raxaul	144	26.59 N	84.51 E
Ray ≃	104	51.48 N	1.15 W
Ray, Cape ▸	172	47.40 N	59.18 W
Raya, Bukit ∧	142	0.40 S	112.41 E
Rāyadrug	148	14.42 N	76.52 E
Rayleigh	104	51.36 N	0.36 E
Raymond Terrace	168	32.46 S	151.44 E
Raymondville	174	26.29 N	97.47 W
Rayner Glacier ◸	87	67.40 S	48.30 E
Rayong	140	12.40 N	101.17 E
R'azan'	130	54.38 N	39.44 E
R'azancevo	130	56.42 N	39.12 E
Razdan	150	40.30 N	44.46 E
Razelm, Lacul ⊜	124	44.54 N	28.57 E
Razgrad	124	43.32 N	26.31 E
R'ažsk	130	53.43 N	40.04 E
Ré, Île de I	118	46.12 N	1.25 W
Rea ≃, Eng., U.K.	104	52.18 N	2.32 W
Rea ≃, Eng., U.K.	104	52.30 N	1.51 W
Reading, Eng., U.K.	104	51.28 N	0.59 W
Reading, Mich., U.S.	176	41.50 N	84.45 W
Reading, Ohio, U.S.	176	39.14 N	84.27 W
Reading, Pa., U.S.	174	40.20 N	75.56 W
Real, Cordillera ⋀	184	17.00 S	67.10 W
Real del Castillo	178	31.58 N	116.19 W
Realicó	188	35.02 S	64.16 W
Réalmont	118	43.47 N	2.12 E
Reay	108	58.33 N	3.47 W
Reay Forest •[3]	108	58.19 N	4.47 W
Rebecca, Lake ⊜	164	29.53 S	122.10 E
Rebouças	188	25.36 S	50.42 W
Rebun-jima I	134a	45.23 N	141.02 E
Recherche, Archipelago of the II	164	34.05 S	122.45 E
Rečica	130	52.22 N	30.25 E
Recife	184	8.03 S	34.54 W
Recinto	188	36.48 S	71.44 W
Recklinghausen	116	51.36 N	7.13 E
Recknitz ≃	116	54.14 N	12.28 E
Reconquista	188	29.10 S	59.40 W
Recovery Glacier ◸	87	81.10 S	28.00 W
Recreo	188	29.20 S	65.04 W
Red (Hong-ha) (Yuanjiang) ≃, As.	140	20.17 N	106.34 E
Red ≃, N.A.	174	50.24 N	96.48 W
Red ≃, U.S.	174	31.00 N	91.40 W
Red ≃, Ky., U.S.	176	37.51 N	84.05 W
Redang, Pulau I	142	5.47 N	103.00 E
Red Bank	176	40.21 N	74.03 W
Redbank Creek ≃	176	40.58 N	79.33 W
Red Bluff	178	40.11 N	122.15 W
Redbourn	104	51.48 N	0.24 W
Redbridge •[8]	104	51.34 N	0.05 E
Redcar	106	54.37 N	1.04 W
Red Cedar ≃	176	42.43 N	84.33 W
Redcliff	158	19.02 S	29.50 E
Redcliffe	168	27.14 S	153.07 E
Redcliffe, Mount ∧	164	28.25 S	121.32 E
Red Cliffs	168	34.19 S	142.11 E
Red Deer	172	52.16 N	113.48 W
Red Deer ≃, Can.	172	52.53 N	101.01 W
Red Deer ≃, Can.	172	50.56 N	109.54 W
Red Deer Lake ⊜	172	52.56 N	101.20 W
Reddersburg	160	29.38 S	26.07 E
Red Dial	106	54.48 N	3.10 W
Redding	178	40.35 N	122.24 W
Redditch	104	52.19 N	1.56 W
Rede ≃	106	55.08 N	2.13 W
Redesdale V	106	55.17 N	2.16 W
Redfield	174	44.53 N	98.31 W
Red Hill, Austl.	164	21.59 S	116.03 E
Redhill, Eng., U.K.	104	51.14 N	0.11 W
Red Hook	176	41.55 N	73.53 W
Redkey	176	40.21 N	85.09 W
Red Lake	172	51.03 N	93.49 W
Red Lake ⊜, Ont., Can.	172	51.01 N	94.05 W
Red Lake ⊜, Ariz., U.S.	178	35.40 N	114.04 W
Redland	108	59.05 N	3.05 W
Redlands, S. Afr.	160	29.52 S	22.57 E
Redlands, Calif., U.S.	178	34.03 N	117.11 W
Red Lion	176	39.54 N	76.36 W
Red Mountain ∧	178	41.35 N	123.06 W
Redon	118	47.39 N	2.05 W
Redonda I	182	16.55 N	62.19 W
Redondo Beach	178	33.51 N	118.23 W
Red Rocks Point ▸	164	32.13 S	127.32 E
Redruth	104	50.13 N	5.14 W
Red Sea (Al-Baḥr al-Aḥmar) ▼[2]	150	25.00 N	36.00 E
Redstone ≃	172	64.17 N	124.33 W
Redstone Lake ⊜	176	45.11 N	78.32 W
Red Wharf Bay C	106	53.18 N	4.10 W
Red Wing	174	44.34 N	92.31 W
Redwood City	178	37.29 N	122.13 W
Redwood Creek ≃	178	41.18 N	124.05 W
Redwood Valley	178	39.16 N	123.12 W
Ree, Lough ⊜	110	53.35 N	8.00 W
Reed City	176	43.53 N	85.31 W
Reedley	178	36.36 N	119.27 W
Reefton	170	42.07 S	171.52 E
Reepham	104	52.46 N	1.07 E
Reese	176	43.27 N	83.42 W
Reese ≃	178	40.39 N	116.54 W
Regen	116	48.59 N	13.07 E
Regen ≃	116	49.01 N	12.06 E
Regensburg	116	49.01 N	12.06 E
Reggane	152	26.42 N	0.10 E
Reggio di Calabria	122	38.07 N	15.39 E
Reggio nell'Emilia	122	44.43 N	10.36 E
Reghin	124	46.47 N	24.42 E
Regina, Sask., Can.	172	50.25 N	104.39 W
Régina, Guy. fr.	184	4.19 N	52.08 W
Registro	188	24.30 S	47.50 W
Reguengos de Monsaraz	120	38.25 N	7.32 W
Rehoboth, S.W. Afr.	156	17.53 S	15.04 E
Rehoboth, S.W. Afr.	160	23.18 S	17.03 E
Rehoboth □[5]	160	23.30 S	17.30 E
Rehoboth Beach	176	38.43 N	75.05 W
Rehoboth Seamount ⚹[3]	90	37.35 N	59.55 W
Reḥovot	150	31.54 N	34.49 E
Reichenbach	116	50.37 N	12.18 E
Reid	164	30.49 S	128.26 E
Reid, Mount ∧	164	17.58 S	130.38 E
Reidsville	174	36.21 N	79.40 W
Reigate	104	51.14 N	0.13 W
Reihoku	134	32.31 N	130.02 E
Reims	118	49.15 N	4.02 E
Reina Adelaida, Archipiélago II	186	52.20 S	74.50 W
Reindeer Lake ⊜	172	57.15 N	102.40 W
Reinga, Cape ▸	170	34.25 S	172.41 E
Reinosa	120	43.00 N	4.08 W
Reisaelva ≃	112	69.48 N	21.00 E
Reiss	108	58.28 N	3.10 W
Reisterstown	176	39.28 N	76.50 W
Reitz	160	27.53 S	28.31 E
Reivilo	160	27.36 S	24.08 E
Remada	152	32.19 N	10.24 E
Remagen	118	50.34 N	7.13 E
Remanso	184	9.41 S	42.04 W
Remarkable, Mount ∧	168	32.48 S	138.10 E
Rembang	142	6.42 S	111.20 E
Remington	176	38.32 N	77.49 W
Remiremont	118	48.01 N	6.35 E
Remscheid	116	51.11 N	7.11 E
Remus	176	43.36 N	85.09 W
Rendova I	162	8.32 S	157.20 E
Rendsburg	116	54.18 N	9.40 E
Rene Reef ⚹[2]	96	16.20 N	178.50 E
Renfrew, Ont., Can.	172	45.28 N	76.41 W
Renfrew, Scot., U.K.	108	55.53 N	4.24 W
Rengat	142	0.24 S	102.33 E
Rengel	142	7.04 S	112.00 E
Rengen ⊜	114	64.05 N	14.03 E
Rengo	188	34.25 S	70.52 W
Reng Tlāng ∧	146	21.59 N	92.36 E
Renhua	136	25.06 N	113.44 E
Renick	176	38.00 N	80.22 W
Renish Point ▸	108	57.44 N	6.59 W
Renkum	116	51.58 N	5.45 E
Renmark	168	34.11 S	140.45 E
Renne, Lac du → Reindeer Lake ⊜	172	57.15 N	102.40 W
Rennell I	162	11.40 S	160.10 E
Rennell Ridge ⚹[3]	96	11.30 S	158.00 E
Renner Springs	164	18.20 S	133.48 E
Rennes	118	48.05 N	1.41 W
Rennick Bay C	87	70.18 S	161.45 E
Rennick Glacier ◸	87	70.30 S	161.45 E
Reno	178	39.31 N	119.48 W
Renovo	176	41.20 N	77.38 W
Rensselaer	176	42.39 N	73.44 W
Rentería	120	43.19 N	1.54 W
Reo	142	8.19 S	120.30 E
Répce ≃	116	47.41 N	17.03 E
Repetek	150	38.34 N	63.11 E
Reporoa	170	38.26 S	176.21 E
Republican ≃	174	39.03 N	96.48 W
Repulse Bay	172	66.32 N	86.15 W
Repulse Bay C	168	20.36 S	148.43 E
Repvåg	112	70.45 N	25.41 E
Reschenpass)(	118	46.50 N	10.30 E
Reserva	188	24.38 S	50.52 W
Resia, Passo di)(	118	46.50 N	10.30 E
Resipol, Beinn ∧	108	56.43 N	5.39 W
Resistencia	188	27.30 S	58.59 W
Reșița	124	45.17 N	21.53 E
Resolute	172	74.41 N	94.54 W
Resolution Island I	172	61.30 N	65.00 W
Resolven	104	51.42 N	3.42 W
Resort, Loch C	108	58.03 N	7.06 W
Resplendor	190	19.20 S	41.15 W
Restinga Sêca	188	29.49 S	53.23 W
Reston	108	55.51 N	2.11 W
Restoule Lake ⊜	176	46.03 N	79.47 W
Rethel	118	49.31 N	4.22 E
Réthimnon	124	35.22 N	24.29 E
Reunion (Réunion) □[2]	161c	21.06 S	55.36 E
Reus	120	41.09 N	1.07 E
Reutlingen	116	48.29 N	9.11 E
Revda	126	56.48 N	59.57 E
Revelstoke	172	50.59 N	118.12 W
Reventazón	184	6.10 S	80.58 W
Revigny-sur-Ornain	118	48.50 N	4.59 E
Revilla del Campo	120	42.13 N	3.32 W
Revillagigedo, Islas de II	180	19.00 N	111.30 W
Revillagigedo Island I	172	55.35 N	131.23 W
Revin	118	49.56 N	4.38 E
Revuè ≃	160	19.49 S	34.00 E
Rewa	146	24.32 N	81.18 E
Rewāri	146	28.11 N	76.37 E
Rey	150	35.35 N	51.25 E
Rey, Isla del I	180	8.22 N	78.52 W
Reyes	184	14.19 S	67.23 W
Reyes, Point ▸	178	38.00 N	123.01 W
Reyhanlı	150	36.18 N	36.32 E
Reykjanes Ridge ⚹[3]	88	60.00 N	28.00 W
Reykjavík	112a	64.09 N	21.51 W
Reynaldo Cullen	188	31.15 S	60.40 W
Reynoldsville	176	41.06 N	78.53 W
Reynosa	180	26.07 N	98.18 W
Rež	126	57.23 N	61.24 E
Reza, Gora Kūh-e Rīzeh) ∧	150	37.47 N	58.05 E
Reẓā'īyeh	150	37.33 N	45.04 E
Reẓā'īyeh, Daryācheh-ye ⊜	150	37.40 N	45.30 E
Rezé	118	47.12 N	1.34 W
Rēzekne	130	56.30 N	27.19 E
Rezovska (Rezve) ≃	124	41.59 N	28.01 E
Rezve (Rezovska) ≃	124	41.59 N	28.01 E
Rhaetian Alps ⋀	118	46.30 N	10.00 E
Rhayader	104	52.18 N	3.30 W
Rhdsneigr	106	53.14 N	4.31 W
Rheda-Wiedenbrück	116	51.50 N	8.18 E
Rheidol ≃	104	52.25 N	4.05 W
Rheims → Reims	118	49.15 N	4.02 E
Rheine	116	52.17 N	7.26 E
Rheinfelden, B.R.D.	116	47.33 N	7.47 E
Rheinfelden, Schw.	118	47.33 N	7.48 E
Rheinhausen	116	51.24 N	6.44 E
Rheinland-Pfalz □[3]	116	50.00 N	7.00 E
Rheydt	116	51.10 N	6.25 E
Rhine (Rhein) (Rhin) ≃	116	51.52 N	6.02 E
Rhinebeck	176	41.56 N	73.55 W
Rhinelander	174	45.38 N	89.25 W
Rhinns of Kells ⋀	106	55.07 N	4.22 W
Rhir, Cap ▸	152	30.38 N	9.55 W
Rhiw ≃	104	52.36 N	3.11 W
Rho	122	45.32 N	9.02 E
Rhode Island □[3]	174	41.40 N	71.30 W
Rhode Island Sound ⩊	176	41.25 N	71.25 W
Rhodesia □[1]	156	20.00 S	30.00 E
Rhodes Salt Marsh ☷	178	38.17 N	118.06 W
Rhodope Mountains ⋀	124	41.30 N	24.30 E
Rhondda	104	51.40 N	3.27 W
Rhône ≃	118	43.20 N	4.50 E
Rhosllanerchrugog	104	53.00 N	3.03 W
Rhos-on-Sea	106	53.19 N	3.45 W
Rhossilli	104	51.34 N	4.17 W
Rhuddlan	106	53.18 N	3.27 W
Rhue ≃	118	45.23 N	2.29 E
Rhum I	108	57.00 N	6.20 W
Rhum, Sound of ⩊	108	56.56 N	6.14 W
Rhyl	106	53.19 N	3.29 W
Rhymney	104	51.46 N	3.18 W
Rhymney ≃	104	51.28 N	3.10 W
Rhynie	108	57.19 N	2.50 W
Riachão	184	7.22 S	46.37 W
Riaño	120	42.58 N	5.01 W
Riau, Kepulauan II	142	1.00 N	104.30 E
Riaza	120	41.17 N	3.28 W
Rib ≃	104	51.48 N	0.04 W
Ribadavia	120	42.17 N	8.08 W
Ribadeo	120	43.32 N	7.02 W
Ribadesella	120	43.28 N	5.04 W
Ribagorza •[1]	120	42.15 N	0.30 E
Ribarroja, Embalse de ⊜[1]	120	41.12 N	0.20 E
Ribble ≃	102	53.44 N	2.50 W
Ribe	114	55.21 N	8.46 E
Ribeira	188	24.40 S	49.01 W
Ribeira de Iguape ≃	188	24.40 S	47.24 W
Ribeirão do Pinhal	190	23.24 S	50.18 W
Ribeirão Prêto	190	21.10 S	47.48 W
Ribera	122	37.30 N	13.16 E
Ribérac	118	45.15 N	0.20 E
Riberalta	184	10.59 S	66.06 W
Ribnitz-Damgarten	116	54.15 N	12.28 E
Riccall	106	53.50 N	1.04 W
Riccarton	170	43.32 S	172.36 E
Riccione	122	43.59 N	12.39 E
Rice Lake ⊜	176	44.08 N	78.13 W
Richard Collinson Inlet C	172	72.45 N	113.45 W
Richard's Bay C	160	28.50 S	32.02 E
Richards Island I	172	69.20 N	134.30 W
Richardson ≃	172	58.30 N	111.30 W
Richardson, Mount ∧	164	28.49 S	119.59 E
Richardson Lakes ⊜	176	44.50 N	70.52 W
Richardson Mountains ⋀, Can.	172	67.15 N	136.30 W
Richardson Mountains ⋀, N.Z.	170	44.45 S	168.31 E
Riche, Pointe ▸	172	50.42 N	57.25 W
Richelieu	118	47.01 N	0.19 E
Richelieu ≃	176	46.03 N	73.07 W
Richfield, Idaho, U.S.	178	43.03 N	114.09 W
Richfield, Pa., U.S.	176	40.41 N	77.07 W
Richfield, Utah, U.S.	174	38.46 N	112.05 W
Richfield Springs	176	42.51 N	74.59 W
Richford	176	45.00 N	72.40 W
Richland, Mich., U.S.	176	42.22 N	85.31 W
Richland, Wash., U.S.	174	46.17 N	119.18 W
Richmond, Austl.	168	20.44 S	143.08 E
Richmond, Ont., Can.	176	45.11 N	75.50 W
Richmond, Qué., Can.	176	45.40 N	72.09 W
Richmond, N.Z.	170	41.20 S	173.11 E
Richmond, S. Afr.	160	31.23 S	23.56 E
Richmond, S. Afr.	160	29.54 S	30.08 E
Richmond, Eng., U.K.	106	54.24 N	1.44 W
Richmond, Calif., U.S.	178	37.57 N	122.22 W
Richmond, Ind., U.S.	176	39.50 N	84.54 W
Richmond, Ky., U.S.	176	37.45 N	84.18 W
Richmond, Maine, U.S.	176	44.05 N	69.48 W
Richmond, Mich., U.S.	176	42.49 N	82.45 W
Richmond, Vt., U.S.	176	44.24 N	72.59 W
Richmond, Va., U.S.	174	37.30 N	77.28 W
Richmond •[8]	104	51.28 N	0.18 W
Richmond, Mount ∧	170	41.29 S	173.24 E
Richmond Hill	176	43.52 N	79.27 W
Richmondville	176	42.38 N	74.34 W
Richwood, Ohio, U.S.	176	40.26 N	83.18 W
Richwood, W. Va., U.S.	176	38.14 N	80.32 W
Rickmansworth	104	51.39 N	0.29 W
Ricobayo, Embalse de ⊜[1]	120	41.30 N	5.55 W
Riddle	178	42.57 N	123.22 W
Riddle Mountain ∧	178	43.07 N	118.30 W
Riddon, Loch C	108	55.58 N	5.12 W
Rideau ≃	176	45.27 N	75.42 W
Ridgecrest	178	35.38 N	117.36 W
Ridgefield	176	41.17 N	73.30 W
Ridgetown	176	42.26 N	81.54 W
Ridgway	176	41.26 N	78.44 W
Ridotta Capuzzo	154	31.35 N	25.03 E
Riecawr, Loch ⊜	106	55.13 N	4.27 W
Riesa	116	51.18 N	13.17 E
Riesco, Isla I	186	52.55 S	72.40 W
Riesi	122	37.17 N	14.05 E
Riet ≃	160	29.00 S	23.54 E
Rietfontein	160	26.44 S	20.01 E
Rieti	122	42.24 N	12.51 E
Rif ⋀	152	35.00 N	4.00 W
Rifle ≃	176	44.00 N	83.49 W
Rift Valley □[4]	158	0.30 N	36.00 E
Rift Valley V	88	3.00 S	29.00 E
Rīga	130	56.57 N	24.06 E
Riga, Mount ∧	164	21.59 S	116.25 E
Rīgestān •[1]	150	31.00 N	65.00 E
Rigi ∧	118	47.05 N	8.30 E
Rigo	166	9.47 S	147.34 E
Rigolet	172	54.20 N	58.35 W
Riihimäki	114	60.45 N	24.46 E
Rijeka	122	45.20 N	14.27 E
Rijssen	116	52.18 N	6.30 E
Rikaze	146	29.17 N	88.53 E
Rikeze	132	29.17 N	88.53 E
Riksgränsen	112	68.24 N	18.12 E
Rikuzen-takata	134	39.01 N	141.38 E
Rillington	106	54.09 N	0.42 W
Rima ≃	152	13.04 N	5.10 E
Rimatara I	96	22.38 S	152.51 W
Rimavská Sobota	116	48.23 N	20.02 E
Rimbo	114	59.45 N	18.22 E
Rimersburg	176	41.02 N	79.30 W
Rimini	122	44.04 N	12.34 E
Rîmnicu-Sărat	124	45.23 N	27.03 E
Rîmnicu-Vîlcea	124	45.06 N	24.22 E
Rinca, Pulau I	142	8.41 S	119.42 E
Rinconada	188	22.26 S	66.10 W
Ringe	114	55.14 N	10.29 E
Ringford	106	54.54 N	4.03 W
Ringkøbing	114	56.05 N	8.15 E
Ringmer	104	50.53 N	0.04 E
Ringsted	114	55.27 N	11.49 E
Ringvassøya I	112	69.55 N	19.15 E
Ringville	110	52.02 N	7.34 W
Ringwood	104	50.51 N	1.47 W
Rinjani, Gunung ∧	142	8.24 S	116.28 E
Rinnes, Ben ∧	108	57.23 N	3.15 W
Rinns of Islay ⋀	108	55.45 N	6.25 W
Rinns Point ▸	108	55.41 N	6.30 W
Río Ariguaisa	182	9.35 N	72.40 W
Rio Azul	188	25.43 S	50.47 W
Riobamba	184	1.40 S	78.38 W
Río Benito	156	1.35 N	9.37 E
Río Blanco	188	32.55 S	70.19 W
Rio Branco	184	9.58 S	67.48 W
Rio Brilhante	190	21.48 S	54.33 W
Río Caribe	182	10.42 N	63.07 W
Rio Casca	190	20.13 S	42.39 W
Rio Claro, Bra.	190	22.24 S	47.33 W
Rio Claro, Trin.	182	10.18 N	61.11 W
Río Colorado	188	39.01 S	64.05 W
Río Cuarto	188	33.08 S	64.20 W
Rio das Antas	188	26.55 S	51.04 W
Rio de Contas	190	13.36 S	41.48 W
Rio de Janeiro	190	22.54 S	43.15 W
Rio de Janeiro □[3]	190	22.00 S	42.30 W
Rio Dell	178	40.30 N	124.07 W
Rio d'Oeste	188	27.12 S	49.48 W
Rio do Prado	190	16.35 S	40.34 W
Rio do Sul	188	27.13 S	49.39 W
Rio Fortuna	188	28.06 S	49.07 W
Río Gallegos	186	51.37 S	69.10 W
Río Grande, Arg.	186	53.50 S	67.40 W
Rio Grande, Bra.	188	32.02 S	52.05 W
Río Grande, Méx.	180	23.50 N	103.02 W
Río Grande, Nic.	182	12.54 N	83.33 W
Rio Grande do Sul □[3]	188	30.00 S	54.00 W
Rio Grande Ridge ⚹[3]	92	31.00 S	35.00 W
Ríohacha	184	11.33 N	72.55 W
Rioja	184	6.03 S	77.05 W
Rio Largo	184	9.29 S	35.51 W
Riom	118	45.54 N	3.07 E
Río Mayo	186	45.40 S	70.15 W
Rional Reef ⚹[2]	96	17.00 N	177.50 E
Rio Negrinho	188	26.15 S	49.31 W
Rio Negro	190	19.27 S	54.58 W
Río Negro □[4]	188	40.00 S	67.00 W
Río Negro, Embalse del ⊜[1]	188	32.45 S	56.00 W
Rionero in Vulture	122	40.56 N	15.41 E
Riópar	120	38.30 N	2.27 W
Rio Pardo	188	29.59 S	52.22 W
Rio Pardo de Minas	190	15.37 S	42.33 W
Rio Pomba	190	21.17 S	43.11 W
Río Segundo	188	31.40 S	63.58 W
Río Tercero	188	32.10 S	64.05 W
Rio Verde, Bra.	190	17.43 S	50.56 W
Rioverde, Méx.	180	21.56 N	99.59 W
Rio Vista	178	38.10 N	121.42 W
Ripley, Eng., U.K.	104	53.03 N	1.24 W
Ripley, N.Y., U.S.	176	42.16 N	79.43 W
Ripley, Ohio, U.S.	176	38.45 N	83.51 W
Ripley, W. Va., U.S.	176	38.49 N	81.43 W
Ripoll	120	42.12 N	2.12 E
Ripon, Qué., Can.	176	45.47 N	75.06 W
Ripon, Eng., U.K.	106	54.08 N	1.31 W
Ripon, Calif., U.S.	178	37.44 N	121.07 W
Ripponden	106	53.41 N	1.57 W
Risbäck	114	64.42 N	15.32 E
Risca	104	51.37 N	3.07 W
Rishiri-suidō ⩊	134a	45.10 N	141.25 E
Rishiri-tō I	134a	45.11 N	141.15 E
Rishiri-zan ∧	134a	45.11 N	141.15 E
Rishon leẒiyyon	150	31.58 N	34.48 E
Rising Sun, Ind., U.S.	176	38.57 N	84.51 W
Rising Sun, Md., U.S.	176	39.42 N	76.04 W
Risingsun, Ohio, U.S.	176	41.16 N	83.25 W
Risle ≃	118	49.26 N	0.23 E
Risør	114	58.43 N	9.14 E
Ristijärvi	114	64.44 N	28.24 E
Ritchie	160	29.02 S	24.38 E
Ritter, Mount ∧	178	37.42 N	119.12 W
Rittman	176	40.58 N	81.47 W
Riva	122	45.53 N	10.50 E
Rivadavia, Arg.	188	33.10 S	68.28 W
Rivadavia, Arg.	188	31.30 S	68.35 W
Rivadavia, Chile	188	29.58 S	70.34 W
Rivanna ≃	176	37.51 N	78.17 W
Rivas	182	11.26 N	85.51 W
Rive-de-Gier	118	45.32 N	4.37 E
Rivera	188	30.54 S	55.31 W
Riverbank	178	37.44 N	120.56 E
River Cess	152	5.28 N	9.32 W
Riverdale	178	36.26 N	119.52 W
Riverhead	176	40.55 N	72.40 W
Riverina •[1]	168	35.30 S	145.30 E
Rivers	172	50.02 N	100.12 W
Riversdale	160	34.07 S	21.15 E
Riverside	178	33.59 N	117.22 W
Rivers Inlet	172	51.41 N	127.15 W
Riversleigh	168	19.02 S	138.44 E
Riverton, Austl.	168	34.09 S	138.45 E
Riverton, N.Z.	170	46.21 S	168.01 E
Riverton, Va., U.S.	176	38.57 N	78.12 W
Rivesville	176	39.32 N	80.07 W
Riviera	178	35.04 N	114.35 W
Rivière-du-Loup	172	47.50 N	69.32 W
Rivière du Rempart	161c	20.06 S	57.41 E
Rivière-Trois-Pistoles	172	48.07 N	69.10 W
Riviersonderend	160	34.09 S	19.55 E
Rivoli	122	45.04 N	7.31 E
Rivoli Bay C	168	37.32 S	140.04 E
Riwaka	170	41.05 S	173.00 E
Riyadh → Ar-Riyāḍ	150	24.38 N	46.43 E
Rīz	150	32.23 N	51.20 E
Rize	144	41.02 N	40.31 E
Rīzeh, Kūh-e (Gora Reza) ∧	150	37.47 N	58.05 E
Rizhao	132	35.27 N	119.29 E
Rjukan	114	59.52 N	8.34 E
Roa, N.Z.	170	42.21 S	171.23 E
Roa, Nor.	114	60.17 N	10.37 E
Roadhead	106	55.04 N	2.46 W
Road Town	182	18.27 N	64.37 W
Roan Fell ∧	106	55.13 N	2.52 W
Roanne	118	46.02 N	4.04 E
Roanoke, Ind., U.S.	176	40.58 N	85.22 W
Roanoke, Va., U.S.	174	37.16 N	79.57 W
Roanoke ≃	174	35.56 N	76.43 W
Roanoke Rapids	174	36.28 N	77.40 W
Roaring Spring	176	40.20 N	78.24 W
Roaringwater Bay C	110	51.25 N	9.35 W
Roatán	182	16.18 N	86.35 W
Roatán, Isla de I	182	16.23 N	86.26 W
Robbins Island I	168	40.41 S	144.57 E
Robbinston	176	45.05 N	67.07 W
Robe	168	37.11 S	139.45 E
Robe ≃, Austl.	164	21.19 S	115.40 E
Robe ≃, Eire	110	53.37 N	9.16 W
Robe, Mount ∧	168	31.40 S	141.20 E
Robertsbridge	104	50.59 N	0.29 E
Roberts Creek Mountain ∧	178	39.52 N	116.18 W
Robertsdale	176	40.11 N	78.07 W
Robertsfors	114	64.11 N	20.51 E
Robertson	160	33.46 S	19.50 E
Roberts Peak ∧	172	52.57 N	120.32 W
Robertsport	152	6.45 N	11.22 W
Robertstown, Austl.	168	34.00 S	139.05 E
Robertstown, Eire	110	53.15 N	6.59 W
Robert Williams	156	12.51 S	15.33 E
Roberval	172	48.31 N	72.13 W
Robin Hood's Bay	106	54.25 N	0.33 W
Robinson ≃	168	16.30 S	137.00 E
Róbinson Crusoe, Isla (Isla Más A Tierra) I	186	33.38 S	78.52 W
Robinson Range ⋀	164	25.45 S	119.00 E
Robinvale	168	34.36 S	142.46 E
Robleda	120	40.23 N	6.36 W
Roblin	172	51.14 N	101.21 W
Roboré	184	18.20 S	59.45 W
Robson, Mount ∧	172	53.07 N	119.09 W
Roca, Cabo da ▸	120	38.47 N	9.30 W
Roçadas	156	16.43 S	15.01 E
Roca Partida, Isla I	180	19.01 N	112.02 W
Rocas, Atol das I[1]	184	3.52 S	33.59 W
Roch ≃	106	53.34 N	2.18 W
Rocha	188	34.29 S	54.20 W
Rochdale	106	53.38 N	2.09 W
Roche	104	50.24 N	4.48 W
Rochechouart	118	45.50 N	0.50 E
Rochefort, Bel.	116	50.10 N	5.13 E
Rochefort, Fr.	118	45.57 N	0.58 W
Rochefort-Montagne	118	45.41 N	2.48 E
Rochester, Austl.	168	36.22 S	144.42 E
Rochester, Eng., U.K.	104	51.24 N	0.30 E
Rochester, Eng., U.K.	106	55.16 N	2.16 W
Rochester, Mich., U.S.	176	42.41 N	83.08 W
Rochester, Minn., U.S.	174	44.02 N	92.29 W
Rochester, N.H., U.S.	176	43.18 N	70.59 W
Rochester, N.Y., U.S.	176	43.10 N	77.36 W
Rochford	104	51.36 N	0.43 E
Rochfort Bridge	110	53.23 N	7.17 W
Rochlitz	116	51.03 N	12.47 E
Rockall Rise ⚹[3]	88	59.00 N	14.00 W
Rockcorry	110	54.07 N	7.01 W
Rock Creek ≃, Nev., U.S.	178	40.39 N	116.54 W
Rock Creek ≃, Oreg., U.S.	178	42.39 N	119.08 W
Rockefeller Plateau ⋀[1]	87	80.00 S	135.00 W
Rockenhausen	116	49.38 N	7.49 E
Rockford, Ill., U.S.	174	42.17 N	89.06 W
Rockford, Mich., U.S.	176	43.07 N	85.33 W
Rockford, Ohio, U.S.	176	40.42 N	84.39 W
Rock Hall	176	39.08 N	76.14 W
Rockhampton	168	23.23 S	150.31 E
Rockhampton Downs	164	18.57 S	135.01 E
Rock Hill	174	34.56 N	81.01 W
Rockingham	164	32.17 S	115.44 E
Rockingham Bay C	168	18.10 S	146.05 E
Rockingham Forest •[3]	104	52.30 N	0.37 W
Rock Island	174	41.30 N	90.34 W
Rockland, Ont., Can.	176	45.33 N	75.17 W
Rockland, Maine, U.S.	176	44.06 N	69.06 W
Rockland, Mass., U.S.	176	42.08 N	70.55 W
Rocklin	178	38.48 N	121.14 W
Rockport, Maine, U.S.	176	44.11 N	69.06 W
Rockport, Mass., U.S.	176	42.39 N	70.36 W
Rock Sound	182	24.54 N	76.12 W
Rock Springs	174	41.35 N	109.13 W
Rockstone	184	5.59 N	58.32 W
Rockville, N.Z.	170	40.44 S	172.38 E
Rockville, Md., U.S.	176	39.05 N	77.09 W
Rockwood, Maine, U.S.	176	45.41 N	69.44 W
Rockwood, Pa., U.S.	176	39.54 N	79.09 W
Rocky Gully	164	34.30 S	116.48 E
Rocky Mount	174	35.56 N	77.48 W
Rocky Mountain House	172	52.22 N	114.55 W
Rocky Mountains ⋀	174	48.00 N	116.00 W
Rodalquilar	120	37.40 N	2.08 W
Rødberg	114	60.16 N	8.58 E
Rødby	114	54.42 N	11.24 E
Rødekro	114	55.04 N	9.21 E
Rodel	108	57.41 N	7.05 W
Roden ≃	104	52.43 N	2.36 W
Rodeo	188	30.13 S	69.08 W
Roderick ≃	164	26.57 S	116.13 E
Rodewisch	116	50.32 N	12.24 E
Rodez	118	44.21 N	2.35 E
Ródhos (Rhodes)	124	36.26 N	28.13 E
Ródhos I	124	36.10 N	28.00 E
Roding	116	49.12 N	12.32 E
Roding ≃	104	51.31 N	0.06 E
Rodinga	164	24.34 S	134.05 E
Rodney	176	42.34 N	81.41 W
Rodniki	130	57.06 N	41.44 E
Rodonit, Kep i ▸	124	41.35 N	19.27 E
Rodrigues I	94	19.42 S	63.25 E
Rodstock, Cape ▸	164	33.12 S	134.20 E
Rødven	114	62.38 N	7.33 E
Roebourne	164	20.47 S	117.09 E
Roebuck Bay C	164	19.04 S	122.17 E
Roermond	116	51.12 N	6.00 E
Roeselare	116	50.57 N	3.08 E
Roes Welcome Sound ⩊	172	64.00 N	88.00 W
Rogačevo	130	56.26 N	37.10 E
Rogagua, Lago ⊜	184	13.43 S	66.54 W
Rogaland □[6]	114	59.00 N	6.15 E
Rogan's Seat ∧	106	54.25 N	2.07 W
Rogart	108	58.00 N	4.08 W
Rogatica	124	43.48 N	19.00 E
Rogen ⊜	114	62.19 N	12.23 E
Rogers, Mount ∧	174	36.39 N	81.33 W
Rogers City	176	45.25 N	83.49 W
Rogers Lake ⊜	178	34.52 N	117.51 W
Roggeveldberge ⋀	160	32.17 S	20.08 E
Rogoaguado, Lago ⊜	184	12.52 S	65.43 W
Rogue ≃, Mich., U.S.	176	43.04 N	85.35 W
Rogue ≃, Oreg., U.S.	178	42.26 N	124.25 W
Rogue River	178	42.26 N	123.10 W
Rohri	146	27.41 N	68.54 E
Rohtak	149	28.54 N	76.34 E
Roi Et	140	16.03 N	103.40 E
Roi Georges, Îles du II	96	14.32 S	145.08 W
Rojas	188	34.15 S	60.44 W
Rojo, Cabo ▸	182	17.56 N	67.12 W
Rokan ≃	142	2.00 N	100.52 E
Rokycany	116	49.45 N	13.36 E
Rolândia	190	23.18 S	51.22 W
Rolla	174	37.57	91.46 W
Rolle	118	46.28 N	6.20 E
Rolleston, Austl.	168	24.28 S	148.37 E
Rolleston, N.Z.	170	43.35 S	172.23 E
Rollingstone	168	19.03 S	146.24 E
Rolvsøya I	112	71.00 N	24.00 E
Roma, Austl.	168	26.35 S	148.47 E
Roma (Rome), It.	122	41.54 N	12.29 E
Romagna □[9]	122	44.30 N	12.15 E
Romaine ≃	172	50.18 N	63.47 W
Roman	124	46.55 N	26.56 E
Roman ≃	104	51.51 N	0.57 E
Romanche Gap ⚹[1]	88	0.10 S	18.15 W
Romang, Pulau I	166	7.35 S	127.26 E
Romania (România) □[1]	100	46.00 N	25.30 E
Roman-Koš, Gora ∧	126	44.37 N	34.15 E
Romano, Cayo I	182	22.15 N	78.00 W
Romanshorn	118	47.34 N	9.22 E
Romans[-sur-Isère]	118	45.03 N	5.03 E
Rombari	158	4.33 N	31.02 E
Rome → Roma, It.	122	41.54 N	12.29 E
Rome, Ga., U.S.	174	34.16 N	85.11 W
Rome, N.Y., U.S.	176	43.13 N	75.27 W
Romeo	176	42.48 N	83.01 W
Romilly-sur-Seine	118	48.31 N	3.43 E
Romney	176	39.21 N	78.45 W
Romney Marsh ☷	104	51.03 N	0.55 E
Romny	126	50.45 N	33.30 E
Romont	118	46.42 N	6.55 E
Romorantin-Lanthenay	118	47.22 N	1.45 E
Romsdalsfjorden C[2]	114	62.39 N	7.15 E
Romsey	104	50.59 N	1.30 W
Rona I, Scot., U.K.	108	59.07 N	5.48 W
Rona I, Scot., U.K.	108	57.34 N	5.59 W
Ronas Hill ∧[2]	108a	60.31 N	1.28 W
Ronas Voe C	108	60.32 N	1.29 W
Ronay I	108	57.29 N	7.11 W
Roncador, Serra do ⋀[1]	184	12.00 S	52.00 W
Roncador Bank ⚹[4]	182	13.32 N	80.03 W
Roncesvalles	120	43.01 N	1.19 W
Ronda	120	36.44 N	5.10 W
Ronda, Serranía de ⋀	120	36.44 N	5.03 W
Rondane ∧	114	61.55 N	9.45 E
Rønde	114	56.18 N	10.29 E
Rondon	190	23.23 S	52.48 W
Rondonópolis	190	16.28 S	54.38 W
Ronge, Lac la ⊜	172	55.10 N	105.00 W
Rongelap I[1]	96	11.20 N	166.50 E
Rongjiang	140	25.52 N	108.37 E
Rongotea	170	40.18 S	175.25 E
Ron-ma, Mui ▸	140	18.07 N	106.22 E
Rønne	114	55.06 N	14.42 E
Ronneburg	116	50.51 N	12.10 E
Ronneby	114	56.12 N	15.18 E
Ronne Entrance C	87	72.30 S	74.00 W
Ronne Ice Shelf ◸	87	78.30 S	61.00 W
Ronse	116	50.45 N	3.36 E
Roodepoort-Maraisburg	160	26.11 S	27.54 E
Rooiboklaagte ≃	160	20.50 S	21.00 E
Roorkee	146	29.52 N	77.53 E
Roosendaal	116	51.32 N	4.28 E
Roosevelt Island I	87	79.30 S	162.00 W
Roper ≃	166	14.43 S	135.27 E
Roper Valley	166	14.56 S	134.00 E
Roquefort	118	44.02 N	0.19 W
Roquemaure	118	44.03 N	4.47 E
Roque Pérez	188	35.23 S	59.22 W
Rora Head ▸	108	58.52 N	3.25 W
Roraima, Mount ∧	184	5.12 N	60.44 W
Rørholtfjorden ⊜	114	59.01 N	9.15 E
Røros	114	62.35 N	11.20 E
Rorschach	118	47.29 N	9.30 E
Rosa	158	9.38 S	31.21 E
Rošal'	130	55.40 N	39.51 E
Rosalind Bank ⚹[4]	182	16.30 N	80.30 W
Rosamond	178	34.52 N	118.10 W
Rosamond Lake ⊜	178	34.50 N	118.04 W
Rosans	118	44.23 N	5.28 E
Rosario, Arg.	188	32.57 S	60.40 W
Rosário, Bra.	184	2.57 S	44.14 W
Rosario, Para.	188	24.27 S	57.03 W
Rosario, Islas de II	182	10.10 N	75.46 W
Rosario de la Frontera	188	25.50 S	64.55 W
Rosario de Lerma	188	24.59 S	65.32 W
Rosario del Tala	188	32.20 S	59.10 W
Rosário do Sul	188	30.15 S	54.55 W
Rosário Oeste	184	14.50 S	56.25 W
Rosarito	178	32.20 N	117.02 W
Rosarito, Embalse de ⊜[1]	120	40.05 N	5.15 W
Rosarno	122	38.29 N	15.59 E
Rosas, Golfo de C	120	42.10 N	3.15 E
Roscoe Glacier ◸	87	66.30 S	95.20 E
Roscommon, Eire	110	53.38 N	8.11 W
Roscommon, Mich., U.S.	176	44.30 N	84.35 W
Roscommon □[6]	110	53.40 N	8.30 W
Roscrea	110	52.57 N	7.47 W
Rose, Mount ∧	178	39.21 N	119.55 W
Roseau	182	15.18 N	61.24 W
Roseberth	168	25.47 S	139.37 E
Rosebery	168	41.46 S	145.32 E
Rosebud	168	38.21 S	144.54 E
Roseburg	174	43.13 N	123.20 W
Rosebush	176	43.42 N	84.46 W
Rose City	176	44.25 N	84.07 W
Rosedale	168	24.38 S	151.55 E
Rosehearty	108	57.42 N	2.07 W
Rose Hill	161c	20.14 S	57.27 E
Rosenheim	116	47.51 N	12.07 E
Rosetown	172	51.33 N	108.00 W
Rosetta → Rashīd	154	31.24 N	30.25 E
Roseville, Calif., U.S.	178	38.45 N	121.17 W
Roseville, Mich., U.S.	176	42.30 N	82.56 W
Roseville, Ohio, U.S.	176	39.49 N	82.05 W
Rosewood	168	27.39 S	152.35 E
Rosignano Marittimo	122	43.24 N	10.28 E
Rosignol	184	6.16 N	57.32 W
Roșiori-de-Vede	124	44.07 N	25.00 E
Roskilde	114	55.39 N	12.05 E
Roslagen •[1]	114	59.30 N	18.40 E
Roslags-Näsby	114	59.26 N	18.04 E
Roslavl'	130	53.57 N	32.52 E
Rosmead	160	31.29 S	25.08 E
Ross	168	42.02 S	147.29 E
Ross ≃	172	61.59 N	132.26 W
Ross, Mount ∧	170	41.28 S	175.21 E
Rossano	122	39.35 N	16.39 E
Rossan Point ▸	110	54.42 N	8.48 W
Rosscarbery	110	51.35 N	9.01 W
Rosseau, Lake ⊜	176	45.10 N	79.35 W
Rossel Island I	162	11.21 S	154.09 E
Rossendale V	106	53.45 N	2.47 W
Rosses Bay C	110	55.10 N	8.27 W
Rosses Point	110	54.18 N	8.33 W
Rossford	176	41.37 N	83.33 W
Ross Ice Shelf ◸	87	81.30 S	175.00 W
Rossijskaja Sovetskaja Federativnaja Socialističeskaja Respublika □[3]	128	60.00 N	100.00 E
Ross Island I	87	77.30 S	168.00 E
Rossiter	176	40.53 N	78.56 W
Rosslare	110	52.17 N	6.23 W
Rosslare Harbour	110	52.15 N	6.22 W
Rosslau	116	51.53 N	12.14 E
Rosslea	110	54.14 N	7.11 W
Rosso	152	16.30 N	15.49 W
Rosso, Cap ▸	122	42.14 N	8.33 E
Ross-on-Wye	104	51.55 N	2.35 W
Ross River	172	61.59 N	132.27 W
Ross Sea ▼[2]	87	76.00 S	175.00 W
Røssvatnet ⊜	112	65.45 N	14.00 E
Røst II	112	67.28 N	11.59 E
Rostavatn ⊜	112	68.45 N	20.30 E
Rosthern	172	52.40 N	106.17 W
Roštkala	126	37.16 N	71.49 E
Rostock	116	54.05 N	12.07 E
Rostock □[5]	116	54.15 N	12.30 E
Rostov	130	57.11 N	39.25 E
Rostov-na-Donu	126	47.14 N	39.42 E
Roswell	174	33.24 N	104.32 W
Rosyth	108	56.03 N	3.26 W
Rota	120	36.37 N	6.21 W
Rota I	138	14.10 N	145.12 E
Rotenburg	116	53.06 N	9.24 E
Rothaargebirge ⋀	116	51.05 N	8.15 E
Rothbury	106	55.19 N	1.55 W
Rothbury Forest •[3]	106	55.18 N	1.54 W
Rothenburg ob der Tauber	116	49.23 N	10.10 E
Rother ≃	104	50.57 N	0.32 W
Rotherham	106	53.26 N	1.20 W
Rothes	108	57.31 N	3.13 W
Rothesay	108	55.51 N	5.03 W
Rothsay	164	29.17 S	116.53 E
Rothwell, Eng., U.K.	104	52.25 N	0.48 W
Rothwell, Eng., U.K.	106	53.46 N	1.29 W
Roti, Pulau I	142	10.45 S	123.10 E
Roto	168	33.03 S	145.28 E
Rotomanu	170	42.39 S	171.32 E
Rotondo, Monte ∧	122	42.13 N	9.03 E
Rotoroa, Lake ⊜	170	41.52 S	172.38 E
Rotorua	170	38.09 S	176.15 E
Rotorua, Lake ⊜	170	38.05 S	176.16 E
Rottenburg	116	48.28 N	8.56 E
Rottenburg an der Laaber	116	48.42 N	12.02 E
Rottenmann	116	47.31 N	14.22 E
Rotterdam, Ned.	116	51.55 N	4.28 E
Rotterdam, N.Y., U.S.	176	42.48 N	74.01 W
Rottingdean	104	50.48 N	0.04 W
Rottweil	116	48.10 N	8.37 E
Rotuma I	96	12.30 S	177.05 E
Roubaix	118	50.42 N	3.10 E
Roudnice	116	50.22 N	14.16 E
Rouen	118	49.26 N	1.05 E
Rouge ≃	176	45.39 N	74.42 W
Rougemont	118	47.29 N	6.21 E
Rouillac	118	45.47 N	0.04 W
Roulers → Roeselare	116	50.57 N	3.08 E
Roulette	176	41.47 N	78.09 W
Round Hill Head ▸	168	24.10 S	151.53 E
Round Island I	161c	19.51 S	57.48 E
Round Lake ⊜	176	45.38 N	77.32 W
Round Mountain	178	38.43 N	117.04 W
Round Mountain ∧[2]	168	30.27 S	152.14 E
Roundstone	110	53.23 N	9.53 W
Roundup	174	46.27 N	108.33 W
Roundwood	110	53.04 N	6.13 W
Rousay I	108	59.10 N	3.02 W
Rouses Point	176	45.00 N	73.22 W
Roussillon □[9]	118	42.30 N	2.30 E
Rouxville	160	30.29 S	26.46 E
Rouyn	172	48.15 N	79.01 W
Rovaniemi	112	66.34 N	25.48 E
Rovato	122	45.34 N	10.00 E
Rovereto	122	45.53 N	11.02 E
Rovigo	122	45.04 N	11.47 E
Rovno	126	50.37 N	26.15 E
Rovuma (Ruvuma) ≃	158	10.29 S	40.28 E
Rowena	168	29.49 S	148.54 E
Rowlands Gill	106	54.54 N	1.45 W
Rowlesburg	176	39.21 N	79.40 W
Rowley ≃	172	70.16 N	77.45 W
Rowley Island I	172	69.08 N	78.50 W
Rowley Regis	104	52.29 N	2.03 W
Rowley Shoals ⚹[2]	164	17.30 S	119.00 E
Roxas (Capiz)	138	11.35 N	122.45 E
Roxborough Downs	168	22.30 S	138.50 E
Roxburgh, N.Z.	170	45.32 S	169.19 E
Roxburgh, Scot., U.K.	108	55.34 N	2.30 W
Royal Canal ☲	110	53.21 N	6.15 W
Royale, Isle I	174	48.00 N	89.00 W
Royal Leamington Spa	104	52.18 N	1.31 W
Royal Oak	176	42.30 N	83.08 W
Royan	118	45.37 N	1.01 W
Roydon	104	51.46 N	0.03 E
Roye	118	49.42 N	2.48 E
Roy Hill	164	22.38 S	119.57 E
Royston, Eng., U.K.	104	52.03 N	0.01 W
Royston, Eng., U.K.	106	53.37 N	1.27 W
Royton	106	53.34 N	2.08 W
Rozel	105b	49.14 N	2.03 W
Rozewie, Przylądek ▸	116	54.51 N	18.21 E
Rožňava	116	48.40 N	20.32 E
Roztocze ∧	116	50.30 N	23.20 E
Rrëshen	124	41.47 N	19.54 E
Rrogozhinë	124	41.05 N	19.40 E
Ruabon	104	52.59 N	3.02 W
Ruacana Falls ↳	160	17.22 S	14.12 E
Ruatahuna	170	38.33 S	176.57 E
Ruatapu	170	42.48 S	170.53 E
Ruathair, Lochan ⊜	108	58.18 N	3.56 W
Ruatoria	170	37.53 S	178.20 E
Ruawai	170	36.08 S	174.02 E
Rubcovsk	128	51.33 N	81.10 E
Rubery	104	52.24 N	2.00 W
Rubeshibe	134a	43.47 N	143.38 E
Rubežnoje	126	49.01 N	38.23 E
Rubicon ≃	178	39.00 N	120.44 W
Rubidoux	178	33.60 N	117.25 W
Rubim	190	16.23 S	40.32 W
Ruby Dome ∧	178	40.37 N	115.28 W
Ruby Lake ☷	178	40.10 N	115.30 W
Ruby Mountains ⋀	178	40.25 N	115.35 W
Ruby Valley V	178	40.30 N	115.15 W
Rucheng	136	25.34 N	113.41 E
Rudall	168	33.41 S	136.16 E
Ruda Śląska	116	50.18 N	18.51 E
Rüdersdorf	116	52.29 N	13.47 E
Rudkøbing	114	54.56 N	10.43 E
Rudn'a	130	54.57 N	31.06 E
Rudnyj	126	52.57 N	63.07 E
Rudolf, Lake ⊜	158	3.30 N	36.00 E
Rudolstadt	116	50.43 N	11.20 E
Rudong	136	32.19 N	121.12 E
Rūd Sar	150	37.08 N	50.18 E
Ruen ∧	124	42.10 N	22.31 E
Ruenya (Luenha) ≃	158	16.24 S	33.48 E
Rufā 'ah	154	14.46 N	33.22 E
Ruffec	118	46.02 N	0.42 E

Symbols in the index entries are identified on page 198.

Rufi – Sand

Name Page Lat Long
Rufino 188 34.16 S 62.40 W
Rufisque 152 14.43 N 17.17 W
Rufunsa 158 15.05 S 29.40 E
Rugao 136 32.25 N 120.36 E
Rugby, Eng., U.K. 104 52.23 N 1.15 W
Rugby, N. Dak., U.S. 174 48.22 N 100.00 W
Rugeley 104 52.46 N 1.55 W
Rügen I 112 54.25 N 13.24 E
Ruhengeri 158 1.30 S 29.38 E
Ruian 136 27.49 N 120.38 E
Ruijin 136 25.50 N 116.00 E
Rukwa, Lake ⊜ 158 8.00 S 32.25 E
Ruma 124 45.00 N 19.49 E
Rumbalara 164 25.20 S 134.29 E
Rumbek 154 6.48 N 29.41 E
Rumbling Bridge 108 56.10 N 3.35 W
Rum Cay I 182 23.40 N 74.50 W
Rumford 176 44.33 N 70.33 W
Rumia 116 54.35 N 18.25 E
Rum Jungle 166 13.01 S 131.00 E
Rummānah 150 31.01 N 32.40 E
Rumney 104 51.31 N 3.07 W
Rumoi 134a 43.56 N 141.39 E
Rump Mountain ∧ 176 45.12 N 71.04 W
Rumula 166 16.35 S 145.20 E
Runan 136 33.01 N 114.22 E
Runanga 170 42.24 S 171.16 E
Runaway, Cape ≻ 170 37.32 S 177.59 E
Runcorn 106 53.20 N 2.44 W
Rungwa 158 6.57 S 33.31 E
Rungwa ≃ 158 7.36 S 31.50 E
Runheji 136 32.30 N 116.05 E
Ruoqiang 132 38.30 N 88.05 E
Ruoshui ≃ 132 41.00 N 100.10 E
Ruovesi 114 61.59 N 24.05 E
Rūpar 149 30.59 N 76.31 E
Rupert, Idaho, U.S. 178 42.37 N 113.41 W
Rupert, W. Va., U.S. 176 37.58 N 80.41 W
Rupert, Rivière de ≃ 172 51.29 N 78.45 W
Rupert Creek ≃ 168 20.53 S 142.23 E
Rupert House 172 51.30 N 78.45 W
Rurrenabaque 184 14.28 S 67.34 W
Rurstausee ⊜[1] 118 50.36 N 6.22 E
Rurutu I 96 22.26 S 151.20 W
Rusape 158 18.32 S 32.07 E
Ruse 124 43.50 N 25.57 E
Rush 110 53.32 N 6.06 W
Rush Creek ≃ 176 39.38 N 82.33 W
Rushden 104 52.17 N 0.36 W
Rusizi (Ruzizi) ≃ 158 3.16 S 29.14 E
Russas 184 4.56 S 37.58 W
Russell, Man., Can. 172 50.47 N 101.15 W
Russell, Ont., Can. 176 45.17 N 75.17 W
Russell, Ky., U.S. 176 38.32 N 82.42 W
Russell, Pa., U.S. 176 41.56 N 79.08 W
Russell, Cape ≻ 172 75.15 N 117.35 W
Russell Island I 172 73.55 N 98.25 W
Russell Islands II 162 9.04 S 159.12 E
Russell Point ≻ 172 73.30 N 115.00 W
Russell Range ∧ 164 33.24 S 123.28 E
Russells Point 176 40.28 N 83.54 W
Russellville 174 35.17 N 93.08 W
Rüsselsheim 116 50.00 N 8.25 E
Russian ≃ 178 38.27 N 123.08 W
Russkaja Gavan' 126 76.10 N 62.35 E
Russkij, Ostrov I 128 77.00 N 96.00 E
Rust 116 47.48 N 16.41 E
Rustavi 126 41.33 N 45.02 E
Rustenburg 160 25.37 S 27.08 E
Rustington 104 50.48 N 0.31 W
Ruston 174 32.32 N 92.38 W
Rutana 158 3.55 S 30.00 E
Ruteng 142 8.36 S 120.27 E
Ruth 178 39.17 N 114.59 W
Rutherglen 108 55.50 N 4.12 W
Ruthin 106 53.07 N 3.18 W
Rutland 174 43.36 N 72.59 W
Rutter 176 46.06 N 80.10 W
Ruukki 114 64.40 N 25.06 E
Ruvubu ≃ 158 2.23 S 30.47 E
Ruvuma □[4] 158 11.00 S 36.00 E
Ruvuma (Rovuma) ≃ 158 10.29 S 40.28 E
Ruwenzori ∧ 158 0.23 N 29.54 E
Ruya (Luia) ≃ 158 16.34 S 33.12 E
Ruyang 136 34.10 N 112.26 E
Ruyigi 158 3.29 S 30.15 E
Ruyton-Eleven-Towns 104 52.48 N 2.54 W
Ružajevka 112 54.04 N 44.57 E
Ruzizi (Rusizi) ≃ 158 3.16 S 29.14 E
Ružomberok 116 49.06 N 19.18 E
Rwanda □[1] 156 2.30 S 30.00 E
Ryan, Loch C 106 54.58 N 5.02 W
Rybačij, Poluostrov ≻[1] 112 69.42 N 32.36 E
Rybačje, S.S.S.R. 126 42.28 N 76.10 E
Rybačje, S.S.S.R. 128 46.27 N 81.32 E
Rybinsk 130 58.03 N 38.52 E
Rybinskoje Vodochranilišče ⊜[1] 130 58.30 N 38.25 E
Rybnik 116 50.06 N 18.32 E
Ryd 114 56.28 N 14.41 E
Ryde 104 50.44 N 1.10 W
Ryder's Hill ∧[2] 104 50.31 N 3.53 W
Rye 104 50.57 N 0.44 E
Rye ≃ 106 54.10 N 0.45 W
Rye Patch Reservoir ⊜[1] 178 40.38 N 118.18 W
Ryes 118 49.19 N 0.37 W
Ryfoss 114 61.09 N 8.49 E
Ryfylke ⁺[1] 114 59.30 N 5.30 E
Ryhope 106 54.52 N 1.21 W
Ryōhaku-sanchi ⋀ 134 36.09 N 136.45 E
Ryōtsu 134 38.05 N 138.26 E
Rysy ∧ 116 49.12 N 20.04 E
Ryton 106 54.59 N 1.46 W
Ryton ≃ 106 53.25 N 1.00 W
Ryton-on-Dunsmore 104 52.22 N 1.26 W
Ryūgasaki 134 35.54 N 140.11 E
Rzeszów 116 50.03 N 22.00 E
Ržev 130 56.16 N 34.20 E

S

Saale ≃ 116 51.57 N 11.55 E
Saalfeld 116 50.39 N 11.22 E
Saar → Saarland □[3] 116 49.20 N 7.00 E
Saar (Sarre) ≃ 116 49.42 N 6.34 E
Saarbrücken 116 49.14 N 6.59 E
Saaremaa I 130 58.25 N 22.30 E
Saarijärvi 114 62.43 N 25.16 E
Saarland □[3] 116 49.20 N 7.00 E
Saarlautern → Saarlouis 116 49.21 N 6.45 E
Saarlouis 116 49.21 N 6.45 E
Saavedra 188 37.45 S 62.23 W
Sab, Tônlé ⊜ 140 13.00 N 104.00 E
Saba I 182 17.38 N 63.10 W
Šabac 124 44.45 N 19.42 E
Sabadell 120 41.33 N 2.06 E
Sabae 134 35.57 N 136.11 E
Sabana, Archipiélago de II 182 23.00 N 80.00 W
Sabana de la Mar 182 19.04 N 69.23 W
Sabana de Mendoza 182 9.26 N 70.46 W
Sabanagrande 182 13.50 N 87.15 W
Sabanalarga 184 10.38 N 74.55 W
Sabang, Indon. 138 0.11 N 119.51 E
Sabang, Indon. 138 5.55 N 95.19 E
Sābarmati ≃ 146 22.18 N 72.22 E
Şāberī, Hāmūn-e ⊜ 150 31.30 N 61.20 E
Sabhah 154 27.03 N 14.26 E
Sabi (Save) ≃ 160 21.00 S 35.02 E
Sabie 160 25.10 S 30.48 E
Sabie (Sábiè) ≃ 160 25.19 S 32.18 E
Sabina 176 39.29 N 83.38 W
Sabina ⁺[1] 122 42.15 N 12.42 E
Sabinal, Cayo I 182 21.40 N 77.15 W
Sabiñánigo 120 42.31 N 0.22 W
Sabinas 180 21.51 N 101.07 W
Sabinas Hidalgo 180 26.30 N 100.10 W
Sabine ≃ 174 30.00 N 93.45 W
Sabine, Mount ∧ 87 71.55 S 169.33 E
Sabine Bay C 172 75.35 N 109.30 W
Sabine Peninsula ≻[1] 172 76.20 N 109.30 W
Sable, Cape ≻, N.S., Can. 172 43.25 N 65.35 W
Sable, Cape ≻, Fla., U.S. 174 25.12 N 81.05 W
Sable, Île de I 162 19.15 S 159.56 E
Sable, Rivière du ≃ 172 55.30 N 68.21 W
Sable Island I 172 43.55 N 59.50 W
Sablé-sur-Sarthe 118 47.50 N 0.20 W
Sabor ≃ 120 41.10 N 7.07 W
Sabres 118 44.09 N 0.44 W
Sabrina Coast ⁺[2] 87 67.00 S 119.30 E
Sabzevār 150 36.13 N 57.42 E
Sacedón 120 40.29 N 2.43 W
Săcele 124 45.37 N 25.42 E
Sachalin, Ostrov (Sakhalin) I 128 51.00 N 143.00 E
Sachalinskij Zaliv C 128 53.45 N 141.30 E
Sachigo ≃ 172 55.06 N 88.58 W
Šachrisabz 126 39.03 N 66.50 E
Sachsen □[9] 116 51.00 N 13.30 E
Sachs Harbour 172 72.00 N 125.00 W
Šachty 126 47.42 N 40.13 E
Šachunja 112 57.40 N 46.37 E
Šack 130 54.01 N 41.43 E
Sackets Harbor 176 43.57 N 76.07 W
Säckingen 116 47.33 N 7.56 E
Sackville 172 45.54 N 64.22 W
Saco 176 43.29 N 70.28 W
Saco Bay C 176 43.30 N 70.15 W
Sacramento 178 38.03 N 121.56 W
Sacramento ≃ 178 38.03 N 121.56 W
Sacramento Mountains ⋀ 174 33.10 N 105.50 W
Sacramento Valley V 178 39.15 N 122.00 W
Sacramento Wash V 178 34.43 N 114.28 W
Şa'dah 144 16.52 N 43.37 E
Sada-misaki ≻ 134 33.20 N 132.01 E
Sada-misaki-hantō ≻[1] 134 33.26 N 132.13 E
Saddleback ∧ 106 54.38 N 3.03 W
Saddleworth 106 53.33 N 1.59 W
Sa-dec 140 10.18 N 105.46 E
Şādiqābād 146 28.18 N 70.08 E
Sadiya 144 27.50 N 95.40 E
Sado I 134 38.00 N 138.25 E
Sado ≃ 120 38.29 N 8.55 W
Sado-kaikyō ⊔ 134 37.50 N 138.40 E
Sadowara 134 32.02 N 131.26 E
Šadrinsk 126 56.05 N 63.38 E
Sādulgarh 149 29.35 N 74.19 E
Saegertown 176 41.43 N 80.09 W
Safājah, Jazīrat I 150 26.45 N 33.59 E
Safed Koh Range ⋀ 149 33.58 N 70.25 E
Säffle 114 59.08 N 12.56 E
Saffron Walden 104 52.01 N 0.15 E
Safi 152 32.20 N 9.17 W
Safid ≃ 146 36.44 N 65.38 E
Safīd Kūh, Selseleh-ye ⋀ 150 34.30 N 63.30 E
Safonovo 130 55.06 N 33.15 E
Saga, Nihon 134 33.15 N 130.18 E
Saga, Zhg. 132 29.30 N 85.22 E
Sagae 134 38.22 N 140.17 E
Sagaing 140 21.52 N 95.59 E
Sagaing □[8] 140 24.00 N 95.00 E
Sagamihara 134 35.32 N 139.23 E
Sagami-nada C 134 35.00 N 139.30 E
Sagan ≃ 158 4.28 N 36.40 E
Saganaga Lake ⊜ 174 48.14 N 90.52 W
Saganoseki 134 33.15 N 131.53 E
Saganthit Kyun I 140 11.56 N 98.29 E
Sāgar 148 14.10 N 75.02 E
Sagara 134 34.41 N 138.12 E
Saginaw 176 43.25 N 83.58 W
Saginaw ≃ 176 43.39 N 83.51 W
Saginaw Bay C 176 43.50 N 83.40 W
Saglek Bay C 172 58.35 N 63.00 W
Saglouc 172 62.14 N 75.38 W
Sagonar 128 51.32 N 92.48 E
Sag Sag 166 5.35 S 148.20 E
Sagua de Tánamo 182 20.35 N 75.14 W
Sagua la Grande 182 22.49 N 80.05 W
Saguenay ≃ 172 48.08 N 69.44 W
Sagunto 120 39.41 N 0.16 W
Sahagún 182 8.57 N 75.27 W
Sahara ⁺[2] 88 26.00 N 13.00 E
Sahāranpur 146 29.58 N 77.33 E
Sahaswān 146 28.05 N 78.45 E
Şahin 124 41.01 N 26.50 E
Sāhīwāl, Pāk. 149 31.58 N 72.20 E
Sāhīwāl (Montgomery), Pāk. 149 30.40 N 73.06 E
Şahrā', Jabal ∧ 150 28.00 N 34.08 E
Sahuaripa 180 29.03 N 109.14 W
Sahul Shelf ⁺[4] 96 12.00 S 127.00 E
Saibai I 166 9.24 S 142.40 E
Saibai Island I 166 9.24 S 142.40 E
Sai Buri 138 6.42 N 101.37 E
Saïda 152 34.50 N 0.09 E
Saidaiji 134 34.39 N 134.02 E
Saidpur 146 25.47 N 88.54 E
Saidu 149 34.45 N 72.21 E
Saigō 134 36.12 N 133.20 E
Sai-gon → Thanh-pho Ho Chi Minh 140 10.45 N 106.40 E
Saijō 134 33.55 N 133.11 E
Saiki 134 32.57 N 131.54 E
Sailor Creek ≃ 178 42.56 N 115.29 W
Saim 126 60.21 N 64.14 E
Saimaa ⊜ 114 61.15 N 28.15 E
Saimaa Canal 114 61.05 N 28.18 E
Saint Abb's Head ≻ 108 55.54 N 2.09 W
Saint-Affrique 118 43.57 N 2.53 E
Sainte-Agathe-des-Monts 172 46.03 N 74.17 W
Saint Agnes 104 50.18 N 5.13 W
Saint Agnes I 104a 49.54 N 6.20 W
Saint-Agrève 118 45.01 N 4.24 E
Saint Albans, Eng., U.K. 104 51.46 N 0.21 W
Saint Albans, Vt., U.S. 176 44.49 N 73.05 W
Saint Albans, W. Va., U.S. 176 38.23 N 81.49 W
Saint Aldhelm's Head ≻ 102 50.34 N 2.04 W
Saint-Amand-les-Eaux 118 50.26 N 3.26 E
Saint-Amand-Mont-Rond 118 46.44 N 2.30 E
Saint-Ambroix 118 44.15 N 4.11 E
Saint-Amour 118 46.26 N 5.21 E
Saint-André 161c 20.57 S 55.39 E
Saint-André, Cap ≻ 161b 16.11 S 44.27 E
Saint-André-Avellin 176 45.43 N 75.03 W
Saint-André-de-Cubzac 118 45.00 N 0.27 W
Saint-André-les-Alpes 118 43.58 N 6.30 E
Saint Andrews 108 56.20 N 2.48 W
Saint Andrews Bay C 108 56.22 N 2.50 W
Saint Anne 105b 49.42 N 2.12 W
Saint Anne's 106 53.45 N 3.02 W
Saint Ann's Bay 182 18.26 N 77.15 W
Saint Ann's Head ≻ 104 51.41 N 5.10 W
Saint Anthony 172 51.22 N 55.35 W
Saint-Antonin 118 44.09 N 1.45 E
Saint Arnaud 168 36.37 S 143.15 E
Saint Arvans 104 51.40 N 2.41 W
Saint Asaph 106 53.16 N 3.26 W
Saint Athan 104 51.24 N 3.25 W
Saint-Auban 118 43.51 N 6.44 E
Saint Aubin 105b 49.11 N 2.10 W
Saint-Aubin-d'Aubigné 118 48.15 N 1.36 W
Saint-Augustin ≃ 172 51.14 N 58.41 W
Saint Augustine 174 29.54 N 81.19 W
Saint-Augustin-Saguenay 172 51.14 N 58.39 W
Saint Austell 104 50.20 N 4.48 W
Saint-Avold 118 49.06 N 6.42 E
Saint-Barthélemy I 182 17.55 N 62.50 W
Saint Bathans, Mount ∧ 170 44.44 S 169.46 E
Saint-Béat 118 42.55 N 0.42 E
Saint Bees Head ≻ 106 54.32 N 3.38 W
Saint-Benoît 161c 21.02 S 55.43 E
Saint Blazey 104 50.22 N 4.43 W
Saint-Bonnet-de-Joux 118 46.29 N 4.27 E
Saint Brides Bay C 104 51.48 N 5.15 W
Saint Bride's Major 104 51.28 N 3.38 W
Saint-Brieuc 118 48.31 N 2.47 W
Saint-Calais 118 47.55 N 0.45 E
Saint Catharines 176 43.10 N 79.15 W
Saint Catherine's Point ≻ 102 50.34 N 1.15 W
Saint-Chamond 118 45.28 N 4.30 E
Saint Charles, Mich., U.S. 176 43.18 N 84.09 W
Saint Charles, Mo., U.S. 174 38.47 N 90.29 W
Saint-Chély-d'Apcher 118 44.48 N 3.17 E
Saint Christopher (Saint Kitts) I 182 17.21 N 62.48 W
Saint-Ciers-sur-Gironde 118 45.18 N 0.37 W
Saint Clair 176 42.49 N 82.30 W
Saint Clair, Lake ⊜ 176 42.25 N 82.41 W
Saint Clair Shores 176 42.30 N 82.54 W
Saint Clairsville 176 40.05 N 80.54 W
Saint-Claud 118 45.53 N 0.23 E
Saint-Claude 118 46.23 N 5.52 E
Saint Clears 104 51.50 N 4.30 W
Saint Cloud 174 45.33 N 94.10 W
Saint Columb Major 104 50.26 N 5.03 W
Saint Combs 108 57.39 N 1.54 W
Sainte-Croix 118 46.49 N 6.31 E
Saint Croix I 182 17.45 N 64.45 W
Saint-Cyprien 118 44.52 N 1.02 E
Saint David's 104 51.54 N 5.16 W
Saint David's Head ≻ 104 51.55 N 5.19 W
Saint-Denis, Fr. 118 48.56 N 2.22 E
Saint-Denis, Réu. 161c 20.52 S 55.28 E
Saint Dennis 104 50.23 N 4.53 W
Saint-Dié 118 48.17 N 6.57 E
Saint-Dizier 118 48.38 N 4.57 E
Saint Dogmaels 104 52.05 N 4.40 W
Sainte → Saint
Saint Elias, Cape ≻ 172 59.52 N 144.30 W
Saint Elias, Mount ∧ 172 60.18 N 140.55 W
Saint-Elie 184 4.49 N 53.17 W
Saint-Étienne 118 45.26 N 4.24 E
Saint-Étienne-du-Rouvray 102 49.23 N 1.06 E
Saint-Eustache 176 45.34 N 73.53 W
Saint-Félicien 172 48.39 N 72.26 W
Saint-Félix-de-Valois 176 46.11 N 73.26 W
Saint Fillans 108 56.23 N 4.07 W
Saint-Florentin 118 48.00 N 3.44 E
Saint-Florent-sur-Cher 118 46.59 N 2.15 E
Saint-Flour 118 45.02 N 3.05 E
Saint Francis, Cape ≻ 160 34.14 S 24.49 E
Saint-François ≃ 176 46.07 N 72.55 W
Saint-François, Lac ⊜ 176 45.55 N 71.10 W
Saint-Gabriel 176 46.17 N 73.23 W
Saint-Gall → Sankt Gallen 118 47.25 N 9.23 E
Saint-Gaudens 118 43.07 N 0.44 E
Saint-Genis-de-Saintonge 118 45.29 N 0.34 W
Saint George, Austl. 168 28.02 S 148.35 E
Saint George, N.B., Can. 176 45.08 N 66.49 W
Saint George, Ont., Can. 176 43.15 N 80.15 W
Saint George, Utah, U.S. 174 37.06 N 113.35 W
Saint George, Point ≻ 178 41.47 N 124.15 W
Saint George's, Gren. 182 12.03 N 61.45 W
Saint-Georges, Guy. fr. 184 3.54 N 51.48 W
Saint George's Bay C 172 48.20 N 59.00 W
Saint George's Channel ⊔, Eur. 102 52.00 N 6.00 W
Saint George's Channel ⊔, Pap. N. Gui. 166 4.30 S 152.30 E
Saint Georges Ranges ⋀ 164 18.40 S 125.00 E
Saint-Germain 118 48.54 N 2.05 E
Saint-Germain-Lembron 118 45.28 N 3.14 E
Saint-Germain-l'Herm 118 45.28 N 3.33 E
Saint Germans 104 50.24 N 4.18 W
Saint-Gervais-les-Bains 118 45.54 N 6.43 E
Saint-Gilles-croix-de-Vie 118 46.42 N 1.57 W
Saint-Girons 118 42.59 N 1.09 E
Saint Govan's Head ≻ 104 51.36 N 4.55 W
Saint-Guénolé 118 47.49 N 4.20 W
Saint Helena 178 38.30 N 122.28 W
Saint Helena □[2] 88 15.57 S 5.42 W
Saint Helena Bay C 156 32.43 S 18.05 E
Saint Helens, Austl. 168 41.20 S 148.15 E
Saint Helens, Eng., U.K. 104 50.42 N 1.06 W
Saint Helens, Eng., U.K. 106 53.28 N 2.44 W
Saint-Helier, Fr. 102 49.12 N 2.37 W
Saint Helier, Jersey 105b 49.12 N 2.37 W
Sainte-Hermine 118 46.33 N 1.04 W
Saint-Hilaire-du-Harcouët 118 48.35 N 1.06 W
Saint-Hippolyte-du-Fort 118 43.58 N 3.51 E
Saint-Hyacinthe 172 45.37 N 72.57 W
Saint Ignace 176 45.52 N 84.43 W
Saint Ignace Island I 172 48.48 N 87.55 W
Saint Ives, Eng., U.K. 104 50.12 N 5.29 W
Saint Ives, Eng., U.K. 104 52.20 N 0.05 W
Saint Ives Bay C 104 50.14 N 5.28 W
Saint James, Mich., U.S. 176 45.45 N 85.31 W
Saint James, N.Y., U.S. 176 40.53 N 73.09 W
Saint James, Cape ≻ 172 51.56 N 131.01 W
Saint-Jean 172 45.19 N 73.16 W
Saint-Jean, Lac ⊜ 172 48.35 N 72.05 W
Saint-Jean-d'Angély 118 45.57 N 0.31 W
Saint-Jean-de-Losne 118 47.06 N 5.15 E
Saint-Jean-de-Luz 118 43.23 N 1.40 W
Saint-Jean-de-Maurienne 118 45.17 N 6.21 E
Saint-Jean-de-Monts 118 46.48 N 2.03 W
Saint-Jean-Pied-de-Port 118 43.10 N 1.14 W
Saint-Jérôme 172 45.47 N 74.00 W
Saint John, N.B., Can. 172 45.16 N 66.03 W
Saint John, Jersey 105b 49.15 N 2.08 W
Saint John I 182 18.20 N 64.45 W
Saint John ≃ 172 45.15 N 66.04 W
Saint John, Cape ≻ 172 50.00 N 55.32 W
Saint Johns, Antig. 182 17.06 N 61.51 W
Saint John's, Newf., Can. 172 47.34 N 52.43 W
Saint Johns, Mich., U.S. 176 43.00 N 84.33 W
Saint Johnsbury 176 44.25 N 72.01 W
Saint-Joseph, Qué., Can. 176 45.37 N 70.52 W
Saint-Joseph, Réu. 161c 21.22 S 55.36 E
Saint Joseph, Mo., U.S. 174 39.46 N 94.51 W
Saint Joseph ≃ 176 42.07 N 86.29 W
Saint Joseph, Lake ⊜ 172 51.05 N 90.35 W
Saint Joseph Channel ⊔ 176 46.16 N 83.51 W
Saint-Jovite 176 46.07 N 74.36 W
Saint-Julien-en-Born 118 44.04 N 1.14 W
Sainte-Julienne 176 45.58 N 73.43 W
Saint-Junien 118 45.53 N 0.54 E
Saint Just 104 50.07 N 5.42 W
Saint-Just-en-Chaussée 118 49.30 N 2.26 E
Saint-Just-en-Chevalet 118 45.55 N 3.50 E
Saint Keverne 104 50.03 N 5.06 W
Saint Kilda 170 45.54 S 170.31 E
Saint Kitts (Saint Christopher) I 182 17.21 N 62.48 W
Saint Kitts-Nevis □[2] 182 17.20 N 62.50 W
Saint Kitts-Nevis-Anguilla → Saint-kitts-Nevis □[2], N.A. 180 17.20 N 62.45 W
Saint Kitts-Nevis-Anguilla → Anguilla □[2], N.A. 180 18.15 N 63.05 W
Saint-Lambert 176 45.30 N 73.30 W
Saint-Laurent-du-Maroni 184 5.30 N 54.02 W
Saint Lawrence 168 22.21 S 149.31 E
Saint Lawrence ≃ 172 49.30 N 67.00 W
Saint Lawrence, Gulf of C 172 48.00 N 62.00 W
Saint-Léonard-d'Aston 176 46.06 N 72.22 W
Saint-Léonard-de-Noblat 118 45.50 N 1.29 E
Saint Leonards 104 50.51 N 0.34 E
Saint-Lô 118 49.07 N 1.05 W
Saint-Louis, Réu. 161c 21.16 S 55.25 E
Saint-Louis, Sén. 152 16.02 N 16.30 W
Saint Louis, Mich., U.S. 176 43.25 N 84.36 W
Saint Louis, Mo., U.S. 174 38.38 N 90.11 W
Saint-Loup-sur-Semouse 118 47.53 N 6.16 E
Saint Lucia □[2] 180 13.53 N 60.58 W
Saint Lucia, Cape ≻ 160 28.25 S 32.25 E
Saint Lucia, Lake ⊜ 160 28.05 S 32.26 E
Saint Lucia Channel ⊔ 182 14.15 N 61.00 W
Saint Magnus Bay C 108a 60.24 N 1.34 W
Saint-Malo 118 48.39 N 2.01 W
Saint-Malo, Golfe de C 118 48.45 N 2.00 W
Saint-Mamert 118 43.53 N 4.12 E
Saint-Mamert[-du-gard] 120 43.53 N 4.12 E
Saint-Marc 182 19.07 N 72.42 W
Saint-Marc, Canal de ⊔ 182 18.45 N 72.40 W
Saint Margaret's at Cliffe 104 51.09 N 1.24 E
Saint Margaret's Hope 108 58.49 N 2.57 W
Sainte-Marguerite ≃ 172 50.09 N 66.36 W
Sainte-Marie, Cap ≻ 161b 25.36 S 45.08 E
Sainte-Marie, Île I 161b 16.50 S 49.55 E
Saint-Martin (Sint Maarten) I 182 18.04 N 63.04 W
Saint Martin, Lake ⊜ 172 51.37 N 98.29 W
Saint-Martin-de-Londres 118 43.47 N 3.44 E
Saint Martin's I 104a 49.58 N 6.20 W
Saint Mary Bourne 104 51.16 N 1.24 W
Saint Mary Peak ∧ 168 31.30 S 138.33 E
Saint Mary's, Austl. 168 41.35 S 148.10 E
Saint Mary's, Ont., Can. 176 43.16 N 81.08 W
Saint Marys, Ohio, U.S. 176 40.33 N 84.23 W
Saint Marys, Pa., U.S. 176 41.26 N 78.34 W
Saint Marys, W. Va., U.S. 176 39.23 N 81.12 W
Saint Mary's I 104a 49.55 N 6.18 W
Saint Marys ≃ 176 41.05 N 85.08 W
Saint Mary's, Cape ≻ 172 46.49 N 54.12 W
Saint Mary's Bay 104 51.00 N 0.58 E
Saint Mary's Bay C 172 46.50 N 53.47 W
Saint-Mathieu 118 45.42 N 0.46 E
Saint-Mathieu, Pointe de ≻ 118 48.20 N 4.46 W
Saint-Maur[-des-Fossés] 118 48.48 N 2.30 E
Sainte-Maure-du-Touraine 118 47.07 N 0.37 E
Saint-Maurice ≃ 172 46.21 N 72.31 W
Saint Mawes 104 50.09 N 5.01 W
Saint Mawgan 104 50.28 N 4.58 W
Saint-Méen-le-Grand 118 48.11 N 2.12 W
Sainte-Mère-Église 118 49.25 N 1.19 W
Saint Merryn 104 50.31 N 4.58 W
Saint Michaels 176 38.47 N 76.14 W
Saint-Mihiel 118 48.54 N 5.33 E
Saint Monance 108 56.12 N 2.46 W
Saint-Moritz → Sankt Moritz 118 46.30 N 9.50 E
Saint-Nazaire 118 47.17 N 2.12 W
Saint Neots 104 52.14 N 0.17 W
Saint-Nicolas → Sint-Niklaas 116 51.10 N 4.08 E
Saint-Omer 118 50.45 N 2.15 E
Saintonge □[9] 118 45.30 N 0.30 W
Saint Paris 176 40.07 N 83.58 W
Saint-Patrick, Lac ⊜ 176 46.22 N 77.21 W
Saint Paul, Alta., Can. 172 53.59 N 111.17 W
Saint-Paul, Réu. 161c 21.00 S 55.16 E
Saint Paul, Minn., U.S. 174 44.58 N 93.07 W
Saint Paul ≃, Can. 172 51.26 N 57.40 W
Saint Paul ≃, Liber. 152 7.10 N 10.00 W
Saint-Paulien 118 45.08 N 3.49 E
Saint Peter Island I 164 32.17 S 133.35 E
Saint Peter Port 105b 49.27 N 2.32 W
Saint Petersburg → Leningrad, S.S.S.R. 130 59.55 N 30.15 E
Saint Petersburg, Fla., U.S. 174 27.46 N 82.38 W
Saint-Pierre, Mart. 182 14.45 N 61.11 W
Saint-Pierre, Réu. 161c 21.19 S 55.29 E
Saint-Pierre, Lac ⊜ 176 46.12 N 72.52 W
Saint Pierre and Miquelon □[2] 172 46.55 N 56.15 W
Saint Pierre Island I 156 9.19 S 50.43 E
Saint-Pierre-le-Moûtier 118 46.48 N 3.07 E
Saint-Pierre-sur-Dives 102 49.01 N 0.02 W
Saint-Pierreville 118 44.49 N 4.29 E
Saint-Pol-de-Léon 118 48.41 N 3.59 W
Saint-Pons 118 43.29 N 2.46 E
Saint-Prosper-de-Dorchester 176 46.13 N 70.29 W
Saint-Quentin 118 49.51 N 3.17 E
Saint-Raphaël 118 43.25 N 6.46 E
Saint Regis, East Branch ≃ 176 44.39 N 74.28 W
Saint Regis, West Branch ≃ 176 44.47 N 74.46 W
Saint Regis Falls 176 44.40 N 74.33 W
Saint-Rémi-d'Amherst 176 46.01 N 74.47 W
Saint-Renan 118 48.26 N 4.37 W
Saintes 118 45.45 N 0.38 W
Saintes, Îles des II 182 15.52 N 61.36 W
Saint Sampson 105b 49.29 N 2.31 W
Saint-Savinien 118 45.53 N 0.41 W
Saint Saviour 105b 49.11 N 2.06 W
Saint-Sébastien, Cap ≻ 161b 12.26 S 48.44 E
Saint-Seine-l'Abbaye 118 47.26 N 4.47 E
Saintes-Maries-de-la-Mer 118 43.27 N 4.26 E
Saint Stephen, N.B., Can. 172 45.12 N 67.17 W
St. Stephen, N.B., Can. 176 45.12 N 67.17 W
Saint-Symphorien 118 44.26 N 0.30 W
Sainte-Thérèse-de-Blainville 176 45.39 N 73.49 W
Saint Thomas, Ont., Can. 172 42.47 N 81.12 W
Saint Thomas → Charlotte Amalie, Vir. Is., U.S. 182 18.21 N 64.56 W
Saint Thomas I 182 18.21 N 64.55 W
Saint Tudy 104 50.33 N 4.43 W
Saint-Valery-en-Caux 118 49.52 N 0.44 E
Saint-Valery-sur-Somme 118 50.11 N 1.38 E
Saint-Vallier 118 45.10 N 4.49 E
Saint-Vallier-de-Thiey 118 43.42 N 6.51 E
Saint-Varent 118 46.53 N 0.14 W
Saint Vincent □[2] 180 13.15 N 61.12 W
Saint-Vincent, Cap ≻ 161b 21.57 S 43.16 E
Saint Vincent, Cape ≻ 168 43.18 S 145.50 E
Saint Vincent, Gulf C 168 35.00 S 138.05 E
Saint-Vincent-de-Tyrosse 118 43.40 N 1.18 W
Saint Vincent Passage ⊔ 182 13.30 N 61.00 W
Saint-Vith 116 50.17 N 6.08 E
Saint-Vivien-de-Médoc 118 45.26 N 1.02 W
Saipan I 138 15.12 N 145.45 E
Saiqi 136 27.00 N 119.43 E
Sairecábur, Cerro ∧ 188 22.43 S 67.54 W
Saitama □[5] 134 35.59 N 139.24 E
Saito 134 32.06 N 131.24 E
Saitula 132 36.21 N 78.02 E
Sajama, Nevado ∧ 184 18.06 S 68.54 W
Sajia 132 28.55 N 88.05 E
Sajó ≃ 116 47.56 N 21.08 E
Sajószentpéter 116 48.13 N 20.44 E
Sak ≃ 160 30.52 S 20.25 E
Sakai 134 34.35 N 135.28 E
Sakaide 134 34.19 N 133.52 E
Sakai-minato 134 35.33 N 133.15 E
Sakākah 150 29.59 N 40.06 E
Sakakawea, Lake ⊜[1] 174 47.50 N 102.20 W
Sakami 172 53.40 N 76.40 W
Sakami, Lac ⊜ 172 53.15 N 76.45 W
Sakania 158 12.45 S 28.34 E
Sakar ⋀ 124 41.59 N 26.16 E
Sakata 134 38.55 N 139.50 E
Sakawa 134 33.30 N 133.17 E
Sakhalin → Sachalin, Ostrov I 128 51.00 N 143.00 E
Šakiai 130 54.57 N 23.03 E
Sakito 134 33.02 N 129.32 E
Sakon Nakhon 140 17.10 N 104.09 E
Sakrivier 160 30.54 S 20.28 E
Sakskøbing 114 54.48 N 11.39 E
Saku 134 36.09 N 138.26 E
Sakuma 134 35.05 N 137.48 E
Sakura 134 35.43 N 140.14 E
Sakurai 134 34.30 N 135.51 E
Sal I 152 16.45 N 22.55 W
Sal, Cay I 182 23.42 N 80.24 W
Sala 114 59.55 N 16.36 E
Salacgrīva 130 57.45 N 24.21 E
Salada, Laguna ⊜ 178 32.20 N 115.40 W
Saladas 188 28.15 S 58.38 W
Saladillo 188 35.38 S 59.48 W
Saladillo ≃ 188 29.07 S 63.23 W
Salado 188 26.25 S 70.19 W
Salado ≃, Arg. 188 35.44 S 57.22 W
Salado ≃, Arg. 188 31.40 S 60.41 W
Salado ≃, Cuba 182 20.38 N 76.57 W
Salado ≃, Méx. 180 26.50 N 99.17 W
Salaguolehe ≃ 132 40.28 N 94.30 E
Sălaj □[4] 124 47.15 N 23.00 E
Salala 188 30.41 S 71.32 W
Şalālah 144 17.00 N 54.06 E
Salamá 182 14.50 N 86.36 W
Salamanca, Chile 188 31.47 S 70.58 W
Salamanca, Esp. 120 40.58 N 5.39 W
Salamanca, Méx. 180 20.34 N 101.12 W
Salamanca, N.Y., U.S. 176 42.09 N 78.43 W
Salamís 124 37.59 N 23.28 E
Salamonie ≃ 176 40.50 N 85.43 W
Salantai 130 56.04 N 21.32 E
Salas de los Infantes 120 42.01 N 3.17 W
Salat ≃ 118 43.10 N 0.58 E
Salatiga 142 7.19 S 110.30 E
Salavat 126 53.21 N 55.55 E
Salaverry 184 8.14 S 78.58 W
Salavina 188 28.48 S 63.26 W
Salawati I 166 1.07 S 130.52 E
Sala y Gómez, Isla I 92 26.28 S 105.28 W
Salcedo 182 19.22 N 70.25 W
Šalčininkai 130 54.18 N 25.23 E
Salcombe 104 50.13 N 3.47 W
Saldanha 160 33.00 S 17.56 E
Saldanhabaai C 160 33.04 S 18.00 E
Sale, Austl. 168 38.06 S 147.04 E
Salé, Magreb 152 34.04 N 6.50 W
Sale, Eng., U.K. 106 53.26 N 2.19 W
Salebabu, Pulau I 138 3.55 N 126.40 E
Salechard 128 66.33 N 66.40 E
Salem, Bhārat 148 11.39 N 78.10 E
Salem, Mass., U.S. 176 42.31 N 70.55 W
Salem, N.H., U.S. 176 42.47 N 71.12 W
Salem, N.J., U.S. 176 39.34 N 75.28 W
Salem, N.Y., U.S. 176 43.10 N 73.20 W
Salem, Ohio, U.S. 176 40.54 N 80.52 W
Salem, Oreg., U.S. 174 44.57 N 123.01 W
Salem, W. Va., U.S. 176 39.17 N 80.34 W
Salen, Scot., U.K. 108 56.43 N 5.47 W
Salen, Scot., U.K. 108 56.31 N 5.57 W
Salerno 122 40.41 N 14.47 E
Salford 106 53.28 N 2.18 W
Salies-de-Béarn 118 43.29 N 0.55 W
Salignac-Eyvignes 118 44.59 N 1.19 E
Salima 158 13.47 S 34.26 E
Salimah, Wāḥat ⁺[4] 154 21.22 N 29.19 E
Salimani 161a 11.47 S 43.17 E
Salina 174 38.50 N 97.37 W
Salina Cruz 180 16.10 N 95.12 W
Salina Point ≻ 182 22.10 N 74.18 W
Salinas, Ec. 184 2.13 S 80.58 W
Salinas, Calif., U.S. 178 36.40 N 121.39 W
Salinas ≃ 178 36.45 N 121.48 W
Salinas, Cabo de ≻ 120 39.16 N 3.03 E
Salinas, Punta ≻ 182 18.13 N 70.30 W
Salinas de Hidalgo 180 22.38 N 101.43 W
Saline ≃ 174 33.10 N 92.08 W
Salisbury, Austl. 168 34.46 S 138.38 E
Salisbury, Rh. 158 17.50 S 31.03 E
Salisbury, Eng., U.K. 104 51.05 N 1.48 W
Salisbury, Md., U.S. 176 38.22 N 75.36 W
Salisbury, N.C., U.S. 174 35.40 N 80.29 W
Salisbury, Pa., U.S. 176 39.45 N 79.05 W
Salisbury Island I 172 63.30 N 77.00 W
Salisbury Plain ⊟ 104 51.12 N 1.55 W
Saljany 150 39.34 N 48.58 E
Sallanches 118 45.56 N 6.38 E
Salling ⁺[1] 114 56.40 N 9.00 E
Salliqueló 188 36.46 S 62.57 W
Sallyāna 146 28.22 N 82.10 E
Salmon ≃, N.A. 176 45.02 N 74.31 W
Salmon ≃, Calif., U.S. 178 41.23 N 123.29 W
Salmon ≃, Idaho, U.S. 174 45.51 N 116.46 W
Salmon ≃, N.Y., U.S. 176 43.35 N 76.12 W
Salmon, North Fork ≃ 178 41.16 N 123.18 W
Salmon, South Fork ≃ 178 41.16 N 123.18 W
Salmon Arm 172 50.42 N 119.16 W
Salmon Falls Creek ≃ 178 42.43 N 114.51 W
Salmon Gums 164 32.59 S 121.38 E
Salmon Mountain ∧ 176 45.14 N 71.08 W
Salmon Mountains ⋀ 178 41.00 N 123.00 W
Salmon River Mountains ⋀ 174 44.45 N 115.00 W
Salo 114 60.23 N 23.08 E
Salo ≃ 176 43.27 N 70.22 W
Salon-de-Provence 118 43.38 N 5.06 E
Salonta 124 46.48 N 21.40 E
Salop □[6] 104 52.40 N 2.40 W
Saloum ≃ 152 13.50 N 16.45 W
Salsipuedes, Punta ≻ 178 32.00 N 116.52 W
Sal'sk 126 46.28 N 41.33 E
Salt ≃, Ariz., U.S. 174 33.23 N 112.18 W
Salt ≃, Ky., U.S. 176 38.00 N 85.01 W
Salta 188 24.47 S 65.24 W
Salta □[4] 188 25.00 S 64.30 W
Saltash 104 50.24 N 4.12 W
Saltburn-by-the-Sea 106 54.35 N 0.58 W
Saltcoats 108 55.38 N 4.47 W
Salt Creek ≃ 178 36.15 N 116.49 W
Saltee Islands II 110 52.07 N 6.36 W
Saltillo 180 25.25 N 101.00 W
Salt Lake City 174 40.46 N 111.53 W
Salto, Arg. 188 34.17 S 60.15 W
Salto, Bra. 190 23.12 S 47.17 W
Salto, Ur. 188 31.23 S 57.58 W
Salto de las Rosas 188 34.43 S 68.14 W
Salto Grande 190 22.54 S 49.59 W
Salton City 178 33.19 N 115.59 W
Salton Sea ⊜ 178 33.19 N 115.50 W
Sālūr 148 18.32 N 83.13 E
Saluzzo 122 44.39 N 7.29 E
Salvado, Mount ∧ 164 25.15 S 121.01 E
Salvador 190 12.59 S 38.31 W
Salviac 118 44.41 N 1.16 E
Salwá, Baḩr as- C 150 25.30 N 50.40 E
Salween ≃ 94 16.31 N 97.37 E
Salyer 178 40.54 N 123.35 W
Salyersville 176 37.45 N 83.04 W
Salza ≃ 116 47.40 N 14.43 E
Salzach ≃ 116 48.12 N 12.56 E
Salzburg 116 47.48 N 13.02 E
Salzburg □[3] 116 47.25 N 13.15 E
Salzgitter 116 52.10 N 10.25 E
Salzkammergut ⁺[1] 116 47.45 N 13.30 E
Salzwedel 116 52.51 N 11.09 E
Sama [de Langreo] 120 43.18 N 5.41 W
Samalanga 138 5.13 N 96.22 E
Sāmalkot 148 17.03 N 82.11 E
Samālūt 154 28.18 N 30.42 E
Samambaia ≃ 190 22.45 S 53.21 W
Samāna, Bhārat 149 30.09 N 76.12 E
Samaná, Rep. Dom. 182 19.13 N 69.19 W
Samaná, Bahía de C 182 19.10 N 69.25 W
Samaná, Cabo ≻ 182 19.18 N 69.10 W
Samana Cay I 182 23.03 N 73.45 W
Samangān □[4] 146 36.15 N 67.40 E
Samani 134a 42.07 N 142.56 E
Samar I 138 12.00 N 125.00 E
Samara ≃ 126 53.10 N 50.04 E
Samarai 166 10.37 S 150.40 E
Samarinda 142 0.30 S 117.09 E
Samarkand 126 39.40 N 66.48 E
Sāmarrā' 150 34.12 N 43.52 E
Samaso 158 3.12 S 43.44 E
Samāstipur 146 25.51 N 85.47 E
Samba 158 4.38 S 26.22 E
Sambalpur 146 21.27 N 83.58 E
Sambas 142 1.20 N 109.15 E
Sambava 161b 14.16 S 50.10 E
Sambe-yama ∧ 134 35.08 N 132.37 E
Sambhal 146 28.35 N 78.33 E
Sāmbhar 144 26.55 N 75.12 E
Samboja 142 1.02 S 117.02 E
Sambor 116 49.32 N 23.11 E
Samborombón, Bahía C 188 36.00 S 57.00 W
Sambre ≃ 118 50.28 N 4.52 E
Samch'ŏk 132 37.27 N 129.10 E
Samch'ŏnp'o 132 34.57 N 128.03 E
Same 158 4.04 S 37.44 E
Samer 102 50.38 N 1.45 E
Samoa → American Samoa □[2] 96 14.20 S 170.00 W
Samo Alto 188 30.25 S 70.58 W
Samoded 112 63.38 N 40.29 E
Samokov 124 42.20 N 23.33 E
Sámos I 124 37.48 N 26.44 E
Samosir, Pulau I 140 2.35 N 98.50 E
Sampacho 188 33.20 S 64.40 W
Sampang 142 7.12 S 113.14 E
Sampford Peverell 104 50.56 N 3.22 W
Sampit 142 2.32 S 112.57 E
Sampués 182 9.11 N 75.23 W
Sam Rayburn Reservoir ⊜[1] 174 31.27 N 94.37 W
Samson I 104a 49.56 N 6.22 W
Samsun 126 41.17 N 36.20 E
Samui, Ko I 140 9.30 N 100.00 E
Samut Prakan 140 13.36 N 100.36 E
Samut Sakhon 140 13.32 N 100.17 E
Samut Songkhram 140 13.24 N 100.00 E
San 152 13.18 N 4.54 W
San ≃, As. 140 13.32 N 105.58 E
San ≃, Eur. 116 50.45 N 21.51 E
Saña 184 6.54 S 79.36 W
Sanaduva 188 27.57 S 51.48 W
Şanāfir, Jazīrat I 150 27.55 N 34.40 E
Sanaga ≃ 152 3.35 N 9.38 E
San Agustin, Cape ≻ 138 6.16 N 126.11 E
San Ambrosio, Isla I 186 26.21 S 79.52 W
Sanana, Pulau I 142 2.12 S 125.55 E
Sanandaj 150 35.19 N 47.00 E
San Andreas 178 38.12 N 120.41 W
San Andrés 182 12.35 N 81.42 W
San Andrés, Isla de I 184 12.33 N 81.42 W
San Andrés de Giles 188 34.26 S 59.28 W
San Andrés Tuxtla 180 18.27 N 95.13 W
San Andrés y Providencia □[8] 182 13.00 N 81.30 W
San Angelo 174 31.28 N 100.26 W
San Anselmo 178 37.59 N 122.34 W
San Antero 182 9.23 N 75.46 W
San Antonio, Chile 188 33.35 S 71.38 W
San Antonio, Tex., U.S. 174 29.28 N 98.31 W
San Antonio ≃ 178 31.00 N 116.15 W
San Antonio, Cabo ≻, Arg. 188 36.40 S 56.42 W
San Antonio, Cabo ≻, Cuba 182 21.52 N 84.57 W
San Antonio, Mount ∧ 178 34.17 N 117.39 W
San Antonio Abad 120 38.58 N 1.18 E
San Antonio del Golfo 182 10.27 N 63.50 W
San Antonio de los Baños 182 22.53 N 82.30 W
San Antonio de los Cobres 188 24.15 S 66.20 W
San Antonio de Tamanaco 182 9.41 N 66.03 W
San Antonio Oeste 186 40.44 S 64.57 W
Şan'ā'yaman 144 15.23 N 44.12 E
San Baudilio de Llobregat 120 41.21 N 2.03 E
San Benedetto del Tronto 122 42.57 N 13.53 E
San Benedicto, Isla I 180 19.18 N 110.49 W
San Benito 180 16.55 N 89.54 W
San Benito ≃ 178 36.53 N 121.34 W
San Benito Mountain ∧ 178 36.22 N 120.38 W
San Bernardino 178 34.06 N 117.17 W
San Bernardino Mountains ⋀ 178 34.10 N 117.00 W
San Bernardino Strait ⊔ 138 12.32 N 124.10 E
San Bernardo 188 33.36 S 70.43 W
San Bernardo, Islas de II 182 9.45 N 75.50 W
San Bernardo del Viento 182 9.21 N 75.57 W
San Blas 180 76.05 N 108.46 W
San Blas, Cape ≻ 174 29.40 N 85.22 W
San Blas, Cordillera de ⋀ 182 9.20 N 78.45 W
San Blas, Golfo de C 182 9.28 N 79.00 W
San Borja 184 14.49 S 66.51 W
San Bruno 178 37.37 N 122.25 W
San Buenaventura → Ventura 178 34.17 N 119.18 W
Sanbuzhen 132 22.23 N 112.35 E
San Carlos, Chile 188 36.25 S 71.58 W
San Carlos, Gui. Ecu. 152 3.27 N 8.33 E
San Carlos, Nic. 182 11.07 N 84.47 W
San Carlos, Pil. 138 15.55 N 120.20 E
San Carlos, Pil. 138 10.30 N 123.25 E
San Carlos, Calif., U.S. 178 37.31 N 122.16 W
San Carlos, Ur. 188 34.48 S 54.55 W
San Carlos, Ven. 184 9.40 N 68.36 W
San Carlos ≃, C.R. 182 10.48 N 84.11 W
San Carlos ≃, Ven. 182 9.07 N 68.25 W
San Carlos, Isla I 182 11.01 N 71.43 W
San Carlos Centro 188 31.44 S 61.05 W
San Carlos de Bariloche 186 41.08 S 71.15 W
San Carlos de la Rápita 120 40.37 N 0.36 E
San Carlos del Zulia 184 9.01 N 71.55 W
San Carlos de Río Negro 184 1.55 N 67.04 W
San Cataldo 122 37.29 N 14.04 E
San Cayetano 188 38.20 S 59.35 W
Sancerre 118 47.20 N 2.51 E
Sancerrois, Collines du ⁺[2] 118 47.25 N 2.45 E
Sanchang 136 31.54 N 121.15 E
Sánchez 182 19.14 N 69.36 W
San Clemente 178 33.26 N 117.37 W
San Clemente Island I 178 32.54 N 118.29 W
Sancoins 118 46.50 N 2.55 E
San Cristóbal, Arg. 188 30.20 S 61.15 W
San Cristóbal, Rep. Dom. 182 18.25 N 70.06 W
San Cristóbal, Ven. 184 7.46 N 72.14 W
San Cristóbal, Volcán ∧[1] 182 12.42 N 87.00 W
San Cristóbal las Casas 180 16.45 N 92.38 W
San Cristobal Trench ⁺[1] 96 11.00 S 161.00 E
Sancti-Spíritus 182 21.56 N 79.27 W
Sand 114 59.29 N 6.15 E
Sand ≃ 160 22.25 S 30.05 E
Sandai 142 1.15 S 110.31 E
Sanda Island I 108 55.18 N 5.34 W
Sandakan 142 5.50 N 118.07 E
Sanday I 108 59.15 N 2.35 W
Sanday Sound ⊔ 108 59.11 N 2.31 W
Sandbach 106 53.09 N 2.22 W
Sandbank 108 55.59 N 4.58 W
Sandefjord 114 59.08 N 10.14 E
Sanderson 174 30.09 N 102.24 W
Sand Fork 176 38.55 N 80.45 W
Sandgate, Austl. 168 27.20 S 153.05 E
Sandgate, Eng., U.K. 104 51.05 N 1.09 E
Sandhurst 104 51.19 N 0.48 W
Sandia 184 14.14 S 69.25 W
San Diego 178 32.46 N 117.13 W
San Diego, Cabo ≻ 186 54.38 S 65.05 W

Symbols in the index entries are identified on page 198.

Name	Page	Lat	Long
San Diego Aqueduct �1	178	32.55 N	116.55 W
Sandness	108a	60.17 N	1.38 W
Sandoa	156	9.41 S	22.52 E
Sandomierz	116	50.41 N	21.45 E
San Donà di Piave	122	45.38 N	12.34 E
Sandovalina	190	22.27 S	51.44 W
Sandover ≈	164	21.43 S	136.32 E
Sandoway	140	18.28 N	94.22 E
Sandown	104	50.39 N	1.09 W
Sandpoint	174	48.16 N	116.33 W
Sandray I	108	56.53 N	7.30 W
Sandringham, Austl.	168	24.05 S	139.04 E
Sandringham, Eng., U.K.	104	52.50 N	0.30 E
Sandstone	164	27.59 S	119.17 E
Sanduo	136	32.49 N	119.42 E
Sanduozhu	136	23.02 N	114.56 E
Sandusky, Mich., U.S.	176	43.25 N	82.50 W
Sandusky, Ohio, U.S.	176	41.27 N	82.42 W
Sandusky ≈	176	41.27 N	83.00 W
Sandvig	114	55.17 N	14.47 E
Sandvika	114	59.54 N	10.31 E
Sandviken	114	60.37 N	16.46 E
Sandwich, Eng., U.K.	104	51.17 N	1.20 E
Sandwich, Mass., U.S.	176	41.46 N	70.30 W
Sandwich Bay C	108a	53.35 N	57.15 W
Sandwick	108a	60.00 N	1.15 W
Sandwick C	108	60.42 N	0.52 W
Sandy	104	52.08 N	0.18 W
Sandy ≈	176	44.45 N	69.52 W
Sandy Bay Mountain ∧	176	45.47 N	70.25 W
Sandy Cape ⪫	168	24.42 S	153.17 E
Sandy Creek ≈, N.Y., U.S.	176	43.44 N	76.15 W
Sandy Creek ≈, Ohio, U.S.	176	40.38 N	81.26 W
Sandy Hook ⪫2	176	38.05 N	83.08 W
Sandykači	150	36.33 N	62.34 E
Sandy Lake	172	53.00 N	93.07 W
Sandy Point	182	17.22 N	62.50 W
San Estanislao	182	10.24 N	75.09 W
San Esteban de Gormaz	120	41.35 N	3.12 W
San Felipe, Chile	188	32.45 S	70.44 W
San Felipe, Méx.	180	31.00 N	114.52 W
San Felipe, Ven.	184	10.20 N	68.44 W
San Felipe, Cayos de II	182	21.58 N	83.30 W
San Felipe, Punta ⪫	178	31.03 N	114.51 W
San Felipe Creek ≈	178	33.09 N	115.46 W
San Feliu de Guíxols	120	41.47 N	3.02 E
San Félix, Isla I	186	26.17 S	80.05 W
San Fernando, Chile	188	34.35 S	71.00 W
San Fernando, Esp.	120	36.28 N	6.12 W
San Fernando, Méx.	180	31.16 N	110.36 W
San Fernando, Pil.	138	15.01 N	120.41 E
San Fernando, Pil.	138	16.37 N	120.19 E
San Fernando, Trin.	182	10.17 N	61.28 W
San Fernando, Calif., U.S.	178	34.17 N	118.26 W
San Fernando de Apure	184	7.54 N	67.28 W
San Fiorenzo	118	49.42 N	9.24 E
Sanford, Fla., U.S.	174	28.48 N	81.16 W
Sanford, Maine, U.S.	176	43.26 N	70.46 W
Sanford, Mich., U.S.	176	43.40 N	84.23 W
San Francisco, Calif., U.S.	188	31.27 S	62.05 W
San Francisco, Calif., U.S.	178	37.48 N	122.24 W
San Francisco, Cabo de ⪫	184	0.40 N	80.05 W
San Francisco Bay C	178	37.43 N	122.17 W
San Francisco del Oro	186	26.52 N	105.51 W
San Francisco del Rincón	180	21.01 N	101.51 W
San Francisco de Macorís	182	19.18 N	70.15 W
San Francisco de Mostazal	188	33.59 S	70.43 W
San Francisco Mountains ∧	174	33.45 N	109.00 W
San Gabriel Mountains ∧	178	34.20 N	118.00 W
Sangamner	148	19.34 N	74.13 E
Sang'angqu	132	29.15 N	96.59 E
Sanga Puitã	190	22.40 S	55.36 W
Sangar	128	63.55 N	127.31 E
Sangay, Volcán ∧1	184	2.00 S	78.20 W
Sangayán, Isla de I	184	13.51 S	76.28 W
Sangchungshih	136	25.04 N	121.29 E
Sangeang, Pulau I	142	8.12 S	119.04 E
Sanger	178	36.42 N	119.27 W
Sangerhausen	116	51.28 N	11.17 E
San Germán, Cuba	182	20.36 N	76.08 W
San Germán, P.R.	182	18.05 N	67.03 W
Sangerville	176	45.10 N	69.21 W
Sangganhe ≈	132	40.21 N	115.21 E
Sanggau	142	0.08 N	110.36 E
Sangha ≈	156	1.13 S	16.49 E
Sanghar	146	26.02 N	68.57 E
Sangihe, Kepulauan II	142	3.00 N	125.30 E
Sangihe, Pulau I	142	3.35 N	125.32 E
San Gil	184	6.33 N	73.08 W
San Giovanni in Fiore	122	39.16 N	16.42 E
San Giovanni in Persiceto	122	44.38 N	11.11 E
San Giovanni Rotondo	122	41.42 N	15.44 E
San Giovanni Valdarno	122	43.34 N	11.32 E
Sàngla	148	31.43 N	73.23 E
Sàngli	148	16.52 N	74.34 E
San Gorgonio Mountain ∧	178	34.06 N	116.50 W
San Gregorio, Passo del ✕	118	46.33 N	8.34 E
San Gregorio, Arg.	188	34.19 S	62.05 W
San Gregorio, Ur.	188	32.37 S	55.40 W
Sangre Grande	182	10.35 N	61.07 W
Sangrür	149	30.14 N	75.50 E
Sanibel Island I	182	26.27 N	82.06 W
San Ignacio, Arg.	182	27.15 S	55.30 W
San Ignacio, Bol.	184	16.23 S	60.59 W
San Ignacio, Bol.	184	14.53 S	65.36 W
San Ignacio, Hond.	182	14.38 N	87.02 W
San Ignacio, Méx.	180	32.45 N	106.25 W
San Ildefonso o La Granja	120	40.54 N	4.00 W
San Isidro, Arg.	188	34.29 S	58.31 W
San Isidro, Arg.	188	28.28 S	65.44 W
San Isidro, C.R.	182	9.22 N	83.42 W
San Jacinto, U.S.	182	9.50 N	75.08 W
San Jacinto, Calif., U.S.	178	33.47 N	116.57 W
San Jacinto Peak ∧	178	33.49 N	116.41 W
San Javier, Bol.	184	16.20 S	62.38 W
San Javier, Chile	184	16.20 S	62.38 W
San Javier, Chile	188	35.35 S	71.45 W
Sanjiang	140	25.42 N	109.23 E
Sanjiangying	136	32.18 N	119.42 E
Sanjō	134	37.37 N	138.57 E
San Joaquín	184	13.04 S	64.49 W
San Joaquín ≈	178	38.03 N	121.50 W
San Joaquín Valley V	178	36.50 N	120.10 W
San Jorge	184	31.54 S	61.50 W
San Jorge, Golfo C	186	46.00 S	66.50 W
San José, Arg.	188	27.45 S	55.45 W
San José, C.R.	182	9.56 N	84.05 W
San José, Pil.	138	12.27 N	121.03 E
San José, Pil.	138	15.48 N	120.59 E
San José, Isla I	180	25.00 N	110.38 W
San José de Chiquitos	184	17.51 S	60.47 W
San José de Feliciano	188	30.25 S	58.45 W
San José de Guanipa	182	8.54 N	64.09 W
San José de Guaribe	182	9.52 N	65.48 W
San José de las Lajas	182	22.58 N	82.09 W
San José del Cabo	180	23.03 N	109.41 W
San José del Guaviare	184	2.34 N	72.38 W
San José de Mayo	188	34.20 S	56.42 W
San José de Ocuné	184	4.09 N	70.20 W
San José de Río Chico	182	10.18 N	65.59 W
San José de Tiznados	182	9.23 N	67.30 W
San Juan, Arg.	188	31.30 S	68.30 W
San Juan, P.R.	182	18.28 N	66.07 W
San Juan □4	188	30.50 S	69.00 W
San Juan ≈, Arg.	188	32.20 S	67.25 W
San Juan ≈, N.A.	182	10.56 N	83.42 W
San Juan ≈, Rep. Dom.	182	18.40 N	71.05 W
San Juan ≈, U.S.	174	37.11 N	110.54 W
San Juan ≈, Ven.	182	10.14 N	62.38 W
San Juan, Embalse de ◙	120	40.30 N	4.15 W
San Juan, Pico ∧	182	21.59 N	80.08 W
San Juan Bautista, Para.	188	26.38 S	57.10 W
San Juan Bautista, Calif., U.S.	178	36.51 N	121.32 W
San Juan Creek ≈	178	35.40 N	120.22 W
San Juan de la Maguana]	182	18.48 N	71.14 W
San Juan del César	182	10.46 N	73.01 W
San Juan del Norte	182	10.56 N	83.42 W
San Juan del Norte, Bahía de C	182	11.15 N	83.45 W
San Juan de los Cayos	182	11.10 N	68.25 W
San Juan de los Morros	184	9.55 N	67.21 W
San Juan del Sur	182	11.15 N	85.52 W
San Juan Mountains ∧	174	37.35 N	107.10 W
San Juan Nepomuceno	182	9.57 N	75.05 W
San Julián	188	49.19 S	67.40 W
San Justo	188	30.47 S	60.35 W
Sankosh ≈	146	26.48 N	89.56 E
Sankt Gallen, Öst.	116	47.41 N	14.37 E
Sankt Gallen, Schw.	118	47.25 N	9.23 E
Sankt Gilgen	116	47.46 N	13.22 E
Sankt Ingbert	118	49.17 N	7.06 E
Sankt Johann in Tirol	116	47.31 N	12.26 E
Sankt Lorenz → Saint Lawrence ≈	172	49.15 N	67.00 W
Sankt Michel → Mikkeli	114	61.41 N	27.15 E
Sankt Moritz	118	46.30 N	9.50 E
Sankt Peter	116	54.18 N	8.38 E
Sankt Pölten	116	48.12 N	15.37 E
Sankt Valentin	116	48.10 N	14.32 E
Sankt Veit an der Glan	116	46.46 N	14.21 E
Sankuru ≈	156	4.17 S	20.25 E
San Lázaro, Cabo ⪫	180	24.50 N	112.18 W
San Leandro	178	37.43 N	122.09 W
San Lorenzo, Arg.	188	28.08 S	58.46 W
San Lorenzo, Arg.	188	32.45 S	60.44 W
San Lorenzo, Ec.	184	1.17 N	78.50 W
San Lorenzo, Nic.	182	12.06 N	86.34 W
San Lorenzo, Ven.	182	9.47 N	71.04 W
San Lorenzo, Isla I	184	12.06 S	77.14 W
San Lorenzo de El Escorial	120	40.35 N	4.09 W
San Lorenzo de la Parrilla	120	39.51 N	2.22 W
Sanlúcar de Barrameda	120	36.47 N	6.21 W
San Lucas	184	20.06 S	65.07 W
San Lucas, Cabo ⪫	180	22.50 N	109.55 W
San Luis, Arg.	188	33.18 S	66.20 W
San Luis, Cuba	182	20.12 N	75.51 W
San Luis, Guat.	180	16.14 N	89.27 W
San Luis, Ariz., U.S.	178	32.29 N	114.47 W
San Luis ≈	188	11.07 N	69.42 W
San Luis □4	188	34.00 S	66.00 W
San Luis, Lago de ◙	184	13.45 S	64.00 W
San Luis, Sierra de ∧	188	32.45 S	66.00 W
San Luis del Palmar	188	27.30 S	58.34 W
San Luis Obispo	178	35.17 N	120.40 W
San Luis Potosí	180	22.09 N	100.59 W
San Luis Reservoir ◙1	178	37.07 N	121.05 W
San Luis Rey ≈	178	33.12 N	117.24 W
San Luis Río Colorado	180	32.29 N	114.48 W
San Marcos, Chile	188	29.53 S	71.03 W
San Marcos, Tex., U.S.	174	29.53 N	97.57 W
San Marcos de Colón	182	13.26 N	86.48 W
San Marino	122	43.55 N	12.28 E
San Marino □1	122	43.56 N	12.25 E
San Martín, Arg.	188	33.10 S	68.25 W
San Martín, Col.	184	3.42 N	73.42 W
San Martín ≈	184	13.08 S	63.43 W
San Martín de los Andes	186	40.10 S	71.20 W
San Mateo, Calif., U.S.	178	37.35 N	122.19 W
San Mateo, Ven.	182	9.45 N	64.33 W
San Matías, Golfo C	186	41.30 S	64.20 W
Sanmen	136	29.06 N	121.24 E
Sanmenxia	132	34.45 N	111.05 E
San Miguel, Arg.	188	28.00 S	57.34 W
San Miguel, El Sal.	180	13.29 N	88.11 W
San Miguel, Calif., U.S.	178	35.45 N	120.42 W
San Miguel ≈	184	13.52 S	63.56 W
San Miguel del Monte	188	35.25 S	58.49 W
San Miguel de Tucumán	188	26.49 S	65.13 W
San Miguel Island I	178	34.02 N	120.22 W
Sanming, Zhg.	136	26.25 N	117.13 E
Sanming, Zhg.	136	26.14 N	117.36 E
San Miniato	122	43.41 N	10.51 E
Sannår	154	13.33 N	33.38 E
Sannicandro Garganico	122	41.50 N	15.34 E
San Nicolás de los Arroyos	188	33.20 S	60.13 W
San Nicolas Island I	178	33.15 N	119.31 W
Sanniehoé ≈	160	26.30 S	25.47 E
Sannikova, Proliv ⥙	128	74.30 N	140.00 E
Sanniquellie	152	7.22 N	8.43 W
Sano	134	36.19 N	139.35 E
Sanok	116	49.34 N	22.13 E
San Onofre	182	9.44 N	75.32 W
San Pablo, Punta ⪫	180	14.04 N	121.19 W
San Pablo Bay C	178	38.06 N	122.22 W
San Pedro, Arg.	188	33.40 S	59.41 W
San Pedro, Arg.	188	24.14 S	64.50 W
San Pedro, Chile	188	21.57 S	68.34 W
San Pedro, Chile	188	33.54 S	71.28 W
San Pedro, Col.	182	9.24 N	75.04 W
San Pedro ≈	188	24.07 S	56.59 W
San Pedro, Punta ⪫	188	24.15 S	56.30 W
San Pedro □5	188	25.30 S	57.38 W
San Pedro, Volcán ∧1	182	21.53 S	68.25 W
San Pedro Channel ⥙	178	33.35 N	118.25 W
San Pedro de Atacama	188	22.55 S	68.13 W
San Pedro de las Colonias	180	25.45 N	102.59 W
San Pedro de Macorís	182	18.27 N	69.18 W
San Pedro Mártir, Sierra ∧	180	30.45 N	115.13 W
San Pedro Sula	180	15.27 N	88.02 W
San Pelayo	182	8.58 N	75.51 W
Sanquhar	108	55.22 N	3.56 W
San Quintín, Cabo ⪫	180	30.21 N	116.00 W
San Rafael, Arg.	188	34.36 S	68.21 W
San Rafael, Chile	188	35.19 S	71.32 W
San Rafael, Calif., U.S.	178	37.59 N	122.31 W
San Rafael, Ven.	182	10.58 N	71.44 W
San Rafael de Arriba	182	31.05 N	116.05 W
San Rafael del Norte	182	13.11 N	86.06 W
San Ramón, Bol.	184	34.45 N	119.50 W
San Ramón, C.R.	182	13.17 S	64.43 W
San Ramón, Nic.	182	10.06 N	84.28 W
San Ramón, Bahía de C	180	12.55 N	85.50 W
San Ramón de la Nueva Orán	188	23.08 S	64.20 W
Sanrao	136	23.59 N	116.50 E
San Remo	122	43.49 N	7.46 E
San Román, Cabo ⪫	182	12.12 N	70.00 W
San Rosendo	188	37.16 S	72.43 W
San Salvador (Watling Island) I	182	24.00 N	74.30 W
San Salvador de Jujuy	188	24.10 S	65.20 W
Sansanné-Mango	152	10.21 N	0.28 E
San Sebastián	182	43.19 N	1.59 W
San Severo	122	41.41 N	15.23 E
Sansha	136	26.58 N	120.12 E
Sanshawan C	136	26.14 N	119.58 E
San Simon	184	13.26 N	80.46 W
Santa ≈	184	8.58 S	78.39 W
Santa Adélia	190	21.16 S	48.48 W
Santa Ana, Arg.	188	27.20 S	55.35 W
Santa Ana, Bol.	184	13.45 S	65.35 W
Santa Ana, Bol.	184	15.31 S	67.30 W
Santa Ana, Col.	182	9.19 N	74.35 W
Santa Ana, El Sal.	180	13.59 N	89.34 W
Santa Ana, Méx.	180	30.33 N	111.07 W
Santa Ana, Calif., U.S.	178	33.43 N	117.54 W
Santa Ana, Cuchilla de (Coxilha de Santana) ∧2	188	30.50 S	55.35 W
Santa Ana de Barcelona	182	9.19 N	64.39 W
Santa Bárbara, Chile	188	37.40 S	72.01 W
Santa Barbara, Méx.	186	26.48 N	105.49 W
Santa Barbara, Calif., U.S.	178	34.25 N	119.42 W
Santa Barbara, Sierra ∧	188	24.10 S	64.25 W
Santa Barbara Channel ⥙	178	34.15 N	119.55 W
Santa Bárbara do Sul	188	28.22 S	53.15 W
Santa Barbara Island I	178	33.28 N	119.02 W
Santa Catalina, Gulf of C	178	33.20 N	117.45 W
Santa Catalina de Armara	120	43.02 N	8.49 W
Santa Catalina Island I	178	33.23 N	118.26 W
Santa Catarina □3	178	31.37 N	115.48 W
Santa Catarina □3	188	27.00 S	50.00 W
Santa Catarina, Ilha de I	188	27.36 S	48.30 W
Santa Cecilio	188	26.56 S	50.27 W
Santa Clara, Cuba	182	22.24 N	79.58 W
Santa Clara, Calif., U.S.	178	37.21 N	121.57 W
Santa Clara ≈	178	38.14 N	119.16 W
Santa Clara, U.S.	188	33.00 S	80.00 W
Santa Comba Dão	120	40.24 N	8.08 W
Santa Cruz, Arg.	186	50.00 S	68.32 W
Santa Cruz, Bol.	184	17.48 S	63.10 W
Santa Cruz, Chile	188	34.38 S	71.22 W
Santa Cruz, C.R.	182	10.16 N	85.36 W
Santa Cruz, Esp.	88	28.41 N	17.45 W
Santa Cruz ≈	186	50.08 S	68.20 W
Santa Cruz Basin ⪫⁊1	96	13.00 S	163.00 E
Santa Cruz de la Zarza	120	39.58 N	3.10 W
Santa Cruz do Rio Pardo	190	22.55 S	49.37 W
Santa Cruz do Sul	188	29.43 S	52.26 W
Santa Cruz Island I	178	34.01 N	119.45 W
Santa Elena	188	31.00 S	59.50 W
Santa Elena, Cabo ⪫	182	10.59 N	85.57 W
Santa Eulalia del Río	120	38.59 N	1.31 E
Santa Fe, Arg.	188	31.40 S	60.40 W
Santa Fé, Bra.	190	23.01 S	51.48 W
Santa Fé, Cuba	182	21.45 N	82.45 W
Santa Fe, N. Mex., U.S.	174	35.42 N	106.57 W
Santa Fe □4	188	31.00 S	61.00 W
Santa Fe Baldy ∧	174	35.50 N	105.46 W
Santa Filomena	184	9.07 S	45.56 W
Santai	132	31.10 N	105.02 E
Santa Inés, Isla I	186	53.40 S	73.00 W
Santa Isabel, Arg.	188	36.14 S	66.54 W
Santa Isabel → Malabo, Gui. Ecu.	152	3.45 N	8.47 E
Santa Isabel I	162	8.00 S	159.00 E
Santa Isabel de las Lajas	182	22.25 N	80.18 W
Santa Juliana	190	19.19 S	47.32 W
Santa Lucía, Arg.	188	28.58 S	59.06 W
Santa Lucía, Cuba	182	21.02 N	76.00 W
Santa Lucía, Ur.	188	34.27 S	56.24 W
Santa Lucía Range ∧	178	36.00 N	121.20 W
Santa Luzia	120	37.44 N	8.24 W
Santa Luzia I	144	16.46 N	24.45 W
Santa Magdalena, Isla I	180	24.50 N	112.15 W
Santa Margarita ≈	178	35.23 N	120.37 W
Santa Margarita, Isla de I	180	24.25 N	111.50 W
Santa Margherita Ligure	122	44.20 N	9.12 E
Santa María, Arg.	188	26.40 S	66.02 W
Santa María, Bra.	188	29.41 S	53.48 W
Santa María, Calif., U.S.	178	34.57 N	120.26 W
Santa María ≈	188	36.58 N	25.06 W
Santa María ≈, Arg.	188	26.05 S	65.49 W
Santa María, Bra.	190	29.48 S	54.56 W
Santa María, Cabo de ⪫, Ang.	156	13.25 S	12.32 E
Santa María, Cabo de ⪫, Port.	120	36.58 N	7.54 W
Santa María, Cape ⪫	182	23.41 N	75.19 W
Santa María Capua Vetere	122	41.05 N	14.15 E
Santa María de Ipire	182	8.49 N	65.19 W
Santa María la Real de Nieva	120	41.04 N	4.24 W
Santa Marta	184	11.15 N	74.13 W
Santa Marta Grande, Cabo de ⪫	188	28.38 S	48.45 W
Santa Monica	178	34.01 N	118.30 W
Santa Monica Bay C	178	33.54 N	118.25 W
Santana	190	12.59 S	44.03 W
Santana, Coxilha de (Cuchilla de Santa Ana) ∧2	188	30.50 S	55.35 W
Santana da Boa Vista	188	30.52 S	53.07 W
Santana do Livramento	188	30.53 S	55.31 W
Santander, Esp.	120	43.28 N	3.48 W
Santander, Pil.	138	9.25 N	123.20 E
Santander, Norte de □4	182	8.00 N	73.00 W
Sant' Antioco	122	39.04 N	8.27 E
Santa Paula	184	34.21 N	119.04 W
Santa Pola, Cabo de ⪫	120	38.12 N	0.31 W
Santarém, Bra.	184	2.26 S	54.42 W
Santarém, Port.	120	39.14 N	8.41 W
Santa Rita, Ven.	182	10.32 N	71.32 W
Santa Rosa, Arg.	186	36.37 S	64.17 W
Santa Rosa, Bol.	184	10.36 S	67.20 W
Santa Rosa, Bra.	188	27.52 S	54.29 W
Santa Rosa, Ec.	184	3.27 S	79.58 W
Santa Rosa, Hond.	180	14.47 N	88.46 W
Santa Rosa, Méx.	178	31.50 N	116.45 W
Santa Rosa, Calif., U.S.	178	38.26 N	122.43 W
Santa Rosa de Río Primero	188	31.10 S	63.23 W
Santa Rosa Island I	178	33.58 N	120.06 W
Santa Rosalía, Méx.	180	27.19 N	112.17 W
Santa Rosalía, Ven.	182	9.02 N	69.01 W
Santa Rosa Range ∧	178	41.45 N	117.40 W
Santárskije Ostrova II	128	55.00 N	137.36 E
Santa Sylvina	182	27.50 S	61.10 W
Santa Teresa, Embalse de ◙1	120	40.40 N	5.30 W
Santa Teresa del Tuy	190	10.14 N	66.40 W
Santa Ynez ≈	178	34.37 N	120.36 W
Santee ≈	174	33.07 N	79.17 W
Santiago, Chile	188	33.27 S	70.40 W
Santiago, Pan.	182	8.06 N	80.59 W
Santiago ≈	184	4.27 S	77.38 W
Santiago de Compostela	120	42.53 N	8.33 W
Santiago de Cuba	182	20.01 N	75.49 W
Santiago del Estero	188	27.50 S	64.15 W
Santiago del Estero □4	188	27.40 S	63.15 W
Santiago [de los Caballeros]	182	19.27 N	70.42 W
Santiago Papasquiaro	180	25.03 N	105.25 W
Santiago Rodríguez	182	19.30 N	71.21 W
San Timoteo	182	9.48 N	71.04 W
Santípur	146	23.15 N	88.26 E
Santis ∧	118	47.15 N	9.21 E
Santisteban del Puerto	120	38.15 N	3.12 W
Santo Amaro	184	12.32 S	38.43 W
Santo Anastácio	190	21.58 S	51.39 W
Santo André	190	23.40 S	46.31 W
Santo Ângelo	188	28.18 S	54.16 W
Santo Antão I	152	17.05 N	25.10 W
Santo Antônio, Bra.	188	26.02 S	53.44 W
Santo Antônio, Bra.	188	29.50 S	50.32 W
Santo Antônio, S. Tom./P.	156	1.39 N	7.26 E
Santo Antônio de Jesus	190	12.58 S	39.16 W
Santo Antônio do Zaire	156	6.07 S	12.18 E
Santo Augusto	188	27.51 S	53.47 W
Santo Cristo	188	27.50 S	54.40 W
Santo Domingo, Nic.	182	12.16 N	84.59 W
Santo Domingo, Rep. Dom.	182	18.28 N	69.54 W
Santo Domingo, Arroyo ≈	178	30.43 N	116.02 W
Santo Domingo de la Calzada	120	42.26 N	2.57 W
Santo Estevão	120	12.26 S	39.13 W
Santo Tomé	182	40.47 N	0.19 W
Santos	190	23.57 S	46.20 W
Santos Dumont	190	21.28 S	43.34 W
Santo Tomás, Col.	182	10.46 N	74.45 W
Santo Tomás, Méx.	178	31.33 N	116.24 W
Santo Tomás, Nic.	182	12.06 N	85.04 W
Santo Tomás, Ven.	182	8.53 N	64.33 W
Santo Tomás, Punta ⪫	178	31.33 N	116.40 W
Santo Tomé, Arg.	188	31.34 N	116.42 W
Santo Tomé, Arg.	188	31.40 S	60.45 W
Santo Tomé, Arg.	188	28.35 S	56.05 W
Sanuki-sammyaku ∧	134	34.05 N	134.00 E
San Vicente, Chile	186	46.40 S	73.25 W
San Vicente, El Sal.	180	13.38 N	88.48 W
San Vicente, Méx.	178	31.20 N	116.15 W
San Vicente de Baracaldo	120	43.18 N	2.59 W
San Vicente de la Barquera	120	43.26 N	4.24 W
San Vicente del Caguán	184	2.07 N	74.46 W
San Vito dei Normanni	122	40.39 N	17.42 E
Sanyō	134	34.02 N	131.10 E
Sanyuan	132	34.35 N	108.54 E
Sanza Pombo	156	7.19 S	15.59 E
São Bento do Sul	188	26.15 S	49.23 W
São Borja	188	28.39 S	56.00 W
São Caetano do Sul	190	23.36 S	46.34 W
São Carlos, Bra.	188	27.04 S	52.59 W
São Carlos, Bra.	190	22.01 S	47.54 W
São Domingos	184	13.24 S	46.19 W
São Francisco	190	15.57 S	44.52 W
São Francisco ≈, Bra.	184	10.30 S	36.24 W
São Francisco ≈, Bra.	188	24.40 S	54.20 W
São Francisco, Baía de C	188	26.10 S	48.34 W
São Francisco de Assis	188	29.33 S	55.08 W
São Francisco de Paula	188	29.27 S	50.35 W
São Francisco do Sul	188	26.14 S	48.39 W
São Gabriel, Bra.	188	30.20 S	54.19 W
São Gabriel, Bra.	190	19.01 S	40.32 W
São Gonçalo do Sapucai	190	21.54 S	45.36 W
Sao Hill	158	8.20 S	35.12 E
São Jerônimo	188	29.58 S	51.43 W
São Jerônimo da Serra	190	23.43 S	50.44 W
São João da Barra	190	21.38 S	41.03 W
São João da Boa Vista	190	21.58 S	46.47 W
São João da Madeira	120	40.54 N	8.30 W
São João da Ponte	190	15.56 S	44.01 W
São João do Caiuá	190	22.43 S	52.17 W
São João do Triunfo	188	25.41 S	50.20 W
São Joaquim	188	28.18 S	49.56 W
São Joaquim da Barra	190	20.35 S	47.53 W
São Jorge	190	23.24 S	52.17 W
São Jorge I	88	38.38 N	28.00 W
São José do Cedro	188	26.30 S	53.30 W
São José do Norte	188	32.01 S	52.03 W
São José do Rio Prêto	190	20.48 S	49.23 W
São José dos Campos	190	23.11 S	45.53 W
São José dos Pinhais	188	25.31 S	49.13 W
São Leopoldo	188	29.46 S	51.09 W
São Lourenço d'Oeste	188	26.22 S	52.48 W
São Lourenço do Sul	188	31.22 S	51.58 W
São Luís	184	2.31 S	44.16 W
São Luís Gonzaga	188	28.24 S	54.58 W
São Manuel	190	22.44 S	48.34 W
São Mateus do Sul	188	25.52 S	50.23 W
São Miguel I	88	37.47 N	25.30 W
São Miguel d'Oeste	188	26.45 S	53.34 W
Saona, Isla I	182	18.10 N	68.40 W
Saône ≈	118	45.44 N	4.50 E
Saône-et-Loire □5	118	46.42 N	4.45 E
São Nicolau I	152	16.35 N	24.15 W
São Paulo	190	23.32 S	46.37 W
São Paulo □3	190	22.00 S	49.00 W
São Paulo de Olivença	184	3.22 S	68.52 W
São Pedro do Ivaí	190	23.51 S	51.51 W
São Pedro do Sul, Bra.	188	29.37 S	54.10 W
São Pedro do Sul, Port.	120	40.45 N	8.04 W
São Raimundo Nonato	184	9.01 S	42.42 W
São Romão	190	16.22 S	45.04 W
São Roque	190	23.32 S	47.08 W
São Roque, Cabo de ⪫	184	5.29 S	35.16 W
Saorre, Mount ∧	172	64.27 N	84.30 W
São Salvador do Congo	156	6.16 S	14.15 E
São Sebastião	190	23.48 S	45.25 W
São Sebastião, Ilha de I	190	23.50 S	45.18 W
São Sebastião, Ponta ⪫	160	22.07 S	35.30 E
São Sepé	188	30.10 S	53.34 W
São Tiago I	152	15.05 N	23.40 W
São Tomé	156	0.20 N	6.44 E
São Tomé I	156	0.12 N	6.39 E
São Tomé, Cabo de ⪫	190	21.59 S	40.59 W
São Tomé and Príncipe □1	156	1.00 N	7.00 E
São Vicente	190	23.58 S	46.23 W
São Vicente I	152	16.50 N	25.00 W
São Vicente, Cabo de ⪫	120	37.01 N	9.00 W
Sapé	184	7.06 S	35.13 W
Sapele	152	5.54 N	5.41 E
Saphwa ∧	158	15.57 S	35.38 E
Sapiranga	188	29.38 S	51.01 W
Sapporo	134a	43.03 N	141.21 E
Sapt Kosi ≈	146	26.31 N	86.58 E
Sapucaí ≈	190	22.00 S	45.54 W
Sapulpa	174	35.59 N	96.06 W
Sapuyán, Ciénega ⊜	182	10.08 N	74.45 W
Saqqar	158	5.20 S	35.30 E
Saráb	150	37.56 N	47.32 E
Saraburi	138	14.32 N	100.55 E
Saragosa → Zaragoza	120	41.38 N	0.53 W
Saraji	168	22.21 S	148.18 E
Sarajevo	122	43.52 N	18.25 E
Saraktaš	126	51.47 N	56.20 E
Saran'	126	49.48 N	72.52 E
Saranac	176	44.20 N	74.08 W
Saranac Lake	176	44.19 N	74.07 W
Sarandë	124	39.52 N	20.00 E
Sarandí	188	27.56 S	52.55 W
Sarangani Islands II	138	5.25 N	125.25 E
Sarangpur	146	23.34 N	76.28 E
Saransk	112	54.11 N	45.11 E
Sarapul	112	56.28 N	53.48 E
Sarare	182	9.47 N	69.10 W
Sarasota	174	27.20 N	82.32 W
Saratoga	178	37.16 N	122.02 W
Saratoga Springs	176	43.04 N	73.47 W
Saratov	112	51.34 N	46.02 E
Saratov □4	112	52.00 N	46.00 E
Saravan	140	15.43 N	106.25 E
Saray	124	41.26 N	27.55 E
Sarayakpınar	124	41.46 N	26.29 E
Sarayevo → Sarajevo	124	43.52 N	18.25 E
Sárbogárd	116	46.53 N	18.38 E
Sarcidano ⁼1	122	39.55 N	9.05 E
Sarclet	108	58.22 N	3.07 W
Sarda (Káli) ≈	146	27.22 N	81.23 E
Sardasht	154	25.46 N	10.34 E
Sardárshahr	146	28.26 N	74.29 E
Sardegna □4	122	40.00 N	9.00 E
Sardegna (Sardinia) I	122	40.00 N	9.00 E
Sardinia → Sardegna I	122	40.00 N	9.00 E
Sarektjåkkå ∧	112	67.25 N	17.46 E
Sar-e-Pol	150	36.14 N	65.55 E
Sargodha	149	32.05 N	72.40 E
Sarh	154	9.09 N	18.23 E
Sári	150	36.34 N	53.04 E
Sarigan I	162	16.42 N	145.47 E
Sarina	168	21.26 S	149.13 E
Sariwŏn	132	38.31 N	125.44 E
Sariyer	124	41.10 N	29.03 E
Sarja	112	58.24 N	45.30 E
Sark I	105b	49.26 N	2.21 W
Šarkóy	124	40.37 N	27.06 E
Sarlat-la-Canéda	118	44.53 N	1.13 E
Särmellék	116	46.42 N	17.10 E
Sarmi	166	1.51 S	138.44 E
Sarmiento	186	45.35 S	69.05 W
Sarmiento, Monte ∧	186	54.25 S	70.50 W
Särna	114	61.41 N	13.08 E
Särnena ∧	124	42.35 N	25.10 E
Sarnia	172	42.58 N	82.23 W
Sarno	122	40.49 N	14.37 E
Sarolangun	142	2.18 S	102.42 E
Saroma-ko ◙	134a	44.08 N	143.50 E
Saron	160	33.11 S	19.01 E
Saronikós Kólpos C	124	37.54 N	23.12 E
Saronno	122	45.38 N	9.02 E
Saros Körfezi C	124	40.30 N	26.15 E
Sárospatak	116	48.19 N	21.34 E
Sarralbe	118	48.59 N	7.01 E
Sarreguemines	118	49.06 N	7.03 E
Sartang ≈	128	67.44 N	133.12 E
Sartène	122	41.36 N	8.59 E
Sarthe □5	118	48.00 N	0.05 E
Sarthe ≈	118	47.30 N	0.32 W
Sartilly	118	48.45 N	1.27 W
Saru ≈	134a	42.30 N	142.00 E
Sarufutsu	134a	45.16 N	142.12 E
Sárvár	116	47.15 N	16.57 E
Saryarka ⁼1	126	49.00 N	72.00 E
Sarykol'skij Chrebet ∧	146	38.00 N	74.30 E
Saryözek	126	44.22 N	77.59 E
Sarysu ≈	126	45.12 N	66.36 E
Sary-Taš	126	39.44 N	73.15 E
Saryžaz ≈	126	42.42 N	80.25 E
Sarzana	122	44.07 N	9.58 E
Sasarām	146	24.57 N	84.02 E
Sasayama	134	35.04 N	135.13 E
Sásd	116	46.15 N	18.06 E
Sasebo	134	33.10 N	129.43 E
Saskatchewan □4	172	54.00 N	105.00 W
Saskatchewan ≈	172	53.12 N	99.16 W
Saskatoon	172	52.07 N	106.38 W
Saskylach	128	71.55 N	114.01 E
Sasolburg	160	26.48 S	27.45 E
Sasovo	112	54.21 N	41.54 E
Sassandra	152	4.58 N	6.05 W
Sassandra ≈	152	4.58 N	6.05 W
Sassari	122	40.44 N	8.33 E
Sassnitz	116	54.31 N	13.38 E
Sassuolo	122	44.33 N	10.47 E
Sastown	152	4.40 N	8.26 W
Sastre	188	31.45 S	61.50 W
Satakunta ⁼1	114	61.30 N	22.30 E
Sata-misaki ⪫	134	30.58 N	130.40 E
Satára, Bhārat	148	17.41 N	73.59 E
Satara, S. Afr.	160	24.29 S	31.47 E
Säter	114	60.21 N	15.45 E
Satka	126	55.03 N	59.01 E
Sátpura Range ∧	148	22.00 N	78.00 E
Satsuma-hantō ⪫	134	31.22 S	51.58 E
Satsuman-shotō II	135b	29.00 N	130.00 E
Sattahip	138	12.40 N	100.54 E
Satu Mare □5	124	47.40 N	23.00 E
Satun	138	6.37 N	100.04 E
Sauce	188	30.05 S	58.45 W
Saucillo	180	28.01 N	105.17 W
Sauda	114	59.39 N	6.22 E
Sauðárkrókur	112	65.45 N	19.38 W
Saudi Arabia □1	150	25.00 N	45.00 E
Sauerland ⁼1	118	51.10 N	8.00 E
Sauger ≈	176	48.01 N	89.06 W
Saugeries	176	42.05 N	73.57 W
Saül	184	3.37 N	53.12 W
Sauldre ≈	118	47.36 N	1.49 E
Sault Sainte Marie	172	46.31 N	84.20 W
Sault Ste. Marie	172	46.30 N	84.21 W
Saumarez Reef ⪫2	168	21.50 S	153.40 E
Saumâtre, Étang ◙	182	18.35 N	72.02 W
Saumon, Rivière au ≈	176	45.41 N	71.27 W
Saumur	118	47.16 N	0.05 W
Saunders Point ∧2	164	27.52 S	125.38 E
Saunderfoot	104	51.43 N	4.42 W
Saurimo (Henrique de Carvalho)	156	9.39 S	20.24 E
Sausalito	178	37.51 N	122.29 W
Sauveterre, Causse de ∧	118	44.20 N	3.10 E
Sauveterre-de-Béarn	118	43.24 N	0.56 W
Sauveterre-de-Guyenne	118	44.42 N	0.05 W
Sauwald ∧3	116	48.28 N	13.40 E
Sava ≈	124	44.50 N	20.26 E
Savage	176	47.27 N	104.20 W
Savai'i I	96	13.35 S	172.25 W
Savalen ◙	114	62.18 N	10.15 E
Savannah	174	32.04 N	81.05 W
Savannah ≈	174	32.02 N	80.53 W
Savannakhét	140	16.33 N	104.45 E
Savanna-la-Mar	182	18.13 N	78.08 W
Savé	152	8.02 N	2.29 E
Save ≈	118	44.07 N	1.09 E
Save (Sabi) ≈	160	21.00 S	35.02 E
Saveh	150	35.01 N	50.20 E
Savenay	118	47.22 N	1.57 W
Savernake Forest ∧3	104	51.23 N	1.37 W
Saverne	118	48.44 N	7.22 E
Savigliano	122	44.38 N	7.40 E
Savino	106	56.35 N	41.13 E
Savitaipale	114	61.12 N	27.42 E
Savoia ⁼1	118	45.30 N	6.25 E
Savolax ⁼1	114	62.30 N	27.45 E
Savona	122	44.18 N	8.29 E
Savonlinna	114	61.52 N	28.53 E
Savory Creek ≈	164	23.22 S	122.37 E
Savu Basin ⪫1	96	9.30 S	122.00 E
Savu Sea → Sawu, Laut ⪫2	142	9.40 S	122.00 E
Sawai Mádhopur	146	26.00 N	76.38 E
Sawankhalok	138	17.19 N	99.53 E
Sawara	134	35.53 N	140.30 E
Sawatch Mountains ∧	174	38.50 N	106.20 W
Sawbridgeworth	104	51.50 N	0.09 E
Sawda', Qurnat as- ∧	150	34.18 N	36.07 E
Sawel Mountain ∧	110	54.49 N	7.02 W
Sawhâj	154	26.33 N	31.42 E
Sawknah	154	29.04 N	15.47 E
Sawmills	158	19.31 S	28.02 E
Sawqarah, Dawhat C	144	18.35 N	57.15 E
Sawston	104	52.07 N	0.10 E
Sawtry	104	52.27 N	0.17 W
Sawu, Laut (Savu Sea) ⪫2	142	9.40 S	122.00 E
Sawu, Pulau I	142	10.30 S	121.54 E
Saxby ≈	168	18.25 S	140.53 E
Saxilby	106	53.17 N	0.40 W
Saxis	176	37.55 N	75.43 W
Saxmundham	104	52.13 N	1.29 E
Saxton	176	40.13 N	78.15 W
Sayaboury	132	19.15 N	101.45 E
Saya de Malha Bank ⁼4	94	10.30 S	61.00 E
Sayan Mountains (Sajany) ∧	126	52.45 N	96.00 E
Saydá (Sidon)	150	33.33 N	35.22 E
Sayhût	144	15.12 N	51.14 E
Sayre	176	41.59 N	76.32 W
Sayreville	176	40.28 N	74.21 W
Sayula	180	29.22 N	111.33 W
Say'ūn	144	15.56 N	48.47 E
Sazanit I	124	40.30 N	19.16 E
Sazlijka ≈	124	42.02 N	25.52 E
Sazonovo	106	59.04 N	35.14 E
Scaddan	164	33.27 S	121.43 E
Scaër	118	48.02 N	3.42 E
Scafell Pikes ∧	102	54.27 N	3.12 W
Scalasaig	108	56.04 N	6.11 W
Scalby	106	54.18 N	0.27 W
Scalloway	108a	60.08 N	1.18 W
Scalpay I, Scot., U.K.	108	57.17 N	5.59 W
Scalpay I, Scot., U.K.	108	57.52 N	6.40 W
Scapa Flow C	108	58.55 N	3.06 W
Scapegoat Mountain ∧	174	47.19 N	112.50 W
Ščapino	128	55.19 N	159.25 E
Scarba I	108	56.11 N	5.43 W
Scarborough, Trin.	182	11.11 N	60.44 W
Scarborough, Eng., U.K.	106	54.17 N	0.24 W
Scarborough Shoal ⁼1	96	15.08 N	117.46 E
Scardroy	108	57.31 N	4.59 W
Scargill	170	42.56 S	172.57 E
Scarinish	108	56.29 N	6.48 W
Scarp I	108	58.02 N	7.08 W
Scartaglin	110	52.10 N	9.26 W
Scavaig, Loch C	108	57.09 N	6.10 W
Scawfell Island I	168	20.52 S	149.36 E
Sceale Bay	164	33.01 S	134.12 E
Scelfjajur	112	65.21 N	53.21 E
Ščelkovo	130	55.55 N	160.30 E
Ščerbakovo	128	65.15 N	160.30 E
Ščerbinka	130	55.31 N	160.31 E
Schaffhausen	118	47.42 N	8.38 E
Schefferville	172	54.48 N	66.50 W
Schelde (Escaut) ≈	116	51.22 N	4.15 E
Schell Creek Range ∧	178	39.10 N	114.40 W
Schenectady	176	42.48 N	73.53 W
Schenevus Creek ≈	176	42.29 N	74.59 W
Schesslitz	116	49.59 N	11.01 E
Schichallion ∧	108	56.40 N	4.06 W
Schiedam	116	51.55 N	4.24 E
Schiermonnikoog I	116	53.28 N	6.15 E
Schiltigheim	118	48.36 N	7.45 E
Schio	122	45.43 N	11.21 E
Schjetman Reef ⪫2	96	15.10 N	178.40 W
Schkeuditz	116	51.24 N	12.13 E
Schladming	116	47.23 N	13.41 E
Schleswig	116	54.31 N	9.33 E
Schleswig-Holstein □3	116	54.00 N	10.30 E
Schlitz	116	50.40 N	9.33 E
Schlüchtern	116	50.20 N	9.31 E
Schmalkalden	116	50.43 N	10.26 E
Schmidmühlen	116	49.16 N	11.56 E
Schmölln	116	50.53 N	12.20 E
Schneeberg	116	50.36 N	12.38 E
Schodn'a	130	55.57 N	37.18 E
Schoharie	176	42.40 N	74.19 W
Schoharie Creek ≈	176	42.57 N	74.18 W
Schönebeck	116	51.55 N	4.24 E
Schongau	116	53.34 N	13.34 E
Schorndorf	116	48.48 N	9.32 E
Schouten Island I	168	42.19 S	148.17 E
Schouwen I	116	51.43 N	3.50 E
Schramberg	116	48.13 N	8.23 E
Schreiber	172	48.48 N	87.15 W
Schrobenhausen	116	48.33 N	11.17 E
Schroon ≈	176	43.49 N	73.49 W
Schroon Lake	176	43.48 N	73.46 W
Schull	110	51.31 N	9.33 W
Schultz Lake ◙	172	64.45 N	97.30 W
Schuyli I	172	64.45 N	97.30 W
Schuylkill Haven	176	40.37 N	76.10 W
Schwaben ⁼9	116	48.20 N	10.30 E
Schwabach	116	49.20 N	11.01 E
Schwäbisch Gmünd	116	48.48 N	9.48 E
Schwäbisch Hall	116	49.06 N	9.45 E
Schwandorf in Bayern	116	49.20 N	12.07 E
Schwaner, Pegunungan ∧	142	0.40 S	112.40 E
Schwarzach im Pongau	116	47.19 N	13.09 E
Schwarze Elster ≈	116	51.45 N	12.50 E
Schwarzenberg	116	50.32 N	12.47 E
Schwarzwald ∧	116	48.00 N	8.15 E
Schwaz	116	47.20 N	11.43 E
Schwechat	116	48.09 N	16.29 E
Schwedt	116	53.04 N	14.17 E
Schweinfurt → Świdnica	116	50.51 N	16.29 E
Schweinfurt	116	50.03 N	10.14 E
Schweizer-Reneke	160	27.11 S	25.18 E
Schwenningen	116	48.03 N	8.32 E
Schwerin	116	53.38 N	11.23 E
Schwerin □5	116	53.30 N	11.33 E
Schweriner See ◙	116	53.45 N	11.28 E
Schwetzingen	116	49.22 N	8.34 E
Schwyz	118	47.02 N	8.40 E
Sciacca	122	37.30 N	13.06 E
Scicli	122	36.47 N	14.43 E
Scilly, Isles of II	104a	49.56 N	6.22 W
Scio	176	40.24 N	81.05 W
Sciota	176	40.58 N	75.20 W
Ščokino	106	54.01 N	37.31 E
Scole	104	52.22 N	1.10 E
Scone	168	32.05 S	150.52 E
Scordia	122	37.18 N	14.51 E
Scotia Ridge ⥙3	87	60.00 S	50.00 W
Scotland □8	102	57.00 N	4.00 W
Scott ≈	172	55.55 N	65.20 W
Scott, Mount ∧	178	42.56 N	122.01 W
Scottburgh	160	30.17 S	30.45 E
Scottdale	176	40.06 N	79.35 W
Scott Glacier ⇓	87	66.15 S	100.05 E
Scott Islands II	172	50.48 N	128.40 W
Scottsbluff	174	41.52 N	103.40 W
Scottsdale, Austl.	168	41.10 S	147.31 E
Scottsdale, Ariz., U.S.	174	33.30 N	111.55 W
Scourie	108	58.20 N	5.09 W
Scramlo	124	41.24 N	25.04 E
Scranton	176	41.24 N	75.39 W
Screw ≈	166	3.55 S	142.50 E
Scridain, Loch C	108	56.21 N	6.08 W
Ščrocoby	106	56.21 N	46.00 E
Ščucinsk	126	52.56 N	70.12 E
Scunthorpe	106	53.36 N	0.38 W
Scurrival Point ⪫	108	57.04 N	7.18 W
Scutari → Shkodër	124	42.05 N	19.30 E
Seaford, Eng., U.K.	104	50.46 N	0.06 E
Seaford, Del., U.S.	176	38.38 N	75.36 W
Seaforth	176	43.33 N	81.24 W
Seaforth, Loch C	108	57.52 N	6.40 W
Seafox Seamount ⪫3	96	30.30 S	172.40 W
Seaham	106	54.52 N	1.21 W
Seahorse Point ⪫	172	63.47 N	80.09 W

Name	Page	Lat°′	Long°′
Seahorse Shoal ✧[2]	142	5.30 N	112.37 E
Seahouses	106	55.35 N	1.38 W
Sea Islands II	174	31.20 N	81.20 W
Sea Isle City	176	39.09 N	74.42 W
Seal ≃	172	59.04 N	94.48 W
Sea Lake	168	35.30 S	142.51 E
Seal Bay C	87	71.40 S	12.25 W
Seal Cove	176	44.39 N	66.51 W
Seal Harbor	176	44.18 N	68.14 W
Seal Lake ⊜	172	54.18 N	61.40 W
Seara	188	27.07 S	52.17 W
Searchlight	178	35.28 N	114.55 W
Searcy	174	35.15 N	91.44 W
Searles Lake ⊜	178	35.43 N	117.20 W
Searsport	176	44.28 N	68.56 W
Seascale	106	54.24 N	3.29 W
Seaside	178	36.37 N	121.50 W
Seaside Park	176	39.55 N	74.05 W
Seaton, Eng., U.K.	104	50.43 N	3.05 W
Seaton, Eng., U.K.	106	54.41 N	3.33 W
Seaton, Eng., U.K.	106	53.54 N	0.14 W
Seaton ≃	104	50.22 N	4.22 W
Seaton Delaval	106	55.04 N	1.31 W
Seattle	174	47.36 N	122.20 W
Seaward Kaikoura Range ⋀	170	42.14 S	173.39 E
Sébaco	182	12.51 N	86.06 W
Sebago Lake ⊜	176	43.50 N	70.35 W
Šebalino	128	51.17 N	85.40 E
Sebastian, Cape ≻	178	42.19 N	124.26 W
Sebastián Vizcaíno, Bahía C	180	28.00 N	114.30 W
Sebastopol	178	38.24 N	122.49 W
Sebatik, Pulau I	142	4.08 N	117.47 E
Sebec Lake ⊜	176	45.18 N	69.18 W
Sebei □[5]	158	1.25 N	34.25 E
Seberi	188	27.29 S	53.24 W
Sebeș	124	45.58 N	23.34 E
Sebes Körös (Crișu Repede) ≃	124	46.55 N	20.59 E
Sebewaing	176	43.44 N	83.27 W
Sebnitz	116	50.58 N	14.16 E
Sebring	176	40.55 N	81.02 W
Sechura, Bahía de C	184	5.35 S	81.00 W
Seco, Arroyo ≃	178	36.25 N	121.20 W
Séd ≃	116	47.00 N	18.31 E
Seda	132	32.20 N	100.41 E
Sedalia	174	38.42 N	93.14 W
Sedan, Austl.	168	34.35 S	139.18 E
Sedan, Fr.	118	49.42 N	4.57 E
Sedano	120	42.43 N	3.45 W
Sedayu	142	6.59 S	112.33 E
Sedbergh	106	54.20 N	2.31 W
Seddon	170	41.40 S	174.05 E
Sedel'nikovo	128	56.57 N	75.18 E
Sederberge ⋀	160	32.23 S	19.20 E
Séderon	118	44.12 N	5.32 E
Sedgefield	106	54.39 N	1.26 W
Sedgley	104	52.33 N	2.08 W
Sedgwick	176	44.18 N	68.37 W
Sedrata	122	36.08 N	7.32 E
Seefeld in Tirol	116	47.20 N	11.11 E
Seeheim	160	26.50 S	17.45 E
Seelow	116	52.32 N	14.23 E
Seemore Downs	164	30.42 S	125.15 E
Sefton	170	43.15 S	172.40 E
Segama ≃	142	5.27 N	118.48 E
Segamat	142	2.30 N	102.49 E
Segeža	112	63.44 N	34.19 E
Segorbe	120	39.51 N	0.29 W
Ségou	152	13.27 N	6.16 W
Segovia	120	40.57 N	4.07 W
Segré	118	47.41 N	0.53 W
Séguédine	152	20.12 N	12.59 E
Segura	120	39.50 N	6.59 W
Segura, Sierra de ⋀	120	38.00 N	2.43 W
Sehore	146	23.12 N	77.05 E
Seil I	108	56.18 N	5.39 W
Seiland I	112	70.25 N	23.15 E
Sein, Île de I	118	48.02 N	4.51 W
Seinäjoki	114	62.47 N	22.50 E
Seine ≃, Ont., Can.	172	48.40 N	92.49 W
Seine ≃, Fr.	118	49.26 N	0.26 E
Seine, Baie de la ≃	118	49.30 N	0.30 W
Seine-et-Marne □[5]	118	48.30 N	3.00 E
Seine-Maritime □[5]	118	49.45 N	1.00 E
Seixal	120	38.38 N	9.06 W
Sejm ≃	126	51.27 N	32.34 E
Sejmčan	128	62.53 N	152.26 E
Seki, Nihon	134	35.29 N	136.55 E
Šeki (Nucha), S.S.S.R.	126	41.12 N	47.12 E
Sekondi-Takoradi	152	4.59 N	1.43 W
Šelagskij, Mys ≻	128	70.06 N	170.26 E
Selama	142	5.13 N	100.42 E
Selaru, Pulau I	166	8.09 S	131.00 E
Selatan, Tanjung ≻	142	4.10 S	114.38 E
Selatpanjang	142	1.00 N	102.43 E
Selayar, Pulau I	142	6.05 S	120.30 E
Selb	116	50.10 N	12.08 E
Selborne	104	51.06 N	0.56 W
Selbusjøen ⊜	114	63.14 N	10.54 E
Selby	106	53.48 N	1.04 W
Selbyville	176	38.28 N	75.13 W
Selemdža ≃	128	51.42 N	128.53 E
Selenga (Selenge Mörön) ≃	128	52.16 N	106.16 E
Selenge Mörön (Selenga) ≃	128	52.16 N	106.16 E
Selenicë	124	40.32 N	19.38 E
Selenn'ach ≃	128	67.48 N	144.54 E
Sélestat	118	48.16 N	7.27 E
Seletyteniz, Ozero ⊜	126	53.15 N	73.15 E
Selfoss	112a	63.56 N	20.57 W
Sélibaby	152	15.10 N	12.11 W
Šelichova, Zaliv C	128	60.00 N	158.00 E
Seliger, Ozero ⊜	130	57.13 N	33.05 E
Selinsgrove	176	40.48 N	76.52 W
Selišče	130	56.53 N	33.16 E
Selkämeri (Bottenhavet) C	114	62.00 N	20.00 E
Selkirk, Man., Can.	172	50.09 N	96.52 W
Selkirk, Scot., U.K.	108	55.33 N	2.50 W
Selkirk Mountains ⋀	172	51.00 N	117.40 W
Selly Oak •[8]	104	52.25 N	1.52 W
Selma, Ala., U.S.	174	32.25 N	87.01 W
Selma, Calif., U.S.	178	36.34 N	119.37 W
Selsey	104	50.44 N	0.48 W
Selsey Bill ≻	104	50.43 N	0.48 W
Selston	104	53.04 N	1.20 W
Selu, Pulau I	166	7.32 S	130.54 E
Selukwe	158	19.40 S	30.00 E
Selva	188	29.50 S	62.02 W
Selvas •[3]	184	5.00 S	68.00 W
Selwyn	168	21.32 S	140.30 E
Selwyn Lake ⊜	172	59.55 N	104.35 W
Selwyn Mountains ⋀	172	63.10 N	130.20 W
Selwyn Range ⋀	168	21.35 S	140.35 E
Šemacha	150	40.38 N	48.39 E
Seman ≃	124	40.56 N	19.24 E
Semara	152	26.44 N	14.41 W
Semarang	142	6.58 S	110.25 E
Semau, Pulau I	142	10.13 S	123.22 E
Semenic, Munții ⋀	124	45.05 N	22.05 E
Semeru, Gunung ∧	142	8.06 S	112.55 E
Semibratovo	130	57.18 N	39.32 E
Seminole, Lake ⊜[1]	174	30.46 N	84.50 W
Semipalatinsk	128	50.28 N	80.13 E
Semitau	142	0.33 N	111.58 E
Semliki ≃	158	1.14 N	30.28 E
Semnān	150	35.33 N	53.24 E
Šemonaicha	128	50.39 N	81.54 E
Sem'onov	112	56.48 N	44.30 E
Semporna	138	4.28 N	118.36 E
Sena	158	17.27 S	35.00 E
Senador Pompeu	184	5.35 S	39.22 W
Senanga	156	16.06 S	23.16 E
Sendai, Nihon	134	31.49 N	130.18 E
Sendai, Nihon	134	38.15 N	140.53 E
Sendai ≃	134	31.51 N	130.12 E
Sendai-heiya ≚	134	38.15 N	141.00 E
Sendai-wan C	134	38.18 N	141.18 E
Seneca, Mount ∧	176	42.01 N	78.49 W
Seneca Falls	176	42.55 N	76.48 W
Seneca Lake ⊜	176	42.40 N	76.57 W
Senecaville Lake ⊜[1]	176	39.55 N	81.25 W
Senegal (Sénégal) □[1]	152	14.00 N	14.00 W
Sénégal ≃	152	15.48 N	16.32 W
Senekal, S. Afr.	156	26.16 S	25.06 E
Senekal, S. Afr.	160	28.30 S	27.32 E
Senetosa, Punta di ≻	122	41.33 N	8.47 E
Senftenberg	116	51.31 N	14.00 E
Senga Hill	158	9.22 S	31.12 E
Sengés	190	24.06 S	49.29 W
Senghenydd	104	51.36 N	3.16 W
Sengilej	112	53.58 N	48.46 E
Sengwa ≃	158	17.07 S	28.05 E
Senhor do Bonfim	184	10.27 S	40.11 W
Senica	116	48.41 N	17.22 E
Senigallia	122	43.43 N	13.13 E
Senj	122	44.59 N	14.54 E
Senja I	112	69.20 N	17.30 E
Senkobo	158	17.38 S	25.58 E
Šenkursk	112	62.08 N	42.53 E
Senlis	118	49.12 N	2.35 E
Senmonorom	140	12.27 N	107.12 E
Sennen	104	50.04 N	5.42 W
Sennestadt	116	51.59 N	8.37 E
Senneterre	172	48.23 N	77.15 W
Sennokura-yama ∧	134	36.49 N	138.50 E
Sennybridge	104	51.57 N	3.34 W
Sens	118	48.12 N	3.17 E
Senta	124	45.56 N	20.04 E
Sentinel Range ⋀	87	78.10 S	85.30 W
Senyavin Islands II	96	6.55 N	158.00 E
Senza	158	3.02 N	26.19 E
Seo de Urgel	120	42.21 N	1.28 E
Seoni	148	22.05 N	79.32 E
Seoul → Sŏul	132	37.33 N	126.58 E
Sepik ≃	166	3.51 S	144.34 E
Sept-Îles (Seven Islands)	172	50.12 N	66.23 W
Sepúlveda	120	41.18 N	3.45 W
Sequeros	120	40.31 N	6.01 W
Serafimovič	126	49.36 N	42.43 E
Seraing	116	50.36 N	5.29 E
Seram (Ceram) I	166	3.00 S	129.00 E
Seram, Laut (Ceram Sea) ⊤[2]	138	2.30 S	128.00 E
Seram, Laut (Ceram Sea) ⊤[2], Indon.	166	2.30 S	128.00 E
Serang	142	6.07 S	106.09 E
Serdobsk	126	52.28 N	44.13 E
Sered'	116	48.17 N	17.44 E
Seremban	142	2.43 N	101.56 E
Serengeti Plain ≚	158	2.50 S	35.00 E
Serenje	158	13.15 S	30.14 E
Sergač	112	55.32 N	45.28 E
Sergeja Kirova, Ostrova II	128	77.12 N	89.30 E
Sergejevka	128	43.21 N	133.22 E
Sergen	124	41.42 N	27.42 E
Seria	142	4.39 N	114.23 E
Serian	142	1.10 N	110.34 E
Sérifos I	124	37.11 N	24.31 E
Sérigny ≃	172	56.47 N	66.00 W
Seringapatam	144	12.25 N	76.42 E
Šerlovaja Gora	128	50.34 N	116.15 E
Sermata, Pulau I	138	8.10 S	128.40 E
Serodino	188	32.37 S	60.57 W
Serov	126	59.29 N	60.31 E
Serowe	160	22.25 S	26.44 E
Serpentine Lakes ⊜	164	28.32 S	129.09 E
Serpuchov	130	54.55 N	37.25 E
Serra do Salitre	190	19.06 S	46.41 W
Sérrai	124	41.05 N	23.32 E
Serrana	190	21.14 S	47.36 W
Serrana Bank ✧[4]	182	14.23 N	80.12 W
Serrania	190	21.33 S	46.03 W
Serranilla Bank ✧[4]	182	15.50 N	79.50 W
Serres	118	44.26 N	5.43 E
Serrezuela	188	30.40 S	65.20 W
Serrières	118	45.19 N	4.45 E
Sêrro	190	18.37 S	43.23 W
Sertaneja	190	23.03 S	50.50 W
Serua, Pulau I	166	6.18 S	130.01 E
Serui	166	1.53 S	136.14 E
Sérvia	124	40.11 N	22.00 E
Servi Burnu ≻	124	41.40 N	28.06 E
Sesayap ≃	142	3.36 N	117.15 E
Sesfontein	160	19.07 S	13.39 E
Sesheke	156	17.19 S	24.18 E
Sespe Creek ≃	178	34.23 N	118.57 W
Sessa Aurunca	122	41.14 N	13.56 E
Sestao	120	43.18 N	3.00 W
Sestri Levante	122	44.16 N	9.24 E
Šešupe ≃	130	55.30 N	22.12 E
Setana	134a	42.26 N	139.51 E
Sète	118	43.24 N	3.41 E
Sete Barras	188	24.23 S	47.55 W
Sete Lagoas	190	19.27 S	44.14 W
Setentrional, Cordillera ⋀	182	19.40 N	70.45 W
Sete Quedas, Salto das (Salto del Guairá) ↳	188	24.02 S	54.16 W
Setesdal V	114	59.25 N	7.25 E
Sétif	152	36.09 N	5.26 E
Seto	134	35.14 N	137.06 E
Seto-naikai ⊤[2]	134	34.20 N	133.30 E
Setouchi	135b	28.10 N	129.15 E
Settat	152	33.04 N	7.37 W
Sette Cama	156	2.32 S	9.45 E
Sette-Daban, Chrebet ⋀	128	62.00 N	138.00 E
Settle	106	54.04 N	2.16 W
Settlers	160	25.02 S	28.30 E
Setúbal	120	38.32 N	8.54 W
Setúbal, Baía de C	120	38.27 N	8.53 W
Seul, Lac ⊜	172	50.20 N	92.30 W
Seul Choix Point ≻	176	45.56 N	85.52 W
Sevagram	144	20.45 N	78.30 E
Sevan, Ozero ⊜	150	40.20 N	45.20 E
Sevastopol'	126	44.36 N	33.32 E
Ševčenko	126	43.35 N	51.05 E
Seven ≃	106	54.11 N	0.52 W
Seven Islands → Sept-Îles	172	50.12 N	66.23 W
Sevenmile Creek ≃	176	39.28 N	84.33 W
Sevenoaks	104	51.16 N	0.12 E
Seven Sisters	104	51.46 N	3.43 W
Sévérac-le-château	118	44.19 N	3.04 E
Severn ≃, Ont., Can.	172	56.02 N	87.36 W
Severn ≃, Eng., U.K.	102	51.35 N	2.40 W
Severn, Mouth of the ≃	104	51.25 N	3.00 W
Severnaja Dvina ≃	112	64.32 N	40.30 E
Severnaja Sos'va ≃	126	64.10 N	65.28 E
Severnaja Zeml'a II	128	79.30 N	98.00 E
Severna Park	176	39.04 N	76.33 W
Severnyje Uvaly ⋀[2]	112	59.30 N	49.00 E
Severočeský Kraj □[4]	118	50.35 N	14.15 E
Severodvinsk	112	64.34 N	39.50 E
Severo-Jenisejskij	128	60.22 N	93.01 E
Severo-Kuril'sk	128	50.40 N	156.08 E
Severomoravský Kraj □[4]	116	49.45 N	17.50 E
Severomorsk	112	69.05 N	33.24 E
Severo-Sibirskaja Nizmennost' ≚	128	73.00 N	100.00 E
Severoural'sk	126	60.09 N	59.57 E
Severo-Zadonsk	130	54.00 N	38.23 E
Severskij Donec ≃	126	48.20 N	40.15 E
Sevettijärvi	112	69.26 N	28.38 E
Sevier ≃	174	39.04 N	113.06 W
Sevier Lake ⊜	174	38.55 N	113.09 W
Sevilla, Col.	184	4.16 N	75.57 W
Sevilla, Esp.	120	37.23 N	5.59 W
Seville → Sevilla, Esp.	120	37.23 N	5.59 W
Seville, Ohio, U.S.	176	41.01 N	81.52 W
Sevlievo	124	43.01 N	25.06 E
Seward, Alaska, U.S.	172	60.06 N	149.26 W
Seward, Nebr., U.S.	174	40.55 N	97.06 W
Seward, Pa., U.S.	176	40.25 N	79.01 W
Sewell	188	34.05 S	70.23 W
Seychelles □[1]	156	4.53 S	55.40 E
Seychelles-Mauritius Ridge ✧[3]	94	14.00 S	61.00 E
Seyðisfjörður	112a	65.16 N	14.00 W
Seymour, Austl.	168	37.02 S	145.08 E
Seymour, S. Afr.	160	32.33 S	26.46 E
Seymour, Conn., U.S.	176	41.24 N	73.04 W
Seyne	118	44.21 N	6.21 E
Seyssel	118	45.57 N	5.49 E
Sézanne	118	48.43 N	3.43 E
Sezela	160	30.24 S	30.42 E
Sfax	152	34.44 N	10.46 E
Sfîntu-Gheorghe	124	45.52 N	25.47 E
Sfîntu Gheorghe, Brațul ≃[1]	124	44.53 N	29.36 E
Sfîntu Gheorghe, Ostrovul I	124	45.07 N	29.22 E
's-Gravenhage (The Hague)	116	52.06 N	4.18 E
Sgritheall, Beinn ∧	108	57.08 N	5.35 W
Shaba □[4]	158	8.00 S	27.00 E
Shabani	158	20.20 S	30.02 E
Shabqadar	149	34.13 N	71.34 E
Shackleton Glacier ⊽	87	84.35 S	176.15 W
Shackleton Ice Shelf ⊽	87	66.00 S	100.00 E
Shackleton Range ⋀	87	80.40 S	26.00 W
Shady Cove	178	42.37 N	122.49 W
Shadyside	176	39.58 N	80.45 W
Shafter	178	29.49 N	104.18 W
Shaftesbury	104	51.01 N	2.12 W
Shagou	136	33.09 N	119.45 E
Shag Rocks II[1]	186	53.33 S	42.02 W
Shāhābād	149	30.10 N	76.53 E
Shah Alam	142	3.00 N	101.33 E
Shahdād, Namakzār-e ≚	144	30.30 N	58.30 E
Shāhdādkot	146	27.51 N	67.54 E
Shāhdādpur	146	25.56 N	68.37 E
Shāhdara	149	31.38 N	74.18 E
Shahdol	146	23.20 N	81.21 E
Shahe	132	40.08 N	116.15 E
Shāhī	150	36.28 N	52.53 E
Shāhjahānpur	146	27.53 N	79.55 E
Shāh Kot	149	31.34 N	73.29 E
Shāhpūr	150	38.11 N	44.47 E
Shāhpura	146	25.38 N	74.56 E
Shahreẕā	150	32.01 N	51.52 E
Shāhrūd	150	36.25 N	55.01 E
Shahsavār	150	36.49 N	50.53 E
Shā'ib al-Banāt, Jabal ∧	150	26.59 N	33.29 E
Shakawe	160	18.23 S	21.50 E
Shaker Heights	176	41.29 N	81.36 W
Shaki	152	8.39 N	3.25 E
Shākir, Jazīrat I	150	27.30 N	33.59 E
Shakotan-hantō ≻[1]	134a	43.20 N	140.30 E
Shala, Lake ⊜	154	7.35 N	38.30 E
Shalatayn, Bi'r ⊤[4]	150	23.08 N	35.36 E
Shaler Mountains ⋀	172	72.35 N	110.45 W
Shām, Bādiyat ash- •[2]	150	32.00 N	40.00 E
Shām, Jabal ash- ∧	150	23.13 N	57.16 E
Shamattawa	172	55.52 N	92.05 W
Shāmli	149	29.27 N	77.19 E
Shamo, Lake ⊜	154	5.49 N	37.35 E
Shamokin	176	40.47 N	76.34 W
Shamva	158	17.18 S	31.34 E
Shan □[3]	140	22.00 N	98.00 E
Shandī	154	16.42 N	33.26 E
Shandong □[4]	132	36.00 N	118.00 E
Shandongbandao ≻[1]	132	37.00 N	121.00 E
Shangani	158	19.47 S	29.22 E
Shangani ≃	158	18.41 S	27.10 E
Shangcai	136	33.16 N	114.15 E
Shangcheng	136	31.48 N	115.24 E
Shangdian	136	34.07 N	112.23 E
Shanggan	136	25.56 N	119.22 E
Shanggang	136	33.30 N	120.04 E
Shanggao	136	28.18 N	114.54 E
Shanghai, Zhg.	136	31.01 N	121.25 E
Shanghai, Zhg.	136	31.14 N	121.28 E
Shanghai Shih □[7]	136	31.10 N	121.30 E
Shanghang	136	25.06 N	116.25 E
Shangqiu, Zhg.	136	34.23 N	115.37 E
Shangqiu, Zhg.	136	34.27 N	115.42 E
Shangrao	136	28.26 N	117.58 E
Shangshui	136	33.39 N	114.39 E
Shangsi	140	22.09 N	107.57 E
Shangxian	132	33.51 N	109.54 E
Shangyou	136	25.51 N	114.30 E
Shangyu	136	30.02 N	120.54 E
Shangzhi	132	45.13 N	127.59 E
Shanhaiguan	132	40.01 N	119.44 E
Shanhe	132	33.38 N	79.50 E
Shanjiang	136	27.32 N	115.08 E
Shanklin	104	50.38 N	1.10 W
Shannon, N.Z.	170	40.33 S	175.25 E
Shannon, S. Afr.	160	29.08 S	26.18 E
Shannon ≃	110	52.36 N	9.41 W
Shannon, Mouth of the ≃[1]	110	52.30 N	9.50 W
Shannon Airport ⊠	110	52.41 N	8.55 W
Shansi → Shānxī □[4]	132	37.00 N	112.00 E
Shantou (Swatow)	136	23.23 N	116.41 E
Shantung Peninsula → Shandongbandao ≻[1]	132	37.00 N	121.00 E
Shǎnxī □[4], Zhg.	132	35.00 N	109.00 E
Shānxī □[4], Zhg.	132	37.00 N	112.00 E
Shanyin	132	39.35 N	112.58 E
Shaobo	136	32.30 N	119.32 E
Shaoguan	136	24.50 N	113.37 E
Shaowu	136	27.20 N	117.28 E
Shaoxing	136	30.00 N	120.35 E
Shaoyang	132	27.06 N	111.25 E
Shap	106	54.32 N	2.41 W
Shapinsay I	108	59.03 N	2.53 W
Sharbatāt, Ra's ash- ≻	144	17.52 N	56.22 E
Sharbot Lake	176	44.46 N	76.41 W
Shari	134a	43.55 N	144.50 E
Shari-dake ∧	134a	43.46 N	144.43 E
Shark Bay C	164	25.30 S	113.30 E
Sharktooth Mountain ∧	172	58.35 N	127.57 W
Sharm ash-Shaykh	150	27.51 N	34.17 E
Sharon	174	41.14 N	80.31 W
Shashi	132	30.19 N	112.14 E
Shashi ≃	160	22.14 S	29.20 E
Shasta	178	40.36 N	122.29 W
Shasta ≃	178	41.50 N	122.35 W
Shasta, Mount ∧[1]	178	41.20 N	122.20 W
Shasta Lake ⊜[1]	178	40.50 N	122.25 W
Shaunavon	172	49.40 N	108.25 W
Shaw ≃	164	20.20 S	119.17 E
Shawanaga Inlet C	176	45.32 N	80.24 W
Shawbury	104	52.47 N	2.39 W
Shawinigan	172	46.33 N	72.45 W
Shawnee, Ohio, U.S.	176	39.36 N	82.13 W
Shawnee, Okla., U.S.	174	35.20 N	96.55 W
Shaw River	164	20.43 S	119.20 E
Shawville	176	45.36 N	76.30 W
Shaxi	136	31.34 N	121.04 E
Shaxian	136	26.24 N	117.47 E
Shayangzhen	136	30.42 N	112.33 E
Shaybārā I	150	25.27 N	36.48 E
Shay Gap	164	20.25 S	120.03 E
Shaykh, Jabal ash- ∧	150	33.26 N	35.51 E
Shaykh 'Uthmān	144	12.52 N	44.59 E
Sheaf ≃	106	53.23 N	1.26 W
Shebele (Shebelle) ≃	154	0.50 N	43.10 E
Sheberghān	146	36.41 N	65.45 E
Sheboygan	174	43.46 N	87.36 W
Shedfield	104	50.55 N	1.12 W
Shediac	172	46.13 N	64.32 W
Sheelin, Lough ⊜	110	53.48 N	7.22 W
Sheenjek ≃	172	66.45 N	144.33 W
Sheep Creek ≃	178	42.27 N	115.36 W
Sheep Haven C	110	55.10 N	7.52 W
Sheep Mountain ∧	178	32.32 N	114.14 W
Sheep Range ⋀	178	36.45 N	115.05 W
Sheepscot ≃	176	44.00 N	69.50 W
Sheerness	104	51.27 N	0.45 E
Sheffield, N.Z.	170	43.23 S	172.01 E
Sheffield, Eng., U.K.	106	53.23 N	1.30 W
Sheffield, Ala., U.S.	174	34.46 N	87.40 W
Sheffield, Pa., U.S.	176	41.42 N	79.02 W
Shefford	104	52.02 N	0.20 W
Shegaon	148	20.47 N	76.41 E
Shehy Mountains ⋀	110	51.48 N	3.15 W
Shekhūpura	149	31.42 N	73.59 E
Shelagyote Peak ∧	172	55.58 N	127.12 W
Shelburne, N.S., Can.	172	43.46 N	65.19 W
Shelburne, Ont., Can.	176	44.04 N	80.12 W
Shelburne Falls	176	42.36 N	72.44 W
Shelby, Mont., U.S.	174	48.30 N	111.51 W
Shelby, Ohio, U.S.	176	40.53 N	82.40 W
Shelbyville	176	38.13 N	85.14 W
Shell, Loch C	108	58.00 N	6.30 W
Shellbrook	172	53.13 N	106.24 W
Shellharbour	168	34.35 S	150.52 E
Shell Lakes ⊜	164	29.21 S	127.25 E
Shelton	176	41.19 N	73.05 W
Shenandoah, Iowa, U.S.	174	40.46 N	95.22 W
Shenandoah, Pa., U.S.	176	40.49 N	76.12 W
Shenandoah, Va., U.S.	176	38.29 N	78.37 W
Shenandoah ≃	176	39.19 N	92.03 W
Shenandoah, North Fork ≃	176	38.57 N	78.12 W
Shenandoah, South Fork ≃	176	38.57 N	78.12 W
Shengfang	132	39.04 N	116.42 E
Shengxian	136	29.36 N	120.48 E
Shengze	136	30.55 N	120.39 E
Shenhou	136	34.08 N	113.13 E
Shenhu	136	24.38 N	118.39 E
Shenjiamen	136	29.58 N	122.17 E
Shenqiu	136	33.24 N	115.02 E
Shenquan	136	22.59 N	116.20 E
Shensi → Shǎnxī □[4]	132	35.00 N	109.00 E
Shenyang (Mukden)	132	41.48 N	123.27 E
Shenzha	132	30.57 N	88.38 E
Sheopur	146	25.40 N	76.42 E
Shepherd	176	43.32 N	84.41 W
Shepherd Bay C	172	68.56 N	93.40 W
Shepherdstown	176	39.26 N	77.48 W
Shepparton	168	36.23 S	145.25 E
Shepperd, Lake ⊜	164	29.55 S	123.09 E
Sheppey, Isle of I	102	51.24 N	0.50 E
Shepshed	104	52.47 N	1.18 W
Shepton Mallet	104	51.12 N	2.33 W
Sheqizhen	136	33.03 N	112.57 E
Sherard, Cape ≻	172	74.36 N	80.25 W
Sherborne	104	50.57 N	2.31 W
Sherborne Saint John	104	51.18 N	1.07 W
Sherbro Island I	152	7.45 N	12.55 W
Sherbrooke	172	45.24 N	71.54 W
Sherburne	176	42.41 N	75.30 W
Shercock	110	54.00 N	6.54 W
Sheridan	174	44.48 N	106.58 W
Sheringa	164	33.51 S	135.15 E
Sheringham	104	52.57 N	1.12 E
Sherlock ≃	164	20.44 S	117.35 E
Sherman, N.Y., U.S.	176	42.10 N	79.36 W
Sherman, Tex., U.S.	174	33.38 N	96.36 W
Sherman Creek ≃	176	40.23 N	77.02 W
Sherman Mills	176	45.52 N	68.23 W
Sherman Station	176	45.54 N	68.26 W
Sherpur	146	25.01 N	90.01 E
Sherridon	172	55.07 N	101.05 W
Sherrill	176	43.04 N	75.35 W
Shertallai	148	9.42 N	76.20 E
's-Hertogenbosch	116	51.41 N	5.19 E
Sherwood	176	41.17 N	84.33 W
Sherwood Forest •[3]	106	53.08 N	1.08 W
Shetland Islands □[4]	108a	60.30 N	0.15 W
Shetland Islands II	108a	60.30 N	1.00 W
Shexian	136	29.53 N	118.26 E
Sheyang (Hede), Zhg.	136	33.46 N	120.18 E
Sheyang, Zhg.	136	33.20 N	119.38 E
Sheyenne ≃	174	47.05 N	96.50 W
Sheykh Sho'eyb, Jazīreh-ye I	144	26.48 N	53.15 E
Shiant, Sound of ⩌	108	57.55 N	6.25 W
Shiant Islands II	108	57.53 N	6.21 W
Shibām	144	15.56 N	48.38 E
Shibarghān	126	36.41 N	65.45 E
Shibata	134	37.57 N	139.20 E
Shibecha	134a	43.17 N	144.36 E
Shibetsu, Nihon	134a	44.10 N	142.23 E
Shibetsu, Nihon	134a	43.40 N	145.08 E
Shibīn al-Kawm	154	30.33 N	31.01 E
Shibotsu-tō I	134a	43.30 N	146.09 E
Shibukawa	134	36.29 N	139.00 E
Shibushi	134	31.28 N	131.07 E
Shicheng	136	26.22 N	116.22 E
Shickshinny	176	41.09 N	76.09 W
Shidao	132	36.53 N	122.23 E
Shiel, Loch ⊜	108	56.47 N	5.35 W
Shiel Bridge	108	57.12 N	5.25 W
Shieldaig	108	57.31 N	5.39 W
Shifnal	104	52.40 N	2.21 W
Shiga □[5]	134	35.15 N	136.00 E
Shiggar ≃	149	34.35 N	75.59 E
Shigu	136	34.10 N	113.39 E
Shijiagang	136	30.41 N	114.32 E
Shijiazhuang	132	38.03 N	114.28 E
Shijushan	132	39.20 N	106.50 E
Shikārpur	146	27.57 N	68.38 E
Shikohābād	146	27.06 N	78.36 E
Shikoku I	134	33.45 N	133.30 E
Shikoku-sanchi ⋀	134	33.47 N	133.30 E
Shikotsu-ko ⊜	134a	42.45 N	141.20 E
Shilbottle	106	55.23 N	1.42 W
Shildon	106	54.38 N	1.39 W
Shillelagh	110	52.45 N	6.32 W
Shillingstone	104	50.54 N	2.14 W
Shillington	176	40.18 N	75.58 W
Shillong	146	25.34 N	91.53 E
Shiloh	176	39.49 N	84.15 W
Shilong	136	23.07 N	113.48 E
Shima	134	34.13 N	136.51 E
Shimabara	134	32.47 N	130.22 E
Shimada	134	34.49 N	138.11 E
Shimane □[5]	134	35.00 N	132.30 E
Shimane-hantō ≻[1]	134	35.30 N	133.00 E
Shimanto ≃	134	32.56 N	133.00 E
Shimian	132	29.18 N	102.22 E
Shimizu, Nihon	134	35.01 N	138.29 E
Shimizu, Nihon	134a	43.01 N	142.53 E
Shimminato	134	36.47 N	137.04 E
Shimoda	134	34.40 N	138.57 E
Shimodate	134	36.18 N	139.59 E
Shimoga	148	13.55 N	75.34 E
Shimokawa	134a	44.18 N	142.39 E
Shimokita-hantō ≻[1]	134	41.15 N	141.00 E
Shimonoseki	134	33.57 N	130.57 E
Shimpuru Rapids ↳	160	17.50 S	19.56 E
Shin, Loch ⊜	108	58.06 N	4.34 W
Shinano ≃	134	37.56 N	139.03 E
Shīndand	150	33.18 N	62.08 E
Shinglehouse	176	41.58 N	78.12 W
Shingū, Nihon	134	34.55 N	134.33 E
Shingū, Nihon	134	33.44 N	135.59 E
Shingwidzi	160	23.05 S	31.25 E
Shinji-ko ⊜	134	35.27 N	132.58 E
Shinjō	134	38.46 N	140.18 E
Shinkolobwe	158	11.02 S	26.35 E
Shinnel Water ≃	106	55.13 N	3.49 W
Shinness	108	58.05 N	4.28 W
Shinnston	176	39.24 N	80.18 W
Shinshiro	134	34.54 N	137.30 E
Shinyanga	158	3.40 S	33.26 E
Shinyanga □[4]	158	3.45 S	33.00 E
Shiogama	134	38.19 N	141.01 E
Shiojiri	134	36.06 N	137.58 E
Shiono-misaki ≻	132	33.26 N	135.45 E
Shiono-zaki ≻	134	33.26 N	135.45 E
Shioya-zaki ≻, Nihon	134	36.59 N	140.59 E
Shioya-zaki ≻, Nihon	134	33.26 N	135.45 E
Shipdham	104	52.37 N	0.53 E
Shiping	140	23.47 N	102.30 E
Shipley	106	53.50 N	1.47 W
Shippensburg	176	40.03 N	77.31 W
Shipston-on-Stour	104	52.04 N	1.37 W
Shipu	136	29.13 N	121.55 E
Shiqiaozhen	136	33.12 N	112.36 E
Shiqu	132	33.04 N	97.45 E
Shira ≃	134	32.12 N	130.37 E
Shirahama	134	33.40 N	135.20 E
Shirakami-saki ≻	134a	41.24 N	140.12 E
Shirakawa	134	37.07 N	140.13 E
Shiranuka, Nihon	134a	41.08 N	141.24 E
Shiranuka, Nihon	134a	42.57 N	144.05 E
Shiraoi	134a	42.33 N	141.21 E
Shirase Glacier ⊽	87	70.10 S	38.35 E
Shīrāz	150	29.36 N	52.32 E
Shire (Chire) ≃	158	17.42 S	35.19 E
Shirebrook	106	53.12 N	1.13 W
Shiretoko-hantō ≻[1]	134a	44.00 N	145.00 E
Shiretoko-misaki ≻[1]	134a	44.14 N	145.17 E
Shiriya-saki ≻	134	41.26 N	141.28 E
Shiroishi	134	38.00 N	140.37 E
Shirone	134	37.46 N	139.01 E
Shirrell Heath	104	50.55 N	1.12 W
Shīrvān	150	37.24 N	57.55 E
Shitan	136	27.44 N	112.42 E
Shitang	136	28.16 N	121.36 E
Shitara	134	35.05 N	137.35 E
Shivpuri	146	25.26 N	77.39 E
Shiwan	136	23.01 N	113.04 E
Shixing	136	24.58 N	114.03 E
Shizhen	136	22.37 N	113.11 E
Shizhenjie	136	28.51 N	116.56 E
Shizugawa	134	38.40 N	141.27 E
Shizunai	134a	42.20 N	142.22 E
Shizuoka	134	34.58 N	138.23 E
Shkodër	124	42.05 N	19.30 E
Shkumbin ≃	124	41.01 N	19.26 E
Shō ≃	134	36.47 N	137.04 E
Shoal Cape ≻	164	33.53 S	121.07 E
Shoalhaven ≃	168	34.52 S	150.44 E
Shoalwater Bay C	168	22.02 S	150.25 E
Shōbara	134	34.51 N	133.01 E
Shōdo-shima I	134	34.30 N	134.17 E
Shoeburyness	104	51.32 N	0.48 E
Sholāpur	148	17.41 N	75.55 E
Shona, Eilean I	108	56.47 N	5.52 W
Shoreham-by-Sea	104	50.49 N	0.16 W
Shortsville	176	42.57 N	77.14 W
Shoshone	178	42.56 N	114.24 W
Shoshone Mountains ⋀	178	39.25 N	117.15 W
Shoshone Peak ∧	178	36.56 N	116.16 W
Shoshone Range ⋀	178	40.20 N	116.50 W
Shoshong	160	22.59 S	26.30 E
Shotley Gate	104	51.58 N	1.15 E
Shotton Colliery	106	54.44 N	1.20 W
Shotts	108	55.49 N	3.48 W
Shouchang	136	29.22 N	119.13 E
Shouning	136	27.27 N	119.30 E
Shournagh ≃	110	51.53 N	8.35 W
Shouxian	136	32.35 N	116.47 E
Shreve	176	40.41 N	82.01 W
Shreveport	174	32.30 N	93.45 W
Shrewsbury, Eng., U.K.	104	52.43 N	2.45 W
Shrewsbury, Mass., U.S.	176	42.18 N	71.43 W
Shrewton	104	51.12 N	1.55 W
Shrivenham	104	51.36 N	1.39 W
Shrule	110	53.30 N	9.08 W
Shuajingsi	132	32.00 N	103.05 E
Shuangcheng	132	45.26 N	126.18 E
Shuanggou, Zhg.	136	34.03 N	117.37 E
Shuanggou, Zhg.	136	33.16 N	118.10 E
Shuanggou, Zhg.	136	32.12 N	112.21 E
Shuangjiang	140	23.37 N	99.41 E
Shuangliao	132	43.31 N	123.30 E
Shuanglin	136	30.47 N	120.19 E
Shuangpai	140	25.57 N	111.32 E
Shuangqiaoji	136	32.28 N	116.11 E
Shuangyashan	132	46.37 N	131.22 E
Shucheng	136	31.27 N	116.57 E
Shuicheng	140	26.41 N	104.50 E
Shuidongzhen	136	30.47 N	118.57 E
Shuiji	136	27.26 N	118.20 E
Shuitou	136	24.43 N	118.25 E
Shuiyang	136	31.14 N	118.47 E
Shujāābād	149	29.53 N	71.18 E
Shulehe ≃	132	40.50 N	94.10 E
Shunchang	136	26.50 N	117.48 E
Shunde	136	22.50 N	113.14 E
Shundian	136	34.15 N	113.20 E
Shuqrah	144	13.21 N	45.42 E
Shushan	136	31.18 N	119.51 E
Shūshtar	150	32.03 N	48.51 E
Shuswap Lake ⊜	172	50.57 N	119.15 W
Shuyang	136	34.08 N	118.47 E
Shwebo	140	22.34 N	95.42 E
Shweli (Longchuanjiang) ≃	140	23.56 N	96.17 E
Shyok ≃	146	35.13 N	75.53 E
Siālkot	149	32.30 N	74.31 E
Siam → Thailand □[1]	138	15.00 N	100.00 E
Siam,, Gulf of → Thailand, Gulf of C	140	10.00 N	101.00 E
Sian → Xi'an, Zhg.	132	34.15 N	108.52 E
Sian, Zhg.	136	30.54 N	119.39 E
Siargao Island I	138	9.53 N	126.02 E
Siasconset	176	41.16 N	69.58 W
Šiaškotan, Ostrov I	128	48.49 N	154.06 E
Siátista	124	40.16 N	21.33 E
Siau, Pulau I	142	2.42 N	125.24 E
Šiauliai	130	55.56 N	23.19 E
Sibā'ī, Jabal as- ∧	150	25.43 N	34.09 E
Sibaj	126	52.42 N	58.39 E
Sibasa	160	22.53 S	30.33 E
Sibayi, Lake ⊜	160	27.20 S	32.40 E
Šibenik	122	43.44 N	15.54 E
Siberia → Sibir' •[1]	128	65.00 N	110.00 E
Siberut, Pulau I	138	1.20 S	98.55 E
Sibi	146	29.33 N	67.53 E
Sibir' (Siberia) •[1]	128	65.00 N	110.00 E
Sibir'akova, Ostrov I	128	72.50 N	79.00 E
Sibiti	156	3.41 S	13.21 E
Sibiu	124	45.48 N	24.09 E
Sibiu □[4]	124	46.00 N	24.15 E
Sible Hedingham	104	51.58 N	0.35 E
Sibolga	140	1.45 N	98.48 E
Sibsāgar	146	26.59 N	94.38 E
Sibu	142	2.18 N	111.49 E
Sibutu Island I	142	4.46 N	119.29 E
Sibuyan Island I	138	12.25 N	122.34 E
Sibuyan Sea ⊤[2]	138	12.50 N	122.40 E
Siccus ≃	164	31.26 S	139.30 E
Sichote-Alin' ⋀	128	48.00 N	138.00 E
Sichuan □[4]	132	31.00 N	105.00 E
Sicié, Cap ≻	118	43.03 N	5.51 E
Sicilia □[4]	122	37.30 N	14.00 E
Sicilia (Sicily) I	122	37.30 N	14.00 E
Sicily → Sicilia I	122	37.30 N	14.00 E
Sicily, Strait of ⩌	122	37.20 N	11.20 E
Sico ≃	182	15.58 N	84.58 W
Sicuani	184	14.15 S	71.15 W
Sidamo □[4]	158	4.30 N	38.50 E
Siddipet	148	18.06 N	78.51 E
Sideròpolis	188	28.35 S	49.26 W
Sidhi	144	24.24 N	81.53 E
Sidhirókastron	124	41.14 N	23.22 E
Sidhpur	146	23.55 N	72.23 E
Sīdī Barrānī	154	31.36 N	25.55 E
Sidi bel Abbès	152	35.13 N	0.10 W
Sidi-Bennour	152	32.30 N	8.30 W
Sidi Ifni	152	29.24 N	10.12 W
Sidlaw Hills ⋀[2]	108	56.30 N	3.10 W
Sidley, Mount ∧	87	77.02 S	126.00 W
Sidmouth	104	50.41 N	3.15 W
Sidney, Mont., U.S.	174	47.43 N	104.09 W
Sidney, Nebr., U.S.	174	41.09 N	102.59 W
Sidney, N.Y., U.S.	176	42.19 N	75.24 W
Sidney, Ohio, U.S.	176	40.17 N	84.09 W
Sidney Lanier, Lake ⊜[1]	174	34.15 N	83.57 W
Sidon → Ṣaydā	150	33.33 N	35.22 E
Sidu	136	23.48 N	117.18 E
Siedlce	116	52.11 N	22.16 E
Siegburg	116	50.47 N	7.12 E
Siegen	116	50.52 N	8.02 E
Siemianowice Śląskie	116	50.19 N	19.01 E
Siĕmréab	140	13.22 N	103.51 E
Siena	122	43.19 N	11.21 E
Sieradz	116	51.36 N	18.45 E
Sierck-les-Bains	118	49.26 N	6.21 E
Sierpc	116	52.52 N	19.41 E
Sierra Colorada	186	40.35 S	67.50 W
Sierra de Outes	120	42.51 N	8.54 W
Sierra Gorda	188	22.54 S	69.19 W
Sierra Leone □[1]	152	8.30 N	11.30 W
Sierra Leone Basin ✧[1]	88	5.00 N	16.00 W
Sierra Leone Rise ✧[3]	88	6.00 N	24.00 W
Sierre	118	46.18 N	7.32 E
Sífnos I	124	36.59 N	24.40 E
Sighetul Marmației	124	47.56 N	23.54 E
Sighișoara	124	46.13 N	24.48 E
Sighty Crag ∧	106	55.07 N	2.37 W
Siglan	128	59.02 N	152.25 E
Sigli	138	5.23 N	95.57 E
Siglufjörður	112a	66.10 N	18.56 W
Sigmaringen	116	48.05 N	9.13 E
Signal Mountain ∧	176	44.12 N	72.20 W
Signy-l'Abbaye	118	49.42 N	4.25 E
Sigsbee Deep ✧[1]	90	23.54 N	91.51 W
Sigsig	184	3.01 S	78.45 W
Sigtuna	114	59.37 N	17.43 E
Siguanea, Ensenada de la C	182	21.40 N	83.05 W
Sigüenza	120	41.04 N	2.38 W
Sigües	120	42.38 N	1.00 W
Siguiri	152	11.25 N	9.10 W
Sihanoukville → Kâmpóng Saôm	138	10.38 N	103.30 E
Sihong	136	33.28 N	118.11 E
Siikajoki ≃	114	64.50 N	24.44 E
Siilinjärvi	114	63.05 N	27.40 E
Siirt	150	37.56 N	41.57 E
Sijunjung	142	0.42 S	100.58 E
Sikalongo	158	16.46 S	27.07 E
Sikandarābād	146	28.27 N	77.42 E
Sikanni Chief ≃	172	58.20 N	121.50 W
Sīkar	146	27.37 N	75.09 E
Sikaram ∧	144	34.50 N	69.55 E
Sikasso	152	11.19 N	5.40 W
Sikéai	124	36.46 N	22.56 E
Sikeston	174	36.53 N	89.35 W
Sikkim □[3]	132	27.35 N	88.35 E
Šikotan, Ostrov (Shikotan-tō) I	134a	43.48 N	146.45 E
Sikt'ach	128	69.55 N	125.02 E
Silay	138	10.48 N	122.58 E
Silchar	146	24.49 N	92.48 E
Silesia □[9]	116	51.00 N	16.45 E
Silhouette I	156	4.29 S	55.14 E
Silifke	150	36.22 N	33.56 E
Silīguri	146	26.42 N	88.26 E
Silistra	124	44.07 N	27.16 E
Şilivri	124	41.04 N	28.15 E
Siljan ⊜	114	60.50 N	14.45 E
Šilka	128	51.51 N	116.02 E
Šilka ≃	128	53.22 N	121.32 E
Silkeborg	114	56.10 N	9.34 E
Sillamäe	130	59.24 N	27.45 E
Sillem Island I	172	70.55 N	71.30 W
Sillon de Talbert ≻[1]	118	48.53 N	3.05 W
Silloth	106	54.52 N	3.23 W
Šilovo	130	54.19 N	40.53 E
Silsden	106	53.55 N	1.55 W
Šilutė	130	55.21 N	21.29 E
Silvânia	190	16.42 S	48.38 W
Silver Bank Passage ⩌	182	20.40 N	70.20 W
Silver City	174	32.46 N	108.17 W
Silver Creek	176	42.33 N	79.10 W
Silver Creek ≃	178	43.16 N	119.13 W
Silverdale	170	36.37 S	174.40 E
Silver Lake	178	43.08 N	120.56 W
Silver Lake ⊜, Oreg., U.S.	178	43.22 N	119.24 W
Silver Lake ⊜, Oreg., U.S.	178	43.06 N	120.53 W
Silvermine Mountains ⋀	110	52.45 N	8.15 W
Silvermines	110	52.47 N	8.13 W
Silver Peak Range ⋀	178	37.35 N	117.45 W
Silver Spring	176	39.02 N	77.03 W
Silverstone	104	52.05 N	1.02 W
Silver Streams	160	28.20 S	23.33 E
Silverton, Austl.	168	31.53 S	141.13 E
Silverton, Eng., U.K.	104	50.48 N	3.28 W
Silves	120	37.11 N	8.26 W
Silvretta ⋀	118	46.50 N	10.10 E
Sima	161a	12.11 S	44.17 E
Simanggang	142	1.15 N	111.26 E
Šimanovsk	128	52.00 N	127.42 E
Simao	132	22.50 N	101.00 E
Simbach	116	48.34 N	12.45 E
Simcoe	176	42.50 N	80.18 W
Simcoe, Lake ⊜	176	44.20 N	79.20 W
Simeria	124	45.51 N	23.01 E
Simeulue, Pulau I	140	2.35 N	96.00 E
Simferopol'	126	44.57 N	34.06 E
Sími	124	36.36 N	27.50 E
Sími I	124	36.35 N	27.52 E
Simití	184	7.58 N	73.57 W
Simi Valley	178	34.16 N	118.47 W
Simla	149	31.06 N	77.10 E
Simoca	188	27.15 S	65.21 W
Simojärvi ⊜	114	66.06 N	27.03 E
Simojoki ≃	114	65.37 N	25.03 E
Simon, Lac ⊜	176	45.58 N	75.05 W
Simonsbath	104	51.09 N	3.45 W
Simonstad	160	34.14 S	18.26 E
Simoom Sound	172	50.45 N	126.45 W
Simpson Desert •[2]	168	25.00 S	137.00 E
Simpson Lake ⊜	172	68.39 N	91.19 W
Simpson Peninsula ≻[1]	172	68.34 N	88.45 W
Simpson Strait ⩌	172	68.27 N	97.45 W
Simrishamn	114	55.33 N	14.20 E
Simsbury	176	41.52 N	72.48 W
Simušir, Ostrov I	128	46.58 N	152.02 E
Sīnā' (Sinai Peninsula), Shib Jazīrat ≻[1]	154	29.30 N	34.00 E
Sinabang	140	2.29 N	96.23 E
Sinai, Mount → Mūsā, Jabal ∧	150	28.32 N	33.59 E
Sinaia	124	45.21 N	25.33 E
Sinai Peninsula → Sīnā', Shibh Jazīrat ≻[1]	154	29.30 N	34.00 E
Sin'aja ≃	128	61.06 N	126.50 E
Sinamaica	182	11.05 N	71.51 W
Sinan	132	27.54 N	108.18 E
Sīnāwan	154	31.02 N	10.36 E
Sincé	182	9.15 N	75.09 W
Sincelejo	184	9.18 N	75.24 W
Sinclair's Bay C	108	58.30 N	3.07 W
Sindal	114	57.28 N	10.13 E
Sindangbarang	142	7.27 S	107.08 E
Sindara	156	1.02 S	10.40 E
Sindelfingen	116	48.42 N	9.00 E
Sindri	144	23.45 N	86.42 E
Siné V	152	14.10 N	16.28 W
Sinekli	124	41.14 N	28.12 E
Sines	120	37.57 N	8.52 W
Sines, Cabo de ≻	120	37.57 N	8.53 W
Sinfães	120	41.04 N	8.05 W
Singânallūr	148	11.00 N	77.01 E
Singapore	140	1.17 N	103.51 E
Singapore □[1]	138	1.22 N	103.48 E
Singapore Strait ⩌	142	1.15 N	104.00 E
Singaraja	142	8.07 S	115.06 E
Sing Buri	140	14.53 N	100.25 E
Singen [hohentwiel]	116	47.46 N	8.50 E
Singida	158	4.49 S	34.45 E
Singida □[4]	158	5.30 S	34.30 E
Singkaling Hkāmti	132	26.00 N	95.42 E
Singkang	142	4.08 S	120.01 E
Singkawang	142	0.54 N	109.00 E
Singkep, Pulau I	142	0.30 S	104.25 E
Singleton, Austl.	168	32.34 S	151.10 E
Singleton, Eng., U.K.	104	50.55 N	0.46 W
Singleton, Mount ∧	164	22.00 S	130.49 E
Singuédeze (Groot Shingwidzi) ≃	160	23.53 S	32.17 E
Sinj	122	43.42 N	16.38 E
Sinjah	154	13.09 N	33.56 E
Sinjai	142	5.07 S	120.15 E
Sinjār	150	36.19 N	41.52 E
Sinkāt	154	18.50 N	36.50 E
Sinkiang → Xinjiang Weiwuer Zizhiqu □[4]	132	40.00 N	85.00 E
Sinking ≃	110	53.37 N	8.52 W
Sinnamahoning	176	41.19 N	78.06 W
Sinnamary	184	5.23 N	52.57 W
Sinnar	148	19.51 N	74.00 E
Sinnes	114	58.56 N	6.50 E
Sînnicolau Mare	124	46.05 N	20.38 E
Sinnūris	154	29.25 N	30.52 E
Sinoe, Lacul ⊜	124	44.38 N	28.53 E
Sinoia	158	17.22 S	30.12 E
Sinop	126	42.01 N	35.09 E
Sinsheim	118	49.15 N	8.53 E
Sinskoje	128	61.08 N	126.48 E
Sintang	142	0.04 N	111.30 E
Sint Eustatius I	182	17.30 N	62.59 W
Sint Marten (Saint-Martin) I	182	18.04 N	63.04 W
Sint-Niklaas	116	51.10 N	4.08 E
Sint-Truiden	116	50.48 N	5.12 E
Sinú ≃	184	9.24 N	75.49 W
Sinŭiju	132	40.05 N	124.24 E

Symbols in the index entries are identified on page 198.

Name	Page	Lat	Long
Siocon	138	7.42 N	122.08 E
Siófok	116	46.54 N	18.04 E
Sion	118	46.14 N	7.21 E
Sionascaig, Loch ⊜	108	58.04 N	5.11 W
Sioule ≏	118	46.22 N	3.19 W
Sioux City	174	42.30 N	96.23 W
Sioux Falls	174	43.32 N	96.44 W
Sioux Lookout	174	50.06 N	91.55 W
Siparia	182	10.08 N	61.30 W
Siping	132	43.12 N	124.20 E
Sipiwesk Lake ⊜	172	55.05 N	97.35 W
Siple, Mount ∧	87	73.15 S	126.06 W
Sipura, Pulau I	142	2.12 S	99.40 E
Siqueira Campos	190	23.42 S	49.50 W
Siquijor Island I	138	9.11 N	123.34 E
Siquirres	182	10.06 N	83.30 W
Siquisique	182	10.34 N	69.42 W
Sira ≏	114	58.17 N	6.24 E
Si Racha	140	13.10 N	100.56 E
Siracusa	122	37.04 N	15.17 E
Sirājganj	146	24.27 N	89.43 E
Sirdalsvatn ⊜	114	58.33 N	6.41 E
Sir Edward Pellew Group II	166	15.40 S	136.48 E
Siret ≏	124	45.24 N	28.01 E
Sirḥān, Wādī as- ∨	150	30.30 N	38.00 E
Sir James MacBrien, Mount ⋀	172	62.07 N	127.41 W
Sir Joseph Banks Group II	168	34.32 S	136.17 E
Sirmūr □[5]	149	30.40 N	77.20 E
Sirohi	146	24.53 N	72.52 E
Sironj	146	24.06 N	77.42 E
Síros → Ermoúpolis	124	37.26 N	24.56 E
Síros I	124	37.26 N	24.54 E
Sīrrī, Jazīreh-ye I	150	25.55 N	54.32 E
Sirsa	149	29.32 N	75.01 E
Sirsi	148	14.37 N	74.51 E
Sirsiri	158	4.24 N	31.53 E
Sir Thomas, Mount ∧	164	27.10 S	129.45 E
Sīrvān (Diyālā) ≏	150	33.14 N	44.31 E
Sisak	122	45.29 N	16.23 E
Sisaket	140	15.07 N	104.20 E
Sishen	160	27.55 S	22.59 E
Siskiyou Mountains ⋀	178	41.55 N	123.15 W
Siskiyou Pass)(	178	42.03 N	122.36 W
Sisquoc ≏	178	34.54 N	120.18 W
Sissonville	176	38.32 N	81.38 W
Sīstān, Daryācheh-ye ⊜	144	31.00 N	61.15 E
Sisteron	118	44.12 N	5.56 E
Sistersville	176	39.34 N	81.00 W
Sistranda	114	63.43 N	8.50 E
Sītāmarhi	146	26.36 N	85.29 E
Sītāpur	144	27.35 N	80.40 E
Sithoniá	124	35.12 N	26.07 E
Sitidgi Lake ⊜	172	68.32 N	132.42 W
Sitionuevo	182	10.47 N	74.43 W
Sitka	172	57.03 N	135.14 W
Sitna ≏	124	47.37 N	27.08 E
Sittang ≏	140	17.10 N	96.58 E
Sittard	116	51.00 N	5.53 E
Sittingbourne	104	51.21 N	0.44 E
Sittwe (Akyab)	140	20.09 N	92.54 E
Siuna	182	13.37 N	84.45 W
Sivakāsi	148	9.27 N	77.49 E
Sivas	150	39.45 N	37.02 E
Siverek	150	37.45 N	39.19 E
Siverskij	130	59.21 N	30.05 E
Sīwah	154	29.12 N	25.31 E
Siwān	146	26.13 N	84.22 E
Sixian	136	33.30 N	117.56 E
Sixmilecross	110	54.34 N	7.08 W
Siyāl, Jazā'ir II	150	22.47 N	36.12 E
Siyang	136	33.43 N	118.41 E
Sjælland I	114	55.30 N	11.45 E
Sjenica	124	43.16 N	20.00 E
Skærbæk	114	55.09 N	8.46 E
Skaftung	114	62.07 N	21.22 E
Skagafjörður C	112a	65.55 N	19.35 W
Skagen	114	57.44 N	10.36 E
Skagerrak ⟗	114	57.45 N	9.00 E
Skaidi	112	70.25 N	24.30 E
Skåne □[9]	114	55.59 N	13.30 E
Skånevik	114	59.44 N	5.59 E
Skaraborgs Län □[6]	114	58.20 N	13.30 E
Skārdu	149	35.18 N	75.37 E
Skarżysko-Kamienna	116	51.08 N	20.53 E
Skaudvilė	130	55.24 N	22.35 E
Skaugum	114	59.51 N	10.26 E
Skawina	116	49.59 N	19.49 E
Skeena ≏	172	54.09 N	130.02 W
Skeena Mountains ⋀	172	57.00 N	128.30 W
Skegness	106	53.10 N	0.21 E
Skeikampen	114	61.20 N	10.07 E
Skeldon	184	5.57 N	57.09 W
Skellefteå	114	64.46 N	20.57 E
Skellefteälven ≏	114	64.42 N	21.06 E
Skelleftehamn	114	64.41 N	21.14 E
Skellig Rocks II[1]	110	51.48 N	10.31 W
Skelmersdale	106	53.33 N	2.48 W
Skelmorlie	108	55.51 N	4.53 W
Skelton, Eng., U.K.	106	54.33 N	0.59 W
Skelton, Eng., U.K.	106	54.43 N	2.51 W
Skene	114	57.29 N	12.38 E
Skerne ≏	106	54.29 N	1.34 W
Skerryvore II[1]	108	56.19 N	7.07 W
Skewen	104	51.40 N	3.51 W
Ski	114	59.43 N	10.50 E
Skíathos	124	39.10 N	23.29 E
Skibbereen	110	51.33 N	9.15 W
Skiddaw ∧	102	54.38 N	3.08 W
Skien	114	59.12 N	9.36 E
Skierniewice	116	51.58 N	20.08 E
Skiftet ⟗	114	60.15 N	21.05 E
Skikda	152	36.50 N	6.58 E
Skilak Lake ⊜	172	60.25 N	150.25 W
Skillingaryd	114	57.26 N	14.05 E
Skipton, Austl.	168	37.41 S	143.22 E
Skipton, Eng., U.K.	106	53.58 N	2.01 W
Skirfare ≏	106	54.07 N	2.01 W
Skive	114	56.34 N	9.02 E
Sklad	128	71.55 N	123.33 E
Skoenmakerskop	160	34.02 S	25.33 E
Škofja Loka	122	46.10 N	14.18 E
Skoganvarre	112	69.47 N	25.06 E
Skokholm Island I	104	51.42 N	5.16 W
Skomer Island I	104	51.44 N	5.17 W
Skópelos	124	39.07 N	23.43 E
Skopin	130	53.51 N	39.33 E
Skopje	124	41.59 N	21.26 E
Skotterud	114	59.59 N	12.07 E
Skövde	114	58.24 N	13.50 E
Skovorodino	128	53.59 N	123.55 E
Skowhegan	176	44.46 N	69.43 W
Skradin	122	43.49 N	15.56 E
Skreen	110	54.15 N	8.45 W
Skukuza	160	25.01 S	31.38 E
Skye, Island of I	108	57.18 N	6.15 W
Skyring, Seno ⟗	186	52.35 S	72.00 W
Slagelse	114	55.24 N	11.22 E
Slamet, Gunung ∧	142	7.14 S	109.12 E
Slancy	130	59.06 N	28.04 E
Slaney ≏	110	52.21 N	6.30 W
Slaný	116	50.11 N	14.04 E
Śląsk → Silesia □[9]	116	51.00 N	16.45 E
Slatina	124	44.26 N	24.22 E
Slautnoje	128	63.00 N	167.59 E
Slav'ansk	126	48.52 N	37.37 E
Slav'ansk-na-Kubani	126	45.15 N	38.08 E
Slave ≏	172	61.18 N	113.39 W
Slavgorod	128	53.00 N	78.40 E
Slavonska Požega	122	45.20 N	17.41 E
Slavonski Brod	124	45.10 N	18.01 E
Sławno	116	54.22 N	16.40 E
Slea ≏	104	53.03 N	0.12 W
Sleaford	104	53.00 N	0.24 W
Slea Head ≻	110	52.06 N	10.27 W
Sleat, Point of ≻	108	57.01 N	6.02 W
Sleat, Sound of ⟗	108	57.06 N	5.49 W
Sledmere	106	54.04 N	0.35 W
Slessor Glacier ⊓	87	79.50 S	28.30 W
Sliabh Gaoil ∧	108	55.55 N	5.28 W
Slide Mountain ∧	176	42.00 N	74.23 W
Sliedrecht	116	51.49 N	4.45 E
Slievenaman ∧	110	52.25 N	7.34 W
Sligo, Eire	110	54.17 N	8.28 W
Sligo, Pa., U.S.	176	41.07 N	79.29 W
Sligo □[6]	110	54.10 N	8.40 W
Sligo Bay C	110	54.20 N	8.40 W
Slioch ∧	108	57.41 N	5.22 W
Slippery Rock	176	41.04 N	80.03 W
Sliven	124	42.40 N	26.19 E
Sloan	178	35.57 N	115.13 W
Slobodskoj	112	58.42 N	50.12 E
Slobozia	124	44.34 N	27.23 E
Slonim	130	53.06 N	25.19 E
Slough	104	51.31 N	0.36 W
Slovakia → Slovensko □[9]	116	48.50 N	20.00 E
Slovenia → Slovenija □[3]	122	46.15 N	15.10 E
Slovenská Socialistická Republika □[3]	116	48.30 N	20.00 E
Slovensko □[9]	116	48.50 N	20.00 E
Sluck	130	53.01 N	27.33 E
Sl'ud'anka	128	51.38 N	103.42 E
Slunj	122	45.07 N	15.35 E
Słupsk (Stolp)	116	54.28 N	17.01 E
Slurry	160	25.49 S	25.52 E
Slyne Head ≻	110	53.24 N	10.13 W
Småland □[9]	114	57.20 N	15.00 E
Smalininkai	130	55.05 N	22.35 E
Smederevo	124	44.40 N	20.56 E
Smela	126	49.14 N	31.53 E
Smerwick Harbour C	110	52.12 N	10.24 W
Smethport	176	41.49 N	78.27 W
Smethwick (Warley)	104	52.30 N	1.58 W
Smidovič	128	48.36 N	133.49 E
Šmidta, Ostrov I	128	81.08 N	90.48 E
Smiltene	130	57.26 N	25.56 E
Smirnovskij	126	54.31 N	69.25 E
Smite ≏	104	52.57 N	0.53 W
Smith ≏	178	41.56 N	124.12 W
Smith, Cape ≻	176	45.48 N	81.35 W
Smith Arm C	172	66.15 N	124.00 W
Smithers, B.C., Can.	172	54.47 N	127.10 W
Smithers, W. Va., U.S.	176	38.11 N	81.18 W
Smithfield, S. Afr.	160	30.09 S	26.30 E
Smithfield, Eng., U.K.	106	54.59 N	2.52 W
Smith Island I	87	63.00 S	62.30 W
Smith Peninsula ≻[1]	87	74.25 S	61.15 W
Smith River	178	41.56 N	124.09 W
Smiths Falls	172	44.54 N	76.01 W
Smithton	168	40.51 S	145.07 E
Smoke Creek Desert •[2]	178	40.30 N	119.40 W
Smokey Dome ∧	178	43.29 N	114.56 W
Smoky ≏	172	56.10 N	117.21 W
Smoky Bay	164	32.22 S	133.56 E
Smoky Cape ≻	168	30.56 S	153.05 E
Smøla I	114	63.24 N	8.00 E
Smolensk	130	54.47 N	32.03 E
Smoljan	124	41.35 N	24.41 E
Smyley, Cape ≻	87	72.26 S	78.10 W
Smyrna → İzmir, Tür.	94	38.25 N	27.09 E
Smyrna, Del., U.S.	176	39.18 N	75.36 W
Smyrna Mills	176	46.08 N	68.10 W
Smythe, Mount ∧	172	57.54 N	124.53 W
Snæfell ∧, Ísland	112a	64.48 N	15.32 W
Snaefell ∧, I. of Man	106	54.16 N	4.27 W
Snag	172	62.24 N	140.22 W
Snake ≏, Yukon, Can.	172	65.58 N	134.10 W
Snake ≏, U.S.	174	46.12 N	119.02 W
Snake Range ⋀	178	39.00 N	114.15 W
Snake River Plain ≚	178	43.00 N	113.00 W
Snake Valley ∨	178	39.20 N	113.55 W
Snap Point ≻	182	23.46 N	77.35 W
Sneek	116	53.02 N	5.40 E
Sneeuberg ⋀	160	31.46 S	24.20 E
Snelling	178	37.31 N	120.26 W
Snettisham	104	52.53 N	0.30 E
Śniardwy, Jezioro ⊜	116	53.46 N	21.44 E
Snina	116	48.59 N	22.07 E
Snizort, Loch C	108	57.34 N	6.28 W
Snodland	104	51.20 N	0.27 E
Snøhetta ∧	114	62.20 N	9.17 E
Snøtinden ∧	112	66.38 N	14.00 E
Snover	176	43.28 N	82.58 W
Snowbird Lake ⊜	172	60.41 N	103.00 W
Snowdon ∧	106	53.04 N	4.05 W
Snowdrift	172	62.23 N	110.47 W
Snow Hill	176	38.11 N	75.24 W
Snow Lake	172	54.53 N	100.02 W
Snow Mountain ∧	178	39.23 N	122.45 W
Snowtown	168	33.47 S	138.13 E
Snow Water Lake ⊜	178	41.07 N	115.00 W
Snowy ≏	168	37.48 S	148.32 E
Snowy Mountain ∧	176	43.42 N	74.23 W
Snowy Mountains ⋀	168	36.30 S	148.20 E
Soaker, Mount ∧	170	45.23 S	167.15 E
Soalala	161b	16.06 S	45.20 E
Soay I	108	57.08 N	6.14 W
Sobat ≏	154	9.22 N	31.33 E
Sobinka	130	55.59 N	40.01 E
Sobradinho	188	29.24 S	53.03 W
Sobral	184	3.42 S	40.21 W
Sobrarbe •[1]	120	42.22 N	0.10 E
Socaire	188	23.36 S	67.51 W
Sochaczew	116	52.14 N	20.14 E
Sochi → Soči	126	43.35 N	39.45 E
Soči	126	43.35 N	39.45 E
Société, Îles de la II	96	17.00 S	150.00 W
Society Islands → Société, Îles de la II	96	17.00 S	150.00 W
Society Ridge ⟡[3]	96	17.00 S	152.00 W
Soco ≏	182	18.28 N	69.14 W
Socopo, Cerro ∧	182	10.28 N	70.48 W
Socorro, Col.	184	6.29 N	73.16 W
Socorro, N. Mex., U.S.	174	34.04 N	106.54 W
Socorro, Isla I	180	18.45 N	110.58 W
Socotra → Suquṭrā I	144	12.30 N	54.00 E
Socuéllamos	120	39.17 N	2.48 W
Soda Lake ⊜	178	35.08 N	116.04 W
Sodankylä	112	67.29 N	26.32 E
Söderhamn	114	61.18 N	17.03 E
Söderköping	114	58.29 N	16.18 E
Södermanland □[9]	114	59.12 N	16.49 E
Södermanlands Län □[6]	114	59.15 N	16.40 E
Södertälje	114	59.12 N	17.37 E
Sodium	160	30.11 S	23.09 E
Sodo	154	6.52 N	37.47 E
Södra Kvarken ⟗	114	60.15 N	19.05 E
Sodražica	122	45.46 N	14.38 E
Sodus	176	43.14 N	77.04 W
Soe	142	9.52 S	124.17 E
Soekmekaar	160	23.28 S	29.58 E
Soest, B.R.D.	116	51.34 N	8.07 E
Soest, Ned.	116	52.09 N	5.18 E
Sofádhes	124	39.20 N	22.06 E
Sofia → Sofija	124	42.41 N	23.19 E
Sofia ≏	161b	15.27 S	47.23 E
Sofija (Sofia)	124	42.41 N	23.19 E
Sogamoso	184	5.43 N	72.56 W
Sognafjorden C[2]	114	61.06 N	5.10 E
Sogne Fjord → Sognafjorden C[2]	114	61.06 N	5.10 E
Sogn og Fjordane □[6]	114	61.30 N	6.50 E
Soham	104	52.20 N	0.20 E
Soignies	116	50.35 N	4.04 E
Soissons	118	49.22 N	3.20 E
Sojat	146	25.55 N	73.40 E
Sŏjosŏn-man C	132	39.20 N	124.50 E
Šokal'skogo, Proliv ⟗	128	79.00 N	100.25 E
Sŏkch'o	132	38.12 N	128.36 E
Sokhós	124	40.49 N	23.21 E
Sokna	114	60.14 N	9.54 E
Sokodé	152	8.59 N	1.08 E
Sokol, S.S.S.R.	128	72.24 N	126.48 E
Sokol, S.S.S.R.	130	59.28 N	40.10 E
Sokółka	116	53.25 N	23.31 E
Sokolov	116	50.14 N	12.40 E
Sokołów	116	52.25 N	22.07 E
Sokoto	152	13.04 N	5.16 E
Sokoto ≏	152	11.20 N	4.10 E
Sol, Costa del •[2]	120	36.30 N	4.30 W
Solander Island I	170	46.34 S	166.53 E
Solbad Hall in Tirol	116	47.17 N	11.31 E
Sol de Julio	188	29.33 S	63.27 W
Soledad, Col.	184	10.55 N	74.46 W
Soledad, Calif., U.S.	178	36.26 N	121.19 W
Soledad Díez Gutiérrez	180	22.12 N	100.57 W
Soledade	188	28.50 S	52.30 W
Soledad Pass)(	178	34.30 N	118.07 W
Solenzara	122	41.51 N	9.23 E
Soleure → Solothurn	118	47.13 N	7.32 E
Solheim	114	60.53 N	5.27 E
Soligorsk	130	52.48 N	27.32 E
Solihull	104	52.25 N	1.45 W
Solikamsk	112	59.39 N	56.47 E
Sol'-Ileck	126	51.10 N	54.59 E
Solimões → Amazon ≏	184	0.05 S	50.00 W
Solingen	116	51.10 N	7.05 E
Sollas	108	57.39 N	7.21 W
Sollefteå	114	63.10 N	17.16 E
Sollentuna	114	59.28 N	17.54 E
Sóller	120	39.46 N	2.42 E
Søln ∧	114	61.55 N	11.30 E
Solna	114	59.22 N	18.01 E
Solnečnogorsk	130	56.11 N	36.59 E
Sologne •[1]	118	47.50 N	2.00 E
Šologoncy	128	66.13 N	114.14 E
Solok	142	0.48 S	100.39 E
Solola	158	0.08 N	41.30 E
Solomon Basin ⟡[1]	96	7.30 S	152.00 E
Solomon Islands □[2]	96	8.00 S	159.00 E
Solomon Sea ⩒[2]	96	8.00 S	155.00 E
Solon	176	44.57 N	69.52 W
Solothurn	118	47.13 N	7.32 E
Solovjevsk	128	49.55 N	115.42 E
Solsona	120	41.59 N	1.31 E
Soltau	116	52.59 N	9.49 E
Solva	104	51.52 N	5.11 W
Solva ≏	104	51.52 N	5.17 W
Solvang	178	34.36 N	120.08 W
Solvay	176	43.04 N	76.12 W
Sol'vyčegodsk	112	61.21 N	46.52 E
Solway Firth C[1]	106	54.50 N	3.35 W
Solwezi	158	12.11 S	26.25 E
Sōma	134	37.48 N	140.57 E
Somabula	158	19.41 S	29.41 E
Somalia □[1]	154	10.00 N	49.00 E
Somali Basin ⟡[1]	94	5.00 N	53.00 E
Somali Republic → Somalia □[1]	154	10.00 N	49.00 E
Sombor	124	45.46 N	19.07 E
Sombrero I	182	18.35 N	63.25 W
Sombrio	188	29.07 S	49.40 W
Sombrio, Lagoa do C	188	29.12 S	49.42 W
Somerset, Ky., U.S.	174	37.05 N	84.36 W
Somerset, Mass., U.S.	176	41.45 N	71.09 W
Somerset, Ohio, U.S.	176	39.48 N	82.18 W
Somerset, Pa., U.S.	176	40.01 N	79.05 W
Somerset □[6]	102	51.08 N	3.00 W
Somerset East	160	32.42 S	25.35 E
Somerset Island I	172	73.15 N	93.30 W
Somerset West	160	34.08 S	18.50 E
Somersham	104	52.23 N	0.01 E
Somers Point	176	39.20 N	74.36 W
Somersworth	176	43.16 N	70.52 W
Somerton, Eng., U.K.	104	51.03 N	2.44 W
Somerton, Ariz., U.S.	178	32.36 N	114.43 W
Somerville	176	40.34 N	74.37 W
Someș (Szamos) ≏	124	48.07 N	22.22 E
Sommariva	168	26.24 S	146.36 E
Somme □[5]	118	49.55 N	2.30 E
Somme ≏	118	50.11 N	1.39 E
Sommen ⊜	114	58.01 N	15.15 E
Sömmerda	116	51.10 N	11.07 E
Somogy □[6]	116	46.25 N	17.35 E
Somoto	182	13.28 N	86.37 W
Somport, Puerto de)(	120	42.48 N	0.31 W
Son ≏	146	25.40 N	84.51 E
Sondags ≏	160	33.44 S	25.51 E
Sønderborg	114	54.55 N	9.47 E
Sondershausen	116	51.22 N	10.52 E
Søndre Strømfjord	172	66.59 N	50.40 W
Søndre Strømfjord C[2]	172	67.30 N	52.00 W
Sondrio	122	46.10 N	9.52 E
Sonepur	144	20.50 N	83.54 E
Songbu	136	31.05 N	114.48 E
Song-cau	140	13.27 N	109.13 E
Songea	158	10.41 S	35.39 E
Songhuahu ⊜[1]	132	43.20 N	127.07 E
Songhuajiang ≏	132	47.44 N	132.32 E
Songjiang	136	31.01 N	121.14 E
Songkhla	140	7.12 N	100.36 E
Songkou	136	24.32 N	116.24 E
Songmen	136	28.19 N	121.34 E
Songming	140	25.24 N	102.59 E
Songnim	132	38.44 N	125.38 E
Songwe	158	12.25 S	29.40 E
Songyang	136	28.27 N	119.29 E
Songzheng	136	27.33 N	118.46 E
Songzong	132	29.45 N	96.10 E
Sonīpat	149	28.59 N	77.01 E
Son-la	140	21.19 N	103.54 E
Sonmiāni Bay C	146	25.15 N	66.30 E
Sonneberg	116	50.22 N	11.10 E
Sonning	104	51.29 N	0.55 W
Sonoma	178	38.17 N	122.28 W
Sonoma Peak ∧	178	40.52 N	117.36 W
Sonora, Méx.	178	32.27 N	115.10 W
Sonora, Calif., U.S.	178	37.59 N	120.23 W
Sonora □[3]	178	29.20 N	110.40 W
Sonora ≏	180	28.50 N	111.33 W
Sonqor	150	34.47 N	47.36 E
Sonseca	120	39.42 N	3.57 W
Sonskyn	160	30.47 S	26.28 E
Sonsón	184	5.42 N	75.18 W
Sonsonate	180	13.43 N	89.44 W
Sonsorol Islands II	138	5.20 N	132.13 E
Sonstraal	160	27.07 S	22.28 E
Son-tay	140	21.08 N	105.30 E
Sonthofen	116	47.31 N	10.17 E
Soochow → Suzhou	136	31.18 N	120.37 E
Sopa Sopa Head ≻	166	1.58 S	146.35 E
Sopockin	130	53.50 N	23.39 E
Sopot	116	54.28 N	18.34 E
Sopron	116	47.41 N	16.36 E
Sopur	149	34.18 N	74.28 E
Sor, Ribeira de ≏	120	39.00 N	8.17 W
Sora	122	41.43 N	13.37 E
Sorbas	120	37.07 N	2.07 W
Sore	118	44.20 N	0.35 W
Sorel	172	46.02 N	73.07 W
Sorell	168	42.47 S	147.33 E
Sorell, Cape ≻	168	42.12 S	145.10 E
Sorel Point ≻	105b	49.16 N	2.10 W
Sørfjorden C[2]	114	60.24 N	6.40 E
Sorgues	118	44.00 N	4.52 E
Soria	120	41.46 N	2.28 W
Sørli	114	64.15 N	13.45 E
Sorn	108	55.30 N	4.18 W
Sorocaba	190	23.29 S	47.27 W
Soročinsk	126	52.26 N	53.10 E
Sorol I[1]	138	8.08 N	140.23 E
Sorong	166	0.53 S	131.15 E
Soroti	158	1.43 N	33.37 E
Sørøya I	112	70.36 N	22.46 E
Sorrento	122	40.37 N	14.22 E
Sorsatunturi ∧	112	67.24 N	29.38 E
Sorsogon	138	12.58 N	124.00 E
Sort	120	42.24 N	1.08 E
Sortat	108	58.33 N	3.13 W
Sortavala	112	61.42 N	30.41 E
Sør-Trøndelag □[6]	114	63.00 N	10.40 E
Sorūbī	146	34.36 N	69.43 E
Sos del Rey Católico	120	42.30 N	1.13 W
Sosnogorsk	112	63.37 N	53.51 E
Sosnovo-Oz'orskoje	128	52.31 N	111.32 E
Sosnovskoje	130	56.32 N	43.16 E
Sosnowiec	116	50.18 N	19.08 E
Sospel	118	43.53 N	7.27 E
Šostka	126	51.52 N	33.30 E
Sos'va, S.S.S.R.	126	63.40 N	62.06 E
Sos'va, S.S.S.R.	126	59.10 N	61.50 E
Sotik	158	0.41 S	35.07 E
Sotkamo	114	64.08 N	28.25 E
Sotonera, Embalse de la ⊜[1]	120	42.05 N	0.48 W
Sotteville	118	49.25 N	1.06 E
Soudan	166	20.05 S	137.50 E
Souderton	176	40.19 N	75.19 W
Soufrière ∧, Guad.	182	16.03 N	61.40 W
Soufrière ∧, St. Vin.	182	13.21 N	61.11 W
Souhegan ≏	176	42.51 N	71.29 W
Souk Ahras	122	36.23 N	8.00 E
Soŭl (Seoul)	132	37.33 N	126.58 E
Sources, Mount aux ∧	160	28.46 S	28.52 E
Soure	120	40.03 N	8.38 W
Souris	172	49.38 N	100.15 W
Souris ≏	174	49.39 N	99.34 W
Sourland Mountain ∧[2]	176	40.29 N	74.43 W
Sousa	184	6.45 S	38.14 W
Sousse	152	35.49 N	10.38 E
Sout ≏	160	31.35 S	18.24 E
South ≏	176	38.18 N	78.49 W
South Africa □[1]	156	30.00 S	26.00 E
South Alligator ≏	166	12.15 S	132.24 E
Southam	104	52.15 N	1.23 W
South America ⚲[1]	92	15.00 S	60.00 W
Southampton, Ont., Can.	176	44.29 N	81.23 W
Southampton, Eng., U.K.	104	50.55 N	1.25 W
Southampton, N.Y., U.S.	176	40.53 N	72.24 W
Southampton, Cape ≻	172	62.09 N	83.40 W
Southampton Island I	172	64.20 N	84.40 W
South Andaman I	140	11.45 N	92.45 E
South Aulatsivik Island I	172	56.45 N	61.30 W
South Australia □[3]	168	31.00 S	138.00 E
South Australian Basin ⟡[1]	96	38.00 S	125.00 E
South Banda Basin ⟡[1]	96	6.30 S	127.00 E
South Barrule ∧[2]	106	54.12 N	4.40 W
South Bay C, N.W. Ter., Can.	172	63.58 N	83.30 W
South Bay C, Ont., Can.	176	45.38 N	81.50 W
South Baymouth	176	45.33 N	82.01 W
South Bend	174	41.41 N	86.15 W
South Benfleet	104	51.33 N	0.34 E
Southborough	104	51.10 N	0.15 E
South Brent	104	50.25 N	3.50 W
Southbridge, N.Z.	170	43.49 S	172.15 E
Southbridge, Mass., U.S.	176	42.05 N	72.02 W
South Bruny I	168	43.23 S	147.17 E
South Burlington	176	44.28 N	73.13 W
South Carolina □[3]	174	34.00 N	81.00 W
South Cave	106	53.46 N	0.35 W
South Channel ⟗	176	45.38 N	84.32 W
South Charleston	176	38.22 N	81.44 W
South China Basin ⟡[1]	94	15.00 N	115.00 E
South China Sea ⩒[2]	138	10.00 N	113.00 E
South Dakota □[3]	174	44.15 N	100.00 W
South Deerfield	176	42.29 N	72.37 W
South Dorset Downs ⋀[1]	104	50.40 N	2.25 W
South Downs ⋀[1]	102	50.55 N	0.25 W
South East □[5]	160	25.00 S	25.45 E
South East Cape ≻	168	43.39 S	146.50 E
Southeast Newfoundland Ridge ⟡[3]	84	40.00 N	47.00 W
Southeast Pacific Basin ⟡[1]	84	60.00 S	115.00 W
Southend	106	55.20 N	5.38 W
Southend-on-Sea	104	51.33 N	0.43 E
Southern □[4], Malawi	158	15.30 S	35.00 E
Southern □[4], Zam.	158	16.00 S	27.00 E
Southern Alps ⋀	170	43.30 S	170.30 E
Southern Cross	164	31.13 S	119.19 E
Southern Indian Lake ⊜	172	57.10 N	98.40 W
Southern Yemen → Yemen, People's Democratic Republic of □[1]	144	15.00 N	48.00 E
Southery	104	52.32 N	0.23 E
South Esk ≏, Austl.	168	41.25 S	147.08 E
South Esk ≏, Scot., U.K.	108	55.53 N	3.04 W
South Esk ≏, Scot., U.K.	108	56.42 N	2.32 W
Southesk Tablelands ⋀[1]	164	20.50 S	126.40 E
South Fallsburg	176	41.43 N	74.38 W
Southfield	176	42.29 N	83.17 W
South Fiji Basin ⟡[1]	96	27.00 S	176.00 E
South Fiji Ridge ⟡[3]	96	23.00 S	179.00 W
South Foreland ≻	102	51.09 N	1.23 E
South Forty Foot Drain ≍	104	52.56 N	0.15 W
South Fox Island I	176	45.25 N	85.50 W
Southgate	176	42.12 N	83.13 W
South Georgia Rise ⟡[3]	92	50.00 S	28.00 W
South Glamorgan □[6]	104	51.30 N	3.25 W
South Hadley Falls	176	42.14 N	72.36 W
South Hams ≚	104	50.22 N	3.50 W
South Hayling	104	50.47 N	0.59 W
South Henik Lake ⊜	172	61.30 N	97.30 W
South Hero	176	44.39 N	73.19 W
South Honshu Ridge ⟡[3]	96	18.00 N	143.00 E
South Indian Basin ⟡[1]	87	60.00 S	120.00 E
South Indian Lake	172	56.46 N	98.57 W
Southington	176	41.36 N	72.53 W
South Island I, Kenya	158	2.38 N	36.36 E
South Island I, N.Z.	170	43.00 S	171.00 E
South Jan Mayen Ridge ⟡[3]	88	68.00 N	10.00 W
South Kirkby	106	53.34 N	1.20 W
South Korea → Korea, South □[1]	132	36.30 N	128.00 E
South Lake Tahoe	178	38.57 N	119.57 W
South Luconia Shoals ⟡[2]	142	5.03 N	112.33 E
South Lyon	176	42.28 N	83.39 W
South Medford	178	42.18 N	122.50 W
Southminster	104	51.40 N	0.50 E
South Molton	104	51.01 N	3.50 W
South Mountain ∧	178	42.44 N	116.54 W
South Nahanni ≏	172	61.03 N	123.20 W
South Nation ≏	176	45.35 N	75.06 W
South Ockendon	104	51.32 N	0.18 E
South Orkney Islands II	87	60.35 S	45.30 W
South Paris	176	44.13 N	70.31 W
South Petherton	104	50.58 N	2.49 W
South Platte ≏	174	41.07 N	100.42 W
South Point ≻, Austl.	168	39.00 S	146.20 E
South Point ≻, Ba.	182	22.52 N	74.50 W
Southport, Austl.	168	27.58 S	153.25 E
Southport, Eng., U.K.	106	53.39 N	3.01 W
Southport, N.Y., U.S.	176	42.03 N	76.49 W
South Portland	176	43.38 N	70.15 W
South River	172	45.45 N	79.25 W
South Rockwood	176	42.04 N	83.16 W
South Ronaldsay I	108	58.46 N	2.58 W
South Sandwich Islands II	92	57.45 S	26.30 W
South Sandwich Trench ⟡[1]	92	57.00 S	25.00 W
South San Francisco	178	37.39 N	122.24 W
South Saskatchewan ≏	172	53.15 N	105.05 W
South Saugeen ≏	176	44.08 N	81.02 W
South Shetland Islands II	87	62.00 S	60.00 W
South Shields	106	55.00 N	1.25 W
South Sound ⟗	110	53.02 N	9.28 W
South Spicer Island I	172	68.06 N	79.13 W
South Taranaki Bight C[3]	170	39.40 S	174.10 E
South Tasmania Ridge ⟡[3]	84	46.00 S	147.00 E
South Tyne ≏	106	54.59 N	2.08 W
South Uist I	108	57.15 N	7.21 W
South Umpqua ≏	178	43.20 N	123.25 W
South Ventana Cone ∧	178	36.17 N	121.38 W
South Vietnam → Vietnam □[1]	138	16.00 N	108.00 E
Southwark •[8]	104	51.30 N	0.06 W
South West Africa □[2]	156	22.00 S	17.00 E
South West Cape ≻, Austl.	168	43.34 S	146.02 E
Southwest Cape ≻, N.Z.	170	47.17 S	167.28 E
Southwestern Pacific Basin ⟡[1]	96	42.00 S	166.00 W
Southwest Harbor	176	44.17 N	68.20 W
Southwest Indian Ridge ⟡[3]	88	38.00 S	50.00 E
Southwest Pacific Basin ⟡[1]	87	55.00 S	180.00 W
Southwest Point ≻	182	25.51 N	77.13 W
Southwick	104	50.50 N	0.13 W
South Windham	176	43.44 N	70.26 W
Southwold	104	52.20 N	1.40 E
South Woodham Ferrers	104	51.39 N	0.37 E
South Yorkshire □[6]	106	53.30 N	1.15 W
South Zeal	104	50.44 N	3.54 W
Soutpansberg ⋀	160	22.55 S	29.30 E
Souvigny	118	46.32 N	3.11 E
Sovetsk (Tilsit)	130	55.05 N	21.53 E
Sovetskaja Gavan'	128	48.58 N	140.18 E
Soviet Union → Union of Soviet Socialist Republics □[1]	128	60.00 N	80.00 E
Sow ≏	104	52.48 N	2.00 W
Sowerby	106	54.13 N	1.21 W
Sowerby Bridge	106	53.43 N	1.54 W
Sōya-misaki ≻	134a	45.31 N	141.56 E
Spa	116	50.30 N	5.52 E
Spain □[1]	100	40.00 N	4.00 W
Spalding, Austl.	168	33.30 S	138.37 E
Spalding, Eng., U.K.	104	52.47 N	0.10 W
Spanish	176	46.12 N	82.21 W
Spanish ≏	176	46.11 N	82.19 W
Spanish North Africa □[2]	152	35.53 N	5.19 W
Spanish Sahara → Western Sahara □[2]	152	24.30 N	13.00 W
Spanish Town	182	18.00 N	76.57 W
Sparkford	104	51.02 N	2.34 W
Sparks	178	39.32 N	119.45 W
Sparlingville	176	42.58 N	82.30 W
Sparrows Point	176	39.13 N	76.29 W
Sparta → Spárti, Ellás	124	37.05 N	22.27 E
Sparta, Ky., U.S.	176	38.41 N	84.55 W
Sparta, N.J., U.S.	176	41.01 N	74.39 W
Spartanburg	174	34.57 N	81.55 W
Spárti (Sparta)	124	37.05 N	22.27 E
Spartivento, Capo ≻	122	38.53 N	8.50 E
Spassk-Dal'nij	128	44.37 N	132.48 E
Spassk-R'azanskij	130	54.24 N	40.23 E
Spean, Glen ∨	108	56.53 N	4.45 W
Spean Bridge	108	56.53 N	4.54 W
Spearfish	174	44.30 N	103.52 W
Spednic Lake ⊜	176	45.38 N	67.38 W
Speightstown	182	13.15 N	59.39 W
Speikkogel ∧	116	47.14 N	15.03 E
Spelve, Loch C	108	56.22 N	5.46 W
Spence Bay	172	69.32 N	93.31 W
Spencer, Iowa, U.S.	174	43.09 N	95.09 W
Spencer, Mass., U.S.	176	42.15 N	71.60 W
Spencer, W. Va., U.S.	176	38.48 N	81.21 W
Spencer, Cape ≻	168	35.18 S	136.53 E
Spencer Gulf C	168	34.00 S	137.00 E
Spencerville	176	40.42 N	84.21 W
Spennymoor	106	54.42 N	1.35 W
Spenser Mountains ⋀	170	42.15 S	172.30 E
Sperillen ⊜	114	60.28 N	10.03 E
Sperrin Mountains ⋀	110	54.50 N	7.05 W
Sperryville	176	38.39 N	78.14 W
Spey ≏	108	57.40 N	3.06 W
Spey Bay C	108	57.41 N	3.00 W
Speyer	116	49.19 N	8.26 E
Speyside	182	11.18 N	60.32 W
Spiekeroog I	116	53.46 N	7.42 E
Spiess Seamount ⟡[3]	84	54.40 S	0.15 E
Spišská Nová Ves	116	48.57 N	20.34 E
Spithead ≻	104	50.45 N	1.05 W
Spit Point ≻	164	20.02 S	119.00 E
Spitsbergen Bank ⟡[3]	88	76.00 N	23.00 E
Spittal an der Drau	116	46.48 N	13.30 E
Spittal of Glenshee	108	56.48 N	3.28 W
Spjelkavik	114	62.28 N	6.23 E
Split	122	43.31 N	16.27 E
Split Lake ⊜	172	56.08 N	96.15 W
Spokane	174	47.40 N	117.23 W
Spoleto	122	42.44 N	12.44 E
Spondon	104	52.54 N	1.25 W
Spornoje	128	62.20 N	151.03 E
Spotsylvania	176	38.12 N	77.35 W
Sprague ≏	178	42.34 N	121.51 W
Sprague, North Fork ≏	178	42.26 N	121.07 W
Sprague, South Fork ≏	178	42.26 N	121.07 W
Spratly Island I	138	8.38 N	111.55 E
Spremberg	116	51.34 N	14.22 E
Springbok	160	29.43 S	17.55 E
Springburn	170	43.40 S	171.28 E
Spring Creek	170	41.28 S	173.58 E
Spring Creek ≏, Austl.	168	24.12 S	140.58 E
Spring Creek ≏, Nev., U.S.	178	39.55 N	117.50 W
Springdale, Newf., Can.	172	49.30 N	56.04 W
Springdale, Pa., U.S.	176	40.33 N	79.46 W
Springe	116	52.12 N	9.32 E
Springfield, N.Z.	170	43.20 S	171.55 E
Springfield, Ill., U.S.	174	39.47 N	89.40 W
Springfield, Mass., U.S.	176	42.07 N	72.36 W
Springfield, Mo., U.S.	174	37.14 N	93.17 W
Springfield, Ohio, U.S.	176	39.56 N	83.49 W
Springfield, Oreg., U.S.	174	44.03 N	123.01 W
Springfield, S. Dak., U.S.	174	42.49 N	97.54 W
Springfield, Vt., U.S.	176	43.18 N	72.29 W
Springfontein	160	30.19 S	25.36 E
Spring Garden	184	6.59 N	58.30 W
Spring Grove	176	39.52 N	76.52 W
Springhill	172	45.39 N	64.03 W
Spring Mountains ⋀	178	36.10 N	115.40 W
Springs	160	26.13 S	28.25 E
Springs Junction	170	42.19 S	172.11 E
Springsure	168	24.07 S	148.05 E
Springvale, Austl.	168	23.33 S	140.42 E
Springvale, Maine, U.S.	176	43.28 N	70.48 W
Spring Valley, Calif., U.S.	178	37.40 N	121.14 W
Spring Valley, N.Y., U.S.	176	41.07 N	74.03 W
Spring Valley ∨	178	39.15 N	114.25 W
Spring Valley Creek ≏	178	39.20 N	114.25 W
Springville, Calif., U.S.	178	36.08 N	118.49 W
Springville, N.Y., U.S.	176	42.31 N	78.40 W
Sprint ≏	106	54.22 N	2.45 W
Spruce Knob ∧	176	38.42 N	79.32 W
Spruce Mountain ∧	178	40.33 N	114.49 W
Spurn Head ≻	102	53.34 N	0.07 W
Squamish	172	49.42 N	123.09 W
Squam Lake ⊜	176	43.45 N	71.32 W
Squinzano	122	40.26 N	18.03 E
Sragen	142	7.26 S	111.02 E
Srbobran	124	45.33 N	19.48 E
Sredinnyj Chrebet ⋀	128	56.00 N	158.00 E
Srednekolymsk	128	67.27 N	153.41 E
Srednerusskaja Vozvyšennost' ⋀[1]	126	52.00 N	38.00 E
Srednesibirskoje Ploskogorje ⋀[1]	128	65.00 N	105.00 E
Srednij Vas'ugan	128	59.16 N	78.15 E
Śrem	116	52.08 N	17.01 E
Sremska Mitrovica	124	44.58 N	19.37 E
Sremski Karlovci	124	45.12 N	19.57 E
Sri Düngargarh	146	28.05 N	74.00 E
Sri Gangānagar	149	29.55 N	73.53 E
Srīkākulam	148	18.18 N	83.54 E
Sri Karanpur	149	29.50 N	73.27 E
Sri Lanka □[1]	144	7.00 N	81.00 E
Srīnagar	149	34.05 N	74.49 E
Srirampur	148	19.34 N	74.34 E
Srīrangam	148	10.52 N	78.41 E
Srīvilliputtūr	148	9.31 N	77.38 E
Środa Wielkopolski	116	52.14 N	17.17 E
Srpska Crnja	124	45.43 N	20.42 E
St. → Saint, Sankt, Sint			
Staaten ≏	166	16.24 S	141.17 E
Stack, Loch ⊜	108	58.20 N	4.55 W
Stackpoie Head ≻	104	51.37 N	4.54 W
Stack Skerry I[2]	108	59.01 N	4.31 W
Stade	116	53.36 N	9.28 E
Stadlandet ≻[1]	114	62.07 N	5.18 E
Stadskanaal	116	53.00 N	6.55 E
Stadthagen	116	52.19 N	9.13 E
Staffa I	108	56.25 N	6.20 W
Staffin	108	57.37 N	6.12 W
Stafford, Eng., U.K.	104	52.48 N	2.07 W
Stafford, Va., U.S.	176	38.25 N	77.24 W
Staffordshire □[6]	106	52.50 N	2.00 W
Stafford Springs	176	41.57 N	72.18 W
Staffordsville	176	37.50 N	82.50 W
Staines	104	51.26 N	0.31 W
Stainforth	106	53.36 N	1.01 W
Stainmore Forest •[3]	106	54.30 N	2.10 W
Staked Plain → Estacado, Llano ≚	174	33.30 N	103.00 W
Stalać	124	43.40 N	21.25 E
Stalbridge	104	50.58 N	2.23 W
Stalham	104	52.47 N	1.31 E
Stalin → Varna, Blg.	124	43.13 N	27.55 E
Stalin → Brașov, Rom.	124	45.39 N	25.37 E
Stalin (Kuçovë), Shq.	124	40.48 N	19.54 E
Stalinabad → Dušanbe	126	38.35 N	68.48 E
Stalinogorsk → Novomoskovsk	130	54.05 N	38.13 W
Stalinogród → Katowice	116	50.16 N	19.00 E
Ställdalen	114	59.56 N	14.56 E
Stalowa Wola	116	50.35 N	22.02 E
Stamford, Austl.	168	21.16 S	143.49 E
Stamford, Eng., U.K.	104	52.39 N	0.29 W
Stamford, Conn., U.S.	176	41.03 N	73.32 W
Stamford, N.Y., U.S.	176	42.25 N	74.37 W
Stamford, Tex., U.S.	174	32.57 N	99.48 W
Stamford Bridge	106	53.59 N	0.55 W
Stanaford	176	37.49 N	81.10 W
Stanardsville	176	38.18 N	78.26 W
Standerton	160	26.58 S	29.07 E
Standish, Eng., U.K.	106	53.36 N	2.41 W
Standish, Mich., U.S.	176	43.59 N	83.57 W
Standon	104	51.53 N	0.02 E
Stanford le Hope	104	51.31 N	0.26 E
Stanger	160	29.27 S	31.14 E
Stanhope	106	54.45 N	2.01 W
Stanislaus ≏	178	37.40 N	121.14 W
Stanislaus, Middle Fork ≏	178	38.09 N	120.21 W
Stanislaus, North Fork ≏	178	38.09 N	120.21 W
Stanke Dimitrov	124	42.16 N	23.07 E
Stanley, Austl.	168	40.46 S	145.18 E
Stanley, Falk. Is.	186	51.42 S	57.51 W
Stanley, Eng., U.K.	106	54.52 N	1.42 W
Stanley, Scot., U.K.	108	56.28 N	3.27 W
Stanley, Va., U.S.	176	38.34 N	78.31 W
Stanley Falls ∟	158	0.30 N	25.12 E
Stanleyville → Kisangani	158	0.30 N	25.12 E
Stanlow	106	53.17 N	2.52 W
Stann Creek	180	16.58 N	88.13 W
Stannington	106	55.06 N	1.40 W
Stanovoj Chrebet ⋀	128	56.20 N	126.00 E
Stanovoje Nagorje (Stanovoy Mountains) ⋀	128	56.00 N	114.00 E
Stansmore Range ⋀	164	21.23 S	128.33 E
Stanstead Abbots	104	51.47 N	0.01 E
Stansted Mountfitchet	104	51.54 N	0.12 E
Stanthorpe	168	28.39 S	151.57 E
Stanton, Eng., U.K.	104	52.19 N	0.53 E
Stanton, Ky., U.S.	176	37.54 N	83.52 W
Stanton, Mich., U.S.	176	43.18 N	85.05 W
Stanwix	106	54.54 N	2.55 W
Stapleford	104	52.56 N	1.16 W
Staplehurst	104	51.10 N	0.33 E
Starachowice	116	51.03 N	21.04 E
Staraja Russa	130	58.00 N	31.23 E
Stara Pazova	124	44.59 N	20.10 E
Stara Planina (Balkan Mountains) ⋀	124	43.15 N	25.00 E
Starav, Ben ∧	108	56.32 N	5.03 W
Stara Zagora	124	42.25 N	25.38 E
Starbuck Island I	96	5.37 S	155.53 W
Starcross	104	50.38 N	3.27 W
Stargard Szczeciński (Stargard in Pommern)	116	53.20 N	15.02 E
Stari Bar	124	42.06 N	19.08 E
Stari Grad	122	43.11 N	16.36 E
Star Mountains ⋀	166	5.05 S	141.05 E
Starnberg	116	48.00 N	11.20 E
Starodub	130	52.35 N	32.46 E
Starogard Gdański	116	53.59 N	18.33 E
Star Peak ∧	178	40.32 N	118.10 W
Start Bay C	104	50.17 N	3.36 W
Start Point ≻	102	50.13 N	3.38 W
Staryj Sambor	116	49.27 N	22.59 E
Stassfurt	116	51.51 N	11.34 E
State College	176	40.48 N	77.52 W
Stateline	178	38.57 N	119.57 W
Station Peak	164	21.10 S	118.11 E
Staunton	174	38.09 N	79.04 W
Stavanger	114	58.58 N	5.45 E
Staveley	106	53.16 N	1.20 W
Staveren	116	52.53 N	5.22 E
Stavropol'	126	45.02 N	41.59 E
Stawell	168	37.04 S	142.46 E
Staxigoe	108	58.28 N	3.04 W
Stayner	176	44.25 N	80.05 W
Steamboat Springs	174	40.29 N	106.50 W
Steenbergen	116	51.35 N	4.19 E
Steenkool	166	2.07 S	133.32 E
Steens Mountain ⋀	178	42.35 N	118.40 W
Steenwijk	116	52.47 N	6.08 E
Steep Holm I	104	51.21 N	3.07 W
Steeping ≏	106	53.06 N	0.18 E
Steep Point ≻	164	26.08 S	113.08 E
Stefansson Island I	172	73.17 N	106.45 W
Stegi	160	26.32 S	31.58 E
Steiermark □[3]	116	47.10 N	15.10 E
Steinach	116	47.05 N	11.28 E
Steinbach	172	49.32 N	96.41 W
Steinkjer	114	64.01 N	11.30 E
Steinkopf	160	29.18 S	17.43 E
Steinshamn	114	62.47 N	6.29 E
Stella	160	26.38 S	24.48 E
Stellarton	172	45.34 N	62.40 W
Stellenbosch	160	33.58 S	18.50 E
Stenay	118	49.29 N	5.11 E
Stendal	116	52.36 N	11.51 E
Stenhousemuir	108	56.02 N	3.48 W
Stenness, Loch of ⊜	108	59.00 N	3.15 W
Stenstrup	114	55.07 N	10.31 E
Stepanakert	150	39.49 N	46.44 E
Stepancevo	130	56.08 N	41.42 E
Stephens, Port C	168	32.45 S	152.05 E
Stephens City	176	39.05 N	78.13 W
Stephens Creek	168	31.50 S	141.30 E
Stephenson, Mount ∧	87	69.49 S	69.43 W
Stephenville	172	48.33 N	58.35 W
Stepn'ak	126	52.50 N	70.50 E
Steptoe Valley ∨	178	39.25 N	114.45 W
Sterkaar	160	31.05 S	23.42 E
Sterkstroom	160	31.32 S	26.32 E
Sterling, Colo., U.S.	174	40.37 N	103.13 W
Sterling, Ill., U.S.	174	41.48 N	89.42 W
Sterling, Mich., U.S.	176	44.02 N	84.02 W
Sterlitamak	112	53.37 N	55.58 E
Šternberk	116	49.44 N	17.18 E
Steubenville	176	40.22 N	80.37 W
Stevenage	104	51.55 N	0.14 W
Stevens, Mount ∧	170	40.48 S	172.50 E
Stevenson Creek ≏	164	27.06 S	135.33 E
Stevens Point	174	44.31 N	89.34 W
Stevenston	108	55.39 N	4.45 W
Stewart	172	55.56 N	129.59 W
Stewart ≏	172	63.18 N	139.26 W
Stewart, Cape ≻	166	11.57 S	134.45 E

Symbols in the index entries are identified on page 198.

Stew – Tane

Name	Page	Lat ° ′	Long ° ′
Stewart Island I	170	47.00 S	167.50 E
Stewarton	108	55.41 N	4.31 W
Stewartstown, N. Ire., U.K.	110	54.35 N	6.41 W
Stewartstown, Pa., U.S.	176	39.45 N	76.35 W
Steyning	104	50.53 N	0.20 W
Steynsburg	160	31.15 S	25.49 E
Steynsrus	160	27.58 S	27.33 E
Steyr	116	48.03 N	14.25 E
Steytlerville	160	33.21 S	24.21 E
Stikine ≃	172	56.40 N	132.30 W
Stikine Ranges ⋀	172	58.45 N	130.00 W
Stilbaai	160	34.24 S	21.26 E
Stilfontein	160	26.50 S	26.50 E
Stilís	124	38.55 N	22.36 E
Stillwater, Minn., U.S.	174	45.04 N	92.49 W
Stillwater, Okla., U.S.	174	36.07 N	97.04 W
Stillwater Range ⋀	178	39.50 N	118.15 W
Stinchar ≃	106	55.06 N	5.00 W
Stinear Nunataks ⋀	87	69.42 S	64.40 E
Štip	124	41.44 N	22.12 E
Stiperstones ∧	104	52.35 N	2.56 W
Stirling, Austl.	164	21.44 S	133.45 E
Stirling, Ont., Can.	176	44.18 N	77.33 W
Stirling, Scot., U.K.	108	56.07 N	3.57 W
Stirling City	178	39.54 N	121.32 W
Stirling Range ⋀	164	34.23 S	117.50 E
Stittsville	176	45.15 N	75.55 W
Stjernøya I	112	70.18 N	22.45 E
Stockbridge	104	51.07 N	1.29 W
Stockerau	116	48.23 N	16.13 E
Stockholm	114	59.20 N	18.03 E
Stockholms Län □[6]	114	59.30 N	18.20 E
Stockport	106	53.25 N	2.10 W
Stocksbridge	106	53.27 N	1.34 W
Stockton	178	37.57 N	121.17 W
Stockton-on-Tees	106	54.34 N	1.19 W
Stockton Plateau ⋀[1]	174	30.30 N	102.30 W
Stockton Springs	176	44.29 N	68.52 W
Stœng Trêng	140	13.31 N	105.58 E
Stoer	108	58.12 N	5.20 W
Stoer, Point of ≻	108	58.15 N	5.21 W
Stoffberg	160	25.29 S	29.49 E
Stoke Golding	104	52.34 N	1.24 W
Stokenchurch	104	51.40 N	0.55 W
Stoke-on-Trent	104	53.00 N	2.10 W
Stokesley	106	54.28 N	1.11 W
Stokes Point ≻	168	40.10 S	143.56 E
Stolac	122	43.05 N	17.58 E
Stolberg	116	50.46 N	6.13 E
Stolbovoj, Ostrov I	128	74.05 N	136.00 E
Ston	122	42.50 N	17.42 E
Stone	104	52.54 N	2.10 W
Stoneboro	176	41.20 N	80.07 W
Stone Harbor	176	39.03 N	74.45 W
Stonehaven	108	56.38 N	2.13 W
Stonehenge	168	24.22 S	143.17 E
Stonehouse, Eng., U.K.	104	51.45 N	2.17 W
Stonehouse, Scot., U.K.	108	55.43 N	4.00 W
Stoneleigh	104	52.21 N	1.31 W
Stone Mountain ∧	176	44.34 N	71.40 W
Stonewall	172	50.09 N	97.21 W
Stoney Creek	176	43.13 N	79.46 W
Stonington	176	44.09 N	68.40 W
Stony Creek ≃	178	39.41 N	121.58 W
Stony Crossing	168	35.05 S	143.35 E
Stony Lake ⊜, Man., Can.	172	58.51 N	98.35 W
Stony Lake ⊜, Ont., Can.	176	44.33 N	78.05 W
Stony Point	176	41.57 N	83.16 W
Stony Rapids	172	59.16 N	105.50 W
Stony Stratford	104	52.04 N	0.52 W
Stora Le ⊜	114	59.05 N	11.53 E
Stora Sotra I	114	60.18 N	5.05 E
Storby	114	60.13 N	19.34 E
Stord I	114	59.53 N	5.25 E
Store Heddinge	114	55.19 N	12.25 E
Storfjorden C[2]	114	62.25 N	6.30 E
Storfors	114	59.32 N	14.16 E
Storkerson Bay C	172	73.00 N	124.50 W
Storkerson Peninsula ≻[1]	172	72.30 N	106.30 W
Storlien	114	63.19 N	12.06 E
Storm Bay C	168	43.10 S	147.32 E
Stormberg ⋀	160	31.27 S	26.55 E
Storm Lake	174	42.39 N	95.13 W
Stormsrivier	160	33.59 S	23.52 E
Stornoway	108	58.12 N	6.23 W
Storrington	104	50.55 N	0.28 W
Storrs	176	41.48 N	72.15 W
Storsjøen ⊜	114	60.23 N	11.40 E
Storsjön ⊜, Sve.	114	62.48 N	13.07 E
Storsjön ⊜, Sve.	114	60.34 N	16.44 E
Storsjön ⊜, Sve.	114	63.12 N	14.18 E
Storskardhøa ∧	114	62.30 N	8.45 E
Storsteinsfjellet ∧	112	68.14 N	17.52 E
Storuman	112	65.06 N	17.06 E
Storvarts gruve	114	62.38 N	11.31 E
Storvreta	114	59.58 N	17.42 E
Stotfold	104	52.01 N	0.14 W
Stoughton	176	42.07 N	71.06 W
Stour ≃, Eng., U.K.	102	50.43 N	1.46 W
Stour ≃, Eng., U.K.	104	51.52 N	1.16 E
Stour ≃, Eng., U.K.	104	52.20 N	2.15 W
Stour ≃, Eng., U.K.	104	51.18 N	1.22 E
Stourbridge	104	52.27 N	2.09 W
Stourport-on-Severn	104	52.21 N	2.16 W
Stow	176	41.10 N	81.27 W
Stowe	176	44.28 N	72.41 W
Stowmarket	104	52.11 N	1.00 E
Stow-on-the-Wold	104	51.56 N	1.44 W
Strabane	110	54.49 N	7.27 W
Strachan	108	57.01 N	2.32 W
Strachur	108	56.10 N	5.04 W
Stradbally	110	53.00 N	7.08 W
Stradbroke	104	52.19 N	1.16 E
Stradella	122	45.05 N	9.18 E
Stradone	110	53.58 N	7.14 W
Strahan	168	42.09 S	145.19 E
Strakonice	116	49.16 N	13.55 E
Stralsund	116	54.19 N	13.05 E
Strand	160	34.06 S	18.50 E
Strandhill	110	54.17 N	8.36 W
Strangford	110	54.22 N	5.34 W
Strangford Lough ⊜	110	54.30 N	5.36 W
Strangways ≃	166	14.52 S	133.50 E
Strangways, Mount ∧	164	23.02 S	133.51 E
Stranorlar	110	54.48 N	7.46 W
Stranraer	106	54.55 N	5.02 W
Strasbourg	118	48.35 N	7.45 E
Strasburg, Ohio, U.S.	176	40.36 N	81.32 W
Strasburg, Pa., U.S.	176	39.59 N	76.11 W
Strasburg, Va., U.S.	176	38.59 N	78.22 W
Stratford, Ont., Can.	176	43.22 N	80.57 W
Stratford, N.Z.	170	39.20 S	174.17 E
Stratford, Calif., U.S.	178	36.11 N	119.49 W
Stratford, Conn., U.S.	176	41.14 N	73.07 W
Stratford-upon-Avon	104	52.12 N	1.41 W
Strathalbyn	168	35.16 S	138.54 E
Strathaven	108	55.40 N	4.04 W
Strathclyde □[4]	108	56.00 N	5.15 W
Strathdearn V	108	57.15 N	4.05 W
Strathdon	108	57.11 N	3.02 W
Strathearn V	108	56.18 N	3.45 W
Strathkanaird	108	57.59 N	5.11 W
Strathminglo	108	56.16 N	3.16 W
Strathmore	178	36.09 N	119.04 W
Strathmore V	108	56.39 N	3.00 W
Strathpeffer	108	57.35 N	4.33 W
Strathroy	176	42.57 N	81.38 W
Strathy ≃	108	58.34 N	4.00 W
Strathy Point ≻	108	58.35 N	4.02 W
Stratton, Eng., U.K.	104	50.50 N	4.31 W
Stratton, Maine, U.S.	176	45.08 N	70.26 W
Stratton Mountain ∧	176	43.05 N	72.56 W
Stratton Saint Margaret	104	51.35 N	1.45 W
Straubing	116	48.53 N	12.34 E
Straumen	114	63.52 N	11.18 E
Strausberg	116	52.35 N	13.53 E
Streaky Bay	164	32.48 S	134.13 E
Streaky Bay C	164	32.36 S	134.08 E
Středočeský Kraj □[4]	116	49.55 N	14.30 E
Stredoslovenský Kraj □[4]	116	48.50 N	19.10 E
Street	104	51.07 N	2.42 W
Streetsboro	176	41.14 N	81.21 W
Streetsville	176	43.35 N	79.42 W
Strelka-Čun'a	128	61.45 N	102.48 E
Strel'na	130	59.51 N	30.02 E
Strenči	130	57.37 N	25.41 E
Stresa	122	45.53 N	8.32 E
Stretensk	128	52.15 N	117.43 E
Stretford	106	53.27 N	2.19 W
Stretton, Austl.	164	32.32 S	117.41 E
Stretton, Eng., U.K.	104	52.44 N	0.35 W
Stretton, Eng., U.K.	106	53.21 N	2.35 W
Strichen	108	57.34 N	2.05 W
Strimón (Struma) ≃	124	40.47 N	23.51 E
Striven, Loch C	108	55.58 N	5.09 W
Strjama ≃	124	42.10 N	24.56 E
Strokestown	110	53.47 N	8.08 W
Stroma I	108	58.41 N	3.08 W
Stromeferry	108	57.21 N	5.34 W
Stromness	108	58.57 N	3.18 W
Strömstad	114	58.56 N	11.10 E
Strömsund	114	63.51 N	15.35 E
Strong	176	44.48 N	70.13 W
Stronsay I	108	59.07 N	2.37 W
Stronsay Firth)(	108	59.02 N	2.41 W
Strontian	108	56.41 N	5.44 W
Strood	104	51.24 N	0.28 E
Stroud	104	51.45 N	2.12 W
Stroud Road	168	32.20 S	151.56 E
Stroudsburg	176	40.59 N	75.12 W
Struer	114	56.29 N	8.37 E
Struga	124	41.11 N	20.40 E
Strule ≃	110	54.43 N	7.25 W
Struma (Strimón) ≃	124	40.47 N	23.51 E
Strumble Head ≻	104	52.02 N	5.04 W
Strumica	124	41.26 N	22.38 E
Strunino	130	56.23 N	38.34 E
Struthers	176	41.04 N	80.38 W
Struy	108	57.24 N	4.39 W
Strydenburg	160	29.58 S	23.40 E
Stryker	176	41.30 N	84.25 W
Stryn	114	61.55 N	6.47 E
Strzegom	116	50.57 N	16.21 E
Strzelce Opolskie	116	50.31 N	18.19 E
Strzelecki Creek ≃	168	29.37 S	139.59 E
Strzelin	116	50.47 N	17.03 E
Stuart ≃	172	54.00 N	123.32 W
Stuart Bluff Range ⋀	164	22.47 S	132.13 E
Stuart Lake ⊜	172	54.32 N	124.35 W
Stuart Range ⋀	164	29.10 S	134.56 E
Stuarts Draft	176	38.01 N	79.02 W
Stubbekøbing	114	54.53 N	12.03 E
Studen Kladenec, Jazovir ⊜[1]	124	41.37 N	25.30 E
Studholme Junction	170	44.44 S	171.08 E
Studland	104	50.39 N	1.58 W
Studley	104	52.16 N	1.52 W
Stupino	130	54.53 N	38.05 E
Sturdee	164	31.52 S	132.23 E
Sturgeon ≃	176	45.24 N	84.38 W
Sturgeon Falls	172	46.22 N	79.55 W
Sturgeon Lake ⊜	176	44.28 N	78.42 W
Sturgis	176	41.48 N	85.25 W
Sturminster Newton	104	50.50 N	2.19 W
Sturry	104	51.18 N	1.07 E
Sturt Creek	164	19.10 S	128.10 E
Sturt Creek ≃	164	20.08 S	127.24 E
Sturt Desert ⊶[2]	168	28.30 S	141.00 E
Stutterheim	160	32.33 S	27.28 E
Stuttgart, B.R.D.	116	48.46 N	9.11 E
Stuttgart, Ark., U.S.	174	34.30 N	91.33 W
Stykkishólmur	112a	65.06 N	22.48 W
Suakin Archipelago II	154	18.42 N	38.30 E
Subah	142	6.58 S	109.52 E
Subang	142	6.34 S	107.45 E
Subansiri ≃	146	26.48 N	93.50 E
Subarnarekha ≃	146	21.33 N	87.12 E
Subata	130	56.01 N	25.56 E
Subotica	124	46.06 N	19.39 E
Sučan	128	43.08 N	133.09 E
Succor Creek ≃	178	43.35 N	117.01 W
Suceava	124	47.39 N	26.19 E
Suceava □[4]	124	47.30 N	25.45 E
Suchana	128	68.45 N	118.00 E
Süchbaatar	132	50.17 N	106.10 E
Suchiniči	130	54.06 N	35.20 E
Suchona ≃	112	60.46 N	46.24 E
Suchumi	126	43.01 N	41.02 E
Suck ≃	110	53.16 N	8.03 W
Sucre	184	19.02 S	65.17 W
Sucre □[3]	182	10.25 N	63.30 W
Sucre □[5]	182	9.00 N	75.00 W
Sud, Canal du)(	182	18.35 N	73.00 W
Sud, Massif du ⋀	182	18.25 N	73.55 W
Sud, Pointe ≻	161a	11.53 S	43.49 E
Sudalsvatnet ⊜	114	59.35 N	6.45 E
Sudan □[1]	154	15.00 N	30.00 E
Sudan ⊶[1]	154	10.00 N	20.00 E
Sudbury, Ont., Can.	172	46.30 N	81.00 W
Sudbury, Eng., U.K.	104	52.02 N	0.44 E
Sude ≃	116	53.22 N	10.45 E
Sudety ⋀	116	50.30 N	16.00 E
Sue ≃	154	7.41 N	28.03 E
Sueca	120	39.12 N	0.19 W
Suez, Gulf of → Suways, Khalīj as- C	154	29.00 N	32.50 E
Suez Canal → Suways, Qanāt as- ≍	154	29.55 N	32.33 E
Suffolk	174	36.44 N	76.35 W
Suffolk □[6]	104	52.10 N	1.20 E
Sugar ≃	176	43.24 N	72.24 W
Sugar Creek	176	41.25 N	79.49 W
Sugarloaf ∧[2]	176	41.24 N	81.06 W
Sugarloaf Mountain ∧	176	45.01 N	70.22 W
Sugarloaf Point ≻	168	32.26 S	152.33 E
Sugoj ≃	128	64.15 N	154.29 E
Şuḥār	150	24.22 N	56.45 E
Suhl	116	50.37 N	10.41 E
Suhl □[5]	116	50.35 N	10.40 E
Suhopolje	122	45.48 N	17.30 E
Suian	136	29.28 N	118.44 E
Suichang	136	28.34 N	119.14 E
Suichuan	136	26.26 N	114.32 E
Suide	132	37.33 N	110.04 E
Suifenhe	132	44.24 N	131.10 E
Suihua	132	46.37 N	127.00 E
Suining, Zhg.	132	30.31 N	105.34 E
Suining, Zhg.	136	33.54 N	117.56 E
Suipacha	188	34.47 S	59.40 W
Suiping	136	33.10 N	113.57 E
Suir ≃	110	52.15 N	7.00 W
Suixi	136	33.56 N	116.46 E
Suixian	136	31.42 N	113.20 E
Şuizhong	132	40.20 N	120.19 E
Šuja	130	56.50 N	41.23 E
Sūjāngarh	146	27.42 N	74.28 E
Sujiabu	136	31.38 N	116.22 E
Sukabumi	142	6.55 S	106.56 E
Sukadana, Indon.	142	1.15 S	109.57 E
Sukadana, Indon.	142	5.05 S	105.33 E
Sukagawa	134	37.17 N	140.23 E
Sukaraja	142	2.21 S	110.37 E
Sukeva	114	63.52 N	27.26 E
Sukhothai	140	17.01 N	99.49 E
Sukkertoppen	172	65.25 N	52.53 W
Sukkozero	112	63.11 N	32.18 E
Sukkur	146	27.42 N	68.52 E
Sukoharjo	142	7.41 S	110.50 E
Sukumo	134	32.56 N	132.44 E
Sul, Baía do C	188	27.40 S	48.35 W
Sula I	114	61.08 N	4.55 E
Sula, Kepulauan II	142	1.52 S	125.22 E
Sulaimān Range ⋀	146	30.30 N	70.10 E
Sulawesi (Celebes) I	142	2.00 S	121.00 E
Sulcis ⊶[1]	122	39.05 N	8.45 E
Sulechów	116	52.06 N	15.37 E
Sule Skerry I[2]	108	59.05 N	4.26 W
Sulina, Braţul ≃[1]	124	45.09 N	29.41 E
Sulitelma ∧	112	67.08 N	16.24 E
Sullana	184	4.53 S	80.42 W
Sullane ≃	110	51.53 N	8.56 W
Sully	118	47.46 N	2.22 E
Sulmona	122	42.03 N	13.55 E
Sulu Archipelago II	142	6.00 N	121.00 E
Sulu Basin ⋄[1]	94	7.30 N	121.00 E
Sulūq	154	31.39 N	20.15 E
Sulu Sea ⊤[2]	138	8.00 N	120.00 E
Sulusi	132	33.08 N	95.08 E
Sulzbach	116	49.18 N	7.07 E
Sulzbach-Rosenberg	116	49.30 N	11.45 E
Sumampa	188	29.20 S	63.30 W
Sumatera (Sumatra) I	138	0.05 S	102.00 E
Sumaúma	184	7.50 S	60.02 W
Sumba I	142	10.00 S	120.00 E
Sumbawa I	142	8.40 S	118.00 E
Sumbawa Besar	142	8.30 S	117.26 E
Sumbawanga	158	7.58 S	31.37 E
Sümber	132	46.21 N	108.25 E
Sumbilla	120	43.10 N	1.40 W
Sumburgh Head ≻	108a	59.53 N	1.20 W
Sumburgh Roost)(	108	59.49 N	1.19 W
Sumedang	142	6.52 S	107.55 E
Sümeg	116	46.59 N	17.17 E
Šumen	124	43.16 N	26.55 E
Sumenep	142	7.01 S	113.52 E
Šumerl'a	112	55.30 N	46.26 E
Sumgait	150	40.36 N	49.38 E
Šumicha	126	55.14 N	63.19 E
Sumisu-jima I	132	31.27 N	140.03 E
Summer Bridge	106	54.03 N	1.41 W
Summerhill	110	53.29 N	6.44 W
Summer Isles II	108	58.02 N	5.28 W
Summer Lake ⊜	178	42.50 N	120.45 W
Summerland	172	49.39 N	119.33 W
Summerside	172	46.24 N	63.47 W
Summersville	176	38.17 N	80.51 W
Summit Lake	172	54.17 N	122.38 W
Summit Mountain ∧	178	39.23 N	116.28 W
Summit Rock ∧	170	45.25 S	170.04 E
Sumner, Lake ⊜	170	42.42 S	172.13 E
Sumoto	134	34.21 N	134.54 E
Šumperk	116	49.58 N	16.58 E
Sumpiuh	142	7.37 S	109.21 E
Šumšu, Ostrov I	128	50.45 N	156.20 E
Sumter	174	33.55 N	80.20 W
Sumy	126	50.55 N	34.45 E
Sumy □[4]	130	52.10 N	33.40 E
Sunagawa	134a	43.29 N	141.55 E
Sunām	149	30.08 N	75.48 E
Sunapee Lake ⊜	176	43.23 N	72.03 W
Sunart, Loch ⊜	108	56.41 N	5.43 W
Sunbury, Austl.	168	37.35 S	144.44 E
Sunbury, Ohio, U.S.	176	40.14 N	82.52 W
Sunbury, Pa., U.S.	176	40.52 N	76.47 W
Sunchales	188	30.57 S	61.35 W
Sunch'ŏn	132	34.57 N	127.28 E
Suncook	176	43.08 N	71.27 W
Suncook ≃	176	43.08 N	71.28 W
Sunda, Selat (Sunda Strait))(	142	6.00 S	105.45 E
Sundarbans ⊶[1]	146	22.00 N	89.00 E
Sunda Strait → Sunda, Selat)(	142	6.00 S	105.45 E
Sundbyberg	114	59.22 N	17.58 E
Sunderland	106	54.55 N	1.23 W
Sundown	164	26.14 S	133.12 E
Sundridge	176	45.46 N	79.24 W
Sundsvall	114	62.23 N	17.18 E
Sunfish Creek ≃	176	39.01 N	83.03 W
Sungaipenuh	142	2.05 S	101.23 E
Sungai Petani	142	5.39 N	100.30 E
Sungguminasa	142	5.12 S	119.27 E
Suniteyouqi	132	42.32 N	112.58 E
Sunjiabu	136	30.55 N	118.54 E
Sunne	114	59.50 N	13.09 E
Sunninghill	104	51.25 N	0.40 W
Sunnylvsfjorden C[2]	114	62.17 N	7.01 E
Sunnyvale	178	37.23 N	122.01 W
Sunset Country ⊶[1]	168	35.00 S	141.30 E
Suntar	128	62.10 N	117.40 E
Suntar-Chajata, Chrebet ⋀	128	62.00 N	143.00 E
Sun Valley	174	43.42 N	114.21 W
Sunyani	152	7.20 N	2.20 W
Suoche (Yarkand)	146	38.25 N	77.16 E
Suolun	132	46.36 N	121.13 E
Suomussalmi	114	64.53 N	29.05 E
Suō-nada ⊤[2]	134	33.50 N	131.30 E
Suonenjoki	114	62.37 N	27.08 E
Suordach	128	66.43 N	132.04 E
Suoxian	144	31.50 N	93.45 E
Suozong	132	31.50 N	93.45 E
Superior	174	46.44 N	92.05 W
Superior, Lake ⊜	174	48.00 N	88.00 W
Superior Upland ⋀[1]	174	46.00 N	90.30 W
Supetar	122	43.23 N	16.33 E
Suphan Buri	140	14.28 N	100.07 E
Sūq ash-Shuyūkh	150	30.53 N	46.28 E
Suqian	136	33.59 N	118.18 E
Suquṭrā I	144	12.30 N	54.00 E
Şūr (Tyre), Lubnān	150	33.16 N	35.11 E
Şūr, 'Umān	144	22.35 N	59.31 E
Sur, Point ≻	178	36.18 N	121.54 W
Sura ≃	112	56.06 N	46.00 E
Surabaya	142	7.15 S	112.45 E
Surakarta	142	7.35 S	110.50 E
Surat, Austl.	168	27.09 S	149.04 E
Surat, Bhārat	146	21.10 N	72.50 E
Surat Thani (Ban Don)	140	9.08 N	99.19 E
Surаž	130	55.25 N	30.44 E
Surdulica	124	42.41 N	22.10 E
Surendranagar	146	22.42 N	71.41 E
Surf City	176	39.40 N	74.10 W
Surfers Paradise	168	28.00 S	153.26 E
Surgères	118	46.07 N	0.45 W
Surgut	128	61.14 N	73.20 E
Suriāpet	148	17.09 N	79.37 E
Surigao	138	9.45 N	125.30 E
Surin	140	14.53 N	103.29 E
Surinam □[1]	184	4.00 N	56.00 W
Sūrmaq	150	31.03 N	52.48 E
Surprise Valley V	178	41.35 N	120.05 W
Surrey □[6]	102	51.10 N	0.20 W
Surt	154	31.12 N	16.35 E
Surt, Khalīj C	154	31.30 N	18.00 E
Surtainville	102	49.25 N	1.50 W
Surtsey I	112a	63.16 N	20.32 W
Surud Ad ∧	154	10.41 N	47.18 E
Suruga-wan C	134	34.51 N	138.33 E
Şurulangun	142	2.37 S	102.45 E
Šuryškary	128	65.54 N	65.22 E
Susa	134	34.37 N	131.36 E
Susaki	134	33.22 N	133.17 E
Susan ≃	178	40.19 N	120.17 W
Sūsangerd	150	31.34 N	48.11 E
Susanville	178	40.25 N	120.39 W
Šušenskoje	128	59.19 N	91.58 E
Susitna ≃	172	61.16 N	150.30 W
Susoh	138	3.43 N	96.50 E
Susong	136	30.09 N	116.06 E
Susquehanna	176	41.57 N	75.36 W
Susquehanna ≃	176	39.33 N	76.05 W
Susquehanna, West Branch ≃	176	40.53 N	76.47 W
Susques	188	23.25 S	66.30 W
Sussex, N.B., Can.	172	45.43 N	65.31 W
Sussex, N.J., U.S.	176	41.13 N	74.36 W
Sussex, East □[6]	102	50.55 N	0.15 E
Sussex, Vale of V	104	50.57 N	0.17 W
Susuman	128	62.47 N	148.10 E
Susuzmüsellim	124	41.06 N	27.03 E
Sutherland	160	32.24 S	20.40 E
Sutherlin	178	43.25 N	123.19 W
Sutlej (Satluj) (Langchuhe) ≃	146	29.23 N	71.02 E
Sutter	178	39.10 N	121.45 W
Sutter Buttes ∧	178	39.12 N	121.50 W
Sutter Creek	178	38.23 N	120.48 W
Sutton, Eng., U.K.	104	52.23 N	0.07 E
Sutton, W. Va., U.S.	176	38.40 N	80.43 W
Sutton ⊶[8]	104	51.22 N	0.12 W
Sutton Bridge	104	52.46 N	0.12 E
Sutton Coldfield	104	52.34 N	1.48 W
Sutton Courtenay	104	51.39 N	1.17 W
Sutton-in-Ashfield	106	53.08 N	1.15 W
Sutton Lake ⊜[1]	176	38.40 N	80.40 W
Sutton-on-Sea	106	53.19 N	0.17 E
Sutton on Trent	106	53.10 N	0.49 W
Suttons Bay	176	44.59 N	85.39 W
Sutton Scotney	104	51.10 N	1.21 W
Sutton Valence	104	51.12 N	0.36 E
Sutton Veny	104	51.11 N	2.08 W
Sutton West	176	44.18 N	79.22 W
Suttor ≃	168	21.25 S	147.45 E
Suttsu	134a	42.48 N	140.14 E
Suurberge ⋀	160	33.18 S	25.32 E
Suurbraak	160	34.00 S	20.39 E
Suure-Jaani	130	58.33 N	25.28 E
Suva	96	18.08 S	178.25 E
Suvorov	130	54.07 N	36.30 E
Suwa	134	36.02 N	138.08 E
Suwa-ko ⊜	134	36.05 N	138.05 E
Suwałki	116	54.07 N	22.56 E
Suwanose-jima I	135b	29.38 N	129.43 E
Suwanose-suidō)(	135b	29.32 N	129.40 E
Suwarrow I[1]	96	13.15 S	163.05 W
Suways, Khalīj as- C	154	29.00 N	32.50 E
Suways, Qanāt as- ≍	154	29.55 N	32.33 E
Suwŏn	132	37.17 N	127.01 E
Suxian	136	33.38 N	116.58 E
Suzak	126	44.07 N	68.28 E
Suzaka	134	36.39 N	138.19 E
Suzdal'	130	56.25 N	40.26 E
Suzhou (Soochow)	136	31.18 N	120.37 E
Suzu	134	37.25 N	137.17 E
Suzuka	134	34.51 N	136.35 E
Suzuka-sammyaku ⋀	134	35.00 N	136.25 E
Suzu-misaki ≻	134	37.31 N	137.21 E
Svalbard and Jan Mayen □[2]	88	71.00 N	8.20 W
Svappavaara	112	67.39 N	21.04 E
Svartenhuk ≻[1]	172	71.55 N	55.00 W
Svartisen ⊓	112	66.38 N	14.00 E
Svataj	128	67.57 N	151.54 E
Sv'atoj Nos, Mys ≻, S.S.S.R.	112	68.10 N	39.45 E
Sv'atoj Nos, Mys ≻, S.S.S.R.	128	72.52 N	140.42 E
Svay Riĕng	140	11.05 N	105.48 E
Sveg	114	62.02 N	14.21 E
Svelvik	114	59.37 N	10.24 E
Şven'	130	53.09 N	34.21 E
Švenčionėliai	130	55.10 N	26.00 E
Svendborg	114	55.03 N	10.37 E
Svenljunga	114	57.30 N	13.07 E
Sverdlovsk, S.S.S.R.	126	48.05 N	39.40 E
Sverdlovsk, S.S.S.R.	126	56.51 N	60.36 E
Sverdrup, Ostrov I	128	74.35 N	74.30 E
Sveti Nikole	124	41.52 N	21.58 E
Svetlaja	128	46.33 N	138.18 E
Svetlyj	128	58.26 N	115.55 E
Svetogorsk	112	61.07 N	28.51 E
Svetozarevo	124	43.58 N	21.16 E
Svilajnac	124	44.14 N	21.13 E
Svilengrad	124	41.46 N	26.12 E
Svir' ≃	130	60.30 N	32.48 E
Svirica	130	60.29 N	32.51 E
Svirsk	128	53.04 N	103.21 E
Svir'stroj	130	60.48 N	33.43 E
Svisloč'	130	53.02 N	24.06 E
Svištov	124	43.37 N	25.20 E
Svitavy	116	49.45 N	16.27 E
Svobodnyj	128	51.24 N	128.08 E
Svolvær	112	68.14 N	14.34 E
Svullrya	114	60.25 N	12.24 E
Svyataya Anna Trough ⋄[1]	94	80.00 N	70.00 E
Swābi	149	34.07 N	72.28 E
Swadlincote	104	52.47 N	1.33 W
Swaffham	104	52.39 N	0.41 E
Swain Reefs ⋄[2]	168	21.40 S	152.15 E
Swains Island I[1]	96	11.03 S	171.05 W
Swakopmund	160	22.41 S	14.34 E
Swakopmund □[5]	160	22.00 S	14.30 E
Swale ≃	102	54.06 N	1.20 W
Swaledale V	106	54.25 N	1.47 W
Swan ≃	164	32.03 S	115.45 E
Swanage	104	50.37 N	1.58 W
Swan Hill	168	35.21 S	143.34 E
Swan Island II	182	17.25 N	83.55 W
Swan Lake ⊜	172	52.30 N	100.45 W
Swanley	104	51.24 N	0.12 E
Swanlinbar	110	54.10 N	7.42 W
Swan River	172	52.06 N	101.16 W
Swansea, Austl.	168	42.08 S	148.04 E
Swansea, Wales, U.K.	104	51.38 N	3.57 W
Swansea Bay C	104	51.35 N	3.52 W
Swans Island I	176	44.10 N	68.25 W
Swanton, Ohio, U.S.	176	41.35 N	83.53 W
Swanton, Vt., U.S.	176	44.55 N	73.07 W
Swartruggens	160	25.40 S	26.42 E
Swartz Creek	176	42.58 N	83.50 W
Swarzędz	116	52.26 N	17.05 E
Swatara Creek ≃	176	40.11 N	76.44 W
Sway	104	50.47 N	1.37 W
Swaziland □[1]	156	26.30 S	31.30 E
Sweden □[1]	100	62.00 N	15.00 E
Swedru	152	5.32 N	0.43 W
Sweetwater	174	32.28 N	100.25 W
Swellendam	160	34.02 S	20.26 E
Świdnica (Schweidnitz)	116	50.51 N	16.29 E
Świdnik	116	51.14 N	22.41 E
Świdwin	116	53.47 N	15.47 E
Świebodzice	116	50.52 N	16.19 E
Świebodzin	116	52.15 N	15.32 E
Świecie	116	53.25 N	18.28 E
Świętokrzyskie, Góry ⋀	116	50.55 N	21.00 E
Swift ≃	104	52.23 N	1.16 W
Swift Current	172	50.17 N	107.50 W
Swilly ≃	110	54.57 N	7.42 W
Swilly, Lough C	110	55.10 N	7.38 W
Swinburne, Cape ≻	172	71.14 N	98.34 W
Swindon	104	51.34 N	1.47 W
Swinford	110	53.57 N	8.57 W
Świnoujście (Swinemünde)	116	53.53 N	14.14 E
Swinton, Eng., U.K.	106	53.28 N	1.20 W
Swinton, Scot., U.K.	108	55.43 N	2.15 W
Switzerland □[1]	100	47.00 N	8.00 E
Swona I	108	58.45 N	3.03 W
Swordfish Seamount ⋄[3]	96	18.30 N	158.25 W
Swords	110	53.28 N	6.13 W
Swords Range ⋀	168	21.57 S	141.32 E
Syalach	128	66.12 N	124.00 E
Sycamore	176	40.57 N	83.10 W
Sycan ≃	178	42.27 N	121.15 W
Syčovka	130	55.50 N	34.17 E
Sydenham	176	44.25 N	76.36 W
Sydney, Austl.	168	33.52 S	151.13 E
Sydney, N.S., Can.	172	46.09 N	60.11 W
Sydney I[1]	96	4.27 S	171.15 W
Sydney Mines	172	46.14 N	60.14 W
Syke	116	52.54 N	8.49 E
Sykesville, Md., U.S.	176	39.22 N	76.58 W
Sykesville, Pa., U.S.	176	41.03 N	78.49 W
Syktyvkar	112	61.40 N	50.46 E
Sylarna ∧	114	63.02 N	12.13 E
Sylhet	146	24.54 N	91.52 E
Sylt I	116	54.54 N	8.20 E
Sylvania	176	41.43 N	83.42 W
Sylvia Grinnell Lake ⊜	172	64.10 N	69.25 W
Sym	128	60.20 N	88.23 E
Symmes Creek ≃	176	38.26 N	82.27 W
Syracuse	176	43.03 N	76.09 W
Syrdarja	126	40.52 N	68.38 E
Syrdarja (Syr-Darya) ≃	126	46.03 N	61.00 E
Syre	108	58.22 N	4.14 W
Syria □[1]	144	35.00 N	38.00 E
Syriam	140	16.46 N	96.15 E
Syston	104	52.42 N	1.04 W
Syzran'	112	53.09 N	48.27 E
Szabadka → Subotica	124	46.06 N	19.39 E
Szabolcs-Szatmár □[6]	116	48.00 N	22.10 E
Szamos (Someș) ≃	124	48.07 N	22.20 E
Szamotuły	116	52.37 N	16.35 E
Szarvas	116	46.52 N	20.34 E
Szczecin (Stettin)	116	53.24 N	14.32 E
Szczecinek (Neustettin)	116	53.43 N	16.42 E
Szczeciński, Zalew (Oderhaff) C	116	53.46 N	14.14 E
Szczytno	116	53.34 N	21.00 E
Szechwan → Sichuan □[4]	132	31.00 N	105.00 E
Szeged	116	46.15 N	20.09 E
Szeghalom	116	47.01 N	21.11 E
Székesfehérvár	116	47.12 N	18.25 E
Szekszárd	116	46.21 N	18.42 E
Szentes	116	46.39 N	20.16 E
Szerencs	116	48.09 N	21.13 E
Szob	116	47.50 N	18.52 E
Szolnok	116	47.10 N	20.12 E
Szolnok □[6]	116	47.12 N	20.11 E
Szombathely	116	47.14 N	16.38 E
Szprotawa	116	51.34 N	15.33 E

T

Name	Page	Lat ° ′	Long ° ′
Taavetti	114	60.55 N	27.34 E
Tabacal	188	23.15 S	64.15 W
Tábara	120	41.49 N	5.57 W
Tabar Islands II	166	2.50 S	152.00 E
Ţabas	150	33.36 N	56.54 E
Tabasco	178	32.35 N	114.50 W
Tabelbala	152	29.23 N	3.15 W
Taber	172	49.47 N	112.08 W
Tabernes de Valldigna	120	39.04 N	0.16 W
Tabiteuea I[1]	96	1.20 S	174.50 E
Tablas, Cabo ≻	188	31.51 S	71.34 W
Tablas Island I	138	12.24 N	122.02 E
Table Bay C	160	33.53 S	18.27 E
Tableland	164	17.17 S	127.00 E
Tabletop ∧	164	22.32 S	123.55 E
Tábor, Česko.	116	49.25 N	14.41 E
Tabor, S.S.S.R.	128	71.16 N	150.12 E
Tabora	158	5.01 S	32.48 E
Tabora □[4]	158	6.00 S	32.00 E
Tabou	152	4.25 N	7.21 W
Tabrīz	150	38.05 N	46.18 E
Tabuaço	120	41.07 N	7.34 W
Tabūk	150	28.23 N	36.35 E
Täby	114	59.30 N	18.03 E
Taché, Lac ⊜	172	64.00 N	120.00 W
Tacheng	132	46.45 N	82.57 E
Tachiataš	126	42.25 N	59.35 E
Tachikawa	134	35.42 N	139.25 E
Tachta-Bazar	150	35.57 N	62.50 E
Tachtamgyda	128	54.06 N	123.34 E
Tacloban	138	11.15 N	125.00 E
Tacna	184	18.01 S	70.15 W
Tacoma	174	47.15 N	122.27 W
Taconic Range ⋀	176	42.40 N	73.15 W
Tacuarembó	188	31.44 S	55.59 W
Tacutu (Takutu) ≃	184	3.01 N	60.29 W
Tadami	134	37.21 N	139.19 E
Tadcaster	106	53.53 N	1.16 W
Tademaït, Plateau du ⋀[1]	152	28.30 N	2.00 E
Tādepallegūdem	148	16.50 N	81.30 E
Tadjoura	154	11.47 N	42.54 E
Tadley	104	51.21 N	1.08 W
Tadotsu	134	34.16 N	133.45 E
Tadoule Lake ⊜	172	58.36 N	98.20 W
Tadoussac	172	48.09 N	69.43 W
Tādpatri	148	14.55 N	78.01 E
Tadworth	104	51.17 N	0.14 W
Tadžikskaja Sovetskaja Socialističeskaja Respublika □[3]	126	39.00 N	71.00 E
T'aebaek-sanmaek ⋀	132	37.40 N	128.50 E
Taegu	132	35.52 N	128.35 E
Taejŏn	132	36.20 N	127.26 E
Tafahi I	96	15.51 S	173.43 W
Tafalla	120	42.31 N	1.40 W
Tafassasset, Oued V	152	21.20 N	10.10 E
Taff ≃	104	51.27 N	3.09 W
Tafí Viejo	188	26.45 S	65.15 W
Taft	178	35.08 N	119.28 W
Tagajō	134	38.20 N	141.00 E
Taganrog	126	47.12 N	38.56 E
Tagaytay	138	14.06 N	120.56 E
Tagbilaran	138	9.39 N	123.51 E
Tagdempt → Tiaret	152	35.28 N	1.21 E
Taghmon	110	52.18 N	6.39 W
Tagish Lake ⊜	172	59.45 N	134.15 W
Taguatinga	190	12.25 S	46.26 W
Taguke	132	32.07 N	84.35 E
Tagula Island I	166	11.30 S	153.30 E
Tagus (Tejo) (Tajo) ≃	120	38.40 N	9.24 W
Tahaa I	96	16.38 S	151.30 W
Tahakopa	170	46.31 S	169.23 E
Tahan, Gunong ∧	142	4.38 N	102.14 E
Tahat ∧	152	23.18 N	5.47 E
Taheke	170	35.27 S	173.39 E
Tahiryuak Lake ⊜	172	70.56 N	112.20 W
Tahiti I	96	17.37 S	149.27 W
Tahlequah	174	35.55 N	94.58 W
Tahoe, Lake ⊜	178	38.58 N	120.00 W
Tahoe City	178	39.10 N	120.09 W
Tahoe Lake ⊜	172	70.15 N	108.45 W
Tahoe Valley	178	38.55 N	120.00 W
Tahoua	152	14.54 N	5.16 E
Tahulandang, Pulau I	142	2.20 N	125.25 E
Tahuna	138	3.37 N	125.29 E
Taian	132	36.12 N	117.07 E
Taibilla, Sierra de ⋀	120	38.10 N	2.10 W
Taicang	136	31.26 N	121.07 E
T'aichung	136	24.09 N	120.41 E
T'aichunghsien	136	24.15 N	120.43 E
Taieri ≃	170	46.03 S	170.11 E
Taihangshan ⋀	132	36.00 N	113.35 E
Taihape	170	39.40 S	175.48 E
Taihe, Zhg.	136	26.49 N	114.55 E
Taihe, Zhg.	136	33.11 N	115.36 E
Taihu	136	30.26 N	116.16 E
Taihu ⊜	132	31.15 N	120.10 E
Taikang	136	34.04 N	114.50 E
Tailai	132	46.23 N	123.27 E
Taimba	128	60.18 N	98.58 E
Tain	108	57.48 N	4.04 W
T'ainan	136	23.00 N	120.11 E
T'ainanhsien	136	23.18 N	120.19 E
Tainaron, Ákra ≻	124	36.22 N	22.30 E
Taining	136	26.54 N	117.09 E
Taiobeiras	190	15.49 S	42.14 W
T'aipei	136	25.03 N	121.30 E
T'aipeihsien	136	25.00 N	121.27 E
Taiping, Malay.	142	4.51 N	100.44 E
Taiping, Zhg.	136	30.18 N	118.12 E
Taira → Iwaki	134	37.03 N	140.55 E
Tais	142	4.06 S	102.34 E
Taisetsu-zan ∧	132	43.30 N	142.57 E
Taisha	134	35.24 N	132.40 E
Taishun	136	27.33 N	119.43 E
Taitao, Península de ≻[1]	186	46.30 S	74.25 W
Taitapu	170	43.40 S	172.33 E
T'aitung	136	22.45 N	121.09 E
Taivalkoski	114	65.34 N	28.15 E
Taiwan (T'aiwan) □[1]	132	23.30 N	121.00 E
Taixing	136	32.11 N	120.01 E
Taiyuan	132	37.55 N	112.30 E
Taizhao	144	32.30 N	119.58 E
Taizhou	136	32.30 N	119.58 E
Ta'izz	144	13.38 N	44.04 E
Tajga	128	56.04 N	85.37 E
Tajgonos, Poluostrov ≻[1]	128	61.20 N	161.00 E
Tajima	134	37.12 N	139.46 E
Tajimi	134	35.19 N	137.08 E
Tajmura ≃	128	63.46 N	98.01 E
Tajmyr, Ozero ⊜	128	74.30 N	102.30 E
Tajmyr, Poluostrov ≻[1]	128	76.00 N	104.00 E
Tajo → Tagus ≃	120	38.40 N	9.24 W
Tajrīsh	150	35.48 N	51.25 E
Tajšet	128	55.57 N	98.00 E
Tajumulco, Volcán ∧[1]	180	15.02 N	91.54 W
Tak	140	16.52 N	99.08 E
Takachiho	134	32.42 N	131.18 E
Takada	134	37.06 N	138.15 E
Takahagi	134	36.43 N	140.43 E
Takahashi	134	34.47 N	133.37 E
Takahe, Mount ∧	87	76.16 S	112.14 W
Takaka	170	40.51 S	172.48 E
Takalar	142	5.28 S	119.24 E
Takamatsu	134	34.20 N	134.03 E
Takanabe	134	32.08 N	131.30 E
Takanosu	134	40.13 N	140.22 E
Takaoka	134	36.45 N	137.01 E
Takapoto I[1]	96	14.38 S	145.12 W
Takapuna	170	36.47 S	174.47 E
Takara-jima I	135b	29.09 N	129.13 E
Takasago	134	34.45 N	134.48 E
Takasaki	134	36.20 N	139.01 E
Takashima	134	32.39 N	129.45 E
Takatsuki	134	34.51 N	135.37 E
Takawa	134	33.38 N	130.49 E
Takayama	134	36.08 N	137.15 E
Takefu	134	35.54 N	136.10 E
Takeo	134	33.12 N	130.01 E
Take-shima I	135b	30.49 N	130.26 E
Taketa	134	32.58 N	131.24 E
Takêv	140	10.59 N	104.47 E
Takhār □[4]	146	36.30 N	69.30 E
Ta Khli	138	15.15 N	100.21 E
Takijuq Lake ⊜	172	66.15 N	113.05 W
Takikawa	134a	43.33 N	141.54 E
Takingeun	138	4.38 N	96.50 E
Takla Lake ⊜	172	55.25 N	125.53 W
Taku	134	33.17 N	130.08 E
Takutea I	96	19.49 S	158.18 W
Talagang	149	32.55 N	72.25 E
Talagante	188	33.40 S	70.56 W
Talamanca, Cordillera de ⋀	182	9.30 N	83.40 W
Talana	160	28.10 S	30.15 E
Talangbetutu	142	2.53 S	104.41 E
Talangpadang	142	5.21 S	104.11 E
Talara	184	4.35 S	81.25 W
Talarrubias	120	39.02 N	5.14 W
Talas	126	42.32 N	72.14 E
Talasea	166	5.20 S	150.05 E
Talata Mafara	152	12.35 N	6.04 E
Talaud, Kepulauan II	138	4.20 N	126.50 E
Talavera de la Reina	120	39.57 N	4.50 W
Talawanta	168	18.38 S	140.16 E
Talawdī	154	10.38 N	30.23 E
Talbot, Cape ≻	166	13.48 S	126.43 E
Talca	188	35.26 S	71.40 W
Talca □[4]	188	35.30 S	71.10 W
Talcahuano	188	36.43 S	73.07 W
Taldom	130	56.44 N	37.32 E
Taldy-Kurgan	126	45.00 N	78.23 E
Talent	178	42.15 N	122.47 W
Talgar	126	43.18 N	77.18 E
Talgarreg	104	52.08 N	4.18 W
Talgarth	104	52.00 N	3.15 W
Talia	164	33.19 S	134.54 E
Taliabu, Pulau I	142	1.48 S	124.48 E
Talica, S.S.S.R.	126	57.00 N	63.43 E
Talica, S.S.S.R.	126	58.01 N	51.30 E
Talimuhe ≃	132	41.05 N	86.40 E
Talimupendi (Takla Makan) ⊶[2]	132	39.00 N	83.00 E
Talisay	138	10.44 N	122.58 E
Talish Mountains (Kūhhā-ye Ţavālesh) ⋀	150	38.42 N	48.18 E
Talisker	108	57.17 N	6.27 W
Taliwang	142	8.44 S	116.52 E
Talladale	108	57.42 N	5.29 W
Talladega	174	33.26 N	86.06 W
Tall 'Afar	150	36.22 N	42.27 E
Tallaght	110	53.26 N	6.21 W
Tallahassee	174	30.25 N	84.16 W
Tallangatta	168	36.13 S	147.15 E
Tallard	118	44.28 N	6.03 E
Talla Reservoir ⊜[1]	108	55.29 N	3.24 W
Tallinn	130	59.25 N	24.45 E
Tallmadge	176	41.06 N	81.27 W
Tallow	110	52.05 N	8.00 W
Tallulah	174	32.25 N	91.11 W
Talmage	178	39.08 N	123.10 W
Tal'menka	128	53.51 N	83.35 E
Talmine	108	58.31 N	4.26 W
Talmont	118	46.28 N	1.37 W
Talo ∧	154	10.44 N	37.55 E
Talok	138	1.03 N	118.48 E
Talon, Lake ⊜	176	46.18 N	79.05 W
Tāloqān	146	36.44 N	69.33 E
Talsarnau	104	52.54 N	4.03 W
Taltal	188	25.24 S	70.29 W
Taltson ≃	172	61.23 N	112.45 W
Talu	142	0.14 N	99.59 E
Taluk	142	0.32 S	101.35 E
Talwood	168	28.30 S	149.30 E
Talybont	104	52.29 N	3.59 W
Tamala	164	26.42 S	113.45 E
Tamale	152	9.25 N	0.50 W
Tamalpais, Mount ∧	178	37.56 N	122.35 W
Tamana	134	32.55 N	130.33 E
Tamana I	96	2.29 S	175.59 E
Tamanaco ≃	182	9.25 N	65.23 W
Tamano	134	34.30 N	133.56 E
Tamanrasset	152	22.56 N	5.30 E
Tamaqua	176	40.48 N	75.58 W
Tamar ≃, Austl.	168	41.04 S	146.47 E
Tamar ≃, Eng., U.K.	102	50.22 N	4.10 W
Tamarite de Litera	120	41.52 N	0.26 E
Tamási	116	46.38 N	18.18 E
Tamatave	161b	18.10 S	49.23 E
Tamatave □[4]	161b	18.00 S	48.40 E
Tamazunchale	180	21.16 N	98.47 W
Tambacounda	152	13.47 N	13.40 W
Tamba-kōchi ⋀[1]	134	35.20 N	135.30 E
Tāmbaram	148	12.55 N	80.07 E
Tambej	128	71.30 N	71.50 E
Tambelan, Kepulauan II	142	1.00 N	107.30 E
Tambellup	164	34.02 S	117.39 E
Tambo ≃, Austl.	168	37.51 S	147.48 E
Tambo ≃, Perú	184	17.10 S	71.52 W
Tamboara	190	23.09 S	52.33 W
Tambohorano	161b	17.30 S	43.58 E
Tamboritha, Mount ∧	168	37.28 S	146.41 E
Tambov	130	52.43 N	41.25 E
Tambura	154	5.36 N	27.28 E
Tamchaket	152	17.15 N	10.40 W
Tame	184	6.28 N	71.44 W
Tame ≃	104	52.44 N	1.43 W
Tâmega ≃	120	41.05 N	8.21 W
Tamel Aike	186	48.20 S	70.58 W
Tamerton Foliot	104	50.26 N	4.08 W
Tamiahua	180	21.16 N	97.27 W
Tamiahua, Laguna de C	180	21.35 N	97.35 W
Tamil Nadu □[3]	148	11.00 N	78.15 E
Tamiš (Timiș) ≃	124	44.51 N	20.39 E
Tam-ky	140	15.34 N	108.29 E
Tampa	174	27.57 N	82.27 W
Tampa Bay C	174	27.45 N	82.35 W
Tampere	114	61.30 N	23.45 E
Tampico	180	22.13 N	97.51 W
Tampin	142	2.28 N	102.14 E
Tamsagbulag	132	47.16 N	117.17 E
Tamworth	168	31.05 S	150.55 E
Tana	112	70.28 N	28.18 E
Tana I	96	19.30 S	169.20 E
Tana ≃, Eur.	112	70.30 N	28.23 E
Tana ≃, Kenya	158	2.32 S	40.31 E
Tana, Lake ⊜	154	12.00 N	37.20 E
Tanabe	134	33.44 N	135.22 E
Tanafjorden C[2]	112	70.54 N	28.40 E
Tanahbala, Pulau I	140	0.25 S	98.25 E
Tanahgrogot	142	1.55 S	116.12 E
Tanahjampea, Pulau I	142	7.05 S	120.42 E
Tanahmasa, Pulau I	140	0.12 S	98.27 E
Tanahmerah, Indon.	166	6.05 S	140.17 E
Tanah Merah, Malay.	142	5.48 N	102.09 E
Tanami	164	19.59 S	129.43 E
Tanami Desert ⊶[2]	164	20.00 S	129.30 E
Tan-an	140	10.32 N	106.25 E
Tanana	172	65.10 N	152.05 W
Tanana ≃	172	65.09 N	151.55 W
Tanarivo → Antanarivo	161b	18.55 S	47.31 E
Tananarive □[4]	161b	19.00 S	47.00 E
Tanat ≃	104	52.46 N	3.07 W
Tanbar	168	25.50 S	141.55 E
Tanchoj	128	51.33 N	105.07 E
Tanch'ŏn	132	40.27 N	128.54 E
Tandaai	158	19.36 S	32.48 E
Tandag	138	9.04 N	126.12 E
Tandil	188	37.20 S	59.05 W
Tāndliānwāla	149	31.02 N	73.08 E
Tando Ādam	146	25.46 N	68.40 E
Tando Allāhyār	146	25.28 N	68.43 E
Tando Muhammad Khān	146	25.08 N	68.32 E
Tandou Lake ⊜	168	32.38 S	142.05 E
Tandragee	110	54.21 N	6.25 W
Taneatua	170	38.04 S	177.01 E
Tanega-shima I	134	30.40 N	131.00 E
Taneichi	134	40.26 N	141.43 E
Taneytown	176	39.40 N	77.10 W

Symbols in the index entries are identified on page 198.

Tane – Tobe

Name	Page	Lat° ′	Long° ′
Tanezrouft ⇀[2]	152	24.00 N	0.45 W
Tanga	158	5.04 S	39.06 E
Tanga □[4]	158	5.00 S	38.15 E
Tangail	146	24.15 N	89.55 E
Tanga Islands II	96	3.30 S	153.15 E
Tanganyika, Lake ⊜	158	6.00 S	29.30 E
Tangará	188	27.08 S	51.13 W
Tanger (Tangier)	152	35.48 N	5.45 W
Tangerang	142	6.11 S	106.37 E
Tangermünde	116	52.32 N	11.58 E
Tanggou	136	34.01 N	118.56 E
Tanggu	132	39.01 N	117.40 E
Tanggulahu ⊜	146	31.00 N	86.20 E
Tanggulashanmai ⋀	146	33.00 N	90.00 E
Tanghe	136	32.43 N	112.48 E
Tangi	149	34.18 N	71.40 E
Tangier → Tanger	152	35.48 N	5.45 W
Tangjiagou	136	30.48 N	117.28 E
Tangjiang	136	25.51 N	114.44 E
Tangjiazha	136	32.05 N	120.49 E
Tangqi	136	30.29 N	120.11 E
Tangshan	132	39.38 N	118.11 E
Tangxi	136	29.04 N	119.23 E
Tanigawa-dake ∧	134	36.50 N	138.56 E
Tanimbar, Kepulauan II	166	7.30 S	131.30 E
Taninges	118	46.07 N	6.36 E
Tanjung	142	8.21 S	116.09 E
Tanjungbalai	140	2.58 N	99.48 E
Tanjungbatu	142	0.38 N	103.26 E
Tanjungkarang	142	5.25 S	105.16 E
Tanjungmengedar	142	2.39 N	100.01 E
Tanjungpandan	142	2.45 S	107.39 E
Tanjungpinang	142	0.55 N	104.27 E
Tanjungraja	142	3.21 S	104.40 E
Tanjungredep	142	2.09 N	117.29 E
Tanjungselor	142	2.51 N	117.22 E
Tännäs	114	62.27 N	12.40 E
Tannila	114	65.29 N	25.59 E
Tannu-Ola, Chrebet ⋀	128	51.00 N	94.00 E
Tannūrah, Ra's at- ›	150	26.40 N	50.30 E
Tânout	152	14.58 N	8.53 E
Tanshui	136	25.10 N	121.26 E
Ṭanṭā	154	30.47 N	31.00 E
Tantou	136	26.03 N	119.35 E
Tanuku	148	16.45 N	81.42 E
Tanworth	104	52.20 N	1.50 W
Tanworth-in-Arden	104	52.39 N	1.40 W
Tanzania □[1]	156	6.00 S	35.00 E
Taoan	132	45.22 N	122.47 E
Taoerhe ≃	132	45.42 N	124.05 E
Taohe ≃	132	32.52 N	103.16 E
Taongi I[1]	96	14.37 N	168.58 E
Taormina	122	37.52 N	15.17 E
Taoudenni	152	22.40 N	4.00 W
Taoxi	136	31.33 N	117.00 E
T'aoyüan	132	25.00 N	121.18 E
Tapachula	180	14.54 N	92.17 W
Tapah	142	4.11 N	101.16 E
Tapajós ≃	184	2.24 S	54.41 W
Tapanahoni ≃	184	4.20 N	54.25 W
Tapanui	170	45.57 S	169.16 E
Tapawera	170	41.24 S	172.49 E
Tapejara	188	28.04 S	52.00 W
Tapera	188	28.38 S	52.52 W
Taperoá	190	13.31 S	39.06 W
Tapes	188	30.40 S	51.23 W
Taphan Hin	140	16.13 N	100.26 E
Tāpi ≃	146	21.06 N	72.41 E
Tapiche ≃	184	5.03 S	73.51 W
Taping (Dayingjiang) ≃	140	24.17 N	97.14 E
Tappahannock	176	37.56 N	76.52 W
Tappi-zaki ›	134	41.15 N	140.21 E
Tapurucuara	184	0.24 S	65.02 W
Taqāṭu' Hayyā	154	18.20 N	36.22 E
Taquara	188	29.39 S	50.47 W
Taquaras, Ponta das ›	188	27.01 S	48.34 W
Taquari	190	17.50 S	53.17 W
Taquari ≃	188	29.56 S	51.44 W
Taquaritinga	190	21.24 S	48.30 W
Tara, Austl.	168	27.17 S	150.28 E
Tara, S.S.S.R.	128	56.54 N	74.22 E
Tara, Zam.	158	16.56 S	26.47 E
Taraba ≃	152	8.30 N	10.15 E
Ṭarābulus (Tripoli), Lībīya	154	32.54 N	13.11 E
Ṭarābulus (Tripoli), Lubnān	150	34.26 N	35.51 E
Ṭarābulus (Tripolitania) ⇀[1]	154	31.00 N	15.00 E
Taradale	170	39.32 S	176.51 E
Tarakan	142	3.18 N	117.38 E
Taralga	168	34.24 S	149.49 E
Tarancón	120	40.01 N	3.00 W
Taranga Island I	170	35.58 S	174.43 E
Taransay I	108	57.54 N	7.01 W
Taranto	122	40.28 N	17.15 E
Taranto, Golfo di C	122	40.10 N	17.20 E
Tarapoto	184	6.30 S	76.20 W
Taraquá	184	0.06 N	68.28 W
Tarare	118	45.54 N	4.26 E
Tarāsa Dwīp I	140	8.15 N	93.10 E
Tarata	184	17.37 S	66.01 W
Tarauacá	184	8.10 S	70.46 W
Taravo ≃	122	41.42 N	8.49 E
Tarawa I[1]	96	1.25 N	173.00 E
Tarawera	170	39.02 S	176.35 E
Tarawera, Lake ⊜	170	38.12 S	176.27 E
Tarazona	120	41.54 N	1.44 W
Tarazona de la Mancha	120	39.15 N	1.55 W
Tarbagataj, Chrebet ⋀	126	47.12 N	83.00 E
Tarbat Ness ›	108	57.51 N	3.47 W
Tarbert, Eire	110	52.32 N	9.23 W
Tarbert, Scot., U.K.	108	57.54 N	6.49 W
Tarbert, Scot., U.K.	108	55.52 N	5.26 W
Tarbert, Loch C	108	55.57 N	6.00 W
Tarbes	118	43.14 N	0.05 E
Tarbet	108	56.12 N	4.43 W
Tarbolton	108	55.31 N	4.29 W
Tarbū	154	26.02 N	15.10 E
Tarcoola	164	30.41 S	134.33 E
Tarcoon	168	30.16 S	146.43 E
Tardajos	120	42.21 N	3.49 W
Tardoki-Jani, Gora ∧	128	48.55 N	138.04 E
Tardun	164	28.48 S	115.45 E
Taree	168	31.54 S	152.28 E
Tareja	128	73.20 N	90.37 E
Tarentum	176	40.36 N	79.45 W
Ṭarfā, Wādī aṭ- V	150	28.15 N	31.45 E
Tarfaya	152	27.58 N	12.55 W
Tarfside	108	56.54 N	2.50 W
Tarf Water ≃	106	54.55 N	4.35 W
Târgovište	124	43.15 N	26.34 E
Tarhūnah	154	32.26 N	13.38 E
Tari	166	5.50 S	143.00 E
Tarifa	120	36.01 N	5.36 W
Tarifa, Punta de ›	120	36.00 N	5.37 W
Tarija	184	21.31 S	64.45 W
Tariki	170	39.14 S	174.15 E
Tariku ≃	166	3.04 S	138.09 E
Taritatu ≃	166	2.54 S	138.27 E
Tarkastad	160	32.00 S	26.16 E
Tarko-Sale	128	64.55 N	77.49 E
Tarkwa	152	5.19 N	1.59 W
Tarlac	138	15.29 N	120.35 E
Tarland	108	57.08 N	2.52 W
Tarleton	106	53.41 N	2.50 W
Tarma	184	11.25 S	75.43 W
Tarn □[5]	118	43.50 N	2.00 E
Tarn ≃	118	44.05 N	1.06 E
Tarna ≃	116	47.31 N	19.59 E
Tärnaby	112	65.43 N	15.16 E
Tarn-et-Garonne □[5]	118	44.05 N	1.20 E
Tarnica ∧	116	49.05 N	22.42 E
Tarnobrzeg	116	50.35 N	21.41 E
Tarnów	116	50.01 N	21.00 E
Tarnowskie Góry	116	50.27 N	18.52 E
Tarn Tāran	149	31.27 N	74.55 E
Tarong	168	26.46 S	151.51 E
Taroom	168	25.39 S	149.49 E
Tarporley	106	53.09 N	2.40 W
Tarrabool, Lake ⊜	164	18.15 S	135.04 E
Tarragona	120	41.07 N	1.15 E
Tarrakoski L	112	68.10 N	20.00 E
Tarraleah	168	42.18 S	146.27 E
Tarran Hills ⋀[2]	168	32.27 S	146.27 E
Tarrant Hinton	104	50.53 N	2.05 W
Tarrasa	120	41.34 N	2.01 E
Tárrega	120	41.39 N	1.09 E
Tarri Mashen	158	0.45 N	41.50 E
Tarsus	150	36.55 N	34.53 E
Tartagal	188	22.32 S	63.50 W
Tartu	130	58.23 N	26.43 E
Ṭarṭūs	150	34.53 N	35.53 E
Tarumizu	134	31.29 N	130.42 E
Tarutung	140	2.01 N	98.58 E
Tarves	108	57.22 N	2.13 W
Tas ≃	104	52.36 N	1.18 E
Taşağıl	124	41.31 N	27.07 E
Tašauz	126	41.50 N	59.58 E
Tašauz □[4]	150	50.15 N	59.00 E
Tasejeva ≃	128	58.06 N	94.01 E
Tasejevo	128	57.12 N	94.54 E
Ṭashk, Daryācheh-ye ⊜	150	29.45 N	53.35 E
Tashkent → Taškent	126	41.20 N	69.18 E
Tāshkurghān, Afg.	126	36.42 N	67.41 E
Tāshkurghān → Kholm, Afg.	146	36.42 N	67.41 E
Tasikmalaya	142	7.20 S	108.12 E
Taškent	126	41.20 N	69.18 E
Taškepri	150	36.18 N	62.38 E
Tasman, Mount ∧	170	43.34 S	170.09 E
Tasman Basin ⌖[1]	96	44.00 S	157.00 E
Tasmania □[3]	162	43.00 S	147.00 E
Tasmania I	168	42.00 S	147.00 E
Tasman Mountains ⋀	170	41.07 S	172.33 E
Tasman Ridge ⌖[3]	96	46.00 S	147.00 E
Tasman Sea ⊤[2]	96	40.00 S	163.00 E
Tassialouc, Lac ⊜	172	59.03 N	74.00 W
Taštagol	128	52.47 N	87.53 E
Tata	116	47.39 N	18.18 E
Tatabánya	116	47.34 N	18.26 E
Tatarlar	124	41.46 N	26.55 E
Tatarsk	128	55.13 N	75.58 E
Tatarskij Proliv ʊ	128	50.00 N	141.15 E
Tatar Strait → Tatarskij Proliv ʊ	128	50.00 N	141.15 E
Tate ≃	168	17.22 S	143.44 E
Tateyama	134	34.59 N	139.52 E
Tate-yama ∧	134	36.35 N	137.37 E
Tathlina Lake ⊜	172	60.32 N	117.32 W
Tathra	168	36.44 S	149.59 E
Tatnam, Cape ›	172	57.16 N	91.00 W
Tatsuno, Nihon	134	35.59 N	137.59 E
Tatsuno, Nihon	134	34.52 N	134.33 E
Tatta	146	24.45 N	67.55 E
Tatvan	150	38.30 N	42.16 E
Taubaté	190	23.02 S	45.33 W
Tauber ≃	116	49.46 N	9.31 E
Tauberbischofsheim	116	49.37 N	9.40 E
Taučik	126	44.21 N	51.19 E
Taujskaja Guba C	128	59.20 N	150.20 E
Taumarunui	170	38.52 S	175.17 E
Taung	160	27.33 S	24.47 E
Taungdwingyi	140	20.01 N	95.33 E
Taunggyi	140	20.47 N	97.02 E
Taunsa	149	30.42 N	70.39 E
Taunton, Eng., U.K.	104	51.01 N	3.06 W
Taunton, Mass., U.S.	176	41.54 N	71.06 W
Taunton, Vale of V	104	51.02 N	3.08 W
Taupo	170	38.41 S	176.05 E
Tauranga	170	37.42 S	176.10 E
Taurianova	122	38.21 N	16.01 E
Tauroa Point ›	170	35.10 S	173.04 E
Tauste	120	41.55 N	1.15 W
Tauu Islands II	96	4.45 S	157.00 E
Tavda	126	58.03 N	65.15 E
Tavda ≃	126	59.20 N	63.28 E
Taveuni I	96	16.51 S	179.58 E
Tavira	120	37.07 N	7.39 W
Tavistock, Ont., Can.	176	43.19 N	80.50 W
Tavistock, Eng., U.K.	104	50.33 N	4.08 W
Tavoliere ⇀[1]	122	41.35 N	15.25 E
Tavolžan	128	52.44 N	77.27 E
Távora ≃	120	41.09 N	7.35 W
Tavoy	140	14.05 N	98.12 E
Tavy ≃	104	50.16 N	4.10 W
Taw ≃	102	51.04 N	4.11 W
Tawa	170	41.10 S	174.51 E
Tawas City	176	44.16 N	83.31 W
Tawau	142	4.15 N	117.54 E
Tawe ≃	104	51.37 N	3.55 W
Ṭawīlah, Juzur II	150	27.35 N	33.46 E
Tawitawi Island I	142	5.10 N	120.00 E
Ṭawkar	154	18.26 N	37.44 E
Taxco de Alarcón	180	18.33 N	99.36 W
Tay ≃	108	56.22 N	3.21 W
Tay, Firth of C[1]	108	56.26 N	3.00 W
Tay, Lake ⊜	164	32.55 S	120.48 E
Tay, Loch ⊜	108	56.31 N	4.10 W
Taymā'	150	27.38 N	38.29 E
Tay-ninh	140	11.18 N	106.06 E
Taynuilt	108	56.25 N	5.14 W
Tayport	108	57.27 N	2.53 W
Tayside □[4]	108	56.30 N	3.30 W
Taytay	138	10.49 N	119.31 E
Taz ≃	128	67.32 N	78.40 E
Taza	152	34.16 N	4.01 W
Tazawa-ko ⊜	134	39.43 N	140.40 E
Tazin ≃	172	60.26 N	110.45 W
Tazin Lake ⊜	172	59.47 N	109.03 W
Tazovskaja Guba C	128	69.05 N	76.00 E
Tazovskij	128	67.28 N	78.42 E
Tazovskij Poluostrov ›[1]	126	68.35 N	76.00 E
Tbilisi	126	41.43 N	44.49 E
Tchibanga	156	2.51 S	11.02 E
Tchien	152	6.04 N	8.08 W
Tczew	116	54.06 N	18.47 E
Te Anau	170	45.25 S	167.43 E
Te Anau, Lake ⊜	170	45.12 S	167.48 E
Teangue	108	57.07 N	5.50 W
Teano	122	41.15 N	14.04 E
Teapa	180	17.33 N	92.57 W
Te Araroa	170	37.38 S	178.22 E
Te Aroha	170	37.33 S	175.43 E
Tea Tree	164	22.11 S	133.17 E
Te Awamutu	170	38.01 S	175.19 E
Teba	120	36.58 N	4.56 W
Tebay	106	54.26 N	2.35 W
Tébessa	152	35.28 N	8.09 E
Tebicuary ≃	188	26.36 S	58.16 W
Tebingtinggi	140	3.20 N	99.09 E
Tebingtinggi, Pulau I	142	0.54 N	102.45 E
Tecate	178	32.34 N	116.38 E
Tech ≃	118	42.36 N	3.03 E
Tecka	186	43.30 S	70.51 W
Tecopa	178	35.51 N	116.13 W
Tecpan de Galeana	180	17.15 N	100.41 W
Tecuci	124	45.50 N	27.26 E
Tecumseh	176	42.00 N	83.57 W
Tedesa	158	5.07 N	37.45 E
Tedžen	150	37.23 N	60.31 E
Tedžen (Harīrūd) ≃	150	37.24 N	60.38 E
Teels Marsh ☷	178	38.12 N	118.21 W
Tees ≃	102	54.34 N	1.16 W
Tees Bay C	106	54.39 N	1.07 W
Teesdale V	106	54.38 N	2.07 W
Teeswater	176	44.00 N	81.17 W
Tefé	184	3.22 S	64.42 W
Tegal	142	6.52 S	109.08 E
Tegernsee	116	47.43 N	11.45 E
Tegid, Llyn ⊜	104	52.53 N	3.36 W
Tegucigalpa	182	14.06 N	87.13 W
Tehachapi	178	35.08 N	118.27 W
Tehachapi Mountains ⋀	178	35.00 N	118.40 W
Tehachapi Pass)(	178	35.06 N	118.18 W
Te Haroto	170	39.08 S	176.36 E
Tehek Lake ⊜	172	64.55 N	95.38 W
Tehrān	150	35.40 N	51.26 E
Tehuantepec	180	16.20 N	95.14 W
Tehuantepec, Golfo de C	180	16.00 N	94.50 W
Tehuantepec, Istmo de ⊥[3]	180	17.00 N	94.30 W
Tehuantepec Ridge ⌖[3]	90	13.00 N	98.45 W
Teifi ≃	104	52.07 N	4.42 W
Teifiside ⇀[1]	104	52.02 N	4.22 W
Teign ≃	104	50.33 N	3.29 W
Teignmouth	104	50.33 N	3.30 W
Teith ≃	108	56.08 N	3.59 W
Teixeira de Sousa	156	10.42 S	22.12 E
Teixeiras	190	20.39 S	42.51 W
Teixeira Soares	188	25.22 S	50.27 W
Tejakula	142	8.08 S	115.20 E
Tejkovo	130	56.52 N	40.34 E
Tejo → Tagus ≃	120	38.40 N	9.24 W
Tejon Pass)(	178	34.48 N	118.52 W
Te Kaha	170	37.44 S	177.41 E
Te Kao	170	34.39 S	172.57 E
Tekapo, Lake ⊜	170	43.53 S	170.31 E
Teke Burnu ›	124	40.02 N	26.10 E
Tekeli	126	44.48 N	78.57 E
Tekeze ≃	154	14.20 N	35.50 E
Tekirdağ	124	40.59 N	27.31 E
Tekirdağ □[4]	124	41.00 N	27.30 E
Tekonsha	176	42.05 N	84.59 W
Te Kopuru	170	36.02 S	173.56 E
Te Kuiti	170	38.20 S	175.10 E
Tela	180	15.44 N	87.27 W
Tel Aviv-Yafo	150	32.04 N	34.46 E
Telechany	130	52.31 N	25.51 E
Teleckoje, Ozero ⊜	128	51.35 N	87.40 E
Telefomin	166	5.10 S	141.35 E
Telegraph Creek	172	57.55 N	131.10 W
Telemark □[6]	114	59.30 N	8.40 E
Telén	188	36.15 S	65.31 W
Telen ≃	142	0.26 S	116.42 E
Teleño ∧	120	42.21 N	6.23 W
Teleorman □[4]	124	44.00 N	25.15 E
Telerig	124	43.51 N	27.40 E
Telertheba, Djebel ∧	152	24.10 N	6.51 E
Telescope Peak ∧	178	36.10 N	117.05 W
Teli	128	51.07 N	90.14 E
Tellicherry	148	11.45 N	75.32 E
Telok Anson	142	4.02 N	101.01 E
Telsen	186	42.25 S	67.00 W
Telšiai	130	55.59 N	22.15 E
Teltow	116	52.23 N	13.16 E
Telukbayur	142	1.00 S	100.22 E
Telukbetung	142	5.27 S	105.16 E
Telukdalem	140	0.34 N	97.49 E
Temagami, Lake ⊜	172	47.00 N	80.05 W
Tematangi I[1]	96	21.41 S	140.40 W
Temax	180	21.09 N	88.56 W
Tembenči ≃	128	64.36 N	99.58 E
Tembesi ≃	142	1.43 S	103.06 E
Tembilahan	142	0.19 S	103.09 E
Temblador	182	8.59 N	62.44 W
Tembleque	120	39.42 N	3.30 W
Temblor Range ⋀	178	35.20 N	119.55 W
Tembuland ⇀[1]	160	31.30 S	28.00 E
Teme ≃	104	52.09 N	2.18 W
Temecula	178	33.46 N	117.29 W
Temerin	124	45.24 N	19.53 E
Temerloh	142	3.27 N	102.25 E
Teminabuan	166	1.26 S	132.01 E
Temir	126	49.08 N	57.06 E
Temirtau, S.S.S.R.	126	50.05 N	72.56 E
Temirtau, S.S.S.R.	128	53.08 N	87.28 E
Temora	168	34.26 S	147.32 E
Tempe	174	33.25 N	111.56 W
Temperance	176	41.47 N	83.34 W
Tempio Pausania	122	40.54 N	9.07 E
Temple	174	31.06 N	97.21 W
Templecombe	104	51.00 N	2.25 W
Temple Ewell	104	51.09 N	1.16 E
Templemore	110	52.48 N	7.50 W
Temple Sowerby	106	54.39 N	2.35 W
Templeton ≃	168	21.14 S	138.13 E
Templin	116	53.07 N	13.30 E
Temuco	188	38.44 S	72.36 W
Tena	184	0.59 S	77.49 W
Tenāli	148	16.15 N	80.35 E
Tenasserim	138	12.05 N	99.01 E
Tenasserim □[8]	140	12.00 N	99.00 E
Tenbury Wells	104	52.19 N	2.35 W
Tenby	104	51.41 N	4.43 W
Tendaho	154	11.48 N	40.52 E
Tende	118	44.05 N	7.36 E
Tende, Col de)(	118	44.09 N	7.34 E
Ten Degree Channel ʊ	140	10.00 N	93.00 E
Tendō	134	38.21 N	140.22 E
Tenente Portela	188	27.22 S	53.45 W
Ténéré ⇀[2]	152	19.00 N	10.30 E
Tenerife I	88	28.19 N	16.34 W
Ténès	120	36.31 N	1.14 E
Tengchong	140	25.04 N	98.29 E
Tenggarong	142	0.24 S	116.58 E
Tengiz, Ozero ⊜	126	50.24 N	68.57 E
Tengtiaohe (Na) ≃	140	22.05 N	103.09 E
Tengxian, Zhg.	132	35.08 N	117.10 E
Tengxian, Zhg.	140	23.21 N	110.53 E
Tenkāsi	148	8.58 N	77.18 E
Tenke, Zaïre	158	11.26 S	26.45 E
Tenke, Zaïre	158	10.35 S	26.07 E
Tenkodogo	152	11.47 N	0.22 W
Tenmile Creek ≃	176	40.08 N	80.22 W
Tennant Creek	164	19.40 S	134.10 E
Tennessee □[3]	174	35.50 N	85.30 W
Tennessee ≃	174	37.04 N	88.33 W
Teno	188	34.52 S	71.11 W
Tenom	138	5.08 N	115.57 E
Tenosique de Pino Suárez	180	17.29 N	91.26 W
Tenryū	134	34.52 N	137.49 E
Tenryū ≃	134	34.39 N	137.47 E
Tenterden	104	51.05 N	0.42 E
Tenterfield	168	29.03 S	152.01 E
Ten Thousand Islands II	182	25.50 N	81.33 W
Teodelina	188	34.10 S	61.34 W
Teófilo Otoni	190	17.51 S	41.30 W
Tepa	166	7.52 S	129.31 E
Tepatitlán	180	20.49 N	102.44 W
Tepelenë	124	40.18 N	20.01 E
Tepic	180	21.30 N	104.54 W
Teplice	116	50.39 N	13.48 E
Te Pohue	170	39.15 S	176.41 E
Te Puia	170	38.04 S	178.18 E
Te Puke	170	37.47 S	176.20 E
Tequendama, Salto de L	184	4.35 N	74.18 W
Ter ≃	104	51.50 N	0.36 E
Téra	152	14.01 N	0.45 E
Teradomari	134	37.38 N	138.46 E
Teramo	122	42.39 N	13.42 E
Terang	168	38.14 S	142.55 E
Terceira I	88	38.43 N	24.13 W
Tercero ≃	188	32.55 S	62.19 W
Terek ≃	126	43.44 N	46.33 E
Teresina	184	5.05 S	42.49 W
Teresópolis	190	22.26 S	42.59 W
Terib'orka	112	69.08 N	35.08 E
Terkos Gölü ⊜	124	41.20 N	28.35 E
Termez	150	37.14 N	67.16 E
Termini Imerese	122	37.59 N	13.42 E
Términos, Laguna de C	180	18.35 N	91.30 W
Termoli	122	42.00 N	15.00 E
Tern ≃	104	52.47 N	2.32 W
Ternate	138	0.48 N	127.24 E
Ternberg	116	47.58 N	14.22 E
Ternej	128	45.03 N	136.37 E
Terneuzen	116	51.20 N	3.50 E
Terni	122	42.34 N	12.37 E
Ternitz	116	47.44 N	16.03 E
Ternopol'	126	49.34 N	25.36 E
Terpenija, Mys ›	128	48.39 N	144.44 E
Terpenija, Zaliv C	128	49.00 N	143.30 E
Terra Alta	176	39.27 N	79.31 W
Terra Bella	178	35.58 N	119.03 W
Terra Boa	190	23.45 S	52.27 W
Terrace	172	54.31 N	128.35 W
Terracina	122	41.17 N	13.15 E
Terra di Bari ⇀[1]	122	41.10 N	16.50 E
Terralba	122	39.43 N	8.38 E
Terra Nova Bay C	87	74.45 S	164.30 E
Terra Rica	190	22.43 S	52.38 W
Terra Roxa d'Oeste	188	24.08 S	53.59 W
Terrasson-la-Villedieu	118	45.08 N	1.18 E
Terre Haute	174	39.28 N	87.24 W
Terrington Saint Clement	104	52.45 N	0.18 E
Terschelling I	116	53.24 N	5.20 E
Teruel	120	40.21 N	1.06 W
Tervola	114	66.05 N	24.48 E
Tésa	116	48.02 N	18.51 E
Tešanj	124	44.37 N	18.00 E
Tes-Chem (Tesijn) ≃	128	50.28 N	93.04 E
Teseney	154	15.07 N	36.41 E
Teshi	152	5.35 N	0.05 W
Teshikaga	134a	43.29 N	144.28 E
Teshio	134a	44.53 N	141.44 E
Teshio ≃	134a	44.53 N	141.44 E
Teshio-sanchi ⋀	134a	44.15 N	142.05 E
Tesijn (Tes-Chem) ≃	128	50.28 N	93.04 E
Teslić	124	44.37 N	17.51 E
Teslin	172	60.09 N	132.45 W
Teslin ≃	172	61.34 N	134.54 W
Teslin Lake ⊜	172	60.15 N	132.57 W
Teso □[5]	158	1.45 N	33.40 E
Tesouro	190	16.04 S	53.34 W
Tessalit	152	20.12 N	1.00 E
Tessaoua	152	13.45 N	7.59 E
Tessik Lake ⊜	172	64.53 N	75.25 W
Test ≃	102	50.55 N	1.29 W
Têt ≃	118	42.44 N	3.02 E
Tetas, Punta ›	188	23.31 S	70.38 W
Tetbury	104	51.39 N	2.10 W
Tete	158	16.13 S	33.35 E
Tete □[5]	158	15.15 S	32.40 E
Te Teko	170	38.02 S	176.48 E
Teterow	116	53.46 N	12.34 E
Tetiaroa I[1]	96	17.05 S	149.32 W
Tetica de Bacares ∧	120	37.15 N	2.25 W
Tétouan	152	35.34 N	5.23 W
Tetovo	124	42.01 N	20.58 E
Tetschen → Děčín	116	50.48 N	14.13 E
Tettenhall	104	52.36 N	2.09 W
Tet'uche	128	44.35 N	135.35 E
Teuco ≃	188	25.35 S	60.11 W
Teun, Pulau I	166	6.59 S	129.08 E
Teuri-tō I	134a	44.25 N	141.19 E
Teuva	114	62.29 N	21.44 E
Tevere (Tiber) ≃	122	41.44 N	12.14 E
Teverya	150	32.47 N	35.32 E
Teviot ≃	108	55.35 N	2.26 W
Teviotdale V	106	55.25 N	2.50 W
Teviothead	108	55.21 N	2.56 W
Te Whaiti	170	38.35 S	176.47 E
Tewkesbury	104	51.59 N	2.09 W
Texarkana	174	33.26 N	94.03 W
Texas	168	28.51 S	151.11 E
Texas □[3]	174	31.30 N	99.00 W
Texas City	174	29.23 N	94.54 W
Texel I	116	53.05 N	4.45 E
Texoma, Lake ⊜[1]	174	33.55 N	96.37 W
Teynham	104	51.20 N	0.50 E
Teyvareh	146	33.21 N	64.25 E
Teziutlán	180	19.49 N	97.21 W
Tezpur	146	26.38 N	92.48 E
Tha-anne ≃	172	60.31 N	94.37 W
Thabana Ntlenyana ∧	160	29.28 S	29.16 E
Thaba Nchu	160	29.17 S	26.52 E
Thabazimbi	160	24.41 S	27.21 E
Thai-binh	140	20.27 N	106.20 E
Thailand □[1]	138	15.00 N	100.00 E
Thailand, Gulf of C	140	10.00 N	101.00 E
Thai-nguyen	140	21.36 N	105.50 E
Thal	149	33.22 N	70.33 E
Thale	116	51.45 N	11.02 E
Thalfang	116	49.45 N	6.59 E
Thallon	168	28.38 S	148.52 E
Thame	104	51.45 N	0.59 W
Thames	170	37.08 S	175.33 E
Thames ≃, Ont., Can.	176	42.19 N	82.28 W
Thames ≃, Eng., U.K.	102	51.28 N	0.43 E
Thamesford	176	43.04 N	81.00 W
Thamesville	176	42.33 N	81.59 W
Thāna	148	19.12 N	72.58 E
Thānesar	149	29.59 N	76.49 E
Thanet, Isle of I	104	51.22 N	1.20 E
Thangoo	164	18.10 S	122.22 E
Thangool	168	24.29 S	150.35 E
Thanh-hoa	140	19.48 N	105.46 E
Thanh-pho Ho Chi Minh (Sai-gon)	140	10.45 N	106.40 E
Thanjāvūr	148	10.48 N	79.09 E
Thaon-les-Vosges	118	48.15 N	6.25 E
Thar Desert (Great Indian Desert) ⇀[2]	146	27.00 N	71.00 E
Thargomindah	168	28.00 S	143.49 E
Tharrawaddy	140	17.39 N	95.48 E
Tharsuinn, Beinn ∧	108	57.47 N	4.21 W
Thásos I	124	40.41 N	24.47 E
Thatcham	104	51.25 N	1.15 W
Thaton	140	16.55 N	97.22 E
Thaungyin ≃	140	17.50 N	97.42 E
Thaxted	104	51.57 N	0.20 E
Thaya (Dyje) ≃	116	48.37 N	16.56 E
Thayetmyo	140	19.19 N	95.11 E
Thazi	132	20.51 N	96.05 E
Theale	104	51.27 N	1.04 W
Thealka	176	37.49 N	82.47 W
The Bight	182	24.19 N	75.24 W
The Brothers II	144	12.09 N	53.12 E
The Cheviot ∧	102	55.28 N	2.09 W
The Dalles	174	45.36 N	121.10 W
The Deeps C	108a	60.09 N	1.23 W
The Downs ⊤[3]	104	51.13 N	1.27 E
Theebine	168	25.57 S	152.33 E
The English Companys Islands II	166	11.50 S	136.32 E
The Everglades ☷	174	26.00 N	80.40 W
The Father ∧	166	5.03 S	151.20 E
The Fens ☷	102	52.38 N	0.02 E
The Glenkens ⇀[1]	106	55.10 N	4.15 W
The Granites	164	20.35 S	130.21 E
The Hague → 's-Gravenhage	116	52.06 N	4.18 E
The Heads ›	178	42.44 N	124.31 W
The Lake ⊜	182	21.00 N	73.30 W
Thelon ≃	172	64.16 N	96.05 W
The Long Mynd ∧	104	52.35 N	2.48 W
The Lynd	168	18.56 S	144.30 E
The Machars □[8]	106	54.50 N	4.30 W
The Machars ⇀[1]	106	55.20 N	4.33 W
The Minch ʊ	108	58.10 N	5.50 W
The Moors ⇀[1]	106	54.56 N	4.40 W
The Mumbles	104	51.34 N	4.00 W
The Naze ›	102	51.53 N	1.16 E
The Needles ›	102	50.39 N	1.34 W
The Oa ⇀[1]	108	55.37 N	6.16 W
Theodore	168	24.57 S	150.05 E
The Paps ∧	110	52.00 N	9.17 W
The Pas	172	53.50 N	101.15 W
The Pilot ∧	168	36.45 S	148.13 E
Thérain ≃	118	49.15 N	2.27 E
The Rand → Witwatersrand ⇀[1]	160	26.00 S	27.00 E
The Range	158	19.00 S	31.04 E
Theresa	176	44.13 N	75.48 W
The Rhins ›[1]	106	54.50 N	5.00 W
Thermopolis	174	43.39 N	108.13 W
The Road C	104a	49.56 N	6.20 W
The Rock	168	35.16 S	147.07 E
Theron Mountains ⋀	87	79.05 S	28.15 W
Thesiger Bay C	172	71.30 N	124.05 W
The Snares II	87	48.00 S	166.30 E
The Solent ʊ	104	50.46 N	1.20 W
The Sound ʊ	114	55.50 N	12.40 E
Thessalon	176	46.15 N	83.34 W
Thessaloníki (Salonika)	124	40.38 N	22.56 E
The Storr ∧	108	57.31 N	6.12 W
The Swale ʊ	104	51.22 N	0.56 E
Thet ≃	104	52.27 N	0.33 E
Thetford	104	52.25 N	0.45 E
Thetford Mines	172	46.05 N	71.18 W
The Thumbs ∧	170	43.36 S	170.44 E
The Twelve Pins ∧	110	53.31 N	9.50 W
Theunissen	160	28.30 S	26.41 E
The Valley	182	18.13 N	63.04 W
Thevenard	164	32.09 S	133.38 E
The Wash C	102	52.55 N	0.15 E
The Weald ⇀[1]	102	51.05 N	0.05 E
The Wrekin ∧[2]	104	52.41 N	2.34 W
Thief River Falls	174	48.07 N	96.10 W
Thiel Mountains ⋀	87	85.15 S	91.00 W
Thielsen, Mount ∧	178	43.09 N	122.04 W
Thiene	122	45.42 N	11.29 E
Thiers	118	45.51 N	3.34 E
Thiès	152	14.48 N	16.56 W
Thika	158	1.03 S	37.05 E
Thimbu	144	27.28 N	89.39 E
Thingvellir	112a	64.17 N	21.07 W
Thionville	118	49.22 N	6.10 E
Thira I	124	36.24 N	25.29 E
Thirlmere ⊜	106	54.33 N	3.04 W
Thirsk	106	54.14 N	1.20 W
Thistle Island I	168	35.00 S	136.09 E
Thívai (Thebes)	124	38.21 N	23.19 E
Thizy	118	46.02 N	4.19 E
Thlewiaza ≃	172	60.28 N	94.45 W
Thoa ≃	172	60.30 N	109.47 W
Thomas	176	39.09 N	79.30 W
Thomas Mountains ⋀	87	75.32 S	70.57 W
Thomaston, Conn., U.S.	176	41.40 N	73.04 W
Thomaston, Maine, U.S.	176	44.05 N	69.10 W
Thomastown	110	52.31 N	7.08 W
Thomasville	174	30.50 N	83.59 W
Thom Bay C	172	70.09 N	92.00 W
Thomes Creek ≃	178	39.59 N	122.06 W
Thompson	172	55.45 N	97.45 W
Thompson Peak ∧	178	41.00 N	123.03 W
Thomsen ≃	172	74.08 N	119.35 W
Thomson ≃	168	25.11 S	142.53 E
Thomson's Falls	158	0.02 N	36.22 E
Thongwa	140	16.46 N	96.32 E
Thonon-les-Bains	118	46.22 N	6.29 E
Thonze	140	17.38 N	95.47 E
Thormanby	106	54.10 N	1.14 W
Thornaby-on-Tees	106	54.34 N	1.18 W
Thornbury, Ont., Can.	176	44.34 N	80.26 W
Thornbury, N.Z.	170	46.17 S	168.06 E
Thornbury, Eng., U.K.	104	51.37 N	2.32 W
Thorndon	104	52.17 N	1.08 E
Thorne	106	53.37 N	0.58 W
Thorney	104	52.37 N	0.07 W
Thornhill	106	55.15 N	3.46 W
Thornton	106	53.53 N	3.02 W
Thornton Dale	106	54.14 N	0.43 W
Thorpe-le-Soken	104	51.52 N	1.10 E
Thorpe Saint Andrew	104	52.38 N	1.20 E
Thorshavn → Tórshavn	100	62.01 N	6.46 W
Thouars	118	46.59 N	0.13 W
Thouin, Cape ›	164	20.20 S	118.12 E
Thousand Oaks	178	34.10 N	118.50 W
Thousand Springs Creek ≃	178	41.17 N	113.51 W
Thrace □[9]	124	41.20 N	26.45 E
Thrapston	104	52.24 N	0.32 W
Three Bridges	104	51.07 N	0.09 W
Three Hummock Island I	168	40.26 S	144.55 E
Three Kings Islands II	96	34.10 S	172.05 E
Three Pagodas Pass)(	140	15.18 N	98.23 E
Three Points, Cape ›	152	4.45 N	2.06 W
Three Rivers	164	25.07 S	119.09 E
Three Sisters	160	31.54 S	23.06 E
Three Springs	164	29.32 S	115.45 E
Threlkeld	106	54.38 N	3.03 W
Throckley	106	54.59 N	1.45 W
Throssel, Lake ⊜	164	27.27 S	124.16 E
Thrushel ≃	104	50.39 N	4.15 W
Thuin	116	50.20 N	4.17 E
Thule	90	76.34 N	68.47 W
Thun	118	46.45 N	7.37 E
Thunder Bay	172	48.23 N	89.15 W
Thunder Bay C	176	45.00 N	83.22 W
Thunder Bay ≃	176	45.04 N	83.25 W
Thunder Bay, North Branch ≃	176	45.08 N	83.35 W
Thüringen □[9]	116	51.00 N	11.00 E
Thüringer Wald ⋀	118	50.30 N	10.30 E
Thurles	110	52.41 N	7.49 W
Thurmont	176	39.37 N	77.25 W
Thurnscoe	106	53.31 N	1.19 W
Thursby	106	54.51 N	3.03 W
Thursday Island	166	10.35 S	142.13 E
Thurso	108	58.35 N	3.32 W
Thurso ≃	108	58.36 N	3.30 W
Thurston Island I	87	72.20 S	99.00 W
Thury-Harcourt	118	48.59 N	0.29 W
Thwaites Ice Tongue ⊼	87	74.45 S	106.30 W
Thy ⇀[1]	114	57.00 N	8.30 E
Thylungra	168	26.04 S	143.28 E
Thysville → Mbanza-Ngungu	156	5.15 S	14.52 E
Tía Juana	182	10.16 N	71.22 W
Tiancang	132	41.09 N	100.17 E
Tianchang	136	32.41 N	119.01 E
Tiandeng	140	23.40 N	106.57 E
Tianjin (Tientsin)	132	39.08 N	117.12 E
Tianjun	132	37.25 N	98.58 E
Tianlin	140	24.14 N	106.03 E
Tianmen	136	30.40 N	113.08 E
Tianmushan ⋀	136	30.25 N	119.30 E
Tianshui	132	34.30 N	105.58 E
Tiantai	136	29.09 N	121.02 E
Tiantaishan ⋀	136	29.22 N	121.10 E
Tianwangsi	136	31.45 N	119.12 E
Tianyang	140	23.51 N	106.34 E
Tianzhu	132	37.14 N	102.59 E
Tiaret	152	35.28 N	1.21 E
Tiaro	168	25.44 S	152.35 E
Tibagi	188	24.30 S	50.24 W
Tibari	158	5.01 N	31.43 E
Tibasti, Sarīr ⇀[2]	154	24.15 N	17.15 E
Tibbermore	108	56.22 N	3.32 W
Tiberias → Teverya	150	32.47 N	35.32 E
Tibesti ⋀	154	21.30 N	17.30 E
Tibet □[9]	146	31.00 N	88.00 E
Tiburón, Isla I	180	29.00 N	112.20 W
Ticehurst	104	51.03 N	0.25 E
Tîchît	152	18.28 N	9.30 W
Tichoreck	126	45.51 N	40.09 E
Tichvin	130	59.39 N	33.31 E
Ticino □[3]	118	46.20 N	8.45 E
Ticino ≃	122	45.09 N	9.14 E
Tickhill	106	53.26 N	1.06 W
Ticonderoga	176	43.51 N	73.26 W
Tidaholm	114	58.11 N	13.57 E
Tidioute	176	41.41 N	79.24 W
Tidjikdja	152	18.33 N	11.25 W
Tidore	138	0.40 N	127.26 E
Tidra, Île I	152	19.44 N	16.24 W
Tiel	116	51.54 N	5.25 E
Tielelihu ⊜	132	44.30 N	85.15 E
Tieli	132	46.59 N	128.02 E
Tieling	132	42.18 N	123.49 E
Tielt	118	51.00 N	3.19 E
T'ienchung	136	23.53 N	120.34 E
Tienen	116	50.48 N	4.57 E
Tien Shan ⋀	132	42.00 N	80.00 E
Tierga	120	41.37 N	1.36 W
Tierp	114	60.20 N	17.30 E
Tierra Amarilla	188	27.29 S	70.17 W
Tierra de Campos ⇀[1]	120	42.10 N	4.50 W
Tierra del Fuego, Isla Grande de I	186	54.00 S	69.00 W
Tietê	190	23.07 S	47.43 W
Tietê ≃	188	20.40 S	51.35 W
Tiffin	176	41.07 N	83.11 W
Tifton	174	31.27 N	83.31 W
Tighvein ∧[2]	108	55.30 N	5.10 W
Tigil'	128	57.48 N	158.40 E
Tigre ≃, Perú	184	4.30 S	74.10 W
Tigre ≃, Ven.	182	9.20 N	62.30 W
Tigris (Dicle) (Dijlah) ≃	150	31.00 N	47.25 E
Tiguabos	182	20.14 N	75.21 W
Tiguentourine	152	27.50 N	9.18 E
Tīh, Jabal at- ⋀[1]	150	29.30 N	34.00 E
Tijesno	122	43.48 N	15.39 E
Tijuana	180	32.32 N	117.01 W
Tijuana ≃	178	32.33 N	117.08 W
Tijucas	188	27.14 S	48.38 W
Tijucas do Sul	188	25.55 S	49.12 W
Tikei I	96	14.58 S	144.32 W
Tikitiki	170	37.48 S	178.24 E
Tiko	152	4.05 N	9.22 E
Tikrīt	150	34.36 N	43.42 E
Tiksi	128	71.36 N	128.48 E
Tilamuta	142	0.30 N	122.20 E
Tilburg	116	51.34 N	5.05 E
Tilbury, Ont., Can.	176	42.16 N	82.26 W
Tilbury, Eng., U.K.	104	51.28 N	0.23 E
Tilcha	168	29.36 S	140.54 E
Tilemsi, Vallée du V	152	16.15 N	0.02 E
Tilhar	146	27.59 N	79.44 E
Till ≃, Eng., U.K.	106	53.16 N	0.37 W
Till ≃, Eng., U.K.	108	55.41 N	2.12 W
Tillabéry	152	14.13 N	1.27 E
Tillanchāng Dwīp I	140	8.30 N	93.37 E
Tillicoultry	108	56.09 N	3.45 W
Tillson	176	41.50 N	74.04 W
Tillsonburg	176	42.51 N	80.44 W
Tillyfourie	108	57.11 N	2.35 W
Tilpa	168	30.57 S	144.24 E
Tilsit → Sovetsk	130	55.05 N	21.53 E
Tilt ≃	108	56.46 N	3.50 W
Tilton	176	43.27 N	71.35 W
Tiltonsville	176	40.10 N	80.42 W
Timanskij Kr'až ∧	126	65.00 N	51.00 E
Timaru	170	44.24 S	171.15 E
Timbédra	152	16.15 N	8.10 W
Timbó	188	26.50 S	49.18 W
Timbuktu → Tombouctou	152	16.46 N	3.01 W
Timimoun	152	29.14 N	0.16 E
Timir'azevskij	128	56.29 N	84.54 E
Timiris, Cap ›	152	19.23 N	16.32 W
Timiș □[5]	124	45.40 N	21.20 E
Timiș (Tamiš) ≃	124	44.51 N	20.39 E
Timișoara	124	45.45 N	21.13 E
Timmendorfer Strand	116	54.00 N	10.46 E
Timmins	172	48.28 N	81.20 W
Timor I	142	9.00 S	125.00 E
Timor Sea ⊤[2]	96	11.00 S	128.00 E
Timor Trough ⌖[1]	96	10.00 S	126.00 E
Timotes	182	8.59 N	70.44 W
Timpton ≃	128	58.43 N	127.12 E
Timšer	126	62.06 N	54.40 E
Tina ≃	160	31.18 S	29.14 E
Tinaca Point ›	142	5.33 N	125.20 E
Tinaco	182	9.42 N	68.26 W
Ṭīnah, Khalīj aṭ- C	150	31.08 N	32.40 E
Tinahely	110	52.47 N	7.26 W
Tinapagee	168	29.28 S	144.23 E
Tinaquillo	182	9.55 N	68.18 W
Tindivanam	148	12.15 N	79.39 E
Tindouf	152	27.50 N	8.04 W
Tineo	120	43.20 N	6.25 W
Tingha	168	29.57 S	151.13 E
Tinglev	114	54.56 N	9.15 E
Tingo María	184	9.09 S	75.56 W
Tingsryd	114	56.32 N	14.59 E
Tingvoll	114	62.54 N	8.12 E
Tingvollfjorden C[2]	114	62.50 N	8.11 E
Tinian I	138	15.00 N	145.38 E
Tinkisso ≃	152	11.21 N	9.10 W
Tinnsjø ⊜	114	59.54 N	8.55 E
Tinogasta	188	28.05 S	67.34 W
Tínos I	124	37.38 N	25.10 E
Tinrhert, Plateau du ⋀[1]	152	29.00 N	9.00 E
Tinsukia	146	27.30 N	95.22 E
Tintagel	104	50.40 N	4.45 W
Tintagel Head ›	104	50.41 N	4.46 W
Tintern Parva	104	51.42 N	2.40 W
Tintina	188	27.02 S	62.45 W
Tinto ∧	108	55.36 N	3.39 W
Tinwald	170	43.55 S	171.43 E
Tioga	176	41.55 N	77.08 W
Tioga ≃	176	42.09 N	77.05 W
Tiojala	112	61.10 N	23.52 E
Tioman, Pulau I	142	2.48 N	104.10 E
Tionesta	176	41.30 N	79.27 W
Tionesta Creek ≃	176	41.28 N	79.22 W
Tioro, Selat ʊ	138	4.40 S	122.20 E
Tioughnioga ≃	176	42.14 N	75.51 W
Tioughnioga, East Branch ≃	176	42.36 N	76.10 W
Tipitapa	182	12.12 N	86.06 W
Tipperary, Austl.	166	13.44 S	131.02 E
Tipperary, Eire	110	52.29 N	8.10 W
Tipperary □[6]	110	52.40 N	8.20 W
Tipton, Eng., U.K.	104	52.32 N	2.05 W
Tipton, Calif., U.S.	178	36.04 N	119.19 W
Tipton, Mount ∧	178	35.32 N	110.12 W
Tip Top Mountain ∧	172	48.16 N	85.59 W
Tiptree	104	51.49 N	0.45 E
Tīrān, Jazīrat I	154	27.56 N	34.34 E
Tīrān, Maḍīq ʊ	150	27.58 N	34.28 E
Tiranë	124	41.20 N	19.50 E
Tiraspol'	126	46.51 N	29.38 E
Tirat Karmel	150	32.46 N	34.58 E
Tirau	170	37.59 S	175.45 E
Tiree I	108	56.30 N	6.55 W
Tîrgoviște	124	44.56 N	25.27 E
Tîrgu-Jiu	124	45.02 N	23.17 E
Tîrgu Mureș	124	46.33 N	24.33 E
Tîrgu-Neamț	124	47.12 N	26.22 E
Tîrgu-Ocna	124	46.15 N	26.37 E
Tirich Mīr ∧	149	36.15 N	71.50 E
Tîrnava Mare ≃	124	46.09 N	23.42 E
Tîrnăveni	124	46.20 N	24.17 E
Tírnavos	124	39.45 N	22.17 E
Tirol □[3]	116	47.15 N	11.20 E
Tiros	190	19.00 S	45.58 W
Tirry ≃	108	58.02 N	4.26 W
Tirschenreuth	116	49.53 N	12.21 E
Tirso ≃	122	39.52 N	8.33 E
Tiruchchirāppalli	148	10.49 N	78.41 E
Tiruchengodu	148	11.23 N	77.56 E
Tirunelveli	148	8.44 N	77.42 E
Tirupati	148	13.39 N	79.25 E
Tiruppattūr	148	12.30 N	78.34 E
Tiruppur	148	11.06 N	77.21 E
Tiruvālūr	148	10.46 N	79.39 E
Tiruvannāmalai	148	12.13 N	79.04 E
Tiruvottiyūr	148	13.09 N	80.18 E
Tisa (Tisza) ≃	124	45.15 N	20.17 E
Tisbury	104	51.04 N	2.03 W
Tisdale	172	52.51 N	104.04 W
Tissemsilt	120	35.35 N	1.50 E
Tista ≃	146	25.23 N	89.43 E
Tisza (Tisa) ≃	124	45.15 N	20.17 E
Tiszafüred	116	47.37 N	20.46 E
Tiszavasvári	116	47.58 N	21.22 E
Tit-Ary	128	71.58 N	127.01 E
Titchfield	104	50.51 N	1.13 W
Titel	124	45.12 N	20.18 E
Titicaca, Lago ⊜	184	15.50 S	69.20 W
Titograd	124	42.26 N	19.14 E
Titova Korenica	122	44.45 N	15.43 E
Titovo Užice	124	43.51 N	19.51 E
Titov Veles	124	41.41 N	21.48 E
Tittabawassee ≃	176	43.23 N	83.59 W
Titterstone Clee Hill ∧[2]	104	52.23 N	2.35 W
Tittling	116	48.44 N	13.23 E
Titule	158	3.17 N	25.32 E
Titusville, Fla., U.S.	174	28.37 N	80.49 W
Titusville, Pa., U.S.	176	41.38 N	79.41 W
Tiumpan Head ›	108	58.16 N	6.09 W
Tiverton	104	50.55 N	3.29 W
Tivoli	122	41.58 N	12.48 E
Tizimín	180	21.10 N	88.10 W
Tizi-Ouzou	152	36.48 N	4.02 E
Tiznados ≃	182	8.16 N	67.47 W
Tjolotjo	158	19.47 S	27.46 E
Tjøme I	114	59.07 N	10.24 E
Tlaxcala	180	19.19 N	98.14 W
Tlaxiaco	180	17.16 N	97.41 W
Tlemcen	152	34.52 N	1.15 W
Toano Draw V	178	41.27 N	114.35 W
Toano Range ⋀	178	40.50 N	114.20 W
Toay	188	36.40 S	64.25 W
Toba	134	34.29 N	136.51 E
Toba, Danau ⊜	138	2.35 N	98.50 E
Tobacco ≃	176	43.49 N	84.24 W
Tobago I	182	11.15 N	60.40 W
Toba Kākar Range ⋀	146	31.15 N	68.00 E
Tobarra	120	38.35 N	1.41 W
Toba Tek Singh	149	30.58 N	72.29 E
Tobe Jube, Bahía C	182	9.15 N	60.45 W
Tobelo	138	1.44 N	128.01 E
Tobercurry	110	54.03 N	8.43 W
Tobermorey	168	22.15 S	138.00 E
Tobermory	108	56.37 N	6.05 W
Toberonochy	108	56.13 N	5.38 W
Tōbetsu	134a	43.13 N	141.31 E

Symbols in the index entries are identified on page 198.

Name	Page	Lat °′	Long °′
Tobi I	138	3.00 N	131.10 E
Tobin, Mount ∧	178	40.22 N	117.32 W
Tobin Lake ⊜	164	21.45 S	125.49 E
Tobi-shima I	134	39.12 N	139.34 E
Toboali	142	3.00 S	106.30 E
Tobol	126	52.40 N	62.39 E
Tobol ≃	126	58.10 N	68.12 E
Toboli	142	0.43 S	120.05 E
Tobol'sk	126	58.12 N	68.16 E
Tobruk → Ṭubruq	154	32.05 N	23.59 E
Tobyhanna	176	41.11 N	75.25 W
Tocantins ≃	184	1.45 S	49.10 W
Tochigi	134	36.23 N	139.44 E
Tochigi □5	134	36.45 N	139.45 E
Tochio	134	37.28 N	139.00 E
Töcksfors	114	59.30 N	11.50 E
Toco	188	22.05 S	69.35 W
Tocoa	182	15.41 N	86.03 W
Toconao	188	23.11 S	68.01 W
Tocopilla	188	22.05 S	70.12 W
Tocumwal	168	35.49 S	145.34 E
Tocuyo ≃	182	11.03 N	68.23 W
Tocuyo de la Costa	182	11.02 N	68.23 W
Toddington	104	51.57 N	0.32 W
Todmorden, Austl.	164	27.08 S	134.48 E
Todmorden, Eng., U.K.	106	53.43 N	2.05 W
Todo-saki ≻	134	39.33 N	142.05 E
Todos Santos	184	16.48 S	65.08 W
Todos Santos, Bahía C	178	31.48 N	116.42 W
Todtnau	116	47.50 N	7.56 E
Toe Head ≻	108	57.50 N	7.08 W
Toetoes Bay C	170	46.38 S	168.43 E
Tofte	114	59.33 N	10.34 E
Togi	134	37.08 N	136.44 E
Togian, Kepulauan II	142	0.20 S	122.00 E
Togo □1	152	8.00 N	1.10 E
Togučin	128	55.16 N	84.23 E
Tōhaku	134	35.30 N	133.40 E
Tohakum Peak ∧	178	40.11 N	119.27 W
Tohāna	149	29.42 N	75.54 E
Toi-misaki ≻	134	31.20 N	131.22 E
Toiyabe Range ⋀	178	39.10 N	117.10 W
Tōjō	134	34.53 N	133.16 E
Tokaanu	170	38.58 S	175.46 E
Tokachi ≃	134a	42.44 N	143.42 E
Tokachi-dake ∧	134a	43.25 N	142.41 E
Tokachi-heiya ≚	134a	43.00 N	143.30 E
Tōkamachi	134	37.08 N	138.46 E
Tokanui	170	46.34 S	168.56 E
Tokara-kaikyō)(	135b	30.10 N	130.10 E
Tokara-rettō II	135b	29.36 N	129.43 E
Tokashiki-shima I	135b	26.11 N	127.21 E
Tokat	150	40.19 N	36.34 E
Tok-dō I	134	37.17 N	131.53 E
Tokelau Islands □2	96	9.00 S	171.45 W
Tokelau Islands II	84	9.00 S	171.45 W
Toki	134	35.21 N	137.11 E
Tokko	128	59.59 N	119.52 E
Tokmak	126	42.55 N	75.18 E
Tokomaru	170	40.28 S	175.30 E
Toko Range ⋀	168	23.05 S	138.20 E
Tokoro ≃	134a	44.07 N	144.05 E
Tokoroa	170	38.14 S	175.52 E
Toku I	96	18.10 S	174.11 W
Tokuno-shima I	135b	27.45 N	128.58 E
Tokushima	134	34.04 N	134.34 E
Tokuyama	134	34.03 N	131.49 E
Tokwe ≃	158	21.09 S	31.30 E
Tōkyō	134	35.42 N	139.46 E
Tokyo Bay → Tōkyō-wan C	134	35.25 N	139.47 E
Tōkyō-wan C	134	35.25 N	139.47 E
Tol I	96	7.22 N	151.37 E
Tolaga Bay	170	38.22 S	178.18 E
Tolbuhin	124	43.34 N	27.50 E
Toledo, Bra.	188	24.44 S	53.45 W
Toledo, Esp.	120	39.52 N	4.01 W
Toledo, Ohio, U.S.	176	41.39 N	83.32 W
Toledo, Montes de ⋀	120	39.33 N	4.20 W
Toledo Bend Reservoir ⊜1	174	31.30 N	93.45 W
Tolima, Nevado del ∧	184	4.40 N	75.19 W
Tolitoli	142	1.02 N	120.49 E
Toljatti	112	53.31 N	49.26 E
Tol'ka	128	64.02 N	81.55 E
Tollense ≃	116	53.54 N	13.02 E
Tollesbury	104	51.46 N	0.50 E
Tølløse	114	55.37 N	11.45 E
Tolmačovo	130	58.52 N	29.55 E
Tolmezzo	122	46.24 N	13.01 E
Tolmin	122	46.11 N	13.44 E
Tolna	116	46.26 N	18.46 E
Tolna □6	116	46.30 N	18.35 E
Tolo, Teluk C	142	2.00 S	122.30 E
Tolob	108a	59.53 N	1.19 W
Tolosa	120	43.08 N	2.04 W
Tolpuddle	104	50.45 N	2.18 W
Tolsta Head ≻	108	58.20 N	6.10 W
Tolstoj, Mys ≻	128	59.10 N	155.12 E
Toltén	186	39.13 S	73.14 W
Tolú	184	9.31 N	75.35 W
Toluca	180	41.00 N	89.08 W
Tolvdalselva ≃	114	58.10 N	8.00 E
Tom' ≃	128	56.50 N	84.27 E
Tomakomai	134a	42.38 N	141.36 E
Tomaszów Lubelski	116	50.28 N	23.25 E
Tomaszów Mazowiecki	116	51.32 N	20.01 E
Tomatin	108	57.20 N	3.59 W
Tomazina	190	23.46 S	49.58 W
Tombigbee ≃	174	31.04 N	87.58 W
Tombos	190	20.55 S	42.02 W
Tombouctou (Timbuktu)	152	16.46 N	3.01 W
Tombstone Mountain ∧	172	64.25 N	138.30 W
Tom Burke	160	23.05 S	28.00 E
Tomdoun	108	57.04 N	5.03 W
Tomé	188	36.37 S	72.57 W
Tomelilla	114	55.33 N	13.57 E
Tomelloso	120	39.10 N	3.01 W
Tomich	108	57.18 N	4.48 W
Tomini	142	0.30 N	120.32 E
Tomini, Teluk C	142	0.20 S	121.00 E
Tomintoul	108	57.14 N	3.22 W
Tomioka	134	36.15 N	138.54 E
Tommot	128	58.58 N	126.19 E
Tomnavoulin	108	57.18 N	3.19 W
Tomo ≃	184	5.20 N	67.48 W
Tom Price	164	22.43 S	117.41 E
Tomptokan	128	57.06 N	133.59 E
Toms ≃	176	39.57 N	74.07 W
Tomsk	128	56.30 N	84.58 E
Toms River	176	39.58 N	74.12 W
Tonalá	180	20.37 N	103.14 W
Tonami	134	36.38 N	136.54 E
Tonawanda	176	43.01 N	78.53 W
Tonbridge	104	51.12 N	0.16 E
Tondabayashi	134	34.30 N	135.36 E
Tondano	142	1.19 N	124.54 E
Tønder	114	54.56 N	8.54 E
Tone ≃	134	35.44 N	140.51 E
Tonga □1	96	20.00 S	175.00 W
Tongaat	160	29.37 S	31.03 E
Tonga Islands II	96	20.00 S	175.00 W
Tong'an	136	24.46 N	118.08 E
Tonga Ridge ∻3	96	22.00 S	175.00 W
Tongariro, Mount ∧	170	39.08 S	175.38 E
Tongatapu I	96	21.10 N	175.10 W
Tongatapu Group II	96	21.10 S	175.10 W
Tonga Trench ∻1	96	22.00 S	173.00 W
Tongbai	136	32.22 N	113.24 E
Tongcheng, Zhg.	136	32.53 N	118.58 E
Tongcheng, Zhg.	136	31.03 N	116.58 E
Tongcheng, Zhg.	136	29.11 N	113.49 E
Tongchuan	132	35.01 N	109.01 E
Tongeren	116	50.47 N	5.28 E
Tonggu	136	28.33 N	114.21 E
Tongguan, Zhg.	132	34.38 N	110.20 E
Tongguan, Zhg.	136	28.29 N	112.48 E
Tonghai	140	24.07 N	102.49 E
Tonghua	132	41.50 N	125.55 E
Tongjing	136	31.47 N	118.33 E
Tongjosŏn-man C	132	39.30 N	128.00 E
Tongli	136	31.10 N	120.43 E
Tongliao	132	43.39 N	122.14 E
Tongling	136	30.53 N	117.46 E
Tonglingzhen	136	30.56 N	117.47 E
Tonglu	136	29.48 N	119.40 E
Tongo	168	30.30 S	143.45 E
Tongololo Creek ≃	164	22.06 S	121.08 E
Tongoy	188	30.15 S	71.30 W
Tongren	132	27.38 N	109.03 E
Tongsa Dzong	144	27.31 N	90.31 E
Tongtianhe ≃	146	33.25 N	96.32 E
Tongtianheyan	132	33.50 N	92.28 E
Tongue	108	58.28 N	4.25 W
Tongue, Kyle of C	108	58.30 N	4.26 W
Tongxian	132	39.55 N	116.39 E
Tongxiang	136	30.38 N	120.32 E
Tongxu	136	34.29 N	114.28 E
Tongzi	132	28.08 N	106.49 E
Tonk	146	26.10 N	75.47 E
Tonkin, Gulf of C	140	20.00 N	108.00 E
Tonle Sap → Sab, Tônlé ⊜	140	13.00 N	104.00 E
Tonneins	118	44.23 N	0.19 E
Tönning	116	54.19 N	8.56 E
Tōno	134	39.19 N	141.32 E
Tonopah	178	38.04 N	117.14 W
Tonoro ≃	182	9.29 N	63.17 W
Tonoshō	134	34.29 N	134.11 E
Tonota	160	21.29 S	27.29 E
Tønsberg	114	59.17 N	10.25 E
Tonyrefail	104	51.36 N	3.25 W
Toobeah	168	28.25 S	149.52 E
Toodyay	164	31.33 S	116.28 E
Tooele	174	40.32 N	112.18 W
Toogoolawah	168	27.06 S	152.23 E
Toomebridge	110	54.45 N	6.27 W
Toomevara	110	52.50 N	8.02 W
Toompine	168	27.13 S	144.22 E
Toora-Chem	128	52.28 N	96.17 E
Toormakeady	110	53.39 N	9.24 W
Toowoomba	168	27.33 S	151.57 E
Topeka	174	39.03 N	95.41 W
Topka, Gora ∧	128	57.08 N	137.24 E
Topki	128	55.16 N	85.36 E
Topocalma, Punta ≻	188	34.08 S	72.01 W
Topol'čany	116	48.34 N	18.10 E
Topolobampo	180	25.36 N	109.03 W
Tops, Mount ∧	164	21.50 S	134.00 E
Topsham, Eng., U.K.	104	50.41 N	3.27 W
Topsham, Maine, U.S.	176	43.56 N	69.58 W
Top Springs	166	16.38 S	131.50 E
Toquima Range ⋀	178	39.00 N	117.00 W
Toquop Wash V	178	36.45 N	114.11 W
Torawitan, Tanjung ≻	142	1.46 N	124.58 E
Torbat-e Ḥeydarīyeh	150	35.16 N	59.13 E
Torbat-e Jām	150	35.14 N	60.36 E
Tor Bay C	104	50.25 N	3.30 W
Torch ≃	172	53.50 N	103.05 W
Torch Lake ⊜	176	45.00 N	85.19 W
Tordesillas	120	41.30 N	5.00 W
Töre	114	65.54 N	22.39 E
Toreno	120	42.42 N	6.30 W
Torez	126	48.01 N	38.37 E
Torgau	116	51.34 N	13.00 E
Torgelow	116	53.37 N	14.00 E
Torhout	116	51.04 N	3.06 E
Torino (Turin)	122	45.03 N	7.40 E
Torit	154	4.24 N	32.34 E
Torment, Point ≻	164	17.02 S	123.36 E
Torne ≃	106	53.36 N	0.44 W
Torneträsk ⊜	112	68.20 N	19.10 E
Torngat Mountains ⋀	172	59.00 N	64.00 W
Tornio	114	65.51 N	24.08 E
Tornquist	188	38.06 S	62.14 W
Toro	120	41.31 N	5.24 W
Toro □5	158	0.30 N	30.30 E
Toro, Cerro del ∧	188	29.08 S	69.48 W
Toro, Punta ≻	188	33.47 S	71.49 W
Törökszentmiklós	116	47.11 N	20.25 E
Toronto, Ont., Can.	172	43.39 N	79.23 W
Toronto, Ohio, U.S.	176	40.28 N	80.36 W
Toro Peak ∧	178	33.32 N	116.25 W
Toropec	130	56.30 N	31.39 E
Tororo	158	0.42 N	34.11 E
Toros Dağları ⋀	150	37.00 N	33.00 E
Torphins	108	57.06 N	2.37 W
Torpoint	104	50.22 N	4.11 W
Torquay (Torbay)	104	50.28 N	3.30 W
Torquemada	120	42.02 N	4.19 W
Torrance	178	33.50 N	118.19 W
Torrão	120	38.18 N	8.13 W
Torre Annunziata	122	40.45 N	14.27 E
Torre Baja	120	40.07 N	1.15 W
Torrecilla ∧	120	37.36 N	2.31 W
Torrecilla en Cameros	120	42.16 N	2.37 W
Torre del Campo	120	37.46 N	3.53 W
Torre de Moncorvo	120	41.10 N	7.03 W
Torredonjimeno	120	37.46 N	3.57 W
Torrejón, Embalse de ⊜1	120	39.50 N	5.50 W
Torrejoncillo	120	39.54 N	6.28 W
Torrejón de Ardoz	120	40.27 N	3.29 W
Torrelaguna	120	40.50 N	3.32 W
Torrelavega	120	43.21 N	4.03 W
Torremaggiore	122	41.41 N	15.17 E
Torremolinos	120	36.37 N	4.30 W
Torrens, Lake ⊜	168	31.00 S	137.50 E
Torrens Creek	168	20.46 S	145.02 E
Torrente	120	39.26 N	0.28 W
Torreón	180	25.33 N	103.26 W
Torreperogil	120	38.02 N	3.17 W
Tôrres	188	29.21 S	49.44 W
Torres Novas	120	39.29 N	8.32 W
Torres Strait)(	166	10.25 S	142.10 E
Torres Vedras	120	39.06 N	9.16 W
Torrevieja	120	37.59 N	0.41 W
Torricelli Mountains ⋀	166	3.25 S	142.20 E
Torridge ≃	102	51.03 N	4.11 W
Torridon	108	57.33 N	5.31 W
Torridon, Loch C	108	57.35 N	5.46 W
Torrijos	120	39.59 N	4.17 W
Torrin	108	57.12 N	6.02 W
Torrington, Conn., U.S.	176	41.48 N	73.08 W
Torrington, Wyo., U.S.	174	42.04 N	104.11 W
Torrinha	190	22.26 S	48.09 W
Torsby	114	60.08 N	13.00 E
Tórshavn	100	62.01 N	6.46 W
Torteval	105b	49.27 N	2.38 W
Tortola I	182	18.26 N	64.37 W
Tortona	122	44.54 N	8.52 E
Tortosa	120	40.48 N	0.31 E
Tortosa, Cabo de ≻	120	40.43 N	0.55 E
Tortue, Île de la I	182	20.01 N	72.50 W
Toruń	116	53.02 N	18.35 E
Torup	114	56.58 N	13.05 E
Tory Island I	110	55.16 N	8.14 W
Tory Sound)(	110	55.14 N	8.14 W
Toržok	130	57.03 N	34.58 E
Tosa	134	33.29 N	133.25 E
Tosa-shimizu	134	32.46 N	132.57 E
Tosa-wan C	134	33.20 N	133.40 E
Tosca	160	25.53 S	23.58 E
Toscaig	108	57.24 N	5.50 W
Toscana □4	122	43.25 N	11.00 E
To-shima I	134	32.12 N	130.05 E
Tosilei	158	1.24 N	41.23 E
Tosno	130	59.33 N	30.53 E
T'osovo-Netyl'skij	130	58.57 N	31.04 E
T'osovskij	130	58.48 N	30.52 E
Tostado	188	29.15 S	61.45 W
Totana	120	37.46 N	1.30 W
Toteng	160	20.22 S	22.58 E
Tôtes	118	49.41 N	1.03 E
Totes Gebirge ⋀	116	47.42 N	13.55 E
Tot'ma	130	59.57 N	42.45 E
Totnes	104	50.25 N	3.41 W
Totness	184	5.53 N	56.19 W
Totoras	188	32.40 S	61.10 W
Totten Glacier ⚑	87	66.45 S	116.10 E
Tottenham, Austl.	168	32.14 S	147.21 E
Tottenham, Ont., Can.	176	44.01 N	79.49 W
Tottington	106	53.37 N	2.20 W
Totton	104	50.56 N	1.29 W
Tottori	134	35.30 N	134.14 E
Touba	152	8.17 N	7.41 W
Toubkal, Jbel ∧	152	31.05 N	7.55 W
Toucy	118	47.44 N	3.18 E
Touggourt	152	33.10 N	6.00 E
Toul	118	48.41 N	5.54 E
Toulnustouc ≃	172	49.35 N	68.24 W
Toulon	118	43.07 N	5.56 E
Toulon Lake ⊜	178	40.01 N	118.40 W
Toulouse	118	43.36 N	1.26 E
Tounan	136	23.41 N	120.28 E
Toungoo	140	18.56 N	96.26 E
Touques ≃	118	49.22 N	0.06 E
Touraine	176	45.34 N	75.47 W
Touraine □9	118	47.12 N	1.30 E
Tourcoing	118	50.43 N	3.09 E
Tourinan, Cabo ≻	120	43.03 N	9.18 W
Tournai	116	50.36 N	3.23 E
Tournus	118	46.34 N	4.54 E
Tours	118	47.23 N	0.41 E
Touside, Pic ∧	154	21.02 N	16.25 E
Touws ≃	160	33.45 S	21.11 E
Touwsrivier	160	33.20 S	20.00 E
Tove ≃	104	52.05 N	0.38 W
Towada	134	40.37 N	141.13 E
Towada-ko ⊜	134	40.28 N	140.55 E
Towanda	176	41.46 N	76.26 W
Towanda Creek ≃	176	41.45 N	76.26 W
Towan Head ≻	104	50.25 N	5.07 W
Towcester	104	52.08 N	1.00 W
Tower City	176	40.35 N	76.33 W
Tower Hamlets ◆8	104	51.32 N	0.03 W
Tower Hill	168	22.03 S	144.36 E
Towerhill Creek ≃	168	22.29 S	144.39 E
Towla, Mount ∧	158	21.22 S	29.52 E
Tow Law	106	54.44 N	1.49 W
Townshend Island I	168	22.15 S	150.30 E
Townsville	168	19.16 S	146.48 E
Towson	176	39.24 N	76.36 W
Towuti, Danau ⊜	142	2.45 S	121.32 E
Toyama	134	36.41 N	137.13 E
Toyama-heiya ≚	134	36.40 N	137.15 E
Toyama-wan C	134	36.50 N	137.10 E
Tōyō	134	33.32 N	134.18 E
Toyohashi	134	34.46 N	137.23 E
Toyokawa	134	34.49 N	137.24 E
Toyonaka	134	34.47 N	135.28 E
Toyooka	134	35.32 N	134.50 E
Toyota	134	35.05 N	137.09 E
Toyoura	134	34.08 N	130.58 E
Tozer, Mount ∧	166	12.45 S	143.13 E
Tozeur	152	33.55 N	8.08 E
Trabiju	190	22.03 S	48.18 W
Trabzon	144	41.00 N	39.43 E
Tracy, Qué., Can.	176	46.01 N	73.09 W
Tracy, Calif., U.S.	178	37.44 N	121.25 W
Trafalgar, Cabo ≻	120	36.11 N	6.02 W
Tragacete	120	40.21 N	1.51 W
Traid	120	40.40 N	1.49 W
Traiguén	188	38.15 S	72.41 W
Trail	172	49.06 N	117.42 W
Trakt	112	62.44 N	51.11 E
Tralee	110	52.16 N	9.42 W
Tralee Bay C	110	52.15 N	9.59 W
Tramore	110	52.10 N	7.10 W
Tranås	114	58.03 N	14.59 E
Trancas	188	26.20 S	65.20 W
Tranebjerg	114	55.50 N	10.36 E
Tranent	108	55.57 N	2.58 W
Trang	140	7.33 N	99.36 E
Trangan, Pulau I	166	6.35 S	134.20 E
Trangie	168	32.02 S	147.59 E
Trani	122	41.17 N	16.26 E
Trannon ≃	104	52.31 N	3.25 W
Transkei □9	160	31.20 S	29.00 E
Transvaal □3	160	25.00 S	29.00 E
Transylvania □9	124	46.30 N	24.00 E
Transylvanian Alps → Carpații Meridionali ⋀	124	45.30 N	24.15 E
Trapani	122	38.01 N	12.31 E
Traralgon	168	38.12 S	146.32 E
Trasimeno, Lago ⊜	122	43.08 N	12.06 E
Trás-os-Montes □9	120	41.30 N	7.15 W
Traun	116	48.13 N	14.14 E
Traun ≃	122	48.16 N	14.22 E
Traunstein	116	47.52 N	12.38 E
Travellers Lake ⊜	168	33.18 S	142.00 E
Traverse City	176	44.46 N	85.37 W
Travnik	122	44.14 N	17.40 E
Trawbreaga Bay C	110	55.17 N	7.18 W
Trawsfynydd	104	52.54 N	3.55 W
Trbovlje	122	46.10 N	15.03 E
Třebíč	116	49.13 N	15.53 E
Trebinje	124	42.43 N	18.20 E
Trebišov	116	48.40 N	21.47 E
Tredegar	104	51.47 N	3.16 W
Tregaron	104	52.13 N	3.55 W
Tregosse Islets II	168	17.41 S	150.43 E
Tréguier	118	48.47 N	3.14 W
Treharris	104	51.41 N	3.16 W
Treig, Loch ⊜1	108	56.50 N	4.44 W
Treinta y Tres	188	33.14 S	54.23 W
Trélazé	118	47.27 N	0.28 W
Trelew	186	43.15 S	65.20 W
Trelleborg	114	55.22 N	13.10 E
Tremadoc	104	52.56 N	4.09 W
Tremblant, Mont ∧	172	46.16 N	74.35 W
Tremont	176	40.38 N	76.23 W
Trenčín	116	48.54 N	18.04 E
Trenggalek	142	8.03 S	111.43 E
Trenque Lauquen	188	35.58 S	62.44 W
Trent ≃, Ont., Can.	176	44.06 N	77.34 W
Trent ≃, Eng., U.K.	104	53.12 N	0.47 W
Trent, Vale of V	104	52.44 N	1.50 W
Trente-et-un-Milles, Lac des ⊜	176	46.12 N	75.49 W
Trentino-Alto Adige □4	122	46.30 N	11.20 E
Trento	122	46.04 N	11.08 E
Trenton, Ont., Can.	172	44.06 N	77.35 W
Trenton, N.J., U.S.	176	40.13 N	74.45 W
Tres Algarrobos	188	35.10 S	62.47 W
Tres Arroyos	188	38.22 S	60.15 W
Tresco I	104a	49.57 N	6.19 W
Três Coroas	188	29.32 S	50.48 W
Três de Maio	188	27.47 S	54.14 W
Tres Esquinas	184	0.43 N	75.16 W
Treshnish Isles II	108	56.30 N	6.24 W
Treshnish Point ≻	108	56.33 N	6.21 W
Tres Isletas	188	26.20 S	60.36 W
Três Lagoas	190	20.48 S	51.43 W
Tres Marías, Islas II	180	21.25 N	106.28 W
Três Marias, Represa ⊜1	190	18.12 S	45.15 W
Tres Picos, Cerro ∧	188	38.09 S	61.57 W
Três Pontas	190	21.22 S	45.31 W
Tres Puntas, Cabo ≻	186	47.05 S	65.50 W
Três Rios	190	22.07 S	43.12 W
Tresta	108	60.14 N	1.21 W
Treuchtlingen	116	48.57 N	10.54 E
Treuen	116	50.32 N	12.18 E
Treviglio	122	45.31 N	9.35 E
Treviño	120	42.44 N	2.45 W
Treviso	122	45.40 N	12.15 E
Trevorton	176	40.47 N	76.41 W
Trevose	176	40.09 N	74.59 W
Trevose Head ≻	102	50.33 N	5.01 W
Trévoux	118	45.56 N	4.46 E
Trgovište	124	42.21 N	22.05 E
Triabunna	168	42.30 S	147.55 E
Triánda	124	36.24 N	28.10 E
Triangle	176	38.33 N	77.20 W
Trichardt	160	26.28 S	29.13 E
Trichūr	148	10.31 N	76.13 E
Trident Peak ∧	178	41.54 N	118.25 W
Trier	116	49.45 N	6.38 E
Trieste	122	45.40 N	13.46 E
Trieste Depth ∻1	96	11.21 N	142.12 E
Triglav ∧	122	46.23 N	13.50 E
Trigo Mountains ⋀	178	33.15 N	114.35 W
Trigueros	120	37.23 N	6.50 W
Trikala	124	39.34 N	21.46 E
Trikora, Puncak (Wilhelmina Peak) ∧	166	4.15 S	138.45 E
Trillick	110	54.27 N	7.30 W
Trim	110	53.34 N	6.47 W
Trincomalee	148	8.34 N	81.14 E
Trindade	190	16.40 S	49.30 W
Třinec	116	49.41 N	18.40 E
Tring	104	51.48 N	0.40 W
Trinidad, Bol.	184	14.47 S	64.47 W
Trinidad, Col.	184	5.25 N	71.40 W
Trinidad, Cuba	182	21.48 N	79.59 W
Trinidad, Colo., U.S.	174	37.10 N	104.31 W
Trinidad, Ur.	188	33.32 S	56.54 W
Trinidad I	182	10.30 N	61.15 W
Trinidad, Isla I	188	39.08 S	62.00 W
Trinidad and Tobago □1	180	11.00 N	61.00 W
Trinity ≃, Calif., U.S.	178	41.11 N	123.42 W
Trinity ≃, Tex., U.S.	174	29.47 N	94.42 W
Trinity, South Fork ≃	178	40.54 N	123.35 W
Trinity Bay C	172	48.00 N	53.40 W
Trinity Mountains ⋀	178	41.00 N	122.30 W
Trinity Peak ∧	178	40.14 N	118.45 W
Triolet	161c	20.03 S	57.32 E
Tripoli → Ṭarābulus, Lībīya	154	32.54 N	13.11 E
Tripoli → Ṭarābulus, Lubnān	150	34.26 N	35.51 E
Trípolis	124	37.31 N	22.21 E
Tripura □4	146	24.00 N	92.00 E
Tristan da Cunha Group II	88	37.15 S	12.30 W
Triste	120	42.23 N	0.43 W
Triste, Golfo C	182	10.40 N	68.10 W
Triton Island I	138	15.47 N	111.12 E
Trivandrum	148	8.29 N	76.55 E
Trnava	116	48.23 N	17.35 E
Troarn	118	49.11 N	0.11 W
Trobriand Islands II	166	8.35 S	151.05 E
Trogir	122	43.31 N	16.15 E
Troick	126	54.06 N	61.35 E
Troicko-Pečorsk	126	62.44 N	56.06 E
Troina	122	37.47 N	14.37 E
Troisdorf	116	50.49 N	7.08 E
Trois-Rivières	172	46.21 N	72.33 W
Trojan	124	42.51 N	24.43 E
Trollhättan	114	58.16 N	12.18 E
Trollheimen ∧	114	62.51 N	9.05 E
Trombudo Central	188	27.18 S	49.47 W
Tromelin I	156	15.52 S	54.25 E
Trompsburg	160	30.01 S	25.46 E
Troms □6	112	69.15 N	19.40 E
Tromsø	112	69.40 N	18.58 E
Trona	178	35.45 N	117.23 W
Tronador, Monte ∧	186	41.10 S	71.54 W
Trondheim	114	63.25 N	10.25 E
Trondheimsfjorden C2	114	63.39 N	10.49 E
Trondheimsleia)(	114	63.30 N	9.00 E
Trooilapspan	160	28.40 S	21.25 E
Troon	108	55.32 N	4.40 W
Tropojë	124	42.24 N	20.10 E
Trosa	114	58.54 N	17.33 E
Trostan ∧	110	55.03 N	6.10 W
Trotwood	176	39.48 N	84.18 W
Trou-du-Nord	182	19.38 N	72.01 W
Troup Head ≻	108	57.41 N	2.18 W
Trout ≃	172	61.19 N	119.51 W
Trout Creek ≃	178	42.23 N	118.36 W
Trout Lake ⊜, N.W. Ter., Can.	172	60.35 N	121.10 W
Trout Lake ⊜, Ont., Can.	172	51.13 N	93.20 W
Trout Lake ⊜, Ont., Can.	176	46.13 N	80.35 W
Trout Lake ⊜, Ont., Can.	176	46.18 N	79.20 W
Trouville [-sur-Mer]	118	49.22 N	0.05 E
Trowbridge	104	51.20 N	2.13 W
Troy, Ala., U.S.	174	31.48 N	85.58 W
Troy, N.H., U.S.	176	42.50 N	72.11 W
Troy, N.Y., U.S.	174		
	176	42.43 N	73.40 W
Troy, Ohio, U.S.	176	40.02 N	84.13 W
Troy, Pa., U.S.	176	41.47 N	76.47 W
Troyes	118	48.18 N	4.05 E
Troy Lake ⊜	178	34.49 N	116.33 W
Troy Peak ∧	178	38.19 N	115.30 W
Trpanj	122	43.00 N	17.17 E
Trstenik	124	43.37 N	21.00 E
Trubč'ovsk	130	52.37 N	33.44 E
Truc-giang	140	10.14 N	106.23 E
Trucial States → United Arab Emirates □1	144	24.00 N	54.00 E
Truckee	178	39.20 N	120.11 W
Truckee ≃	178	39.51 N	119.24 W
Truim ≃	108	57.02 N	4.10 W
Trujillo, Esp.	120	39.28 N	5.53 W
Trujillo, Hond.	182	15.55 N	86.00 W
Trujillo, Perú	184	8.10 S	79.02 W
Trujillo, Ven.	184	9.22 N	70.26 W
Trujillo □3	182	9.25 N	70.30 W
Truk Islands II	96	7.25 N	151.47 E
Trumansburg	176	42.33 N	76.40 W
Trumbull	176	41.15 N	73.12 W
Trumon	140	2.49 N	97.38 E
Trundle	168	32.55 S	147.43 E
Truro, N.S., Can.	172	45.22 N	63.16 W
Truro, Eng., U.K.	104	50.16 N	5.03 W
Trutnov	116	50.34 N	15.55 E
Truyère ≃	118	44.39 N	2.34 E
Trwyn Cilan ≻	104	52.46 N	4.30 W
Trysilelva (Klarälven) ≃	114	59.23 N	13.32 E
Tryweryn ≃	104	52.24 N	3.35 W
Trzcianka	116	53.03 N	16.28 E
Trzebinia	116	50.10 N	19.18 E
Tržič	122	46.22 N	14.19 E
Tsaratanana	161b	16.47 S	47.39 E
Tsaratanana, Massif du ⋀	161b	14.00 S	49.00 E
Tsau	160	20.12 S	22.22 E
Tsavo	158	2.59 S	38.28 E
Tsévié	152	6.25 N	1.13 E
Tshabong	160	26.03 S	22.29 E
Tshane	160	24.05 S	21.54 E
Tshangalele, Lac ⊜	158	10.55 S	27.03 E
Tshela	156	4.59 S	12.56 E
Tshidilamolomo	160	25.50 S	24.41 E
Tshikapa	156	6.25 S	20.48 E
Tshofa	158	5.14 S	25.15 E
Tshuapa ≃	158	0.14 S	20.42 E
Tshwaane	160	22.29 S	22.03 E
Tsiafajavona ∧	161b	19.21 S	47.15 E
Tsihombe	161b	25.18 S	45.29 E
Tsineng	160	27.06 S	23.04 E
Tsinghai → Qinghai □4	132	36.00 N	96.00 E
Tsiribihina ≃	161b	19.42 S	44.31 E
Tsiroanomandidy	161b	18.46 S	46.02 E
Tsolo	160	31.18 S	28.37 E
Tsomo ≃	160	32.25 S	27.50 E
Tsoying	136	22.41 N	120.17 E
Tsu	134	34.43 N	136.31 E
Tsubame	134	37.39 N	138.56 E
Tsuchiura	134	36.05 N	140.12 E
Tsugaru-hantō ≻1	134	41.00 N	140.30 E
Tsugaru-heiya ≚	134	40.49 N	140.27 E
Tsugaru-kaikyō)(	134a	41.35 N	141.00 E
Tsukumi	134	33.04 N	131.52 E
Tsukushi-sanchi ⋀	134	33.30 N	130.30 E
Tsumeb	160	19.13 S	17.42 E
Tsumeb □5	160	19.00 S	17.30 E
Tsumis Park	160	23.43 S	17.28 E
Tsuruga	134	35.39 N	136.04 E
Tsurugi-san ∧	134	33.51 N	134.06 E
Tsuruoka	134	38.44 N	139.50 E
Tsushima	134	35.10 N	136.43 E
Tsushima II	134	34.30 N	129.22 E
Tsushima-kaikyō)(	134	34.00 N	129.00 E
Tsuwano	134	34.28 N	131.46 E
Tsuyama	134	35.03 N	134.00 E
Tua ≃	120	41.13 N	7.26 W
Tuakau	170	37.16 S	174.57 E
Tual	166	5.40 S	132.45 E
Tuam	110	53.31 N	8.50 W
Tuamarina	170	41.26 S	173.57 E
Tuamotu, Îles II	96	19.00 S	142.00 W
Tuanfeng	136	30.38 N	114.51 E
Tuapse	126	44.07 N	39.05 E
Tuatapere	170	46.08 S	167.41 E
Tuath, Loch)(	108	56.30 N	6.12 W
Tuban	142	6.54 S	112.03 E
Tubarão	188	28.30 S	49.01 W
Tübingen	116	48.31 N	9.02 E
Ṭubruq	154	32.05 N	23.59 E
Tucacas	184	10.48 N	68.19 W
Tucacas, Punta ≻	182	10.50 N	68.14 W
Tuckanarra	164	27.07 S	118.05 E
Tuckerton	176	39.36 N	74.20 W
Tucson	174	32.13 N	110.58 W
Tucumán → San Miguel de Tucumán	188	26.49 S	65.13 W
Tucumán □4	188	27.00 S	65.30 W
Tucumcari	174	35.10 N	103.44 W
Tucunduva	188	27.39 S	54.27 W
Tucupido	182	9.17 N	65.47 W
Tucupita	184	9.04 N	62.03 W
Tud ≃	104	52.38 N	1.15 E
Tudela	120	42.05 N	1.36 W
Tudela de Duero	120	41.35 N	4.35 W
Tudmur (Palmyra)	150	34.33 N	38.17 E
Tudweiliog	104	52.54 N	4.35 W
Tufi	166	9.05 S	149.20 E
Tugela ≃	160	29.14 S	31.31 E
Tuguegarao	138	17.37 N	121.44 E
Tugur	128	53.48 N	136.48 E
Tuirc, Beinn an ∧2	108	55.34 N	5.34 W
Tujmazy	126	54.36 N	53.42 E
T'ukalinsk	128	55.52 N	72.12 E
Tukangbesi, Kepulauan II	142	5.40 S	123.50 E
Tuktoyaktuk	172	69.27 N	133.02 W
Tukums	130	57.00 N	23.10 E
Tula, Méx.	180	23.00 N	99.43 W
Tula, S.S.S.R.	130	54.12 N	37.37 E
Tulaghi	162	9.06 S	160.09 E
Tulancingo	180	20.05 N	98.22 W
Tulangbawang ≃	142	4.24 S	105.52 E
Tulare	178	36.13 N	119.21 W
Tulare Lake Bed ⊜	178	36.03 N	119.49 W
Tulbagh	160	33.17 S	19.09 E
Tulcán	184	0.48 N	77.43 W
Tulcea	124	45.11 N	28.48 E
Tulcea □4	124	45.00 N	29.00 E
Tule ≃	178	36.03 N	119.50 E
Tuléar	161b	23.21 S	43.40 E
Tuléar □4	161b	24.00 S	45.00 E
Tulelake	178	41.57 N	121.29 W
Tule Lake Sump ⊜	178	41.54 N	121.32 W
Tuli	158	21.59 S	29.15 E
Tuli ≃	158	21.48 S	29.04 E
Ṭūlkarm	150	32.19 N	35.02 E
Tulla	110	52.52 N	8.45 W
Tullahoma	174	35.22 N	86.11 W
Tullamore, Austl.	168	32.38 S	147.34 E
Tullamore, Eire	110	53.16 N	7.30 W
Tulle	118	45.16 N	1.46 E
Tullibigeal	168	33.25 S	146.44 E
Tullow	110	52.48 N	6.44 W
Tulsa	174	36.09 N	95.58 W
Tulsequah	172	58.35 N	133.35 W
Tulsk	110	53.47 N	8.16 W
Tuluá	184	4.06 N	76.11 W
Tulufan	132	42.56 N	89.10 E
Tulufanpendi ⊜	132	42.40 N	89.10 E
Tulum	182	20.13 N	87.28 W
Tulun	128	54.35 N	100.33 E
Tulungagung	142	8.04 S	111.54 E
Tuma ≃	182	13.06 N	84.35 W
Tumaco	184	1.49 N	78.46 W
Tuman-gang ≃	132	42.18 N	130.41 E
Tumany	128	60.56 N	155.56 E
Tumba, Lac ⊜	156	0.48 S	18.03 E
Tumbarumba	168	35.47 S	148.01 E
Tumbes	184	3.30 S	80.25 W
Tumbes, Punta ≻	188	36.37 S	73.07 W
Tumbur	158	4.20 N	31.34 E
Tumby Bay	168	34.22 S	136.06 E
Tumča ≃	112	66.36 N	30.48 E
T'umen', S.S.S.R.	126	57.09 N	65.32 E
Tumen, Zhg.	132	42.58 N	129.49 E
Tumeremo	184	7.18 N	61.30 W
Tumkūr	148	13.21 N	77.05 E
Tummel ≃	108	56.38 N	3.40 W
Tummo	154	22.40 N	14.10 E
Tumoteqi	132	40.52 N	111.28 E
Tumpat	142	6.12 N	102.10 E
Tumsar	146	21.23 N	79.44 E
Tumuc-Humac Mountains ⋀	184	2.20 N	55.00 W
Tumut	168	35.18 S	148.13 E
Tunas de Zaza	182	21.38 N	79.33 W
Tunbridge Wells	104	51.08 N	0.16 E
Tunca (Tundža) ≃	124	41.40 N	26.34 E
Tunchang	140	19.28 N	110.08 E
Tunduru	158	11.07 S	37.21 E
Tundža (Tunca) ≃	124	41.40 N	26.34 E
T'ung ≃	128	63.46 N	121.35 E
Tunga ≃	148	14.00 N	75.41 E
Tungabhadra ≃	148	15.57 N	78.15 E
Tungchiang	136	22.28 N	120.26 E
Tungla	182	13.21 N	84.21 W
Tungshih	136	24.16 N	120.50 E
Tuni	148	17.21 N	82.33 E
Tunis	152	36.48 N	10.11 E
Tunis, Golfe de C	152	37.00 N	10.30 E
Tunisia □1	152	34.00 N	9.00 E
Tunja	184	5.31 N	73.22 W
Tunkhannock	176	41.32 N	75.57 W
Tunnelton	176	39.24 N	79.45 W
Tunnsjøen ⊜	112	64.43 N	13.24 E
Tunstall	104	53.05 N	2.13 W
Tunungayualok Island I	172	56.05 N	61.05 W
Tunuyán	188	33.35 S	69.00 W
Tunuyán ≃	188	34.03 S	66.45 W
Tunxi	136	29.44 N	118.18 E
Tuobuja	128	62.00 N	122.02 E
Tuoj-Chaja	128	62.32 N	111.18 E
Tuojiang ≃	132	28.57 N	105.27 E
Tuokusidawanling ∧	146	37.14 N	85.47 E
Tuolumne	178	37.58 N	120.14 W
Tuolumne ≃	178	37.36 N	121.10 W
Tuorong (Tuoyang)	136	27.16 N	119.54 E
Tupã	190	21.56 S	50.30 W
Tupaciguara	190	18.35 S	48.42 W
Tupanciretã	188	29.05 S	53.51 W
Tupelo	174	34.16 N	88.43 W
Tupi Paulista	190	21.24 S	51.34 W
Tupiza	184	21.27 S	65.43 W
Tupper Lake	176	44.13 N	74.29 W
Tupuai, Île I	96	23.18 S	149.30 W
Tupungato	188	33.20 S	69.10 W
Tupungato, Cerro ∧	188	33.22 S	69.47 W
Túquerres	184	1.05 N	77.37 W
Tura, Bhārat	144	25.31 N	90.13 E
Tura, S.S.S.R.	128	64.17 N	100.15 E
Tura ≃	126	57.12 N	66.56 E
Turakina	170	40.02 S	175.13 E
Turakina ≃	170	40.04 S	175.08 E
Turan	128	52.08 N	93.55 E
Turangi	170	39.00 S	175.49 E
Turbaco	182	10.20 N	75.25 W
Turbacz ∧	116	49.33 N	20.08 E
Turbat	150	25.59 N	63.04 E
Turbo	184	8.06 N	76.43 W
Turda	124	46.34 N	23.47 E
Turee Creek	164	23.37 S	118.39 E
Turek	116	52.02 N	18.30 E
Turfan Depression → Tulufanpendi ⚲7	132	42.40 N	89.10 E
Turgaj	126	49.38 N	63.28 E
Turgaj ≃	126	48.01 N	62.45 E
Turgajskaja Dolina V	126	51.00 N	64.30 E
Turgajskaja Stolovaja Strana ⋀1	126	51.00 N	64.00 E
Turginovo	130	56.30 N	36.00 E
Turgwe ≃	158	20.28 S	32.18 E
Türi	130	58.48 N	25.26 E
Turia ≃	120	39.27 N	0.19 W
Turimiquire, Cerro ∧	182	10.07 N	63.53 W
Turin → Torino	122	45.03 N	7.40 E
Turinsk	126	58.03 N	63.42 E
Turka	116	49.10 N	23.02 E
Turkestan	126	43.18 N	68.15 E
Túrkeve	116	47.06 N	20.45 E
Turkey □1, As., Eur.	100	39.00 N	35.00 E
Turkey Creek	166	17.02 S	128.12 E
Turkmenskaja Sovetskaja Socialističeskaja Respublika □3	126	40.00 N	60.00 E
Turk Mine	158	19.45 S	28.50 E
Turks and Caicos Islands □2	180	21.45 N	71.35 W
Turks Island Passage)(	182	21.30 N	71.20 W
Turks Islands II	182	21.24 N	71.07 W
Turku (Åbo)	114	60.27 N	22.17 E
Turkwel ≃	158	3.06 N	36.06 E
Turlock	178	37.30 N	120.51 W
Turnagain ≃	172	59.06 N	127.35 W
Turnagain, Cape ≻	170	40.29 S	176.37 E
Turnagain Island I	166	9.34 S	142.18 E
Turnbull, Mount ∧2	164	21.03 S	131.57 E
Turnbull Dry Lake ⊜	178	43.10 N	118.00 W
Turneffe Islands II	180	17.22 N	87.51 W
Turner ≃	164	20.21 S	118.25 E
Turners Falls	176	42.36 N	72.33 W
Turnhout	116	51.19 N	4.57 E
Türnitz	116	47.57 N	15.30 E
Turnor Lake ⊜	172	56.32 N	108.38 W
Turnov	116	50.35 N	15.10 E
Turnu-Măgurele	124	43.45 N	24.53 E
Turnu-Severin → Drobeta-Turnu-Severin	124	44.38 N	22.39 E
Turquino, Pico ∧	182	19.59 N	76.51 W
Turriff	108	57.32 N	2.28 W
Turritano ◆1	122	40.48 N	8.30 E
Turu ≃	128	64.38 N	100.00 E
Turua	170	37.14 S	175.34 E
Turuchan ≃	128	65.56 N	87.42 E
Turuchansk	128	65.49 N	87.59 E
Turvo	188	28.56 S	49.41 W
Turvo ≃	188	27.16 S	54.06 W
Tuscaloosa	174	33.13 N	87.33 W
Tuscarora Mountain ∧	176	40.10 N	77.45 W
Tuscarora Mountains ⋀	178	41.00 N	116.20 W
Tushanzhen	136	34.14 N	117.51 E
Tusker Rock II1	104	51.27 N	3.40 W
Tustumena Lake ⊜	172	60.12 N	150.50 W
Tutajev	130	57.53 N	39.32 E
Tuticorin	148	8.47 N	78.08 E
Tutin	124	42.59 N	20.20 E
Tutóia	184	2.45 S	42.16 W
Tutoko, Mount ∧	170	44.36 S	168.00 E
Tutrakan	124	44.03 N	26.37 E
Tutuila I	96	14.18 S	170.42 W
Tutupaca, Volcán ∧1	184	17.02 S	70.22 W
Tuupovaara	114	62.29 N	30.36 E
Tuurun ja Poorin lääni □4	114	61.20 N	22.30 E
Tuusniemi	114	62.49 N	28.30 E
T'uva-Guba	112	69.08 N	33.32 E
Tuvalu □2	96	8.00 S	178.00 E
Ṭuwayq, Jabal ⋀	144	23.00 N	46.00 E
Tuxiaqiao	136	28.47 N	121.29 E
Tuxpan	180	21.57 N	105.18 W
Tuxpan de Rodríguez Cano	180	20.57 N	97.24 W
Tuxtla Gutiérrez	180	16.45 N	93.07 W
Túy	120	42.03 N	8.38 W
Tuy ≃	182	10.24 N	65.59 W
Tuya ≃	172	58.05 N	130.50 W
Tuyen-hoa	140	17.50 N	106.10 E
Tuyenquang	138	21.49 N	105.13 E
Tuy-hoa	140	13.05 N	109.18 E
Tuz Gölü ⊜	150	38.45 N	33.25 E
Tuzla	124	44.32 N	18.41 E
Tveitsund	114	59.01 N	8.32 E
Tweed	176	44.29 N	77.19 W
Tweed ≃	108	55.46 N	2.00 W
Tweeddale V	108	55.37 N	2.55 W
Tweed Heads	168	28.10 S	153.31 E
Tweedmouth	106	55.45 N	2.01 W
Tweeling	160	27.38 S	28.31 E
Tweespruit	160	29.11 S	27.01 E
Twentynine Palms	178	34.08 N	116.03 W
Twilight Cove C	164	32.16 S	126.03 E
Twin Creek ≃	176	39.33 N	84.21 W
Twin Falls	178	42.34 N	114.28 W
Twin Heads ⋀	164	20.13 S	126.30 E
Twinsburg	176	41.19 N	81.27 W
Twitchell Reservoir ⊜1	178	35.00 N	120.19 W
Twitya ≃	172	64.10 N	128.12 W
Two Thumb Range ⋀	170	43.45 S	170.43 E
Twrch ≃, Wales, U.K.	104	51.46 N	3.46 W
Twrch ≃, Wales, U.K.	104	52.42 N	3.29 W
Twyford, Eng., U.K.	104	51.01 N	1.19 W
Twyford, Eng., U.K.	104	51.29 N	0.53 W
Twymyn ≃	104	52.38 N	3.44 W
Tychy	116	50.09 N	18.59 E
Tyin ⊜	114	61.17 N	8.13 E
Tyldesley	106	53.31 N	2.28 W
Tyler	174	32.21 N	95.18 W
Tym ≃	128	59.25 N	80.04 E
Tynagh	110	53.09 N	8.22 W
Tyndinskij	128	55.10 N	124.43 E
Tyndrum	108	56.27 N	4.44 W
Tyne ≃, Eng., U.K.	102	55.01 N	1.26 W
Tyne ≃, Scot., U.K.	108	56.01 N	2.37 W
Tyne and Wear □6	106	54.55 N	1.35 W
Tynemouth	106	55.01 N	1.24 W
Tyre → Ṣūr	150	33.16 N	35.11 E
Tyrifjorden ⊜	114	60.02 N	10.08 E
Tyrma	128	50.03 N	132.12 E
Tyrone	176	40.40 N	78.14 W
Tyrrell, Lake ⊜	168	35.21 S	142.50 E
Tyrrellspass	110	53.23 N	7.22 W
Tyrrhenian Sea (Mare Tirreno) ⚲2	122	40.00 N	12.00 E
Tysnesøy I	114	60.00 N	5.35 E
Tyssedal	114	60.07 N	6.34 E
Tywardreath	104	50.22 N	4.41 W
Tywi ≃	104	51.46 N	4.22 W
Tywyn	104	52.35 N	4.05 W
Tzaneen	160	23.50 S	30.09 E

U

Name	Page	Lat °′	Long °′
Uaupés	184	0.08 S	67.05 W
Ubá	190	21.07 S	42.56 W
Ubangi (Oubangui) ≃	154	1.15 N	17.50 E
Ubatã	190	14.12 S	39.31 W
Ubayyiḍ, Wādī al- V	150	32.34 N	43.48 E
Ube	134	33.56 N	131.15 E
Úbeda	120	38.01 N	3.22 W
Uberaba	190	19.45 S	47.55 W
Uberlândia	190	18.56 S	48.18 W
Ubly	176	43.43 N	82.56 W
Ubombo	160	27.33 S	32.00 E
Ubon Ratchathani	140	15.14 N	104.54 E
Ubrique	120	36.41 N	5.27 W
Ubundi (Ponthierville)	158	0.21 S	25.29 E
Učami	128	63.50 N	96.29 E
Ucayali ≃	184	4.30 S	73.30 W
Uchinoura	134	31.16 N	131.05 E
Uchiura-wan C	134a	42.20 N	140.40 E
Uchiza	184	8.25 S	76.20 W
Uchta	112	63.33 N	53.38 E
Uckermark □9	116	53.10 N	13.35 E
Uckfield	104	50.58 N	0.06 E
Učur ≃	128	58.48 N	130.35 E
Uda ≃, S.S.S.R.	128	56.05 N	99.34 E
Uda ≃, S.S.S.R.	128	54.42 N	135.14 E
Uda ≃, S.S.S.R.	128	51.47 N	107.33 E
Udaipur	146	24.35 N	73.41 E
Udamalpet	148	10.35 N	77.15 E
Udbina	122	44.32 N	15.46 E
Uddevalla	114	58.21 N	11.55 E
Uddingston	108	55.50 N	4.06 W
Udgīr	148	18.23 N	77.07 E
Udhampur	149	32.56 N	75.08 E
Udine	122	46.03 N	13.14 E
Udipi	148	13.21 N	74.45 E
Udoml'a	130	57.52 N	35.01 E
Udono	134	33.44 N	136.01 E
Udon Thani	140	17.26 N	102.46 E
Udor, Mount ∧	164	23.30 S	131.01 E
Udskaja Guba C	128	54.50 N	135.45 E
Udža	128	71.14 N	117.10 E
Ueckermünde	116	53.44 N	14.03 E
Ueda	134	36.24 N	138.16 E
Uele ≃	158	4.09 N	22.26 E
Uelen	128	66.10 N	169.48 W
Uel'kal'	128	65.32 N	179.17 W
Uelzen	116	52.58 N	10.33 E
Ueno	134	34.45 N	136.08 E
Uere ≃	158	3.42 N	25.24 E
Uetersen	116	53.41 N	9.39 E
Ufa	126	54.44 N	55.56 E
Uffculme	104	50.54 N	3.20 W
Uffenheim	116	49.32 N	10.14 E
Ugalla ≃	158	5.08 S	30.42 E
Uganda □1	156	1.00 N	32.00 E

Symbols in the index entries are identified on page 198.

Ugie – Vill

Name	Page	Lat °′	Long °′
Ugie	160	31.10 S	28.13 E
Ugie ≃	108	57.30 N	1.47 W
Ugíjar	120	36.57 N	3.03 W
Uglegorsk	128	49.02 N	142.03 E
Uglič	130	57.32 N	38.19 E
Ugoma ∧	158	4.00 S	28.45 E
Uh (Už) ≃	116	48.34 N	22.00 E
Uherské Hradiště	116	49.05 N	17.28 E
Uhrichsville	176	40.24 N	81.20 W
Uig, Scot., U.K.	108	58.12 N	7.00 W
Uig, Scot., U.K.	108	57.35 N	6.22 W
Uíge	156	7.37 S	15.03 E
Uil ≃	126	48.36 N	52.30 E
Uitenhage	160	33.40 S	25.28 E
Uithuizermeeden	116	53.24 N	6.42 E
Uj ≃	126	54.17 N	64.58 E
Ujae I[1]	96	9.05 N	165.40 E
Ujandina ≃	128	68.23 N	145.50 E
Ujar	128	55.48 N	94.20 E
Ujedinenija, Ostrov I	126	77.28 N	82.28 E
Ujelang I[1]	96	9.49 N	160.55 E
Újfehértó	116	47.48 N	21.40 E
Uji	134	34.53 N	135.48 E
Uji-guntō II	134	31.11 N	129.27 E
Ujiji	158	4.55 S	29.41 E
Ujjain	146	23.11 N	75.46 E
Ujung Pandang (Makasar)	142	5.07 S	119.24 E
Uka	128	57.50 N	162.06 E
Ukerewe Island I	158	2.03 S	33.00 E
Ukiah	178	39.09 N	123.13 W
Ukmergė	130	55.15 N	24.45 E
Ukyr	128	49.28 N	108.52 E
Ulaanbaatar	132	47.55 N	106.53 E
Ulaangom	132	49.58 N	92.02 E
Ulan Bator → Ulaanbaatar	132	47.55 N	106.53 E
Ulan-Ude	128	51.50 N	107.37 E
Ulcinj	124	41.55 N	19.11 E
Ulco	160	28.21 S	24.15 E
Ulfborg	114	56.16 N	8.20 E
Ulhāsnagar	148	19.13 N	73.07 E
Uliastaj	132	47.45 N	96.49 E
Ulindi ≃	158	1.40 S	25.52 E
Ulithi I[1]	138	9.58 N	139.40 E
Ulja	128	58.51 N	141.50 E
Uljanovsk	112	54.20 N	48.24 E
Ulla	130	55.14 N	29.15 E
Ulladulla	168	35.21 S	150.29 E
Ulladulla Trough ⩫[1]	96	34.00 S	154.00 E
Ullapool	108	57.54 N	5.10 W
Ullswater ⊜	106	54.34 N	2.54 W
Ullŭng-do I	134	37.29 N	130.52 E
Ulm	116	48.24 N	10.00 E
Ulmer, Mount ∧	87	77.35 S	86.09 W
Ulrum	116	53.22 N	6.20 E
Ulsan	132	35.34 N	129.19 E
Ulsta	108	60.30 N	1.09 W
Ulsteinvik	114	62.20 N	5.53 E
Ulster □[9]	110	54.37 N	7.15 W
Ulster Canal ≚	110	54.08 N	7.22 W
Ulu	128	60.19 N	127.24 E
Uluguru Mountains ⋀	158	7.10 S	37.40 E
Ulul I	96	8.35 N	149.40 E
Ulva I	108	56.29 N	6.14 W
Ulverston	106	54.12 N	3.06 W
Ulverstone	168	41.09 S	146.10 E
Ulzë	124	41.41 N	19.54 E
Umag	122	45.25 N	13.32 E
Uman'	126	48.44 N	30.14 E
Umanak	172	70.40 N	52.07 W
Umanak Fjord C[2]	172	70.55 N	53.00 W
Umarkot	144	25.22 N	69.44 E
Umba	112	66.41 N	34.15 E
Umbria □[4]	122	43.00 N	12.30 E
Ume ≃	158	16.40 S	28.26 E
Umeå	114	63.50 N	20.15 E
Umeälven ≃	114	63.47 N	20.16 E
Umfolozi ≃	160	28.25 S	32.26 E
Umfuli ≃	158	17.30 S	29.23 E
Umhlanga Rocks	160	29.43 S	31.06 E
Umkomaas	160	30.15 S	30.42 E
Umm al-Qaywayn	150	25.35 N	55.34 E
Umm Durmān (Omdurman)	154	15.38 N	32.30 E
Umniati	158	18.39 S	29.49 E
Umniati ≃	158	16.49 S	28.45 E
Um'ot	130	54.08 N	42.42 E
Umpqua ≃	178	43.42 N	124.03 W
'Umrān	144	15.50 N	43.56 E
Umrer	148	20.51 N	79.20 E
Umreth	146	22.42 N	73.07 E
Umtali	158	18.58 S	32.40 E
Umtata	160	31.35 S	28.47 E
Umtentweni	160	30.42 S	30.28 E
Umuarama	190	23.45 S	53.20 W
Umvukwe Range ⋀	158	17.20 S	30.40 E
Umvuma	158	19.19 S	30.35 E
Umzimkulu	160	30.16 S	29.56 E
Umzingwane ≃	158	22.12 S	29.56 E
Umzinto	160	30.22 S	30.33 E
Unadilla	176	42.20 N	75.19 W
Unadilla ≃	176	42.20 N	75.25 W
Unaí	190	16.23 S	46.53 W
Unare ≃	182	10.03 N	65.14 W
'Unayzah	150	26.06 N	43.56 E
Uncia	184	18.27 S	66.37 W
Uncompahgre Peak ∧	174	38.04 N	107.28 W
Underberg	160	29.50 S	29.22 E
Uneča	130	52.50 N	32.40 E
Ungarie	168	33.38 S	146.58 E
Ungava, Péninsule d' ≻[1]	172	60.00 N	74.00 W
Ungava Bay C	172	59.30 N	67.30 W
União	184	4.35 S	42.52 W
União da Vitória	188	26.13 S	51.05 W
União dos Palmares	184	9.10 S	36.02 W
Union, Maine, U.S.	176	44.13 N	69.17 W
Union, N.J., U.S.	176	40.42 N	74.16 W
Union, S.C., U.S.	174	34.43 N	81.37 W
Union City, Mich., U.S.	176	42.04 N	85.08 W
Union City, Ohio, U.S.	176	40.10 N	84.48 W
Union City, Pa., U.S.	176	41.54 N	79.51 W
Union City, Tenn., U.S.	174	36.26 N	89.03 W
Uniondale	160	33.40 S	23.08 E
Unión de Reyes	182	22.48 N	81.32 W
Union of Soviet Socialist Republics □[1], As., Eur.	128	60.00 N	80.00 E
Union Seamount ⩫[3]	90	49.35 N	132.40 W
Union Springs	176	42.50 N	76.42 W
Uniontown	174	39.54 N	79.44 W
Unionville	176	43.39 N	83.28 W
United	176	40.13 N	79.31 W
United Arab Emirates □[1]	144	24.00 N	54.00 E
United Kingdom □[1]	100	54.00 N	2.00 W
United States □[1]	174	38.00 N	97.00 W
Unity, Sask., Can.	172	52.27 N	109.10 W
Unity, Maine, U.S.	176	44.40 N	69.14 W
Unjha	146	23.48 N	72.24 E
Unna	116	51.32 N	7.41 E
Unquillo	188	31.15 S	64.20 W
Unst I	108a	60.45 N	0.53 W
Unstrut ≃	116	51.10 N	11.48 E
Unža ≃	130	57.20 N	43.08 E
Unzen-dake ∧	134	32.45 N	130.17 E
Uozu	134	36.48 N	137.24 E
Upata	184	8.01 N	62.24 W
Upavon	104	51.18 N	1.49 W
Upemba, Lac ⊜	158	8.36 S	26.26 E
Upernavik	172	72.47 N	56.10 W
Up Holland	106	53.33 N	2.44 W
Upington	160	28.25 S	21.15 E
Upire ≃	182	11.27 N	68.58 W
Upleta	146	21.44 N	70.17 E
Upolu I	96	13.55 S	171.45 W
Upolu Point ≻	179a	20.16 N	155.51 W
Upper Arlington	176	40.00 N	83.03 W
Upper Arrow Lake ⊜	172	50.30 N	117.55 W
Upper Hutt	170	41.08 S	175.04 E
Upper Klamath Lake ⊜	178	42.23 N	122.55 W
Upper Lake	178	39.10 N	122.54 W
Upper Lake ⊜	178	41.44 N	120.08 W
Upper Moutere	170	41.16 S	173.00 E
Upper Red Lake ⊜	174	48.10 N	94.40 W
Upper Sandusky	176	40.50 N	83.17 W
Upper Tean	104	52.57 N	1.58 W
Upper Volta □[1]	152	13.00 N	2.00 W
Uppingham	104	52.35 N	0.43 W
Uppland □[9]	114	59.59 N	17.48 E
Uppsala	114	59.52 N	17.38 E
Uppsala Län □[6]	114	60.00 N	17.45 E
Upsala → Uppsala	114	59.52 N	17.38 E
Upstart, Cape ≻	168	19.42 S	147.45 E
Upton	106	53.13 N	2.52 W
Upton upon Severn	104	52.04 N	2.13 W
Upwell	104	52.36 N	0.12 E
Uracoa	182	9.00 N	62.21 W
Urahoro	134a	42.48 N	143.39 E
Uraj	126	60.08 N	64.48 E
Urakawa	134a	42.09 N	142.47 E
Ural ≃	126	47.00 N	51.48 E
Uralla	168	30.39 S	151.30 E
Ural Mountains → Ural'skije Gory ⋀	126	60.00 N	60.00 E
Ural'sk	126	51.14 N	51.22 E
Ural'skije Gory (Ural Mountains) ⋀	126	60.00 N	60.00 E
Urana	168	35.20 S	146.16 E
Urandangi	168	21.36 S	138.18 E
Urangan	168	25.18 S	152.54 E
Uranium City	172	59.34 N	108.36 W
Urarey	164	27.26 S	122.18 E
Ura-T'ube	126	39.55 N	68.59 E
Urawa	134	35.51 N	139.39 E
Urbana	176	40.07 N	83.45 W
Urbiña, Peña ∧	120	43.01 N	5.57 W
Urbino	122	43.43 N	12.38 E
Urdoma	112	61.47 N	48.32 E
Ure ≃	102	54.01 N	1.12 W
Urenui	170	39.00 S	174.23 E
Ures	180	29.26 N	110.24 W
Ureshino	134	33.06 N	129.59 E
Urfa	150	37.08 N	38.46 E
Urgenč	126	41.33 N	60.38 E
Ürgüp	150	38.38 N	34.56 E
Uribia	184	11.43 N	72.16 W
Urie ≃	108	57.19 N	2.30 W
Urlingford	110	52.42 N	7.35 W
Urmar Tanda	149	31.42 N	75.38 E
Urmston	106	53.27 N	2.21 W
Uroševac	124	42.22 N	21.09 E
Urquhart, Glen V	108	57.20 N	4.35 W
Urrao	184	6.20 N	76.11 W
Urr Water ≃	106	54.53 N	3.49 W
Ursus	116	52.12 N	20.53 E
Uruana	190	15.30 S	49.41 W
Uruapan	180	31.38 N	116.15 W
Urubamba ≃	184	10.43 S	73.48 W
Urubici	188	28.02 S	49.37 W
Uruçuca	190	14.35 S	39.16 W
Uruçuí, Serra do ⋀[2]	184	9.00 S	44.45 W
Uruguaiana	188	29.45 S	57.05 W
Uruguay □[1]	186	33.00 S	56.00 W
Uruguay (Uruguai) ≃	188	34.12 S	58.18 W
Urukthapel I	138	7.15 N	134.24 E
Ur'ung-Chaja	128	72.48 N	113.23 E
Urun-Islāmpur	148	17.03 N	74.16 E
Urup, Ostrov I	128	46.00 N	150.00 E
Ur'upinsk	126	50.47 N	41.59 E
Urussanga	188	28.31 S	49.19 W
Uruti	170	38.57 S	174.32 E
Uržum	112	57.08 N	50.00 E
Usa	134	33.31 N	131.22 E
Usa ≃	112	65.57 N	56.55 E
Ušači	130	55.11 N	28.37 E
Usakos	160	22.01 S	15.32 E
Ušće	124	43.28 N	20.37 E
Usedom I	116	54.00 N	14.00 E
Ushibuka	134	32.11 N	130.01 E
Ushuaia	186	54.47 S	68.20 W
Usk	104	51.43 N	2.54 W
Usk ≃	104	51.36 N	2.58 W
Uskedal	114	59.56 N	5.52 E
Üsküb → Skopje	124	41.59 N	21.26 E
Uslar	116	51.39 N	9.38 E
Usman'	130	52.02 N	39.44 E
Usolje-Sibirskoje	128	52.47 N	103.38 E
Uspallata	188	32.37 S	69.22 W
Ussel	118	45.33 N	2.18 E
Ussurijsk	128	43.48 N	131.59 E
Ustaoset	114	60.30 N	8.04 E
Ust'-Barguzin	128	53.27 N	108.59 E
Ust'-Belaja	128	65.30 N	173.20 E
Ust'-Bol'šereck	128	52.48 N	156.14 E
Ust'-Čaun	128	68.47 N	170.30 E
Ust'-Cil'ma	112	65.27 N	52.06 E
Uster	118	47.21 N	8.43 E
Ústí nad Labem	116	50.40 N	14.02 E
Ústí nad Orlicí	116	49.58 N	16.24 E
Ust'-Išim	128	57.42 N	71.10 E
Ustka	116	54.35 N	16.50 E
Ust'-Kamčatsk	128	56.15 N	162.30 E
Ust'-Kamenogorsk	128	49.58 N	82.38 E
Ust'-Katav	126	54.56 N	58.10 E
Ust'-Koksa	128	50.18 N	85.36 E
Ust'-Kut	128	56.46 N	105.40 E
Ust'-Maja	128	60.25 N	134.32 E
Ust'-Manja	126	62.11 N	60.20 E
Ust'-Nera	128	64.34 N	143.12 E
Ust'-N'ukža	128	56.34 N	121.37 E
Uštobe	126	45.16 N	78.00 E
Ust'-Omčug	128	61.09 N	149.38 E
Ust'-Ordynskij	128	52.48 N	104.45 E
Ust'-Oz'ornoje	128	58.54 N	87.48 E
Ust'-Tym	128	59.26 N	80.08 E
Ustupo	182	9.25 N	78.36 W
Ust'urt, Plato ⋀[1]	126	43.00 N	56.00 E
Ust'-Usa	112	65.59 N	56.54 E
Ust'užna	130	58.51 N	36.26 E
Usu-dake ∧	134a	42.32 N	140.51 E
Usuki	134	33.08 N	131.49 E
Usumacinta ≃	180	18.22 N	92.40 W
Usumbura → Bujumbura	158	3.23 S	29.22 E
Ušumun	128	52.49 N	126.27 E
Utah □[3]	174	39.30 N	111.30 W
Utah Lake ⊜	174	40.13 N	111.49 W
Utashinai	134a	43.31 N	142.03 E
Utembo ≃	156	17.06 S	22.01 E
Utena	130	55.30 N	25.36 E
Utersum	116	54.43 N	8.24 E
Utete	158	7.59 S	38.47 E
Uthai Thani	140	15.22 N	100.03 E
Utica, Mich., U.S.	176	42.38 N	83.02 W
Utica, N.Y., U.S.	176	43.05 N	75.14 W
Utica, Ohio, U.S.	176	40.14 N	82.27 W
Utila	182	16.06 N	86.54 W
Utila, Isla de I	182	16.05 N	86.55 W
Utirik I[1]	96	11.15 N	169.48 E
Utmānzai	149	34.11 N	71.46 E
Uto	134	32.41 N	130.40 E
Utopia	164	22.14 S	134.33 E
Utrecht, Ned.	116	52.05 N	5.08 E
Utrecht, S. Afr.	160	27.38 S	30.20 E
Utrera	120	37.11 N	5.47 W
Utsira	114	59.18 N	4.54 E
Utsjoki	112	69.53 N	27.00 E
Utsunomiya	134	36.33 N	139.52 E
Uttaradit	140	17.38 N	100.06 E
Uttar Pradesh □[3]	146	27.00 N	80.00 E
Uttoxeter	104	52.54 N	1.51 W
Utuado	182	18.16 N	66.42 W
Uudenmaan lääni □[4]	114	60.30 N	25.00 E
Uusikaupunki (Nystad)	114	60.48 N	21.25 E
Uusimaa ◆[1]	114	60.30 N	25.00 E
Uvá ≃	184	3.41 N	70.03 W
Uvalde	174	29.13 N	99.47 W
Uvarovka	130	55.32 N	35.37 E
Uvat	128	59.09 N	68.54 E
Uvéa, Île I	96	20.30 S	166.35 E
Uvinza	158	5.06 S	30.22 E
Uvongo Beach	160	30.51 S	30.23 E
Uvs Nuur ⊜	128	50.20 N	92.45 E
Uwa	134	33.20 N	132.30 E
Uwajima	134	33.13 N	132.34 E
'Uwaynāt, Jabal al- ∧	154	21.54 N	24.58 E
Uxbridge	176	44.06 N	79.07 W
Uyuni	184	20.28 S	66.50 W
Uyuni, Salar de ⩧	184	20.20 S	67.42 W
Už (Uh) ≃	116	48.34 N	22.00 E
Uzbekskaja Sovetskaja Socialističeskaja Respublika □[3]	126	41.00 N	64.00 E
Uzdin	124	45.12 N	20.38 E
Uzès	118	44.01 N	4.25 E
Užgorod	116	48.37 N	22.18 E
Uzlovaja	130	53.59 N	38.10 E
Uzunköprü	124	41.16 N	26.41 E
Užur	128	55.20 N	89.50 E
Užventis	130	55.47 N	22.39 E
V			
Vaal ≃	160	27.40 S	26.09 E
Vaala	114	64.26 N	26.48 E
Vaalserberg ∧	116	50.46 N	6.01 E
Vaalwater	160	24.20 S	28.03 E
Vaasa (Vasa)	114	63.06 N	21.36 E
Vaasan lääni □[4]	114	63.00 N	23.00 E
Vác	116	47.47 N	19.08 E
Vacacaí ≃	188	29.55 S	53.06 W
Vacaria	188	28.30 S	50.56 W
Vacaville	178	38.21 N	121.59 W
Vach ≃	128	60.45 N	76.45 E
Vache, Île à I	182	18.05 N	73.38 W
Vachš ≃	146	37.06 N	68.18 E
Vacoas	161c	20.18 S	57.29 E
Vadheim	114	61.13 N	5.49 E
Vadsø	112	70.05 N	29.46 E
Vaduz	116	47.09 N	9.31 E
Værøy I	112	67.40 N	12.39 E
Vaga ≃	112	62.48 N	42.56 E
Vagaj	128	57.56 N	69.01 E
Vågåmo	114	61.53 N	9.06 E
Váh ≃	116	47.55 N	18.00 E
Vahsel Bay C	87	77.48 S	34.39 W
Vaich, Loch ⊜	108	57.43 N	4.46 W
Vaila I	108a	60.12 N	1.37 W
Vailly-sur-Aisne	118	49.25 N	3.31 E
Vaison-la-Romaine	118	44.14 N	5.04 E
Vaitupu I	96	7.28 S	178.41 E
Vajgač	126	70.25 N	58.46 E
Vajgač, Ostrov I	126	70.00 N	59.30 E
Vākhān ◆[1]	146	37.00 N	73.00 E
Valaisannes, Alpes ⋀	118	46.00 N	7.30 E
Valandovo	124	41.19 N	22.34 E
Valašské Meziříčí	116	49.28 N	17.58 E
Valatie	176	42.25 N	73.41 W
Valcheta	186	40.40 S	66.10 W
Valdagno	122	45.39 N	11.18 E
Valdaj	130	57.59 N	33.14 E
Valdajskaja Vozvyšennost' ⋀[2]	112	57.00 N	33.30 E
Valdecañas, Embalse de ⊜[1]	120	39.45 N	5.30 W
Val-de-Marne □[5]	118	48.47 N	2.29 E
Valdepeñas	120	38.46 N	3.23 W
Valderas	120	42.05 N	5.27 W
Valderrobres	120	40.53 N	0.09 E
Valdés, Península ≻[1]	186	42.30 S	64.00 W
Val-des-Bois	176	45.54 N	75.35 W
Valdez	172	61.07 N	146.16 W
Val di Mazara ◆[1]	122	37.50 N	13.00 E
Val di Noto ◆[1]	122	37.05 N	14.40 E
Val-d'Isère	118	45.27 N	6.59 E
Valdivia	186	39.48 S	73.14 W
Valdobbiadene	122	45.54 N	12.00 E
Val-d'Oise □[5]	118	49.10 N	2.10 W
Val-d'Or	172	48.07 N	77.47 W
Valdosta	174	30.50 N	83.17 W
Valdres V	114	60.55 N	9.10 E
Vale	105b	49.29 N	2.31 W
Valença, Bra.	190	13.22 S	39.05 W
Valença, Port.	120	42.02 N	8.38 W
Valence	118	44.56 N	4.54 E
Valencia, Esp.	120	39.28 N	0.22 W
Valencia, Ven.	184	10.11 N	68.00 W
Valencia □[9]	120	39.30 N	0.40 W
Valencia, Golfo de C	120	39.50 N	0.30 E
Valencia, Lago de ⊜	182	10.15 N	67.45 W
Valencia de Alcántata	120	39.25 N	7.14 W
Valencia de Don Juan	120	42.18 N	5.31 W
Valencia Island I	110	51.52 N	10.20 W
Valenciennes	118	50.21 N	3.32 E
Valentine	174	42.52 N	100.33 W
Valenza	122	45.01 N	8.38 E
Våler	114	60.40 N	11.50 E
Valera	184	9.19 N	70.37 W
Valga	130	57.47 N	26.02 E
Valiente, Península ≻[1]	182	9.05 N	81.50 W
Valjevo	124	44.16 N	19.53 E
Valkeakoski	114	61.16 N	24.02 E
Valkenburg	116	50.52 N	5.50 E
Valkenswaard	116	51.21 N	5.28 E
Valladolid, Esp.	120	41.39 N	4.43 W
Valladolid, Méx.	180	20.41 N	88.12 W
Vallauris	118	43.35 N	7.03 E
Vall de Uxó	120	39.49 N	0.14 W
Valle d'Aosta □[4]	122	45.45 N	7.25 E
Valle de Guanape	182	9.54 N	65.41 W
Valle de la Pascua	184	9.13 N	66.00 W
Valledupar	184	10.29 N	73.15 W
Valle Fértil, Sierra de ⋀	188	30.20 S	68.00 W
Vallegrande	184	18.29 S	64.06 W
Vallejo	178	38.07 N	122.14 W
Vallenar	188	28.35 S	70.46 W
Valle Redondo	178	32.31 N	116.46 W
Valletta	122	35.54 N	14.31 E
Valley Bend	176	38.46 N	79.56 W
Valley City	174	46.55 N	97.59 W
Valleyfield	176	45.15 N	74.08 W
Valley Head	176	38.33 N	80.02 W
Valleyview	172	55.04 N	117.17 W
Vallgrund I	114	63.12 N	21.14 E
Vallon-Pont-d'Arc	118	44.24 N	4.24 E
Valls	120	41.17 N	1.15 E
Valmaseda	120	43.12 N	3.12 W
Valognes	118	49.31 N	1.28 W
Valona → Vlorë	124	40.27 N	19.30 E
Valongo	120	41.11 N	8.30 W
Valoria la Buena	120	41.48 N	4.32 W
Valparai	148	10.22 N	76.58 E
Valparaíso, Bra.	190	21.13 S	50.51 W
Valparaíso, Chile	188	33.02 S	71.38 W
Valparaíso, Méx.	180	22.46 N	103.34 W
Valparaíso □[4]	188	33.00 S	71.15 W
Valpovo	124	45.39 N	18.26 E
Valréas	118	44.23 N	4.59 E
Vals ≃	160	27.23 S	26.30 E
Vals, Tanjung ≻	166	8.26 S	137.38 E
Valsbaai C	160	34.12 S	18.40 E
Valsjöbyn	114	64.04 N	14.08 E
Valtimo	114	63.40 N	28.48 E
Valujki	126	50.13 N	38.08 E
Valverde	182	19.34 N	71.05 W
Valverde del Camino	120	37.34 N	6.45 W
Van	150	38.28 N	43.20 E
Vanavana I[1]	96	20.47 S	139.09 W
Vanavara	128	60.22 N	102.16 E
Van Buren	174	35.26 N	94.21 W
Vanč	126	38.23 N	71.26 E
Vanceboro	176	45.34 N	67.26 W
Vanceburg	176	38.36 N	83.19 W
Vancouver, B.C., Can.	172	49.16 N	123.07 W
Vancouver, Wash., U.S.	174	45.39 N	122.40 W
Vancouver, Cape ≻	164	35.01 S	118.12 E
Vancouver Island I	172	49.45 N	126.00 W
Vandalia	176	39.53 N	84.12 W
Vanderbijlpark	160	26.42 S	27.54 E
Vanderbilt	176	45.09 N	84.40 W
Vandergrift	176	40.36 N	79.34 W
Vanderhoof	172	54.01 N	124.01 W
Vanderlin Island I	166	15.44 S	137.02 E
Van Diemen, Cape ≻	166	11.10 S	130.23 E
Van Diemen Gulf C	166	11.50 S	132.00 E
Van Duzen ≃	178	40.33 N	124.08 W
Vänern ⊜	114	58.55 N	13.30 E
Vänersborg	114	58.22 N	12.19 E
Vang, Mount ∧	87	73.56 S	68.39 W
Vangaindrano	161b	23.21 S	47.36 E
Van Gölü ⊜	150	38.33 N	42.46 E
Vangunu I	162	8.38 S	158.00 E
Vangviang	132	18.56 N	102.27 E
Vanier	176	45.26 N	75.40 W
Vanimo	166	2.40 S	141.20 E
Vanino	128	49.05 N	140.15 E
Vāniyambādi	148	12.41 N	78.37 E
Vankarem	128	67.51 N	175.50 W
Vankleek Hill	176	45.31 N	74.39 W
Van Lear	176	37.46 N	82.46 W
Vanna I	112	70.09 N	19.51 E
Vannes	118	47.39 N	2.46 W
Vanoise, Massif de la ⋀	118	45.20 N	6.40 E
Van Reenen	160	28.22 S	29.24 E
Van Rees, Pegunungan ⋀	166	2.35 S	138.15 E
Vanrhynsdorp	160	31.36 S	18.44 E
Vanrook	168	16.57 S	141.57 E
Vansittart Island I	172	65.50 N	84.00 W
Vanstadensrus	160	29.59 S	27.02 E
Vanua Lava I	96	13.48 S	167.28 E
Vanua Levu I	96	16.33 S	179.15 E
Vanua Mbalavu I	96	17.40 S	178.57 W
Van Wert	176	40.52 N	84.35 W
Vanwyksdorp	160	33.46 S	21.28 E
Vanwyksvlei	160	30.18 S	21.49 E
Vanzylsrus	160	26.52 S	22.04 E
Var □[5]	118	43.30 N	6.20 E
Varades	118	47.23 N	1.02 W
Varaklāni	130	56.37 N	26.44 E
Varāmīn	150	35.20 N	51.39 E
Vārānasi (Benares)	146	25.20 N	83.00 E
Varangerfjorden C[2]	112	70.00 N	30.00 E
Varangerhalvøya ≻[1]	112	70.25 N	29.30 E
Varaždin	122	46.19 N	16.20 E
Varazze	122	44.22 N	8.34 E
Varberg	114	57.06 N	12.15 E
Vardak □[4]	146	34.15 N	68.00 E
Vardar (Axiós) ≃	124	40.31 N	22.43 E
Varde	114	55.38 N	8.29 E
Vardø	112	70.21 N	31.02 E
Varegovo	130	57.47 N	39.17 E
Varel	116	53.22 N	8.10 E
Varėna	130	54.13 N	24.34 E
Varennes	102	50.03 N	2.32 E
Varennes-sur-Allier	118	46.19 N	3.24 E
Vareš	124	44.09 N	18.19 E
Varese	122	45.48 N	8.48 E
Varginha	190	21.33 S	45.26 W
Varkaus	114	62.19 N	27.55 E
Värmland □[9]	114	59.48 N	13.03 E
Värmlands Län □[6]	114	59.45 N	13.15 E
Varna	124	43.13 N	27.55 E
Värnamo	114	57.11 N	14.02 E
Varnsdorf	116	50.52 N	14.40 E
Varsinais-Suomi ◆[1]	114	60.40 N	22.30 E
V'artsil'a, S.S.S.R.	112	62.11 N	30.41 E
Värtsilä, Suomi	114	62.15 N	30.40 E
Varvarin	124	43.43 N	21.19 E
Várzea, Rio da ≃	188	27.13 S	53.19 W
Varzeão	188	24.34 S	49.26 W
Vas □[6]	116	47.05 N	16.45 E
Vasai (Bassein)	148	19.21 N	72.48 E
Vascão ≃	120	37.31 N	7.31 W
Vascongadas □[9]	120	43.00 N	2.45 W
Vasiliká	124	40.28 N	23.08 E
Vaslui	124	46.38 N	27.44 E
Vaslui □[4]	124	46.30 N	27.45 E
Vassar	176	43.22 N	83.35 W
Vassdalsegga ∧	114	59.46 N	7.10 E
Västerås	114	59.37 N	16.33 E
Västerbotten □[9]	114	64.36 N	20.04 E
Västerbottens Län □[6]	114	64.00 N	17.30 E
Västergötland □[9]	114	58.01 N	13.03 E
Västernorrlands Län □[6]	114	63.00 N	17.30 E
Västervik	114	57.45 N	16.38 E
Västmanland □[9]	114	59.38 N	15.15 E
Västmanlands Län □[6]	114	59.45 N	16.20 E
Vasto	122	42.07 N	14.42 E
Vas'ugan ≃	128	59.07 N	80.46 E
Vas'uganje ≡	128	58.00 N	77.00 E
Vasvár	116	47.03 N	16.49 E
Vatan	118	47.05 N	1.48 E
Vaternish Point ≻	108	57.36 N	6.38 W
Vatersay I	108	56.55 N	7.32 W
Vathí	124	37.45 N	26.59 E
Vatican City □[1]	122	41.54 N	12.27 E
V'atka ≃	112	55.36 N	51.30 E
Vatnajökull ◸	112a	64.25 N	16.50 W
Vatneyri	112a	65.38 N	23.57 W
Vatomandry	161b	19.20 S	48.59 E
Vatra Dornei	124	47.21 N	25.21 E
V'atskije Pol'any	112	56.14 N	51.04 E
Vättern ⊜	114	58.24 N	14.36 E
Vaucluse □[5]	118	44.00 N	5.10 E
Vaucouleurs	118	48.36 N	5.40 E
Vaughan	176	43.50 N	79.32 W
Vaughn	174	34.36 N	105.13 W
Vaupés (Uapés) ≃	184	0.02 S	67.16 W
Vavau I	96	18.36 S	174.00 W
Vavau Group II	96	18.40 S	174.00 W
Växjö	114	56.52 N	14.49 E
V'azemskij	128	47.32 N	134.48 E
V'az'ma	130	55.13 N	34.18 E
V'azniki	130	56.15 N	42.10 E
Veazie	176	44.51 N	68.42 W
Vechta	116	52.43 N	8.16 E
Vecsés	116	47.25 N	19.16 E
Veddige	114	57.16 N	12.19 E
Vedia	188	34.30 S	61.32 W
Veendam	116	53.06 N	6.58 E
Veenendaal	116	52.02 N	5.34 E
Vega I	112	65.39 N	11.50 E
Vegreville	172	53.30 N	112.03 W
Veil, Loch ⊜	108	56.20 N	4.25 W
Veinticinco de Mayo	188	35.25 S	60.11 W
Vejen	114	55.29 N	9.09 E
Vejer de la Frontera	120	36.15 N	5.58 W
Vejle	114	55.42 N	9.32 E
Vela Luka	122	42.58 N	16.43 E
Velas, Cabo ≻	182	10.21 N	85.52 W
Velasco, Sierra ⋀	188	29.00 S	67.10 W
Velbert	116	51.20 N	7.02 E
Velddrif	160	32.47 S	18.11 E
Velden	116	48.19 N	12.16 E
Veldhoven	116	51.24 N	5.24 E
Veleka ≃	124	42.04 N	27.58 E
Velencei-tó ⊜	116	47.12 N	18.35 E
Velenje	122	46.21 N	15.06 E
Velestínon	124	39.23 N	22.45 E
Velet'ma	130	55.20 N	42.25 E
Vélez-Málaga	120	36.47 N	4.06 W
Vélez Rubio	120	37.39 N	2.04 W
Velika Gorica	122	45.43 N	16.05 E
Velikaja ≃, S.S.S.R.	128	64.40 N	176.20 E
Velikaja ≃, S.S.S.R.	130	57.48 N	28.20 E
Velika Plana	124	44.20 N	21.04 E
Velike Lašče	122	45.50 N	14.38 E
Velikije Luki	130	56.20 N	30.32 E
Velikij-ust'ug	112	60.48 N	46.18 E
Veliko Gradište	124	44.45 N	21.32 E
Velikookt'abr'skij	130	57.26 N	33.49 E
Veliko Tărnovo	124	43.04 N	25.39 E
Veli Lošinj	122	44.31 N	14.30 E
Vélingara	152	13.09 N	14.07 W
Veliž	130	55.38 N	31.12 E
Vella Lavella I	162	7.45 S	156.40 E
Velletri	122	41.41 N	12.47 E
Vellore	148	12.56 N	79.08 E
Vel'sk	112	61.05 N	42.05 E
Vemdalen	114	62.27 N	13.52 E
Venachar, Loch ⊜	108	56.13 N	4.19 W
Venaco	122	42.14 N	9.10 E
Venado Tuerto	188	33.46 S	61.58 W
Venâncio Aires	188	29.36 S	52.11 W
Vence	118	43.43 N	7.07 E
Venceslau Braz	190	23.51 S	49.48 W
Venda Nova	190	19.49 S	43.58 W
Vendas Novas	120	38.41 N	8.28 W
Vendée □[5]	118	46.40 N	1.20 W
Vendeuvre-sur-Barse	118	48.14 N	4.28 E
Vendôme	118	47.48 N	1.04 E
Vendsyssel ◆[1]	114	57.20 N	10.00 E
Venecia	182	10.22 N	84.17 W
Veneto □[4]	118	45.30 N	11.45 E
Venev	130	54.21 N	38.16 E
Venezia (Venice)	122	45.27 N	12.21 E
Venezuela □[1]	184	8.00 N	66.00 W
Venezuela, Golfo de C	184	11.30 N	71.00 W
Venezuelan Basin ⩫[1]	90	14.30 N	68.00 W
Vengerovo	128	55.41 N	76.45 E
Venice → Venezia	122	45.27 N	12.21 E
Venice, Gulf of C	122	45.15 N	13.00 E
Vénissieux	118	45.41 N	4.53 E
Venjan	114	60.57 N	13.55 E
Venlo	116	51.24 N	6.10 E
Venosa	122	40.57 N	15.49 E
Venraij	118	51.32 N	5.59 E
Vent	116	46.52 N	10.56 E
Ventersburg	160	28.09 S	27.08 E
Ventersdorp	160	26.17 S	26.48 E
Venterstad	160	30.47 S	25.48 E
Ventimiglia	122	43.47 N	7.36 E
Ventnor	104	50.36 N	1.11 W
Ventry	110	52.08 N	10.22 W
Ventspils	130	57.24 N	21.36 E
Ventuari ≃	184	3.58 N	67.02 W
Ventura	178	34.17 N	119.18 W
Ver ≃	104	51.42 N	0.20 W
Vera	120	37.15 N	1.52 W
Verá, Laguna ⊜	188	26.05 S	57.39 W
Veracruz	180	32.25 N	115.05 W
Veranópolis	188	28.57 S	51.33 W
Verāval	146	20.54 N	70.22 E
Vercelli	122	45.19 N	8.25 E
Verchn'aja Amga	128	59.30 N	126.08 E
Verchn'aja Salda	126	58.02 N	60.33 E
Verchn'aja Tajmyra ≃	128	74.15 N	99.48 E
Verchn'aja Tura	126	58.22 N	59.49 E
Verchneimbatskoje	128	63.11 N	87.58 E
Verchnevil'ujsk	128	63.27 N	120.18 E
Verchnij Ufalej	126	56.04 N	60.14 E
Verchojansk	128	67.35 N	133.27 E
Verchojanskij Chrebet ⋀	128	67.00 N	129.00 E
Verchoturje	126	58.52 N	60.48 E
Vercors □[9]	118	44.57 N	5.25 E
Verden	116	52.55 N	9.13 E
Verdi	178	39.31 N	119.59 W
Verdun, Qué., Can.	176	45.27 N	73.34 W
Verdun, Fr.	118	43.52 N	1.14 E
Verdun, Fr.	118	49.10 N	5.23 E
Verdun-sur-Meuse	116	49.10 N	5.23 E
Vereeniging	160	26.38 S	27.57 E
Vereja	130	55.21 N	36.11 E
Vereščagino, S.S.S.R.	112	58.05 N	54.40 E
Vereščagino, S.S.S.R.	128	64.14 N	87.37 E
Vergara	120	43.07 N	2.25 W
Vergemont Creek ≃	168	24.12 S	143.17 E
Vergennes	176	44.10 N	73.15 W
Vergt	118	45.02 N	0.43 E
Verín	120	41.56 N	7.26 W
Verísimo Sarmento	156	8.10 S	20.39 E
Verme Falls L	158	5.20 N	40.16 E
Vermenton	118	47.40 N	3.44 E
Vermilion	176	41.25 N	82.22 W
Vermillion	174	42.47 N	96.56 W
Vermont □[3]	174	43.50 N	72.45 W
Verneuil	118	48.44 N	0.56 E
Verneukpan ⩧	160	30.00 S	21.10 E
Vernon, B.C., Can.	172	50.16 N	119.16 W
Vernon, Fr.	118	47.48 N	1.38 E
Vernon, Conn., U.S.	176	41.52 N	72.27 W
Verny	118	49.01 N	6.12 E
Vero Beach	174	27.38 N	80.24 W
Véroia	124	40.31 N	22.12 E
Verona, Ont., Can.	176	44.29 N	76.42 W
Verona, It.	122	45.27 N	11.00 E
Verran	168	33.51 S	136.18 E
Verrettes	182	19.04 N	72.27 W
Versailles, Fr.	118	48.48 N	2.08 E
Versailles, Ky., U.S.	176	38.03 N	84.44 W
Versailles, Ohio, U.S.	176	40.13 N	84.29 W
Veršino-Darasunskij	128	52.20 N	115.32 E
Veršino-Šachtaminskij	128	51.21 N	117.50 E
Vert, Cap ≻	152	14.43 N	17.30 W
Verteillac	118	45.21 N	0.22 E
Vertientes	182	21.16 N	78.09 W
Vertou	118	47.10 N	1.29 W
Verulam	160	29.45 S	31.02 E
Verviers	116	50.35 N	5.52 E
Verwoerd Reservoir ⊜[1]	160	30.40 S	25.40 E
Verwood	104	50.53 N	1.52 W
Veryan	104	50.13 N	4.54 W
Vesanto	114	62.56 N	26.25 E
Vescovato	122	42.30 N	9.26 E
Vesjegonsk	130	58.40 N	37.16 E
Vesoul	118	47.38 N	6.10 E
Vesta	182	9.43 N	83.03 W
Vest-Agder □[6]	114	58.30 N	7.10 E
Vesterålen II	112	68.45 N	15.00 E
Vestfjorden C[2]	112	68.08 N	15.00 E
Vestfold □[6]	114	59.15 N	10.10 E
Vestmannaeyjar	112a	63.26 N	20.12 W
Vestvågøya I	112	68.15 N	13.50 E
Vesuvio ∧[1]	122	40.49 N	14.26 E
Vesuvius → Vesuvio ∧[1]	122	40.49 N	14.26 E
Veszprém	116	47.06 N	17.55 E
Veszprém □[6]	116	46.50 N	17.30 E
Vésztő	116	46.55 N	21.16 E
Vetlanda	114	57.26 N	15.04 E
Vetluga	112	57.51 N	45.47 E
Vetrino	130	55.25 N	28.28 E
Vetschau	116	51.47 N	14.04 E
Vettisfossen L	114	61.22 N	7.55 E
Veurne	116	51.04 N	2.40 E
Vevay	176	38.45 N	85.04 W
Vevey	118	46.28 N	6.51 E
Vézelise	118	48.29 N	6.05 E
Vézère ≃	118	44.53 N	0.53 E
Viacha	184	16.39 S	68.18 W
Viadana	122	44.56 N	10.31 E
Viadutos	188	27.34 S	52.01 W
Viamão	188	30.05 S	51.02 W
Viana	190	20.23 S	40.30 W
Viana del Bollo	120	42.11 N	7.06 W
Viana do Alentejo	120	38.20 N	8.00 W
Viana do Castelo	120	41.42 N	8.50 W
Viangchan (Vientiane)	140	17.58 N	102.36 E
Viareggio	122	43.52 N	10.14 E
Viaur ≃	118	44.08 N	2.23 E
Viborg	114	56.26 N	9.24 E
Vibo Valentia	122	38.40 N	16.06 E
Vic-en-Bigorre	118	43.06 N	0.05 E
Vicente López	188	34.32 S	58.29 W
Vicente Noble	182	18.23 N	71.11 W
Vicenza	122	45.33 N	11.33 E
Vich	120	41.56 N	2.15 E
Vichada ≃	184	4.55 N	67.50 W
Vichadero	188	31.48 S	54.43 W
Vichun	136	27.49 N	114.23 E
Vichuquén	188	34.53 S	72.00 W
Vichy	118	46.08 N	3.26 E
Vicksburg, Mich., U.S.	176	42.06 N	85.32 W
Vicksburg, Miss., U.S.	174	32.14 N	90.56 W
Viçosa	190	20.45 S	42.53 W
Victor Harbor	168	35.34 S	138.37 E
Victoria, Arg.	188	32.40 S	60.10 W
Victoria, Cam.	152	4.01 N	9.12 E
Victoria, B.C., Can.	172	48.25 N	123.22 W
Victoria, Chile	188	38.13 S	72.20 W
Victoria, Gren.	182	12.12 N	61.42 W
Victoria (Xianggang), H.K.	136	22.17 N	114.09 E
Victoria, Malay.	138	5.17 N	115.15 E
Victoria, Sey.	156	4.38 S	55.27 E
Victoria, Tex., U.S.	174	28.48 N	97.00 W
Victoria □[3]	162	38.00 S	145.00 E
Victoria □[4]	158	20.54 S	31.21 E
Victoria ≃	166	15.12 S	129.43 E
Victoria, Lake ⊜, Afr.	158	1.00 S	33.00 E
Victoria, Lake ⊜, Austl.	168	34.00 S	141.16 E
Victoria, Mount ∧, Austl.	162	8.55 S	147.35 E
Victoria, Mount ∧, Mya.	140	21.14 N	93.55 E
Victoria, Mount ∧, Pap. N. Gui.	166	8.55 S	147.35 E
Victoria de las Tunas	182	20.58 N	76.57 W
Victoria Falls	158	17.56 S	25.50 E
Victoria Falls L	158	17.55 S	25.51 E
Victoria Harbour	176	44.45 N	79.46 W
Victoria Island I	172	71.00 N	114.00 W
Victoria Land ◆[1]	87	75.00 S	163.00 E
Victoria Nile ≃	158	2.14 N	31.26 E
Victoria Peak ∧	180	16.47 N	88.36 W
Victoria River Downs	166	16.24 S	131.00 E
Victoria Strait ⩏	172	69.15 N	100.30 W
Victoriaville	172	46.03 N	71.57 W
Victoria West	160	31.25 S	23.04 E
Victorville	178	34.32 N	117.18 W
Vičuga	130	57.13 N	41.56 E
Vicuña	188	30.02 S	70.44 W
Vicuña Mackenna	188	33.55 S	64.25 W
Vidal Ramos	188	27.23 S	49.22 W
Vidauban	118	43.26 N	6.26 E
Videbæk	114	56.05 N	8.38 E
Videira	188	27.00 S	51.08 W
Vidin	124	43.59 N	22.52 E
Vidisha	146	23.32 N	77.49 E
Vidsel	112	65.51 N	20.24 E
Vidzy	130	55.24 N	26.38 E
Viechtach	116	49.05 N	12.53 E
Viedma	186	40.50 S	63.00 W
Viedma, Lago ⊜	186	49.40 S	72.30 W
Vienna → Wien, Öst.	116	48.13 N	16.20 E
Vienna, Md., U.S.	176	38.29 N	75.49 W
Vienna, W. Va., U.S.	176	39.20 N	81.26 W
Vienne	118	45.31 N	4.52 E
Vienne □[5]	118	46.35 N	0.30 E
Vientiane → Viangchan	140	17.58 N	102.36 E
Vieques	182	18.09 N	65.27 W
Vieques, Isla de I	182	18.08 N	65.25 W
Vieremä	114	63.45 N	27.01 E
Vierfontein	160	27.03 S	26.46 E
Viersen	116	51.15 N	6.23 E
Vierzon	118	47.13 N	2.05 E
Vieste	122	41.53 N	16.10 E
Vietnam □[1], As.	138	16.00 N	108.00 E
Viet-nam → Vietnam □[1], As.	140	16.00 N	108.00 E
Viet-tri	140	21.18 N	105.26 E
Vieux Fort	182	13.44 N	60.57 W
Vigan, Fr.	120	43.59 N	3.35 E
Vigan, Pil.	138	17.34 N	120.23 E
Vigevano	122	45.19 N	8.51 E
Vigneulles-lès-Hattonchâtel	118	48.59 N	5.43 E
Vignola	122	44.29 N	11.00 E
Vigo	120	42.14 N	8.43 W
Vigo, Ría de C[1]	120	42.15 N	8.45 W
Vigrestad	114	58.34 N	5.42 E
Vihāri	149	30.02 N	72.21 E
Vihti	114	60.25 N	24.20 E
Viinijärvi	114	62.39 N	29.14 E
Viinijärvi ⊜	114	62.44 N	29.17 E
Vijāpur	144	23.34 N	72.45 E
Vijayapuri	144	16.52 N	79.35 E
Vijayawāda	148	16.31 N	80.37 E
Vijosë (Aóös) ≃	124	40.37 N	19.20 E
Vikajärvi	112	66.37 N	26.12 E
Viken	114	56.09 N	12.34 E
Vikna	112	64.57 N	10.58 E
Vikramasingapuram	148	8.43 N	77.24 E
Vila Arriaga	156	14.46 S	13.21 E
Vila Brasil	190	22.22 S	54.34 W
Vila Cabral	158	13.18 S	35.14 E
Vila Coutinho	158	14.37 S	34.19 E
Vila de João Belo	156	25.02 S	33.34 E
Vila de Manica	160	18.56 S	32.53 E
Vila do Conde	120	41.21 N	8.45 W
Vila Flor	120	41.18 N	7.09 W
Vila Fontes	160	17.50 S	35.21 E
Vilafranca del Panadés	120	41.21 N	1.42 E
Vila Franca de Xira	120	38.57 N	8.59 W
Vila Glória	190	22.21 S	54.13 W
Viļaka	130	57.11 N	27.41 E
Vilanculos	160	22.01 S	35.19 E
Viļāni	130	56.33 N	26.57 E
Vila Nova de Famalicão	120	41.25 N	8.32 W
Vila Nova de Gaia	120	41.08 N	8.37 W
Vila Novo de Ourém	120	39.39 N	8.35 W
Vila Pery	160	19.08 S	33.29 E
Vila Real	120	41.18 N	7.45 W
Vila Velha	190	20.20 S	40.17 W
Vila Velha de Ródão	120	39.38 N	7.40 W
Vila Verde	120	41.39 N	8.26 W
Vila Viçosa	120	38.47 N	8.13 W
Vilcabamba, Cordillera ⋀	184	13.00 S	73.00 W
Vîlcea □[4]	124	45.19 N	24.00 E
Vildbjerg	114	56.12 N	8.46 E
Vilhelmina	114	64.37 N	16.39 E
Viljandi	130	58.22 N	25.36 E
Viljoensdrif	160	26.44 S	27.55 E
Viljoenskroon	160	27.12 S	27.00 E
Vil'kickogo, Ostrov I	126	73.29 N	75.50 E
Vil'kickogo, Proliv ⩏	128	77.55 N	103.00 E
Vilkija	130	55.03 N	23.35 E
Villa Ahumada	180	30.37 N	106.31 W
Villa Alberdi	188	27.36 S	65.40 W
Villa Alemana	188	33.03 S	71.23 W
Villa Ángela	188	27.35 S	60.43 W
Villa Bella	184	10.23 S	65.24 W
Villablino	120	42.56 N	6.19 W
Villa Bruzual	182	9.20 N	69.06 W
Villa Cañás, Arg.	188	34.01 S	61.30 W
Villacañas, Esp.	120	39.38 N	3.20 W
Villacarriedo	120	43.14 N	3.48 W
Villacarrillo	120	38.07 N	3.05 W
Villacastín	120	40.47 N	4.25 W
Villach	116	46.36 N	13.50 E
Villacidro	122	39.27 N	8.44 E
Villa Colón (Caucete)	188	31.40 S	68.20 W
Villa de Cura	182	10.02 N	67.29 W
Villa del Río	120	37.59 N	4.17 W
Villa del Rosario	182	10.19 N	72.19 W
Villa Diego	188	33.02 S	60.37 W
Villa Dolores	188	31.58 S	65.12 W
Villafranca del Bierzo	120	42.36 N	6.48 W
Villafranca de los Barros	120	38.34 N	6.20 W
Villafranca di Verona	122	45.21 N	10.50 E
Villagaracía	120	42.36 N	8.45 W
Villaguay	188	31.55 S	59.00 W
Villa Hayes	188	25.06 S	57.34 W
Villahermosa	180	17.59 N	92.55 W
Villa Hidalgo	178	30.59 N	116.10 W
Villaines-la-Juhel	118	48.21 N	0.17 W
Villajoyosa	120	38.30 N	0.14 W
Villa Krause	188	31.35 S	68.35 W
Villalón de Campos	120	42.06 N	5.02 W
Villalonga	186	39.55 S	62.40 W
Villalpando	120	41.52 N	5.24 W
Villa María	188	32.25 S	63.15 W
Villa Montes	184	21.15 S	63.30 W
Villa Nora	160	23.34 S	28.01 E
Villanueva	182	10.37 N	72.59 W
Villanueva de Córdoba	120	38.20 N	4.37 W
Villa Nueva de Guaymallén → Guaymallén	188	32.54 S	68.47 W
Villanueva de la Serana	120	38.58 N	5.48 W
Villanueva de la Sierra	120	40.12 N	6.24 W
Villanueva de los Infantes	120	38.44 N	2.59 W
Villanueva del Río y Minas	120	37.39 N	5.42 W
Villanueva y Geltrú	120	41.14 N	1.44 E
Villa Ocampo	188	28.30 S	59.20 W
Villa Quinteros	188	27.15 S	65.30 W
Villard-de-Lans	118	45.04 N	5.33 E
Villardefrades	120	41.43 N	5.15 W
Villar del Arzobispo	120	39.44 N	0.49 W
Villa Regina	188	39.05 S	67.05 W
Villarreal	120	39.56 N	0.06 W
Villarrica, Chile	186	39.16 S	72.13 W
Villarrica, Para.	188	25.45 S	56.26 W
Villarrobledo	120	39.16 N	2.36 W
Villarrubia de los Ojos	120	39.13 N	3.36 W
Villas	176	39.02 N	74.56 W
Villa San Martín	188	28.20 S	64.10 W
Villasayas	120	41.21 N	2.37 W
Villa Somoza	182	12.08 N	84.58 W
Villa Unión, Arg.	188	29.24 S	62.47 W
Villa Unión, Méx.	180	28.15 N	100.43 W
Villa Vásquez	182	19.45 N	71.27 W
Villavicencio	184	4.09 N	73.37 W
Villaviciosa	120	43.29 N	5.26 W
Villaviciosa de Córdoba	120	38.05 N	5.01 W
Villazón	184	22.06 S	65.36 W
Ville-de-laval → Laval	172	45.35 N	73.44 W
Villedieu	118	48.50 N	1.13 W
Villefort	118	44.26 N	3.56 E
Villefranche	118	45.59 N	4.43 E
Villefranche-de-Rouergue	118	44.21 N	2.02 E

Symbols in the index entries are identified on page 198.

Symbols in the index entries are identified on page 198.

Name	Page	Lat	Long
Weymouth, Eng., U.K.	104	50.36 N	2.28 W
Weymouth, Mass., U.S.	176	42.13 N	70.58 W
Weymouth, Cape ⌐	166	12.37 S	143.27 E
Whakatane	170	37.58 S	177.00 E
Whakatane ≈	170	37.57 S	177.00 E
Whales, Bay of C	87	78.30 S	164.20 W
Whaley Bridge	106	53.20 N	1.59 W
Whalley	106	53.50 N	2.24 W
Whalsay I	108a	60.20 N	0.59 W
Whangamata	170	37.12 S	175.52 E
Whangamomona	170	39.09 S	174.44 E
Whangarei	170	35.43 S	174.19 E
Whaplode	104	52.48 N	0.02 W
Wharfe ≈	106	53.51 N	1.07 W
Wharfedale V	106	54.01 N	1.56 W
Wharton	176	37.55 N	81.40 W
Wharton Lake ⊜	172	64.00 N	99.55 W
Whauphill	106	54.49 N	4.29 W
Wheao ≈	170	38.34 S	176.39 E
Wheathampstead	104	51.49 N	0.17 W
Wheatland	178	39.01 N	121.25 W
Wheatley	176	46.24 N	82.27 W
Wheatley Hill	106	54.45 N	1.23 W
Wheaton	178	39.03 N	77.03 W
Wheelbarrow Peak ⋀	178	37.27 N	116.05 W
Wheeler ≈	172	57.02 N	67.13 W
Wheeler Peak ⋀, Calif., U.S.	178	38.25 N	119.17 W
Wheeler Peak ⋀, Nev., U.S.	178	38.59 N	114.19 W
Wheeler Peak ⋀, N. Mex., U.S.	174	36.34 N	105.25 W
Wheeling	174	40.05 N	80.42 W
Wheelock ≈	106	53.12 N	2.26 W
Whela Creek ≈	164	26.17 S	116.50 E
Whelan, Mount ⋀[2]	168	23.25 S	138.54 E
Whernside ⋀	106	54.14 N	2.23 W
Whidbey Islands II	164	34.45 S	135.04 E
Whiddon Down	104	50.43 N	3.51 W
Whim Creek	164	20.50 S	117.50 E
Whinham, Mount ⋀	164	26.04 S	130.15 E
Whiston	106	53.25 N	2.50 W
Whitburn	106	55.52 N	3.42 W
Whitby, Ont., Can.	176	43.52 N	78.56 W
Whitby, Eng., U.K.	106	54.29 N	0.37 W
Whitchurch, Eng., U.K.	104	51.52 N	2.39 W
Whitchurch, Eng., U.K.	104	52.58 N	2.41 W
Whitchurch, Eng., U.K.	104	51.53 N	0.51 W
Whitchurch, Eng., U.K.	104	51.14 N	1.20 W
Whitchurch, Wales, U.K.	104	51.33 N	3.14 W
Whitchurch-Stouffville	176	43.58 N	79.15 W
White ≈, N.A.	172	63.10 N	139.36 W
White ≈, U.S.	174	43.45 N	99.30 W
White ≈, U.S.	174	33.53 N	91.03 W
White ≈, Ind., U.S.	176	38.25 N	87.44 W
White ≈, Nev., U.S.	178	37.42 N	115.10 W
White ≈, Vt., U.S.	176	43.27 N	72.20 W
White, Lake ⊜	164	21.05 S	129.00 E
White Bay C	172	50.00 N	56.30 W
White Cap Mountain ⋀	176	45.35 N	69.13 W
White Cliffs	168	30.51 S	143.05 E
White Cloud	174	43.33 N	86.46 W
White Coomb ⋀	106	55.26 N	3.20 W
Whitecourt	172	54.09 N	115.41 W
White Esk ≈	106	55.12 N	3.10 W
Whiteface, Mount ⋀	176	44.22 N	73.54 W
Whitefield, Maine, U.S.	176	44.10 N	69.38 W
Whitefield, N.H., U.S.	176	44.22 N	71.36 W
Whitefish	178	48.25 N	114.20 W
Whitefish Lake ⊜	172	62.41 N	106.48 W
Whitegate	110	53.50 N	8.14 W
Whitehall, Scot., U.K.	108	59.07 N	2.37 W
Whitehall, N.Y., U.S.	176	43.33 N	73.25 W
Whitehaven, Eng., U.K.	106	54.33 N	3.35 W
White Haven, Pa., U.S.	176	41.04 N	75.47 W
Whitehead	110	54.46 N	5.43 W
Whitehorse	172	60.43 N	135.03 W
White Horse, Vale of V	104	51.37 N	1.37 W
Whitehorse Hill ⋀[2]	104	51.34 N	1.34 W
Whitehouse	106	57.13 N	2.37 W
White Island I	172	65.50 N	84.50 W
White Lake ⊜	176	45.18 N	76.31 W
Whitemark	168	40.07 S	148.01 E
White Mountain Peak ⋀	178	37.38 N	118.15 W
White Mountains ⋀, U.S.	178	37.38 N	118.15 W
White Mountains ⋀, N.H., U.S.	176	44.10 N	71.35 W
White Head I	108	58.34 N	4.36 W
White Nile (Al-Bahr al-Abyad) ≈	154	15.38 N	32.31 E
White Plains	176	41.02 N	73.46 W
White River Junction	176	43.39 N	72.19 W
White Sea → Beloje More ⌐[2]	112	65.30 N	38.00 E
White Umfolozi ≈	160	27.59 S	31.32 E
White Umfolozi ≈	160	28.22 S	31.58 E
White Volta (Volta Blanche) ≈	152	9.10 N	1.15 W
Whitewater ≈, U.S.	178	39.10 N	84.47 W
Whitewater ≈, Calif., U.S.	178	33.30 N	116.03 W
Whitewater, East Fork ≈	176	39.24 N	85.01 W
Whitewood	168	21.28 S	143.36 E
Whitford Point ⌐	104	51.38 N	4.14 W
Whithorn	106	54.44 N	4.25 W
Whitianga	170	36.50 S	175.42 E
Whiting Bay	106	55.29 N	5.06 W
Whitland	104	51.50 N	4.37 W
Whitley Bay	106	55.03 N	1.25 W
Whitmore	176	50.00 N	70.56 W
Whitmore Mountains ⋀	87	82.35 S	104.30 W
Whitney	178	45.30 N	78.14 W
Whitney, Mount ⋀	178	36.35 N	118.18 W
Whitney Point	176	42.20 N	75.58 W
Whitstable	104	51.22 N	1.02 E
Whitsunday Island I	168	20.17 S	148.59 E
Whittemore	176	44.14 N	83.48 W
Whittingham	106	55.24 N	1.54 W
Whittington	104	52.52 N	3.00 W
Whittle, Cap ⌐	172	50.11 N	60.08 W
Whittlesea, Austl.	168	37.31 S	145.07 E
Whittlesea, S. Afr.	160	32.10 S	26.50 E
Whittlesey	104	52.34 N	0.08 W
Whitwick	104	52.44 N	1.21 W
Whitworth	106	53.39 N	2.11 W
Wholdaia Lake ⊜	172	60.43 N	104.10 W
Whyalla	168	33.02 S	137.35 E
Wiarton	176	44.45 N	81.09 W
Wiay I	108	57.23 N	7.13 W
Wichita	174	37.41 N	97.20 W
Wichita Falls	174	33.54 N	98.30 W
Wick ≈	108	58.26 N	3.06 W
Wick ≈	108	58.27 N	3.05 W
Wickepin	164	32.46 S	117.30 E
Wickford	104	51.38 N	0.31 E
Wickham	104	50.54 N	1.10 W
Wickham, Eng., U.K.	166	16.22 S	131.06 E
Wickham, Cape ⌐	168	39.35 S	143.56 E
Wickham Market	104	52.09 N	1.22 E
Wicklow	110	52.59 N	6.03 W
Wicklow □[6]	110	52.59 N	6.30 W
Wicklow Head ⌐	110	52.58 N	6.00 W
Wicklow Mountains ⋀	110	53.02 N	6.24 W
Widecombe in the Moor	104	50.35 N	3.48 W
Widemouth Bay	104	50.47 N	4.32 W
Widen	176	38.28 N	80.52 W
Widerøe, Mount ⋀	87	72.08 S	23.30 E
Widgiemooltha	164	31.30 S	121.34 E
Widnes	106	53.22 N	2.44 W
Wieczka	116	51.59 N	20.04 E
Wieliczka	116	50.00 N	20.05 E
Wielkopolska ≈[1]	116	52.00 N	17.00 E
Wieluń	116	51.14 N	18.34 E
Wien (Vienna)	116	48.13 N	16.20 E
Wiener Neustadt	116	47.49 N	16.15 E
Wienerwald ⋀	116	48.08 N	16.00 E
Wierden	116	52.22 N	6.35 E
Wiesbaden	116	50.05 N	8.14 E
Wiesloch	116	49.17 N	8.42 E
Wigan	106	53.33 N	2.38 W
Wigglesworth	106	54.01 N	2.17 W
Wight, Isle of I	104	50.40 N	1.20 W
Wigmore	104	52.19 N	2.51 W
Wigston Magna	104	52.36 N	1.05 W
Wigton	106	54.49 N	3.09 W
Wigtown	106	54.52 N	4.26 W
Wigtown Bay C	106	54.46 N	4.15 W
Wil	118	47.27 N	9.03 E
Wilberforce Falls ⌐	172	67.07 N	108.47 W
Wilcannia	168	31.34 S	143.23 E
Wilcox	176	41.35 N	78.41 W
Wilder Shoal ⋇[2]	96	8.30 N	174.05 W
Wildon	116	46.53 N	15.31 E
Wildspitze ⋀	116	46.53 N	10.52 E
Wildwood	176	38.59 N	74.49 W
Wilge ≈	160	27.03 S	28.20 E
Wilgena	164	30.46 S	134.44 E
Wilhelm, Mount ⋀	166	5.45 S	145.05 E
Wilhelmina Peak → Trikora, Puncak ⋀	166	4.15 S	138.45 E
Wilhelm-Pieck-Stadt Guben	116	51.57 N	14.43 E
Wilhelmshaven	116	53.31 N	8.08 E
Wilkes-Barre	176	41.14 N	75.53 W
Wilkes Lake ⊜	176	46.01 N	79.00 W
Wilkes Land ⋇[1]	87	69.00 S	120.00 E
Wilkhaven	108	57.52 N	3.45 W
Wilkie	172	52.25 N	108.43 W
Wilkinson Basin ⋇[1]	90	42.30 N	69.30 W
Wilkins Sound ⊔	87	70.15 S	73.00 W
Willard	176	41.03 N	82.44 W
Willemstad	182	12.06 N	68.56 W
Willenhall	104	52.36 N	2.02 W
Willerby	106	53.46 N	0.27 W
Willeroo	166	15.17 S	131.35 E
William Creek	168	28.55 S	136.21 E
Williams	178	39.09 N	122.09 W
Williams ≈	164	20.04 S	141.08 E
Williams, Cape ⌐	87	70.29 S	164.05 E
Williamsburg	176	40.28 N	78.12 W
Williams Lake	172	52.08 N	122.09 W
Williamson, N.Y., U.S.	176	43.13 N	77.11 W
Williamson, W. Va., U.S.	174	37.41 N	82.17 W
Williamson ≈	178	42.28 N	121.57 W
Williamsport	174	41.14 N	77.00 W
Williamston	174	42.41 N	84.17 W
Williamstown, Ky., U.S.	176	38.38 N	84.34 W
Williamstown, Mass., U.S.	176	42.43 N	73.12 W
Williamstown, N.J., U.S.	176	39.41 N	74.60 W
Williamstown, W. Va., U.S.	176	44.07 N	72.33 W
Willich	118	51.16 N	6.33 E
Willimantic	176	41.43 N	72.13 W
Willingboro	176	40.03 N	74.53 W
Willingdon	104	50.47 N	0.15 E
Willingham	104	52.19 N	0.04 E
Willington	106	54.43 N	1.41 W
Willis Group II	166	16.18 S	150.00 E
Williston, S. Afr.	160	31.20 S	20.53 E
Williston, N. Dak., U.S.	174	48.09 N	103.37 W
Williston Lake ⊜[1]	172	55.40 N	123.40 W
Willits	178	39.25 N	123.21 W
Willmar	174	45.07 N	95.03 W
Willoughby ≈	178	41.38 N	81.25 W
Willoughby, Cape ⌐	168	35.51 S	138.07 E
Willow Brook ≈	104	52.32 N	0.24 W
Willow Creek	178	40.56 N	123.38 W
Willowick	178	38.10 N	116.35 W
Willowlake ≈	172	62.11 N	119.10 W
Willowmore	160	33.17 S	23.29 E
Willows	178	39.31 N	122.12 W
Willow Tree	168	31.40 S	150.43 E
Willowvale	160	32.16 S	28.30 E
Wills, Lake ⊜	164	21.25 S	128.51 E
Wills Creek ≈, Austl.	168	22.43 S	140.02 E
Wills Creek ≈, Ohio, U.S.	176	40.09 N	81.55 W
Willshire	176	40.45 N	84.48 W
Willunga	168	35.17 S	138.33 E
Wilmette	176	42.04 N	87.42 W
Wilmington, Austl.	168	32.39 S	138.07 E
Wilmington, Del., U.S.	176	39.44 N	75.33 W
Wilmington, N.C., U.S.	174	34.13 N	77.55 W
Wilmington, Ohio, U.S.	176	39.27 N	83.50 W
Wilmington, Vt., U.S.	176	42.52 N	72.52 W
Wilmore	176	37.52 N	84.40 W
Wilmslow	106	53.20 N	2.15 W
Wilna → Vilnius	130	54.41 N	25.19 E
Wilnecote	104	52.36 N	1.40 W
Wilshamstead	104	52.05 N	0.27 W
Wilson, Austl.	168	32.00 S	138.22 E
Wilson, N.C., U.S.	176	35.44 N	77.55 W
Wilson, N.Y., U.S.	176	43.19 N	78.50 W
Wilson, Cape ⌐	172	66.59 N	81.28 W
Wilson, Mount ⋀, Calif., U.S.	178	34.13 N	118.04 W
Wilson, Mount ⋀, Nev., U.S.	178	38.15 N	114.23 W
Wilson Range ⋀	168	28.50 S	124.15 E
Wilsons Promontory ⌐	176	44.56 N	66.56 W
Wilton, Eng., U.K.	104	51.05 N	1.52 W
Wilton, Maine, U.S.	176	44.35 N	70.14 W
Wilton, N.H., U.S.	176	42.51 N	71.44 W
Wiltshire □[6]	104	51.15 N	1.50 W
Wiluna	164	26.36 S	120.13 E
Wimborne Minster	104	50.48 N	1.59 W
Winburg	160	28.37 S	27.00 E
Wincanton	104	51.04 N	2.25 W
Winchcombe	104	51.57 N	1.58 W
Winchelsea	104	50.55 N	0.42 E
Winchendon	176	42.41 N	72.03 W
Winchester, Ont., Can.	176	45.06 N	75.21 W
Winchester, Eng., U.K.	104	51.04 N	1.19 W
Winchester, Ind., U.S.	176	40.10 N	84.59 W
Winchester, Ky., U.S.	176	37.59 N	84.11 W
Winchester, N.H., U.S.	176	42.46 N	72.23 W
Winchester, Va., U.S.	176	39.11 N	78.10 W
Wind ≈	172	65.49 N	135.19 W
Windera	168	26.03 S	151.50 E
Windermere	106	54.23 N	2.54 W
Windermere ⊜	106	54.22 N	2.56 W
Windhoek	160	22.34 S	17.06 E
Windhoek □[5]	160	22.30 S	17.00 E
Windorah	168	25.26 S	142.39 E
Windrush ≈	104	51.42 N	1.25 W
Windsor, Austl.	168	33.37 S	150.49 E
Windsor, N.S., Can.	172	44.59 N	64.08 W
Windsor, Ont., Can.	176	42.18 N	83.01 W
Windsor, Que., Can.	176	45.34 N	72.00 W
Windsor, Eng., U.K.	104	51.29 N	0.38 W
Windsor, Calif., U.S.	178	38.33 N	122.49 W
Windsor, Vt., U.S.	176	43.29 N	72.23 W
Windsor Forest ≈[3]	104	51.27 N	0.40 W
Windsor Locks	176	41.55 N	72.38 W
Windsorton	160	28.16 S	24.44 E
Windward Islands II	182	13.00 N	61.00 W
Windward Passage ⊔	182	20.00 N	73.50 W
Winnipesaukee, Lake ⊜	176	43.35 N	71.20 W
Winona	174	44.03 N	91.39 W
Winooski	176	44.29 N	73.11 W
Winooski ≈	176	44.30 N	73.15 W
Winschoten	118	53.08 N	7.02 E
Winsford, Eng., U.K.	104	51.06 N	3.33 W
Winsford, Eng., U.K.	106	53.12 N	2.32 W
Winshill	104	52.48 N	1.36 W
Winslow, Eng., U.K.	104	51.57 N	0.54 W
Winslow, Ariz., U.S.	174	35.01 N	110.42 W
Winslow, Maine, U.S.	174	44.32 N	69.38 W
Winslow Seamount ⋇[3]	96	1.35 N	174.55 W
Winsted	176	41.55 N	73.04 W
Winston	178	45.07 N	123.25 W
Winston-Salem	174	36.06 N	80.15 W
Winterberg ⋀	160	32.28 S	26.15 E
Winterbourne Abbas	104	50.43 N	2.34 W
Winter Harbor	172	44.24 N	68.05 W
Winter Haven, Fla., U.S.	174	28.01 N	81.44 W
Winter Island I	172	66.14 N	83.04 W
Winterport	176	44.38 N	68.51 W
Winters	178	38.31 N	121.58 W
Winterswijk	116	51.58 N	6.44 E
Winterthur	118	47.30 N	8.43 E
Winterton-on-Sea	104	52.43 N	1.42 E
Winthrop	176	44.18 N	69.59 W
Wintinna	164	27.44 S	134.07 E
Wintinna Creek ≈	164	27.47 S	134.14 E
Winton, Austl.	168	22.23 S	143.02 E
Winton, N.Z.	170	46.09 S	168.20 E
Wipperfürth	116	51.07 N	7.23 E
Wirral ≈[1]	102	53.20 N	3.03 W
Wirrannna	164	32.24 S	136.15 E
Wirrulla	164	32.24 S	134.31 E
Wisbech	104	52.40 N	0.10 E
Wisconsin □[3]	174	44.00 N	89.30 W
Wisconsin ≈	174	43.00 N	91.15 W
Wisconsin Rapids	174	44.23 N	89.49 W
Wishaw	108	55.47 N	3.56 W
Wisła	116	54.22 N	18.55 E
Wisła ≈	116	54.22 N	18.55 E
Wisłoka ≈	116	50.27 N	21.23 E
Wismar, D.D.R.	116	53.53 N	11.28 E
Wismar, Guy.	184	5.59 N	58.18 W
Wissembourg	118	49.02 N	7.57 E
Wissey ≈	104	52.33 N	0.21 E
Witbank	160	25.56 S	29.07 E
Witdraai	160	26.58 S	20.45 E
Witham	104	51.48 N	0.38 E
Witham ≈	106	53.06 N	0.13 W
Witherbee	176	44.05 N	73.32 W
Withernsea	106	53.44 N	0.02 E
Witley	104	51.09 N	0.38 W
Witney	104	51.48 N	1.29 W
Wittdün	116	54.38 N	8.23 E
Wittenberg	116	51.52 N	12.39 E
Wittenberge	116	53.00 N	11.44 E
Wittenburg	116	53.31 N	11.04 E
Wittenoom	164	22.17 S	118.19 E
Wittingen	116	52.43 N	10.44 E
Wittlich	116	49.59 N	6.53 E
Wittmund	116	53.34 N	7.47 E
Wittstock	116	53.09 N	12.29 E
Witwatersrand ⋇[1]	160	26.00 S	27.00 E
Witzenhausen	116	51.20 N	9.51 E
Wiveliscombe	104	51.03 N	3.19 W
Wivenhoe	104	51.52 N	0.58 E
Wkra ≈	116	52.27 N	20.44 E
Włocławek	116	52.39 N	19.02 E
Wnion ≈	104	52.44 N	3.53 W
Woburn	176	42.31 N	71.12 W
Woburn Sands	104	52.01 N	0.39 W
Wodgina	164	21.11 S	118.40 E
Wodonga	168	36.07 S	146.54 E
Wodzisław Śląski	116	50.00 N	18.28 E
Wokam, Pulau I	166	5.37 S	134.30 E
Woking	104	51.20 N	0.34 W
Wokingham	104	51.25 N	0.51 W
Wokingham Creek ≈	168	19.12 S	142.30 E
Wolcott	176	43.13 N	76.49 W
Wolcottville	176	41.32 N	85.22 W
Woleai I[1]	138	7.21 N	143.52 E
Wolf ≈	176	48.17 N	8.13 E
Wolf Creek	178	42.42 N	123.24 W
Wolfeboro	176	43.35 N	71.12 W
Wolfe Island I	176	44.12 N	76.26 W
Wolfen	116	51.40 N	12.16 E
Wolfenbüttel	116	52.10 N	10.32 E
Wolf Rock I[2]	104	49.56 N	5.48 W
Wolfsberg	116	46.51 N	14.51 E
Wolfsburg	116	52.25 N	10.47 E
Wolf's Castle	104	51.54 N	4.58 W
Wolgast	116	54.03 N	13.46 E
Wollaston, Cape ⌐	172	71.04 N	118.07 W
Wollaston, Islas II	186	55.45 S	67.40 W
Wollaston Lake ⊜	172	58.15 N	103.20 W
Wollaston Peninsula ⌐[1]	172	70.00 N	115.00 W
Wollogorang	168	17.13 S	137.57 E
Wollongong	168	34.25 S	150.54 E
Wolmaransstad	160	27.12 S	26.13 E
Wolomin	116	52.21 N	21.14 E
Wolseley, Sask., Can.	172	50.25 N	103.15 W
Wolseley, S. Afr.	160	33.26 S	19.12 E
Wolsingham	106	54.44 N	1.52 W
Wolverhampton	104	52.36 N	2.08 W
Wolverine	176	45.16 N	84.36 W
Wolverton	104	52.04 N	0.50 W
Wombwell	106	53.31 N	1.24 W
Wonarah	166	19.55 S	136.20 E
Wondai	168	26.19 S	151.52 E
Wonderland	178	36.18 N	119.06 W
Wongan Hills	164	30.53 S	116.42 E
Wŏnju	132	37.22 N	127.58 E
Wonogiri	142	7.49 S	110.55 E
Wonosari	142	7.58 S	110.35 E
Wonosobo	142	7.22 S	109.54 E
Wŏnsan	132	39.09 N	127.25 E
Wonthaggi	168	38.36 S	145.35 E
Woocalla	168	31.42 S	137.13 E
Woodbine	176	39.14 N	74.49 W
Woodbridge, Eng., U.K.	104	52.06 N	1.19 E
Woodbridge, Va., U.S.	176	38.39 N	77.15 W
Woodbury, Eng., U.K.	104	50.40 N	3.24 W
Woodbury, Conn., U.S.	176	41.33 N	73.13 W
Woodbury, N.J., U.S.	176	39.50 N	75.09 W
Woodchurch	104	51.05 N	0.46 E
Woodcock, Mount ⋀	166	13.25 S	131.47 E
Wood Buff ⋀[4]	160	29.22 S	153.22 E
Woodford Halse	104	52.10 N	1.12 W
Woodlake	178	36.25 N	119.06 W
Woodland, Calif., U.S.	178	38.41 N	121.46 W
Woodland, Maine, U.S.	176	45.09 N	67.24 W
Woodlark Island I	166	9.05 S	152.50 E
Woodley	104	51.27 N	0.54 W
Woodmansey	106	53.50 N	0.29 W
Woodrarung Range ⋀	164	23.48 S	132.30 E
Woodroffe, Mount ⋀	164	26.20 S	131.45 E
Woods, Lake ⊜	166	17.50 S	133.30 E
Woods, Lake of the ⊜	174	49.15 N	94.45 W
Woods Hole	176	41.31 N	70.40 W
Woodside	168	38.31 S	146.52 E
Woodstock, Austl.	168	19.35 S	146.50 E
Woodstock, N.B., Can.	172	46.09 N	67.34 W
Woodstock, Ont., Can.	176	43.08 N	80.45 W
Woodstock, Eng., U.K.	104	51.52 N	1.21 W
Woodstock, N.Y., U.S.	176	42.02 N	74.07 W
Woodstock, Va., U.S.	176	38.53 N	78.31 W
Woodsville	176	44.09 N	72.02 W
Woodville, N.Z.	170	40.20 S	175.52 E
Woodville, Ohio, U.S.	176	41.27 N	83.22 W
Woodward	174	36.26 N	99.24 W
Woodward Reservoir ⊜[1]	178	37.51 N	120.52 W
Wool	104	50.41 N	2.14 W
Woolacombe	104	51.10 N	4.13 W
Wooler	106	55.33 N	2.01 W
Woolgangie	164	31.10 S	120.32 E
Woolgoolga	164	30.07 S	153.12 E
Woolpit	104	52.13 N	0.54 E
Woomera	168	31.31 S	137.10 E
Woonsocket	176	42.00 N	71.31 W
Woorabinda	168	24.08 S	149.28 E
Wooramel	164	25.44 S	114.17 E
Wooramel ≈	164	25.47 S	114.10 E
Wooster	176	40.48 N	81.56 W
Wootton Bassett	104	51.33 N	1.54 W
Wootton Wawen	104	52.16 N	1.47 W
Worcester, S. Afr.	160	33.39 S	19.27 E
Worcester, Eng., U.K.	104	52.11 N	2.13 W
Worcester, Mass., U.S.	176	42.16 N	71.48 W
Workington	106	54.39 N	3.35 W
Worksop	106	53.18 N	1.07 W
Worland	174	44.01 N	107.57 W
Wormit	108	56.25 N	2.59 W
Worms	116	49.38 N	8.22 E
Worms Head ⌐	104	51.34 N	4.20 W
Worthen	104	52.38 N	3.00 W
Wörther See ⊜	116	46.37 N	14.10 E
Worthing	104	50.48 N	0.23 W
Worthington, Minn., U.S.	174	43.37 N	95.36 W
Worthington, Ohio, U.S.	176	40.05 N	83.01 W
Worthington Peak ⋀	178	37.55 N	115.37 W
Wotho I[1]	96	10.06 N	165.59 E
Wotje I[1]	96	9.27 N	170.02 E
Wotton-under-Edge	104	51.39 N	2.21 W
Wowan	168	23.55 S	150.12 E
Wowoni, Pulau I	142	4.08 S	123.06 E
Woy Woy	168	33.30 S	151.20 E
Wragby	106	53.17 N	0.19 W
Wrangell	172	56.28 N	132.23 W
Wrangell Mountains ⋀	172	62.00 N	143.00 W
Wrath, Cape ⌐	108	58.37 N	5.01 W
Wreck Reef ⋇[2]	166	22.13 S	155.17 E
Wrentham	104	52.23 N	1.40 E
Wrexham	106	53.03 N	3.00 W
Wright Peak ⋀	178	38.59 N	122.46 W
Wrightwood	178	34.21 N	117.38 W
Wrigley	172	63.16 N	123.37 W
Wrigley Gulf C	87	74.00 S	129.00 W
Writtle	104	51.44 N	0.26 E
Wrocław (Breslau)	116	51.06 N	17.00 E
Wrotham	104	51.19 N	0.19 E
Wroughton	104	51.31 N	1.46 W
Wroxham	104	52.42 N	1.24 E
Września	116	52.20 N	17.34 E
Wubin	164	30.06 S	116.38 E
Wuchang → Wuhan	136	30.36 N	114.17 E
Wuchang[8]	140	44.54 N	127.08 E
Wuchuan	140	21.25 N	110.40 E
Wudangshan ⋀	136	32.24 N	111.08 E
Wudian	136	32.42 N	117.18 E
Wuding	140	25.32 N	102.23 E
Wudina	168	33.03 S	135.28 E
Wudu	132	33.21 N	105.00 E
Wuershunhe ≈	132	49.00 N	117.41 E
Wugang	136	26.40 N	110.31 E
Wugongshan ⋀	136	27.21 N	113.50 E
Wuhai	136	39.36 N	106.49 E
Wuhe	136	33.10 N	117.54 E
Wuhu	136	31.21 N	118.22 E
Wuhua	136	23.57 N	115.48 E
Wujiang, Zhg.	136	31.10 N	120.39 E
Wujiang ≈, Zhg.	136	29.42 N	107.26 E
Wujin	136	31.49 N	119.59 E
Wukang	136	30.33 N	119.59 E
Wulanhaote	140	46.05 N	122.05 E
Wuliangshan ⋀	140	24.30 N	100.45 E
Wuliaru, Pulau I	166	7.27 S	131.04 E
Wuluhan	142	8.15 S	113.33 E
Wulumuqi (Urumchi)	132	43.48 N	87.35 E
Wulumuguhe ≈	132	46.59 N	87.27 E
Wuming	140	23.10 N	108.18 E
Wundowie	164	31.46 S	116.22 E
Wuneba	158	4.50 N	30.20 E
Wuning	136	29.17 N	115.06 E
Wunnummin Lake ⊜	172	52.55 N	89.10 W
Wunsiedel	116	50.02 N	12.00 E
Wuping	136	25.08 N	116.06 E
Wuppertal, B.R.D.	116	51.16 N	7.11 E
Wuppertal, S. Afr.	160	32.15 S	19.15 E
Wurarga	164	28.25 S	116.17 E
Würzburg	116	49.48 N	9.56 E
Wurzen	116	51.21 N	12.44 E
Wushan	132	31.05 N	109.48 E
Wushenqi	132	38.58 N	109.01 E
Wusong	136	31.23 N	121.29 E
Wusu	132	44.27 N	84.37 E
Wusulijiang (Ussuri) ≈	128	48.27 N	135.04 E
Wutai	132	38.44 N	113.17 E
Wutaishan ⋀	132	39.04 N	113.35 E
Wutongqiao	132	29.26 N	103.51 E
Wuvulu Island I	166	1.45 S	142.50 E
Wuwei	136	31.18 N	117.54 E
Wuxi (Wuhsi)	136	31.35 N	120.18 E
Wuxi, Zhg.	136	31.26 N	119.18 E
Wuyang	136	33.26 N	113.26 E
Wuyi, Zhg.	136	28.54 N	119.50 E
Wuyi, Zhg.	136	38.28 N	115.54 E
Wuyishan ⋀	136	27.40 N	117.40 E
Wuyuan, Zhg.	136	29.15 N	117.49 E
Wuyuan, Zhg.	132	41.06 N	108.28 E
Wuzhong	132	37.57 N	106.10 E
Wuzhou (Wuchow)	140	23.30 N	111.27 E
Wyaaba ≈	168	16.27 S	141.35 E
Wyaaba Creek ≈	168	16.27 S	141.27 E
Wyalkatchem	164	31.10 S	117.22 E
Wyalusing	176	41.40 N	76.16 W
Wyandotte	176	42.12 N	83.10 W
Wyandra	168	27.15 S	145.59 E
Wycheproof	168	36.05 S	143.14 E
Wydgee	164	28.51 S	117.49 E
Wye	104	51.11 N	0.56 E
Wye ≈, Eng., U.K.	104	51.37 N	2.39 W
Wye ≈, Eng., U.K.	106	53.15 N	1.40 W
Wyk	116	54.42 N	8.34 E
Wylye ≈	104	51.08 N	1.52 W
Wymondham	104	52.34 N	1.07 E
Wynberg	160	34.02 S	18.28 E
Wynbring	164	30.33 S	133.32 E
Wyndham	166	15.28 S	128.06 E
Wynniatt Bay C	172	72.55 N	110.30 W
Wynyard	168	41.00 S	145.44 E
Wyoming □[3]	174	43.00 N	107.30 W
Wyong	168	33.17 S	151.25 E
Wyre ≈	106	53.55 N	3.00 W
Wyre I	108	59.07 N	2.58 W
Wyre Forest ≈[3]	104	52.23 N	2.23 W
Wyszków	116	52.36 N	21.28 E
Wytopitlock	176	45.38 N	68.05 W
Wyvis, Ben ⋀	108	57.42 N	4.35 W
Xambrê ≈	190	24.02 S	53.59 W
Xam Nua	140	20.25 N	104.02 E
Xánthi	124	41.08 N	24.53 E
Xanxerê	190	26.56 S	52.31 W
Xapuri	184	10.39 S	68.31 W
Xarrama ≈	120	38.14 N	8.20 W
Xau, Lake ⊜	160	21.15 S	24.38 E
Xaxim	190	26.56 S	52.31 W
Xenia	176	39.41 N	83.56 W
Xeres → Jerez de la Frontera	120	36.41 N	6.08 W
Xertigny	118	48.03 N	6.24 E
Xiaguan	140	25.36 N	100.14 E
Xiamen (Amoy)	136	24.28 N	118.07 E
Xi'an (Sian)	136	34.15 N	108.52 E
Xiang ≈	136	31.12 N	117.46 E
Xiangcheng, Zhg.	136	33.28 N	114.53 E
Xiangcheng, Zhg.	136	33.53 N	113.29 E
Xiangfan	136	32.03 N	112.01 E
Xiangjiang ≈	136	29.00 N	112.56 E
Xiangkhoang	140	19.20 N	103.22 E
Xiangride	132	36.02 N	98.08 E
Xiangshan	136	29.28 N	121.51 E
Xiangtan	136	27.51 N	112.54 E
Xiangtan	136	28.26 N	115.58 E
Xiangyin	136	28.40 N	112.53 E
Xiangyun	140	25.30 N	100.30 E
Xianju	136	28.51 N	120.44 E
Xianning	136	29.53 N	114.17 E
Xianyang	132	34.23 N	108.40 E
Xianyou	136	25.23 N	118.40 E
Xiaoao	136	26.14 N	119.39 E
Xiaodanyang	136	31.38 N	118.43 E
Xiaofeng	136	30.36 N	119.32 E
Xiaogan	136	30.55 N	113.54 E
Xiaoji	136	32.38 N	119.48 E
Xiaolan	136	22.41 N	113.14 E
Xiaoshan	136	30.10 N	120.16 E
Xiaoxian	136	34.11 N	116.56 E
Xiaoxing'anlingshan ⋀	132	48.45 N	127.00 E
Xiapu	136	26.52 N	120.01 E
Xiashi	136	30.32 N	120.42 E
Xiayang	136	26.46 N	117.59 E
Xichang	132	34.14 N	114.11 E
Xichong	140	27.53 N	102.16 E
Xigeer ≈	146	28.38 N	87.04 E
Xihe	132	41.44 N	121.30 E
Xihua	136	33.47 N	114.31 E
Xihuashan ⋀	136	23.10 N	115.22 E
Xijiang ≈, Zhg.	136	23.10 N	115.02 E
Xijiang ≈, Zhg.	136	22.25 N	113.23 E
Xilinhaote	132	43.58 N	116.04 E
Xilókastron	124	38.05 N	22.38 E
Ximakou	136	30.33 N	113.47 E
Xinavane	160	25.02 S	32.47 E
Xincai	136	32.44 N	114.59 E
Xinchang	136	29.30 N	120.53 E
Xincheng	132	39.15 N	115.59 E
Xindian	136	33.07 N	112.38 E
Xindianji	136	33.33 N	114.50 E
Xinfeng, Zhg.	136	25.24 N	114.56 E
Xinfeng, Zhg.	136	24.04 N	114.12 E
Xingguo	136	26.21 N	115.19 E
Xinghe	132	40.48 N	113.58 E
Xinghua	136	32.57 N	119.50 E
Xingkathu (Ozero Chanka) ⊜	132	45.00 N	132.24 E
Xingning	136	24.09 N	115.45 E
Xin'gouzui	136	29.15 N	115.59 E
Xingtai	132	37.04 N	114.29 E
Xingu ≈	184	1.30 S	51.53 W
Xingyi	140	25.06 N	104.58 E
Xinhailian	132	34.39 N	119.16 E
Xinhe	136	37.21 N	115.15 E
Xinhui	136	22.32 N	113.02 E
Xinjian, Zhg.	136	28.46 N	120.02 E
Xinjian (Shengmi), Zhg.	136	34.20 N	115.47 E
Xinjiang	132	35.40 N	111.11 E
Xinjiang Weiwuer Zizhiqu (Sinkiang) □[4]	132	40.00 N	85.00 E
Xinning	140	26.19 N	110.45 E
Xinping	140	24.06 N	101.58 E
Xinshi	136	30.37 N	120.19 E
Xintian	136	25.58 N	112.12 E
Xinxian	136	31.38 N	114.51 E
Xinxiang	136	35.20 N	113.51 E
Xinyang	136	32.19 N	114.01 E
Xinyi (Xin'anzhen)	136	34.22 N	118.21 E
Xinyu	136	27.49 N	114.57 E
Xinzheng	136	34.24 N	113.44 E
Xinzhuang	136	31.07 N	121.22 E
Xiping	136	33.23 N	114.02 E
Xique-Xique	184	10.50 S	42.44 W
Xishui	136	29.47 N	115.13 E
Xiuning	136	29.47 N	118.10 E
Xiushui	136	29.10 N	114.34 E
Xixian	136	32.21 N	114.44 E
Xixiang	136	33.00 N	107.46 E
Xizang Zizhiqu □[4]	146	31.42 N	89.30 E
Xukehu ⊜	146	31.42 N	89.30 E
Xuancheng	136	30.57 N	118.45 E
Xuanfeng	136	27.42 N	114.08 E
Xuanhua	132	40.37 N	115.03 E
Xuanwei	140	26.14 N	104.04 E
Xuchang	136	34.01 N	113.49 E
Xuefeng	136	27.44 N	110.19 E
Xuefengshan ⋀	136	27.44 N	110.19 E
Xunwu	136	24.58 N	115.38 E
Xuyi	136	32.58 N	118.30 E
Xuyong	140	28.10 N	105.24 E
Xuzhou (Süchow)	136	34.16 N	117.11 E
Y			
Yaan	140	30.03 N	103.02 E
Yaapeet	168	35.46 S	142.03 E
Yabelo	158	4.54 N	38.05 E
Yablis	182	14.06 N	83.45 W
Yacuiba	184	22.02 S	63.45 W
Yádgir	146	16.46 N	77.08 E
Yadong	146	27.29 N	88.55 E
Yafran	152	32.04 N	12.31 E
Yagoua	152	10.20 N	15.14 E
Yaguajay	182	22.19 N	79.14 W
Yaguaraparo	182	10.34 N	62.50 W
Yahualica	180	21.11 N	102.53 W
Yai, Khao ⋀	140	8.48 N	99.49 E
Yainax Butte ⋀	178	42.20 N	121.16 W
Yaita	132	36.48 N	139.56 E
Yaizu	132	34.52 N	138.20 E
Yajalón	180	17.12 N	92.20 W
Yaka	158	6.31 N	23.15 E
Yakima	174	46.36 N	120.30 W
Yakima ≈	178	46.15 N	119.02 W
Yakumo	134a	42.15 N	140.16 E
Yaku-shima I	134a	30.20 N	130.30 E
Yakutat	172	59.33 N	139.44 W
Yakutat Seamount ⋇[3]	90	54.52 N	150.16 W
Yala	140	6.33 N	101.18 E
Yalahán, Laguna de ⊜	180	21.27 N	87.40 W
Yalata	164	31.29 S	131.52 E
Yalgoo	164	28.21 S	116.41 E
Yalinga	154	6.31 N	23.15 E
Yalongjiang ≈	140	26.35 N	101.44 E
Yalta	130	44.30 N	34.10 E
Yaluijang (Amnok-kang) ≈	126	39.55 N	124.20 E
Yanai	134	33.58 N	132.07 E
Yanam	144	16.40 N	82.10 E
Yan'an	136	36.41 N	109.19 E
Yanbu'	150	24.05 N	38.03 E
Yancheng	136	33.30 N	110.15 E
Yancheng, Zhg.	136	33.24 N	120.09 E
Yanchi	132	37.52 N	107.22 E
Yanco	168	34.36 S	146.25 E
Yandal	164	27.33 S	121.07 E
Yandama ≈	168	27.02 S	139.59 E
Yandina	168	26.33 S	152.57 E
Yangambi	154	0.47 N	24.28 E
Yangcheng	136	35.29 N	112.24 E
Yangchun	140	22.09 N	111.48 E
Yanghe	136	33.47 N	118.23 E
Yangjiang	136	21.51 N	111.56 E
Yangjiaqiao	132	32.51 N	116.52 E
Yangquan	132	37.52 N	113.36 E
Yangsheng	136	31.52 N	120.32 E
Yangshuo	140	24.45 N	110.24 E
Yangxin	136	29.51 N	115.12 E
Yangzhong (Sanmaozhen)	136	32.16 N	119.49 E
Yangzhou	136	32.24 N	119.26 E
Yangzhuoyonghu ⊜	146	28.58 N	90.44 E
Yanji	132	42.57 N	127.00 E
Yankton	174	42.53 N	97.23 W
Yanling	136	34.07 N	114.11 E
Yanna	168	26.58 S	146.00 E
Yanqi	132	42.00 N	86.15 E
Yanrey	164	22.32 S	114.48 E
Yantabulla	168	29.21 S	145.00 E
Yantai (Chefoo)	132	37.33 N	121.20 E
Yanzhou	132	34.37 N	135.36 E
Yao	134	34.37 N	135.36 E
Yaoan	140	25.32 N	101.12 E
Yaoundé	152	3.52 N	11.31 E
Yap I	138	9.31 N	138.06 E
Yapen, Pulau I	166	1.45 S	136.15 E
Yapeyú	188	29.28 S	56.50 W
Yaque del Norte ≈	182	19.50 N	71.40 W
Yaque del Sur ≈	182	18.18 N	71.05 W
Yaqui ≈	180	27.37 N	110.39 W
Yaracuy □[3]	182	10.20 N	68.90 W
Yaracuy ≈	182	10.33 N	68.15 W
Yaraka	168	24.53 S	144.04 E
Yarcombe	104	50.52 N	3.05 W
Yare ≈	102	52.35 N	1.44 E
Yari ≈	184	0.22 S	72.16 W
Yariga-take ⋀	134	36.20 N	137.39 E
Yarim	144	14.29 N	44.21 E
Yaring	140	6.52 N	101.22 E
Yaritagua	182	10.05 N	69.08 W
Yarle Lakes ⊜	164	30.15 S	131.27 E
Yarloop	164	32.57 S	115.54 E
Yarmouth, N.S., Can.	172	43.50 N	66.07 W
Yarmouth, Eng., U.K.	104	50.42 N	1.29 W
Yarmouth, Maine, U.S.	176	43.48 N	70.12 W
Yarram	168	38.33 S	146.41 E
Yarraman	168	26.50 S	151.59 E
Yarrawonga	168	36.01 S	146.00 E
Yarrow	108	55.32 N	3.01 W
Yarty ≈	104	50.47 N	3.01 W
Yarumal	184	6.58 N	72.24 W
Yashiro-jima I	134	33.55 N	132.15 E
Yasothon	140	15.47 N	104.08 E
Yass	168	34.50 S	148.55 E
Yasugi	134	35.26 N	133.15 E
Yata ≈	184	10.29 S	65.26 W
Yatate-yama ⋀	134	39.29 N	140.40 E
Yateley	104	51.21 N	0.49 W
Yatesboro	176	40.48 N	79.20 W
Yathkyed Lake ⊜	172	62.41 N	98.00 W
Yatsuga-take ⋀	134	35.59 N	138.23 E
Yatsuo	134	36.34 N	137.08 E
Yatsushiro	134	32.30 N	130.36 E
Yatsushiro-wan C	134	32.30 N	130.20 E
Yatta Plateau ≈[1]	154	2.00 S	38.00 E
Yatton	104	51.24 N	2.49 W
Yauco	182	18.02 N	66.51 W
Yavari (Javari) ≈	184	4.21 S	70.02 W
Yavatmál	148	20.24 N	78.08 E
Yavi, Cerro ⋀	184	5.32 N	65.59 W
Yawata → Kitakyūshū	134	33.53 N	130.50 E
Yawatahama	134	33.27 N	132.24 E
Yaxian	132	18.20 N	109.30 E
Yaxley	104	52.31 N	0.16 W
Yazd	150	31.53 N	54.25 E
Yazoo ≈	174	32.22 N	91.00 W
Ybbs	116	48.10 N	15.06 E
Ydstebøhavn	114	59.08 N	5.15 E
Yeadon	106	53.52 N	1.41 W
Yealmpton	104	50.21 N	3.59 W
Yecheng	146	37.54 N	77.25 E
Yeelanna	164	34.09 S	135.45 E
Yeerqianghe (Yarkand) ≈	132	40.28 N	80.52 E
Yei	158	4.05 N	30.40 E
Yei ≈	154	6.15 N	30.13 E
Yelets → Jelec	130	52.37 N	38.30 E
Yélimané	152	15.08 N	10.34 W
Yell I	108a	60.36 N	1.06 W
Yellow → Huanghe ≈	132	37.32 N	118.19 E
Yellow Creek	176	40.40 N	80.40 W
Yellowhead Pass)(	172	52.53 N	118.28 W
Yellowknife	172	62.27 N	114.21 W
Yellowknife ≈	172	62.23 N	114.19 W
Yellow Mountain ⋀	168	32.30 S	146.51 E
Yellow Sea ⋝[2]	132	36.00 N	123.00 E
Yellowstone ≈	174	47.58 N	103.59 W
Yellowstone Lake ⊜	174	44.25 N	110.22 W
Yelma	164	26.30 S	121.40 E
Yelverton	104	50.29 N	4.05 W
Yelvertoft	168	20.13 S	138.53 E
Yemen, People's Democratic Republic of □[1]	144	15.00 N	48.00 E
Yenangyaung	140	20.28 N	94.52 E
Yendéré	152	10.12 N	4.58 W
Yendi	152	9.26 N	0.01 W
Yenshui	136	33.23 N	120.08 E
Yeo ≈	104	51.02 N	2.49 W
Yeo, Lake ⊜	164	28.03 S	124.30 E
Yeola	148	20.02 N	74.29 E
Yeo Lake ⊜	164	28.03 S	124.30 E
Yeovil	104	50.57 N	2.39 W
Yeppoon	168	23.08 S	150.45 E
Yerevan → Jerevan	130	40.11 N	44.30 E
Yerington	178	38.59 N	119.10 W
Yerilla	164	29.24 S	121.47 E
Yerupajá, Nevado ⋀	184	10.16 S	76.54 W
Yerushalayim (Jerusalem)	150	31.46 N	35.14 E
Yesa, Embalse de ⊜	120	42.37 N	1.09 W
Yeşilköy	124	40.57 N	28.49 E
Yes Tor ⋀	104	50.41 N	3.59 W
Yetminster	104	50.57 N	2.35 W
Yeu, Île d' I	118	46.42 N	2.20 W
Yexian	136	37.10 N	119.57 E
Yian	132	47.55 N	125.18 E
Yibin	140	28.47 N	104.38 E
Yichang	136	30.42 N	111.17 E
Yichuan	136	36.02 N	110.03 E
Yichun, Zhg.	132	47.42 N	128.55 E
Yichun, Zhg.	136	27.49 N	114.23 E
Yifeng	136	28.24 N	114.46 E
Yilan	132	46.20 N	129.34 E
Yiliang	140	24.57 N	103.09 E
Yiliang	140	27.35 N	104.03 E
Yilliminning	164	32.54 S	117.22 E
Yima	136	34.44 N	111.53 E
Yimen, Zhg.	140	24.41 N	102.10 E
Yimen, Zhg.	136	33.39 N	116.02 E

Name Page Lat Long

Yimen, Zhg. 140 24.43 N 102.10 E
Yinchuan 132 38.30 N 106.18 E
Yindarlgooda, Lake ⊜ 164 30.45 S 121.55 E
Yingcheng 136 30.57 N 113.32 E
Yingde 136 24.12 N 113.24 E
Yinggen 140 19.04 N 109.48 E
Yinghe ≐ 136 32.30 N 116.32 E
Yingheji 136 32.16 N 116.31 E
Yingjisha 132 38.57 N 76.03 E
Yingkou 132 40.40 N 122.14 E
Yingqiao 136 33.58 N 113.39 E
Yingshan, Zhg. 136 31.38 N 113.50 E
Yingshan, Zhg. 136 30.45 N 115.39 E
Yingshang 136 32.38 N 116.15 E
Yingtan 136 28.14 N 117.00 E
Yining (Kuldja) 132 43.55 N 81.14 E
Yinkanie 168 34.20 S 140.19 E
Yinnietharra 164 24.39 S 116.11 E
Yinxianji 136 32.07 N 116.32 E
Yirga Alem 154 6.52 N 38.22 E
Yirrkala Mission 166 12.14 S 136.56 E
Yishan 140 24.40 N 108.35 E
Yishui 132 35.50 N 118.41 E
Yisuhe 136 27.46 N 112.54 E
Yithion 124 36.45 N 22.34 E
Yituline 132 50.38 N 121.57 E
Yiwu 136 29.18 N 120.04 E
Yixian 136 29.55 N 117.56 E
Yixing 136 31.22 N 119.50 E
Yixu 136 26.02 N 119.16 E
Yiyang, Zhg. 136 28.36 N 112.20 E
Yiyang, Zhg. 136 28.23 N 117.25 E
Yizhang 136 25.26 N 112.56 E
Yizheng 136 32.16 N 119.12 E
Ylikitka ⊜ 114 66.08 N 28.30 E
Ylivieska 114 64.05 N 24.33 E
Ylöjärvi 114 61.33 N 23.36 E
Ynykčanskij 128 60.15 N 137.43 E
Yoco 182 10.36 N 62.24 W
Yodo ≐ 134 34.41 N 135.25 E
Yogyakarta 142 7.48 S 110.22 E
Yoichi 134a 43.12 N 140.41 E
Yōka 134 35.24 N 134.46 E
Yōkaichi 134 35.06 N 136.12 E
Yōkaichiba 134 35.42 N 140.33 E
Yokkaichi 134 34.58 N 136.37 E
Yokoate-shima I 135b 28.48 N 129.00 E
Yokohama 134 35.27 N 139.39 E
Yokosuka 134 35.18 N 139.40 E
Yokote 134 39.18 N 140.34 E
Yola 152 9.12 N 12.29 E
Yom ≐ 140 15.52 N 100.16 E
Yonago 134 35.26 N 133.20 E
Yonaha-dake ʌ2 135b 26.43 N 128.13 E
Yoneshiro ≐ 134 40.13 N 140.01 E
Yonezawa 134 37.55 N 140.07 E
Yongan 136 25.58 N 117.22 E
Yongcheng, Zhg. 136 34.26 N 115.05 E
Yongcheng, Zhg. 136 33.58 N 116.21 E
Yongchun 136 25.21 N 118.21 E
Yongdeng 132 36.48 N 103.14 E
Yongding 136 24.46 N 116.43 E
Yongdinghe ≐ 132 39.39 N 116.13 E
Yongdingzhen 136 26.08 N 101.40 E
Yongfeng 136 27.19 N 115.24 E
Yongjia 136 28.11 N 120.42 E
Yongkang 136 28.53 N 120.02 E
Yongning, Zhg. 136 24.43 N 118.42 E
Yongning, Zhg. 140 22.42 N 108.50 E
Yongping 140 25.28 N 99.33 E
Yongshan 132 28.15 N 103.24 E
Yongsheng 136 26.42 N 100.43 E
Yongtai 136 25.54 N 118.58 E
Yongxin 136 26.56 N 114.18 E
Yongxing 136 26.08 N 113.06 E
Yongxiu 136 29.04 N 115.49 E
Yongyang 136 26.57 N 114.46 E
Yonkers 176 41.00 N 73.52 W
Yonne □5 118 47.55 N 3.45 E
Yonne ≐ 118 48.23 N 2.58 E
York, Austl. 164 31.53 S 116.46 E
York, Eng., U.K. 106 53.58 N 1.05 W
York, Pa., U.S. 174 39.58 N 76.44 W
York ≐ 176 37.15 N 76.23 W
York, Cape ≻ 166 10.42 S 142.31 E
York, Kap ≻ 90 75.53 N 66.12 W
York, Vale of ∨ 106 54.10 N 1.20 W
Yorke Peninsula ≻1 168 35.00 S 137.30 E
Yorketown 168 35.02 S 137.36 E
York Factory 172 57.00 N 92.18 W
Yorkshire Wolds ʌ2 106 54.00 N 0.40 W
York Sound U 162 14.50 S 125.05 E
Yorkton 172 51.13 N 102.28 W
Yorkville 176 43.07 N 75.16 W
Yoro 182 15.09 N 87.07 W
Yoron-jima I 135b 27.02 N 128.26 E
Yosemite National Park 178 37.45 N 119.35 W
Yoshii ≐ 134 34.36 N 134.03 E
Yoshino ≐ 134 34.05 N 134.36 E
Yos Sudarsa, Pulau (Frederik Hendrik-Eiland) I 166 7.50 S 138.30 E
Yŏsu 132 34.46 N 127.44 E
Yōtei-zan ʌ 134a 42.49 N 140.49 E
Youanmi 164 28.37 S 118.49 E
Youghal 110 51.51 N 7.50 W
Youghal Bay C 110 51.52 N 7.50 W
Youjiang ≐ 140 22.50 N 108.06 E
Young 168 34.19 S 148.18 E
Youngstown, N.Y., U.S. 176 43.15 N 79.03 W
Youngstown, Ohio, U.S. 176 41.06 N 80.39 W
Youngsville 176 41.51 N 79.19 W
Yountville 178 38.24 N 122.22 W
Youssoufia 152 32.16 N 8.33 W
Youxi 136 26.11 N 118.09 E
Youxian 136 27.00 N 113.21 E
Youyang 132 28.58 N 108.41 E
Yoweragabbie 164 28.13 S 117.39 E
Yozgat 150 39.50 N 34.48 E
Ypres → Ieper 116 50.51 N 2.53 E
Ypsilanti 176 42.15 N 83.36 W
Yreka 178 41.44 N 122.38 W
Ysbyty Ystwyth 104 52.20 N 3.48 W
Yscir ≐ 104 51.57 N 3.27 W
Yssingeaux 118 45.08 N 4.07 E
Ystad 114 55.25 N 13.49 E
Ystalyfera 104 51.47 N 3.47 W
Ystrad ≐ 106 53.13 N 3.20 W
Ystrad Aeron 104 52.11 N 4.11 W
Ystradfellte 104 51.48 N 3.34 W
Ystradgynlais 104 51.47 N 3.45 W
Ystwyth ≐ 104 52.24 N 4.05 W
Ythan ≐ 108 57.18 N 2.00 W
Yu'alliq, Jabal ʌ 150 30.22 N 33.31 E
Yuanlin 136 23.58 N 120.34 E
Yuanling 136 28.28 N 110.16 E
Yuanmou 140 25.38 N 101.54 E
Yuantan 136 32.47 N 112.53 E
Yuasa 134 34.02 N 135.11 E
Yuba ≐ 178 39.07 N 121.36 W
Yuba City 178 39.08 N 121.37 W
Yūbari 134a 43.04 N 141.59 E
Yūbari-sanchi ʌ 134a 43.15 N 142.20 E
Yūbetsu 134a 43.13 N 144.05 E
Yūbetsu ≐ 134a 44.14 N 143.37 E
Yucaipa 178 34.02 N 117.02 W
Yucatán □3 182 20.40 N 89.00 W
Yucatan Channel U 182 21.45 N 85.45 W
Yucatan Peninsula ≻1 180 19.30 N 89.00 W
Yucca 178 34.52 N 114.09 W
Yucca Lake ⊜ 178 36.59 N 116.01 W
Yucca Valley 178 34.07 N 116.35 W
Yucheng 136 34.24 N 115.52 E
Yuci 132 37.45 N 112.41 E
Yuda 134 39.20 N 140.50 E
Yudu 136 25.59 N 115.24 E
Yuekou 136 30.32 N 113.03 E
Yuendumu 164 22.16 S 131.49 E
Yuexi 136 30.50 N 116.24 E
Yueyang 136 29.23 N 113.06 E
Yugan 136 28.41 N 116.41 E
Yugoslavia □1 100 44.00 N 19.00 E
Yugou 136 33.42 N 118.55 E
Yuhang 136 30.17 N 119.56 E
Yuin 164 27.58 S 116.02 E
Yujiang ≐ 140 23.24 N 110.05 E
Yukon □4 172 64.00 N 135.00 W
Yukuhashi 134 33.44 N 130.59 E
Yule ≐ 164 20.41 S 118.17 E
Yule Bay C 87 70.44 S 166.40 E
Yuli 136 23.20 N 121.19 E
Yulin, Zhg. 132 38.20 N 109.29 E
Yulin, Zhg. 140 22.36 N 110.07 E
Yuma 178 32.43 N 114.37 W
Yuma, Bahia de C 182 18.20 N 68.35 W
Yumare 182 10.37 N 68.41 W
Yumbel 188 37.08 S 72.32 W
Yumbi 158 1.14 S 26.14 E
Yumen 132 39.56 N 97.51 E
Yuna 164 28.20 S 115.00 E
Yuna ≐ 182 19.13 N 69.35 W
Yunan (Ducheng) 140 23.11 N 111.29 E
Yuncao 136 31.26 N 118.04 E
Yuncheng 132 35.00 N 110.59 E
Yundamindra 164 29.07 S 122.02 E
Yungay 188 37.07 S 72.01 W
Yunhe (Grand Canal) ≚ 132 32.12 N 119.31 E
Yunlin 136 23.43 N 120.33 E
Yunlong 140 25.50 N 99.17 E
Yunmeng 136 31.02 N 113.41 E
Yunnan □4 140 24.00 N 101.00 E
Yunta 168 32.35 S 139.33 E
Yunxian 132 32.49 N 110.49 E
Yunxiao 136 24.04 N 117.20 E
Yunyang 136 33.28 N 112.42 E
Yupanyang C 136 30.30 N 121.46 E
Yurimaguas 184 5.54 S 76.05 W
Yürük 124 40.56 N 27.04 E
Yuscarán 182 13.55 N 86.51 W
Yushan 136 28.41 N 118.15 E
Yu Shan ʌ 136 23.28 N 120.57 E
Yushu 132 33.28 N 96.18 E
Yutian 132 36.51 N 81.40 E
Yuty 188 26.32 S 56.18 W
Yūwan-dake ʌ 135b 28.18 N 129.21 E
Yuxi 140 24.21 N 102.34 E
Yuxian 136 34.10 N 113.28 E
Yuyao 136 30.04 N 121.10 E
Yuza 134 39.01 N 139.54 E
Yuzawa 134 39.10 N 140.30 E
Yvelines □5 118 48.50 N 1.50 E
Yverdon 118 46.47 N 6.39 E

Z

Zaandam 116 52.26 N 4.49 E
Zabajkal'sk 128 49.38 N 117.19 E
Zabari 124 44.21 N 21.13 E
Zabarjad, Jazirat I 154 23.37 N 36.12 E
Zabid 144 14.10 N 43.17 E
Zabkowice Śląskie 116 50.36 N 16.53 E
Žabljak 124 43.09 N 19.07 E
Zābol 150 31.02 N 61.30 E
Zābol □4 146 32.00 N 67.15 E
Zabrze 116 50.18 N 18.46 E
Zacapa 182 14.58 N 89.32 W
Zacatecas 180 22.47 N 102.35 W
Zadar 122 44.07 N 15.14 E
Zadetkyi Kyun I 140 9.58 N 98.13 E
Za'farānah, Bi'r ⊤4 150 29.07 N 32.33 E
Zafra 120 38.25 N 6.25 W
Zagabria → Zagreb 122 45.48 N 15.58 E
Żagań 116 51.37 N 15.19 E
Zagorsk 130 56.18 N 38.08 E
Zagreb 122 45.48 N 15.58 E
Zagros, Kūhhā-ye ʌ 150 33.40 N 47.00 E
Zagubica 124 44.13 N 21.48 E
Zagyva ≐ 116 47.10 N 20.13 E
Zāhedān 150 29.30 N 60.52 E
Zahlah 150 33.51 N 35.53 E
Zaire □1 88 4.00 S 25.00 E
Zaječar 124 43.54 N 22.17 E
Zajsan 128 47.28 N 84.55 E
Zajsan, Ozero ⊜ 128 48.00 N 84.00 E
Zaka 158 20.20 S 31.29 E
Zakamensk 128 50.23 N 103.17 E
Zakarpatskaja Oblast' □4 124 48.20 N 23.30 E
Zākhū 150 37.08 N 42.41 E
Zákinthos 124 37.47 N 20.53 E
Zákinthos I 124 37.52 N 20.44 E
Zakopane 116 49.19 N 19.57 E
Zala □6 116 46.45 N 16.50 E
Zala ≐ 116 46.43 N 17.16 E
Zalaegerszeg 116 46.51 N 16.51 E
Zalalövő 116 46.51 N 16.35 E
Zalamea de la Serena 120 38.39 N 5.39 W
Zalău 124 47.11 N 23.03 E
Žalec 122 46.15 N 15.10 E
Žaltyr 128 51.40 N 69.50 E
Zambezi (Zambeze) ≐ 156 18.55 S 36.04 E
Zambezia □5 160 16.15 S 37.30 E
Zambezi Escarpment ●4 158 16.20 S 30.00 E
Zambia □1 156 15.00 S 30.00 E
Zamboanga 142 6.54 N 122.04 E
Zambrano 182 9.45 N 74.49 W
Zambrów 116 53.00 N 22.15 E
Zamfara ≐ 152 12.05 N 4.02 E
Zamora 120 41.30 N 5.45 W
Zamora de Hidalgo 180 19.59 N 102.16 W
Zamość 116 50.44 N 23.15 E
Zamuro, Punta ≻ 182 11.26 N 68.50 W
Zanaga 156 2.51 S 13.50 E
Zandvoort 116 52.22 N 4.32 E
Zanesville 176 39.56 N 82.01 W
Zanjān 150 36.40 N 48.29 E
Zanjón ≐, Arg. 188 27.55 S 64.15 W
Zanjón ≐, Arg. 188 31.16 S 67.41 W
Zannetty, Ostrov I 128 76.43 N 158.00 E
Zanthus 164 31.02 S 123.34 E
Zanzibar 158 6.10 S 39.11 E
Zanzibar I 158 6.10 S 39.20 E
Zanzibar Mjini □4 158 6.10 S 39.11 E
Zanzibar Shambini □4 158 6.08 S 39.14 E
Zaohe 136 34.03 N 118.07 E
Zaō-san ʌ 134 38.08 N 140.26 E
Zaoshi, Zhg. 136 26.22 N 112.50 E
Zaoshi, Zhg. 136 30.51 N 113.20 E
Zaouia el Kahla 152 28.09 N 6.43 E
Zaoyang 136 32.10 N 112.43 E
Zaoz'ornyj 128 55.58 N 94.42 E
Zapadnaja Dvina (Daugava) ≐ 130 57.04 N 24.03 E
Zapadno-Sibirskaja Nizmennost' ≚ 126 60.00 N 75.00 E
Zapadnyj Sajan ʌ 128 53.00 N 94.00 E
Zapala 188 38.55 S 70.05 W
Zapallar 188 32.33 S 71.28 W
Zapata, Peninsula de ≻1 182 22.20 N 81.45 W
Zapatosa, Ciénaga de ⊜ 182 9.05 N 73.50 W
Zapl'usje 130 58.26 N 29.43 E
Zapol'arnyj 112 69.26 N 30.48 E
Zapolje 130 58.23 N 29.41 E
Zaporožje 126 47.50 N 35.10 E
Zaprudn'a 130 56.34 N 37.26 E
Zaragoza 120 41.38 N 0.53 W
Zarajsk 130 54.46 N 38.53 E
Zaranj 150 31.06 N 61.53 E
Zarasai 130 55.44 N 26.15 E
Zárate 188 34.05 S 59.02 W
Zaraza 182 9.21 N 65.19 W
Zard Kūh ʌ 150 32.22 N 50.04 E
Zarghūn Shahr 146 32.51 N 68.25 E
Zaria 152 11.07 N 7.44 E
Žarkovskij 130 55.52 N 32.17 E
Žarma 128 48.48 N 80.50 E
Žary (Sorau) 116 51.38 N 15.09 E
Zāskār Mountains ʌ 146 33.00 N 78.00 E
Zastavna 124 48.31 N 25.50 E
Zastron 160 30.18 S 27.07 E
Žatec 116 50.18 N 13.32 E
Zavidoviči 124 44.27 N 18.09 E
Zavitinsk 128 50.07 N 129.27 E
Zavodovski Island I 92 56.20 S 27.35 W
Zavolžje 130 56.37 N 43.26 E
Zavolžsk 130 57.30 N 42.10 E
Zawiercie 116 50.30 N 19.25 E
Zāwiyat al-Bayḍā' 154 32.46 N 21.43 E
Zaza ≐ 182 21.37 N 79.33 W
Ždanov 126 47.06 N 37.33 E
Zduńska Wola 116 51.36 N 18.57 E
Zebediela 160 24.19 S 29.21 E
Zedang 132 29.16 N 91.46 E
Zeehan 168 41.53 S 145.20 E
Zeerust 160 25.33 S 26.06 E
Zeguo 136 28.32 N 121.20 E
Zehdenick 116 52.59 N 13.20 E
Zeil, Mount ʌ 164 23.24 S 132.23 E
Zeila 154 11.21 N 43.30 E
Zeist 116 52.05 N 5.15 E
Zeitz 116 51.03 N 12.08 E
Zeja 128 53.45 N 127.15 E
Zeja ≐ 128 50.15 N 127.35 E
Zele 116 51.04 N 4.02 E
Zelengora ʌ 124 43.15 N 18.45 E
Zelenogorsk 130 60.12 N 29.42 E
Zelenogradsk 130 54.58 N 20.29 E
Železnik 124 44.43 N 20.23 E
Železnogorsk 130 52.22 N 35.23 E
Železnogorsk-Ilimskij 128 56.37 N 104.08 E
Zelienople 176 40.48 N 80.08 W
Zelina 122 45.58 N 16.15 E
Zella-Mehlis 116 50.39 N 10.39 E
Zell am See 116 47.19 N 12.47 E
Zel'onodol'sk 112 55.51 N 48.33 E
Zemgale □9 130 56.30 N 25.00 E
Zemio 154 5.02 N 25.08 E
Zendeh Jān 150 34.21 N 61.45 E
Zengcheng 136 23.19 N 113.49 E
Zenica 124 44.12 N 17.55 E
Zentsūji 134 34.14 N 133.47 E
Zeravšan ≐ 126 39.22 N 63.45 E
Zerbst 116 51.58 N 12.04 E
Zerdevka 130 51.51 N 41.28 E
Zereh, Gowd-e ⊜ 150 29.45 N 61.50 E
Zermatt 118 46.02 N 7.45 E
Zernograd 126 46.50 N 40.19 E
Zerqan 124 41.30 N 20.21 E
Zeulenroda 116 50.39 N 11.58 E
Zeven 116 53.18 N 9.16 E
Zevenaar 116 51.56 N 6.05 E
Zêzere ≐ 120 39.28 N 8.20 W
Zgierz 116 51.52 N 19.25 E
Zgorzelec 116 51.12 N 15.01 E
Zhaiqiao 136 31.35 N 119.55 E
Zhalinghu ⊜ 132 34.53 N 97.58 E
Zhalinhu ⊜ 146 31.10 N 88.15 E
Zhalutegi 132 44.37 N 120.58 E
Zhangbei 136 34.07 N 113.27 E
Zhangguangcailing ʌ 132 45.25 N 129.20 E
Zhangjiakou (Kalgan) 132 40.50 N 114.53 E
Zhangjiegang 136 30.34 N 112.51 E
Zhangliantang 136 31.01 N 121.02 E
Zhangmutou 136 22.55 N 114.05 E
Zhangping 136 25.19 N 117.25 E
Zhangpu 136 24.09 N 117.36 E
Zhangyan 136 30.48 N 121.16 E
Zhangye 132 38.56 N 100.27 E
Zhangzhou (Longxi) 136 24.33 N 117.39 E
Zhanjiang 140 21.16 N 110.28 E
Zhanyi 132 25.38 N 103.43 E
Zhaoan 136 23.44 N 116.11 E
Zhaoping 140 24.03 N 110.52 E
Zhaoqing 138 23.03 N 112.27 E
Zhaotong 132 27.19 N 103.48 E
Zhapu 136 30.36 N 121.05 E
Zhaxigang 132 32.32 N 79.41 E
Zhecheng 136 34.06 N 115.19 E
Zhegao 136 31.46 N 117.45 E
Zhejiang □4 136 29.00 N 120.00 E
Zhelin 136 28.52 N 115.36 E
Zhengding 132 38.10 N 114.34 E
Zhengfeng 140 25.23 N 105.41 E
Zhenghe 136 27.22 N 118.50 E
Zhengyang 136 32.37 N 114.23 E
Zhengzhou 132 34.48 N 113.39 E
Zhenhai 136 29.57 N 121.42 E
Zhenjiang 136 32.13 N 119.26 E
Zhenning 140 26.05 N 105.46 E
Zhenping 136 33.08 N 112.19 E
Zhentong 136 32.39 N 120.08 E
Zhenyu 136 27.08 N 120.18 E
Zhenyuan 132 26.53 N 108.19 E
Zhenze (Dongshan) 136 31.04 N 120.24 E
Zhide 136 30.04 N 116.58 E
Zhijin 140 26.41 N 105.37 E
Zhob ≐ 146 32.04 N 69.50 E
Zhongba 132 29.54 N 83.40 E
Zhongcungang 136 32.38 N 115.45 E
Zhongdian 132 27.50 N 99.40 E
Zhongning 132 37.27 N 105.38 E
Zhongshan (Shiqi) 136 22.31 N 113.22 E
Zhongtou 136 34.00 N 113.21 E
Zhongxiang 136 31.11 N 112.33 E
Zhoucun 132 36.47 N 117.48 E
Zhouning 136 27.16 N 119.12 E
Zhoupu 136 31.07 N 121.34 E
Zhoushan 136 30.02 N 122.06 E
Zhoushanqundao II 136 30.00 N 122.00 E
Zhouxiang 136 30.10 N 121.08 E
Zhuangaerpendi ≚1 132 45.00 N 88.00 E
Zhucikou 136 29.17 N 112.41 E
Zhuhonggang 136 32.52 N 119.58 E
Zhuji 136 29.43 N 120.14 E
Zhujiahe 136 29.44 N 113.06 E
Zhujiangkou ≐ 136 23.36 N 113.44 E
Zhumadian 136 33.00 N 114.01 E
Zhungeerqi 132 39.49 N 111.10 E
Zhuoxian 132 39.30 N 115.58 E
Zhushan 132 32.10 N 110.19 E
Zhuzhou 136 27.50 N 113.09 E
Žiar nad Hronom 116 48.36 N 18.52 E
Zibo 132 36.47 N 118.01 E
Zicavo 122 41.54 N 9.08 E
Zielona Góra (Grünberg) 116 51.56 N 15.31 E
Zierikzee 116 51.38 N 3.55 E
Žigalovo 128 54.48 N 105.08 E
Zigana Dağları ʌ 144 40.37 N 39.30 E
Žigansk 128 66.45 N 123.20 E
Zigong 132 29.24 N 104.47 E
Ziguinchor 152 12.35 N 16.16 W
Žigulevsk 112 53.25 N 49.27 E
Zihuatanejo 180 17.38 N 101.33 W
Zijin 136 23.40 N 115.11 E
Žilina 116 49.14 N 18.46 E
Zillah 154 28.33 N 17.35 E
Zillertaler Alpen ʌ 116 47.00 N 11.55 E
Zilwaukee 176 43.28 N 83.55 W
Zima 128 53.55 N 102.04 E
Zimnicea 124 43.39 N 25.21 E
Zinder 152 13.48 N 8.59 E
Zinnik → Soignies 116 50.35 N 4.04 E
Zipaquirá 184 5.02 N 74.00 W
Zirbitzkogel ʌ 116 47.04 N 14.34 E
Zishui ≐ 132 28.45 N 112.25 E
Žitomir 126 50.16 N 28.40 E
Zittau 116 50.54 N 14.47 E
Ziway, Lake ⊜ 154 8.00 N 38.50 E
Zixi 136 27.42 N 117.02 E
Zixing 136 26.00 N 113.23 E
Ziyun 132 25.43 N 106.05 E
Zizhong 132 29.48 N 104.50 E
Zlarin 122 43.42 N 15.50 E
Zlatar 122 46.06 N 16.05 E
Zlatoust 126 55.10 N 59.40 E
Zlitan 152 32.28 N 14.34 E
Žlobin 130 52.54 N 30.03 E
Złotoryja 116 51.08 N 15.55 E
Złotów 116 53.22 N 17.02 E
Zmeinogorsk 128 51.10 N 82.13 E
Žminj 122 45.09 N 13.55 E
Znamensk 130 54.37 N 21.13 E
Znamenskoje 128 57.08 N 73.55 E
Znojmo 116 48.52 N 16.02 E
Zoar 160 33.30 S 21.28 E
Žochova, Ostrov I 128 76.04 N 152.40 E
Žoltyje Vody 126 48.21 N 33.31 E
Žolymbet 128 51.45 N 71.44 E
Zomba 158 15.23 S 35.18 E
Zone Point ≻ 104 50.08 N 5.00 W
Zonza 122 41.45 N 9.10 E
Zouar 154 20.27 N 16.32 E
Zrenjanin 124 45.23 N 20.24 E
Zubova Pol'ana 130 54.04 N 42.51 E
Zuckerhütl ʌ 116 46.58 N 11.09 E
Zudañez 184 19.06 S 64.44 W
Zug 118 47.10 N 8.31 E
Zugdidi 126 42.30 N 41.53 E
Zugspitze ʌ 116 47.25 N 10.59 E
Zuiderzee → IJsselmeer ⊤2 116 52.45 N 5.25 E
Zujar, Embalse del ⊜1 120 38.50 N 5.20 W
Zujevka 112 58.25 N 51.10 E
Žukovskij 130 55.35 N 38.08 E
Zulia □3 182 10.00 N 72.10 W
Zulia □5 158 3.00 N 32.30 E
Zulueta 182 22.22 N 79.34 W
Zululand □9 160 28.10 S 32.00 E
Zumbo 158 15.36 S 30.25 E
Zunyi 132 27.39 N 106.57 E
Županja 124 45.04 N 18.42 E
Zuqar, Jazirat I 144 14.00 N 42.45 E
Zurich, Ont., Can. 176 43.26 N 81.37 W
Zürich, Schw. 118 47.23 N 8.32 E
Zürichsee ⊜ 118 47.13 N 8.45 E
Zutphen 116 52.08 N 6.12 E
Zuwārah 154 32.56 N 12.06 E
Žužemberk 122 45.50 N 14.56 E
Zvenigorod 130 55.44 N 36.51 E
Zvolen 116 48.35 N 19.08 E
Zvornik 124 44.23 N 19.06 E
Zweibrücken 116 49.15 N 7.21 E
Zwettl 116 48.37 N 15.10 E
Zwickau 116 50.44 N 12.29 E
Zwiesel 116 49.01 N 13.14 E
Zwischenahn 116 53.11 N 8.00 E
Zwolle 116 52.30 N 6.05 E
Zyr'anka 128 65.45 N 150.51 E
Zyr'anovsk 128 49.43 N 84.20 E
Żyrardów 116 52.04 N 20.25 E
Żywiec 116 49.41 N 19.12 E

General acknowledgements

A great many people and institutions have given advice and assistance during the preparation of this book. The publishers wish to extend their thanks to them all, and in particular to the following:

Air Pollution Research Unit (M.R.C.), London. Bedford College, London. British Antarctic Survey. British Leyland, Coventry. British Museum of Natural History. Brookhaven National Laboratory, U.S.A. California Academy of Sciences. Chevron Oil (U.K.) Ltd. Cranfield Institute of Technology. *The Daily Telegraph*. Deep Sea Venture Inc. (U.S.A.). Directorate of Overseas Surveys (U.K.). *The Economist*. The Economist Intelligence Unit, London. Embassies and Cultural Offices of Australia, Canada, Denmark, Egypt, Finland, India, Japan, Netherlands, New Zealand, Pakistan, South Africa, U.S.A., U.S.S.R. Environmental Science Services Administration (U.S.A.). Fairey Surveys Ltd, Maidenhead. *The Financial Times*. Food and Agricultural Organization (U.N.). The Galton Foundation, London. *Geographical Magazine*. Geological Survey and Museum, London. The Hale Observatories (Mt. Wilson and Palomar, U.S.A.). The Harvard Center for Population Studies, U.S.A. Huntings Surveys Ltd. London Imperial Chemical Industries, London. Institute of Psychiatry, London. Laboratory of Human Mechanics (M.R.C.), London. The Laboratory of Molecular Evolution, Miami, U.S.A. London School of Economics. The London School of Hygiene and Tropical Medicine. Marine Biological Association of the United Kingdom. Medical Research Council, London. Meteorological Office, London. Ministries of H.M. Government. National Aeronautics and Space Administration (U.S.A.). National Coal Board. The National Institute of Oceanography, Surrey. *New Scientist* and *Science Journal*. *The Observer*. The Ordnance Survey of Great Britain. Pilkington Bros. Ltd., London. Queen Mary College, London. Royal Aircraft Establishment, Farnborough. The Royal Astronomical Society, London. Royal Institute of Netherlands Architects. The Royal Society for the Protection of Birds, London. The Science Museum, London. *Scientific American*. Shell Petroleum Co., London. The Soil Association, Suffolk. The Stockholm Peace Research Institute. Survival Service Commission of the International Union for the Conservation of Nature. Unilever, London. Union for the Conservation of Nature. United Kingdom Atomic Energy Authority. United States Department of the Interior. United States Geological Survey. Universities of Cambridge, Liverpool, Newcastle upon Tyne, Oxford, Reading, Sheffield, Strathclyde. The Water Research Association. The White Fish Authority (U.K.). World Health Organization (U.N.). *Weather* Magazine. The Zoological Society of London.

The Ordnance Survey of Great Britain and the Landuse Surveys of Japan and Canada for permission to reproduce the landuse maps on pp 44–45.

Illustrators

Section symbols throughout by Jim Bulman.

10–11 Diagram; 12–13 Diagram, Colin Rose (time clock); 14–15 Diagram; 17 Diagram, Colin Rose; 18–19 Diagram; 20–21 Diagram, Sheilagh Noble (line drawing); 22–23 Diagram; 24–25 Diagram; 26–27 Diagram; 28 David Fryer & Centrum (map), Richard Lewis; 29 David Fryer & Centrum (map), Centrum (clouds), Colin Rose, Eric Jewel; 32 Karel Thole Artist Partners, Michael Ricketts, Richard Lewis; 33 Richard Lewis; 34 Diagram, Karel Thole Artist Partners; 35 Diagram, Sheilagh Noble, Karel Thole Artist Partners; 36–37 Diagram, Karel Thole Artist Partners; 38–39 Diagram, Karel Thole Artist Partners; 40–41 Colin Rose (maps), Diagram, Michael Ricketts, Peter Barrett Artist Partners; 44–45 Colin Rose (diagrams), Richard Lewis; 46 Colin Rose, Richard Lewis; 47 Colin Rose, Richard Lewis; 48–49 David Fryer; 50 Diagram; 51 David Fryer; 52 David Fryer & Centrum (map), Richard Lewis, David Cook (line drawings); 53 Malcolm Topp, David Cook, Richard Lewis; 54–55 David Fryer (map), Centrum (diagrams), David Cook; 56–57 David Fryer (maps), Centrum (diagrams), David Cook; 58–59 David Fryer; 60–61 Giovanni Casselli Artist Partners, Colin Rose, Diagram; 62–63 Diagram, Colin Rose (maps); 64–65 Colin Rose (time scale), Roy Coombs Artist Partners.

Photographers

Photographs on each page are credited in descending order of the base line of each photograph. Where two or more photographs rest on the same level credits read left to right.

1–5 John Moyes; 6 Camera Press Ltd, John Moyes; 7 The Mansell Collection; 8–9 The Hale Observatories (Mt. Wilson and Palomar); 11 The Royal Greenwich Observatory; 14 The Hale Observatories (Mt. Wilson and Palomar); 16 N.A.S.A.; 17 N.A.S.A., H. Brinton, W. Zunti; 20 Solarfilma (Iceland); 21 Gerald Warhurst Associated Press; 29 Ken Pillsbury, Ken Pillsbury, Ken Pillsbury, M. J. Bramwell NHPA, Ken Pillsbury, Ken Pillsbury, Ken Pillsbury, M. J. Bramwell NHPA, Ken Pillsbury, J. Allen Cash, Picturepoint Ltd, Frank Lane, Ken Pillsbury; 30–31 Institute of Molecular Evolution, University of Miami; 42–43 Fairey Surveys Ltd.; 44 Colorific Photo Library; 45 Prof. G. S. Nelson London School of Tropical Medicine, W. MacQuitty, N.A.S.A.; 46 A. Loftas; 49 N.E.R.C. Copyright, reproduced by permission of the Director of the Institute of Geological Sciences; 50 Picturepoint Ltd.; 51 National Coal Board, Peter Keen, Shell International Petroleum Co., U.K.A.E.A.; 54 Picturepoint Ltd.; 56 Picturepoint Ltd.; 58 Picturepoint Ltd, Spectrum Colour Library, remainder Picturepoint Ltd.; 60 John Moss Oxfam, Gerard Klijn-Novib/Oxfam, Gerard Klijn-Novib/Oxfam; 61 Mike Busselle; 62 *Daily Telegraph*, The Mansell Collection; 63 Tom Kay.

Cartography

All maps in the sections The Great Cities of the Earth 66–81; The Face of the Earth 82–97; and Systematic Atlas of the Earth 98–178 by Rand McNally & Company. World Political Information Table, Largest Metropolitan Areas and Cities of the World and Geographical Index also by Rand McNally & Company.
Jacket designed by Mitchell Beazley. Map projections used by kind permission of Rand McNally & Company.

Symbols in the index entries are identified on page

To Richard
from Mum & Dad
Xmas 79.